WITHDRAWN

Hawaii

Kim Grant, Glenda Bendure,
Conner Gorry

Contents

Destination Hawaii

For millions, the Hawaiian Islands define paradise: palm trees keeping time to trade winds; crystal-clear waters pulsing with sea life; tropical blooms hurling intoxicating fragrances into the air; buff young men (and more women every day) riding surfboards at sunset; *paniolo* (cowboys) riding the open range; and even snow. Yes, snow – on Mauna Kea in winter.

Thousands of gems fashion the archipelago's necklace, but only six islands welcome visitors. Each is as different as the multiethnic complexion of the local population. Ah, the residents: talking story and sharing their passions about Hawaii as if you're long-lost pals.

Kaua'i is the eldest sibling – an outdoorsy playground with jagged cliffs, the glorious Waimea Canyon, and a marvelously lush landscape.

O'ahu hosts 80% of the state's population, mostly in cosmopolitan Honolulu, and has its most famous beach (Waikiki) and winter surfing on the monster waves of the North Shore. Maui, a playground of manicured oceanfront hotels and world-class golf, also boasts dusty, treasure-filled shops and superb ethnic eats.

The most Hawaiian of the main islands is Moloka'i, where children go to school barefoot and there are no stoplights. Lana'i is a private island of pineapples and posh resorts.

And then there's the Big Island, the youngest and largest member of the island *'ohana* (family) – and one that's growing all the time, thanks to the endless lava fields and expansive spirit of active Kilauea Volcano.

Hawaii isn't simply the definition of paradise – it's a state of mind. Aloha.

JOHN BORTHWICK

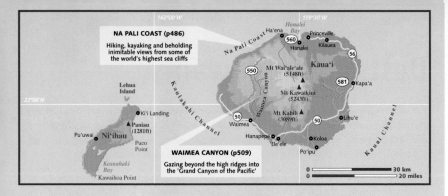

NA PALI COAST (p486)

Hiking, kayaking and beholding inimitable views from some of the world's highest sea cliffs

WAIMEA CANYON (p509)

Gazing beyond the high ridges into the 'Grand Canyon of the Pacific'

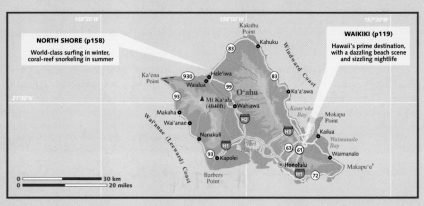

NORTH SHORE (p158)

World-class surfing in winter, coral-reef snorkeling in summer

WAIKIKI (p119)

Hawaii's prime destination, with a dazzling beach scene and sizzling nightlife

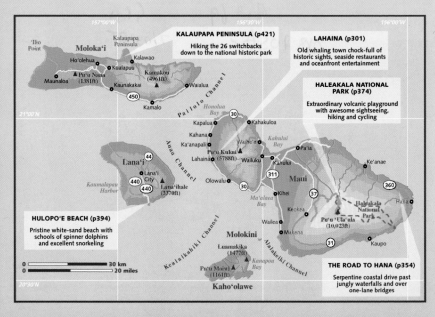

KALAUPAPA PENINSULA (p421)

Hiking the 26 switchbacks down to the national historic park

LAHAINA (p301)

Old whaling town chock-full of historic sights, seaside restaurants and oceanfront entertainment

HALEAKALA NATIONAL PARK (p374)

Extraordinary volcanic playground with awesome sightseeing, hiking and cycling

HULOPO'E BEACH (p394)

Pristine white-sand beach with schools of spinner dolphins and excellent snorkeling

THE ROAD TO HANA (p354)

Serpentine coastal drive past jungly waterfalls and over one-lane bridges

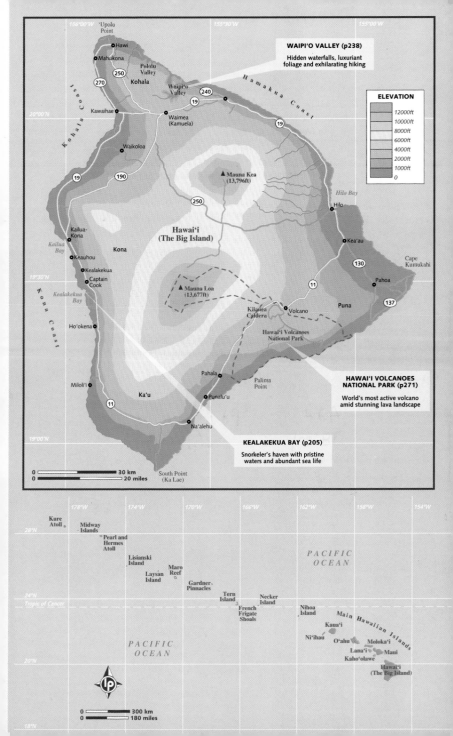

ELEVATION

	12000ft
	10000ft
	8000ft
	6000ft
	4000ft
	2000ft
	1000ft
	0

WAIPI'O VALLEY (p238)
Hidden waterfalls, luxuriant foliage and exhilarating hiking

HAWAI'I VOLCANOES NATIONAL PARK (p271)
World's most active volcano amid stunning lava landscape

KEALAKEKUA BAY (p205)
Snorkeler's haven with pristine waters and abundant sea life

'Upolu Point
Hawi
Mahukona
Pololu Valley
Kohala
Waipi'o Valley
Kawaihae
Waimea (Kamuela)
Waikoloa
Hamakua Coast
Kohala Coast
▲ Mauna Kea (13,796ft)
Hilo Bay
Hilo
Hawai'i (The Big Island)
Kailua-Kona
Kailua Bay
Keauhou
Kona
Kealakekua
Captain Cook
Kealakekua Bay
Kea'au
Cape Kumukahi
Ho'okena
Kona Coast
▲ Mauna Loa (13,677ft)
Pahoa
Puna
Kilauea Caldera
Volcano
Hawai'i Volcanoes National Park
Miloli'i
Pahala
Palima Point
Ka'u
Punalu'u
Na'alehu
South Point (Ka Lae)

0 30 km
0 20 miles

Kure Atoll
Midway Islands
Pearl and Hermes Atoll
Lisianski Island
Laysan Island
Maro Reef
Gardner Pinnacles
Tern Island
French Frigate Shoals
Necker Island
Nihoa Island
PACIFIC OCEAN
Tropic of Cancer
PACIFIC OCEAN
Main Hawaiian Islands
Kaua'i
Ni'ihau
O'ahu
Moloka'i
Lana'i
Kaho'olawe
Maui
Hawai'i (The Big Island)

0 300 km
0 180 miles

LP

From dripping jungles to dry volcanic summits, from vertical rushes of water to verdant plateaus, Hawaii has her natural bases covered thoroughly. Step back in time to **Waipi'o Valley** (p238), where only 50 or so hearty souls inhabit the almost-inaccessible terrain. Hike to the summit of **Haleakala National Park** (p378) to feel and hear the crunch of volcanic soil underfoot. Take in a North Shore sunset on O'ahu from **Sunset Beach** (p164) or **Ka'ena Point** (p171). Dunk your head under a **Kaua'i waterfall** (p452) and, on Moloka'i, admire the cliff-top views of **Halawa Valley** (p415) and **Kalaupapa Peninsula** (p421).

Soak in the calm turquoise waters of Kailua Beach on the Windward Coast of O'ahu (p147)

RICHARD CUMMINS

ANN CECIL

Take in a sunset at 'Anaeho'omalu Bay on the Big Island (p181)

Drive along the Chain of Craters Rd (p278), where you may see lava heading toward the sea

ANN CECIL

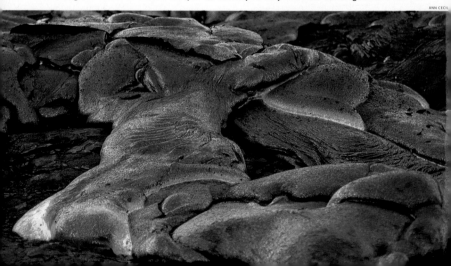

Whether it's shimmering at sunset or cascading 100ft to a valley floor, the seawater surrounding these islands and fresh water pulsing through them beckons thirsty travelers. Whet your appetite with phenomenal surfing at **Tunnels Beach** (p483) on the North Shore of Kaua'i or the **North Shore** (p78) of O'ahu. On Kaua'i, float on a calm, navigable river or get your heart racing in a seaworthy boat along the rugged **Na Pali Coast** (p486). To snorkel amid vibrantly colored fish, try paddling to sparkling **Kealakekua Bay** (p205) on the Big Island or the even more pristine **Hulupo'e Bay** (p393) on Lana'i.

CASEY & ASTRID WITTE MAHANEY

Experience some of the world's best surfing (p57) in the place that invented it

Get up close and personal with an amazing array of colorful fish (p55)

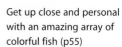

CASEY & ASTRID WITTE MAHANEY

ANN CECIL

Check out the waves at the famous Banzai Pipeline on O'ahu's North Shore (p158)

Explore Hawaii's past – from the saga of sugar and the religious fervor of missionaries, to the ancient Hawaiian customs kept alive with zeal and appreciation. Tour the leprosy colony isolated on Kalaupapa Peninsula on **Moloka'i** (p421). For a tutorial in whaling, boisterous sailors and conversion to Christianity, nothing beats the well-restored sights of **Lahaina** (p301). The old plantation town of **Waimea** (p504) on Kaua'i dishes up sweet sugar chronicles alongside a past peppered with Polynesians, kings, Cook and missionaries. For more about Captain Cook, head to **Kealakekua Bay** (p205) on the Big Island.

KARL LEHMANN

Lay a lei on the statue of Kamehameha the Great at the Ali'iolani Hale in Honolulu (p92)

JOHN BORTHWICK

Ride the historic sugarcane train between Lahaina and Ka'anapali on Maui (p308)

KARL LEHMANN

Discover what life was like in Hawaii before Western development swept the land at the Hale Kahiko on Maui (p304)

Diversity is Hawaii's middle name. From the cultural purists who populate **'Heavenly Hana'** (p358) and plantation villages such as **Lana'i City** (p389) to the bustling cosmopolitan crowds of downtown **Honolulu** (p84), Hawaiian residents come from all corners of the Pacific Rim. Whether it's a young Hawaiian girl performing hula on the edge of a volcano or the Filipino sumo wrestler who has has become that Japanese sport's first foreign-born grand champion, Hawaii's multicultural mix is the secret ingredient in making the islands *no ka oi* (the best).

Planting taro near the town of Hana on Maui (p358)

ANN CECIL

ANN CECIL

Girl of Japanese descent (p40)

Stallholders playing ukeleles at a local craft fair (p43)

ANN CECIL

Island flavors are seductive, by turns sweet, savory, salty and simply smashing. Start your morning at one of the many markets in **Honolulu** (p105), on **Kaua'i** (p491) or **Lana'i** (p390). Take a lunchtime break at a casual *kaukau* wagon, chill out with shave ice on a sticky afternoon or kick back at dusk with an island microbrew. At night, please your palate with some tantalizing **Hawaii Regional Cuisine** (p65) or make reservations for a slice of culture at a Polynesian **luau** (p66). With a bit of luck, your island sojourn might coincide with a fabulous food and wine celebration, such as the **Taste of Lahaina Festival** (p308).

ANN CECIL

Crunch on a colorful shave ice (p69)

Wander through the bustling produce markets in Honolulu's Chinatown (p106)

LEE FOSTER

ANN CEC

Indulge in the deep aromatic flavor of 100% Kona coffee from the Big Island (p204)

Hawaii offers enough action to keep even the highest-flying adrenaline junkies jacked. After all, this is the place that invented surfing – now taken to extremes like kiteboarding, tow-in surfing and the one-and-only **Ironman Triathalon** (p60). You don't have to go quite that far to get your thrills, though. Anyone can learn to surf, snorkel or dive on any island. If turf grounds you more than surf, try cycling down **Haleakala** (p380), hiking across an active lava field in **Hawai'i Volcanoes National Park** (p280), exploring the jaw-dropping **Na Pali Coast** (p486) on Kaua'i or four-wheel driving on the **Munro Trail** (p397).

Take a cycling tour of Honolulu (p80) to really see the sights

Kayak off tranquil Lanikai Beach (p147) near the town of Kailua on O'ahu's Windward Coast

ANN CECIL

Experience some of the world's best windsurfing off Ho'okipa Beach, Maui (p352)

ANN CECIL

Although the Hawaiian archipelago comprises only about 1% of the USA's total land mass, it's a wildly fertile place. Boasting more than 10,000 endemic species of flora and fauna, Hawaii is a fragile paradise that also claims 75% of the nation's extinct species. Consider yourself fortunate to encounter **green sea turtles** (p48) or **Hawaiian monk seals** (p48). Other more common, but no less spectacular, species include the **Hawaiian owl** (p48) and **hawk** (p49), wild horses on the Big Island, fragrant sandalwood forests or hardy ohia plants – the first to colonize new lava flows in **Hawai'i Volcanoes National Park** (p271).

ANN CECIL

The rare silversword (p49) can grow for up to half a century, but blooms only once in a lifetime

Hawaii's state bird, the nene (p48), is currently endangered, with only 800 left in all of Hawaii

ANN CECIL

Spinner dolphins (p48) are frequent visitors to calm bays

CASEY & ASTRID WITTE MAHANEY

Getting Started

Without some advance planning, the Hawaiian adventure of your dreams could well fall short of your lofty expectations. The more specific your desires are and the shorter your holiday, the more work you'll want to do before departing. If an occasional downpour will ruin your day, avoid staying on the windward sides of the islands.

The biggest decision? Choosing your island destination. If you feel out of step with your island, it's not like you can hop in your car and drive to the adjacent Neighbor Island. Yes, interisland flights are frequent enough for you to be somewhere else within hours, but you'll pay more for a last-minute flight. And speaking of cars, unless you have time to kill, rent one. (The only island where you may be able to disregard that advice is O'ahu.)

Avoid the temptation to see and do too much. Unless you're a repeat visitor, try to visit just one or two islands to better appreciate Hawaii's rich variety and texture. Although reservations for activities can be made after arrival in Hawaii, there are exceptions, such as the Old Lahaina Luau (p312), which is booked weeks in advance. The moral of the story? If something is critically important, make your reservations before departing for the islands. This couldn't be more true for booking accommodations well in advance of your trip, especially during high season.

Hawaii is often thought of as out of reach because of costs. While you can crop a wad of cash, you don't have to; all budgets can be accommodated here. Thinking about bringing the kids? Don't think twice: *na keiki* (children) are beloved in Hawaii, and each of the island destination chapters has a boxed text with ideas about what they'll like (see also p521).

WHEN TO GO

Hawaii is a great place to visit any time of the year. Although the busiest season is winter (mid-December through March), that has more to do with weather *elsewhere*. It's a bit rainier in winter and a bit hotter in summer (June through August) here, but there are no extremes and cooling trade winds modify the heat throughout the year.

Big holidays like Thanksgiving, Christmas, New Years and Easter (see p526) mean lodging vacancies are tight and prices a bit higher. In terms of cost, visiting between mid-April and mid-November can be a bargain

See climate charts (pp521-2) for more information.

DON'T LEAVE HOME WITHOUT...

- A bathing suit – regardless of how comfortable you are in your own skin (p55)
- A light jacket or sweater (think lots of layers if you're lingering on Big Island or Maui volcano summits)
- Accommodations reservations in your pocket (p518)
- Binoculars for whale watching and birding, and flashlights for exploring lava tubes
- Footwear with good traction for hiking on wet trails and dry lava
- Lightweight rain gear for sudden downpours (p521)
- Snorkel gear if you're going to be underwater on more than a day or two (p55)

because some hotel prices drop in the off-season. Hotels and resorts catering to summertime vacationing families do not lower their rates significantly.

Naturally, certain participatory and spectator activities have their peak seasons. For instance, if you're a board surfer, you'll find the biggest waves in winter, whereas if you're a windsurfer, you'll find the best wind conditions in summer. Football freaks will want to plan holidays around the Hula and Pro Bowls, while cowboys might plan an adventure around big rodeos (p232). Alternatively, you might want to *avoid* big-time events. For example, unless you've scored tickets to the Merrie Monarch Festival (p259), visit Hilo another time. For details of island-wide festivals and events, see p524. Each island destination chapter also features listings of island-specific festivals.

COSTS & MONEY

HOW MUCH?

Condo per night
$100-150

Cup of Kona coffee
$2

Haute 'Pacific Rim' dinner
for two
$75+

Local phone call
25-50¢

Movie ticket
$8

LONELY PLANET INDEX

US gallon of gas
$2.50

Liter of bottled water
$1.75

Bottle of Kona Brewing
Co's Longboard Lager
$4

Souvenir T-shirt
$12

Hawaiian plate lunch
$4-5

The amount of cash you'll need directly correlates to your traveling style. You can get by cheaply by eating plate lunches (see p63) and camping. Or you can dine on haute Pacific Rim cuisine, sleep at plush resorts and rack up beefy balances on your credit card. Or you could always take the Buddha's 'middle way.'

Airfare is usually one of the heftier budget items. Expect to spend at least $400 for a roundtrip flight from the USA's west coast, $600 from the east coast (see p533). Interisland flights (p533) cost from $70 to $115 one way. Cashing in frequent flyer miles for flights to Hawaii is usually good value.

O'ahu, which boasts a good, inexpensive bus system (p535), is the only place you can do without a car (although it's still a treat to have one for a couple of days). Renting a car (p536) usually costs from $175 to $250 per week.

As for sleeping (see Accommodations, p518), each main island has absurdly inexpensive state and county campgrounds. (We're talking fees in the single digits!) Maui and the Big Island have excellent national parks with free camping. The main islands also have a couple of hostel-style places with dormitory beds for under $20 and either B&Bs or spartan hotels for around $50 per double. For standard middle-class hotels expect to pay at least $125 nightly. If your tastes tend toward deluxe beachfront hotels, get ready to pay about $200 a night. And for a splurge at some of the world's finest hostelries, rates generally begin around $300.

If you're staying a while and looking for better value, ask about weekly and monthly condo rentals. Besides having more space than the typical hotel room, condos have full kitchens so you can cook and save a bundle on food costs. Since much of Hawaii's food is shipped in, grocery prices average 25% higher than on the mainland. Food in neighborhood restaurants is good value in Hawaii, with prices generally as cheap as you'll find on the mainland (see Food, p63).

TRAVEL LITERATURE

Use the long flight to Hawaii for doing some illuminating background reading and boning up on the rich island culture.

Two classics seem destined to remain on the short list of 'required reading' for those embarking on a Hawaii holiday. *Hawaii*, James Michener's ambitious saga of the islands, traces the trajectory of the Polynesian settlers, the arrival of the missionaries and whalers, the emergence of the sugar barons and the development of Hawaii's multiethnic society. The other is Paul Theroux's *Hotel Honolulu*, a charming book about a washed-up writer, an aging prostitute and a handful of semiliterates who call the Hotel Honolulu their home.

Garrett Hongo's *Volcano*, an honest account of a native son returning to his family's homeland, reads as a lyrical and visceral portrayal of revelation that could only be written by a poet. *A World Between Waves*, compiled by Frank Stewart, is an essay collection about Hawaii and the Pacific by such writers as Diane Ackerman, Peter Matthiessen, John McPhee, WS Merwin, and Maxine Hong Kingston.

For a rare glimpse into the year before the United States annexed Hawaii, turn the pages of *A Story by Hawaii's Queen*. Queen Lili'uokalani's graceful autobiography was written during the last year of her monarchy and couldn't be more eloquent. The first book to recount Hawaiian history from the native Hawaiian perspective, *A Call for Hawaiian Sovereignty* by Michael Kioni Dudley and Keoni Kealoha Agard, has been rightly dubbed the 'handbook on Hawaiian sovereignty.'

For more recommended reading, see p43. Just be sure to put your tray table and seat back in their upright position when you're done.

TOP FIVES

Fave Festivals & Events
Hawaiians love a good celebration, and there's almost always something interesting going on. For a comprehensive listing of festivals and events, see p524 and the Festivals & Events sections for major destinations that appear in the island chapters later in this guide.

- **Cherry Blossom Festival** February (O'ahu)
- **Merrie Monarch Festival** begins Easter week (Big Island)
- **May Day** (aka Lei Day) May (all main islands)
- **Aloha Week** mid-September to early October (all main islands)
- **Triple Crown of Surfing** November (O'ahu)

Fave Flicks
Vacation planning and dreaming is best done in a comfy chair with a bowl of popcorn in one hand and a remote in the other. Head to your local video store for these feature flicks filmed in Hawaii, as well as scores of others that have used Hawaii as a backdrop. For more movies, see p44.

- *Hawaii* (1966) Starring: Julie Andrews and Max von Sydow
- *Picture Bride* (1993) Starring: Yuki Kudoh
- *Blue Hawaii* (1961) Starring: Elvis Presley
- *Godzilla* (1998) Starring: Matthew Broderick
- *Molokai: The Story of Father Damien* (1999) Starring: Peter O'Toole

Fave Activities
You could spend 14 days in Hawaii and become utterly exhausted by doing 14 different superlative activities. Choose your method of play wisely; for more ideas, see p55.

- Hike within Hawai'i Volcanoes National Park, the Big Island (p271)
- Snorkel at Hulopo'e Beach, Lana'i (p393)
- Windsurf at Kanaha Beach, Maui (p328)
- Paddle the Wailua River, Kaua'i (p452)
- Hike to the top of Diamond Head, O'ahu (p138)

INTERNET RESOURCES

Alternative Hawaii (www.alternative-hawaii.com) An ecotourism site that promotes, preserves and perpetuates Hawaiian culture.

Hawaii State Vacation Planner (www.hshawaii.com) Everything you need for planning an aloha vacation.

Hawaii Visitors & Convention Bureau (www.gohawaii.com) The state's official tourism site.

Honolulu Advertiser (www.honoluluadvertiser.com) The state's main daily newspaper.

LonelyPlanet.com (www.lonelyplanet.com) Succinct summaries on traveling to Hawaii, travel news and the subwwway section with links to useful web resources.

Search Hawaii (www.search-hawaii.com) Searches Hawaiian websites by topic or word.

Itineraries
CLASSIC ROUTES

O'AHU
A Long Weekend

Start in **Waikiki** (p119), the mecca of tourist activities. An early-morning stroll at less-populated **Kapiolani Park** (p126) leads past locals practicing tai chi, with **Diamond Head** (p138) silhouetted in the background. Join the crowds at Waikiki later to sunbathe or people-watch. Check out some hula dancers at sunset. Make the most of the weekend by heading out of town for the **North Shore** (p158). If it's winter, check out the world-class surfing at the **Banzai Pipeline** (p164), **Waimea Bay** (p163) and **Sunset Beach** (p164) where waves can reach 30ft. In summer, snorkel with sea turtles over coral reefs. In nearby **Hale'iwa** (p158), enjoy a fresh mahimahi sandwich followed by a shave ice. Check out the **Surf Museum** (p159) in Hale'iwa, before heading back to Honolulu to take in some contemporary Hawaiian music at Waikiki hotels for the price of a drink and some *pupu* (snacks). The next day, take the short drive over the **Nu'uanu Pali Lookout** (p144) to **Kailua Beach Park** (p147), rent a tandem kayak and paddle out to **Popoi'a Island** (p147), a pristine bird sanctuary. Head back to Waikiki for dinner and drinks on the beach, or splurge on a lavish luau.

In one long weekend you can go from living it up, big-city style, in Honolulu, to chilling out with surfer dudes on the North Shore, to paddling a kayak in Kailua Bay, to taking a romantic walk on Waikiki Beach. The drive covers about 90 miles.

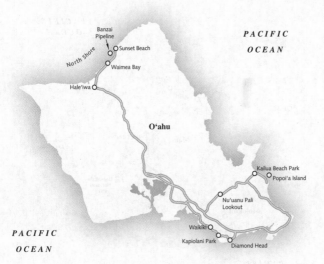

MAUI   Four Days

Start off in the old whaling town of **Lahaina** (p301) and enjoy the bustling scene, poking into galleries and exploring its treasure trove of historic sites, then cap off the day with a seafood dinner at one of the waterfront restaurants along **Front Street** (p309) or make it a night out at the superb **Old Lahaina Luau** (p312). Set aside day two for **Haleakala** (p374), Maui's looming volcano – get up early to catch an inspiring sunrise on the crater rim, then hike or take a horseback ride down to the cinder-covered crater floor. Time left in the afternoon? Swing through the **Upcountry** (p366), stopping to stroll its bountiful gardens, and stop off at **Pa'ia** (p354) in the afternoon where you can visit art and crafts shops. By day three the water should be beckoning, and depending on your interests, there is plenty to choose from: whale-watching cruises, kayaking along the stunning **south Maui coast** (p337), windsurfing or kiteboarding at **Kanaha Beach** (p328), snorkeling along one of the island's glorious beaches or heading out by boat to dive or snorkel **Molokini** (p297) volcanic crater. That leaves a day to work your way down the coast along Hawaii's premier drive – the jungly, cliff-hugging **Road to Hana** (p354), with its 600 twists and turns, dozens of cascading waterfalls and scores of one-lane bridges.

Four days on Maui provides just enough time to get a sense of what this terrific island is all about, from exploring its splendid beaches to setting foot on its highest summit. Depending on where you're staying, expect to travel about 300 miles in all …120 miles of which would be the day-long Road to Hana adventure.

THE BIG ISLAND   One Week

With a week, you can get a taste of the entire Big Island. Start out by car from Kailua-Kona and rid yourself of jet lag the first day at **Kahalu'u Beach** (p198), great for snorkeling, or **Kealakekua Bay** (p205), if you're up for a little kayaking. If you have the energy, visit **Pu'uhonua O Honaunau National Historical Park** (p209) to imagine old Hawai'i. On the second day, stop at the galleries of **Holualoa** (p200) on your way to overnight at **Hawai'i Volcanoes National Park** (p271), where you can see the main sights around **Halema'uma'u Crater** (p276) and perhaps trek toward the flow (p279). Begin your third day with a hike, then drive around Hwy 137, nicknamed **Red Road** (p269), in laid-back **Puna** (p266) before heading to **Hilo** (p249), preferably staying near the historic downtown or verdant **Lili'uokalani Park** (p255). On day four, cruise north along the scenic **Hamakua Coast** (p234), ending with a hike down **Waipi'o Valley** (p238). Spend day five in **Waimea** (p229), where you can go horseback riding or cycling over endless rolling hills. On day six, chill out in rustic **North Kohala** (p224), visiting **Pololu Valley** (p229) and **Mo'okini Heiau** (p226). End by relaxing at a white-sand crescent along the Gold Coast – like **Hapuna Beach** (p222) or **Kauna'oa Bay** (p223) – or driving up Saddle Rd to the summit of **Mauna Kea** (p243).

On the Big Island, you'll find a microcosm of a continent, including tropical rain forests, vast lava deserts, rolling hills of pastureland and an active volcano. Circling the island, you'll cover 220 miles, passing through longtime towns that remain hang-loose local. Visitors typically flock to the balmy Kona Coast, but a week will let you sample the island's staggering diversity instead.

ISLAND HOPPING

MAUI, MOLOKA'I & LANA'I   One Week

You can enjoy a fine slice of Maui – including daylong outings as well as beach time – in four days and then catch the highlights of Lana'i in one day. Then fly or ferry to Moloka'i, the 'most Hawaiian' island, to combine ocean and trail fun for a couple of days. Expect to cover about 375 miles total.

Spend your first day on Maui exploring the old whaling town of **Lahaina** (p301) and watch the sunset while dining at a waterfront restaurant. On day two, drive to **Haleakala National Park** (p374) to see the sun rise over the world's largest dormant volcano and then hike into the crater's awesome belly. On day three, take a morning **whale-watching** or **snorkel cruise** (p306) out of Lahaina, head to a gorgeous beach in the afternoon, and enjoy Hawaii's best luau, the **Old Lahaina Luau** (p312) in the evening. On day four, drive the lush **Road to Hana** (p354) or, alternatively, opt for a morning kayak trip with the turtles along Maui's south coast, then kick around **Pa'ia** (p351) with its fun shops and scrumptious cafés. Follow it up with a driving tour of **Upcountry** (p366). On day five, pack a swimsuit and hop the early ferry in Lahaina to Lana'i. Catch the shuttle to **Lana'i City** (p389), rub elbows with the locals over breakfast at **Blue Ginger Café** (p392), stroll the town and head back to **Hulopo'e Beach** (p394) to swim and snorkel before catching the sunset sail back to Lahaina. On day six, fly to Moloka'i, poking around the eastern and northern portions, snorkeling at **Twenty-Mile Beach** (p413) and exploring **Halawa Valley** (p411). Devote your final day to the **Kalaupapa Peninsula** (p421) and watch the sunset with the locals at the **Hotel Moloka'i** (p410).

See the Transportation chapter (p532) for details on island-hopping, whether by air or boat.

O'AHU, THE BIG ISLAND & KAUA'I

Two Weeks

Begin on O'ahu by exploring historic **downtown** (p88) and colorful **Chinatown** (p93). Catch a hotel hula show at sunset and enjoy the nightlife in **Waikiki** (p134). Wake to snorkel at **Hanauma Bay** (p139) or kayak or windsurf at **Kailua Beach** (p146). Stop at the **Valley of the Temples** (p150) in Kane'ohe for a spiritual change of pace. On day three, visit **Pearl Harbor** (p116) before heading to the **North Shore** (p158) to check out the surf action. Finally, hike **Diamond Head** (p138) and reward yourself with a sunset mai tai afterward.

Fly to the Big Island, get a buzz with Kona coffee in **Holualoa** (p200) and snorkel the clear, warm waters along the Kona Coast at **Kealakekua Bay** (p205). Check out the ancient coastal Hawaiian sights, such as **Pu'uhonua O Honaunau National Historical Park** (p209) and the **Puako Petroglyph Preserve** (p221). On day three, head to **Hawai'i Volcanoes National Park** (p271), where you can hike across awesome lava flows. Spend a day exploring **Hilo** (p249). Top it off with a hike into **Waipi'o Valley** (p238).

End up on Kaua'i's **North Shore** (p469), swimming at **Ha'ena Beach** (p484), snorkeling at **Ke'e Beach** (p485) and hiking to **Hanakapi'ai Falls** (p486). The following day, hit some good waterfalls like **'Opaeka'a** (p455), before paddling up the **Wailua River** (p452). You could spend another day catching some rays and snorkeling near **Po'ipu** (p492). Save a day for **Waimea Canyon** (p509) and **Koke'e State Park** (p510), where hiking and breathtaking vistas await.

With just a few days, O'ahu (110 miles) bursts with Waikiki nightlife, hiking and sunset mai tais. The Big Island (220 miles) offers every vista imaginable, from tropical rain forests to vast lava deserts to rolling pastureland. With only four days on Kaua'i (125 miles), you can easily dip into the water before lacing up your hiking shoes on the North Shore.

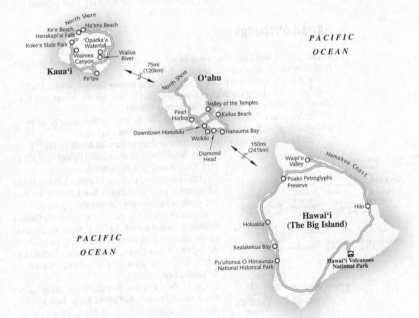

TAILORED TRIPS

HAWAII WITH KIDS

Don't leave home without them! On Kaua'i, the boogie boarding, horse-back riding and snorkeling at **Po'ipu Beach** (p492) are all accessible to wee ones. Hiking isn't just for big kids in **Waimea Canyon** (p509), where the Canyon Trail is great for little boots.

Kids love the **Maui Ocean Center** (p336), where you can touch a sea cucumber and walk through a see-through tunnel alongside sharks. In the winter, ogle giant humpback whales on tours from **Lahaina** (p308).

Over on Lana'i, watch spinner dolphins frolic off **Hulopo'e Beach** (p394).

Beach days rule on lazy Moloka'i. Pack a picnic and set off to snorkel and swim at **Twenty-Mile Beach** (p413).

On the Big Island, choices are as varied as the island is big. Walk through a lava tube at **Hawai'i Volcanoes National Park** (p271), ride horses across rolling hills in **Waimea** (p229) or head to **North Kohala** (p227) to get wet kayaking 'da ditch.'

On O'ahu, the small **Honolulu Zoo** (p124) entertains, while the **Waikiki Aquarium** (p123) has a touch tank with colorful tropical fish. And at the fine **Bishop Museum** (p122), families can watch hula performances or quilting and lei-making demonstrations.

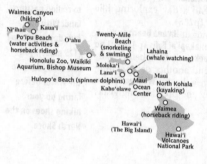

HAWAII OUTDOORS

What? Don't feel like lying on a beach all day? You name it and you can probably do it outdoors in Hawaii.

On Kaua'i, swim with sea turtles around **Ha'ena Beach** (p484). Mellow paddles await along the **Wailua River** (p452). Or feast on the views and hike above the plunging waterfalls of **Waimea Canyon** (p509).

On Moloka'i, hiking and mountain biking enthusiasts can head deep into the rugged backcountry at **Kamakou Preserve** (p416).

On Maui, try windsurfing or kiteboarding at **Kanaha Beach** (p328). Back on dry land, drive to the top of **Haleakala** (p374) and hike down to the crater floor.

Little Lana'i boasts big-time snorkeling. Head straight for pristine **Hulopo'e Beach** (p394) or dive the grottoes at nearby **Cathedrals** (p393).

On the Big Island, there's no ignoring **Hawai'i Volcanoes National Park** (p271), with trails that cross desolate lava rock and thriving rain forest. Along the Kona Coast, kayak across **Kealakekua Bay** (p205) and snorkel the pristine waters of **Ka'awaloa Cove** (p205).

On O'ahu, visitors flex different muscles on the relatively easy **Kuli'ou'ou Ridge Trail** (p138), with 360-degree views of Honolulu and the Windward Coast.

The Authors

KIM GRANT
Coordinating Author

Timing is everything. Flying from Boston to Honolulu for a three-month research trip, Kim made a fortuitous layover in the Bay Area to have coffee with Catherine Direen and say hello to Lonely Planet contacts. On the spot Kim was asked to lend her name to the project. Perhaps her passion for the islands was obvious. Her answer was as clear as a Hawaiian night sky: Yes. Any excuse to spend more time wrapped in a Hawaiian state of mind is welcome. Working in Hawaii annually since the mid-1990s, Kim Grant's love of the aloha spirit is as boundless as the energy flow beneath Kilauea crater.

My Favorite Trip

I'm an end-of-the-road kind of girl. I need the stillness of places that tell me, when I arrive, that I'm home. Points along the Kahekili Hwy (p150) always beckon, and if given the choice, I'd live my last month on this planet at Hotel Hana-Maui (p361). Nu'uanu Pali Lookout (p145) always elicits gasps, and Hale'iwa (p158), the only place I wear a bikini in public, reminds me to take life less seriously. No place is more romantic than Hanalei Bay (p479), but desolate Polihale State Park (p509) is also compelling. Nothing beats Hawai'i Volcanoes National Park (p271) – not even washing away the past at Hapuna Beach (p222).

GLENDA BENDURE & NED FRIARY
Maui, Lana'i, Kaho'olawe, Northwestern Hawaiian Islands

After having lived for a time on both Kaua'i and the Big Island, Ned Friary and Glenda Bendure explored each island from top to bottom before writing Lonely Planet's first guidebook to Hawaii in 1990. They returned to the islands again and again, driving the back roads, hiking remote trails and snorkeling hidden coves while working on the next five editions of *Hawaii*. They're also the authors of LP's guide to O'ahu. Ned and Glenda live on Cape Cod, Massachusetts.

MICHAEL CLARK
O'ahu

Michael's first trip to Hawaii was as a deckhand aboard a tanker crossing the Pacific. When the ship dropped anchor in Honolulu, he was hooked. Later, a master's degree program in second-language studies at the University of Hawai'i included a hula class to help keep things in perspective. When not visiting Hawaii, Michael teaches international students in Berkeley and San Francisco.

CONNER GORRY
Moloka'i, Kaua'i, Ni'ihau

Conner knows a little about the salt spray and slow motion of tropical islands: her virgin domestic assignment for Lonely Planet was the first edition of *Hawai'i: The Big Island,* which really is the best Hawaiian island and where she danced hula, ate from *ti* leaves, drank 'awa and got spooked by ancient spirits. Conner has bitten lots of red dust on these guidebook assignments for LP, but still hasn't learned to appreciate slack-key guitar.

LUCI YAMAMOTO
The Culture, Food & Drink,
Hawai'i (The Big Island)

Luci Yamamoto is a third-generation native of the Big Island. Thus she's not fazed by rain, pidgin or Hawaiian street names. After college in Los Angeles, she moved to Berkeley for law school and spent two summers working in Honolulu, contemplating practicing land-use law in Honolulu. Ultimately she remained in California, where she's now a freelance writer. But she regularly returns to Hilo, the only place she's ever called 'home.'

CONTRIBUTING AUTHORS

Nanette Naioma Napoleon wrote the History chapter and the Language chapter. Nanette is a freelance researcher and writer from Kailua, O'ahu. She has written a daily history column for the *Honolulu Star-Bulletin* newspaper and currently writes historical features for the *'Oiwi Files,* a Native Hawaiian news journal. She is also the state's leading authority on historic graveyards.

Dr David Goldberg wrote the Health chapter. David completed his training at Columbia-Presbyterian Medical Center in New York City. He is an infectious diseases specialist and the editor-in-chief of www .mdtravelhealth.com.

Snapshot

As Charles Dickens famously penned in *A Tale of Two Cities*, 'It was the best of times, it was the worst of times.' It's also the tale of two Hawaiis: the one visitors enjoy and the one locals live in (and, frankly, many struggle with).

At its heart, Hawaii is the homeland of a foreign culture – to Westerners, anyway. The differences between Hawaiian and Western views of the universe are galactic (see p37). Hawaii is the only state in the union with two official languages: English and Hawaiian. Hawaii was a monarchy (many wish it still was) and it is home to the only royal palace on American soil. It is stunningly beautiful and, for the most part, it is an absolutely joyful place. But it's not without its conflicts.

The state of the state can be simply stated in real-estate terms – location, location, location. (There are more realtors per capita here than in most places on the US mainland, except for places like California and New York City.) Further from any other landmass than any place else on earth, Hawaii is the gateway to the Pacific Rim and a base for much international business. Its biggest industry is tourism, and its location between the US mainland and Asia means massive marketing efforts in both directions.

As an island state, Hawaii also has its own set of transportation and growth challenges, separate from growing the tourist industry (you obviously can't drive from Kona to Kaua'i!). There's only so much land on which to spread out. And, most important to Hawaiians, there's only so much fresh water. Speaking of the environment (p46), water use is but one issue of concern. Cruise ships and other industries are arguably polluting the surrounding ocean, and landfills are almost overflowing. Because Hawaii is basically a closed eco-system, issues of endangered and introduced species are of utmost concern.

If you're eavesdropping (ever so politely) on a conversation between locals, or reading the *Honolulu Advertiser* on a regular basis, two words will come up with greater frequency than others: development and sovereignty. The median house price on Maui exceeded $500,000 in 2004. 'Affordable housing' translates to $250,000 houses, which makes home ownership inaccessible to locals working at $10-an-hour hotel jobs. Many feel that too much land has been gobbled up by developers and speculators. The tremendous influx of extremely wealthy mainlanders – many of them dot-commers from the boom times – has also resulted in a political shift. Ever a 'blue' state, Hawaii's current governor is a Republican, as well as being a Jewish woman from the mainland. The state legislature, however, remains Democratic, at least for the time being.

As for sovereignty, the Hawaiian culture was at tremendous risk until the 1970s when a renaissance (p34) began. It's thriving today: there are more Hawaiian language speakers, more hula dancers, more taro farmers, and more Hawaiian entertainers making it big than ever before. And there are more, and stronger, voices that want to curtail development and the encroachment of all things haole (Caucasian) – foreign to Hawaiians, anyway. With each passing year, a tenuous balance is refigured and a more steely spirit forged.

FAST FACTS

Population: 1,245,000

Distance from Los Angeles: 2250 miles

GDP: $33 billion

Miles of coastline: 750

State fish: Humuhumunukunukuapua'a

Average personal income: $27,800

Unemployment rate: 3.0%

It is illegal in Hawaii to appear in public wearing only swim trunks.

All residents of Hawaii may be fined as a result of not owning a boat.

History

ANCIENT HAWAI'I

Hawaii is the northern point of the huge triangle of Pacific Ocean islands known as Polynesia, which means 'many islands.' The other two points of the triangle are Rapa Nui (Easter Island) to the southeast and Aotearoa (New Zealand) to the southwest. Island cultures within this region share many similarities of language, religious beliefs, social structure, legends, myths, musical traditions and tools.

Ancient Hawaii (1998) is a short book about ancient Hawaiian culture and community life that is written – and stunningly illustrated – by internationally acclaimed artist and author Herb Kawainui Kane.

The exact origins of the first settlers in Hawai'i is unknown. Whether they had their roots in Southeast Asia, as has been thought traditionally, or whether they originated in Melanesia, as archaeologists now believe, is a matter of ongoing debate. Either way, their eastward migratory path took them to the southern Polynesian islands of Tonga and Samoa in about 1000 BC. Over the next 1500 years, they migrated to more far-flung areas of Polynesia, with Hawai'i being the last settled.

The early Hawaiian settlers came in two waves. The first group began arriving around AD 500 in large voyaging canoes. It is hypothesized they first came ashore at Ka Lae (South Point) on the Big Island (p288). What their intentions were in making this 2000-mile trek across the Pacific in search of new lands is unknown. It may have been because of overpopulation, to escape from famine or war, or out of a pure sense of exploration and discovery. Whatever the reason, the voyages were one-way ventures.

The second group came primarily from Tahiti around AD 1000. Over the next hundred years, a two-way migratory route was established. Most of these settlers were of *ali'i* (chiefly) rank. It is speculated that these individuals were interested mainly in establishing their own ruling domains in an island group that was largely unpopulated.

Society

The ancient Hawaiian social structure comprised four groups. The people of the highest rank were the *ali'i*. The chiefs ruled over land divisions

---

HOKULE'A: STAR OF GLADNESS

Until about three decades ago, most anthropologists did not think it was possible for ancient people from the western Pacific to make long-distance ocean journeys, since ocean voyaging by most Europeans did not begin until the 15th century, with the aid of navigational equipment such as sextons, chronometers and other instruments for plotting and mapping.

This prevailing theory was shattered in 1976 when the Polynesian Voyaging Society, based in Honolulu, launched the *Hokule'a*, a modern reproduction of an ancient Hawaiian voyaging canoe. The *Hokule'a* made a 4800-mile return voyage to Tahiti using only traditional Polynesian navigational aids such as the sun, the moon and the stars, wind directions, ocean current systems, cloud and wave patterns.

Today the *Hokule'a*, which has sailed more than 100,000 miles on eight major voyages across the Pacific, has become an important symbol of cultural pride for Hawaiians and other Pacific Islanders.

TIMELINE **AD 4–5**   **1000**

| Earliest settlers arrive in Hawai'i | Second group of settlers arrive, primarily from Tahiti |

called *ahupua'a*, which were pie-shaped wedges of land that ran from the mountains to the sea. Sometimes an *ali'i nui* (high chief) would emerge to rule over several *ahupua'a* or an entire island. These chiefs did not own land, but were considered to be the caretakers of the land and the people who lived there. Their responsibility was to make sure that all of the natural resources of the land and the sea were not depleted and that religious laws were obeyed. The *ali'i* were also believed to be the direct descendants of the gods, and therefore were considered to be sacred.

One's rank as an *ali'i* was determined by the mother's lineage, making Hawai'i a matriarchal society. Although there were some arranged marriages, most *ali'i* were allowed to marry anyone of their choosing, as long as they were of *ali'i* rank. Otherwise, their mana (spiritual essence) would be lessened through marriage to a person from one of the lower classes.

The kahuna class comprised of individuals trained in specific skills, such as canoe building, temple construction, religious and ceremonial protocol, healing arts, warfare, astronomy, navigation and agriculture.

The third class of people in the social hierarchy was the *maka'ainana* (commoners), who lived independently on the land, but had major obligations to the *ali'i* who governed the district within which they lived. One of these obligations was to pay annual tributes, or taxes, to the chiefs. These tributes were mostly food, but could also be objects such woven mats, weapons, fishing spears and the like. The *maka'ainana* were also obligated to help build communal structures such as heiau (temples) and *lokoi'a* (fishponds), which required massive labor efforts. Some of Hawai'i's most impressive *lokoi'a* are strung along the eastern shore of Moloka'i (p412), while Mo'okini Heiau (p226) on the Big Island remains active today.

In times of warfare, the *maka'ainana* were required to fight. They are often compared to serfs in medieval European society, or slaves in other societies, but they were neither. The *maka'ainana* were free to travel from district to district and utilize any unused land for as long as they desired, as long as they cared for the land and its resources in a prudent manner. Chiefs often set regulations for land and ocean resources to ensure that they would not be depleted.

The lowest class were the *kauwa* (outcasts), who were looked down upon and generally did not mix with the other classes, except as slaves.

Religion

Religion in ancient Hawaiian civilization was the cornerstone of society. All individual, family and community activities were governed by strict religious laws and regulations, known commonly as the *kapu* (taboo, or prohibition) system, in order to assure peace and harmony. These laws governed what people ate, how they prayed, whom they married, what food they ate, and just about every other aspect of daily living.

The breaking of a *kapu* could result in banishment for a brief period for a minor infraction – such as stealing or eating a prohibited food – or death, if it was a major infraction, such as murder or temple desecration.

It was believed that religious laws were not determined by humans, but by the gods. Hawai'i was a polytheistic society, one that believed in many gods of many ranks. The four major gods were Ku, the god of war

Learn more about Polynesian migration and the settlement of Hawaii, as well as the famous contemporary voyaging canoe, *Hokule'a*, at http://leahi.kcc.hawaii.edu/org/pvs.

DID YOU KNOW?

In Hawaiian mythology, the taro plant is considered to be the older brother of man.

1778	1810
Captain James Cook, the first Westerner to 'discover' Hawai'i, lands	Kamehameha the Great completes the unification of the islands, becomes king

Explore the epic saga of *Holo Mai Pele*, as performed by *hula halau* Halau o Kekuhi, at www .pbs.org/holomaipele.

and male generating power; Kane, the god of fresh water, winds, sunlight, procreation and fertility; Kanaloa, the god of the ocean and ocean winds; and Lono, the god of peace, agriculture and fertility.

In addition to these major gods, there were dozens of demigods and deities who reigned over the natural and supernatural worlds. Among those who are still worshipped today are Pele, goddess of volcanoes (p275); Laka, goddess of the hula; and Hina, goddess of the moon. Most land features, such as valleys, beaches, mountains and rivers also still have their own protector gods.

Most of the deities had earthly counterparts *(kinolau)*, which could be animate or inanimate objects, such as rocks, animals, and trees; or other natural elements, such as wind and rain. Virtually all things in the earthly world were the *kinolau* of one of the many deities, therefore, all things were considered to have mana, to one degree or another.

Ancient Hawaiians also believed that when humans die, their spirits live on in the form of *'aumakua* (guardian spirits). These spirits also take on earthly forms such as sharks, owls, geckos, birds, fish and other animate and inanimate objects. *'Aumakua* were acknowledged for providing guidance and protection to living family members; in turn, the living had the responsibility to revere and protect these things on earth.

THE FOREIGN INVASION

In July of 1776, Captain James Cook of the British Navy set out on his third voyage to the Pacific in search of the elusive Northwest Passage, which reputedly ran from the northern Pacific across the North American continent to the Atlantic. Quite by accident, on January 18, 1778, Cook and his crews aboard the HMS *Resolution* and *Discovery* sighted the island of O'ahu, thus becoming the first Westerners to 'discover' the

THE HAWAIIAN CREATION CHANT

Kumulipo (The Source of Life), a 2102-line epic genealogy chant, was created in the 18th century in honor of the birth of high chief Lonoikamakahiki. It describes the creation of the earth and its life forms and reveals the connections of the earth and sky, the ocean and land, and humans to all these elements and to the gods. The chant was passed on orally through the generations until the late 1800s, when it was written down in Hawaiian for the first time, then translated into English.

The First Era

At the time that turned the heat of the earth,
At the time when the heavens turned and changed,
At the time when the light of the sun was subdued
To cause light to break forth,
At the time of the night Makali'i (Winter),
Then began the slime which established the earth,
The source of deepest darkness
Of the depth of darkness, of the depth of darkness,
Of the darkness of the sun, in the depth of the night,
It is night, so was the night born.

1819	1820
The ancient *kapu* system is abolished after the death of King Kamehameha I	First Christian missionaries arrive from Boston

islands. Cook promptly named the Hawaiian archipelago the Sandwich Islands in honor of his patron, the Earl of Sandwich. The story of Captain Cook's arrival in the islands at Waimea Bay (p504), and his subsequent death at Kealakekua Bay (p206), is a compelling one. After Cook's ships returned to Great Britain, news of his discovery quickly spread throughout Europe and America, opening the floodgates to a foreign invasion of other explorers, traders, adventurers, missionaries and fortune seekers.

Like their explorer counterparts, the American, British, French and Russian traders – who began arriving in the islands in the late 1800s – had different ideas about the value of the islands to themselves and their home countries. Hawai'i became a key factor in the development of the China trade route. These traders picked up furs in the Pacific Northwest and sandalwood (p416) in Hawai'i, then traded them in China for exotic spices, silk cloth and furniture, which commanded high prices in their home ports.

The whalers similarly found Hawai'i to be the perfect mid-ocean way station where they could transfer their catch to trade ships bound primarily for the eastern seaboard of America. Pausing in the islands allowed them to stay in the Pacific for longer periods of time without having to return home with their payload, resulting in greater catch and higher profits. By the 1840s Hawai'i had become the whaling capital of the Pacific, with hundreds of ships stopping in Hawaiian ports each year.

On April 19, 1820, the brig *Thaddeus* arrived from Boston at Kaliua Bay on the Big Island with the first group of Christian missionaries, comprised of 22 men, women and children sent by the American Board of Commissions for Foreign Missions, who spread the Congregational Church throughout the Americas and the Pacific. By a twist of fate, the missionaries arrived just 11 months after the death of King Kamehameha I (see p31), which had precipitated the overthrow of the traditional *kapu*.

Into this religious chaos came the missionaries, who were determined to save the natives from themselves. They prohibited the dancing of hula because of its 'lewd and suggestive' movements. They prohibited most of the traditional Hawaiian chants and songs that paid homage to the old gods. They taught the women to sew Western-style clothing so they could cover their mostly naked bodies. And they abolished polygamy, despite the fact that it was accepted, and necessary, in the isolated island group.

The missionaries were also zealous in their efforts to teach Hawaiians how to read and write. As the Hawaiians had no written language, the missionaries established one using the Roman alphabet, allowing them to translate the Bible. They also established as many schools as they did churches. The first of these churches was Kawaiaha'o Church in Honolulu (p92). Hawaiians took these lessons in great numbers, leading to a higher literacy rate than that on the US mainland. The first secondary school west of the Rocky Mountains, Lahainaluna (p305), was established in 1831. As Hawaiians became more proficient in reading and writing, they established over 100 Hawaiian-language newspapers. Despite this, the Hawaiian language nearly became extinct. When public schools were instituted in 1840, English became the standard language, as it did later in the government sector, leading to the slow decline of the Hawaiian language at home and in the community. This trend would not change until the 1970s (see p34).

Missionary Album (1820–1970), published by the Hawaiian Mission Children's Society in 1969, provides profiles and portraits of over a hundred American Protestant missionaries in Hawaii.

DID YOU KNOW?

In Captain Cook's day, one iron nail would trade for two grown pigs.

1831	1835
First secondary school established in Hawai'i	First sugar plantation, Koloa Plantation, is founded

Because missionaries became cozy with many of the chiefs, they were often given land and other resources. Many children of the pioneer missionaries married into Hawaiian families. Subsequently, many of these missionaries left the church to become highly influential merchants, plantation owners and government officials. Many say that the missionaries came to do good, and did very well.

Because of the economic stranglehold of King Sugar (see below), virtually all of the sugar planters became highly influential in the business community as well as in government circles. These influential 'sugar barons' made concerted efforts to bring the kingdom of Hawai'i into the political and economic sphere of the USA, which would of course greatly enhance their bottom line. In 1876 they successfully lobbied the USA to ratify a reciprocity treaty, which allowed sugar from Hawai'i to enter the USA duty-free. This not only increased the planter's economic power, but solidified their political influence as well. In 1893, a small group of sugar barons desperate for US annexation successfully overthrew the Hawaiian government by deposing Queen Lili'uokalani (see p33), ending the independent Kingdom of Hawai'i.

By this time Hawai'i's native population was in severe decline, as the result of the introduction of deadly diseases such as smallpox, influenza and syphilis by foreigners, for which the Hawaiians had no natural immunity. It is estimated that when Captain Cook arrived, there were approximately 500,000 Hawaiians in the islands. By 1820 when the missionaries arrived, this number had dropped to 100,000; that number was less than 50,000 in 1875.

Sugar barons and government officials alike worried about the shortage of Hawaiian labor. Minister of Foreign Affairs Robert C Wyllie lamented, 'Unless we get more population, we are a doomed nation.' To expand their operations, plantation owners, with the help of the government, began to look overseas for a labor supply. In 1850 the Act for the Government of Masters and Servants was passed, which included rules and regulations for the importation and treatment of foreign labor.

Shortly thereafter, plantation owners began recruiting laborers from China. In 1868 recruiters went to Japan, and in the 1870s, they brought in Portuguese workers from Madeira and the Azores Islands. However, by the 1880s, the Chinese population had grown so much that plantation owners, who were almost exclusively haole (Caucasians), began to fear Chinese

DID YOU KNOW?

One of the Hawaiian words for leprosy is *mai ho'oka'awale* (the separating sickness), called such because individuals with the disease were taken from their families starting in 1865 and sent into exile for the remainder of their lives.

KING SUGAR

Ko (sugarcane) arrived in Hawai'i with the early Polynesian settlers. While Hawaiians enjoyed chewing the cane for its juices, they never refined it into sugar. The first known attempt to produce sugar in Hawai'i was in 1802, when a Chinese immigrant on the island of Lana'i boiled crushed sugarcane in iron pots. Other Chinese soon set up small sugar mills on the scale of neighborhood bakeries. In 1835, a young Bostonian, William Hooper, founded Hawai'i's first sugar plantation, Koloa Plantation (p489), on the island of Kaua'i, which operated for 113 years. By 1850, the number of plantations had grown to seven, and the industry was beginning to take off. Less than four decades later, there were 80 plantations in the islands and 'King Sugar' was the backbone of the Hawaiian economy.

1840	1855
First constitution is promulgated, creating a constitutional monarchy	First contract laborers arrive from China

domination and power in the labor force. In 1882 the Chinese Exclusion Act limited the number of Chinese immigrants to the islands. After Hawai'i's 1898 annexation to the USA, the contract-labor system was abolished. Plantation owners then turned their recruiting efforts to Puerto Rico and Korea. In the early 20th century, Filipinos were the last group of immigrants brought to Hawai'i to work in the fields and mills. A number of Pacific Islanders, Scots, Scandinavians, Germans, Galicians, Spaniards and Russians came as well.

Most of the labor contracts typically lasted for two to three years, with wages as low as $1 per week, plus housing. Workers usually lived in ethnically divided 'camps' set up by the plantations that included modest housing, a company store, a social hall and other recreational amenities. These camps provided a strong social-support network for the workers. At the end of their contracts, some returned to their homelands, but most remained in the islands, integrating into the multicultural mainstream.

MONARCHY ERA

Before the time of Kamehameha the Great, the Hawaiian Islands were divided into independent chiefdoms. This all changed in 1790, when Kamehameha, the high chief of the Big Island (p175), began his campaign to conquer and unite all of the islands under one rule. Through a combination of warfare and diplomacy, Kamehameha accomplished his goal in 1810. He ruled as *mo'i* (king) of all the islands until his death in 1819.

Under his rule, the government structure consisted of himself, as supreme ruler, and a council of chiefs, who gave him advice but did not have any direct power. His leadership abilities and dedication to peaceful coexistence among the former warring chiefs led to a time of abundance and stability throughout the kingdom, although he was beset with a myriad of influences and changes brought in by the foreigners who were arriving in droves (see p28), seeking a foothold in a place that was considered by most to be 'paradise on earth.'

Following the death of Kamehameha I, his 23-year-old son Liholiho became Kamehameha II. However, because of inexperience, he shared rule with Ka'ahumanu, the favorite wife of Kamehameha I, who was named *kuhina nui* (regent). Liholiho's short reign of four years was marked by the overthrow of the *kapu* system, primarily at the instigation of Ka'ahumanu, who had embraced the tenets of Christianity espoused by the missionaries. Ka'ahumanu and Liholiho intentionally ate a meal together, although it was *kapu* for men and women to do so. This event was made public to show the people that the *kapu* laws were no longer valid.

Tragically, this young king died at the age of 27 while on a diplomatic mission to England in 1824, where he and some of his entourage, including his wife Kamamalu, were stricken with the measles. Liholiho's younger brother Kauikeaouli ascended to the throne, at the age of nine, as King Kamehameha III. Like Liholiho, he was named coruler with Ka'ahumanu, but unlike his brother, Kauikeaouli reigned for 30 years.

During Kauikeaouli's long rule, many landmark political events occurred. In 1840 Hawai'i's first constitution, primarily based on the American model, was instituted. The Council of Chiefs was replaced with the House of Nobles (Hawaiians of chiefly descent) and a Cabinet of

Hawaii, The Royal Legacy (1992), written and photographed by Allan Seiden, covers the life and times of Hawai'i's ruling monarchs. More than just short profiles, but less than official biographies, the book also contains good photos and illustrations.

1866	1876
First leprosy victims are sent into exile on Moloka'i	Hawai'i's 'sugar barons' successfully lobby the USA to allow sugar from Hawai'i to enter the USA duty-free

Ministers, primarily foreigners experienced in Western-style government structure and policies. Just as this new structure gave power to foreign residents, who were hungry for land and a greater voice in government, it also lessened the power of the king.

In 1848 the Great Mahele allowed, for the first time, the fee simple ownership of land. This would have far-reaching implications for both Westerners and Hawaiians. For foreigners who had money to buy land, this meant greater political power. For Hawaiians, who had little or no money, this meant a loss of land-based self-sufficiency and forced entry into the low-wages labor market primarily run by Westerners.

Next to ascend the throne was Prince Alexander Liholiho (King Kamehameha IV), the grandson of King Kamehameha I. He is noted, along with his wife Emma, for raising the funds to build Queen's Hospital, Hawai'i's first public medical institution, and for helping to establish the Anglican Church in the islands. In 1862, the royal household suffered a tragic blow when Liholiho and Emma's four-year-old son (and heir to the throne) died after a brief, undetermined illness. Liholiho himself died the following year at the age of 29. He was followed by his older brother Prince Lot (Kamehameha V), who ruled for nine years until his death at the age of 42.

As Lot grew to manhood, he saw the decline, in health and in power, of his native people, and worked hard to balance the scales, fearing that the Hawaiians would become second-class citizens in their own homeland. In 1864, he promulgated a new constitution, which was intended to restore some of the power that had been relinquished under the 1852 constitution. His new constitution abolished the position of *kuhina nui* and consolidated the legislative branch to include hereditary *ali'i*, those elected to represent the commoners and also resident foreigners. As sugar replaced whaling as the economic engine of the islands, Lot was in constant conflict with sugar planters and others over the sovereignty of the kingdom and the power of the crown.

When Lot – who was the last of the Kamehameha dynasty in lineage – died in 1872, leaving no heir or successor, for the first time the office was open for public election. However, only Hawaiians of high rank were eligible to run for office. William Charles Lunalilo won a decided victory over his opponent, David Kalakaua. Lunalilo's reign was marked by heated debates and controversy over the proposal to cede Pearl Harbor to the USA in return for a reciprocity treaty (see p30) that would allow sugar from Hawai'i to enter the USA mainland duty-free. Many royalists condemned Lunalilo for supporting this proposal, and the conflict exacerbated his already-poor health.

When Lunalilo died in 1874, after a rule of only one year, David Kalakaua was elected to office after a heated campaign against Queen Emma, the widow of King Kamehameha IV. In 1876, under Kalakaua's rule, a reciprocity treaty was signed, but without Pearl Harbor being ceded. In 1887, Kalakaua was forced by his political opponents to sign a new constitution that stripped the crown of many of its remaining powers. This so-called 'Bayonet Constitution' led to a brief, but unsuccessful, rebellion led by Hawaiian pro-monarchy activist Robert Wilcox, a young, educated Hawaiian *ali'i* who was vehemently opposed to annexation.

1893	1894
Queen Lili'uokalani is deposed, provisional government is declared	Hawai'i declared a republic

Kalakaua, who was nicknamed the 'Merrie Monarch,' was instrumental in reviving the open practice of traditional Hawaiian cultural activities, such as hula, that had been prohibited by the missionaries (see p29). He was also responsible for the building of 'Iolani Palace, which replaced the original, small wooden palace. When King Kalakaua died in California in 1891, his younger sister Lili'uokalani, who was designated heir apparent, ascended the throne.

ANNEXATION & STATEHOOD

Queen Lili'uokalani, who was determined to restore the power of the crown that had been lost by her brother, planned to proclaim a new constitution that would strengthen the monarchy. However, this plan was usurped in 1893 when a small group of resident foreigners, primarily led by Americans, and supported by a unit of visiting US marines, stormed 'Iolani Palace and demanded that the queen step down.

Because the Kingdom of Hawai'i had no standing army and the queen wanted to avoid bloodshed, she abdicated under protest. After the coup, a provisional government was declared, thus ending 83 years of the Hawaiian monarchy. In 1894, the Republic of Hawai'i was established and almost immediately envoys were sent to Washington to seek annexation, which sugar planters and others had been advocating for some years.

In 1895, while annexation was debated in Washington, a group of Hawaiian royalists attempted a counterrevolution, which was easily squashed. The deposed queen was accused of being a conspirator and sentenced to five years of hard labor, later reduced to nine months under house arrest at 'Iolani Palace and a $5000 fine. After serving her term, Lili'uokalani lived out her days at her husband's family home, Washington Place (p89). Although she continued to lobby for the restoration of the monarchy, her efforts were in vain. She died in 1917, 14 years after her overthrow, a tragic, but heroic, figure to the Hawaiian people and other supporters.

In 1887, as a protest of the overthrow and the petition for annexation, more than 21,000 people – almost half of the population of Hawai'i at that time – signed an anti-annexation petition that was sent to Washington. Despite this overwhelming show of support for home rule, President William McKinley signed a joint congressional resolution approving the annexation of the five-year-old Republic of Hawai'i on July 7, 1898.

Although annexation had been sought by factions of resident foreigners since the 1870s, it was not until April 1898, when the USA declared war on Spain to redress the Spanish occupation of Cuba and the Philippines, that Hawaii (in particular, Pearl Harbor) become a strategic military focal point in the Pacific. With the tide of 'Manifest Destiny' still in motion, the USA easily rationalized its colonial presence in the Pacific Rim and Asia. However, even with annexation a fait accompli, the next logical push, for statehood, would be a long and arduous one.

Between 1900, when Hawaii formally became a territory, and 1959, when Hawaii was finally declared a state, numerous statehood bills were introduced in Congress, only to be shot down. One of the primary reasons for this lack of support was racial prejudice against Hawaii's multicultural population. Many congressional delegates, particularly in the South, feared that statehood would open the doors to Asian immigration

Nation Within: The Story of America's Annexation of the Nation of Hawaii (2003), by Tom Coffman, provides compelling historic details about the overthrow of the Hawaiian monarchy, annexation and the drive for statehood.

Photos enhance this feature story published by the *Honolulu Star-Bulletin* about Hawaii's long road to statehood – http://star bulletin.com/1999/10/18 /special/story4.html.

1898	1900
Hawai'i annexed to the USA	Hawai'i becomes a US territory

to the mainland, where US citizens were being inundated with threatening media reports about the 'Yellow Peril.'

In the 1920s and '30s, two nationally publicized murder cases involving local residents of Hawaiian and Asian descent and haole individuals – the Jamieson case of 1928 and the Massie case of 1931 – led US lawmakers to conclude (unjustly) that Hawaii was a 'lawless outpost' where the nonwhite population could not be controlled. Hawaii's growing labor unions were also a cause for concern. Several worker riots had taken place during the early 1900s, and Congress feared that these unions, which were considered to be Communist-controlled, would be a threat to US businesses interested in expanding their enterprises in the Pacific and Asian markets.

In 1936, Pan American flew the first passenger flights from the US mainland to Hawaii, an aviation milestone that ushered in the transpacific air age and mass tourism. But it was not until after the Korean War ended in 1953 that the USA began to take Hawaii seriously as a contender for statehood. The strategic role of Pearl Harbor during WWII and the Korean War was a main reason for this change of attitude. Hawaii was finally admitted to the union, as its 50th state, on August 21, 1959.

DID YOU KNOW?

After the overthrow of the monarchy in 1893, 'Iolani Palace, the royal residence, was significantly altered to accommodate government offices. In the 1980s, it took more than 10 years and millions of dollars to restore it to its former glory.

HAWAIIAN RENAISSANCE

In the early 1970s, Hawaii began to experience a resurgence of Hawaiian cultural pride and ethnic identity, not seen since the reign of King Kalakaua (see p33) in the 1880s. It is difficult to pinpoint one event or

HAWAIIAN HOME LANDS

In 1920, under the sponsorship of Prince Jonah Kuhio Kalaniana'ole, the Territory of Hawaii's congressional delegate, the US Congress passed the Hawaiian Homes Commission Act. The act set aside almost 200,000 acres of land for homesteading by native Hawaiians. Despite this apparently generous gift, the land was but a small fraction of the crown lands that were taken from the Kingdom of Hawai'i when the USA annexed the islands in 1898.

Under the legislation, people of at least 50% Hawaiian ancestry were eligible for 99-year leases at $1 a year. Originally, most of the leases were for 40-acre parcels of agricultural land, although more recently residential lots as small as a quarter of an acre have been allocated under the plan. Hawaii's prime land, already in the hands of the sugar barons, was excluded from the act. Much of what was designated for homesteading was on far more barren turf.

Still, many Hawaiians were able to make a go of it. Presently, there are about 6500 native Hawaiian families living on about 30,000 acres of homestead lands. As with many projects intended to help native Hawaiians, administration of the Hawaiian Home Lands has been controversial. The majority of the land has not been allocated to native Hawaiians but has been leased out to big business, ostensibly as a means of creating an income for the administration of the program, but in reality, most of these revenues go into the state general fund. In addition, the federal, state and county governments have, with little or no compensation, taken large tracts of Hawaiian Home Lands for their own use.

In recent years, many Hawaiian organizations have participated in protest marches, sit-ins and legislative initiatives to correct these injustices. In 2003, after years of lobbying, state senate Bill 476 was enacted, mandating the state to pay the office of Hawaiian affairs an amount equivalent to the pro rata share of ceded land lease revenues obtained from the Honolulu International Airport. Revenues from other homestead lands being leased out are still in dispute.

1941	1959
Japanese forces attack Pearl Harbor and other military sites on O'ahu	Hawaii becomes the 50th state of the USA

activity that caused this resurgence, but the building of the long-distance voyaging canoe, *Hokule'a*, was certainly a catalyst. This project (see p26) required the learning of ancient navigational skills and sailing techniques that had been nearly forgotten. Simultaneously, a small group of people on the island of Moloka'i, the Protect Kaho'olawe 'Ohana (PKO), began to protest the US Navy's bombing practice on the nonpopulated island of Kaho'olawe (p382). This group rapidly gained support, and became a focal point of political awareness and activism.

Eddie Would Go (2002), by Stuart Holmes Coleman, is a biography of notable professional surfer and lifeguard Eddie Aikau, including his tragic death. It describes the Hawaiian renaissance of the 1960s and '70s from a personal perspective.

Greater interest in the hula also began to be seen in the 1970s, especially among young men. New *hula halau* (hula schools) began to open, many of which revived interest in ancient hula techniques and dances that had been subjugated in favor of more modern, Western-style hula dances. The Merrie Monarch Festival (p259), which was founded in 1971, has become the Olympics of hula, and has an international following. Today, there are many such hula festivals on all of the islands, featuring dozens of *hula halau* and thousands of dancers. In 2001, the stage production of *Holo Mai Pele*, the epic tale of the rivalry between Pele (the goddess of fire) and her sister Hi'iaka, performed by the famed *hula halau*, Halau o Kekuhi, was broadcast nationwide on PBS.

Revival of the Hawaiian language has also been a focal point of the Hawaiian renaissance. By the 1970s, the pool of native Hawaiian speakers had dropped to under 1000 individuals statewide. In an effort to reverse this trend, Hawaiian language immersion schools began to emerge. The

MARTIAL LAW DECLARED!

The surprise bombing of Pearl Harbor and other military installations on the island of O'ahu on December 7, 1941, will forever be remembered as the 'Day of Infamy' in American history. On that quiet Sunday morning, 354 Japanese aircraft, launched from six aircraft carriers stationed 230 miles north of O'ahu, invaded peaceful Hawaii. More than 2000 US military personnel were killed. Tragically, almost 70 civilians also died, by either enemy fire or inadvertent friendly fire. This sudden and devastating attack propelled the USA into the Pacific theater of WWII against Japan and changed the course of history.

Unlike the US mainland, Hawaii was placed under marshall law and actions 'vital to national security' were initiated. Nightly blackouts and gas rationing were strictly enforced. Mail was censored. All residents, adults and children alike, were issued gas masks. 'Victory Gardens' were established to make up for the shortfall of food supplies, and many of the beaches were lined with barbed wire to prevent Japanese troop landings via submarines.

About 300 to 400 Japanese residents in Hawaii were arrested as enemy sympathizers and sent to mainland internment camps, some for the duration of the war. Although the Japanese community, many of whom were born and raised in the islands and were loyal US supporters, protested this action vehemently, their protests fell on deaf ears. Many of these families not only suffered the indignity of incarceration, but had their personal property (land, homes, businesses and boats) confiscated as well.

The enlistment of hundreds of men of Japanese ancestry into the US armed forces, and national recognition of the all-Japanese 442nd Regimental Combat Team and the 100th Infantry Battalion (both of which were mostly made up of soldiers from Hawaii) during the war, went a long way toward changing mainstream America's attitude toward the resident Japanese population, both in Hawaii and on the mainland.

1971	1976
Inaugural Merrie Monarch Festival is held, which is to become the 'Olympics' of hula	The voyaging canoe *Hokule'a* makes a historic trip to Tahiti

University of Hawai'i began offering Hawaiian language classes for the first time in the 1970s. In 2003 the school graduated its first student with a master's degree in Hawaiian language studies.

Contemporary music has also been affected by the ongoing Hawaiian renaissance. There is interest in preserving old songs, particularly pro-test songs, as well as new compositions. Many people have also become interested in relearning nearly lost arts, such as the making of *kapa* (bark cloth), drums, gourds, feather lei, fish hooks, wooden bowls and many other items. Many people feel that if this renaissance had not occurred, Hawaiian language and culture would be nearly extinct by now.

There has also been a resurgence of interest in genealogy, and in tradi-tional ancestral connections. Hui Malama I Na Kupuna 'O Hawai'i Nei, literally 'a group caring for the ancestors of Hawai'i,' helped enact the Native American Grave Repatriation Act of 1990, which allows claims for repatriation of designated human remains and artifacts from museums and other public repositories around the world. Islandwide burial coun-cils now oversee the disposition of human remains found inadvertently during construction projects or land erosion.

Beginning in the early 1990s, the topic of Hawaiian sovereignty (or self-determination) has become a highly debated and controversial issue, not only for Hawaiians, but the general community as well. It has been a hot topic of media coverage, local meetings and household discussions. Many groups have formed, and they all have differing ideas about what model of sovereignty, if any, should be adopted.

The Culture

While Hawaii boasts year-round sunshine, sandy beaches and tropical fruits galore, calling it 'paradise' is an oversimplification. Beyond the undeniable natural beauty of the islands, it's the distinct 'local' culture that makes Hawaii unique.

REGIONAL IDENTITY

At first glance, being 'local' in Hawaii means talking pidgin and wearing a T-shirt and *rubbah slippah*. But underneath it's a mindset that comes from living 2500 miles from the nearest continent, in communities where everyone knows everyone. Here, family background and connections are important – not to be snooty, but to find common bonds. Especially on the Neighbor Islands (ie any of the main islands other than O'ahu), it's no surprise for locals to run into long-ago schoolmates at the supermarket. People cannot be anonymous, but most prefer blending into the crowd rather than standing out.

Locals tend to be easygoing and low-key. Most avoid embarrassing confrontations and prefer to 'save face' by keeping quiet. Public conversations, both among friends and strangers, are typically kept to casual topics; if you hear an intense discussion on international politics, Greek philosophy or sex and relationships, it's likely the speakers are mainland transplants or tourists. That said, locals do have opinions – they just don't broadcast them. Politically, Hawaii is a middle-of-the-road Democratic state; voters and legislators generally support progressive causes, but they've so far nixed legalized gambling, physician-assisted suicide and same-sex marriage.

Those with little in common will nevertheless band together to support fellow locals. If an athlete or musician from Hawaii becomes a national celebrity, everyone rejoices over the coup. During the 2004 season of the Fox network's *American Idol*, thousands of Hawaii fans went wild and catapulted O'ahu native Jasmine Trias to the top three.

Though adored by visitors, Hawaii sometimes struggles to be taken seriously – which can exasperate locals. The stereotype of easygoing (if not lazy) islanders whiling away their days at the beach is a Hollywood concept. Daily life includes careers in high-rises, long hours at the office, shopping trips to Wal-Mart and Costco, killing time in traffic jams, poverty and homelessness and, yes, wearing long pants and leather shoes.

Indeed, Hawaii people are drawn to mainstream American culture and follow national trends. Kids watch the same TV and listen to the same music – and they emulate hip-hop stars, to the chagrin of those who see local culture getting diluted. The highly educated and upper-income classes also might fall outside the usual definition of 'local-ness,' as they speak no pidgin and aspire to the same Ivy League dreams as their mainland counterparts.

Underlying local consciousness are long-standing native Hawaiian issues. The 1970s Hawaiian cultural renaissance (p34) initiated changes hailed by all locals. In 1978, the state re-established Hawaiian as an official language, and the US government stopped bombing Kaho'olawe (p382). But there is no cohesive political group and no consensus regarding larger sovereignty issues (p36). In the islands, only native Hawaiians are called 'Hawaiian,' to recognize the existence of the indigenous people. Hawaiian identity and local identity are related, but be careful not to confuse the two.

Translate your name into Hawaiian at www .alohafriends.com/names .html.

DID YOU KNOW?

In 1874 King David Kalakaua wrote 'Hawai'i Pono'i,' which in 1967 became Hawaii's state song (and the only state song not in English).

LIFESTYLE

Hawaii has a carefree, party-time image, but most locals steer clear of Waikiki nightlife. Family is the predominant force. The 'ohana (family) is central to islanders' interactions with each other and with outsiders. Weekends are generally reserved for family – you'll often see locals gathered together for all-day picnics and cookouts. You need not be related by blood or marriage to be considered 'ohana, and lots of 'uncles' and 'aunties' are not relatives at all. While locals are friendly and approachable, however, those looking to hook up with an island girl or guy might find it hard to penetrate their tight social circles.

The workday starts and ends early, and most find a comfortable work-home balance. It's not surprising to see professionals running or surfing before hitting the office. Childcare is shared with grandparents and relatives, typically eager babysitters. Honolulu is a relatively fast-paced city, but towns on the Neighbor Islands remain relaxed. Throughout the state, the business 'uniform' for men is a cotton Reyn Spooner aloha shirt with dark slacks. (Believe it or not, Honolulu lawyers and businessmen always wear their aloha shirts tucked in, while the untucked style is favored by retirees, blue-collars and the with-it young crowd.) For women, the muumuu has been passé since the 1980s, unless worn by Hawaiian *tutu* (grandmothers) or hula teachers.

DID YOU KNOW?

Captain Cook wrote Hawaii as Owy-hee, Maui as Mowee, O'ahu as O-ahoo, Kaua'i as Atowai and Ni'ihau as Neehau.

Much of what's considered local lifestyle are working-class customs lingering from plantation days. Today, socioeconomic class determines whether a Hawaii person follows the typical pattern (which parallels the mainstream 'American dream') or adopts more-cosmopolitan mores. The less educated usually marry early and stick to traditional male and female domestic roles (it's still odd for a wife not to take her husband's surname). But those who study or travel outside the islands are less likely to fit the mold. For the story of the Hawaiian Home Lands, see p34.

Politically and socially, the state of Hawaii today displays many contradictions. While Hawaii is predominantly Democratic, voters in 2002 elected a Republican governor, Linda Lingle (also the state's first female or Jewish governor). On the whole, sexual orientation is a nonissue, following traditional Hawaiians' acceptance of homosexuality. But many gays and lesbians remain closeted and there are pockets of extreme conservatives in the islands, especially in rural areas. On Maui, local elders pushed

GOT LUCKY?

When locals go on vacation, they go to…Las Vegas. Perhaps blasé about tropical scenery, a surprising number enjoy the man-made glitz, theme-park casinos, nearby golf courses, all-you-can-eat buffets and chance to win big (gambling is illegal only in two states: Hawaii and Utah).

Mostly, however, Hawaii people go to Vegas to hang out with other locals. On any given trip, locals are bound to spot folks they recognize from home. While the Vegas habit crosses ethnic and age lines, seniors are particularly frequent returnees.

The Honolulu–Vegas circuit has become a well-oiled machine, and companies such as Sam Boyd's Vacations-Hawaii offer discounted packages that keep locals coming back – often multiple times a year. Most stay downtown at the California Hotel, rather than at the upscale resorts on the Strip.

Over the years, Hawaii has considered ending its gambling ban, but opposition abounds from a bipartisan coalition of politicians, religious groups and the general public. Despite the state's financial woes and the local penchant for playing the slots, island gambling remains taboo.

A sizable community of Hawaii expatriates lives in Vegas, largely due to the low cost of living. But most locals shake their heads in disbelief. Vegas is fun but there's no place like Hawaii.

to abolish the 'clothing optional' status of the predominantly gay Little Beach and their actions were deemed an attempt to shut down the only well-known meeting place for gay people on the island. In 1998, Hawaii made national headlines when a whopping 70% of Hawaii voters passed a measure granting the legislature, not the courts, the power to define marriage – essentially advocating the prohibition on same-sex marriage.

The Aloha Shirt: Spirit of the Islands, by Dale Hope and Gregory Tozian, is a gloriously illustrated picture book that reveals the rich history behind this modern Hawaii icon.

Pakalolo (marijuana) remains a billion-dollar underground industry (and Hawaii's most profitable crop) and the use of 'ice' (crystal methamphetamine) has become rampant since the 1990s, especially in rural communities. Some attribute the ice epidemic to dropping prices for the drug and crackdowns on marijuana cultivation. Whatever the cause, ice-related crime is rising and social-service agencies are struggling to provide treatment for addicts.

POPULATION

Hawaii's population of 1.2 million is heavily concentrated on O'ahu, and Honolulu remains the state's only 'city.' Comparing the population density of the islands paints a clear picture: roughly 1470 people per sq mile on O'ahu; 162 on Maui; 106 on Kaua'i; and 37 on the Big Island. The density on Lana'i and Moloka'i is lower still.

For the first time in 2000, respondents could select more than one race for the US census. The new 'mixed-race' category made a huge difference in Hawaii, where the multiracial population is 24% (compared to only 2.4% nationwide). Most of the mixed-race people in Hawaii have Asian (mainly Chinese) and Hawaiian ancestry, or that combination plus Caucasian.

The number of native Hawaiians has dropped steadily ever since Captain Cook's arrival, and today roughly 80,000 (5%) of Hawaii's people identify themselves as native Hawaiian. This figure is misleading, however, and experts estimate the number of pure native Hawaiians to be under 5000, less than half of 1% of the population.

The haole (Caucasians) comprise the largest ethnic group, averaging 22% of the population in the islands, but their numbers are higher on Maui and the Big Island, where the influx of mainlanders, many from the West Coast, is booming. The Japanese are the second-largest ethnic group in the state with 16%, closely followed by the Filipinos at 14%. The Chinese comprise only 3% of the population overall, and the vast majority lives in Honolulu County.

The latest wave of newcomers to Hawaii is wealthy mainland transplants – 'gentleman farmers' and second-home millionaires – who are scooping up prime real estate throughout the islands, thus driving prices beyond the reach of most locals. Another trend is the 'graying' of the state population, due to an influx of retirees over 65. From 1990 to 2000, Honolulu's over-65 population increased by 53%, while its under-35 population decreased by 7%.

MULTICULTURALISM

It's a common misconception that Hawaii is a 'melting pot' of races and ethnicities. Certainly the island population is diverse, with no ethnic majority, and locals are generally tolerant of differences. But lines do exist. The old plantation stereotypes and hierarchies continue to influence social interaction in Hawaii. Caucasians have historically held the most power, but early immigrant groups, particularly the Chinese and Japanese, have proven upwardly mobile. Later immigrants, including Filipinos, Southeast Asians and other Polynesians, have had less time to advance and often hold low-level service jobs.

Among themselves, locals good-naturedly joke about what are admittedly island stereotypes: Portuguese talk too much, Chinese are tight with money, Japanese are uptight do-gooders, haole act like know-it-alls, Hawaiians are huge and lazy, Filipinos eat dog and so forth. Hawaii's much-loved comedians of the 1970s and 1980s – Andy Bumatai, Frank DeLima and Rap Reiplinger – used such stereotypes to comic effect appreciated by all. Locals seem slightly perplexed at the emphasis on 'political correctness' on the mainland. Schoolchildren might stick together by race or ethnicity, especially Japanese and haole kids. But half of all marriages in Hawaii are mixed race.

Interestingly, while locals recognize the different Asian ethnicities, they lump all whites into one group: haole. If someone calls you haole, don't worry. There's usually no negative subtext. But depending on the tone of voice (and any accompanying adjectives), it can be an insult or a threat. Generally, prejudice against haole depends on personal factors, such as whether they are local or longtime residents and, above all, whether they respect island ways.

RELIGION

In ancient Hawai'i, religion permeated daily life, determining one's livelihood, marriage and diet. Religion was intertwined with government, and chiefs ruled based on God-given rights. Almost all the ancient historical sites – pu'uhonua (place of refuge), heiau (place of worship), petroglyphs – are religious sites, chosen for the mana of the land. Some sites have little or no man-made adornment, such as Halema'uma'u Crater (p276) on the Big Island, where traditionalists perform rituals and leave offerings.

To hear pidgin spoken by fo' real kine locals, go to www.extreme-hawaii .com/pidgin.

When King Liholiho broke the kapu (taboo) by dining with Queen Ka'ahumanu yet suffered no divine punishment, many Hawaiians rejected the entire tradition and were willing converts to Christianity (see p32). But others took the Hawaiian religion underground. While the traditional beliefs never regained their former command, the philosophy endured, often expressed as aloha 'aina (reverence for the land's sanctity).

DID I CATCH THE WRONG PLANE?

Some visitors to Hawaii are surprised at the number of Japanese residents. While not the majority, they often appear to be as they number 200,000 (or nearly 300,000 counting mixed Japanese). The Japanese first arrived in Hawaii in the mid-1880s, and by 1900 there were over 60,000 Japanese residents in Hawaii.

The first generation of immigrants, the issei, remained loyal to Japan, but their children, the nisei, wanted full recognition as Americans. After the bombing of Pearl Harbor during WWII, Hawaii was placed under martial law for the duration of the war. With suspicion surrounding all Japanese in the USA, they were not accepted as soldiers. But eventually the government called for combat volunteers and over 10,000 came forth. Americans of Japanese Ancestry (AJAs) from Hawaii and the mainland formed the 100th Infantry Battalion and the 442nd Regimental Combat Team, the most decorated unit in US military history.

Back in the USA, AJAs earned college degrees through the GI bill and got hired by the 'Big Five' corporations, thus escaping the yoke of plantation work. Politics was the next step and upon Hawaii's statehood in 1959, Senator Daniel Inouye, who served in WWII and lost an arm, was elected as Hawaii's first US congressman, becoming the first Japanese American in Congress. Elected to the US senate in 1962, Inouye has served seven consecutive terms to date. Another notable AJA from Hawaii is General Eric Shinseki, who served as US army chief of staff from 1999 to 2003, when he was 'retired' by the Bush administration after he testified to Congress that the 2003 Iraq War would require more troops than the administration predicted.

In part, the Hawaiian sovereignty movement is rooted in *aloha 'aina*, to reclaim the land regarded as abused by outsiders.

Today the term kahuna (Hawaiian priest, physician or sage) is often misused by nonlocals as a catchword for any hotshot, hence the 'big kahuna' moniker. But true kahuna are few in number and must possess a deep knowledge of Hawaiian culture. *Kahuna nui* (high priests) must be chosen by their teacher, be properly trained and often belong to an official bloodline to gain the title (see p226).

Today, most Hawaii people remain devoted Christians. While the majority of locals do not claim adherence to a particular faith, religion plays a strong role in Hawaii. Undoubtedly the largest group in Hawaii is Roman Catholic, with roughly 240,000 adherents, a large percentage of whom are Filipino immigrants. The next largest group is the Church of Jesus Christ of Latter-Day Saints, with around 43,000 adherents, including many converts from the South Pacific. As for Protestant Christianity, the mainstream, less conservative groups – including the United Church of Christ, which arrived with the early missionaries – are struggling with declining membership. Conversely, nondenominational and often-fundamentalist evangelical churches are burgeoning. Buddhists number an estimated 100,000 in Hawaii, the highest statewide percentage of Buddhists in the USA, but the number of younger adherents is dwindling.

Different religious groups overlap: Christian sermons often include both Hawaiian and English words and public ceremonies, such as ground breaking, include a kahuna to bless the land. Occasionally a religious festival will cross over to become a community event, such as the Japanese Buddhist Obon summer season to honor the deceased. In Hawaii the Obon season spans weeks and, while only a few attend the temple services, people of all faiths join in the festive communal dances.

ARTS
Music
Integral to Hawaiian music is the guitar, first introduced by Spanish cowboys in the 1830s. In 1885 Joseph Kekuku, a native Hawaiian, began to evolve the steel guitar, one of only two major musical instruments invented in what is now the USA. (The other is the banjo.) Hawaiian steel guitar of the 1880s used a Spanish guitar with raised strings, slack-key tunings and anything from a knife to a comb to, eventually, a steel bar to stop the strings. For the slack-key method (*ki ho'alu*, which means 'loosen the key'), the six strings are slacked from their standard tuning to facilitate a full sound on a single guitar – the thumb plays the bass and rhythm chords, while the fingers play the melody and improvisations, in a picked style. Hawaiian slack-key is little documented because of its folkloric origins. Traditionally, slack-key tunings were closely guarded family secrets.

The most influential slack-key artist was Gabby Pahinui (1921–80), who launched the modern slack-key era with his first recording in 1946. Over the years, he played with the legendary Sons of Hawaii and later formed the Gabby Pahinui Hawaiian Band with four of his sons; his home in Waimanalo on O'ahu was a mecca for backyard jam sessions. Other pioneering slack-key masters were Sonny Chillingworth, Leonard Kwan and Atta Isaacs. Today the tradition lives on in Dennis Kamakahi, Keola Beamer, Led Ka'apana and Cyril Pahinui, among others.

The instrument most commonly associated with Hawaii is the ukulele, though it's derived from the *braguinha*, a Portuguese instrument introduced to Hawaii in the late 19th century. Ukulele means 'jumping flea' in Hawaiian, referring to the way players' deft fingers would swiftly 'jump'

DID YOU KNOW?

If you spot a Union Jack lookalike in the Hawaii state flag, you're right. It symbolizes the friendship between the British and King Kamehameha I, who commissioned the flag in 1816.

For an overview of Hawaiian slack-key music and artists, click to www .dancingcat.com.

around the strings. Hawaii's ukulele masters include Eddie Kamae, Herb Ohta and Jake Shimabukuro.

Over the years, Hawaiian music has progressed from the lighthearted, novelty music of the 1930s to '50s, such as 'Lovely Hula Hands' and 'Sweet Leilani,' to a more sophisticated sound. In the 1970s, Hawaiian music enjoyed a rebirth, and artists such as the Sunday Manoa, Cecilio & Kapono and the Beamer Brothers remain icons in Hawaii. Over the years the Hawaiian sound has spurred offshoots like reggae-inspired 'Jawaiian,' but the traditional style lives on in gifted contemporary voices, such as award-winning Keali'i Reichel, also a hula master, and Kainani Kahaunaele, a Hawaiian-language instructor considered one of Hawaii's rising stars. Perhaps the most famous island musician is the late Israel Kamakawiwo'ole, whose *Facing Future* is Hawaii's all-time bestselling album. 'Bruddah Iz' died in 1997 at age 38, due to morbid obesity, but he remains a driving force in putting Hawaiian music on the map. The genre is now breaking out of the niche market, with online sales mounting and a new Grammy Award for Best Hawaiian Music Album established in 2005.

www.store.mountain applecompany.com is a one-stop shop for classic and contemporary Hawaiian music.

Hula

In ancient Hawaii, hula was not entertainment, but religious expression. Dancers used hand gestures, facial expression and rhythmic movement to illustrate historical events and legendary tales and to venerate the gods. They wore *kapa* (bark cloth), never the stereotypical grass skirts. When the Christian missionaries arrived, they viewed hula dancing as too licentious and suppressed it. The hula might have been lost forever if King Kalakaua, the 'Merrie Monarch' (see p33), had not revived it in the late 1800s.

Today's commercial hula shows, which emphasize swaying hips and nonstop smiling, might be compelling but they're not 'real' hula. Serious students join a *hula halau* (school), where they undergo rigorous training and adopt hula as a life practice. Dancers learn to control every part of the body, as subtle differences in gestures can change the meaning entirely.

The best event at which to watch authentic hula is the Merrie Monarch Festival (p259), a fierce competition in Hilo that starts on Easter Sunday. *Halau* from all the islands compete in *kahiko* (ancient) and *'auana* (modern) categories. The only catch: shows sell out by January. Free shows are held four times a year at Hawai'i Volcanoes National Park (p283). Other hula festivals include the Prince Lot Hula Festival held each July on O'ahu

---

SONGS THAT MAKE LOCALS HOMESICK

- 'Honolulu City Lights,' Keola and Kapono Beamer
- 'Hi'ilawe,' Gabby Pahinui
- 'Lifetime Party,' Cecilio & Kapono
- 'I'll Remember You,' Don Ho
- 'Naturally,' Kalapana
- 'Wahine 'Ilikea,' Sons of Hawaii
- 'Home in the Islands,' the Brothers Cazimero
- 'Kanaka Wai Wai,' Melveen Leed
- 'Over the Rainbow,' Israel Kamakawiwo'ole (featured in the movies *Meet Joe Black*, *Finding Forrester*, *50 First Dates* and *The Big Bounce* and during a key episode of *ER!*)
- 'Room Service' from *Poi Dog*, Rap Reiplinger (a classic comedy album)

and two shows in January and May on Moloka'i, which was the site of Hawai'i's first *hula halau* (see p425).

Hawaiian Arts & Crafts

Ancient Hawaiians relied on manual handiwork for everything, from clothing to canoes. Thus, almost all traditional objects have an aesthetic component, being handmade according to exacting detail. Today, a small group of artisans and craftspeople perpetuate the old traditions, such as woodworking, which ideally uses Hawaii's prized koa. In old Hawai'i, the best craftspeople used giant logs to build canoes. The usual creations are hand-turned wooden bowls and furniture, impossibly smooth and polished, made from a variety of hardwood (since koa has grown scarce).

Lauhala weaving is another craft perpetuated only by a few. Weaving the *lau* (leaves) of the *hala* (pandanus) tree is actually the easy part, while preparing the leaves, which have razor-sharp spines, is difficult, messy work. Traditionally *lauhala* served as mats and floor coverings, but today smaller items such as hats, placemats and baskets are most common. Cheap imitations abound, so look for a specialty shop, such as Kimura Lauhala Shop (p200) on the Big Island.

Christian missionaries introduced patchwork quilting to Hawaiians. But because they'd only recently adopted Western dress, Hawaiians didn't have a surplus of cloth scraps – and the idea of chopping up fabric simply to sew it back together in small squares seemed absurd. Instead they created their own designs, which typically feature stylized tropical flora on a contrasting background. A handcrafted Hawaiian quilt is painstakingly stitched and costs thousands of dollars.

Lei making remains a popular craft, as people continue to wear lei on a regular basis. Today's popular tourist lei feature flashy or fragrant flowers, such as plumeria or dendrobium orchids. In fact, many orchid lei originate in Thailand and are not 'Hawaiian' at all. Traditionally, lei were subtler in their beauty, made of *mokihana* berries, *maile* leaves and other greenery. Intricate collectors' lei are sewn with shells and seeds. The prized 'Ni'ihau shell lei' is required by state law to include genuine shells from Ni'ihau for at least 80% of the lei. Because the shells are tiny and rare, a lei often requires months or years to complete and can cost as much as $25,000.

Contemporary artists typically do painting or sculpture, and some have garnered worldwide fame, such as Wyland and his underwater seascapes; but those pieces are generally considered touristy and would not grace a connoisseur's wall. Often, low-key artisans in Hawaii's 'artist colony' villages such as Hui No'eau (p368), Hanapepe (p503) and Holualoa (p200) do the most exquisite, sophisticated work. If buying, be careful to check for authenticity. A rule of thumb is the price: you get what you pay for.

Literature

For years, 'Hawaii literature' referred to fiction set in Hawaii, typically by nonlocal writers. Oft-cited examples include *Hawaii*, James Michener's ambitious saga of Hawaii's history, and *Hotel Honolulu*, Paul Theroux's novel about a washed-up writer who becomes the manager of a rundown Waikiki hotel. Also widely read is Isabella Bird, the 19th-century British adventurer, who captures the exoticism of the islands for outsiders. Today, however, a growing body of local writers is redefining the meaning of Hawaii literature.

Local literature doesn't consciously highlight Hawaii as an exotic setting but instead focuses on the lives and attitudes of universal characters. Bamboo Ridge Press (www.bambooridge.com), which publishes contemporary

Kids of all ages will get *chicken skin* (ie goose bumps) from the classic island legends in *Hawaii's Best Spooky Tales* and its sequels, edited by Rick Carroll.

local fiction and poetry in a biannual journal, *Bamboo Ridge*, has launched many local writers' careers. Some have hit the national scene, such as Nora Okja Keller, whose first novel, *Comfort Woman*, won the 1998 American Book Award, and Lois-Ann Yamanaka, who introduced pidgin to literary circles with *Saturday Night at the Pahala Theatre* – winner of the 1993 Pushcart Prize for poetry – and critically acclaimed novels including *Wild Meat and the Bully Burgers* and *Heads by Harry*.

Today, local writing often includes pidgin English, especially in dialogue. If you're new to pidgin, *Growing Up Local: An Anthology of Poetry and Prose from Hawaii* is a good introduction. While four-letter words pepper many local works, this collection contains none and is widely used in high school and college ethnic-literature classes nationwide.

Cinema & TV

Since the 1930s, Hollywood has embraced Hawaii as a sultry paradise in film classics such as Bing Crosby's *Waikiki Wedding*, Elvis Presley's *Blue Hawaii*, and a spate of WWII dramas like the 1953 classic *From Here to Eternity*. Today, over 100 films and TV shows have been shot in Hawaii, but the same themes and stereotypes (and fake pidgin accents) prevail. In the 2004 release starring Adam Sandler, *50 First Dates*, which was shot in Kailua and Kane'ohe on O'ahu, island life is distilled down to swaying palms and lapping waves, acres of pineapple fields and local characters whose vocabulary seems limited to 'aloha' and 'mahalo.'

Often, Hawaii stands in for places like Costa Rica, Africa or Vietnam. Kaua'i, the most prolific island 'set,' has appeared in over 70 films, such as *Raiders of the Lost Ark*, *Jurassic Park* and *South Pacific*. Diehard fans can even visit their favorite Kaua'i sites through **Hawaii Movie Tours** (www .hawaiimovietour.com).

On TV during the 1960s, *Hawaii Five-O* (and it's inimitable theme song) became synonymous with Honolulu urban life, while the 1980s' *Magnum*

You'll laugh till you hurt reading the illustrated pidgin dictionary, *Pidgin to da Max* by Douglas Simonson – a local classic available at www .besspress.com.

NO TALK LI' DAT

The Hawaii educational system has traditionally pushed local kids to use standard English and not pidgin in the classroom. State department of education leaders (and many parents) often blame low scores on standardized tests on local kids' speaking, thinking and writing in pidgin. But a movement to legitimize pidgin as a language is afoot. Da Pidgin Coup, a group of University of Hawai'i faculty and graduate students, asserts that pidgin can coexist with standard English and should not be forbidden if its use facilitates the learning process. As the argument goes, *what* you say is more important than *how* you say it.

The most well-known champion for pidgin use is Lee Tonouchi, a lecturer in Kapiolani at O'ahu's Community College's English Department, who was hired with an application written entirely in pidgin. A prolific writer and playwright, he makes an intriguing, subversive argument for legitimizing pidgin. His books include *Da Word* and *Living Pidgin: Contemplations on Pidgin Culture*.

This debate parallels the 1996 debate over Ebonics (black English) in Oakland, California, where the local school board recognized Ebonics, a term derived from ebony and phonics, as a separate language. The board concluded that most African American children come to school fluent in their vernacular, and to condemn it would be counterproductive.

Granted, pidgin use is not universal among locals and is determined by socioeconomic class. At the top schools such as Punahou and Iolani on O'ahu, you'll hear little, if any, pidgin. But all locals clearly understand it – and they regard pidgin as social glue, bonding one another to a shared identity and sense of humor. Most locals straddle the two languages, using either pidgin or standard English when it's most appropriate.

For more on pidgin, see the Language chapter (p546).

PI made Tom Selleck and his red Ferrari famous. Recently O'ahu has enjoyed the spotlight as the location for two major network series: Fox's *North Shore* (a spinoff of *The OC*) and ABC's *Lost*.

SPORTS

Locals are avid sports fans, especially for sports they know firsthand. Thus surfing is a hot event, especially in November and December, when top surfers head to O'ahu's North Shore (p158) to compete in the legendary Triple Crown of Surfing Championship and the prestigious In Memory of Eddie Aikau competition (held only if wave heights exceed 20ft!). Golf is everyperson's sport in Hawaii, and premier courses across the islands in January host major PGA events, such as the Mercedes Championships held at Kapalua Plantation Course (p324). 'Extreme' sports such as the Ironman Triathlon Championship (p191) garner worldwide attention.

Due to the islands' remoteness and relatively small population, no professional sports team has lasted here. Thus locals rally around the University of Hawai'i (UH) teams. The UH women's volleyball team is a longstanding powerhouse, with NCAA championship titles in 1982, 1983 and 1987. In 2003, they made an eighth appearance (and second in a row) in the NCAA Final Four. In 2002, the men's volleyball team won a milestone NCAA championship in a four-game rout of Pepperdine – their first UH men's national title ever. However, it was later revoked because star player Costas Theocharidis had played 22 games with professionals in his native Greece. UH Football, the only NCAA Division I program statewide, might rank as the biggest draw, attracting thousands of fans to the 50,000-seat Aloha Stadium on O'ahu. The stadium is also home to the Hawaii Bowl, a post-season college game held on Christmas Day, and the all-star Pro Bowl, which draws sell-out crowds the first week in February.

For an insider's look at surf culture, don't miss Stacy Peralta's 2004 Sundance Film Festival opener, *Riding Giants*, which features three titans in big-wave surfing: Greg Noll, Jeff Clark and Laird Hamilton.

Hawaii's Sports Hall of Fame (www.alohafame .org) honors the state's champion athletes and outstanding coaches.

HAWAII'S SPORTS SUPERSTARS

- 'Duke' Paoa Kahanamoku (1890–1968) – champion surfer and first Olympic gold medallist from Hawaii (three gold and two silver medals for swimming)

- Rell Kapolioka'ehukai Sunn (1950–98) – top-ranking longboard surfer who established the first professional tour for women (featured in an excellent documentary, *Heart of the Sea: Kapolioka'ehukai*, by Lisa Denker and Charlotte Lagarde, available at www.swellcinema.com)

- Tom Pohaku Stone (1951–) – native Hawaiian expert surfer and waterman who single-handedly revitalized *he'e holua* – the ancient sport of sledding down mountainsides at speeds up to 50mph

- Russ Francis (1953–) – NFL football player, three-time Pro Bowl tight end with the New England Patriots and SF 49ers

- Sid Fernandez (1962–) – pro baseball player, NY Mets, World Series winner and two-time All-Star

- Chad 'Akebono' Rowan (1969–) – first foreigner to win the highest rank of *yokozuna* (grand champion) in Japan's 2000-year sumo history

- Lokelani McMichael (1977–) – 'extreme sports' athlete and Nike model who at 18 became the youngest female to finish the Ironman Triathlon (and who completed her ninth Ironman finish in 2004!)

- Michelle Wie (1989–) – golf phenomenon who at 12 became the youngest player to qualify for an LPGA tournament, and at 13, the youngest winner of the US Women's Amateur Public Links

Environment

The Hawaiian Islands are actually the tips of massive shield volcanoes, created not by explosions but by a crack in the earth's mantle that has been spewing out molten rock for more than 25 million years. Dramatic and solid, to be sure, yet, utterly fragile and Darwinian. Even though the islands make up only 1% of the total US landmass, Hawaii accounts for 75% of extinct species in the USA and one third of its endangered flora and fauna. The majority of Hawaii's more than 10,000 endemic species of flora and fauna are found nowhere else on earth. It's a rich system, a system that's as inter dependent as an interlocking jigsaw puzzle. And it's one with devoted protectors.

THE LAND

The Hawaiian Islands chain is 2500 miles from the nearest continental landmass, making it the most geographically isolated place in the world. The islands form the apex of the Polynesian triangle and stretch from remote Kure Atoll in the northwest to the Big Island's South Cape (Ka Lae), the southernmost point of the USA.

Hawaii: The Islands of Life (1989) has strikingly beautiful photos of the flora, fauna and landscapes being protected by the Nature Conservancy of Hawaii (TNC), with text by Gavan Daws.

The equator lies 1470 miles south of the state capital Honolulu and all of the major Hawaiian Islands are south of the Tropic of Cancer. Hawaii shares approximately the same latitude as Hong Kong, Bombay, Mexico City and Cuba. The total landmass of all the Hawaiian Islands (6423 sq miles) is slightly smaller than Fiji but larger than the state of Connecticut. The remote Northwestern Hawaiian Islands (p516), which lie scattered across a thousand miles of ocean west of Kaua'i, contribute a total landmass of just under 5 sq miles.

Any discussion of the land should really begin and end with volcanoes. Although 95% of the world's volcanoes are located on plate edges, Hawaii's

HAWAII BY NUMBERS

- 5: Haleakala volcano (Maui), when measured from the ocean floor, is this many miles high
- 18: Degrees of latitude north at Ka Lae (Big Island), the southernmost point in the USA
- 40 plus: Kilauea volcano (Big Island) has buried this many sq miles under lava since 1983
- 486: Mt Waialeale (Kaua'i), the world's wettest spot, averages this many inches of rainfall per year
- 560: Average number of acres of new land added to the Big Island annually
- 800: Number of nene (Hawaiian geese) remaining in Hawaii (but the population is increasing each season)
- 200: Average number of Big Island earthquakes weekly
- 5000: Number of varieties of Hawaiian hibiscus
- 33,476: Mauna Kea (Big Island), technically the world's highest mountain when measured from the ocean floor, is this many feet at the summit
- 60,000: The Lo'ihi Seamount will poke above the ocean surface, if it continues apace, in this many years
- 70 million: The Hawaiian Island–Emperor Seamount chain has been in the making for this many years (at least)

are not. They're part of the Hawaiian Island–Emperor Seamount chain, created by hot spots in the earth's mantle. The Big Island straddles the hot spot and so has active, dormant and extinct volcanoes, while all of the other, older Hawaiian islands have shifted away from the hot spot. Experts estimate that the Big Island is a youthful one million years old, while Kaua'i is the wizened *kupuna* (elder) of the group at six million years old.

As weak spots in the earth's crust pass over the hot spot, molten lava rises and bursts through, slowly piling up and building underwater mountains. Some of these shield volcanoes finally emerge above the water-line as islands. Kilauea (p271), on the Big Island, sits directly over the hot spot. In its latest eruptive phase, Kilauea has pumped out more than two billion cu yd of lava. And just about 20 miles southeast of the Big Island, a new seamount named Loihi has already risen almost 12,500ft off the ocean floor – that's within 3200ft of the surface of the sea.

Roadside Geology of Hawaii (1996), by Richard Hazlett and Donald Hyndman, is a layperson's science textbook for the volcanic and other awesome natural forces that shaped the islands.

WILDLIFE
All living things that reached Hawaii's shores were carried across the ocean on wing, wind or wave – seeds clinging to a bird's feather, a float-ing *hala* (pandanus) plant or insect eggs in a piece of driftwood. The first Polynesian settlers brought chickens and pigs, along with medicinal plants and fruit. On the islands these species evolved in relative isolation.

The legacy of Western contact has been the destruction of many of Hawaii's fragile ecosystems. Since the arrival of Europeans, invasive plants and animals have endangered, and even caused the extinction of, many Hawaiian species, which previously had few natural predators and only limited defenses.

Animals
Countless species of native birds and Hawaii's two native mammals, the Hawaiian monk seal and a subspecies of hoary bat, are endangered. While Hawaii has *no* snakes (although there are reports of recent sight-ings), it more than makes up for it with cockroaches and geckos, those green-and-tan lizards that scamper across ceilings. You're well advised to become fast friends with the geckos – they eat bugs.

An Underwater Guide to Hawaii (1987), by Ann Fielding and Ed Robinson, is a brilliantly photo-graphed and annotated guide for anything dwell-ing in Poseidon's realm.

LAND MAMMALS
The reclusive Hawaiian hoary bat (*'ope'ape'a*) has a heavy coat of brown-and-grayish fur, making it appear 'hoary.' With a wingspan of around a foot, these tree-dwellers are thought to exist predominantly around forests on the leeward sides of the Big Island, Maui and Kaua'i.

Wild horses roam free in the uplands of many islands, dropped off by Western explorers two centuries ago. The axis deer that run around

---

ANIMAL 911

Even short-term visitors can help Hawaiian conservation efforts in a variety of ways. Do not ap-proach or otherwise disturb any endangered creatures, especially marine species such as whales, dolphins, seals and sea turtles; doing so is not only illegal, but subjects trespassers to a hefty fine. And please slow down while driving around the islands. Many nene (native Hawaiian goose) have been backed over by careless drivers in parking lots or run over along park roads; others have been tamed by too much human contact, so do not feed them. Report any sightings of Hawaiian monk seals, or any wild animal in distress, to the State of Hawaii's **Division of Conservation & Resource Enforcement** (DOCARE; ☎ 587-0077).

Hawaii's Birds (1997), by the Hawaii Audubon Society, is the best pocket-sized guide to the native and endangered birds of Hawaii.

Moloka'i, Lana'i and Maui are descendants of eight deer sent from India in 1868 as a gift to King Kamehameha V. Most insidious of all is the mongoose, a commonly seen ferretlike creature that was originally introduced to control sugarcane rats.

MARINE MAMMALS

The Hawaiian monk seal – so named for its solitary habits and cowl-like neck fold – was almost wiped out last century. The seals breed and give birth primarily in the remote Northwestern Hawaiian Islands.

It is the islands' most frequent visitor, the migrating North Pacific humpback whale (p316), that everyone wants to see. Before an international ban on their slaughter came into force, these whales were hunted almost to extinction. As the fifth largest of the great whales, the endangered humpback can reach lengths of 45ft and weigh up to 45 tons. Hundreds of whales migrate to the shallow waters between Maui, Lana'i and Kaho'olawe during breeding season (January through March).

Intelligent and wild, spinner dolphins are nocturnal feeders that often come into calm bays during the day to rest. Because they're easily disturbed by noise, it's illegal to swim out and join them.

AMPHIBIANS

All three Hawaiian sea turtle species are endangered, as poaching and other human disturbance to nesting grounds have killed uncountable numbers. In ancient Hawai'i, sea turtles served as *'aumakua* (family gods and guardians) and their form often appears in petroglyphs. The green sea turtle *(honu)* and Hawksbill sea turtle *(honuea)* weigh up to 200lb when mature, while the soft-shelled leatherback can weigh 10 times that amount and grow up to 8ft long. Green sea turtles migrate hundreds of miles every few years to breed and nest in the remote Northwestern Hawaiian Islands.

DID YOU KNOW?

There were no nene left inside Haleakala National Park until Boy Scouts carried junior birds back into the crater inside their backpacks in 1946.

BIRDS

Native Hawaiian birdlife is so varied, it deserves a book of its own.

Many of Hawaii's birds may have evolved from a single species in a spectacular display of adaptive radiation. Left vulnerable to new predatory species and infectious avian diseases after Europeans arrived, half of Hawaii's native bird species are already extinct, and more than 30 of those remaining are still under threat.

One of the most critically endangered is the Hawaiian crow *('alala)*, of which only a handful of birds remain in captive breeding programs on Maui and the Big Island. Hawaiians believe that the Hawaiian short-eared owl (pueo) has protective powers and represents a physical manifestation

FOOD & MEDICINE

The common Hawaiian taro *(kalo)* plant has green heart-shaped leaves and purplish-white roots, which are pounded into the traditional dietary staple called poi. Waxy yellow-green leaves from Polynesian *ti* plants are used to wrap food, as well as to cure headaches when laid flat against the forehead. Polynesian breadfruit *('ulu)*, a green, spiky football-sized fruit, can be a treatment for skin diseases, cuts and scratches. But unparalleled among traditional restoratives is Indian mulberry *(noni)*, which is said to be effective against almost anything – and certainly tastes bad enough to prove it! A petite tree with knobby berries, *noni* often thrives on the mineral-rich soil of lava flows.

For an in-depth look at the connection between traditional Hawaiian medicine and native species, Beatrice Krauss's books, published by University Press of Hawai'i, are good references.

of ancestors' spirits. Seeing one is a good omen and the most likely place is atop volcanic peaks where it soars at high altitudes. From a distance some mistake it for the Hawaiian hawk ('io), a symbol of royalty, but the Hawaiian hawk is only found on the Big Island's volcanoes.

The endangered nene, Hawaii's state bird, is a long-lost cousin of the Canada goose. Nene generally nest in high cliffs from 6000ft to 8000ft, surrounded by sparse vegetation and rugged lava flows, on the slopes of Haleakala, Mauna Kea and Hawai'i Volcanoes National Park. Their feet have gradually adapted by losing most of their webbing. Nene have black heads, light-yellow cheeks, a white underbelly and dark gray feathers. Currently, there are only 800 nene in Hawaii, but breeding programs are raising that number every year.

Finches, early ancestors of today's rainbow variety of Hawaiian honeycreepers, are theorized to be the first birds to colonize the islands. Native waterfowl include the Hawaii coot ('alae ke'oke'o), which is all black except for its white bill and the front of its head, which can be white, yellow or blood-red. Although it's seen on all islands, it's most populous in fresh- or brackish-water ponds on O'ahu. The endangered Hawaiian stilt (aeo), a black-necked wading bird with a white underbelly and long orange legs, feeds along the marshy edges of ponds. Even though the stilt population in all Hawaii is estimated at just 1500, the birds can still be spotted on Maui (p336) and Kaua'i (p477).

> Check out some great photos of Hawaiian plants at www.hear.org/starr /hiplants/images/index .html.

Plants

With climate zones varying from dry alpine desert to lush tropical rain forest, visitors will find a wide variety of flora. Still, less than half of the islands' original forest cover remains today, due to widespread overgrazing, logging, erosion, invasive species and watershed pollution.

FLOWERS

Found only on the volcanoes of Maui and the Big Island, the striking silversword ('ahinahina) is a distant relative of the sunflower. Now endangered, the silversword was nearly wiped out in the early 20th century by grazing feral goats, pigs and cattle, as well as by people who cut them down for souvenirs. Each plant can grow for up to half a century, but blooms only once in a lifetime. In the summer of its final year, the silversword shoots up a flowering stalk with hundreds of maroon and yellow blossoms. When the flowers go to seed in late fall, the plant dies.

> **DID YOU KNOW?**
>
> A stalk of bamboo can grow over six inches in a single day.

Common native plants include the royal ilima, used for making leis, and the seed-filled passion fruit (liliko'i). More than 5000 varieties of hibiscus grow in Hawaii. The koki'o ke'oke'o, a native white hibiscus tree that grows up to 40ft high, is the only Hawaiian hibiscus with a fragrance.

Hawaii is abloom with scores of other exotic tropical flowers, including blood-red anthuriums with heart-shaped leaves, brilliantly orange-and-blue (or lily-white) bird-of-paradise and a myriad of heliconia. The

---

NOT NATIVE?

Many cultivated crops thought of as uniquely Hawaiian today are actually exotic imports, eg macadamia nuts from Australia. Pineapples, which came from Brazil, belong to the bromeliad family of plants, some of which have showy decorative flowers. Sugarcane (ko) was first planted by Polynesian settlers. Now cane stalks often grow wild alongside island highways, especially since many of Hawaii's commercial sugar operations have been shut down.

ever-exotic night-blooming cereus has exquisitely fragrant white flowers that only bloom one night a year. Hundreds of varieties of both cultivated and native wild orchids and ornamental ginger varieties exist, including the white 'shampoo' ginger ('awapuhi), which has a fragrant, soapy juice that is squeezed from its flowers.

Hawaii's protea, native to South Africa, comes in more than 1500 varieties – from macadamia nuts to spiky carnations to artichoke blossoms. Hawaiian protea account for 90% of the world market, with 85 species alone situated solely on the slopes of Haleakala (Maui).

FERNS

There are about 200 varieties of Hawaiian ferns and fern allies (such as mosses) found in rain forests and colonizing recent lava flows. Among them are hapu'u and 'ama'u ferns, false staghorn ferns (uluhe), hare's foot fern (laua'e haole) and the fragrant, glossy maile-scented fern (laua'e), which are favored by lei makers (p41) and resort gardeners.

SHRUBS & TREES

The most bewitching of native Hawaiian forest trees is koa, nowadays found only at higher elevations and even then rarely. Growing up to 100ft

HAWAII'S TOP 20 NATURAL AREAS

Natural Area	Features	Activities	Visit	Page
O'ahu				
Hanauma Bay Nature Preserve	Hawaii's only underwater park	snorkeling, swimming	year-round	p139
Ka'ena Point State Park	O'ahu's westernmost point, only accessible by foot	hiking, mountain biking, solitude-seeking	May–Oct	p171
Malaekahana State Recreation Area	sandy beach, Moku'auia (Goat Island) bird sanctuary	swimming, snorkeling, camping, bird-watching	May–Oct	p155
Big Island				
Akaka Falls State Park	lush rainforest boardwalk to an impressive waterfall	walking	year-round	p242
Hawai'i Volcanoes National Park	lava fields, lunar landscapes and fern forests	hiking, camping	year-round	p271
Mauna Kea	Hawaii's highest peak	hiking, star gazing, ancient Hawaiian sites	May–Oct	p246
Pu'uhonua O Honaunau National Historical Park	ancient 'place of refuge'	hiking, snorkeling, exploring tide pools	year-round	p209
Waipi'o Valley	remote, fertile tangle of jungle, taro and waterfalls	hiking	year-round	p239
Mo'okini Heiau	ancient temple, haunting in its magnitude and isolation	hiking, whale watching	year-round	p226
Maui				
Haleakala National Park (Summit Section)	large dormant volcano	hiking, camping	year-round	p374
Haleakala National Park (Kipahulu Section)	towering waterfalls, cascading pools and ancient sites	hiking, swimming, camping	year-round	p362

high, this rich hardwood is traditionally used to make canoes, surfboards and even ukuleles.

Hawaii was once rich in fragrant sandalwood ('iliahi) forests, but these were sold off to foreign traders by the mid-19th century. Rare nowadays, these tall trees are found in Hawai'i Volcanoes National Park. The dark green leaves of false (or 'bastard') sandalwood (naio) appear twisted, with tiny white or pinkish flowers, and the tree is most common on Maui.

The versatile ohia, one of the first plants to colonize lava flows, is found everywhere. Its distinctive tufted flowers consist of petalless groups of red, orange, yellow and (rarely) white stamens.

Brought by early Polynesian settlers, the candlenut tree (kukui) has light silver-tinged foliage that stands out brightly in the forest. The oily nuts from Hawaii's state tree are used for making lei, dyes and candles.

Stands of ironwood, a nonnative conifer with drooping needles, act as natural windbreaks and prevent erosion from beaches. Majestic banyan trees have a canopy of hanging aerial roots with trunks large enough to swallow small children; they're also shady and a haven for birdlife. Rainbow eucalyptus, imported from Australia, proves its name when its bark is peeled away; paperbark eucalyptus has layered white bark.

Natural Area	Features	Activities	Visit	Page
Makena State Park	glorious, unspoiled, expansive beaches (one is clothing-optional)	swimming, sunset watching	year-round	p349
Wai'anapanapa State Park	lava tubes, trail over rugged sea cliffs to Hana	hiking, camping	year-round	p358
Moloka'i				
Kalaupapa National Historic Park	historic and remote leprosy colony	mule riding, hiking, touring	year-round	p421
Lana'i				
Hulopo'e Beach	dolphins frolic offshore in a pristine, perfect bay	swimming, snorkeling	year-round	p394
Kaua'i				
Kilauea Point NWR	wildlife refuge at the northernmost point of Hawaii	birding	year-round	p470
Koke'e State Park	waterfalls, trails for overnighters and daytrippers	hiking	year-round	p510
Na Pali Coast	beaches, waterfalls, classic 11-mile backpack trek	hiking, camping, swimming, snorkeling	May-Oct	p486
Polihale State Park	remote, miles-long white-sand beach	sunset-watching, partying, camping	year-round	p509
Waimea Canyon State Park	unbeatable views of 'Grand Canyon of the Pacific'	hiking, mountain biking, camping	Apr-Nov	p509

Legacy of the Landscape (1996), by Patrick Vinton, provides dramatic photos and a detailed written treatment of 50 of the most important Hawaiian archaeological sites, including heiau, fishponds and petroglyphs.

Often mistakenly called Norfolk pines, stately Cook pines came to the islands from the South Pacific. The pesky and intrusive mangrove has a twisted root system that has completely choked natural ponds and entire sections of coastline. A member of the alien mesquite family, kiawe is a nuisance to beachgoers, as its sharp thorns easily pierce soft soles. Coastal kiawe often form shade cover with their long branches, compound leaves and dense flowers with white spikes.

Monkeypod, a common shade tree, sports dark glossy green leaves, puffy pink flowers and longish seed pods. Jacaranda trees burst with blue and purple blooms in spring and summer, their tubular flowers carpeting upcountry roads.

NATIONAL, STATE & COUNTY PARKS

Hawaii has two national parks, Haleakala National Park on Maui and Hawai'i Volcanoes National Park on the Big Island. You could have a perfectly splendid hiking vacation without leaving the parks. Each is uniquely fascinating, covering a variety of environments and natural phenomena. Both were nominated as international biosphere preserves in the 1980s and Hawai'i Volcanoes has been declared a Unesco World Heritage site.

Prince Jonah Kalanianaole, the man who could've been king if the Hawaiian monarchy hadn't been overthrown, first proposed Haleakala as a national park. When the bill was signed into law in 1916, Hawai'i National Park officially comprised both Haleakala and its Big Island siblings, Mauna Loa and Kilauea. In the 1960s, Haleakala National Park and Hawai'i Volcanoes National Park were separated and became independent entities.

Across the islands there are dozens of registered national historic parks, sites and landmarks (see table on pp50-1), notably Pu'uhonua O Honaunau (Place of Refuge) on the Big Island and Kalaupapa Peninsula on Moloka'i. Some of Hawaii's **national wildlife refuges** (NWR; www.refugenet .org) are open to the public. Birders will delight in James Campbell NWR (p156), Kealia Pond NWR (p336), and Hanalei NWR (p477).

Each island also has its own system of state parks and recreation areas; county beach parks; forest reserves, petroglyph preserves and marine sanctuaries; and arboretums and botanical gardens, all of which protect at least equal diversity, if much smaller natural areas, than the national parks. Some are just stops on the 'headless chicken' tour-bus circuit, while others are wild and natural.

Many organizations (p53) and agencies (p53) work to preserve Hawaii's state and county parks. In addition to the government agencies on O'ahu, all of which have regional offices on many of the Neighbor Islands, check the blue section of the local White Pages telephone directory. The **Department of Land & Natural Resources** (DLNR; ☎ 587-0320; www.state .hi.us/dlnr/; Kalanimoku Bldg, 1151 Punchbowl St, Honolulu) issues camping permits and has many useful publications and online information about safe hiking, conservation and aquatic safety. The DLNR oversees all of the following divisions and programs, which have their own offices in the same building in Honolulu (Map pp86-7).

Division of Forestry & Wildlife (DOFAW; www.dofaw.net) Supervises public land management of Hawaii's forests and natural area reserves (NARs). Public outreach focuses on outdoor recreation, conservation and watershed protection.

Division of State Parks (☎ 587-0300; www.hawaii.gov/dlnr/dsp) Administers over 50 state parks on five islands, and also handles permits for camping, housekeeping cabins and A-frame shelters on various islands.

Na Ala Hele Trail & Access Program (☎ 587-0062; www.hawaiitrails.org) Na Ala Hele ('Trails to Go On') coordinates public access to hiking trails, as well as historical trail preservation and maintenance. The excellent website contains useful island overview maps, guidelines for safe hiking and announcements of recently developed or reopened trails.

ENVIRONMENTAL ISSUES

Hawaii's native ecosystems have been decimated by the introduction of exotic flora and fauna since Europeans arrived. Erosion – caused by free-ranging cattle, goats and pigs and the monocrop cultures of sugarcane and pineapple – have destroyed native ground covers, resulting in washouts that sweep prime topsoil into the sea and choke near-shore reefs. Beach resorts and 'condoville' areas that sprang up from the mid-20th century were poorly planned, if they were even planned at all. This trend reached its epitome with the mainly Japanese-driven golf-course megaresorts of the 1980s. When the Japanese economic bubble burst, many resorts went belly up, or suffered through environmental misman- agement. Today many groups are in cutthroat competition for Hawaii's land and natural resources, including agriculture, ranching, forestry, tourism and resort development.

From the mountaintops to the coral reefs, the Conservation Council for Hawai'i (www.conser vation-hawaii.org) is dedicated to preserving Hawaii's biodiversity and to restoring the integrity of native ecosystems.

On a more positive note, the Hawaiian islands have no polluting heavy industry and not a single roadside billboard to blight natural vistas. The islands boast examples of virtually all of the world's ecological zones and some of the only tropical rain forest in the USA. On a grassroots level, a wide coalition of environmentalists, scientists, activists and residents has made island conservation efforts a slow, but steady success. They help fight invasive weeds, pulling up one plant at a time; monitor migrating

RESPONSIBLE TOURISM

Hawaii's natural ecosystem has been ravaged by nonnative plants and animals ever since the first contact with foreign ships. Seeds caught in the soles of your shoes or bugs left hiding out in the bottom of your backpack can potentially be a threat – as much as anything that the US Department of Agriculture specifically forbids and confiscates from travelers during airport inspections (see p522).

You'll see countless 'No Trespassing – Kapu' signs around the islands. Although you may be tempted to push on through that closed gate just to see what's beyond it, don't – unless of course a trustworthy local says it's actually OK. Respect the privacy of residents, whose quality of life is continually being encroached upon by tourist development. Practice respect for the 'aina (land). Leave nothing but footprints when walking in the rain forest or along beaches (snorkelers and divers shouldn't leave so much as a single toe print on fragile coral). Take out all your garbage.

Don't take cuttings of native plants, stuff your shoes full of pretty black sand or steal lava rock for souvenirs. Unless you'd like to feel the wrath of Pele, the mythical creator-destroyer goddess of the Hawaiian islands, that is. (Remember what happened to the Brady Bunch when they took the idol from the temple in the epic three-part 'Hawaii Bound' episode? Tarantulas in their hotel beds were the least of their troubles.) In fact, every year Hawaii national parks staff receive hundreds of letters from visitors bemoaning the bad luck they've had after taking a hunk of lava home, and pleading for the lava (enclosed) to be returned to placate the goddess (see p275).

There are plenty of informal ways for a visitor to assuage their environmental conscience. Look into volunteer programs (see p531) at Hawaii's national parks; lend a helping hand to the **Protect Kaho'olawe Ohana** (www.kahoolawe.org); or hook up with the Sierra Club (p531). For environmental news and more volunteer opportunities – everything from public awareness campaigns to counting migrating whales – contact **Malama Hawaii** (www.malamahawaii.org), a partnership network of community groups and other nonprofit organizations.

whale and nesting turtle populations; advocate for the protection of coral reefs and tide pools; and protest against potentially harmful tourism, such as cruise ships visiting Moloka'i. Kaho'olawe (p382) is an activists' success story.

One of the most tooth-and-nail battles waged on the islands today is over watershed resources. All the greenery of well-manicured resorts and golf courses comes with a price tag. It is mostly paid by Hawaiian farmers, whose water is drained through irrigation ditches to provide the millions of gallons required by resort guests daily. But as one activist slogan points out, 'No one can eat golf balls.'

Conservation also focuses on archaeological sites, such as heiau (temples), petroglyph fields and traditional fishponds. In recent years, efforts have been made to rebuild and restock a few fishponds, mostly with *ama'ama* (mullet) and *awa* (milkfish). Some impressive ones lie along the shores of east Moloka'i (p412), Maui and Kaua'i.

For a great source of news, check with the broadest-based environmental organization in the state: the **Sierra Club** (☎ 538-6616; www.hi.sierraclub .org). With groups on all main islands, its activities range from political activism on local environmental issues to weekend outings aimed at eradicating invasive plants from native forests. The **Nature Conservancy of Hawaii** (☎ 537-4508; www.nature.org; 923 Nu'uanu Ave, Honolulu) has opted for a different approach: it protects Hawaii's rarest ecosystems by buying up vast tracts of land and working out long-term stewardships with some of Hawaii's biggest landholders.

The **Earthjustice Legal Defense Fund** (☎ 599-2436; www.earthjustice.org; 4th fl, 223 S King St, Honolulu) plays a leading role in protecting Hawaii's fragile environment through court action. Together with the Center for Marine Conservation and the Sea Turtle Restoration Project, it also successfully sued to stop the killing of endangered sea turtles by the longline fishing industry. Most longline ships arrived in Hawaii's waters in the 1990s after depleting fishing stocks in the Atlantic Ocean. Although these operations targeted swordfish or tuna, they laid fishing lines up to 30 miles long, carrying thousands of baited hooks that caught anything that went for the bait, including marine mammals and hundreds of sea turtles. At the time the industry was banned in 2001, Earthjustice estimated the population of adult leatherback turtles in the eastern Pacific had dropped from about 250,000 in 1980 to just 3000.

The investigative journal Environment Hawai'i (www.environment-haw aii.org) is the single most important source of environmental concerns as they relate to the sensitive issue of development.

Hawaii Outdoors

You made it to Hawaii. Now what are you gonna do? The sky – or the sea – is the limit. The Hawaiian islands are rife with outdoor activities, and there's something about paradise that spurs people to try new things. Only a few activities require planning before landing in the islands. Most of the time you can just show up, look around and decide. Details on gear rentals, lessons and specific locations for each activity are found on p99 (O'ahu), p189 (Big Island), p294 (Maui), p391 (Lana'i), p402 (Moloka'i) and p437 (Kaua'i).

WATER ACTIVITIES

These islands sit in the middle of the vast Pacific Ocean, so it makes sense that playing in, on, and under the water would be central to any Hawaiian adventure.

SWIMMING

Hawaii is endowed with so many phenomenal beaches that it would take the better part of a year to sample them all just once.

The islands have four distinct coastal areas – north shore, south shore, leeward (west) coast and windward (east) coast – each of which has its own peculiar water conditions. As a general rule, the best places to swim in the winter are along the south shores, and in the summer, the north shores. When it's rough on one side, it's usually calm on another, so you can generally find a suitable place.

Many people argue Maui has the best beaches. Who can argue with mile-long strands? But each island boasts different kinds of gems. For instance, the Big Island's beaches are like little white oases surrounded by a sea of black lava and turquoise water.

For more information on dive spots in Hawaii, pick up Lonely Planet's Diving & Snorkeling Hawaii, *which includes color photos illustrating sites and fish.*

DIVING & SNORKELING

Hawaii's underwater world is spectacular and its waters offer excellent visibility, with temperatures ranging from 72°F to 80°F year-round.

Of the 700 fish species that call Hawaii home, a full one-third of these aren't found anywhere else in the world. You can often see spinner dolphins, green sea turtles, manta rays and moray eels. Although it's rare for snorkelers or divers to see humpback whales, you may get lucky and hear them singing underwater – you'll never forget it.

Snorkeling

By simply donning a mask and snorkel and putting your face in the water, the ocean can become an underwater aquarium. And the best part? Snorkeling doesn't take extensive training or expensive equipment. Snorkel and mask rentals cost about $8 per day (or $25 per week).

Hanauma Bay (p139) offers the best snorkeling on O'ahu's south shore. Maui's best snorkeling is found at Black Rock (p317), while Kapalua (p323) usually has calm waters for snorkeling year-round. Countless cruises leave for the partly submerged volcanic crater of Molokini (p297) from Ma'alaea (p336) and Lahaina Harbor (p306).

The Big Island's sweetest spots include Kahalu'u Beach (p198), Two-Step (p210), Kealakekua Bay (p207) and the Kapoho tide pools (p269).

Snorkeling at Hulopo'e Beach (p394), on Lana'i will guarantee an abundance of reef fish and vibrant corals.

Scuba Diving

Hawaii is a great place for learning to dive, as many dive operations offer reasonably short introductory courses. O'ahu and the Big Island's Ka'awaloa Cove (p205) are particularly good places for diving novices. Open-water certification courses are offered by many companies. Dive-trip prices start at $55 for a one-tank boat dive or $75 for two tanks. Experienced divers needn't bring anything other than a swimsuit and certification card.

O'ahu's waters don't offer the greatest visibility, but they do have the best wreck diving. On the Big Island, the leeward Kona side has the island's best overall diving conditions, with sites ranging from shallow beginner dives to challenging nighttime and lava tube dives. A hot spot for night diving is around Kailua-Kona (p189). Dive shops in Hilo (p257) offer trips on the windward side, but the shores are usually buffeted by trade winds.

Off Maui, the granddaddy of dives is crescent-shaped Molokini (p297). Otherwise, head to the island's Makena State Park (p349) to find sea turtles or Black Rock (p317) for live coral.

Divers Alert Network (DAN; 919-684-8111, 800-446-2671; www .diversalertnetwork.org) gives advice on diving emergencies, insurance, decompression services, illness and injury.

RESPONSIBLE DIVING

The popularity of diving is placing immense pressure on many sites. Please consider the following tips when diving to help preserve the ecology and beauty of reefs.

- Do not use reef anchors and take care not to ground boats on coral. Encourage dive operators to establish permanent moorings at popular sites.

- Avoid touching living marine organisms with your body or dragging equipment across the reef. Polyps can be damaged by even the gentlest contact. Never stand on coral. If you must hold on to the reef, only touch exposed rock or dead coral.

- Be conscious of your fins. Even without contact, the surge from heavy fin strokes near the reef can damage delicate organisms. When treading water in shallow reef areas, take care not to kick up clouds of sand. Settling sand can easily smother the delicate organisms of the reef.

- Practice and maintain proper buoyancy control. Major damage can be done by divers descending too fast and colliding with the reef. Make sure you are correctly weighted and that your weight belt is positioned so that you stay horizontal. Be aware that buoyancy can change over the period of an extended trip: initially you may breathe harder and need more weight; a few days later you may breathe more easily and need less weight.

- Take care in underwater caves. Spend as little time within them as possible, as your air bubbles may be caught within the roof and thereby leave previously submerged organisms high and dry.

- Resist the temptation to collect or buy coral or shells. Aside from the ecological damage, taking home marine souvenirs depletes the beauty of a site and spoils the enjoyment of others.

- Ensure that you take home all your rubbish and any litter you may find as well. Plastics in particular are a serious threat to marine life. Turtles can mistake plastic for jellyfish and eat it.

- Resist the temptation to feed fish. You may disturb their normal eating habits, encourage aggressive behavior or feed them food that is detrimental to their health.

- Minimize your disturbance of marine animals. It is illegal to approach endangered marine species too closely; these include many whales, dolphins, sea turtles and the Hawaiian monk seal. In particular, do not ride on the backs of turtles, as this causes them great anxiety.

On Lana'i set out for Manele Bay off Hulopo'e Beach (394). Cathedrals (p394) offers intriguing geological grotto formations, including caves, arches and connecting passageways.

Kaua'i has excellent diving, but weather conditions are fickle. The water is rough for most of the winter along the island's majestic North Shore, which makes many dive sites inaccessible.

The **Professional Association of Diving Instructors** (PADI; ☎ 800-729-7234; www.padi .com) and the **National Association of Underwater Instructors** (NAUI; www.naui.org) certify scuba divers.

Paddling Hawaii by Audrey Sutherland is an indispensable guide for everything from cleaning your fresh octopus dinner to making safe surf landings.

Snuba

If you aren't ready for a full-on dive, how about a hybrid snorkel-scuba dive? You wear a snorkel mask and stay connected by an air hose to an oxygen tank floating 20ft above. No certification is needed, but a 20-minute introductory lesson is a good idea. Many dive operators also offer snuba opportunities. Costs are similar to that of scuba diving.

KAYAKING

The first Polynesian settlers in Hawaii arrived by outrigger canoe and we're still following in their wake. Island kayaking is gaining fans as rental outfits, tours and enthusiasts spread the gospel of paddling fun.

On O'ahu, the most well-deservedly popular spot is Kailua Bay (p147), where you can rent kayaks on the beach and paddle across to a deserted island.

On the Big Island, set out for Kealakekua Bay (p203), a haven for dolphins, a splendid snorkeling locale and the spot where Captain Cook met his maker.

On Maui, many people kayak near La Perouse Bay (p350), which is particularly special during the winter whale-watching season. Another favorite spot is the area north of Kapalua Bay (p323), particularly placid during the summer.

Kaua'i offers both navigable rivers and ocean kayaking along the Na Pali Coast (p486). In winter, when north side surf gets rough, ocean kayaking moves to Kaua'i's less spectacular but still pleasant south side.

Molokai offers expert-level kayaking along its remote northeast shore.

SURFING

Hawaii lies smack in the path of all major swells that race across the Pacific. Even in ancient times, when the waves were up, everyone in Hawaii

---

OCEAN SAFETY

Drowning is the leading cause of accidental death for visitors. If you're not familiar with water conditions, please ask around. It's best not to swim alone in unfamiliar places.

Rip Currents Rips, or rip currents, are fast-flowing ocean currents that can drag swimmers out into deeper water. Anyone caught in one should either go with the flow until it loses power or swim parallel to shore to slip out of it.

Rogue Waves Never turn your back on the ocean. Waves don't all come in with equal height or strength, and sometimes, one can sweep over a shoreline ledge and drag sunbathers from the beach into the ocean.

Shorebreaks If waves that are breaking close to the shore are only a couple of feet high, they're generally fine for novice bodysurfers. Large shorebreaks, though, can hit hard with a slamming downward force.

Undertows Common along steeply sloped beaches, undertows occur where large waves wash back directly into incoming surf. If caught up you can be pulled under. Don't panic; go with the current until you get beyond the wave.

For information about tsunami, see p523.

was out in the water, and at some surfing locales today, you can still find the remains of coastal heiau where Hawaiians paid their respects to the surfing gods before hitting the waves.

Hawaii's biggest waves roll into the north shores of the islands from November through February. Summer swells, which break along the south shores, aren't as frequent or large as their winter counterparts.

O'ahu's North Shore attracts championship surfers from around the world and hosts big-name competitions. Winter swells at Waimea Bay (p163), Sunset Beach (p164) and the Banzai Pipeline (p164) can bring in towering 30ft waves and create conditions through which legends are made. Waikiki Beach (p125) boasts O'ahu's most popular south-shore surfing.

Maui and Kaua'i also have some very good surfing spots, particularly in the winter along their north shores. The best spots are Honolua Bay (p125) on Maui and Hanalei Bay (p479) on Kaua'i. Big Island swells will leave adrenaline junkies jonesing, but surfing conditions are better on the leeward side and winter brings in bigger sets than summer.

Surfing lessons and board rentals are available from surf shops on all of the islands. A three-hour group lesson typically costs $85.

Hawaii Surfing News (www.holoholo.org/surfnews) lists everything from surf conditions to upcoming events.

Bodysurfing & Boogie Boarding

Brennecke's Beach (p495) on Kaua'i and White Sands Beach (p189) on the Big Island are top spots for bodysurfing and boogie boarding. Kihei (p337) on Maui is decent when the waves are right. On O'ahu, head to either Sandy Beach Park (p141) or Makapu'u Beach Park (p141).

Kiteboarding

Kind of like skateboarding or snowboarding on water, kiteboarding is actually a kind of surfing. If you can wakeboard or windsurf, that'll help. So will lots of muscles and stamina. While it may be impressive to watch, it's harder to master. Instruction is given in three hour-long lessons (around $85). First you learn how to fly the kite, then you practice bodydragging (letting the kite pull you across the water) and finally you step on board.

On Maui, where it's most popular, the action centers on Kite Beach at the western end of Kahului's Kanaha Beach Park (p328), which is not to be confused with Kahana Beach in West Maui.

In Girl in the Curl: A Century of Women in Surfing, Andrea Gabbard gives long overdue recognition to the role of wahine (female) surfers.

SURFSPEAK

Don't know the difference between a stick and a tube? Surfers everywhere have their own lingo. Hit the waves in Hawaii, and you're likely to hear some of these terms:

brah or cuz friend, surfing buddy
da kine a great wave, top quality (in many contexts beyond surfing, too)
goofy-footing surfing with the right foot forward
keiki waves small, gentle waves suitable for kids
macked to get clobbered by a huge wave, as if by a Mack truck
ne'e nalu traditional Hawaiian term for board surfing
pau quitting time
snake steal; as in 'that dude's snaking my wave'
stick local slang for a surfboard
tube also tubing; when the crest of a wave seems to fall over a hollow barrel
wahine female surfer
wipeout get knocked down by a big wave

WHALE-WATCHING

Many species of whale are found in Hawaiian waters, including sperm whales, false killer whales, pilot whales and beaked whales. Nonetheless, it's the migrating humpbacks (see also p48) with their acrobatic displays that attract tourists. Peak whale-watching season is from January through March, although whales are usually around for a month or so on either side of those dates.

The western coastline of Maui and the eastern shore of Lana'i are the chief birthing and nursing grounds for wintering North Pacific humpbacks. Luckily for whale watchers, humpbacks are coast-huggers, preferring shallow offshore waters for nursing their newborn calves.

Maui's finest shoreline whale-watching spots are the stretches from Olowalu (p314) to Ma'alaea Bay (p336) and near Makena Beach (p349). On the Big Island, whale-watching tours depart from Honokohau Harbor (p213).

Humpbacks are highly sensitive to human disturbance and noise. Coming within 100yd of a humpback (300yd in 'cow/calf waters') is prohibited by federal law and can result in a hefty $25,000 fine.

WINDSURFING

In general, the best winds blow from June through September. Gear rentals and lessons are available on the main islands, but many hardcore devotees arrange package tours that include accommodations, car rental and airfare.

Maui's Ho'okipa Beach (p352) hosts top international windsurfing competitions. For experts only, Ho'okipa's death-defying conditions include dangerous shorebreaks and razor-sharp coral. Tamer spots are found in Kihei (p337).

On O'ahu, Kailua Bay (p146), suitable for all levels, attracts the biggest crowds because of year-round trade winds and consistent wave conditions in different sections of the bay.

Kaua'i has some fairly good windsurfing spots, most notably 'Anini Beach (p147), with good conditions for all skill levels.

For everything you want to know about humpback whales, consult the National Marine Sanctuary (www.hihwnms.nos .noaa.gov).

LAND ACTIVITIES

These tiny specks of land, jutting more than 10,000ft from the bottom of the ocean, offer some of the richest ecosystems on the planet. Hiking is extraordinary. But you needn't be limited to your own two feet: try two wheels or a four-legged creature. Or take a swing with racquets and clubs.

HIKING

The hiking in Hawaii is top-notch, and there's enough diverse terrain to sate even the shortest attention spans. Hikes range from brief, laid-back nature strolls perfect for kids and seniors to multiday backcountry treks that will set anyone's calves quaking. And despite all the development in Hawaii, it's amazing how much land is still in a natural state. There are places where you could walk for days without seeing another soul. Just pick your place: blistering desert treks or lush rain-forest walks, nature preserves or botanical gardens, beach strolls or snowy ridgelines – it's all here.

The premier hike in all of Hawaii is on Kaua'i's Na Pali coast (p486), where the Kalalau Trail follows an ancient Hawaiian footpath along the edges of the most spectacularly fluted coastal cliffs in Hawaii. But unparalleled Hawai'i Volcanoes National Park (p271) on the Big Island

Lonely Planet's *Hiking in Hawaii* is a comprehensive, independent hiking guide with good maps and clear directions. What else would you expect?

contains the world's most active volcano. The park offers cool jaunts through mystical ohia forests as well as breathtaking hikes into steaming craters. Hardcore hikers won't want to miss the 18-mile trek to the snowcapped summit of Mauna Loa (p282).

On Maui, the volcano at Haleakala National Park (p374) is sleepier but equally awe-inspiring, and boasts the world's largest crater. Hikes into the moonscapelike caldera can take half a day, while hikes across its floor can take half a week. You can also trek into the ancient, fabled Waipi'o and Waimanu Valleys (p239), on the Big Island, or follow footpaths along old 'king's trails' – footpaths worn into the lava over hundreds of years by the bare feet of travelers on Maui and the Big Island.

O'ahu's most popular trail by far leads to the summit of Diamond Head (p139). But the island also has a wealth of more challenging trails to the top of peaks in the Ko'olau range, as well as the spectacular waterfalls and rolling switchbacks of the Maunawili Falls & Demonstration Trail (p143).

Safety

Hawaii has no snakes (although there are some reports of recent sights), no poison ivy, no poison oak and few wild animals that will fuss with hikers. But hiking around volcanoes presents a variety of dangers. Fumes can lead to respiratory problems; lava flows can unexpectedly collapse; crevasses can wrench ankles. Heed all posted warnings and hike with a buddy.

Flash floods are a real danger in many of the steep, narrow valleys that require stream crossings. Warning signs include a distant rumbling, the smell of fresh earth and a sudden increase in the river's current. If the water begins to rise, get to higher ground immediately. A walking stick is good for bracing yourself on slippery approaches, gaining leverage and testing the depth of rivers and streams.

To learn more about the Ironman Triathlon World Championship visit the website at www .ironmanlive.com.

Darkness falls fast once the sun sets and ridge-top trails are no place to be caught unprepared in the dark. Always carry a flashlight just in case. Long pants offer protection from overgrown parts of the trail, and sturdy footwear with good traction is a must (and lava will still chew right

---

EXTREME HAWAII

The Ironman Triathlon World Championship is a grueling, nonstop combination of a 2.4-mile swim, 112-mile bike race and 26.2-mile run. And it all has to be done in 17 hours, although the top athletes cross the finish line in about half that time. Luc van Lierde of Belgium set the current men's record at eight hours and four minutes in 1996, while the women's record, set by Paula Newby-Fraser of the USA in 1992, is eight hours and 55 minutes.

Harsh *kona* (leeward) conditions make the event the ultimate endurance test, even by triathlon standards. Heat reflected off the lava landscape commonly exceeds 100°F, making dehydration and heat exhaustion major challenges. Many contenders arrive weeks before the race just to acclimatize themselves. On the day of the race, nearly 7000 volunteers line the 140-mile course to hand out some 12,500 gallons of water – more than 8 gallons for each triathlete!

For all this punishment, the top male and female winners walk (or crawl) away with $100,000 each. Perhaps you'd like to keep your day job? In all, a total of $325,000 is given to competitors. The race takes place each October on the Big Island's Kona Coast (p191).

Begun in 1978 with just 15 participants, the Ironman was labeled 'lunatic' by *Sports Illustrated* after the second race. By 1980, the Ironman had enough participants to receive TV coverage on ABC's *Wide World of Sports,* and the numbers continue to grow. These days, some 50,000 triathletes compete in a couple of dozen qualifiers in hopes of earning one of the 1500 entry berths for the main event. The athletes represent each US state, Canadian province and approximately 50 other countries.

NA ALA HELE

Of special interest to hikers and naturalists is the work of Na Ala Hele, a group affiliated with Hawaii's Division of Forestry & Wildlife. Na Ala Hele was established with the task of documenting public access to trails as part of a movement to preserve Hawaii's natural environment and cultural heritage. Throughout the state, the group has negotiated with private landowners and the military to gain access to previously restricted areas and reestablish abandoned trails.

The Na Ala Hele logo signpost – a brown sign that features a yellow hiking petroglyph figure – is marking an increasing number of trailheads as the organization's work continues. Na Ala Hele is headquartered at the **Division of Forestry & Wildlife** (DOFAW; Map p86; ☎ 587-0062; www .hawaiitrails.org; Suite 132, 567 S King St) in downtown Honolulu.

through it). Pack 2L of water per person for a day hike, carry a whistle and something bright to alert rescue workers should the need arise, wear sunscreen, tote a first aid kit and above all, start out early.

Check out the Sierra Club (www.hi.sierraclub.org) for information on guided hikes on the major islands.

MOUNTAIN BIKING

Mountain biking is an increasingly hip adventure sport in Hawaii and rentals are plentiful. Generally speaking, local biking communities are well organized, host group rides, build new trails and promote responsible and safe cycling. Aside from established trails, you'll also find miles of 4WD roads to scream through and scratchy trails leading to little secret beaches that will surely catch the passing fancy of a cyclist or two.

Head Upcountry on Maui to the Skyline Trail (p373) in the Polipoli Spring State Recreation Area. Or join the crowds by biking down Haleakala (p374) at sunrise.

On the Big Island, the county has designated a number of areas that bikers can use and has funded the publication of a mountain-biking trail map. The routes (p233) include the 45-mile Mana Rd loop circling Mauna Kea and the 6.5-mile beach trail to Pine Trees on the Kona Coast.

On Kaua'i, you can pedal the Waimea Canyon Trail (p510) and Powerline Trail (p458), a picturesque ridge-top route from Wailua to Princeville.

John Alford's *Mountain Biking the Hawaiian Islands* should be your bible.

HORSEBACK RIDING

All of the main islands offer memorable horseback riding. But since ranches, rodeos, cattle and cowboys are a big part of the Big Island and Maui, save your serious riding for these spots. Maui has the most unique offering: guides lead horses down crunchy cinder-rock trails into Haleakala (p298). On the Big Island, head to Parker Ranch and the Kohala Mountains (p231). Two-hour trail rides with drop-dead gorgeous scenery and trusty steeds typically start at $75 per person.

GOLF & TENNIS

If you feel like teeing off in paradise, you'll have more than 80 choices, ranging from modest county-operated courses to elitist world-class links.

Some of the more spectacular courses in Hawaii include the Francis I'i Brown Course (p221), sculpted from a jet-black Big Island lava field; Princeville's Prince Course (p475), overlooking scenic Hanalei Bay on Kaua'i; the mountainside Ko'olau Golf Course (p156); and West Maui's Kapalua Bay Course (p324), with a tee on one side of the bay and the green on the other. Lana'i has two top-notch courses: the waterside Challenge at Manele (p394) overlooking Hulopoe Bay and the rolling Experience at Koele course (p391). Expect to shell out $100 to $175 per round at the better courses (less if it's later in the day).

GUILTY PLEASURES

Spa tourism is hot – hot as in 'ili'ili therapy (with hot lava stones), that is. Modern Hawaiian spa treatments often sound a bit whimsical, but are loosely based on herbal traditions. Popular body wraps use wild ginger to remedy colds or jet-lag and seaweed to detoxify. Body scrubs make use of coffee or sea salts to exfoliate and ti leaf or aloe to heal sunburns.

Other tropical treatments sound good enough to eat: lomilomi (the name of a salmon preparation) is also a type of traditional Hawaiian massage. Then there are coconut-milk baths, Kona-coffee scrubs, kukui-nut reflexology and awapuhi (wild ginger) or limu (seaweed) body wraps.

If you don't have the necessary $100 or so to spend on these delights, pick up a bottle of coconut oil to try at home. Otherwise, head to these top picks:

Grand Wailea Spa Grand Wailea Resort Hotel & Spa, Maui (p347)
Spa at Kea Lani Fairmont Kea Lani Hotel, Maui (p347)
Anara Spa Hyatt Regency Kaua'i, Kaua'i (p497)
Spa Four Seasons Resort Hualalai, the Big Island (p217)
Mandara Spa Hilton Hawaiian Village, O'ahu (p130)

All islands have free public tennis courts (first come, first served), but you'll need to bring your own equipment. Many resort hotels have tennis clubs with equipment rentals; they charge court fees (around $15 per hour per person) and sometimes offer lessons to nonguests. You won't find tennis courts at Waikiki hotels, however, where space is at a premium. Maui has a full-service club in Wailea (p346).

SKYDIVING & HANG GLIDING
With skydiving, after receiving an hour of instruction, you're attached by the hips and shoulders to an experienced jumper. Then step out of a plane at 13,000ft, freefall for a minute, and float with a chute for 10 to 15 minutes. Sound fun? Now there's a view you won't soon forget! Glider rides are tamer: you board an engineless but piloted glider that's towed up by an airplane and then released to quietly glide back to earth. Rides are offered at Dillingham Airfield (p167) on O'ahu and from Birds in Paradise (p502) on Kaua'i.

Food & Drink

In Hawaii, the locals don't eat for survival – they eat for sheer pleasure. You'll find an array of cuisines, introduced by the first Polynesians and the succession of immigrants who followed. It took human settlers to create Hawaii's modern-day cornucopia, as the only indigenous edibles were ferns, *ohelo* berries and other barely sustaining plants. The Polynesians brought *kalo* (taro), *'ulu* (breadfruit), *'uala* (sweet potato), *mai'a* (banana), *ko* (sugarcane), *niu* (coconut) and mountain apple, plus chickens, pigs and dogs for meat – and they discovered an abundance of seafood.

Today native staples remain popular in dishes such as poi (a sticky paste made from steamed taro) and *kalua* pig, and Asian basics dominate the local palate with rice, noodles, shoyu (soy sauce) and ginger. Hawaii's ethnic cuisines, from Thai to Japanese to Italian, often break free of tradition when chefs can't resist adding an island tang to old favorites.

Bear in mind that 'local' fare is a broad term. You can go highbrow at five-star restaurants serving Hawaii Regional Cuisine, which highlights Pacific Rim flavors and island-grown produce, seafood and meat. Or you can sample everyday local *kine grinds* – hearty, flavorful and, most important, plenty! Local street food is often fried, salty, gravy-laden and meaty. But a trend toward healthy cooking in Hawaii is afoot, and you can find plate lunches featuring grilled fish and brown rice. Vegetarians will find lots of options: luscious fresh papaya and pineapple, organic greens, tofu delicacies and more. No one in Hawaii goes hungry.

DID YOU KNOW?

Restaurants that top pizzas with pineapple and call it 'Hawaiian' are way off. The pineapple was introduced to Hawaii in 1813 and grown commercially only after 1900.

STAPLES & SPECIALTIES

Nowadays you can find haute cuisine and imported haole (Caucasian) supplies (like olive oil, artisan bread and balsamic vinegar) anywhere in the islands. But at heart, Hawaii is a 'beer and rice' type of place – the 'wine and cheese' crowd has a long way to go. A meal is incomplete without the foremost local staple: sticky, medium-grain, white rice. The rice pot accompanies even pasta or potato meals, and 20lb bags of rice are typical raffle prizes. (Granted, the Atkins low-carb diet is a phenomenon in Hawaii, too.) While ketchup and salsa might be the mainland's top condiments, the local essential is soy sauce, always called by its Japanese name, shoyu.

HOMAGE TO TARO

To locals, describing poi as 'wallpaper paste' is not only absurd, it's an insult. Taro is a sacred food, considered the root of all life. The taro stem is called *'oha*, from which *'ohana* (family) is derived. In old Hawai'i, only men could tend the taro fields because women menstruate and were considered unclean. Traditional Hawaiian households always show respect for taro: when the poi bowl sits on the table, one is expected to refrain from arguing or speaking in anger.

In the 1970s, a cultural resurgence pushed taro cultivation into the mass commercial market, but production has ebbed and flowed over the years. Until recently, taro farms struggled in part because younger generations showed less interest in farming, and fungus disease and snail infestation devastated crops.

Lately taro has made a comeback. Terry Shintani, a University of Hawai'i MD, has developed a 'Hawaii Diet' that emphasizes taro over rice (half the calories!) and celebrity chefs are featuring taro at their upscale restaurants. At supermarkets you can find many brands of poi on sale, along with taro chips and baked goods. The Hawaii Taro Company based in Maui sells taro burgers throughout the islands and even at whole-foods supermarkets on the mainland.

Native Hawaiian

The centerpiece of a native Hawaiian meal is *kalua* pig, baked underground in an *imu* (a pit of red-hot stones). To cook the pig, layers of crushed banana trunks and *ti* leaves are placed over the stones. The pig, stuffed with hot stones, is laid atop the bed, along other foods wrapped in *ti* and banana leaves. Everything receives another covering of *ti* leaves, a layer of mats and dirt to seal in the hot steam. To *kalua* means to cook using this method. Cooking time is four to eight hours, depending on the quantity of food. Traditional *kalua* cooking is hard to find nowadays, as few resorts still cook pork underground for luau. At home, it's hard to find folks willing to sacrifice their backyard for an *imu*, which scorches all surrounding vegetation.

Wetland taro was the Hawaiians' primary starch, usually eaten as poi, a paste pounded from cooked taro. The paste is thinned to a desired consistency by adding water. You might hear locals describe poi texture by the number of fingers needed to scoop it into the mouth: one-, two- and three-finger poi. Poi is highly nutritious and easily digestible, but for most nonlocals it's an acquired taste. Poi highlights and balances the flavor of richer foods, and if you first taste it by itself, you might find it bland and gooey.

Homesick locals living on the mainland share their recipe collections online at www.alohaworld.com/ono.

Other commonly eaten Hawaiian foods are *laulau* (bundle of pork, chicken or butterfish, wrapped in taro leaf, which cooks to a soft texture similar to spinach, and steamed in a covering of *ti* leaf); *lomi* salmon (a dish of minced, salted salmon, diced tomato and green onion); baked *'ulu* (breadfruit); raw *opihi* (limpets picked off the reef at low tide); *pipi kaula* (beef jerky); *haupia* (a stiff pudding made of coconut cream and arrowroot); and raw *'a'ama* (black crab).

Local Food

While 'destination' restaurants might show off Hawaii's finest flavors, the soul of island food resides in cheap everyday eats, including the following:

Bento – A remnant of plantation days, this prepackaged Japanese-style box lunch includes rice and your choice of meat or fish, along with pickles, *kamaboko* (a cake of puréed, steamed fish) and cooked vegetables.

Crack seed – A Chinese snack food made with dried fruit, often plums or lemon. Crack seed can be sweet, sour, salty or a combination of all. The most popular – and most overwhelming to the uninitiated – is *li hing mui*. Today locals use *li hing* flavoring to spice up everything from fresh apples to margaritas!

Hawaii's Best Local Desserts by Jean Watanabe Hee reveals dozens of recipes for gotta-be-homemade desserts, from haupia chocolate pie to macadamia nut angels.

Loco moco – For an only-in-Hawaii experience, try this amalgamation of rice, fried egg and hamburger patty topped with gravy and a dash of shoyu. It's surprisingly appetizing, and meatless versions are available.

Okazu-ya – If you want to cobble together your own meal, Japanese 'fast food' is sold individually (by the piece) at *okazu-ya* (lunch counters). There are dozens of options, including *musubi* (rice ball), *maki* (hand-rolled) sushi, tofu patties, shrimp tempura, *nishime* (stew of root vegetables) and Japanese-style fried chicken.

Plate lunch – This fixed-plate meal (akin to a 'blue-plate special') comprises 'two scoop rice,' a scoop of macaroni salad and an entrée, such as beef stew, *tonkatsu* (pork cutlets), grilled mahimahi or teriyaki chicken.

Pupu – 'Anykine' snacks or appetizers. An irresistibly savory favorite is *poke* (poh-kay), which contains cubed raw fish (often *'ahi*) typically marinated in shoyu, sesame oil, salt, green onion and chili pepper. Traditional *poke* includes *ogo* (seaweed) and *inamona*, a flavoring made of roasted and ground *kukui* (candlenut), while countless current renditions might use oysters, tofu or fruit. Also worth trying are boiled peanuts in the shell, which are similar to the *edamame* (boiled soybeans) popular at sushi bars and taste fresher than the usual dry-roasted nuts.

Saimin – Found only in Hawaii, this noodle soup is garnished with your choice of toppings, such as green onion, dried nori (seaweed), slices of *kamaboko*, egg roll and *char siu* (Chinese roast pork).
Shave ice – Called 'ice shave' on the Big Island, this is a mainland 'snow cone' taken to the next level: the ice is shaved fine like powdered snow, packed into a paper cup and drenched with syrups in eye-popping hues. For a change, try sweet adzuki bean paste or ice cream underneath.

Hawaii Regional Cuisine

Less than two decades ago, Hawaii was not exactly a foodie destination. Sure, locals savored their Spam *musubi* (see p65) and enjoyed decent ethnic fare, but fine dining typically meant imitation 'continental' fare that ignored the bounty of locally grown produce, seafood and meat.

In the late 1980s and early 1990s, top island chefs finally showed off local ingredients and multicultural influences – and quickly hit the gourmet radar. The movement was dubbed 'Hawaii Regional Cuisine' and the pioneering chefs became celebrities. Roy Yamaguchi is the forerunner who opened his original Roy's restaurant (p141) in 1988, but today's culinary connoisseurs seem rather jaded by his ever-growing empire of 30 restaurants across the USA. Alan Wong's namesake restaurant (p109), founded in 1995, is widely considered Hawaii's finest, and critics nationwide marvel at his imaginative signature starter – a shot glass filled with *opihi* (limpet) in a light bath of tomato broth, fennel and basil.

DRINKS
Non-Alcoholic

The best-known drink in Hawaii is world-renowned Kona coffee, which typically costs $20 per pound. The upland slopes of Mauna Loa and Hualalai on the Big Island's Kona district offer the ideal climate – sunny mornings and rainy afternoons – for coffee cultivation (see p204). Recently coffee farms have reappeared on O'ahu, Maui, Moloka'i and especially Kaua'i, where 4000 acres were recently set aside for growing coffee. However, only 100% Kona has gourmet cachet.

Traditionally, Hawaiians had no alcoholic drinks, but whalers introduced liquor and taught them to make their own, *'okolehao*, distilled from the *ti* root. Instead they used *'awa* (kava) as a mild intoxicant, and in recent years, *'awa* (kava) 'bars' have popped up (see p194). *'Awa* is found throughout the Pacific and used as medicine and for rituals. Typically, the root of the plant is chewed or pulverized and mixed with water to produce a milky concoction that numbs the mouth and has a

Never trust a skinny chef? That's the motto of celebrity chef Sam Choy, who shares a few favorite recipes at www.samchoy.com.

For Spam trivia, history, events, recipes and more, go to www.hormel.com (and search the site for Spam).

HAWAII'S COMFORT FOOD IN A CAN

Hawaii is the Spam capital of the USA, and locals consume a whopping 4 million cans per year, or 10,958 cans per day (3.5 times more than any other state consumes). While US foodmaker Hormel's Spam, a pork-based luncheon meat, is the butt of jokes almost everywhere, there's little stigma in Hawaii. Rather, Spam is a comfort food – always eaten cooked, not straight from the can.

Why Spam? No one knows exactly. Some say it simply goes well with rice, Hawaii's ubiquitous starch. Others claim it's a legacy of plantation cookery, when fresh meat was not always available. Even today, whenever the islands are threatened by a hurricane or a dockworkers' strike, locals stock up on water, batteries, toilet paper, 20lb bags of rice and…Spam.

A local favorite is Spam *musubi*: a block of rice with a slice of fried Spam on top (or in the middle), wrapped with a strip of black sushi nori. Originated in the 1960s or '70s, it has become a classic, and thousands of *musubi* are sold daily at grocers, lunch counters and convenience stores. The Spam *musubi* phenomenon has even reached Hormel, which in 2004 released a collector's edition can called 'Hawaiian Spam' with a recipe for you-know-what on the back.

sharp and earthy flavor. Truth be told, the stuff tastes awful. But the lactones in kava are believed to relieve anxiety, fatigue and insomnia, while fostering restful sleep and vivid dreams. The effect from an 8oz glass is mildly narcotic, but not mind-altering. 'Awa is not recommended for pregnant women or for daily use.

Fruit drinks are everywhere, but inexpensive canned drinks are generally not pure juice. One native Hawaiian fruit-juice tonic is *noni* (Indian mulberry), which grows with wild abandon alongside roads. Proponents claim that *noni* reduces inflammation, boosts energy and helps cure everything from arthritis to cancer. All that's known for sure: *noni* tastes and smells nasty. Sold commercially, it's usually mixed with other juices. On Kaua'i you'll see roadside smoothie stands selling $2 *noni* 'shots.'

Alcoholic
In general, drinking is a social pastime rather than a daily habit. The drinking age in Hawaii is 21, and shopkeepers will card baby faces. Beer is the drink of choice, due to habit and cost (it's cheap). Coors Light, nicknamed 'bullets,' tends to be a local favorite.

The microbrew trend is thriving in Hawaii, though craft brewers tend to come and go. Most of the established companies have lively brewpubs, such as Kona Brewing Company (p188) on the Big Island, Fish & Game Brewing Company & Rotisserie (p322) on Maui, Sam Choy's Big Aloha Brewery (p110) on O'ahu and Waimea Brewing Company (p508) on Kaua'i. Mehana Brewing Company on the Big Island is strictly a brewery (no pub) but it supplies its beer to upscale restaurants and even produces a mild ale called 'Roy's Special Reserve' for Roy Yamaguchi's restaurants.

While locals are predominantly beer drinkers, wine is gaining in popularity among the upper-income classes. Wine-tasting parties and clubs are not uncommon, and wine sales have skyrocketed, both at Costco and at specialty wine shops. In 2003 Lyle Fujioka opened a wine bar called **Formaggio** (☎ 739-7719; Market City Shopping Center, 2919 Kapiolani Blvd, Honolulu; ⏰ 5-10:30pm Tue-Thu, 5pm-1am Fri & Sat), where you can pick from over 40 selections by the glass. Chuck Furuya, Hawaii's only 'master sommelier,' does the wine lists for top restaurants like Alan Wong's and Roy's. At upscale restaurants, you'll find extensive wine lists of California and European vintages. On Maui and the Big Island, you can sample only-in-Hawaii tropical wines, such as the popular pineapple wine of Tedeschi Vineyards (p374) or the imaginative guava or macadamia nut honey concoctions of **Volcano Winery** (☎ 967-7772; www.volcanowinery.com; 35 Pi'i Mauna Dr, Volcano; ⏰ 10am-5:30pm).

As for the kitschy 'umbrella' drinks often associated with Hawaii, be forewarned that no self-respecting local would ever order a *chi chi* or, worse, any blue beverage. But if you can't resist, three tourist favorites are: piña colada with rum, pineapple juice and cream of coconut; mai tai, a mix of rum, grenadine, and lemon and pineapple juices; and Blue Hawaii, a vodka drink colored with blue curaçao.

CELEBRATIONS
The best-known local celebration is the luau, the native Hawaiian feast that's become a household word across the USA. Early Hawaiians celebrated auspicious occasions – such as a child's birth, war victory or successful harvest – with a feast to honor the gods and share their bounty. Called *aha 'aina* (gathering for a meal) in ancient times, the term luau became common much later; it also refers to the young edible taro leaves that traditionally were used to wrap food cooked in the underground *imu*.

In *The Best of the Best from Hawaii Cookbook*, Gwen McKee and Barbara Moseley carefully compile 300 recipes from Hawaii's most-popular community cookbooks. With plastic spiral binding, this is a neo-retro masterpiece.

Today there are two types of luau: private and commercial. Private luau are family affairs, thrown for a Hawaiian wedding or a baby's first birthday, sans fire-eaters and Tahitian dancers and the rousing 'Aloooooooooooha!' greeting. Guests feast on raw shellfish delicacies never served at commercial luau, and the entertainment is a lively local band, which might spur the *tutu* (grandmothers) to get up and dance hula with their grandchildren.

But unless you have connections, your only option is a hotel luau performance. These are well-choreographed shows that include an all-you-can-eat buffet and flashy Polynesian performances. The food tends to be mediocre, featuring the Hawaiian standards like poi and *kalua* pig – plus roast beef, teriyaki beef, fried rice and motley options designed to please all. Predictably, top-end resorts offer the best luau.

Other festivals showcase island specialties, such as the Big Island's Kona Coffee Cultural Festival (p191), when parades, farm tours and a coffee-tasting competition are spread over 10 days in early November. Also on the Big Island, the Aloha Festival Poke Weekend (p223) lets guests sample both professional and amateur *poke* entries in a contest founded in 1992 by Sam Choy. Beer lovers mark their calendars for the Kona Brewers Festival (p191), hosted each March by Kona Brewing Company. In Hana, the East Maui Taro Festival (p360) is a three-day event in late March, featuring poi-making demonstrations and a range of taro-containing foods, such as taro tempura, taro burgers, taro bread, taro seafood chowder and poi *mochi* (*mochi* is a Japanese sticky rice cake).

Recently, high-end culinary events have appeared across the islands, but they can vary widely in price and atmosphere. Entry to some costs around $5 with individual fees at carnival-type food booths; others charge $100 per person, often with funds donated to charities. If you want to support a cause, go for it – otherwise you might as well blow the $100 on dinner you can order yourself. Maui boasts a spate of gourmet events, including A Taste of Lahaina (p308) and the Kapalua Wine & Food Festival (p324).

Locals also find lots of informal occasions to celebrate, and you're bound to see large family gatherings at beaches and parks. Families and other groups often reserve a park pavilion for potluck dinners, where numerous tables are literally covered with food. All milestone events invariably involve a massive spread. You'll also see locals celebrating the standard American holidays much as mainlanders do, with elaborate birthday and wedding cakes, Easter egg hunts, Super Bowl beer parties and Thanksgiving turkey dinners. The difference lies in the nontraditional variety of food served. Sure, you'll see a whole turkey on the table for Thanksgiving, but you'll also see rice (no mashed potatoes), teriyaki-barbecued meat, fried whole shrimp, *maki* sushi and much more.

WHERE TO EAT & DRINK

If nothing else, you'll have the gamut of dining options in Hawaii. For a quick meal, the best places are open-air, '70s-style drive-ins or *okazu-ya* lunch shops. Often queued up at lunchtime, the folks in line behind you might get impatient if you dawdle at the counter. *Kaukau* wagons (lunch vans) are another to-go option, primarily on O'ahu. Typically found at beaches or busy streets, the vendors park in the same spot daily and serve plate lunches to go.

Diner-style restaurants abound. Often with formica tables and vinyl chairs, no view and no decor, these restaurants are the mainstays of everyday dining out because you get quick service and decent food at decent prices. If you've got an appetite or want variety, all-you-can-eat

DID YOU KNOW?

It takes 300 pounds of pressure to crack the outer shell of a macadamia nut.

If making your own sushi sounds way too daunting, use *DK's Sushi Chronicles from Hawaii* as a guide. Dave 'DK' Kodama is the owner-chef of the renowned Sansei Seafood Restaurant & Sushi Bars in Honolulu and on Maui (p343).

seafood and prime rib buffets are a good option. Such buffets are common at hotels, and they're popular for local family gatherings. The better buffets serve *nigiri* sushi and sashimi.

If you want to sample Hawaii's finest offerings, top-end restaurants are impressive and distinct. But don't expect the smooth, sophisticated service you might receive at a comparable place in New York or San Francisco. Hawaii is not a white-tablecloth-and-silver type of place, and service might seem lackadaisical. But the casual air can be refreshing.

For an online restaurant-review blog by a local in the know (complete with photos!), click to http://onokinegrindz .typepad.com.

Locals are early-bird eaters, and typical restaurant hours are 6am to 10am for breakfast, 11:30am to 2pm for lunch and 5pm to 9:30pm for dinner. Most places shut down by 10pm. For late-night dining, you'll have to seek out 24-hour places like Zippy's. In general, locals tip slightly less than mainlanders do, but still up to 20% for good service and at least 15% for the basics.

If you want to dine in, try locally owned supermarkets such as Foodland and KTA. You might be tempted to head to Safeway, a mainland chain, but prices are generally higher there and you won't find the local specialties. Groceries can be inexpensive (sashimi-grade 'ahi is less than $10 per pound) or costly (a box of cereal might be $5), usually depending on whether it's been shipped from the mainland. Supermarkets often include full delis offering hot entrées, plus conventional sandwiches to go. Even better on the run are the *bento*, sushi and other individually packaged meals.

VEGETARIANS & VEGANS

While most locals are omnivores, vegetarians and vegans can feast in Hawaii, too. The Asian influence in local cuisine guarantees lots of vegetable and tofu options, even when you're 'out country' in rural towns. The vast majority of restaurants offer a variety of entrées (main courses), rather than proclaiming themselves a steakhouse or rib joint. So, even if you forgo the oxtail soup, you're sure to find stir-fried veggies or fresh tossed greens on the menu.

That said, vegetarians aren't the target market: a plate lunch without meat or fish is not quite a plate lunch, and high-end restaurants do tend to highlight seafood. You'll have to seek out the few exclusively vegetarian eateries, such as Blossoming Lotus (p466) and Hanapepe Café (p504) on Kaua'i. A good alternative is to forage for yourself at the numerous farmers markets and health food stores islandwide, but be warned, they aren't cheap.

The trend toward meatless diets is growing slowly, mostly among young women and mainland transplants (hippie or otherwise). Most people eat everything in moderation and might view vegetarianism as extreme. Locals have a 'live and let live' attitude and if you start admonishing others about the evils of meat eating, you won't make any friends. As you'd expect, the most ardent supporters of meatless diets and organic, local and sustainable farming are haole newcomers, especially from the west coast.

When ordering at a restaurant, be sure to ask whether a dish is indeed meatless, as local cooks might inadvertently overlook those bacon bits on the spinach salad or that chicken broth in the risotto.

WHINING & DINING

Hawaii's family-oriented, extremely casual atmosphere means kids are welcome almost everywhere. Restaurants are usually quick to accommodate children with high chairs and booster seats, though too much noise or unruliness is inappropriate for the upscale establishments (locals are courteous to the nth degree and might not complain, but why stick out like an obnoxious tourist?). Often the most popular places with local families are the nondescript eateries at minimalls – and at such places, you'll see kids at every other table.

Families should also take advantage of the daily opportunity to eat outdoors. The balmy weather allows for impromptu plate lunch at the beach or fresh fruit at a roadside stand. If you really want to act local, buy a *goza* (inexpensive roll-up straw mat sold at ABC and Longs Drug stores), pack a picnic and head to the nearest park.

Kids will find lots of treats, such as homemade ice cream, shave ice, sweet bread and an assortment of chips. As for main dishes, the local palate tends toward the sweet and straightforward side, without too much garlic, bitter greens, pungent cheeses and strong spices – which typically agrees with kid tastes.

HAWAII'S TOP FIVE

No doubt, there are many other excellent eateries throughout the islands. But you can't go wrong here:

Hawaii Regional Cuisine

- A Pacific Café (p463)
- Chef Mavro (p109)
- Merriman's (p233)
- Alan Wong's (p109)
- I'o (p311)

Local Food

- Hamura Saimin (p449)
- Helena's Hawaiian Food (p110)
- Sam Choy's Kaloko (p214)
- Hana Hou Restaurant (p370)
- Ono Hawaiian Food (p133)

Luau

- Feast at Lele (p312)
- Old Lahaina Luau (p312)
- Polynesian Cultural Center's Ali'i Luau (p154)
- Kona Village Resort (p217)
- Royal Hawaiian Hotel (p134)

Plate Lunch

- Café 100 (p261)
- Kaka'ako Kitchen (p107)
- Pono Market (p466)
- Ichiban Okazuya (p334)
- Kamuela Cookhouse (p418)

Shave Ice

- Itsu's Fishing Supplies (p263)
- Jo-Jo's Shave Ice (p507)
- Local Boys Shave Ice (p342)
- Matsumoto Shave Ice (p163)
- Waiola Bakery & Shave Ice (☎ 949-2269; 2135 Waiola Ave, Honolulu, O'ahu; ⊙ 7:30am-6:30pm)

At hotel luaus, kids get a discount (and sometimes free admission with a paid adult). Commercial luaus might seem like a cheesy Vegas show to adults, but kids will probably enjoy the flashy dances and fire tricks. For more advice on traveling with children, see p521.

HABITS & CUSTOMS

Locals eat meals early and on the dot: typically 6am breakfast, noon lunch and 6pm dinner. Restaurants are jammed around the habitual mealtimes, but they clear out an hour or two later, as locals are not lingerers. If you dine at 8:30pm you might not have to wait at all! But bear in mind that restaurants also close early and night owls must hunt for places.

Locals tend to consider food quantity as important as quality – and the portion sizes are telling (more so at budget and mid-range restaurants than at ritzy ones). If you're a light eater, feel free to split a meal or to take home the leftovers.

Home entertainment for Hawaiians always revolves around food, which is usually served 'potluck style' with all the guests adding to the anything-goes smorgasbord. Most locals never serve dinner in one-at-a-time courses. Rather, meals are served 'family style,' where diners help themselves. Throwaway paper plates and wooden chopsticks make for an easy cleanup, and the rule is 'all you can eat' (and they definitely mean it!).

If you're invited to someone's home, show up on time and bring a dish, preferably homemade (but a bakery cake or pie is always appreciated). Remove your shoes at the door. And don't be surprised if you're forced to take home a plate or two of leftovers.

For pau hana (after work) meals, Joan Namkoong's Go Home, Cook Rice features everyday recipes that originally appeared in the Honolulu Advertiser, for which she was a food writer.

EAT YOUR WORDS

If someone offered you a *broke da mout malasada* would you try it? Don't miss out because you're stumped by the lingo. Here's a list of common food terms; for pidgin and Hawaiian pronunciation tips, see p546.

Food Glossary

'a'ama – black crab
'awa – kava, a native plant used to make an intoxicating drink
bento – Japanese-style box lunch

WHERE'S MY OMIYAGE?

Whenever locals travel to another island or beyond, they lug big boxes along with suitcases. The boxes are stuffed with *omiyage* (oh-mee-yah-geh, which means 'gift' in Japanese) for the people they'll visit. Usually inexpensive and edible, the gifts are chosen because they're unique to the home island. In return, they receive reciprocal *omiyage* from their hosts – and they buy more *omiyage* for the folks back home. (The boxes serve double duty.) The custom might be waning among younger generations who refuse to be bothered on vacation, however.

Of course, who needs a reason to enjoy each island's specialties? Try them while you're here and you'll understand why locals can't get enough.

O'ahu – Coco Puffs from Liliha Bakery (☎ 531-1651; 515 North Kuakini St; ⏰ 24hr btwn 6am Tue & 8pm Sun, closed Mon); Royal Kitchen manapua (p106); Ted's Bakery (p166) pies
Big Island – Big Island Candies (p263) macadamia and chocolate treats; 100% Kona coffee (p204); Sputnik buttermilk doughnuts (p263)
Maui – Tasaka Guri-Guri (p330) sherbet; Sam Sato's (p334) *manju;* Home Maid Bakery (p342) coconut turnovers; Komoda Store & Bakery (p369) cream puffs; Kitch'n Cook'd potato chips
Moloka'i – Kanemitsu Bakery (p409) sweet bread
Kaua'i – *Liliko'i* chiffon pie or fresh saimin noodles from Hamura Saimin (p449)

broke da mout – delicious
crack seed – Chinese preserved fruit; a salty, sweet or sour snack
donburi – large bowl of rice and main dish
grind – to eat
grinds – food; *ono kine grinds* is good food
guava – green-yellow fruit with moist pink flesh and lots of edible seeds
gyoza – grilled dumpling usually containing minced pork or shrimp
haupia – coconut pudding
imu – underground earthen oven used to cook *kalua* pig and other luau food
inamona – ground and roasted *kukui* (candlenut), used to flavor dishes such as *poke*
kaiseki ryori – formal Japanese meal consisting of a series of small dishes
kaki mochi – shoyu-flavored rice crackers
kalo – taro
kalua – traditional method of cooking in an underground pit
kaukau – food
kamaboko – a cake of puréed, steamed fish
katsu – deep-fried fillets
laulau – a bundle made of pork or chicken and salted butterfish, wrapped in taro and *ti* leaves and steamed
li hing mui – sour crack seed
liliko'i – passion fruit
loco moco – dish of rice, fried egg and hamburger patty topped with gravy or other condiments
lomilomi salmon – minced, salted salmon, diced tomato and green onion
luau – Hawaiian feast
mai'a – banana
mai tai – alcoholic drink made from rum, grenadine, and lemon and pineapple juices

---

WHAT'S THE CATCH?

Locals usually use Hawaiian or Japanese names of fish

- *'ahi* – yellowfin tuna
- *aku* – skipjack tuna (called *katsuo* in Japanese)
- *akule* – big-eyed scad
- *a'u* – swordfish, marlin
- mahimahi – white-fleshed fish also called 'dolphin' (not the mammal)
- *mano* – shark
- *onaga* – mild-tasting red snapper
- *ono* – white-fleshed wahoo
- *'opae* – shrimp
- *opah* – moonfish
- *'opakapaka* – snapper
- *'opelu* – pan-sized mackerel scad
- *papio* or *ulua* – jack fish
- *tako* – octopus
- *uhu* – parrotfish
- *uku* – strongly flavored gray snapper
- *ula* – Hawaiian lobster
- *wana* – sea urchin

malasada – Portuguese fried dough, served warm and sugar-coated

manju – Japanese cake filled with sweet bean paste

mochi – Japanese sticky-rice cake

nishime – stew of root vegetables and seaweed

noni – type of mulberry with smelly yellow fruit used medicinally

nori – Japanese seaweed, usually dried

ogo – seaweed

ohelo – shrub with edible red berries similar in tartness and size to cranberries

'ono – delicious

'ono kine grinds – good food

'opihi – edible limpet

pho – Vietnamese soup, typically beef broth, noodles and fresh herbs

pipi kaula – Hawaiian beef jerky

poha – gooseberry

poi – staple Hawaiian starch made of steamed, mashed taro

poka – a fruit in the passion-fruit family

poke – cubed raw fish mixed with shoyu, sesame oil, salt, chili pepper, *inamona* or other condiments

ponzu – Japanese citrus sauce

pupu – snack or appetizer; also a type of cowry shell

saimin – local-style noodle soup

shoyu – soy sauce

soba – buckwheat noodles

star fruit – translucent yellow-green fruit with five ribs like the points of a star and sweet, juicy pulp

taro – plant with edible corm used to make poi and with edible leaves eaten in *laulau*; also called *kalo*

teishoku – fixed, multicourse Japanese meal

teppanyaki – Japanese style of cooking with an iron grill

tonkatsu – breaded and fried pork cutlets, also prepared as chicken *katsu*

tsukemono – pickled vegetables

'uala – sweet potato

'ulu – breadfruit, a fruit starchy like a potato and prepared much the same way

ume – Japanese pickled plum

O'ahu

Waikiki, Diamond Head, Pearl Harbor, Sunset Beach: these images of O'ahu are the Hawaii tourist industry's stock and trade. But the reality beneath the images is rich – and even the briefest exploration can reveal unexpected finds.

The most developed of the Hawaiian islands, O'ahu is home to nearly 75% of the state's population. It's an urban scene, with high-rises and downtown traffic jams. Despite its development, the island has a scenic beauty that rivals the best of the Neighbor Islands: dramatic mountain cliffs, aqua-blue coral bays and deep valleys teeming with rich flora and fauna.

O'ahu's beaches and bays are legendary, from the surfing meccas of Sunset and Waimea to windsurfing favorite Diamond Head. Just east of Waikiki, Hanauma Bay Nature Preserve is the most-visited snorkeling spot in Hawaii.

Ready for the urban scene? You'll find Honolulu offers a rich blend of Eastern and Western influences. There is no ethnic majority here and the mix of people from around the Pacific is one of O'ahu's greatest assets. Honolulu has the only royal palace in the USA, outstanding parks and beaches, and spectacular hilltop views. The city is also a diner's delight.

Step out of Waikiki to really get what O'ahu is about. Wander through the bustling markets in Honolulu's Chinatown, hike along a quiet mountain trail near Tantalus and get your feet wet on a North Shore beach. Along the way, let the living spirit of aloha guide you.

HIGHLIGHTS

- Catch waves at **Sunset Beach** (p164)
- Relax on the beaches of **Hale'iwa** (p158) on the North Shore
- Munch on tasty shrimp scampi from the shrimp trucks at **Kahuku** (p156)
- Cruise the hotel beach bars of **Waikiki** (p134)
- Explore the **Valley of the Temples** (p150)
- Count your lucky stars at the luxurious **Turtle Bay Resort** (p168)
- Hike to **Makiki Valley Loop Trail** (p101)
- Glider ride over the **North Shore** (p167)
- Rise up for sunrise from **Diamond Head Crater** (p138)
- See Spinner dolphins up close on the **Wai'anae (Leeward Coast)** (p170)

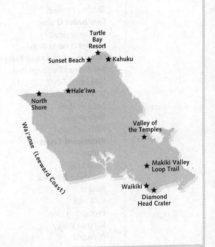

| POPULATION: 902,700 | NICKNAME: THE GATHERING PLACE | AREA: 608 SQ MILES |

Climate

Between O'ahu's Windward Coast and the dryer Wai'anae Coast lies Honolulu, where the average daily temperature ranges from 70°F to 84°F. Temperatures are a bit higher in summer and a few degrees lower in winter. Average afternoon water temperatures in Waikiki are 77°F in March and 82°F in August; mid-afternoon humidity averages 56%. Waikiki has an average annual rainfall of 25 inches; whereas the Lyon Arboretum, only four miles north in the Manoa Valley, averages 158 inches.

The National Weather Service provides **recorded weather forecasts** (☎ 973-4381) and **marine conditions** (☎ 973-4382) for all of O'ahu. See p521 for climate charts.

State & County Parks

Recreation opportunities in O'ahu's state and county parks range from sparkling public beaches and picnic grounds to ancient fishponds and wetland bird sanctuaries.

At O'ahu's far northwest corner, hikers and birdwatchers can follow the coastal cliffs of Kaena Point State Park (p171), the nesting home to several Pacific seabirds – boobies and shearwaters among them. Near the north tip of O'ahu, the protected wetlands at James Campbell National Wildlife Refuge (p156) attract winter birdwatchers who can glimpse several endangered waterbirds, including the striking Hawaiian stilt.

Popular spots like Malaekahana State Recreation Area (p155) or Kualoa Regional Park (p152) occupy beautiful stretches of the Windward Coast. Kailua Beach Park (p147) is justifiably famous, and a mecca for swimmers and windsurfers.

On O'ahu's south shore, Hanauma Bay (p139) boasts the state's only underwater park. Inland, highlights include Diamond Head State Monument (p138).

Closer to Honolulu, Sans Souci Beach Park (p126), opposite Kapiolani Park, attracts serious swimmers and sunbathers. Just opposite Ala Moana Center, the combination of shallow shore and grassy shade make Magic Island beach (p95) one of O'ahu's best for children. Nearby Kaka'ako Waterfront Park (p93) is great for picnics, and watching surfers and boogie boarders up close.

The protected bay at Hale'iwa Ali'i Beach Park (p160) offers the best year-round swimming on the North Shore, and the nearby marine preserve at Pupukea Beach Park (p164) attracts divers and snorkelers during the summer. Swing over to Poka'i Bay Beach Park (p169), just north of the boat harbor, to find the only year-round swimming on the leeward side of O'ahu.

CAMPING

Although O'ahu has no national parks to camp in, you can pitch a tent at numerous county beach parks, four state parks and one botanical garden. You'll find the highest concentration of facilities on the Windward Coast, beneath the majestic Ko'olau range.

All county and state campgrounds on O'ahu are closed on Wednesday and Thursday nights. At Malaekahana (p155), a private non-profit group operates a campground that is open daily.

Although thousands of visitors to O'ahu use campsites each year without incident, rip-offs and car break-ins, especially at roadside and beachfront campgrounds, are not unknown. The Wai'anae Coast is best reserved for day trips, as campers can run into turf issues with locals living on the beach there.

State Parks

Camping is allowed by permit at Kea'iwa Heiau State Park (p118) and Sand Island State Recreation Area (p99), both in the greater Honolulu area, as well as at Malaekahana State Recreation Area (p155) and Ahupua'a 'O Kahana State Park (formerly Kahana Valley State Park; p153), both on the Windward

---

TOP 10 BEACHES

- **Kailua Beach Park** (p147)
- **Sunset Beach Park** (p164)
- **Waikiki Beach** (p125)
- **Malaekahana State Recreation Area** (p155)
- **Hale'iwa Ali'i Beach Park** (p160)
- **Ala Moana Beach Park** (p95)
- **Sans Souci Beach** (p126)
- **Waimanalo Beach Park** (p142)
- **Waimea Bay Beach Park** (p163)
- **Sandy Beach** (p141)

O'AHU

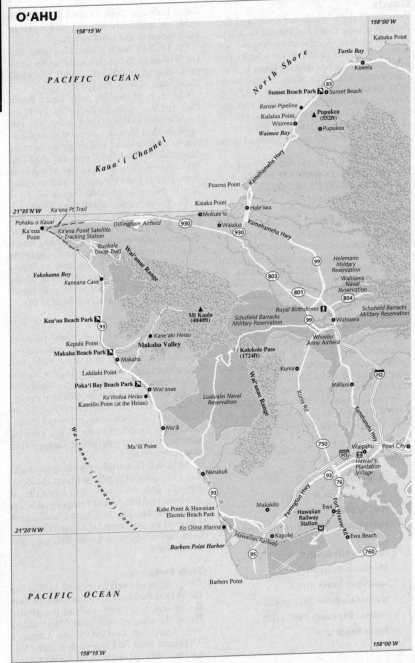

PACIFIC OCEAN

158°15'W

158°00'W

Kahuku Point

Turtle Bay

Kawela

North Shore

Sunset Beach Park 🏠 Sunset Beach

83

Banzai Pipeline

Kulalua Point ▲ **Pupukea**

Waimea (552ft)

● Pupukea

Waimea Bay

Kaua'i Channel

Puaena Point

Kamehameha Hwy

Kaiaka Point

● Hale'iwa

21°35'N W   Ka'ena Pt. Trail   ● Mokule'ia

Pohaku o Kauai   *Dillingham Airfield*   930

Ka'ena   Ka'ena Point Satellite   ● Waialua

Point   Tracking Station   930   Kamehameha Hwy

Kuokala   *Wai'anae Range*   99

Troop Trail

Helemano

Military

Yokohama Bay   Reservation

Kaneana Cave   803   Wahiawa

Naval

801   Reservation   804

Royal Birthstones   Schofield Barracks

Kea'au Beach Park 🏠   ▲ **Mt Kaala**   Schofield Barracks   Military Reservation

93   (4040ft)   Military Reservation

● Kane'aki Heiau   99   ● Wahiawa

Kepuhi Point   **Makaha Valley**   Wheeler

Makaha Beach Park 🏠   ● Makaha   Army Airfield

Kolekole Pass   H2

Lahilahi Point   (1724ft)

Poka'i Bay Beach Park 🏠   Kunia ●   Mililani ●

Ku'ililoa Heiau   ● Wai'anae   *Luaualei Naval*

Kaneilio Point (at the Heiau)   *Reservation*   Kunia

Rd

● Ma'ili   750   Waipahu   Pearl City

H1

Ma'ili Point   *Wai'anae Range*   **Hawai'i's**   ◆

Plantation

Village

Wai'anae (leeward) Coast   ● Nanakuli   93   76

Farrington Hwy

93

Kahe Point & Hawaiian   Makakilo ●   Ewa   Fort Weaver Rd

Electric Beach Park   **Hawaiian**   ●

21°20'N W   ● Ko Olina Marina   **Railway**   Ewa Beach

Hawaiian Railway   **Station**   760

Barbers Point Harbor   ● Kapolei

95

PACIFIC OCEAN   Barbers Point

158°15'W   158°00'W

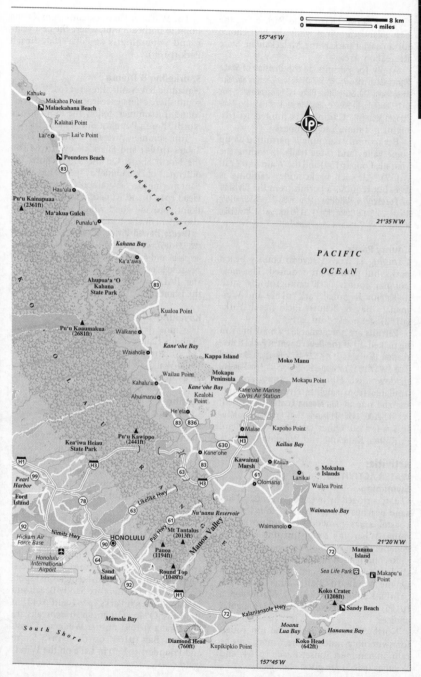

0 _____ 8 km
0 _____ 4 miles

157°45'W

Kahuku
Makahoa Point
Malaekahana Beach
Kalahai Point
Lai'e — Lai'e Point

Pounders Beach
(83)
Hau'ula

Pu'u Kainapuaa
(2361ft)
Ma'akua Gulch
Punalu'u

21°35'N'W

Windward Coast

Kahana Bay
Ka'a'awa

Ahupua'a 'O
Kahana
State Park
(83)

Kualoa Point

Pu'u Kaaumakua
(2681ft)
Waikane

Waiahole

Kane'ohe Bay
Kappa Island

Moko Manu

Wailau Point
Mokapu
Peninsula
Mokapu Point

Kahalu'u
Ahuimanu
Kane'ohe Bay
Kealohi
Point
Kane'ohe Marine
Corps Air Station

He'eia
(83) (836)
Malae
Kapoho Point

Kea'iwa Heiau
State Park
Pu'u Kawippo
(2441ft)
Kane'ohe
(630)
Kailua Bay

(H1)
(99)
(H3)
(63)
(83)
Kawainui
Marsh
Kailua

Mokulua
Islands

Pearl
Harbor
Ford
Island
(78)
(63)
(H3)
(61)
Olomana
Lanikai
Wailea Point

Likelike Hwy
Nu'uanu Reservoir

Waimanalo Bay

(92)
Hickam Air
Force Base
Nimitz Hwy
Pali Hwy
(61)
Mt Tantalus
(2013ft)
Manoa Valley
Waimanalo

21°20'N'W

HONOLULU
(90)
Pauoa
(1194ft)
(72)
Manana
Island

Honolulu
International
Airport
(64)
Sand
Island
(92)
Round Top
(1048ft)
(H1)
Sea Life Park
Makapu'u
Point

Koko Crater
(1208ft)
Sandy Beach

Mamala Bay
(72)
Kalanianaole Hwy
Moana
Lua Bay
Hanauma Bay

South Shore
Diamond Head
(760ft)
Kupikipkio Point
Koko Head
(642ft)

PACIFIC

OCEAN

157°45'W

Coast. Kea'iwa Heiau State Park offers the best inland camping, while the best choice for a coastal park is the Malaekahana State Recreation Area.

Apply for permits at the **Division of State Parks** (Map pp86-7; ☎ 587-0300; www.hawaii.gov/dlnr /dsp; Room 310, State Office Bldg, 1151 Punchbowl St, Box 621, Honolulu, HI 96809; campsite per night $5; ◷ 8am-3:15pm Mon-Fri). Camping is limited to five nights per month in each park.

Backcountry camping is permitted along some valley and ridge trails, including the Hau'ula Loop (p154) and the Waimano Trail (p117). All such backcountry camping is free, but requires a permit from the **Division of Forestry & Wildlife** (Map pp86-7; ☎ 587-0166; Room 325, State Office Bldg, 1151 Punchbowl St, Honolulu, HI 96813; ◷ 7:45am-4:15pm Mon-Fri).

County Parks

Camping is free at several county beach parks, but permits are required. The most popular county park campgrounds, such as Kualoa Regional Park (p152) and Waimanalo Bay & Bellows Field Beach Parks (p142), get booked up early.

Permits are not available by mail, but can be picked up at the **Department of Parks & Recreation** (Map pp86-7; ☎ 523-4525; Honolulu Municipal Bldg, 650 S King St, cnr Alapai St; ◷ 7:45am-4pm Mon-Fri) in downtown Honolulu. Permits are also available from satellite city halls, including the one at **Ala Moana Center** (Map pp90-1; ☎ 973-2600; 1450 Ala Moana Blvd; ◷ 9am-5pm Mon-Fri, 8am-4pm Sat). Other satellite city halls are in Kailua, Kane'ohe and Wahiawa.

Activities
WATER ACTIVITIES
Swimming

O'ahu is ringed by over 50 gorgeous white-sand beaches and the island's four distinct coastal areas provide year-round swimming. When it's rough on one side, it's generally calm on another.

Recommended south shore beaches include Waikiki (p125) and Ala Moana (p95). On the Windward Coast, Kailua Beach Park (p147), Kualoa Point (p152), Malaekahana (p155) and Waimanalo Bay (p142) are good choices.

North Shore beaches, while too rough for swimming much of the winter, can be calm in summer; Sunset Beach (p164) and Waimea (p163) are good choices.

The Wai'anae Coast extends from Ka'ena Point to Barbers Point, where the best year-round swimming is at Poka'i Bay Beach Park (p169).

Snorkeling & Diving

Hanauma Bay Nature Preserve (p139) on the south shore offers excellent snorkeling year-round. In summer, follow the locals to the North Shore's Pupukea Beach Park (p164).

Top summer dive spots include Three Tables (p164) and Shark's Cove (p164) on the North Shore. On the south shore, the outer part of Hanauma Bay (p140) has abundant marine life. Several spots between Koko Head (p140) and Kupikipiki'o Point (Black Point) provide good winter diving. O'ahu also offers the best wreck diving in Hawaii.

Breeze Hawaii Diving Adventure (Map pp86-7; ☎ 735-1857; www.breezehawaii.com; 3014 Kaimuki Ave, Honolulu) and **Aaron's Dive Shop** (☎ 262-4158; www .hawaii-scuba.com; 307 Hahani St, Kailua) are both five-star PADI operations and operate around the island.

Kayaking

The most popular place for kayaking on O'ahu is Kailua Bay (p147). Diamond Head (p138) attracts more advanced paddlers, while Waikiki's Fort DeRussy Beach (p124) area offers a good introduction to the sport.

Surfing

Come winter on O'ahu's North Shore, Sunset Beach (p164), Waimea Bay (p163) and the Pipeline (p164) are host to some of the world's top surfing competitions. There's also good winter surfing at Makaha Beach (p169) on the Wai'anae Coast. In summer, Waikiki (p125), Diamond Head (p138) and Kaka'ako Waterfront Park (p93) have some of the best breaks.

The best boogie-boarding in Waikiki is The Wall (p125) by Kuhio Beach.

In southeast O'ahu, Waimanalo Beach Park (p142) and Bellows Field Beach Park (p143) are best for beginner bodysurfers. The two hottest (and most dangerous) spots for expert bodysurfers are Sandy Beach and Makapu'u Beach Parks (p141 and p142) in southeast O'ahu. Other top shorebreaks are at Makaha (p169) on the Wai'anae Coast, Waimea Bay (p163) on the North Shore and Pounders (p155) in Lai'e on the Windward coast.

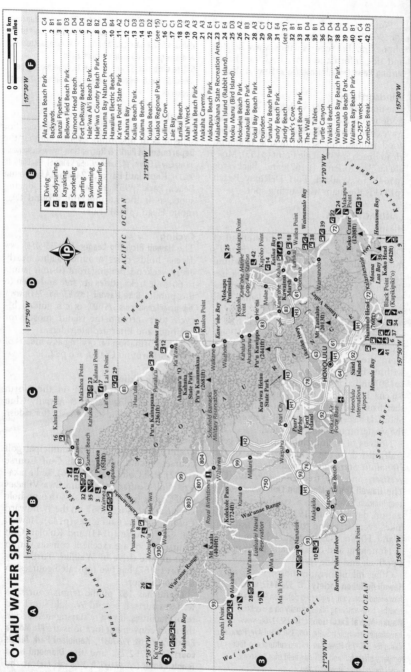

O'AHU WATER SPORTS

0   4 miles
0   8 km

Legend:
- Diving
- Bodysurfing
- Kayaking
- Snorkeling
- Surfing
- Swimming
- Windsurfing

O'AHU

For surf reports, call **Surf News Network** (☎ 596-7873), a recorded surf-condition telephone line that reports winds, wave heights and tide information, or check out **Hawaii Surfing News** (www.holoholo.org/surfnews) online.

Windsurfing

The number one spot, with good year-round trade winds along with good flat-water and wave conditions, is Kailua Bay (p147). Other good windsurfing spots include Diamond Head Beach (p138), Laie Point (p155), Mokule'ia Beach Park (p167) and Backyards (p164). In Waikiki, Fort DeRussy Beach (p124) is the main windsurfing spot.

LAND ACTIVITIES

Hiking

The short-but-steep trail to the summit of Diamond Head crater (p138) is the island's most popular hike. But the far more natural Tantalus & Makiki Valley (p100) area has the most extensive trail network around Honolulu. There the Manoa Falls Trail (p99) is a popular day hike.

On the Windward coast, you'll find a pleasant hour-long hike to Makapu'u Point Lighthouse (p141). There are also short walks from the Nu'uanu Pali Lookout (p145), within Ho'omaluhia Botanical Garden (p150) and along many of O'ahu's beaches. Ka'ena Point Trail (p172), approached either from the Wai'anae Coast or the North Shore, is a scenic hike through a reserve on the westernmost point of O'ahu.

Notices of hiking-club outings are generally listed in the Friday editions of the *Honolulu Star-Bulletin* and *Honolulu Advertiser*, and the free *Honolulu Weekly*. The **Hawaii Trail & Mountain Club** (www.geocities .com/htmclub; donation $2), a volunteer organization dating from 1910, leads informal hikes every weekend to one of 80 trails on O'ahu. Hikers usually meet at 'Iolani Palace in Honolulu, and occasionally team up for a potluck and slide show.

Other hiking organizations:

Hawaii Audubon Society (☎ 528-1432; www .hawaiiaudubon.com; suggested donation $2) Leads monthly bird-watching hikes, usually on a weekend.

Mauka-Makai Excursions (☎ 255-2206; www .hawaiianecotours.net; Suite 106, 350 Ward Ave, Honolulu; hiking fee $40-75) Hawaiian-owned cultural eco-tour company offers full and half-day field trips to scenic archeological sites around O'ahu.

O'ahu Nature Tours (☎ 924-2473; www.oahunature tours.com; per person $20-40) Small half-day tours to hidden rain forest waterfalls and coastal seabird sanctuaries, and easy guided hikes up Diamond Head.

Sierra Club (☎ 538-6616; www.hi.sierraclub.org; per person $5) Leads hikes and other outings around O'ahu on weekends.

Running

O'ahu has about 75 road races each year. For schedules of upcoming events, contact the **Department of Parks & Recreation** (www.co.honolulu .hi.us; City & County of Honolulu, 650 S King St, Honolulu, HI 96813). Kapiolani Park (p124) and Ala Moana Beach Park (p95) are two favorite jogging spots, as is the 4.6-mile run around Diamond Head (p138) crater.

Cycling

The **Hawaii Bicycling League** (☎ 735-5756; www .hbl.org) holds rides around O'ahu nearly every weekend, ranging from 10-mile jaunts to 60-mile treks. Rides are free and open to the public. **Bike Hawaii** (☎ 877-682-7433; www .bikehawaii.com; tours $75-100) offers guided bicycle tours around the island, mostly for beginner and intermediate riders.

For information on cycling as a means of transport around O'ahu, see p82.

Horseback Riding

Turtle Bay Resort (p168) on the North Shore and Kualoa Ranch & Activity Club (p152) on the Windward coast offer rides.

Golf & Tennis

O'ahu has several 18-hole municipal golf courses, including Ala Wai Golf Course (p102), Pali Golf Course (p156), Ted Makalena Golf Course (p102) and Ewa Villages Golf Course (p102). There's also a nine-hole course at Kahuku (p156), on the Windward Coast. Olomana Golf Links (p143), Hawai'i Kai Golf Course (p143) and Ko'olau Golf Course (p156) are excellent courses within a 30-minute drive of Waikiki. Turtle Bay Resort (p167) has two top-rated courses on the North Shore.

O'ahu has 182 public tennis courts, as well as courts at several Waikiki hotel and resort facilities. If you're staying in Waikiki, the most convenient locations are **Ala Moana Beach Park** (☎ 592-7031), **Kapiolani Park Tennis Courts** (☎ 971-2525), and the **Diamond Head Tennis Center** (☎ 971-7150; 3908 Paki Ave) at the

Diamond Head end of Kapiolani Park. The top-rated Turtle Bay Resort (p167) on the North Shore has 10 courts.

Hang Gliding & Skydiving
Skydiving and glider rides are offered at Dillingham Airfield near Mokule'ia on the North Shore; for details, see p167.

Getting There & Away
AIR
The vast majority of flights into Hawaii land at Honolulu International Airport, the only commercial airport on O'ahu. See p532 for information on flights to O'ahu from the mainland and abroad.

Honolulu also serves as the hub for the main interisland air carriers and has frequent services to all of the Neighbor Islands. For details on interisland flights, see p533.

Honolulu International Airport
Modern and easy to navigate, the **Honolulu International Airport** (HNL; www.state.hi.us/dot/airports /oahu/hnl) has all the expected services, including fast-food restaurants, lounges, newsstands, sundry shops, flower lei stands, gift shops, duty-free shops and a medical clinic with a nurse on duty 24 hours a day.

You'll find a **visitor information booth** (☎ 836-6413), car-hire counters and hotel courtesy phones in the baggage-claim area. A free shuttle called Wiki Wiki connects several terminals of the airport. It can be picked up in front of the main lobby (on the upper level) and in front of the inter-island gates.

If you need to exchange money, Thomas Cook has booths in the international arrival area and the central departure lobby next to Gate 24. You can also find a small Bank of Hawaii on the ground level of the terminal, across the street from baggage claim D. ATMs can be found near gates 12, 13 and 14, all inside the security area. There is one ATM outside security, near the H2 baggage area.

If you arrive early for a flight, check out the free Pacific Aerospace Museum in the main departure lobby, or relax at the garden on the concourse level.

Getting Around
O'ahu is an easy island to get around, whether you travel by public bus, private car, moped or taxi. See p114 for information about the various options available.

TO/FROM THE AIRPORT
From the airport you can get to Waikiki by local bus, airport shuttle services, taxi or hire car. A taxi to Waikiki from the airport will cost about $28.

O'AHU FLORA & FAUNA

Most of the islets off O'ahu's Windward Coast are sanctuaries for seabirds, including terns, noddies, shearwaters, Laysan albatrosses, tropic birds, boobies and frigate birds. Moku Manu (Bird Island) off Mokapu Peninsula has the greatest number of species.

The 'elepaio, a brownish bird with a white rump, and the 'amakihi, a small yellow-green bird, are the most common endemic forest birds on O'ahu. The 'apapane, a vibrant red honeycreeper, and the 'i'iwi, a bright vermilion bird, are less common.

The only other endemic forest bird, the O'ahu creeper, may already be extinct. This small yellowish bird looks somewhat like the 'amakihi, which makes positive identification difficult. The last sighting of the O'ahu creeper was in 1985 on the Poamoho Trail. The James Campbell National Wildlife Refuge (p156) provides limited viewing of several endangered seabirds.

O'ahu has wild pigs and goats in its mountain valleys. Brush-tailed rock-wallabies, accidentally released in 1916, reside in the Kalihi Valley. Although rarely seen, the wallabies are of interest to zoologists because they are thought to be an extinct subspecies in their native Australia.

O'ahu boasts several excellent botanical gardens, each in a different ecological setting. The largest and most diverse, Foster Botanical Garden (p94), on the edge of Honolulu's Chinatown, features orchids and palms, many bordering on the science-fiction variety. Among the stars of this garden is a Bo tree, a descendant of the tree under which the Buddha sat. The nearby Lili'uokalani Botanical Garden, named for the last reigning monarch of Hawaii, is devoted to native plants. At the Ho'omaluhia Botanical Garden (p150) in Kane'ohe, you can enjoy a stroll or drive through a lush rain forest garden.

O'AHU

Travel time between the airport and Waikiki on city bus No 19 or 20 is about an hour; the fare is $2. The buses run every 20 to 30 minutes from 5am to 11:15pm Monday to Friday, to 11:45pm on weekends. The bus stops at the roadside median on the terminal's 2nd level, in front of the airline counters. There are two stops, in front of Lobby 4, and between Lobby 6 and 7. Luggage is limited to what you can hold on your lap or store under your seat, the latter space comparable to the space under an airline seat. For more information on public buses, see right.

The easiest way to drive to Waikiki from the airport is via the Nimitz Hwy (92), which turns into Ala Moana Blvd. Although this route hits more local traffic, it's hard to get lost on it; follow the signs 'To Waikiki.' If you're into life in the fast lane, connect instead with the H1 Fwy heading east.

On the return trip to the airport from Waikiki, beware of the poorly marked interchange where H1 and Hwy 78 split; if you're not in the right-hand lane at that point, you could easily end up on Hwy 78. It takes about 25 minutes to get from Waikiki to the airport via H1 *if* you don't hit traffic.

Hawaii Super Transit (☎ 841-2928, 877-247-8737) and **Reliable Shuttle** (☎ 924-9292) offer shuttle services from 6am to 10pm between the airport and Waikiki hotels. The ride averages 45 minutes, but it could be as much as twice that long if you're the last person to be dropped off. Board with your luggage at the roadside median on the ground level, in front of the baggage-claim areas. The charge is $6 to $8 one way or $10 to $14 return. You don't need a reservation from the airport to Waikiki, but you do need to call at least a few hours in advance for the return van to the airport.

BICYCLE
It's possible to cycle your way around O'ahu, but cyclists should consider taking the bus to get beyond the greater Honolulu traffic. Most buses are equipped with bicycle racks, which can carry two bicycles, at no extra charge.

The state's **Highways Division** (www.state.hi.us /dot/highways/bike/oahu) publishes a *Bike O'ahu* map with biking trails, including clear road-safety categories. The map is on the website, and can be found at the Hawaii Visitors and Convention Bureau's (HVCB) visitor information center (p122) in Waikiki and most island bike shops.

BUS
O'ahu's public bus system, called **TheBus** (☎ 848-5555; www.thebus.org), is extensive and easy to use. TheBus has about 80 routes, which collectively cover most of O'ahu. You can take the bus to watch windsurfers at Kailua or surfers at Sunset Beach, visit Chinatown or the Bishop Museum, snorkel at Hanauma Bay or hike Diamond Head.

Ala Moana Center is Honolulu's central transfer point. Each bus route can have a few different destinations, and buses generally keep the same number whether inbound or outbound. If you're in doubt, ask the bus driver. They're used to disoriented and jet-lagged visitors.

All buses are wheelchair accessible, and all can accommodate two bicycles at no extra charge. Be prepared for the frigid air-conditioning. A bus in Honolulu is probably the coldest place on O'ahu, regardless of the season.

Fares
The one-way fare for all rides is $2 for adults, $1 for children aged six to 18 and

---

ROAD DISTANCES & DRIVE TIMES

Although actual times may vary depending upon traffic conditions, the average driving times and distances from Waikiki to points of interest around O'ahu are as follows:

destination	miles	time
Hale'iwa	29	50 min
Hanauma Bay	11	25 min
Honolulu Airport	9	20 min
Ka'ena Point State Park	43	1¼ hr
Kailua	14	25 min
Laie	34	1 hr
Makaha Beach	36	1 hr
Mililani	15	30 min
Nu'uanu Pali Lookout	11	20 min
Sea Life Park	16	35 min
Sunset Beach	37	65 min
USS *Arizona* Memorial	12	30 min
Waimea	34	1 hr

for seniors 65 years and older with a valid Medicare card; children under the age of six ride free. You can use either coins or $1 bills; bus drivers don't give change.

Transfers, which have a two-hour time limit stamped on them, are given free when more than one bus is required to get to a destination. If you're unsure, ask the driver if you'll need one.

Four-day visitor passes are valid for unlimited rides and can be purchased at any of the ubiquitous ABC Stores for $20. Monthly bus passes, valid for unlimited rides in a calendar month, cost $40 and can be purchased at satellite city halls, 7-Eleven stores, and Foodland, Star and Times supermarkets.

Schedules & Information
Bus schedules vary depending on the route; many operate from about 5:30am to 8pm daily, though some main routes, such as Waikiki, continue until around midnight. Buses run reasonably close to scheduled times, although waiting for the bus anywhere between Ala Moana and Waikiki on a Saturday night can be a particularly memorable experience, with full buses passing you by.

BE YOUR OWN TOUR GUIDE

It's possible to make a cheap day excursion circling the island by bus, beginning at the Ala Moana Center. The No 52 Wahiawa-Circle Island bus goes clockwise up Hwy 99 to Hale'iwa and along the North Shore. At the Turtle Bay Resort, on the northern tip of O'ahu, it switches signs to No 55 and comes down the scenic Windward Coast to Kane'ohe and back over the Pali Hwy to Ala Moana. The No 55 Kane'ohe-Circle Island bus does the same route in reverse. These buses operate every 30 minutes from 5am to around 11pm daily. If you take the circle-island route nonstop, it takes about four hours.

For a shorter excursion from Waikiki, you can make a loop around southeast O'ahu by taking bus No 58 to Sea Life Park and then bus No 57 up to Kailua and back into Honolulu. Because you'll need to change buses, ask the driver for a transfer when you first board.

TheBus has a great **telephone service** (☎ 848-5555; ☽ 5:30am-10pm). As long as you know where you are and where you want to go, the staff will tell you not only which bus to catch, but also when the next one will arrive. This same service also has a TDD service for the hearing impaired.

You can get printed timetables for individual routes free from any satellite city hall, including the one at the Ala Moana Center. Timetables can also be picked up from the Hawaii State Library in downtown Honolulu, and from the McDonald's restaurant on the corner of Kalia Rd and Lewers St in Waikiki.

CAR
The main car-hire agencies have booths or courtesy phones in the airport baggage-claim area. **Budget** (☎ 800-527-7000), **National** (☎ 831-3800), **Hertz** (☎ 831-3500), **Avis** (☎ 834-5536) and **Dollar** (☎ 800-800-4000) all have desks inside the airport and cars at adjacent lots. **Alamo** (☎ 833-4585; cnr Nimitz Hwy & Ohohia St) has its operations outside the airport, about a mile northeast of the airport terminal. For toll-free reservations numbers and websites, see p537.

TOURS
Island sightseeing tours by van or bus are offered by the following:
Discover Hidden Hawaii Tours (☎ 737-3700, 800-946-4432; www.discoverhawaiitours.com)
E Noa Tours (☎ 591-2561, 800-8804; www.enoa.com)
Polynesian Adventure Tours (☎ 833-3000, 800-622-3011; www.polyad.com)
Roberts Hawaii (☎ 539-9400, 800-831-5541; www.robertshawaii.com)

All four companies offer a variety of tours, including full-day circle-island tours that average $55/40 per adult/child. The circle-island tours typically include Diamond Head and other southeast O'ahu sights, Byodo-In temple, Sunset Beach, the Waimea Valley Audubon Center and a drive past the pineapple fields of central O'ahu on the return to Waikiki. There are also several half-day tours on offer, which cost around half the price of the circle-island tours. The most popular half-day tour includes downtown Honolulu, Punchbowl crater and the USS *Arizona* Memorial at Pearl Harbor.

O'AHU

HONOLULU

pop 378,000

Honolulu, the only big city in Hawaii, is the state's center of business, culture and politics. It has been the capital of Hawaii since 1845. Home to people from throughout the Pacific, Honolulu is a city of ethnic minorities. Its diversity can be seen on almost every corner – the sushi shop next door to the Vietnamese bakery, the Catholic church around the block from the Chinese Buddhist temple and the rainbow of school children waiting for the bus.

Honolulu offers a range of things to see and do. It boasts a lovely city beach, some excellent museums, elegant public gardens and an abundance of good restaurants. Architecturally, the city is a striking mix of sleek high-rises and Victorian-era buildings, visually connected only by swaying palm trees.

HISTORY

The fall of O'ahu to Kamehameha the Great in 1795 signaled the beginning of a united Hawaiian kingdom. The new king moved to Honolulu in 1809 to control the vigorous international trade taking place in the harbor.

In the 1820s Honolulu's first bars and brothels opened up to crews of whaling ships; Christian missionaries began arriving about the same time, presumably for different purposes. Sugar plantations, established in the 1830s, soon asserted themselves as Hawaii's major industry. Contract workers from Asia, North America and Europe were brought in to fill the labor shortage, marking a surge in immigration exemplified by today's ethnic diversity.

Honolulu replaced Maui as capital of the Kingdom of Hawai'i in 1845. Increasingly, Western expatriates dominated Hawaiian affairs. In 1893 a small group of these new Hawaiian citizens seized control of Hawai'i from Queen Lili'uokalani and declared it their own 'republic'; in 1898 Hawaii was formally annexed by the USA as its newest territory (p33).

Honolulu continued to grow as a commercial center. In 1901 electric streetcars were introduced. Then the next decades saw

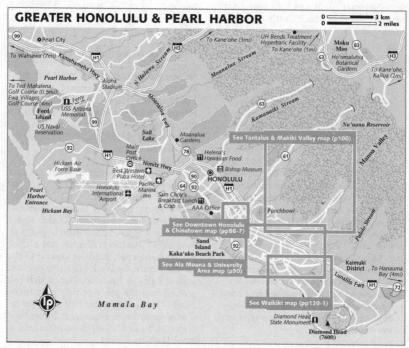

GREATER HONOLULU & PEARL HARBOR

a revival of Hawaiian culture as the sounds of falsetto voices and steel guitars filled the airwaves of territorial radio.

Following the Japanese attack on Pearl Harbor in 1941 Honolulu became the site of a harsh cultural, political and economic clampdown on the resident Japanese American population by military leaders. The 1950s closed with a plebiscite on statehood in which 90% of islanders voted 'yes.' (See the boxed text, p35.)

ORIENTATION

Honolulu's boundaries are not cut and dried. Still, the city proper is generally considered to extend west to the airport and east to Kaimuki.

Downtown Honolulu contains all of O'ahu's state and federal government buildings, including the state capitol and 'Iolani Palace, once home to Hawaii's last few monarchs and still the only royal palace in the USA. Chinatown is a few blocks northwest of the palace; the Aloha Tower and cruise ship terminals are a few blocks west.

Chinatown is immediately north of downtown Honolulu, roughly bounded by Honolulu Harbor, Bethel St, Vineyard Blvd and River St. Ala Moana Blvd (Hwy 92) connects the Nimitz Hwy and the airport with downtown Honolulu and Waikiki. Kapiolani Blvd and University Ave are the main thoroughfares connecting the Ala Moana area and the University of Hawaii, situated in beautiful Manoa Valley beneath the southern Ko'olau range.

Southeast of downtown Honolulu, Waikiki is the tourist epicenter; the big resorts and much of the city's nightlife are found there. Just southeast of Waikiki, 760ft (230m) Diamond Head rises up as the city's favorite geological landmark. All of these sites are within the boundaries of greater Honolulu, but are covered in separate sections later in this chapter.

H1, the main south shore freeway, passes east–west through Honolulu, connecting it to the airport and all other freeways on the island. Interestingly enough, it's a US interstate freeway – no small achievement for an island in the middle of the Pacific.

Maps

The free tourist magazines contain simple island maps, but if you plan to explore the island in a hire car or spend time in Honolulu, it's worth picking up a good road map.

The **American Automobile Association** (AAA; Map p84; ☎ 593-2221; Suite A170, 1130 N Nimitz Hwy, Honolulu) puts out reliable road maps of Honolulu and O'ahu. You can buy a similar map published by Rand McNally in convenience stores throughout O'ahu. The most comprehensive map is the 200-page *Phears O'ahu Mapbook*, which shows and indexes virtually every street on the island. *Franko's Map of O'ahu* is a sturdy one-page fold-out map with surprising detail, including the best locations for water sports throughout the island.

INFORMATION

The **Ala Moana Center** (Map pp90-1; 1450 Ala Moana Blvd) has airline offices, a post office, a couple of banks and ATMs, and a satellite city hall where you can get bus schedules. For more details, see p114.

Bookstores

Bestsellers (Map pp86-7; ☎ 528-2378; 1001 Bishop St; ☒ 7:30am-5:30pm Mon-Fri, 9am-3pm Sat) Good selection of travel guides, novels and maps.

Borders Books & Music (Map pp90-1; ☎ 591-8995; 1200 Ala Moana Blvd, Ward Centre; ☒ 9am-11pm Mon-Thu, 9am-midnight Fri & Sat, 9am-10pm Sun) Extensive news and travel sections.

Native Books/Na Mea Hawaii (Map pp90-1; ☎ 596-8885; Ward Warehouse, cnr Ala Moana Blvd & Ward Ave; ☒ 10am-9pm Mon-Sat, 10am-5pm Sun) Specializes in Hawaiiana titles.

Rainbow Books & Records (Map pp90-1; ☎ 955-7994; 1010 University Ave; ☒ 10am-10pm Sun-Thu, 10am-11pm Fri & Sat) Carries both new and used books.

UH Manoa Campus Bookstore (Map pp90-1; ☎ 956-8022; 2465 Campus Rd; ☒ 8:15am-4:45pm Mon-Fri, 8:15am-11:45am Sat) In the Campus Center.

Emergency

Police (☎ 529-3111) For non-emergencies.

Police, Fire & Ambulance (☎ 911) For all emergencies.

Suicide & Crisis Line (☎ 832-3100) Operates 24 hours.

Internet Access

Coffeeline (Map pp90-1; ☎ 778-7909; cnr University & Seaview Aves; ☒ 7am-3:30pm Mon-Fri, 9am-noon Sat & Sun) A wireless Internet hotspot where customers can link up their own device free of charge.

Coffee Talk (☎ 737-7444; 3601 Waialae Ave; per hr $5; ☒ 5am-11pm Sun-Thu, 5am-midnight Fri & Sat) This Internet café has it all – four fast terminals for web mail, plus a free-use wireless setup. If nothing else, you can get

O'AHU

DOWNTOWN HONOLULU & CHINATOWN

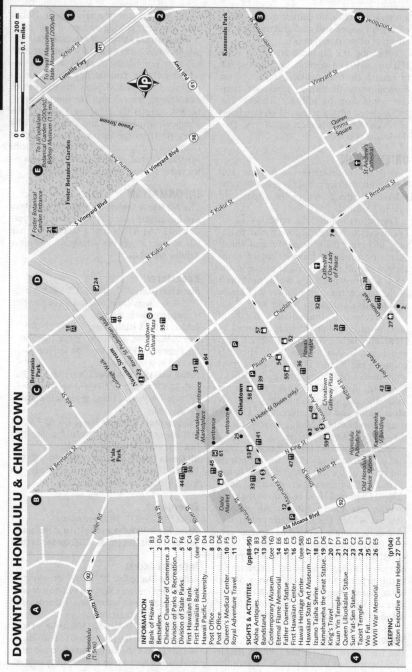

INFORMATION	
Bank of Hawaii....................................	1 B3
Bestsellers...	2 D4
Chinese Chamber of Commerce..	3 C4
Division of Parks & Recreation....	4 F7
Division of State Parks...................	5 F6
First Hawaiian Bank.........................	6 C4
First Hawaiian Bank...................	(see 16)
Hawaii Pacific University................	7 D4
Post Office..	8 D2
Queen's Medical Center.................	9 D6
Royal Adventure Travel..................	10 F5
	11 C5

SIGHTS & ACTIVITIES	(pp88-95)
Aloha Antiques.................................	12 B3
Bandstand...	13 D6
Contemporary Museum..............	(see 16)
Eternal Flame Memorial..................	14 E6
Father Damien Statue.....................	15 E5
First Hawaiian Center..................	(see 58)
Hawaii Heritage Center.................	16 C5
Hawaiian State Art Museum..........	17 D5
Izumo Taisha Shrine........................	18 D1
Kamehameha the Great Statue..	19 D6
King's Travel.......................................	20 F7
Kuan Yin Temple...............................	21 D1
Queen Liliuokalani Statue.............	22 E5
Sun Yat-Sen Statue..........................	23 C2
Taoist Temple.....................................	24 D1
Wo Fat..	25 C3
WWII War Memorial.........................	26 E5

SLEEPING	(p104)
Aston Executive Centre Hotel...	27 D4

O'AHU

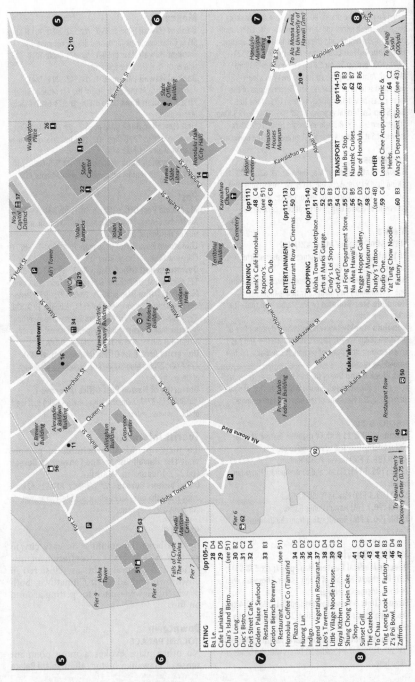

DRINKING   (pp111)
Hank's Café Honolulu.............48 C4
Kapono's...........................(see 51)
Ocean Club........................49 C8

ENTERTAINMENT   (pp112-13)
Restaurant Row 9 Cinemas....50 C8

SHOPPING   (pp113-14)
Aloha Tower Marketplace........51 A6
Arts at Marks Garage.............52 C3
Cindy's Lei Shop...................53 B3
Got Art?.............................54 C3
Lai Fong Department Store.......55 C3
Na Mea Hawai'i....................56 B5
Pegge Hopper Gallery............57 D3
Ramsay Museum...................58 C3
Sharky's Tattoo...................(see 48)
Studio One..........................59 C4
Yat Tung Chow Noodle
   Factory............................60 B3

TRANSPORT   (pp114-15)
Main Bus Stop......................61 B3
Nanatek Cruises...................62 B7
Star of Honolulu...................63 B6

OTHER
Leanne Chee Acupuncture Clinic &
   Herbs...............................64 C2
Macy's Department Store.......(see 43)

EATING   (pp105-7)
Ba Le...................................28 D4
Cafe Laniakea.......................29 D5
Chai's Island Bistro..............(see 51)
Cuu Long.............................30 B2
Duc's Bistro.........................31 C2
Fort Street Cafe....................32 D4
Golden Palace Seafood
   Restaurant.........................33 B3
Gordon Biersch Brewery
   Restaurant.......................(see 51)
Honolulu Coffee Co (Tamarind
   Plaza)................................34 D5
Huong Lan............................35 D2
Indigo.................................36 B2
Legend Vegetarian Restaurant...37 C2
Leo's Taverna........................38 D4
Little Village Noodle House......39 C3
Royal Kitchen.......................40 D2
Shung Chong Yuein Cake
   Shop.................................41 C3
Sunset Grill..........................42 C8
The Gazebo..........................43 C4
To Chau...............................44 B2
Ying Leong Look Fun Factory...45 B3
Z's Poi Bowl.........................46 D4
Zaffron...............................47 B3

wired on the coffee drinks, all of which are double shots. Breakfast, fresh juices and sandwiches are offered through the day and evening, and the peanut-butter cookies rock.

Honolulu Coffee Company (Map pp86-7; ☎ 521-4400; 1001 Bishop St, cnr S King St; ☾ 6am-5:30pm Mon-Fri, 7am-12:30pm Sat) Tucked away in a leafy courtyard setting at Tamarind Square, this is one of the more pleasant wireless places in town to surf the Net.

Net Stop Coffee (Map pp90-1; ☎ 955-1020; 2615 S King St; per min 9¢; ☾ 8:30am-midnight Mon-Fri, 9:30am-midnight Sat & Sun) A casual cybercafé near the university.

Libraries

Hawaii State Library (Map pp86-7; ☎ 586-3500; 478 S King St; ☾ 9am-5pm Tue, Fri & Sat, 10am-5pm Wed, 9am-8pm Thu) Adjacent to 'Iolani Palace, with a central courtyard and selection of international periodicals.

Media

NEWSPAPERS & MAGAZINES

101 Things to Do A good source of visitor information, similar to *This Week O'ahu*.

Honolulu Advertiser (www.honoluluadvertiser.com) One of Honolulu's two main daily newspapers.

Honolulu Star-Bulletin (www.starbulletin.com) The other main daily.

Honolulu Weekly (www.honoluluweekly.com) One of the more useful weekly papers, it's progressive and has an extensive entertainment section. It's available for free around the island.

This Week O'ahu One of the free tourist magazines available at the airport and all around Waikiki. It's full of paid advertising, but has some of the best discount coupons.

RADIO & TV

Channels 10 & 11 Both TV channels feature 24-hour visitor information and ads geared to tourists.

KHPR (88.1 FM) Hawaii Public Radio.

KINE (105.1 FM) Classic and contemporary Hawaiian music.

KIPO (89.3 FM) Hawaii Public Radio.

KKUA (90.7 FM) Hawaii Public Radio.

KTUH (90.3 FM) Broadcasting from the University of Hawaii.

Medical Services

Queen's Medical Center (Map pp86-7; ☎ 538-9011; 1301 Punchbowl St) One of O'ahu's several hospitals with 24-hour emergency services.

Straub Clinic & Hospital (Map pp90-1; ☎ 522-4000; 888 S King St, cnr Ward Ave) Offers 24-hour emergency services.

UH Bends Treatment Hyperbaric Facility (Map p84; ☎ 587-3425; 347 N Kuakini St) Divers with the bends are taken here.

Money

Bank of Hawaii (Map pp86-7; ☎ 532-2480; 101 N King St) In Chinatown, look for the red dragon columns.

Bank of Hawaii (Map pp90-1; ☎ 973-4460; 1010 University Ave) Near the university.

Bank of Hawaii (Map pp90-1; ☎ 942-6111; 1441 Kapiolani Blvd) At the north side of the Ala Moana Center.

First Hawaiian Bank (Map p100; ☎ 973-6481; Manoa Marketplace)

First Hawaiian Bank (Map pp86-7; ☎ 844-4444; First Hawaiian Center, 999 Bishop St) Classic building, convenient location, with a 24-hour ATM.

First Hawaiian Bank (Map pp86-7; ☎ 525-6888; 2 N King St) A 19th-century retro-interior with 24-hour ATM.

Post

Ala Moana Post Office (Map pp90-1; ☎ 800-275-8777; Ala Moana Center, 1450 Ala Moana Blvd) On the inland side on the ground floor.

Chinatown Post Office (Map pp86-7; ☎ 800-275-8777; Chinatown Cultural Plaza, River St)

Downtown Post Office (Map pp86-7; ☎ 800-275-8777; 335 Merchant St, cnr Richards St) In the old Federal Building.

Main Post Office (Map pp86-7; ☎ 800-275-8777; Honolulu International Airport, 3600 Aolele St, Honolulu, HI 96820; ☾ 7:30am-8pm Mon-Fri, 8am-4pm Sat) If you're expecting to receive mail by general delivery (poste restante), it is only accepted at this location and then held for 30 days.

University Area Post Office (Map pp90-1; ☎ 800-275-8777; 2700 S King St) Mo'ili'ili branch is a block east of University Ave.

University of Hawaii Post Office (Map pp90-1; ☎ 800-275-8777; Administrative Services Bldg) Just west of the Campus Center.

Tourist Information

To pick up tourist brochures in person, visit the **Hawaii Visitors and Convention Bureau** (p122), located in Waikiki.

O'ahu Visitors Bureau (☎ 523-8802, 877-525-6248; www.visit-oahu.com) An excellent website. Can answer questions over the phone.

SIGHTS

By and large, Honolulu is an easy city to explore. The largest concentration of historical and cultural sights are clustered in downtown and adjacent Chinatown, both of which are well-suited for getting around on foot.

Downtown

'IOLANI PALACE

No other place evokes a more poignant sense of Hawaiian history than **'Iolani Palace**

O'AHU

(Map pp86-7; ☎ 522-0832; tour adult/child $20/5; ⏱ 9am-2pm Tue-Sat), where royalty feasted, the business community steamed and plots and counterplots simmered, all within its regal walls.

The only royal palace in the USA, 'Iolani was the residence of King Kalakaua and Queen Kapiolani from 1882 to 1891, and of Queen Lili'uokalani for two years after that. Following the overthrow of the Hawai'ian kingdom in 1893, the palace became the capitol of the republic, then the territory and later the state of Hawaii.

The government moved out of their cramped palace quarters in 1969 into the current state capitol, leaving 'Iolani Palace a shambles. In 1978, after a lengthy multi-million dollar reconstruction project had restored the palace to its former glory, it reopened as a museum, where today visitors must wear booties over their shoes to preserve the polished wooden floors.

At the heart of the palace, the red and gold **throne room** features the original thrones of the king and queen. The site of celebrations that were full of pomp and pageantry, it was also where King Kalakaua danced his favorite Western dances – the polka, the waltz and the Virginia reel – into the wee hours of the morning.

In a move calculated to humiliate the Hawaiian people, two years after she was dethroned by American businessmen, Queen Lili'uokalani was brought back to the throne room and convicted of treason, spending nine months as a prisoner in 'Iolani Palace, her former home.

The interior of the palace can only be seen on a guided tour, which lasts about an hour; children under five are not admitted. Tours start every half-hour; sometimes you can join a tour on the spot, but it's advisable to call ahead for reservations.

The palace grounds, which are free and open to the public during daylight hours, pre-date the palace. A simpler house on these grounds was used by King Kamehameha III, who ruled from 1825 to 1854, and in ancient times a Hawaiian temple stood here. The former Royal Household Guards **barracks** has a gift shop and is where the palace ticket window is found. The domed **pavilion**, originally built for the coronation of King Kalakaua in 1883, is still used for the inauguration of governors, and on every Friday afternoon

concerts by the Royal Hawaiian Band are performed here (see p113 for details).

King Kamehameha II and Queen Kamamalu lay buried in the **grassy mound** surrounded by a wrought-iron fence until 1865, when their remains were moved to the Royal Mausoleum in Nu'uanu. The huge **banyan tree** between the palace and the state capitol is thought to have been planted by Queen Kapiolani.

HAWAII STATE ART MUSEUM
Opening in 2002, **Hawaii State Art Museum** (Map pp86-7; ☎ 586-0900; www.state.hi.us/sfca; 250 S Hotel St; admission free; ⏱ 10am-4pm Tue-Sat) was a long-over-due addition to Honolulu's museum scene. The downtown museum is housed in the Capitol District Building, a Spanish Mission–style gem that dates from 1928 when it was home to the Army & Navy YMCA. Today, the museum showcases the best of traditional and contemporary art from Hawaii's diverse ethnic artistic community. A variety of artistic styles are on display, from fine art and sculpture to contemporary photography and mixed-media. Revolving exhibits reveal how a blending of Western, Asian and traditional Pacific folk art forms have shaped a unique island aesthetic.

QUEEN LILI'UOKALANI STATUE
The bronze **statue** (Map pp86–7) of Hawaii's last queen stands between 'Iolani Palace and the capitol, facing Washington Place, Lili'uokalani's place of exile for more than 20 years. Lili'uokalani holds the Hawaii constitution, which she wrote in 1893 (fear of which caused US businessmen to depose her); *Aloha Oe*, a popular hymn she composed; and *Kumulipo*, the Hawaiian chant of creation.

WASHINGTON PLACE
The governor's official residence, **Washington Place** (Map pp86–7), is a large colonial-style building surrounded by stately trees, built in 1846 by US sea captain John Dominis. The captain's son, also named John, became the governor of O'ahu and married the Hawaiian princess who later became Queen Lili'uokalani. After the queen was dethroned, she lived at Washington Place in exile until her death in 1917. A plaque near the side-walk on the left side of Washington Place is inscribed with the words to *Aloha Oe*.

O'AHU

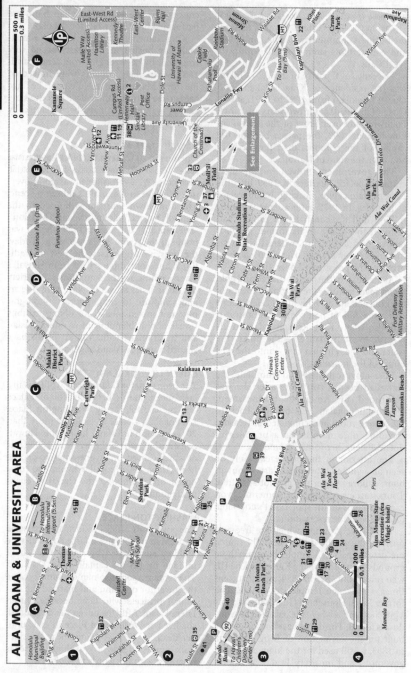

ALA MOANA & UNIVERSITY AREA

STATE CAPITOL

Built in the 1960s, Hawaii's **state capitol** (Map pp86-7; ☎ 587-0666; 415 S Beretania St) is an acquired architectural taste for some, and certainly not your standard gold dome. Its two cone-shaped legislative chambers represent volcanoes; the supporting columns symbolize palm trees. Trade winds blow gently through an open rotunda, and a large pool representing the ocean surrounding Hawaii encircles the entire structure. Visitors are free to walk through the rotunda and peer through viewing windows into the legislative chambers.

In front of the capitol stands a statue of **Father Damien**, the Belgian priest who in 1873 volunteered to work among leprosy victims on Molokai (see p421). The stylized sculpture was created by Venezuelan artist Marisol Escobar. Directly opposite on S Beretania St, an **eternal torch** memorializes soldiers who died in WWII.

HAWAII MARITIME CENTER

Near the Aloha Tower, the **Hawaii Maritime Center** (Map pp86-7; ☎ 536-6373; Pier 7; admission adult/child under 6-17 yrs $7.50/free/4.50; ☉ 8:30am-5pm) is a great place to get a sense of Hawaii's history. The museum covers everything from the arrival of Captain Cook to modern-day windsurfing, with lots of details you won't find anywhere else.

Displays on early tourism include a reproduction of a Matson liner stateroom and photos of Waikiki – this was a time when the Royal Hawaiian and the Moana hotels shared the shore with Diamond Head. Matson built both in the early 1900s to accommodate cruise passengers, selling the hotels to Sheraton in 1959, just before tourism became a booming industry.

The maritime center is home to the 266ft *Falls of Clyde*, the world's last four-masted four-rigger. Built in 1878 in Glasgow, the *Falls* first carried sugar and passengers between Hilo (Big Island) and San Francisco; then oil; and finally was stripped down to a barge. Just before she was to be sunk to form part of a breakwater off Vancouver, a Hawaiian group raised funds to rescue and restore her. Visitors can stroll the deck and explore the cargo holds of this National Historic Landmark.

The center is also home to 60ft *Hokule'a*, a double-hulled sailing canoe constructed to resemble boats used by Polynesians in their migrations. *Hokule'a* has made voyages from Hawaii to the South Pacific, retracing the routes of the early Polynesian seafarers, using only traditional methods of navigation, such as wave patterns and the position of the stars (see Hokule'a: a Star of Gladness, p26).

ALOHA TOWER

Built in 1926 at the edge of the downtown district, the 10-story **Aloha Tower** (Map pp86-7; ☎ 537-9260; Pier 9; admission free; ☉ 9am-sunset) is a Honolulu landmark that for years was the city's tallest building. Today cruise ships still disembark at the terminal beneath the tower. Take a peek through the terminal windows to see colorful murals depicting bygone Honolulu.

The Aloha Tower's top-floor **observation deck** offers a sweeping 360-degree view of Honolulu's large commercial harbor.

INFORMATION		EATING 🍴 (pp107-10)		Yanagi Sushi...............................**32** A1
Bank of Hawaii.................................**1** B3		Alan Wong's...............................**14** D2		
Bank of Hawaii..........................(see 36)		Auntie Pasto's............................**15** B1		DRINKING (p111)
Borders Books & Music...............(see 40)		Big City Diner...........................(see 35)		Brew Moon................................(see 40)
Campus Center.............................**2** F2		Bubbies.......................................**16** B3		
Longs Drugs.................................**3** E2		Cafe Maharani.............................**17** A4		ENTERTAINMENT 🎭 (pp112-13)
Native Books / Na Mea Hawaii.......(see 41)		Chef Mavro..................................**18** D2		Academy Doris Duke Theatre.........(see 8)
Net Stop Cafe...............................**4** B4		Coffeeline...................................**19** E1		Anna Bannanas.............................**33** E2
Post Office....................................**5** B3		Compadres..................................(see 40)		Rumours.......................................(see 9)
Rainbow Books & Records.............**6** B3		Down to Earth Natural Foods..........**20** A4		Varsity Twins...............................**34** B3
Straub Clinic & Hospital.................**7** A1		El Burrito.....................................**21** B2		Ward Stadium 16...........................**35** A2
UH Monoa Campus Bookstore.........(see 2)		Foodland Supermarket...................**22** F3		
		Imanas Tei...................................**23** B4		SHOPPING 🛍 (p114)
SIGHTS & ACTIVITIES (p96)		Kincaid's Fish, Chop & Steakhouse....(see 41)		Ala Moana Center..........................**36** B3
Honolulu Academy of Arts..............**8** B1		Kokua Natural Foods Market...........**24** B4		Hula Supply Center........................**37** E2
		L'Uraku..**25** B2		
SLEEPING 🏠 (pp104-5)		Montien Thai...............................**26** B4		TRANSPORT (pp114-15)
Ala Moana Hotel...........................**9** C3		Pavilion Café..............................(see 8)		Bus Stop.......................................**38** E2
Central Branch YMCA....................**10** C3		Side Street Inn.............................**27** B2		Bus Terminal.................................**39** B3
Hostelling International		The Greek Corner.........................**28** B3		
Honolulu.................................**11** E1		The Willows..................................**29** A4		OTHER
Manoa Valley Inn..........................**12** E1		Viet Cafe.....................................**30** D3		Ward Centre..................................**40** A3
Pagoda Hotel................................**13** C2		Well Bento...................................**31** A3		Ward Warehouse...........................**41** A2

Beneath the tower is the **Aloha Tower Marketplace**, a shopping center with numerous kiosks, stores and eateries.

ST ANDREW'S CATHEDRAL

King Kamehameha IV, attracted by the royal trappings of the Church of England, decided to build his own cathedral in Hawaii. He and his consort, Queen Emma, founded the Anglican Church of Hawaii in 1858. King Kamehameha V had the cornerstone laid in 1867 four years after the death of Kamehameha IV on St Andrew's Day – hence the name.

Today the architecture of **St Andrew's Cathedral** (Map pp86-7; ☎ 524-2822; cnr Alakea & S Beretania Sts; admission free; ☒ 9am-5pm) is French Gothic, the construction stone and glass shipped from England. The impressive window of hand-blown stained glass forms the western facade reaching from the floor to the eaves. In the right section of the stained glass the Reverend Thomas Staley, the first bishop sent to Hawaii by Queen Victoria, stands with Kamehameha IV and Queen Emma.

KAWAIAHA'O CHURCH

O'ahu's oldest church, **Kawaiaha'o Church** (Map pp86-7; ☎ 522-1333; cnr Punchbowl & S King Sts; admission free; ☒ 8am-4pm Mon-Fri) was built on the site where the first missionaries constructed a grass thatch church shortly after their arrival in 1820. The original structure seated 300 people on *lauhala* mats, woven from *hala* (pandanus) leaves.

This New England–style Gothic Congregational church, completed in 1842, is constructed of 14,000 coral slabs, each weighing about 1000lbs, which Hawaiian divers chiseled out of Honolulu's underwater reef – a task that took four years. The clock tower was donated by Kamehameha III, and the old clock, installed in 1850, still keeps accurate time. The rear seats of the church, marked by *kahili* (feather staffs) and velvet padding were for royalty and are still reserved for their descendants.

The **tomb of King Lunalilo**, the successor to Kamehameha V, is at the main entrance. Lunalilo ruled for only one year before his death in 1874 at the age of 39. The **cemetery** at the rear of the church is a bit like a who's who of colonial history. Early missionaries are buried alongside other notables of the day, including the infamous Sanford Dole,

who became the first territorial governor of Hawaii after the overthrow of Queen Lili'uokalani.

MISSION HOUSES MUSEUM

Containing three of the original buildings of the Sandwich Islands Mission headquarters, the **Mission Houses Museum** (Map pp86-7; ☎ 531-0481; 553 S King St; 1-hr guided tour adult/child $10/6; ☒ 10am-6pm Tue-Sat, noon-5pm Sun) is authentically furnished with handmade quilts on the beds, settees in the parlor and iron cooking pots in the stone fireplaces.

The first missionaries packed more than their bags when they left Boston: they actually brought a prefabricated wooden house, now called the **Frame House**, around the Horn with them! Designed to withstand cold New England winter winds, the small windows instead block out Honolulu's cooling trade winds, keeping the two-story house hot and stuffy. Erected in 1821, it's the oldest wooden structure in Hawaii.

The coral-block **Chamberlain House** was the early mission storeroom, a necessity as Honolulu had few shops in those days. Upstairs are hoop barrels, wooden crates packed with dishes, and the desk and quill pen of Levi Chamberlain. He was appointed by the mission to buy, store and dole out supplies to the missionary families, who survived on a meager allowance – as the account books on his desk testify.

The **Printing Office** housed a lead-type press used to print the Bible in Hawaiian.

Tours of the museum are 11am, 1pm, 2:45pm and 4:30pm Tuesday to Saturday.

ALI'IOLANI HALE

The first major government building constructed by the Hawaiian monarchy in 1874, **Ali'iolani Hale** (House of Heavenly Kings; Map pp86–7) has housed the Hawaii Supreme Court and the state legislature. It was originally designed by Australian architect Thomas Rowe to be a royal palace, although it was never used as such. It was on the steps of Ali'iolani Hale, in January 1893, that Sanford Dole proclaimed the provisional government and the overthrow of the Hawaiian monarchy.

A **statue** of Kamehameha the Great, cast in Florence in the 1880s, stands in front of Ali'iolani Hale. Each year on June 11, the state holiday honoring the king, the statue is ceremoniously draped with colorful layers of 12ft lei.

HONOLULU HALE

City Hall, also known as **Honolulu Hale** (Map pp86-7; ☎ 523-2489; 530 S King St), was designed and built in 1927 as a Spanish mission by CW Dickey, Honolulu's then famous architect. Now on the National Register of Historic Places, it has a tiled roof, decorative balconies, arches and pillars, some ornate frescoes, and an open-air courtyard sometimes used for concerts and art exhibits. On the front lawn, an **eternal-flame memorial** honors the victims of the September 11 terrorist attacks on the US mainland.

FIRST HAWAIIAN CENTER

The headquarters of the First Hawaiian Bank houses the downtown gallery of the **Contemporary Museum** (Map pp86-7; ☎ 526-0232, 525-7000; 999 Bishop St; admission free; ☻ 8:30am-4pm Mon-Thu, 8:30am-6pm Fri), which features changing exhibits of modern Hawaiian art (p98). The building is Honolulu's newest, tallest highrise, and includes a four-story-high glass wall with 185 prisms designed by famed New York glass artist Jamie Carpenter.

HAWAII CHILDREN'S DISCOVERY CENTER

The 37,000-sq-ft **Hawaii Children's Discovery Center** (Map pp90-1; ☎ 524-5437; www.discoverycenterhawaii.org; 111 Ohe St; admission adult/child under 2 yrs/child 2-17 yrs $8/free/6.75; ☻ 9am-1pm Tue-Fri, 10am-3pm Sat & Sun) is a hands-on children's museum occupying the waterfront site of the city's old incinerator, although the only hint of its past is the towering smokestack reaching skyward from the building's center.

It's part of an ambitious redevelopment plan to return the neighborhood to recreational use, and adjacent to a new 30-acre waterfront park. Although older kids may find some exhibits interesting, the museum is principally geared toward pre-teens. The museum has five main sections extending over three stories. The **Toy Box**, just off the entry, introduces visitors to the museum via a video puppet show. **Fantastic You** explores the human body, allowing kids to walk through a mock stomach. More traditional displays are found in the **Your Town** section, where kids can drive an interactive fire engine, or be bank tellers or TV interviewers. The other two sections, **Hawaiian Rainbows**

and the **Rainbow World**, relate specifically to Hawaii, and allow children to navigate a ship and swim with dolphins.

You can get here from Waikiki via bus No 8 or 20; it's a five-minute walk from the nearest bus stop on Ala Moana Blvd to the museum, and just opposite Kaka'ako Waterfront Park.

ROYAL MAUSOLEUM STATE MONUMENT

Housing the remains of Kings Kamehameha II, III, IV and V, as well as King David Kalakaua and Queen Lili'uokalani (Hawaii's last reigning monarchs), is the **Royal Mausoleum** (Map pp86-7; ☎ 587-0300; 2261 Nu'uanu Ave; admission free; ☻ 8am-4:30pm Mon-Fri). Conspicuously absent are the remains of Kamehameha the Great, the last king to be buried in secret in accordance with Hawaii's old religion. Built in 1864, the original mausoleum is now a chapel; the caskets are in nearby crypts. Other gravestones honor Kamehameha I's British confidant John Young and American Charles Reed Bishop, husband of Princess Bernice Pauahi Bishop.

The Royal Mausoleum is on Nu'uanu Ave, just before it meets the Pali Hwy. You can get there by taking the No 4 Nu'uanu Dowsett bus from Waikiki. Guided tours are available by reservation.

KAKA'AKO WATERFRONT PARK

Near downtown Honolulu and just off Ala Moana Blvd at the end of Cooke St, little Kaka'ako Waterfront Park is protected from much of the city noise by a small grassy rise. Roller bladers cruise along the rock-fringed promenade, which offers clear views of Diamond Head, Waikiki and Honolulu Harbor. The 28-acre park attracts experienced surfers in the morning and picnickers in the afternoon. It's not a safe swimming beach, but the tricky surf break is near the shore, making Kaka'ako a great place to watch surfers and boogie boarders up close. Facilities include a modern pavilion, picnic tables, showers, restrooms and free parking.

Chinatown

A walk through Chinatown is a bit like a quick trip across Asia. Although predominantly Chinese, there are Vietnamese, Thai and Filipino influences.

Chinese immigrants who had worked off their sugarcane plantation contracts began settling in Chinatown and opening up small businesses around 1860. In December 1899 bubonic plague broke out in the area. The 7000 Chinese, Hawaiians and Japanese who made the crowded neighborhood their home were cordoned off and forbidden to leave.

When more plague cases arose, the all-powerful Board of Health ordered the Honolulu Fire Department to burn the wooden buildings on the *mauka* side of Beretania St, between Nu'uanu Ave and Smith St, on January 20, 1900. But the wind suddenly picked up and the fire spread out of control, racing toward the waterfront. Nearly 40 acres of Chinatown burned to the ground, leaving four thousand residents homeless.

Despite the adverse climate, the Chinese held their own and a new Chinatown has arisen from the ashes.

MAUNAKEA ST

An outstanding example of 'Pidgin Chinese' architecture in Hawaii, **Wo Fat** (Map pp86-7; ☎ 521-5355; cnr N Hotel & Maunakea Sts) is a signature Chinatown building, twice decimated by fire – the last time in 1900. The upstairs section is home to a seafood restaurant.

If you're up for a snack, visit **Shung Chong Yuein Cake Shop** (Map pp86-7; ☎ 531-1983; 1027 Maunakea St), an old-fashioned Chinese sweets shop (for full review, see p114).

Cindy's Lei Shop (Map pp86-7; ☎ 536-6538; 1034 Maunakea St; ☺ 6am-8pm Mon-Sat, 6am-6pm Sun), just across the street, is a gorgeous place selling a variety of leis (see p114 for full review).

CHINATOWN CULTURAL PLAZA

This plaza (Map pp86-7), covering most of the block, is bordered by N Beretania St, Mau-

---

> #### FLOWER POWER
>
> Chinatown herbalists are both physicians and pharmacists, with walls full of small wooden drawers each filled with a different herb. They'll size you up, feel your pulse and listen to you describe your ailments before deciding which drawers to open, mixing herbs and flowers and wrapping them for you to take home and boil together. The object is to balance yin and yang forces. You can find herbalists at the Chinatown Cultural Plaza, and along N King and Maunakea Sts.

---

nakea and River Sts. The modern complex doesn't have the character of Chinatown's older shops, but inside it's still quintessential Chinatown, with tailors, acupuncturists and calligraphers alongside travel agents and restaurants. In a small courtyard, people light incense and leave mangoes at a statue of the goddess Kuan Yin.

RIVER ST PEDESTRIAN MALL

The River St pedestrian mall (Map pp86-7) has covered tables beside Nu'uanu Stream, where old-timers play mah-jongg and checkers. A **statue** of Chinese revolutionary leader Sun Yat-Sen stands watch at the end of the pedestrian mall near N Beretania St.

Along the mall are several eateries, including a couple of hole-in-the-wall family businesses and Chinatown's largest vegetarian restaurant, Legend (p107). River St terminates opposite the entrance of Foster Botanical Garden.

FOSTER BOTANICAL GARDEN

At the north side of Chinatown, **Foster Botanical Garden** (Map pp86-7; ☎ 522-7066; 180 N Vineyard Blvd; admission adult/child $5/1; ☺ 9am-4pm) is O'ahu's main botanical garden. In 1850 German botanist William Hillebrand purchased five acres of land from Queen Kalama and planted the trees now towering in its center. In 1867 Captain Thomas Foster bought the property, continuing to plant the grounds. In the 1930s the garden became the property of Honolulu.

An impressive 14-acre collection of tropical flora, the garden is laid out according to plant groups: palms, plumeria and poisonous plants. The **economic garden** has nutmeg, allspice and cinnamon, as well as a black pepper vine that climbs 50ft up a gold tree, a vanilla vine, and other herbs and spices. The **herb garden** was the site of the first Japanese-language school in O'ahu and where many Japanese immigrants sent their children to learn Japanese, hoping to maintain their cultural identity and the possibility of someday returning to Japan. During the bombing of Pearl Harbor a stray artillery shell exploded in a room full of students. A memorial marks the site. At the other end of the park, the **wild orchid garden** makes a good place for close-up photography.

Among the garden's many extraordinary plants is a tree so rare it has no common name – the East African *Gigasiphon macrosiphon*. It is thought to be extinct in the wild. The native Hawaiian *loulu* palm, taken long ago from O'ahu's upper Nu'uanu Valley, may also be extinct in the wild. The garden's chicle, New Zealand kauri tree and Egyptian doum palm are all reputed to be the largest of their kind in the USA. Oddities include the cannonball tree, the sausage tree and the double coconut palm capable of producing a 50lb nut.

All of the trees are labeled, and a free self-guided tour booklet is available at the entrance. Included in the admission price is an hour-long tour, given at 1pm on weekdays.

KUAN YIN TEMPLE

Near the entrance of Foster Botanical Garden, the **Kuan Yin Temple** (Map pp86-7; ☎ 533-6361; 170 N Vineyard Blvd; ☯ during daylight) is a bright red Buddhist temple with a green ceramic-tile roof. The ornate interior is richly carved and filled with the sweet, pervasive smell of burning incense.

The temple is dedicated to Kuan Yin Bodhisattva, Goddess of Mercy, whose statue is the largest in the prayer hall. Devotees burn paper 'money' for prosperity and good luck. Offerings of fresh flowers and fruit are placed at the altar. The large citrus fruit that is stacked pyramid-style is the pomelo, considered a symbol of fertility because of its many seeds.

Honolulu's multiethnic Buddhist community worships at the temple, and respectful visitors are welcome.

TAOIST TEMPLE

Founded in 1889, the Lum Sai Ho Tong Society was one of more than 100 societies started by Chinese immigrants in Hawaii to help preserve their cultural identity. This one was for the Lum clan, which hails from an area west of the Yellow River. At one time the society had more than 4000 members, and even now there are nearly a thousand Lums in the Honolulu phone book.

The society's **Taoist temple** (Map pp86-7; cnr River & Kukui Sts) honors the goddess Tin Hau, a Lum child who rescued her father from drowning and was later deified. Many Chinese claim to see her apparition when they travel by boat. The temple is not usually open to the general public, but you can admire the building from the outside.

IZUMO TAISHA SHRINE

Across the river from the Taoist temple, this **shrine** (Map pp86-7; ☎ 538-7778, 522-7060; 215 N Kukui St; ☯ 9am-4pm) is a small wooden Shinto shrine built by Japanese immigrants in 1923. During WWII the property was confiscated by the city of Honolulu and wasn't returned to its congregation until 1962. Incidentally, the 100lb sacks of rice that sit near the altar symbolize good health, while ringing the bell at the shrine entrance is considered an act of purification for those who come to pray.

Ala Moana & University Area

Ala Moana means 'Path to the Sea.' It is also the name of the area west of Waikiki, which includes Honolulu's largest beach park and the state's largest shopping center.

ALA MOANA BEACH PARK

Opposite the Ala Moana Center, this fine park (Map pp90–1) is fronted by a broad, golden beach, nearly a mile long, and buffered from the noise of Ala Moana Blvd by a spacious, grassy area with shade trees. Honolulu residents go jogging here, play volleyball and enjoy weekend picnics. It has full beach facilities, several softball fields, tennis courts, and free parking. It's very popular, yet big enough not to feel crowded.

Ala Moana is safe for swimming and a good spot for distance swimmers. However, at low tide the deep channel running the length of the beach can be a hazard to poor swimmers who don't realize it's there. A former boat channel, it drops off suddenly to overhead depths. If you measure laps, it's 500m between the lifeguard tower at the Waikiki end and the white post in the water midway between the third and fourth lifeguard towers.

The 43-acre peninsula jutting from the east side of the park, the Aina Moana State Recreation Area, more commonly known as **Magic Island**, is where high-school outrigger-canoe teams often practice in the late afternoon during the school year. In summer this is also a hot surf spot. There's a nice walk around the perimeter of Magic Island, and picturesque sunsets, with sailboats pulling in and out of the adjoining Ala Wai Yacht Harbor.

If you're taking the bus from Waikiki, bus Nos 8 and 20 stop on Ala Moana Blvd opposite the beach park.

O'AHU

HONOLULU ACADEMY OF ARTS

An exceptional **museum** (Map pp90-1; ☎ 532-8700; www.honoluluacademy.org; 900 S Beretania St; admission adult/child under 13 yrs/concession $7/free/4; ☯ 10am-4:30pm Tue-Sat, 1-5pm Sun) with solid Asian, European and Pacific art collections, this is Hawaii's only comprehensive fine arts museum, housing nearly 40,000 pieces of artwork.

The museum has a predominantly classical facade, with some 30 galleries branching off a series of garden courtyards. The splendid Asian gallery exhibits peaceful Buddhas and samurai armor. Considered one of the finest Asian art collections in the USA, it gives almost equal weight to both Japanese and Chinese works, ranging from scenes of Kyoto, painted by the renowned Japanese artist Kano Motohide, to the extensive Ming dynasty collection. The latter includes pivotal works by Shen Zhou, credited with establishing a composition technique that significantly influenced Ming painting styles.

In 2001, the museum opened the **Henry R Luce Pavilion**, a 10,000-sq-ft contemporary section, containing Hawaiian artifacts and paintings on the upper level, and modern art, by such modernist luminaries as Henry

---

SHANGRI OOH LA LA

In 2002 the Honolulu Academy of Art began conducting small group tours of **Shangri La** (☎ 866-385-3849; www.shangrilahawaii.org; admission adult/child 12-17 yrs $25; ☯ Wed-Sun), the 1930s-era home of wealthy heiress and philanthropist Doris Duke, who transformed five acres of property overlooking the Pacific Ocean and Diamond Head into a serene palace of graciousness and beauty.

Duke's 14,000-sq-ft home has architectural features from the Islamic world and houses her extensive collection of Islamic art, ranging from glazed ceramic paintings to silk *suzanis*, intricate needlework tapestries that were part of young women's dowries. Throughout the estate, gardens and courtyards weave in and out of cool interiors and symmetrical fountains.

Advance reservations are required, and no children under 12 are admitted. Small-group tours begin at the Honolulu Academy of Arts (p96) and last around two hours, including transportation.

Moore and Georgia O'Keeffe, on the lower level.

A gallery of European art of the 19th and 20th centuries exhibits paintings by Henri Matisse, Paul Cezanne, Claude Monet, Paul Gauguin, Vincent van Gogh and Camille Pissarro. The museum also contains works of 16th- to 18th-century European artists Pieter de Hotch, Sir Thomas Lawrence and Carlo Bonavia, and a number of Madonna-and-child oils from 14th-century Italy.

Pacific art collections include ceremonial carvings, war clubs and masks from Papua New Guinea, and body ornaments and navigational stick charts from Micronesia. The museum owns some fine eclectic pieces, sculptures and miniature figurines from India, and fertility figures and ceremonial carvings from Africa.

A large museum gift shop and an appealing café overlook a fountain courtyard. Bus No 2 from Waikiki stops out front. In addition to metered parking, there is a museum parking lot between S Beretania and S King Sts. The cost is $1 with validation.

UNIVERSITY OF HAWAII AT MANOA

The central campus of the statewide university system, the **University of Hawaii at Manoa** (UH; Map pp90-1; ☎ 956-8111; cnr University Ave & Dole St) is just two miles north of Waikiki.

UH has strong programs in astronomy, second-language studies, geophysics, marine sciences, and Hawaiian and Pacific studies. The campus attracts students from islands throughout the Pacific. It has approximately 19,000 students and offers degrees in 90 fields of study.

Staff at the **information center** (☎ 956-7235; Room 212, Campus Center) provide campus maps and can answer questions you have about the university. Free one-hour **walking tours** of the campus, emphasizing history and architecture, leave from the Campus Center at 2pm on Monday, Wednesday and Friday; to join a tour, simply arrive 10 minutes early.

At the east side of campus is the **East-West Center** (☎ 944-7111; 1777 East-West Rd), an internationally recognized education and research organization established by the US Congress in 1960 to promote mutual understanding among the peoples of Asia, the Pacific and the USA. Some 2000 professional and student researchers work and study at the center, examining development policy, the environment and other Pacific issues. Changing exhibits on Asian art and culture are displayed in the East-West Center's **Burns Hall** (☎ 944-7111; 1601 East-West Rd; admission free; ☺ 8am-5pm Mon-Fri, noon-4pm Sun). The center often has other multicultural programs open to the public, including seminars, concert and dance performances.

Ka Leo O Hawaii, the free student newspaper, lists lectures, music performances and other campus happenings. Pick it up at university libraries and other places around campus.

Bus No 4 runs between the university and Waikiki; bus No 6 travels between the university and Ala Moana.

Elsewhere in Honolulu
BISHOP MUSEUM

Considered the finest Polynesian anthropological museum in the world, the **Bishop Museum** (Map p84; ☎ 847-3511; www.bishopmuseum .org; 1525 Bernice St; admission adult/child under 4 yrs/child 4-12 yrs $15/free/12; ☺ 9am-5pm) boasts an impressive array of exhibits.

The main gallery, **Hawaiian Hall**, has three floors of exhibits covering the cultural history of Hawaii. The 1st floor displays include a full-sized *pili*-grass thatched house, carved temple images and shark-toothed war clubs.

One of the museum's most impressive holdings is a feather cloak once worn by Kamehameha the Great, created entirely of the yellow feathers of the now-extinct *mamo,* a predominately black bird with a yellow upper tail. Some 80,000 birds were caught and plucked before they were released to create this single cloak. To get a sense of just how few feathers each bird had, look at the nearby taxidermic *mamo,* to the left of the Queen Lili'uokalani exhibit.

The 2nd floor is dedicated to 19th-century Hawaii. Here you will find traditional tapa (cloth made by pounding the bark of the paper mulberry tree) robes, missionary-inspired quilt work and barter items Yankee traders brought to the islands; there's also a small whaling exhibit, and Princess Bernice Pauahi Bishop's whimsical hat collection.

The third floor displays artifacts of the ethnic groups that comprise Hawaii today. Like Hawaii itself, it has a bit of everything, including samurai armor, Portuguese festival costumes, Taoist fortune-telling sticks and a

Hawaiian ukulele made of coconut shells. An impressive 55ft sperm whale skeleton hangs from the ceiling, opposite a koa royal racing canoe.

The **Kahili Room**, a small gallery off the main hall, features portraits of Hawaiian royalty and a display of *kahili,* the feathered staffs used at coronations and royal funerals. Other exhibits cover the cultures of Polynesia, Micronesia and Melanesia.

The museum is also home to O'ahu's only **planetarium**, which highlights traditional Polynesian methods of navigation, such as wave patterns and the position of the stars. Shows are held at 11:30am, 1:30pm, 2:30pm and 3:30pm, and are included in the museum admission price.

The museum's modern wing, the **Castle Building**, has changing natural-history exhibits, some interactive, designed for children.

The gift shop off the lobby sells books on the Pacific not easily found elsewhere, as well as some quality Hawaiian crafts and souvenirs. A snack shop is open until 4pm.

To get to the Bishop Museum by bus from Waikiki or downtown Honolulu, take the No 2 School St bus to Kapalama St and turn right on Bernice St. By car, take exit 20B off the H1, go inland on Houghtailing St and turn left on Bernice St.

TANTALUS & MAKIKI VALLEY

Just two miles from downtown Honolulu, a narrow switchback road cuts its way up the lush green forest reserve land of Tantalus and Makiki Valley. The road climbs up almost to the top of 2013ft Mt Tantalus, with swank mountainside homes tucked in along the way. Although the road is one continuous loop, the west side is called Tantalus Dr and the east side is Round Top Dr. The 8.5-mile circuit is Honolulu's finest scenic drive, offering splendid views of the city below.

The route is winding, narrow and steep, but it's in good condition. Among the profusion of dense tropical growth, bamboo, ginger, elephant-ear taro and fragrant eucalyptus trees are easily identified. Vines climb to the top of telephone poles and twist their way across the wires.

The Makiki Heights area below the forest reserve is one of the most exclusive residential areas in Honolulu. There's a bus service as far as Makiki Heights, but none around the Tantalus–Round Top loop road.

CONTEMPORARY MUSEUM

Occupying an estate with 3.5 acres of tropical and meditative gardens, the **Contemporary Museum** (Map p100; ☎ 526-0232; www.tcmhi.org; 2411 Makiki Heights Dr; admission adult/child 12 yrs & under/concession $5/free/3; ⏱ 10am-4pm Tue-Sat, noon-4pm Sun) is an engaging modern art museum, with views of Honolulu below. Admission is free every third Thursday of the month.

The estate house was constructed in 1925 for Mrs Charles Montague Cooke, whose other former home is the present site of the Honolulu Academy of Arts (p96). A patron of the arts, she played a founding role in both museums.

The main galleries feature changing exhibits of paintings, sculpture, and other contemporary artwork by local, national and international artists. A newer building on the lawn holds the museum's most prized piece, a vivid environmental installation by David Hockney based on sets for *L'Enfant et les Sortilèges*, Ravel's 1925 opera.

Docent-led tours, conducted at 1:30pm, are included in the admission price. An excellent courtyard café serves lunch.

The museum, near the intersection of Mott-Smith and Makiki Heights Drs, can be reached by bus No 15 from downtown Honolulu.

LYON ARBORETUM

At the time of research, this highly regarded **arboretum** (Map p100; ☎ 988-0456; 3860 Manoa Rd; admission adult/child/concession $7/3/5; ⏱ 9am-4pm Mon-Sat), founded in 1918, was closed until further notice. The Univeristy of Hawaii, which oversees the facility, expressed safety and health concerns. At press time, negotiations with the Division of Land & Natural Resources were underway, with hopes of soon reopening this state landmark.

Dr Harold Lyon, after whom the arboretum is named, is credited with introducing 10,000 exotic trees and plants to Hawaii. Approximately half of these are represented in this 193-acre arboretum. This is not a landscaped tropical flower garden, but a mature and largely wooded arboretum where related species are clustered in a seminatural state.

Among the plants in the Hawaiian ethnobotanical garden are mountain apple, breadfruit and taro; *ko*, the sugarcane brought by early Polynesian settlers; *kukui*, which was used to produce lantern oil; and *ti*, which was used for medicinal purposes during ancient times and for making moonshine after Westerners arrived.

PU'U 'UALAKA'A STATE PARK

For a marvelous panoramic view over Honolulu, visit **Pu'u 'Ualaka'a State Park** (Map p100; ⏱ 7am-6:45pm). The park entrance is 2.5 miles up Round Top Dr from Makiki St. It's half a mile in to the lookout; bear to the left when the road forks.

The sweeping view extends from Kahala and Diamond Head on the far left, across Waikiki and downtown Honolulu, to the Wai'anae Range on the right. To the southeast is the University of Hawaii at Manoa, easily recognized by its sports stadium; to the southwest you can see clearly into the green mound of Punchbowl crater; the airport is visible on the coast, with Pearl Harbor beyond that.

If you're taking photos, the best time is during the day; however, this is also a fine place to watch the evening settle over the city. Arrive half an hour before sunset to see the hills before they're in shadow.

NATIONAL MEMORIAL CEMETERY OF THE PACIFIC

Punchbowl, the bowl-shaped remnant of a long-extinct volcanic crater, sits a mile north of downtown Honolulu at an elevation of 500ft and offers a fine view of the city, out to Diamond Head and the Pacific beyond.

The early Hawaiians called the crater Puowaina, the 'hill of human sacrifices.' It's believed there was a heiau (an ancient stone temple) at the crater and that the slain bodies of *kapu* (taboo) breakers were brought to Punchbowl to be cremated upon the altar.

Today it's the site of a 114-acre **cemetery** (Map p100; ☎ 532-3720; 2177 Puowaina Dr; admission free; ⏱ 8am-5:30pm Oct-Feb, 8am-6:30pm Mar-Sep), where the remains of over 25,000 US soldiers are interred, more than half of whom were killed in the Pacific during WWII.

The remains of Ernie Pyle, the distinguished war correspondent who covered both world wars and was hit by machine gun fire on Ie Shima during the final days of WWII, lie in section D, grave 109. Five stones to the left, at grave D-1, is the marker for astronaut Ellison Onizuka, the Big Island native (p215) who perished in the 1986 *Challenger* space-shuttle disaster. Their resting places are marked with the same style of flat granite stone that marks each of the cemetery's graves.

A huge marble court **memorial** at the rear of the cemetery is inscribed with the names of the 26,289 Americans missing in action from WWII and the Korean War. An adjacent court displays the names of another 2489 soldiers missing from the Vietnam War. For a good view of the city, walk to the **lookout**, 10 minutes' south of the memorial.

If you're driving to Punchbowl, take the H1 to the Pali Hwy. There's a marked exit as you start up the Pali Hwy; watch closely, because it comes up quickly! From there, follow signs through a series of narrow streets on the short route up to the cemetery.

Or take bus No 2 from Waikiki to downtown Honolulu and get off at Beretania and Alapai Sts, where you transfer to bus No 15. Ask the driver where to get off; from there it's about a 15-minute walk to Punchbowl.

SAND ISLAND STATE RECREATION AREA
If you like plane-spotting or watching ships enter and leave Honolulu Harbor, this popular coastal park near the flight path of Honolulu International Airport has it all. It's a popular local destination, with camping and picnic tables. Facilities include restrooms and showers, along with a boat ramp used by fishing crews. The park is at the end of Sand Island Access Road, off Nimitz Hwy (92) at the western edge of Honolulu Harbor.

ACTIVITIES
Many first-time visitors to Honolulu are surprised by the city's boundaries; there don't seem to be any! But head inland, and within a few miles you are winding up the lush green valleys, accompanied by passing showers and rainbows. Excellent hiking trails cover the area.

Hiking
MANOA FALLS
The Upper Manoa Valley, inland (or *mauka*) from the university, ends at forest reserve land in the hills above Honolulu. Manoa Rd runs into the valley through the well-to-do residential neighborhood Woodlawn before reaching the trailhead to Manoa Falls and the Lyon Arboretum.

Manoa Falls Trail is a beautiful hike. The trail runs for three-quarters of a mile above

a rocky streambed before ending at the falls. It's an easy hike, about 30 minutes one way, with a 400ft gain in elevation. The trail can be a bit muddy and slippery, so shoes or walking sandals are advised.

Surrounded by lush, damp vegetation, moss-covered stones and tree trunks, you get the feeling you're walking through a thick rain forest a long way from anywhere. The only sounds come from chirping birds and the rushing stream and waterfall. All sorts of trees line the path, including tall *Eucalyptus robusta*, with their soft, spongy, reddish bark; flowering orange African tulip trees; and other lofty varieties that creak like wooden doors in old houses. Many of them were planted by the Lyon Arboretum, which at one time held a lease on the property.

Wild purple orchids and red ginger grow near the falls, adding a colorful element to the tranquil scene. The falls are steep, dropping about 100ft into a small shallow pool. Occasional falling rocks make swimming inadvisable and the local health department warns against swimming in the water for fear of leptospirosis (see p541)! About 50ft before reaching Manoa Falls, a marked trail starts to the left of a chain-link fence. Well worth a 15- to 20-minute side trip, the **Aihualama Trail** offers a broad view of the Manoa Valley, just a short way up the path, which can be muddy. After about a five-minute walk, you'll enter a bamboo forest with some massive old banyan trees.

DETOUR: MANOA VALLEY

Close to Waikiki but unknown to most tourists, the Manoa Valley makes for a surprising morning or afternoon detour. Drive or take bus No 4 or 6 beyond the university, continuing past the Manoa Marketplace to the Woodlawn residential area, where many of the elegant homes and lush gardens date from Hawaii's territorial days. On your way back, near the intersection of E Manoa Rd and Pakanu Rd, stop in front of the red arches of the Chinese Cemetery, where gifts and food are left for the ancestors. To finish off your detour with a dash of aloha, stop for afternoon tea or a passion fruit spritzer at the Waioli Tea Room (p111) on Manoa Rd, set in a tropical garden reminiscent of Manoa's early days.

When the wind blows, the forest releases eerie crackling sounds. It's an engaging forest – enchanted or spooky, depending on your mood.

You can return the same way to the Manoa Falls Trail or continue another mile to **Pauoa Flats** (opposite), where the trail connects with the **Pu'u 'Ohi'a Trail** (opposite) in the Tantalus area.

TANTALUS & MAKIKI VALLEY TRAILS

A network of hiking trails runs between Tantalus Dr and Round Top Dr and throughout the forest reserve, and there are many marked trailheads off both roads. The trails are seldom crowded, which seems amazing considering how accessible they are.

Perhaps because the drive itself is so nice, the only walking most people do is between their car and the scenic lookouts.

Naturalists from the **Hawaii Nature Center** (Map p100; ☎ 955-0100; www.hawaiinaturecenter.org; hiking fee $8) at the forestry base-yard camp in Makiki conduct family programs and lead hikes on most weekends. The state **Division of Forestry & Wildlife** (☎ 587-0166; www.hawaiitrails .org; 2135 Makiki Hts Dr; ⏰ 7:45am-4:30pm Mon-Fri) maintains a small branch office just uphill from the Hawaii Nature Center. It distributes a free photocopied Honlulu Mauka Trail System handout with an accurate topographic map of the Tantalus–Makiki area along with brief hiking notes. The map (and others) can be downloaded from the

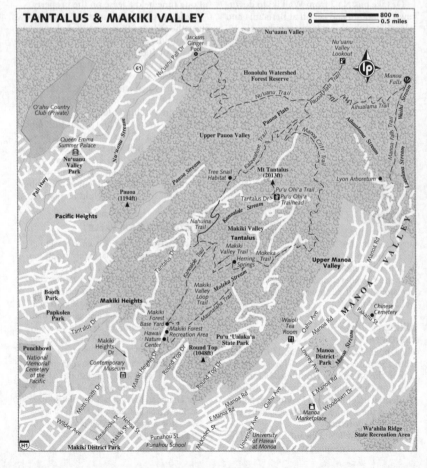

website. There's also a drinking fountain, next to a soda vending machine, good for filling empty water bottles.

To get started at the Makiki Forest baseyard, turn left off Makiki St and go half a mile up Makiki Heights Dr. Where the road makes a sharp bend, proceed straight ahead through a gate into the Makiki Forest Recreation Area and continue until you reach the baseyard. There's a parking lot nearby which serves both offices.

You can also take bus No 15, which runs between downtown and Pacific Heights. Get off near the intersection of Mott-Smith and Makiki Heights Drs and walk one mile down Makiki Heights Dr to the baseyard.

Makiki Valley Loop Trail

Three of the Tantalus area hiking trails – Maunalaha Trail, Makiki Valley Trail and Kanealole Trail – can be combined to make the Makiki Valley Loop Trail, a popular 2.5-mile hike. The loop cuts through a lush and varied tropical forest that begins and ends in Hawaii's first state nursery and arboretum, where hundreds of thousands of trees were grown to replace the sandalwood forests that were leveled in Makiki Valley and elsewhere in Hawaii in the 19th century to match the demand from China. Kanealole Trail is usually muddy, so wear shoes with good traction and pick up a walking stick.

Maunalaha Trail begins at the restrooms below the parking lot of the Makiki Forest baseyard. It crosses a bridge, passes taro patches and climbs up the eastern ridge of Makiki Valley, passing Norfolk pine, bamboo, and fragrant allspice and eucalyptus trees, with some clear views along the way.

JEWELS OF THE FOREST

O'ahu has an endemic genus of tree snail, the *Achatinella*. In former days the forests were loaded with these colorful snails, which clung like gems to the leaves of trees. They were too attractive for their own good, however, and hikers collected them by the handfuls around the turn of the 20th century. Even more devastating has been the deforestation of habitat and the introduction of a cannibal snail and predatory rodents. Of 41 *Achatinella* species, only 19 remain today and all are endangered.

After three-quarters of a mile, you'll come to a four-way junction, where you'll take the left fork and continue on the **Makiki Valley Trail**. The trail goes through small gulches and across gentle streams bordered with patches of ginger. Near the Moleka Stream crossing, there are mountain apple trees (related to allspice and guava) that flower in the spring and bear fruit in the summer. Edible yellow guava and strawberry guava also grow along the trail, which offers great glimpses of the city below.

The **Kanealole Trail** begins as you cross Kanealole Stream and then follows the stream back to the baseyard, three-quarters of a mile away. The trail leads down through a field of Job's tears; the beadlike bracts of the female flowers of this tall grass are often used for leis.

An alternative is to hike just the Makiki Valley Trail, which you can reach by going up Tantalus Dr two miles from its intersection with Makiki Heights Dr. As you come around a sharp curve, look for the wooden post marking the trailhead on the right. You can take this route in as far as you want and backtrack out, or link up with other trails along the way.

PU'U 'OHI'A TRAIL

The Pu'u 'Ohi'a Trail, in conjunction with the Pauoa Flats Trail, leads up to a lookout with a view of the Nu'uanu reservoir and valley. It's nearly two miles one way and makes a hardy hike. The trailhead is at the very top of Tantalus Dr, 3.6 miles up from its intersection with Makiki Heights Dr. There's a large turnoff opposite the trailhead where you can park.

Pu'u 'Ohi'a Trail begins with reinforced log steps, and leads past ginger, lush bamboo groves and lots of eucalyptus, a fast-growing tree planted to protect the watershed. About a half-mile up, the trail reaches the top of 2013ft **Mt Tantalus** (Pu'u 'Ohi'a).

From below Mt Tantalus, the trail leads to a service road. Continue on the road to its end, where there's a telephone company. The trail picks up again behind the left side of the building. Continue down the trail until it reaches the **Manoa Cliff Trail** and go left. Walk on for a short distance until you come to another intersection, where you'll turn right onto the **Pauoa Flats Trail**. This trail leads down into Pauoa Flats and on to the lookout. The flats area can be muddy; be careful not to trip on exposed tree roots.

You'll pass two trailheads before reaching the lookout. The first is Nu'uanu Trail, on the left, which runs three-quarters of a mile along the western side of Upper Pauoa Valley, and offers views of Honolulu and the Wai'anae Range. The second is **Aihualama Trail**, a bit further along on the right, which takes you 1.3 miles through tranquil bamboo groves and past huge old banyan trees to Manoa Falls. If you follow this route, you can hike down **Manoa Falls Trail** (p99), a distance of about a mile, to the end of Manoa Rd. From there catch a bus back to town.

Golf

Honolulu has several 18-hole municipal golf courses, including **Ala Wai Golf Course** (Map pp120-1; ☎ 733-7387; 404 Kapahulu Ave), **Ted Makalena Golf Course** (☎ 675-6052; 93-059 Waipio Point Access Rd, Waipahu) and **Ewa Villages Golf Course** (☎ 681-0220; 91-1760 Park Row, Ewa), west of Honolulu.

Green fees for 18 holes at any of these municipal courses are $42 per person; rental carts ($16) and clubs ($25) are available.

The reservation system is the same for all municipal courses: call ☎ 296-2000 and key information into the recorded system as prompted. For the busy Ala Wai golf course, the earliest bookings are taken just three days in advance for visitors and one week in advance for resident golfers.

There are also several excellent courses within a 30-minute drive of Waikiki. See p80 for information on courses on the Windward Coast and for southeast O'ahu.

WALKING TOUR

Chinatown is one of the most intriguing quarters of the city, and the adjacent downtown neighborhood is a mother lode of historical buildings.

A good place to start is **Chinatown Gateway Plaza (1)**, where stone lions, male and female,

Start Chinatown Gateway Plaza
Finish YWCA
Distance 1.6 miles
Duration 2–3 hours

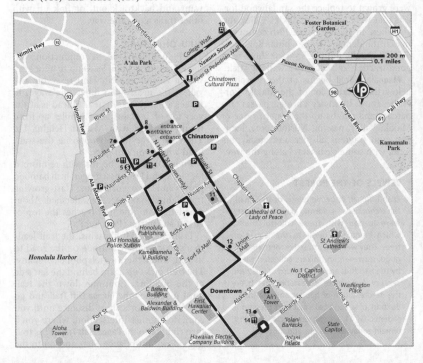

mark the official entrance. Turn left onto Nu'uanu Ave, where the granite-block sidewalks were built with the discarded ballasts of trade ships that brought tea from China in the 19th century in exchange for sandalwood, to the corner of N King St, and peek into the **First Hawaiian Bank** (2; p93), where the retro-architecture includes wooden teller cages with bars.

Turn right on N King St, then after a block turn right on Smith St, passing the Shaolin Society Kung Fu School, until you reach N Hotel St, where X-rated peep shows and strip bars recall Chinatown's seedier past. Turn left on N Hotel St, and go one block to Maunakea St, the heart of Chinatown. **Wo Fat** (3; p94), on the corner, Chinatown's signature building, was twice rebuilt after the fires of 1886 and 1900. Walk down Maunakea St, stopping at **Shung Chong Yuein cake shop** (4; p114) on your left. Here you can buy *jung*, a mixture of sticky rice and shredded pork wrapped in bamboo leaves, or a sweet treat of candied ginger.

Turn right again onto N King St, past the red dragon columns guarding the **Bank of Hawaii** (5). If you're hungry, sample the $1.50 dim sum at the **Golden Palace Seafood Restaurant** (6; p107) before proceeding to the corner of Kehaulike St and the bustling **O'ahu Market** (7; p113), where boxes of iced fish and fresh produce await morning shoppers. Cross the street and wander up the short Kehaulike St pedestrian mall.

On the opposite side of N Hotel St, poke your nose into the bustling **Maunakea Marketplace** (8; p107), where the fish is still jumping around in large buckets. You can continue on Hotel St or walk right through the marketplace's dozen ethnic lunch counters, turning left as you emerge onto Pauahi St. Either way, you'll end up on River St, home to several Vietnamese eateries and shops.

Walking up River St pedestrian mall, notice the **bronze statue** (9; p94) of Chinese revolutionary leader Dr Sun Yat-sen, and Chinatown seniors playing checkers or mah-jongg on stone benches. Take the short bridge across the Nu'uanu Stream to the century-old **Izumo Taisha shrine** (10; p95), to which school children from Japan journey each year as a gesture of peace.

On the corner of Kukui St, begin to circle back and make your way to the corner of Maunakea and Pau'ahi Sts, where O'ahu's thriving lei industry is in full bloom. You'll pass clusters of tiny shops where skilled lei makers, some with glasses studiously tilted down, string and braid blossom after blossom, filling the air with the scents of pikake and ginger.

Continue southeast until the corner of Bethel St, home to the **Hawaii Theater** (11; p112), a restored 1920s neoclassical masterpiece. Continue one block to Fort St Mall. Turn right and go another block to S Hotel St, turning left at watery **Tamarind Plaza (12)**, marked by a modern sculpture *(Upright Motive 9)*, the work of American Henry Moore. Walk another block to Richards St and turn left, arriving at the 1927 Julia Morgan–designed **YWCA (13)**, opposite 'Iolani Palace. Finish at **Cafe Laniakea (14**; p105) for a well-deserved iced passion-fruit tea or tangy *haupia* coconut sorbet.

TOURS

Although Chinatown is a fun place to poke around on your own, tour guides provide chatty commentary with historical insights and often take you to a few places you're unlikely to visit yourself. With either of the following groups, there's no need for reservations – just show up.

The **Hawaii Heritage Center** (Map pp86-7; ☎ 521-2749; Ramsay Galleries, 1117 Smith St; tour $10) leads walking tours of Chinatown, beginning at the Ramsay Galleries. Tours take place from 9:30am to 11:30am Wednesday and Friday. The **Chinese Chamber of Commerce** (Map pp86-7; ☎ 533-3181; 42 N King St; tour $5) leads walking tours of Chinatown from 9:30am to 11:30am on Tuesday. Tours begin at the chamber office on the 2nd floor.

Treat your taste buds to one of O'ahu's treasures – great food – compliments of **Hawaii Food Tours** (☎ 926-3663, 800-715-2468; www .hawaiifoodtours.com; tour $50-150), the creation of the former restaurant critic for the *Honolulu Advertiser*. What sets this operation apart is variety. A four-hour lunchtime tour samples Honolulu's ethnic hole-in-the-wall eateries; another focuses on traditional Hawaiian favorites, like *kalua* pork and *lomilomi* salmon (minced, salted salmon, diced tomatos and green onion). A third visits three top gourmet restaurants for appetizers, dinner and dessert, each course paired with a fine wine. Prices include transportation.

Mauka Makai Excursions (☎ 255-2206; www .hawaiianecotours.net; 350 Ward Ave, Suite 109, Honolulu; tour adult/child $75/60), a Hawaiian owned and operated cultural ecotour company, does Saturday-only day hikes to several ancient Hawaiian sites on the North Shore, including a fishing shrine, Kaneaukai Ko'a, above Waimea Bay. The hike is five miles long, usually with a swim in the middle. Rates include hotel pick-ups.

FESTIVALS & EVENTS

Follow the hungry locals to Honolulu's own tribute to the art of eating, **Taste of Honolulu** (www.taste808.com; Honolulu Civic Center) an annual three-day food and music affair sampling the city's best cooking, held on the last weekend in June. There's a bit of everything, from top-of-the-food-chain to humble mom-and-pop eateries. Over 30 musical groups keep the place jumping, but island *grinds* (food) are what bring thousands of locals to this one-of-a-kind event.

If you're in town on the first Friday of the month, join the locals at the city's **Gallery Walk**, a self-guided stroll through the happening downtown Honolulu and Chinatown art scene, complete with free *pupu* (snacks) and entertainment. It's on between 5pm and 9pm. Walking maps can be picked up at the 19 featured galleries, any of which can be contacted for more information:

Got Art? (Map pp86-7; ☎ 521-1097; 1136 Nu'uanu Ave)
Hanks Cafe Honolulu (Map pp86-7; ☎ 526-1410; 1038 Nu'uanu Ave)
Pegge Hooper Gallery (Map pp86-7; ☎ 524-1160; 1164 Nu'uanu Ave)
Sharky's Tattoo (Map pp86-7; ☎ 585-0076; 1038 Nu'uanu Ave)
Studio 1 (Map pp86-7; ☎ 550-8701; 1 N King St)
The Arts at Marks Garage (Map pp86-7; ☎ 521-2903; 1159 Nu'uanu Ave)

SLEEPING
Downtown
TOP END

Aston at the Executive Centre Hotel (Map pp86-7; ☎ 539-3000, 800-922-7866; www.astonhotels.com; 1088 Bishop St; ste $195-270 incl continental breakfast; 🅿 🖭) Honolulu's only downtown hotel, the Aston is geared for businesspeople. It has 94 suites, each large and comfortable, with three phones, voice mail, two TVs, a refrigerator and a room safe. The hotel is on the upper floors of a high-rise, so most of the rooms

have fine city views. Pricier rooms have ocean views and kitchen facilities. There's a fitness center, a heated lap pool, and a business center with secretarial services and laptop rentals. Overnight parking is $15.

Ala Moana & University Area
BUDGET

Central Branch YMCA (Map pp90-1; ☎ 941-3344; www .ymcahonolulu.org; 401 Atkinson Dr; s/d with shared bathroom $33/45, s/d $41/55; 🖭) Conveniently located on the east side of the Ala Moana Center, just outside Waikiki. The rooms with shared bathroom are available to men only and are small and simple, resembling those in a student dorm. Rooms with bathrooms, which are a bit nicer, are open to both men and women. Guests receive YMCA privileges, including free use of the sauna, pool and gym. There's a coin laundry, TV lounge and snack bar. Overnight parking is $5.

Hosteling International Honolulu (Map pp90-1; ☎ 946-0591; hihostel@lava.net; 2323A Seaview Ave; members/nonmembers dm $14/17, r $44/38; 🕒 8am-noon & 4pm-midnight; 🅿) This small, well-run hostel, in a quiet residential neighborhood near the university, has seven dorm rooms with bunk beds. It can accommodate up to 43 travelers, with men and women in separate dorms, and two rooms for couples. If you're not an HI member, there's a three-night maximum stay. HI membership is sold on-site; the cost is $25 for Americans, $18 for foreign visitors. The hostel has a TV lounge, guest kitchen, laundry room, lockers and bulletin boards.

MID-RANGE

Manoa Valley Inn (Map pp90-1; ☎ 947-6019; www .manoavalley.inn.com; 2001 Vancouver Dr; r with shared bathroom $100-120, r $140-160, incl continental breakfast; 🅿 🟊) Located on a quiet side street just near the university, this restored Victorian inn is on the National Register of Historic Places. The inn's common areas and eight guest rooms are furnished with antiques, and the whole place simply drips with colonial character. Best suited for those who prefer to be outside the main tourist scene.

Pagoda Hotel (Map pp90-1; ☎ 941-6611, 800-367-6060; www.pagodahotel.com; 1525 Rycroft St; r $110, studio $170; 🟊) North of the Ala Moana Center, the Pagoda Hotel has two sections. Rooms in the 12-story main hotel unit are quiet and have the expected amenities, including

TV and refrigerator. An adjacent five-story complex features studios with kitchenettes, but they can feel a bit removed from the main hotel – especially if you're checking in at night. A busy restaurant with a koi pond is open all day. The hotel is especially popular with visitors from the Neighbor Islands, mainly as an alternative to jumping into the bustling Waikiki scene. Overnight parking is $5.

TOP END

Ala Moana Hotel (Map pp90-1; ☎ 955-4811, 800-367-6025; www.alamoanahotel.com; 410 Atkinson Dr; r $170-260; ☒) Looming above the Ala Moana Center, just west of Waikiki and near the Hawaiian Convention Center, this hotel offers 1262 well-appointed, but fairly identical rooms. Amenities include cable TV, small refrigerators and room safes. The lower rates are for lower-floor city-view rooms, with prices rising as you climb, topping out at ocean-view rooms on the 35th floor. The hotel is popular with business travelers, especially overnighting airline crews. Overnight parking is $10.

Elsewhere in Honolulu

If you have some dire need to be near Honolulu international airport, there are mid-range hotels outside the airport along a busy highway and beneath flight paths. All provide free 24-hour transport to/from the airport, about 10 minutes' away.

Best Western Plaza Hotel (Map pp84 ☎ 836-3636, 800-800-4683; www.bestwesternhonolulu.com; 3253 N Nimitz Hwy; r $109-125; ℗ ☒ ☒) The most comfortable option near the airport, this modern hotel boasts 274 pleasant rooms, each with a king-size bed or two double beds, cable TV and refrigerator. The only drawback is the noise from the heavy traffic on the adjacent overpass – ask for a rear room. The hotel has a lounge and restaurant. Within walking distance is the Nimitz Mart center, which has a handful of fast-food places.

Pacific Marina Inn (Map p84; ☎ 836-1131, 800-548-8040; www.castleresorts.com; 2628 Waiwai Loop; r $80; ℗ ☒ ☒) A mile east of the airport, with less traffic noise, this three-decker motel has small, straightforward rooms with cable TV. There's often an 'airport special' of $70; call from its courtesy phone in the airport's baggage-claim area.

EATING

Honolulu has an incredible variety of restaurants that mirror the city's multiethnic composition, and if you know where to look it can also be quite cheap. Get out of the tourist areas and join the locals.

Downtown
BUDGET

There's a cluster of inexpensive restaurants at the north side of the downtown area within easy walking distance of 'Iolani Palace. There are some good choices here, and the variety will only increase as more college students move into this area.

Ba-Le (Map pp86-7; ☎ 521-4117; 1154 Fort St Mall; snacks $2-5; ❂ 7am-6pm Mon-Fri, 7am-3pm Sat) This Fort St eatery is one of an island-wide Vietnamese bakery/café chain and good for a quick, inexpensive bite. Options range from more than a dozen sandwiches to shrimp rolls and noodles. For a caffeine jolt, there's sweet, strong French coffee with milk, either hot or iced.

The Gazebo (Map pp86-7; ☎ 945-5130; Macy's, cnr Fort St Mall & N King St; dishes $5-8; ❂ 8:30am-3:30pm Mon-Sat) Follow the downtown office workers on their lunch break to the 2nd floor of Macy's Department Store for first-rate cafeteria fare, including fresh salads, grilled fish and pastries.

Cafe Laniakea (Map pp86-7; ☎ 524-8789; 1040 Richards St; dishes $4-10; ❂ 11am-2pm Mon-Fri) Menu highlights at this casual courtyard café at the Julia Morgan–designed YWCA range from

---

TOP 10 EATS

- **Indigo** (p107), Chinatown
- **Duke's Canoe Club** (p132), Waikiki
- **Kaka'ako Kitchen** (p107), Honolulu
- **Hale'iwa Joe's** (p162), Hale'iwa
- **Imanas Tei** (p108), Honolulu
- **L'Uraku** (p109), Honolulu
- **Duc's Bistro** (p107), Chinatown
- **Little Village Noodle House** (p106), Chinatown
- **Hale Vietnam** (p110), Honolulu (Kaimuki)
- **Lei Lei's Bar & Grill** (p168), North Shore

salmon bisque soup and Tuscan meatloaf to chocolate mousse and passionfruit iced tea.

Z's Poi Bowl (Map pp86-7; ☎ 545-4225; 1108 Bishop St; lunch $4-6; ⏰ 6:30am-2pm Mon-Fri) A little hole-in-the-wall that scores with take-out plate lunches of traditional Hawaiian food. A typical plate includes *kalua* pig, *lomilomi* salmon, poi or rice.

Leo's Taverna (Map pp86-7; ☎ 550-8443; 1116 Bishop St; dishes $4-8; 8am-6pm Mon-Fri, 10am-3pm Sat) Popular Greek restaurant with an extensive menu. Vegetarians can choose from falafel, Greek salad, stuffed grape leaves and the like. For meat eaters, there are kebabs, moussaka and tasty gyros of marinated beef and lamb.

MID-RANGE

The Aloha Tower Marketplace, on Pier 8, is a waterfront complex, immediately west of the downtown district, easily recognized by its landmark clock tower. It boasts some of Honolulu's trendiest seaside restaurants and bars. It's one of the most user-friendly venues in Honolulu, easily reached by bus and with plenty of validated parking.

Gordon Biersch Brewery Restaurant (Map pp86-7; ☎ 599-1405; 1st fl, Aloha Tower Marketplace; mains $10-23; ⏰ 11am-11:30pm Sun-Thu, 11:30am-1am Fri & Sat) On the seaside, this is another great spot for a drink (see p111). The food is also good: Hawaiian *pupu*, creative salads, sandwiches and pizza are available for under $10; mains include specialty pasta dishes and grilled seafood. There's live entertainment on Wednesday to Saturday nights.

Chai's Island Bistro (Map pp86-7; ☎ 585-0011; Aloha Tower Marketplace; lunch $12-20, dinner $28-45; ⏰ 11am-10pm Mon-Fri, 4-10pm Sat & Sun) You'll find award-winning Pacific Rim cuisine – crispy duck spring rolls, macadamia-crusted prawns and brandy-glazed Mongolian lamb. It's pricey and there's no water view, but the food and presentation are winners. Some of Hawaii's top musicians perform at dinner.

Sunset Grill (Map pp86-7; ☎ 521-4409; cnr Ala Moana Blvd & Punchbowl St; lunch/dinner around $10/20; ⏰ 11am-11pm Mon-Fri, 5-11pm Sat & Sun) Next to the cinemas in the Restaurant Row complex, this is a good spot for a bite and a glass of wine before catching a movie. The varied menu includes salads, fresh fish, pasta and grills for dinner, and hearty sandwiches at lunch.

Chinatown
BUDGET

Royal Kitchen (Map pp86-7; ☎ 524-4461; River St, Chinatown Cultural Plaza; dishes $3-7; ⏰ 6:30am-5pm) This lively open-front eatery is famous for some of the best baked *manapua* (pork buns) around. And pork is just one of the choices, along with chicken curry, vegetarian, sweet potato, *kalua* pig and more. Each *manapua* is only 89¢.

To Chau (Map pp86-7; ☎ 533-4549; 1007 River St; dishes $3-6; ⏰ 8am-2:30pm) This Vietnamese restaurant serves fantastic *pho*, a delicious soup of beef broth, rice noodles and thin slices of beef. It comes with a second plate of fresh basil and hot chili peppers that you add to your liking. A bowl of soup is a meal in itself, and the shrimp rolls are also excellent. It's so popular that even at 10am you may have to line up outside the door for one of the 16 tables. It's well worth the wait.

Cuu Long (Map pp86-7; ☎ 585-3663; 1001 River St; dishes $4-7; ⏰ 8am-8pm) If the line at To Chau

---

THE AUTHOR'S CHOICE

Little Village Noodle House (Map pp86-7; ☎ 545-3008; 1113 Smith St; dishes $5-12; ⏰ 10:30am-10:30pm Sun-Thu, 10:30am-midnight Fri-Sat) A quiet and air-conditioned restaurant in Chinatown? That's only the beginning at this outstanding Chinese eatery just *mauka* of Hotel St. The food at Little Village is prepared in an open kitchen and covers several regions in China, mostly Canton and the northern provinces. The eclectic menu ranges from spicy Szechwan chicken and plump Shanghai noodles to chicken and chive dumplings simmered in olive oil. And if you enjoy anything in black bean sauce, this is the gold standard for Honolulu. Try the sizzling butterfish ($13) or stir-fried clams ($10). Unusual noodle dishes include duck noodle O'ahu style ($6.30), hot and sour cold noodles ($5) and fish-cake noodles ($5). Other fusion touches include stir-fried lamb with leek and chile ($11) and roasted pork with taro ($7). The unusual menu extends to tea and dessert. Choose from chrysanthemum honey herbal tea or carrot tea, both served cold. For sweets, the fresh crepe with red bean paste is as good as it gets. Little Village is clean, friendly and full of surprises, not the least of which is free parking just behind the restaurant.

is too daunting, this is a good alternative. While this restaurant is relatively large and blandly modern, it too specializes in *pho* and does a good job of it. The menu also includes other Vietnamese noodle and rice dishes.

Huong Lan (Map pp86-7; ☎ 538-6707; 100 N Beretania St; dishes $4-7; ☉ 8am-5pm) Vietnamese folk come to this hidden gem in the Chinatown Cultural Plaza for the excellent *pho* soup, and yummy appetizers, like the delicate summer spring rolls, and iced French coffee.

Golden Palace Seafood Restaurant (Map pp86-7; ☎ 521-8268; 111 N King St; dishes $5-7; ☉ 7am-10pm) It says seafood on the sign outside, but the $1.50 dim sum is what brings Chinatown's mid-morning regulars here, unless it's the pink tablecloths and kitschy art. Have a seat and wait for the carts filled with bamboo steamer boxes to roll by. You have to choose quickly, but keep an eye out for the steamed pork with bean curd and deep-fried shrimp-and-seaweed roll.

Maunakea Marketplace (Map pp86-7; N Hotel St; meals $5; ☉ 7am-3:30pm) For a quintessentially local dining option, head to the food court in this marketplace, where you'll find about 20 stalls with mom-and-pop vendors dishing out home-style Chinese, Filipino, Thai, Vietnamese, Korean and Japanese food. You can chow down at tiny wooden tables crowded into the central walkway.

MID-RANGE & TOP END

Indigo (Map pp86-7; ☎ 521-2900; 1121 Nu'uanu Ave; dinner $16-26; ☉ 11:30am-2pm Tue-Fri, 6-9:30pm Tue-Sat) Indigo has a relaxed, open-air courtyard and very good contemporary Eurasian cuisine. Located on the Chinatown-downtown border behind the Hawaii Theatre, it's a favorite dinner spot for theatergoers, and the crowd is a happy, eclectic mix. Creative dim sum appetizers, such as tempura *'ahi* (yellowfin tuna) rolls and goats cheese wontons, are a special treat. Dinner features such dishes as tangerine-glazed ribs, ginger-miso salmon and mahogany duck. An award-winning wine list matches the inspired menu. See p111 for a review of its bars.

Duc's Bistro (Map pp86-7; ☎ 521-2900; 1188 Maunakea St; lunch $10-17; complete dinners $14-30; ☉ 11:30am-1:30pm Mon-Fri, 5:30-10pm nightly) This swank upscale Chinatown bistro is mostly Paris, part Saigon, with a tiny Manhattan-like bar. French-Vietnamese fusion highlights include noodles in lime sauce, seafood

paella, vermicelli with spring rolls, and avocado and green papaya salad. A small jazz combo performs on most evenings.

Legend Vegetarian Restaurant (☎ 532-8218; Chinatown Cultural Plaza; mains $7-12; ☉ 10:30am-2pm Thu-Tue) A curious place with a loyal following on the River St side. This health-oriented, Chinese, lunch-only spot is known for several fish and pork analogs that even meat eaters acknowledge as tasty! Favorites include the vegetarian butter fish and sweet-and-sour vegetarian pork, along with a huge selection of dim sum offerings.

Zaffron (Map pp86-7; ☎ 533-6635; 69 N King St; lunch/dinner $8/13; ☉ 11am-2pm Mon-Sat, 5-9pm Wed-Sat) This simple, home-style Indian eatery at the southwest side of Chinatown offers a variety of hearty plate lunches and a good dinner buffet. You can choose from vegetarian mains, tandoori chicken or fish curries. Each plate lunch includes rice, naan and a number of side dishes.

Ala Moana & University Area

Not surprisingly, the area around the University of Hawaii at Manoa supports an interesting collection of reasonably priced ethnic restaurants, coffee shops and health-food stores. You'll also find worthy eats in and around the Ala Moana area malls.

BUDGET

Kaka'ako Kitchen (Map pp90-1; ☎ 596-7488; Ward Centre, 1200 Ala Moana Blvd; meals $6-10; ☉ 7am-10pm Mon-Sat, 7am-5pm Sun) A spin-off of the upscale restaurant 3660 On the Rise, Kaka'ako uses the same fresh ingredients and creative flair as its pricier parent operation. Here, however, the food is served plate-lunch style on Styrofoam with brown or white rice and an organic salad. You can choose from local favorites, such as shoyu chicken, or for a bit more, order a gourmet plate such as sautéed wild salmon (a great choice) or ginger-sake *'ahi* steak. Eat here at patio tables or take it across the street to Ala Moana Beach for a picnic.

Bubbies (Map pp90-1; ☎ 949-8984; 1010 University Ave, cnr S Beretania St; ☉ noon-midnight, noon-1am Fri & Sat, noon-11:30pm Sun) This ice-cream shop is a great place to go for homemade ice cream in luscious tropical flavors, such as papaya-ginger. Just as many people come to Bubbies for its chocolate mochi-with-espresso ice cream.

Coffeeline (Map pp90-1; ☎ 778-7909; cnr University & Seaview Aves; dishes $3-6; ☺ 7am-3:45pm Mon-Fri, 8am-noon Sat) A casual student hangout with good coffee and vegetarian food, it proudly serves 'slow food.' Coffeeline offers vegan soup, 'big hippie' sandwiches, hearty salads and a few hot dishes, such as spinach lasagna. Blues and jazz play all day and there's a large stack of alternative magazines to browse through; it's also a wireless Internet hotspot.

Well Bento (Map pp90-1; ☎ 941-5261; 2570 S Beretania St, 2nd fl; dishes $6-10; ☺ 10:30am-8pm, closed Sat) This inconspicuous hole-in-the-wall serves the most unusual dishes without the benefit of sugar or dairy products. The surprising menu ranges from Zen macrobiotic veggies and grilled tofu ($7) to flank steak or Cajun chicken ($8). There are only a few tables, so consider it a great take-out or picnic option. Cash only.

Mekong I (Map pp90-1; ☎ 591-8841; 1295 S Beretania St; appetizers $4-7, mains $7-10; ☺ 11am-2pm Mon-Fri, 5-9:30pm daily) One of the oldest Thai restaurants in Honolulu, it's a small unpretentious place with a reputation for good food and fair prices. The menu includes excellent spring rolls, tasty noodle dishes and a variety of vegetarian and meat curries.

Montien Thai (Map pp90-1; ☎ 949-2679; 2671-D S King St; dishes $7-10; ☺ 11am-9pm Thu-Tue, 4-9pm Sun) A small family restaurant that serves authentic northeastern Thai cuisine with a local touch, like Penang curry with mahimahi ($9), and a tasty veggie pad Thai with tofu ($7).

Down to Earth Natural Foods (Map pp90-1; ☎ 947-7678; 2525 S King St; salad bar per lb $6; ☺ 7:30am-9pm) Honolulu's largest natural foods supermarket is a great place to shop, as it carries everything from Indian chapatis to local organic produce. The store also has a vegetarian deli with a salad bar and hot dishes, such as tahini tofu balls or vegetable curry.

Kokua Natural Foods Market (Map pp90-1; ☎ 941-1922; 2643 S King St; ☺ 8:30am-8:30pm) This cozy health food co-op, just south of the university, is stocked with quality local produce, fresh juices and sandwiches, even a good selection of micro-brewed beers.

The **Ala Moana Center** (Map pp90-1; 1450 Ala Moana Blvd) has a small **Foodland** (☎ 949-5044) supermarket and a food court with scores of ethnic fast-food stalls. There's another **Foodland** (Map pp90-1; ☎ 734-6303), north of Waikiki, at the eastern intersection of S King St and Kapiolani Blvd.

MID-RANGE

Brew Moon (Map pp90-1; ☎ 593-0088; Ward Centre, 1200 Ala Moana Blvd; pub grub $6-10, lunch/dinner $12/20; ☺ 11am-1am) This stylish, high-energy place brews its own ales (see p111) and serves a wide variety of snacks, including fried calamari, grilled pizza and sandwiches. Dishes available at lunch and dinner include jambalaya chicken or sautéed fish.

The Willows (Map pp90-1; ☎ 952-9200; 901 Hausten St; lunch/dinner buffet $17/28, per child $9/14; ☺ 11am-2pm & 5:30-9pm; ℗ valet parking) Follow the locals to this Honolulu landmark for authentic all-you-can-eat Hawaiian buffets. Few restaurants have a more loyal following than this one, where a chef carves prime rib and suckling pig to accompany 'ahi poke (cubed raw fish mixed with soya, sesame oil, salt, chili pepper and other condiments), crab legs and more. The open garden setting, complete with lily ponds and ginger blossoms, is family friendly throughout.

Side Street Inn (Map pp90-1; ☎ 591-0253; 1225 Hopaka St; dishes $7-18; ☺ 10am-1:30pm Mon-Fri, 4pm-1am daily) This late-night mecca near Ala Moana Center attracts Honolulu's best chefs, along with a faithful following who come for Hawaiian standards, like fried rice ($9), pan-fried pork chops ($17) and poke-style ocean clams ($7). The portions are big, and the ambiance ranges from smoky karaoke mellow to jukebox diner.

Pavilion Cafe (Map pp90-1; ☎ 532-8734; 900 S Beretania St; dishes $8-13; ☺ lunch Tue-Sat) Located in the Honolulu Academy of Arts, this upscale café has a lovely courtyard setting overlooking the museum's water fountains. The kitchen specializes in gourmet salads and sandwiches, but also makes an innovative pasta of the day. It's a good place to relax and a wonderfully indulgent way to support the arts. Reservations are suggested, particularly if there's a special exhibition at the museum.

Imanas Tei (Map pp90-1; ☎ 941-2626; 2626 S King St; dishes $3-12; ☺ 5-11:30pm Mon-Sat) They call it an izakaya (pub), but visitors from Japan know it for what it is: an upscale eatery serving excellent sushi and Japanese grills, mostly à la carte style.

El Burrito (Map pp90-1; ☎ 596-8225; 550 Piikoi St; dishes $8-10; ☺ 11am-8pm Mon-Thu, 11am-9pm Fri & Sat) Near the Ala Moana Center, this could be a neighborhood hole-in-the-wall on a back street in Mexico City. It squeezes in about a dozen tables and serves authentic Mexican

Bustling Waikiki (p123), O'ahu

ANN CECIL

Hanauma Bay (p139) in Southeast O'ahu

ANN CECIL

Aerial view of Waikiki and Kapiolani Park from Diamond Head (p138), O'ahu

ANN CECIL

Waikiki Trolley (p137), Honolulu, O'ahu

GLENDA BENDURE

RICHARD CUMMINS

A night passage on a cruise ship in the Honolulu Harbor (p99), O'ahu

Waimanalo Bay (p142), O'ahu

ANN CECIL

People swimming at a Waikiki beach (p124), O'ahu

RICHARD I'ANSC

food: fellow diners are as likely to be chatting in Spanish as English. Expect queues at dinnertime, especially on weekends.

Auntie Pasto's (Map pp90-1; ☎ 523-8855; 1099 S Beretania St; mains $8-12; ☻ 11am-10:30pm Mon-Fri, 4-11pm Sat & Sun) Pasta is the specialty here, with a number of vegetarian varieties such as eggplant parmesan, as well as a full range of seafood and meat choices. Although it's off the tourist track, this popular spot serves good Italian food that attracts a crowd. You may have to wait for a table – particularly on weekends.

Yanagi Sushi (☎ 537-1525; 762 Kapiolani Blvd; à la carte sushi $2-5, meals $10-20; ☻ 11am-2pm & 5:30pm-2am, 5:30pm-10pm Sun) Yanagi is one of Honolulu's most popular late-night places for sushi, along with other Japanese dishes prepared to perfection. Ask about the 'late birds' – $8 meal specials available after 10:30pm.

Kincaid's Fish, Chop & Steak House (Map pp90-1; ☎ 591-2005; Ward Warehouse, 1050 Ala Moana Blvd; lunch $10-15, complete dinners $18-30; ☻ 11am-10pm) It's a smart upmarket place with good food and a harbor view. A favorite lunch spot for downtown businesspeople, the restaurant specializes in creative seafood dishes and steaks. The best deal is the soup-to-dessert 'early bird' that's available from 5pm to 6pm and offers a choice of several mains ($19).

Viet Cafe (Map pp90-1; ☎ 949-8268; 1960 Kapiolani Blvd; dishes $8-12; ☻ 10am-midnight) Within walking distance of the Ala Moana end of Waikiki via the McCully Bridge, this busy Vietnamese eatery is a favorite among Honolulu's Vietnamese community for its traditional sour soups, barbequed pork chops and late hours.

Cafe Maharani (Map pp90-1; ☎ 951-7447; 2509 S King St; dishes $9-12; ☻ 5-10pm) Along with standard northern-Indian dishes, like Tandoori chicken and chicken masala curry, this simple family restaurant also serves several excellent vegetarian dishes like dal and eggplant tikka masala. When it comes to spiciness, most dishes can be ordered hot, medium or mild.

The Greek Corner (Map pp90-1; ☎ 942-5503; 1025 University Ave; mains $10-12; ☻ 11am-9:30pm Mon-Fri, 5-9:30pm Sat & Sun) This is an inviting eatery, and being near the university, prices are cheaper than they'd be in a trendier part of town. Main dishes (which come with Greek salad, rice and pita bread) include popular standards like lamb kebabs, moussaka and stuffed

grape leaves, as well as plenty of choices for vegetarians and carnivores alike.

Pagoda Restaurant (Map pp90-1; ☎ 941-6611; 1525 Rycroft St; breakfast $4-9, lunch buffet $11, dinner buffet $19-21; ☻ breakfast 6:30-11am Mon-Sat, lunch 11am-2pm Mon-Fri, dinner 4:30-9:30pm daily) The restaurant at the Pagoda Hotel (p104) offers a pleasant garden-like setting bordering a carp pond. The breakfast menu is extensive, and there's a lunch buffet of Japanese and American dishes, and a fancier dinner buffet with a spread that includes prime rib, crab legs, sashimi, a salad bar and dessert.

Compadres (Map pp90-1; ☎ 591-8307; Ward Centre, 1200 Ala Moana Blvd; appetizers $5-8, dishes $10-20; ☻ 11am-11pm Mon-Thu, 11am-midnight Fri & Sat, 11am-10pm Sun) On the Ward Centre's upper level, this bustling Mexican restaurant draws a crowd and wins plenty of local dining awards. It not only offers the expected enchilada, fajita and taco dishes, but also has some interesting cross-cultural fare like spicy peanut Thai quesadillas.

TOP END

Alan Wong's (Map pp90-1; ☎ 949-2526; 1857 S King St; appetizers $8-12, mains $26-38; ☻ 5-10pm) One of Hawaii's top restaurants, this high-energy place specializes in upmarket Hawaiian regional cuisine. Chef Wong, who won accolades at the Big Island's exclusive Mauna Lani Resort before striking out on his own, offers a creative menu with an emphasis on fresh local ingredients. Appetizers include tempura *'ahi*, while mains feature fresh seafood – such as Wong's signature dish, ginger-crusted *onaga* (red snapper). Each night there's also a five-course 'tasting menu' ($65). Reservations are recommended.

L'Uraku (Map pp90-1; ☎ 955-0552; 1341 Kapiolani Blvd; mains $20-35; ☻ 11am-2pm, 5:30pm-10pm) Perhaps the best value of the top-end Honolulu restaurants, this sparkling Japanese-European fusion eatery blends flavors East and West with local ingredients, like pan-seared *moi* (Pacific threadfin) fish with a light soy butter sauce served over wilted chard ($20). For unbeatable value, try the four-course 'weekender' lunch ($16) or the 'dinner tasting' for a generous sampling of the best in the house ($34, with wine pairings $47).

Chef Mavro (Map pp90-1; ☎ 944-4714; 1969 S King St; 4-course dinner $56-66) When you're ready to mix a green-tea dusted zucchini blossom tempura appetizer with a glass of German

O'AHU

mosel wine, you're ready for one of Honolulu's most elegant restaurants, known in particular for its food and wine pairings. Entrées include catch-of-the-day fish with braised radicchio, roasted pork with lentil puree, along with assorted cheeses and desserts. Three- and four-course dinners with wine pairings cost $78 to $98.

Kaimuki & Waialae Ave

Honolulu's off-the-beaten-path neighborhood 'restaurant row' is at the end of the Kaimuki district, on the way to the Kahala Mall. If you're driving, follow Kapiolani Blvd, which turns into Waialae Ave. From Waikiki, take bus No 2 or 13, and transfer to bus No 1 on S King St.

MID-RANGE

Sis Kitchen (☎ 732-0902; 1137 11th Ave; lunch specials $6, mains $10-14; ☺ 11am-9pm Mon-Sat) This excellent Korean eatery is the stylish creation of four sisters whose menu combines traditional and modern flavors. As quickly as you're seated, a complimentary plate of *ban chahn* ('small tastes') will appear. Entrées include Korean standards, like *bulgogi* (thinly sliced rib-eye steak) and *dak gui* (barbecued chicken), and jazzier dishes like sautéed garlic shrimp ($13) and *boochoo jopchae* (sautéed shredded pork with fresh chives; $10).

Hale Vietnam (☎ 735-7581; 1140 12th Ave; mains $6-11; ☺ 11am-10pm) This top-notch local favorite has delicious Vietnamese food at moderate prices. A delightful starter is the temple rolls ($5), a combination of fresh basil, mint, tofu and yam rolled in rice paper. The yellow curries are also excellent, and come in vegetarian, beef and chicken variations.

Days of Aloha (☎ 735-5166; 1137 11th Ave; dishes 4-7; ☺ 11am-9pm Tue-Fri, 9am-9pm Sat, 9am-6pm Sun) Tucked away behind a string of restaurants on Waialae Ave, this vintage Hawaiian-style café serves tasty salads and sandwiches, Italian sodas and coffee drinks. On Saturday night, there's live Hawaiian music, and you can bring your own beer!

Maguro-ya (☎ 732-3775; 3665 Waialae Ave; mains $12-15; ☺ 11am-1:45pm Tue-Sat, 5-9:30pm Tue-Sun) This handsome Japanese eatery is among the town's best for sushi and traditional *teishoku* (combination) dinners of fresh fish, tempura and sashimi ($14 to $19).

AN ACQUIRED TASTE?

Admit it, you don't like poi, or so you say.

Of the many Hawaiian foods to try, from briny *lomilomi* salmon and *kalua* pig, to raw sashimi and crunchy seaweed, one Hawaiian staple still remains off-limits to most island visitors – the pasty, slightly sour, pounded taro root known as poi. It has been relegated to a culinary outpost for things bland and purplish.

But poi is mainly used as a tangy dipping sauce for nearly everything on the table, never as a dish on its own. And the best poi is slightly aged, not the fresh (and bland) stuff of the tourist luau (traditional Hawaiian feast).

So it may be time for another try. Really, all we are saying is: give poi a chance.

TOP END

3660 On the Rise (☎ 737-1177; 3660 Waialae Ave; appetizers $7-10, mains $20-28; ☺ 5:30-9pm Tue-Sun) A trendy restaurant with a loyal Honolulu following, 3660 features 'Euro-Island' cuisine. Popular mains include red snapper steamed in a Hawaiian *ti* leaf, macadamia nut-crusted lamb and Black Angus garlic steak. Appetizers include escargot, spicy crab cakes and specialty salads. The restaurant is three miles northeast of Waikiki on Waialae Ave between 12th and 13th Aves; reservations are recommended.

Elsewhere in Honolulu
BUDGET

Helena's Hawaiian Food (☎ 845-8044; 1240 North School St; per person $5-9; ☺ 10am-7:30pm Tue-Fri) West of downtown and close to the Bishop Museum, this Honolulu institution can claim its own history, dating to 1946. Owner Helena Chock still runs the kitchen, handles the cash register and chats with customers. The menu is mostly à la carte dishes, some smoky and salty, others sweet or spicy. You start with poi or rice, then add a couple of small plates of *lomilomi* salmon, briny shortribs or *kalua* pig, and you've got a mini-luau for under $10.

MID-RANGE

Sam Choy's Breakfast, Lunch & Crab (☎ 545-7979; 580 N Nimitz Hwy; lunch mains $8-16, dinner mains $18-40, Sat & Sun brunch buffet $15; ☺ 6:30am-10pm) Its menu offers huge portions of local specialties, such as fried noodles or *loco moco* (three hamburger patties and more, buried in gravy) for breakfast, along with mainland staples such as bacon and eggs, and fresh crab, crabcakes or other sandwiches for lunch, and more crab for dinner. There's also a steak-and-lobster combo ($34). The food is great, a high-quality change from overpriced hotel fare. Dinner reservations recommended. The restaurant's on-site Big Aloha Brewery pours some of the best microbrews in town, with $2 *pupu* from 3pm to 6pm.

Contemporary Cafe (Map p100; ☎ 523-3362; Contemporary Museum, 2411 Makiki Heights Dr; lunch mains $8-10; ☺ 11am-2:30pm Tue-Sat, noon-2:30pm Sun) This is a genteel treat, with a pleasant lawn setting at the Contemporary Museum in Makiki Valley. There are healthy salads, such as chicken Caesar or soba noodle with watercress, and creative sandwiches, including grilled eggplant with feta or tapenade and boursin cheese on a baguette. It's not necessary to pay museum admission if you're just having lunch – simply let the staff at the door know that you're visiting the café.

DRINKING

For more options in nearby Waikiki, see p134.

Indigo (Map pp86-7; ☎ 521-2900; 1121 Nu'uanu Ave; ☺ 11:30am-2pm Tue-Fri, 6pm-midnight Tue-Sun) The Opium Den and Champagne Bar offer drink specials ($3 for a huge variety of flavored, vodka-based drinks, like its signature sake martini or a Mandarin cosmo), plus live music and DJs (see p112). The courtyard bar has an impressive, free spread at happy hour (food at 5pm, drink specials from 4pm to 7pm Tuesday to Friday). See p107 for the restaurant review.

Kapono's (Map pp86-7; ☎ 536-2161; Aloha Tower Marketplace; ☺ 11am-midnight) In the marketplace's waterfront courtyard, this is not only a happening place for Hawaiian music, but a good spot for a drink and light eats. The menu includes snacks, sandwiches and fried calamari ($5 to $11). Happy 'hour' is a day-long event (11am to 8pm) featuring $2 draft beers. There's also live Hawaiian music (see p112) nightly.

Hank's Cafe Honolulu (Map pp86-7; ☎ 526-1410; 1038 Nu'uanu St; ☺ noon-midnight Mon-Fri, 3pm-1am Sat & Sun) You can't get more low-key than at this friendly neighborhood bar on the edge of Chinatown. There's very good live music most nights, and the dim walls are brightened with the paintings of owner Hank Taufaasau; the bar is always listed on the 'Gallery Walk' (p104). For tattoo-related artwork, check out Sharky's Tattoo upstairs.

Gordon Biersch Brewery Restaurant (Map pp86-7; ☎ 599-1405; 1st fl, Aloha Tower Marketplace; mains $10-23; ☺ 11am-11:30pm Sun-Thu, 11:30am-1am Fri & Sat) Hawaii's first and most successful microbrewery restaurant (see p106), this outpost of the San Francisco brewpub features fresh lagers made according to Germany's centuries-old purity laws.

Brew Moon (Map pp86-7; ☎ 593-0088; Ward Centre, 1200 Ala Moana Blvd ☺ 11am-1am) Brewed on-site, ales range from a low-calorie 'moonlight' brew to the copper-colored 'Hawaii 5' malt. Tantalize the taste buds with the 24oz sampler ($6) of six different ales. Snacks are also served. See p108 for restaurant review.

THE AUTHOR'S CHOICE

Waioli Tea Room (Map p100; ☎ 988-5800; 2950 Manoa Rd; à la carte dishes $8-12; ☺ 8am-4pm) Toward the back of Manoa Valley, near O'ahu Ave, this is a different sort of place, a bit like stepping back 100 years when it was the kitchen for the Salvation Army Young Ladies' Orphanage. Its bakery truck was so successful that it threatened to put local shops out of business, so the girls had to back off. The open-air restaurant looks out onto gardens of red ginger and birds-of-paradise. In one of the gardens is the restored grass hut that author Robert Louis Stevenson stayed in during his retreat at Waikiki Beach; the cottage was dismantled and moved to this site in 1926. The main event here is the afternoon high tea (per person $18.50), which is served on the veranda at 2:30pm Tuesday to Sunday. It's an elegant affair served on fine china, offering a dozen-plus teas and a selection of homemade scones and pastries. You can also get breakfast here, with waffles and omelets, as well as lunchtime sandwiches, such as chicken curry with mango chutney, and specialty salads such as fresh 'ahi on Island greens. For high tea, reservations are required and usually need to be made at least a day in advance.

O'AHU

ENTERTAINMENT

Honolulu has lively entertainment scene, with most of the action occurring in Waikiki (p134), around the university and the Aloha Tower Marketplace. For up-to-the-minute information, check out the free *Honolulu Weekly*, which comes out on Wednesday and the Friday *Honolulu Advertiser's* TGIF section. Free tourist magazines often have discount coupons.

Live Music & Nightclubs

Hawaii's gay scene revolves around Honolulu. For more venues, Waikiki is the hub (p135).

Kapono's (Map pp86-7; ☎ 536-2161; Aloha Tower Marketplace) Live music is performed from 9pm to 2am Tuesday to Saturday, featuring jazz, rock and top Hawaiian musicians, including the club's namesake, Henry Kapono.

Anna Bannanas (Map pp90-1; ☎ 946-5190; 2440 S Beretania St) Not far from the university, this is a hot dance place that features blues, ska, punk and reggae bands from 9pm to 2am Thursday to Sunday.

Indigo (Map pp86-7; ☎ 521-2900; 1121 Nu'uanu Ave; admission free; ⏰ 11:30am-2pm Tue-Fri, 6pm-midnight, Tue-Sun) This popular downtown Honolulu restaurant has live music Tuesday and Thursday nights. The multilevel restaurant's Green Room has late-night ambient DJ music and dancing on Friday and Saturday. A bar menu is served until midnight.

Gordon Biersch Brewery Restaurant (Map pp86-7; ☎ 599-1405; 1st fl, Aloha Tower Marketplace; mains $10-23; ⏰ 11am-11:30pm Sun-Thu, 11:30am-1am Fri & Sat) A popular waterfront microbrewery (see p111 and p106) that hosts live rhythm and blues.

TOP 10 ENTERTAINMENT SPOTS

- **Brew Moon** (p111), Honolulu
- **Kukio Beach Torch Lighting & Hula Show** (p134), Waikiki
- **Paradise Lounge** (p134), Waikiki
- **Wonder Lounge** (p134), Waikiki
- **Anna Bannana's** (p112), Honolulu
- **Kapono's** (p111), Waikiki
- **Hank's Cafe Honolulu** (p111), Waikiki
- **Waikiki Shell** (p134), Waikiki
- **Doris Duke Theater** (p113), Honolulu Academy of Arts
- **Royal Hawaiian Hotel**, **Sheraton Moana Surfrider** and **Outrigger Waikiki** hotel beach bars (p120-30)

It also features contemporary Hawaiian and soft rock from 9pm to midnight Thursday to Saturday.

Rumours (☎ 955-4811; Ala Moana Hotel, 410 Atkinson Dr) Dancing and DJs from 9pm to 4am Thursday to Saturday, with Latin music on Thursday, Top 40 on Friday, and hip hop and R&B on Saturday.

Theater, Dance & Concerts

Honolulu boasts a symphony orchestra, an opera company, ballet troupes, chamber orchestras and community theater groups.

Hawaii Theatre (Map pp86-7; ☎ 528-0506; 1130 Bethel St) In a beautifully restored historic building on the edge of Chinatown, this is a major venue for dance, music and theater.

SUNSET ON THE BEACH

How can you go wrong in a city where the mayor throws a beach party every weekend? Each Saturday and Sunday evening the Mayor's Office of Culture and the Arts (p113) for the City and County of Honolulu turns Queen's Surf Beach into a festive scene that attracts an equal measure of locals and visitors. Dubbed 'Sunset on the Beach,' it's as much fun as a luau and everything is free – except for the food and that's a bargain.

Hawaiian bands perform on a beachside stage from 4pm to sunset, and then when darkness falls a huge screen is unscrolled above the stage and a feature movie is shown. Sometimes they opt for a movie with island connections, such as *Blue Hawaii* – the 1961 classic starring Elvis Presley – while other nights it's a popular first-run Hollywood flick.

Tables and chairs are set up on the beach and out along the beachfront by The Wall. The area's eateries operate food stalls along the boardwalk, serving great Honolulu plate-lunch picnic fare, from Panang chicken curry to Greek gyros. Nothing is over $6, and there's popcorn, too. It's all plenty of good fun and a great community experience.

Performances range from top contemporary Hawaiian musicians, such as Hapa and Hookena, to modern dance and film festivals.

Blaisdell Center (Map pp90-1; ☎ 591-2211; 777 Ward Ave) The center presents concerts, Broadway shows and family events, such as the Honolulu Symphony, the Ice Capades, the American Ballet Theatre and occasional big-name rock musicians, like Sting.

The **Academy Theatre** (Map pp90-1; ☎ 532-8768; 900 S Beretania St), at the Honolulu Academy of Arts, and the **East-West Center** (Map pp90-1; ☎ 944-7111), adjacent to the university, both present multicultural theater performances and concerts.

Cinemas

Varsity Twins (Map pp90-1; ☎ 973-5833; 1006 University Ave) The two-screen theater near the university usually shows foreign, arthouse and other alternative films.

Doris Duke Theatre (Map pp90-1; ☎ 532-8768; 900 S Beretania St) At the Honolulu Academy of Arts, this theater showcases American independent cinema, foreign films and avantgarde shorts.

Movie Museum (☎ 735-8771; 3566 Harding Ave, Kaimuki) This Kaimuki-district gem is a fun place to watch classic oldies, such as *Citizen Kane* and *Casablanca*, in a theater with just

---

FREE ENTERTAINMENT IN HONOLULU

Except during August, the **Royal Hawaiian Band** performs from noon to 1pm on Friday at the bandstand on the 'Iolani Palace lawn. It's a quintessential Hawaiian scene that caps off with the audience joining hands and singing Queen Lili'uokalani's *Aloha Oe* in Hawaiian.

In the **Ala Moana Center**, a courtyard area called Centerstage is the venue for free performances by hula dancers, gospel groups, ballet troupes, local bands and the like. There's something happening almost daily – look for the schedule in Ala Moana Center's free shopping magazine.

The **Mayor's Office of Culture & Arts** (☎ 527-5666) also sponsors numerous free performances, art exhibits and musical events, ranging from street musicians in city parks to band concerts in various locales around Honolulu. Call for current events.

---

20 comfy chairs. Movies are shown Thursday to Monday evenings and weekend afternoons. Reservations are recommended.

Honolulu also has several movie theaters showing first-run feature films:

Restaurant Row 9 Cinemas (Map pp86-7; ☎ 526-4171; 500 Ala Moana Blvd) This nine-screen multiplex is at the Restaurant Row complex.

Ward Stadium 16 (Map pp90-1; ☎ 594-7000; 1020 Auahi St) O'ahu's biggest theater has 16 screens.

SHOPPING

Aloha Tower Marketplace (☎ 566-2337; 1 Aloha Tower Dr; www.aloha-tower.com; ☷ 9am-9pm Mon-Sat, 9am-7pm Sun) This handsome harborfront shopping center is anchored by the 184ft Aloha Tower. Today, the two-story marketplace, with over 75 open-air shops and kiosks, is one of the best one-stop shopping destinations in town. Some of Hawaii's best musicians perform at several waterfront restaurants and lounges. It's walking distance from downtown Honolulu, and there's validated parking.

International Market Place (☎ 971-2080; 2330 Kalakaua Ave; ☷ 10am-10pm) For the ultimate in tourist trinket shopping, try this busy and rambling open air collection of clothing and jewry stalls, palm trees and snack shops, all in the heart of Waikiki. You'll find everything from seashell necklaces and refrigerator magnets to T-shirts and Hawaiian music CDs.

Chinatown

Maunakea Marketplace (1120 Maunakea St; ☷ 7am-5pm) Test your bargaining skills at this bustling bazaar in the heart of Chinatown. A combination of ramshackle stalls and inviting shops compete for space around a sunny courtyard, and it's a good place to pick up Chinese crafts and calendars, jewelry and souvenirs. Follow the downtown lunch crowd inside to the foodcourt with a variety of excellent and cheap ethnic eateries.

Lai Fong Department Store (Map pp86-7; 537-3497; 1118 Nu'uanu Ave) For antiques, junk and kitsch, this is a great place to browse. It sells a variety of antiques and knickknacks, including Chinese silk clothing, Oriental porcelain and old postcards of Hawaii dating back to the first half of the 20th century.

O'ahu Market (Map pp86-7; cnr Kekaulike & N King Sts) The heart of Chinatown is in this lively open-air market. Everything a Chinese cook needs is on display: pig heads, ginger root, fresh octopus, quail eggs, slabs of tuna, jasmine rice, long beans and salted jellyfish. The market has been an institution since 1904. In 1984 the tenants organized and purchased the market themselves to save it from falling into the hands of developers. Today it gets a lot of competition from the bustling Maunakea Marketplace (p107).

Cindy's Lei Shop (Map pp86-7; ☎ 536-6538; 1034 Maunakea St; ☼ 6am-8pm Mon-Sat, 6am-6pm Sun) A friendly and inviting place with leis made of *maile* (a native twining plant), lantern *ilima* (a native ground cover) and Micronesian ginger, in addition to more common orchids and plumeria.

Chinatown has several good art galleries and antique shops. **Pegge Hopper Gallery** (Map pp86-7; ☎ 524-1160; 1164 Nu'uanu Ave) showcases the works of Pegge Hopper, whose prints of voluptuous Hawaiian women adorn many a wall in the islands. Also notable is the **Ramsay Museum** (Map pp86-7; ☎ 537-2787; 1128 Smith St), featuring finely detailed pen-and-ink drawings by the artist Ramsay and changing exhibits of high-quality works by other local artists.

Shung Chong Yuein (Map pp86-7; ☎ 531-1983; 1027 Maunakea St) Sells delicious moon cakes, almond cookies and other pastries at bargain prices. This is also the place to buy dried and sugared foods – everything from

candied ginger and pineapple to candied squash and lotus root.

If you look inside one of the half-dozen noodle factories in Chinatown, you'll see clouds of white flour hanging in the air and thin sheets of dough running around rollers. One easy-to-find shop, **Yat Tung Chow Noodle Factory** (Map pp86-7; ☎ 531-7982; 150 N King St), makes nine sizes of noodles, from skinny golden threads to fat *udon*.

Ala Moana & University Area

Ala Moana Center (Map pp90-1; 1450 Ala Moana Blvd) Hawaii's biggest shopping center has some 230 shops and over 50 eateries. When outer islanders fly to Honolulu to shop, they go to Ala Moana. It's also Honolulu's major bus terminal and tens of thousands of passengers transit through daily, so even if you weren't planning to go to the center, you're likely to end up there anyway.

Ala Moana has typical mall anchor stores, such as Sears, Macy's and Neiman Marcus, as well as specialty shops. A favorite for local color is the Crack Seed Center, where you can just scoop from jars full of pickled mangoes, candied ginger, dried cuttlefish and *banzai* (rice crackers, nuts and dried fish) mix.

To get to the Ala Moana Center from Waikiki by car, simply head west on Ala Moana Blvd. Bus Nos 8, 19, 20 and 58 connect Waikiki with the Ala Moana Center.

Ward Warehouse (Map pp90-1; ☎ 591-8411; cnr Ward Ave & Kamakee St; ☼ 10am-9pm Mon-Sat, 10am-6pm Sun) Just across the street from Ala Moana Beach Park, this is the original shopping center of the Victoria Ward complex that today takes in the adjacent, upscale Ward Centre, the rambling Wards Farmers Market and Ward Entertainment Center, a movie and restaurant complex. The renovated Ward Warehouse is an accessible two-story complex with specialty clothing shops, music and bookstores, several courtyard eateries and free parking.

GETTING THERE & AROUND

For information on flights to/from Honolulu, see p81. Honolulu International Airport is a 9-mile (15km), 25-minute drive northwest of downtown via Ala Moana Blvd/Nimitz Hwy (92) or the H1. For more information on transport and driving directions to/from Honolulu International Airport, see p81.

TOP 10 SHOPPING SPOTS

▪ **Ala Moana Center** (p114), Honolulu

▪ **Ward Warehouse** (p114), Honolulu

▪ **International Market Place** (p113), Waikiki

▪ **North Shore Marketplace** (p162), Hale'iwa

▪ **Nu'uanu Swap Meet** (p115), Aloha Stadium

▪ **Royal Hawaiian Shopping Center** (p136), Waikiki

▪ **Maunakea Marketplace** (p113), Chinatown

▪ **Kalakaua Ave**, Waikiki

▪ **Island Treasures Antiques** (p136), Waikiki

▪ **Kahala Mall** (p139), Koko Head Regional Park

BARGAIN HUNTING

OK, so where's the best place to hunt for pineapple-shaped ukuleles, cheap Hawaiian CDs and '50s kitsch ceramics? Hands-down the honors go to the **Nu'uanu Meet** (Map pp86-7; ☎ 486-6704; Aloha Stadium, 99-500 Salt Lake Blvd; ☑ 6am-3pm Wed, Sat & Sun) in the Pearl Harbor area. The Aloha Stadium, best known as the host to nationally televised football games and top-name music concerts, transforms itself three days a week into Hawaii's biggest and best swap meet. For local flavor, this flea market is hard to beat, with some 1500 vendors selling an amazing variety of items, from beach gear and bananas to T-shirts and old Hawaii license plates.

This is such a big event that there are private shuttle bus services from Waikiki ($8 to $10 return) that operate every hour or so on swap meet days; for information, call **Affordable Shuttle** (☎ 479-3447) or **Reliable Shuttle** (☎ 924-9292).

To reach Aloha Stadium by bus, take the No 20 from Waikiki, or the No 42 from Ala Moana Shopping Center. By car, take the H1 Fwy west, get off at Stadium/Halawa exit, and follow signs for 'Stadium.'

Bus

The Ala Moana Center, on Ala Moana Blvd just northwest of Waikiki, is the central bus terminal for TheBus (p82), the island's public bus network.

From Ala Moana you can connect with a broad network of buses to points around the island:

Bus Nos 2, 13, 19 and 20 Between Waikiki and downtown Honolulu.
Bus Nos 20 and 42 Between Pearl Harbor and the USS *Arizona* Memorial.
Bus No 4 Between Waikiki and the University of Hawaii at Manoa.
Bus No 22 ('Beach Bus') and 58 From Waikiki to Diamond Head, then on to Hanauma Bay and Sea Life Park.
Bus Nos 56, 57 and 70 Over the Pali Hwy to Kailua and return.
Bus No 52 ('Circle Isle Bus') To the North Shore and continues back via the Windward Coast and the Pali Hwy (approximately four hours).

For details of buses to/from Waikiki, see p136.

Car

Parking is available at several municipal parking lots in the downtown Honolulu area. Chinatown is full of one-way streets, traffic is thick and parking can be tight, so consider taking the bus even if you have a car. However, there are public parking garages at the Chinatown Gateway Plaza on Bethel St and the Alii Center on Alakea St. Note that N Hotel St is open to bus traffic only.

Traffic in Honolulu can jam up during rush hour, from 7am to 9am and 3pm to 6pm Monday to Friday. You can also expect heavy traffic when heading toward Honolulu in the morning and away in the late afternoon on the Pali and Likelike Hwys. The airport is nine miles northwest of Waikiki; if you're heading there during rush hour, give yourself extra time.

The H1, the main south-shore freeway, is the key to getting around the island. It connects with the Kalanianaole Hwy (72), which runs along the southeast coast; with the Pali (61) and Likelike (63) Hwys, which lead to the Windward Coast; with the Farrington Hwy (93), which leads up the Wai'anae (leeward) Coast; with H2 and the Kamehameha Hwy (99, 83) on the way to the North Shore; and with H3, which runs from Pearl Harbor through the Ko'olau Range, ending on the Windward Coast.

Directions on O'ahu are often given by using landmarks, in addition to the Hawaii-wide terms *mauka* (toward the mountains) and *makai* (toward the ocean). If someone tells you to go 'Ewa' (a land area west of Honolulu) or 'Diamond Head' (east of Honolulu), it simply means to head in the direction of these areas.

Taxi

Taxis are readily available at the airport and larger hotels, but are otherwise generally hard to find. Phone **TheCab** (☎ 422-2222), **Charley's** (☎ 955-2211) or **City Taxi** (☎ 524-2121) to book a taxi. They have meters and charge a flag-down fee of $2.25 to start. From there, fares increase in 30¢ increments at a rate of $2.40 per mile. There's an extra charge of 40¢ for each suitcase or backpack.

O'AHU

AROUND HONOLULU
Pearl Harbor

Originally known for its stocks of pearl oysters, Pearl Harbor became synonymous with the attacks of December 7, 1941, which launched the USA into WWII. At 7:55am that morning, a wave of more 350 Japanese planes swooped over the Ko'olau Mountains to attack the US Pacific Fleet.

In addition to the USS *Arizona* Memorial site, two other nearby visitor sites are worth a look – the USS *Bowfin* Submarine Museum & Park, which is adjacent to the USS *Arizona* Memorial, and the Battleship *Missouri*, where General Douglas MacArthur accepted the Japanese surrender marking the end of WWII. Together, for the US, these three sites represent the beginning, middle and end of the war.

For those looking for a little peace and quiet, the greater Pearl Harbor area also has two low-key sights: Hawaii's Plantation Village, which depicts the lifestyle of the various ethnic groups that worked the sugar plantations, and Kea'iwa Heiau State Park, which holds an ancient medicinal temple and hiking trails, and yields excellent views of the harbour and of Diamond Head crater to the southeast.

USS ARIZONA MEMORIAL

Over 1.5 million people 'remember Pearl Harbor' each year by visiting the USS *Arizona* Memorial. Run by the National Park Service (NPS), the memorial is Hawaii's most visited attraction.

The NPS **visitor center** (☎ 422-2771, 24hr recorded information 422-0561; admission free; ☯ 7:30am-5pm, closed Thanksgiving, Christmas & New Year's Day) includes a museum, snack bar, theater and the offshore memorial at the sunken USS *Arizona*. The park service provides a 1¼-hour program that includes a short documentary on the attack and a boat ride to the memorial. There's a large gift shop with interesting photos (from both Japanese and US military archives). One photo is of Harvard-educated Admiral Yamamoto, the brilliant military strategist who planned the attack on Pearl Harbor, and afterwards stated that he feared Japan had 'awakened a sleeping giant and filled him with a terrible resolve.'

Weather permitting, programs run every 15 minutes from 8am to 3pm (from 7:45am in summer) on a first-come, first-served basis. Pick up a ticket at the information booth (each person in the party must pick up his or her own ticket); the number printed on the ticket corresponds to the time the tour begins. Generally, the shortest waits are in the morning. However, as the day goes on, waits of a couple of hours are not uncommon. The summer months are the busiest, with an average of 4500 people taking the tour daily, and the day's allotment of tickets is often gone by noon.

All facilities have disabled access.

SURPRISE ATTACK

On December 7, 1941, a wave of more than 350 Japanese planes attacked Pearl Harbor, home of the US Pacific Fleet.

Some 2335 US soldiers were killed during the two-hour attack. Of those, 1177 died in the battleship USS *Arizona* when it took a direct hit and sank in less than nine minutes. Twenty other US ships were sunk or seriously damaged and 347 airplanes were destroyed on that fateful day.

The attack upon Pearl Harbor, which jolted the USA into WWII, caught the US fleet totally by surprise. There had been two warnings, although the first occurred only 75 minutes before the attack. Both were dismissed.

At 6:40am on December 7, the USS *Ward* spotted a submarine conning tower approaching the entrance of Pearl Harbor. The *Ward* immediately attacked with depth charges and sank what turned out to be one of five midget Japanese submarines launched to penetrate the harbor.

At 7:02am a radar station on the north shore of O'ahu reported planes approaching. Even though they were coming from the west rather than the east, they were assumed to be American planes from the US mainland.

At 7:55am Pearl Harbor was hit. The USS *Arizona* went down in a fiery inferno, trapping its crew beneath the surface. It wasn't until 15 minutes after the bombing started that American anti-aircraft guns began to shoot back at the Japanese warplanes.

O'AHU

CHECK YOUR BAGS

Recent security measures were enacted at the USS *Arizona* and the USS *Missouri* Memorials. Visitors now face strict restrictions on what they can bring into the visitors center or ship tours. You are not allowed to bring any items that allow concealment, including purses, camera bags, fanny packs, backpacks, diaper bags, shopping bags and the like. Also, cameras or video cameras larger than 12 inches can not be brought into the sites at all. You may, of course, bring normal-sized cameras. Storage lockers ($2) are available across the parking lot, in front of the USS *Missouri* site.

USS BOWFIN SUBMARINE MUSEUM & PARK

If you have to wait an hour or two for your USS *Arizona* Memorial tour to begin, you might want to stroll over to the adjacent **USS Bowfin Submarine Museum & Park** (Map p84; ☎ 423-1341; park admission free, admission to submarine & museum adult/child $8/3, combination ticket with USS Missouri $20/10; ☉ 8am-5pm). The park contains the moored WWII submarine the USS *Bowfin*, as well as the Pacific Submarine Museum, which traces the development of submarines from their early origins to the nuclear age.

Commissioned in May 1943, the *Bowfin* sank 44 ships in the Pacific before the end of WWII. Visitors take a self-guided tour using a 30-minute recorded cassette tape that corresponds with items seen along the walk through the submarine. There's no charge to enter the park and view the missiles and torpedoes spread around the grounds. Look through the periscopes or inspect the Japanese *kaiten*, a suicide torpedo.

As the war was closing in on the Japanese homeland, the *kaiten* was developed in a last-ditch effort to ward off invasion. It was the marine equivalent of the kamikaze pilot and his plane. A volunteer was placed in the torpedo before it was fired. He then piloted it to its target. At least one US ship, the USS *Mississinewa*, was sunk by a *kaiten*. It went down off Ulithi Atoll in November 1944.

BATTLESHIP MISSOURI MEMORIAL

In 1998 the decommissioned battleship **USS Missouri** (Map p84; ☎ 973-2494; self-guided tour adult/child $16/8, combination ticket with USS Bowfin $20/10; ☉ 9am-5pm), nicknamed 'Mighty Mo,' was brought to Ford Island by the nonprofit USS *Missouri* Memorial Association to provide a third element to Pearl Harbor's WWII commemorative sites. The 887ft-long USS *Missouri*, a powerful battleship launched near the end of WWII, served as a flagship during the battles of Iwo Jima and Okinawa. On September 2, 1945, the formal Japanese surrender that ended WWII took place on the battleship's deck. The USS *Missouri* is now docked just a few hundred yards from the sunken remains of the USS *Arizona*; together, the ships provide a unique set of historical bookends.

A tour of the ship takes approximately two hours. You can poke about the officers' quarters, visit the wardroom that now houses exhibits on the ship's history and walk the deck where General Douglas MacArthur accepted the Japanese surrender. The tour is that it provides access to a 'combat engagement center' where you can watch a simulated naval battle.

It's not possible to drive directly to Ford Island, because it's an active military facility. Instead, a trolley bus shuttles visitors to the USS *Missouri* from USS *Bowfin* Park, where the tickets are sold. If you're a history buff the USS *Missouri* is a worthwhile sight, but if your time or money is more limited visit the USS *Arizona* Memorial instead.

WAIMANO TRAIL

The trailhead for another popular windward hike begins above Pearl City and ends at a spectacular *pali* lookout atop the Ko'olau Range. The challenging Waimano Trail covers 7 miles in each direction, and it's a stretch to do it in one day. A better approach is to set up at the campsite about 2 miles in, hike to the *pali* lookout the next morning, and back to the trailhead in the afternoon. You'll go boulder-hopping, ridge-scaling and stream-crossing through a relatively untouched native Hawaiian forest, all in pursuit of the *pali* views at the summit.

To reach the trailhead, take the H1 freeway to Moanalua Rd (exit 10), then to Waimano Home Rd. Park at the end of the road on a dirt pull-out.

GETTING THERE & AWAY

The USS *Arizona* Memorial visitor center and USS *Bowfin* Park are off Kamehameha

O'AHU

Hwy (99) on the US Naval Reservation just south of the Aloha Stadium.

If you're coming from Honolulu, take H1 west, past the airport, to exit 15A (Stadium/ USS *Arizona* Memorial). Make sure you follow the highway signs for the USS *Arizona* Memorial and not the signs for Pearl Harbor. There's plenty of free parking at the visitor center.

It's easy to get there by public bus. Bus Nos 20, 42 and City Express-A are the most direct from Waikiki to the visitor center, taking about an hour. Bus No 20 makes a stop at the airport, adding about 15 minutes to the travel time.

Hawaii Super Transit (☎ 841-2989) and **VIP Shuttle** (☎ 839-0911) both pick up from Waikiki hotels several times a day, charging $4/8 one way/return for a van ride to the visitor center. The ride takes around 40 minutes.

Beware of private boat cruises to Pearl Harbor that leave from Kewalo Basin and cost about $25; they don't stop at the visitor center and passengers are not allowed to board the USS *Arizona* Memorial.

Hawaii's Plantation Village

Five miles northeast of Pearl Harbor, **Hawaii's Plantation Village** (Map pp76-7; ☎ 677-0110; 94-695 Waipahu St, Waipahu; admission adult/child 5-17 yrs $10/4; Ⓨ 9am-4pm Mon-Fri, 10am-4pm Sat) rewards visitors with insights into Hawaii's multiethnic heritage. The setting is particularly evocative, as Waipahu was one of O'ahu's last plantation towns, and its rusty sugar mill, which operated until 1995, still looms on a knoll directly above this site.

The site encompasses 30 homes and buildings typical of plantation villages of the early 20th century. Period furnishings illustrate the lifestyles of the different ethnic groups – Hawaiian, Japanese, Chinese, Korean, Portuguese, Puerto Rican and Filipino. The Chinese cookhouse (c 1909) was originally on this site, and the Japanese shrine (1914) was moved here; the other structures are authentic replicas. One-hour guided tours of the village begin on the hour (last tour at 3pm).

To get there by car, take the H1 Fwy to exit 7, turn left onto Paiwa St, then right onto Waipahu St, continue past the sugar mill. The village is on the left. Bus No 42 runs between Waikiki and Waipahu every 30 minutes and takes about 1½ hours.

Kea'iwa Heiau State Park

This 334-acre **park** (Map pp76-7; ☎ 587-0300; Aiea Heights Dr; admission free; Ⓨ 7am-sunset) in Aiea, 3 miles northeast of Pearl Harbor, contains an ancient medicinal temple, campgrounds, picnic facilities and a scenic hiking trail. To get to Keaiwa from Honolulu, head west on Moanalua Hwy (78) and take the Stadium/ Aiea turnoff onto Moanalua Rd. Turn right onto Aiea Heights Dr at the second traffic light. The road winds up through a residential area 2.5 miles to the park.

KEAIWA HEIAU

At the park entrance is Keaiwa Heiau, a 100ft-by-160ft, single-terraced, stone temple built in the 1600s and used by *kahuna lapaau* (herbalist healers). The kahuna used hundreds of medicinal plants and grew many on the grounds surrounding the heiau. Among those still found here are noni (Indian mulberry), whose pungent yellow fruits were used to treat heart disease; kukui, the nuts of which were an effective laxative; breadfruit, the sap of which soothed chapped skin; and *ti* leaves, which were wrapped around a sick person to break a fever.

Not only did the herbs have medicinal value, but the temple itself was considered to possess life-giving energy. The kahuna was able to draw from the powers of both. Today, people wishing to be healed visit the heiau, leaving offerings that reflect the multiplicity of Hawaii's cultures: rosary beads, New Age crystals and sake cups set beside flower leis and rocks wrapped in *ti* leaves.

AIEA LOOP TRAIL

The 4.5-mile Aiea Loop Trail begins at the top of the park's paved loop road next to the restrooms and comes back out at the campground, about a third of a mile below the start of the trail. This easy-to-moderate trail starts off in a forest of eucalyptus trees and runs along the ridge, along the way passing Norfolk Island pines, ironwood, edible guava and native *ohia lehua*, which has feathery red flowers.

There are sweeping urban vistas of Pearl Harbor, Diamond Head and the Ko'olau Range. About two-thirds of the way in, the wreckage of a C-47 cargo plane that crashed in 1943 can be spotted through the foliage on the east ridge.

SLEEPING

The park can accommodate 100 campers, in tent sites that mostly have their own picnic table and barbecue. Sites are not crowded together, but because many are open, there's not a lot of privacy either. If you're camping in winter, make sure your gear is waterproof, as it rains frequently at this 880ft elevation. The park has restrooms, showers and drinking water. There's a resident caretaker by the front gate, and the gate is locked at night for security.

As with all O'ahu public campgrounds, camping is not permitted on Wednesday and Thursday, and permits (p75) must be obtained in advance.

WAIKIKI

Waikiki is one of those sunny meccas that people dream of when they think of a tropical vacation. And why not? It has a picture-perfect seaside location, phenomenal year-round weather and plenty to do when you're not spending a lazy day at the beach.

Waikiki fronts a glimmering white-sand beach that's lined with high-rise hotels and set against the backdrop of scenic Diamond Head. Waikiki has some 65,000 visitors on any given day, mingling with 25,000 permanent residents – all in an area roughly 1.5 miles long and half a mile wide. It boasts 34,000 hotel rooms, 450 restaurants, 350 bars and clubs, and more shops than you'd want to count. There are sunset hula shows, outrigger canoe rides and lively bars. Like any city scene, the deeper you dig, the more you'll find. You can also join in a Japanese tea ceremony, take a surfing lesson from an aging beach boy, or listen to a free concert by the Royal Hawaiian Band.

Although the beaches are packed during the day, at night most of the action is along the streets, where window-shoppers, time-share touts and street performers all go about their business. A variety of live music, from mellow Hawaiian to rock, wafts from clubs and hotel lounges. And there's always the sand, the velvet breeze and the night sky overrun with stars.

ORIENTATION

Waikiki is bounded on two sides by the Ala Wai Canal, on another by the ocean

and on the fourth by Kapiolani Park. Three parallel roads cross Waikiki: Kalakaua Ave, the beach road named after King David Kalakaua; Kuhio Ave, the main drag for Waikiki's buses, which is named after Prince Jonah Kuhio Kalanianaole; and Ala Wai Blvd, which borders the Ala Wai Canal.

City buses are not allowed on Kalakaua Ave, and the traffic on this multilane road is one way, so it's relatively smooth for driving. However, pedestrians need to be cautious, as cars tend to zoom by fairly fast.

Walking along the beach is an alternative to using the crowded sidewalks. It's possible to walk the full length of Waikiki along the sand and the seawalls. Although it's rather hot and crowded at midday, it's pleasant at other times. The beach can be romantic to stroll along at night, enhanced by the city skyline and the surf lapping at the shore.

INFORMATION

Bookstores

Bestsellers (☎ 953-2378; Hilton Hawaiian Village, 2005 Kalia Rd; ☻ 8am-10pm) Hawaiian books, travel guides and paperback fiction.
Borders Express (☎ 922-4154; Waikiki Shopping Plaza, 2270 Kalakaua Ave; ☻ 9:30am-9:30pm)

Emergency

Police, Fire & Ambulance (☎ 911) For all emergencies.
Police Substation (☎ 529-3801; 2405 Kalakaua Ave; ☻ 24hr) If you need help, or just friendly directions, there's a small police station at Kuhio Beach.

Internet Access

Daily Buzz Internet Cafe (☎ 924-2223; 150 Kaiulani Ave; 1st 10 min $3, then per min 15¢; ☻ 6am-2pm)
Hokondo Waikiki Beachside Hostel (☎ 923-9566; 2556 Lemon Rd; per 10 min $1; ☻ 24hr) Offers an Internet shop, with access available to non-guests also.
Hula's Bar & Lei Stand (☎ 923-0669; 134 Kapahulu Ave; ☻ 10am-2am) In the Waikiki Grand hotel, opposite Kapiolani Park, a bar with a few free Internet computers (presumably for customers). This is one of Waikiki's most popular gay venues, but it's definitely straight-friendly.
Surfsite Internet (☎ 778-4270; 2nd fl, 159 Kaiulani Ave; per hr $5, weekly pass $10; ☻ 9am-11pm) One-hour minimum, but you can use your hour in several increments over an extended period.

Laundry

The great majority of Waikiki hotels and hostels offer coin-operated laundry facilities

O'AHU

WAIKIKI

Ala Moana Center **A**   Kona St   **B**   Hawaii Convention Center   Kapiolani Blvd   **C**   Fern St   Date St   **D**

To Downtown Honolulu (2mi)   Mahukona St   Atkinson Dr   Hauoli St   Pumehana St   McCully St   Wiliwili St   Lime St   Paani St   Kona St

1 Ala Moana Beach Park (92)   Hobron Lane   Ena Rd   Ala Wai Blvd   Ala Wai Park   Hoawa St   Isenberg St

Ala Wai Canal   Niu St   Pau St   Keeaumoku St   Kuamoo St   Namahana St   Olohana St   Kalakaua Ave

Ala Wai Yacht Harbor   Holomoana St   Ala Moana Blvd   Hobron Lane   74   Kalakaua Ave   56   Ala Wai Park

Kalia Rd   53   72   88   92   61   33   89   62   48   78   Kuhio Ave   Kalaimoku St   Launiu St   Kaiolu St   17

Hilton Lagoon   25   Dewey Court   Maluhia Rd   83   Lewers St   Kaiulani Ave   35   Nahua St

Kahanamoku Beach   Fort DeRussy Military Reservation   Saratoga Rd   24   8   46   65   1   Royal Hawaiian Way   86   Seaside Ave

Fort DeRussy Beach   90   Kalia Rd   Beach Walk   31   34   14   Helumoa Rd   36   50   84   Duke's

Gray's Beach   23   45   42   37

INFORMATION
Bank of Hawaii	1 D3
Bestsellers	(see 25)
Breeze Hawaii Diving Adventure	2 H2
Campbell Highlander Laundry	3 H4
Daily Buzz Internet Cafe	4 E4
Doctors on Call	(see 44)
First Hawaiian Bank	5 D3
Hawaiian Visitors and Convention Bureau	(see 86)
Panda Travel	6 H2
Police Substation	7 E4
Post Office	8 C3
Surfsite Internet	9 E4
Tours-4-Less Discount Tours	(see 9)
Waikiki Beach Center	(see 7)
Waikiki-Kapahulu Public Library	10 G5
Waldenbooks	(see 86)

SIGHTS & ACTIVITIES   (pp123–6)
Bishop Museum at Kalia	(see 25)
Duke Kahanamoku Statue	(see 15)
Hula Mound	11 E5
Kapiolani Bandstand	12 F6
St Augustine's Church	13 E5
US Army Museum of Hawaii	14 C4
Wizard Stones	15 E4

SLEEPING   (pp126–31)
Aston Aloha Surf Hotel	16 E3
Aston Coconut Plaza Hotel	17 D3
Aston Waikiki Banyan	18 F5
Aston Waikiki Beach Hotel	19 F5
Bamboo	20 E4
Cabana at Waikiki	21 F5
Celebrity Resorts Waikiki	22 E3
Halekulani Hotel	23 D4
Hawaiiana Hotel	24 D4
Hilton Hawaiian Village	25 B2
Hokondo Waikiki Beachside Hostel	26 F5
Hostelling International Waikiki	27 E4
Hyatt Regency Waikiki	28 E4
Ilima Hotel	29 E4
Ocean Resort Hotel Waikiki	30 F5
Ohana Coral Seas	31 D3
Ohana East	32 E4
Ohana Maile Sky Court	33 D2
Ohana Reef Towers	34 D3
Ohana Waikiki Surf East	35 D3
Outrigger Reef Hotel	36 C4
Outrigger Waikiki	37 D4
Polynesian Hostel Beach Club	38 F5
Queen Kapiolani Hotel	39 F5
Radisson Prince Kuhio	40 F4
Royal Grove Hotel	41 E4
Royal Hawaiian Hotel	42 D4
Sheraton Moana Surfrider	43 E4
Sheraton Princess Kaiulani	44 E4
Sheraton Waikiki	45 D4
The Breakers	46 D4
Waikiki Beach Marriott Resort	47 F5

Waikiki Gateway Hotel	48 D2
Waikiki Grand	49 F5
Waikiki Parc Hotel	50 D4
Waikiki Prince Hotel	51 E4
Waikiki Sand Villa Hotel	52 E4

EATING   (pp131–4)
Aloha Sushi	53 B2
Banyan Veranda	(see 43)
Bogart's Cafe	54 H6
Chuck's Steak House	(see 36)
Diamond Head Market & Grill	55 H6
Duke's Canoe Club	(see 37)
Eggs 'n Things	56 C2
Ezogiku	57 F5
Fatty's Chinese Kitchen	58 E4
Food Pantry	59 E4
Golden Dragon	(see 25)
Irifune	60 H4
Keo's	61 C2
Keoni's	(see 32)
Kyo-ya	62 C2
La Cucaracha	63 E3
La Mer	(see 23)
Leonard's	64 H2
Moose McGillycuddy's	65 D3
Oceanarium Restaurant	66 E5
Ono Hawaiian Food	67 H3
Orchid's	(see 23)
Rainbow Drive-In	68 G4
Saint Germain	69 E3
Shore Bird Beach Broiler	(see 36)
The Banyan Grill	(see 43)
The Pyramids	70 H3
Tokkuri Tei	71 H4
Wailana Coffee House	72 B2

DRINKING   (p134)
Coconut Willy's Bar	73 E4
Harry's Bar	(see 28)
Mai Tai Bar	(see 42)

Paradise Lounge	(see 25)
Tiki's Grill & Bar	(see 19)
Wave Waikiki	74 C1
Zanzabar Nightclub	75 E3

ENTERTAINMENT   (pp134–6)
Angles Waikiki	76 E3
Fusion Waikiki	(see 76)
House Without a Key	(see 23)
Hula's Bar & Lei Stand	(see 49)
Scruples	77 E3
Sharkey's Comedy Club	78 D3
Sunset on the Beach	79 F5
Waikiki Shell	80 G6

SHOPPING   (p136)
Bailey's Antique Shop	81 H4
International Market Place	82 E4
Island Treasures Antiques	83 D3
Little Hawaiian Craft Shop	(see 84)
Royal Hawaiian Shopping Center	84 D4
Snorkel Bob's	85 H3
Waikiki Shopping Plaza	86 D4
Waikiki Trade Center	87 E3

TRANSPORT   (pp136–8)
Blue Sky Rentals	88 C2
Gas Station	89 C2

OTHER
Prime Time Sports	90 C3

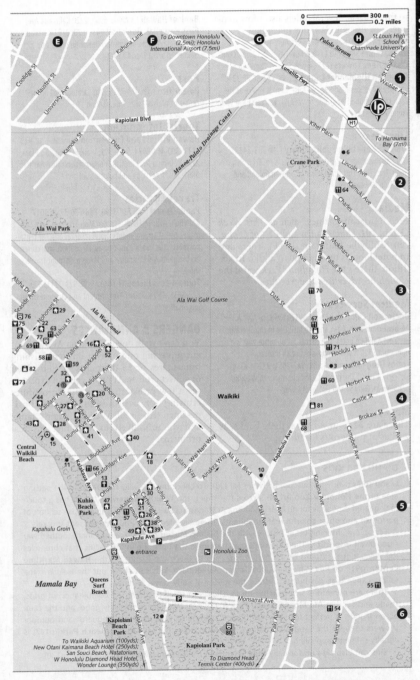

to their guests. Several hotels also allow non-guests to use coin laundry machines:

Ohana East (150 Kaiulani Ave; ☻ 7am-10pm)
Ohana Maile Sky Court (2058 Kukio Ave; ☻ 7am-10pm)
Ohana Reef Towers (227 Lewers St; ☻ 7am-10pm)
Campbell Highlander Laundry (☎ 732-5630; 3340B Campbell Ave; per load $9; ☻ 7am-8pm) If you're at the eastern (Diamond Head) side of Waikiki, you can have your laundry done here.

Libraries

Waikiki-Kapahulu Public Library (☎ 733-8488; 400 Kapahulu Ave; ☻ 10am-5pm Tue, Wed, Fri & Sat, noon-7pm Thu) This small library carries mainland and Honolulu newspapers.

Media

Free tourist magazines, such as *This Week O'ahu*, *101 Things to Do* and *Best of O'ahu*, can readily be found on street corners and in hotel lobbies throughout Waikiki. In addition, there's the *Honolulu Weekly* and the *Honolulu Advertiser* free weeklies.

Medical Services

Doctors on Call (☎ 971-6000; 120 Kaiulani Ave) A 24-hour clinic with X-ray and lab facilities in the Sheraton Princess Kaiulani hotel. The charge for an office visit is a minimum $120 if you don't have health insurance.
Longs Drug (Map pp90-1; ☎ 947-2651; 2220 S King St; ☻ 24-hour) The nearest 24hr pharmacy to Waikiki, between McCully St and University Ave.

Money

There are 24-hour ATMs at these banks, as well as at numerous locations:

Bank of Hawaii (☎ 543-6900; 2220 Kalakaua Ave)
First Hawaiian Bank (☎ 943-4670; 2181 Kalakaua Ave) Displays some interesting Hawaiian murals by renowned artist Jean Charlot.

Post

Post Office (☎ 973-7515; 330 Saratoga Rd) In the center of Waikiki, with free parking.

Tourist Information

Hawaii Visitors and Convention Bureau (☎ 923-1811, 800-464-2924; Suite 801, Waikiki Shopping Plaza, 2270 Kalakaua Ave) Its visitor information office has tourist brochures, free maps and helpful staff.

Travel Agencies

Panda Travel (☎ 738-3898, 888-726-3288; 1017 Kapahulu Ave; ☻ 8am-5:30pm Mon-Fri, 9am-1pm Sat) Makes travel arrangements, hotel reservations, car rentals, passports, package deals, cruises, all connections, currency exchange, travel insurance and it has a discount travel shop.
Tours-4-Less Discount Tours (☎ 923-2211, 800-823-8535; 159 Kaiulani Ave) Student and discount travel information.

DANGERS & ANNOYANCES

You can't walk down Kalakaua Ave without encountering one or two hustlers pushing time-shares or $5 discounts to clubs, luau or sunset cruises. At night you can expect to see a few provocatively dressed prostitutes cruising for well-dressed Japanese businessmen. All in all, Waikiki is fairly tame, and you're unlikely to encounter any real problems.

O'AHU FOR KIDS

O'ahu spills over with outdoor activities for kids. To check out the wild side, head to the petting area of the **Honolulu Zoo** (p124). Across the street, the **Waikiki Aquarium** (p123) has a touch tank geared especially for *na keiki* (children). At **Hanauma Bay** (p139), kids can glimpse schools of parrotfish and other colorful reef inhabitants. There are lifeguards, and you can rent snorkels.

For an enlightening bit of history, visit the **Bishop Museum** (p123), where shark-toothed war clubs await inspection. The museum's planetarium is the only one in the Pacific that chronicles the navigational systems of the first Polynesians to reach the islands. At the **Hawaii Maritime Center** (p91), on Pier 7 by the Aloha Tower Marketplace, kids can check out the *Hokule'a*, the sailing canoe that was built to retrace the routes of early clever seafarers.

There are numerous safe beaches for families with small children. The combination of grass, shade and sand at **Ala Moana Beach Park** (p95), near Waikiki, is especially good, and the calm ocean lagoon is perfect for easy wading and swimming, plus there are lifeguards and outdoor showers to wash the sand off little feet. On the Windward Coast, **Kailua Beach Park** (p147) is equally safe and appealing.

Kids can also sign up for daily **hula lessons** at the Hilton Hawaiian Village hotel (p130).

SIGHTS

Historic Hotels

Waikiki's two historic hotels, the Royal Hawaiian and the Sheraton Moana Surfrider, both retain their period character and are well worth a visit. These beachside hotels, which are on the National Register of Historic Places, are a short walk from each other on Kalakaua Ave.

With its pink turrets and Moorish architecture, the **Royal Hawaiian Hotel** (☎ 923-7311, 800-325-3535; www.sheraton-hawaii.com; 2259 Kalakaua Ave) is a throwback to the era when Rudolph Valentino was *the* romantic idol and travel to Hawaii was by luxury liner. Inside, the hotel (p129) is lovely and airy, with high ceilings and chandeliers, and everything in rose colors. Free tours are held at 2pm Monday, Wednesday and Friday.

The restored **Sheraton Moana Surfrider** (☎ 922-3111, 800-325-3535; www.sheraton.com/hawaii; 2365 Kalakaua Ave) has the aura of an old plantation inn (p130). On the 2nd floor, just up the stairs from the lobby, there's a display of memorabilia from the early hotel days, with scripts from the 'Hawaii Calls' radio show, period photographs and a short video. Historical tours are free of charge and take place at 11am and 5pm Monday, Wednesday and Friday.

Waikiki Aquarium

Located next to a living reef on the Waikiki shoreline, this modern university-managed **aquarium** (☎ 923-9741; http://waquarium.otted.hawaii .edu; 2777 Kalakaua Ave; adult/child under 4 yrs/child 4-13 yrs/child over 13 yrs $9/free/2/4; ☯ 9am-5pm) dates from 1904, and includes an impressive shark gallery where visitors can watch circling reef and zebra sharks through a 14ft-wide window.

The aquarium is a great place to identify colorful coral and fish you've seen while snorkeling or diving. Tanks recreate various Hawaiian reef habitats, including those found in a surge zone, a sheltered reef, a deep reef and an ancient reef. There are rare Hawaiian fish with names like the bearded armorhead and the sling-jawed wrasse, along with moray eels, giant groupers and flash-back cuttlefish wavering with pulses of light.

In addition to Hawaiian marine life, you'll find exhibits on other Pacific ecosystems. Noteworthy are the giant Palauan clams that were raised from dime-sized hatchlings in 1982 and now measure over 2ft, the largest in the USA. The aquarium's outdoor tank is home to a pair of rare Hawaiian monk seals (p48).

Bishop Museum at Kalia

This small **branch museum** (☎ 947-2458; 2005 Kalia Rd; admission adult/child $7/free; ☯ 10am-5pm) in the Hilton Hawaiian Village is for people who can't make it over to the main Bishop Museum (p97), on the west side of Honolulu. Though the Waikiki collection is significantly smaller, it is nonetheless high quality, including Hawaiian artifacts such as stone adzes, hair ornaments, feather capes, a replica *pili*-grass hut, one of Duke Kahanamoku's 10ft wooden surfboards, and some insightful displays on the Hawaiian monarchy, Polynesian migration and the early days of Waikiki tourism.

Fort DeRussy Military Reservation

Fort DeRussy is a US Army post used mainly as a recreation center for the armed forces. This large chunk of Waikiki real estate was acquired by the US Army a few years after Hawaii was annexed to the USA. Prior to that it was swampy marshland and a favorite duck-hunting spot for Hawaiian royalty. The Hale Koa Hotel on the property is open only to military personnel, but there's public access to the beach (p50) and the adjacent military museum. The section of Fort DeRussy between Kalia Rd and Kalakaua Ave has public footpaths that provide a shortcut between the two roads.

Battery Randolph, a reinforced concrete building erected in 1911 as a coastal artillery battery, houses the **US Army Museum of Hawaii** (☎ 955-9552; admission free; ☯ 10am-4:15pm Tue-Sun) at Fort DeRussy. The battery once held two formidable 14-inch disappearing guns with an 11-mile range, designed to recoil into the concrete walls for reloading after firing, which shook the whole neighborhood. A 55-ton lead counterweight then returned the carriage to position. Today, the battery exhibits a wide collection of weapons, from Hawaiian shark-tooth clubs to WWII tanks, as well as exhibits – dioramas, scale models, photos – on military history as it relates to Hawaii. There are historic displays on Kamehameha the Great and on Hawaii's role in WWII.

Kapiolani Park

At the Diamond Head end of Waikiki is Hawaii's first public park, the nearly 200-acre Kapiolani Park, a gift from King Kalakaua to the people of Honolulu in 1877. The king dedicated the park to his wife, Queen Kapiolani. In its early days, horse racing and band concerts were the park's big attractions.

Although the racetrack is gone, the park is home to sports fields, tennis courts, huge lawns, broad banyan trees, Kapiolani Beach Park, Waikiki Aquarium and the Honolulu Zoo. Concerts are held at the Waikiki Shell, an outdoor amphitheater that serves as a venue for symphony, jazz and rock concerts, and Kapiolani Bandstand, where the Royal Hawaiian Band performs free concerts on Sunday afternoon (p135), as well as dance competitions. Hawaiian music concerts and other activities occur throughout the year.

Honolulu Zoo

This respectable **zoo** (☎ 971-7171; admission adult/child 6-12 yrs $6/1; ☼ 9am-4:30pm), at the northern end of Kapiolani Park, features some 300 species spread across 42 acres of tropical greenery. A highlight is the naturalized African Savanna section, which has lions, cheetahs, white rhinos, giraffes, zebras, hippos and monkeys. The zoo also has an interesting reptile section, a good selection of tropical birds (including native Hawaiian birds) and a small petting zoo for children.

Oceanarium

Pacific Beach Hotel houses an impressive three-story 280,000-gallon **aquarium** (☎ 922-1233; 2490 Kalakaua Ave) that forms the backdrop for two of its restaurants. Even if you're not dining here, you can view the aquarium from the hotel lobby. Divers enter the Oceanarium to feed the tropical fish at noon and 1pm, 6:30pm and 8pm. Bon appetit!

Ala Wai Canal

At dawn, people jog and power walk along the Ala Wai Canal, which forms the northern boundary of Waikiki. Late in the afternoon, outrigger canoe teams paddle along the canal and out to the Ala Wai Yacht Harbor. In 1922 the Ala Wai Canal was dug to divert the streams that flowed in the wetland marsh of Waikiki. Old Hawaii lost out, as farmers had the water drained out from under them.

Beaches

The two-mile stretch of white sand running from Hilton Hawaiian Village to Kapiolani Park is commonly called Waikiki Beach, although different sections have their own names and characteristics.

In the early morning, the surprisingly quiet beach belongs to walkers and joggers. Strolling down the beach toward Diamond Head at sunrise can actually be a meditative experience. By midmorning it looks like a normal resort beach – boogie board and surfboard concessionaires setting up shop and catamarans offering $15 sails. By noon it's challenging to walk along the packed beach without stepping on anyone.

As the beachfront developed, landowners haphazardly constructed seawalls and offshore barriers (called 'groins') to protect their properties, blocking the natural forces of sand accretion, making erosion a serious problem at Waikiki. So most of Waikiki's beautiful white sands have been barged in from Papohaku Beach on Molokai over the years, filling channels and depressions, and altering surf breaks along the way.

Waikiki is good for swimming, boogie boarding, surfing, sailing and other beach activities most of the year, and there are lifeguards and showers interspersed along the beach. Between May and September, summer swells make the water a little rough for swimming, but great for surfing. The best snorkeling is in the area toward Diamond Head at Sans Souci Beach.

KAHANAMOKU BEACH

Fronting the Hilton Hawaiian Village, Kahanamoku Beach is the westernmost section of Waikiki. It was named for Duke Kahanamoku, a surfer and swimmer who won an Olympic gold medal in the 100m freestyle in 1912, and went on to become a Hawaiian celebrity and legend.

Kahanamoku Beach is protected by a breakwater at one of its ends and a pier at the other, with a coral reef running between the two. It's a calm swimming area with a gently sloping sandy bottom.

FORT DERUSSY BEACH

One of the least-crowded Waikiki beaches, Fort DeRussy Beach borders 1800ft of the Fort DeRussy Military Reservation (p123). Like all beaches in Hawaii, it's public. In addition to lifeguards and showers, you'll find an inviting grassy lawn with palm trees offering some sparse shade, providing an alternative to frying on the sand.

The water is usually calm and good for swimming. When conditions are right, the beach is used by windsurfers, boogie boarders and board surfers. There are two beach huts, open daily, which rent windsurfing equipment, boogie boards, kayaks and snorkel sets.

GRAY'S BEACH
Located near the Halekulani Hotel (p130), Gray's Beach was named for a boarding house called Gray's-by-the-Sea that stood on the site in the 1920s. In the 1930s it was home to the original Halekulani Hotel, the predecessor to today's swank high-rise. Because the seawall in front of the Halekulani was built so close to the waterline, the part of the beach facing the hotel is often totally submerged, though the waters off the beach are shallow and calm.

CENTRAL WAIKIKI BEACH
Between the Royal Hawaiian Hotel and the Moana Surfrider Hotel, Waikiki's busiest section of sand and surf is great for sunbathing, swimming and people watching.

Most of the beach has a shallow bottom with a gradual slope. The only drawback for swimmers is the beach's popularity with other swimmers, beginner surfers and the occasional catamaran, so be careful. **Queen's Surf** (p125) and **Canoe's Surf**, Waikiki's best-known surf breaks, are offshore.

WAIKIKI BEACH CENTER
Opposite the Hyatt Regency Waikiki is the Waikiki Beach Center, which has rest rooms, showers, surfboard lockers, rental concessions and a small police station.

On the Diamond Head side of the police station, four boulders, the **Wizard Stones of Kapaemahu**, are said to contain the secrets and healing powers of four sorcerers, Kapaemahu, Kinohi, Kapuni and Kahaloa, who visited from Tahiti in ancient times, and before returning transferred their powers to these stones.

Just east of the stones is a bronze **statue** of Duke Kahanamoku (1890–1968), Hawaii's most decorated athlete (p45), standing with one of his long-boards. Considered the 'father of modern surfing,' Duke, who lived in Waikiki, gave surfing demonstrations around the world, from Sydney, Australia, to Rockaway Beach, New York. Many local surfers took issue with the placement of the statue, Duke standing with his back to the sea, a position they say he never would have assumed in real life. So, the city moved the statue as close to the sidewalk as possible, thus moving it further from the water.

KUHIO BEACH PARK
This park is marked on its east end by **The Wall** (see below), a walled storm drain with a walkway on top that juts out into the ocean. Paralleling the beach, a low breakwater seawall running about 1300ft out from The Wall, was built to control sand erosion, forming two nearly enclosed swimming pools. Local kids walk out on the breakwater, but it can be dangerous to the uninitiated due to a slippery surface and breaking surf.

The pool closest to The Wall is best for swimming, with the water near the breakwater reaching depths of 5ft and greater. However, because circulation is limited, the water gets murky, acquiring a noticeable film of suntan oil. The 'Watch Out Deep Holes' sign refers to holes in the pool's sandy bottom created by swirling currents. Be cautious in the deeper areas of the pool, as the holes can take waders by surprise.

The park, incidentally, is named after Prince Kuhio, who maintained his residence here. His house was torn down in 1936, 14 years after his death, in order to expand the beach. The old-timers gathering each afternoon playing chess and cribbage on sidewalk pavilions and the kids boogie boarding off the **Groin** give this section of the beach a real sense of Hawaiian life.

The city recently spent millions of dollars removing one lane of Kalakaua Ave fronting the park to extend the beach and adding water fountains, landscaping and a grassy hula mound, making it a pleasant place to hang out.

THE WALL
Directly opposite Denny's, on the corner of Kapahulu and Kalakaua Aves, you'll find Waikiki's hottest boogie-boarding spot. If the surf's high enough, you're sure to find a few dozen boogie boarders, mostly teenage boys and girls, riding the waves. The kids

O'AHU

ride straight for the wall and then veer away at the last moment, drawing 'oohs' and 'ahs' from the tourists who gather to watch them on the little pier above.

KAPIOLANI BEACH PARK
Starting at The Wall and extending down to the Natatorium, beyond Waikiki Aquarium, is Kapiolani Beach Park.

However, **Queen's Surf** is the common name given to the wide midsection of Kapiolani Beach. The stretch in front of the pavilion is popular with the gay community, and its sandy bottom offers decent swimming. The beach between Queen's Surf and The Wall is shallow and has broken coral.

Kapiolani Beach Park is a relaxed place with far less of the frenzied activity by Waikiki's beachfront hotels. It's a popular weekend picnicking spot for local families who unload the kids to splash in the water as they line up the barbecue grills.

There are restrooms and showers at the Queen's Surf pavilion. The surfing area offshore is called **Public's** and sees some good waves in winter.

NATATORIUM
At the Diamond Head end of Kapiolani Beach Park, this 100m-long saltwater swimming pool was built in 1927 to honor Hawaii's WWI veterans. There were once hopes of hosting an Olympics on O'ahu, with this pool as the focal point. Although Olympic competitions were never held here, two Olympic gold medallists – Johnny Weissmuller and Duke Kahanamoku – both trained in this tide-fed pool.

The Natatorium is on the National Register of Historic Places. The pool has been plagued by circulation problems, however, despite an $11 million restoration project.

SANS SOUCI BEACH
Also known as **Kaimana Beach** because of its proximity to the New Otani Kaimana Beach Hotel, Sans Souci attracts sunbathers and swimmers keen to avoid the main tourist scene. Despite being by itself, it also has a lifeguard station and outdoor showers.

Many residents come to Sans Souci to swim their daily laps out to a wind sock marker and back. A shallow coral reef close to the shore makes for calm, protected waters and provides reasonably good snorkeling.

More coral can be found by following the Kapua Channel as it cuts through the reef, although if you swim here beware of currents that can pick up. Check conditions with the lifeguard before venturing out.

SLEEPING
Waikiki's main beachfront strip, Kalakaua Ave, is lined with high-rise hotels with $300-plus rooms. Many of these hotels cater to package tourists, driving the prices up for individual travelers.

Better value is generally found at the smaller hostelries on the back streets. There are hotels in the Kuhio Ave area and up near the Ala Wai Canal that are as nice as some of the beachfront hotels, but half the price. If you don't mind walking 10 minutes to the beach, you can save a bundle. Ask about discounts and promotional deals when making reservations; it's rare to pay published rates in competitive Waikiki.

At many hotels, especially the Ohana and Aston chains, the rooms themselves are the same, with only the views varying; generally the higher the floor, the higher the price. If you're paying extra for a view, you might want to ask to see the room first. While some 'ocean views' are the real thing, others are merely glimpses of the water as seen through a series of high-rises.

Waikiki has more hotel rooms than condos, though condos are catching up due to an increasing number of hotel-to-condo conversions. The best way to find a condo in Waikiki is to look in the 'Vacation Rentals' section of the two daily newspapers, or one of several vacation rental agencies, among them **Pacific Islands Reservations** (☎ 808-262-8133; www.waikiki-condo-rentals.com).

Budget
HOSTELS
In addition to the one HI hostel, there are a few private hostel-style dormitory accommodations. They all cater to backpackers and draw an international crowd. There are no curfews or other restrictions, except the usual requirement for travelers to show a passport or an onward ticket.

Inquire about refund policies before dishing out any money at a private hostel – you can sometimes get a discount on stays of a week or more, but these typically require advance payment and allow no refunds.

Hostelling International Waikiki (☎ 926-8313; www.hostelsaloha.com; 2417 Prince Edward St; dm/d $23/54; ⏰ reception 7am-3am; ▣) Located on a backstreet a few blocks from Waikiki Beach, this well-managed 60-bed hostel is in an older, converted low-rise apartment complex. Along with the dorms, there are also five private rooms, each with a small refrigerator and bathroom. A large community kitchen is for everyone to use, and a good place to meet travelers. The maximum stay is seven nights and there's a $3 surcharge if you're not an HI member; HI membership can be purchased on-site for $28 for US citizens, $18 for foreign visitors. Unlike most other HI hostels, there's no dormitory lockout or curfew. Reservations are recommended. Overnight parking is $5.

Hokondo Waikiki Beachside Hostel (☎ 923-9566, 866-478-3888; www.hokondo.com; Suite B101, 2556 Lemon Rd; dm $20-30, semi-private r $55-65; ▣) This is a 175-bed condo complex that's been converted into hostel-style accommodations, with dorms, semi-private and private rooms. Each unit has a refrigerator, a stove, cable TV and a bathroom. Along with running a 24-hour Internet room, there are lots of activities to sign up for, like cheap island tours, where you can meet like-minded travelers. Overnight parking is $5.

Polynesian Hostel Beach Club (☎ 922-1340; www.hawaiihostels.com; 2584 Lemon Rd; dm $21, semi-private s/d $40/46, studio d $64) A Lemon Rd bargain, this clean, cheery hostel features co-ed dorms, cable TV, shared kitchen and bathroom. A good place to hang out with fellow travelers, it also arranges cheap island tours, like a sunset sail for $12. Overnight parking is $5.

HOTELS

Royal Grove Hotel (☎ 923-7691; www.royalgrovehotel.com; 151 Uluniu Ave; r in old/new wing $45/60; ▣ ▣) This charming pink low-rise hotel has so many retirees returning each winter to its 85 rooms that it's often impossible to get a room in the high season without advance reservations. Rooms in the oldest wing are small, have no air-con and are exposed to traffic noise. Rooms in the main wing are simple but have air-con and small lanai. Both types of rooms have TV, kitchenette and bathroom. This is an older, no-frills hotel, where Canadian snowbirds play canasta and gather around the piano in the evening. Overnight parking is $6.

The Breakers (☎ 923-3181, 800-426-0494; www.breakers-hawaii.com; 250 Beach Walk; studio $95-100, d $95-135; ▣ ▣ ▣) This older Polynesian-style hotel is a throwback to earlier times, and stands out in a neighborhood dominated by high-rises. The rooms are large with kitchenettes, TV, safes and phones; the 2nd-floor units add a lanai for $6 more.

Waikiki Prince Hotel (☎ 922-1544; www.waikikiprince.com; 2431 Prince Edward St; r $45-55, with kitchenette $55-65; ▣) A superb-value hotel, with 24 units in a six-story building. The rooms are simple but cheery and equipped with TV and bathroom; for $10 extra you can opt for one with cooking facilities and a bit more space. For weekly stays, the seventh night is free. It's a couple of minutes' walk to the beach. Overnight parking is $5.

Mid-Range

Sheraton Princess Kaiulani (☎ 922-5811, 800-325-3535; www.sheraton-hawaii.com; 120 Kaiulani Ave; r from $165; ▣ ▣) The Sheraton's best-value

---

THE AUTHOR'S CHOICE

New Otani Kaimana Beach Hotel (☎ 923-1555, 800-356-8264; www.kaimana.com; 2863 Kalakaua Ave; r/studios from $135/160; ▣) The rooms are small, but the view is big and the location is perfect. Just half a mile from the throbbing hub of Waikiki, the oasis-like New Otani Kaimana Beach Hotel sits oceanside, with little Sans Souci Beach Park just beyond the open lobby and patio restaurant. Across the street is Kapiolani Park and Diamond Head is so close you can easily overlook it. This may be the best value in Honolulu for a beachfront hotel. The rooms, even the suites, are smallish, though many have kitchenettes and all have roomy lanais with views of the park, the ocean or Diamond Head. But this isn't a place to stay indoors all day. A short walk will bring you to the Waikiki Aquarium and the small bay in front of the hotel is a mecca for morning and afternoon swimmers along with mid-day sunbathers. Adjacent, Kapiolani Park offers jogging, tennis and bicycling. The hotel has two restaurants, a beachside bar, a mini-mart and fitness room; it even offers babysitting, at a price. Overnight parking is $12.

O'AHU

Waikiki property, the 'PK' was built in the 1950s by Matson Navigation to help turn Waikiki into a middle-class destination, and from the outside it looks rather like a huge apartment complex. However, the interior is more appealing; the 1150 rooms are modern and inviting. It's in the busy heart of Waikiki across the street from the beach and overlooking the grand Sheraton Moana Surfrider. Overnight parking is $10.

Ilima Hotel (☎ 923-1877, 800-801-9366; www .ilima.com; 445 Nohonani St; s $85-105, d $95-125, studio $105-150; P ⊠ ⊠) Although it lacks ocean views, the Ilima offers outstanding value, with service and amenities only found in beachfront hotels. It's in a less hurried section of Waikiki, between the Ala Wai Canal and the International Marketplace. All 99 units are roomy and bright, with large lanai, two double beds, tasteful rattan furnishings and fully equipped kitchens; the deluxe studios have free DSL connection, and there's a fitness room. Popular with business travelers and other return visitors, the Ilima offers free local phone calls, which is a rarity in Waikiki.

Bamboo (☎ 922-7777, 866-406-2782; www.aquabam boo.com; 2425 Kuhio Ave; d $155, studios d $175-215, 1-bedroom studio $230; ⊠ ⊠) An intimate boutique oasis in the heart of Waikiki, this Eurasian-style small hotel is lovely throughout, with service to match. Rooms are small, but well appointed, and there is a complimentary poolside continental breakfast. The one-bedroom studio sleeps four. Internet specials and weekly discounts can slash rates by as much as half. Overnight parking is $12.

Hawaiiana Hotel (☎ 923-3811, 800-367-5122; www .hawaiianahotelatwaikiki.com; 260 Beachwalk; d $95-125; ⊠ ⊠) The 93 rooms at this old-fashioned garden hotel are similar in low-key charm and comfort to The Breakers next door, with slightly brighter styling, like the lavender door jams, rattan furnishings and ceiling fans. Overnight parking is $10.

Celebrity Resorts Waikiki (☎ 923-7336, 800-423-8604; www.celebrityresorts.com; 431 Nohonani St; studios $95-120, 1-bedroom studio $120-150; P ⊠) Despite the easy-to-overlook name, this low-key, three-story hotel merits a look. It's clean and friendly, in a quieter low-rise section of Waikiki, and offers unusual free amenities, like weekly hula lessons, coconut painting and a barbeque with live Hawaiian music. Look for the small sign and green awning.

Aston Coconut Plaza Hotel (☎ 923-8828, 800-922-7866; www.astonhotels.com; 450 Lewers St; r/studio from $100/135; ⊠) This quiet 80-room Aston-chain hotel near Ala Wai Blvd offers smallish rooms with tiled floors and contemporary decor. Overnight parking is $9.

Waikiki Sand Villa Hotel (☎ 922-4744, 800-247-1903; www.waikiki-hotel.com; 2375 Ala Wai Blvd; r low/high season $76/84, studio $156/166; ⊠ ⊑ ⊠) A good mid-range choice just opposite the Ala Wai Canal, this hotel has a friendly laid-back atmosphere. The rooms are compact, but most have both a double and a twin bed, and all have TV, refrigerator and lanai. For the best views, ask for a corner unit. The studios have kitchenettes and can sleep up to four people. Overnight parking is $9.

Queen Kapiolani Hotel (☎ 922-1941, 800-367-2317; www.queenkapiolani.com; 150 Kapahulu Ave; r $75, r with ocean view $85, studio with ocean view & kitchenette $120; ⊠) One of the best-value options in Waikiki, this 19-story hotel at the quieter Diamond Head end of Waikiki has a regal theme: chandeliers, high ceilings and faded paintings of Hawaiian royalty. The standard rooms vary greatly in size, with some very pleasant and others quite cramped. The simplest way to avoid a closet-sized space is to request a room with two twin beds instead of a single queen. Most ocean-view rooms have lanai with unobstructed views of Diamond Head. Overnight parking is $8.

Cabana at Waikiki (☎ 926-5555, 877-902-2121; www.cabana-waikiki.com; 2551 Cartwright Rd; ste incl continental breakfast $100-175; ⊠ ⊠) The well-appointed Cabana caters to the gay community and is only minutes from Hula's, Waikiki's bustling gay bar. Each of the 15 units can sleep four people, and comes with a queen bed, queen sofa bed, fully equipped kitchen, lanai, DSL service, TV and VCR. Furnishings are on the tropical side, the bathrooms sport dimmer switches, and you can choose between air-con or overhead fan. Rates include use of an eight-person hot tub and access to a men's gym. Overnight parking is $8.

Ohana Waikiki Surf East (☎ 923-7671; 422 Royal Hawaiian Ave; studios/ste $130/180; ⊠) Unusual for an Ohana chain hotel, this converted apartment building, a block above Kuhio Ave, features family-friendly kitchenettes in all 102 units. Both the studios and one-bedroom suites are large, and most have a sofa bed, as well as a king or two double beds. The accommodations are superior to many higher-priced Ohanas – the lower price simply reflects the distance from the beach. Overnight parking is $10.

Ocean Resort Hotel Waikiki (☎ 922-3861, 800-367-2317; www.oceanresort.com; 175 Paoakalani Ave; standard/deluxe r $90/160; ☒ ☙) Although it hosts a fair number of patrons on low-end package tours, the 451 rooms have the same amenities as more expensive resort hotels, such as cable TV, refrigerators and room safes. When things are slow, it sometimes offers walk-in rates as low as $60, an unbeatable deal for a hotel of this standard. Overnight parking is $8.

Aston Waikiki Beach Hotel (☎ 922-2511, 800-922-7866; www.astonhotels.com; 2570 Kalakaua Ave; r from $140, r with ocean view $245; ☒ ☙) Nearly a reflection of the larger Marriott across the street, the 713 rooms here are comparable, but less expensive. The hotel's annex, the Mauka Tower, is a bit drab looking, but offers the lowest rates plus larger and quieter rooms than in the main hotel unit. Ask about discounts that can cut the standard rates by nearly half. Overnight parking is $13.

Waikiki Gateway Hotel (☎ 955-3741, 800-247-1903; www.waikiki-gateway-hotel.com; 2077 Kalakaua Ave; d $100) Near Ala Moana, this friendly 177-room Waikiki staple is great value, especially the ocean-view rooms overlooking green Fort DeRussey. Overnight parking is $9.

Also recommended:

Waikiki Grand (☎ 923-1511, 800-321-2558; www.waikikigrand.com; 134 Kapahulu Ave; r $90, with kitchenette $130; ☒ ☙) Close to the beach, opposite the zoo. Has a popular gay bar. Overnight parking is $8.

Aston Aloha Surf Hotel (☎ 923-0222, 800-922-7866; www.astonhotels.com; 444 Kanekapolei St; r low/high season $115/145; ☒ ☙) Though it has a lively lobby surf theme, most rooms in this 200-unit hotel are standard fare and on the small side. The beach is a 10-minute walk away. Overnight parking is $8.

Aston Waikiki Banyan (☎ 922-0555, 800-321-2558; www.astonhotels.com; 201 Ohua Ave; r $160-250; ☒ ☙) Offers fully equipped kitchens, tennis court and a children's playground. Overnight parking is $7.

Ohana East (☎ 922-5353, 800-462-6262; www.ohanahotels.com; 150 Kaiulani Ave; d $190; ☒ ☙) One of the Ohana chain's more upscale hotels. Larger rooms with kitchenettes and mountain views. Overnight parking is $10.

Ohana Maile Sky Court (☎ 947-2828; www.ohanahotels.com; 2058 Kuhio Ave; r $110, with kitchenette $120; ☒) This 596-unit high-rise hotel has a central location convenient to restaurants, shops and entertainment. One

of Ohana's better deals if you don't mind being away from the beach. Overnight parking is $10.

Ohana Reef Towers (☎ 924-8844; www.ohanahotels.com; 227 Lewers St; r with/without kitchenette $130/120; ☒ ☙) Close to the beach and a regular on the package circuit. The kitchenette units add a sofa bed. Back rooms are away from noisy Lewers St. Overnight parking is $10.

Radisson Prince Kuhio (☎ 922-0811, 800-333-3333; www.radisson.com/waikikihi; 2500 Kuhio Ave; d $175, with ocean view $225; ☒ ☙) Smart-looking hotel with large rooms, well appointed and good value in this range. Restaurant features a popular seafood dinner buffet. Overnight parking is $9.

Top End

The following hotels all have excellent first-class amenities, in-house fine dining restaurants and large swimming pools, and are either on the beach or across the street.

Royal Hawaiian Hotel (☎ 923-7311, 800-325-3535; www.sheraton-hawaii.com; 2259 Kalakaua Ave; r in historic wing/tower from $380/625; ☒ ☙) Now a Sheraton property, the Royal was Waikiki's first true luxury hotel. Despite being overshadowed by modern high-rises, the pink, Moorish-style building remains the class act of Waikiki, a beautiful place, cool and airy, and loaded with charm and aloha. The historic section maintains a classic appeal, with some of the rooms having quiet garden views. The hotel

---

TOP 10 SLEEPS

- **Ke Iki Beach Bungalows** (p165), North Shore
- **Bamboo** (p128), Waikiki
- **Ilima Hotel** (p128), Waikiki
- **New Otani Kaimana Beach Hotel** (p127), Waikiki
- **Royal Hawaiian Hotel** (p129), Waikiki
- **Kahala Mandarin Oriental** (p138), Kahala area
- **Ohana Waikiki Surf East** (p128), Waikiki
- **Sheraton Princess Kaiulani** (p130), Waikiki
- **Manoa Valley Inn** (p104), Ala Moana & University Area
- **Central Branch YMCA** (p104), Ala Moana & University Area

also hosts the best luau on the island. Overnight parking is $10.

Halekulani Hotel (☎ 923-2311, 800-367-2343; www.halekulani.com; 2199 Kalia Rd; r with ocean view $325, r with ocean view $455, ste $775; ⊠ ⊇) The Halekulani collects awards for best service year after year from both *Condé Nast Traveler*'s 'Best Pacific Rim Hotels' and *Travel & Leisure*'s 'World's Best Service.' What's really impressive about the service is how effortless it seems. Pleasantly subdued rather than posh, the hotel's 455 rooms have large balconies, marble vanities and personal touches, like bathrobes and fresh flowers. The staff know how to pamper: there are no check-in lines; instead, guests are registered in the privacy of their own room. Overnight parking is $16.

Sheraton Moana Surfrider (☎ 922-3111, 800-325-3535; www.sheraton.com/hawaii; 2365 Kalakaua Ave; r $270, with ocean view $450; ⊠ ⊇) Built in 1901, the Moana was Hawaii's first beachfront hotel. Several restorations and a couple of modern wings later, it manages to maintain its original colonial character. The lobby is open and airy, with high plantation-like ceilings and Hawaiian artwork. The rooms in the original building have been restored to their early-20th-century appearance, with woods such as koa and cherry adding to the understated motif. TVs and refrigerators are discreetly hidden inside armoires. Overnight parking is $10.

Waikiki Parc Hotel (☎ 921-7272, 800-422-0450; www.waikikiparc.com; 2233 Helumoa Rd; r $190, with ocean view $270; ℗ ⊠ ⊇) Across the street from its more upmarket sister operation, the Halekulani, the 298-room Parc has a pleasantly understated elegance. The rooms are average in size, but have nice touches, such as ceramic-tiled floors, shuttered lanai doors and bathtubs. The hotel offers various specials, including a 50% discount on the second room for families traveling together, and a three-night 'Parc Sunrise' package that includes free breakfast and parking, and costs about 30% less than the regular room rates.

Outrigger Reef Hotel (☎ 923-3111, 800-688-7444; www.outrigger.com; 2169 Kalia Rd; r $240, with ocean view $370; ⊠ ⊇) The well-appointed Outrigger Reef claims a great beach location, though the 883-room hotel lacks the charm of its historical neighbors to either side. There's a fitness center, wheelchair-accessible rooms and some floors are designated for nonsmokers only. Overnight parking is $13.

Waikiki Beach Marriott Resort (☎ 922-6611, 800-367-5121; www.marriotthotels.com; 2552 Kalakaua Ave; r $230, with ocean view $390; ⊠ ⊇) One of Waikiki's largest hotels, with 1308 rooms in a huge block-long complex, this rambling resort commands a prime spot opposite the beach. It also features weekly pool-side performances by the grand lady of Hawaiian falsetto, Auntie Genoa Kiawe. Steep discounts off the standard rates are common. Overnight parking is $14.

Outrigger Waikiki (☎ 923-0711, 800-688-7444; www.outrigger.com; 2335 Kalakaua Ave; r $230, with ocean view $335; ⊠ ⊇) This 522-room beachfront Outrigger was the first of the hotel's chain and remains its flagship property. Set on a prime stretch of sand, there's lots of activity here, from beach events to seaside dining, including Duke's Canoe Club (p132). Overnight parking is $15.

Sheraton Waikiki (☎ 922-4422, 800-325-3535; www.sheraton-hawaii.com; 2255 Kalakaua Ave; r $290, with ocean view $440; ⊠ ⊇) This 1695-room mega-hotel looms over the historic Royal Hawaiian Hotel. The bustling lobby resembles an exclusive Tokyo shopping center, lined with expensive jewelry stores, and boutiques with French names and designer labels. Overnight parking is $10.

Hyatt Regency Waikiki (☎ 921-6026, 800-233-1234; www.hyattwaikiki.com; 2424 Kalakaua Ave; r $265, with mountain/ocean view $290/410; ⊠ ⊇) From the outside, it's hard to miss the Hyatt's twin 40-story towers with a combined 1230 rooms. But inside, with a maximum of 18 rooms per floor, it's quieter and feels more exclusive than other mega-hotels. Rooms are tastefully decorated, and a ground-floor atrium resplendent with cascading waterfalls and tropical plants adds to the plush *Blade Runner*–meets-the-rain-forest affect. Overnight parking is $12.

W Honolulu Diamond Head (☎ 922-1700, 888-528-9465; www.whotels.com; 2885 Kalakaua Ave; r with Diamond Head/ocean view $375/450; ⊠ ⊇) This is a fashionable boutique hotel right on Sans Souci Beach, on the quieter Diamond Head side of Waikiki. Recently renovated and upgraded, it has 48 stylish, contemporary rooms with high-end amenities, such as 27-inch web-TVs and down-feather bedding. Overnight parking is $15.

Hilton Hawaiian Village (☎ 949-4321, 800-445-8667; www.hawaiian village.hilton.com; 2005 Kalia Rd; r $210, with ocean view $430; ⊠ ⊇) Hawaii's largest hotel, with some 3250 rooms in high-rise towers, this is the ultimate in mass tourism, and a package-tour city unto itself. Indeed, with its own beach, 21 restaurants and more than 100 shops, there's little reason to move. Despite its size, the Hilton maintains a good reputation, and offers some of the best Hawaiian entertainment as well. Overnight parking is $12.

EATING
Budget

Eggs 'n Things (☎ 949-0820; 1911 Kalakaua Ave; dishes $3-10; ✆ 11pm-2pm) Never empty, this bustling all-nighter specializes in excellent breakfast fare, from fish and eggs to a variety of waffles, crepes and omelets. The most popular deal is the 'early riser' special of three pancakes and two eggs that's offered from 5am to 9am for just $3.75.

Tokkuri Tei (☎ 739-2800; 611 Kapahulu Ave; à la carte dishes $3-10, dinners $13-18; ✆ 5:30pm-midnight Mon-Sat) Bring your sense of adventure to this cozy Japanese sushi den, with upbeat versions of sushi standards. The decor is Japanese lanterns and bookcases with customers' favorite bottles of drink. Standout offerings range from grilled *shiso maki* (shiso leaf and pork; $3) to salmon and soft-shell crab drizzled with a sweet chili vinaigrette ($11).

Diamond Head Market & Grill (☎ 732-0077; 3158 Monsarrat Ave; dishes $6-10; ✆ grill 1:30am-8pm, market 7:30am-9pm) At the deli side of this upscale neighborhood gem, you can choose from salads like fennel-citrus or cucumber-mint, or from entrées like peanut chicken stirfry or Mexican lasagna. Prices are by the pound, and you order as much as you want. It's freshly made and ready to take back to your apartment or hotel, or to nearby Kapiolani Park for a picnic. Adjacent to the deli is the Grill, a take-out window setup where you can order mini-plates ranging from teriyaki chicken ($6) to grilled 'ahi salad ($8.50), including salad and rice.

Fatty's Chinese Kitchen (☎ 922-9600; 2345 Kuhio Ave; mains $1-3.50; ✆ 10:30am-10:30pm) Have a seat at this hole-in-the-wall eatery next to the Miramar hotel for some of the cheapest food to be found in these parts, with rice or chow mein plus one hot main for only $3.50. Add $1 for each additional main. The atmosphere is purely local, with a dozen seats lining a long bar and the cook on the other side chopping away.

Moose McGillycuddy's (☎ 923-0751; 310 Lewers St; snacks & mains $6-12; ✆ meals served 7:30am-10pm) Perhaps best known as a late-night dance spot (p135), Moose's also serves reasonably priced burgers, steaks, Mexican fare and sandwiches. A great breakfast deal is the early-bird special (until 9:30am) of two eggs, bacon and toast for $1.99. Moose also has salads.

Ezogiku Noodle Cafe (☎ 923-2013; cnr Lemon Rd & Paoakalani Ave; dishes $5-7; ✆ 11am-11pm) This is where many Waikiki hotel employees go during their lunch and dinner breaks for steaming bowls of Japanese ramen, curries and fried rice. It's cheap, fast and the closest you'll get to a subway noodle shop this side of Tokyo.

Bogart's Cafe (☎ 739-0999; 3045 Monsarrat Ave; dishes $5-10; ✆ 6am-8pm Mon-Fri, 6am-6pm Sat & Sun) This eatery is a hot breakfast spot, with everything from thick Belgian waffles ($5.50) to crab and avocado omelets ($9). Lunch ranges from veggie wraps ($5) to a spinach and strawberry salad ($7.50).

Waliana Coffee House (☎ 955-1764; 1860 Ala Moana Blvd; meals $6-12; ✆ 24hr) Opposite Hilton Hawaiian Village, this vintage coffee shop serves heaped portions with plenty of aloha around the clock.

Food Pantry (☎ 923-9831; 2370 Kuhio Ave; ✆ 6am-1am) This is the best place to get groceries in Waikiki. Its prices are higher than those of the chain supermarkets, which are all outside Waikiki, but lower than those of Waikiki's numerous ABC convenience stores.

For locations of supermarkets outside Waikiki, see p108.

Also recommended:

Saint Germain (☎ 924-4305; 2301 Kuhio Ave; snacks $5; ✆ 7am-9pm) Starting with delicious croissants, this little French bakery presents a tasty variety of soups, salads and hearty baguette sandwiches, all made fresh to order with a dozen vegetarian and meat fillings to select from.

Aloha Sushi (☎ 955-5223; 1178 Ala Moana Blvd; meals $5; ✆ 9am-9pm) Find out what spam sushi really tastes like at this fast-food alternative in the Discovery Bay Center. Mix and match dozens of varieties of sushi to your taste or order a pre-arranged *bento* (lunchbox).

Leonard's (☎ 737-5591; 933 Kapahulu Ave; pastries 65¢-$1; ✆ 6am-9pm) Portuguese bakery known throughout Honolulu for its *malasadas*, a type of sweet, fried dough rolled in sugar and served warm – like a doughnut without the hole. Try the *haupia malasada*, with a coconut cream filling, and you'll be hooked.

Rainbow Drive-In (☎ 737-0177; cnr Kapahulu & Kanaina Aves; ⏱ 7:30am-9pm) Closer to central Waikiki if you're on foot, this old-fashioned local favorite serves malts and burgers, saimin (local-style noodle soup) and inexpensive breakfast fare.

Mid-Range

The Banyan Grill (☎ 922-3111; Sheraton Moana Surfrider Hotel, 2365 Kalakaua Ave; snacks $5-13; ⏱ 4-9:30pm) Sit back in your lounge chair at this open-air grill in the beachside courtyard at this upscale hotel, while the chef cooks up your order over a barbecue pit. The simple, but tasty, fare includes baby back ribs, teriyaki chicken and grilled shrimp – and the location, beneath the historic hotel's sprawling banyan tree, is particularly engaging, with local musicians performing daily.

Shore Bird Beach Broiler (☎ 922-2887; Outrigger Reef Hotel, 2169 Kalia Rd; breakfast buffet $10, dinner $9-20; ⏱ 7am-11am & 6pm-1am) On the beach, the Shore Bird makes you work for your dinner, but only at the long common grill where you barbecue your own fish, steak or chicken and chat with your fellow cooks. Meals come with salad, chili, rice and fresh fruit from a buffet bar. Get seated for dinner before 6pm and you can enjoy the sunset and take advantage of early-bird price specials.

Keo's (☎ 922-9355; 2028 Kuhio Ave; mains $10-18; ⏱ 5-11pm) Keo's Thai restaurant has long been a favorite with visiting celebs from Jimmy Carter to Keanu Reeves, but has a loyal local following as well. Owner Keo Sananikone liberally spices the dishes with organically grown herbs. A house specialty is the Evil Jungle Prince, a spicy curry with basil and coconut milk. The main drawback

is the sometimes noisy location on busy Kuhio Ave.

Keoni's (☎ 922-9888; Ohana East, 2375 Kuhio Ave; dishes $8-30; ⏱ 7am-11pm) Keoni's, a branch of nearby Keo's Thai restaurant, adds a twist to its menu, which is evenly divided between Thai and American dishes, and perfect for families who can't agree on where to go. There are good breakfast and lunch specials, too.

La Cucaracha (☎ 922-2288; 2310 Kuhio Ave; dishes $10-16; ⏱ 2pm-midnight) Who would expect an authentic family Mexican restaurant in the heart of Waikiki? Yet the food is excellent. Along with south-of-the-border standards, daily specials included home-made tamales and chicken molé and fresh Pacific salmon or *ono* (white-fleshed wahoo) smothered in salsa verde. Wash it all down with a potent margarita, or Mexican beer on tap.

Oceanarium Restaurant (☎ 921-6111; Pacific Beach Hotel, 2490 Kalakaua Ave; breakfast buffet $16, lunch $8, dinner $13-26; ⏱ 6am-9:30pm) This place has standard hotel fare, but a one-of-a-kind view. Its dining room wraps around a stunning three-story aquarium brimming with colorful tropical fish, including some impressive sharks and rays. A breakfast buffet includes everything but the aquarium fish. Lunch and dinner mains range from pasta and seafood salads to lobster and steak.

Chuck's Steak House (☎ 923-1228; 2nd fl, Outrigger Waikiki Hotel, 2335 Kalakaua Ave; dinner $17-28; ⏱ 5-10pm) Chuck's has an attractive sunset water view and some good early bird specials. From 5pm to 6pm you can get a teriyaki chicken or grilled mahimahi dinner for $16 and down a few mai tais (alcoholic drinks

---

THE AUTHOR'S CHOICE

Duke's Canoe Club (☎ 922-2268; 2335 Kalakaua Ave; breakfast & lunch buffet $12, dinner $15-27; ⏱ 7am-11:30pm) By local consent, Duke's is the most popular beachfront restaurant in Waikiki, located beachside at the Outrigger Waikiki hotel. Named in honor of Hawaiian surfing legend Duke Kahanamoku, the open air restaurant caters to a constant stream of locals and visitors alike, and features live Hawaiian music afternoons and evenings. The breakfast and lunch buffets are a bargain at $12, and range from made-to-order omelets and bacon & eggs to *kalua* pig and cabbage and Thai chicken pizza. Dinner stand-outs include prime rib ($24) and at least two fresh catch-of-the-day choices ($18). For dessert, order Duke's signature Hula Pie, a killer chocolate concoction. Portions are generous and there's a great collection of Hawaiian memorabilia to check out, from a koa wood outrigger canoe and several surfboards to vintage Hawaiian posters and black-and-white photos. The restaurant eventually spills out to the Barefoot Bar, perfect for happy-hour sunsets, with tiki-lamps flickering in the breeze. You can sit under an umbrella and play with one in your mai tai at the same time.

made from rum, grenadine, and lemon and pineapple juices) at just $3.50 each.

You'll also find some great neighborhood restaurants in this price category along Kapahulu Ave, the road that starts in Waikiki near the zoo and runs up to the H1 Fwy.

Irifune (☎ 737-1141; 563 Kapahulu Ave; lunch $7, dinner $10-15; 11:30am-1:30pm, 5:30-9:30pm Tue-Sat) Follow the locals to this bustling eatery, decorated with Japanese country kitsch, and serving up creative appetizers like *gyoza* stuffed with tofu and cheese ($4). A top dinner choice is the *tataki 'ahi*, a delicious fresh tuna that's seared lightly on the outside and sashimi-like inside. Or opt for a combination dinner that pairs tempura with sashimi and other Japanese standards. Alcohol is not served, but you can bring your own beer.

Ono Hawaiian Food (☎ 737-2275; 726 Kapahulu Ave; meals $8-10; 11am-7:45pm Mon-Sat) For a local meal, you can't do better than Ono's, a simple little diner crowded with aging tables and decorated with sports paraphernalia. At night people line up on the sidewalk waiting to get in. A favorite is the *kalua* pig plate, which comes with *lomilomi* salmon, *pipi kaula* beef jerky, *haupia* coconut pudding and either rice or poi. Arrive by 6pm to avoid a long wait.

The Pyramids (☎ 737-2900; 758 Kapahulu Ave; lunch buffet $10, dinner $13-18; 11am-2pm & 5.30-10pm Mon-Sat, 5-9pm Sun) This atmospheric Egyptian restaurant offers a scrumptious lunch buffet of Mediterranean treats, including falafels, tahini, tabouleh and *shwarma*, a spiced meat dish cooked on a spit. Dinner is à la carte, with main dishes such as shish kebab, moussaka and marinated lamb. The Greek salad of sliced tomato and cucumber over crunchy greens, sprinkled with crumbled creamy-sharp feta cheese is a winner. Belly dancers entertain diners nightly.

Top End

La Mer (☎ 923-2311; Halekulani Hotel, 2199 Kalia Rd; mains $35-135, 4-/9-course dinner $85/125; 6-10pm) With a superb 2nd-floor ocean view, La Mer is regarded by many as Hawaii's ultimate fine-dining restaurant. A neoclassical French menu puts the emphasis on Provençal cuisine. The dining is formal, though men are no longer required to wear jackets; long sleeved shirts will do. The menu changes daily but typically features items like *'ahi* with caviar, bouillabaisse and filet mignon.

Orchid's (☎ 923-2311; Haekulani Hotel, 2199 Kalia Rd; breakfast buffet $38; 7:30am-2pm) This mainstay features a popular upscale Sunday brunch buffet, a grand spread that includes sashimi, sushi, prime rib, smoked salmon, roast suckling pig, an array of salads and fruits, and a rich dessert bar. It's a pampering treat, with a fine ocean view, orchid sprays on the tables, and a soothing flute and harp duo. Reservations are highly recommended.

Banyan Veranda (☎ 922-3111; Sheraton Moana Surfrider, 2365 Kalakaua Ave; 3-course dinner $52; 5:30-9pm) For a romantic dinner, visit the hotel's historic courtyard veranda. The menu, which changes nightly, features French and Pacific Rim influenced dishes, such as seared marlin and bouillabaisse, accompanied by Hawaiian music and hula dancing. Another Veranda highlight is afternoon tea (adult/child $25/12.50), with finger sandwiches, scones and traditional sweets.

Kyo-ya (☎ 947-3911; 2057 Kalakaua Ave; lunch $14-20, dinner $20-55; 11am-1:30pm & 5:30-8:30pm) Kyo-ya is the full deal, a formal Japanese restaurant with kimono-clad waitresses and Waikiki's fanciest Japanese cuisine. The eight-page menu includes several sasihmi and tempura pairings, along with butterfish misoyaki and a traditional Kyoto-style grill served with several small courses ($32). Both the setting and food presentation are elegant, and it's a favorite spot among islanders for a special night out.

Golden Dragon (☎ 946-5336; Hilton Hawaiian Village, 2005 Kalia Rd; mains $15-30; 6-9:30pm Tue-Sat) This is a top choice for fine Chinese dining, with both good food and an ocean view. Although the varied menu has some

TEA CEREMONIES

Ensconced in a mellow Japanese teahouse, the **Urasenke Foundation of Hawaii** (☎ 923-3059; 245 Saratoga Rd) presents a traditional tea ceremony at 10am on Wednesday and Friday mornings, bringing a rare bit of serenity to busy Saratoga Rd. Students dressed in kimonos perform the ceremony on tatami mats in a formal tearoom; for those participating, it can be a meditative experience. It costs $3 to be served green tea made from 400-year-old bushes. Guests are asked to wear socks, as they must leave their shoes at the door.

expensive specialties, many dishes, including a tasty Cantonese roast duck and a deliciously crispy lemon chicken, are priced under $20.

DRINKING

Tiki's Grill & Bar (☎ 923-8454; Aston Waikiki Beach Hotel, 2570 Kalakaua Ave; ☯ 10:30am-midnight) At the top of the Aston Waikiki Beach Hotel, Tiki's is a good place to enjoy a drink and pupu, or catch live music in the afternoon (4:30pm to 6:30pm) and again from 9pm to 11pm.

Moana Terrace Bar (☎ 922-6611; 2552 Kalakaua Ave; ☯ 11am-11pm) Just opposite Kuhio Beach at the Waikiki Beach Marriott Hotel, this mellow open-air poolside bar features live Hawaiian music from 6pm to 9pm.

Paradise Lounge (☎ 949-4321; Hilton Hawaiian Village, 2005 Kalia Rd; ☯ 5:30pm-10pm Sun-Thu, 5:30pm-midnight Fri & Sat) For the price of a drink on Friday or Saturday night, head to the Hilton Hawaiian Village's Rainbow Tower to catch Jerry Santos and Olomana, one of the best Hawaiian groups performing today.

Mai Tai Bar (☎ 923-7311; 2259 Kalakaua Ave; ☯ 10am-1am) At the Royal Hawaiian's low-key bar you can catch great local groups, like Augie Roy's Trio and Kelly Boy DeLima, from 4pm to 10pm nightly by the beach. Other local musicians occasionally sit in.

Wonder Lounge (☎ 922-1700; W Honolulu Hotel, 2885 Kalakaua Ave; cover Fri & Sat $10; ☯ 5:30pm-1am) This is easily the swankiest bar around Waikiki, with well-dressed patrons sipping at an elegant bar featuring over 350 wines, munching great *pupu*, and dancing to live music on Friday and Saturday nights, or DJs on Wednesday and Thursday.

Coconut Willy's Bar (☎ 923-9454; International Market Place, 2330 Kalakaua Ave; ☯ 11am-1am) This bar gets loud and it's a great place to watch people. There's plenty of night action, with cover bands playing on and off from 3pm to midnight.

ENTERTAINMENT

For up-to-date information, check out the free *Honolulu Weekly*, which comes out on Wednesday, and the Friday *Honolulu Advertiser's* TGIF section. Those free tourist magazines often have discount coupons, too.

The Waikiki Shell, a beautiful outdoor amphitheater in Kapiolani Park, hosts classical and contemporary twilight musical concerts, with Diamond Head in the background.

For current schedules, call the **Blaisdell Center box office** (☎ 591-2211).

Hawaiian Music & Hula

Waikiki has lots of Hawaiian entertainment, from Polynesian shows with hula dancers to mellow duos playing slack-key guitar.

Duke's Canoe Club (☎ 922-2268; Outrigger Waikiki, 2335 Kalakaua Ave; ☯ 4-6pm & 10pm-midnight) This beachside courtyard is Waikiki's most popular venue for contemporary Hawaiian music. There's entertainment featuring the biggest names – including Kapena and Henry Kapono – appearing on weekend afternoons. It's a great scene, so don't miss it.

House Without a Key (☎ 923-2311; Halekulani Hotel, 2199 Kalia Rd) Attracts a nostalgic crowd who gather from 5pm to 8pm at this open-air bar for sunset cocktails, Hawaiian music and hula dancing by a former Miss Hawaii.

Banyan Veranda (☎ 922-3111; Sheraton Moana Surfrider, 2365 Kalakaua Ave) You can listen to music beneath the same old banyan tree where 'Hawaii Calls' broadcast its nationwide radio show for four decades beginning in 1935. The performance schedule varies, but typically there's Hawaiian music and a hula dancer from 5:30pm to 10:30pm.

Royal Hawaiian Hotel (☎ 923-7311; 2259 Kalakaua Ave; admission adult/child 5-12 yrs $81/48; ☯ 5:30-8:30pm

---

TINY BUBBLES

Want a jolt of 1960s nostalgia? If sing-alongs and getting invited on stage to be razzed with jokes sounds like fun, Don Ho is the way to go. This saucy Honolulu musician has been playing the Waikiki tourist scene since 1962. Sitting behind an organ, he bounces between witty banter, chatting with the audience and singing his classic pop hits, like *Tiny Bubbles* and *I'll Remember You* – offering a good dose of kitsch in the process. Ho's fans, however, range from old-timers like himself to a younger crowd who enjoy his cool brand of humor. Even touring musicians, like Green Day and the Foo Fighters, stop by when they're in town to check out the old master. Reservations are recommended for the **show** (☎ 923-3981; Waikiki Beachcomber Hotel, 2300 Kalakaua Ave; admission $32, with dinner $52; ☯ 8pm Sun, Tue & Thu), where the admission price includes a cocktail.

FREE ENTERTAINMENT IN WAIKIKI

A pleasant way to pass the evening is to stroll along Waikiki Beach at sunset and sample the outdoor Hawaiian shows that take place at the beachfront hotels (p134). You can wander past the musicians playing at the Sheraton Moana Surfrider's Banyan Veranda, watch bands performing beachside at Duke's Canoe Club, see the poolside performers at the Sheraton Waikiki and so on down the line.

The **Royal Hawaiian Shopping Center** (☎ 922-0588; 2201 Kalakaua Ave) offers free events at its fountain courtyard, including a nightly torch lighting ceremony from 6pm to 6:15pm, followed by a 30-minute Polynesian show on Monday, Wednesday and Friday evenings. The same show takes place from 10am to 11:30am on Tuesday, Thursday and Saturday. In addition, the shopping center sponsors various daytime activities; all are free and last one hour. Hula lessons are given at 10am Monday and Friday; lei-making lessons at 11am Monday and Wednesday; and ukulele lessons at 10am Tuesday and Thursday, and 11:30am Monday, Wednesday and Friday.

Except during August, the **Royal Hawaiian Band** (see p113) performs from 2pm to 3pm on Sunday at the Kapiolani Park Bandstand.

The Kapiolani Park Bandstand is also the site of free **Friday Bandstand Concerts** held from 5:30pm to 6:30pm each Friday. A different Hawaiian group performs each week – anything from top-notch slack-key guitar masters to blues and jazz bands.

For an enlightening stroll back in time, join one of the free **Waikiki Historic Trail walking tours** (☎ 737-6442; www.waikikihistorictrail.com). Led by Native Hawaiian guides, these two-hour walks are peppered with interesting tidbits on Hawaiian royalty who lived and played in Waikiki in days past. The walks begin in front of the Royal Hawaiian Shopping Center stage, near the fountain at the corner of Kalakaua and Seaside Ave, at 9am Tuesday, Thursday and Saturday.

There are also free historical tours of Waikiki's two classic hotels, the Royal Hawaiian and the Sheraton Moana Surfrider (see p123 for details).

Mon) This beachside luau includes a bar, buffet-style dinner and Polynesian show.

Sand Bar (☎ 922-4422; 2255 Kalakaua Ave; music 6pm-8:30pm) This cabana-like bar at the Sheraton Waikiki Hotel has views of Diamond Head, and live Hawaiian music nightly, including 'keiki hula' every Sunday, when a children's hula group displays its stuff.

You can watch some of O'ahu's best hula troupes performing for free at a couple of Waikiki venues. The most scenic is the city-sponsored show at Kuhio Beach Park's hula mound, the **Kuhio Beach Torch Lighting & Hula Show** (admission free; ☯ 6:30-7:30pm). Another hula show takes place at the food court of the **International Market Place** (2330 Kalakaua Ave; admission free; ☯ 7:30pm most nights).

Nightclubs

Wave Waikiki (☎ 941-0424; 1877 Kalakaua Ave; admission $5; ☯ 8pm-4am) Waikiki's hottest dance club has Waikiki's edgiest scene, with the emphasis on trance, hip hop, hard rock and alternative music. The minimum age is 21.

Moose McGillycuddy's (☎ 923-0751; 310 Lewers St; admission $3-5; ☯ 9pm-1am Mon-Sat) A restaurant by day, this place turns into a raucous night-

spot, with live Top 40 bands from Monday to Thursday and DJs mixing it up on Friday and Saturday. Minimum age is 21.

Zanzabar Nightclub (☎ 924-3939; 2255 Kuhio Ave; admission $10; ☯ 9pm-4am) In the Waikiki Trade Center, the scene here is more upscale, ranging from R&B and Latin to disco and Top 40, with an occasional bikini contest thrown into the mix. Partiers aged 18 to 21 are admitted on Thursday and Sunday nights for $15.

Scruples (☎ 923-9530; 2310 Kuhio Ave; admission $5, aged 18-21 $15; ☯ 8pm-4am) A busy, disco-style, Top-40 dance club in the center of Waikiki.

Gay & Lesbian Venues

What the Waikiki scene may lack in venues, it makes up for in aloha. Two local monthly magazines, *DaKine* and *Odyssey*, keep up with gay and lesbian events. The *Honolulu Weekly* also carries listings.

Hula's Bar & Lei Stand (☎ 923-0669; 2nd fl, Waikiki Grand Hotel, 134 Kapahulu Ave; ☯ 10am-2am) Waikiki's main gay venue, this friendly open-air bar is a popular place for gays and lesbians to meet, dance and have a few drinks. It also has a great ocean view of Diamond Head.

Also recommended:

Angles Waikiki (☎ 926-9766; 2256 Kuhio Ave; ⊗ 10am-2am) A bar by day, a nightclub by night, with dancing, a pool table and video games.

Fusion Waikiki (☎ 924-2422; 2260 Kuhio Ave; ⊗ 10pm-4am Sun-Thu, 8pm-4am Fri & Sat) This place has karaoke and female impersonator shows.

In-Between (☎ 926-7060; 2155 Lauula St; ⊗ 4pm-2am Mon-Sat, 2pm-2am Sun) A gay karaoke bar where drama reigns.

All of these places welcome both gay men and lesbians, though Hula's and In-Between are frequented more by gay men, while Angles and Fusion tend to have a more mixed crowd.

SHOPPING

Waikiki has no shortage of souvenir stalls, swimsuit and T-shirt shops, quick-stop convenience marts or fancy boutiques.

You'll never be far from one of the ubiquitous ABC Discount Marts, which stand on nearly every other street corner. They're often the cheapest place to pick up vacation necessities, such as beach mats, sunblock and sundry goods.

International Market Place (☎ 971-2080; 2330 Kalakaua Ave) For cheap souvenirs, visit this market under a sprawling banyan tree in the center of Waikiki, where nearly a hundred stalls sell everything from seashell necklaces and refrigerator magnets to T-shirts and sarongs.

Royal Hawaiian Shopping Center (☎ 922-0588; 2201 Kalakaua Ave) Waikiki's biggest shopping center, the Royal Hawaiian has dozens of shops selling jewelry and designer clothing. It also has Hawaiian gift shops, including **Little Hawaiian Craft Shop** (☎ 926-2662), which carries a range of local crafts, from *kukui*-nut key chains and quilt-pattern kits to high-quality koa bowls.

Bailey's Antique Shop (☎ 734-7628; 517 Kapahulu Ave) For antique and used aloha shirts, this shop has the island's widest selection. It's a great place to go and look around – almost like a museum.

Island Treasures Antiques (☎ 922-8223; 2145 Kuhio Ave) For eclectic antiques, try this place, which has lots of odds and ends, including jewelry, period glassware, old posters and Asian porcelain.

Waikiki Shopping Plaza (☎ 923-1191; 2250 Kalakaua Ave) Just oppposite the Royal Hawaiian Shopping Center, the Waikiki Shopping Plaza features close to 75 shops and eateries, most with an Asian theme, along with drop-in weekend classes in the art of making leis and shell necklaces.

GETTING AROUND
To/From the Airport

See p81 for transport options to/from Honolulu International Airport.

Bus

O'ahu's public bus system, **TheBus** (☎ 848-5555; www.thebus.org), runs frequent routes in Waikiki. Most of the Waikiki bus stops are along Kuhio Ave. Bus Nos 8, 19, 20 and 58 run between Waikiki and Ala Moana Center. It's hardly worth checking timetables; one comes by every few minutes. If you're heading to the 'Iolani Palace area from Waikiki, the most frequent and convenient bus is No 2. To go directly to Aloha Tower Marketplace or the Hawaii Maritime Center from Waikiki, take bus No 19 or 20. To get to Chinatown by bus from Waikiki, you can take bus No 2 or 13 to N Hotel St in the center of Chinatown, or bus No 19 or 20 to River St on the western edge of Chinatown. For more details about TheBus, see p82.

Car & Moped

Parking cheaply in Waikiki can be a challenge. Many hotels charge $7 to $15 a day for guest parking. There is four-hour metered parking next to the Waikiki Zoo. However, on the outskirts of Waikiki, you can find free parking. There's a large public parking lot at Ala Wai Yacht Harbor at the west end of Waikiki, with a 24-hour limit. At the east end of Waikiki, there's a parking lot along Monsarrat Ave at Kapiolani Park with no time limit.

In addition to the airport branches (p83), several car-hire companies also have branch locations in Waikiki, many in the lobbies of larger hotels. For general rental information and toll-free numbers, see p536.

Mopeds can be another great way of getting around Waikiki, but they're really best suited to people who already have experience riding in city traffic. **Blue Sky Rentals** (☎ 947-0101; 1920 Ala Moana Blvd), on the

WHO KNEW? HULA LYRICS REVEALED

In traditional hula, poems, stories and prayers were interpreted by a dancer's stylized movements of hands and arms, hips and eyes. But unless you spoke Hawaiian, the lyrics remained a mystery. The latest CDs from **Hula Records** (www.hularecords.com), however, include several re-issued classics from the 1960s and earlier, often with revealing translations of the original lyrics.

But don't count on a straight story. This is the stuff of poetry where subtle suggestion reigns like royalty. The prow of a ship cutting through the bay may be just that, or something else that is longer than it is wide. The morning mist, a sudden wildfire, a sweet smelling flower can all suggest passion or yearning.

Many hula lyrics are part of a tongue-in-cheek Hawaiian tradition known as *kaona*, famous for double entendres such as 'dainty cheeks' and 'plucked flowers.' It was also a way to bypass disapproving missionaries. Watch the dancers for more clues about what you've been missing!

Genoa Keawe, now in her 80s, remains the Queen of Hawaiian Music and can still be heard every week at the Waikiki Beach Marriott Resort (p130).

Some lyrics and translations from songs recorded by Aunty Genoa Keawe:

'Ahulili (c Hula Records; Genoa Keawe, Party Hulas; words & music by Scott Ha'i; translation by Jean Sullivan)

He aloha no 'Ahulili	'Ahulili is loved
He lili paha ko ia ala	But perhaps is jealous
I ke kau mau 'ole ia	When (loving) isn't there all the time
E ka 'ohu kau kuahiwi.	Like mist that settles on the mountains.
Eia no e ka 'olu	Here's what will satisfy
Ke 'ala kupaha'o.	The mysterious fragrance.
A lawa ko makemake	When you have what you want
E manene ai ko kino.	Your whole being trembles.
Pa'a iho 'oe a pa'a	Hold on tight
Ka 'i'ini me ka 'ano'i	To the desire, the longing
Ka 'ano'i no kau pua.	The yearning for your flower.
Ka beauty a'o Mauna Hape.	The beauty of Happy Mountain.

ground floor of Inn on the Park Hotel, is the most reliable place in Waikiki to hire a moped. Hire per four/eight/24 hours costs $20/30/40.

Trolley

There are three trolley-style buses that offer services between Waikiki and Honolulu's main tourist sights. Other companies do city bus tours.

The **Waikiki Trolley** (☎ 593-2822; www.waikiki trolley.com; ◷ 8:30am-4:30pm) extends far beyond Waikiki. The color-coded route system can seem puzzling, but the main thing to know is that an all-day pass (adult/child $25/12) allows you to jump on and off the trolley as often as you like. Its main 'red

line' has about 30 stops between Waikiki and the Bishop Museum; the 'blue line' goes out to Sea Life Park; the 'pink line' to Ala Moana Center; and the 'yellow line' to the shops at Ward Warehouse. Trolleys come by every 20 to 30 minutes between 8:30am and 4:30pm.

For Honolulu and Waikiki, **Red Line Trolley** (☎ 591-2561, 800-824-8804; www.enoa.com), operated by E Noa Tours, offers self-guided trolley tours. The day pass (adult/children 4–12 $25/12) allows you to jump on and off at the more than 20 stops around the city.

Hilo Hattie Trolley (☎ 537-2926) is a free shopping shuttle designed to get you from your Waikiki hotel to the retailer's superstore on Nimitz Hwy, with stops at Ala Moana Center and Aloha Tower Marketplace. It runs every 20 minutes between ten Waikiki hotels and the shopping centers, though you can end up waiting longer for one that's not full.

SOUTHEAST O'AHU

Some of O'ahu's finest scenery is along the southeast coast, which curves around the tip of the Ko'olau Range. Diamond Head, Hanauma Bay and the island's most famous bodysurfing beaches are all just a 20-minute ride from Waikiki.

East of Diamond Head, H1 turns into the Kalanianaole Hwy (72), passing the exclusive Kahala residential area, a run of shopping centers and some housing developments that creep into the mountain valleys.

The highway rises and falls as it winds its way around the Koko Head area and Makapu'u Point, with beautiful coastal views along the way. The area is geologically fascinating with boldly stratified rock formations, volcanic craters and lava sea cliffs.

DIAMOND HEAD

Seven hundred and sixty-three feet at the summit, **Diamond Head** (admission $1; ☼ 6am-6pm) is a tuff cone and crater formed by a violent steam explosion deep beneath the earth's surface long after most of O'ahu's volcanic activity had stopped. The backdrop to Waikiki, it's one of the best-known landmarks in the Pacific.

Today Diamond Head is a state monument with picnic tables, restrooms and drinking water. Be sure to hike the trail to the crater rim for the best panoramic views.

Just east of Diamond Head is the posh neighborhood of Kahala – notable for its luxury homes around Black Point, the Kahala Mandarin Oriental Hotel and the convenient Kahala Mall.

History

The Hawaiians called it Le'ahi and built a *luakini* (temple for human sacrifices) on the top. But ever since 1825, when British sailors found calcite crystals sparkling in the sun and mistook them for diamonds, it's been called Diamond Head.

In 1909 the US Army began Fort Ruger at the edge of the crater, building a network of tunnels, topping the rim with cannon emplacements, bunkers and observation posts. Reinforced during WWII, the fort has been a silent sentinel whose guns have never fired.

Activities

HIKING

The trail to the summit was built in 1910 to service the military observation stations along the crater rim. Although a fairly steep hike, with an elevation gain of 560ft, it's only three-quarters of a mile to the top and plenty of people of all ages hike up. The return trip takes about an hour, and you should definitely pack your own water.

The crater is dry and scrubby with kiawe (a relative of the mesquite tree), grasses, koa trees and wildflowers. The small yellow-orange flowers along the way are native *ilima,* O'ahu's official flower.

Starting up the trail, the summit lies ahead a bit to the left, at roughly 11 o'clock. About 20 minutes up the trail, hikers enter a long, dark tunnel. The roof is high enough to walk without bumping your head (there is a handrail), and your eyes should adjust enough to make out shadows in the darkness. The tunnel curves, and no light is visible until close to the end making it little spooky; the park advises hikers to use a flashlight.

The tunnel should be the climax of this long climb, but coming out into the light hikers face a steep 99-step staircase, followed by a shorter tunnel, a narrow spiral staircase inside an unlit bunker and the last of the trail's 271 steps. And when you reach the top, be careful – there are steep drops.

From the summit there's a fantastic 360-degree view – the southeast coast to Koko Head and Koko Crater, and leeward coast to Barbers Point and the Wai'anae Range, with Kapiolani Park and the Waikiki Shell below. The lighthouse, coral reefs, sailboats and sometimes even surfers waiting for a wave at Diamond Head Beach are also visible. The summit can be quite windy, as evidenced by the several caps and hats you'll see scattered just below the lookout. So hold on!

Sleeping & Eating

Accommodations and eating options are available nearby in the swanky neighborhood of Kahala.

Kahala Mandarin Oriental (☎ 739-8888, 800-367-2525; www.mandarin-oriental.com; 5000 Kahala Ave; r $330, with ocean view $530, presidential ste $3700; ⊠ ⊠) One of the state's most exclusive luxury hotels. This is where the rich and famous go when they want to avoid the Waikiki scene, a 15-minute drive away. The guest list is Hawaii's most regal and includes Britain's Prince Charles, Spain's King Juan Carlos and several recent US presidents. The hotel has two restaurants and a poolside snack bar, along with its own quiet stretch of beach and an enclosed lagoon where dolphins swim and play.

Olive Tree Cafe (☎ 737-0303; 4614 Kilauea Ave; salads $5, mains $10) The motto on the wall says it all at this busy eatery next to the Kahala Mall: 'Mostly Greek – not so fast food.' Highlights include red and yellow tomato salad with feta, and fresh fish or lamb souvlaki. Order at the register, then wait for your name to be called. As is typical on O'ahu, it's BYO (Bring Your Own beer or wine). The Greek deli next door has a surprising selection of imported Greek wines.

Shopping
Kahala Mall (☎ 732-7736; 4211 Waialae Ave; ⊗ 10am-9pm Mon-Sat, 10am-5pm Sun) This air-conditioned surburban mall has a bit of everything, from an eight-screen movie complex and weekend entertainment stage to nearly 100 shops, including a supermarket, Macy's department store and Barnes & Noble bookshop.

Getting There & Away
To reach Diamond Head from Waikiki, take bus No 22 or 58, both of which run about twice an hour. It's a 20-minute walk from the bus stop to the trailhead at the parking lot. By car from Waikiki, take Monsarrat Ave to Diamond Head Rd and then take the right turn after Kapiolani Community College into the crater.

DIAMOND HEAD BEACH
Diamond Head Beach draws both surfers and windsurfers, plus a few picnickers. Conditions are suitable for intermediate to advanced windsurfers, and when the swells are up it's a great place for wave riding. This little beach has showers, but no other facilities.

As there's not much to see here unless the wind and surf are up, most people coming this way are touring by car. To get there from Waikiki, follow Kalakaua Ave to Diamond Head Rd. There's a parking lot just beyond the lighthouse. Walk east past the end of the lot and you'll find a paved trail down to the beach. If you don't have your own transport, bus No 14 runs from Waikiki about once an hour.

HANAUMA BAY NATURE PRESERVE
A wide, sheltered bay of sapphire and turquoise waters set in a rugged volcanic ring, Hanauma (Curved Bay) was designated a marine life conservation district in 1967. Once a popular fishing spot, it had nearly been fished out. Now that the fish are protected instead of eaten, they swarm in by the thousands. From the overlook, view the entire coral reef that stretches across the width of the bay. You're bound to see schools of glittering silver fish, the bright blue flash of parrotfish and perhaps a sea turtle. To see an even more colorful scene, put on a mask, jump in and view it from beneath the surface.

While it's teeming with fish, Hanauma is far from pristine. Being loved to death by over a million visitors a year has gradually damaged the shallow coral reef. Efforts are being made to right the wrongs; you can help by not standing on the reef. Feeding the fish is also prohibited for the same reasons.

Information
Hanauma is both a county nature preserve and a **state underwater park** (☎ 396-4229; www .hanaumabayhawaii.org; admission adult/child $5/free; ⊗ 6am-6pm Wed-Mon, 6am-7pm Apr-Oct; Ⓟ $1). It has a snack bar, lifeguards, showers, restrooms and access for the disabled. The beachside **concession stand** (⊗ 8am to 4:30pm) rents snorkel sets for $6.

Sights & Activities
TOILET BOWL & WITCHES BREW
These once-popular natural wonders have been closed to the public since 2002, following hundreds of rescues and dozens of tragic drownings within a five-year period.

Toilet Bowl, a small natural pool in the lava rock, is connected to the sea by an underwater channel, which enables water to surge into the bowl and then flush out from beneath.

The cove at the southern side of the point is the treacherous Witches Brew, so named for its swirling, turbulent waters, where rogue waves have caught a number of un-suspecting hikers.

SNORKELING
Conditions at Hanauma Bay are favorable for snorkeling year-round. The large, sandy opening in the middle of the coral, known as the **Keyhole**, is the best place for novice snorkelers. The deepest water is 10ft, though it's very shallow over the coral – bring diving gloves if you have them. The Keyhole is well protected and usually very calm.

For confident snorkelers, it's better on the outside of the reef, where there are large coral heads, bigger fish and fewer people; to get there follow the directions on the signboard or ask the lifeguard at the southwest end of the beach. Keep in mind that because of the channel current it's generally easier going out than getting back. Don't attempt to swim outside the reef when the water is rough or choppy. Not only will the channel current be strong, but the sand will be stirred up and the visibility poor anyway.

WATER SAFETY: SNORKELING 101
Here's a scary question. Which is safer – snorkeling in a peaceful bay on the surface, or diving with air tanks to depths of 40ft or more? Believe it or not, far more snorkelers drown in Hawaiian waters than do scuba divers. A scuba diver in distress is usually apparent, and help is at hand, generally the dive group leader. Snorkelers, however, are a solitary lot. When floating in a face-down position, even the smallest wave can flood the breathing tube of a snorkeling mask. Fins can make it difficult to get upright quickly, especially if the snorkeler has started to panic. What to do? Snorkel with a partner and check on each other frequently.

Getting There & Away
Hanauma Bay is about 10 miles from Waikiki along Kalanianaole Hwy (72). The parking lot sometimes fills up by midmorning, so the earlier you get there the better. If the lot is full, you could park at Koko Marina Shopping Center and walk uphill to the entrance.

Bus Nos 22 and 58 both go to Hanauma Bay (No 58 goes on to Sea Life Park). However, No 22 is slightly preferable, as it stops at the entrance to Hanauma Bay; No 58 lets you off about a quarter of a mile below the entrance.

Buses travel to Hanauma Bay from Kuhio Ave in Waikiki from 8:15am to 3:55pm. The last bus returning from Hanauma Bay departs at 5:40pm bound for Waikiki, and at 5:55pm on Saturday and Sunday.

KOKO HEAD REGIONAL PARK
The entire Koko Head area is a county regional park, and includes Hanauma Bay, Koko Head, Halona Blowhole, Sandy Beach and Koko Crater. Koko Crater and Koko Head are both tuff cones created about 10,000 years ago in O'ahu's last gasp of volcanic activity. Koko Head is backed by Hawai'i Kai, an expansive development of condos, houses, shopping centers, a marina and Hawai'i Kai Golf Course (p143) – basically, it's a suburban scene with great weather.

Sights & Activities
KOKO HEAD
Not to be confused with Koko Crater, Koko Head overlooks and forms the southwest side of Hanauma Bay. There are two craters atop Koko Head, as well as radar facilities on the 642ft summit. The mile-long summit road is closed to casual visitors. The Nature Conservancy maintains a preserve inside the shallow 'Ihi'ihilauakea Crater, the larger of the two craters. The crater has a unique vernal pool and a rare fern, the Marsilea villosa. The site can only be visited with a guide. For information on work parties and weekend excursions to the preserve, call **The Nature Conservancy** (TNC; ☎ 537-4508) in Honolulu.

HALONA BLOWHOLE AREA
Here the water surges through a submerged tunnel in the rock and spouts up through a hole in the ledge. It's preceded by a gushing sound, created by the air that's being forced out by the rushing water. The action depends on water conditions – sometimes it's barely discernible, while at other times it's a showstopper. The blowhole is 1.75 miles past Hanauma Bay; on the way, a lookout offers striking views of coastal rock formations and crashing surf. Down to the right of the parking lot is Halona Cove,

LEE FOSTER

Fish for sale at one of Honolulu's bustling markets (p105)

ANN CECIL

Green bananas, papayas, plumeria and ukulele

ANN CECIL

Indigo restaurant (p107) in the heart of Chinatown, Honolulu

Pounding poi – a sticky paste made from steamed taro (p63)

ANN CECIL

Young hula dancers from Halau Hula 'O Hokulani (p42)

ANN CECIL

ANN CE

Wooden *ki'i* stand guard at Pu'uhonua o Honaunau National Historical Park (p209), the Big Island

Hawaiian woven bowls (p43) for sale

CLINT LUC

the little beach where the classic risqué love scene with Burt Lancaster and Deborah Kerr in *From Here to Eternity* was filmed in the 1950s. A small stone monument atop Halona Point was erected by Japanese fishers to honor those lost at sea.

SANDY BEACH

Sandy Beach is one of the most dangerous beaches on the island, if measured in terms of lifeguard rescues and broken necks. It has a punishing shorebreak, a powerful backwash and strong rip currents.

Needless to say, it's extremely popular with bodysurfers who know their stuff. It's equally popular with spectators, who gather to watch the bodysurfers being tossed around in the transparent waves.

Sandy Beach is wide, very long and, yes, sandy. It's frequented by sunbathers, young surfers and admirers of both. When the swells are big, board surfers hit the left side of the beach.

Red flags flown on the beach indicate hazardous water conditions. Even if you don't notice the flags, always check with the lifeguards before entering the water.

Not all the action is in the water. The grassy strip on the inland side of the parking lot is used by people looking skyward for their thrills – it's both a hang-glider landing site and a popular locale for flying kites.

The park has restrooms and showers. Bus No 22 from Waikiki stops in front of the beach. On weekends, you can usually find a food wagon in the parking lot, selling plate lunches and drinks.

KOKO CRATER

According to Hawaiian legend, Koko Crater is the imprint left by the vagina of Pele's sister Kapo, which was sent here from the Big Island to lure the pig-god Kamapua'a away from Pele. Inside the crater, the city and county of Honolulu maintains a simple dryland **botanical garden** (☎ 522-7060; admission free; ✹ 9am-4pm) with plumeria trees, oleander and cacti, which are maintained by the county.

To get there, take Kealahou St off Kalanianaole Hwy (72) opposite the northern end of Sandy Beach. Just over half a mile in, turn left onto the one-lane road to Koko Crater Stables and continue 0.3 miles to the garden.

Eating

Kona Brewing Company (☎ 394-5662; 7192 Kalanianaole Hwy; snacks $5-8, dinner $11-15, pizza $12-22; ✹ 11am-11pm) This hip eatery is known for its good brews, like Longboard Lager and Castaway IPA. There's plenty to eat with your beer, from 'ahi appetizers to fresh fish dinners and wood-fired pizzas.

Roy's (☎ 396-7697; 6600 Kalanianaole Hwy; appetizers $8-13, mains $16-38; ✹ 5:30-9:30pm Sun-Thu, 5-10pm Fri & Sat) The best upmarket option in Southeast O'ahu. Chef Roy Yamaguchi is a prominent force behind the popularity of Hawaiian regional cuisine, which emphasizes fresh local ingredients and blends European, Asian and Polynesian flavors. A superb main dish is the cilantro pesto tiger shrimp, seared and blackened, and served with somen noodles and *lomilomi* tomato. For dessert, the chocolate soufflé is a decadent treat. Reservations are recommended; request a sunset view.

The Greek Marina (☎ 396-8441; 7192 Kalanianaole Hwy; dishes $6-12; ✹ 11am-9pm) *Mezedes* (appetizers), gyros, feta salad, souvlaki and *marides* (small fried fish) are among the offerings at this snappy café.

Koko Marina Shopping Center (cnr Lunalilo Home Rd & Kalanianaole Hwy) In Hawai'i Kai, this shopping center is home to more than a dozen eateries, ranging from fast food to waterfront dining.

Two other shopping centers help maintain Hawai'i Kai's suburban pulse, the Hawai'i Kai Town Center and the Kawaii Kai Shopping Center.

MAKAPU'U POINT

About 1.3 miles north of Sandy Beach, the 647ft Makapu'u Point and its coastal **lighthouse** mark the easternmost point of O'ahu. The gate to the mile-long service road is locked to keep out private vehicles, but hikers can park off the highway just beyond and walk in. Although not difficult, it's an uphill walk, and conditions can be hot and windy. The path and the lighthouse lookout give fine coastal views and, during winter, whales are sometimes visible offshore.

About a third of a mile further along the highway, a scenic **roadside lookout** has a view down onto Makapu'u Beach, its aqua-blue waters bounded by white sand and black lava – an even more spectacular sight when hang-gliders take off from the cliffs, O'ahu's top hang-gliding spot.

From the lookout you can see two off-shore islands, the larger of which is **Manana Island**, also known as Rabbit Island. This aging volcanic crater is populated by edge-tailed shearwaters, coexisting so closely that birds and rabbits sometimes share the same burrows. The island looks vaguely like the head of a rabbit, ears folded back. You could also try to imagine it as a whale.

In front of it is the smaller, flat **Kaohikaipu Island**. There's a coral reef between the two islands that divers sometimes explore, but to do so requires a boat.

MAKAPU'U BEACH PARK

Makapu'u Beach is one of the island's top winter bodysurfing spots, with waves reaching 12ft and higher. It also has the island's best shorebreak. As with Sandy Beach, Makapu'u is strictly the domain of experienced bodysurfers who can handle rough water and dangerous currents. Surfboards are prohibited. In summer the waters can be calm and good for swimming.

The beach is opposite Sea Life Park in a pretty setting, with cliffs in the background and a glimpse of the lighthouse. Two native Hawaiian plants are plentiful – *naupaka* by the beach and yellow-orange *ilima* by the parking lot.

SEA LIFE PARK

At Hawaii's only **marine park** (☎ 259-7933; 41-202 Kalanianaole Hwy; admission adult/child under 4/child 4-12 yrs \$26/free/13; ☯ 9:30am-5pm), the highlight is an enormous 300,000-gallon aquarium filled with sea turtles, eels, eagle rays, hammerhead sharks and thousands of colorful reef fish. A spiral ramp circles the 18ft-deep aquarium, allowing you to view the fish from different depths.

Along with several interactive displays, the usual theme-park entertainment presides, with shows featuring Atlantic bottlenose dolphins giving choreographed perform-ances at 12:30pm daily. The dolphins do the hula and give rides to a 'beautiful island maiden' – it all borders on kitsch.

The park has a large pool of California sea lions and a smaller pool with rare Hawaiian monk seals, including a few pups rescued from the wild; once they reach maturity, they're released back into their natural habi-tat. The park also has a penguin habitat, a turtle lagoon with green sea turtles, and

a seabird sanctuary that holds red-footed boobies, albatrosses and great frigate birds.

You can visit the park's cafeteria and gift shop without paying admission, and from there you can also get a free glimpse of the seal and sea lion pools. Though a parking fee (\$3) is charged in the main lot, if you continue past the ticket booth to the area marked 'additional parking', there's no fee. Bus Nos 22 (Beach Bus), 57 (Kailua/Sea Life Park) and 58 (Hawai'i Kai/Sea Life Park) all stop at the park.

WAIMANALO

Waimanalo Bay has the longest continu-ous stretch of beach on O'ahu: 5.5 miles of white sand that stretches from Makapu'u Point to Wailea Point. A long coral reef breaks about a mile offshore breaks up the biggest waves, protecting much of the shore.

Waimanalo has three beach parks, all with camping facilities. The setting is scenic, al-though the area isn't highly regarded for safety.

Sights
WAIMANALO BEACH PARK
Waimanalo Beach Park has an attractive beach of soft white sand and the water is excellent for swimming. This is an in-town county park with a grassy picnic area, restrooms, changing rooms, showers, ball fields, basketball and volleyball courts, and a playground. The park has ironwood trees, but overall it's more open than the other two parks to the north. The scalloped hills of the lower Ko'olau Range rise up on the inland side of the park, and Manana Is-land and Makapu'u Point are visible to the south. Camping is allowed in an open area near the road. (For information on obtain-ing camping permits, see p75.) Bus No 57 stops at the park entrance.

WAIMANALO BAY BEACH PARK
This county park, about a mile north of Waimanalo Beach Park, has Waimanalo Bay's biggest waves, and is very popular with board surfers and bodysurfers. The park itself is quite appealing, with beachside campsites shaded with ironwood trees. (For information on obtaining permits, see p75.) There's a lifeguard station, barbecue grills, drinking water, showers and restrooms. Bus No 57 stops on the main road in front of the

park, which has something of a reputation for car break-ins and rip-offs – keep an eye on your belongings.

BELLOWS FIELD BEACH PARK
The **beach** (☺ noon Fri-8am Mon) fronting Bellows Air Force Base is open to civilian beachgoers and campers on weekends only. This long beach has fine sand and a natural setting backed by ironwood trees. The small shorebreak waves are good for beginner bodysurfers and board surfers. There's a lifeguard, showers, restrooms and drinking water; the 50 campsites are set out among the trees. Although it's military property, camping permits are issued through the county Department of Parks and Recreation. See p78 for obtaining permits.

The marked entrance is a quarter of a mile north of Waimanalo Bay Beach Park. Bus No 57 stops in front of the entrance road, and from there it's 1.5 miles to the beach.

Activities

DIVING
Many O'ahu dive shops operate along the south shore. One local company, **Aloha Dive Shop** (☎ 395-5922; www.alohadiveshop.com; No1 Marina Bldg, 377 Keahole St, Hawai'i Kai; 2-tank dives $100) leads dives around Moana Lua Bay. It's catamaran takes up to 15 divers. Two-tank dives cost $100 and run from 8:30am to 1:30pm.

HIKING
The safe, usually dry and relatively easy **Kuli'ou'ou Ridge Trail** offers 360-degree views of Honolulu and the Windward Coast. Along this 5.4-mile trail, you can ramble along forest switchbacks before making a short but stiff climb to the windy summit of the Ko'olau Range for great ocean views. To reach the trail, take bus No 1 (Hawai'i Kai) to Kuli'ou'ou Rd, from where it's a one-mile walk inland to the trailhead.

Closer to Waikiki, and above Diamond Head and the Kahala area, the **Wa'ahila Ridge Trail** offers a cool retreat amid Norfolk pines, native plants, and ridge views to Waikiki, Manoa Valley and adjacent Palolo Valley. The 4.8-mile trail covers a variety of terrain in a short time, making for an enjoyable afternoon stroll. The trail begins at the back of St Louis Heights subdivision, east of Manoa Valley. Take the No 14 bus to Peter Place, and walk about 15 minutes to the trailhead.

Just outside Waimanalo, you'll find the start of the very popular **Maunawili Falls & Demonstration Trail**. This 10-mile hike gently contours around a series of *pali* lookouts with views down to the Windward Coast.

Although most hikers refer to the entire route as simply the Maunawili Trail, the trail is actually composed of several sections. From the west trailhead (near Pali Hwy) to the east trailhead (near Waimanalo town), the sections are the Maunawili Falls Connector Trail, the Maunawili Falls Trail, the Maunawili Demonstration Trail and the Maunawili Ditch Trail. The best views are between the Connector Trail and the Ditch Trail. Most hikers begin at either trailhead, hike as far as they want, then turn around.

To reach the trail from the Waimanalo side, by car or bus No 57, go to Waimanalo town center along the Kalanianaole Hwy (72). Turn inland onto Kumuhau St, then turn right onto Waikupanaha Rd. About a quarter mile along this road, look for a break in the fence at a gravel pull-out and the familiar Na Ala Hele trailhead sign.

To reach the trail from the Pali Hwy (61) side by car, look for a hairpin turn just after the tunnels, and a parking area marked 'scenic lookout', where the trailhead begins. Via the No 57 bus, get off at Maunawili Rd, near Castle Medical Center. From there, follow Maunawili Rd about 1.8 miles to the trailhead.

GOLF
Hawai'i Kai Golf Course (☎ 395-2358; 8902 Kalanianaole Hwy, Hawai'i Kai; executive course green fees $37-42, championship course green fees $60-100) also features two nine-hole courses: the 2323yd Robert Trent Jones Sr–designed executive course, and a 6614yd championship course. It also offers a driving range and restaurant.

Olomana Golf Links (☎ 259-7926; 41-1801 Kalanianaole Hwy, Waimanalo; green fees $80-125) offers two distinctive, challenging nine-hole courses. Facilities include a clubhouse, snack bar, restaurant and pro shop.

Sleeping & Eating
For information on camping in the beach parks in this area, see p142.

Keneke's (lunch $5) is a local eatery just north of Waimanalo Beach Park, on Kalanianaole Hwy (72) near the post office.

O'AHU

There are food marts and fast-food eateries just south of Waimanalo Bay Beach Park and in a shopping cluster about a mile north of Bellows Field.

Nearby Kailua (p149) has more to offer hungry travelers.

PALI HIGHWAY

The Pali Hwy (61) runs between Honolulu and Kailua, cutting through the lush, spectacular Ko'olau Range. It's a very scenic little highway, and if it has been raining heavily every fold and crevice in the mountains will have a lacy waterfall streaming down its face. Past the four-mile marker, look up and to the right to see two notches cut about 15ft deep into the crest of the *pali*. These notches are thought to have been dug as cannon emplacements by Kamehameha I.

The original route between Honolulu and windward O'ahu was via an ancient footpath that wound its way perilously over these cliffs. In 1845, the path was widened into a horse trail and, later again, into a cobblestone road that would allow carriage traffic to pass. In 1898, the **Old Pali Hwy** was built following the same route. It was abandoned in the 1950s after tunnels were blasted through the Ko'olau Range. The present multilane Pali Hwy was then opened.

You can still drive a loop of the Old Pali Hwy (Nu'uanu Pali Dr) and hike another mile of it from the Nu'uanu Pali Lookout.

Sights & Activities
QUEEN EMMA SUMMER PALACE

At the Pali Hwy's two-mile marker is this **summer palace** (☎ 595-3167; 2913 Pali Hwy; admission adult/child $5/1; ☺ 9am-4pm, closed holidays), the former residence of Queen Emma, consort of Kamehameha IV.

Emma was three-quarters royal Hawaiian and a quarter English. She was a granddaughter of the captured British sailor John Young, who became a friend and adviser to Kamehameha I. The house is also known as Hanaiakamalama, the name of John Young's home in Kawaihae on the Big Island, where he served as governor.

The Youngs left the luxurious home to Queen Emma, who often slipped away from her more formal downtown home to spend time at this retreat – a bit like an old Southern plantation house – columned porch, high ceilings and louvered windows catching the cool breeze.

Forgotten after Emma's death in 1885, the home was to be razed in 1915, because the estate was being turned into a public park. The Daughters of Hawaii, whose members are descendants of early missionaries, rescued it and now operate it as a museum.

The interior looks much as it did in Queen Emma's day – decorated with period furniture collected from five of her homes, including a koa cabinet displaying a set of china from Queen Victoria; Emma's

---

THE BATTLE OF NU'UANU

O'ahu was the final island conquered by Kamehameha the Great in his campaign to unite Hawaii under his rule. Prior to that, Kahekili, the aging king of Maui, seemed the most likely candidate to grasp control of the entire island chain, having already killed his stepson in order to take O'ahu. But when the king died in 1794, a family feud among his heirs broke out, creating a rift that Kamehameha quickly acted upon. In 1795 Kamehameha conquered Maui and Moloka'i, before crossing the channel to O'ahu. On the quiet beaches of Waikiki he landed his fleet of canoes to battle Kalanikupule, the new king of O'ahu.

Heavy fighting started around the Punchbowl, and continued up Nu'uanu Valley. But the O'ahu warriors were no match for Kamehameha's troops. Prepared for the usual spear-and-stone warfare, the defenders panicked when they realized Kamehameha had brought in a handful of Western sharpshooters, who picked off the O'ahu generals and blasted into their defenses. The defenders made their last stand at the narrow ledge along the current-day Nu'uanu Pali Lookout. Hundreds were driven over the top of the *pali* to their deaths. A hundred years later, during the construction of the Old Pali Hwy, more than 500 skulls were found at the base of the cliffs.

Some O'ahu warriors, including their king, escaped into the upland forests. But when Kalanikupule surfaced a few months later, he was sacrificed by Kamehameha to the war god, Ku. Kamehameha's taking of O'ahu marked the last battle ever fought between Hawaiian troops.

tiger-claw necklace, a gift from a maharaja of India; and feather cloaks and capes once worn by Hawaiian royalty.

To get here, take bus No 4 (Nu'uanu Dowsett Ave), which runs about every 15 minutes from Waikiki, or bus No 55, 56, or 57 from Ala Moana Center. Be sure to let the bus driver know where you're going, so you don't miss the stop.

NU'UANU PALI DRIVE

For a scenic side trip through a shady green forest, turn off the Pali Hwy onto Nu'uanu Pali Dr, half a mile past the Queen Emma Summer Palace. The two-mile road runs parallel to the Pali Hwy and then comes back out to it before the Nu'uanu Pali Lookout, so you don't miss anything by taking this side loop – in fact, quite the opposite is true.

The drive is through mature trees that form a canopy overhead, all draped with hanging vines and wound with philodendrons. The lush vegetation along Nu'uanu Pali Dr includes banyan trees with hanging aerial roots, tropical almond trees, bamboo groves, impatiens, angel trumpets and golden cup – a tall climbing vine with large golden flowers.

NU'UANU PALI LOOKOUT

Don't miss the Nu'uanu Pali Lookout with its broad view of the Windward Coast from a height of 1200ft. From the windy lookout you can see Kane'ohe straight ahead, Kailua to the right, and Mokoli'i Island (Chinaman's Hat) and the coastal fishpond ('Apu'u Fishpond) at Kualoa Park to the far left.

The abandoned Old Pali Hwy winds down from the right of the lookout, ending abruptly at a barrier near the current highway about a mile away. Few people realize the road is here, let alone venture down it. It makes a nice walk and takes about 20 minutes one way. There are good views looking back up at the jagged Ko'olau Range and out across the valley.

As you get back on the highway, it's easy to miss the sign leading you out of the parking lot, and instinct could send you in the wrong direction. As you drive out of the parking lot, go to the left if you're heading toward Kailua, to the right if heading toward Honolulu.

WINDWARD COAST

Windward O'ahu, the island's eastern side, follows the Ko'olau Range along its entire length. The mountains looming inland are lovely, with scalloped folds and deep valleys. In places, they come so near to the shore that they almost seem to crowd the highway into the ocean.

The Windward Coast runs from Kahuku Point in the north to Makapu'u Point in the south. The two main towns are Kane'ohe and Kailua, both bedroom communities for workers who commute to Honolulu, about 10 miles away. North of Kane'ohe, the Windward Coast is rural Hawaii, where many Hawaiians toil close to the earth, making a living with small papaya, banana and vegetable farms. The windward side of the island is generally wetter than other parts of the island, and the vegetation is lush and green.

Because the Windward Coast is exposed to the northeast trade winds, it's a popular area for anything that requires a sail – from windsurfing to yachting. There are attractive swimming beaches on the Windward Coast – notably Kailua, Kualoa and Malaekahana – although many other sections of the coast are too silted to be much good for swimming. Swimmers should keep a careful eye out for the stinging Portuguese man-of-wars that are sometimes washed in during storms.

Most of the offshore islets that you'll see along this coast have been set aside as bird sanctuaries. These tiny islands are vital habitat for ground-nesting seabirds, which have largely been driven off the populated islands by the introduction of mongooses, cats and other predators.

Three highways cut through the Ko'olau Range from central Honolulu to the Windward Coast. The Pali Hwy (61) goes straight into Kailua center. The Likelike Hwy (63) runs directly into Kane'ohe, and, although it doesn't have the scenic stops the Pali Hwy has, it is in some ways more dramatic. The newest route to the windward side is the H3 freeway, which begins near Pearl Harbor and cuts a scenic path through the mountains to Kailua.

If you're heading to/from windward O'ahu through the Ko'olau Range, take the

Pali Hwy (p144) up from Honolulu and the Likelike Hwy back for the best of both.

KAILUA
pop 38,000

Kailua is windward O'ahu's largest town. Although the inland section may appear to be little more than a pretty suburban community, Kailua's shoreline is graced with miles of lovely beach protected by a coral reef, a shaded beach park and a lagoon where outrigger canoe teams practice. Kailua has long been known as a windsurfing and kayaking mecca, and today it draws increasing numbers of kitesurfers, too. The town has a fine variety of restaurants, supported in part by a steady stream of Honolulu residents. The agreeable mix of locals and visitors makes it a refreshing alternative to Waikiki.

History

In ancient times Kailua (meaning 'two seas') was a place of legends and home to several Hawaiian chiefs and, allegedly, the island's first *menehune* (the 'little people' who built many of Hawaii's fishponds, heiaus and other stonework, according to legend). Kailua once served as a political and economic center for the region. Rich in stream-fed agricultural land, fertile fishing grounds and protected canoe landings, the area supported at least three temples, one of which, Ulupo Heiau (p147), you can still visit today.

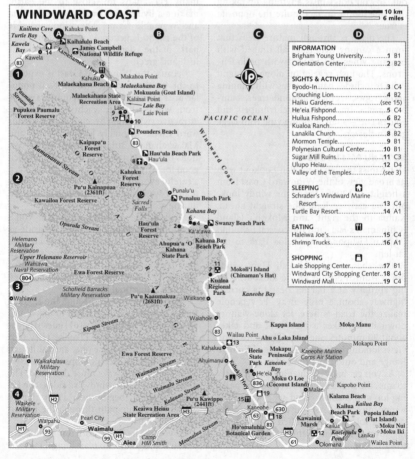

WINDWARD COAST

0 ————— 10 km
0 ————— 6 miles

INFORMATION
Brigham Young University.............1 B1
Orientation Center........................2 B2

SIGHTS & ACTIVITIES
Byodo-In......................................3 C4
Crouching Lion.............................4 B2
Haiku Gardens....................(see 15) C4
He'eia Fishpond...........................5 C4
Huilua Fishpond...........................6 B2
Kualoa Ranch................................7 C3
Lanakila Church............................8 B2
Mormon Temple...........................9 B1
Polynesian Cultural Center...........10 B1
Sugar Mill Ruins..........................11 C3
Ulupo Heiau................................12 D4
Valley of the Temples............(see 3)

SLEEPING
Schrader's Windward Marine
  Resort....................................13 C4
Turtle Bay Resort........................14 A1

EATING
Haleiwa Joe's..............................15 C4
Shrimp Trucks............................16 A1

SHOPPING
Laie Shopping Center...................17 B1
Windward City Shopping Center...18 C4
Windward Mall............................19 C4

Information

Bank of Hawaii (☎ 266-4600; 636 Kailua Rd) On the town's main road.

Bookends (☎ 261-1996; 590 Kailua Rd; ☽ 9am-8pm Mon-Sat, 9am-5pm Sun) Next to the Times Supermarket, selling books, maps and a few mainland newspapers.

Kailua Information Center & Chamber of Commerce (☎ 261-2727; www.kailuachamber.com; Suite 103, 600 Kailua Rd; ☽ 10am-4pm Mon-Fri) Located next to Lanikai Juice in the Kailua Shopping Center, the office has free maps, and information on accommodations and outdoor activities around Kailua.

Kailua Laundromat (cnr Aulike & Uluniu Sts; ☽ 6am-10pm)

Kailua Post Office (☎ 266-3996; 335 Hahani St) In the town center.

Kailua Public Library (☎ 266-1996; 239 Kuulei Rd; ☽ 10am-5pm Mon, Wed & Fri, 1-8pm Tue & Thu) A good place to find kids' books.

Morning Brew (☎ 262-7770; 572 Kailua Rd; per 30 min $3; ☽ 7am-8pm) Offers Internet access and wireless connections for laptops.

Sights & Activities

KAILUA BEACH PARK

Kailua Beach Park is a postcard-perfect stretch of white sand and ironwood trees at the southeastern end of Kailua Bay. The beach is long and broad with turquoise waters. It's popular for walking, family outings and a full range of water activities.

Kailua Beach has a gently sloping sandy bottom with generally calm waters. Swimming is good year-round, but be aware that the breeze propels sand as well as windsurfers. The park has restrooms, showers, lifeguards, snack shop, volleyball court and large grassy expanses shaded by ironwood trees.

Kaelepulu Canal divides the park into two sections, although a sandbar sometimes prevents the waters from emptying into the bay. Windsurfing activities center on the west side of the canal; there's a small boat ramp on the east side, toward the lighthouse. Just offshore at the bird sanctuary of **Popoi'a Island** (Flat Island), kayak landings are permitted.

Onshore trade winds provide windsurfers with year-round sailboarding. Around the bay, water conditions vary, some good for jumps and wave surfing, others for flat-water sailing. Three windsurfing companies, **Naish Hawaii** (☎ 262-6068, 800-767-6068; 155A Hamakua Dr), **Kailua Sailboards & Kayaks** (☎ 262-2555; 130 Kailua Rd) and **Hawaiian Watersports** (☎ 262-5483; 354 Hahani St), give lessons and rent boards at the

beach park Monday to Friday and on Saturday morning; on Sunday, however, they must bring the equipment to you from their nearby shops (due to city regulations).

Kalama Beach, just north, has the roughest shorebreak on the bay, and is popular with experienced boogie boarders. Surfers usually head for the northernmost end of Kailua Bay at Kapoho Point or further still to Zombies Break.

To get to Kailua Beach Park, take bus No 56 or 57 from Ala Moana Center in Honolulu and transfer to bus No 70 in Kailua. If you're driving, simply stay on Kailua Rd, which begins at the end of the Pali Hwy (61) and continues as the main road through town, ending at the beach park.

ULUPO HEIAU

The building of Ulupo Heiau, a sizable open-platform temple of stones piled 30ft high and 140ft long, is attributed to *menehune*, the little people who legends say created much of Hawaii's stonework, finishing each project in one night. Fittingly, Ulupo means 'night inspiration.' In front of the temple, thought to have been a *luakini* (place for human sacrifice), is an artist's rendition of the site as it probably looked in the 18th century. From the path across the top of the heiau, hikers get a view of **Kawainui Marsh**, one of Hawaii's largest habitats for endangered waterbirds. Legend says the edible mud of the ancient fishpond was home to a *mo'o* (lizard spirit).

Ulupo Heiau is a mile south of Kailua Rd, behind the YMCA. Coming up the Pali Hwy from Honolulu, take Uluoa St, the first left after passing the Hwy 72 junction. Turn right on Manu Aloha St and right again onto Manu O'o St.

LANIKAI BEACH

If you follow the coastal road as it continues east of Kailua Beach Park, you'll shortly (after 0.3 miles) come to Lanikai, an exclusive residential neighborhood, fronted by Lanikai Beach, one of the prettiest stretches of powdery white sand in Hawaii. The sandy bottom slopes gently, offering safe swimming conditions similar to those at Kailua. The twin **Mokulua Islands**, Moku Nui and Moku Iki, sit directly offshore.

From Kailua Beach Park, the road turns into the one-way Aalapapa Dr, which comes

O'AHU

back around as Mokulua Dr to make a 2.5-mile loop. There are 11 narrow beach access walkways off Mokulua Dr. For the best stretches of beach, start at the walkway opposite Kualima Dr. There is no public parking in Lanikai and street parking is scarce, so consider parking at Kailua Beach Park.

Sleeping

Kailua has no hotels, but there are many self-contained beachfront homes, cottages and private studios, along with B&B-style rooms in private homes. There is usually a three- to five-night minimum stay, and often a cleaning fee ($75 to $150).

In Kailua, B&Bs operate under antiquated local regulations, some dating back to the 1930s. As a result, there's often a pleasant tropical-underground feeling to them. For example, most cannot display signs and none are permitted to offer a hot breakfast; fresh bakery muffins and local fruit are the usual substitute. Most places also provide beach gear, barbeque facilities and the like. And most prefer ceiling fans and trade winds to air-conditioning.

RESERVATIONS

The **Kailua Information Center & Chamber of Commerce** (☎ 261-2727; www.kailuachamber.com; Suite 103, 600 Kailua Rd; ☉ 10-4pm Mon-Fri) is especially good for last-minute reservations. The **Kailua Bed & Breakfast Association** (www.stayoahu.com) monitors accommodation standards and guest satisfaction.

The vacation rental services that follow collectively book over 500 different Kailua-area accommodations (including their own), ranging from private beachfront homes to modest studio or one- and two-bedroom apartments in and around Kailua:

Affordable Paradise Bed & Breakfast (☎ 261-1693; www.affordable-paradise.com) Offers a good range of budget, mid-range and top-end places.

All Islands Bed & Breakfast (☎ 263-2342, 800-542-0344; www.all-islands.com; 823 Kainui Dr, Kailua, HI 96734) Collects your requirements and presents several matches, mostly budget and mid-range in price.

Pacific Islands Reservations (☎ 262-8133; www.oahu-hawaii-vacation.com; 571 Pauku St, Kailua, HI 96734) Lists both upscale beachfront homes and mid-range studios.

Although the majority of Kailua accommodations are booked by the vacation rental services listed above, the following places that we review can be booked directly with the owners, often at lower prices than those listed online.

MID-RANGE

Beachlane (☎ 262-8286; www.beachlane.com; 111 Hekili St; d $95-250) Just a minute's walk to the beach, this in-house B&B with shared bathroom and kitchen is all yours most of the time. Behind the main house, two studios and a separate cottage fill out the offerings. These rooms have a bathroom, kitchenette, queen-size beds, fans, cable TV and Internet connections. The owner speaks Danish, German, Norwegian, Swedish and English.

Tee's at Kailua (☎ 261-0771; www.teesinn.com; 771 Wanaao Rd; d $145-195; ☒) Located in a private home, this luxury place is a five-minute walk from the beach, and among the best of Kailua's home-style B&Bs. There are two rooms, each with queen-size beds and furnishings, bathroom and shared kitchen.

Linda's Tree Tops (☎ 262-8286; periwinkle@hawaii.rr.com; d $135) This attractive upstairs residential studio features a fully equipped kitchen that opens to a large wooden deck overlooking the Kaelepulu canal. You can walk to the beach in about five minutes, and also arrange for a kayak to be delivered.

Sheffield House (☎ 262-0721; rachel@sheffieldhouse.com; 131 Kuulei Rd; r $75-85) A five-minute walk to the beach, this kid-friendly home consists of two cozy rental units in the home of the Sheffield family. There's a guest room with a wheelchair-accessible bathroom, and a one-bedroom suite that has a queen-size bed and a separate sitting area. Each unit has a private entrance and bathroom, TV and small kitchenette. There's a three-day minimum stay; a basket of pastries, coffee and tea are provided on the first day.

Lanikai Plantations (☎ 561-1851; 1436 Aalapapa Dr; r $125, cottage $150; ☐) About 500ft from the beach in secluded and upscale Lanikai, this large plantation-style house has one private room that sleeps two, and one cottage that sleeps three. A well-equipped outdoor kitchen is available for cooking, and guests can freely use the house bicycles, kayaks, beach gear, and they can even check email. Families with kids sometimes rent both rooms.

Joe's Kailua Hale (☎ 384-4604; joe96734@aol.com; 2-bedroom house $220) You can hear the surf from this roomy house on a private lane half a block from Kailua Beach. The furnishings are basic, but clean and beach friendly. With two bathrooms, a king-sized bed, two doubles and a twin, you can sleep six comfortably, and not bump into each other in the large kitchen.

Kailua Tradewinds (☎ 262-1008; www.kailuaoahu hawaii.com/kt.htm; 391 Auwinala Rd; d $85; 😩) A side gate leads to two private studio units at the home of Jona Williams. Breakfast isn't provided, but each unit has a refrigerator, microwave and coffeemaker, as well as a king-size bed or two twin beds, TV and phone. Beach gear is available for guests. The minimum stay is three days.

Also recommended:

Hale Ihilani (☎ 261-6220; gnsapp@hawaii.rr.com; 174 Kaiholu St; d $195) A spacious and handsome two-room cottage near the beach that sleeps five comfortably, and offers a fully equipped kitchen.

Manu Mele Bed & Breakfast (☎ 262-0016; manu mele@pixi.com; 153 Kailuana Pl; d $80-90) An attractive contemporary home with private entrance, a few minutes' walk to the beach.

Papaya Paradise Bed & Breakfast (☎ 261-0316; www.kailuaoahuhawaii.com/papaya.htm; 395 Auwinala Rd; d $85) Similar to Kailua Tradewinds next door, and owned by the same family.

Paradise Palms Bed & Breakfast (☎ 254-4234; www.paradisepalmshawaii.com; 804 Mokapu Rd; r $75-85) Two private studios at the northwest end of Kailua, and near a grocery.

Eating
NEAR THE BEACH
Kalapawai Market & Deli (☎ 262-4359; 305 S Kalaheo Ave; snacks $2-6; 😊 6am-9pm) A local landmark,

this is the place to pick up coffee, bagels or made-to-order sandwiches with a choice of breads (turkey cranberry or veggie-avocado, $5). Early morning customers often toast their own bagels while helping themselves to fresh coffee (12oz cup for $1). There's also a broad selection of wine and beer.

Buzz's (☎ 261-4661; 413 Kawailoa Rd; lunch $8-12, complete dinners $14-32) Opposite Kailua Beach Park, the lunch menu at this local hangout includes fresh fish sandwiches, kiawe charcoal burgers with fries, and Caesar or Thai chicken salads. However, Buzz's is most popular as an evening steak and lobster house, along with rack of lamb and scampi; all dinners include a salad bar. Credit cards are not accepted.

TOWN CENTER
All of the following are in the town center.

Agnes Portuguese Bake Shop (☎ 262-5367; 46 Hoolai St; snacks $2-3; 😊 6am-6pm Tue-Sat, 6am-2pm Sun) This great bakery makes whole-grain breads, inexpensive pastries and tempting Portuguese malasadas. The malasadas, which are served hot, take about 10 minutes to fry up and cost 60¢ each. The shop also sells coffee, tea and Portuguese bean soup. It has half a dozen café tables where you can sit.

Lanikai Juice (☎ 262-2383; 572 Kailua Rd; snacks $2-4; 😊 6am-8pm Mon-Fri, 8am-7pm Sat & Sun) A great place for a full range of fresh fruit smoothies, it also offers freshly squeezed pineapple, orange and apple juice.

Cinammon's Restaurant (☎ 261-8724; 315 Uluniu St; breakfast $4-9, lunch $6-10; 😊 7am-2pm Sun-Wed, 7am-8:30pm Thu-Sat) Breakfast with a local touch

---

THE AUTHOR'S CHOICE

Lucy's Grill & Bar (☎ 230-8188; 33 Aulike St; appetizers $7-12, dinners $16-26; 😊 5-10pm) Nestled in windward Kailua at the end of the Pali Hwy, this contemporary bistro is one of the best dining and drinking options outside of Honolulu. The menu is classic Hawaiian-Euro-Asian eclectic, ranging from salt-crusted rib-eye steak to a spinach and carmelized onion pizza with *liliko'i* (passion fruit) puree. The food, from presentation to flavor, is upscale but the prices are on the moderate side. Appetizers such as lobster pot stickers ($10) and fresh fish tacos ($13) are a meal in themselves. Pricier and more generous fish mains range from pan-seared *'ahi* to a classic cioppino with saffron broth (both $24). There's a nightly early-bird special from 5pm to 6:30pm for $12 that includes Mongolian BBQ ribs, half a teriyaki chicken, a plate of crispy calamari and salad of greens and gorgonzola. Still hungry? Desserts range from a classic *creme brulee* to dark chocolate souffles. Along with a breezy outdoor patio, there's a full bar that overlooks the dining area and open kitchen. And if you like exotic bar drinks, check out local concoctions like the pineapple martini (with vodka-soaked fresh pineapple chunks) or Li Hing Mui (from a famous sweet and sour 'crackseed' candy) margarita.

is the attraction at this busy Kailua eatery, with eggs Benedict mahimahi ($9) and banana pancakes ($6) among the standouts.

Maui Tacos Kailua (☎ 261-4155; Suite 102, 539 Kailua Rd; dishes $3-6; ✆ 9am-9pm) This island-wide chain serves fresh fish tacos (soft or crispy, $3.75) and hearty burritos ($6), along with a help-yourself assortment of semi-spicy salsas.

Boston's North End Pizza (☎ 263-7757; 29 Hoolai St; pizza $12-18; ✆ 11am-8pm Mon-Fri, 11am-9pm Sat & Sun) In addition to whole pizzas, it offers huge slices, each equal to a quarter of a 19-inch pizza, for $3 to $4.75 depending on the toppings. The spinach and fresh garlic version is awesome.

Assaggio (☎ 261-2772; 354 Uluniu St; lunch $9-14, complete dinners $12-22; ✆ closed Sun & Mon) This restaurant serves very good Italian dishes in a somewhat upmarket setting. The menu is extensive, with more than 50 pasta, seafood, steak and chicken dishes, including chicken Assaggio, a tasty dish brimming with garlic ($14).

Brent's Restaurant & Deli (☎ 262-8588; 629A Kailua Rd; dishes $5-11; ✆ 7am-2pm) From lox and eggs ($11) to sandwiches like the Banker and Gone to Brooklyn ($10), this New York-style deli is the closest you'll get to Manhattan, plus the weather's better.

Champa Thai (☎ 263-8281; 306 Kuulei Rd; dishes $7-10) This small family-run eatery offers authentic versions of several Thai standards, including a knockout Penang curry, with coconut milk and shrimp, along with good noodle dishes and Thai salads.

Down To Earth (☎ 262-3838; 201 Hamakua Dr; ✆ 8am-10pm) This large natural food store has everything from organic produce to power bars, plus a hot veggie and vegan deli.

For supermarkets, try **Times** (☎ 266-4004; 590 Kailua Rd; ✆ 7am-10pm) or **Safeway** (☎ 266-5222; 200 Hamakua Dr; ✆ 24hr).

KANE'OHE

pop 35,000

Kane'ohe is windward O'ahu's second largest town. Kane'ohe Bay, which stretches from Mokapu Peninsula all the way to Kualoa Point, seven miles north of Kane'ohe, is the state's largest bay and reef-sheltered lagoon. Although inshore it's largely silted and not good for swimming, the near-constant trade winds that sweep across the bay are ideal for sailing.

Orientation

Two highways run north to south through Kane'ohe. Kamehameha Hwy (836) is closer to the coast and goes by He'eia State Park. The Kahekili Hwy, which is more inland, intersects the Likelike Hwy and continues on north past the Byodo-In temple. The highways merge into a single route, Kamehameha Hwy (83), a few miles north of Kane'ohe.

Kane'ohe Marine Corps Air Station occupies the whole of Mokapu Peninsula. The H3 Fwy terminates at its gate.

Sights & Activities

HO'OMALUHIA BOTANICAL GARDEN

The county's youngest and largest **botanical garden** (☎ 233-7323; 45-680 Luluku Rd; admission free; ✆ 9am-4pm), a 400-acre park in the uplands of Kane'ohe, is planted with trees and shrubs from the world's tropical regions, and was originally designed by the US Army Corps of Engineers as flood protection for the valley.

This peaceful natural preserve is networked by trails winding through the lush green park up to a 32-acre lake (no swimming). A small **visitor center** features displays on the park's history, flora and fauna, and Hawaiian ethnobotany. Guided two-hour nature hikes are offered at 10am Saturday and 1pm Sunday.

The park is at the end of Luluku Rd, 2.25 miles north of the Pali Hwy via the Kamehameha Hwy. Bus Nos 55 and 56 stop at the Windward City Shopping Center, opposite the start of Luluku Rd, from where the visitor center is a 1.5-mile walk uphill.

VALLEY OF THE TEMPLES & BYODO-IN

The **Valley of the Temples** (☎ 239-8811; adult/child $2/1; ✆ 8am-5pm) is an interdenominational cemetery in a stunning setting just off the Kahekili Hwy. For most visitors the main attraction is Byodo-In, the 'Temple of Equality.' Dedicated in 1968 to commemorate the 100th anniversary of Japanese immigration to Hawaii, Byodo-In is a replica of the 950-year-old temple in Kyoto, Japan. The temple's symmetry is a classic example of Japanese Heian architecture and garden design symbolizing the Pure Land of Mahayana Buddhism. The seated 9ft-tall tall Buddha in the main hall is positioned to catch the first rays of morning sunlight.

The reds of the elegant temple against the deep green of the Ko'olau Range is strikingly

O'AHU

picturesque, especially when mist settles over the *pali*. A three-ton brass bell beside the large pond is said to bring tranquility and good fortune to those who ring it. It's all very Japanese, right down to the gift shop selling imported sake cups, *daruma* (good luck) dolls and happy Buddhas. For a panoramic view of the valley, head up to the hilltop mausoleum with the cross.

There are no buses directly to Byodo-In, but bus No 55 can drop passengers off near the cemetery entrance on Kahekili Hwy, 1.5 miles north of Haiku Rd. From there, it's 0.75 miles to the temple.

HE'EIA STATE PARK
He'eia State Park on Kealohi Point, just off Kamehameha Hwy, has a good view of He'eia Fishpond on the right and He'eia-Kea Harbor on the left. The **fishpond**, an impressive survivor from the days when stone walled ponds of fish raised for royalty were common on Hawaiian shores, remains largely intact despite the invasive mangroves.

Coconut Island, just offshore to the southeast, was once a royal playground, named for the coconut trees planted there by Princess Bernice Pauahi Bishop. In the 1930s it was the estate of Christian Holmes, heir to the Fleischmann fortune, who dredged the island, doubling its size to 25 acres. During WWII it was also used as an R&R facility. In the 1960s the island was used in the filming of the popular *Gilligan's Island* TV series. Today the Hawaii Institute of Marine Biology of the University of Hawaii occupies part of the island.

Sleeping
Ho'omaluhia Botanical Garden (☎ 233-7323; 45-680 Luluku Rd) You're allowed to camp here between 9am on Friday and 4pm on Monday. With a resident caretaker and gates that close at night to noncampers, the park is one of the safest places to camp on O'ahu. Like other county campgrounds, there's no fee. You can get a permit in advance at any satellite city hall, or simply go to the park between 9am and 4pm daily to get one; be sure to call first to confirm that space is available. For more information on obtaining camping permits, see p78.

Alii Bluffs Windward Bed & Breakfast (☎ 235-1124, 800-235-1151; www.hawaiiscene.com/aliibluffs; 46-251 Ikiiki St; r $60-75; 🖾) Hospitality is the

attraction at this cozy home filled with Old World furnishings, oil paintings and collectibles. Scottish host Don Munro and his partner De, a retired New York fashion designer, give guests the run of the house, along with breakfast and afternoon tea. Each of the two available rooms have a bathroom. There's a view of Kane'ohe Bay, although it's a drive to the beach.

K-Bay Vacation Rental (☎ 285-1137; silverecp@aol.com; d $110) This upscale one-bedroom private studio overlooks Kane'ohe Bay, and is a five-minute walk to the Kane'ohe Bay Yacht Club. It has a kitchenette, and sleeps two to four people, with two twin beds, a sofa bed, and two futons. As with most Windward Coast rentals, there is no air-conditioning, but the ceiling fans and trade winds are all you need.

Eating
BUDGET
Chao Phya Thai Restaurant (☎ 235-3555; Windward Coast Shopping Center, 45-480 Kane'ohe Bay Dr; dishes $6-10; 🕓 11am-2pm Mon-Sat, 5-9pm daily) This family-run eatery serves very decent northeastern Thai food, including green papaya salad and sticky rice, along with Thai standards like pad Thai (stir-fried rice noodles) and curries. No liquor, but you can BYO.

Zia's Caffe (☎ 235-9427; 45-620 Kamehameha Hwy; dishes $7-12; 🕓 11am-10pm Mon-Fri, 4-10pm Sat & Sun) Opposite Windward City Shopping Mall, Zia's is popular with local families looking for good value and decent portions of Italian standards, like spaghetti and meatballs and shrimp scampi, along with mussels marinara, vegetable lasagna and Caesar salad. The place has an open feel and a kids' menu.

If you're looking for something convenient, the city's two main shopping centers – **Windward City Shopping Center** (45-480 Kane'ohe Bay Dr) and **Windward Mall** (46-056 Kamehameha Hwy) – have lots of inexpensive food options.

MID-RANGE
Hale'iwa Joe's (☎ 247-6671; 46-336 Haiku Rd; appetizers $5-10, lunch $7-12, complete dinners $14-28; 🕓 11:30am-10pm) The Haiku Gardens location is half the attraction here – a romantic, open-air setting overlooking a large lily pond tucked beneath the Ko'olau Range, and dating from the mid-1800s. The restaurant features excellent Pacific Rim fare, including ceviche ($5) and coconut shrimp tempura ($10),

O'AHU

along with hearty meat dishes and prime rib ($28). You can also drop by the gardens during the day, or just before sunset when it closes for a happy-hour (4:30 to 6:30pm) drink and a pre-dinner stroll. (See p162 for review of the original Hale'iwa Joe's.) To get there from Kamehameha Hwy, turn west on Haiku Rd just past Windward Mall; after crossing Kahekili Hwy, continue on Haiku Rd a quarter of a mile.

WAIAHOLE & WAIKANE

The area north of Kane'ohe has a sleepy, local feel to it, with some lovely beaches, interesting hiking opportunities and fine scenery. The Kamehameha Hwy, really just a modest two-lane road, runs the length of the entire coast, doubling as Main St for each of the small towns along the way. Waiahole and Waikane mark the beginning of rural O'ahu. The area is home to family-run orchid nurseries, and small coconut, banana, papaya and lemon farms.

Large tracts of Waikane Valley, just inland from the town of Waikane, were taken over by military training and target practice during WWII, that continued until the 1960s. The government now claims the land has so much live ordnance that it can't be returned to the families it was leased from. This is a source of ongoing contention with local residents, who are upset that much of the inner valley remains off-limits.

KUALOA
Sights & Activities
KUALOA REGIONAL PARK

This 153-acre county park on Kualoa Point is bounded on its southwestern side by Moli'i Fishpond, visible through the trees as a distinct green line in the bay. The park is largely open lawn with a few palm trees shading a long, thin strip of beach with safe swimming. Pali-ku (Vertical Cliffs) – the mountains looming precipitously across the road – look like a scene from a classic Chinese watercolor when the mist settles.

According to Hawaiian legend, the main offshore island, **Mokoli'i**, is the tail of a nasty lizard slain by a god and thrown into the ocean. Following the immigration of Chinese laborers to Hawaii, this conical-shaped island also came to be called Papale Pake (Chinaman's Hat).

Apua Pond, a three-acre brackish salt marsh on the point, is a nesting area for the endangered *aeo* bird (Hawaiian stilt). Beyond the park, you'll see a bit of **Moli'i Fishpond**, where the rock walls are covered with mangrove, *milo* (a native shade tree) and pickleweed. There are picnic tables, restrooms, showers and a lifeguard. Camping is allowed from Friday through Tuesday, with a county permit. See p78 for information on obtaining permits.

KUALOA RANCH

The horses grazing on the green slopes across the road from Kualoa Regional Park belong to **Kualoa Ranch & Activity Club** (☎ 237-8515; 49-560 Kamehameha Hwy, Kualoa). The ranch offers all sorts of activities, from horseback riding (one- and two-hour trail rides along the foot of the Ko'olau Range for $47 to $87) and target practice, to All Terrain Vehicle (ATV) rides and a one-hour 'ranch and movie set tour'. Part of the scenic ranch property was used as a backdrop for the movies *Jurassic Park* and *George of the Jungle*.

Back in 1850 Kamehameha III leased about 625 acres of this land for $1300 to Dr Judd, a missionary doctor who became one of the king's advisers. Judd planted the land with sugarcane, built flumes to transport it and imported Chinese laborers to work the fields. You can still see the remains of the mill's stone stack and a bit of the crumbling walls, half a mile north of the beach park alongside the road.

KA'A'AWA

In the Ka'a'awa area, the road hugs the coast and the *pali* moves right on in, with barely enough space to squeeze a few houses between the base of the cliffs and the road.

SACRED GROUND

In ancient times, Kualoa was one of the most sacred places on O'ahu. When a chief stood on the point, passing canoes lowered their sails in respect. The children of chiefs were brought here to be raised, and it may also have been a place of refuge where *kapu* (taboo) breakers and escaped warriors could seek reprieve from the law. Because of its rich significance to Hawaiians, Kualoa Regional Park is listed in the National Register of Historic Places.

Swanzy Beach Park, a narrow neighborhood beach used mainly by fishers, is fronted by a shore wall. Across the road from the park is a convenience store, a gas station and a hole-in-the-wall post office – pretty much the center of town, such as it is.

CROUCHING LION

The Crouching Lion is a rock formation at the back of the restaurant of the same name, which comes up just north of the 27-mile marker.

The legend goes, the rock is a demigod from Tahiti who was cemented to the mountain during a jealous struggle between the volcano goddess Pele and her sister Hiiaka. When he tried to free himself by crouching, he was turned to stone. To find him, stand at the Crouching Lion Inn sign with your back to the ocean and look straight up to the left of the coconut tree and the cliff above.

Crouching Lion Inn (☎ 237-8511; 51-666 Kamehameha Hwy; lunch $5-12, dinner $15-33; ☽ 11am-9pm) is a swank seaside eatery popular for its sunset views from the terrace bar, and the early-bird dinner specials (five to seven) for just $11. Expect decent versions of standard steak and seafood dishes. The views to the ocean are great, but be prepared for a tour bus in the picture.

KAHANA VALLEY

In old Hawaii the islands were divided into *ahupua'a* – pie-shaped land divisions reaching from the mountains to the sea – providing everything the Hawaiians needed for subsistence. Kahana Valley is the only publicly owned *ahupua'a* in Hawaii.

Before Westerners arrived, Kahana Valley was planted with wetland taro. Archaeologists have identified the remnants of more than 130 agricultural terraces and irrigation canals, as well as the remains of a heiau, fishing shrines and numerous house sites.

In the early 20th century the area was planted with sugarcane, which was hauled north to the Kahuku Mill via a small railroad. During WWII the upper part of Kahana Valley was taken over by the military and used for training soldiers in jungle warfare. In 1965 the state bought Kahana Valley from the Robinson family of Kaua'i (owners of the island of Ni'ihau) in order to preserve it from development, and today it is home to about 30 Hawaiian families.

Sights & Activities
AHUPUA'A 'O KAHANA STATE PARK
The signposted entrance to Ahupua'a 'O Kahana State Park (formerly Kahana Valley State Park) is one mile beyond the Crouching Lion Inn, between Kane'ohe and Lai'e. Kahana is a relatively unspoiled valley. The park's most impressive site, **Huilua Fishpond** on Kahana Bay, is visible from the main road.

You can walk through the valley on either of two hiking trails. The **orientation center** (☎ 237-7766; ☽ 7:30am-4pm Mon-Fri) provides a map and has the latest information on trail conditions, which tend to be poor. Kahana is one of the wettest valleys on O'ahu; the trails can be slippery whether it's raining or not, and heavily overgrown anytime.

The most accessible of the park trails, 1.25-mile **Kapa'ele'ele Ko'a and Keaniani Lookout Trail**, begins at the orientation center, and continues along the old railroad route, past the Kapa'ele'ele Ko'a fishing shrine to Keaniani Kilo, a lookout that was used in ancient times for spotting schools of fish. The longer **Nakoa Trail**, named for the koa trees found along the 2.5-mile loop through a tropical rain forest, crosses the Kahana Stream twice, passing a swimming hole.

Sleeping
There are 10 beachside campsites at the park, but they're primarily used by island families. Camping is allowed with a permit from the state. For information on obtaining permits, see p75.

PUNALU'U
This inconspicuous seaside community doesn't draw much attention from tourists. Nonetheless, it has a couple of low-key places to stay and a decent beach.

Punalu'u Beach Park has a long, narrow beach offering fairly good swimming, with an offshore reef that protects the shallow inshore waters in all but stormy weather. Be cautious near the mouth of the Waiono Stream and in the channel leading out from it, as currents are strong when the stream is flowing quickly or when the surf is high.

Sleeping & Eating
Punalu'u Guesthouse (☎ 946-0591; 53-504 Kamehameha Hwy; dm per person with shared bathroom $25) Located in the center of Punalu'u, this three-room home is managed by the excellent

Hostelling International Honolulu, which pre-screens potential guests. As a result, people mostly come here after staying in either the Waikiki or Manoa Valley HI hostel. There's a communal kitchen, and guests often get together at dinnertime.

Pat's at Punalu'u (53-567 Kamehameha Hwy) This 136-unit condominium is largely residential and a bit neglected, but on the plus side, it's on the water with the rooms facing the ocean. There's no front desk, instead privately owned rentals are handled by realtors, some of whom post their listings on the condo bulletin board.

Paul Comeau Condo Rentals (☎ 293-2624, 800-467-6215; PO Box 589, Ka'a'awa, HI 96730; studios $90, 1-bedroom/3-bedroom units $105/190, plus cleaning fee $50) Handles several units at Pat's at Punalu'u with a three-day minimum stay.

Punalu'u Restaurant (☎ 237-8474; 53-146 Kamehameha Hwy; meals $6-17; ⏰ 11am-9pm Mon-Sat, 11am-8pm Sun) To find Punalu'u's only restaurant look for the small green wooden building a third of a mile north of the 25-mile marker. There's a lot of aloha spirit here, plus a good selection of fresh fish (ono, mahimahi) and shrimp dishes, like scampi and shrimp tempura. Lunch offerings include burgers and fish sandwiches.

HAU'ULA

This small, coastal town sits against a scenic backdrop of hills and majestic Norfolk pines. Aside from a couple of gas pumps, a general store and a 7-Eleven store, the main landmark in town is the stone ruins of **Lanakila Church** (c 1853), perched on a hill next to the newer Hau'ula Congregational Church. Across the road is **Hau'ula Beach Park**, protected by a coral reef and generally safe, if unappealing, for swimming. Camping is allowed, though it's mostly local families that camp there. For information on obtaining camping permits, see p78.

The Division of Forestry & Wildlife maintains two trails – **Hau'ula Loop** and **Ma'akua Ridge** – in the forest reserve above Hau'ula. Both trails share the same access point and head into beautiful hills in the lower Ko'olau Range. The Hau'ula Loop, which clambers through Waipilopilo Gulch and onto a ridge over Kaipapa'u Valley, is not only better maintained but more rewarding, both for its views and the native flora along the way, including sweet-smelling guava, ohia trees

with feathery red blossoms, as well as thick groves of shaggy ironwood trees and towering Norfolk pines. The 2.5-mile hike is a popular path with locals and families, and usually takes between one and two hours. The signposted trailhead for both hikes is at a bend in Hau'ula Homestead Rd, about a quarter of a mile up from Kamehameha Hwy. Hau'ula Homestead Rd is in town, at the north end of Hau'ula Beach Park.

LAI'E

Lai'e is thought to have been the site of an ancient *pu'uhonua* (place of refuge) – a place where kapu breakers and fallen warriors could seek refuge. Today, Lai'e is the center of the Mormon community in Hawaii.

The first Mormon missionaries to Hawaii arrived in 1850. After an attempt to establish a Hawaiian 'City of Joseph' on the island of Lana'i (p387) failed amid a land scandal, the Mormons moved to Lai'e. In 1865 they purchased 6000 acres of land in the area and slowly expanded their influence.

In 1919 the Mormons constructed a **temple**, a smaller version of the one in Salt Lake City, at the foot of the Ko'olau Range. This stately temple, at the end of a wide promenade, appears like nothing else on the Windward Coast. Nearby is the Hawaii branch of Brigham Young University, with scholarship programs attracting students from islands throughout the Pacific.

Information

Bank of Hawaii (☎ 293-9238; Lai'e Shopping Center, 55-510 Kamehameha Hwy) Has a 24-hour ATM.
Lai'e Washerette (☎ 293-2821; Lai'e Shopping Center, 55-510 Kamehameha Hwy; ⏰ 6am-9pm Mon-Sat) Coin laundromat with an attendant on duty.
Post Office (☎ 293-0337; Lai'e Shopping Center, 55-510 Kamehameha Hwy; ⏰ 9am-3:30pm Mon-Fri, 9:30-11:30am Sat)

Sights & Activities

Although there's a visitors center at the temple where enthusiastic guides will tell you about Mormonism, tourists are not allowed to enter the temple itself.

POLYNESIAN CULTURAL CENTER

Belonging to the Mormon Church, the **Polynesian Cultural Center** (PCC; ☎ 293-3333, 800-367-7060; www.polynesia.com; 55-370 Kamehameha Hwy; admission adult/child 3-11 yrs $35/24, admission & evening show $49/33; admission, Ali'i Luau (buffet) & evening show $79-109/75; noon-9pm Mon-Sat) is a nonprofit organization covering 42 acres and drawing about 900,000 tourists a year, more than any other attraction on O'ahu, with the exception of the USS *Arizona* Memorial.

The park has seven theme villages representing Samoa, New Zealand, Fiji, Tahiti, Tonga, the Marquesas and Hawaii. The 'villages' contain authentic-looking huts and ceremonial houses, many elaborately built with twisted ropes and hand-carved posts. The huts hold weavings, tapa, feather work and other handicrafts. People of Polynesian descent dressed in native garb demonstrate poi pounding, coconut-frond weaving, dances and games. There's a replica of an old mission house and missionary chapel representative of those found throughout Polynesia in the mid-19th century.

Many of the people working here are Pacific Island students from nearby Brigham Young University, who pay their college expenses with jobs at PCC. The interpreters are amiable and you could easily spend a few hours wandering around chatting or trying to become familiar with a craft or two.

The basic admission also includes winding boat rides through the park, the Pageant of the Long Canoes, a sort of floating talent show at 2:30pm; an optional 45-minute tram tour of the Mormon temple grounds and BYU campus; and ocean-theme movies at the IMAX theater. Crowds of tourists are the norm here, and most visits usually fill the day and evening. If you want to stay for the Ali'i Luau (buffet), your best option is the all-inclusive package for $79/55.

BEACHES

The 1.5 miles of beach fronting the town of Lai'e between Malaekahana State Recreation Area and Lai'e Point are used by surfers, bodysurfers and windsurfers.

Pounders, half a mile south of the main entrance to PCC, is an excellent bodysurfing beach, but the shorebreak, as the name of the beach implies, can be brutal. Summer swimming is generally good, but watch out for a strong winter current. The area around the old landing is usually the calmest.

From **Lai'e Point** there's a good view of the mountains to the south and of tiny offshore islands. The islet to the left with the hole in it is **Kukuiho'olua**, otherwise known as Puka

Rock. To get to Lai'e Point, head seaward on Anemoku St, opposite the Lai'e Shopping Center, then turn right on Naupaka St and go straight to the end.

Sleeping & Eating

Laie Inn (293-9282, 800-526-4562; www.laieinn.com; 55-109 Laniloa St; d $95;) This unassuming two-story motel next to the Polynesian Cultural Center is nothing special from the outside, but all 49 rooms surround an attractive courtyard swimming pool, and each room has a lanai, cable TV and mini-refrigerator. Rates include a continental breakfast. Please note that the inn is scheduled to be remodeled and enlarged in 2006; it will will be closed during construction.

Hukilau Cafe (293-8616; 55-662 Wahinepe'e St; dishes $4-5; 7am-2pm Tue-Fri, 7-11:30am Sat) Follow the locals to this friendly hole-in-the-wall just off the highway for Hawaiian-sized breakfast and lunch offerings, like sweet bread french toast ($4), or roast pork, salad and rice ($5).

Laie Chop Suey (293-8022; 55-510 Kamehameha Hwy; dishes $5-8; 10am-8:45pm Mon-Sat) This small family eatery in the Lai'e Shopping Center serves decent portions of Chinese menu standards, including veggie and seafood dishes, along with local favorites, like pot roast pork.

The Lai'e Shopping Center also has a **Foodland supermarket** (293-4443), which does not sell alcohol, and fast-food chain eateries selling plate lunches and pizza.

MALAEKAHANA STATE RECREATION AREA

Malaekahana Beach is a beautiful strand that stretches between Makahoa Point to the north and Kalanai Point to the south. The long, narrow, sandy beach is backed by ironwoods. Swimming is generally good year-round, although there are occasionally strong currents in winter. This popular family beach is also good for many other water activities, including bodysurfing, board surfing and windsurfing. Kalanai Point, the main section of the state park, is less than a mile north of Lai'e, and has picnic tables, barbecue grills, camping, restrooms and showers.

Moku'auia (Goat Island), a state bird sanctuary just offshore, has a small sandy cove with good swimming and snorkeling. It's possible to wade over to the island – best when the tide is low and the water's calm. Be careful of the shallow coral (sharp) and sea urchins (sharper). When the water is deeper, you can also swim across to the island, but beware of a rip that's sometimes present off the windward end of the island. Be sure to ask the lifeguard about water conditions and whether it's advisable to cross.

Sleeping

Malaekahana has the best campgrounds on the Windward Coast, with two campsites to choose from. You can pitch a tent for free in the park's main Kalanai Point section if you have a state park permit (see p78).

You can rent a rustic cabin or camp without needing a permit in the Kahuku section (Makahoa Point) of the park, which has a separate entrance off Kamehameha Hwy, half a mile north of the main park entrance. **Friends of Malaekahana** (☎ 293-1736; www.alternative-hawaii.com/fom; tent site per person $5, 4-6 person yurts $40-60, 4-10 person cabins $66-80, 2-night minimum stay) maintains this end of the park. This well-managed location features 24-hour security and hot showers. Best of all, this is the only place on O'ahu that allows Wednesday and Thursday overnight camping. Reservations strongly recommended.

KAHUKU

Kahuku is a former sugar town with little wooden cane houses lining the road. The mill that once stood in the center of town belonged to the Kahuku Plantation, which produced sugar from 1890 until it closed in 1971. The operation was a relatively small concern, unable to keep up with the increasingly mechanized competition. When the mill shut down, Kahuku's economy skidded into a slump that still lingers today.

A post office, a bank, a local plate-lunch eatery, food mart and gas station occupy the area next to Kahuku's old sugar mill. In 2004 operations began to tear down the mill, with the exception of the signature smokestack.

Kahuku also has a **hospital** (☎ 293-9221; 56-156 Pualalea St).

Sights & Activities
JAMES CAMPBELL NATIONAL WILDLIFE REFUGE

Half a mile southeast of the Turtle Bay Resort turnoff, this **refuge** (☎ 637-6330; http://pacific islands.fws.gov) encompasses a rare freshwater wetlands that provides habitat for Hawaii's four endangered waterbirds – the Hawaiian coot, the Hawaiian stilt, the Hawaiian duck and the Hawaiian moor hen. During stilt nesting season, normally mid-February to October, the refuge is off-limits to all visitors. The rest of the year, it can only be visited on a 1½-hour guided tour, which is provided by refuge staff (at 4pm every Thursday, 9am on the first two Saturdays of the month and 3:30pm on the remaining Saturdays of the month from October 1 to February 15). Tours are free, but reservations are required and can be made by calling the refuge itself, or the Honolulu office of the **US Fish & Wildlife Service** (☎ 792-9540).

GOLF

Kahuku Golf Course (☎ 293-5842; 56-501 Kamehameha Hwy, Kahuku; green fees $21; ☽ 7am-5pm) has stunning coastal views that more than make up for the somewhat rough greens at this nine-hole public course. There's no shop or restaurant, but you can rent pull carts and golf clubs. Did we mention the wind?

Other golfing options are the challenging **Ko'olau Golf Course** (☎ 236-4653; 45-550 Kionaole Rd, Kane'ohe; green fees $80-125), rated as a top-100 US golf course, and **Pali Golf Course** (☎ 266-7612; 45-050 Kamehameha Hwy, Kane'ohe; green fees $42), one of O'ahu's several 18-hole municipal courses. Rental carts ($16) and clubs ($25) are available at Pali. The reservation system is the same for all municipal courses: call ☎ 296-2000 and key information into the recorded system.

Sleeping & Eating

For hotel, condominium and dining options at nearby Turtle Bay, see p168. Rental agencies for condominiums at Turtle Bay are located in Kahuku, however.

Giovanni's Shrimp Truck (☎ 293-1839; dishes $9-12; ☽ 11am-6pm) A truck-wagon that parks along the highway just south of the Kahuku Sugar Mill is the place to go if you like shrimp and garlic. Popular with locals and sightseers from Honolulu, Giovanni's sizzles up a tasty half-pound of shrimp scampi smothered in garlic and butter for $11. There's a covered picnic area where you can sit and eat.

Although Giovanni's may be the first shrimp wagon on the block, several spin-offs have popped up around the Sugar Mill, including **Kahuku Famous Shrimp** (☎ 455-1803; dishes $8-12; ☺ 10am-6pm), which offers a few more choices, like spicy squid, and a tasty shrimp and veggie stirfry.

CENTRAL O'AHU

Central O'ahu forms a saddle between the Wai'anae Range on the west and the Ko'olau Range on the east. Aside from a few historical areas and scenic vistas, most people just zoom up through central O'ahu on their way to the North Shore.

Three routes lead north from Honolulu to Wahiawa, the region's central town. The freeway, H2, is the fastest route, whereas Kunia Rd (750), the furthest west, is the most scenic. The least interesting of the options, Farrington Hwy (99), catches local traffic as it runs through Mililani, a nondescript residential community. From Wahiawa two routes, Kaukonahua Rd (803) and Kamehameha Hwy (99), lead through scenic pineapple country to the North Shore.

KUNIA ROAD (HIGHWAY 750)

Kunia Rd is a worthwhile detour, and only adds a few miles to the drive through central O'ahu. The first mile, after turning from H1, winds through creeping suburbia, soon followed by vast plantation lands. The route runs along the foothills of the Wai'anae Range and the countryside remains solidly agricultural all the way to Schofield Barracks Military Reservation, along the way passing the most scenic pineapple fields in Hawaii. There is little development – just red earth carpeted with long green strips of pineapples stretching to the edge of the mountains.

The little town of **Kunia**, in the midst of the pineapple fields, is home to the field workers employed by Del Monte. If you want to see what a current-day plantation village looks like, turn west off Hwy 750 onto Kunia Dr, which makes a 1.25-mile loop through the town.

A few miles further north, **Kolekole Pass** (elevation 1724ft) occupies the gap in the Wai'anae Range that Japanese fighter planes once flew through on December 7, 1941 just minutes before attacking Pearl Harbor. This flight scene was recreated here in 1970 for the shooting of the popular war film *Tora! Tora! Tora!*.

Kolekole Pass sits above Schofield Barracks Military Reservation. The pass can be visited providing the base isn't on military alert. Access to the pass is through Foote Gate at Schofield Barracks Military Reservation. The five-mile drive takes you past the barracks, a golf course and bayonet assault course to a parking lot, just opposite a large white cross. The five-minute walk to the top of the pass ends at a clearing with a view straight down to the Wai'anae Coast.

In Hawaiian mythology, the large, ribbed stone that sits atop the ridge here is said to be the embodiment of a woman named Kolekole who took the form of this stone in order to become the perpetual guardian of the pass.

WAHIAWA

Wahiawa, whose name means 'place of noise' in Hawaiian, is home to a botanical garden and an interesting historical area, but Wahiawa is best known as a military town. Tattoo parlors and pawn shops are the town's main refinements.

Sights & Activities

DOLE PINEAPPLE PAVILION

Halfway between Wahiawa and Hale'iwa on the North Shore, this touristy **complex** (☎ 621-8408; 64-1550 Kamehameha Hwy; ☺ 9am-6pm) in the heart of O'ahu's pineapple country consists of a bustling gift shop, well-tended bromeliad gardens and an expansive hibiscus hedge maze. Dole's processing plant sits across the street.

Miles of pineapple fields surround the complex. The gift shop sells pineapple juice, pineapple freezes, pineapple ice cream, pineapple pastries, pineapple key chains and even pineapples boxed up to take home.

The **bromeliad gardens** (admission adult/child $3.50/2.50) are lovely and make for a quiet detour. The Pavilion's most popular activity is a little **steam train** (admission adult/child $7.50/5.50; ☺ every 15 min 9am-5:45pm) that encircles the entire complex. If you feel like doing it all, go for the train/garden combo ticket, which costs $9/7 per adult/child.

If you like wandering in circles, or being embarrassed by your kids, take on the **'world's largest maze'** (admission adult/child $5/3), which covers nearly two acres and contains 1.7 miles of pathways, but truth be told, there's a certain monotony to it. Most people take 15 to 30 minutes to get through, or give up in boredom. The posted record is six minutes.

WAHIAWA BOTANICAL GARDEN

A mile east of the Kamehameha Hwy, the **botanical garden** (☎ 621-7321; 1396 California Ave; admission free; 🕑 9am-4pm) started out in the 1920s as a site for forestry experiments by the Hawaii Sugar Planters' Association. It's now a 27-acre county park with shady paths, grand old trees, a wooded ravine and mature exotics, such as cinnamon, chicle and allspice. Tree ferns, *loulu* palms and other Hawaiian natives are among the highlights.

ROYAL BIRTHSTONES

Just north of Wahiawa is the area known as **Kukaniloko**, which marks a group of royal birthstones where Hawaiian queens gave birth to generations of royalty. The stones date to the 12th century. Legend held that if a woman lay properly against the stones while giving birth, her child would be blessed by the gods, and indeed, many of O'ahu's great chiefs were born at this site.

These stones are one of only two documented birthstone sites in Hawaii (the other is on Kaua'i; p455). Many of the petroglyphs on the stones are of recent origin, but the eroded circular patterns are original.

To get to the site from town, go three-quarters of a mile north on Kamehameha Hwy from its intersection with California Ave. Turn left onto the red dirt road directly opposite Whitmore Ave. The stones, marked with a state monument sign, are a quarter of a mile down the road, through a pineapple field, among a stand of eucalyptus and coconut trees.

NORTH SHORE

If frenetic Waikiki is the popular image of O'ahu, the North Shore is the stuff of legend. In many ways, the North Shore is the very soul of the island, with its map-dot towns and dazzling beaches in summer, and its 30ft swells in winter. North Shore beaches like Banzai Pipeline (or Pipeline), Waimea and Sunset Beach attract top surfers from around the globe and show up in every surf movie since the 1960s, starting with Bruce Brown's 1964 classic, *Endless Summer*. But whatever the season, it's a world apart from bustling

Honolulu. Drivers cruise along, usually with one eye veering toward the sea. Along the Kamehameha Hwy, pebble-floored roadside diners and lunch wagons share the same sunset view as upscale eateries.

The earliest Polynesians to arrive on O'ahu were drawn to the North Shore not by the surf, but by the region's rich fishing grounds, cooling trade winds and moderate rain. The areas around Mokuleia, Hale'iwa and Waimea were once sizable Hawaiian settlements. By the early 1900s the O'ahu Railroad & Land Company had linked the North Shore with Honolulu, bringing in the first beachgoers from the city. Hotels and private beach houses sprang up for a time, but largely disappeared by the 1940s when the railroad pulled out. By the 1950s Waikiki surfers started taking on North Shore waves and big-time surf competitions followed a few years later.

Today surfing continues to light up the public imagination. Of course, some North Shore surf breaks are more famous than others, but with names like Avalanche, Hammer Heads, Pyramids, Fujis, Glass Doors, Log Cabins, Himalayas and Left-Overs, they're obviously not for neophytes.

From November to February, the giant waves roll in and quickly grab headlines in Honolulu, when the word spreads, 'Surf's up!' That's when half the population of the North Shore shows up to either take on the waves or stand awe-struck at a safe distance. To avoid the weekend traffic jams, head up to the North Shore on a weekday, when the other half of the population goes to Honolulu to make a living.

HALE'IWA

pop 2300

Hale'iwa, the gateway to the North Shore, is the main town catering to the day-trippers who make the circle-island trip. The folk are a multiethnic mix: families who have lived in Hale'iwa for generations and more recently arrived surfers, artists and New Agers.

Orientation

Most of Hale'iwa's shops are along Kamehameha Ave, the main street. Hale'iwa has a picturesque boat harbor bounded on both sides by beach parks, including Hale'iwa Ali'i Beach Park, known for the North Shore's safest year-round swimming conditions.

The Anahulu River, flowing out along the boat harbor, is spanned by the Rainbow Bridge. In 1832, John and Ursula Emerson, the first missionaries to come to the North Shore, built Hale'iwa, meaning house *(hale)* of the great frigate bird *(iwa)*, a grass house and missionary school on the riverbank which gave its name to the village.

Information

Coffee Gallery (☎ 637-5571; North Shore Marketplace, 66-250 Kamehameha Ave; per 10 min $1; 8am-8:30pm) Internet access also available at this café (p162).

First Hawaiian Bank (☎ 637-5034; 66-135 Kamehameha Ave) At the north side of Hale'iwa Shopping Plaza.

Hale'iwa Pharmacy (☎ 637-9393; 66-149 Kamehameha Hwy) In Hale'iwa Shopping Plaza.

Post Office (☎ 637-1711; 66-437 Kamehameha Ave) At the south side of town.

Sights
NORTH SHORE SURF & CULTURAL MUSEUM

You can get a sense of how integral surfing is to the town's character by visiting this funky **museum** (☎ 637-8888; North Shore Marketplace, 66-250 Kamehameha Ave; admission by donation; most afternoons), where the tone is marked by a key North Shore word, 'usually' – it's staffed by volunteers, so the hours are flexible. The volunteers are into surfing, of course, so when the surf's up expect the place to be closed up! There's a good collection of vintage surfboards, period photos

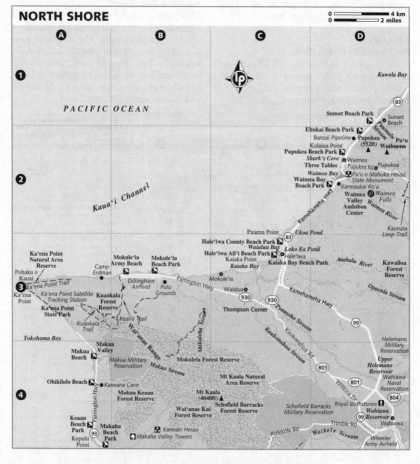

and classic surf posters, along with reasonably priced lost beach jewelry.

LILI'UOKALANI CHURCH

Lili'uokalani Church (☎ 637-9364; 66-090 Kamehameha Ave; ☺ most mornings) is a Protestant church named for Queen Lili'uokalani, who spent summers on Anahulu River and attended services here. Although the church dates from 1832, the current building was constructed in 1961. Services were held entirely in Hawaiian until the 1940s.

In 1892 Queen Lili'uokalani gave the church its seven-dial clock, which shows the hour, day, month and year, as well as the phases of the moon. The queen's 12-letter name replaces the numerals on the clock face. The church is open whenever the minister is in, usually mornings.

BEACHES

Hale'iwa Ali'i Beach Park

Surfing is king at Hale'iwa Ali'i Beach, an attractive park with a generous white-sand beach, and the site of several surfing tournaments in winter, when north swells bring waves as high as 20ft. When waves are 5ft and under, lots of younger kids bring their boards out. Waves 6ft or better bring strong currents, making conditions more suited to experienced surfers. (See Measuring Waves, Hawaiian Style, p161.)

The 20-acre beach park has restrooms, showers, picnic tables and a lifeguard tower. The shallow areas on the southern side of the beach are the calmest for swimming. The park's knotty-pine beachfront community building may look familiar as it served as the lifeguard headquarters in the TV series *Baywatch Hawaii,* which used this beach park as its main setting during filming in Hawaii from 1999 to 2001.

Hale'iwa Beach Park

This park is on the north side of Waialua Bay, where the beach is protected by shallow shoals and a breakwater. The waters are usually calm, though north swells occasionally ripple the bay. This 13-acre park has full beach facilities, as well as basketball and volleyball courts, an exercise area, a softball field and a good view of Ka'ena Point.

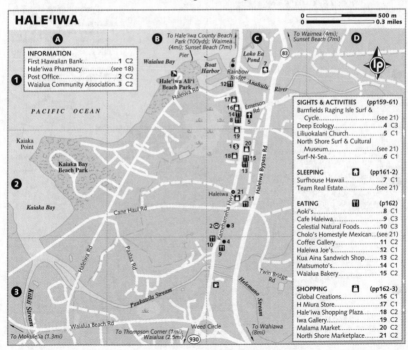

HALE'IWA

0 ___ 500 m
0 ___ 0.3 miles

INFORMATION
First Hawaiian Bank...................1 C2
Hale'iwa Pharmacy..............(see 18)
Post Office..................................2 C2
Waialua Community Association..3 C2

SIGHTS & ACTIVITIES (pp159-61)
Barnfields Raging Isle Surf &
  Cycle.................................(see 21)
Deep Ecology.............................4 C3
Liliuokalani Church....................5 C1
North Shore Surf & Cultural
  Museum............................(see 21)
Surf-N-Sea.................................6 C1

SLEEPING (pp161-2)
Surfhouse Hawaii.......................7 C1
Team Real Estate.................(see 21)

EATING (p162)
Aoki's...8 C1
Cafe Haleiwa..............................9 C3
Celestial Natural Foods.............10 C1
Cholo's Homestyle Mexican...(see 21)
Coffee Gallery...........................11 C2
Haleiwa Joe's............................12 C1
Kua Aina Sandwich Shop.........13 C2
Matsumoto's..............................14 C1
Waialua Bakery..........................15 C2

SHOPPING (pp162-3)
Global Creations.......................16 C1
H Miura Store............................17 C1
Hale'iwa Shopping Plaza..........18 C2
Iwa Gallery...............................19 C2
Malama Market..........................20 C2
North Shore Marketplace..........21 C2

Kaiaka Bay Beach Park

The 53-acre Kaiaka Bay Beach Park is on Kaiaka Bay, about a mile west of town. This is a good place for a picnic, as there are shady ironwood trees, but the in-town beaches are better for swimming. Two streams empty out into Kaiaka Bay, muddying up the beach after heavy rainstorms. Kaiaka has restrooms, picnic tables, showers, and campsites (p162) from Friday to Tuesday.

Activities

DIVING

At the southern end of Hale'iwa, **Deep Ecology** (☎ 637-7946, 800-578-3992; www.deepecology hawaii.com; 66-456 Kamehameha Hwy; 1-tank shore dive $65, 2-dive boat trip $119) offers a full range of scuba and beach gear. This small North Shore family operation is well regarded by local divers. Divers, experienced or novice, generally meet at the shop or at the site.

Like most dive shops, it offers both certified and non-certified (40ft limit) dives. A two-dive boat trip includes all equipment and lunch, with no more than six divers aboard. A simpler shore dive is offered, usually at Shark's Cove (Pupukea Beach Park; p164).

Surf-N-Sea (☎ 637-9887; www.surfnsea.com; 62-595 Kamehameha Ave; 1-tank dive $65; ☑ 9am-7pm), north of the Rainbow Bridge, rents surfboards, boogie boards, windsurfing equipment, diving gear and snorkel sets, and offers surfing and windsurfing lessons. It also has a good dive operation. The one-tank dives usually take place at nearby Shark's Cove.

CYCLING & MOUNTAIN BIKING

Bike riding on the North Shore ranges from paved bike paths next to the Kamehameha Hwy to challenging tracks above Waimea Bay and wider trails around Ka'ena Point (p172). For hire and trail conditions, head to **Barnfield's Raging Isle Surf & Cycle** (☎ 637-7707; www.ragingisle.com; 66-250 Kamehameha Hwy, North Shore Marketplace, 66-250 Kamehameha Ave; bike rental per day $40-60; ☑ 10am-6:30pm). Quality mountain bikes come complete with helmets, gloves and tool kits.

Sleeping

People occasionally rent out rooms in their homes. You can often find room-for-rent notices on the bulletin boards at Malama Market in Hale'iwa, or Foodland supermarket (p166) up the road in Pupukea.

BUDGET

Surfhouse Hawaii (☎ 637-7146; www.surfhouse.com; 62-203 Lokoea Pl; camp site $9.50-16, dm $15, semi-private bungalow s/d $41/47, private bungalow $52/57) This well-managed hide-away is a popular budget option, especially during the busy winter months. A backpacker's haven situated on two acres at the north side of Hale'iwa, it offers three options: eight tent sites in a shaded citrus grove, complete with starfruit, swaying palms and a few mosquitoes; a basic dormitory-style cabin with six beds; and two bungalows, each with their own little garden. All guests share a common kitchen area, and sometimes meals and surf stories as well. Some water-sports equipment is available

---

MEASURING WAVES, HAWAIIAN STYLE

Say you're in the water, when you turn around to notice, a bit late perhaps, a very large wave coming your way. Didn't you hear on the radio that the surf was going to be about 3ft to 4ft today? OK, so where did this massive seven-footer come from that is about to change your life? If it's any consolation, your question is the subject of a long-brewing debate that centers around two competing methods for measuring the height of an approaching wave.

Hawaiian surfers measure the height of the wave from the back; the rest of the world, including California to Australia, measures its height from the front, or face (officially, the distance from the trough in front of a wave to its peak). On average, the face height is nearly double the back height.

The difference is dramatic enough to have convinced the Honolulu office of the National Weather Service to lobby for adopting the international standard in reporting local wave conditions; they cite 60 ocean drownings during high-surf periods since 1980. Many surfers are bummed by the new standard, but lifeguards and rescue squads are relieved. They want people to have a realistic idea of what to expect when they hit the beach – so the next time you get creamed by a six-footer, you won't be able to say you weren't warned.

for hire, along with a few tents. Just a quarter of a mile from the Rainbow Bridge, the site is within walking distance of both the beach and town center. French is spoken.

Hale'iwa's only camping option is at **Kaiaka Bay Beach Park**, where the county allows camping on Friday to Tuesday nights. See p78 for details on obtaining a permit.

MID-RANGE & TOP END

Privately owned condos are increasingly being offered throughout Hawaii as vacation rentals, represented by realty agents or rental associations. Reservations are often made through a website or by phone, and occasionally by walking in to the realty office. These companies rely on repeat visitors, and the satisfaction level is high. There is usually a three- to seven-night minimum stay, and often a cleaning fee surcharge cost $75 to $175. The following companies get reliably good feedback:

Sand Sea Vacation Homes (☎ 637-2568, 800-442-6901; www.sandsea.com; PO Box 239, Haleiwa, Hi 96712; 2-bedroom beachfront house $150-250, 3-bedroom beachfront house $350-650) This outfit specializes in renting privately owned beachfront homes along the North Shore. There are usually about 20 to choose from, and all come with fully equipped kitchen and bathroom, TV, washer, dryer and phone.

Team Real Estate (☎ 637-3507, 800-982-8602; teamrealestate.com; Suite 103, North Shore Marketplace, 66-250 Kamehameha Ave; 1-bedroom condo unit in low/high season $110/135, 2-bedroom house $165-240, 3-bedroom house $235-295) This company represents about 20 condo and home owners stretching from Hale'iwa to Turtle Bay. Nearly all units have bathrooms and fully equipped kitchens, washer and dryer, TV/VCR and phone, and sleep from four to eight people. There's typically a five- to seven-night minimum, but shorter stays can often be arranged.

Eating
BUDGET

Cafe Hale'iwa (☎ 637-5516; 66-460 Kamehameha Ave; breakfast $3-7, lunch $5-8; ⏰ 7am-2pm) An unpretentious joint with formica tables and walls plastered with surf memorabilia, Cafe Hale'iwa is a popular haunt for both local surfers and day-trippers. It offers good food at cheap prices. A popular breakfast choice is the egg sandwich or mahi and eggs. Lunch is mostly sandwiches and Mexican fare.

Coffee Gallery (☎ 637-5571; North Shore Marketplace, 66-250 Kamehameha Ave; snacks $2-6; ⏰ 8am-8:30pm) Follow your nose to this café, with

a mellow setting, good coffees roasted on the spot, pastries (chocolate chip banana bread sells out fast) and hearty sandwiches. Internet access is also available (p159).

Kua Aina Sandwich Shop (☎ 636-6067; 66-214 Kamehameha Ave; snacks $4-7; ⏰ 11am-8pm) Many locals swear that this cool eatery grills up the island's best burgers along with big salads and fresh fish sandwiches. It's a North Shore favorite, and with luck, you'll find a table on the shady lanai.

Wailua Bakery (☎ 637-9079; 66-200 Kamehameha Hwy; snacks $2-6; ⏰ 8am-4pm Mon-Sat) In addition to the usual morning goodies, it serves great smoothies and sandwiches.

Malama Market (☎ 637-4520; 66-190 Kamehameha Ave; ⏰ 7am-9pm), next to Kua Aina Sandwich, this is the place for general grocery items, while **Celestial Natural Foods** (☎ 637-6729; 66-443 Kamehameha Ave; ⏰ 9am-6pm Mon-Sat, 10am-6pm Sun) carries a good variety of fresh produce and health foods and has a vegetarian deli.

MID-RANGE & TOP END

Cholo's Homestyle Mexican (☎ 637-3059; North Shore Marketplace, 66-250 Kamehameha Ave; meals $8-14; ⏰ 8am-9pm) Cholo's has decent Mexican food with a North Shore touch, such as fresh 'ahi tacos with rice and beans for $10. All the usual Mexican standards are available as well, including *gorditas* (literally 'little fat ones,' thick corn pocket tortilla filled with meat and beans) and *chimi changas* (spiced meat and refried beans in crispy flour shell).

Hale'iwa Joe's (☎ 637-8005; 66-001 Kamehameha Ave; appetizers $5-10, lunch $8-15, dinner $12-26; ⏰ 11:30am-9:30pm) Easily the best upmarket restaurant on the North Shore, with an innovative menu, good service and a pleasant open bayside setting. Favorites include Emma's Poke (marinated raw 'ahi), aged New York steak and crunchy coconut shrimp.

Shopping

Hale'iwa shopping ranges from the trendy to the quirky, and most of the shops and galleries are located either in or nearby the **North Shore Marketplace** (66-250 Kamehameha Ave).

Jungle Gems (☎ 637-6609; North Shore Marketplace, 66-250 Kamehameha Ave) For unusual jewelry and elaborate beadwork.

Global Creations (☎ 637-1505; 66-079 Kamehameha Hwy) For furnishings, clothing, Hawaiian trinkets and last-minute gift shopping.

H Miura Store (☎ 637-4845; 66-057 Kamehameha Hwy) For a taste of old Hawaii, stroll into this friendly shop, owned by the same Hale'iwa family since 1918. You'll find yourself in another era, with a tailor filling custom orders, and bolts of colorful fabric and dry goods sharing the cool wooden interior with dashboard hula dancers and old postcards.

At least half a dozen art galleries can be found in Hale'iwa, mostly displaying the work of local island artists. Check out **Hale'iwa Art Gallery** (☎ 637-3368; 66-252 Kamehameha Hwy), inside the North Shore Marketplace, and nearby **Iwa Gallery** (☎ 637-4865; 66-119 Kamehameha Hwy).

WAIMEA
pop 2300
Waimea is a slow-paced beach community spread along the seashore, dotted with open-air boutiques, funky lunch wagons with colorful sarongs flapping in the wind and most everyone wearing dark shades. The beaches are virtual community centers, with friends meeting up, hanging out or just hitting the water on good days – or for that matter, on bad days!

History
The Waimea Valley was once heavily settled, the lowlands terraced in taro, the valley walls dotted with house sites and the ridges topped with heiau sites. Waimea River, now blocked at the beach, originally opened into the bay and was a passage for canoes traveling to villages upstream. Surfing has been associated with Waimea since

the 15th century, when Hawaiians took to *he'e nalu* (wave-sliding).

Sights & Activities
WAIMEA VALLEY AUDUBON CENTER
Across from Waimea Bay Beach Park, this elegant **botanical garden** (☎ 638-9199; www.audubon.org; 59-864 Kamehameha Hwy; admission adult/child under 4 yrs/child 4-12 yrs $8/free/5; 9:30am-5pm) has more than 5000 species. There are sections of ginger, hibiscus, heliconia, native food plants and medicinal species, including many that are endangered. **Waihe'e Falls** sits at the end of the main path through the park, 0.8 miles from the park entrance. The park has several ancient stone platforms and terraces dating back hundreds of years, as well as replicas of thatched buildings similar to those used by early Hawaiians.

Bus No 52 stops on the highway in front on the park, from where it's nearly a half-mile walk inland to the entrance. (From Haleiwa town, you can catch the bus to the Audubon Center from the bus stop opposite Bank of Hawaii on Kamehameha Hwy.) There is a good snack bar, with hot lunches and assorted sandwiches. There is no transportation inside the park.

WAIMEA BAY BEACH PARK
Beautiful, deeply set with turquoise waters and a wide white-sand beach almost 1500ft long, Waimea Bay was sacred to the ancient Hawaiians. Waimea Bay's mood changes with the seasons – as tranquil as a lake in summer, then savage with high surf and mean rips in winter. As at Sunset Beach, the huge north swells bring out crowds of

---

SWEET TREAT
For many people, the circle-island drive isn't complete without lining up for shave ice at **Matsumoto's** (☎ 637-4827; 66-087 Kamehameha Hwy; snacks $2-5) tin-roofed general store. Often Honolulu families drive to the North Shore with one purpose: to stand in line here and walk out with a dripping delicious shave ice cone, drenched with island flavors, like *likikoi* (passion fruit), banana, mango and pineapple.

Hawaiian shave ice is drenched with industrial-strength sweet syrup like the snow cones found on the US mainland, but it's much better, because the ice is more finely shaved. A medium-sized cone with a combination of flavors usually costs about $2, a bit more if you add a local favorite, red adzuki beans. The entire concoction begins dripping into a sticky mess the second you get it, so don't dawdle.

Although most tourists flock to Matsumoto's, many locals prefer **Aoki's** (66-117 Kamehameha Hwy; snacks $1.50-3), or the lesser-known **H Miura Store** (☎ 637-4845; 66-057 Kamehameha Hwy; snacks $1.50-3), an unassuming spot just up the road where coconut cream is a favorite topping.

spectators who throng to watch surfers perform their near-suicidal feats on waves over 30ft.

On winter's calmer days the boogie boarders are out in force, but even then sets come in hard and people get pounded. Winter water activities here are not for novices. The water is usually calm enough for swimming and snorkeling from June to September. There are showers, restrooms and picnic tables, and a lifeguard is on duty daily.

PUPUKEA BEACH PARK

The park includes Three Tables and Shark's Cove, where an array of jagged rock formations and tide pools exposed at low tide invite exploring. But be careful; the razor-sharp rocks can inflict deep cuts if you slip.

There are also showers and restrooms to left of Shark's Cove, as you face the ocean. The beach entrance is opposite an old gas station and auto repair shop; bus No 52 stops out front. Snorkel sets and other water sports equipment can be rented from Planet Surf beside Foodland supermarket.

Three Tables

Three Tables, which gets its name from the flat ledges rising just above the water, has good snorkeling and diving in summer when it's calm. While there is some action around the tables, the best fish, coral caves, lava tubes and arches are in deeper water further out. This is a summer-only spot; in winter, dangerous rips flow between the beach and the tables. Beware of sharp rocks and coral.

Shark's Cove

This cove is beautiful both above and below the water's surface. The origin of the cove's name is uncertain, but sharks are no more common here than anywhere else on the island. The tidepools merit exploring, depending on wave conditions. Shark's Cove is part of the Pupukea Marine Life Conservation District, dedicated to conserving the unusual coral reef here, noteworthy because it is resistant to the impact of big winter waves.

From May to October, when the seas are generally calm, Shark's Cove offers excellent snorkeling and scuba diving. A fair number of beginning divers take lessons here, while the underwater caves and caverns will thrill advanced divers. The caves can be found around the cove's northeast point. There

have been a number of drownings in these caves, and divers in particular should only explore them with a local expert. Most caves have little natural light, and if sediment is stirred up from swells, the result can be zero visibility and disorientation.

The large boulders out on the end of the point to the far right of the cove are said to be followers of Pele, the volcano goddess. As an honor, she gave them immortality by turning them to stone.

EHUKAI BEACH PARK

Further along the coast, look for the park sign opposite the Sunset Beach Elementary School for Ehukai Beach Park. Facing the ocean, walk 300ft to the left to find the world-famous Banzai Pipeline, or **Pipeline**, or just plain Pipe. This is where surfing pros come to compete in winter, riding glassy tubes that break over a dangerously shallow reef. Boogie boarders and bodysurfers also brave hazardous currents to ride the waves. Conditions mellow out in summer, when it's good for swimming. The beach has a lifeguard, restrooms and showers.

SUNSET BEACH PARK

Just south of the nine-mile marker is Sunset Beach Park, a pretty white-sand oasis whose main attraction is the monster waves and challenging breaks that make it a classic winter surfing destination. The tremendous surf activity causes the slope of the beach to become increasingly steep as the season goes on.

Backyards, the surf break off Sunset Point at the northern end, draws a lot of top windsurfers. There are a shallow reef and strong currents, but Backyards often has the island's biggest waves for sailing. Winter swells create a powerful rip, but come summer, the shoreline begins to smooth out and the waves mellow. The beach has restrooms, showers and a lifeguard tower.

PU'U O MAHUKA HEIAU
STATE MONUMENT

Attributed to the legendary *menehune*, Pu'u o Mahuka Heiau, a long, low-walled platform temple perched on a bluff above Waimea, is the largest heiau on O'ahu. The terraced stone walls are a couple of feet high, although most of the heiau is now overgrown. It's an excellent site for a temple, with a commanding view of both Waimea Valley and Waimea Bay. West, the view extends along the coast to Ka'ena Point.

To get to the heiau, turn up Pupukea Rd at Foodland supermarket. The marked turnoff is about half a mile up the road; from there it's three-quarters of a mile in. There's a good view of Pupukea Beach Park on the drive up.

KAUNALA LOOP TRAIL

The little-known **Kaunala Loop** trail sits quietly above Waimea Valley, a good place to mix an easy valley walk with a moderate ridge climb for sweeping views of Waimea Bay. Ancient Hawaiians believed the waters of Waimea were sacred, and after seeing the bay from viewpoints high atop this trail, it would be hard not to agree.

To get to the trailhead, turn up Pupukea Rd at the Foodland supermarket and continue for 2.5 miles. This 4.5-mile hike averages about two hours. This trail is officially open to the public only on weekends and state holidays. Hunting is allowed, so hikers should wear bright colors and don't go wandering off the trail. Also bring water. No permit is required.

Sleeping

The bulletin board at Pupukea's Foodland supermarket has notices of roommates wanted and the occasional vacation rental listing, so check it out if you're thinking of staying a while. There are also a number of private home owners that rely on word-of-mouth advertising, as well as vacation rental agencies (p162).

BUDGET

Shark's Cove Rentals (☎ 779-8535, 888-883-0001; www.sharkscoverentals.com; 59-672 Kamehameha Hwy; s $45-75, d $85-150) This well-managed property consists of four adjacent three-bedroom houses across from Pupukea Beach Park. One of the houses features a setup with bunk beds – only two people to a room, so it's relatively quiet. The other houses have three bedrooms, each clean and spacious, all with ceiling or floor fans; the more expensive rooms have their own TV and refrigerator. All guests have access to a fully equipped kitchen, which doubles as a gathering place for guests and fellow travelers.

Backpackers (☎ 638-7838; www.backpackers-hawaii .com; 59-788 Kamehameha Hwy; dm $20-23, r $55, cabin $65-75, studio $110-130) Located opposite Three Tables, this one-time surfers' hangout has expanded to a collection of cabins, studios and cramped dorm-style rooms, which get very mixed reviews from readers. Most of the dorm rooms are near the office; private studios are across the road next to the beach, and another group of cabins are further along up the road. Because rooms vary in quality, the best advice is to see your room before making a deposit. If you have to make a reservation prior to arrival, ask for a room with a ceiling fan and good ventilation.

MID-RANGE & TOP END

Ironwoods (☎ 293-2554; richard27@hawaii.rr.com; 57-531 Kamehameha Hwy; studio per day/week $75/450) Two miles north of Sunset Beach is this ocean-view studio in a beachside home with

---

THE AUTHOR'S CHOICE

Ke Iki Beach Bungalows (☎ 638-8229, 866-638-8229; www.keikibeach.com; 59-579 Ke Iki Rd; hwy-side 1-bedroom units in low/high season $75/110, beachside 1-bedroom units $140/195, beachside 2-bedroom units $175/195; 1-time cleaning fee $50-100) Make the most of a North Shore visit at this small hide-away oceanfront retreat. Snuggled between two legendary surfing spots, Waimea Bay and Sunset Beach, this quaint collection of duplex cottages and rustic studios faces its own stretch of beach, perfect for summer swimming. Come winter time, however, it's strictly for viewing at a safe distance when the big surf rolls into the North Shore. Nearby Shark's Cove offers snorkeling and tide pool exploring in a small semi-protected bay, and it's gentle enough for kids most of the year. Ke Iki's 12 rooms are not lavish, but are smartly adorned with rattan furniture, along with wonderful ocean views. Every apartment has a full kitchen, TV and phone. Tropical touches include overhead ceiling fans and outdoor hammocks and showers. There are also jogging and bike paths nearby. Craig, the owner-manager, supplies everything from snorkel sets and bicycles to information about nearby Hale'iwa and Waimea.

private entrance. The loft bedroom features one king-size bed (or two twin beds) and is reached via a steep ladder staircase; a downstairs sitting area has cable TV, bathroom, kitchenette and a couch that converts into a single bed, perfect for a child. The beach is just footsteps from the house. There's a three-night minimum stay.

Ulu Wehi B&B (☎ 638-7924; tj4dogs@aol.com; 59-416 Alapio Rd; r $95; 🐾) This B&B is located 1.5 miles up the hill from Pupukea Beach Park. The owners operate a small nursery at their home, and rent out a simple studio unit that has both a double and single bed plus kitchenette. Breakfast includes fresh fruit from the garden, and homemade muffins. The house features a 75ft lap pool in the backyard and a barbecue.

Eating

Sunset Pizza (☎ 638-7660; 59-174 Kamehameha Hwy; pizza $9-18; 🕙 7am-9pm) Opposite Sunset Beach Park, this place has great pizza and slow service, plus $6 meatball subs and $3 pizza slices.

Shark's Cove Grill (☎ 638-8300; snacks $5-7; 🕙 11am-7pm) This little white trailer that parks along the highway 100yd north of Foodland has good burgers, fish sandwiches and chicken teriyaki plates. There are a few sunny tables, and a view of the beach.

Taste of Paradise (☎ 638-0855; 59-254 Kamehameha Hwy; sandwiches $6-7, dinners $9-11; 🕙 11am-9:30pm) Look for the giant wooden *ki'i* (Tiki) figure on the highway 1½ miles north of Waimea. It's open-air picnic style, complete with gravel floor and wobbly plastic tables. Fresh fish plates and veggie sandwiches dominate a menu with a Brazilian touch. 'Ahi tuna with rice and beans fetches $9.50, a veggie sandwich $6. Cash only.

Ted's Bakery (☎ 638-8207; 59-024 Kamehameha Hwy; 🕙 7am-6pm) A sweet-tooth mecca opposite Sunset Beach, Ted's often sells out of its cinnamon rolls and butter buns ($1) by 9am, in which case you'll have to get by with a slice of chocolate *haupia* (coconut) pie or moist carrot cake ($2).

Foodland (☎ 638-8081; 59-720 Kamehameha Hwy; 🕙 6am-10pm) This supermarket opposite Pupukea Beach Park has the best grocery prices and selection on the North Shore. It also has a good deli selling fresh 'ahi poke and inexpensive fried chicken, perfect for a beachside picnic.

WAIALUA

Waialua, a former plantation town about a mile west of Hale'iwa, is centered on the dusty Waialua Sugar Mill, which closed down in 1996, bringing an end to the last commercial sugar operation on O'ahu.

Although the Waialua area remains economically depressed, with many of the surrounding fields overgrown with feral sugarcane, other sections are newly planted with coffee trees – a labor-intensive crop that holds out promise for new jobs. You can see the coffee trees, planted in neat rows, as you come down the slopes into Waialua.

The old sugar mill, which now serves as the coffee operation's headquarters, is chock full of racks where the coffee beans are sorted and dried. You can poke around the place a bit, but there's not much to see, as the visitors center has closed. As for other sights, this sleepy town has a couple of period buildings, the most interesting being the local watering hole, the Sugar Bar & Grill (see below), which occupies the old Bank of Hawaii building down by the mill.

Halfway between Hale'iwa and Dillingham Airfield, the church-owned **Camp Mokule'ia** (☎ 637-6241; www.campmokuleia.com; 68-729 Farrington Hwy, Waialua; campsite per person $7) is open to the public with reservations. The camp is spread out through a partially shaded ironwood grove facing the ocean. Facilities are clean and basic, including showers, toilets and cooking areas.

Mostly a local hangout, the **Sugar Bar & Grill** (☎ 636-2220; 67-069 Kealohanui St) is a funky plantation town bar that draws tourists, surfers and island bikers, a weird mix that seems to work most nights, especially in the busier winter months.

MOKULE'IA & AROUND

The Farrington Hwy (930) runs west from Thompson Corner to Dillingham Airfield and Mokule'ia Beach. Both this road and the road along the Wai'anae Coast are called Farrington Hwy, but they don't connect, as each side reaches a dead end about 2½ miles short of Ka'ena Point.

Mokule'ia Beach is a six-mile stretch of white sand running from Kaiaka Bay toward Ka'ena Point. Although some GIs and locals come this way, the beaches don't draw too much of a crowd. The only beach facilities are at Mokule'ia Beach Park; the nearest store is back in Waialua. Dillingham Airfield is the take-off site for glider rides and skydiving.

Mokule'ia Beach Park

Opposite Dillingham Airfield, Mokule'ia Beach Park has a large open grassy area with picnic tables, restrooms and showers. Mokule'ia is sandy, but has a lava rock shelf along much of its shoreline. The fairly consistent winds make it a very popular spot with windsurfers, particularly in spring and autumn. In the winter there are dangerous currents. Camping is allowed with a county camping permit. For information on obtaining permits, see p78.

Dillingham Airfield

If you fancy sailing with the wind over the scenic North Shore, head to Dillingham Airfield at the west end of the Farrington Hwy, just past Mokule'ia Beach Park, for a one- or two-person glider (sailplane) ride with either **Mr Bill's Original Glider Rides** (☎ 677-3404; Dillingham Airfield; 30-min glide $100) or **Soar Hawaii Sailplanes** (☎ 637-3147; Dillingham Airfield; 30-min glide $70). Both companies offer introductory rides lasting from 10 to 20 minutes for about $35 per person.

Skydive Hawaii (☎ 637-9700; Dillingham Airfield; hawaiiskydiving.com; per person $225) offers tandem jumps with an instructor, usually a friendly stranger with whom you jump out of a perfectly good airplane, free fall for a minute and float down for another 10 minutes. The whole process, including basic instruction, takes about 1½ hours. Participants must be at least 18 years of age and weigh less than 200lb. Planes take off daily, weather permitting.

The five-mile **Kealia Trail** ascends from Dillingham Airfield above Ka'ena Point over a mile of cliff-face switchbacks. Although the segment of dirt 4WD road that follows the initial stretch, which gently switchback up with ocean views, isn't very interesting, the Kealai Trail later joins forces with the **Kuaokala Trail** to bring hikers to a justly celebrated viewpoint over Makua Valley and the high Wai'anae Range. This trail is best for those wishing to avoid the hassle of securing a permit and driving around the Wai'anae Coast just to hike the Kuaokala Trail, accessible from the Ka'ena Point Satellite Tracking Station (p171).

Mokule'ia Army Beach to Ka'ena Point

Mokule'ia Army Beach, opposite the western end of Dillingham Airfield, has the widest stretch of sand on the Mokule'ia shore. Once reserved exclusively for military personnel, the beach is now open to the public, although it is no longer maintained and there are no facilities. The beach is unprotected and has very strong rip currents, especially during high surf in winter.

From Army Beach you can proceed another 1.5 miles down the road, passing still more white-sand beaches with aqua-blue waters. You'll usually find someone shorecasting and occasionally a few local people camping. The terrain is scrub land reaching up to the base of the Wai'anae Range, while the shoreline is wild and windswept. The area is not only desolate, but can also be a bit trashed, and this is certainly not a must-do drive.

The **Ka'ena Point Trail** is a relatively easy coastal trail beginning at the end of a paved road west of Dillingham Airfield. For details about the trail, see p172.

TURTLE BAY TO KAHUKU POINT
Sights & Activities
BEACHES

Shallow **Kuilima Cove** is fronted by the Turtle Bay Resort, three miles west of Kahuku Point, which generally marks the dividing line between the North Shore and Windward Coast. Protected by a shallow reef, Kuilima is one of the area's best swimming spots, and the nearby coral is perfect for snorkeling.

Just a mile east of Kuilima Cove is **Kaihalulu Beach**, a beautiful, curved, white-sand beach backed by ironwoods. The rocky bottom makes for poor swimming, but the shoreline attracts morning beachcombers. Go another mile east to reach scenic **Kahuku Point**, where local fishers cast throw-nets and pole fish from the rocks.

GOLF & TENNIS

The **Turtle Bay Resort** (☎ 293-6000; www.turtlebay resort.com; 57-091 Kamehameha Hwy, Kahuku) features two top-rated 18-hole courses; one designed by George Fazio, and the other by Arnold Palmer. Facilities include a pro shop, club house and restaurant; golf lessons are available. Call the **pro shop** (☎ 293-8574) for more information or reservations.

The tennis center at the resort is rated by *Tennis Magazine* as one of their Top 50 tennis resort picks. Turtle Bay has 10 tennis courts, four of them lighted. The center provides tennis lessons and equipment hire. Call ☎ 293-6024 for more information or reservations.

HORSEBACK RIDING
The **Turtle Bay Resort** (☎ 293-6000; www.turtlebay resort.com; 57-091 Kamehameha Hwy, Kahuku; trail rides adult/child 7-12 yrs $45/30) offers slow-paced trail and sunset rides. The 40- to 45-minute trail ride takes you along beaches and through tropical forests. Several departure times are offered daily. More advanced rides for qualified riders depart at 7:30am (per person $50), as well as 90-minute evening rides for two to six people (per person $65). Horse-drawn carriage rides are also on the menu (30 minutes, per person $15).

Sleeping
Most condo accommodations bookings are handled by either **Turtle Bay Condos** (☎ 293-2800, 888-266-3690; www.turtlebaycondos.com) or **Estates at Turtle Bay** (☎ 293-0600, 888-200-4202; www.turtlebay -rentals.com). Both rental offices, however, are 3.5 miles southeast of the where the condos are located, next to the Kahuku sugar mill. The complex has two tennis courts and five pools.

MID-RANGE
Kuilima Estates (57-101 Kuilima Dr; studios/lofts $85/110, 1-2-3-bedroom apt $130/155/205) For a cheaper alternative to Turtle Bay Resort, try this adjacent condominium complex. Bookings are handled by the rental offices of Turtle Bay Condos or Estates at Turtle Bay.

TOP END
Turtle Bay Resort (☎ 293-8811, 800-203-3650; www .turtlebayresort.com; 57-091 Kamehameha Hwy, Kahuku; r $240-360; 🏃 🏊) Perched atop Kuilima Point between Turtle Bay and Kuilima Cove, this self-contained luxury resort offers several restaurants (see right) and bars and an impressive array of outdoor and indoor activities including two excellent golf courses, two swimming pools, horse stables and 10 tennis courts (see above). Each of the 485 luxurious rooms has a lanai with ocean view, as well as a cable TV and Internet access.

Eating
Turtle Bay Resort (☎ 293-8811; 57-091 Kamehameha Hwy) Between Sunset Beach and Kahuku, your choices are limited to this resort, with several bars and restaurants offering everything from happy-hour appetizers to breakfast buffets and fine dining.

Lei Lei's Bar & Grill (☎ 293-8811; Turtle Bay Resort, 57-091 Kamehameha Hwy; meals $8-22) Of the resort's several eateries facing the golf course, this is a destination all on its own for locals in the know. The eclectic menu includes oyster shooters, sandwiches, baby back ribs and several Japanese-accented dishes, such as seafood scampi with udon noodles ($19).

WAI'ANAE COAST

In 1793, when English captain George Vancouver dropped anchor on the Wai'anae Coast on the leeward side of O'ahu, he found a barren wasteland with only a few scattered fishing huts. In 1795 Kamehameha invaded, swelling the population with refugees fleeing their homes elsewhere on O'ahu.

The Wai'anae Coast still stands separate from the rest of the island – few tourists, no gift shops or sightseeing buses. The area has a history of resisting development and a reputation for not being receptive to outsiders. Although assaults and muggings are no longer common, thefts from cars and campsites still occur.

Farrington Hwy (93) runs the length of the coast beside stretches of white-sand beaches, some quite attractive. In winter most have treacherous swimming conditions, but some of the island's more challenging surfing. Although the towns are ordinary, lovely cliffs and valleys cut into the Wai'anae Range.

At road's end, hike the undeveloped mile-long beach and do a fine nature hike out to scenic Ka'ena Point.

KAHE POINT
A sandy beach north of Kahe Point, **Hawaiian Electric Beach Park** (aka Tracks) is a calm place to swim in summer and frequented by surfers in winter. To get there, take the first turnoff after the power plant and drive over the abandoned railroad tracks.

NANAKULI

Nanakuli, the biggest town on the Wai'anae Coast, is the site of a Hawaiian Homesteads settlement, having one of the largest native Hawaiian populations on O'ahu. It also has supermarkets, a courthouse, a bank and fast-food joints.

Lined by a broad sandy beach park, Nanakuli attracts swimmers, snorkelers and divers during the calmer summer season. In winter, high surf creates rip currents and dangerous shorebreaks. To get to this park, with a playground, sports fields, full facilities and campsites, turn left at the traffic lights on Nanakuli Ave. For information on camping permits, see p78.

MA'ILI

Ma'ili has a long, grassy roadside park with a seemingly endless stretch of white beach. Like other places on this coast, the water conditions are often treacherous in winter, but calm enough for swimming in summer. There's a lifeguard station, a playground and facilities; coconut palms provide shade.

WAI'ANAE

Wai'anae, the second-largest town on the Wai'anae Coast, has a beach park, protected boat harbor, satellite city hall, police station, supermarkets and fast-food joints.

Protected by Kane'ilio Point and a long breakwater, **Poka'i Bay Beach Park** features the calmest year-round swimming on the Wai'anae Coast. Waves seldom break inside the bay, and the sandy seafloor slopes gently, making the beach a popular spot for families. Snorkeling is fair near the breakwater, where fish gather around the rocks. You can watch local canoe clubs rowing in the late afternoon. There are showers, restrooms and picnic tables, and a lifeguard on duty daily.

Kane'ilio Point, along the south side of the bay, is the site of **Ku'ilioloa Heiau**. Partly destroyed by the army during WWII, this stone temple has been reconstructed by local conservationists. To get there, turn onto Lualualei Homestead Rd, heading seaward, at the traffic light immediately north of the Wai'anae post office.

MAKAHA

Makaha means 'ferocious,' and in days past the valley was notorious for the bandits who waited along the cliffs to ambush passing travelers. Today Makaha is best known for its world-class surfing, fine beach, golf course, condominiums and O'ahu's best-restored heiau.

Sights
MAKAHA BEACH PARK

Makaha Beach, a broad, sandy crescent with some of the most daunting winter surf in the islands, attracts experienced surfers and has hosted a number of surf events. Although the biggest surfing events have since shifted to O'ahu's North Shore, Makaha Beach hosts the Buffalo Surf Meet each March, with competitors using old-style 'tankers' reaching 15ft.

Makaha is a popular swimming beach, but when the surf is up, rip currents and a strong shorebreak make swimming hazardous. In summer the slope of the beach is relatively flat, while in winter the wave action results in a steeper drop. As much as half the beach washes away during winter, but even then Makaha is still impressive. Snorkeling is good offshore during the calmer summer months. The Makaha Caverns feature underwater arches and tunnels at depths of 30ft to 50ft. Makaha Beach has showers and restrooms, and lifeguards are on duty.

MAKAHA VALLEY

Inland from Kili Dr, opposite Makaha Beach Park, the road follows scalloped green cliffs into Makaha Valley to one of Hawaii's most authentically restored heiau, situated on a private estate. An estimated 3000 wild peacocks live here, including about two dozen albinos. They can be heard throughout the upper valley and seen performing their courting rituals in the field near the heiau.

Originally a Lono temple, **Kaneaki Heiau** (☎ 695-8174; admission free) was dedicated to the god of agriculture. It later became a *luakini* (a type of temple dedicated to the war god Ku and used for human sacrifices). Kamehameha used it as a place of worship, and it remained in use until the time of his death in 1819.

Restoration, undertaken by the Bishop Museum and completed in 1970, added two prayer towers, a taboo house, drum house, altar and god images. The heiau was reconstructed using traditional ohia tree logs and *pili* (a bunchgrass, commonly used for thatching houses) from the Big Island. The immediate setting surrounding the heiau remains undisturbed, though it's in the midst of a residential estate.

To get there, take Kili Dr to the Makaha Valley Towers condominiums, and turn right onto Huipu Dr. Half a mile down on the left is Mauna Olu St, leading into Mauna Olu Estates and up to Kaneaki Heiau. The guard at the Mauna Olu Estates gatehouse usually lets visitors go through to the heiau, a short drive past the gatehouse, between 10am and 2pm Tuesday to Sunday. Following rain, access is difficult, so call in advance.

Activities

HIKING
The Nature Conservancy (☎ 587-6220; nature.org /hawaii) leads monthly hikes to two trails in Honouliuli Preserve on the southeast slope of the Wai'anae Range. Palikea Ridge Trail is the easier of the two trips, while the Kalua'a Loop Trai is considered intermediate. Honouliuli Preserve is home to nearly 70 rare and endangered plant and animal species. The land once belonged to Hawaiian royalty and was named Honouliuli – meaning dark harbor – for the dark fertile lands that stretch from the waters of Pearl Harbor to the summit of the Wai'anae Range.

GOLF
To get to the **Makaha Valley Country Club** (☎ 695-9578; 84-627 Makaha Valley Rd, Wai'anae), follow the Farrington Hwy through Wai'anae; turn right on Makaha Valley Rd, and go 1.5 miles until the road forks. Take the right fork into the parking lot. Green fees are $65 on weekends, and $55 Monday to Friday, when it's easiest to get a tee time. The views to the ocean are worth the fees alone.

Tours
For the snorkel of a lifetime, **Wildside Specialty Tours** (☎ 306-7273; www.wildsidehawaii.com; per person $95) is it. This well-managed outfit, with a marine biologist aboard, lets you snorkel alongside spinner dolphins off the Wai'anae Coast, alternating among three sandy-bottomed resting grounds. Captain Russell Amamoto is also watch captain on the *Hokule'a*, the double-hulled sailing canoe constructed to retrace the routes of early Polynesians (see Hokule'a: a Star of Gladness, p26). The 42ft catamaran, *Island*

Spirit, only takes 12 to 16 passengers; continental breakfast is served on board. It also offers evening stargazing sails and whale watching trips in winter. Reservations are essential, usually two weeks in advance.

Sleeping & Eating
Makaha doesn't have many accommodations for short-term visitors. There are a handful of condos geared primarily to permanent residents, but none are terribly appealing and they generally require you to stay for at least a week. However, if you're keen to be on the leeward side, **Hawaii Hatfield Realty** (☎ 696-7121, 696-4499; Suite 201, 85-833 Farrington Hwy, Wai'anae) arranges long-term rentals for Makaha Shores, a condo complex at the northern end of Makaha Beach.

You can make a good day at the beach better by stopping at **Aloha'Aina Cafe & Natural Foods** (☎ 697-8808; 85-773 Farrington Hwy; dishes $3-5; 🕑 7am-3pm Mon-Sat), a friendly roadside café in Wai'anae. Have a taro veggie burger or a *kalua* pig quesadilla and wash it down with a fresh fruit smoothie. Eat inside, or at the shaded porch tables.

MAKAHA TO KA'ENA POINT
Keaau Beach Park
Keaau Beach Park is a long, open, grassy strip, bordering a rocky shore, with campsites, showers, drinking water, picnic tables and restrooms. A sandy beach begins at the very northern end of the park, with a rough reef, sharp drop and high seasonal surf. For information on obtaining camping permits, see p78.

North along the coast, you'll see lava sea cliffs, white-sand beaches and patches of kiawe, while, on the inland side, you'll glimpse a run of little valleys.

Kaneana Cave
Massive Kaneana Cave, on the right-hand side of the road about two miles north of Keaau Beach Park, was once underwater. It's impressive size is the result of wave action that wore away loose rock around an earthquake crack and expanded the cavern over the millennia as the ocean slowly receded.

Hawaiian *kahuna* (priests) once performed their rituals inside the cave's inner chamber. Older Hawaiians consider it a sacred place and some won't enter for fear it's haunted.

Ka'ena Point Satellite Tracking Station

Immediately before the gate to Ka'ena Point State Park, a road leads right up to Ka'ena Point Satellite Tracking Station, operated by the US Air Force.

There are hiking trails above the tracking station, including the 2.5-mile **Kuaokala Trail** that follows a high ridge to Mokule'ia Forest Reserve. At the trail's highest point (1960ft) is an overlook with great views. On a clear day hikers can see Mt Ka'ala, the highest peak on O'ahu, and part of the Wai'anae Range. The final lookout can also be accessed via the Kealia Trail (p167) from the North Shore. Obtain a hiking permit in advance from the **Division of Forestry & Wildlife** (☎ 587-0166) to present at the guard station.

KA'ENA POINT STATE PARK

Ka'ena Point State Park is an undeveloped 853-acre coastal strip that runs along both sides of Ka'ena Point, the westernmost point of O'ahu. Until the mid-1940s the O'ahu Railroad ran up here from Honolulu and continued around the point, carrying passengers on to Hale'iwa on the North Shore.

In addition to being a state park, Ka'ena Point has been designated a natural area reserve because of its unique ecosystem. The extensive dry, windswept coastal dunes that rise above the point are the habitat of many rare native plants, including the endangered *Kaena akoko* – found nowhere else.

More common plants are the beach *naupaka*, with white flowers that look like they've been torn in half; *pau-o-Hiiaka*, a vine with blue flowers; and beach morning glory, sometimes found wrapped in the parasite *kaunaoa*.

SLIPPING AWAY

Early Hawaiians believed that when people went into a deep sleep or lost consciousness, their souls would wander. Souls that wandered too far were drawn west to Ka'ena Point. If they were lucky, they were met here by their *'aumakua* (ancestral spirit helper), who led their souls back to their bodies. If unattended, their souls would be forced to leap from Ka'ena Point into the endless night, never to return.

On clear days, Kaua'i is visible from the point. According to legend, it was at Ka'ena Point that the demigod Maui attempted to cast a huge hook into Kaua'i and pull it next to O'ahu to join the islands. But the line broke and Kaua'i slipped away, with just a small piece remaining near O'ahu. Today this splintered rock, off the end of Ka'ena Point, is known as Pohaku o Kauai.

Seabirds seen at Ka'ena Point include shearwaters, boobies and the common noddy – a dark-brown bird with a grayish crown. You can often see schools of spinner dolphins off the beach, and in winter, humpback whales. The reserve is a nesting site for the rare Laysan albatross, and Hawaii's endangered monk seals occasionally bask in the sun here.

Sights & Activities
YOKOHAMA BAY

The attractive mile-long sandy beach on this side of the point is Yokohama Bay, named for the large numbers of Japanese fishers who came here during the railroad days.

ESCAPING THE CROWDS: KA'ENA POINT STATE PARK

A deserted beach on O'ahu? You can walk for miles on island beaches and barely encounter another soul. For a taste of solitude, head to the northwest tip of the island at Ka'ena Point, which can only be reached on foot. During the summer months, this often deserted stretch of sand and lava rock is perfect for beachcombing, exploring tidepools or watching windsurfers zoom across the whitecaps.

During the week, you'll have most of this 4.5-mile stretch of rocky coast and turquoise sea to yourself. Along the way, dozens of small trails run down to sandy coves and coral sea beds. Further out toward the point, winter swells can crest at 30ft to 40ft, and are considered unrideable. Take a picnic, but sit well back from the shore!

Although you can get there from the Wai'anae Coast, the simplest way is via the North Shore (see p167). Leave your car (no buses go this far) at the end of the paved road (Farrington Hwy), past Dillingham Airfield, about 10 miles west of Hale'iwa.

Winter brings huge pounding waves, making Yokohama a popular seasonal surfing and bodysurfing spot best left to the experts because of the submerged rocks, strong rips and dangerous shorebreak.

Swimming is limited to the summer, and then only when calm. When the water's flat, it's possible to snorkel; the best spot with the easiest access is at the south side of the park. Restrooms, showers and a lifeguard station are at the south end of the park.

KA'ENA POINT TRAIL

A 2.5-mile (one-way) coastal hike runs from the end of the paved road at Yokohama Bay

to Ka'ena Point, following the old railroad bed. You'll see tide pools, sea arches, fine coastal views and the lofty sea cliffs of the Wai'anae Range. The hike is unshaded, so take plenty of water, even if you plan on a short hike; there are no facilities in this hot and dry corner of the island.

Don't leave anything valuable in your car unless you're prepared to lose it. Shattered windshield glass at the road's-end parking area warns hikers to leave nothing of value in their cars, park closer to the restrooms or leave their doors unlocked.

You can also access the trail from the North Shore, west of Dillingham Airfield (see p167).

Hawai'i
(The Big Island)

174

Hawai'i is a microcosm of a continent, with astounding diversity in geography and climate. The landscape changes from seemingly lifeless lava desert to dense ohia rain forest, from rolling pastureland to subarctic mountain peaks. You'll find miles of land undeveloped and remote spots void of other humans. That's the beauty of the Big Island – it's a vast frontier.

Of course, urban development is ever encroaching: Hilo and Kailua-Kona are the island's population centers, each with unique appeal. On the leeward coast, Kona attracts the lion's share of tourists, who come seeking sunshine and white-sand beaches. Since the 1960s, the 'Gold Coast' has boomed with luxury resorts and multimillion-dollar oceanfront homes.

On the windward coast, Hilo's average annual rainfall of 130in deters visitors, but it's actually a blessing. East Hawai'i is stunningly lush and green, with rain forests hiding unexpected waterfalls and dramatic gulches cutting into the shore.

Much of the island remains rural, where a relaxed, 'hang loose, brah' atmosphere still prevails. But recently second-home buyers and mainland transplants have flocked to this relatively affordable island, creating pockets of gentrification not welcomed by all locals.

The most unique attraction on the island is the active volcano Kilauea at Hawai'i Volcanoes National Park. The endless stretches of lava terrain are humbling and, depending on nature's whims, you might even witness fiery-red molten lava glowing – earth in the making.

HIGHLIGHTS

- Dive the night away with giant manta rays along the **Kona Coast** (p189)
- Take it easy anywhere in rural North Kohala's hidden **Pololu Valley** (p229)
- Devour fresh whole fish in old-town **Hilo** (p249)
- Imbibe 100% pure **Kona coffee** (p204)
- Spread out in secluded **Waipi'o Valley** (p238)
- Make a Luddite getaway at **Kona Village** (p217)
- Hike to **Waimanu Valley** (p240)
- Kayak the **Kohala ditch** (p227)
- Marvel at the world's most active **volcano** (p271)
- Snorkel among tropical fish and coral reefs in **Kealakekua Bay** (p205)

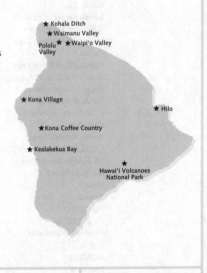

- POPULATION: 158,423
- NICKNAME: THE ORCHID ISLE
- AREA: 4028 SQ MILES

Climate

Big Island climate varies much more by location than by season. The western Kona Coast lives up to its reputation for perennial sunshine, especially at sea level. The heat can be overwhelming, but a few miles upland in coffee country, the air is considerably cooler. Kona's rainfall and temperature hardly changes throughout the year, but the seasons can significantly affect the tides and sand along the coast. White Sands Beach (p189) and Manini'owali (p216) regularly lose most of their sand during winter, though it washes back during summer. In general Big Island waters are calmer in summer and rougher in winter, but conditions are unpredictable so use your best judgment once you're there.

On the eastern coast, Hilo is much wetter, with an annual rainfall of over 100in. But except during rainstorms the typical drizzle is innocuous, especially because temperatures are still balmy. Volcano village is slightly cooler, and many visitors to Hawai'i Volcanoes National Park are caught off guard during pouring rain or chilly nights. But the coolest populated area on the island is Waimea, where the fog rolls in daily.

On the windward side of Mauna Kea, near the 2500ft elevation, around 300in of rain falls annually. So much rain is squeezed out of the clouds as they rise up Mauna Kea and Mauna Loa that only about 15in of precipitation reaches the summits, much of it as snow. Heavy subtropical winter rainstorms in Hilo occasionally bring blizzards to the mountains as low as the 9000ft level.

In January, the average daily high temperature is 65°F at Hawai'i Volcanoes National Park, 79°F in Hilo and a toasty 81°F in Kailua-Kona. August temperatures rise only

HOME OF KAMEHAMEHA THE GREAT

Kamehameha the Great was born on the Big Island in 1758 near Mo'okini Heiau (p226). As a young boy, he was brought to Kealakekua Bay (p205) to live at the royal court of his uncle, Kalaniopu'u, high chief of the island.

Kamehameha became Kalaniopu'u's fiercest general, and the chief appointed him guardian of the war god, Kuka'ilimoku, the 'snatcher of land.' The deity was embodied in a coarsely carved wooden image with a bloody red mouth and a helmet of yellow feathers. Kamehameha carried an image of Kuka'ilimoku into battle with him, and according to legend it would screech out terrifying battle cries during the fiercest fighting.

Immediately after Kalaniopu'u's death in 1782, Kamehameha led his warriors against Kalaniopu'u's son, Kiwalao, who had taken the throne. Kiwalao was killed, and Kamehameha emerged as ruler of the Kohala region and one of the ruling chiefs of the Big Island.

But Kamehameha was too ambitious to share control of the islands. In 1790, with the aid of a captured foreign schooner and two shipwrecked sailors, Isaac Davis and John Young, whom he used as gunners, Kamehameha attacked and conquered the island of Maui.

Kamehameha was on Moloka'i preparing for an invasion of O'ahu when he learned that Keoua Kuahu'ula, his cousin and chief of the Ka'u region, was attacking the Hamakua Coast. Keoua boldly pillaged Waipi'o Valley (p238), the most sacred area on the Big Island and the site where Kamehameha had ceremonially received his war god a decade earlier.

As an angry Kamehameha set sail for home, Keoua's soldiers beat a quick retreat back to Ka'u. But when the withdrawing troops passed beneath the slopes of Kilauea Crater, the volcano suddenly erupted. Toxic fumes and ash engulfed many of the warriors, who were instantly killed. In the midst of these power struggles, the prophet Kapoukahi from Kaua'i told Kamehameha that if he built a new heiau (a stone temple) to honor his war god, Kuka'ilimoku, he would become ruler of all the islands.

Kamehameha thus built Pu'ukohola Heiau (p223) in Kawaihae in 1791. Then he sent word to Keoua that his appearance was requested at the heiau for reconciliation. Keoua, well aware that this was a *luakini* (a temple used for human sacrifices), probably knew his fate was sealed, but he sailed to Kawaihae anyway. Upon landing, Keoua and his party became the heiau's first sacrifices. With Keoua dead, Kamehameha became sole ruler of the Big Island.

Over the next few years, Kamehameha conquered all the islands except Kaua'i, over which he established suzerainty. He named the entire kingdom after his home island, Hawai'i.

HAWAI'I (THE BIG ISLAND)

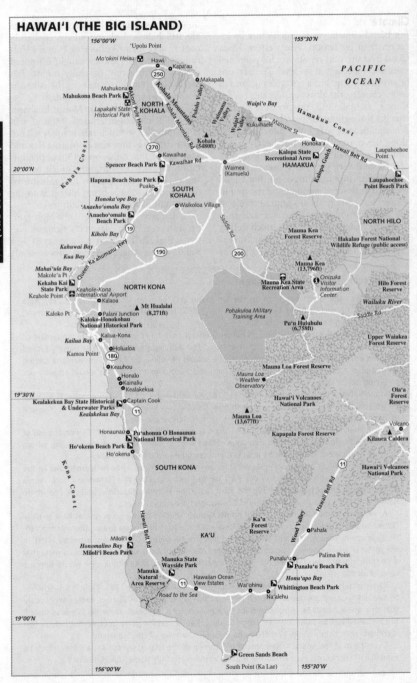

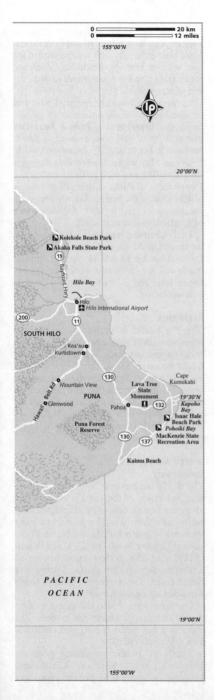

0 [————] 20 km
0 [————] 12 miles

155°00'N

20°00'N

🏕 Kolekole Beach Park
🏕 Akaka Falls State Park
(19)
Bayfront Hwy
Hilo Bay
● Hilo
🛬 Hilo International Airport
(200) (11)
SOUTH HILO
Kea'au ●
Kurtistown ●
(130)   Cape
                     Kumukahi
Mountain View   **Lava Tree**
                State   19°30'N
PUNA   **Monument** Kapoho
Glenwood   🏚 Bay
         Pahoa (132)
                    🏕 Isaac Hale
Hawai'i Belt Rd   Beach Park
Puna Forest   🏚 Pohoiki Bay
Reserve (130)   **MacKenzie State**
              (137) **Recreation Area**
        Kaimu Beach

**PACIFIC
OCEAN**

19°00'N

155°00'W

5°F or so. Nighttime lows are about 15°F less. For more on climate, see p521.

The National Weather Service Hilo provides recorded forecasts for the Big Island (☎ 961-5582), Hilo and surrounds (☎ 935-8555) and for the water conditions (☎ 935-9883). **Hawaii Volcanoes National Park** (☎ 985-6000) has recorded information on eruption activity and viewing points.

National, State & County Parks

Among the Big Island's many parks, Hawai'i Volcanoes National Park (HAVO; p271) is undeniably the headliner. Numerous trails accommodate all levels of hiking, and most major sites are conveniently located along a single loop around Halema'uma'u Crater. Unlike any other park on the island, it's difficult to cover HAVO in just a day.

If you're lucky you'll see a nene, the state bird, which lives on upland volcanic slopes. Just a hundred years ago, an estimated 25,000 nene lived on the Big Island. Today, 1000 or fewer remain in the wild.

The most established historical park is Pu'uhonua o Honaunau (p209), an ancient place of refuge south of Kailua-Kona. However remote Mo'okini Heiau (p226) is haunting in its magnitude and isolation in North Kohala.

Many of the island's finest beaches lie on parkland, such as world-renowned Hapuna Beach (p222). The row of beaches within Kekaha Kai State Park (p215) remains less trafficked, due to difficult access and the lack of amenities, but the state is paving a new road to Manini'owali and it's likely these once-secret beaches will eventually attract crowds.

In east Hawai'i, Akaka Falls State Park (p242) has a paved path that is easily walkable and winds through a lush rain forest. Two other waterfalls are found in Waipi'o Valley (p238), for those who brave the steep trek to the bottom. Hilo's Lili'uokalani Park (p255) and nearby Mokuola (p255) are spacious and ideal for picnics.

CAMPING
The Big Island offers camping at all levels of 'roughin' it.' Some campgrounds, such as Laupahoehoe Point Park (p241), are within view of houses, while others, such as those way up on Mauna Loa (p283), are miles from civilization. For camping supplies, the

**HAWAI'I
(THE BIG ISLAND)**

big-box retailers like Wal-Mart are economical and convenient; in Hilo, visit **Hilo Surplus Store** (Map p253; ☎ 935-6398; 148 Mamo St; ☷ 8am-5pm Mon-Sat), which sells rain gear, stoves, sleeping bags, tents and backpacks.

National Parks
The only national park suitable for camping on the Big Island is Hawai'i Volcanoes National Park, where both campgrounds and cabins are available. See p283 for more information.

State Parks
Camping is allowed at Kalopa State Recreation Area (p241), which has good facilities and a caretaker, and at MacKenzie State Recreation Area (p270), which is rather desolate (many believe powerful spirits dwell in the Mackenzie bluffs, and a camper was murdered there in 1980). Permits are required; the fee is $5 per family campsite.

Cabins cost more: the A-frame cabins at Hapuna Beach State Park (p222) sleep up to four and cost $20 per night; the larger cabins at Kalopa State Recreation Area (p241) cost $55 per night for eight people.

To make a reservation and obtain a permit, contact the **Division of State Parks** (Map p250; ☎ 974-6200; www.hawaii.gov/dlnr/dsp; PO Box 936, Hilo, HI 96721; ☷ 8am-noon Mon-Fri), which accepts reservations in order of priority: first walk-ins, then mail requests, then phone requests. Be warned that the phone is rarely answered and no long-distance calls are returned. The maximum length of stay allowed per permit is five consecutive nights. You can obtain another permit for the same park only after 30 days have passed.

The cabins and shelters are popular with island families and require booking well in advance. Cancellations do occur, however, and if you're flexible with dates, you might be get one without advance reservations.

County Parks
The county allows camping at 10 of its beach parks: Kolekole (p242) and Laupahoehoe (p241), north of Hilo; Isaac Hale (p269) in Puna; Spencer (p223), Mahukona (p225), Ho'okena (p211) and Miloli'i (p211), all on the Kona coast; and Whittington (p286) and Punalu'u (p286), both in Ka'u.

With the exception of Spencer, which is patrolled by a security guard, the county

parks can be rough and noisy areas, as they're popular among late-night drinkers. Isaac Hale especially isn't recommended for solo women. Remote sites in Ka'u don't see much traffic, and are sometimes closed during winter storms.

Camping permits are required, and can be obtained by mail, online or in person from the **Department of Parks & Recreation** (Map p250; ☎ 961-8311; www.co.hawaii.hi.us; Suite 6, 101 Pauahi St, Hilo, HI 96720; ☷ 7:45am-4pm Mon-Fri). You can also make reservations through the Hilo office and pick up the permit at the Department of Parks & Recreation branch offices around the island. Ask whether your specific park currently offers drinking water or treatable catchment water.

Daily camping fees are $5 for adults, $2 for teens and $1 for children 12 and under; Internet booking costs $1 more. Camping is allowed for up to two weeks, except between June and August, when the limit is one week only.

Activities
The Big Island is perfect for outdoorsy types who favor vast, open spaces and vistas of rugged lava rock. While other islands might be better for surfing and windsurfing, the Kona Coast's crystal-clear waters make for ideal snorkeling and respectable diving conditions. And hiking the seemingly endless trails at Hawaii Volcanoes National Park is an experience you'll find nowhere else on earth!

WATER ACTIVITIES
Swimming
The Big Island has over 300 miles of shoreline, but much of the coast is rocky. Only along the Kona Coast will you find powdery white-sand beaches. The best swimming spots are in South Kohala and North Kona, such as Hapuna Beach (p222), Manini'owali (p216) and the perfect crescent-shaped Kauna'oa Bay (p220) by the Mauna Kea Beach Hotel. The snorkeling areas in south Kona are also good for swimming.

On the eastern coast, the seas are often rough and inappropriate for novices. But there is a hot pond (p269) and countless lava tide pools (p269).

There are public swimming pools in Honoka'a, Hilo, Kapa'au, Kealakekua, Laupahoehoe and Pahoa. For directions and open-swim schedules, call the county **Aquatics Division** (☎ 961-8694).

Snorkeling
The waters south of Kailua-Kona are heaven for snorkelers. A popular easy-access snorkeling haunt and a good place for beginners is Kahalu'u Beach (p198) in Keauhou. Two-Step (p210), north of Pu'uonua o Honaunau National Historic Park, is another terrific drive-up snorkeling spot. There's also beautiful snorkeling in the pristine 30ft-deep waters near Captain Cook's monument at the north end of Kealakekua Bay (p205), but you must get there by foot, kayak or horseback.

The cheapest places to rent snorkel gear are in Kailua-Kona. Check out the freebie magazines for coupons. Prices generally run $7 per day and $15 to $40 per week. Snorkeling tours, typically from $80 to $90, can make life easy, transporting you to prime spots and providing gear and food. They depart mainly from Keauhou Bay, Kailua Pier or Honokohau Harbor. It's best to book in advance, especially during high season.

Scuba Diving
Along the Kona Coast, diving conditions are excellent, with warm, calm waters and frequent 100ft visibility. One of the best spots is Ka'awaloa Cove in the Kealakekua Bay State Historical & Underwater Parks (p205). In Kailua-Kona, you can also arrange a thrilling night dive to see manta rays (p189). The best conditions are in spring and summer, but diving is decent year-round. On the Hilo side, the water tends to be cloudy from river runoff, and diving conditions are mediocre.

Most dive outfits are located in Kailua-Kona and charge from $90 to $120 for a two-tank dive (see p189).

Kayaking
Kayaking in lovely **Kealakekua Bay** (p205) is a must. The most popular launching spot is Napo'opo'o Beach, where you paddle across the bay toward the Captain Cook Monument, where you can snorkel and explore.

Surfing
Big Island surf spots often have rugged lava-rock shorelines that require nimble maneuvering. Another hindrance is *wana* (sea urchins that resemble pin-cushions), which abound at some beaches.

Don't expect the monster waves of O'ahu's North Shore. Still, there are a few decent

HAWAI'I (THE BIG ISLAND)

THE BIG ISLAND IN...

Three Days
Assuming you arrive in **Kona** (p185), start by taking it easy at the beach, for example **Kahalu'u Beach** (p198) for snorkeling or **Kealakekua Bay** (p205), for kayaking, too. Later visit **Pu'uhonua o Honaunau** (p209) to imagine old Hawai'i.

On the second day, go for an early swim or visit the galleries in **Holualoa** (p200), then head to **Hawai'i Volcanoes National Park** (p271) for a night. See the main sights around **Halema'uma'u Crater** (p276) and perhaps trek toward the flow. Start your third day with a hike, then loop around **Red Rd** (p269) in laid-back Puna before returning to Kona.

Five Days
Spend your third night in **Hilo** (p249) preferably near the historic downtown. On day four, enjoy a relaxing picnic at **Liliu'okalani Park** (p255), then cruise north along the scenic **Hamakua Coast** (p234), ending with a hike down **Waipi'o Valley** (p238). On your last day, stop at **Puako** (p221) to see tide pools and petroglyphs.

One Week
Follow the five-day itinerary, but spend day five in **Waimea** (p229), where you can go horseback riding or cycling over endless rolling hills. On day six, chill out in rustic **North Kohala** (p224), visiting **Pololu Valley** (p229) and **Mo'okini Heiau** (p226). End your trip either relaxing at a white-sand beach along the Gold Coast – like **Hapuna** (p222) or, better yet, **Kauna'oa Bay** (p222) – or driving up Saddle Rd to the summit of **Mauna Kea** (p243).

HAWAI'I
(THE BIG ISLAND)

THE BIG ISLAND WATER SPORTS

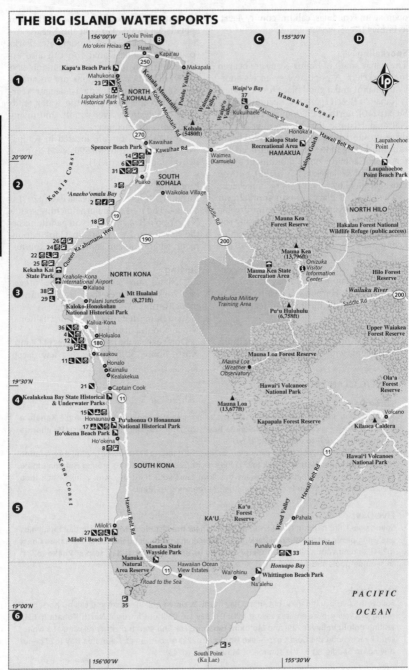

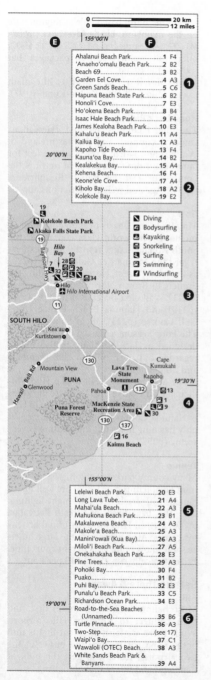

surf breaks where you'll find throngs of dedicated surfers. East Hawai'i's best spots are Honoli'i Cove (p256) and Kolekole Beach Park (p242), both north of Hilo. Pohoiki Bay at Isaac Hale Beach Park (p242) is for experts. Along the Kona Coast, try Kahalu'u Beach (p198) in Keauhou, Banyans (p190) near White Sands Beach, and Pine Trees (p215) near Wawaloli (OTEC) Beach.

Top spots for boogie boarding and body surfing include Hapuna Beach (p222), White Sands Beach (p189), and the beaches at Kekaha Kai State Park (p215).

You can rent a surfboard from local surf shops (per day $10 to $20) or stands near beaches (per day $25, for two hours about $15).

Windsurfing

If windsurfing's your only interest, try another island. But beginner windsurfers will find an ideal spot to learn at 'Anaeho'omalu Bay (p218) in Waikoloa, where you can rent equipment and take lessons. Things get more exciting when the spring trade winds kick up, but novices are warned off at that time.

Fishing

Deep-sea fishing is an obsession on the Kona Coast, which is the world's No 1 spot for catching Pacific blue marlin, a spectacular fighting fish with a long swordlike bill. The waters are also rich with *'ahi* (yellowfin tuna) and *aku* (bonito or skipjack tuna), swordfish, spearfish and mahimahi (dolphin). June to August typically sees the biggest hauls for blue marlin, while January to June is the best for striped marlin. Most of the world records for catches of such fish belong to Kona fishers, with at least one marlin weighing 1000lb or more reeled in virtually every year. For charter tours, see p190.

LAND ACTIVITIES

Hiking

All levels of hikers will find awesome trails on the Big Island. The widest variety of hiking is found at Hawai'i Volcanoes National Park (p271), where trails lead across steaming crater floors, through lush native forests and up to the peak of Mauna Loa.

Along the steep coastal cliffs and deep valleys of the Kohala Mountains, you can take short hikes at Pololu Valley (p229) and

Waipi'o Valley (p239), or backpack deep into remote Waimanu Valley (p240).

North of Kona, you can hike in from the highway to secluded beaches or explore portions of ancient footpaths and petroglyph fields. **Na Ala Hele** (☎ 331-8505; www.hawaiitrails .org), a state-sponsored group of volunteers, is currently working to re-establish the entire 50-mile historic trail system that once ran between Kailua-Kona and Kawaihae. South of Kona, the simple Captain Cook Monument Trail (p207) leads to the spot where he died at Kealakekua Bay, and a jumping-off point for snorkeling (p189).

The most arduous hikes scale the summits of Mauna Kea (p246) and Mauna Loa (p282), where the altitude of almost 14,000ft can be daunting.

For tours, **Hawaiian Walkways** (☎ 775-0372, 800-457-7759; hawaiianwalkways.com) and **Hawaii Forest & Trail** (☎ 331-8505, 800-464-1993; www.hawaii -forest.com) are the Big Island's best outfits, each offering guided hikes to places you might not see otherwise. The Sierra Club's **Big Island Moku Loa Group** (☎ 965-9695; www .hi.sierraclub.org/Hawaii/outings.html; $3 suggested donation for nonmembers) offers low-cost hiking tours, ranging from trekking over new lava rock in Kalapana to backpacking in Pololu Valley. If your heart is set on a particular tour or day, reserve a spot in advance. If you call only a day or two ahead, it might be sold out.

Cycling & Mountain Biking

With wide-open spaces, the Big Island is ideal for both road and mountain biking. In addition to established routes, which include the 45-mile Mana Rd loop (p233) circling Mauna Kea and the 6.5-mile beach trail to Pine Trees (p215) on the Kona Coast, there are also miles of 4WD roads and rocky trails to whip through. To learn more about Big Island mountain biking, contact **People's Advocacy for Trails Hawaii** (☎ 326-9495) in Kona or **Big Island Mountain Bike Association** (☎ 961-4452; www.interpac.net/~mtbike) in Hilo.

For cycling tours of the Big Island, contact **Kona Coast Cycling Tours** (☎ 345-3455, 877-592-2453; www.cyclekona.com; tour ½-day $60-75, full-day $100-155), which allow older kids (12 to 16 years) on many rides at a reduced rate. You can also request custom-designed tours ($150 for the tour) on which a guide will accompany you for the ride (and carry all the supplies!).

Another outfit based in Washington state on the mainland, **Bicycle Adventures** (☎ 800-443-6060; www.bicycleadventures.com; 7-day trip $2400), offers full cycling-vacation packages that traverse the island.

For bicycle rentals, head to the main towns, Hilo (p264) or Kailua-Kona (p197).

Horseback Riding

The Big Island is *paniolo* (Hawaiian-cowboy) country, and the pastureland of Waimea and North Kohala are perfect for horseback riding. An efficient outfit is the family-run Dahana Ranch Roughriders (p231). Age and weight restrictions apply.

Golf

The Big Island boasts over 20 golf courses, including the world-class courses at the South Kohala luxury resorts. Most experts regard the Mauna Kea Golf Course (p223) as the island's best, closely followed by the Francis I'i Brown North & South Courses (p221) Waikoloa Beach & Kings' Courses (p219) and Hapuna Beach Prince Hotel Golf Course (p223), all in South Kohala. The Four Seasons Hualalai Course (p217), designed by Jack Nicklaus, is also highly regarded but open only to club members and hotel guests.

For a sweet deal, head to the Hilo Municipal Golf Course (p257), where the locals play, rain or shine. The other option in Hilo is Naniloa Country Club Golf Course – it only has nine holes but the location is very scenic (p257).

Tennis

Many county parks on the Big Island have municipal tennis courts that are well maintained, with fresh nets and night lighting. Call the **Department of Parks & Recreation** (☎ 961-8311) in Hilo for a list of public tennis courts. Also check with the large hotels as some allow nonguests to rent court time. Prices typically run about $10 per hour.

Getting There & Away
AIR

Most visitors fly into Honolulu first, and then connect to Kona or Hilo airport. While there are fairly frequent flights into both, Kona has become the busier of the two airports. Kona also gets the bulk of mainland and international flights.

ROAD DISTANCES & TIMES

From Hilo

destination	miles	time
Hawi	86	2¼ hr
Honoka'a	40	1 hr
Kailua-Kona	92	2½ hr
Na'alehu	64	1¾ hr
Pahoa	16	½ hr
Volcanoes NP	28	¾ hr
Waikoloa	80	2¼ hr
Waimea	54	1½ hr
Waipi'o Lookout	50	1¼ hr

From Kailua-Kona

destination	miles	time
Hawi	51	1¼ hr
Hilo	92	2½ hr
Honoka'a	61	1½ hr
Na'alehu	60	1½ hr
Pahoa	108	3 hr
Volcanoes NP	98	2½ hr
Waikoloa	18	¾ hr
Waimea	43	1 hr
Waipi'o Lookout	70	1¾ hr

Hilo International Airport (ITO; ☎ 935-5707) Off Hwy 11, just under a mile south of the intersection of Hwys 11 and 19.

Kona International Airport at Keahole (KOA; ☎ 329-3423) On Hwy 19, 7 miles north of Kailua-Kona. A relatively busy airport, but it's all open-air and you disembark directly onto the tarmac. For directions to/from the airport, see right.

See p532 for airline contact details, and more information on flights to the Big Island, from both the mainland and abroad.

The two major interisland carriers are **Hawaiian Airlines** (☎ 800-367-5320; www.hawaiianair .com) and **Aloha Airlines** (☎ 800-367-5250; www.aloha airlines.com). All of Hawaiian and Aloha Airlines' interisland flights require a stopover in Honolulu (except one Hawaiian Airlines flight from Kailua-Kona to Maui). Service through Honolulu is regular, with about 10 flights daily from both Hilo and Kailua-Kona; fares run almost $100 each way.

Another option is **Island Air** (☎ 800-323-3345; www.islandair.com), which is also the only carrier that flies between Kailua-Kona and Hilo (most Big Island tourist opt to drive around the island). But Island Air offers only two to four flights daily. Fares range between about $85 and $110, depending on when you book your flight. (Expect a long wait if you call the 800 number!) See p532 for more on interisland flights.

Getting Around

The Big Island is divided up into six districts: Kona, Kohala, Waimea, Hilo, Puna and Ka'u. The Hawai'i Belt Rd circles the island, covering the main towns and sights. If you really want to explore the Big Island and get to off-the-beaten-path sights, you'll need your own wheels. Public transportation is limited outside of the main towns and tourist resorts.

The best map for getting around the island is the encyclopedic *Ready Mapbook* series, which has separate books for east and west Hawai'i, but admittedly they're bulky. A good lightweight, foldout map is Nelles' *Hawai'i: The Big Island*. The colorful Franko's Map of *Hawai'i, the Big Island* features water sports and is sold at dive shops; its plastic is waterproof and rip-resistant.

TO/FROM THE AIRPORTS

Most Big Island visitors rent cars, and car-hire booths for the major agencies (see p197) line the road outside the arrivals area at both airports.

Hilo International Airport

Taxis can also be found curbside; the approximate fare from Hilo airport to downtown Hilo is $15.

Kona International Airport at Keahole

Taxis can be found curbside; the approximate fare from the airport to Kailua-Kona is $20, and to Waikoloa it's $40.

Shuttle-bus services typically cost nearly as much as taxis. **Speedi Shuttle** (☎ 329-5433; www.speedishuttle.com) charges $17/30 per single person and $18/32 per pair to Kailua-Kona/ Waikoloa (plus tax for all fares). Call 48 hours in advance. If you make a round-trip booking, the return fare is discounted 10%.

BICYCLE

It's possible to cycle around the Big Island, but both sides of the island, and their climactic extremes, can present challenges. The Hilo side is windy and wet, while the Kona and Kohala coasts seesaw between hot and hellishly hot.

What's more, the terrain is almost never flat, with quick, steep elevation gains that will tax even stalwart cyclists – and there are few highway bicycle lanes. However, determined cyclists *do* successfully traverse the island.

Bike shops that rent bicycles also rent safety equipment and carracks and handle repairs and sales. As Kona is the center of activity for the Ironman Triathlon, there are shops that sell and repair high-caliber equipment there.

BUS

A Big Island bus journey just isn't practical, but with a little planning you can get yourself between major towns and attractions. Between Kailua-Kona and Keauhou, the Ali'i Shuttle (p197) bus has several departures daily but only one bus.

Hele-On Bus (☎ 961-8744; www.co.hawaii.hi.us /mass_transit/heleonbus.html; ☻ 7:45am-4:30pm Mon-Fri), the county public bus, offers minimal islandwide service from Monday to Friday, with an even more limited service on Saturday. Schedules are available at the Big Island Visitors Bureau (p252) and the information kiosk at Hilo's Mo'oheau bus terminal (p264). All buses originate from Mo'oheau terminal, unless otherwise noted. Drivers will accept only the exact fare. You can buy a sheet of 10 bus tickets (which normally cost 75¢ each) for $5. You need permission from the driver to board with a surfboard, boogie board or bicycle and you will be charged an extra $1. Luggage and backpacks also entail an additional $1 fee.

CAR & MOTORCYCLE

From Kona to Hilo, the northern half of the belt road is 92 miles, and the nonstop journey takes over two hours. The southern Kona–Hilo route is 125 miles and takes approximately three hours nonstop.

Note that Hwy 19 is called the Queen Ka'ahumanu Hwy from Kawaihae toward Kealakekua. Instead of taking Hwy 19 between Kailua-Kona and Waimea, you can also take a quicker inland route along Hwy 190, the Mamalahoa Hwy.

There are car-hire booths at Kona and Hilo airports:

Alamo Hilo (☎ 961-3343), Kona (☎ 329-8896)
Avis Hilo (☎ 935-1290), Kona (☎ 327-3000)
Budget Hilo (☎ 935-6878), Kona (☎ 329-8511)
Dollar Hilo (☎ 961-6059), Kona (☎ 329-2744)
Hertz Hilo (☎ 935-2896), Kona (☎ 329-3566)
National Hilo (☎ 935-0891), Kona (☎ 329-1674)
Thrifty Hilo (☎ 961-6698), Kona (☎ 329-1339)

For more information on the national chains, including toll-free numbers and websites, see p536.

Harper Car & Truck Rentals (Map p250; ☎ 969-1478, 800-852-9993; www.harpershawaii.com; 456 Kalaniana'ole Ave, Hilo) is the local car-hire agency. Only Harper puts no restrictions on driving their 4WDs to Mauna Kea's summit, or almost anywhere on the island, except Waipi'o Valley and Green Sands Beach.

But bear in mind that if you damage a vehicle you'll pay a high deductible. Rental costs are about $66 per day and $276 per week (including taxes) for a compact car. Renting a 4WD vehicle costs – brace yourself – $138 per day and $709 per week (including taxes).

TAXI

On the Big Island, cab drivers are typically locals who are familiar with the island, and often act as tour guides. It's easy to find a cab at either airport, but most companies are small, with no advertisements or *Yellow Pages* listings. Cabs don't run all night or cruise for passengers, so in town you'll need to call ahead. The standard flag-down fee is $2, plus $2 per mile thereafter.

TOURS
Bus & Van

Several longtime tour operators offer around-the-island tours, which are essentially a mad dash through Kailua-Kona, Hawai'i Volcanoes National Park (focusing on sights along Crater Rim Dr), Punalu'u black-sand beach, Hilo's Rainbow Falls, the Hamakua Coast and Waimea. Trust us, you'll get only a quick glimpse of the island and might be better off watching a PBS documentary instead.

Roberts Hawaii (☎ 329-1688, 800-831-5411; www .roberts-hawaii.com), **Jack's Tours** (☎ 961-6666, 800-442-5557; www.jackshawaii.com) and **Polynesian Adventure Tours** (☎ 329-8008, 800-622-3011; www.polyad .com) offer daylong circle-island bus tours that cost from $55. Both companies pick up passengers at hotels in Waikoloa, Kailua-Kona and Keauhou; the exact time varies by location, but expect to leave at around sunrise and get back around sunset.

Helicopter

If buses are not enough for you, catch a bird's-eye view of the island in a helicopter. The most popular helicopter tours fly over Kilauea Caldera, and the live lava flows of the East Rift Zone (before booking, ask specifically whether they fly over the active Pu'u 'O'o vent or not). Other helicopter tours buzz around the valleys of the Kohala and Hamakua coasts. Expect to pay $120 or more for each 45-minute flight, or up to $350 for a combined two-hour flight.

Helicopter tours are cancelled during inclement weather, but may fly when it's overcast, which limits visibility. Wait for a sparkling clear day, if you can, and remember that even if it's sunny in Kona, it may be hazy over Volcano. Check the free tourist magazines, which are widely available, for discount coupons. Call around to compare prices, especially if you're willing to fly standby:

Blue Hawaiian Helicopters (☎ 961-5600, 800-786-2583; www.bluehawaiian.com)

Safari Helicopters (☎ 969-1259, 800-326-3356; www.safariair.com)

Sunshine Helicopters (www.sunshinehelicopters.com) Hilo (☎ 969-7501, 800-621-3144), Kona (☎ 882-1223)

Tropical Helicopters (☎ 961-6810; www.tropicalhelicopters.com)

Island Hoppers (☎ 969-2000, 800-538-7590; www.fly-hawaii.com/above) Has cheaper 50-minute 'flightseeing tours' by small prop plane.

KAILUA-KONA

pop 10,000

At first glance, Kailua-Kona might seem a kitschy tropical town, with colorful shopping bazaars, sunburnt tourists and a nonstop swath of beachfront hotels. Its tropical heat and central location, on the Kona Coast, attract hundreds of thousands of visitors annually (well over double the number drawn to Hilo).

But take a closer look at Kailua and the Kona district, and you'll find yourself immersed in Hawaiian history. In old Hawai'i,

---

NAME THAT TOWN

Often confusing to nonlocals are Kailua-Kona's alternative names, so here's the scoop. The town started out as simply Kailua. But when the post office discovered there was a Kailua on O'ahu and another on Maui, they renamed the Big Island town Kailua-Kona. Kona means 'leeward' and the Kona Coast refers to dry, sunny west Hawai'i. Locals call the town both Kailua and Kona (and also Kailua-Kona). If they refer to Kona, they *usually* mean Kailua, but they *might* mean any of the towns or beaches along the Kona Coast. Got it?

Kailua Bay was a leisurely retreat for royalty and the site of significant events in the reign of King Kamehameha the Great.

While Hilo is the governmental seat of the island, Kailua's economic clout has skyrocketed since the 1960s, when resorts and condos mushroomed along the coast. With the end of the sugar industry in Hawaii by the mid-1990s, tourism and other crops, including world-renowned Kona coffee, took center stage.

Kailua might feel a tad commercial, but here you'll find an abundance of affordable lodging and beaches literally bordering the highway – a convenient home base for exploring the Kona Coast.

HISTORY

By and large, the Big Island's history, especially along the Kona Coast, is the history of all of the Hawaiian Islands. The first Polynesians arrived here between AD 500 and AD 700. The first *luakini* and the *kapu* (taboo) system emerged here in the 12th century. Seven centuries later, Kamehameha the Great lived his last years here, worshipping at his personal heiau. The traditional belief in Hawaiian gods collapsed here in 1819, when King Kamehameha's son, Liholiho, broke the *kapu* by dining with women, and no godly wrath ensued. A year later, the first missionaries sailed into Kailua Bay and transformed the Hawaiian islands into a Christian society.

ORIENTATION

Kailua-Kona is south of the airport on Hwy 19, which becomes Hwy 11 at Palani Rd, the primary entry to Kailua town. The highways and major roads in the Kona district parallel the coastline, so navigating is easy. Ali'i Dr is Kailua's main street, with the vast majority of hotels and condos abutting the 5-mile coastal road that runs south to Keauhou.

Ali'i Dr is usually bustling with pedestrian traffic, a welcome change from the typical Big Island streets dominated by cars. At dawn, power walkers and joggers take advantage of the scenic strip, which serves as the finish line of the legendary Ironman Triathlon each October. Kailua's shopping malls and supermarkets are found slightly inland, within the 'downtown' area between Ali'i Dr and the highway.

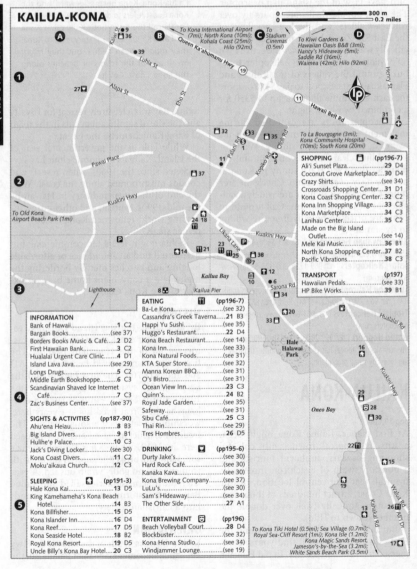

KAILUA-KONA

INFORMATION
Bank of Hawaii.....................................1 C2
Bargain Books..............................(see 37)
Borders Books Music & Café......2 D2
First Hawaiian Bank......................3 C2
Hualalai Urgent Care Clinic......4 D1
Island Lava Java.........................(see 29)
Longs Drugs....................................5 C3
Middle Earth Bookshoppe.........6 C3
Scandinavian Shaved Ice Internet
  Café...7 C3
Zac's Business Center..............(see 37)

SIGHTS & ACTIVITIES   (pp187-90)
Ahu'ena Heiau.................................8 B3
Big Island Divers............................9 B1
Hulihe'e Palace..............................10 C3
Jack's Diving Locker...................(see 30)
Kona Coast Divers.......................11 C3
Moku'aikaua Church....................12 C3

SLEEPING   (pp191-3)
Hale Kona Kai................................13 D5
King Kamehameha's Kona Beach
  Hotel...14 B3
Kona Billfisher................................15 D5
Kona Islander Inn.........................16 D4
Kona Reef..17 D5
Kona Seaside Hotel.......................18 B2
Royal Kona Resort........................19 D5
Uncle Billy's Kona Bay Hotel......20 C3

EATING   (pp196-7)
Ba-Le Kona.................................(see 32)
Cassandra's Greek Taverna.......21 B3
Happi Yu Sushi...........................(see 35)
Huggo's Restaurant.....................22 D4
Kona Beach Restaurant...........(see 14)
Kona Inn.....................................(see 33)
Kona Natural Foods..................(see 31)
KTA Super Store........................(see 32)
Manna Korean BBQ...................(see 31)
O's Bistro...................................(see 31)
Ocean View Inn...........................23 C3
Quinn's...24 B2
Royal Jade Garden....................(see 35)
Safeway.....................................(see 31)
Sibu Café......................................25 C3
Thai Rin.....................................(see 29)
Tres Hombres...............................26 D5

DRINKING   (pp195-6)
Durty Jake's...............................(see 30)
Hard Rock Café..........................(see 30)
Kanaka Kava..............................(see 30)
Kona Brewing Company..........(see 37)
LuLu's..(see 30)
Sam's Hideaway.........................(see 34)
The Other Side.............................27 A1

ENTERTAINMENT   (pp196)
Beach Volleyball Court................28 D4
Blockbuster................................(see 32)
Kona Henna Studio...................(see 34)
Windjammer Lounge................(see 19)

SHOPPING   (pp196-7)
Ali'i Sunset Plaza.........................29 D4
Coconut Grove Marketplace......30 D4
Crazy Shirts...............................(see 34)
Crossroads Shopping Center......31 D1
Kona Coast Shopping Center......32 C2
Kona Inn Shopping Village.........33 C3
Kona Marketplace........................34 C3
Lanihau Center.............................35 C2
Made on the Big Island
  Outlet......................................(see 14)
Mele Kai Music.............................36 B1
North Kona Shopping Center......37 B2
Pacific Vibrations.........................38 C3

TRANSPORT   (p197)
Hawaiian Pedals.......................(see 33)
HP Bike Works..............................39 B1

To Kona International Airport
(7mi); North Kona (10mi);
Kohala Coast (25mi); Hilo (92mi)

To Stadium
Cinemas
(0.5mi)

To Kiwi Gardens &
Hawaiian Oasis B&B (3mi);
Nancy's Hideaway (5mi);
Saddle Rd (36mi);
Waimea (42mi); Hilo (92mi)

To La Bourgogne (3mi);
Kona Community Hospital
(10mi); South Kona (20mi)

To Old Kona
Airport Beach Park (1mi)

Kailua Bay
Kailua Pier
Lighthouse

Hale
Halawai
Park

Oneo Bay

To Kona Tiki Hotel (0.5mi); Sea Village (0.7mi);
Royal Sea-Cliff Resort (1mi); Kona Isle (1.2mi);
Kona Magic Sands Resort,
Jameson's-by-the-Sea (3.2mi);
White Sands Beach Park (3.5mi)

0   300 m
0   0.2 miles

INFORMATION

Bookstores

Bargain Books (☎ 326-7790; North Kona Shopping Center, 75-5629 Kuakini Hwy; ⏰ 10am-9pm Mon-Sat, to 6pm Sun) Well-organized selection of new and used books; good for bargain hunters.

Borders Books Music & Café (☎ 331-1668; 75-1000 Henry St, at Hwy 11; ⏰ 9am-9pm Sun-Thu, to 10pm Fri & Sat) Largest bookseller in Kailua-Kona, with many US and foreign newspapers.

Middle Earth Bookshoppe (☎ 329-2123; 75-5719 Ali'i Dr; ⏰ 9am-9pm Mon-Sat, to 6pm Sun) Indie bookstore tucked in a quiet alley; excellent Hawaiiana and travel sections.

Emergency

Police (☎ 935-3311) For nonemergencies.
Police, Fire & Ambulance (☎ 911) For emergencies.
Sexual Assault Hotline (☎ 935-0677)
Suicide Prevention Hotline (☎ 800-784-2433)

Internet Access

Island Lava Java (☎ 327-2161; Ali'i Sunset Plaza, 75-5799 Ali'i Dr; per 15 min $3; ⏰ 6am-10pm) Popular café but computers are inside, where it can get stuffy.

Scandinavian Shaved Ice Internet Café (☎ 331-1626; 75-5699 Ali'i Dr; per 15 min $2.25; ⏰ 10am-9:30pm Mon-Sat, noon-9pm Sun) Small, closetlike space, saved by the wafting aroma of ice cream and waffle cones.

Zac's Business Center (☎ 329-0006; North Kona Shopping Center, 75-5629 Kuakini Hwy; per 15 min $2.75; ⏰ 8am-6pm Mon-Fri, 9am-5pm Sat) All-purpose center for faxing, copying, scanning and Internet access.

Media

NEWSPAPERS

Hawaii Island Journal (www.hawaiiislandjournal.com) Free bimonthly alternative paper with excellent coverage of current (and often controversial) Big Island issues, plus comprehensive arts and entertainment listings.

Hawaii Tribune-Herald (www.hilohawaiitribune.com) Published Sunday through Friday.

West Hawaii Today (www.westhawaiitoday.com) Kona Coast's daily newspaper.

The free tourist guides can also be surprisingly informative. In Kona, look for *Coffee Times* (www.coffeetimes.com).

RADIO

Due to the Big Island's size and mountainous terrain, west Hawai'i stations broadcast only in the vicinity. Often a station will simulcast shows at different frequencies on either side of the island. Check out www .hawaiiradiotv.com/BigIsleRadio for a complete listing.

KAGB 99.1 FM Island hits on station voted the best in *Hawaii Island Journal*.
KAOY 101.5 FM (www.kwxx.com) Island and pop hits.
KKON 790AM Oldies station.
KLEO 106.1 FM (www.kbigfm.com) Hawaii's big hits.
KLUA 93.3 FM 'Kiss FM' contemporary pop.
KRTR 105.5 FM (www.krater96.com) Adult contemporary.

Medical Services

Hualalai Urgent Care Clinic (☎ 327-4357; 75-1028 Henry St; ⏰ 8am-5pm Mon-Fri, 9am-5pm Sat) For non-emergency medical care. Appointments are recommended. It's across from Wal-Mart.

Kona Community Hospital (☎ 322-9311; www.kch .hhsc.org; 79-1019 Haukapila St, Kealakekua) Located about 10 miles south of Kailua-Kona, off Hwy 11.

Longs Drug (☎ 329-1380; Lanihau Center, 75-5595 Palani Rd; ⏰ 8am-9pm Mon-Sat, to 6pm Sun) For prescriptions, this one is centrally located.

Money

Bank of Hawaii (☎ 326-3903; Lanihau Center, 75-5595 Palani Rd) and **First Hawaiian Bank** (☎ 329-2461; Lanihau Center, 74-5593 Palani Rd) have branches with 24-hour ATMs.

Post

Post office (☎ 331-8307; Lanihau Center, 74-5577 Palani Rd, Kailua-Kona; ⏰ 8:30am-4:30pm Mon-Fri, 9:30am-1:30pm Sat) Holds general-delivery mail for 10 days.

Tourist Information

Be wary of 'tourist information' booths along Ali'i Dr, because they often are fronts for aggressive salespeople, who try to lure visitors into buying a time-share. The best information sources are in neighboring Kona towns: the **Kona Historical Society** (p203) has a small museum and office in Kealakekua; the nearest **Big Island Visitors Bureau** (p218) is in Waikoloa. See also p529.

SIGHTS

Many historic sites are still standing in Kailua. You can see the place where King Kamehameha's heiau was built, the first Christian church in Hawaii, and a stone palace that served as a vacation home for Hawaiian royalty.

Kailua-Kona's downtown area, starting at the north end of Ali'i Dr, includes a handful of historic buildings and landmarks, and popular (often too popular) family beaches at both the north and south ends. Ancient Hawaiian sites are seldom ornate, and you might need to take a second glance to appreciate their significance. Try to observe the setting, which is always carefully chosen, and the power of the *'aina* (land) might reveal itself.

Ahu'ena Heiau

Kamehameha the Great established his kingdom's royal court in Lahaina on Maui, but he returned to his Kamakahonu ('Eye of the Turtle') residence, on the north side of Kailua Bay, where he died in May 1819. His personal temple, **Ahu'ena Heiau** (admission free), lies just *makai* (seaward) of King Kamehameha's Kona Beach Hotel (p192). Hotel permission is not necessary to view the site.

Moku'aikaua Church

On April 4, 1820, Hawai'i's first Christian missionaries sailed into Kailua Bay. When they landed, they were unaware that Hawai'i's old religion had been abolished on that very spot just a few months before. Their timing couldn't have been more auspicious. King Liholiho gave them this site, just a few minutes' walk from Kamehameha's Ahu'ena Heiau, to establish Hawai'i's first Christian church.

Completed in 1836, **Moku'aikaua Church** (☎ 329-1589; 75-5713 Ali'i Dr; admission free; ⏲ services 8am & 10:30am Sun, 7pm Wed) is a handsome building with walls of lava rock held together by a mortar of sand and coral lime. The posts and beams, hewn with stone adzes, and smoothed down with chunks of coral, are made from resilient ohia, and the pews and pulpit are made of koa, the most prized native hardwood. The steeple tops out at 112ft, making the church the tallest structure in Kailua. The interior is cool and serene, and specially built to take advantage of trade winds that blow through its length.

Hulihe'e Palace

Hawaii's second governor, 'John Adams' Kuakini, commissioned this simple but elegant two-story house in 1838 as his private residence. Used as a vacation getaway for Hawaiian monarchs, the house, originally built with lava rock in 1885, was plastered over inside and out by King Kalakaua, who preferred a more polished style after his travels abroad.

Prince Kuhio, who inherited the palace from his uncle Kalakaua, auctioned off the furnishings and artifacts to raise money, but his wife and other female royalty meticulously numbered each piece and recorded the name of the bidder. Eventually the Daughters of Hawai'i, a group founded in 1903 by daughters of missionaries, tracked down the owners and persuaded many to donate the pieces for display in the **museum** (☎ 329-1877; 75-5718 Ali'i Dr; www.huliheepalace.org; adult/child/senior $6/1/4; ⏲ 9am-4pm Mon-Fri, 10am-4pm Sat & Sun) they established at the palace.

The two-story palace has both Western antiques, collected on royal jaunts to Europe, and Hawaiian artifacts, such as a table inlaid with 25 kinds of native Hawaiian wood, some now extinct, and a number of Kamehameha the Great's war spears.

There's no charge to take a peek at the **fishpond** behind the palace. Although no longer stocked, the pond holds a few colorful tropical fish. Curiously, it also once served as a queen's bath and a canoe landing.

Photography is prohibited in the museum to protect the pieces from light, and to keep people from duplicating the designs. Admission includes a 40-minute tour, which provides interesting anecdotes about past royal occupants. The walking tour (p190) offered by the Kona Historical Society also includes museum admission.

Kailua Pier

Kailua Bay, just across the street from Ahu'ena Heiau, was once a major cattle-shipping area. Cattle driven down from hillside ranches were stampeded into the water and forced to swim out to waiting steamers, where they were hoisted aboard by sling and shipped to Honolulu slaughterhouses.

Built in 1915, the pier was long the center of sportfishing on Hawai'i, but it became too crowded. Now Kona's charter fishing boats use the larger Honokohau Harbor north of town. Kailua Pier is mainly used by dive boats and cruise ships, though its hoist and scales are still used for weigh-ins during billfish tournaments.

Kona Brewing Company

Located in the nondescript North Kona Shopping Center, the **Kona Brewing Company** (☎ 334-2739; North Kona Shopping Center, 75-5629 Kuakini Hwy; www.konabrewingco.com; admission & tour free; ⏲ 11am-10pm, to 11pm Fri & Sat, tours 10:30am & 3pm Mon-Fri) is a Kona icon and the Big Island's first microbrewery. Started in 1994 by Cameron Healy and his son Khalsa, this little family-run operation now ships its brew to outer islands and local grocers. Specialty ales include Big Wave Golden, which blends traditional pale and honey malts, and Liliko'i Wheat, with a light, passion-fruit accent. Handcrafted ales can be sampled at the conclusion of the tour.

Old Kona Airport Beach Park

With its unglamorous (but apt) name, the **Old Kona Airport Beach** is often bypassed. However the spacious beach, which became a state park on the site of the old Kona airport, is worth visiting. You'll find solitude here, amid the sound of waves rather than traffic noise. To get here, take the Kuakini Hwy to its end, 1 mile north of downtown.

The old runway skirts a long sandy beach, but lava rocks also run the length of the shore between the sand and the ocean. Swimming is poor here but the beach is perfect for fishing and exploring tide pools. At low tide, the rocks reveal countless aquariumlike pockets holding tiny sea urchins, crabs and bits of coral. A couple of breaks in the lava, including one in front of the first picnic area, allow entry into the water.

The **Garden Eel Cove**, which can be reached by a short walk from the north end of the beach, is a good area for scuba divers and confident snorkelers. The reef fish are large and plentiful, and a steep coral wall in deeper waters harbors moray eels and a wide variety of other sea creatures.

When the surf's up, local surfers flock to an offshore break at 'Shark Rocks.' In high surf, though, it's too rough for other water activities.

Facilities include restrooms, showers and covered picnic tables on a lawn dotted with beach heliotrope and short coconut palms. The Kailua-Kona end of the park contains a gym, soccer and softball fields, four night-lit tennis courts and a horseshoe-toss pit. Next to the old runway is a mile-long loop that locals use as a track. Last but surely not least, there's ample parking.

White Sands Beach Park

Just south of Kailua you'll find a popular county beach park called **White Sands**, **Magic Sands** or **Disappearing Sands**. All the same beach, it earned its moniker because the sand can disappear literally overnight during high surf in winter. The exposed rocks and coral make the beach too treacherous for average swimmers. Eventually however the sand magically returns, transforming the shore back into a white-sand beach. White Sands is known as an ideal boogie-boarding and bodysurfing spot. Facilities include restrooms, showers, picnic tables and a volleyball court; a lifeguard is on duty.

ACTIVITIES

For information on hiring a bicycle see p197.

Swimming

The beaches in and around Kailua-Kona are small and scarce, especially in contrast with the long expanse of sandy shore in South Kohala. Kailua-Kona beaches are convenient, and popular, but they face the same fate of all city beaches: crowds and zooming highway traffic nearby.

The miniature **beach** in front of King Kamehameha's Kona Beach Hotel (p192) is Kailua-Kona's only downtown swimming spot. The waters are calm and safe for children, and the hotel's beach hut rents snorkels, kayaks, beach chairs and umbrellas.

Just beyond Kailua, however, your options increase dramatically on the North Kona Coast (p211) and the South Kona Coast (p201). Check out Old Kona Airport Beach (p189) and White Sands Beach (p189) if you need to stay close to Kailua-Kona.

Snorkeling & Diving

Near the shore, divers can see steep dropoffs with lava tubes, caves and diverse marine life. In deeper waters there are 40 popular boat-dive areas, including an airplane wreck off Keahole Point.

One well-known dive spot is **Red Hill**, an underwater cinder cone about 10 miles south of Kona. It has beautiful lava formations – including ledges and lots of honeycombed lava tubes nicely lit by streaks of sunlight – as well as coral pinnacles and many brightly colored nudibranchs (mollusks).

Coral and other marine life flourish in nearby **Kealakekua Bay** (p205), a protected cove that's calm year-round.

For a unique underwater thrill, go night diving to see giant manta rays. With 'wing' spans of 8ft to 12ft wide, the sheer size of these gentle creatures will amaze you. Divers hold lights that attract plankton, which draws the manta rays to come to feed.

Many dive shops operate from Kailua-Kona. The cost of a two-tank dive ranges from $90 to $120, depending on whether you also need to rent gear. Night dives to see manta rays cost between $65 and $120. The larger five-star PADI operations offer certification courses for around $500.

There are plenty of top-dive operations in Kailua-Kona:

Aloha Dive Company (☎ 325-5560, 800-708-5662; www.alohadive.com) A personable small company run by locals Mike and Buffy Nakachi and Earl Kam. Groups are limited to six on the 28ft boat.

Big Island Divers (☎ 329-6068; 800-488-6068; www .bigislanddivers.com; 74-5467 Kaiwi St; ☺ 8am-6pm) More personable staff with expansive shop (No 1 Aqua Lung dealer on the island). Offers manta-ray dives nightly either with six or eight divers (with one guide) or twelve divers (two guides).

Dive Makai (☎ 329-2025; www.divemakai.com) A small, friendly operation run by a husband-and-wife team with a 31ft boat. In business for nearly three decades, they provide thorough predive briefings, limit groups to 12 people and keep dives unstructured.

Jack's Diving Locker (☎ 329-7585, 800-345-4807; www.jacksdivinglocker.com; Coconut Grove Marketplace, 75-5819 Ali'i Dr; ☺ 8am-9pm) One of the best outfits for introductory dives, as well as night dives to see the manta rays. Housed at a 5000ft facility, with a store, classrooms, a tank room and a 12ft-deep dive pool. There are also two 38ft boats and one 23ft craft, with up to 12 divers each.

Surfing

White Sands Beach (p189) is a favorite spot for boogie boarding, while board surfers prefer **Banyans**, near the banyan tree north of White Sands Beach, and nearby **Kahalu'u Beach** (p198), as well as **Pine Trees** near **Wawaloli (OTEC) Beach** (p215).

For expert advice on surfing and Kona beaches, visit **Pacific Vibrations** (☎ 329-4140; pacvibe@hawaii.rr.com; 75-5702 Likana Ln, at Ali'i Dr; ☺ 10am-5:30pm Mon-Fri, to 3:30pm Sat), the first surf shop in west Hawai'i. Still family-run, the friendly staff includes professional surfers and an Ironman triathlete. You can also buy or rent boards ($10 to $20 per day).

Fishing

Kona has more than 100 charter fishing boats; many are listed in the *Fishing* freebie,

which can be picked up at tourist offices and airports. The standard cost for joining an existing party starts at $60 per person for a half-day (four-hour) trip ($40 if you don't fish). Otherwise, if you charter a whole boat, you can take up to six people for between $200 and $425 for a half-day, and $495 and $750 for a full day, depending upon the boat. Prices include fishing equipment but not food or drink.

You can also catch the boats coming in and ogle at the fish weighed at Honokohau Harbor from 11am for the morning charters and around 3pm for the afternoon and full-day charters. Boats flying white flags scored 'ahi, blue flags mean marlin, and inverted flags signify a catch-and-release excursion.

There are centers that each book numerous boats:

Charter Services Hawaii (☎ 334-1881, 800-567-2650; www.konazone.com)

Fins & Fairways (☎ 325-6171; www.fishkona.com)

Kona Charter Skippers Association (☎ 329-3600, 800-762-7546; www.konabiggamefishing.com)

Charter Desk (☎ 329-5735, 888-566-2487; www .charterdesk.com)

TOURS

Atlantis Submarines (☎ 329-6626, 800-548-6262; www.atlantisadventures.com; 45-min ride adult/child $80/40; ☺ departures 10am, 11:30am & 1pm) Submarines dive down about 100ft in a coral crevice in front of the Royal Kona Resort. The sub has 26 portholes, carries 48 passengers and the outing lasts one hour, including the boat ride to the sub. Japanese-speaking guides are available.

Kailua Bay Charter Company (☎ 324-1749; www .konaglassbottomboat.com; 50-min tour adult/child $25/10; ☺ departures 10:30am, 11:30am & 12:30pm Mon-Sat) Ralph Jewell's 36ft glass-bottom-boat cruise shows off Kona's underwater reef in more vivid colors than you'd see down below. Because you're skimming the waters, you can also see the coastline and perhaps dolphins or whales. An onboard naturalist and pleasant crew, plus easy boarding for elderly or mobility-impaired travelers.

Kona Historical Society (☎ 323-3222; www .konahistorical.org; 75-min tour incl palace admission $15; ☺ 9:30am & 1:30pm Tue & Fri) Offers a walking tour that starts at King Kamehameha's Kona Beach Hotel and covers historical sites such as Hulihe'e Palace, Moku'aikaua Church and the Kona Inn.

FESTIVALS & EVENTS

Kailua's two main festivals highlight the region's specialty commodities: beer and coffee.

Kona Brewers Festival (2nd Saturday in March; ☎ 334-2739; www.konabrewingco.com; admission $40) A food-and-beer event geared for 'just folks' rather than the connoisseur crowd, the Kona Brewers Festival feature 30 craft breweries annually. Beer tasters can also try gourmet samples from a couple dozen local restaurants. The owners of the Kona Brewing Company (p188) established the festival in 1995, and funds go to local environmental and cultural organizations. Tickets are usually sold out by the day before the festival, so order in advance.

Hawaiian International Billfish Tournament (early August; ☎ 329-6155; www.konabillfish.com) Of the numerous fishing tournaments held in Kona, the grand-daddy of them all is this one, accompanied by a week of festive entertainment.

Ironman Triathlon World Championship (3rd Saturday in October; ☎ 329-0063; www.ironmanlive.com; Ste 101, 75-5722 Kuakini Hwy, Kailua-Kona, HI 96740) The legendary event combines a 2.4-mile ocean swim, 112-mile bike race and 26.2-mile marathon into the granddaddy of races. About 1700 men and women from around the world qualify to compete each year. Start time is 7am (6:45am for the pros) at the Kailua Pier, and top triathletes cross the finish line around 3pm; the finish line stays open to stragglers until midnight (kudos!).

Kona Coffee Cultural Festival (early November; ☎ 326-7820; www.konacoffeefest.com; admission $3, surcharges apply for some events) For 10 days during coffee harvest season, the community celebrates the Kona coffee pioneers and their gourmet brew. The dozens of events include a cupping competition (akin to wine tasting), art exhibits, farm tours, parades and a race to pick the most coffee beans in three minutes (a recent winner picked over 23lb!).

SLEEPING

In the heart of Kailua-Kona, you won't find the luxury resorts or cozy B&Bs, but you will find convenience and proximity to shops. Ali'i Dr feels like a small-scale Waikiki, with ABC stores selling cheap tourist souvenirs, vacationers in matching aloha attire, and a surplus of hotels and condominiums, restaurants and people-watching venues.

Here, condos outnumber hotels many times over. Condos tend to be cheaper than hotels if you're staying a while, and most condo units have fully equipped kitchens. Reservations are recommended in the high season. The year-round heat in Kailua-Kona can be brutal, so air-con is virtually indispensable wherever you stay.

Bookings in most of Kona's condominiums are managed by local agencies: guests contract with the agency and not the office staff at the condo (which generally deals

only with grounds maintenance). If you have your heart set on a particular condo, call each agency for availability. Also do a Google search of the condo to find other management companies (that might handle one or two units) and individual owners. Prices in the same condo might vary since units are separately owned. The most often–used agencies are listed below:

Hawaii Resort Management (☎ 329-9393, 800-622-5348; www.konahawaii.com; Ste 105C, 75-5776 Kuakini Hwy)

Knutson & Associates (☎ 329-6311, 800-800-6202; www.konahawaiirentals.com; Ste 8, 75-6082 Ali'i Dr)

SunQuest Vacations & Property Management Hawaii (☎ 329-6488, 800-367-5168; www.sunquest-hawaii.com; 77-6435 Kuakini Hwy)

ATR Properties (☎ 329-6020, 888-311-6020; www.konacondo.com; Ste A-5, 75-5660 Kopiko St)

For more information on condo bookings, minimum-stay requirements and how to get the best rates, see p519 in the Directory chapter.

Budget

Kona Tiki Hotel (☎ 329-1425; 75-5968 Ali'i Dr; r incl breakfast $61, plus kitchenette $84; P ☒ ☒) A sweet deal for a vintage three-story complex near the ocean, if you want a no-frills room (sans TV, phone and air-con). Most of the rooms have a queen-size and a twin bed, and all have a refrigerator and a breezy oceanfront lanai. It's perennially popular with return visitors. No credit cards accepted.

Kona Isle (75-6100 Ali'i Dr; 1-bedroom units $60-115; P ☒ ☒) If the Kona Islander Inn is like the party dorm in college, this complex is the studious dorm, a reputation that gives the place plenty of repeat business and long-term residents. Units enjoy amenities including picnic tables, barbecue grills and chaise lounges overlooking the ocean. There's also a small saltwater pool near the beach.

Kona Islander Inn (☎ 329-9393, 800-622-5348; www.konahawaii.com; 75-5776 Kuakini Hwy; studio units $60-90; P ☒ ☒) You can't get any closer to the Ali'i Dr hub than the Islander, managed almost entirely by Hawaii Resort Management. Ground-floor rooms have a cavernous feel and furnishings are rather worn, but for the price, they're a bargain, with TV, kitchenette (the sink is shared with the bathroom) and phone with free local calls. The Islander draws a local crowd as well, and you might find a high-school band or club occupying whole wings. The cons: rampant mosquitoes in the garden lobby and a major lack of parking (roughly 50 spaces for 150 units!).

Mid-Range

Hale Kona Kai (☎ 329-2155, 800-421-3696; hkk .kona@verizon.net; 75-5870 Kahakai Rd; 1-bedroom units $125-135; P ⊠ ⚲) Just south of the Royal Kona Resort, Hale Kona Kai is a 22-unit gem right at the water's edge – ideal if you want to avoid the high-rise masses and enjoy the sound of the surf all night. The units aren't new, but they're comfortable, often upgraded, and with a full kitchen and cable TV. All have waterfront lanai and the corner units enjoy a wraparound lanai. A $150 security deposit is required, and there's no holiday check-in.

King Kamehameha's Kona Beach Hotel (☎ 329-2911, 800-367-2111; www.konabeachhotel.com; 75-5660 Palani Rd; r $135-200; P ⊠ ⚲) At the very north end of Ali'i Dr, this 460-room hotel is very convenient to restaurants and shops, but less so for beaches. Locals often stop to browse the shops and cool off after driving to Kailua-Kona from other towns. The furnishings are showing their age, but each room includes two double beds, private lanai, refrigerator, TV and phone. Hotel staff quickly solve any problems. The lobby is a well-used oasis with refreshingly chilly air-con and a modest collection of showcases displaying traditional Hawaiian artifacts. Parking costs $7 per day.

Sea Village (☎ 329-6438 75-6002 Ali'i Dr; 1-bedroom units $95-160; P ⊠ ⚲) One of the most popular Ali'i Dr condos, the Sea Village, about 2 miles outside town, features well-kept grounds that include a tennis court and pool. Call the front desk to fax a list of management agencies that handle bookings.

THE AUTHOR'S CHOICE

Kona Magic Sands Resort (☎ 329-3333; 77-6452 Ali'i Dr; studio units $95-125; P ⊠ ⚲) If it's true that location is everything, Magic Sands has it all, with White Sands Beach to the south and Pahoehoe Park to the north. Units in the all-concrete building (which keeps out noise and heat) are compact studios, but they have full kitchen, TV, phone, rattan furnishings and oceanfront lanai. It's great value for being right on the water.

Kona Billfisher (75-5841 Ali'i Dr; 1-/2-bedroom units $90-105/115-135; P ⊠ ⚲) Although located on the *mauka* side of Ali'i Dr, the clean, low-key Billfisher feels more like an apartment complex than a tourist hotel with decor that's more consistent and better upkept than that at similarly priced complexes. The timeshare units include a queen-size sofa bed, a king-size bed in the bedroom, both a ceiling fan and air-con, plus full kitchen and lanai. There's an extra charge for a telephone ($5 per week) and for air-con ($5 per day). All units close for maintenance monthly from 10am on the 13th to 3pm on the 15th.

Nancy's Hideaway (☎ 325-3132, 866-325-3132; www.nancyshideaway.com; 73-1530 Uanani Pl; studio/ 1-bedroom cottage d incl breakfast $110/130; P) Driving 6 miles upland to Nancy's, you enter a whole different world, where the air is moist and cool, banana trees grow wild, and you can gaze upon Kailua town in the distance. Free-standing, immaculate cottages have private lanai, phone, TV, VCR and ample breakfast fixings. Perfect for visitors who want a home base far from the Ali'i Dr bustle. To maintain peace and quiet for all guests, Nancy prefers guests over age 12.

Kiwi Gardens (☎ 326-1559; www.kiwigardens.com; 74-4920 Kiwi St; d/ste incl breakfast $85/95; P) Located in a gorgeous upland neighborhood, 3 miles northeast of Kailua-Kona, Kiwi Gardens offers rooms in a contemporary home with a fridge, shared guest phone and a large common area with '50s decor, complete with a vintage soda fountain and a jukebox. Breakfast includes seasonal fruits from the 80 trees in the yard, where guests may spot doves and quail.

Hawaiian Oasis B&B (☎ 327-1701; www.hawaiian oasis.com; 74-4958 Kiwi St; d incl breakfast ste $140-190, cottages $170-190; P ⚲) If you can't decide between a B&B's intimacy and a hotel's amenities, this is the perfect combination. On a lush 2-acre estate, you'll find a 40ft lap pool, hot tub, wet bar and grill, tennis court, workout room and free wi-fi Internet access. Hosts Mike and Carol Weaver also offer a range of activities such as Harley-Davidson tours led by Mike and personal-fitness training with Carol, a body builder with 25 titles!

If you want to cut costs, and don't mind joining the tourist herds, here are some good local standbys:

Kona Seaside Hotel (☎ 329-2455, 800-560-5558; www.konaseasidehotel.com; 75-5646 Palani Rd; r $120-140;

P ⊠ ⛽) Attracts an older clientele or locals traveling for work (ask for the upgraded new wing).

Uncle Billy's Kona Bay Hotel (☎ 329-1393, 800-367-5102; www.unclebilly.com; 75-5744 Ali'i Dr; r $90-100; P ⊠ ⛽) A 133-room branch of the Uncle Billy family of hotels, it's popular with tour groups, offering rooms with TV, refrigerator and phone.

Top End

Royal Sea-Cliff Resort (☎ 329-8021, 800-688-7444, www.outrigger.com; 75-6040 Ali'i Dr; studios $185-235, 1-bedroom units $215-320; P ⊠ ⛽) A condo complex that's run just like a hotel by the ubiquitous Outrigger chain, the Royal Sea-Cliff feels like an upscale hotel, with an impressive atrium of giant sago palms and a gurgling (albeit artificial) stream. The modern units have stylish furnishings, full kitchen, washing machine and dryer. The complex offers tennis courts, freshwater and saltwater pools, a sauna and covered parking (once you arrive in Kona, you'll appreciate this benefit). No minimum stay. Check the website for discount specials.

Kona Reef (☎ 329-2959, 800-367-5004; www.castleresorts.com; 75-5888 Ali'i Dr; 1-bedroom units $180-260; P ⊠ ⛽) Most units at this condo are run by Castle Resorts, which offers all the services of a hotel. Though prices slightly higher than other mid-range options, the Reef is more modern and spacious, and Castle Resorts definitely takes care of its guests; if you lock yourself out or face a plumbing disaster, the on-site staff will come to your rescue. There's no guarantee that other management agencies' staff will arrive immediately, but it can be considerably cheaper to book through the agencies listed at the beginning of this section. Also check the website for the $130 Internet-booking specials.

Royal Kona Resort (☎ 329-3111, 800-774-5662; www.royalkona.com; 75-5852 Ali'i Dr; r $160-260; P ⊠ ⛽) Formerly a Hilton property, the Royal Kona Resort is an oceanfront hotel with excellent, spacious rooms, all with a balcony; rooms are spread across three airy towers. At the south end, there's a charming saltwater lagoon, perfect for kids, and numerous tennis courts are available.

EATING

Kailua-Kona dining runs the gamut, from tropical-theme restaurants devoid of locals to fun, touristy hangouts that buzz with energy. If you want an ocean view, stay in the commercial strip along Ali'i Dr, where you can window-shop and stroll (and perhaps get a dousing of sea spray) into the night.

You'll pass numerous open-air, balcony restaurants overlooking the water along Ali'i Dr, but in most cases, the setting will have to compensate for mediocre steak-and-seafood fare. If you want more options and a sample of local favorites, you might end up at a shopping mall with no view. Kailua is the major residential center on the Kona coast, so you'll find numerous malls just a few blocks from Ali'i Dr. This might not be the Hawaii you envisioned, but don't forget that great local cuisine might come in quite conventional settings.

Budget

Island Lava Java (☎ 327-2161; Ali'i Sunset Plaza, 75-5799 Ali'i Dr; meals $4-8; ☺ 6am-10pm) A popular hangout with both locals and tourists, who while away the hours at outdoor tables perfect for people-watching. The café scene hasn't quite hit the Big Island yet, but this comes close. Along with real Kona coffee, Lava Java offers the gamut of sandwiches and salads, plus enticing banana-nut pancakes and fresh-baked desserts.

Ocean View Inn (☎ 329-9998; 75-5683 Ali'i Dr; breakfast $3-6, lunch & dinner $5-11; ☺ 6:30am-2:45pm & 5:15-9pm Tue-Sun) Nothing fancy, but this fixture in the Ali'i Dr strip offers a comprehensive sampler of cheap local food. The endless menu is eclectic, and you'll find Chinese, Hawaiian, Japanese and American dishes side by side – usually a red flag – but Ocean View is good value.

TOP 10 EATS

- **Restaurant Kaikodo** (p262)
- **Merriman's** (p233 & p220)
- **Hualalai Grille by Alan Wong** (p217)
- **Hilo Bay Café** (p262)
- **O's Bistro** (p195)
- **Café Pesto** (p262 & p224)
- **Daniel Thiebaut** (p233)
- **Teshima Restaurant** (p201)
- **Maha's Café** (p233)
- **Ke'ei Café** (p205)

HAWAI'I (THE BIG ISLAND)

THE AUTHOR'S CHOICE

Kanaka Kava (☎ 327-1660, 866-327-1660; Coconut Grove Marketplace, 75-5803 Ali'i Dr; ☯ 11am-10pm Sun-Wed, to 11pm Thu-Sat) You won't find any beer or wine at Kanaka Kava – instead, you drink the juice from 'awa (kava), a native plant and mild relaxant used by ancient Hawaiians (see p65). The outdoor tables are always jammed, and the owner, Zachary Gibson, is constantly in motion as chef, host and kava server. He grows his own 'awa in Waipi'o Valley, and patrons drink it either plain or fruit juice–flavored from coconut-shell cups (it's an acquired taste).

Locals know Gibson is a marvelous chef and they repeatedly come for his satisfying salads – a choice of fish, shellfish, chicken, tofu or poke (chopped raw fish marinated in soy sauce, oil and chili pepper) over a bed of fresh organic greens and veggies, marinated seaweed and baby bamboo. His Hawaiian à la carte items, including haupia, sweet-potato pie and taro steamed with coconut milk, rival the fare at any upscale place.

Ba-Le Kona (☎ 327-1212; Kona Coast Shopping Center, 74-5588 Palani Rd; $3-7; ☯ 10am-9pm Mon-Sat, 11am-7pm Sun) A local Vietnamese chain, Ba-Le serves satisfying sandwiches made with freshly baked French bread or croissants, with interesting fillings like lemongrass chicken or tofu. Popular Vietnamese fare includes green papaya salad topped with shrimp, rice-paper summer rolls and traditional pho noodle soups.

Happi Yu Sushi (☎ 895-1151; Lanihau Center, 75-5595 Palani Rd; sushi meals $5-8; ☯ 10am-4pm, 10am-5pm Fri & Sat) Don't miss this small stand (near Longs Drugs) serving take-out sushi and bento (Japanese-style boxed lunches). Choose from a wide range of nigiri and maki sushi rolls.

Manna Korean BBQ (☎ 334-0880; Crossroads Shopping Center, 75-1027 Henry St; mains $6-9; ☯ 10am-8:30pm Mon-Sat) A hole-in-the-wall that packs 'em in, despite the lack of ambience. Manna plates come with four 'veggies' and two scoops of rice. The most popular dish is charbroiled, marinated short ribs. No credit cards.

If you want to eat on the run, **KTA Super Store** (☎ 329-1677; Kona Coast Shopping Center, 74-5594 Palani Rd; ☯ 5am-midnight), the Big Island's best grocery chain, has a deli and bakery,

and sells local edibles you won't find at Safeway. Try the bento boxes of sushi and grilled mackerel or salmon. Kona's biggest supermarket, **Safeway** (☎ 329-2207; Crossroads Shopping Center; 75-1027 Henry St; ☯ 24hr) has more standard fare. **Kona Natural Foods** (☎ 329-2296; Crossroads Shopping Center, 75-1027 Henry St; ☯ 8:30am-9pm Mon-Sat, to 7pm Sun), next to Safeway, stocks organic wines and produce, a good selection of dairy and bulk items.

Mid-Range

Sibu Café (☎ 329-1112; Banyan Court, 78-5695 Ali'i Dr; mains $13-17; ☯ lunch & dinner) The chef can spice your dishes from mild to outrageously hot, using chili peppers grown on Mauna Kea. For pupu (snacks), try the spring rolls with fresh 'ahi or black tiger shrimp. Save room for the house specialty dessert: ohelo berries over haupia (coconut pudding) ice cream. The entire menu is available for take-out.

Quinn's (☎ 329-3822; 75-5864 Palani Rd; meals $9-20; ☯ 11am-11pm) Many locals are devoted fans of this seemingly conventional restaurant nad keep coming back for the consistently good seafood and steak dinners. It's one of few Kona restaurants that stays open late.

Kona Brewing Company (☎ 329-2739; 75-5629 Kuakini Hwy; sandwiches & salads $8-11, small/large pizza $13/22; ☯ 11am-10pm Mon-Thu, to midnight Fri & Sat, 1-9pm Sun) This restaurant-pub serves creative Greek, spinach and Caesar salads and thin-crust pizzas. Enjoy with one of the fresh brews made on-site (p188), or opt for the four-beer sampler ($6.50).

Cassandra's Greek Taverna (☎ 334-1066; 75-5669 Ali'i Dr; lunch $7-9, dinner $15-30; ☯ 11am-10pm) The setting is rather touristy, but Cassandra's serves authentic Greek fare, including an impressive souvlaki, moussaka, or gyros plate for $18; appetizers include calamari, pickled octopus and the ubiquitous Greek salad. If you just want to hang out, there's a bar, a pool table and a clear view of canoe paddlers in the bay.

Tres Hombres (☎ 329-2173; 75-5864 Walua Rd; mains $9-15; ☯ 11:30am-9pm) It beats Pancho & Lefty's (a busier Mexican joint on Ali'i Dr), with its fine margaritas and fresh chips. Menu items include steak fajitas, chile relleno (green peppers stuffed with cheese) and fish tacos. Service is inconsistent (some say it's attentive, others say slow).

Thai Rin (☎ 329-2929; Ali'i Sunset Plaza, 75-5799 Ali'i Dr; mains $9-14; ☯ 11am-2:30pm & 5-8:30pm Mon-Sat)

For an inexpensive, sit-down dinner, Thai Rin offers a range of traditional dishes, from red, green or yellow curries to whole fish steamed in ginger black-bean sauce. Most dishes offer choice of tofu, seafood or meat, so vegetarians will have a good selection.

Royal Jade Garden (☎ 326-7288; Lanihau Center, 75-5595 Palani Rd; mains $7-10; ☺ 10:30am-9pm) A family business that many locals consider their favorite Chinese restaurant in Kona. The vinyl-chair, formica-table setting is nondescript, but the food is tasty and the servings ample. Ask the server for daily specials that don't appear on the menu. Kids are welcome at this casual, family-style restaurant.

Top End

O's Bistro (☎ 327-6565; Crossroads Shopping Center, 75-1027 Henry St; dinner $15-32; ☺ 10am-9pm) Formerly known (and acclaimed) as Oodles of Noodles, the restaurant relaunched a new urban-chic look in July 2004. Still run by Amy Ferguson, the bistro has introduced an eclectic menu of island fish and meats prepared with an Asian-fusion flavor, along with almost a dozen noodle dishes ($10 to $12). For brunch, try their version of the *loco moco* – grilled fish over veggie fried rice ($9). (*Loco moco* is traditionally a hamburger topped with rice, fried egg and gravy.)

Kona Inn (☎ 329-4455; 75-5744 Ali'i Dr; lunch mains $10, dinner mains $17-28; ☺ 11:30am-9:30pm) The namesake inn first opened in 1929 as the Big Island's first hotel. Now it's a restaurant surrounded by an outdoor pedestrian mall, but the interior is handsome, with koa furnishings and gleaming hardwood floors – and the water view can't be beat. American steak and seafood dinners are livened up with island-style *pupu*, like seared 'ahi dusted with rice paper and a salad of Maui onion, vine-ripened tomato and feta cheese.

La Bourgogne (☎ 329-6711; Kuakini Plaza, 77-6400 Nalani St, at Hwy 11; mains $24-32; ☺ 6-10pm Tue-Sat) For many Kona residents, this intimate French restaurant is the hands-down choice for special occasions. The location is a minimall (roughly 3 miles south of Kailua) with no ocean views, but the food is impeccable and unlike any other dining experience in Kona. Specialties include roast duck with raspberries and pine nuts, and lobster braised with shallots, tomato, brandy and cream. Staff can help you navigate the extensive wine list. Reservations are a must.

For a spectacular oceanfront view, there are other fine-dining options that serve decent steak and seafood. Both of the following restaurants are longstanding Kailua destinations:

Huggo's Restaurant (☎ 329-1493; 75-5828 Kahakai Rd; mains $25-30; ☺ 11:30am-2:30pm Mon-Fri & 5:30-10pm)
Jameson's-by-the-Sea (☎ 329-3195; 77-6452 Ali'i Dr; mains $20-25; ☺ 11am-2:30pm Mon-Fri & 5-9pm)

DRINKING

There's no shortage of bars, featuring happy hours and island *pupu* in a mixed bag of hangouts, from lonely-hearts dives to touristy spots that haul 'em in. Luckily Kailua is a compact town, and an easy stroll down Ali'i Dr lets you check out most of your options before stepping inside (though the two best options are off the main drag).

Kona Brewing Company (☎ 329-2739; 75-5629 Kuakini Hwy; ☺ 11am-10pm Mon-Thu, to midnight Fri & Sat, 1-9pm Sun) Here there's no view and mediocre service by young, flippant servers, but the Big Island's first microbrewery is considered by beer aficionados to be the island's (and perhaps the state's) best. Now an established commercial venture (with the requisite logo T-shirts and gear), Kona Brewing continues to produce flavors unique to the island (ask for seasonal brews not on the menu). For information about tours, see p188.

Other Side (☎ 329-7226; 74-5484 Kaiwi St; ☺ 1pm-2am) Away from the hubbub of Ali'i Dr, you'll finally find a bar with many more locals than tourists. You can request tunes from over 400 CDs (from rap to Steely Dan), and join a diverse, laid-back crowd for darts, foosball, pool and an insanely long happy hour that lasts from opening time until 6pm!

Huggo's Restaurant (☎ 329-1493; 75-5828 Kahakai Rd; ☺ 11:30am-2:30pm Mon-Fri & 5:30-10pm daily, bar open to midnight) A longstanding fixture on the Ali'i Dr circuit, Huggo's might strike you as a bit predictable, but the prime waterfront location and decent *pupu* menu appeal to those past the college-party crowd. There's live jazz music on Saturday nights.

LuLu's (☎ 331-2633; Coconut Grove Marketplace, 75-5819 Ali'i Dr; ☺ 11am-10pm) An outdoor sports bar with 13 TV screens, and a lively (either touristy or young) crowd. But LuLu's is spacious (with a view) and ideal during play-off seasons.

Durty Jake's (☎ 329-7366; Coconut Grove Marketplace, 75-5819 Ali'i Dr; ☺ 11-1am, to 2am Fri & Sat)

Downstairs from LuLu's, Jakes offers eight TVs plus live music or karaoke on most nights. You'll find an older, less raucous clientele here. Jake's also serves full meals, but they're mediocre. Go to hang out.

Hard Rock Café (☎ 329-8866; Coconut Grove Marketplace, 75-5815 Ali'i Dr; ☾ 11am-11pm) Does anyone still get excited about this anymore? Apparently, recently-legal 20-somethings still do. The Kailua branch, which draws mainly a tourist crowd, keeps up the Hard Rock tradition of blasting rock music and plastering the walls with memorabilia. The best part is the splendid ocean view.

Sam's Hideaway (☎ 326-7267; Kona Marketplace, 75-5725 Ali'i Dr; ☾ 10-1:30am) Located in the back of an alley off Ali'i Dr, it's smoky, dimly lit and totally untouristy. The nightly karaoke is for diehard fans.

ENTERTAINMENT
Hula & Luau
Kailua-Kona's big hotels offer colorful, albeit hokey, evening luau (p66). The Royal Kona Resort's **Windjammer Lounge** also puts on a pleasant sunset show at 6pm from Tuesday to Sunday.

King Kamehameha's Kona Beach Hotel (☎ 326-4969; www.konabeachhotel.com; 75-5660 Palani Rd; adult/child $34.50/17.50, with dinner $60/24; ☾ 5-8:30pm Tue-Thu & Sun) This beachfront luau starts with a shell-lei greeting, followed by a torch lighting, buffet dinner and Polynesian dance show. On luau days at 10am you can watch staff bury the pig in the *imu* (underground oven) right on the beach. Drinks are included with or without dinner.

Royal Kona Resort (☎ 329-3111, 800-774-5662; www.royalkona.com; 75-5852 Ali'i Dr; adult/child $32/22, with dinner $59/27, 1 child admitted free per adult; ☾ 6pm Mon, Wed & Fri) This luau also has an open bar, buffet dinner and a cast of flamboyant dancers, musicians and fire performers. It's hard to differentiate between the two – choose the more convenient location.

Cinemas
For the most populated city along the Kona Coast, Kailua is surprisingly sedate at night. This is no mecca for film or theater, but you can find first-run movies on 10 screens at **Stadium Cinemas** (☎ 327-0444; Makalapua Shopping Center; 74-5475 Kamaka'eha Ave). If you want to hole up with a video or DVD (as most condos come with players), try **Blockbuster**

(☎ 326-7694; Kona Coast Shopping Center; 74-5588 Palani Rd; ☾ 10am-10pm, to midnight Fri & Sat).

Sports
If you're walking down Ali'i Dr at night, you can watch **beach-volleyball matches** at the sand pit next to the Coconut Grove Marketplace. Watch locals of all shapes and sizes play pickup games, or join in yourself.

SHOPPING
Downtown Kailua is jammed with small shops selling souvenirs, aloha shirts, surf gear, island crafts and beach accessories. If you check carefully, you can find quality art and clothing sellers amid the tourist traps.

Pacific Vibrations (☎ 329-4140; pacvibe@hawaii .rr.com; 75-5702 Likana Ln, at Ali'i Dr; ☾ 10am-5:30pm Mon-Fri, to 3:30pm Sat) Surfers (and wannabe surfers) can find the latest in shorts, swimsuits, rash guards, boards and other gear here.

Made on the Big Island Outlet (☎ 326-4949; 75-5660 Palani Rd; ☾ 10am-6pm) At King Kamehameha's Kona Beach Hotel (p192), this store stocks a huge selection of top-notch island crafts, edibles, clothing and oddities, including take-home potted bonsai.

Mele Kai Music (☎ 329-1454; Ka'ahumanu Plaza, 74-5467 Kaiwi; ☾ 10am-7pm Mon-Fri, to 6pm Sat) Visit here for a wide selection of contemporary and classic and Hawaiian CDs. Instruments, such as guitars and ukuleles, are also sold.

A SOUVENIR TO WEAR HOME
Along Ali'i Dr you'll find more tattoo parlors than you might expect. If you want to go home with a cool island design like a *honu* (turtle) on your arm, but don't want anything permanent, try a henna tattoo at **Kona Henna Studio** (☎ 329-2919; Kona Marketplace, 75-5725 Ali'i Dr; ☾ 11am-8pm Wed-Mon). Henna is a natural plant dye that marks the skin reddish-brown and designs last one to four weeks (those on hands and feet are the darkest and last longest). Shadow and Maria Diessner, the young husband-and-wife owners, will help you choose a design from literally hundreds, both contemporary and traditional *mehndi* (designs from India and the Middle East), or you can custom-design your own. Prices depend on size: a small design costs $5, but on average they cost between $15 and $20.

Crazy Shirts (☎ 329-2176; Kona Marketplace, 75-5719G Ali'i Dr; ⏲ 9am-9pm) The iconic T-shirt company, founded in 1964, offers unique island designs on heavyweight cotton. A Kilauea motif is made from volcanic-ash dye and the Kona Brewing Company line features shirts colored tan using…beer!

If you're seeking the **Hula Heaven** (www .hulaheaven.net), a source for authentic Hawaiian collectibles since the 1970s, you'll have to shop online. The Kailua walk-in store is gone, and has been replaced by a website. However you can still find top-quality vintage aloha shirts, plus antique maps and prints, on sale via the website.

GETTING THERE & AWAY
Air
Most visitors arrive on the Big Island at Kona International Airport at Keahole (p183).

Bus
The Hele-On Bus (p184) runs weekday routes from Kailua to Captain Cook. Fares are 75¢ to $2.25 per ride. The southbound bus departs four times a day from 9:30am to 4:25pm at the Lanihau Center. It stops at Wal-Mart, Macy's/Kmart, Keauhou, Honalo/Kainaliu, Kealakekua and Captain Cook. The northbound bus runs three times a day (first departure 6am, last at 2:15pm).

The Hele-On Bus also offers a three-hour ride to Hilo from the Lanihau Center at 6:45am on the No 7 Downtown Hilo bus. If you're coming to Kailua-Kona from Hilo, take the No 16 Kailua-Kona bus. The one-way fare in either direction is $5.25.

Between Kailua and Keauhou, **Ali'i Shuttle** (☎ 938-1112) has one (yes, only one!) bus running daily, except Sunday. The one-way fare anywhere along this 45-minute route is $2, or you can get a daily/weekly/monthly pass for $5/20/40. The bus leaves Keauhou Bay starting at 8:30am, then runs every 1½ hours thereafter, with the last run at 7pm. Stops include Keauhou Shopping Center, Kahalu'u Beach Park, Royal Kona Resort, Kona Inn Shopping Village, King Kamehameha's Kona Beach Hotel and the Lanihau Center. In the southbound direction, the bus leaves the Lanihau Center every 1½ hours from 9:10am to 6:10pm. (If you miss the bus, flag down the driver anywhere along the route.)

Car
If you're driving to Kona from Hilo, the distance is 92 miles and the trip takes 2½ hours; for other driving times and distances, see p183. Note that Hwy 19 (Queen Ka'ahumanu Hwy) becomes Hwy 11 (Hawai'i Belt Rd) at Palani Rd.

GETTING AROUND
For directions to/from the airport, see p183.

Bicycle
Renting a bike to get around Kailua town will save you time and parking costs. A good rental outfit, **Hawaiian Pedals** (☎ 329-2294; Kona Inn Shopping Village, 75-5744 Ali'i Dr; per day $20; ⏲ 9am-9pm), rents mountain and hybrid bikes. Go to affiliated **HP Bike Works** (☎ 326-2453; www.hpbikeworks.com; 74-5599 Luhia St; per day $35-40; ⏲ 9am-6pm) for higher-end bikes.

Car
Kailua-Kona gets congested. Free public parking is available in the lot behind Kona Seaside Hotel, between Likana Ln and the Kuakini Hwy. Kona Inn Shopping Village provides complimentary parking for patrons in the lot behind the Kona Bay Hotel. Patrons of Kona Marketplace can park for free at the rear of that center. The Coconut Grove Marketplace and Ali'i Sunset Plaza share an enormous free parking lot.

At the north end of Ali'i Dr, the big parking lot behind King Kamehameha's Kona Beach Hotel offers free parking for the first 15 minutes; it costs $1 per half-hour after that. If you patronize a hotel shop or restaurant, you can get a limited amount of free parking (from 30 minutes to two hours).

Public Transportation
The Hele-On Bus and Ali'i Shuttle (see p184) make stops within Kailua, so they're an in-town option. However service is so limited that you'd make better time walking!

Taxi
In town, you must call ahead for a pickup. There are a couple of reliable companies:
Aloha Taxi (☎ 329-7779; ⏲ 5am-10pm)
D&E Taxi (☎ 329-4279; ⏲ 6am-9pm)

AROUND KAILUA-KONA
Just south of Kailua-Kona, you'll find a resort area that's generally ritzier than Kailua

but not as extravagant as the South Kohala Coast.

Keauhou

Keauhou is the coastal area immediately south of Kailua-Kona (Map p202). It starts at Kahalu'u Bay and runs south beyond Keauhou Bay and the Kona Surf Resort. Bishop Estate, Hawaii's biggest private landholder, owns the land. The area was once the site of a major Hawaiian settlement. Although several historical sites can still be explored, they now share their grounds with a planned community of three hotels, nine condo complexes, a shopping center and a 27-hole golf course, all with a country-club atmosphere.

INFORMATION

The following are at the **Keauhou Shopping Center** (cnr Ali'i Dr & Kamehameha III Rd):

Bank of Hawaii (☎ 888-643-3888; 10am-7pm Mon-Fri, to 3pm Sat & Sun) Has a 24-hour ATM.

Keoki's Surfin' Ass Café (☎ 322-9792; per 5 min $3; 6:30am-8pm Mon-Fri, to 6pm Sat & Sun) Internet access, plus 100% Kona coffee and the Donkey Balls line of chocolate and mac-nut treats.

KTA Super Store (☎ 322-2311; 7am-10pm)

Longs Drug (☎ 322-5122; 8am-10pm Mon-Sat, to 6pm Sun)

Post office (☎ 322-7070; 9am-4pm Mon-Fri, 10am-3pm Sat)

SIGHTS & ACTIVITIES
St Peter's Church

The 'Little Blue Church' is one of Hawai'i's most photographed small churches and a favorite choice for weddings (despite the $150 fee). Made of clapboard with a corrugated-tin roof, it practically sits on the water; a beautiful etched-glass window casts soft light over the entire church, especially at sunset.

Built in the 1880s, it was moved from White Sands Beach to this site in 1912. The church now sits on an ancient Hawaiian religious site, Ku'emanu Heiau. Hawaiian royalty, who surfed the waters at the northern end of Kahalu'u Bay, paid their respects at this temple before hitting the waves. Several tidal waves and hurricanes have unsuccessfully attempted to relocate it.

The church is located on the *mauka* side of Ali'i Dr, just north of the 5-mile marker.

Kahalu'u Beach Park

The island's best easy-access snorkeling spot, **Kahalu'u Bay** is like a giant natural aquarium, and loaded with colorful marine life. If you haven't tried snorkeling, this is a great place to learn. Rainbow parrotfish, silver needlefish, brilliant yellow tangs, Moorish idol and butterfly fish are among the numerous tropical fish often seen here. At high tide, green sea turtles often swim into the bay to feed.

An ancient breakwater, which according to legend was built by the *menehune* (little people), is on the reef and protects the bay. Still, when the surf is high, Kahalu'u can harbor strong rip currents that pull in the northward direction of the rocks near St Peter's Church. Experienced local surfers challenge the waves offshore, but they're too much for beginners. It's easy to drift away without realizing it – check your bearings occasionally to make sure you're not being pulled by the current. Also check out water-condition reports posted on the weathered display board by the picnic pavilion.

Located right along Ali'i Dr, Kahalu'u's main drawback is traffic noise and throngs of tourists. The locals joke that 'if you forget sunscreen, take a dip in Kahalu'u Bay and you'll be covered with more than enough!'

The park has a salt-and-pepper beach composed of black lava and white coral sand. Facilities include showers, restrooms, changing rooms, picnic tables and grills. A lifeguard is on duty.

Ohana Keauhou Beach Resort

The grounds of this **resort** (see p199), immediately south of Kahalu'u Beach, contain a number of easily explored historical sites. Ask the front desk for a site map and any tours offered.

On the resort's north end you can see the ruins of **Kapuanoni**, a fishing heiau, and the reconstructed **summer beach house of King Kalakaua** next to a spring-fed pond that was once used as a royal bath. Peek into the simple three-room cottage and see a portrait of the king in his preferred European-style royal dress, a Hawaiian quilt on the bed and *lauhala* (pandanus-leaf) mats on the floor.

Toward the south end you'll see other heiau sites, including the remains of the **Ke'eku Heiau**, a probable *luakini*, just beyond the footbridge that leads to the now-defunct Kona Lagoon Hotel.

The resort is airy and overlooks a *pahoehoe* (smooth lava) rock shelf containing scads of **tide pools**. You'll see not only sea urchins and small tropical fish but also green sea turtles. When the tide is at its very lowest, you can walk out onto a flat lava tongue carved with numerous **petroglyphs**. The site is directly in front of the Kona Lagoon Hotel's northern side, with most of the petroglyphs about 25ft from the shore.

Keauhou Bay

This **bay**, which has a launch ramp, and space for two dozen small boats, is one of the most protected bays on the west coast. If you come by on weekdays in the late afternoon, you can watch the local outrigger canoe club practicing in the bay.

In a small clearing, just south of the harborside dive shacks, a stone marks the site where Kamehameha III was born in 1814. The young prince was said to have been stillborn and brought back to life by a visiting kahuna (priest).

To get to the bay, turn toward the ocean off Ali'i Dr onto Kamehameha III Rd. There are restrooms and showers.

Original Hawaiian Chocolate Factory

A tiny **chocolate factory** (☎ 322-2626; www.original hawaiianchocolatefactory.com; 78-6772 Makenawai St; ⏰ tours by appointment only) on the slopes of Mt Hualalai, Bob and Pam Cooper's mom-and-pop company is unique in its exclusive use of Big Island cocoa beans, and offers free tours. You might find it hard to believe that the sinfully sweet bars of chocolate come from beans that smell like stinky socks. However, the chocolate pods are lovely shades of yellow, gold and fuchsia, and they're harvested by hand every two weeks year-round.

SLEEPING

Ohana Keauhou Beach Resort (☎ 322-3441, 800-462-6262; 78-6740 Ali'i Dr; www.outrigger.com; r $190-250; P ⊠ ⃟) Run by the Outrigger chain, this spacious resort adjoins Kahalu'u Beach Park and its grounds, which include historical sites and tide pools. Tastefully furnished rooms each include a refrigerator, TV and lanai. Throughout the year an outstanding $120 'value rate' applies to garden-view rooms. Parking costs $5 per day.

Keauhou Resort Condominiums (☎ 322-9122, 800-367-5286; 78-7039 Kamehameha III Rd; 1-bedroom units $85-125; P ⊠ ⃟) Although these units are three decades old, most are well maintained and come with full kitchens, washers and dryers. Besides, the property is the cheapest in Keauhou. Add another $25 for a two-bedroom unit for up to four people.

Keauhou Surf & Racquet Club (☎ 329-3333, 800-622-5348; 78-6800 Ali'i Dr; 2-bedroom units $125-195, plus $75 cleaning fee per stay; P ⊠ ⃟) One of the most popular condos in the Kailua area, this is a large, modern complex located near the Keauhou Shopping Center, with tennis courts, grass volleyball court and pool. Not all units have views, but each is spacious and comes equipped with lanai, full kitchen, washer, dryer, TV and VCR.

Outrigger Kanaloa at Kona (☎ 322-9625, 800-688-7444; 78-261 Manukai St; www.outrigger.com; 1-bedroom units $240-300; P ⊠ ⃟) A condo property, 80% of which is run by Outrigger, the Kanaloa offers units with all the standard amenities; oceanfront units have whirlpool spas. There are three pools and two lighted tennis courts.

EATING

Edward's at Kanaloa (☎ 322-1434; Kanaloa at Kona, 78-261 Manukai St; dinner mains $30; ⏰ 8am-3pm, 5-8:30pm) A truly spectacular sunset view and knowledgeable service.

Keauhou isn't really a restaurant town, but you'll find a few mall-quality restaurants at the Keauhou Shopping Center. **Drysdale's Two** (☎ 322-0070; mains $7-16; ⏰ 11am-midnight) is a well-known sports bar and eatery with the requisite steaks, burgers and buffalo wings. Its specialty is sandwiches and burgers. **Royal Thai Café** (☎ 322-8424; mains $6-10; ⏰ 11am-10pm) is dominated by Asian statuary and a large aquarium, but the food holds its own.

ENTERTAINMENT

Verandah Lounge (☎ 322-3441; Ohana Keauhou Beach Resort) Sedate venue featuring jazz on Tuesday night and mellow Hawaiian music Wednesday to Saturday. Drink prices are reasonable, considering the oceanfront location.

Keauhou Cinema (☎ 324-7200; Keauhou Shopping Center, 78-6831 Alii Dr) Multiscreen, shows first-run movies.

GETTING AROUND

Keauhou has a free on-call **shuttle service** (☎ 322-3500) that runs around the resort environs between 9am and 4pm.

HAWAI'I (THE BIG ISLAND)

Holualoa

pop 6000

Holualoa is a sleepy village perched in the hills, 1400ft above Kailua-Kona. The slopes catch afternoon showers, so it's lusher and cooler than at the coast. It's an enviable location, with a fine view of Kailua Bay's sparkling turquoise waters below. This tiny, upland, off-the-beaten-track community might be Kona's best-kept secret, though relentless west Hawai'i development is making inroads. Simple, old homes, half hidden by jungly gardens, now stand side by side with sprawling new ones. A longstanding artists community supports craft shops, galleries and a nonprofit art center.

ORIENTATION & INFORMATION

This is pretty much a one-road village, with everything lined up along Hwy 180. There's a general store, a Japanese cemetery, an elementary school, a couple of churches and a library. From Kailua-Kona, it's a winding but scenic 4 miles up Hualalai Rd to Holualoa, passing poinsettia flowers, coffee bushes and a variety of fruit trees.

SIGHTS

Kona Blue Sky Coffee Company

The Twigg-Smith Estate's Kona Blue Sky Coffee farm covers over 400 acres on Mt Hualalai's slopes. As other large farms have done, Kona Blue Sky established a small **visitors center** (☎ 322-1700; www.konablueskycoffee.com; 76-973A Hualalai Rd; ⏰ 9am-3:30pm Mon-Sat) offering free guided walking tours and sampling. Visitors watch a short video before learning more about the meticulous handpicking, sun-drying and careful roasting of the precious beans. Free samples of coffee and chocolate-covered beans are offered.

Kimura Lauhala Shop

Don't be fooled by the cheap *lauhala* (pandana plant) imposters, whose products are probably made in Southeast Asia of low-grade leaves. For the real deal, visit the Kimura family's **shop** (☎ 324-0053; cnr Hualalai Rd & Hwy 180; ⏰ 9am-5pm Mon-Fri, 9am-4pm Sat) for top-quality, handmade *lauhala* crafts (see p43).

Originally the family ran an old plantation store that sold salt and codfish. Then in the 1930s, during the Great Depression, Mrs Kimura started weaving *lauhala* hats and coffee baskets and selling them at the plantations.

Today, three generations of Kimuras still weave *lauhala* here, assisted by the wives of local coffee farmers, who do piecework at home when it's not coffee season. The most common items are placemats, open baskets and hats of a finer weave. One of the Kimuras' signature pieces is their tote – an elegant, sturdy bag with bamboo handles and cotton lining. They've had to fend off buyers who want to mass-distribute their creations, for they have no intention of filling bulk orders or even selling online.

Donkey Mill Art Center

Sponsored by the Holualoa Foundation for Arts & Culture, this **art center** (☎ 322-3362; 78-6670 Hwy 180), 3 miles south of Holualoa village, offers classes on drawing, ceramics, papermaking and a variety of other arts and crafts. Guests can see exhibits by local artists and attend slide shows and lectures.

In case you're baffled by the name, the building is an historic coffee mill that was built in 1954 and with a donkey painted on the roof. The 'Donkey Mill' has been a landmark since then.

Galleries

Thanks to Holualoa's longstanding community of artists, here you'll find galleries displaying unique, sophisticated (although expensive) art that's a cut above the stereotypical 'tropical' motifs. Most galleries are open 10am to 4pm, Tuesday to Saturday.

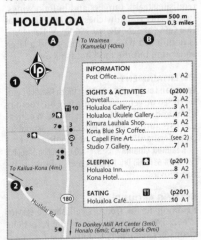

HOLUALOA

0 ——— 500 m
0 ——— 0.3 miles

To Waimea
(Kamuela) (40mi)

To Kailua-Kona (4mi)

Hualalai Rd

(180)

To Donkey Mill Art Center (3mi);
Honalo (6mi); Captain Cook (9mi)

Studio 7 Gallery (☎ 324-1335; Hwy 180) show-cases the work of prominent artist and owner Hiroki Morinoue, whose media include watercolor, oil, woodblock and sculpture. Setsuko, his wife, is an accomplished potter herself and also the gallery director. Like a little museum, the gallery is serene, showcasing pieces that blend Hawaiian and Japanese influences, with wooden walkways over lava stones.

In the historic Holualoa post-office building, the **Holualoa Ukulele Gallery** (☎ 324-1688; Hwy 180) sells ukulele crafted by the owner, Sam Rosen (also a longtime goldsmith), as well as other craftsmen. The average cost of a handmade ukulele is between $450 and $950. Signed portraits of local ukulele legends Jake Shimabukuro and 'Ohta-san' give the gallery a professional seal of approval.

Adjacent to the old post office, **Dovetail** (☎ 322-4046; Hwy 180) displays the elegant work of local artist and custom furniture designer Gerald Ben, and **L Capell Fine Art** (☎ 937-8893; Hwy 180) features abstract paintings.

SLEEPING & EATING

In Holualoa, you have two lodging options. One's luxurious and one's not, but both represent authentic Hawai'i.

Kona Hotel (☎ 324-1155; Hwy 180; s/d with shared bathroom $25/30) You can't miss the Inaba family's Kona Hotel, a bright pink wooden building in Holualoa village. Built in 1926, it's an old-time, family-run hostelry with a lobby full of photos and memorabilia from a bygone era. Rooms are spartan with just a bed and a dresser, but they're clean. A window in the men's rest room upstairs (perfectly positioned above the urinal) is an underground legend for its splendid ocean view. With only 11 rooms, the place is often full so book ahead.

Holualoa Inn (☎ 324-1121, 800-392-1812; www .holualoainn.com; 76-5932 Mamalahoa Hwy; r incl breakfast

$175-225; 🖳) Perched atop 40 acres of sloping meadows, with grand views of the coast, this is a spectacular inn. The exterior of the 6000-sq-ft contemporary house is all western red cedar and the interior floors are red eucalyptus from Maui. If you're traveling with more than two people, go for the Bali suite, which has absolutely unbeatable views. Guest amenities include a tiled swimming pool, a Jacuzzi, a billiard table, a rooftop gazebo, a living room with fireplace, a TV lounge, and facilities for preparing light meals.

Holualoa Café (☎ 322-2233; Hwy 180; 🕑 6:30am-3pm Mon-Sat) At this relaxing café you'll find fresh pastries, sandwiches, salads, plus daily chalkboard specials.

SOUTH KONA COAST

Beyond Kailua-Kona, Hwy 11 meanders south through a line of upland villages: Honalo, Kainaliu, Captain Cook and Honaunau. At a higher elevation, the foliage is verdant, with towering palms and wild fruit trees. Here lies the acclaimed 22-mile 'Kona Coffee Belt,' (see boxed text on p204) where you'll see coffee farms and macadamia-nut groves along the highway. The area is cooled by frequent afternoon showers, which you'll find refreshing after the lowland heat.

Keep your eyes peeled as you drive along the highway, as you might miss the sights. The towns rush by, and it's easy to miss a turn (backtracking is a pain on a two-lane road!). The South Kona Coast is short on beaches, but there are excellent spots for snorkeling and diving.

HONALO
pop 2000

Don't blink or you'll miss Honalo, at the intersection of Hwys 11 and 180. **Daifukuji Soto Mission**, on the *mauka* side of Hwy 11, is a large Buddhist temple with two altars, gold brocade, large drums and incense burners. If you're lucky, the *taiko* (Japanese drum) group will be practicing. As in all Buddhist temples, leave your shoes at the door.

Teshima Restaurant (☎ 322-9140; Hwy 11; mains $9-12; 🕑 6:30am-1:45pm & 5-9pm) is a casual, family-run place that has been serving delicious Japanese food since the 1940s. A good sampler is the *teishoku* (set meal) of miso soup, sashimi, fried fish, sukiyaki, *tsukemono*

TOP FIVE SHOPS

- **Volcano Art Center** (p276)
- **Holualoa galleries** (p200)
- **Giggles** (p230)
- **Elements** (p228)
- **Kimura Lauhala Shop** (p200)

HAWAI'I (THE BIG ISLAND)

(pickled vegetables) and rice. If you're lucky, 'Grandma' Teshima, the almost 100-year-old family matriarch, will stop at your table and refill your rice bowl. No credit cards accepted. Extra parking is available in the Daifukuji Soto Mission lot next door.

KAINALIU

Kainaliu is another barely-there town that you can't help liking. Shops along Hwy 11, such as **Kimura Store** (☎ 322-3771; 9am-6pm Mon-Sat, 10:30am-4:30pm Sun) – which carries the breadth of fine island fabrics – mingle with 'new' antique shops and art galleries. **Island Books** (☎ 322-2006; 79-7360 Mamalahoa Hwy) is a well-stocked used bookstore with plenty of titles on travel and Hawaii.

The town's focal point is the **Aloha Theatre** (☎ 322-2323; www.alohatheatre.com), home of the Aloha Community Players. Check the bulletin board for current performances, which range from indie film screenings to live music and dance.

Undoubtedly the best eatery in town, **Aloha Angel Café** (☎ 322-3383; Hwy 11; breakfast & lunch $6-13, dinner $14-22; 8am-2:30pm daily, 5-9pm Wed-Sun) has a distant ocean view from its skinny terrace outside. Choose among vegetarian dishes and fresh fish tacos, hearty salads and sandwiches, fruit smoothies, fresh-squeezed juices, espresso and heavenly cookies.

Another healthy choice, **Evie's Natural Foods** (☎ 322-0739; Hwy 11; snacks $3-8; 9am-9pm Mon-Fri, to 5pm Sat & Sun) is located on the *makai* side of

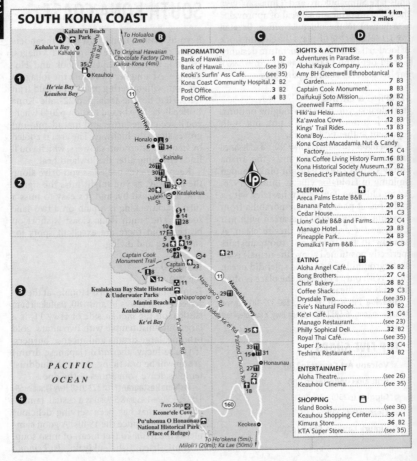

SOUTH KONA COAST

0 ——— 4 km
0 ——— 2 miles

Kahalu'u Beach Park
Kahalu'u Bay
Kahalu'u
He'eia Bay
Keauhou Bay
Keauhou
To Holualoa (2mi)
To Original Hawaiian Chocolate Factory (2mi); Kailua-Kona (4mi)
Honalo
Kainaliu
Kealakekua
Haleki St
Captain Cook Monument Trail
Captain Cook
Kealakekua Bay State Historical & Underwater Parks
Manini Beach
Kealakekua Bay
Ke'ei Bay
Napo'opo'o
Napo'opo'o Rd
Middle Ke'ei Rd
Pu'uhonua Rd
Painted Church Rd
Mamalahoa Hwy
Kuakini Hwy
Honaunau
PACIFIC OCEAN
Two Step
Keone'ele Cove
Pu'uhonua O Honaunau National Historical Park (Place of Refuge)
Keokea
To Ho'okena (5mi); Miloli'i (20mi); Ka Lae (50mi)

Hwy 11, Evie's sells organic produce, fruit juices, smoothies, salads and sandwiches.

KEALAKEKUA
pop 1700
Kealakekua means 'Path of the Gods,' to recognize a chain of 40 heiau that once ran from Kealakekua Bay all the way to Kailua-Kona. Today the town is a tropical jungle of plumeria, banana, lychee and papaya trees growing wild. Lush and balmy, with stunning views of the ocean, this is the Hawai'i of people's fantasies. It's still small and laid-back, not built up like the South Kohala coast, and you cannot find a better snorkeling and kayaking spot on the island.

Orientation & Information
Although tiny, Kealakekua (population 1650) is the commercial center of Kona's upland towns with a **post office** (☎ 322-1656; cnr Hwy 11 & Haleki'i Rd; ☼ 9am-4:30pm Mon-Fri, 9:30am-12:30pm Sat) and banks. The main hospital serving the entire Kona Coast, **Kona Community Hospital** (☎ 322-9311; 79-1019 Haukapila St; www .kch.hhsc.org), is here.

Sights
KONA HISTORICAL SOCIETY MUSEUM
While modest in size, the Kona Historical Society's one-room **museum** (☎ 323-3222; suggested donation $2; ☼ 9am-3pm Mon-Fri) contains interesting displays of period photos and other memorabilia, plus a good selection of Hawaii-themed books, from history to children's literature. The stone-and-mortar building (1875) was once a general merchandise store and post office. Helpful staff will answer questions about nearby sights.

GREENWELL FARMS
This **farm** (☎ 323-2275; Hwy 11; ☼ 8am-5pm Mon-Fri, 8am-4pm Sat), between the 110- and 111-mile markers, has been open for business since the 1850s. Aided by the young volcanic soil of Kona, handpicked coffee trees can yield a million pounds of beans annually. Coffee samples and short tours are free.

AMY GREENWELL ETHNOBOTANICAL GARDEN
The Big Island's only **ethnobotanical garden** (☎ 323-3318; www.bishopmuseum.org/exhibits/greenwell greenwell.html; suggested donation $4; ☼ 8:30am-5pm Mon-Fri, free guided tours 1pm Wed & Fri, 10am 2nd Sat of

the month) displays the flora of Hawai'i before Western contact. Located just south of the 110-mile marker, the 15-acre garden features landscaped walking paths amid three types of plants: endemic (native and exclusive), indigenous (native but found elsewhere) and Polynesian (introduced by the islands' original settlers). The garden is arranged as an *ahupua'a*, (land division) with the lowland species planted at a lower elevation than those naturally found upland.

Though sponsored by the Bishop Museum, this is a small operation with few staff. This is a blessing because your tour guide might be the actual groundskeeper, who gives a minidiscourse on each plant's habitat and traditional usage. The islanders made the most of their limited resources, and plants provided raw material not only for food but for medicine, canoes and dye. Beware of voracious mosquitoes.

KONA COFFEE LIVING HISTORY FARM
Another Kona Historical Society project, the former D Uchida **farm** (☎ 323-2006; adult/child $15/7.50; ☼ tours on the hr 9am-2pm Mon-Fri) gives a close look at rural immigrant life on the Big Island from the early 1900s to 1945. The tour price is rather steep, but the docents are knowledgeable locals who walk you through the historic 1913 Uchida homestead, processing mill, drying roofs and traditional Japanese bathhouse. Free coffee samples (and mosquito repellent) are provided.

Sleeping
Areca Palms Estate B&B (☎ 323-2276, 800-545-4390; www.konabedandbreakfast.com; Hwy 11; r incl breakfast $90-125) The owners, from Oregon, prove you need not be local-born to epitomize the aloha spirit. Outgoing and clued into their community, they go out of their way to help guests enjoy Hawai'i. Their immaculate house resembles an airy cedar lodge, with lots of natural wood, country-style furnishings and exposed-beam ceilings. All rooms have private bathroom, cable TV and big closets stocked with luxurious robes. Guests can use the common living room, with guest phone and outdoor Jacuzzi amid the sprawling lawn and – you guessed it – giant areca palms. Full breakfasts, which might include homemade pancakes, eggs and fresh papaya and pineapple, get rave reviews. It's between the 110- and 111-mile markers.

KONA COFFEE

On the slopes of Hualalai and Mauna Loa sit roughly 650 coffee farms on a strip of land just 2 miles wide and 22 miles long. Most farms are modest 3-acre, independent farms. But from this unassuming region comes the world-renowned Kona coffee.

Missionaries introduced the coffee tree to Hawaii in 1828. By the turn of the century, coffee was an important cash crop throughout the state. However the instability of coffee prices eventually drove island farmers out of business – except on the Big Island, where Kona coffee was extraordinary enough to sell at a profit during gluts in world markets.

Why is Kona coffee so special? First, *Coffea arabica* flourishes with a climate of sunny mornings and rainy afternoons, which is typical in Kona at elevations between 500ft and 2800ft. Second, coffee thrives in rich volcanic soil and mild, frost-free temperatures. Third, only a select variety of *arabica* called 'Kona Typica' (and never the inferior *robusta*) qualifies to produce the superior beans. Finally, Kona farmers use exceptionally meticulous methods to cultivate their crops, with all planting and picking done by hand.

The fruit of the coffee plant starts as green berries, turning yellow, orange, and then deep red (called 'cherry') when ripe. The cherries don't ripen all at once, so they must be picked several times from August to late January. It takes 8lb of cherry (about 4000 beans) to produce 1lb of roasted coffee.

Unassuming visitors are sometimes fooled by cheap coffee labeled 'Kona Coffee' in giant lettering, followed by the miniscule word 'blend' – which means it is probably only 10% Kona coffee. Quality depends not only on the label, but factors such as roasting, grade of the beans, and whether the beans are 'estate' (all from one farm) or a blend of Kona beans from different farms. You might also care about whether beans are organically grown or not. Genuine Kona coffee can be found in several ways:

- Look for the **Kona Coffee Council** (www.kona-coffee-council.com) seal of approval on the bag.
- Expect to pay around $20 per pound.
- Check for a 'purge valve' on the bag (another sign it's the real deal), which allows air and heat to escape from freshly roasted beans (the bag should be well inflated).

There are over 100 private labels for 100% Kona coffee. From Holualoa to Honaunau, tiny 'backyard' growers abound, and every mom-and-pop outfit has a side business selling its family-farm beans. The pioneering coffee farmers of the early 1900s were mostly entrepreneurial Japanese families, who wanted to escape the yoke of sugarcane-plantation life by leasing the coffee lands then being abandoned. They kept the industry alive, but today most of those family farms are gone – the next generations of Japanese Americans had no desire to continue as farmers.

In recent years there has been an explosion of 'gentleman farms' run by mainland transplants. Coffee estates, it seems, have developed a cachet similar to that of Napa Valley vineyards. This might be good news for the Big Island: while Kona coffee production had dropped to a low point by 1980, the gourmet-coffee craze during the past two decades has spurred sales of the highly aromatic Kona beans. Today Kona coffee is the most commercially successful coffee grown in the USA.

Banana Patch (☎ 322-8888, 800-988-2246; www .bananabanana.com; Mamao St; r $55; 1-/2-bedroom cottage d $145/165) Here you'll find two comfortable and secluded vacation cottages set amid thick, unruly foliage (watch out for spiderwebs) for guests who consider clothing optional. Tastefully decorated, both cottages have a full kitchen and a Jacuzzi. The grounds can get muddy during the rainy season.

Pineapple Park (☎ 323-2224, 877-865-2266; www .pineapple-park.com; Hwy 11; dm $20, r with/without bathroom $85/45) Pineapple Park is a popular hostel (with another branch in Puna, p267) run by Doc and Annie Park. Not surprisingly, the hostel primarily draws hang-loose European or younger travelers. The hostel has a guest kitchen, laundry facilities and a large common lounge. You can't miss the hostel, located between the 110- and 111-mile markers, because dozens of rentable kayaks (single/double $20/40) front the building.

Eating

Ke'ei Café (☎ 322-9992; mains $11-19; 🕑 dinner Tue-Sat) One of the best restaurants around, the Ke'ei Café is a touch more elegant than most others in South Kona. You can't go wrong with the fresh catch prepared in your choice of three creative ways, including sautéed on miso salad with green papaya slivers. It's located just south of the 113-mile marker.

Chris' Bakery (☎ 323-2444; Hwy 11; snacks $1-5; 🕑 6am-1pm) Sweetly irresistible offerings great for on-the-road snacking.

Philly Sophical Deli (☎ 322-6607; Hwy 11; mains $5-8; 🕑 7am-6pm Mon-Fri, 7:30am-4pm Sat) Inside a warehouse, this East Coast–style deli caters to carnivores, with liverwurst and pastrami and Philly-cheese steak, though veg sandwiches are also available. Generous eggs, pancakes and other breakfasts, too.

CAPTAIN COOK

pop 3200

This town, named for the ill-fated British navigator, commands grand views: verdant greenery stretching for miles toward the ocean and the brilliant bay beyond. The town itself is small and unpretentious, with modest government offices and a shopping center, a hotel, a gas station and a handful of restaurants. As you continue south, you'll pass numerous roadside coffee-tasting rooms that sell locally grown beans and offer free freshly brewed samples.

Sights

KEALAKEKUA BAY STATE HISTORICAL & UNDERWATER PARKS

Kealakekua Bay is one of the island's (and Hawaii's!) premier snorkeling spots. In the pristine waters, there's a spectacular diversity of marine life. The bay is both a state park and a marine-life conservation district. Among the protected species are spinner dolphins. Note that it's illegal to remove or damage coral, sand and rock, and fishing is restricted.

To reach the park, take Napo'opo'o Rd, off Hwy 11, for 4.5 miles. At the end of the road you'll see **Napo'opo'o Beach**. While the beach is a poor swimming and snorkeling spot, the **Napo'opo'o Wharf** is the best place to launch a kayak to reach outstanding snorkeling

waters. You can't miss it, as kayakers arrive en masse every morning.

From Napo'opo'o Beach, the **Captain Cook Monument** is visible at the far north end of the bay. The area near the monument is **Ka'awaloa Cove**, a decent diving and excellent snorkeling spot that's accessible only by sea or by a dirt trail beginning inland near the town of Captain Cook.

Captain Cook died in Ka'awaloa Cove, at the hands of the Hawaiians during a 1779 skirmish. In 1878 Cook's countrymen erected a 27-foot monument in Cook's honor near the site of his death. The ruins of the ancient village of Ka'awaloa sit on the land behind the monument.

If you turn right at the end of Napo'opo'o Rd, you'll see **Hiki'au Heiau**, a large platform temple above the beach. Nearby facilities include bathrooms and showers. It's forbidden to launch kayaks around the heiau.

South of Kealakekua Bay, there are two mediocre beaches: **Manini Beach** is a small, remote beach that lacks a safe entry point. The shoreline is rocky and exposed to regular northwest swells, so swimming and snorkeling conditions are poor. When the surf's up, you can catch waves off the point just south of Manini Beach. The best point of entry is to your right, just after entering the beach. There are no facilities except a portable toilet.

Further south is **Ke'ei Bay**, which isn't worth visiting (especially with Ka'awaloa Cove just north). To get there, you must take a rough dirt road, just past Manini Beach (if you reach Ke'ei Transfer Station, you've gone too far). At the bay, you'll find a beach and a small canoe launch, a few shacks, but no facilities – and residents who prefer not to be disturbed. Surfers and paddlers test the waters, but swimming is poor.

Finally, if you keep following Napo'opo'o Rd to the end and turn left, you can go 4 miles south through scrub brush to Pu'uhonua o Honaunau (p209). But be warned: the road is barely one lane and roadside grasses conceal trenches.

Activities

SNORKELING

The best place to snorkel is Ka'awaloa Cove, along the 200yd adjacent to the Captain Cook Monument. The water is protected from ocean swells and exceptionally clear.

THE FINAL DAYS OF CAPTAIN COOK

After first landing in what he called the 'Sandwich Islands' (see p28) Captain Cook's expedition continued its journey into the North Pacific. Failing to find the fabled passage through the Artic, Cook sailed back to Hawaii, landing at Kealakekua Bay on January 17, 1779, one year after his first sighting of O'ahu, and once again at the time of the annual *makahiki* festival.

Cook's initial arrival at Waimea Bay (p504) on Kaua'i had coincided with the *makahiki*, a period when all heavy work and warfare was suspended in order to pay homage to Lono (the god of agriculture and peace) and to participate in games and festivities. To the Hawaiians, Cook appeared to be the *kinolau* (earthly form) of the great god, and was thus revered. Dozens of canoes ventured out to greet the tall ship, and when ushered to shore, every effort had been made to accommodate this god on earth.

Since word of Captain Cook's arrival the previous year had spread to all the other islands, his welcome at Kealekekua Bay was even more spectacular, with more than 1000 canoes in the water surrounding his ships, and 9000 people on shore to greet him. Cook later wrote in his journal, 'I had nowhere in the course of my voyages seen so numerous a body of people assembled in one place,' quite unaware that he was seen as the second coming of Lono.

Once landed, Cook and his men were greeted by Chief Kalaniopu'u and feted in grand Hawaiian style, with a big luau accompanied by hula dancing, boxing demonstrations and an abundance of the local brew, *'awa*.

After two weeks of R and R, including sexual indulgences, Cook restocked his ships and departed the Kealakekua on February 4 and headed north once again. En route they ran into a storm off the northwest coast of the Big Island, where the *Resolution* broke a foremast. Uncertain of finding a safe harbor in the area, Cook returned to Kealakekua Bay on February 11.

Although Cook was welcomed back to the island, Kalaniopu'u was concerned about Cook's reappearance because it meant that he would again need to provide the crew's food supplies, which had become nearly depleted from Cook's first stay. This time mutual respect and admiration turned to animosity as parties on both sides began to go beyond the bounds of diplomacy and goodwill. Thievery and insult issued from both sides and tensions escalated.

After a cutter (rowboat) was stolen, Cook ordered a blockade of Kealakekua Bay and went to shore to take Kalaniopu'u as a hostage until the boat was returned, a tactic that had worked well for him in other island groups. As a ruse, Cook told Kalaniopu'u that he wanted to return to the *Resolution* with him to talk about the recent disputes. This plan sat well with the chief, whose culture dictated that disputes be settled by *ho'oponopono*, where everyone airs their grievances and does not leave until a mutual resolution to the dispute is found.

En route to the shore with Cook, Kalaniopu'u received word that the Englishmen on the big ships had shot and killed a lower chief, who had been attempting to exit the bay in his canoe. Eyewitness accounts on both the British and Hawaiian sides differ as to exactly what happened next, but reports generally agree that after hearing about the death of the chief at the hands of the sailors, a brutal battle ensued along the shore, resulting in the death of five Englishmen, including Captain Cook, and 17 Hawaiians.

The death of Cook stunned both sides into ending the battle. The sailors wanted nothing more than to leave, but the Hawaiians had taken Cook's body from the area and the British wanted to retrieve it. Over the next two weeks both sides negotiated the release of Cook's body, which had been dismembered in the fashion accorded high chiefs. Several skirmishes during that time resulted in the death of about 50 indigenous Hawaiians. Some, but not all, of Cook's remains were returned to his ship, after which they were buried at sea according to naval tradition.

You can see coral gardens, a stunning underwater cliff dropping off 70ft to 100ft, tropical fish and, perhaps, sea turtles.

A big draw is the chance (about 30% on any given day) to see spinner dolphins. Some believe that human contact with dolphins harms their sleep habits and health; thus it is advised to keep a distance and to be passive (don't follow them). The more humans push the limits, the more local, state and federal officials will crack down on access to see such species in the wild.

If you reach the Ka'awaloa Cove by land, you can slip into the ocean from the rocks on the left side of the cement dock fronting the monument. The water starts out at 5ft deep and gradually deepens to 30ft.

If you don't want to paddle or hike to the cove, you can catch a snorkeling cruise.

Snorkeling Cruises

The most popular destination is Kealakekua Bay, where most cruises arrive in the morning when waters are calmer, leave around noon, and generally stay offshore. Prices for the following tours include snorkeling gear, beverages and food:

Captain Zodiac (☎ 329-3199, 800-422-7824; www .captainzodiac.com; adult/child $80/65; departures 8am & 12:45pm) Four-hour tours aboard bouncy 16-passenger, 24ft Zodiac rubber rafts depart from Honokohau Harbor, with pickups possible at the Kailua-Kona and Keauhou piers. Tours include about an hour of snorkeling time at Kealakekua Bay followed by visits to sea caves and lava tubes.

Fairwind (☎ 322-2788, 800-677-9461; www.fair-wind .com; adult/child 4½hr tour $90/55, 3½hr tour $60/35; departures 9am & 2pm) Sail into Kealakekua Bay aboard a comfortable 100-passenger, 60ft catamaran fully equipped with showers, restroom, bar and fully covered cabin. The trips leave from Keauhou Bay, which allows for more snorkeling time than other boats. For more excitement, you can also book a four-hour 'Orca Raft Adventure Cruise' (adult/child 4-hr tour $77/69, 3-hr tour $55/45) for a thrilling fast ride through sea caves and lava tubes aboard a 14-passenger, 28ft inflatable boat with diesel engine and a shade canopy.

Sea Quest (☎ 329-7238; www.seaquesthawaii.com; 3-/4-hr tour $60/80; departures 8am & 1pm) For a personal touch, Sea Quest takes a maximum of six people out in rigid-hull inflatable boats. Check website for Internet discounts.

DIVING

Within the bay, the Napo'opo'o area is shallow with little coral, but diving conditions improve if you swim further out. Between the Napo'opo'o landing and the southern tip of Manini Beach, marine life abounds amid coral, caves, crevices and ledges in waters up to about 30ft deep. But the bay's best diving spot is **Ka'awaloa Cove**, where depths range from about 5ft to 120ft – the diversity of coral and fish is exceptional.

The aptly named **Long Lava Tube**, just north of Kealakekua Bay, is an intermediate dive site. Lava 'skylights' allow light to penetrate through the ceiling, yet nocturnal species

may still be active during the day, and you may see crustaceans, morays and even Spanish dancers. Outside are countless lava formations sheltering critters such as conger eels, triton's trumpet shells and schooling squirrelfish. Bring your dive light!

KAYAKING

Most snorkelers reach Ka'awaloa Cove by a 30- to 45-minute kayak ride from the Napo'opo'o landing. No kayak hire is available, but you'll see countless kayaks for rent along Hwy 11, especially between the 110- and 111-mile markers. Guided kayaking tours are prohibited in Kealakekua Bay, though some outfits offer them:

Adventures in Paradise (☎ 323-3005; 888-371-6035; www.bigislandkayak.com; 81-6367 Hwy 11, at Keopuka Rd; kayak s $25, d $45-50; 7:30am-5pm) Friendly, professional and remarkably thorough, the owner goes the extra mile in sharing his firsthand familiarity with Big Island waters. Novice kayakers get detailed instructions on technique and safety, which practically guarantees a successful voyage. He's also mindful of the backlash against snorkelers seeking to swim with dolphins and thus advises visitors to respect wildlife and not to disturb their habitat. He also offers snorkeling cruises and manta ray night dives.

Aloha Kayak Company (☎ 322-2868; www.alohakayak .com; Hwy 11; s/d kayak $25/40; 8am-5pm) Opposite Teshima Restaurant in Honalo, this popular Hawaiian-owned outfit also conducts adventure tours to go cliff-jumping and paddling in sea caves. They try to include a mini Hawaiian-history lesson in their tours.

Kona Boy (☎ 323-1234; www.konaboys.com; 79-7491 Hwy 11; s/d kayak $27/47; 7:30am-5pm) A decent outfit half a mile north of Kealakekua town, run by laid-back guys who give surfing and diving lessons.

HIKING

If you're up for a hardy hike, the **Captain Cook Monument Trail** to the cove, at the north end of Kealakekua Bay, would make even a triathlete sweat. The trail is not particularly steep or uneven, but it's not well maintained. You might find a jungly path through tall elephant grasses, or a distinct trail cleared by horseback riders, to the monument.

To get to the trailhead, turn *makai* off Hwy 11, onto Napo'opo'o Rd, and drive past two telephone poles. On the third pole, you'll see an orange arrow pointing toward a dirt road toward the sea. Start walking down the dirt road (not the chained asphalt road) and after 200yd it will fork – stay to the left, which is essentially a continuation of the road you've been walking on. The route is fairly simple, and in most places runs between two rock fences on an old jeep road. When in doubt, stay to the left.

Eventually the coast becomes visible and the trail veers to the left along a broad ledge, goes down the hill and then swings left to the beach. An obelisk **monument** a few minutes' walk to the left marks the spot where Captain Cook was killed at the water's edge.

Queen's Bath, a little lava pool with brackish spring-fed water, lies at the edge of the cove, a few minutes' walk from the monument toward the cliffs. The water is cool and refreshing, and this age-old equivalent of a beach shower is a great way to wash off the salt before hiking back – although the mosquitoes can get a bit testy here.

A few minutes beyond Queen's Bath, the path ends at **Pali Kapu o Keoua**, the 'sacred cliffs of Keoua,' a chief and rival of Kamehameha. Numerous caves in the cliffs were the burial places of Hawaiian royalty, and it's speculated that some of Captain Cook's bones were placed here as well. A few lower caves are accessible, but they contain nothing more than beer cans. Those higher up are hard to access and probably still contain bones. These caves are sacred sites and should be left undisturbed.

The hike takes about an hour down. It's hot and largely unshaded, and it's a longer uphill climb all the way back. Don't miss the trail's right-hand turn back up onto the lava ledge, as another 4WD road continues straight from the intersection north along the coast – for miles. Note there are no facilities at the bottom of the trail. Bring snorkeling gear and lots of water.

HORSEBACK RIDING

Kings' Trail Rides (☎ 323-2388; www.konacowboy .com; 81-6420 Mamalahoa Hwy; weekday/weekend rides $135/150) takes horseback riders down the Captain Cook Trail to Kealakekua Bay for lunch and snorkeling. Prior riding experience is preferable for this steep, rocky trail. It's near the 111-mile marker.

Sleeping

Manago Hotel (☎ 323-2642; Hwy 11; s $46-51, d $49-54, tatami r $68, s/d with shared bathroom $27/30) Now run by the family's third generation, the Manago Hotel is ideal for no-frills lodging: spare but clean rooms (no TV) in an unpretentious

wooden building. The hotel started in 1917 as a restaurant, serving bowls of *udon* (thick Japanese noodles) to salesmen on the then-lengthy journey between Hilo and Kona. The tatami rooms include a *furo* (Japanese bathtub) and traditional woven floor mats. On the grounds, the koi pond and collection of potted cacti, succulents and ornamentals resemble a well-tended backyard garden. It's between the 109- and 110-mile markers.

Cedar House (☎ 328-8829; 866-328-8829; www .cedarhouse-hawaii.com; Bamboo Rd; r $85-95, 2-bedroom ste $110, r with shared bathroom $70-75) If you're into coffee, you'll appreciate the vista of coffee trees practically right outside your window. The gracious hosts are actual coffee growers (guests can sample their farm's brew), and have firsthand information about Kona's prized commodity. The aptly named cedar-and-redwood house is handsome and airy, with lots of windows and an ocean-view deck. To reach Cedar House, you must drive 1 mile on a winding road (what else is new in upland Kona?). It's off Hwy 11 between the 109- and 110-mile markers.

Pomaika'i Farm B&B (☎ 328-2112, 800-325-6427; www.luckyfarm.com; Hwy 11; $60-75) Also known as Lucky Farm, this B&B is surrounded by dense foliage that brings the outdoors…in. You'll find a degree of homey, 'lived-in' disarray in the common kitchen area, with a refrigerator, microwave and barbecue grill. The two duplex units behind the house are the best deal, but for a more rustic experience, try the converted coffee barn with simple outdoor shower. Watch out for the extremely steep driveway. It's between the 106- and 107-mile markers.

Eating

Manago Restaurant (☎ 323-2642; Manago Hotel, Hwy 11; mains $7.50-13.50; 7-9am, 11am-2pm & 5-7:30pm Tue-Sun) Just like the hotel, the Manago Restaurant is nothing fancy; rather it's the island-Japanese version of a meat-and-potatoes eatery. You won't be disappointed by its famous pork chops ($9) or fried whole *opelu* (scad mackerel; $8.75). Mains come with self-serve sides, including pickled *ogo* (seaweed), potato salad, white rice, and forgettable cafeteria-style peas and carrots.

Coffee Shack (☎ 328-9555; 83-5799 Hwy 11; meals $6.25-7.25; 7am-sunset) A local favorite for its generous Caesar, Greek and Cobb salads, as well as take-out sandwiches from smoked

Alaskan salmon to hot pastrami and Swiss. Don't miss it. The Shack is located between the 108- and 109-mile markers.

Super J's (Hwy 11; mains $6; ☺ 10am-6pm Mon-Sat) If you're craving Hawaiian take-out, Super J's, south of the 107-mile marker, is your best bet for *kalua* pig (pig cooked traditionally in an underground oven) with cabbage.

HONAUNAU

The main attraction around Honaunau is Pu'uhonua o Honaunau National Historical Park, commonly called the 'Place of Refuge.' Many residents in the Honaunau and Napo'opo'o area (population 2400) are small coffee and macadamia-nut growers.

Sights
ST BENEDICT'S PAINTED CHURCH

John Berchmans Velghe, a Catholic priest who came to Hawai'i from Belgium in 1899, is responsible for the unusual painted interior of the **church** (☎ 328-2227; Painted Church Rd; admission free; ☺ mass at 4pm Sat, 7:15am Sun). When Father John arrived, the church was on the coast near the Place of Refuge. He decided to move the church 2 miles up the slopes to its present location. It's not clear whether he did this as protection from tsunami, or as an attempt to rise above – both literally and symbolically – the Place of Refuge and the old gods of 'pagan Hawai'i.'

Father John then painted the walls with a series of biblical scenes as an aid in teaching the Bible to 'natives' who couldn't read. He designed the wall behind the altar to resemble the Gothic cathedral in Burgos, Spain. In true Hawaiian style, painted palm leaves look like an extension of the slender columns that support the roof of the church.

KONA COAST MACADAMIA NUT & CANDY FACTORY

Most coffee and mac-nut 'visitors centers' are covers for gift stores. The Kamigaki family's Kona Coast **factory** (☎ 328-8141; www.konaoftheworld.com; Middle Ke'ei Rd; admission free; ☺ 8am-4:30pm Mon-Fri, to 4pm Sat, 11am-3pm Sun) is no exception. The main attraction is a modest historical display with a husking machine and nutcracker. You can try it out, one macadamia nut at a time. The showroom overlooks the real operation out back, where nuts by the bagful are husked and sorted. That said, the mac nuts here

are delicious and, at under $8 a pound, a real bargain!

Sleeping & Eating
Lions' Gate B&B & Farms (☎ 328-2335, 800-955-2332; www.konabnb.com; Hwy 11; incl breakfast r $110, ste $175-180) Located on a family-run, 10-acre working macadamia-nut and coffee farm, Lions' Gate is a secluded getaway. The two rooms have a private entrance and lanai, TV, DVD and a refrigerator; an adjoining bedroom can be added to form suites. Guests also have access to wi-fi or Ethernet access, a microwave, snorkeling gear, a BBQ grill, a Jacuzzi and a gazebo. There are excellent ocean views from every room, and for breakfast you'll sample the hosts' own coffee and nuts. It's at the 105-mile marker.

Restaurants are scarce in Honaunau proper, and your best bet is take-out from **Bong Brothers** (☎ 328-9289; www.bongbrothers.com; Hwy 11; ☺ 9am-6pm Mon-Fri, 10am-6pm Sun, closed Sat) Located in an historic 1929 building, Bong Brothers is the name of both a small market and a coffee mill next door. The market displays good, farmers-market produce outside, where you can find deals on local favorites like fresh lychee. Inside, you can buy organic produce, smoothies and deli dishes; a vegetarian chef cooks up homemade soups and healthy specials (around $5) for lunch.

Whatever you do, avoid Wakefield Gardens Restaurant, just west of Painted Church Rd. It's often closed when the sign says 'open' and the grounds are usually a mess.

PU'UHONUA O HONAUNAU NATIONAL HISTORICAL PARK

In ancient Hawai'i, the *kapu* system regulated all daily life. A common person could not look at the *ali'i* (chief) or walk in his footsteps. Women could not prepare food for men or eat with them. One could not fish, hunt or gather timber except during certain seasons.

If one broke the *kapu*, the penalty was always death. After all, they believed, the violation had angered the gods, who might retaliate with volcanic eruptions, tidal waves, famine or earthquakes. Thus, to appease the gods, they hunted down and killed the violator.

However there was one escape. Commoners who broke a *kapu* could get a second chance, if they reached the sacred ground of a *pu'uhonua* (place of refuge). Similarly, a *pu'uhonua* also gave sanctuary to defeated warriors and wartime 'noncombatants' (men who were too old, young, or unable to fight).

To reach the *pu'uhonua* was more challenging that it might seem. Since royals and their warriors lived on the grounds immediately surrounding the refuge, *kapu* breakers had to swim through open ocean, braving currents and sharks, to reach safety. Once inside the sanctuary, priests performed ceremonies of absolution that apparently placated the gods. *Kapu* breakers could then return home for a fresh start.

Information

Nowadays the *pu'uhonua* is an impressive **national park** (☎ 328-2288; www.nps.gov/puho; 1-week pass adult/family $3/5; ✆ 6am-8pm Mon-Thu, to 11pm Fri-Sun) fronting Honaunau Bay. The park's tongue twister of a name simply means 'place of refuge at Honaunau.' The rangers here seem especially numerous and helpful; get a brochure from the entrance station.

Early morning or late afternoon is the optimum time to visit the park to avoid the beating midday heat. Twenty-minute orientation talks are given at 10am, 10:30am, 11am, 2:30pm, 3pm and 3:30pm. Every summer, on the weekend closest to July 1, a **cultural festival** gives visitors a chance to see traditional displays and food, *hukilau* (net fishing) and a 'royal court.'

Sights

The half-mile **walking tour** is easy to navigate using the brochure map. While most of the sandy trail is accessible by wheelchair, the sights near the water traverse rough lava rock and require walking.

Pu'uhonua o Honaunau comprises two sections: the royal grounds, where Kona *ali'i* lived, and the place of refuge, separated by a massive stone wall. **Hale o Keawe Heiau**, the temple on the point of the cove, was built around 1650. Buried there are the bones of 23 chiefs. It was believed that the mana (spiritual power) of the chiefs remained in their bones, and bestowed sanctity on those who entered the grounds.

The reconstructed heiau appears authentic, with a carved wooden *ki'i* (statue) standing almost 15ft high beside it. Leading up to the heiau is the **Great Wall** separating the *pu'uhonua* to the west, and the royal grounds to the east. Built around 1550, this stone wall is more than 1000ft long and 10ft high. You'll also pass two older heiau, a petroglyph, legendary stones, a fishpond, lava tree molds, a hand-carved koa canoe and a few thatched huts and shelters.

At the southern end of the park, **tide pools** in *pahoehoe* (smooth-flowing) lava rock contain tiny black *pipipi* (tiny black mollusk). Near the picnic area at the southern end, tide pools contain coral, black-shelled crabs, small fish and eels, sea hares, and sea urchins with rose-colored spines.

Activities

Near the park are two popular snorkeling areas and an easy trail.

SWIMMING & SNORKELING

Swimming is allowed at shallow **Keone'ele Cove** inside the Place of Refuge. The cove was once the royal canoe landing. Snorkeling is best when the tide is rising, as the water is deeper and the tide brings in fish. Sunbathing is discouraged, and visitors cannot leave towels or mats on the ground.

Just north of the Place of Refuge is **Two-Step**, a terrific place to snorkel. It's also popular with kayakers and canoe paddlers. From the park's parking lot, take the narrow one-way road marked with a 15mph sign (to the left as you exit the park).

Snorkelers step off a lava ledge immediately north of the boat ramp into about 10ft of water. It then drops off fairly quickly to about 25ft. Some naturally formed lava steps make it fairly easy to get in and out of the water, but there's no beach here. In winter, high surf can create rough waters.

Visibility is excellent, especially at noon with the sun overhead, with good-sized reef fish and a fine variety of corals close to shore. The predatory 'crown of thorns' starfish can be seen here feasting on live coral polyps. Divers can investigate a ledge a little way out that drops off about 100ft.

HIKING

Hiking the **1871 Trail** to Ki'ilae Village is a two-mile-return trip starting at the park. Ask a ranger to direct you to the nearby trailhead (off the road toward the picnic grounds) and to borrow a booklet describing the marked sights along the way.

On the way to the abandoned village you'll pass a collapsed lava tube and temple **ruins** before reaching the steep **Alahaka Ramp**, which once allowed riders on horseback to travel between villages. Halfway up the ramp is **Waiu-O-Hina lava tube**, which opens to the sea; bring a flashlight, if you want to explore it, because the floor is rough and jagged rocks jut from overhead.

At the top of the ramp, incredible vistas spread out below. Keep going to the spot where Ki'ilae Village once stood, heading back where the trail ends at a fence. The trail is tree-lined but not shaded, so a morning or late-afternoon excursion is advised.

HO'OKENA

If you have time to explore south Kona, Ho'okena is a worthwhile detour. The locals are friendlier than their neighbors in Miloli'i, but they often view tourists with a touch of wariness. The village is just over 2 miles down a narrow road that turns off Hwy 11 between the 101- and 102-mile markers.

Ho'okena was once a bustling village with two churches, a school, courthouse and post office. King Kalakaua sent his friend Robert Louis Stevenson here in 1889 to show him a typical Hawaiian village. Stevenson stayed a week with the town's judge and wrote about Ho'okena in *Travels in Hawaii*.

In the 1890s, Chinese immigrants began to move into Ho'okena, setting up shops and restaurants. A tavern and a hotel opened, and the town got rougher and rowdier. In those days, Big Island cattle were shipped from the Ho'okena landing to market in Honolulu. When the circle-island road was built, the steamers stopped coming and people moved away. By the 1920s, the town was all but deserted.

Today Ho'okena is a tiny fishing community with an attractive **beach**, that's been designated a county park. It has soft black sand and calm waters for snorkeling, however, it has a reputation for drug activity. When the winter surf is up, local kids with boogie boards hit the waves. When it's calm, kayakers paddle around, and you can snorkel straight out from the landing. It drops off pretty quickly, and there's lots of coral, but don't go too far out or you may encounter strong currents. There are picnic tables, but no drinking water. **Camping** is allowed with a county permit (p178).

MILOLI'I

Miloli'i means 'fine twist.' Historically, the village was known for its skilled sennit twisters, who used bark from the *olona* (a native shrub) to make fine cord and highly valued fishnets. Many villagers continue to make a living from the sea.

While Miloli'i is one of the most traditional fishing villages in Hawai'i, this is more in spirit than in appearance. Old fishing shacks have been replaced with a row of makeshift homes that seem incongruous to the surrounding lava rock and beach beyond. Nowadays fishermen zip out in motorized boats to do their fishing. Miloli'i residents generally prefer their isolation and are not enthusiastic about tourists poking around.

The village sits at the edge of an expansive 1926 lava flow that covered the nearby fishing village of Ho'opuloa. The turnoff is just south of the 89-mile marker on Hwy 11, 5 miles down a steep and winding paved single-lane road that cuts across the long-ago flow. At the end of the road, you'll reach a peaceful, deserted beach park with an expanse of tide pools. Camping is allowed (see p178), but while there are picnic tables, the restrooms are locked.

NORTH KONA COAST

From Kailua-Kona, Hwy 19 (Queen Ka'ahumanu Hwy) runs north through miles of arid lava terrain. From the coast you can look inland and see Mauna Kea and Mauna Loa, both often snowcapped in winter. Along the road, clumps of red bougainvillea look striking against the jet black rock, but vegetation is mainly sparse tufts of grass that can survive the dry winds. Along the highway you'll see a unique version of graffiti – messages spelled out in white coral against a black lava background.

The shoreline from Kailua-Kona to Waikoloa was once dotted with tiny fishing villages, but most were wiped out by the 1946 tsunami. A string of beautiful, secluded beaches and coves lies along this sparsely populated coastline, but they're hidden from the road and most are accessible only by foot or 4WD.

Hwy 19 is flat, straight and easy to zoom along, but it's also a hot spot for radar speed traps, particularly on the stretch between

NORTH KONA & SOUTH KOHALA COASTS

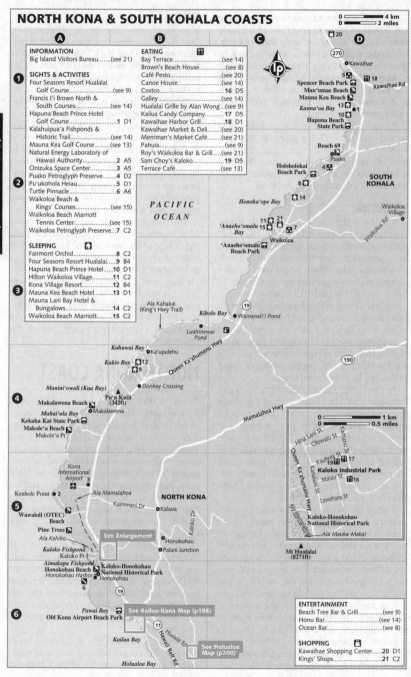

INFORMATION
Big Island Visitors Bureau.......(see 21)

SIGHTS & ACTIVITIES
Four Seasons Resort Hualalai
Golf Course.............................(see 9)
Francis I'i Brown North &
South Courses.........................(see 14)
Hapuna Beach Prince Hotel
Golf Course.........................**1** D1
Kalahuipua'a Fishponds &
Historic Trail.........................(see 14)
Mauna Kea Golf Course.........(see 13)
Natural Energy Laboratory of
Hawaii Authority.................**2** A5
Onizuka Space Center............**3** A5
Puako Petroglyph Preserve.....**4** D2
Pu'ukohola Heiau...................**5** D1
Turtle Pinnacle......................**6** A6
Waikoloa Beach &
Kings' Courses.......................(see 15)
Waikoloa Beach Marriott
Tennis Center........................(see 15)
Waikoloa Petroglyph Preserve..**7** C2

SLEEPING 🏠
Fairmont Orchid....................**8** C2
Four Seasons Resort Hualalai..**9** B4
Hapuna Beach Prince Hotel....**10** D1
Hilton Waikoloa Village.........**11** C2
Kona Village Resort...............**12** B4
Mauna Kea Beach Hotel........**13** D1
Mauna Lani Bay Hotel &
Bungalows...........................**14** C2
Waikoloa Beach Marriott.......**15** C2

EATING 🍴
Bay Terrace..........................(see 14)
Brown's Beach House............(see 8)
Café Pesto............................(see 20)
Canoe House.........................(see 14)
Costco................................**16** D5
Galley.................................(see 14)
Hualalai Grille by Alan Wong...(see 9)
Kailua Candy Company...........**17** D5
Kawaihae Harbor Grill...........**18** D1
Kawaihae Market & Deli..........(see 20)
Merriman's Market Café.........(see 21)
Pahuia...............................(see 9)
Roy's Waikoloa Bar & Grill.....(see 21)
Sam Choy's Kaloko................**19** D5
Terrace Café.........................(see 13)

ENTERTAINMENT
Beach Tree Bar & Grill............(see 9)
Honu Bar.............................(see 14)
Ocean Bar...........................(see 8)

SHOPPING 🛍
Kawaihae Shopping Center.....**20** D1
Kings' Shops.......................**21** C2

Kailua and the airport. Be warned that Big Island police cruise in anything from Grand Ams to Explorers, so they're tough to spot. The highway is bordered with wide, smooth bike lanes because it's part of the Ironman Triathlon route.

HONOKOHAU HARBOR

In 1970, this **harbor** was built to alleviate traffic off Kailua Pier. These days, almost all of Kona's catch comes here. To reach the harbor, turn *makai* on Kealakehe Rd just north of the 98-mile marker. You'll pass dozens of boat launches.

Sights

If you want to see the charter fishing boats pull up and weigh their catches of marlin and yellowfin tuna, drive straight in, park near the gas station and walk to the dock behind the adjacent building. The best times to see the weigh-ins are around 11:30am and 3:30pm.

KALOKO-HONOKOHAU NATIONAL HISTORICAL PARK

This **national historical park** (☎ 329-6881; www .nps.gov/kaho; 🕐 7:30am-3:30pm) covers 1160 acres of fishponds, ancient heiau and house sites, burial caves, petroglyphs, *holua* (sled courses), a restored one-mile segment of the ancient King's Trail footpath, and the entire oceanfront between Kaloko and Honokohau Harbor. It is speculated that the bones of Kamehameha the Great were buried in secret near Kaloko.

Yet the park is virtually unknown, even by locals, who recognize the Kaloko name only because Costco is located in the nearby Kaloko Light Industrial Area. The park is worth exploring, but it might seem desolate at first glance: a seemingly endless expanse of lava rock. Temperatures are unbearable during the midday heat. Go in the early morning or late afternoon (or when it's overcast), so you can enjoy the interpretive trails.

The entrance is between the 96- and 97-mile markers, down a newly paved road leading to a small visitors center that was built in 2003 (having been 'in development' since 1978). A ranger and information brochures are available.

On the northern end of the coast is **Kaloko Fishpond**. Before the park took over the land from Huehue Ranch, mangrove had invaded

the fishpond and proliferated, causing native birds to abandon the habitat. The park service eradicated the mangrove in a labor-intensive process that involved cutting and torching the trees, then tearing the new shoots up one by one and burning the roots.

Aimakapa Fishpond, just inland from Honokohau Beach on the park's southern end, is the largest pond on the Kona Coast and a habitat for endangered waterbirds. Like Kaloko, a mangrove invasion required intensive eradication efforts. If you visit this brackish pond, you're likely to see the *aeo* (Hawaiian black-neck stilt) and *'alae ke'oke'o* (Hawaiian coot), both endangered native waterbirds that have thrived since the pond was cleared.

Kahinihiniula (Queen's Bath) is a brackish spring-fed pool in the middle of a lava flow. Although inland, the water level changes with the tide; at high tide, saltwater seeps in and the water in the pool rises. To get there, walk inland from the northern end of Honokohau Beach. The pool is marked by stone cairns and Christmas berries, always a good sign that freshwater is nearby.

HONOKOHAU BEACH

Just north of the harbor, Honokohau Beach used to be a favorite of nudists. But now, under control of the park, swimsuits are de rigueur.

The sand is large-grained and a mix of black lava, white coral and rounded shell fragments. The water is acceptable for swimming and snorkeling, although the bottom is a bit rocky. The only facilities are pit toilets at the end of the trail. Bring mosquito repellent in case they're biting.

Take Honokohau Harbor Rd from Hwy 19, turning right in front of the marina complex. Follow the road for 400yd, until the dry dock boatyard; pull off to the right and look for the trailhead at a break in the lava wall on the right, near the end of the road. A well-beaten path leads to the beach.

Activities

SNORKELING

The area between Honokohau Harbor and Kailua Bay is a marine-life conservation district. **Kamanu Sail & Snorkel** (☎ 329-2021; adult/ child $55/35; 🕐 departures 9am & 1:30pm) sails a 36ft catamaran out of Honokohau Harbor for snorkeling at Pawai Bay, just north of the

Old Kona Airport Beach Park. The boat, which motors down and sails back, takes a maximum of 24 people.

DIVING

Accessible by boat, off the coast of Honokohau Harbor, **Turtle Pinnacle** is a premier dive site for spotting turtles, which congregate here to clean their shells (small fish feed off the algae and parasites on the turtles' shells). The turtles are accustomed to divers, so they don't shy away from photo opportunities. Other frequent sightings in the water include frogfish, octopi and pipefish.

Another good spot is off **Kaiwi Pt**, south of Honokohau Harbor, where sea turtles, large fish and huge eagle rays swim around some respectable drop-offs. Nearby is **Suck 'Em Up**, a couple of lava tubes you can swim into and let the swell pull you through, like an amusement-park ride.

For gear rentals, **Kona Coast Divers** (☎ 329-8802; www.konacoastdivers.com; 74-381 Kealakeha Parkway, Honokohau Harbor; ❉ 8am-5pm) is conveniently located. Its boat is custom-designed for diving, and it offers thrilling manta-ray night dives.

Tours

Although the best whale-watching is found off Maui, the Big Island is another prime spot. The season for humpback whales usually starts around January and runs to March or April. However sperm, false killer, dolphin and melon-headed whales, plus five dolphin species, can be seen in Kona waters year-round. Some of the snorkeling or fishing cruises also offer whale-watching tours during humpback season, but marine-mammal biologist Dan McSweeney of **Whale Watch** (☎ 322-0028; www.ilovewhales.com; adult/child $60/40; ❉ seasonal departures 7:10am & 1:30pm) specializes in whales. He leads three-hour whale-watching cruises leaving from Honokohau Harbor. Hydrophones allow passengers to hear whale songs. The tours have a 24-hour nonrefundable cancellation policy.

Eating

North Kona is a region rather than a town, so restaurants and shops are scarce. But you'll find a few options at the Kaloko Light Industrial Area on the *mauka* side of Hwy 19.

Costco (☎ 334-0770; 73-5600 Maiau St; annual membership $45; ❉ 11am-8:30pm Mon-Fri, 9:30am-6pm Sat, 10am-6pm Sun) If you're a member of the bulk discount retailer and you want a cheap meal, the snack bar here serves pizza and concession fare. If you're traveling with a group for over a week, you'll save a bundle on bulk groceries and discount gas, too.

Sam Choy's Kaloko (☎ 326-1545; 73-5576 Kauhola St; meals under $10; ❉ 6am-2pm Mon-Sat, 7am-2pm Sun) This is the famous Big Island chef's first restaurant. The setting is surprisingly casual, with Formica tables and 1950s-style diner chairs. Try the Hawaii 'comfort food': to-

---

TOP 10 BEACHES

- **Kauna'oa Bay** (p222) for sheer perfection and calm waters.
- **'Anaeho'omalu Beach Park** (p218) for the best (and perhaps only) windsurfing on the island.
- **Kealakekua Bay** (p205) for kayaking and snorkeling amid astounding marine life.
- **Kahalu'u Beach** (p198) for the best place to learn to snorkel.
- **Hapuna Beach** (p222) for a party beach where you can see and be seen (if you can find parking).
- **Kiholo Bay** (p217) for a taste of desert-island paradise.
- **Kehena Beach** (p270) for an alternative, hippie-friendly, clothing-optional beach with spectacular black sand.
- **Old Kona Airport Beach** (p189) for tide pools to explore in solitude.
- **Ho'okena Beach** (p211) for being among locals (if they don't give you *da stink eye* – a dirty look).
- **Kekaha Kai State Park** (p215) for a choice of beaches 'off the beaten track' (4WD only).

mato beef, teriyaki steak, chicken stir-fry, fried fish, *laulau* (bundles of pork or beef, with salted fish, that are wrapped in leaves and steamed) and *lomilomi* salmon (raw diced salmon marinated with tomato and onion). It's still family-run; you might even see Sam here when he's in town.

Kailua Candy Company (☎ 329-2522, 800-622-2462; www.kailua-candy.com; 73-5512 Kauhola St; gift shop ☑ 8am-6pm Mon-Sat, to 4pm Sun) Founded in 1977, this is ranked by *Bon Appetit* magazine as one of the 'top 10 chocolate shops in America.' Specialties include handmade 'tropical truffles' (try the guava-rum in dark chocolate or the coffee-cinnamon in milk chocolate) and macadamia-nut *honu* (turtle), made of buttery caramel over dry-roasted macs, covered by luscious chocolate. The company president, Cathy Smoot Barrett, who took over her parents' company almost two decades ago, is a lively fount of information on all things chocolate.

KEAHOLE POINT

At Keahole Point, the seafloor drops steeply just offshore, providing a continuous supply of both cold water from 2000ft depths and warm surface water. These are ideal conditions for – you'll never guess it – ocean thermal-energy conversion (OTEC).

Sights & Activities
NATURAL ENERGY LABORATORY OF HAWAII AUTHORITY

In 1974 the Hawaii State Legislature created the Natural Energy Laboratory of Hawaii Authority (NELHA) to provide a support facility for OTEC research and related technologies. Electricity has been successfully generated at the site, and research continues into ways to make this an economically viable energy resource. **Public lectures** (☎ 329-7341; www.nelha.org; per person $5; ☑ 10-11:30am Wed & Thu) are held here and require reservations.

Today NELHA also sponsors a variety of commercial ventures, including aquaculture production of *ogo*, algae, abalone, lobster and black pearls. One of NELHA's tenants is a Japanese company that desalinates pristine Hawaiian seawater and sells it as a tonic, Ma Ha Lo Hawaii Deep-Sea Water, in Japan.

The turnoff to NELHA is 1 mile south of Kona airport, between the 94- and 95-mile markers.

WAWALOLI (OTEC) BEACH

The NELHA access road leads to **Wawaloli Beach**, a great spot for exploring tide pools covering the rocky lava coastline. Swimming conditions are poor, but the beach is uncrowded and good for watching the horizon or eating outdoors. There are picnic tables, restrooms and showers. The drawback: planes occasionally drone overhead.

PINE TREES

To see one of the best **surfing breaks** in west Hawai'i, drive about 2 miles further south to Pine Trees. When the access road to Nelha veers to the right, look leftward for a well-worn 4WD road leading south.

On weekends, local surfers flock to Pine Trees in a continuous procession of SUVs (sports utility vehicles). While appreciated by surfers, swimmers will find the shoreline too rocky and inaccessible. Go for the show. You need a 4WD; otherwise, walking is possible, if you can stand the heat. Gates are closed between 8pm and 6am.

Why Pine Trees? Early surfers spied mangrove trees near the break, which they thought were pines. No mangroves (or pines) are visible today but the name stuck.

ONIZUKA SPACE CENTER

Astronaut Ellison S Onizuka Space Center (☎ 329-3441; adult/child $3/1; ☑ 8:30am-4:30pm), opposite the car-hire booths at the Kona airport, pays tribute to the Big Island native who perished in the 1986 *Challenger* space-shuttle disaster. The little museum features exhibits and educational films about space and astronauts. Items on display include a moon rock, a NASA space suit and scale models of spacecraft.

KEKAHA KAI STATE PARK

Formerly known as Kona Coast State Park, **Kehaka Kai** (☑ 9am-7pm Thu-Tue) is a 1600-acre park comprising pristine beaches that remain relatively secluded, mostly due to rough access. Shaded picnic tables, barbecue grills and portable toilets are available on the main site but most of the park is completely undeveloped.

Mahai'ula Beach

The largest and easiest to reach, **Mahai'ula Beach** has salt-and-pepper sand, along with coral rubble. The inshore waters are shallow, and the bottom is gently sloping. Snorkeling and swimming are usually good, but during periods of high surf, which are not infrequent in winter, surfing is the sport of choice on the bay's north side.

To reach Mahai'ula Beach, take the *makai* access road off Hwy 19, about 2.5 miles north of Kona airport, between the 90- and 91-mile markers. The unpaved road (barely passable in a 2WD) runs for 1.5 miles across a vast lava flow that's totally devoid of trees and greenery. From the first parking area, take a five-minute walk north.

Remember, walking even 15 minutes can be punishing at high noon. Be prepared for the heat, or plan your trek in the morning.

Manini'owali (Kua Bay)

Manini'owali, also called Kua Bay, is what many consider to be a perfect, crescent-shaped beach, with turquoise waters and white sand. Most of the year, the surf is suited to swimmers, and in winter, the waves kick up for boogie boarders and bodysurfers. Winter storms can generate currents that temporarily strip the beach of its sand.

State officials plan to complete a $2.5 million paved access road (just south of the 88-mile marker) and facilities by spring 2005 – a controversial decision because Mahai'ula is the larger beach and can accommodate more visitors.

Currently there are no trees or awnings to provide shade and very little vegetation and no facilities. Prior to 2005, people accessed Manini'owali by taking the turnoff just north of both the 88-mile marker and **Pu'u Ku'ili**, the 342ft grassy cinder cone *makai* of the highway. The road, marked by a stop sign and gate, is 1 mile to the beach. Even a 4WD can't make it the whole way.

Makalawena & Makole'a Beaches

These beaches require either a 4WD or a hike. Occasionally campers have been harassed or assaulted by hostile locals at these deserted beaches, so be alert to trouble.

To the north lies **Makalawena Beach,** a pristine, white-sand beach owned by the Kamehameha Schools Bishop Estate. To reach this beach, you must hike in about 1.25 miles, which takes roughly half an hour. To start the trek, park by the service road that's cabled off, and walk toward the old house on the beach. Find the coastal trail further *makai* and hike north.

You'll be walking on lava rock, and the sun will get your blood pumping en route. The payoff is a dip in clear waters, ideal for swimming and snorkeling and especially for boogie boarding. At the southern end, behind the dunes, a brackish pond lets you rinse off before hiking back. There are no facilities and almost no crowds on weekdays.

Another hidden treasure, **Makole'a Beach**, south of Kekaha Kai, is a small black-sand beach, where you probably won't encounter another soul. If you're walking from the park, find the easy-to-navigate 'path' along the lava fields; follow the coastline and you can't lose your way. With a 4WD, turn left at the first parking lot in the park; drive for about 1000yd until you reach a path, which is marked by coral and goes to the ocean; from here it's probably wise to walk rather than drive to the beach.

This beach might be less breathtakingly impressive than the others within park grounds, but black sand near Kona is rare. There's no shade and the lava rock and black sand add to the heat, so bring plenty of water. Again, there are no facilities.

KA'UPULEHU

After the 1946 tsunami, this fishing village, accessible only by boat, was abandoned until the early 1960s, when a wealthy yachter who had anchored offshore concluded Ka'upulehu would be the perfect place for a hideaway hotel.

The Kona Village Resort opened in 1965. It was so isolated it had to build its own airstrip to shuttle in guests – the highway that now parallels the Kona Coast wasn't built for another decade. In 1996 a second upscale hotel, the Four Seasons Resort, opened at Ka'upulehu Beach, about a 10-minute walk south of Kona Village Resort.

The new hotel exposed the shoreline, making the white-sand beach at **Kukio Bay**, and a string of pristine easily accessible little coves further south. There are showers, restrooms, drinking water and parking. A mile-long coastal footpath through the lava connects Kukio Bay with the Four Seasons via an area of reddish lava and brackish water, where turtles can be seen.

The PGA-tour **Four Seasons Hualalai Course** (☎ 325-8000), designed by Jack Nicklaus, is open only to members and resort guests of the Four Seasons.

Sleeping

Kona Village Resort (☎ 325-5555, 800-367-5290; www .konavillage.com; 1 Kahuwai Bay Dr; hale 1-r $515-910, 2-r $850-1125; ☒) If you want to escape the modern-day world, but still enjoy fine dining and gorgeous settings, one-of-a-kind Kona Village fits the bill. You'll escape phones, clocks, radios, TVs or air-con. And you'll sleep in a 'village' of thatched-roof *hale* (houses) standing on stilts around an ancient fishpond or along a sandy beach. However the interiors are modern and comfortable, with a high ceiling, fan, rattan furnishings, refrigerator and probably a Jacuzzi. Excellent restaurants are a stroll away, as are a spa, fitness center, two swimming pools and a glass-bottom boat. Rates include meals and activities. Kona Village is a favorite of wealthy CEOs, movie stars, and others who normally live at just the opposite pace of this place. Management keeps the 82-acre grounds off-limits to nonguests except during guided tours at 11am. If you simply can't get over the irony of paying big bucks to 'go native,' you can drop in for the spectacular Friday-evening luau (see right).

Four Seasons Resort Hualalai (☎ 325-8000; 800-332-3442; www.fourseasons.com; 100 Ka'upulehu Dr; r $540-780, 1-bedroom ste $935-3450; ☒ ☒) Known for its impeccable service and classy luxury, the newest resort on the Gold Coast is also the only five-diamond resort on the Big Island. If you're here, go for the full treatment at the world-class spa. The adjacent beach isn't great for swimming; an underwater reef drops off steeply, causing currents that can carry you far out to sea. Hollywood stars, such as Denzel Washington and Heather Locklear, have been spied here. Resort guests can enjoy the Jack Nicklaus–designed golf course. The course is not open to nonguests.

Eating

Hualalai Grille by Alan Wong (☎ 325-8525; Golf Clubhouse, Four Seasons Resort Hualalai, 100 Ka'upulehu Dr; mains $30-38; ☒ 11:30am-2:30pm & 5-9pm) Nicknamed the '19th Hole,' the Hualalai Grille reopened under the direction of celebrity chef Alan Wong in early 2004, with signature dishes like the 'New Wave' Opihi Shooter appetizer – a tall glass of local limpets in spicy tomato water, fennel basil and *ume*

shiso (Japanese plum) essences – plus creative fish mains and intriguing Hawaii-style versions of American classics, like the 'soup and sandwich' appetizer with chilled red-and-yellow-tomato soup and fois gras, *kalua* pig and grilled cheese sandwich.

Pahuia (☎ 325-8000; Four Seasons Resort Hualalai; mains $25-48; ☒ 6:30-11:30am & 6pm-9:30pm) The more formal, elegant oceanfront restaurant featuring consistent Hawaii regional cuisine.

Entertainment

Kona Village Resort (☎ 325-5555; 1 Kahuwai Bay Dr per person $78; ☒ 5:30pm Fri) The best commercial luau on Hawai'i. The old-world Polynesian setting gives an authentic feel, and the fire-eaters, dancers and singers certainly earn their pay. Reservations are required.

Beach Tree Bar & Grill (☎ 325-8000; Four Seasons Resort Hualalai, 100 Ka'upulehu Dr) Sitting at a bar, watching the sunset: this is the perfect setting for it. There's live music from Tuesday to Saturday.

KIHOLO BAY

Halfway up the coast, just south of the 82-mile marker, you'll come to a lookout that commands a great view of Kiholo Bay. With its pristine turquoise waters and shoreline fringed with coconut trees, the bay is an oasis in the midst of the lava.

An inconspicuous trail down to the bay starts about 100yd south of the 81-mile marker (see the cars parked along the highway). Walk straight in for about 10ft, then veer left and follow a 4WD road, the beginning of which has been blocked off by boulders to keep vehicles out. Near the end of the trail, look for a faint footpath toward the left. Allow 20 to 30 minutes in total.

Kiholo Bay, almost 2 miles wide, has a lovely, large spring-fed pond called Luahinewai at the southern end of the bay. It's refreshingly cold and fronted by a black-sand beach, which is great for swimming when it's calm. As you walk to the freshwater pond, check out the **Queen's Bath**, a freshwater swimming hole that appears deceptively small but actually extends back into the rock for about 40ft. Look for a *makai* opening in the trees after you pass the gargantuan yellow estate and tennis courts. On the northern end, you can actually walk across a shallow channel to a small island with white sand. In the water, you might see green sea turtles.

DONKEY CROSSING

In the evenings, donkeys come down from the hills to drink at spring-fed watering holes and to eat seedpods from the kiawe (mesquitelike trees) along the coast between Kua and Kiholo Bays. The donkeys are descendants of the pack animals that were used on coffee farms until the 1950s, when jeeps replaced them.

Growers, who had become fond of these 'Kona nightingales,' as the braying donkeys were nicknamed, chose to release many of them into the wild rather than turn them into glue. The donkeys were largely forgotten until Hwy 19 went through in 1974.

Keep an eye out for the donkeys at night. They need to cross the road for their evening feedings, and often ignore the 'Donkey Crossing' signs on the highway!

SOUTH KOHALA COAST

From Waikoloa to Kawaihae, the endless vista of lava rock is probably unlike anything you've seen. This was an important area in Hawaiian history, and ancient trails, heiau, fishponds and petroglyph sites still remain. In the middle of the desolate lava terrain, however, you'll see an incongruous bunch of lush, green oases. These are the swanky resorts and pro golf courses that have sprung up since the 1960s. Now known as Big Island's Gold Coast, this shoreline stretch reflects both old and new Hawaii.

WAIKOLOA RESORT AREA

After crossing into the South Kohala district, a turnoff just south of the 76-mile marker leads to the Waikoloa Beach Marriott and Hilton Waikoloa Village hotels. The Kohala branch of the **Big Island Visitors Bureau** (☎ 886-1655, 800-648-2441; www.gohawaii.com; Suite B15, King's Shops, 250 Waikoloa Beach Dr; ☼ 8am-4:30pm Mon-Fri) is here.

While rack rates typically range from $350 to $1000, you can almost always find special deals at the resorts' websites.

Sights & Activities
'ANAEHO'OMALU BEACH PARK
Dubbed 'A Bay' by the linguistically challenged, **'Anaeho'omalu Beach** (☼ 6am-8pm) is long

and sandy, and curves along an attractive bay. Popular with families, swimmers and picnickers, this is perhaps the only beach suited to windsurfing. Winter weather can produce rip currents, but the water is usually quite calm.

Both ends of the bay are composed of prehistoric lava flows from Mauna Kea, with 'a'a (rough, jagged lava) to the north and smoother *pahoehoe* to the south. The southern end of the beach has public facilities, with showers, toilets, changing areas, drinking water and parking.

The northern end of the beach, which fronts the Outrigger Waikoloa Beach, has a little fitness area with swing ropes, chin-up bars and a volleyball net. The **Ocean Sports beach hut** (☎ 886-6666, ext 2; www.hawaiioceansports .com) announces the latest water conditions, and hires out windsurfing equipment and kayaks (at rip-off prices of $15 per hour for a single and $22 per hour for a double). Ocean Sports also offers (more reasonably priced) windsurfing and scuba-diving lessons, boat dives, catamaran and glass-bottom-boat cruises.

For snorkeling, there's a decent spot at the north end, directly in front of the sluice gate. Here you'll find coral formations, a fair variety of tropical fish and, if you're lucky, sea turtles.

'Anaeho'omalu was once the site of royal fishponds, and archaeologists from the Bishop Museum have found evidence here of human habitation dating back more than a thousand years. Two large fishponds lie just beyond the line of coconut trees on the beach. A short footpath starts near the showers and bypasses fishponds, caves, ancient house platforms and a shrine. Check the interpretive plaques along the way.

To get there, drive along Waikoloa Beach Dr toward the resorts and make a left turn opposite the entrance to the Kings' Shops

WAIKOLOA PETROGLYPH PRESERVE
On Waikoloa Beach Dr, a lava field etched with impressive petroglyphs is off to the right, immediately before the Kings' Shops complex. If you park at the shopping complex, it's a five-minute walk along a signposted path to the first of the etchings.

Stay on the path at all times. Do not walk atop the petroglyphs and cause irreparable damage, as careless tourists do. Many date back to the 16th century; some are graphic (humans, birds, canoes) and others, cryptic (dots, lines). Western influences appear in the form of horses and English initials.

HILTON WAIKOLOA VILLAGE

When it opened in 1988, at a cost of $360 million, this hotel (then a Hyatt) billed itself as the world's most expensive resort. Aptly nicknamed 'Disneyland,' the ostentatious 62-acre Hilton Waikoloa Village is, if nothing else, eye candy.

Most of the hotel's glamour lies in its manmade enormity. Even the beach is artificial, with a saltwater lagoon stocked with tropical fish and fantasy swimming pools with a 175ft twisting waterslide (kids adore it). You'll see lots of families riding kayaks or paddling pedal boats in the 'lake,' oblivious to the natural wonders nearby.

Perhaps the biggest draw is the dolphin pool, where guests can get thrillingly close to one of them. **DolphinQuest** (☎ 800-248-3316; www.dolphinquest.org; adult/child $150/125, family up to 5 $700) even sponsors a 'dolphin training adventure' for $295. The dozen or so cetaceans seem healthy as they leap and swim in large tanks, and are carefully supervised during guest programs.

If you don't feel like walking, you can navigate the sprawling grounds in canopied boats that cruise artificial canals, or on a modernistic tram like the Monorail. The lobby showcases a multimillion-dollar art collection of museum-quality pieces from Melanesia, Polynesia and Asia. It's particularly big on Papua New Guinea, along with replicas, such as a giant Buddha sculpture.

GOLF & TENNIS

Golfers can head for the **Waikoloa Beach & Kings' Courses** (☎ 886-7778, 877-924-5656), both at the Waikoloa Beach Marriott. Nonguests are charged green fees of $150, but at all the premier South Kohala courses you can beat the nonguest prices by waiting until mid-afternoon to tee off for a 50% discount. Carts are mandatory.

Tennis courts are available at the **Waikoloa Beach Marriott Tennis Center** (☎ 886-6789; per court 1st hr $10, subsequent per hr $5). Six courts rent for a surprisingly reasonable cost. Nonguests are welcome, too.

Festivals & Events

Great Waikoloa Food, Wine & Music Festival (☎ 886-1234; www.dolphindays.com; Hilton Waikoloa Village; admission $100; ☼ 3rd weekend Jun) combines over 30 of the state's best chefs with an array of fine wines and boutique brews, plus world-class jazz artists. This festival is part of the three-day **Dolphin Days Summer Fest**, established in 1994 to celebrate the first birthday of the first dolphin born at the resort.

Sleeping

Waikoloa Beach Marriott (☎ 886-6789, 888-924-5656; www.waikoloabeachmarriott.com; 69-275 Waikoloa Beach Dr; r $325-535; 🅿 🛈) Formerly the Royal Waikoloan, the 15-acre Marriott is an older resort, but the best choice in the Waikoloa resort area. Its beachside location is far superior to the Hilton's, and the rooms are comfortable, with private lanai. The Kings' Shops are within walking distance, so you're not captive to resort fare for all your meals.

Hilton Waikoloa Village (☎ 886-1234, 800-221-2424; www.hiltonwaikoloavillage.com; 425 Waikoloa Beach Dr; garden-view r $200-470, ocean-view r $240-690; 🅿 🛈) This megaresort might be over the top, but the sheer magnitude can make an impression – and it's more affordable than the other resorts. Kids seem to enjoy the 'rides' and parents might appreciate the safe, waveless waters. Grounds are plush, with all the usual Hilton amenities and two 18-hole golf courses.

GOLD COAST RESORT REPORT

▪ **Four Seasons Resort Hualalai** (p217) for impeccable service and dining

▪ **Kona Village Resort** (p217) for privacy and a taste of old Hawai'i

▪ **Hilton Waikoloa Village** (p219) for an extravagant, larger-than-life playground for kids

▪ **Mauna Kea Beach Hotel** (p223) for a beach that'll take your breath away and the island's premier golf course

▪ **Hapuna Beach Prince Hotel** (p223) for virtually the same features as the Mauna Kea (they're 'sister' hotels)

▪ **Mauna Lani Bay Hotel & Bungalows** (p221) for the prettiest architecture on grounds that contain ancient Hawaiian sites

HAWAI'I (THE BIG ISLAND)

Eating

Two famous island chefs have outposts at the Kings' Shops.

Merriman's Market Café (☎ 886-1700; dinner mains $15-25; ☉ 11am-9:30pm) The second location of the well-known Merriman's in Waimea, the Market Café serves flavorful Mediterranean-influenced dishes featuring organic island-grown produce, fresh fish caught locally, and the finest artisan breads, cheeses and wines. The setting is casual, and lunch mains stay under $15.

Roy's Waikoloa Bar & Grill (☎ 886-4321; mains $22-25; ☉ 11:30am-2pm & 5:30-9:30pm) This branch of the world-famous Roy's restaurants serves excellent regional Hawaii cuisine. At dinner, expect creative main courses such as rack of lamb in a liliko'i (passion fruit) Cabernet sauce or blackened 'ahi with pickled ginger.

Entertainment

If you can afford the Kona Village luau (p217), go for it. Otherwise, there are places that give you the standard colorful show:

Hilton Waikoloa Village (☎ 886-1234; adult/child $72/36; ☉ 6pm Fri) Presented by 'Legends of the Pacific,' this luau show includes a dinner buffet and one cocktail.

Waikoloa Beach Marriott (☎ 886-6789, 888-924-5656; www.waikoloabeachmarriott.com; 69-275 Waikoloa Beach Dr; adult/child $67/33; ☉ 5:30pm Sun & Wed) This poolside luau is the typical commercial show with Hawaiian-style dinner buffet, open bar and Polynesian dances.

Shopping

Kings' Shops is the Big Island's most upscale shopping mall, where Bulgari, Burberry and Louis Vuitton sit beside Macy's and a food court.

MAUNA LANI RESORT AREA

Built in 1983 by a Japanese company, the Mauna Lani Resort truly resembles an oasis. Once you turn off the highway onto Mauna Lani Dr (at the splash of coconut palms and bougainvillea), you pass a long stretch of lava with virtually no vegetation. Halfway along there's a strikingly green golf course sculpted in the black lava. Drive to the end to reach Mauna Lani Bay; the Fairmont Orchid and Holoholokai Beach Park are to the north.

Sights & Activities

Built on a historic site, the Mauna Lani Bay Hotel & Bungalows is accessible to non-guests who wish to explore the trails and fishponds. The beach fronting the hotel is protected, but the water is rather shallow; snorkelers might prefer exploring a coral reef beyond the inlet. A less frequented cove is down by the Beach Club restaurant, a 15-minute walk to the south.

HONOKA'OPE BAY

One mile south of the hotel is this **bay**, which is protected at the southern end, and good for swimming and snorkeling when the seas are calm. You can reach the bay either on foot, by an old coastal trail that passes an historic fishing and village site, or by taking a new access road.

KALAHUIPUA'A FISHPONDS

These ancient **fishponds** lie along the beach just south of the hotel, partly under a shady grove of coconut palms and milo (native hardwood) trees. They are among the few still-working fishponds in Hawai'i, and are stocked, as in ancient times, with awa (Hawaiian milkfish). Water circulates from the ocean through traditional makaha (sluice gates), which allow small fish to enter but keep mature, fattened catch from leaving. You might notice fish sporadically jumping into the air and slapping down on the water, an exercise that knocks off parasites.

KALAHIPUA'A HISTORIC TRAIL

This **trail** begins on the inland side of the Mauna Lani Bay Hotel, at a marked parking lot, opposite the resort's little grocery store. Pick up a free, self-guided trail map from the concierge desk.

The first part of the trail meanders through a former Hawaiian settlement that dates from the 16th century, passing lava tubes once used as cave shelters and a few other archaeological and geological sites marked by interpretive plaques. Keep an eye out for quail, northern and red-crested cardinals, saffron finches and Japanese white-eyes.

The trail then skirts fishponds lined with coconut palms and continues out to the beach, where you'll find a thatched shelter with an outrigger canoe and an historic cottage with a few Hawaiian artifacts on display. If you continue southwest past the cottage, you can loop around the fishpond and back to your starting point – a round trip of about 1.5 miles.

Take a break en route, at the cove near the southern tip of the fishpond, where the swimming is good and a restaurant offers simple lunches.

HOLOHOLOKAI BEACH PARK

North of the Fairmont Orchid, this **beach** has a rocky shoreline composed of coral chunks and lava. While not great for swimming, the waters are fine for snorkeling during calm surf. Facilities include showers, drinking water, restrooms, picnic tables and grills.

To get there, take Mauna Lani Dr and turn right at the rotary, then right again on the beach road immediately before the Fairmont Orchid. The park also features the petroglyphs described below.

PUAKO PETROGLYPH PRESERVE

With more than 3000 petroglyphs, this **petroglyph preserve** is one of the largest collections of ancient lava carvings in Hawai'i and definitely worth a visit.

To see the petroglyphs, you must walk about 1300yd from the beach park. From the *mauka* end of the Holoholokai Beach parking lot, a well-marked trail leads to the preserve. The walk is easy, but don't wear 'rubbah slippah' because the thorny foliage along the way can pierce your feet and the ground is rocky. The path is only partly shaded so the midday heat can be stifling.

The human figures drawn in simple linear forms are among the oldest examples of such drawings in Hawai'i. Like all petroglyphs in Hawaii, the meaning of the symbols remains enigmatic. The aging petroglyphs are fragile, as the ancient lava flow into which they're carved is brittle and cracking. Stepping on the petroglyphs can damage them – don't step over the boundary!

If you want to make rubbings, use the authentically reproduced petroglyphs at the start of the trail that have been created for that purpose. Bring rice paper and charcoal, or cotton cloth and crayons.

GOLF

The **Francis I'i Brown North & South Courses** (☎ 885-6655; Mauna Lani Bay Hotel & Bungalows) are considered among the Big Island's top world-class courses. Nonguests pay green fees of $185 to play either course, but the south course, considered more scenic and challenging, is more popular.

Sleeping

Mauna Lani Bay Hotel & Bungalows (☎ 885-6622, 800-367-2323; www.maunalani.com; 68-1400 Mauna Lani Dr; mountain-/ocean-view r $390/575; 🛇 🔌) Although over two decades old, this place remains one of the finest resorts in the islands. The hotel is ritzy but still classily low-key. The modern, open-air building is centered around a spacious atrium that has sleek water sculptures, colorful orchid sprays and towering coconut trees. The historic sites on the grounds are meticulously maintained; a saltwater stream and ponds around the hotel hold colorful reef fish, small black-tipped sharks and a few turtles. Check the website for promotional packages.

Fairmont Orchid (☎ 885-2000, 800-845-9905; www .orchid-maunalani.com; 1 N Kaniku Dr; garden-/ocean-view r $435/605) Just north of the Mauna Lani Bay Hotel, the Orchid is an elegant hotel with an upscale air. Service is always impeccable and the large swimming pool is a hit with kids.

Eating

Brown's Beach House (☎ 885-2000; Fairmont Orchid; mains $24-37; 🕙 11:30am-2pm & 6-9:30pm) Brown's, a longtime favorite, serves flavorful island dishes like seared foie gras, *unagi* sushi, sautéed grilled *moi* (Pacific threadfin, which in ancient Hawaii was reserved only for royalty), and soft-shell crab. (The chef de cuisine, Etsuji Umezu, moved to head the Four Seasons Hualalai Grille, p217, in spring 2004, but the quality seems to be holding.)

Canoe House (☎ 885-6622; mains $27-50; Mauna Lani Bay Hotel & Bungalows; 🕙 6-9pm) Mauna Lani Bay Hotel's most upscale restaurant has a romantic, oceanfront setting and a menu that blends Asian and Hawaiian influences, with an emphasis on seafood. Dishes include grilled lemon-pepper scallops or pancetta-wrapped mahimahi with coconut-and-spinach risotto.

Gallery (☎ 885-7777; Mauna Lani Bay Hotel & Bungalows; lunch $8-15, dinner $25-30; 🕙 11am-2pm daily, 6-9pm Tue-Sat) At the Mauna Lani Bay Hotel's golf clubhouse (Francis I'i Brown North & South Courses), the Gallery serves continental and Pacific Rim dishes. The fresh fish is a specialty; try the *onaga* (red snapper) encrusted with macadamia nuts.

Bay Terrace (☎ 885-6622; Mauna Lani Bay Hotel; breakfast mains $8-20, breakfast buffet $24; 🕙 6:30-10:30am) Delicious breakfasts and a generous buffet, if you're hungry.

Entertainment

The resorts offer the expected level of night-time amusement, but a couple of places are recommended.

Honu Bar (☎ 885-6622; Mauna Lani Bay Hotel; ☾ 6pm-midnight) Billiards, cigars, and occasional live entertainment accompany the premium wines, cocktails and liqueurs. The hotel **atrium** also has live Hawaiian music and hula dancing nightly from 6pm to 9pm.

Ocean Bar (☎ 885-2000; The Fairmont Orchid; ☾ 11:30am-10pm) Here you'll find live music nightly, and awesome sunset views from the chaise lounges.

PUAKO

Puako is a one-road beach town (population 430) that's lucky to remain off the beaten tourist track. The town is simply a mile-long row of houses, with many marked 'shoreline access' points. To get here, take either the marked turnoff from Hwy 19, or a bumpy side road from Hapuna Beach State Park.

The main attraction at Puako is giant tide pools, set in the swirls and dips of *pahoehoe* coastline. Some pools are deep enough to shelter live coral and other marine life. A narrow beach of pulverized coral and lava lines much of the shore. Snorkeling can be excellent off Puako but the surf is usually too rough in winter.

For the easiest beach access, go to the south end of the village, stopping just before the 'Road Closed 500 Feet' sign. Take the short dirt road toward the water. There is no beach per se, but there is a small cove that's used for snorkeling and shore diving; be careful of the undertow. A couple of minutes' walk north brings you to a few petroglyphs, a board for *konane* (a game similar to checkers) chinked into the lava, and tide pools deep enough to cool off in.

Nearby, beautiful **Beach 69** has easy access and gentle waves. There's plenty of shade, and boundary trees make it feel like each group of sunbathers has a private little plot. There are no facilities. Turn down Puako Rd between the 70- and 71-mile markers; take the first right turn (the road quickly becomes one lane). Look for telephone pole No 71 to the left and park. Follow the 'road' to its end, and then tramp along the footpath that runs parallel to a wooden fence. In case you're wondering, telephone pole No 71 was once No 69, hence the beach's nickname.

HAPUNA BEACH STATE PARK

Already legendary as the Big Island's most popular and accessible **beach**, Hapuna is also ranked among the world's best beaches by *Condé Nast Traveler*. The clear waters and deep, white sand that gently slopes into the ocean won't disappoint you. But be warned that Hapuna gets jammed on weekends, and if you wait till noon, you'll be stuck in the parking lot forever.

When calm, Hapuna affords good swimming, snorkeling and diving. When the surf's up in winter, the bodysurfers and boogie boarders get their turn. High winter surf can produce strong currents close to the shore and a pounding shorebreak, and waves over 3ft should be left for the experts. Hapuna has had numerous drownings, and many of the victims have been tourists who were unfamiliar with the water conditions.

A tiny cove with a small sandy beach lies about five minutes' walk north of the park. The water is a bit calmer there and, in winter, less sand is kicked up by the waves. The park has a landscaped picnic area, showers, pay phones, drinking water and pitiable restrooms. Lifeguards are on duty. Be sure to lock your car.

Just up from the beach are six state-owned A-frame **cabins** (q $20) with million-dollar views. Each sleeps four people on two platforms (you sleep head to head) and has lights and electricity. They are also surprisingly bug-free. Amenities include shared bathrooms with showers and a cooking pavilion with a stove and fridge. See p178 for reservation information.

MAUNA KEA RESORT AREA

In the early 1960s, the late Laurance Rockefeller obtained a 99-year lease on the land around Kauna'oa Bay from his friend Richard Smart, owner of Parker Ranch (p231). Five years later, Rockefeller opened Mauna Kea Beach Hotel, the first luxury hotel on the Neighbor Islands.

The hotel, located just north of the 68-mile marker, remains a first-class act as the respected granddaddy of them all. The lobby and grounds have displays of Asian and Pacific artwork, including bronze statues, temple toys and Hawaiian quilts. The north garden holds the most prized possession: a 7th-century pink granite Buddha from a temple in southern India.

The **Mauna Kea Golf Course** (☎ 882-5400) consistently ranks among the top 10 courses in the world. Nonguests pay green fees of $195, while guests pay $130 and also have privileges at **Hapuna Beach Prince Hotel Golf Course** (☎ 880-3000).

But the prize of the Mauna Kea Beach Hotel is a gift from nature: **Kauna'oa Bay** (nicknamed 'Mauna Kea Beach') might be the most visually stunning beach on the Big Island. The crescent-shaped cove has fine white sand and a gradual slope that fosters excellent swimming conditions most of the year. On the north end, snorkeling conditions are good during calm waters.

The beach is open to the public, but only 30 parking spaces are set aside daily for nonguests. By noon, you'll probably be too late. If you're having a drink or lunch at the hotel, you can handily bypass the issue of obtaining a parking pass.

Just north of Mauna Kea Beach is delightful **Mau'umae Beach**, with soft white sand, shady trees and protected waters. Locals are proprietary about this beach (for good reason) so don't overstep your welcome. To get here, go toward the Mauna Kea Beach Hotel, turn right on Kamahoi and cross two wooden bridges. Look for telephone pole No 22 on the left and park. Walk down the trail to the Ala Kahakai sign and turn left toward the beach. You can also get here from nearby Spencer Beach, by walking 10 minutes on the Ala Kahakai Trail, a shady coastal path.

Locals flock to the Hapuna Beach Prince Hotel for the Aloha Festival **Poke Weekend** (☎ 880-3424; www.pokecontest.com; admission $5; ☺ late Sep), which is the 'signature event' of the Aloha Festival in September. Professional chefs and amateurs compete in various categories, such as *poke* with soy sauce or tofu or macadamia nuts! The weekend ends with a craft fair and celebrity golf tournament for charity.

Sleeping & Eating

Mauna Kea Beach Hotel (☎ 882-7222, 800-882-6060; www.maunakeabeachhotel.com; 62-100 Mauna Kea Beach Dr; mountain-/ocean-view r $360/565) After 40 years, the hotel is showing signs of age, but you can't go wrong here. Kauna'oa Bay is guaranteed to satisfy any beach fantasy. Check the website for hot deals (eg mountain-view room for $250 per night).

If you're spending an evening here, don't miss the luminous manta ray 'show' at the lookout point near the lobby between 7pm and 10pm, when lights are shone to attract the sea creatures into the bay. Also try to catch the decadent Sunday brunch at the **Terrace Café** (☎ 882-7222; brunch buffet $38; ☺ 11am-2pm Sun), where you can feast on sushi, dim sum, prime rib, lobster bisque, domestic and imported cheeses, and Belgian waffles (from the waffle station), plus the usual array of bacon, eggs, made-to-order omelets and fresh fruit.

Hapuna Beach Prince Hotel (☎ 880-1111; 866-774-6236; www.princeresortshawaii.com; terrace-/oceanview r $360/460) The Mauna Kea Beach Hotel's 'sister' resort, open since 1994, tends to be overshadowed, but the two share the same amenities and buses transport guests between the two. It's a good option, if you want a particular type of room.

SPENCER BEACH PARK

Spencer Beach Park, off Hwy 270 south of Kawaihae, is a low-key place for visitors with children, with a shallow, sandy beach that's protected by a reef and the jetty to the north. The waters are calm but they tend to be silty. The rocky south end of the beach past the pavilion is better for snorkeling, although entry is not as easy; kayaking is prohibited.

The park has a lifeguard station, picnic tables, barbecue grills, restrooms, showers, drinking water and both basketball and volleyball courts. A footpath leads south to Mau'umae Beach near the Mauna Kea Beach Resort.

Camping is allowed, and though the campsites are exposed and crowded together, it's still the best beach north of Kona to sleep under the stars. See p178 for information on obtaining a county permit.

PU'UKOHOLA HEIAU NATIONAL HISTORIC SITE

By 1790 Kamehameha the Great had conquered Maui, Lana'i and Moloka'i. However power over his home island of Hawai'i proved to be a challenge. When told by a prophet that if he built a heiau dedicated to his war god Kuka'ilimoku atop Pu'ukohola (Whale Hill) in Kawaihae he'd rule all the islands, Kamehameha built **Pu'ukohola Heiau**, a structure that's 224ft by 100ft, with 16ft to 20ft walls.

HAWAI'I
(THE BIG ISLAND)

It is believed that men formed a human chain 20 miles long, transporting rocks hand to hand from Pololu Valley in North Kohala – and with Kamehameha laboring alongside his men. After finishing the heiau by summer 1791, Kamehameha held a dedication ceremony and invited his rival and cousin, Keoua, the chief of Ka'u. When Keoua came ashore, he was killed and taken to the *luakini* as the first offering to the gods. With Keoua's death, Kamehameha took sole control of the Big Island, eventually ruling all the islands by 1810.

Back then Pu'ukohola Heiau was adorned with wooden *ki'i* and thatched structures, including an oracle tower, altar, drum house and shelter for the high priest. After Kamehameha's death in 1819, his son Liholiho and powerful widow Ka'ahumanu destroyed the deity images and the heiau was abandoned.

Today, only the basic rock foundation remains, but it's still impressive and has been designated a **national historic site** (☎ 882-7218; admission free; ❧ 7:30am-4pm). A two-minute trail to the heiau starts at the visitors center, which has a few simple displays and pamphlets. If you arrive after hours, you can park at Spencer Beach Park and walk to the heiau along an old entrance road that's closed to vehicle traffic.

Just beyond Pu'ukohola Heiau are the ruins of **Mailekini Heiau**, which predates Pu'ukohola, and was later turned into a fort by Kamehameha. **Hale o Kapuni Heiau**, a third temple dedicated to shark gods, lies submerged just offshore; nearby, on land, you can see the stone leaning post, where the high chief watched sharks bolt down offerings.

The trail leads across the highway to the site of **John Young's homestead**. Young, a shipwrecked British sailor, served Kamehameha as a military advisor and island governor. Today, all that remains are partial foundations for two of Young's buildings.

KAWAIHAE

While the Big Island's second-largest deepwater commercial harbor is in Kawaihae, the town is just a stopping point between North Kohala and the Kona Coast. In town, there's little more than a harbor, fuel tanks, cattle pens and a tiny beach park. You won't starve, however.

Café Pesto (☎ 882-1071; Kawaihae Shopping Center, Hwy 270; lunch/dinner mains $11/20, large/small pizza $11/18; ❧ 11am-9pm, to 10pm Fri & Sat) is sure to please with gourmet thin-crust pizza and inspired seafood salads and pastas. It's across from the harbor.

About 400yd south of Café Pesto, **Kawaihae Harbor Grill** (☎ 882-1368; dinner mains $18; ❧ 11am-2:30pm & 5:30-9:30pm) has a huge local following (especially Waimea residents) due to the reliable seafood, kid-friendly service and lively upstairs seafood bar. It's off Hwy 270.

If you're looking for sundries or deli take-out, the **Kawaihae Market & Deli** (☎ 880-1611; Kawaihae Shopping Center, Hwy 270; ❧ 4:30am-9pm Mon-Fri, 5:30am-8pm Sat & Sun) offers standard convenience items plus pasta and tofu salads that are better than you might expect. It's also across from the harbor.

NORTH KOHALA COAST

If you bypass North Kohala, as too many visitors do, you'll miss one of the most untouched, striking areas of the Big Island. Here there are significant historical sites, quaint towns to explore, and a breathtaking valley at the end of the road. The Kohala Mountains form a central ridge on this northernmost tip of the island: the leeward side is dry desert, while the windward side features coastal cliffs and spectacular valleys.

There are two fully paved routes into the district: an inland road (Hwy 250, Kohala Mountain Rd) and a coastal road (Hwy 270, Akoni Pule Hwy), which starts in Kawaihae, takes in the coastal sights of Lapakahi State Historical Park and Mo'okini Heiau, and ends at a lookout above Pololu Valley, where a trail descends to the valley floor.

Hwy 250 runs for 20 miles between Hawi and Waimea. As you head south, the road peaks at 3564ft and Maui rises out of the mist. Mauna Kea and Mauna Loa are also visible. Views of the coast and Kawaihae Harbor unfold below, and there's a roadside scenic lookout near the 8-mile marker, where you can appreciate the vastness of the Big Island. The road then winds through rolling green hills dotted with grazing cattle.

LAPAKAHI STATE HISTORICAL PARK

This **park** (admission free; ❧ 8am-4pm, closed most holidays) was a remote fishing village 600 years ago. The terrain was rocky and dry, so the ancient villagers turned to the sea for their food. Fish were plentiful, and the cove fronting the village provided a safe year-round canoe landing. Eventually some of the villagers moved to the wetter uplands and began to farm, trading their crops for fish with those who had stayed on the coast. In the process, Lapakahi grew into an *ahupua'a*, a wedge-shaped division of land radiating from the mountainous interior out to the sea. When the freshwater table dropped in the 19th century, the village was abandoned.

The 262-acre park encourages visitors to imagine traditional life here. A one-mile **loop trail** leads to the remains of stone walls, house sites, canoe sheds and fishing shrines. Displays show how fishers used lift nets to catch *opelu*, a technique still practiced today, and how the salt used to preserve the fish was dried in stone salt pans. Visitors can try their hands at Hawaiian games, with game pieces and instructions laid out for *'o'o ihe* (spear throwing), *konane* and *'ulu maika* (stone bowling).

Lapakahi's waters are part of a marine-life conservation district. The fish are so plentiful and the water so clear that you can stand above the shoreline and watch yellow tangs and other colorful fish swim around in the cove below. It is illegal to swim with them, however, and there's no easy beach access.

The park, which is largely unshaded, is just south of the 14-mile marker. Brochures are available at the trailhead.

MAHUKONA BEACH PARK

A mile north of Lapakahi, this **beach park** is a low-key fishing and swimming spot. Once a key port for the Kohala Sugar Company, you can still see the abandoned landing, which connected to the sugar mills by rail.

Beyond the landing, you can find interesting snorkeling and diving spots, although they're usually too rough in winter. Entry, via a ladder, is in about 5ft of water. Heading north, it's possible to follow an anchor chain out to a submerged boiler and the remains of a ship in about 25ft of water. You'll find a shower near the ladder, where you can rinse off. There is no sandy beach, however.

HAWAI'I (THE BIG ISLAND)

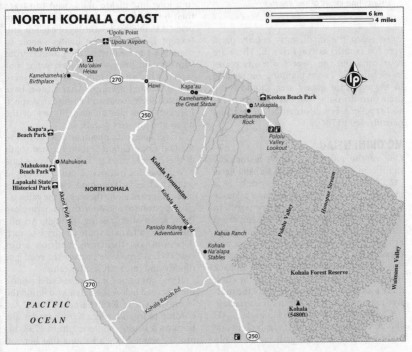

NORTH KOHALA UPCOUNTRY RIDES

The upcountry drive along Hwy 250, between Waimea and Hawi, crosses acres of rolling ranchland that's easy to appreciate from the car. To take a closer look, a horseback ride is a bit pricey but kids enjoy it. Companies typically don't allow those under 4ft tall, children under eight, or those who weigh more than 230lb.

Paniolo Riding Adventures (☎ 889-5354; www.panioloadventures.com; Hwy 250; rides $75-125) Offers a variety of horseback rides over 11,000-acre Ponoholo Ranch, a working cattle ranch. Horses are selected for the rider's experience, but they're all riding horses, not trail horses, and you can canter with the lead wrangler. Dress up like a *paniolo* (cowboy) with the boots, hats and chaps provided free of charge.

Kohala Na'alapa Stables (☎ 889-0022; www.naalapastables.com; Kohala Ranch Rd; rides $55-75) Tour guides allow open-range rather than head-to-tail riding so they don't feel like kiddie rides. Rides cross the pastures of Kahua Ranch, which spans 8500 acres, and affords fine views of the coast.

To reach the small, ratty county park, veer left (south) as you drive in. There are restrooms, but they won't win any prizes in cleanliness. Those planning on **camping** in the unkempt grassy area should bring their own drinking water and plenty of insect repellent. For information on camping permits, see p178.

MO'OKINI HEIAU

One of the oldest and most historically significant heiau in Hawaii, **Mo'okini Heiau** (☎ 373-8000; admission free; ⏰ dawn-dusk) is a massive place of worship, set atop a grassy knoll on the Big Island's solitary northern tip. This windswept, desolate site imparts a sense of timelessness and overarching mana. From here, you have a clear view out across the ocean to Maui. During the winter season this is a fantastic spot to observe humpback whales; at the northernmost tip of the coast there's an area of freshwater, where the massive mammals swim to clean off barnacles.

Chants date Mo'okini Heiau back to AD 480. According to legend, it was built in one night with basalt stones gathered in Pololu Valley, and passed along a human chain stretching 14 miles. For nearly 15 centuries, the heiau was reserved exclusively for *ali'i* to fast, pray and give offerings, including human sacrifices dedicated to the god Ku.

A *kapu* that once banned commoners from the heiau grounds wasn't lifted until recent times, and the site still remains isolated, though it was deemed a national historic landmark in 1963. Few come this way, and you'll probably be alone with the wind and the spirits here. Restrooms are not available, and the site is not wheelchair-accessible.

The heiau is 250ft by 125ft, with rock walls reaching 25ft high. The entrance is through the wall on the western side. A large scallop-shaped altar at the north end of the heiau is thought to have been added by Pa'ao, the Tahitian priest who arrived around the 12th century, and introduced human sacrifice to Hawaiian worship. Understandably, islanders tried to live a safe distance from Mo'okini.

The current *kahuna nui* (wise person, commonly a priest, healer or sorcerer), Leimomi Mo'okini Lum, is the most recent in a long line of Mo'okini, who can trace their lineage back to the temple's first high priest. On the third Saturday of each month (except December), she invites people to the temple to help weed the grounds from 9am to noon; bring work gloves, water, sunscreen, a brown-bag lunch and a lei to leave as a *ho'okupu* (offering). After visitors have invested their sweat and a sense of respect, Leimomi provides an oral history of the heiau and answers questions.

To get here, turn *makai* off Hwy 270 onto the Old Coast Guard Station Rd, just south of the 19-mile marker. Follow the one-lane paved road for just over a mile. Turn right onto a wide red-cinder road. Two cattle gates block this road along the way; if the gates are closed, go ahead and open them but do close them again after passing through. An oft-mentioned alternate route (to drive toward 'Upolu airport then turn south on a dirt road) is less accessible because the road gets muddy and impassable after rains.

If you continue for about 600yd down on the dirt road below the heiau, you'll find the legendary site of Kamehameha's birth. According to legend, when Kamehameha was born on a stormy winter night in 1758, his mother was told by a kahuna that her son would become a destroyer of chiefs and a powerful ruler. The high chief of the island didn't take well to the prophecy, and in a King Herod–like scenario, he ordered the newborn be killed. Thus, immediately after birth, the baby was taken to Mo'okini Heiau for his birth rituals, and then into hiding in the nearby mountains.

HAWI

Less than a thousand people live in **Hawi** (hah-*vee*), but they certainly enjoy a variety of charming shops and eateries. Today there's a mixture of old-timers and newcomers drawn by the low-key village flavor and cheaper real estate. North Kohala used to be sugar country, and Hawi was the biggest of half a dozen sugar towns. Kohala Sugar Company, which had incorporated all of the mills, closed down its operations in 1975. You can still see the occasional strip of feral cane among the pastures outside town.

Information

Entering town via Hwy 270, you'll pass the small **visitors center** (Hwy 270; ☽ 9am-5pm Mon-Fri), which has a few area brochures and sketch maps. Hawi also has a post office, grocery store, gas station and a few restaurants.

Sights, Activities & Tours

The park on Hwy 250, in front of the post office, is cool and shady with giant banyan trees. Behind the park is the old sugar-mill tower, a remnant of the town's former mainstay.

One activity you'll find nowhere else on the island is **Flumin' da Ditch** (☎ 889-6922, 877-449-6922; www.flumindaditch.com; adult/child & senior $85/65; ☽ departures 8:15am & 12:15pm), three-hour kayaking tours of Kohala Ditch, the area's historic irrigation system. Kayaks sit four or five people (depending on size). Don't expect rapids or whitewater on the journey, but be prepared to get soaked.

Kohala Ditch, built in 1906, is an intricate series of ditches, tunnels and flumes used to irrigate Kohala sugarcane fields. Water from the rugged wet interior of the Kohala Forest Reserve flowed out to the drier Hawi area. The ditch runs 22.5 miles and was built by Japanese immigrant laborers, who were paid about $1 a day for very hazardous work that killed over a dozen during construction. The last Kohala cane

was cut in the 1970s, but the ditch continues to be a source of water for Kohala ranches and farms.

Sleeping

Kohala Village Inn (☎ 889-0404; www.kohalavillage inn.com; 55-514 Hawi Rd; d $60, ste $90-95) In a motel-style building located right off the highway, you'll find rooms that are plain and clean but no fan, air-con or phone. The attached restaurant is decent but the others just down the street are better.

Cardinals' Haven (winter ☎ 884-5550, summer ☎ 425-822-3120; r $60; ☽ mid-Nov–mid-May) During winter only, you can join the owners in their lovely rural home 3 miles from central Hawi. From the yard, you can look across cattle pastures clear out to Maui. The guest unit comes with a TV, a kitchenette and a sofa bed. Originally from Switzerland, the owners speak fluent German and French.

Eating

Sushi Rock (☎ 889-5900; Hwy 270; nigiri $4-5, sushi rolls $7-10; ☽ 12-8pm) In a small but charming space (shared with the gift shop, Without Boundaries), Sushi Rock offers impressive, island-influenced sushi. The setting is personal and the youthful owner-chef Rio Miceli, a Hawi native, serves creative rolls such as the Kohala, with *'ahi poke*, fresh papaya and cucumber, rolled in macadamia nuts – plus all the traditional *nigiri* sushi.

Bamboo (☎ 889-5555; Hwy 270; lunch/dinner $8/10; ☽ 11:30am-2:30pm & 6-9pm Tue-Sat, 11am-2pm Sun) A longtime favorite, and the only fine-dining option in North Kohala, Bamboo serves excellent island food amid tourist-tropical but pleasant decor. Savor the coconut grilled chicken or sesame-nori-crusted tiger shrimp, and save room for the homemade desserts. There's live music on Friday and Saturday nights. Reservations are recommended.

Aunty's Place (☎ 889-0899; Hwy 270; meals $10; ☽ 11am-3:30pm & 5-9pm Mon-Sat, noon-9pm Sun) Gerda 'Aunty' Medeiros makes pizzas all day, and traditional hearty German dinners at night, served in a casual diner setting. While the owner doesn't like to compare her 'housewife cooking' to Waimea's Edelweiss restaurant's 'hotel cooking,' she shouldn't be so modest. Hawi's main nightlife attraction happens here on Friday evening, when the karaoke mikes are open from 9:30pm until 2am.

Hula La's Mexican Kitchen & Salsa Factory
(☎ 889-5668; Hwy 270; meals $5-10; ☻ 10am-8pm)
Tasty Mexican fare, including filling burritos and homemade tropical salsa, are on offer, but there's only a smattering of tables in close quarters or on the lanai. Credit cards aren't accepted.

If you want to pick up food to go, try the **farmers market** (☻ 7:30am-1pm Sat) held at the park on Hwy 250. **Kohala Health Food** (☎ 889-0277; Hwy 270; ☻ 10am-5pm Mon-Fri, to 4pm Sat) sells tea, organic juices and packaged natural-food items. **Kohala Coffee Mill** (☎ 889-5577; Hwy 270; snacks $3-5; ☻ 6:30am-6pm) is a comfy place to hang out and treat yourself to muffins, fresh-brewed Kona coffee and heavenly Tropical Dreams ice cream.

Shopping
Without Boundaries (☎ 889-5900; Hwy 270; ☻ 11am-5pm) A find for unusual artsy gifts.

KAPA'AU
pop 1000
The largest town in North Kohala, Kapa'au has a courthouse, police station, library and bank. During the King Kamehameha Day festivities in June (a statewide holiday), the park hosts a parade and Hawaiian dancing, music and food.

Sights & Activities
Kamehameha Park boasts a large, modern gymnasium, and everything from a ballpark to a swimming pool, all free and open to the public.

KAMEHAMEHA THE GREAT STATUE
This **statue** on the front lawn of the North Kohala Civic Center may look familiar. Its lei-draped and much-photographed twin stands opposite Honolulu's Iolani Palace (p88).

The statue was made in 1880 in Florence, Italy, by American sculptor Thomas Gould. When the ship delivering it sank off the Falkland Islands, a second statue was then cast from the original mold. The duplicate statue arrived at the islands in 1883 and took its place in downtown Honolulu. Later the sunken statue was recovered from the ocean floor and completed its trip to Hawaii. This original statue was then sent here, to Kamehameha's childhood home, where it now stands.

KALAHIKIOLA CHURCH
Protestant missionaries Elias and Ellen Bond, who arrived in Kohala in 1841, built **Kalahikiola Church** in 1855. The church itself is usually locked, but the detour through lush foliage with its chirping birds is pleasant. The land and buildings on the drive in are part of the vast Bond estate (proving that missionary life wasn't one of total deprivation).

If you want to take a look, turn inland off Hwy 270 onto a narrow road 900yd east of the Kamehameha statue, between the 23- and 24-mile markers. The church is another 900yd up from the highway.

KAMEHAMEHA ROCK
The rock is on the inland side of the road, about 2 miles east of Kapa'au, on a curve just over a small bridge. According to legend, Kamehameha carried this rock up from the beach below to demonstrate his strength.

When a road crew attempted to move the rock to a different location, they managed to get it up onto a wagon, but the rock stubbornly fell off – a sign that it wanted to stay put. Not wanting to upset Kamehameha's mana, the workers left it in place.

Eating
Takata Store (☎ 889-5413; Hwy 270; ☻ 8am-7pm Mon-Sat, to 1pm Sun) The largest market in North Kohala is stocked with produce, meat and all kinds of other edibles.

Kohala Rainbow Café (☎ 889-0099; Hwy 270; sandwiches & salads $8; ☻ 11am-5pm) Just opposite the Kamehameha statue, this really is *the* place to eat in town. Jen's has tasty chicken Caesar salads, good chili and a recommendable Greek wrap sandwich with organic greens. Also on the menu are fresh fruit smoothies, deli sandwiches and soups.

Shopping
In the historic **Nambu Hotel Building**, a handful of shops and galleries makes for pleasant browsing. **Kohala Book Shop** (☎ 889-6400; Hwy 270; ☻ 11am-5pm Mon-Sat) is not only the biggest and best used bookstore on the island, but also a gathering place for local authors and literary luminaries from abroad. **Elements** (☎ 889-0760; Hwy 270; ☻ 10am-6pm Mon-Fri, to 5pm Sat) showcases a sophisticated collection of fine jewelry, ceramics and other art pieces made by local artists.

MAKAPALA

The little village of Makapala has only a few hundred residents. If you're hiking down to Pololu Valley, the town's little store is the last place to get a drink or snack – if it's open.

While located along a scenic rocky coast, **Keokea Beach Park** isn't a big draw because there's no sandy beach. Signs warn about dangerous shorebreaks and strong currents, though a protected cove allows for decent swimming. The park has restrooms, showers, drinking water, picnic pavilions and barbecue grills, but no camping.

The park is about 1 mile in from the highway; take the marked turnoff about 1.5 miles before Pololu Valley Lookout. On the way down to the beach, you'll pass an old **Japanese cemetery**. Most of the gravestones are in kanji (Japanese script), and in front of a few, there are filled sake cups.

POLOLU VALLEY

Hwy 270 ends at a viewpoint that overlooks secluded Pololu Valley, with its scenic backdrop of steeply scalloped coastal cliffs spreading out to the east. The lookout has the kind of strikingly beautiful angle that's rarely experienced without a helicopter tour – and it's just as stunning as the more famous Waipi'o Valley Lookout.

Pololu was once thickly planted with wetland taro. Pololu Stream fed the valley, carrying water from the remote, rainy interior to the valley floor. When the Kohala Ditch was built, it siphoned off much of the water and put an end to the taro production. The last islanders left the valley in the 1940s, and the valley slopes are now forest-reserve land.

Sights & Activities

The **Pololu Valley Trail**, from the lookout down to Pololu Valley, takes less than 30 minutes to walk. It's steep, but not overly strenuous, and you'll be rewarded with lovely vistas throughout. Be cautious with your footing – much of the trail is rocky or packed clay, which gets slippery when wet. The uphill climb might actually be easier than the trek downhill because of the loose rocks. At the trailhead, Good Samaritans leave walking sticks for your assistance. Cool breezes and a canopy of trees keep the walk comfortable.

The black-sand **beach** fronting the valley stretches for about 900yd and can make an enjoyable stroll. Driftwood collects in great

---

THE BIG ISLAND FOR KIDS

- Picnic at **Lili'uokalani Park** (p255)
- Go **horseback riding** in Waimea (p231)
- Hike with walking sticks in **Pololu Valley** (see left)
- Meet a **dolphin** up close (p219)
- Scream on carnival rides at Hilo's annual **county fair** (p259)
- See the moon and planets from atop **Mauna Kea** (p246)
- Walk through a **lava tube** (p277)
- Catch a **matinee** (p263) and sample the island's best **ice cream** (p263) in Hilo (p249)
- Get wet kayaking the **Kohala ditch** (p227)
- Go snorkeling in **Kealakekua Bay** (p205)

---

quantities here. Cattle and horses roam the valley; a gate at the bottom of the trail keeps them in. The surf is usually intimidating in winter, and there can be rip currents year-round. This is not a swimming beach: much of the shoreline is rocky. There are no facilities.

Tours

Another way to explore Pololu Valley is by mule. **Hawaii Forest & Trail** (☎ 331-8505, 800-464-1993; www.hawaii-forest.com) offers morning mule rides (adult/child $95/75, departing at 8am and noon Monday to Saturday), which cross streams towards the waterfall and valley lookouts, though not into the valley itself. Mules are used for a few reasons: the surefooted creatures are steadier than horses and can handle heavier loads. In the early 1900s they helped Japanese laborers build the Kohala Ditch, which you'll also see on the tour. It's best to book in advance.

WAIMEA (KAMUELA)

pop 7000

Amid rolling pastureland and cool mist, Waimea shows off another face of the Big Island. This is former cowboy country, and headquartered here is Parker Ranch,

Hawai'i's largest cattle ranch, which spreads across about 10% of the Big Island. Almost everything in Waimea is owned, run or leased by Parker Ranch (see the boxed text on p231).

Waimea certainly has its cowboy influences, but it's also rapidly growing in size and sophistication. Wealthy mainlanders have moved in, and the town also serves the upscale subdivisions emerging on former ranches in the Kohala Mountains. Waimea's relative proximity to the Mauna Kea summit has also attracted a growing number of astronomers and engineers to settle here.

For most visitors Waimea is just a stopover between Kona and Hilo, but the town does boast first-rate art galleries and excellent restaurants, including Merriman's, a forerunner in the Hawaii Regional Cuisine movement. Don't be caught off guard by Waimea's chilly weather, which includes daily fog and brisk winds.

ORIENTATION

Waimea is also referred to as Kamuela, which is the Hawaiian spelling of Samuel. Although some say the name comes from an early postmaster named Samuel Spencer, most claim it's for Samuel Parker of Parker Ranch fame. Regardless, the result is the same: confusion.

Hwy 190 is commonly called the Mamalahoa Hwy. From Hilo, Hwy 19 is also called the Mamalahoa Hwy, but once it intersects with Hwy 190, it is called Kawaihae Rd. Further east, there's the Old Mamalahoa Hwy, which intersects Hwy 19 at both ends.

INFORMATION

North Hawaii Community Hospital (☎ 885-4444; 67-1125 Mamalahoa Hwy; ☺ 24hr emergency services)

Post office (☎ 885-6239; 67-1197 Mamalahoa Hwy) Located southwest of Parker Ranch Center. Address all Waimea mail to Kamuela.

Waimea visitors center (☎ 885-6707; 65-1291 Kawaihae Rd; ☺ 8:30am-3:30pm Mon-Fri) Amiable staff and located in the Lindsey House, which was built in 1909 by Parker Ranch for a five-star employee.

SIGHTS

Most of Waimea's sights are along the Mamalahoa Hwy, around three consecutive stoplights. Prominently located in Waimea's center, near a grove of cherry-blossom trees, is the **WM Keck Observatory office** (☎ 885-7887; 65-1120 Mamalahoa Hwy; ☺ 8am-4:30pm Mon-Fri). But it's a working office, so there's little for visitors to see besides a short video and simple displays about the Mauna Kea telescopes. For more about the observatory, see p244.

Parker Ranch Museum & Visitors Center

If you know little about the Big Island's history, this small **museum** (☎ 885-7655; www .parkerranch.com; Parker Ranch Center, 67-1185 Mamalahoa Hwy; adult/child/senior $6.50/5/5.50; ☺ 9am-5pm Mon-Sat, last entry 4pm) provides a manageable introduction. In just a few displays, you'll learn

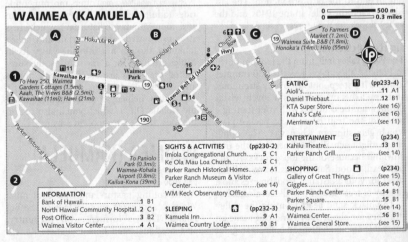

WAIMEA (KAMUELA)

0 ———— 500 m
0 ———— 0.3 miles

To Farmers Market (1.2mi);
Waimea Suite B&B (1.8mi);
Honoka'a (14mi); Hilo (55mi)

To Hwy 250, Waimea Gardens Cottages (1.5mi); Aaah, The Views B&B (2.5mi); Kawaihae (11mi); Hawi (21mi)

To Paniolo Park (0.3mi); Waimea-Kohala Airport (0.8mi); Kailua-Kona (39mi)

INFORMATION	
Bank of Hawaii	1 B1
North Hawaii Community Hospital	2 C1
Post Office	3 B2
Waimea Visitor Center	4 A1

SIGHTS & ACTIVITIES	(pp230-2)
Imiola Congregational Church	5 C1
Ke Ola Mau Loa Church	6 C1
Parker Ranch Historical Homes	7 A1
Parker Ranch Museum & Visitor Center	(see 14)
WM Keck Observatory Office	8 C1

SLEEPING	(pp232-3)
Kamuela Inn	9 A1
Waimea Country Lodge	10 B1

EATING	(pp233-4)
Aioli's	11 A1
Daniel Thiebaut	12 B1
KTA Super Store	(see 16)
Maha's Café	(see 16)
Merriman's	(see 11)

ENTERTAINMENT	(p234)
Kahilu Theatre	13 B2
Parker Ranch Grill	(see 14)

SHOPPING	(p234)
Gallery of Great Things	(see 15)
Giggles	(see 16)
Parker Ranch Center	14 B1
Parker Square	15 B1
Reyn's	(see 14)
Waimea Center	16 B1
Waimea General Store	(see 15)

about the ranch's history through Parker-family memorabilia, such as portraits, lineage charts, traditional Hawaiian quilts and cowboy gear, including saddles and branding irons. Also displayed are Hawaiian artifacts such as stone adzes, poi pounders and *kapa* (bark-cloth) bedcovers. However if you plan to visit other Big Island museums, the admission fee might seem a bit steep for the size of the collection. A worthwhile feature is the 25-minute movie on Parker Ranch, which shows footage of *paniolo* rushing cattle into the sea, and lifting them by slings onto the decks of waiting steamers.

Parker Ranch Historic Homes

See how wealthy landowners lived in these two 19th-century **homes** (☎ 885-5433; www .parkerranch.com; Mamalahoa Hwy; adult/child/senior $8.50/6.50/8; ⏰ 10am-5pm, last entry 4pm), less than a mile south of the intersection of Hwys 190 and 19.

Built in 1962, **Pu'uopelu** is the estate's sprawling 8000-sq-ft grand manor, which showcases the collection of European and Chinese art owned by the last Parker Ranch owner Richard Smart. One room is French provincial, with chandeliers, skylights and master impressionist paintings. Another room is covered with playbills and photos of Smart, who studied theater and performed on Broadway and in Europe. The local scoop is that this theatrical eccentric greeted tourists in his bathrobe on more than one occasion before his death in 1992.

Next door is the modest **Mana Hale**, a recreation of the original 1840s home built by John Parker in the hills outside Waimea. Parker constructed his home in the same saltbox style that was popular in his native Massachusetts, except he used koa wood. The original interior was dismantled board by board and rebuilt here. It's now decorated with period furnishings and old photos of the hardy-looking Parker clan.

Church Row

Waimea's first Christian church was a grass hut built in 1830. It was replaced in 1838 by a wooden structure that was also built using coral stones carved out of the reef. They named it Imiola, which means 'seeking salvation.'

The current **Imiola Congregational Church** (admission free; ⏰ services 8:30am & 10:15am) was

PARKER RANCH

Parker Ranch claims to be the nation's largest privately owned ranch, and some impressive numbers back those words. It has more than 35,000 cattle on 175,000 acres, contained by 850 miles of fence; the ranch produces more than 10 million pounds of beef annually.

Parker Ranch owes its beginnings to John Palmer Parker, a 19-year-old who arrived from New England on the Big Island in 1809 aboard a whaler. He took one look at Hawaii and jumped ship. Parker soon gained the favor of Kamehameha, who commissioned him to bring the cattle under control.

Parker managed to domesticate some of the cattle and butchered others, cutting the herds down to size. Later, he married one of Kamehameha's granddaughters, and, in the process, landed himself a tidy bit of land. He eventually gained control of the entire Waikoloa *ahupua'a* (traditional land division) clear down to the sea.

Descendants of the Mexican-Spanish cowboys, who were brought over to help round up the cattle, still work the ranches today. Indeed, the Hawaiian word for cowboy, *paniolo*, is a corruption of the Spanish word *españoles*.

constructed in 1857, and restored in 1976. The interior is simple and beautiful; it's built entirely of koa, most of it dating back to the original construction. In the churchyard is the grave of missionary Lorenzo Lyons, who arrived in 1832 and spent 54 years in Waimea. Lyons wrote many of the hymns, including the popular 'Hawai'i Aloha,' that are still sung in Hawaiian here each Sunday. Also in the garden is the church bell, which is too heavy for the church roof to support.

The green-steepled church next door is the all-Hawaiian **Ke Ola Mau Loa Church**. Buddhists, Baptists and Mormons also have places of worship in this row.

ACTIVITIES

Waimea is just the place for horseback riding, and the island's best outfit is right near town. **Dahana Ranch Roughriders** (☎ 885-0057, 888-399-0057; www.dahanaranch.com; ride per ½/2½hr $55/100; ⏰ 9am, 11am, 1pm & 3pm) is owned and operated by a native Hawaiian family – and it's both a working ranch and the most established horseback tour company on the Big Island. It breeds, raises, trains and uses only its own American quarter horses for its tours. Horses cross the open range of a working cattle ranch rather than follow trails, and you can trot, canter and gallop. Rides are by appointment only. For a special 'city slicker' adventure (and with a minimum of four people), you can help drive a 100-head herd of cattle ($100). Dahana is also the only outfit that lets very young children (aged three and up) join in. It's located 7.5 miles east of Waimea, off Old Mamalahoa Hwy.

COURSES

In early November the annual **Waimea 'Ukulele & Slack Key Guitar Institute** (☎ 885-6017; www .kahilutheatre.org) brings prominent local musicians together for a concert at the Kahilu Theatre (p234). A series of workshops ($40 to $60 each) is also held, ranging from beginner to master classes, including songwriting and improvistaion. Such greats as Led Ka'apana and Dennis Kamakahi have taught at the institute. Evening *kanikapila* (open-mike jam sessions) charge just $5 admission.

TOURS

Kids typically enjoy the novelty of a horse-drawn **wagon ride** (☎ 885-7655; www.parkerranch .com; Parker Ranch Center, 67-1185 Mamalahoa Hwy; adult/ child & senior $15/12; ☼ departures every hr 10am-2pm, Tue-Sat). The guides are lively showmen and tell stories of life on the range, as you see acres of cattle country. Rain is no problem because the wagon is covered.

FESTIVALS & EVENTS

Small rodeo events occur year-round on the Big Island.
Fourth of July Rodeo A uniquely Waimea event (with cattle roping, bull riding and other hoopla), which celebrated its 42nd anniversary in 2004.
Round-Up Rodeo (Labor Day weekend, 1st Monday in September) Another whip-cracking event.
Aloha Festivals Ho'olaule'a During the statewide Aloha Festivals in August and September, with food, games, art and crafts, and entertainment, along with the
Aloha Festival Paniolo Parade, which honors local cowboys with marching bands, elaborately decorated floats and equestrian units.

SLEEPING

Waimea's reasonably priced accommodations and central location makes it a good alternative for travelers who prefer upcountry scenery, cooler weather and open spaces.

Waimea Suite B&B (☎ 937-2833; cookshi@aol.com; Iokua St; ste incl breakfast $145) If you stay at this immaculate, spacious suite, you'll have the added benefit of meeting your host, who knows *everything* about Waimea and the Big Island. Located 2 miles east of town off Hwy 19, the suite sleeps up to four people. Amenities include a huge kitchen stocked with local snacks and condiments, dining lanai, cable, TV, VCR, telephone and stereo.

Aaah, the Views B&B (☎ 885-3455; www.aaah theviews.com; 66-1773 Alaneo St; incl breakfast s $65-75, d $75-85, ste $115-125) A longtime B&B that's been under new ownership since 2004, this place has a playful air, like a treehouse. Guests are welcome to use the common kitchen, yoga and meditation rooms, and hammocks on the porch overlooking a stream. The Dream Room is a loft-style suite with multiple windows and a skylight, a Jacuzzi tub and an outdoor shower on a private deck, while the Treetop Suite, also with a private deck and entrance, can accommodate up to six people. All rooms have cable TV, VCR, phone, fridge, microwave and coffeemaker.

Waimea Gardens Cottages (☎ 885-8550; www .waimeagardens.com; studio $140, cottage d $150-160 both incl breakfast) Just 2 miles west of town (near the intersection of Kawaihae Rd & Hwy 250), two charming cottages offer more upscale lodging, with polished hardwood floors, antique furnishings, patio French doors and a deck. One has a fireplace, the other has a Japanese-style soaking tub adjacent to a private garden. There's also a spacious studio unit near the lawn, where a seasonal stream flows.

Kamuela Inn (☎ 885-4243, 800-555-8968; www .kamuelainn.com; 1600 Kawaihae Rd; r $60-85, ste $90-185) For clean, simple lodging, the Kamuela Inn is a deal. All rooms have TV and a private bathroom, but only 'new wing' rooms have phones; suites sleep up to four people and resemble a modest apartment unit, with a refrigerator, a stove and cooking equipment.

Waimea Country Lodge (☎ 885-4100, 800-367-5004; www.castleresorts.com; 65-1210 Lindsey Rd; r $100-105, with kitchenette $115) Rooms at this small motel all have a phone, TV and a view of the Kohala hills out back. Standard rooms have two double beds; superior rooms have two kings or queens, plus a fridge. However there can be early-morning noise from trucks unloading at the nearby shopping center.

EATING

Merriman's (☎ 885-6822; Opelo Plaza, 65-1227 Opelo Rd; lunch mains $7-12, dinner mains $17-33; ☽ 11:30am-1:30pm Mon-Fri, 5:30-9pm daily) This longstanding gem still ranks among the Big Island's best. Chef and owner Peter Merriman pioneered the use of fresh, organically grown and chemical-free products from Big Island farmers and fishers. A specialty is the delicious wok-charred 'ahi, blackened on the outside and sashimi-like inside.

Daniel Thiebaut (☎ 887-2200; 65-1259 Kawaihae Rd; mains lunch $9-15, dinner $20-30; ☽ 10:30am-2pm & 5:30-9pm) Another foodie destination, Thiebaut features French-Asian cuisine, and a pleasing plantation-style setting in the historic Chock In Store building. Inspired dishes include sweet-corn crabcakes with lemongrass-coconut lobster sauce, and rack of lamb with eggplant compote. Vegetarians have a nice selection of tofu-and-veg dishes.

Maha's Café (☎ 885-0693; Waimea Center, 65-1158 Mamalahoa Hwy; breakfast $3-5, lunch under $10; ☽ 8am-4:30pm Thu-Mon) The former resort chef whips up delicious island-style fare. Guaranteed to please are the poi pancakes with coconut syrup, and grilled fish with taro and greens. It has a cozy setting inside Waimea's first frame house, which was built in 1852.

Aioli's (☎ 885-6325; Opelo Plaza, 65-1227 Opelo Rd; dinner mains $13-21; ☽ 11am-8pm Tue-Thu, to 9pm Fri & Sat) Frequented by locals, Aioli's bakes its own breads, cakes and pastries, and at lunch serves well-made sandwiches, salads and soups. Dinners vary from goat-cheese enchiladas to fresh seafood and steaks.

HAWAI'I
(THE BIG ISLAND)

DETOUR: HAKALAU FOREST NATIONAL WILDLIFE REFUGE

To go off the beaten path and see real Big Island wilderness, drive to the Hakalau Forest National Wildlife Refuge – a place few locals have ever ventured. This extremely remote wildlife refuge protects a portion of the state's largest koa-ohia forest, which provides habitat for endangered bird species, including the native hoary bat and Hawaiian hawk. About 7000 acres are open to public access, but only on weekends and state holidays.

The drive takes two hours from either Waimea or Hilo; 4WD is absolutely necessary and the road might be closed after rains. You'll be roughin' it, as there are no facilities, signage or trails. The only folks who typically come here are ranchers and hunters, and you're far from anywhere, if you get stuck en route.

To get here from Waimea, drive east on Hwy 19 until you reach the 55-mile marker; turn onto Mana Rd, which leads around the eastern flank of Mauna Kea. After 15 miles, the road becomes Keanakolu Rd and continues about 25 miles to Summit Rd (the access road to Mauna Kea summit) and then connects with Saddle Rd (which is another starting point, if you're coming from Hilo). Along the way, you'll pass through private ranches, and numerous cattle gates must be opened and closed.

About halfway between Waimea and Saddle Rd, you'll pass a stone monument to David Douglas, the famed Scottish botanist, for whom the Douglas fir tree is named. Douglas planted trees here and in 1834 died under mysterious circumstances: his gored body was found trapped with an angry bull in a pit, on the slopes of Mauna Kea. Hunters commonly dug and camouflaged pits to trap feral cattle, but the probability of both Douglas and a bull falling in together seemed unlikely. A key suspect was an Australian convict named Ned Gurney, who had been hiding out nearby, and was the last person to see Douglas alive.

You need a permit, which you can obtain by calling or writing to the **refuge manager** (☎ 933-6915; 32 Kino'ole St, Hilo, HI 96720; ☽ 8am-4pm Mon-Fri). An ideal time to visit is during the second week in October, which is National Wildlife Refuge Week, when Hawaiian ornithological experts and rangers are on hand. Another possibility is to do volunteer tree planting on weekends, but you'd have to arrange this beforehand. Staff numbers are very limited, and the first priorities are birds and plants, not tourists, but interested visitors are welcome. **Hawaii Forest & Trail** (☎ 331-8505, 800-464-1993; www.hawaii-forest.com; tours $145) offers a birding adventure tour in the Hakalau refuge.

There's no liquor license, but you can bring your own beer or wine (no corkage fee). Take-out is also available.

For the freshest organic produce, cheeses, flowers and lei, island-made jams and home-made goods, check out the **farmers market** (☙ 7am-noon Sat) at the Hawaiian Home Lands office, near the 55-mile marker. The best grocer is **KTA Super Store** (☎ 885-8866; 65-1158 Mamalahoa Hwy; ☙ 9am-7pm Mon-Fri, to 5pm Sat & Sun) at Waimea Center.

ENTERTAINMENT

Kahilu Theatre (☎ 885-6017, box office 885-6868; www.kahilutheatre.org; Parker Ranch Center, 67-1185 Mamalahoa Hwy; $15-45; ☙ showtimes vary) Waimea isn't exactly hopping with nightlife, but this headlines an impressive list of performances including classic and contemporary music, dance and theater, featuring performers from George Winston to the Paul Taylor Dance Company to the Harlem Gospel Choir. A big draw is the annual Waimea 'Ukulele & Slack Key Guitar Institute concert (p232).

Parker Ranch Grill (☎ 887-2624; Parker Ranch Center; 67-1185A Mamalahoa Hwy; ☙ 8am-3pm & 4-10:30pm, to 1am Sat) For casual, nightly live music, head here. You can hear country and western, acoustic rock or karaoke, depending on the night. The best shows happens on Hawaiian *kanikapila* nights (Thursday and Sunday), when you can hear or jam with guitarist 'Braddah Smitty' (Smitty Colburn), who played with the legendary group Sons of Hawaii in its final years. Crowds can top 100 people, and fellow musicians bring everything from guitars and ukulele to harps and violins!

SHOPPING

Parker Square (65-1279 Kawaihae Rd) A mecca for quality gifts, from art to handicrafts to edibles. The main shopping malls, Parker Ranch Center and Waimea Center, both off Hwy 19, are convenient for groceries and basics.

Gallery of Great Things (☎ 885-7706; Parker Square, 65-1279 Kawaihae Rd; ☙ 9am-5:30pm Mon-Sat, 10am-4pm Sun) A standout among Waimea's antiques, art and collectibles galleries. Browse for Hawaiian, Polynesian and Asian art, furnishings and photographs.

Waimea General Store (☎ 885-4479; Parker Square, 65-1279 Kawaihae Rd; ☙ 9am-5:30pm Mon-Sat,

10am-4pm Sun) Don't let the name fool you: this store sells everything from Hawaiian cookbooks to toys to locally made jams and candy. The kitchen department is especially popular and carries items that are hard to find elsewhere.

Giggles (☎ 885-2151; Parker Ranch Center, 67-1185 Mamalahoa Hwy; ☙ 9am-5:30pm Mon-Sat, to 3pm Sun) A local children's boutique featuring toddler-sized aloha shirts, colorful cloth books, bath toys and Hello Kitty items available only in Hawaii.

Reyn's (☎ 885-4493; Parker Ranch Center, 67-1185 Mamalahoa Hwy; ☙ 9am-5pm Mon-Sat, to 3pm Sun) At this local version of Brooks Brothers you'll find the understated aloha shirts that islanders wear in lieu of suits. The classic Reyn's look uses Hawaiian fabrics in reverse.

GETTING THERE & AWAY

While there's a Waimea-Kohala Airport south of Waimea, it's quite unlikely you'll fly here. The Hele-On Bus (p184) goes from Waimea to Kailua-Kona on its No 16 Kailua-Kona route ($3, 65 minutes), and to Hilo on its No 7 Downtown Hilo route ($4.50, one hour 40 minutes). The bus stops at the Parker Ranch Center.

The drive from Kailua-Kona is 40 miles along Hwy 190, which becomes Old Mamalahoa Hwy in town. Along the way, the highway climbs out of the residential areas into a mix of lava flows and dry, grassy rangeland studded with prickly-pear cacti. You'll see distant coastal views, wide-open spaces, awe-inspiring cloud formations and tall roadside grasses that have an incredible golden hue in the morning light. From Hilo, the drive is 55 miles along Hwy 19 around the Hamakua Coast.

GETTING AROUND

A car is indispensable in Waimea, though it's a compact, three-stoplight town. There is ample parking here.

HAMAKUA COAST

The Hamakua Coast winds along the island's verdant northern shoreline, from the dramatic cliffs of Waipi'o Valley down toward the Laupahoehoe area. In the heart of a defunct Hawaiian sugar industry, wild cane stalks, up to 8ft tall, blow in the trade winds.

Alongside the highway, the ocean alternates between deep aquamarine on sunny days, and stormy green during showers.

The entire Hawai'i Belt Rd (Hwy 19) is an impressive engineering feat spanning lush ravines that locals call gulches – Maulua Gulch, Laupahoehoe Gulch and Ka'awali'i Gulch, from east to west – traversed on sweeping cantilevered bridges. If you look inland, you'll see streams and waterfalls. The setting is very picturesque, with inviting back roads if you have time to dawdle. If you're just passing through, at least make time for the Waipi'o Valley Lookout and a hot *malasada* (Portuguese doughnuts) from longtime local favorite Tex Drive Inn.

HONOKA'A

pop 2200

The town of Honoka'a has had to reinvent itself over and over, and it's gone from cattle to sugar to tourism. However it's a survivor, and makes a relaxing stop along Hwy 19. Most of the people living here are descendants of sugarcane-plantation workers, from the first Scottish and English immigrants to the Chinese, Portuguese, Japanese, Puerto Ricans and Filipinos. The Honoka'a Sugar Company mill, dating from 1873, processed its last harvest in 1993.

Honoka'a's main street, Mamane St, runs just a block or two, but it's worth a trip to see traditional plantation-western-style architecture. If nothing else, Honoka'a will transport you back to late-19th- and early-20th-century Hawai'i. The town remains the largest on the Hamakua Coast, and residents of Waipi'o Valley (often driving muddy trucks with hounds scrambling around in the back) come 'topside' to stock up on supplies here – but for major shopping, residents head to Waimea or Hilo.

Information

In town you'll find all the basics: banks with ATMs, a grocery store, a coin laundry and a **post office** (☎ 800-275-8777; 45-490 Lehua St; 🕒 9am-4pm Mon-Fri, 8:15-9:45am Sat). For Internet access, the **Virtual Lounge** (☎ 775-9355; www.vlhawaii.com; Mamane St; per 30 min $3, unlimited wi-fi $5; 🕒 9am-6pm Mon-Sat) is simple but roomy.

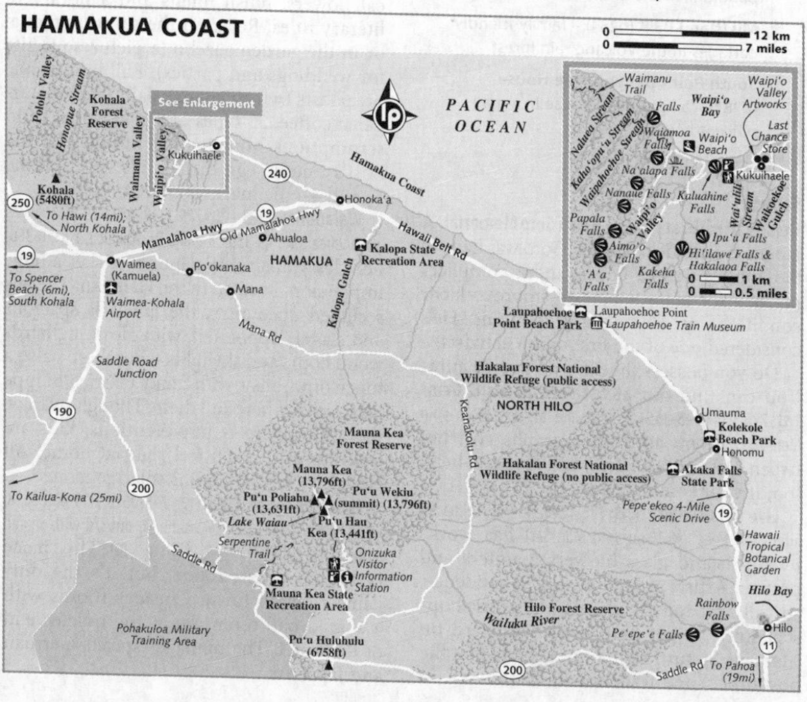

TOP 10 SLEEPS

- **Dolphin Bay Hotel** (p260) – no-frills home away from home

- **Mauna Kea Beach Hotel** (p223) – 'original' Gold Coast resort with still-the-best golf and beach

- **Hawaiian Oasis B&B** (p192) – the perfect combination of a B&B's intimacy and a hotel's amenities

- **Ohana Keauhou Beach Resort** (p199) – affordably upscale neighbor to a premier snorkeling beach

- **Areca Palms Estate B&B** (p203) – impeccable bedrooms and delicious breakfasts

- **Mountain Meadow Ranch** (p237) – misty pastureland, pristine air, peace and quiet

- **Mauna Lani Bay Hotel & Bungalows** (p221) – luxurious comfort amidst ancient Hawaiian ponds and trails

- **Cliff House Hawaii** (p238) – astounding panoramic view of the Pacific

- **My Island B&B** (p284) – family-friendly cottages in the Volcano rain forest

- **South Point Banyan Tree House** (p287) – a light-filled house in a magnificent banyan

---

Sights

Beside the library is the **Katsu Goto Memorial**. A Japanese cane-field worker, Goto was hanged by Honoka'a sugar bosses and accomplices in 1889 for his attempts to improve labor conditions on Hamakua plantations. He's considered one of the first union activists.

Do you possess the coveted purple aura? You can find out at **Starseed Beads & Gems** (☎ 775-9344; 45-3551A2 Mamane St; ⏰ 10am-5pm Mon-Sat), where aura photographs cost between $10 and $20. They sell espresso here, too, if your soul needs a jolt.

Live Arts Gallery (☎ 775-1240; 45-368 Lehua St; admission free; ⏰ 10am-5pm Mon-Sat) has works by Big Island glass blowers, painters and potters. Artists are not always in residence, so call first for the events-and-workshops schedule. To get here, walk westward on Mamane St, turn right onto Lehua St (at the post office) and walk downhill.

Festivals & Events

Hamakua Music Festival (mid-May & early October; ☎ 775-3378; www.hamakuamusicfestival.org; Honoka'a People's Theater, Mamane St; admission $20-30) A premier music event bringing world-class Hawaiian music, jazz, classical and more to. The festival also awards scholarships to music students islandwide, presents student workshops with visiting celebrities, and provides the only funding for music teachers in public schools.

Honoka'a Western Weekend (late May; ☎ 933-9772; Mamane St; admission free) An annual event that awakens the usually sleepy Mamane St with a barbecue, parade, country dance, rodeo and entertainers such as local icon Melveen Leed.

Sleeping

Near Honoka'a, you'll find a handful of B&B gems that let you escape it all.

Waipi'o Wayside B&B (☎ 775-0275, 800-833-8849; www.waipiowayside.com; Hwy 240; r incl breakfast $95-175) If you appreciate fine furnishings and attention to detail, this 1932 plantation house, nestled in a macadamia-nut orchard, couldn't be more perfect. There are five elegant and cozy rooms, each with genuine antique furnishings, sprays of tropical flowers, plush linens and a library of literary titles. Relax on the sprawling lanai or in the garden gazebo (a picturesque site for weddings and parties). Full homemade breakfasts (which change daily) include organic coffee, 30 types of tea, seasonal fruit, scrumptious homemade muffins and the host's unique egg dishes. It's between the 3- and 4-mile markers on Hwy 240.

Waianuhea B&B (☎ 775-1118, 888-775-2577; www.waianuhea.com; 45-3503 Kahana Dr, Ahualoa; r $170-350) For classy luxury, Waianuhea makes a huge impression. Located in the Hamakua Coast's secluded upcountry, the house is spacious and classily appointed, with gleaming hardwood floors and skylights – but there's also a touch of whimsy, with funky plastic Philippe Starck chairs here and there. Though swanky, the atmosphere is unpretentious, kids are welcome and you'll feel right at home. All electricity for the B&B is solar-generated.

Hotel Honokaa Club (☎ 775-0678, 800-808-0678; www.hotelhonokaa.com; Mamane St; dm/s/d with shared bathroom $15/20/35, r $45-65, ste $80) This place is on the tattered side, but it's the only game right in town. Cheaper rooms with a shared bathroom are at the quieter end of the hotel. The manager speaks German and Japanese.

THE AUTHOR'S CHOICE

Mountain Meadow Ranch (☎ 775-9376; www.mountainmeadowranch.com; 46-3895 Kapuna Rd, Ahualoa; ste/cottage d incl breakfast $85/135) Located 3 miles southwest of Honoka'a, Mountain Meadow is a peaceful retreat on 7 acres of green rolling hills (complete with horses in the distance). At its 2200ft elevation, the air is refreshingly crisp and often swathed in misty fog. The warm and gracious hosts designate the lower level of their redwood home for a guest suite, which includes two bedrooms, a large tiled bathroom, a dry-heat sauna, TV/VCR, a refrigerator and a microwave. The bedrooms aren't rented separately – so if you book only one bedroom, the other one won't be rented during your stay! The nearby cottage is private and spacious, with two bedrooms, a full kitchen and a washer/dryer.

Eating

Near Honokaa Trading Company, a farmers market is held on Saturday from 10am to 2pm.

Tex Drive Inn (☎ 775-0598; Hwy 19; sandwiches & plate lunches $4-7; ☆ 6am-8:30pm) For many, Tex is reason enough to drive between Hilo and Kona. Its famous *malasada* cost 85¢ plain. For a quarter extra you can get a delicious filling of flavor – perhaps papaya-pineapple or classic Bavarian creme. Island-style sandwiches, fresh fish burgers and plate lunches are also served. The owner is from Holland but she has turned Tex into a little empire, with a gift shop, a garden shop and a garden on the property.

Café il Mondo (☎ 775-7711; 45-3626A Mamane St; sandwiches $5.50, pizza $9-18; ☆ 11am-8pm Tue-Sat) This casual Italian restaurant serves tasty sandwiches, soups, salads and pizza (available by the slice before 5pm). A house specialty is fresh-squeezed lemonade. Outdoor seating lets you watch the world amble by.

Mamane Street Bakery Café (☎ 775-9478; Mamane St; baked goods $2; ☆ 6am-noon Mon-Fri) If you walk in, the aroma will compel you to try the delectable cookies, cinnamon rolls, cakes or breads. The pastries sold at all the Starbucks cafés on the Big Island come from this bakery.

Jolene's Kau Kau Korner (☎ 775-9498; 45-3625 Mamane St; lunch $4.50-8; ☆ 10am-8pm Mon, Wed & Fri,

to 3pm Tue & Thu) This local-style eatery represents the local beef industry very generously on its menu, but there are also mushroom burgers.

Entertainment

Honoka'a People's Theater (☎ 775-0000; Mamane St; adult/child/senior $6/3/4) In a historic building dating from 1930, movies show each weekend. It also hosts jazz, classical and Hawaiian performing artists during the Hamakua Music Festival (p236).

Shopping

Honokaa Trading Company (☎ 775-0808; Mamane St) Open since 1986, this is the island's best antique store. It's jam-packed with vintage aloha wear, antiques, used books, rattan and koa furniture and hand-selected Hawaiian artifacts. Near the ceiling, the display of genuine old-time business signs is a history lesson in itself.

Bamboo Gallery (☎ 775-0433; 45-3490 Mamane St; ☆ 10am-5pm Mon-Sat) Photographer Nick Kato shows off a wide selection of island art and crafts, from Japanese antiques to Hawaiian collectibles. Kato, who grew up in Japan, also publishes attractive Japanese-language travel books.

Mohala Pua (☎ 775-7800; Tex Drive Inn, Hwy 19; ☆ 9am-6pm) Well-kept and well-stocked with its namesake 'blossoming flowers,' this garden shop will ship orchids, bromeliads, hibiscus and many other plants to your home for you.

A HARD NUT TO CRACK

Hawaii's first macadamia trees were planted in Honoka'a in 1881 by William Purvis, a sugar-plantation manager who brought seedlings from Australia. For 40 years the trees were grown in Hawaii, as in Australia, mainly for ornamental purposes, because the nutshells were once considered too hard to crack.

Hawaii's first large-scale commercial macadamia orchard was planted in Honoka'a in 1924. Macadamia nuts have proven to be one of the most commercially viable agricultural crops in Hawaii. They are high in fat (*da good kine*), protein and carbohydrates and are an excellent source of several essential vitamins and minerals.

Getting There & Away

The Hele-On Bus (p184) arrives in Honoka'a from Kona on the No 7 Downtown Hilo route, then continues on to Hilo ($3.75); from Hilo you can reach Honoka'a either by the No 31 Honoka'a route or the No 16 Kailua-Kona route, which continues to Kona. Fares run $3.75 to $4.50. It takes 1¼ hours from either direction.

KUKUIHAELE

pop 300

Outside Honoka'a, about 7 miles toward Waipi'o Valley, a loop road off Hwy 240 leads right down to the tiny village of Kukuihaele. Its name means 'traveling light' in Hawaiian, referring to the 'night marchers,' ghosts of Hawaiian warriors passing through, carrying torches on their way to Waipi'o. Night marchers are believed to walk through ancient battle fields on the night of Huaka'ipo (27th phase of the moon). According to legend, if you look directly at them or if you're in their way, you'll die. It's possible to survive if one of your ancestors is a marcher – or if you lie face down on the ground.

There's not much to Kukuihaele. Its 'commercial center' consists of the Last Chance Store and Waipi'o Valley Artworks gallery and bookshop. Kukuihaele is also the jumping-off point for tour operators into Waipi'o Valley.

Sleeping

Cliff House Hawaii (☎ 775-0005, 800-492-4746; www .cliffhousehawaii.com; Hwy 240; 2-bedroom house $195) Gorgeously set on 40 private acres, the aptly named Cliff House is perched above the stunning cliffs of Waipi'o Valley. With sweeping windows and a wraparound lanai, you'll have unforgettable views of the verdant valley and endless Pacific. The Cliff House has two bedrooms with queen-size beds, a living-dining room and a full bathroom and kitchen. It's near the end of Hwy 240.

Hale Kukui Orchard Retreat (☎ 775-7130; 800-444-7130; www.halekukui.com; 48-5460 Kukuihaele Rd; studios $125, 2-bedroom cottage d $160-175) Tranquil and secluded in a thriving orchard, all units (even the spacious 400-sq-ft studio) include a full kitchen and a dining area, plus a private jet tub on the deck. Here you'll have enough space and privacy to feel as if you own the place (if only!). For $5, guests can

pick as much fruit as they can eat: there are 26 varieties to choose from, including lychee, pomelo, papaya, banana and star fruit.

Waipio Ridge Vacation Rental (☎ 775-0603; rlasko3343@aol.com; Hwy 240; trailers $75, 1-bedroom cottage d $85) Located right at the Waipi'o Valley trailhead (at the end of Hwy 240), these units offer the view of a lifetime. The cottage has a casual feel, with island-style decor and wooden furnishings made by the owner, queen-size bed and sofa bed, full kitchen, TV and VCR. If you want to 'rough it,' you might try the funky, scruffy 24ft Airstream trailer turned vacation shelter, with a kitchenette and an outdoor shower.

Eating

In the village, the **Last Chance Store** (☎ 775-9222; ☺ 9am-3:30pm Mon-Sat) is just that – no food or supplies are available in Waipi'o Valley. This small grocery store has snacks, canned chili, beer, water and wine. **Waipio Valley Artworks** (☎ 775-0958, 800-492-4746; ☺ 8am-5pm) sells Tropical Dreams ice cream, muffins, inexpensive sandwiches and coffee (plus fine koa and ceramic art).

WAIPI'O VALLEY

Hwy 240 ends abruptly at the edge of cliffs overlooking Waipi'o Valley, the largest of seven spectacular amphitheater valleys on the windward side of the Kohala Mountains. Down in Waipi'o (Curving Water) grows a fertile tangle of jungle, flowering plants, taro patches and waterfalls, fronted by a black-sand beach cleaved by a stream. Some of the near-vertical *pali* (cliffs) wrapping around the valley reach heights of 2000ft. The whole place pulsates with mana, and on clear days the dark outline of Maui is visible in the distance.

Many of the valley's 50 or so residents have taro patches, and you may see farmers knee-deep in the muddy ponds. Other Waipi'o crops include lotus root, avocados, breadfruit, oranges, limes and *pakalolo* (marijuana). You'll also find *kukui* (candlenut) trees and Turk's cap hibiscus.

History

In ancient times, Waipi'o Valley was the political and religious center of Hawai'i and home to the highest *ali'i*. Umi, the Big Island's ruling chief in the early 16th century, is credited with laying out Waipi'o's taro fields, many of which are still in production today. Waipi'o is also the site where Kamehameha the Great received the statue of his fearsome war god, Kuka'ilimoku.

According to oral histories, several thousand people lived in this fertile valley before the arrival of Westerners. Waipi'o's sacred status is evidenced by a number of important *heiau*. The most sacred, Paka'alana, was also the site of one of the island's two major *pu'uhonua* (the other place of refuge, is now a national historic park, see p209), but today its location has been lost.

In 1823 William Ellis, the first missionary to visit Waipi'o Valley, guessed the population to be 1300. Later in that century, immigrants, mainly Chinese, began to settle in Waipi'o. At one time, the valley had schools, restaurants and churches as well as a hotel, a post office and a jail.

In 1946, Hawai'i's most devastating tsunami slammed great waves far back into the valley. Coincidentally or not, no one in this sacred place perished (every valley resident was also spared during the great 1979 flood). But, afterwards, most people resettled 'topside,' and Waipi'o has been sparsely populated ever since.

Dangers & Annoyances

Avoid hiking during the winter rainy season, when streams in Waipi'o and Waimanu Valleys can swell, usually for just a few hours, to impassable. It's dangerous to attempt crossing swollen streams, if the water reaches above your knees. Such rising waters should be considered life-threatening obstacles, as flash floods are possible. Just be patient and wait for the water to subside.

If you decide it's essential to cross (eg near sundown), look for a wide, relatively shallow stretch of stream rather than a bend. Before stepping off the bank, unclip your backpack chest strap and belt buckle. This lets you easily slip out and swim to safety, if you lose your balance and get swept away. Use a walking pole, grasped in both hands, on the upstream side, as a third leg, or go arm in arm with a companion, clasping at the wrist, and cross side-on to the flow, taking short steps.

Don't drink from *any* creeks or streams without first boiling or treating the water. Feral animals roam the area, making leptospirosis a real threat (see p541).

Activities

For a challenging two-day hike, the 9.5-mile **Muliwai Trail** leads you from the Waipi'o Valley Overlook down to Waipi'o Beach, and then all the way to the adjacent Waimanu Valley. Most people do just part of the Muliwai Trail, hiking down to Waipi'o Beach and back up, roughly 1½ hours return.

If you plan to hike the whole Muliwai Trail, bear in mind that it can take seven or eight hours one way – and getting to Waimanu Valley and back in a day is unrealistic, even for hard-core hikers. The last mile or so of the trail is precipitous and irregularly maintained, making this one of the most technically challenging hikes on the Big Island. The final switchbacks are especially tough because hikers will probably be carrying a heavy backpack with camping gear.

Most people hike all the way into Waimanu Valley on the first day, camp for two nights and then walk back out on the third day. You can get a head start by camping at Waipi'o Beach the night before.

WAIPI'O VALLEY HIKE

From beside the lookout, a 1-mile paved road leads down into Waipi'o Valley. It's so steep (25% grade) that only hikers and 4WD vehicles are allowed. The hike takes roughly 30 minutes down and 45 minutes back up. Only the bottom of the valley is shaded, and you'll definitely work up a sweat trekking uphill, so carry plenty of water.

From the bottom of the hill, if you detour five or 10 minutes to the left, you may see wild horses grazing along the stream – a beautiful Hawaiian tableau with precipitous cliffs as a backdrop. Walk until you get a distant view of **Hi'ilawe Falls**, which at over 1200ft is Hawai'i's highest free-fall waterfall. Hiking to the falls is possible but challenging. There's no trail and it's mainly a lot of bushwhacking. Only goats will make it to the falls in the heart of the rainy season.

Keep in mind that many valley residents, who tolerate visitors trekking down to visit the beach, aren't keen on their exploring the valley interior. A lot of 'Private Property' and 'Kapu – No Trespassing' signs are posted, and the further back in the valley you go, the scarier the dogs become.

If you turn right at the bottom of the hill, **Waipi'o Beach** is only 10 minutes away (but tack on an extra 10 minutes if it's rained recently). The beach is lined with graceful ironwood trees, which serve as a barrier against the winds that sometimes whip through here. Surfers catch wave action at Waipi'o, but mind the rip currents, rogue waves and a treacherous undertow. When it's calm, Waipi'o Beach is sublime and you might encounter spinner dolphins.

Walk toward the stream mouth for a good view of **Kaluahine Falls**, which cascade down the cliffs to the east. Getting to the falls is more challenging than it looks, as the intervening coast is made up of loose, ankle-twisting lava. High surf breaking over the uppermost rocks can be very dangerous. Local lore holds that night marchers periodically come down from the upper valley to the beach and march to Lua o Milu, a hidden entrance to the netherworld.

MULIWAI TRAIL TO WAIMANU VALLEY

To continue on, cross the stream and walk toward the far end of the beach; there's a shaded path just inland of the rocks that passes by fishing boats and grazing land. The path turns left before reaching the cliffs, then veers right and ascends under thick forest cover.

The Muliwai Trail then rises over 1200ft in a mile of hard laboring up steep switchbacks on the cliff face. The hike is exposed and hot, so hike this stretch in the early morning. Eventually the trail moves into ironwood and Norfolk pine forest, and tops a little knoll before gently descending, and becoming muddy and frequented by mosquitoes. You lose sight of the ocean and instead you hear a rushing stream.

The trail crosses a gulch and ascends past a trail sign for Emergency Helipad No 1 on the *mauka* side of the trail. For the next few hours, the trail finds a steady rhythm of wet and dry gulch crossings and forest ascents. A waterfall at the third gulch is a source of freshwater, but it must treated before drinking. Mostly the trail is covered in squashed guava, ferns and buzzing gnats and even bees. For a landmark, look for Emergency Helipad No 2 at about the halfway point from Waipi'o Beach. Then look for an open-sided trail shelter with pit toilets that might be littered with trash.

Rest here before making the final difficult descent. Leaving the shelter, hop across three more gulches and pass Emergency Helipad

No 4, from where it's less than a mile to Waimanu Valley. Over a descent of 1200ft, this final section of switchbacks starts out innocently enough, with some artificial and natural stone steps set in the mud, but the trail is poorly maintained and extremely hazardous later. A glimpse of a waterfall on the far side of the valley wall might inspire hikers to press onward. The trail is very narrow and washed out in parts, with sheer drop-offs hundreds of feet into the ocean, and nothing to hold onto apart from mossy rocks and spiny plants. Dense leaves underfoot hide centipedes and slippery *kukui*. If the descent proves impossible, head back to the trail shelter for the night instead, stopping at a stream gulch for water.

If you make it, Waimanu Valley is a mini-Waipi'o, minus the tourists. On any given day, you'll bask alone amid a stunning deep valley framed by cliffs, waterfalls and a black-sand beach. From the bottom of the switchbacks, the boulder-strewn beach is 10 minutes past the camping regulations signboard. When safe, ford the stream to reach the campsites on its western side.

On the return trip, be careful to take on the correct trail. Walking inland from Waimanu Beach, do not veer left on a false trail-of-use that attempts to climb a rocky streambed. Instead keep heading straight inland past the camping regulations sign to find the trail to the switchbacks. It takes about two hours to get to the trail shelter, and about two more hours to reach the waterfall gulch: refill your water here. Exiting the ironwood forest soon after, the trail descends back to the floor of Waipi'o Valley.

Tours

Other options for getting into the valley:
Hawaiian Walkways (☎ 775-0372, 800-457-7759; http://hawaiianwalkways.com; guided hikes $95) If you're up for a hiking adventure, it leads you to waterfalls and pools, where you can swim.

Waipio Ridge Stables (☎ 775-1007, 877-757-1414; www.waipioridgestables.com; rides $75-145; ☉ departures 9:30am) For horseback riding tours, this follows a 2½-hour valley floor route, or a five-hour trot out to Hi'ilawe Falls that ends with a picnic and a swim at a hidden waterfall.

Waipi'o Na'alapa (☎ 775-0419; www.naalapastables .com; ride $75; ☉ departures 9:30am & 1pm) This outfit also offers a 2½-hour horseback ride, but children must be at least eight years.

Waipio Valley Shuttle (☎ 775-7121; www.waipio valleytour.com; adult/child $45/20; ⊙ departures 9am, 11am, 1pm & 3pm Mon-Sat) Runs two-hour 4WD taxi tours, although the driver does point out waterfalls, identify plants and throw in a bit of history.

Waipio Valley Wagon Tours (☎ 775-9518; www .waipiovalleywagontours.com; adult/child $45/22.50; ⊙ departures 9:30am, 11:30am, 1:30pm & 3:30pm Mon-Sat) For a quaint experience, this one-hour jaunt in an open mule-drawn wagon carts visitors over rutted roads and rocky streams.

Sleeping

Kamehameha Schools Bishop Estate which owns most of Waipi'o Valley, allows **camping** at four primitive sites in a wooded area near Waipi'o Beach. There are no amenities: no drinking water, no showers and no toilets (campers are required to bring chemical toilets). The maximum stay is four days, and you must apply for a permit at least two weeks in advance, and even earlier for weekend dates and in summer. Each camper is required to sign a liability waiver, but the permits are free. Contact the **Kamehameha Schools Bishop Estate** (☎ 776-1104; PO Box 495, Pa'auilo, HI 96764).

Backcountry camping in Waimanu Valley, which is managed by the state, is allowed by free permit for up to six nights. Facilities include fire pits and a couple of composting outhouses. Reservations are taken no more than 30 days in advance by the **Division of Forestry & Wildlife** (☎ 974-4221; 19 E Kawili St, PO Box 4849, Hilo, HI 96720; ⊙ 7:45am-4:30pm Mon-Fri). With two weeks' advance notice, the permit can be mailed to you.

KALOPA STATE RECREATION AREA

This 100-acre state park is a native forest, containing mainly the trees, shrubs and ferns that were already present when the Polynesians arrived. Hawaii's native plants are extremely precious because almost 90% are endemic. At an elevation of 2000ft, the Kalopa forest is cooler and wetter than the coast, and normal precipitation is 100in per year. To get here, turn *mauka* off Hwy 19 at the Kalopa Dr sign and drive in 3 miles. You'll pretty much have the park to yourself.

A **nature trail**, beginning near the cabins, loops for three-quarters of a mile through old ohia forest, where some of the trees measure more than 3ft in diameter. The woods are inhabited by the *elepaio*, an easily spotted native forest bird that's brown and white, about the size of a sparrow, and has a loud whistle.

A longer **hiking trail** heads into the adjoining forest reserve. Begin trekking along Robusta Lane, on the left between the caretaker's house and the campground. It's about 600yd to the edge of Kalopa Gulch, through a thick eucalyptus forest. The gulch was formed eons ago by the erosive movement of melting glaciers that originated at Mauna Kea. The trail continues along the rim of the gulch for another mile, while side trails along the way branch off and head west back into the recreation area.

Tent camping is available in a grassy area surrounded by tall trees. There are restrooms and covered picnic pavilions with electricity, running water and barbecue grills – the works! Simple group **cabins** have bunk beds, linens and blankets, plus hot showers and a fully equipped kitchen. Permits are required for the cabins and *technically* for the campsites, too. For details see p178.

LAUPAHOEHOE

pop 470

Laupahoehoe means 'leaf of pahoehoe lava,' an apt name for the landmark **Laupahoehoe Point**, a flat peninsula formed by a late-stage Mauna Kea eruption. It's located midway between Honoka'a and Hilo; a highway sign points to the steep winding road that leads 1.5 miles to the coast. It's a scenic drive, with spectacular cliffs in the distance and dense foliage all around.

On April 1, 1946, tragedy hit Laupahoehoe, a small plantation town, when a tsunami up to 30ft high wiped out the schoolhouse on the point, killing 20 children and four adults. Today a monument, listing the names and ages of the victims, stands at Laupahoehoe Pt. After the tsunami, the whole town moved uphill. Along the way to the point, however, you can see the giant banyan tree that once stood at the school's center, still standing. Every April there's a community festival with food, music and old-timers who 'talk story.'

Laupahoehoe is a rugged coastal area that's not suitable for swimming. The surf is usually rough, and sometimes crashes up over the rocks and onto the lower parking lot (roll up those windows!). Interisland boats once landed here, and many of the immigrant plantation laborers first set foot on the Big Island at Laupahoehoe.

The county beach park on the point has restrooms, showers, drinking water, picnic pavilions and electricity. Both local and tourist families often camp here. For permit information, see p178. Watch out for strong gusts of wind when pitching your tent!

Up by the highway, the **Laupahoehoe Train Museum** (☎ 962-6300; adult/child $3/2; ☯ 9am-4:30pm Mon-Fri & 10am-2pm Sat & Sun) has all the ephemera, knick-knacks and nostalgia of the bygone Hawaiian railroad era. Knowledgeable docents burst with pride when speaking of the restored length of track, ol' Rusty the switch engine, and other pieces of rail history that keep turning up. The museum is visible from Hwy 19 between the 25- and 26-mile markers. Call first because opening hours can vary.

KOLEKOLE BEACH PARK

Beneath a highway bridge, this grassy park sits at the side of Kolekole Stream, which flows down from Akaka Falls. It has small waterfalls, picnic tables, barbecue pits, restrooms and showers. Locals sometimes surf and boogie board here, but ocean swimming is dangerous.

Tent camping is allowed with a county permit, but be aware that the park is crowded with picnicking local families on weekends and in summer. For permit information, see p178.

To get here, turn inland off Hwy 19 at the southern end of the Kolekole Bridge, about 1300yd south of the 15-mile marker.

HONOMU
pop 540

Honomu is an old sugar town that might be forgotten today, if not for its proximity to Akaka Falls. Of course, life here remains rural and slow-paced. Among the village's old wooden buildings, you'll find a shop selling vintage glass bottles and a few worthy galleries. The two lodging options are direct opposites, and your choice will depend on your creature-comfort needs.

Akiko's Buddhist Bed & Breakfast (☎ 963-6422; www.alternative-hawaii.com/akiko; s/d with shared bathroom & incl breakfast $40/55, per week $265/355, studio s/d $420/590 for 2 weeks) Nothing fancy, just

basic, well-worn rooms especially suited to the spiritually inclined (but you need not be Buddhist). You can either sleep on Japanese monastery-style folding futons in the main house, or on regular beds in the house next door. A self-contained studio on the grounds requires a two-week minimum stay. Silence is observed between 6:30pm and 6am in the main house, and guests are welcome to join in Zen meditation at 5am on Monday, Wednesday and Friday.

Palms Cliff House Inn (☎ 963-6076; www.palms cliffhouse.com; 28-3514 Mamalahoa Hwy; r incl breakfast $175-375) Clearly one of the Big Island's most lavish B&Bs, Palms Cliff House has upscale rooms, all with plush linens, marble baths and private lanai overlooking Pohakumanu Bay and the vast horizon beyond; corner suites have indoor Jacuzzis. A gourmet breakfast is served on the lanai, and thoughtful amenities (from room safe to yoga mat) are tucked away in each room. This B&B has garnered rave reviews from national and local magazines. Some say it's rather pretentious, but no one can deny the luxury.

AKAKA FALLS STATE PARK

No one should miss a visit to the Big Island's most impressive 'drive-up' waterfall. Along a half-mile rain-forest loop, an unevenly paved **trail** passes through dense and varied foliage, including massive philodendrons, fragrant ginger, dangling heliconia, orchids and gigantic bamboo groves.

If you start by going to the right, you'll come first to the 100ft **Kahuna Falls**, which, while attractive, is a bit wimpy when compared to its neighbor. Up ahead **Akaka Falls** drops a sheer 420ft down a fern-draped cliff. Its mood depends on the weather – sometimes it rushes with a mighty roar, and at other times it gently cascades. With a little luck, you'll catch a rainbow winking in the spray.

To get here, turn onto Hwy 220 between the 13- and 14-mile markers.

PEPE'EKEO 4-MILE SCENIC DRIVE

Between Honomu and Hilo, a four-mile scenic loop off Hwy 19 between the 7- and 8-mile markers is a majestic tropical drive. At the north end of the drive, **What's Shakin'** (☯ 10am-5pm) serves luscious smoothies.

The road crosses a string of one-lane bridges over little streams and through lush jungle. In places you'll be almost canopied with African tulip trees, which drop their orange flowers on the road, and with *liliko'i*, guava and tall mango trees. The fruit can be picked up along the roadside in season. There are also many small paths leading to babbling rivers and the coast. Look for one of these on the right, about 2.5 miles along, just after the one-lane wooden bridge.

Hawaii Tropical Botanical Garden (☎ 964-5233; www.hawaiigarden.com; adult/child $15/5; ⊙ 9am-4pm) is a nature preserve with 2000 species of tropical plants amid streams and waterfalls. Buy your ticket at the yellow building on the *mauka* side of the road. The half-mile, self-guided walk should take a couple hours. Bear in mind that the vibrant flowers and exotic ornamentals are all non-native, so the original Hawaiians saw a whole different landscape. For an example of pre–Captain Cook vegetation, visit the Amy Greenwell Ethnobotanical Garden (p203).

For a quick, pretty hike down to the bay, find the **Na Ala Hele** trailhead on the *makai* side of the road, just north of the botanical garden. After a 10-minute hike down a slippery jungle path, you'll come to a finger of lava jutting into the sea. A spur to the right goes to a couple of small waterfalls and a cove. Otherwise continue straight on, and look for a rope tied to an almond tree for low-tide beach access. Beware of voracious mosquitoes.

SADDLE ROAD

True to its name, Saddle Rd (Hwy 200) runs along a saddle-shaped valley between the island's two highest points, Mauna Kea to the north and Mauna Loa to the south. At sunrise and sunset there's a gentle glow on the mountains, and a light show on the clouds. In the early morning, it's crisp enough to see your breath, and if you take the spur road up to Mauna Kea, you'll reach permafrost.

Although the 50-mile, two-lane road is paved, it's narrow, winding and hilly, with blind turns, no lights and frequent thick fog. Most car-hire contracts prohibit travel on this road; Harper's is the only company with no restrictions on Saddle Rd. On this remote route, accidents are quite frequent, especially from dusk until just after dawn. There are no gas stations or facilities along the way.

If you're coming from Kona, the road starts off in cattle ranchland with rolling grassy hills and eucalyptus groves. A gated subdivision called Waiki'i Ranch has divided more than 2000 acres into million-dollar house lots for wealthy urban cowboys. After 10 miles, the land starts getting rougher, and the pastures and fences become fewer. The military takes over where the cows leave off, and you'll eventually come to the Quonset huts of the Pohakuloa Military Training Area. Most vehicles here are military-owned, although in hunting season you'll come across a fair number of pickup trucks.

From Hilo, the terrain of Saddle Rd is ohia-fern forest, shrubby near the mountain, thicker and taller toward Hilo. This section of road has been upgraded but it's winding; beware of oncoming drivers hogging the center of the road to cut curves.

MAUNA KEA

Mauna Kea (White Mountain) is Hawai'i's highest peak, and its 13,796ft summit now houses 13 astronomical observatories, considered the greatest collection of major astronomical telescopes in the world. To reach the summit and the Onizuka Visitor Information Station, first take the Mauna Kea Access Rd, which begins off Saddle Rd, just past the 28-mile marker opposite a hunters' check station. Nearby is a 20-minute **hiking trail** up a cinder cone called Pu'u Huluhulu (Shaggy Hill), which is covered with bushy foliage.

The access road starts off passing through open range with grazing cattle, where you'll probably see Eurasian skylarks in the grass. If you're lucky, you might see an 'io (Hawaiian hawk), soaring overhead. The grassy mountain slopes are the habitat of many birds, including the nene and the *palila*, a small yellow honeycreeper that lives nowhere else in the world. Mouflon (mountain sheep) and feral goats roam freely. Silversword, a distant relative of the sunflower, is also found at this high elevation. For more information about wildlife in Hawaii see p47 in the environment chapter.

Environmental protection is paramount here because the mountain is the exclusive home of numerous plants, birds and insects – and the introduction of non-native species upsets the existing ecology. A predominant invasive plant here is mullein, which has soft woolly leaves and shoots up a tall stalk. In spring, the stalks get so loaded down with flowers that they bend over from the weight of big yellow 'helmets.' Ranchers inadvertently introduced mullein as a freeloading weed in grass seed.

Dangers & Annoyances

At altitudes above the Onizuka Visitor Information Station's 9200ft level, your body might not adjust properly to the low atmospheric pressure (roughly half the pressure at sea level). Altitude sickness is common, and the symptoms include nausea, headaches, drowsiness, impaired reason, loss of balance, shortness of breath and dehydration. If you feel ill at the summit, the only way to recover is to descend. Kids under 16, pregnant women, and those with high blood pressure or circulatory conditions should not go to the summit.

Absolutely all travelers to the summit should stop first at the Onizuka center for at least 30 minutes to acclimatize before continuing on.

Information

Bear in mind that the Mauna Kea summit is not a national, state or county park. There are no facilities, restaurants, gas stations or emergency services anywhere on Mauna Kea. It's strongly recommended that 4WD vehicles are used beyond the Onizuka Visitor Information Station (see p244).

Weather conditions can change rapidly, and daytime temperatures range from the 50s to below freezing. The summit can be windy, and temperatures are just as low in observatory viewing rooms as outside. Bring warm clothing, sunglasses and sunscreen. Call the **recorded hotline** (☎ 935-6268) for info on weather and road conditions.

Sights

ONIZUKA VISITOR INFORMATION STATION

Officially the Onizuka Center for International Astronomy, the **center** (Map p235; ☎ 961-2180; www.ifa.hawaii.edu/info/vis; ☽ 9am-10pm) was named for Ellison Onizuka, a Big Island native, and one of the astronauts who perished in the 1986 Challenger space-shuttle disaster.

The center is approximately one hour's drive from Hilo, Waimea or Waikoloa, and two hours from Kailua-Kona. The drive to

DIMMING THE LIGHTS

You might notice, as you tour around the Big Island, that the streetlights have an unusual orange glow. In order to provide Mauna Kea astronomers with the best viewing conditions possible, streetlights on the island have been converted to low-impact sodium. Rather than using the full iridescent spectrum, these orange lights use only a few wavelengths, which the telescopes can be adjusted to remove.

the Onizuka Visitor Information Station from the Saddle Rd intersection is just over 6 miles, plus 2500ft in elevation. Along the way you'll see majestic clouds spread out below you. Mauna Kea doesn't appear as a single main peak but rather a jumble of lava-rock peaks, some black, some red-brown, some seasonally snowcapped.

More than 100,000 tourists visit Mauna Kea annually, and most pass through the Onizuka Visitor Information Station. Stopping here is a must – to acclimatize for at least a half-hour for the journey to the summit. The rangers, interpretive guides, and volunteers are extremely knowledgeable on all aspects of the Mauna Kea, including hiking, historical and cultural significance, road access and astronomy.

The center is modest: just a room with photo displays of the observatories, information on discoveries made from the summit, computer-driven astronomy programs and exhibits of the mountain's history, ecology and geology. You can watch a PBS-produced video about Mauna Kea's observatories or pick another of many astronomy videos to watch while you acclimatize, perhaps with a steaming cup of coffee, hot chocolate, instant noodles or freeze-dried astronaut food, which are all sold here.

Across from the visitors center, a 10-minute uphill hike on a well-trodden trail crests **Pu'u Keonehehe'e**, a cinder cone, and offers glorious sunset views.

SUMMIT OBSERVATORIES

Visitors may go up to the summit in the daytime, but vehicle headlights are not allowed between sunset and sunrise because they interfere with astronomical observation. Driving on the summit after sunset is strongly discouraged. See p248 for important information on driving to the summit.

About 4.5 miles up from the visitor information station, on the east side of the road, is an area dubbed 'moon valley,' because it's where the Apollo astronauts rehearsed with their lunar rover before their journey to the real moonscape.

If you drive to the summit instead of attempting the grueling hike, you'll miss a few important Mauna Kea sights. But nonhikers have another option to see the adze quarry Keanakakoi and Lake Waiau (see Hiking, p246). As you near the summit, you can park at the hairpin turn just before the final ascent to the observatories (look for the 10mph sign and you'll see the trailhead signs), then walk down and over to see the lake (turn right at the trail junction) or to the quarry (keep heading straight downhill). It'll take an hour or so to see both, depending on your level of fitness and acclimatization.

Once you're at the summit, you'll see massive dome-shaped observatories rise up from the vast, stark terrain. The juxtaposition is striking: you'll feel as if you've found a futuristic human colony on another planet. These observatories constitute the greatest collection of state-of-the-art optical, infrared and millimeter-submillimeter telescopes on earth. Viewing conditions on Mauna Kea are optimal with clear, dry and stable air that is also relatively free of dust and smog. At almost 14,000ft, the summit is above 40% of the earth's atmosphere, and over 90% of its water vapor. Only the Andes Mountains can match Mauna Kea for cloudless nights.

You can't see much inside the observatories. Currently only two have visitor galleries

ON THE SUMMIT

The University of Hawai'i (UH) holds the lease on the 'Mauna Kea Science Reserve,' which comprises approximately 11,216 acres above the 12,000ft level – essentially the entire summit. The university built the summit's first telescope in 1968 with a 24in mirror, and now leases property to others. Under one of the lease provisions UH receives observing time at each telescope. Of the 13 telescopes currently in operation, all have base stations in Hilo, except WM Keck and the Canada-France-Hawaii Telescope, which have bases in Waimea.

The **WM Keck Observatory** (www2.keck.hawaii.edu), a joint project of the California Institute of Technology (Caltech), the University of California and NASA, houses the world's largest and most powerful optical-infrared telescope. Keck featured a breakthrough in telescope design. Previously, the sheer weight of the glass mirrors was a limiting factor in telescope construction. The Keck telescope has a unique honeycomb design with 36 hexagonal mirror segments (each 6ft across) that function as a single piece of glass.

In January 1996, the 390in Keck I telescope discovered the most distant galaxy ever observed, at 14 billion light-years away. The discovery of this 'new galaxy,' in the constellation Virgo, has brought into question the very age of the universe itself, because the stars making up the galaxy seemingly predate the 'big bang' that is thought to have created the universe.

A replica of the first telescope, Keck II became operational in October 1996. The two interchangeable telescopes can function as one – 'like a pair of binoculars searching the sky' – allowing them to study the cores of elliptical galaxies. The cost for the twin Keck observatories, each weighing 300 tons and reaching a height of eight stories, was approximately $200 million.

Just 150yd west is Japan's **Subaru Telescope** (www.naoj.org), which opened in 1999 after a decade of construction. Its $300-million price tag makes this the most expensive observatory yet constructed, and its 22-ton mirror, reaching 27ft in diameter, is the largest optical mirror in existence. In case you're wondering, Subaru is the Japanese word for the Pleiades constellation (and the telescope has nothing to do with the automaker!). The Subaru Telescope offers free tours (see p247).

Recently completed is the Submillimeter Array, sponsored by the Smithsonian Astrophysical Observatory and a Taiwanese institute, and UH is envisioning future projects to maintain Mauna Kea's status as the premier site for astronomical research. In coming years, some existing telescopes might become obsolete and lose funding, resulting in fewer but superior telescopes. Learn more about all the observatories at www.ifa.hawaii.edu.

HAWAI'I
(THE BIG ISLAND)

but they're unmanned and minimal: the **WM Keck Observatory visitor gallery** (www2.keck.Hawaii .edu; admission free; ☽ 10am-4pm Mon-Fri) includes a display, 12-minute video screening, public bathrooms and a viewing area inside the Keck I dome; and the **University of Hawai'i 2.2m Telescope** (admission free; ☽ 10am-4pm Mon-Thu).

At the summit, sunsets and moonrises are breathtaking. If you look toward the east at sunset, you can see the 'the shadow,' which is a gigantic silhouette of Mauna Kea looming over Hilo. Moonrises at such a high altitude causes unusual sights, depending on the clouds and weather: the moon might appear squashed and misshapen, or it might resemble a brushfire.

Activities
STARGAZING
The Onizuka Visitor Information Station (p244) offers a **free stargazing program** from 6pm to 10pm, weather permitting (bad weather prevents stargazing only two to three nights per month). Visitors need not call ahead, but if you'd like to confirm that the program is on, call the Visitor Information Station. There is no prerecorded message about the status. At 9200ft the skies are among the clearest, driest, and darkest on the planet. In fact, at the station you're above the elevation of most major telescopes worldwide. This is the *only* place you can use telescopes on Mauna Kea; there are no public telescopes on the summit. Remember that stargazing is hit-or-miss depending on cloud cover and moon phase. The busiest nights are Friday and Saturday.

HIKING
The daunting 6-mile **Mauna Kea Summit Trail** starts at an altitude of 9200ft and climbs almost 4600ft. High altitude, steep grades and brisk weather make the hike very strenuous. Don't attempt it in inclement weather. Get an extremely early start, if you're braving this climb, and give yourself the maximum number of daylight hours; most people need at least five hours to reach the summit, slightly less for the return trip (10 hours total). Before you start, go to the visitor-information station to get a hiking map and sign the hiker registration form; rangers are available to answer any questions.

The hike starts near the end of the paved road above the Onizuka Center. Park at the

center and walk up the road about 200yd. Before it curves to the right and becomes gravel, an old jeep track leads off to the left. Follow the **Humu'ula Trail** signs and start climbing uphill, taking a right at the next fork. After another 100yd you'll see another trail sign pointing uphill. From here on, the trail continues doggedly upward, while numerous false spur trails only lead back to the access road. The first mile of the trail is marked with signs, and starts out roughly parallel to the summit road, then diverges around cinder cones.

At about 45 minutes to an hour, the summit road comes back into view, approximately 100yd to your right. Remember to take time to acclimatize as you go, with frequent rest breaks if necessary. Vegetation begins to disappear and the path is marked intermittently with red painted poles, and sometimes with reflectors. The trail continues upward through ash-and-cinder terrain. Past the two-hour point, the trail starts to ascend more gradually as it weaves among giant cinder cones. After a level traverse over some basalt flows and glacial till, the trail rises through white boulders and the summit of Mauna Kea looms far ahead.

Along the way you'll pass the **Mauna Kea Ice Age Natural Area Reserve**. A Pleistocene glacier once moved down this slope, carrying earth and stones that carved grooves, which are still visible in the rocks. Entering a broad valley after about three hours, the battering winds die down temporarily. A sharp, short ascent on crumbly soil takes you over a rise. **Keanakakoi**, an ancient adze quarry, comes into view off to the right; look for large piles of bluish black chips. From this spot, extremely dense and hard basalt was quarried by ancient Hawaiians to make tools and weapons that were traded throughout the islands. As this is a protected area, nothing should be removed. The quarry is about two-thirds of the way up the trail.

After a steep mile-long ascent, the trail meets another jeep road from the right. Continue straight past the intersection until you reach a four-way junction, where a 10-minute detour to the left brings you to **Lake Waiau**. This unique alpine lake, sitting inside Pu'u Waiau at 13,020ft, is the third-highest lake in the USA. Set on porous cinder, in desert conditions of less than 15in of rainfall annually, the lake is only 10ft deep, yet it's never dry. It's fed by permafrost (leftover from the last Ice Age) and meltwater from winter snows, which elsewhere on Mauna Kea quickly evaporate. Hawaiians used to place umbilical stumps in the lake to give their babies the strength of the mountain.

Back at the four-way junction, head north (uphill) and make a final push upward to meet the Mauna Kea Access Rd at an impromptu parking lot. Suddenly the observatories are visible up on the summit, and straight ahead is Millimeter Valley, nicknamed for the three submillimeter observatories on the summit. The trail ends here at the 7-mile marker of the access road, just below the hairpin turn. But the top of the mountain is still snickering at you another 1.5 miles further up the road.

A few hikers will want to turn back before reaching the summit. If you're in that category, you have a choice of either backtracking along the same 5-mile trail you just came up (only if the weather and visibility are good) or walking down along the shoulders of the road, which is faster and easier even though it's 2 miles longer. Below the 5-mile marker, the road leaves the pavement and returns to gravel on its final leg back to the visitor-information station.

To reach the summit from the hairpin turn described previously, follow the main road up to the right (not the spur road into Millimeter Valley) for over a mile. Past the 8-mile marker, where the road forks, veer right and look for an unofficial trail that starts opposite the University of Hawai'i's 2.2m telescope observatory. This 200yd trail-of-use descends steeply east, crosses a saddle, and scrambles up Pu'u Wekiu to Mauna Kea's true summit, which is marked by a USGS summit benchmark sticking out of the ground. Given the biting winds, high altitude and extreme cold, most people don't linger long before retracing their steps back down.

The trail's steep grade and crumbling cinders make for a most unnerving walk down, especially as daylight fades and afternoon clouds roll in. If you walk back down along the paved road instead of the trail, you'll not only save time but you'll increase your chances of getting a lift. If, however, you're tempted to hitch a ride up from the Onizuka Center...don't. Unless you spent the previous night on the mountain, you won't be properly acclimatized.

SKIING

Skiing in Hawai'i is a curiosity event. Snow does fall on the upper slopes of Mauna Kea each winter, and while there's no guarantee, the ski season usually starts between early January and late February, and can continue for two months. After major snowstorms, locals (who are generally non-skiers) sometimes attempt to slide down the mountain on surfboards, boogie boards and inner tubes!

Skiing Mauna Kea is a notch on your novelty belt. The altitude is tough, and the slopes can harbor exposed rocks and ice sheets. Don't expect any ski lodges, lifts, trails, patrols, equipment or grooming on the mountain. The slopes can be very steep, and there are vertical drops of 5000ft. Commercial ski tours on Mauna Kea are prohibited. You might see tours offered by a company called Ski Hawaii, but officials have warned them to stop all operations on Mauna Kea.

Tours

Free summit tours (admission free; ⊙ 1pm Sat & Sun). The Onizuka Visitor Information Station offers this tour. You must provide your own 4WD transportation to the summit. To join the tour, arrive at the visitors center by 1pm; the first hour is spent watching videos about astronomy on Mauna Kea as you acclimatize. After the orientation, you caravan up to the summit, where you hear a talk on the summit telescopes, including their history, ownership, mirror size, and the type of work they do. The tours visit one or two of the summit telescopes, most commonly the University of Hawai'i's 2.2m telescope and WM Keck's 10m telescope. Pregnant women, children under 16, and those with circulatory and respiratory conditions are not allowed. Tours depart from the summit at about 4:30pm and are subject to cancellation at any time when there's inclement weather at the summit, so call ahead.

Subaru Telescope (www.naoj.org/Information/Tour/Summit; ⊙ tours at 10:30am, 11:30am & 1:30pm) offers 30-minute summit tours up to 15 days per month, in English and in Japanese. You must make advance reservations (by Internet only), and you need your own transportation to the summit.

If you prefer not to drive, a handful of companies offers sunset tours, typically arriving at the Onizuka Center around 4:30pm. Hawaii Forest & Trail and Arnott's Lodge offer similar tours, and require participants to be at least 16 years old.

Arnott's Lodge (☎ 969-7097; www.arnottslodge.com; 98 Apanane Rd, Hilo; tours guests/nonguests $60/90) For active types, with the option to hike around Onizuka Center and even the last few hundred feet to the summit. Tours depart from the hostel in Hilo, with an extra pickup stop at the nearby Hilo Hawaiian Hotel (p260) between noon and 3pm (depending on the season) and return between 9pm and 11pm.

Hawaii Forest & Trail (☎ 331-8505, 800-464-1993; www.hawaii-forest.com; tours $155) Hosts a hot picnic dinner at a Parker Ranch outpost before its sunset 'Mauna Kea Summit and Stars Adventure,' which also includes gloves and parka. There are pickups in Kailua-Kona and Waikoloa.

Mauna Kea Summit Adventures (☎ 322-2366, 888-322-2366; www.maunakea.com; tours $165) Has been leading tours to the summit for two decades, and soup and sandwich, hot beverages, gloves and a hooded parka are provided. There are pickups in Kailua-Kona, Waikoloa and Waimea. Children aged between 10 and 12 can only be taken as far as the Onizuka Center, and those 13 and older to the top. You get a 15% discount for Internet bookings made two weeks in advance.

Sleeping

At the 35-mile marker you'll find a campground and cabins at the **Mauna Kea State Recreation Area**, but they were closed at the time of research. For an update call the **Division of State Parks** (Map250; ☎ 974-6200; www.hawaii .gov/dlnr/dsp; PO Box 936, Hilo, HI 96721; ⏰ 8am-noon Mon-Fri). Facilities include picnic tables and restrooms, but there is no water and the site is used mainly as a waystation for Big Island hunters.

Getting There & Around

From Kona, Saddle Rd (Hwy 200) starts just south of the 6-mile marker on Hwy 190. From Hilo, drive *mauka* on Kaumana Dr, which becomes Saddle Rd (Hwy 200). All drivers should start with a full tank of gas, as there are no gas stations on Saddle Rd.

Driving to the summit is suitable only for 4WD vehicles. Once you pass Hale Pohaku, the residential complex for scientists just above the Onizuka center, the 8 miles to the summit are unpaved gravel for the first 5 miles, then pavement for the last 3 miles. The drive takes about 25 minutes. You should drive in low gear and loosen the gas cap to prevent vapor lock. The upper road can be covered with ice, and loose cinder is always a problem. Be particularly careful on the way down, especially if you develop any signs of altitude sickness at the top. Driving when the sun is low – in the hour after sunrise or before sunset – can create extremely hazardous blinding conditions.

SACRED SITE

Astronomers marvel at Mauna Kea's extraordinary viewing conditions and local businesses appreciate the economic boom from the observatories. But native Hawaiians see Mauna Kea – a sacred temple – being desecrated by science and development.

Traditionally, Mauna Kea is translated not only as White Mountain but also as Wakea's Mountain. Wakea is the sky-father of the islands and the Big Island is considered his first-born child. Lake Waiau is the *piko* (umbilicus) connecting the islands to the heavens.

Mauna Kea is also associated with the goddess Poliahu, the embodiment of snow, whose home is Pu'u Poliahu, a hill near the summit. According to legend, Poliahu is more beautiful than her sister Pele. During catfights over men, Pele would erupt Mauna Kea, then Poliahu would pack it over with ice and snow. Then an angry Pele would erupt again. Back and forth they would go. Interestingly, the legend is metaphorically correct. As recently as 10,000 years ago, there were volcanic eruptions up through glacial ice caps here. Because of its spiritual significance, Pu'u Poliahu is off-limits to astronomical domes.

Native Hawaiians have allied with some environmentalists to oppose development on Mauna Kea, asserting that observatories dump tens of thousands of gallons of human waste at the summit. Further, some observatories use mercury to float mirrors used in telescope operations, and spills have occurred. Reputedly neither the EPA nor the State Department of Health keeps records or follows any baseline standards. The Office of Hawaiian Affairs is currently challenging the approval of a $50 million Keck project for lacking an environmental-impact statement.

MAUNA LOA'S NORTHERN FLANK

The road to Mauna Loa starts near the 28-mile marker, roughly 200yd east of the Mauna Kea Access Rd. Turn south onto the red asphalt road and proceed 17.5 miles up the northern flank of Mauna Loa to a weather observatory at 11,150ft. There are no visitor facilities or bathrooms.

The narrow road is gently sloping and passable in a standard car, but it's a winding, nearly single-lane drive with blind spots, so give yourself 45 minutes to drive up. To avoid vapor-lock problems, loosen your gas cap before starting. Park in the lot below the weather station; the equipment used to measure atmospheric conditions is highly sensitive to vehicle exhaust. The summit and domes of Mauna Kea are visible from here.

Sights & Activities

The Mauna Lea Weather Observatory (Map p272) is the trailhead for the very steep and difficult **Observatory Trail**. If you haven't been staying in the mountains, altitude sickness (p542) is very likely. Anyone who is not in top shape shouldn't even consider it. Overnight hikers need to register in advance with the Kilauea Visitor Center in Hawai'i Volcanoes National Park (see p273).

After about 4 miles, the trail connects up with the Mauna Loa Summit Trail (p282), which starts down in the main section of the national park. From the trail junction, it's just over 2.5 miles around the caldera's western side to Mauna Loa summit at 13,677ft, or about 2 miles along the caldera's eastern side to Mauna Loa cabin at 13,250ft. All told, the hike to the cabin will take at least four to six hours.

HILO

pop 41,000

With a classically crescent-shaped bay and lush rain-forest terrain, Hilo is undeniably scenic. But though it's the county capital and commercial center, it has by and large remained 'old Hilo town.' Here, you'll find relatively few tourists among the longtime locals – probably because measurable rain falls on 278 days per year. Heavy rains have deterred both developers and tourists, and resorts have never really caught on anywhere in east Hawai'i. The 'rainiest city in

the USA' just can't compete with the sun-drenched beaches of the Kona Coast.

Thus Hilo has remained a well-kept secret. The population has remained stable over the years, and residents of Japanese, Korean, Filipino, Portuguese, Puerto Rican, Hawaiian and Caucasian descent live together. Town residents enjoy easy access to Hawai'i Volcanoes National Park, relatively affordable housing and a diverse cultural scene. The copious rainfall only means gushing waterfalls, lush valley gardens, orchids growing wild and tropical fruits aplenty.

Recently, however, Hilo has been discovered, and the influx of newcomers from the mainland has somewhat changed its boondocks reputation and unpretentious vibe. For better or worse, upscale restaurants, chic yoga studios and high-end art galleries are springing up downtown, and 'new money' is pouring in from mainland transplants.

Natural forces have long been a threat to the town – lava from one side, tidal waves from the other. In 1984 a lava flow from Mauna Loa volcano stopped short just 8 miles above town, and during the post-WWII era, two devastating tsunami flattened the coastal town. Hilo is a survivor, however, and the historic buildings that remain have been beautifully restored. Hilo's downtown is a 'pedestrian heaven,' with manageable distances, courteous drivers and inviting backstreets for strolling.

HISTORY

Hilo has a long history as a harbor town, starting with the first Polynesians settlers who farmed, fished and traded goods along the Wailuku River. By the 1900s, numerous wharves dotted the bay, a railroad connected Hilo with the Hamakua Coast, and the breakwater was under construction. Hilo has been the Big Island's center of commerce since then, though the departure of the sugar industry has shifted the balance of economic and political power between east and west Hawai'i.

ORIENTATION

Hilo's charming and compact 'downtown' lies between Kamehameha Ave and Kino'ole St (both parallel to the bay) and between Waianuenue Ave and Mamo St. Hilo's modest hotel row is on Banyan Dr toward the

HILO

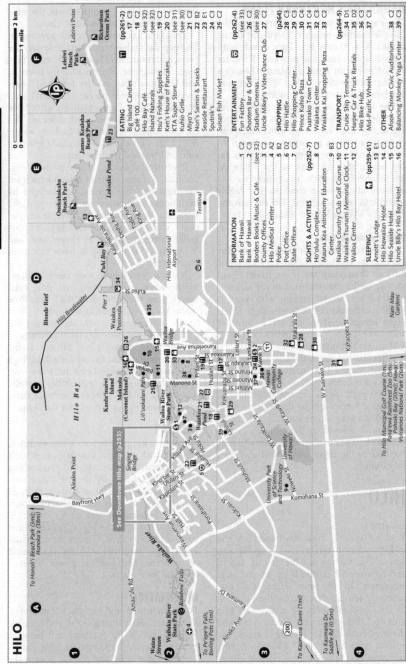

INFORMATION
Bank of Hawaii.....................................1	C2
Bank of Hawaii.....................................2	C2
Borders Books Music & Café...........(see 32)	
County Offices....................................3	A2
Hilo Medical Center.............................4	B2
Police..5	B2
Post Office...6	D2
State Offices..7	C2

SIGHTS & ACTIVITIES (pp252-7)
Ho'olulu Complex.................................8	B3
Mauna Kea Astronomy Education	
Center...9	B3
Naniloa Country Club Golf Course....10	C2
Waiakea Tsunami Memorial Clock....11	C2
Wailoa Center....................................12	C2

SLEEPING (pp259-61)
Arnott's Lodge.................................13	E1
Hilo Hawaiian Hotel..........................14	C2
Hilo Seaside Hotel............................15	D2
Uncle Billy's Hilo Bay Hotel.............16	C2

EATING (pp261-2)
Big Island Candies............................17	C3
Café 100..18	C2
Hilo Bay Café.............................(see 32)	
Island Naturals................................19	C2
Itsu's Fishing Supplies......................20	C2
Ken's House of Pancakes..................21	C2
KTA Super Store........................(see 31)	
Kuhio Grille.............................(see 30)	
Miyo's...22	B2
Nori's Saimin & Snacks.....................23	E1
Seaside Restaurant...........................24	C3
Sputnik's...25	C2
Suisan Fish Market...........................26	C2

ENTERTAINMENT (pp262-4)
Fun Factory...............................(see 33)	
Shooters Bar & Grill.........................26	C2
Stadium Cinemas......................(see 32)	
Uncle Mikey's Video Dance Club.....27	C2

SHOPPING (p264)
Hilo Hattie......................................28	C3
Hilo Shopping Center.......................29	C3
Prince Kuhio Plaza...........................30	C4
Puainako Town Center......................31	C4
Waiakea Center................................32	C3
Waiakea Kai Shopping Plaza.............33	C2

TRANSPORT (pp264-5)
Cruise Ship Terminal........................34	D1
Harper Car & Truck Rentals..............35	D2
Hilo Bike Hub..................................36	C3
Mid-Pacific Wheels..........................37	C3

OTHER
Afook-Chinen Civic Auditorium........38	C2
Balancing Monkey Yoga Center........39	C3

east, but most B&B are located in residential neighborhoods closer to downtown.

For the most scenic drive from the airport to downtown Hilo, head north along Kanoelehua Ave and turn left on to Kamehameha Ave. South of the airport, the shopping malls along Kanoelehua Ave resemble mainland suburban sprawl, but this is Hilo's main retail district, complete with a Wal-Mart and other big-box stores.

INFORMATION
Bookstores

Basically Books (Map p253; ☎ 961-0144, 800-903-6277; 160 Kamehameha Ave; ☺ 9am-5pm Mon-Thu & Sat, to 6pm Fri, 11am-4pm Sun) Longtime indie bookseller that specializes in maps, travel guides and Hawaiian and out-of-print titles.

Borders Books Music & Café (Map p250; ☎ 933-1410; Waiakea Center, 301 Maka'ala; ☺ 9am-9pm Sun-Thu, to 10pm Fri & Sat) Full-service chain selling books, CDs and a range of newspapers and magazines, and where you can hang out for hours.

Emergency

Police (☎ 935-3311; 349 Kapiolani St) For nonemergencies.
Police, Fire & Ambulance (☎ 911) For emergencies.
Sexual Assault Hotline (☎ 935-0677)
Suicide Prevention Hotline (☎ 800-784-2433)

Internet Access

Beach Dog Rental & Sales (Map p253; ☎ 961-5207; 62 Kino'ole St; per 20 min $2.50; ☺ 8am-10pm Mon-Fri, 10am-10pm Sat, to 6pm Sun) Airy space near the federal building, post office and Kalakaua Park.

Bytes & Bites (Map p253; ☎ 935-3520; 223 Kilauea Ave; per 15 min $2.50; ☺ 10am-10pm) The largest Internet spot with 14 computers, in the midst of downtown.

Library

Hilo Public library (Map p253; ☎ 933-8888; 300 Waianuenue Ave; ☺ 11am-7pm Tue & Wed, 9am-5pm Thu & Sat, 10am-5pm Fri) Internet terminals and an impressive selection of Hawaiian volumes, CDs and rental movies.

Media
NEWSPAPERS & MAGAZINES

The *Hawaii Tribune-Herald* (www.hilohawaiitribune.com), the Big Island's main paper, is published Sunday through Friday. In addition, the free tourist guides that you find at airports, hotels and on sidewalk racks can be surprisingly informative. The best:

101 Things to Do (www.101thingstodo.com)
This Week Big Island (www.thisweek.com/bigisland)

RADIO

The vast majority of radio stations are based in Hilo. These stations can be heard only in

---

HILO IN...

One Day

Start at the **Lyman House Memorial Museum** (p254) for a crash course on Hawaiian history, then stroll around the **galleries** and **historical buildings** (p257) downtown. For lunch, picnic under shady trees at **Lili'uokalani Park** (p255). If it's sunny, visit Hilo's rocky but still-appealing **beaches** (p256): Onekahakaha for kids or Richardson for snorkeling. In a good ol' Hilo downpour, a $1 movie at **Kress Cinemas** (p263) is a good option. For dinner, enjoy fresh-caught fish from **Seaside Restaurant** (p262).

Two Days

Start early the next morning with a visit to the **farmers market** (p254), or get active with a round of **golf** (p257) at the Hilo Municipal or Naniloa course, a **yoga class** (p257) or a brisk **walk** across the bayfront. Then head to the Hamakua Coast, stopping at **Akaka Falls** (p242) and rural **Honoka'a** (p235) town, before ending the day at spectacular **Waipi'o Valley** (p238).

Four Days

Follow the two-day itinerary, and on your third day head to **Hawai'i Volcanoes National Park** (p271), only 45 minutes from Hilo. On a day trip, you can visit the main sights and hike to see the **lava flow** if it's visible). If you spend a night in Volcano village, **hike** the Kilauea Iki or Halema'uma'u Trail the next day. Driving back to Hilo, detour to **Red Rd** (p269) to see a 'hot pond' and a brand-new black sand beach and stop for **ice shave** (p263) at Itsu's, when you get back to town.

the east of the Big Island, due to the island's geography. Check out the website www.haw aiiradiotv.com/BigIsleRadio for a complete listing.

KANO 91.1 FM (www.hawaiipublicradio.org) Hawai'i Public Radio featuring classical music and news.

KAPA 100.3 FM Island hits on the station voted the best station in *Hawaii Island Journal*.

KHBC 1060AM (www.khbcradio.com) Hawaiian, country, rock and jazz standards; features longtime DJ Mel 'Mynah Bird Medeiros' 6am to 10am Monday to Saturday.

KHLO 850AM Oldies (simulcast with Kona's KKON 790AM).

KKBG 97.9 (kbigfm.com) Hawai'i's big hits.

KPUA 670AM (www.kpua.net) News, sports and talk radio (including…Rush Limbaugh).

KPVS 95.9 FM 'Kiss FM' contemporary pop.

KWXX 94.7 FM (www.kwxx.com) Island and pop hits.

Medical Services

Hilo Medical Center (Map p250; ☎ 974-4700, emergency room ☎ 974-6800; 1190 Waianuenue Ave; ☒ 24hr emergency) Located near Rainbow Falls.

KTA Super Store (☎ 959-8700; Puainako Town Center, 50 E Puainako St; ☒ 5:30am-midnight) For prescriptions; south of the airport.

Money

All banks in Hilo have 24-hour ATMs.

Bank of Hawaii (Map p250) Kawili St (☎ 961-0681; 417 E Kawili St); Pauahi St (☎ 935-9701; 120 Pauahi St)

First Hawaiian Bank (Map p253; ☎ 969-2222; 120 Waianuenue Ave)

Post

Main post office (Map p250; ☎ 933-3019; 1299 Kekuanaoa St; ☒ 8am-4:30pm Mon-Fri, 8:30am-12:30pm Sat) Holds general delivery mail.

Downtown post office (Map p253; ☎ 961-2976; 154 Waianuenue Ave; ☒ 8am-4pm Mon-Fri, 12:30-2pm Sat) Conveniently located in the Federal Building downtown.

Tourist Information

Big Island Visitors Bureau (Map p250; ☎ 961-5797, 800-648-2441; www.gohawaii.com; 250 Keawe St; ☒ 8am-4:30pm Mon-Fri) Check the website for a detailed events calendar with links.

SIGHTS

In downtown Hilo, the charming early-20th-century architecture remains, and many of the buildings on the National Register of Historic Places now house restaurants, stores and galleries. You'll also see aging wooden storefronts and backstreets with old pool halls and barbershops still using hand-pumped chairs. Locals refer to the coastal stretch along Hilo bay as 'bayfront.' Outside the downtown area, the main sights are on Banyan Dr and the beaches further south.

LITTLE TOKYO & BIG TSUNAMI

On April 1, 1946, Hilo Bay was inundated by a tsunami that had raced across the Pacific from an earthquake epicenter in the Aleutian Islands. It struck at 6:54am without warning.

Fifty-foot waves jumped the seawall and swept over the city. They ripped the first line of buildings from their foundations, carrying them inland and smashing them into the rows behind. As the waves pulled back, they sucked splintered debris and a number of people out to sea.

By 7am the town was littered with shattered buildings. The ground was not visible through the pile of rubble. Throughout Hawaii the tsunami killed 159 people and caused $25 million in property damage. The hardest hit was Hilo, with 96 fatalities.

Hilo's bay-front 'Little Tokyo' bore the brunt of the storm. Shinmachi, which means 'new town' in Japanese, was rebuilt on the same spot.

Fourteen years later, on May 23, 1960, an earthquake off the coast of Chile triggered a tsunami that sped toward Hilo at 440mph. A series of three waves washed up in succession, each one sweeping further into the city.

Although the tsunami warning speakers roared this time, many people didn't take them seriously. The tiny tsunami incidents of the 1950s had been relatively harmless, and some people actually went down to the beach to watch the waves.

Those along the shore were swept inland, while others further up were dragged out into the bay. A few lucky people, who managed to grab hold of floating debris, were rescued at sea. In the end, this tsunami caused 61 deaths and property damage of over $20 million.

Once more the Shinmachi area was leveled, but this time, instead of being redeveloped, the low-lying bayfront property was turned into parks, and survivors relocated to higher ground.

DOWNTOWN HILO

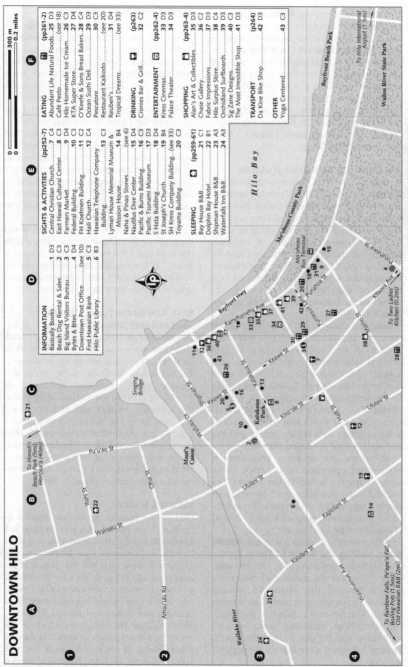

INFORMATION
Basically Books.................1 D3
Beach Dog Rental & Sales.....2 C3
Big Island Visitors Bureau.....3 C3
Bytes & Bites.....................4 D4
Downtown Post Office.....(see 10)
First Hawaiian Bank.............5 C3
Hilo Public Library..............6 B3

SIGHTS & ACTIVITIES (pp252-7)
Central Christian Church.......7 C4
East Hawaii Cultural Center....8 C3
Farmers Market..................9 D4
Federal Building................10 C4
FH Koehnen Building...........11 C2
Haili Church....................12 C4
Hawaiian Telephone Company
  Building.......................13 C3
Lyman House Memorial Museum &
  Mission House...........(see 6)
Naha & Pinao Stones...........14 B4
Nautilus Dive Center...........15 D4
Pacific & Burns Building........16 C3
Pacific Tsunami Museum........17 D3
S Hata Building.................18 D4
St Joseph's Church.............19 B4
SH Kress Company Building...(see 33)
Toyama Building................20 C3

SLEEPING (pp259-61)
Bay House B&B..................21 C1
Dolphin Bay Hotel..............22 B1
Shipman House B&B.............23 A3
Waterfalls Inn B&B..............24 A3

EATING (pp261-2)
Abundant Life Natural Foods...25 D3
Café Pesto....................(see 18)
Hilo Homemade Ice Cream....26 C3
KTA Super Store................27 D4
O'Keefe & Sons Bread Bakers..28 C4
Ocean Sushi Deli...............29 D3
Pescatore......................30 C3
Restaurant Kaikodo............31 D4
Reuben's......................(see 20)
Tropical Dreams................(see 33)

DRINKING (p263)
Cronies Bar & Grill.............32 C2

ENTERTAINMENT (pp262-4)
Kress Cinemas.................33 D3
Palace Theater.................34 D3

SHOPPING (pp263-4)
Alan's Art & Collectibles.......35 D3
Chase Gallery..................36 C2
Fabric Impressions.............37 D3
Hilo Surplus Store.............38 C4
Orchidland Surfboards.........39 D3
Sig Zane Designs...............40 C3
The Most Irresistible Shop.....41 D3

TRANSPORT (p264)
Da Kine Bike Shop.............42 D3

OTHER
Yoga Centered.................43 C3

At the time of writing, **Mauna Kea Astronomy Education Center** (Map p250) was set to open in late 2005 at the University of Hawai'i at Hilo's **University Park of Science and Technology** (Map p250; N Aohoku Pl), off Komohana Dr, where most of the astronomical observatories are actually headquartered. This $28 million, 40,000 sq ft project will include a planetarium, exhibit hall, classrooms, a restaurant and a gift shop – and is expected to be the Big Island's second-biggest tourist draw (after Hawai'i Volcanoes National Park).

LYMAN HOUSE MEMORIAL MUSEUM

A great place to spend a rainy afternoon, this **museum** (Map p253; ☎ 935-5021; www.lymanmuseum .org; 276 Haili St; adult/child/senior $10/3/8; ☽ 9:30am-4:30pm Mon-Sat) will teach you all about ancient Hawaiian life, such as the making of adzes from rare types of volcanic rock, and candles by skewering *kukui* nuts on coconut-frond spines. You can wander past displays of feather lei, *kapa,* and the framework of a traditional thatched house, as the mysteries of mana, kahuna and *'awa* (kava) are revealed.

You pass through a lava tube, escorted by the sights and sounds of volcanic eruptions, curtains of fire, and molten lava. Science exhibits take you through Hawai'i's geological history, from the first volcanic cone that broke the sea's surface to modern-day Lo'ihi Seamount, with artifacts of spatter, olivine, Pele's tears (solidified drops of volcanic glass) and Pele's hair (fine strands of volcanic glass). Pele is the volcano goddess and so lava rock is named after her.

Elsewhere the museum showcases a world-class collection of minerals, along with computers linked to the Mauna Kea summit astronomical observatories, and displays on the varied lifestyles of the indentured immigrants, who eventually created Hawaii's multiethnic society.

Adjacent to the museum is the **Mission House,** built by the Reverend David Lyman and his wife, Sarah, in 1839. The two missionaries had seven children of their own, and, in the attic, they boarded a number of island boys who attended their church school. The house has many of the original furnishings, including Sarah Lyman's melodeon, rocking chair, china and quilts. Docent-led tours leave hourly throughout the day.

PACIFIC TSUNAMI MUSEUM

This modern multimedia **museum** (Map p253; ☎ 935-0926; www.tsunami.org; 130 Kamehameha Ave; adult/student/senior $7/2/6; ☽ 9am-4pm Mon-Sat) captures the destructive horror and triumphant survival left in the wake of Pacific Ocean tsunami. The docents are well-informed, probably because some are tsunami survivors themselves (see the boxed text Little Tokyo & Big Tsunami on p252).

Tsunami have killed more Hawaiians than all other natural disasters combined, and this museum covers the entire Pacific region. Videos of oral histories and documentary pieces are projected on screens inside a minitheater, built in an old bank vault. Computers are available for those who want to know more about these gigantic waves.

The building itself, completed in 1930 and designed by CW Dickey, is a survivor. Both the 1946 and 1960 tsunami failed to wash it away. Look up at the tsunami-cam on the roof of the building, which projects live surf images online every day of the year.

EAST HAWAII CULTURAL CENTER

The **East Hawaii Cultural Center** (Map p253; ☎ 961-5711; www.ehcc.org; 141 Kalakaua St; suggested donation $2; ☽ 10am-4pm Mon-Sat) showcases the work of local artists, most of whom are professionals, but local schoolkids' masterpieces also appear. Ongoing workshops and classes on a range of creative forms (including painting, drawing, ukulele and glasswork) are also held here. The building is a registered historic landmark that served as the Hilo police station until 1975. The hipped roof, which resembles a Hawaiian *hale,* covered lanai and other distinct features were common in 19th-century island homes.

FARMERS MARKET

One of the pioneering farmers market in Hawaii, Hilo **market** (Map p253; cnr Mamo St & Kamehameha Ave; ☽ 7am-noon Wed & Sat) is a sight to behold. Dozens of local farmers, mostly Filipino immigrants, sell the gamut of island produce. Try both the solo (traditional yellow) and sunrise (strawberry pink) papayas, tart-flavored apple bananas, sweet Ka'u oranges, and lychee and mango in season. Here you'll see the real locals, for whom the market is a 'town square' of sorts. On the east side of Mamo St you'll find T-shirt and craft sellers; beware of fake 'Hawaiian' woven

COUNT THE KING KAMEHAMEHA STATUES

On the bayfront side of Wailoa River State Park, a 14ft, Italian-made bronze **statue** of Kamehameha the Great was erected in 1997. This statue, which underwent a $30,000 gold-leaf restoration in 2004, is not a copy of the 'identical' statues in Honolulu (p92) or Kapa'au (p228) – it's larger and the face is different (one Kamehameha Schools alumnus quipped that it looks like President Clinton!). The other two statues have an interesting history (see p228), and the Honolulu statue is gilded, while the Kapa'au statue is painted. And don't forget the fourth Kamehameha statue, another replica of the original, which stands at the US Capitol in Washington, DC.

baskets, wood carvings and shell jewelry (though the real stuff can be found, too!). Flowers are an especially amazing deal, where $2 can buy you a huge protea bloom, or a bunch of vibrant anthuriums.

WAILOA RIVER STATE PARK

The arc-shaped bridges at this **state park** (Map p250) are ideal for a quiet stroll. The Wailoa River flows through the park, ending at **Waiakea Pond**, a spring-fed estuarine pond with saltwater and brackish-water fish species (mostly mullet). There's a boat launch ramp, near the mouth of the river, for motorless boats. The park features two **memorials**: a tsunami memorial dedicated to the 1946 and 1960 victims; and a Vietnam War memorial, an eternal flame dedicated to the war casualties.

The **Wailoa Center** (Map p250; ☎ 933-0416; admission free; ⏰ 8:30am-4:30pm Mon, Tue, Thu & Fri, noon-4:30pm Wed) is an eclectic state-run art gallery with striking photographs of tsunami damage displayed downstairs. Multicultural exhibits change monthly and might include woodwork, bonsai, Chinese watercolors or *oshibana* (Japanese dried-flower art), all done by locals who are both novices and professionals. It's best to arrive early, as the gallery staff sometimes lock up by 4pm.

CHURCHES

Haili St was once called Church Street for the churches lining it. Catholic **St Joseph's**

Church (Map p253; cnr Haili & Kapiolani Sts) is a pink paean of Spanish-mission design. Built in 1919, it has stained-glass windows and trumpeting angels. **Haili Church** (Map p253; ☎ 935-4847; 211 Haili St) was built in 1859 and looks as if it were airlifted straight out of the New England countryside. Services are held in Hawaiian and English. Downhill toward the bay, the Victorian-style **Central Christian Church** (Map p253; ☎ 935-8025; 109 Haili St) was built by Portuguese immigrants in the early 1900s.

BANYAN DRIVE

Hilo's short but scenic 'hotel row,' **Banyan Dr** (Map p250), is best known for the enormous banyan trees lining the road. Royalty and celebrities planted the trees in the 1930s, and, if you look closely, you'll find plaques beneath the trees identifying Babe Ruth, Amelia Earhart and Cecil B DeMille, among them. The road wraps around the edge of Waiakea Peninsula, which juts into Hilo Bay. The road skirts the 9-hole Naniloa Golf Course (p257).

Nearby on Kamehameha Ave, near Manono St, time stands still at the **Waiakea Tsunami Memorial Clock**. The clock is stuck at 1:05, the exact moment, in the predawn hours of May 23, 1960, when Hilo's last major tsunami swept ashore.

LILI'UOKALANI PARK

Hilo's 30-acre Japanese-style **park** (Map p250), named for Hawai'i's last queen, is a lovely green oasis with koi ponds, patches of bamboo, quaint arched bridges and a teahouse. Many of the lanterns and pagoda were donated by Japanese regional governments and sister cities in honor of the 100th anniversary of Japanese immigration to Hawai'i. The 2 miles of paths here are perfect for a sunset stroll or an early-morning jog.

MOKUOLA (COCONUT ISLAND)

A tiny island connected to land by a footbridge, **Mokuola** (Map p250), which means 'Island of Life,' is just opposite Lili'uokalani Gardens. The site is a county park with picnic tables and swimming, but it's most popular as a recreational fishing spot.

In ancient times, this little island was a *pu'uhonua*, and a powerful healing stone on the island was used by kahuna to cure the sick. Mokuola also had pure spring water, which was said to bring good health, and a birthing stone that instilled mana in the children born on the island.

BEACHES Map   p250

Make no mistake: Hilo is not a beach town. Though there are some decent pockets for snorkeling, catching a break or watching the sunrise along **Kalaniana'ole Ave**, a 4-mile coastal road on the eastern side of Hilo. All of these beaches can get fairly rough with rip currents and surf, so assess conditions carefully before venturing out.

About 1.5 miles east of the intersection of Kalaniana'ole Ave and Kanoelehua Ave, **Puhi Bay** is a good beginner dive site. If you enter from the grassy outcropping on the eastern side, you'll come to an interesting reef, 'Tetsu's Ledge,' at 30ft. The teeth-rattling waters are too cold for swimming, however.

Further east, **Onekahakaha Beach Park**, about 450yd north of Kalaniana'ole Ave, has restrooms, showers and a picnic area. A broad sandy-bottomed pool here is formed by a large boulder enclosure. As the water is just 1ft or 2ft deep in most places, it's popular

---

ROCKS OF AGES

On the front lawn of the Hilo Public Library (Map p253) are the Naha and Pinao Stones. The **Pinao Stone** was an entrance pillar to an old heiau. The **Naha Stone**, from the same temple grounds, is estimated at 3.5 tons. According to Hawaiian legend, anyone who had the strength to budge the stone would also have the strength to conquer and unite all the Hawaiian Islands. Kamehameha the Great reputedly met the challenge, overturning the stone in his youth.

From the Pu'ueo St Bridge, at the north end of Keawe St just beyond Wailuku Dr, you can see the current swirling around **Maui's Canoe** (Map p253) a large rock in the upstream Wailuku River. Legend has it that the demigod Maui paddled his canoe with such speed across the ocean that he crash-landed here and the canoe turned to stone. Ever the devoted son, Maui was rushing to save his mother, Hina, from a water monster that was trying to drown her by damming the river and flooding her cave beneath Rainbow Falls.

---

with families with young children. On the Hilo side, an unprotected cove attracts snorkelers on calm days, but mind the seaward current. Swimmers and snorkelers should never venture beyond the breakwater.

James Kealoha Beach Park is a roadside county park that's known locally as 'Four Miles' (the distance between the park and the downtown post office). There are showers and restrooms. For swimming and snorkeling, most people head for the eastern side of the park, which is sheltered by an island and a breakwater. It's generally calm there, with clean, clear water and pockets of white sand. The west side of the park is open ocean and much rougher. Locals sometimes net fish here and it's a popular winter surfing spot, although there are strong rips.

Almost another mile eastward, **Leleiwi Beach Park** is the best shore-dive site in Hilo, but the entrance is a bit trickier than at Puhi Bay. The best place to enter is to the left of the third pavilion, where the wall jogs toward the ocean. From there, walk to the level area beyond the gap in the wall.

Richardson Ocean Park, just before the end of the road, has a small black-sand beach fronting Hilo's most popular snorkeling site. When the waves get bumpy, it's also boogie-boarding territory. On the Hilo side, the bay tends to be cooler, due to subsurface freshwater springs. The water is warmer and the snorkeling better on the eastern side of the park, which also has a lava shoreline for exploring. There are restrooms, showers, picnic tables and a lifeguard.

On the northern side of town, the cove at **Honoli'i Beach Park** is a protected pocket with Hilo's best surfing. There are showers and toilets. To get there, take Hwy 19 north out of Hilo. Between the 4- and 5-mile markers, make a right onto Nahala St and a left onto Kahoa St. Join all the other cars parked on the side of the road and head down to the park. You can return to Hwy 19 by following Kahoa St downhill onto a one-lane road that winds through an enchanting forest.

ACTIVITIES
Swimming

Hilo is not exactly a drawcard for swimmers, as the beaches are rocky and often rough. Along Kalaniana'ole Ave, **James Kealoha Beach** (Map p250) offers the calmest waters for swimming; for toddlers and young kids,

Onekahakaha Beach (Map p250) is shallow and ideal for learning to swim.

For lap swimming, the **Ho'olulu Complex** (Map p250; ☎ 961-8698) has an impressive, Olympic-sized, open-air pool that is generally uncrowded during the day. Phone for opening hours.

Diving

The best spot near Hilo is **Leleiwi Beach** (Map p250), with depths of 10ft to 70ft. You can see lava arches, coral reef, turtles, dolphins, fish and whales in season. In the nearby Puna district, **Pohoiki Bay** is the best dive site in east Hawai'i, with depths of 20ft to 100ft and an impressive variety of marine life.

For equipment and firsthand advice, **Nautilus Dive Center** (Map p253; ☎ 935-6939; www.nautilusdivehilo.com; 382 Kamehameha Ave; scuba package or kayak per day $25) is a reliable outfit that organizes dives and courses in the Hilo area at competitive rates.

Surfing

By far the best surfing spot near Hilo is Honoli'i Cove at Honoli'i Beach Park, which draws crowds when the surf's up.

Stop by **Orchidland Surfboards** (Map p253; ☎ 935-1533; www.orchidlandsurf.com; 262 Kamehameha Ave; ☺ 9am-5pm Mon-Sat, 10am-3pm Sun) for board rentals (per day $20) or surf gear. Owner Stan Lawrence is an expert surfer, and he opened the Big Island's first surf shop in 1972. Check his website for surf reports and cool videos.

To learn to surf, especially if you're female, **Big Island Girl Surf** (☎ 326-0269; www.bigislandgirlsurf.com; 1-hr group/private lesson $50/60, day camp $55-125) offers safe lessons and day camps at Honoli'i Beach. Weeklong overnight camps (for both novices and advanced surfers) include accommodations, healthy meals, yoga classes, surf lessons and island excursions. Lessons are offered for boys, too, but the overnighters are all *wahine* (women). The average age range is 14 to 30 but they say 'attitude is more important than age!'

Golf

In Hilo, you can golf practically for nothing at **Hilo Municipal Golf Course** (☎ 959-7711; 340 Haihai St; Mon-Fri $29, Sat & Sun $34) or at the nine-hole **Naniloa Country Club Golf Course** (Map p250; ☎ 935-3000; Mon-Fri 9-/18-hole green fees $20/25 Sat & Sun $25/30).

Yoga

Yoga Centered (Map p253; ☎ 934-7233; www.yogacentered.com; 37 Waianuenue Ave; drop-in class $12) An attractive 'heated' studio offering mostly Ashtanga and *vinyasa* (flowing sequences of poses) classes, plus the latest yoga fashions.

Balancing Monkey Yoga Center (Map p250; ☎ 936-9590; www.balancingmonkey.com; 65 Mohouli St; drop-in class $11) Owned by the director of the UH Hilo yoga program, this studio offers 90-minute classes in either the Ashtanga or Iyengar method.

HILO WALKING TOUR

Old Hilo town is perfect for a leisurely stroll along historic buildings, unique shops and the panoramic bay. This 2-mile (one way) walking tour starts in downtown Hilo and ends at Lili'uokalani Park near Banyan Dr. First stop by the **East Hawaii Cultural Center** (**1**; p254), a public art gallery located in the historic former police station, then check out the **Hawaiian Telephone Company Building (2)** next door. Designed by renowned Honolulu architect CW Dickey in the 1920s, this is the jewel in Hilo's architectural crown. Influenced by Spanish, Italian and Californian missions, the building features handsome terracotta tiles, high-hipped roof and metalwork detailing on the windows.

Next cross Kalakaua St into **Kalakaua Park (3)**, which features a bronze statue of 19th-century King David Kalakaua (the 'Merrie Monarch') under a majestic banyan tree. The taro leaf by the King's side symbolizes his connection with the land, while the *ipu* (gourd instrument) on his right stands for the traditional Hawaiian cultural arts that he helped to revive. The lily-filled pool is a Korean War veterans memorial, and buried under the grass is a time capsule, sealed on the last total solar eclipse, and to be opened on the next one.

Look further north at the neoclassical **Federal Building (4)**, across the street. Built in 1919 in a style typical of early-20th-century government buildings, it now houses government offices and a post office. Next head *makai* on Waianuenue Ave, and see the traditional **Burns Building (5**; 1911) and **Pacific Building (6**; 1922) to your right. Across the street is the **Toyama Building (7**; 1908), which was meticulously restored and now has become a destination, with Restaurant Kaikodo (p262) downstairs. Keep heading

HAWAI'I (THE BIG ISLAND)

makai until you reach the **Koehnen's Building** (**8**) at Kamehameha Ave. This eye-catching blue 1910 building has interior koa walls and ohia floors; since 1957 the Koehnen family has owned the building and its fine furnishings store.

Now you're on downtown Hilo's main street with a lovely view of the bay. You'll pass a handful of excellent galleries, such as the spacious **Chase Gallery** (**9**; p264). Just before you cross Kalakaua St, stop at the **Pacific Tsunami Museum** (**10**; p254) in the old First Hawaiian Bank Building. Another CW Dickey creation, this sturdy concrete building with fluted columns and wrought-iron detailing was built in 1930.

In the next block, you'll hit the art deco **SH Kress Company Building** (**11**; 1932), which until 1980 was a bustling department store. In the 1980s it fell into disrepair until former US Senator Hiram Fong bought and restored it in 1990. Now the building houses a first-run movie theater, a 245-student public-charter school and small shops. When you reach Haili St, turn *mauka* to see Hilo's old-time **Palace Theater** (**12**; p263), which in 1925 was the first deluxe playhouse on the Big Island.

> **Start** Downtown Hilo
> **Finish** Lili'uokalani Park
> **Duration** 1 hour
> **Distance** 2 miles

Keep walking southeast along Kamehameha Ave until you reach the **S Hata Building** (**13**; 1912), a fine example of renaissance revival architecture that was seized from the original Japanese owner by the US government during WWII. After the war, the owner's daughter bought the building back for $100,000. Today the restored building houses Café Pesto (p262) and other restaurants, shops and offices.

On Saturday and Wednesday, the open space at Mamo St is a **farmers market** (**14**; p254), teeming with more varieties of island produce than you can try on vacation. Prices are amazingly cheap and you can cobble together a delectable snack of fresh fruit and to-go sushi and *bento*.

Now cross Kamehameha Ave to walk along the **Bayfront Beach Park** (**15**). The breakwater was built between 1908 and 1929 to provide a safe port for Hilo, using 951,273 tons of rock. Before the 1946 and 1960 tsunami, there were many businesses and houses on the grassy area lined with coconut palms. Watch for canoe paddlers training in the bay.

At Manono St, head left toward the unmistakable **Suisan Fish Market** (**16**), where you can come back and watch fish being auctioned at 7am. Now you can picnic and hang out at Hilo's peaceful **Lili'uokalani Park** (**17**; p255), which at 30 acres is rarely crowded. Just a short walk away is **Mokuola** (**18**; p255), easily accessible by a modern bridge. If you still have energy, a quick stroll

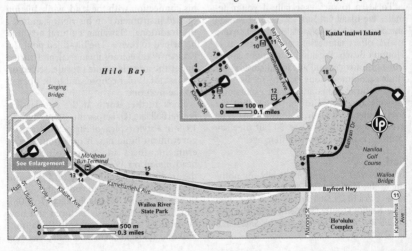

down Banyan Dr is very scenic, past Hilo's handful of 'high-rise' hotels, giant banyan trees and a golf course.

HILO FOR CHILDREN

Hilo is kid-friendly, with many outdoor spots where kids can freely romp and parents can enjoy the scenery. A day spent picnicking or netting guppies at **Lili'uokalani Park** (p255) and walking across the bridge to **Mokuola** (p255) to pole-fish is sure to please. **Onekahakaha Beach** (p256) is small, calm, close to town and very easy to manage. The grassy areas alongside Kamehameha Ave are Hilo's soccer fields and an ideal place to kick around a ball or play catch with a football or baseball. If you visit Hilo in September, the annual **Hawai'i County Fair** (p259) is a great, old-fashioned event with carnival rides, petting zoo, cotton candy and ring-toss games.

Fun Factory (Map p250; ☎ 935-3444; Waiakea Kai Shopping Plaza, 88 Kanoelehua Ave; token 25¢; ☷ 10am-10pm Sun-Thu, to midnight Fri & Sat) If your kid is a gamer who needs a fix, the Fun Factory is Hilo's main video-game arcade. Unfortunately the shopping-plaza location has lost its cinemas and become deserted over the years – it used to be a bustling teen hangout in the 1980s.

Pana'ewa Rainforest Zoo (Map p265; ☎ 959-9233; www.hilozoo.com; admission free; ☷ 9am-4pm, petting zoo 1:30-2:30pm Sat) Hilo's 12-acre zoo has seen better days but zoos never fail to excite kids, and if you have an hour or two, it's a convenient diversion. Free-roaming peacocks have the run of the place. Caged monkeys, reptiles, a pygmy hippo and an axis deer look a bit cramped. But a white Bengal tiger (shipped in from Las Vegas) has a generous grassy arena – and if an unknowing peacock lands inside, you'll witness a bloody feast worthy of a PBS documentary. You can also see some of Hawai'i's endangered birds, such as the nene and the Hawaiian duck, hawk and owl. To get here, turn off Hwy 11 at W Mamaki St, just past the 4-mile marker; the zoo is another mile west.

TOURS

Arnott's Adventure Tours (Map p250; ☎ 969-7097; www.arnottslodge.com; 98 Apapane Rd; tour per guest/ nonguest $50-60/75-90), run by the same folks who run Arnott's Lodge, offers popular backpacker-oriented day tours to Mauna Kea (p247), Waipi'o Valley (p238) and Hawai'i Volcanoes National Park (p271). These are geared for active people who prefer to do some hiking and/or swimming during their outings, rather than just sitting on a bus.

FESTIVALS & EVENTS

For a complete listing of Big Island events, click to www.gohawaii.com.

Merrie Monarch Festival (March or April; ☎ 935-9168; www.merriemonarchfestival.org; 2-night admission general/reserved $10/15; ☷ starts Easter Sunday) Hilo's biggest event is a weeklong cultural event that culminates with a spirited hula competition. The islands' best hula troupes vie in *kahiko* (ancient) and *auana* (modern) categories – and if you've seen only hotel hula shows, these dancers' skill and seriousness will give you a whole new perspective. Other events include a *ho'olaule'a* (celebration), a Miss Aloha Hula contest and a parade. Tickets go on sale at the end of December and sell out within a month.

Big Island Hawaiian Music Festival (mid-July; Map p250; ☎ 961-5711; Afook-Chinen Civic Auditorium; adult/child $10/free) A two-day concert featuring accomplished ukulele, steel-guitar and slack-key-guitar players from across the islands.

Hawai'i County Fair (September) The fair comes to town on the grounds of the Afook-Chinen Civic Auditorium. It's sure to spur nostalgia, with carnival rides and games and the aroma of grilled corn, popcorn, chili and cotton candy, plus only-in-Hawaii treats like *malasada*. Also featured are orchid and cactus shows, agricultural exhibits including live animals, and political-campaign booths during major election years.

SLEEPING

Hilo is not a beach town, so the glut of resorts and 'vacation rental' condos on the Kona Coast is nonexistent here. Instead you'll find a handful of standard hotels and numerous B&Bs, including elegant old-style manors (the best option if you want a bit of extravagance).

Budget

Hilo Bay Hostel (Map p253; ☎ 933-2771; www.hawaii hostel.net; 101 Waianuenue Ave; dm $18, r without/with bathroom $38/58; ☐) In a prime location smack dab in the middle of downtown Hilo, this hostel, in the 1911 Burns Building, is clean and airy. The crowd is diverse and from all over the world, and the vibe is low-key (less backpackers than at Arnott's). Dorm rooms sleep four to eight, and there's one room with a private bathroom. All rooms have ceiling fans and windows that let in the refreshing Hilo breezes. Guests can use three computers and a TV in the common area. There's free coffee and tea. No drugs or alcohol are permitted. Internet access costs per $2 per 15 minutes.

Arnott's Lodge (Map p250; ☎ 969-7097; www.arnottslodge.com; 98 Apapane Rd; tent sites $9, dm/s/d with shared bathroom $19/39/49, r/ste $62/125; 🚫 💻) This is the place for the outdoorsy, backpacking crowd; the only downside is its location on the outskirts of town. There are wheelchair-accessible portions, sex-segregated dorms, camping in the front yard and private rooms. Amenities at this laid-back hostel include a TV and DVD room, Internet access ($2 per 20 minute), air-con ($3 per day in private rooms only) and coin laundry. Guests can hop cheap shuttles into town or rent bicycles (under $10 per day). Adventure island tours cost $50 to $60 ($75 to $90 for nonguests). Free airport pickups are available (until 8pm). If you're driving, head east of Hwy 11 on Kalaniana'ole Ave about 1.5 miles, then turn left onto Keokea Loop Rd. The lodge is about 100yd further.

Mid-Range & Top End

Old Hawaiian B&B (☎ 961-2816; www.thebigislandvacation.com; 1492 Wailuku Dr; r incl breakfast $75-95) In a scenic neighborhood above Hilo Medical Center, just 10 minutes' drive from downtown, these three attractive rooms with private entrances are amazing deals. A full breakfast, including homemade bread and island fruit, is served on the shared lanai, where there's a microwave and refrigerator you can use. Military discounts are offered.

THE AUTHOR'S CHOICE

Dolphin Bay Hotel (Map p253; ☎ 935-1466; www.dolphinbayhotel.com; 333 Iliahi St; studios $80-90, 1-/2-bedroom units $110/130) Located right near downtown, this popular, family-run hotel is the best deal in Hilo. All rooms resemble comfy apartment units – with full kitchen, color TV, fan and sliding glass doors. This is an ideal place for a 'home base' to explore east Hawai'i, and the down-to-earth staff are generous with insider advice. The owner is an experienced hiker and a fount of information on the entire Big Island outdoors, especially Hawai'i Volcanoes National Park – check out his photos and daily volcano update at the reception desk. Fresh-picked fruit from the backyard and free morning coffee are available to guests. Reduced weekly rates are also available.

Bay House B&B (Map p253; ☎ 961-6311, 888-235-8195; www.bayhousehawaii.com; 42 Pukihae St; r incl breakfast $105-120) Located just across the 'Singing Bridge' from downtown Hilo, the Bay House offers immaculate, spacious rooms, literally overlooking the bay, in a separate guest wing. Each room has a private lanai, cable TV, phone and king- or queen-size beds, with a shared kitchenette and a hot tub. The hosts are friendly, longtime residents, and they serve a delicious breakfast buffet that you eat on your lanai.

Shipman House B&B (Map p253; ☎ 934-8002, 800-627-8447; www.hilo-hawaii.com; 131 Kaiulani St; r incl breakfast $170-215) Set on a knoll just outside downtown Hilo, this graceful Victorian mansion has been in the Shipman family since 1901. Past visitors to this B&B, which is on the National Register of Historic Places, have included Queen Lili'uokalani and Jack London. All rooms, whether in the main house or the 1910 guest cottage, have baths (with gorgeous tubs), high ceilings, small refrigerators, hardwood floors covered with lauhala mats and genuine vintage furnishings. The congenial owners have added appealing touches, such as guest kimonos, fresh flowers, a library and a Steinway grand piano.

Waterfalls Inn B&B (Map p253; ☎ 969-3407, 888-808-4456; www.waterfallsinn.com; 240 Kaiulani St; r incl breakfast $145-175) From your first glimpse of the French doors and spacious verandah, it's clear that this plantation home (also on the National Register of Historic Places) is magnificent. The added bonus is that it's also relaxed and unpretentious. There's a large antique soaking tub and wi-fi access, too. In the backyard, the sounds of Wailuku River and rain-forest birds add to the serenity.

Hilo Hawaiian Hotel (Map p250; ☎ 935-9361, 800-367-5004; www.castleresorts.com; 71 Banyan Dr; r $125/180; 🚫 💻) If you'd prefer a hotel, the Hilo Hawaiian is definitely Hilo's best. Located on scenic Banyan Dr, overlooking Coconut Island, the crescent-shaped building is pleasant and airy. Rooms are comfortable (with TV and phone), and most have a private lanai. There's also the popular Queen's Court restaurant (p262) here.

Uncle Billy's Hilo Bay Hotel (Map p250; ☎ 935-0861, 800-442-5841; www.unclebilly.com; 87 Banyan Dr; r $85/105; 🚫) This Hawaiian-owned hotel is a fixture in Hilo, and though the Polynesian decor is a cliché, the rooms are decent and overlook a pleasant courtyard of palms, red ginger and talkative mynah birds. The adjacent restaurant is popular with senior-citizen breakfast gangs and offers a free nightly hula show at 6pm. You can save over 25% if you book on the Internet.

Hilo Seaside Hotel (Map p250; ☎ 935-0821, 800-560-5557; www.hiloseasidehotel.com; 126 Banyan Dr; r $100-120; 🔀 🥤) A surprisingly sprawling complex of two-story motel-style buildings, the Seaside is good, if you simply want a room and a bit of anonymity. Rooms include air-con, ceiling fan, TV, louvered windows and refrigerator. Avoid those around the swimming pool and the noisy streetside Hukilau wing; better rooms in the deluxe ocean wing have balconies overlooking a carp pond. Internet specials go as low as $62.

EATING
Budget
For real local-style *grinds* (food) or late-night eats, Hilo's casual restaurants are the ticket.

Café 100 (Map p250; ☎ 935-8683; specials hotline 935-6368; 969 Kilauea Ave; loco moco $2-4, plate lunches $4-6; 🕑 6:45am-8:30pm Mon-Sat) This legendary drive-in, named for the Japanese-American WWII 100th Battalion, popularized the *loco moco*, which is rice topped with hamburger, fried egg and a cardiac-arresting amount of brown gravy, and now available in 20 different varieties (including veg).

Nori's Saimin & Snacks (Map p250; ☎ 935-9133; Ste 124, 688 Kino'ole St; noodle soups $4-7; 🕑 11:30am-3pm Mon, 10:30am-3pm & 4pm-midnight Tue-Sat, to 11pm Sun) Despite the strip-mall setting, Nori's is a great place to try Japanese noodle soups such as saimin, *udon*, *ramen* or *soba*. Other specialties include a whole fried-fish plate ($7 to $9) and gift-ready sweets and snacks. The proprietor, Beth-An Nishijima, hosts a cooking show called *Two Skinny Chefs* (a play on restaurateur Sam Choy's 'Never Trust a Skinny Chef' motto) on the local cable channel.

Kuhio Grille (Map p250; ☎ 959-2336; Prince Kuhio Plaza Suite A106; mains $5.50-8.50; 🕑 6am-10pm Sun-Thu, 6am-midnight Fri & Sat) Always packed at local mealtimes, Kuhio Grille is a family-run place known for filling breakfasts, for fried-rice *loco moco* and especially 1lb *laulau* plates ($7) and other Hawaiian favorites such as *poi, lomilomi, kalua* pig and *haupia*. The *laulau* is also available packed for travel. It's behind Prince Kuhio Plaza.

Ken's House of Pancakes (Map p250; ☎ 935-8711; 1730 Kamehameha Ave; meals $6-12; 🕑 24hr) The perfect spot after Mauna Kea stargazing. A family-friendly diner, Ken's offers hundreds of menu combos, including giant Spam omelettes, macadamia-nut pancakes and milkshakes. Dinners such as *kalua* pig and cabbage come with all the trimmings.

SELF-CATERING
In Hilo, your best meals might be the picnics and to-go meals you cobble together yourself. First pick up the freshest raw materials at the extensive **farmers market** (p254), then try **Suisan Fish Market** (Map p250; ☎ 935-9349; 93 Lihiwai St; 🕑 8am-5pm Mon-Sat) for just-caught fish. You can't buy wholesale anymore, due to health regulations, but the retail store sells the whole range plus an *ono* (delicious) selection of *poke*. **O'Keefe & Sons Bread Bakers** (Map p253; ☎ 934-9334; 374 Kino'ole St; snacks $3-7; 🕑 6am-5pm Mon-Fri, to 3pm Sat) bakes gorgeous artisan breads, as well as pastries and sandwiches that will make your mouth water.

For natural foods, the best place in the downtown area is **Abundant Life Natural Foods** (Map p253; ☎ 935-7411; 292 Kamehameha Ave; 🕑 8:30am-7pm Mon, Tue, Thu & Fri, 7am-7pm Wed & Sat, 10am-5pm Sun), which carries the expected cheeses, juices and bulk foods, plus a simple smoothie and sandwich bar. Near the malls toward the airport, **Island Naturals** (Map p250; ☎ 935-5533; Waiakea Center, 303 Ma'akala St; 🕑 8:30am-8pm Mon-Sat, 10am-7pm Sun) is considerably larger and newer (and also a bit more expensive), with a smoothie counter, and a deli serving hot selections such as 'ahi with coconut, vegetarian pad Thai and curries.

By far the best grocer on the Big Island is **KTA Super Store** Downtown (Map p253; ☎ 935-3751; 323 Keawe St; 🕑 7am-9pm, to 6pm Sun); Puainako Town Center (☎ 959-9111; 50 E Puainako St; 🕑 5:30am-midnight). It carries appetizing *bento* such as grilled mackerel or salmon, teriyaki beef or *maki* (rolled) sushi, plus hot selections and an amazing variety of *poke*. But don't go there after mid-morning – all the good stuff is sold out by then!

Mid-Range
Miyo's (Map p250; ☎ 935-2273; Waiakea Village, 400 Hualani St; mains $8-12; 🕑 11am-2pm & 5:30-8:30pm Mon-Sat) On the inland bank of Waiakea Pond, Miyo's resembles a rustic Japanese teahouse. The daily fish specials are excellent and all

HAWAI'I
(THE BIG ISLAND)

mains, from tempura to *tonkatsu* (lean pork cutlets), include fresh baby-lettuce salad, miso soup, rice, pickles and hot tea. Savory tofu and vegetable selections will satisfy any vegetarian. Save room for the homemade ice cream.

Hilo Bay Café (Map p250; ☎ 935-4939; Waiakea Center, 315 Maka'ala; mains $8-12; ☑ 11am-5pm Mon-Sat, 5pm-8:30pm daily) Don't be deterred by the mall environment. Once you're inside, the modern urban decor and gourmet sensibility will make you forget the Wal-Mart outside. The eclectic menu is not only health-conscious (organically grown produce and free-range meats) but also delicious and creative, from foie gras with glazed apples to bacon-infused chicken breast to vegan dishes like coconut tofu kebabs and grilled eggplant Napoleon.

Ocean Sushi Deli (Map p253; ☎ 961-6625; 239 Keawe St; items $1.50-20; ☑ 10am-2:30pm & 4:30-9pm Mon-Sat) It's fantastic: scores of inventive specials include nut rolls made with *'ahi*, avocado and *kukui*, and sushi rolls with *poke* and macadamia nuts. Meat eaters – we dare you to try the plantation roll (with hamburger, onions and gravy). Vegetarian options are also plentiful.

Reuben's (Map p253; ☎ 961-2552; 336 Kamehameha Ave; combination plates $8-9.50; ☑ 11am-9pm Mon-Fri, noon-9pm Sat) Resembling an Oaxaca cantina, with festively painted cinder block, piñatas galore and folding tables and chairs, Reuben's keeps the locals coming back with authentic Mexican fare, including classic enchiladas and rellenos (chilies stuffed with cheese), freshly fried chips, salsa that'll make you speechless, and an unforgettable fish taco-and-tamale combination plate.

Top End
Restaurant Kaikodo (Map p253; ☎ 961-2558; 60 Keawe St; lunch mains $10; dinner mains $22-27; ☑ 11am-2:30pm, 5-9:30pm) The most talked-about restaurant in years, Kaikodo brings a touch of upscale elegance (plus inevitable yuppie-ism) to formerly sleepy Hilo. Executive chef Michael Fennelly is meticulous about both quality and presentation, with inspired dinner entrées such as *'opakapaka* (pink snapper) steamed in lemongrass and sake, and grilled mint-and-pomegranate rack of lamb. For such a lavish setting, however, service can be unpolished. The owners have a Manhattan art gallery, and they've filled the restaurant

> **THE AUTHOR'S CHOICE**
> **Seaside Restaurant** (Map p250; ☎ 935-8825; 1790 Kalaniana'ole Ave; meals $18-24; ☑ 5pm-8:30pm Tue-Thu, to 9pm Fri & Sat) Certainly there are swankier restaurants in Hilo, but if you want urban chic, go to the mainland. In Hilo, try the longtime, family-run Seaside Restaurant, where you know the fish is fresh because the mullet, *aholehole* (flagtail) and other island fish are raised in Hawaiian-style fishponds right outside. The setting is unremarkable, but outdoor tables have a nice view of the aqua-farm. The simple preparation of the fish (steamed in *ti* leaves with lemon and onions) is delicious, with all meals generously including rice, salad, apple pie and coffee.

and banquet rooms with antiques and collectibles; a fine-art museum is in the works.

Café Pesto (Map p253; ☎ 969-6640; 308 Kamehameha Ave; lunch mains $8-12, dinner mains $10-30; ☑ 11am-9pm Sun-Thu, to 10pm Fri & Sat) It's impossible not to like Café Pesto. Located in a beautifully renovated historical building, Pesto uses local ingredients to create inspired dishes, like a seafood risotto featuring Kona lobster tail and charbroiled Kamuela beef tenderloin. There are 10 flavors of crispy-crust pizza, plus numerous vegetarian selections. If you peer through the expansive windowed facade, it looks rather fancy, but the core local crowd is casual and very diverse.

Pescatore (Map p253; ☎ 969-9090; 235 Keawe St; breakfast $4-6, lunch mains $6-12, dinner mains $20; ☑ 11am-2pm & 5:30-9pm Mon-Sat, 7:30-11am Sat & Sun) If you're craving authentic Italian fare, most Big Island 'spaghetti' mains will disappoint. So head to Pescatore for impressive classically prepared seafood and pasta (plus a Little Italy social-club atmosphere).

Queen's Court (Map p250; ☎ 935-9361, 800-367-5004; www.castleresorts.com; Ground Fl, Hilo Hawaiian Motel, 71 Banyan Dr) This restaurant offers a popular Friday seafood dinner buffet ($24.50), along with daily prime-rib dinner buffets.

DRINKING & ENTERTAINMENT
Bars & Nightclubs
Shooters Bar & Grill (Map p250; ☎ 969-7069; 121 Banyan Dr; admission $5, drinks $5-7; ☑ 3pm-2am Mon-Wed, to 3am Thu-Sat) Popular with the local 20-something set, Shooters attracts both locals

and tourists from Banyan Dr. From 10pm, the bar turns into a nightclub with a DJ and dancing. Thursday is 'college night,' permitting 18-to-20 year olds to join the party (no alcohol is served to minors).

Uncle Mikey's Video Dance Club (Map p250; ☎ 933-2667; Waiakea Village, Bldg 22, 400 Hualani St; cover charge $5; 🕒 9pm-1:30am Wed, Fri & Sat) Tucked in a woodsy condo-and-commercial complex, Uncle Mikey's is jammed with 600 people on Saturday nights. DJs play everything from 'old' 1970s tunes to current hits, and Wednesday night is 'college night' (with a separate room for the under-21s).

Uncle Billy's Hilo Bay Hotel (Map p250; ☎ 935-0861; 87 Banyan Dr; live-music & hula show 6-7:30pm & 8-9:30pm) The standard hula show offered during dinnertime at the restaurant (which serves mains comparable to the fare at a low-budget wedding) at least features enthusiastic performers.

Cronies Bar & Grill (Map p253; ☎ 935-5158; 11 Waianuenue Ave; 🕒 11-2am Mon-Sat) One of Hilo's few late-night hangouts, Cronies has an atmosphere about as stimulating as its name, but the live local music and dirt-cheap drink specials are worth checking out.

Cinemas

If the bars and clubs are too much like '80s throwbacks, head to the cinemas. The two located downtown offer a pleasantly old-fashioned atmosphere, while Stadium Cinemas is the shopping-mall standby you'd find anywhere in the USA.

Kress Cinemas (Map p253; ☎ 961-3456; 174 Kamehameha Ave; tickets $1) An atmospheric place to take in a little celluloid (after 6pm you pay only 50¢). It screens standard first-run Hollywood films, as do the **Stadium Cinemas** (☎ 961-3456; Prince Kuhio Plaza, 111 E Puainako St; adult/child/matinee $8/5/5.50).

Palace Theater (Map p253; ☎ 934-7010, box office 934-7777; 38 Haili St; tickets $6) Shows foreign films, documentaries and director's cuts. The local intelligentsia comes out of the woodwork

THERE'S ALWAYS ROOM FOR DESSERT

If you have a sweet tooth, Hilo won't let you down. The best ice cream and sorbet on the island comes from a Kawaihae creamery that produces two equally yummy premium lines: Hilo Homemade (classic single flavors) and Tropical Dreams (novel fusion flavors). Do your own taste test at **Hilo Homemade Ice Cream** (Map p253; ☎ 933-1520; 41 Waianuenue Ave; per scoop $2; 🕒 10:30am-7:30pm Mon-Fri, noon-6pm Sat, to 4pm Sun) and **Tropical Dreams** (Map p253; ☎ 935-9109; 174 Kamehameha Ave; per scoop $2.50; 🕒 9am-6pm Mon-Thu, to 9:30pm Fri & Sat).

For an island take on traditional Japanese *mochi* (sweet rice dessert) and *manju* (baked adzuki bean–filled cake), stop at **Two Ladies Kitchen** (Map p253; ☎ 961-4766; 274 Kilauea Ave; 8-piece boxes $5.60; 🕒 11am-5pm Wed-Sat), where you can find temptingly golden *liliko'i mochi* made with fresh passion fruit, purple sweet-potato *mochi,* and its specialty, fresh strawberries wrapped in a sweet bean paste and *mochi* – all handmade by two Hilo-born ladies.

You haven't tasted buttermilk doughnuts until you've tried the moist, satisfying beauties from **Sputnik's** (Map p250; ☎ 961-2066; 811 Laukapu St; doughnuts 80¢; 🕒 6:30am-2pm Mon-Fri), a third-generation family business. But go before 11am because they bake less than 100 doughnuts daily and they're often sold out by then!

Chocoholics can get their fix from **Big Island Candies** (Map p250; ☎ 935-8890; 800-935-5510; www.bigislandcandies.com; 585 Hinano St; 🕒 8:30am-5pm), a 30-year-old company that produces perhaps the best confections in Hawaii (the chocolate-dipped shortbread is a classic). You'll be tempted to buy everything in the store, and the classy packaging makes for impressive gifts (a big cut above store-bought brands and available only at the factory or online). Free cookie, candy and coffee samples are given as you watch the white-outfitted workers hand-dipping cookies and macadamia nuts in chocolate.

And no visit to Hilo is complete without a stop at **Itsu's Fishing Supplies** (Map p250; ☎ 935-8082; 810 Pi'ilani; snacks under $5; 🕒 5am-5pm) – yes, a fishing-supply store! – which sells Hilo's best ice shave (note: Hilo folks call it 'ice shave,' not 'shave ice') and concession snacks like gravy burgers and hot dogs. The ice shave is neither too fine nor too grainy, and there's no skimping on the dozens of sweet syrups that you have to choose from. And for a real blast from the past, buy a bag of sweetened, colored popcorn ($2.50 to $4.50 per bag).

for special events including concerts, plays and readings.

SHOPPING

Most locals do the bulk of their shopping at **Prince Kuhio Plaza** (Map p250; ☎ 959-3555; 111 E Puainako St; 10am-9pm Mon-Fri, 9:30am-7pm Sat; 10am-6pm Sun), a standard suburban mall located on Hwy 11, just south of Hilo airport. Downtown Hilo makes for much better browsing, with a host of fine galleries and unique boutiques.

Chase Gallery (Map p253; ☎ 934-9101; www .chasedesigns.com; 100 Kamehameha Ave; 11am-5pm Tue-Sat) Exquisite original art including koa furniture, island-influenced sculpture, artistic glass pieces and bronzes.

Sig Zane Designs (Map p253; ☎ 935-7077; 122 Kamehameha Ave; 9am-5pm Mon-Fri, to 4pm Sat) Unique Hawaii attire featuring custom-designed fabrics and styles.

Alan's Art & Collectibles (Map p253; ☎ 969-1554; 202 Kamehameha Ave; 10am-5pm Mon, Wed, Thu & Fri, 1-5pm Tue, to 3pm Sat) Catch a glimpse of Hawaii 'back in the day' amid this eye-popping collection of vintage island artifacts, including

---

CLOWN PRINCESS OF HAWAII

In 1936 Clara Inter was a Hawaiian schoolteacher on a glee-club trip to Canada when she first performed 'Hilo Hattie (Does the Hilo Hop)' to a delighted Canadian crowd. A year later in the Monarch Room at Waikiki's Royal Hawaiian Hotel, Clara approached bandleader (and the song's composer) Don McDiarmid Sr and asked him to play it. McDiarmid wondered whether the 'low-class hula' was appropriate at the ritzy hotel, implying it was a dance that 'no law would allow.'

With a taste of applause under her muu-muu from her Canadian hit, Clara would not be deterred. She convinced him to play the tune and the rest, as they say, is history. Clara Inter rose to international stardom on the wings of this song (with worldwide tours and appearances in movies such as *Song of the Islands* and *Ma & Pa Kettle in Waikiki*), legally changed her name to **Hilo Hattie** (☎ 961-3077; www.hilohattie.com; Prince Kuhio Plaza, cnr Kanoelehua Ave and Maka'ala St; 8:30am-6pm) and eventually lent it to the now-famous chain of Hawaiian stores.

---

glassware, household doodads, plantation-era clothing, aloha shirts and old magazines and records.

Fabric Impressions (Map p253; ☎ 961-4468; 206 Kamehameha Ave; 9:30am-5pm Mon-Fri, to 4:30pm Sat) Wide selection of fabrics, including cotton Hawaiian prints hard to find elsewhere, for clothing and quilts.

Most Irresistible Shop (Map p253; ☎ 935-9644; 256 Kamehameha Ave; 9am-5pm Mon-Fri, to 4pm Sat) This longstanding gift shop lives up to its name, offering handcrafted jewelry, children's books, fragrant soaps and candles, koa objects, artsy greeting cards and much more.

Orchidland Surfboards (Map p253; ☎ 935-1533; 262 Kamehameha Ave; 9am-5pm Mon-Sat, 10am-3pm Sun) A great selection of shorts, swimsuits, rash guards and other gear, plus one-of-a-kind boards in back.

GETTING THERE & AWAY
Air

Although most Big Island visitors fly into the Kona airport, the Hilo airport (p183) is also busy.

Bus

The main Hilo station for the **Hele-On Bus** (☎ 961-8744; www.co.hawaii.hi.us/mass_transit/heleon-bus.html; 7:45am-4:30pm Mon-Fri) is at Mo'oheau terminal (329 Kamehameha Ave). All intra-island buses originate here, and routes go to Waikoloa, Honoka'a, Waimea, Kona, Pahoa, Ka'u and other small towns along the way. See individual destinations in this chapter for details on available routes to/from Hilo.

GETTING AROUND

For directions to/from the airport, see p183.

Bicycle

Getting around by bike is doable, if you don't mind occasional rain showers.

Da Kine Bike Shop (Map p253; ☎ 934-9861; 12 Furneaux Ln; 1-6pm Mon-Sat) Rents $5-a-day rusty cruisers and $50 pro models. It also offers island cycling tours.

Hilo Bike Hub (Map p250; ☎ 961-4452; 318 E Kawili St) Rents cruisers, rock hoppers as well as full-suspension mountain bikes for $20 to $45 per day. Ask about the phenomenal weekly discounts.

Mid-Pacific Wheels (Map p250; ☎ 935-6211; 1133-C Manono St; 9am-6pm Mon-Sat, 11am-5pm Sun) Rents 21-speed bikes for $15 per day.

Car

Hilo is a car-oriented town, so shopping malls and businesses usually have ample parking lots. Downtown, all street parking is free but limited to two hours. On most days, it's easy to find a space, but the entire bayfront area is jammed during the Sunday and Wednesday farmers market (p254).

Public Transport

The Hele-On Bus (p184) has a few intracity routes, all costing 75¢ and operating Monday to Friday only:

No 4 Kaumana Goes five times a day (from 7:35am to 2:20pm) to Hilo Library and Hilo Medical Center (near Rainbow Falls).

No 6 Waiakea-Uka Goes to the University of Hawai'i at Hilo and also Prince Kuhio Plaza and Wal-Mart; to return to Hilo catch the No 7 Downtown Hilo bus.

No 7 Downtown Hilo Goes five times a day (from 8am to 3:05pm) to Prince Kuhio Plaza and Wal-Mart.

Taxi

In Hilo, call **Marshall's Taxi** (☎ 936-2654) or **Percy's Taxi** (☎ 969-7060).

AROUND HILO
Rainbow Falls

Five-minute's drive from Hilo, **Rainbow Falls** is worth seeing for the massive banyan tree alone. You can get a straight-on view of the falls from the lookout in front of the parking lot. The falls are usually seen as a double drop, with the two streams flowing together, before hitting the large pool at the bottom.

Waianuenue, which literally means 'rainbow seen in water,' is the Hawaiian name for this lovely 80ft cascade ringed by palm, ohia and African tulip trees. The gaping cave beneath the falls is fit for a goddess, and is said to have been the home of Hina, mother of Maui. The best time for seeing rainbows is morning, although they're by no means guaranteed – both the sun and mist need to be accommodating.

For a cool little diversion, take the short loop trail, to the left of the falls, that continues for about five minutes past a giant banyan tree, which supports a canopy so thick that it blocks the sun and has roots so vast it swallows children. The jungle trail ends at the water's edge: swimmers and rock hoppers can explore upriver for private aquatic delights. Be prepared for voracious mosquitoes.

Pe'epe'e Falls & Boiling Pots

Up Waianuenue Ave, about 1.5 miles past Rainbow Falls, **Pe'epe'e Falls** drops over a sheer rock face. Water cascades in a series of waterfalls, swirling in bubbling pools (hence the 'boiling pots' name). The viewpoints here are accessible by wheelchair. Swimming is not advised. You'll see locals trekking to the water on a well-beaten path just past the 'No Swimming' sign, but frequent drownings occur.

Kaumana Caves

These caves are actually a large lava tube that was formed by an 1881 lava flow from Mauna Loa. As the flow subsided, the outer edges of the deep lava stream cooled and crusted over to form a tube. When the hot molten lava inside then drained out, these caves were created. The caves are wet, mossy and thickly covered with ferns and impatiens. If you have a flashlight, you might want to explore them. They are signposted, about 3 miles up Kaumana Dr (Hwy 200) on the right, en route to Mauna Kea (p243) via Saddle Rd.

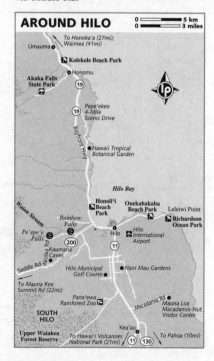

AROUND HILO

0 — 5 km
0 — 3 miles

Mauna Loa Macadamia-Nut Visitor Center

While essentially a 'tourist trap' that caters mainly to bus tours, **Mauna Loa Macadamia-Nut Visitor Center** (Map p265; ☎ 966-8618, 888-628-6256; www.maunaloa.com; Macadamia Rd; ☻ 8:30am-5:30pm) is a decent diversion. On the grounds you'll see a working factory with windows that allow visitors to view the large, fast-paced assembly line, where the nuts are roasted and packaged. The little garden behind the visitors center, with labeled fruit trees and flowering bushes, is worth strolling through, if you've come this far. C Brewer Co, which owns the Mauna Loa company, produces most of Hawaii's macadamia nuts. To get here, turn left off Hwy 11 just over 5 miles south of Hilo. A 2.5-mile access road, Macadamia Rd, then cuts across row after row of macadamia trees, as far as the eye can see.

Nani Mau Gardens

Encompassing more than 20 acres of flowering plants, these rather contrived **gardens** (☎ 959-3500; 421 Makalika St; adult/child $10/6; ☻ 8am-5pm) are another stop on the tour-bus circuit.

Nevertheless, the orderly plots for different flowers (including the hibiscus, anthurium, orchid, bromeliad and gardenia) and fruit trees might impress those unfamiliar with such species. About 3 miles south of Hilo, the turnoff from Hwy 11 onto Makalika St is marked with a small sign.

PUNA

Pocketed with hidden treasures, the Puna district is the easternmost point of the Big Island. Its main attractions all revolve around lava, whether that means black-sand beaches, lava-rock tide pools, ancient forests of lava-tree molds or red-hot molten stuff flowing this way. Kilauea's active East Rift Zone slices clear across Puna. Today Hwy 130 ends abruptly at the 1990 lava flow that buried the village of Kalapana.

While not known for its beaches, an awesome surf spot called Drainpipe near the village of Kalapana was a beacon for expert surfers until the 1990 flow changed the shape of the coastline and obliterated 12

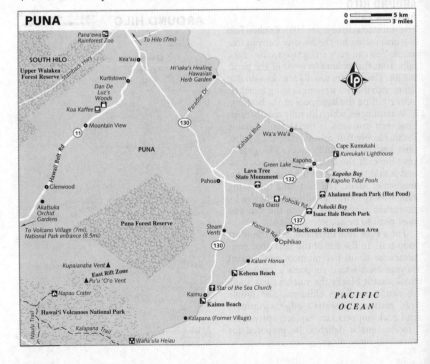

irreplaceable surf breaks. The waters along the coast in Puna are subject to strong currents and dangerous riptides, so it's not for novices.

Today Puna is the fastest growing district in the state, and home prices have doubled and even tripled since the late 1990s. Most newcomers are mainlanders, many of whom are gay. It's a maverick district, well represented by hippies, Hawaiian sovereignty activists and *pakalolo* growers. Police raids, aerial sprayings and infrared surveillance have not prevented marijuana harvests, and Puna remains the Big Island's pot capital. Other crops also thrive in lava, and here you'll find the best anthuriums, papayas and prize-winning orchids.

The sultry air and hang-loose attitude makes Puna a great place to ditch your guidebook and poke around. For a few sights mentioned in this section, you'll pass 'No Trespassing' signs that folks seem to ignore, but do respect landowners if you're on private property and you're asked to leave.

From Hwy 11, the first town in Puna is Kea'au. If you continue southwest along Hwy 11, you pass a few small towns before reaching Hawai'i Volcanoes National Park (p271). From Kea'au, Hwy 130 (also known as Kea'au-Pahoa Rd, Pahoa-Kalapana Rd and Kalapana Hwy) goes south to Pahoa and continues almost to the coast, ending at Kaimu and Kalapana, which was buried under the 1990 lava flow.

KEA'AU

Formerly known as Ola'a, Kea'au is the main town in Puna. While Kea'au's population is only 2000, it serves the burgeoning nearby subdivisions: Hawaiian Paradise Park, Hawaiian Beaches, Hawaiian Acres and Orchidland Estates. The **Kea'au Shopping Center**, off Hwy 11 at the main crossroads, has a post office, a laundry and ATM. Across the street is the island's cheapest gas station.

Hi'iaka's Healing Hawaiian Herb Garden (☎ 966-6126; www.hiiakas.com; 15-1667 2nd St, Hawaiian Paradise Park; adult/senior & child $10/8, with guided tour $15/10; ☺ 1-5pm Tue, Thu & Sat) is a lovingly tended acre of Hawaiian, Western and ayurvedic herbs set in a sprawling dirt-road subdivision southeast of town. The good-humored herbalist here sells tinctures, teaches workshops and rents out a fully equipped **cottage** (s/d $50/75).

Feel hungry? **Keaau Natural Foods** (☎ 966-8877; Keaau Shopping Center, 16-586 Old Volcano Rd; ☺ 8:30am-8pm Mon-Fri, to 7pm Sat, 9:30am-5pm Sun) is convenient. For a sit-down meal, **Charley's Bar & Grill** (☎ 966-7589; Keaau Shopping Center, 16-586 Old Volcano Rd; pub grub $5-10; ☺ 11am-midnight Mon & Tue, to 2am Wed-Sat, 9-1am Sun) serves decent burgers, pizza and ice-cold beers, and offers **live music** (admission $3), which attracts folks all the way from Hilo, from Thursday to Saturday nights.

Verna's Drive Inn (☎ 966-9288; 16-566 Hwy 130; snacks $2.50-7.50; ☺ 6am-10pm) is the original of four Verna's locations islandwide, serving the same artery-clogging-but-popular breakfasts and plate lunches.

Mountain View

For more sleeping options than Kea'au, check out nearby Mountain View, further southeast along Hwy 11.

Pineapple Park (☎ 968-8170, 800-865-2266; www.pineapple-park.com; dm $20, r without/with bathroom $45/$85) is very basic but it's a soothingly quiet escape. Amenities include a big guest kitchen, laundry facilities, common room with TV, VCR and pool table, plus outdoor horseshoes and badminton. Pineapple Park has a sister hostel in Captain Cook on the Kona Coast (p204).

Just across the way, **Bed & Breakfast Mountain View** (☎ 968-6868, 888-698-9896; www.bbmtview.com; r with breakfast $55-95) offers clean, peaceful rooms in the home of two well-known Big Island artists, Jane and Linus Chao. At the 4-acre estate, there is a sprawling lawn and custom-made fishpond filled with mullet.

PAHOA
pop 1000

Deep in Puna's heart, Pahoa is a ragamuffin town with raised wooden sidewalks, cowboy architecture and an untamed bohemian edge. It is caught in a wrinkle in time, where alternative vibes left over from the 1960s mix with the beeps of ATMs.

Orientation & Information

Roads in and around Pahoa are known by many names. For example, the main road through town is signposted as Pahoa Village Rd but also called Government Main Rd, Old Government Rd, Main St, Puna Rd and Pahoa Rd – but Hwy 130 is also known as Pahoa Rd!

In town you'll find a convenience store, banks and a **post office** (☎ 965-1158; 15-2859 Pahoa Village Rd; ☯ 8:30am-4pm Mon-Fri, 11am-2pm Sat). In the Pahoa Village Center, **Pahoa Home Video** (☎ 965-1199; 15-2872 Pahoa Village Rd; ☯ 9am-8pm Mon-Thu, to 9pm Fri & Sat, 11am-8pm Sun) sells new and used Hawaiiana books, local activity guides and maps.

Sights & Activities

At Pahoa's weekend **farmers market** (☯ 8am Sat & Sun) you can sip a cup of kava, indulge in a massage or palm reading, buy quality used books and organic goat cheese or boogie to a local band well into the afternoon. It's best to ask around for the exact location.

Sleeping & Eating

Pahoa Orchid Inn (☎ 965-9664; www.pahoaorchidinn .com; 15-2942B Pahoa Village Rd; r with shared bathroom $40-50, r $60) In a historic wooden building smack in the heart of town (right above Luquin's), the inn offers small but nicely furnished antique-filled rooms arranged around an inner lanai. Most have cable TV.

Pahoa Natural Groceries (☎ 965-8322; 15-1403 Pahoa Village Rd; ☯ 7:30am-7:30pm Mon-Sat, to 6pm Sun) This is a nexus for Pahoa's hippie-and-healthy contingent. Don't miss the satisfying sandwiches and hot-food bar ($6 per pound).

Luquin's Mexican Restaurant (☎ 965-9990; 15-2942 Pahoa Village Rd; mains $8-15; ☯ 7am-9pm) This Pahoa institution can't be beat for hanging out and talking story, but do locals think this is real Mexican food? Never you mind. The atmosphere and cocktail bar let you check out a slice of life, Puna style.

Paolo's Bistro (☎ 965-7033; Pahoa Village Rd; mains $10-20; ☯ 5:30-9pm Tue-Sun) Paolo's offers decent Northern Italian fare in an intimate atmosphere, but the waitstaff can get overwhelmed quickly. Save room (and time) for dessert.

Pahoa's Village Café (☎ 965-0072; 15-2471 Pahoa Village Rd; mains $8; ☯ 8am-8pm Wed-Sat, to 2pm Tue & Sun) It has a pleasant café atmosphere with delicious custom omelets, organic waffles and ample veggie sandwiches with Brie, plus steak and prime rib for meat eaters.

Drinking & Entertainment

Pahoa nightlife is nonexistent, except when a special event flares up. **Full-moon parties** exemplify events that run under the radar. Locals know what's happening, so ask around.

TOP FIVE ENTERTAINMENT SPOTS

- **Kahilu Theatre** (p234) – world-class music and dance performances
- **Kona Village Resort luau** (p217) – taste of ancient Hawaii
- **Parker Ranch Grill** (p234) – rousing local jam sessions
- **Lava Zone** (see below) – casual gay-friendly, tourist-friendly hangout
- **Palace Theater** (p263) – venue for artsy and indie films

---

For hanging out, **Lava Zone** (☎ 965-2222; 15-2929 Pahoa Village Rd; ☯ noon-midnight Sun-Thu, to 2am Fri & Sat) is a lively, eclectic bar with outdoor pool tables and a mixed gay-and-straight crowd. It alternates between karaoke, DJ music and live bands, and the bartenders are great sources on local secret spots.

Getting There & Away

The Hele-On Bus (p184) goes from Hilo to Kea'au and Pahoa on the No 9 Pahoa route ($2.25, one hour).

LAVA TREE STATE MONUMENT

The approach to this, through a tight-knit canopy of monkeypod trees, is like a dreamscape. Once inside the **park**, a 20-minute trail loops through thickets of bamboo and orchids, past 'lava trees' created in 1790, when a rain forest was engulfed in *pahoehoe* from Kilauea's East Rift Zone. A flood of lava up to 10ft deep flowed through the forest, enveloping moisture-laden ohia trees and then receding. The lava hardened around the trees, which themselves burned away, creating molds of lava that remain today. In this 'ghost forest' of lava shells, you'll see some 10ft high and others so short you can peer down into the ferns and frogs sheltered inside their hollows. Be careful if you walk off the path, as in places the ground is crossed by deep cracks, some hidden by new vegetation.

Recently much of the dense foliage was woefully thinned when locals tried to eradicate the proliferating coqui frog and other invasive species. To get here, follow Hwy 132 about 2.5 miles east of Hwy 130.

KARL LEHMANN

Lava from Hawai'i's Kilauea Caldera (p271) flows into the Pacific Ocean under a full moon

The road to Akaka Falls (p242) passes through the old sugar town of Honomu, the Big Island

ANN CECIL

ERIC L WHEATER

East Hawai'i's lush interior is thick with rain forests and waterfalls (p249)

Outrigger canoe on the sand at Pu'uhonua o Honaunau National Historical Park (p209), the Big Island

ANN CE

NED FRIARY

View from Pololu Valley (p229), the Big Island

Offerings to the goddess of snow Poliahu, and the astronomical observatories at Mauna Kea Summit (p244), the Big Island

KARL LEHMA

KAPOHO

Hwy 132 heads east through orchards of papaya and thick ohia forest to Kapoho, a former farming town of about 300 people. The old lighthouse is less than 2 miles down a dirt road east of 'Four Corners,' where Hwys 132 and 137 intersect.

On January 13, 1960, a fissure opened and a half-mile-long curtain of fire shot up in the midst of a sugarcane field just above Kapoho. The main flow of *pahoehoe* lava ran toward the ocean but a slower moving offshoot of *'a'a* lava crept toward the town, burying orchid farms in its path. Two weeks later, the lava entered Kapoho and buried the town. A hot-springs resort and nearly 100 homes and businesses disappeared beneath the flow.

Amazingly, when the lava approached the sea at **Cape Kumukahi**, it parted into two flows around the lighthouse, sparing it from destruction. Cape Kumukahi, which means 'first beginning' in Hawaiian, is the easternmost point in the state. Breathe deeply: the air here is among the verifiably freshest in the world.

RED ROAD (HIGHWAY 137)

Near sea level, Hwy 137 (the Kalapana to Kapoho Beach road) passes under a canopy of milo and *hala* (pandanus) trees that are so dense they create a tunnel effect. The pleasantly winding highway is nicknamed Red Rd because it's paved with red cinder in its northern stretch.

Green Lake

Placid green waters surrounded by breadfruit, guava, avocado and rustling bamboo plants make this freshwater crater **lake** seem ideal for swimming but beware: the water is stagnant. In spite of this, people can't seem to resist this clothing-optional swimming hole. To get here, park just after the 8-mile marker, opposite the unmarked Kapoho Beach Rd. On the inland side of the road, you'll see a locked gate marked 'Keep Out.' You can, however, enter from an unlocked entrance on the right. Once inside, walk along the grassy road for five minutes, always bearing right. Once you pass between the garden and homestead, the downhill path turns muddy and overgrown. It's slippery toward the bottom, where the lake sits prettily.

Kapoho Tide Pools

Spend a lazy afternoon exploring the sprawling network of **tide pools** formed in Kapono's lava-rock coastline. Some pools are deep enough for snorkeling (except during low tide). Rich spots are on the windward side, with coral gardens supporting saddle wrasses, Moorish idols, butterfly fish, sea urchins and cucumbers.

The nearby houses form the Kapoho Vacationland subdivision, where all everyone seems to have a swimming pool. To get here, turn off Hwy 137 a mile south of the lighthouse onto Kapoho Kai Dr, then left at the end on Wai Opae, and park near the house festooned with found art objects and coconut shells.

Ahalanui Beach Park

Known simply as 'the hot pond' to locals, the star attraction is a spring-fed **thermal pool** set in lava rock. It's deep enough for swimming, with water temperatures averaging around 90°F. The pool has an inlet to the ocean, which pounds upon the seawall on the *makai* side of the pool, bringing in many tropical fish during high tide and keeping the water clean. Nighttime soaks under the moon and stars are also a possibility.

The park has picnic tables, pit toilets and a lifeguard. There's plenty of parking, but, as always, don't leave valuables in your car.

Isaac Hale Beach Park

Isaac Hale Beach (*ha*-lay) at Pohoiki Bay is mainly a locals' hangout. On weekends, there's usually a frenzy of local activity, with family picnics and fishing. Local kids like to swim inside the breakwater near the boat ramp, which is the only place to launch in Puna. Surfers find breaks toward the south, but they're for experts only due to rough conditions and tons of *wana* everywhere. Soaking fans are in for a treat as there's a small hot pond hiding in the growth along the shore. To reach this 10ft oasis, pick up the beaten path just beyond the house decked with 'No Trespassing' signs.

The park has toilets, but no drinking water or showers. **Camping** is allowed (see p178 for information on permits), but it's not a very attractive option, as the campground is virtually in the parking lot and subject to long-term squatters.

Pohoiki Road

As you veer around the bend along Red Rd, you have the option of staying straight on **Pohoiki Rd**, a good shortcut to Pahoa. Yet another of Puna's shaded, mystical roads, Pohoiki Rd winds through thick forest dotted with papaya orchards and wild *noni* (Indian mulberry).

Yoga Oasis (☎ 965-8460, 800-274-4446; www.yoga oasis.org; 13-678 Pohoiki Rd; s/d $75/100, cabins $100-145) For a personalized retreat experience, Yoga Oasis is the ticket. On average, there are just eight to 12 guests (the maximum is 18), and the 26-acre retreat center is sprawling and utterly secluded. All rates include daily yoga and an organic breakfast. Finely furnished rooms share a spectacular marble bath, while the cabins have equally impressive private facilities. The founder, a yogi since 1972, is a professional acrobat who studied mime with Marcel Marceau and Etienne Decroux. He is also trained in Tibetan Buddhism and Thai massage; retreats are offered monthly. To get here, keep your eyes peeled for a driveway on your left, 2 miles up from Red Rd, with colorful flags over the driveway and a yellow fire hydrant on the opposite side.

MacKenzie State Recreation Area

Set in a grove of ironwood trees, this **park** is eerily quiet and secluded. There's no beach here, only dramatic 40ft cliffs and pounding surf far below. It's a peaceful picnic spot, but crime has been a problem here, however, and locals tend to steer clear.

Camping is allowed with a state permit (p178), but facilities are shabby, trash cans are often overflowing and drinking water is unavailable.

Opihikao

The village of Opihikao is marked by a little Congregational church and a handful of houses.

Kalani Oceanside Retreat (☎ 965-7828, 800-800-6886; www.kalani.com; tent sites $20, r & cottage d $105-155, tree house s/d $210/240) Located between the 17- and 18-mile markers, Kalani is the Big Island's largest New Age retreat center, offering a range of yoga, meditation, dance, adventure and alternative-healing classes and workshops. The setting feels like a casual resort, with a café, a 25m swimming pool, a sauna and Jacuzzis (clothing optional after 5pm). Many programs are geared exclusively to gay guests. The **dining room** serves healthy buffet-style meals (mostly veg with fish and chicken options) and is open to anyone who drops by.

Kehena Beach

At the base of a cliff, this **black-sand beach** was created by a 1955 lava flow. Shaded by coconut and ironwood trees, it's a free-spirited, nude sunbathing spot that attracts a mixed crowd of hippies, Hawaiians, families and seniors. On Sunday it pulsates to the beat of an open drum circle. Nearby subdivisions (Puna Beach Palisades, Kalapana Seaview Estates and Kehena Beach Estates) are budding gay communities.

Even when it rains in Pahoa, it's usually sunny here. In the morning, it's not unusual for dolphins to venture close to shore. When the water is calm, swimming is usually safe, but mind the currents and undertows. Good, strong swimmers die at Kehena every year, especially in winter. Do not venture beyond the rocky point at the southern end.

Kehena is on Red Rd, immediately south of the 19-mile marker. Look for the little parking lot on the right, and you'll see the path down to the beach; it's a five-minute walk over jagged lava rock. Don't leave any valuables in your car.

Kalapana (Former Village)

For years, the village of Kalapana sat precariously downshore of Kilauea's restless East Rift Zone. When the latest series of eruptions began in 1983, the main lava flow moved downslope west of Kalapana. However, lava flows are quick to change direction, and it changed course toward Kalapana in 1990. It's also believed that the earlier flow had passed through a series of lava tubes, which shunted the molten lava toward the sea. But during pauses in the 1990 eruption, the lava tubes to the ocean had cooled long enough to harden and block up. Thus when the eruption resumed, the flow was redirected toward Kalapana. By the end of 1990 most of the village, including 100 homes, was buried.

Today Hwy 137 ends abruptly at **Kaimu Beach** on the eastern edge of what used to be Kalapana. Formerly Hawai'i's most famous black-sand beach, Kaimu is now buried under a sea of hardened lava that flowed clear into the bay. A few houses were spared,

DETOUR: HIGHWAY 11 TO VOLCANO

Why stop along the highway from Kea'au to Hawai'i Volcanoes National Park? No reason unless you want to see sleek koa bowls and eye-popping orchids, and sample tried-and-true 'stone cookies.' The stops along the villages of Kurtistown, Mountain View and Glenwood might not be major, but this is the real Big Island.

Just after the 12-mile marker, **Dan De Luz's Woods** (☎ 968-6607; Hwy 11; 🕑 9am-5pm) sells hand-turned bowls, platters and furniture made by a master craftsman from native hardwoods, including koa, sandalwood, mango and banyan. Adjacent **Koa Kaffee** (☎ 968-1129; Hwy 11; 🕑 5am-8pm Wed-Mon, to 2pm Tue) is a home-style diner cooking up excellent Portuguese bean soup and hearty breakfasts.

If you want to stock up on treats for the road, **Mountain View Bakery** (☎ 968-6353; Old Volcano Rd; 🕑 7:30-11am Thu, to 1pm Sat), near the 14-mile marker, bakes glazed doughnuts that put Krispy Kreme to shame, along with its iconic 'stone cookies' ($4.50 per bag). Yes, they are rock hard but now come in original, soft, extra-crispy and chocolate-chip flavors! The bakery's only open twice a week.

Though just another conventional tour-bus stop, **Akatsuka Orchid Gardens** (☎ 967-8234, 888-967-6669; www.akatsukaorchid.com; Hwy 11; admission free; 🕑 8:30am-5pm) is also the best place to order orchids that can be shipped to your door (cut flowers $30 to $40, plants $40 to $54). Inside the store, cattleyas, dendrobiums and phelonopsis orchids are perennially in bloom. It's halfway between the 22- and 23-mile markers.

including **Uncle Robert's** (admission by donation), where you can take a nature walk and peruse photos of the devastating volcanic event.

Tourist buses arrive constantly here, and a handful of shops and a branch of **Verna's Drive Inn** (☎ 965-8234; burgers/plate lunches $2/6; 🕑 10am-5pm), at the end of Hwy 137, have joined Uncle Robert's. From here, a 10-minute walk across lava leads to a new **black-sand beach**. At the end of the flow, the *pahoehoe* turns to coarse granules and hundreds of baby coconut palms form a natural promenade to the sea. The lonely beach is only an apostrophe of sand. Wear shoes, otherwise glass-sharp lava shards will cut your feet. While the walk is easy, the midday sun is punishing.

HIGHWAY 130

Red Rd intersects Hwy 130 (Old Kalapana Rd), which leads north to Pahoa. Along the highway, at the 20-mile marker, you'll see **Star of the Sea Church**, a tiny 1929 Catholic church, noted for its interior trompe l'oeil murals that give visitors the impression of being in a large cathedral. The style is primitive, but the illusion of depth amazingly effective. Even if it's locked, you're free to walk up and peek at the interior through the front windows. The church will eventually become a community cultural center.

At the 15-mile marker, roughly 3.5 miles south of Pahoa, a big blue 'Scenic View'

highway sign points into the undergrowth. There's absolutely zilch to view, unless you know what you're looking for: puffs of steam from several low spatter cones signaling **natural steam baths**. Follow the well-beaten track for a few minutes, taking the right fork for a two-person sauna with wooden planks. Further back there's a much-larger hollow that can accommodate a few people lying down. Beware of bugs, including hundreds of voracious cockroaches after dark. In spite of this, it's relaxing and – in the spirit of Puna – clothing is optional.

HAWAI'I VOLCANOES NATIONAL PARK

Hawai'i Volcanoes National Park (HAVO) is unique among US national parks. The huge preserve contains two active volcanoes and terrain ranging from tropical beaches to the subarctic Mauna Loa summit. The centerpiece is steaming Kilauea Caldera, at the summit of the youngest and most active volcano on earth.

The landscape is phenomenal, with dozens of craters and cinder cones, hills piled high with pumice, and hardened oceans of lava. Here and there, amid the bone-cracking lava, are *kipuka* (rain forests and fern groves

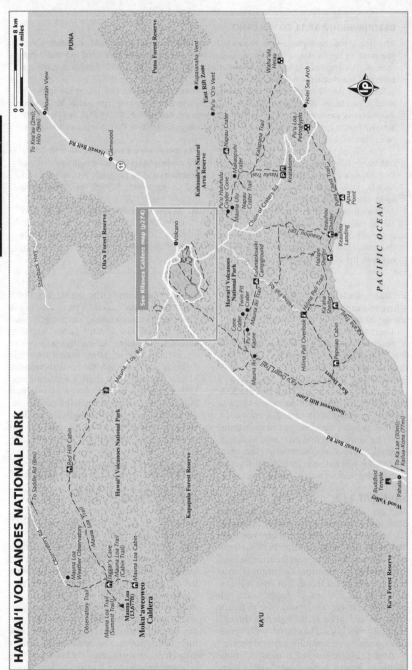

HAWAI'I VOLCANOES NATIONAL PARK

HAWAI'I (THE BIG ISLAND)

See Kīlauea Caldera map (p274)

spared by lava flows) and other oases that have since grown over them, all protected habitats for native bird species.

The park is one of Hawai'i's best places for camping and hiking. It has 140 miles of amazingly varied hiking trails, and both drive-up campsites and backcountry camping. HAVO encompasses roughly 333,000 acres of land – more than the entire island of Moloka'i – and it's still growing, as lava pouring from Kilauea has added more than 600 acres in the past 15 years.

Kilauea's East Rift Zone has been erupting since 1983, destroying everything in its path. The coastal road to Puna was blocked by lava in 1987. The Wahaula Visitor Center on the south coast was buried the next year, and the entire village of Kalapana disappeared under lava in 1990. Since that time, the flows have crept further west, engulfing Kamoamoa Beach in 1994, and later claiming an additional mile of road and most of sacred Wahaula Heiau.

The current series of eruptions has spewed out more than 2.5 billion cu yd of lava. Central to the action is the Pu'u 'O'o Vent, a smoldering cone in the northeastern section of the park. Although many visitors expect to see geyserlike fountains of lava, this is certainly the exception rather than the rule. Hawai'i's shield volcanoes lack the explosive gases of those that dramatically spew ash or lava into the air. Here lava is hotter and more fluid, so it mostly oozes and creeps along. In Hawai'i, people generally run *to* volcanoes, not away from them. When Pele sends up curtains of fire, bright red spattering and flaming lava orbs, cars stream in from all directions.

Don't visit the park with a set idea of what you'll see. Lava flows are unpredictable, and your vantage point depends on current volcanic activity. From near the end of Chain of Craters Rd, you might see slight ribbons of lava pouring into the sea or only steam clouds billowing above. Once the sun is down, you might see the mountainside glow red in the night sky.

ORIENTATION

The park's main road is Crater Rim Dr, which circles the moonscape of Kilauea Caldera. You can buzz through the drive-up sites in an hour – and if that's all you have time for, it's unquestionably worth it.

The park's other scenic drive is Chain of Craters Rd, which leads south 20 miles to the coast, ending at the site of the most recent lava activity. Allow about three hours down and back, with stops along the way.

While you can get a feel for the place in a full day, you'll probably want more time to explore this vast and varied park. Escaping the crowds is often as simple as leaving your car in the nearest lot. Some of the sites and shorter trails are accessible by wheelchair.

The village of Volcano, a mile east of the park, is a mystical place of giant ferns, giant *sugi* (Japanese evergreen) and ohia trees full of puffy red blossoms. The cool mist and pristine air are invigorating, and many artists seclude themselves here.

Maps

Blame Mother Nature, but topographical maps can't keep up with the park's dynamic landscape. National Geographic's *Trails Illustrated Hawaii Volcanoes National Park* is a large-format, prefolded, waterproof and rip-resistant topographic hiking map. It covers the most popular hiking and wilderness areas and adds features of special interest, such as campsites and trail distances. For specific hikes, the USGS 1:24,000 maps *Kilauea*, *Volcano* and *Ka'u Desert* are also helpful. But remember that all maps are likely to be outdated, especially when it comes to hiking trails in the active rift zones.

A free full-color visitors guide, containing basic driving maps, is given out at the park entrance station. While these maps are meant for navigating around by car, they also outline the park's major networks of hiking trails, showing important trailheads, key junctions and distances. Topographic detail is lacking, but it's just barely enough to keep most hikers from getting lost.

INFORMATION

The **park** (☎ 985-6000; www.nps.gov/havo; 7-day pass per car $10, per person on foot, bicycle or motorcycle $5) never closes. An annual HAVO pass costs only $20, and the toll station also sells annual national-parks passes ($50).

Rangers at the park's **Kilauea Visitor Center** (Map p274; ☎ 985-6017; ☼ 7:45am-5pm) provide updates on volcanic activity and backcountry trail conditions. They have free pamphlets for a few of the park trails, and sell an excellent selection of books and videos

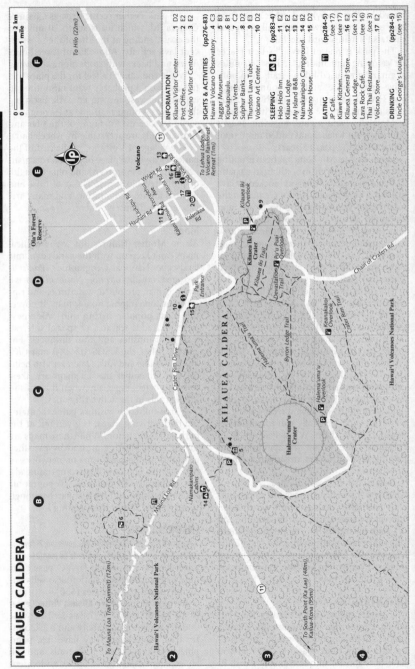

KILAUEA CALDERA

INFORMATION
Kilauea Visitor Center....................1	D2
Post Office.....................................2	E2
Volcano Visitor Center...................3	E2

SIGHTS & ACTIVITIES   (pp276-83)
Hawaii Volcano Observatory..........4	C3
Jaggar Museum..............................5	B3
Kipukapuaulu................................6	B1
Steam Vents..................................7	C2
Sulphur Banks...............................8	D2
Thurston Lava Tube.......................9	E3
Volcano Art Center......................10	D2

SLEEPING   🄰 🄰
Holo Holo Inn..............................11	E2
Kilauea Lodge...............................12	E2
My Island B&B..............................13	E2
Namakanipaio Campground.........14	B2
Volcano House..............................15	D2

EATING   🄰   (pp284-5)
JP Café....................................(see 17)	
Kiawe Kitchen.............................16	E2
Kilauea General Store..............(see 12)	
Kilauea Lodge..........................(see 16)	
Lava Rock Café.........................(see 3)	
Thai Thai Restaurant...................17	E2
Volcano Store.........................(see 15)	

DRINKING   (pp284-5)
Uncle George's Lounge............(see 15)	

on volcanoes, flora and hiking. Ask about guided walks and the fun junior-ranger program for kids. There's also a 24-hour ATM here.

The park's **hotline** (☎ 985-6000; ☽ 24hr) tells you what the volcanoes are doing that day, and where to best view the action. Updates on eruptions, weather conditions and road closures are available at 530AM on your radio. During periods of prolonged drought, both Mauna Loa Rd and Hilina Pali Rd are subject to closure due to fire-hazard conditions. Drivers should note that the nearest gas is in Volcano village.

Get a **recorded weather forecast** (☎ 961-5582): the park has a range of climatic conditions that vary with elevation. Chilly rain, wind and fog typify the moody weather; on any given day it can change from hot and dry to a soaking downpour in a flash. Near Kilauea Caldera, temperatures average 15°F cooler than in Kona. Add a layer of long pants and a jacket, just in case.

In Volcano village, there's a small, unmanned **Volcano Visitor Center** (Map p274; Volcano Rd; ☽ 8am-5pm) in front of Thai Thai restaurant, but it offers just racks of glossy tourist brochures. Nearby is the tiny **post office** (Map p274; ☎ 967-7611; 19-4030 Old Volcano Rd; ☽ 7:30am-3:30pm Mon-Fri, 11am-noon Sat).

DANGERS & ANNOYANCES

Several violently explosive eruptions are known to have occurred at Kilauea, but the most recent was in 1924. Fatalities are rare but they do happen. Most recent deaths happened because people ventured too close to the flow – onto unstable 'benches' of new land that collapse, or near steam explosions where lava is flowing into the ocean. Other potential hazards include deep cracks in the earth and thin lava crusts, which mask hollows and unstable lava tubes.

For you own safety, follow the rules: stay on marked trails and take all park warning signs seriously. Don't venture off on your own, as you're almost certain to get lost. Watch your step on undulating terrain; if you fall, you'll definitely suffer abrasions from the glass-sharp lava rock.

Another hazard, if lava reaches the sea, is the toxic cocktail of sulfuric and hydrochloric acid, as well as minute glass particles. Everyone should take care, but especially those with respiratory and heart conditions, pregnant women and those with infants or young children. High concentrations of sulfuric fumes (which smell like rotten egg) permeate the air at Halema'uma'u Overlook and Sulphur Banks.

If you're hiking, it's important to come prepared: wear hiking shoes, long pants and a hat, if you're planning to walk over lava rock. Park officials are often amused, if not exasperated, when tourists show up in tanks and 'rubbah slippah,' or wrapped in beach towels. Drink lots of water, as dehydration is another common-but-preventable malady.

NO NO'S AT THE VOLCANO

We've all heard about folks who pocket chunks of Pele's lava, only to regret it when bad luck strikes them once they're home. Park officials receive countless boxes of lava rock, along with handwritten tales of woe, mailed back by visitors. Some pay up to $50 in postage! Hawaiians discount the bad-luck myth but emphasize that it is indeed disrespectful to take lava souvenirs without Pele's permission. Regardless, it is illegal to remove anything from a national park, so whatever your superstition quotient, don't touch the rocks. This also goes for the *ahu* (rock cairns) along the trails – don't remove any or build more.

Likewise, don't leave anything around Kilauea Caldera either. Traditionally Hawaiians did leave plants and fish as offerings to Pele. More recently, however, bottles of gin have appeared – apparently following the example of George Lycurgus, the owner of Volcano House during the early 20th century. Many Southeast Asians, who have adopted Pele as their goddess, burn incense and throw 'hell money' and pigs' heads into the caldera. Anonymous locals leave 'rock *laulau*' – a rock wrapped in *ti* leaves to resemble the Hawaiian dish – at trailhead and historical sites, though the gesture holds absolutely no traditional significance. Park visitors have also started leaving white coral 'graffiti' on black lava rock, imitating what you see along Hwy 19 in Kona.

To rangers, such offerings are just litter – a case of 'monkey see, monkey do.' Take the high road and leave no trace of yourself at the park.

The park service suggests each person carry a minimum of a quart of water, a flashlight with extra batteries, binoculars, a first-aid kit and sunscreen.

SIGHTS
Crater Rim Drive   Map p274

Many HAVO sights are conveniently located along Crater Rim Dr, an amazing 11-mile loop road that skirts the rim of Kilauea Caldera, and has marked stops at steam vents and smoking crater lookouts. Natural forces have rerouted the drive more than a few times. Earthquakes in 1975 and 1983 rattled it hard enough to knock sections of road down into the caldera. Quakes come with the territory: there are more than 1200 earthquakes of measurable magnitude on this island every week. If you take Crater Rim Dr in a counterclockwise direction, you'll start off at the visitors center. Unlike the Chain of Craters Rd, Crater Rim Dr is relatively level, making it a good road for cyclists.

KILAUEA VISITOR CENTER

Inside the park visitors center (p273) is a tiny **theater** showing (on the hour from 9am to 4pm) a free 20-minute film on Kilauea Volcano. Footage typically includes flowing rivers of lava, and some of the most spectacular lava fountains ever to be caught on film. Commercial videos of recent eruptions run continuously in the center's equally small **museum**, where volcano-related exhibits are due to be upgraded.

Restrooms, water fountains and pay phones are found outside.

VOLCANO ART CENTER

Next door to the visitors center, inside the 1877 Volcano House lodge, this **gallery shop** (☎ 967-7565; www.volcanoartcenter.org; ⏱ 9am-5pm) sells high-quality island pottery, paintings, woodwork, sculpture, jewelry, Hawaiian quilts and more. Many are one-of-a-kind items, and it's worth a visit just to admire the workmanship. The nonprofit arts organization that runs the gallery also puts together craft and cultural workshops, music concerts, plays and dance recitals, all listed in its free monthly *Volcano Gazette*.

SULPHUR BANKS

Next up is Sulphur Banks, where piles of steaming rocks come in shades of yellow

and orange. This is one of many areas where Kilauea lets off steam, releasing hundreds of tons of sulfuric gases daily. As the steam reaches the surface, it deposits sulfur, which crystallizes in fluorescent yellow around the mouths of the vents. The pervasive smell of rotten eggs is from the hydrogen sulfide wafting from the vents. Don't breathe deeply! Other gases in the toxic cocktail include carbon dioxide and sulfur dioxide.

STEAM VENTS

There are a few nonsulfurous steam vents at the next pull-off, though they're puny compared to the sulfur banks nearby. Rainwater that percolates into the earth is heated by the hot rocks below, and released upward as steam. More interesting is the two-minute walk beyond the vents, out to a part of the crater rim aptly called **Steaming Bluff**. Go early in the morning because the steam is impressive only when the air is cool.

JAGGAR MUSEUM

This small, one-room **museum** (☎ 985-6049; ⏱ 8:30am-5pm) has real-time seismographs and tiltmeters, a mural of the Hawaiian pantheon and a short history of the museum's founder, Dr Thomas A Jaggar.

It's worth stopping, if only for the fine view of Pele's house, at Halema'uma'u Crater. Sitting within Kilauea Caldera, it's sometimes referred to as the 'crater within the crater.' Detailed interpretive plaques at the lookout explain the geological workings of volcanoes. When the weather is clear, there's a rapturous view of Mauna Loa to the west, 20 miles away.

Drivers should be careful of the endangered nene that congregate in the parking lot. Feeding them contributes to the road deaths of these endangered birds, and is strictly prohibited. After leaving the museum, you'll pass the **Southwest Rift**, where you can stop and take a look at the wide fissure slicing across the earth, from caldera summit out to the coast and under the ocean floor.

HALEMA'UMA'U OVERLOOK

For at least a hundred years (from 1823, when missionary William Ellis first recorded the sight in writing), Halema'uma'u was a boiling lake of lava, overflowing its banks and then receding.

This fiery lake has enchanted travelers from all over the world. Some observers compared it to the fires of hell, while others saw primeval creation. Of staring down at it, Mark Twain wrote:

Circles and serpents and streaks of lightning all twined and wreathed and tied together...I have seen Vesuvius since, but it was a mere toy, a child's volcano, a soup kettle, compared to this.

In 1924 the floor of Halema'uma'u subsided rapidly, causing groundwater to react with hot lava rock, touching off a series of explosive eruptions. Boulders and mud rained down for days. When it was over, the crater had doubled in size (to about 300ft deep and 3000ft wide) and lava activity ceased. The crust has since cooled, although the pungent smell of sulfur persists.

The last time Halema'uma'u erupted, on April 30, 1982, geologists at the Hawaiian Volcano Observatory watched as their seismographs and tiltmeters went haywire in early morning, warning of an imminent eruption. The park service quickly closed off Halema'uma'u Trail and cleared hikers from the crater floor. Before noon a half-mile fissure broke open in the crater and began spewing out 1.3 million cu yd of lava – and nothing since.

All of the Big Island is Pele's territory, but Halema'uma'u is her home. Ceremonial hula is performed in her honor on the crater rim, and throughout the year those wishing to appease Pele leave flowers, bottles of gin and other offerings. The overlook is at the start of the **Halema'uma'u Trail**. Although few people who aren't hiking the full trail venture past the overlook, it's an easy half-mile walk to a 1982 lava-flow site.

THURSTON LAVA TUBE
On the east side of the Chain of Craters Rd intersection, Crater Rim Dr passes through the rain forest of native tree ferns and ohia that covers Kilauea's windward slope.

The **Thurston Lava Tube Trail** is an enjoyable 15-minute loop walk that starts out in ohia forest, passing through an impressive lava tube. All the tour buses stop here, so don't expect peace and quiet. A soundtrack of birdsong accompanies this walk, especially in early morning. The *'apapane*, a native honeycreeper, is easy to spot. With a red body, silvery white underside and black tail and wings, it flies from flower to flower, gathering nectar.

Lava tubes are formed when the outer crust of a river of lava starts to harden but the liquid lava beneath the surface continues to flow on through. After the flow has drained out, the hard shell remains. Dating back perhaps 500 years, Thurston Lava Tube is a grand example – it's tunnellike and almost big enough to run a train through. If you bring a flashlight, you can walk beyond the lighted area, further into the tube.

KILAUEA IKI CRATER
When Kilauea Iki (Little Kilauea) burst open in a fiery inferno in November 1959, the whole crater floor turned into a bubbling lake of molten lava. Its fountains reached record heights of 1900ft, lighting the evening sky with a bright orange glow for miles around. At its peak, it gushed out 2 million tons of lava an hour.

From the overlook there's a good view of the mile-wide crater below, which was used for filming the 2001 remake of *Planet of the Apes*. Crossing the crater is like walking on ice – here, too, there's a lake below the hardened surface, although in this case it's molten magma, not water. Recent plumb tests reveal that the lava is a mere 230ft beneath the surface.

DEVASTATION TRAIL
Crater Rim Dr continues across the barren Ka'u Desert, and through the fallout area of the 1959 eruption of Kilauea Iki Crater.

The **Devastation Trail** is a half-mile walk across a former rain forest that was devastated by cinder and pumice from that eruption. Everything green was wiped out. What remains today are dead ohia trees, stripped bare and sun-bleached white, and some tree molds. You can't keep good flora down, however; ohia trees, native *ohelo* bushes and ferns have already started colonizing the area anew.

The trail is paved and has parking lots on each end. The prominent cinder cone along the way is Pu'u Puai (Gushing Hill), formed during the 1959 eruption. The northeastern end of the trail looks down into Kilauea Iki Crater.

Chain of Craters Rd intersects Crater Rim Dr opposite the west-side parking area for the Devastation Trail.

Chain of Craters Road

Chain of Craters Rd winds 20 miles down the southern slopes of Kilauea Volcano, ending abruptly at the latest East Rift Zone lava flow on the Puna Coast. It's a good paved two-lane road, although there are no services along the way. Allow a few hours for the round-trip, to navigate around curves and slow-moving sightseers.

From the road you'll have striking vistas of the coastline far below, and for miles the predominant view is of frozen fingers of lava heading toward the sea, occasionally crossing the road. You can sometimes find thin filaments of volcanic glass, known as Pele's hair, in the lava cracks and crevices. The best time to photograph the unique landscape is before 9am or after 3pm, when sunlight slants off the lava.

In addition to endless lava expanses, the road takes in an impressive collection of sights, including a handful of craters that you can literally peer into. Some are so new there's no sign of life, while others are thickly forested with ohia, wild orchids and ferns.

Chain of Craters Rd once connected to Hwys 130 and 137, allowing traffic between the volcano and Hilo via Puna. Lava flows closed the road in 1969, but by 1979 it was back in service, albeit slightly rerouted. Then Kilauea's active flows cut the link again in 1988, burying a 9-mile stretch of the road.

MAUNA ULU

In 1969, eruptions from Kilauea's east rift began building a new lava shield, which eventually rose 400ft above its surroundings. It was named Mauna Ulu (Growing Mountain). By the time the flow stopped in 1974, it had covered 10,000 acres of parkland and added 200 acres of new land to the coast.

It also buried a 12-mile section of Chain of Craters Rd in lava up to 300ft deep. A half-mile portion of the old road survives, and you can follow it to the lava flow by taking the turnoff on the left, 3.5 miles down Chain of Craters Rd. Just beyond this is Mauna Ulu itself.

The **Pu'u Huluhulu Overlook Trail**, a 3-mile round-trip hike, begins at the parking area,

crosses over lava flows from 1974, and climbs to the top of a 150ft cinder cone, where you'll have a panoramic view of Mauna Loa, Mauna Kea, Pu'u 'O'o vent, Kilauea, the East Rift Zone and ocean beyond. This beautiful, moderate hike takes about two hours return.

KEALAKOMO

As you continue down Chain of Craters Rd, you'll be passing over Mauna Ulu's extensive flows. About halfway along the road, at an elevation of 2000ft, is this covered **shelter** with picnic tables and a superb ocean view. In 1975, a 7.2-magnitude earthquake rocked Kealakomo, and portions of the south flank sank up to 12ft, touching off a tsunami that killed two people at Halape.

After Kealakomo, the road begins to descend along a series of winding switchbacks, some deeply cut through lava flows.

PU'U LOA PETROGLYPHS

The gentle Pu'u Loa Trail leads less than a mile to a field of petroglyphs chiseled into *pahoehoe* lava by early Hawaiians. The site, which is along an ancient trail that once ran between Ka'u and Puna, has more than 20,000 drawings. The marked trailhead begins on the Chain of Craters Rd midway between the 16- and 17-mile markers.

At the site, stay on the boardwalk at all times – the views of the petroglyphs are good, and there's no need to wear them down by trampling over the rocks. At **Pu'u Loa** (Long Hill), toward the southeast, ancient Hawaiians pecked out thousands of dimpled depressions in the petroglyph field to serve as receptacles for the umbilical stumps of babies. By placing the umbilical stumps inside the cupules and covering them with stones, they hoped to bestow their children with longevity.

HOLEI SEA ARCH

Just before the 19-mile marker, look for the sign marking the **Holei Sea Arch**. This rugged section of the coast has sharply eroded lava cliffs, called Holei Pali, which are constantly being pounded by the crashing surf. The high rock arch, carved out of one of the cliffs, is impressive, although the wave action of Namakaokahai, goddess of the sea and sister to Pele, has numbered its days.

THE END OF THE ROAD

Chain of Craters Rd ends abruptly wherever hardened lava covers the road. Park rangers try to mark a trail over the hardened lava with small reflectors leading to a safe observation point. There's a simple info board and portable toilets here, but no water or other facilities.

Mauna Loa Road   Map p272

Also known as the 'Bird Park,' **Kipukapuaulu** is a unique 100-acre sanctuary for native flora and fauna, and worth the short drive 1.5 miles up Mauna Loa Rd. Visitors often overlook this peaceful, easy walk because it's outside the park entrance. On clear days, the panoramic view of Mauna Loa will make you appreciate its size.

Along the 1-mile loop trail, you'll hear only silence and birdsong, especially in early morning. About 400 years ago, a major lava flow from Mauna Loa's northeastern rift covered most of the surrounding area. Pele spared this bit of land when the flow parted, creating an island forest in a sea of lava. In Hawaiian, it's known as a *kipuka,* though the term can mean any variation in form, such as a fertile oasis, a patch of blue sky amid clouds or even the manmade resorts on the South Kohala lava terrain.

Today Kipukapuaulu is an official Special Ecological Area of rare endemic plants, insects and birds, where there is intensive management to remove alien plants and to restore native plant species. You'll see lots of koa trees, which provide a habitat for the ferns and peperomia that take root in its moist bark. You'll also pass a **lava tube** where a unique species of big-eyed spider was discovered in the dark depths of 1973. A free flora-and-fauna trail guide is available at the visitors center (p273) inside the park.

If you keep driving on Mauna Loa Rd, you'll pass other heavily forested *kipuka* as you approach Mauna Loa. Mauna Loa has erupted more than 18 times in the past century – the last eruption, in March 1984, lasted 21 days. The onerous **Mauna Loa Summit Trail** (p282) begins at the end of the road after 13.5 miles.

GO TO THE FLOW

The National Park Service welcomes visitors to see the active lava flow at the end of Chain of Craters Rd, but officials also emphasize the dangers of the hike and the proximity to molten lava. The trek toward the flow is strenuous, crossing hardened lava, and the 'trail' is not only unmarked, except for temporary reflectors, but it's unpatrolled and potentially dangerous. Hikers should stay at least 400yd inland because of unstable land at the coastline.

The trek leads as close to the lava as safety allows, and often toward the point where lava flows into the sea. However, what you'll find at the end of the trek is unpredictable. You might hike *mauka* or *makai* of Chain of Craters Rd, and you might see molten lava just a few feet away, or only steam rising in the distance. The round-trip hike can take anywhere from 20 minutes to several hours.

During the day, the black lava reflects the sun's heat and temperature, often reaching the high 90s (°F). Many visitors begin late in the afternoon, to view the orange glow after dark, but it's inadvisable to be on the trail after sunset without a knowledgeable guide. Many adventure tour companies, such as Arnott's Lodge (p259) or Hawaii Forest & Trail (p247), lead guided treks a few days a week.

While the steam plumes are impressive to see from afar, they are extremely dangerous up close. The explosive clash between seawater and 2100°F molten lava can spray scalding water hundreds of feet into the air and can throw chunks of lava up to a half-mile inland.

The lava crust itself forms in unstable ledges called lava benches, which can collapse into the ocean without warning. In 1993, a collapsing lava bench sent one islander to his fiery death and burned more than a dozen people in the ensuing steam explosion. In March 1999, the scene almost repeated itself when seven onlookers scattered to safety, after a series of explosions began blasting lava bombs into the air, and then collapsed the 25-acre lava bench they'd been standing on.

Volcanic activity and viewing conditions are always subject to change, so call the park visitors-center **hotline** (☎ 985-6000) for updates.

ACTIVITIES

To join a ranger-led guided walk, see the bulletin board at the Kilauea Visitor Center (p273). You can also join a guided hike with outdoor-adventure companies Hawaii Forest & Trail or Hawaiian Walkways (p181).

If you're not a hiker and golf's your pleasure, the **Volcano Golf & Country Club** (☎ 967-7331; Pi'i Mauna Dr; green fees $62.50) has majestic links sitting beneath Mauna Kea and Mauna Loa volcanoes.

Hiking

The park has an extensive network of hiking trails, rising from sea level to over 13,000ft. Trails strike out in a number of directions – across crater floors, down to secluded beaches, through native forests, around the Ka'u Desert and up to the snow-capped summit of Mauna Loa. The trails often intersect, so you can create your own loops and paths, but the most common are described here.

The following hikes range from an easy 1-mile walk to multiday backcountry treks. Remember that except at the cabins and shelters, no drinking water is available anywhere. Trail signs are not reliable, and often contradicting each other in distance and direction.

HALEMA'UMA'U TRAIL

One of the park's best day hikes, this 6-mile loop (Map p274) starts in a moist ohia forest and descends almost 400ft to the floor of Kilauea Caldera, and crosses the surface of the active volcano. The trailhead is located diagonally across the road from the visitors center. Most of the counterclockwise loop is entirely exposed, making it either a hot, dry hike or chillingly damp.

You'll traverse flow after flow, beginning with one from 1974 and continuing over others from 1885, 1894, 1954, 1971 and 1982, each distinguished by a different shade of black. The trail, which is marked by *ahu*, ends about 3 miles from the visitors center at the steaming Halema'uma'u Overlook (see Sights p276). On the way back, you'll take the Byron Ledge Trail, which heads toward Pu'u Puai and the **Devastation Trail** (p277), which you can add as a side trip. On the last stretch, you'll return to damp, cool forest air and birdsong breaking the silence.

KILAUEA IKI TRAIL

Perhaps the most popular hike, this trail (Map p274) leads you though a microcosm of the park. The 4-mile, counterclockwise loop begins near the Thurston Lava Tube parking lot, quickly descending 400ft through fairy-tale ohia forest and then cutting across the milewide crater, passing the main vent. Like many trails in the park, the way is delineated with *ahu*. On the crater surface, colorful native flora grows stubbornly.

Much of the trail is unshaded but heading generally northwest across the crater floor, the path over *pahoehoe* is not taxing. Soft black cinders reveal the footprints of previous hikers, aiding navigation. Don't wander off-trail to explore without an experienced guide.

Keep to the right to ascend the crater wall on the far side. You'll be on Byron Ledge, the ledge that separates Kilauea Iki from Kilauea Caldera. Turn around for good views of Kilauea Iki Crater and gold-topped Pu'u Puai, which looks much more jagged than when viewed from the Halema'uma'u Trail. From there you'll pass two junctions; if you turn right at both, you'll continue along the Kilauea Iki trail back to the parking lot; if you turn left, you'll connect with the Crater Rim Trail or the Byron Ridge Trail, which hooks up with Halema'uma'u Trail after 1 mile.

CRATER RIM TRAIL

This 11-mile trek (Map p274) skirts the crater rim, running roughly parallel to Crater Rim Dr (p276) – on the north side, the trail skirts the crater rim, while on the south side, it runs outside the paved road. For most of the trail you won't see the road. But because Crater Rim Dr is meant to pass the main sights, you'll actually miss a few by hiking. Yet quick side trips are possible and overall you'll gain a range of views and environments unseen along the other trails – and you'll leave the park crowds behind. From the Southwest Rift Zone area, you should also take the short 1¼-mile side trip to see Halema'uma'u Crater (p276). Allow five or six hours for the entire Crater Rim Trail, with a leisurely lunch break.

MAUNA IKI TRAIL

The Ka'u Desert is a land of arid beauty and expansive horizons. Most hikers find the trails here to be long, hot and rather dull –

though the sense of solitude and oneness with nature can be mesmerizing. But the 7-mile Mauna Iki Trail (Map p272) is doable and exceptionally varied.

To reach the trailhead, go down Chain of Craters Rd for 2 miles and turn right on Hilina Pali Rd, which can be hazardous due to blind curves, sharp rises and fog. About 4.5 miles down Hilina Pali Rd, shortly after Kulanaokuaiki Campground, look for a trailhead sign on the right. A large *ahu* signals the trail's beginning.

The trail crosses *pahoehoe* that appear in a range of colors, from shiny gray to muted brown to metallic red. Mind the lava crevices. From a distance to your left you'll see double-peaked Pu'ukaone (3250ft) on the right, a tawny cinder cone with a rust-colored 'chimney' formation on its top.

As you approach a set of twin pit craters, you'll see warning signs reading 'Danger Overhanging Edge, Stay Back.' Carefully peer into the pits, which hide a surprising amount of plantlife.

The trail 'ends' around Pu'ukaone, though you can venture further down the trail, turning left at the Ka'u Desert Trail junction to reach Mauna Iki (3032ft) lava shield, about 3 miles away. If you continue west along the trail, you'll hit Hwy 11, which is another starting point.

BACKCOUNTRY TRAILS

Free **hiking shelters** and rustic **cabins** are available along some of the park's backcountry trails. All have pit toilets and limited catchment water that must be treated before drinking. The current level of water at each site is posted on a board at the visitors center. There are also two primitive **campgrounds**, which have pit toilets, but no shelter or water, at Apua Point along the Puna Coast Trail, and Napau Crater campground, 3 miles west of the Pu'u 'O'o vent, reached via the Napau Crater Trail.

Overnight hikers are required to register for permits, which are free, at the visitors center (p276) before heading out. Rangers have updates on trail and cabin conditions. Permits are issued on a first-come, first-served basis, beginning no earlier than noon on the day before your intended hike. There's a three-day limit at each backcountry campsite, and each site has a limit of eight to 16 campers.

Essential backpacking equipment includes a first-aid kit, a flashlight with extra batteries, a minimum of a gallon of water, extra food, a mirror (for signaling), a stove with fuel (open fires are prohibited), broken-in boots, sunscreen, rain gear and a hat. Note that the desert and coastal trails can make for extremely hot hiking. More information on backcountry hiking, including basic trail maps and hiking books, can be obtained at the visitors center.

On the Mauna Loa Summit and Observatory Trails (for the latter, see p249), it's critically important to acclimatize. Altitude sickness is a danger (see p542 for more information). Hypothermia from the cold and wind is another hazard. A good windproof jacket, wool sweater, winter-rated sleeping bag and rain gear are all essential. Sunglasses and sunscreen will provide protection from snow glare and the strong rays of the sun that prevail in the thin atmosphere.

Napau Crater Trail

For spectacular views of Pu'u 'O'o, the source of Kilauea's current spectacle, the 18-mile Napau Crater Trail (Map p272) can't be beat. Day-trippers will see giant plumes of steam arising from the active vent, while fiery red 'skylights' allow glimpses of the molten lava to campers. Due to ongoing volcanic activity, however, this trail is subject to change. Note: if you've got only a couple hours, you can do just the first leg of this hike, the Pu'u Huluhulu Overlook Trail (p278), without a permit.

The Napau trailhead is at the 3.5-mile marker along Chain of Craters Rd, near the Mauna Ulu parking area. The trail's first 5 miles follow what was formerly Chain of Craters Rd, before *pahoehoe* lava covered it in 1973. There are great examples of reticulite and Pele's hair strewn here.

You'll pass lava trees and the 150ft Pu'u Huluhulu (Shaggy Hill) cinder cone before veering left toward the east. On clear days the view is magnificent, with Mauna Loa off to the northwest, Mauna Kea to the north and the ever-changing Pu'u 'O'o vent straight ahead. After descending across *pahoehoe* terrain, you'll reach the south rim of Makaopuhi crater, a jaw-dropping 1 mile wide and 500ft deep.

After less than half an hour cooling off in a fern forest of purple fiddleheads, you reach the Naulu Trail fork, leading to the Keala-komo parking area on Chain of Craters Rd. However, you should continue straight across this junction. Upon exiting the fern forest, you'll come to the rock walls of an old depository for *pulu*, the golden, silky 'hair' found at the base of *hapu'u* (tree fern) fid-dlehead stems. The ancient Hawaiians used *pulu* to embalm their dead. In the late 1800s, *pulu* was exported for use as mattress and pillow stuffing, until it was discovered to quickly decompose and turn to dust.

Ten minutes past the '*pulu* factory' there are fantastic views of the partially collapsed Pu'u 'O'o cone. Beyond the junction for the **Napau Crater lookout** is a primitive **camp-ground**. Hike past this toward the toilet, swing around it to the right, and follow the almost indistinguishable trail to the floor of the Napau Crater. The *ahu* here are hard to distinguish from natural piles of lava. Keep an eye out for where the indistinct 'trail' plunges over the crater wall in a daringly steep fashion. There crumbling switch-backs have been forced onto '*a'a* rockslides and intermittent scree. Although relatively short, the switchbacks are difficult – even more so on the way back.

After making this precipitous descent, there's a barely discernible trail snaking across Napau Crater. Step lightly and keep as close to the cairns as possible. On the far eastern side of the crater, another set of short but steep switchbacks ascend the crater wall. Wherever the cairns end is the de facto terminus of the trail. Use your best judgment in deciding how closely to approach this ex-tremely active volcanic area. Don't linger too long, to avoid more exposure than necessary to hazardous fumes.

Kahaualeʻa Trail

Park officials strongly discourage hikers from taking this unofficial trail-of-use to-ward the Pu'u 'O'o vent, mainly because people seeking 'adventure' are frequently unprepared and get lost or injured. The 8.5-mile hike (nicknamed the 'Pu'u 'O'o Trail') is not located on HAVO land but on the Kahaualeʻa Natural Area Reserve. The trail is barely marked and poorly maintained; ex-pect mud and glassy *pahoehoe* terrain. Dense fog often shrouds the trail, disorienting hik-ers who end up unexpectedly spending the night outside and spurring a rescue.

To get to the trailhead, take Hwy 11 north of Volcano village and turn east onto S Glenwood Rd immediately before the 20-mile marker. Wind through the Fern Forest subdivision to the end of the dirt road. Beyond the Kahaualeʻa Natural Area Reserve sign, a footpath wanders for about 4.5 miles through lush ohia-*hapu'u* forest, then forges ahead one last mile over deso-late volcanic desert toward Pu'u 'O'o. Don't go further than the edge of the forest – the terrain is unstable and treacherous.

Before starting out, check to see if the winds are blowing predominantly toward the trailhead – if that's the case, don't hike, since volcanic fumes can seriously impair breathing. Lock your car doors as break-ins are common. Wear bright clothing, as the trail passes through an area that's open year-round for game hunting. Be cautious and don't proceed beyond the sign at the end of the trail.

Mauna Loa Summit Trail

Only those who are extremely fit and pre-pared to camp should attempt to climb Mauna Loa – the high elevation and subarc-tic conditions can be surprisingly daunt-ing. The summit trail (Map 272) begins at the end of Mauna Loa Rd, about an hour's drive from the visitors center. The road is occasionally closed due to fire danger but if you have a backcountry permit you'll be al-lowed in. The rugged 19-mile trail gradually ascends 6600ft. It takes a minimum of three days, but four is better for proper acclimati-zation. Two simple cabins, with a dozen or fewer bunks, are available on a first-come, first-served basis at Red Hill and Mauna Loa summit. Potable water might be available and must be treated (inquire at the visitors center, p276).

At first the trail rises through an ohia for-est and above the tree line. After 7.5 miles and about four to six hours, you reach **Red Hill** (Pu'u'ula'ula) at 10,035ft. There are fine views of Mauna Kea to the north and Maui's venerable Haleakala to the northwest.

It's a full day's hike from Red Hill to the summit cabin at 13,250ft. The route traverses a stark, stirring landscape of multi-colored fields of cinder, '*a'a* and *pahoehoe*, with gaping fissures cleaving the landscape that includes spatter cones. If you look closely, you'll see amazing variations in the lava, which ranges from iridescent black to matte clay red to olivine green.

After 9.5 miles, you come to **Moku'aweoweo Caldera** and a fork in the trail. It's another 2 miles along the **Cabin Trail** to your night's resting place. If you absolutely can't push on, **Jaggar's Cave** (just beyond the fork) can serve as a windbreak – but it's a small niche rather than an actual cave.

The other fork is for the 2.5-mile **Summit Trail**. The last 2 miles are especially challenging and will seem to last forever (no one can believe it's only 2 miles!). At 13,677ft, Mauna Loa's summit has a subarctic climate, and temperatures normally drop to freezing every night. Winter snowstorms can last for days, bringing whiteout conditions. Occasionally, snow falls as low as Red Hill and covers the upper end of the trail. Consult park rangers about weather conditions before setting out.

Puna Coast Trail

This trail (Map p272) starts almost at the end of the Chain of Craters Rd, at about the 19.5-mile mark at the Pu'u Loa Petroglyphs. The entire stretch of this hike is on gorgeous coastal cliffs, but it's also both hot and windy, crossing miles of barren lava fields from Mauna Ulu's early-1970s eruptions.

While not as colorful as the other hikes, the volcanic textures are interesting, and you'll pass *kipuka* along the way. **Apua Point campground** is 6.5 miles along a flat, decently marked trail. Remember that this is an endangered turtle-nesting ground. Further west, the Keauhou and Halape **hiking shelters** could be incorporated into a multiday loop that returns via the 7-mile Keauhou Trail. Water is available only at the shelters, not the campground.

FESTIVALS & EVENTS

Regular park programs include **After Dark in the Park** (Kilauea Visitor Center Auditorium; admission free; ☺ 7pm Tue), a series of free talks by experts on cultural, historic and geological matters, held two or three times monthly.

Annual special events that are free with park admission include the following:

Na Mea Hawaii Hula Kahiko Series A series of outdoor hula *kahiko* performances four times throughout the year.

Annual Dance & Music Concert (last weekend in March) An event hosted by the Volcano Art Center,

presenting works by Big Island choreographers, dancers and musicians.

Kilauea Volcano Wilderness Runs (late July) Held at Hawai'i Volcanoes National Park. There are four separate events: a 10-mile run around the rim of Kilauea Caldera; both a 5-mile run and a 5-mile walk that go down into Kilauea Iki Crater; and a 26-mile marathon through the Ka'u Desert. For information, contact the **Volcano Art Center** (☎ 985-8725; www.volcanoartcenter.org).

Aloha Festivals Ka Ho'ola'a o Na Ali'i (September) A brilliant royal court procession and celebration on the Halema'uma'u Crater rim during the Aloha Festival.

SLEEPING
Budget

Holo Holo Inn (Map p274; ☎ 967-7950, 800-671-2999; www.enable.org/holoholo; 19-4036 Kalani Honua Rd; dm $17-19; r $44) This small, sociable lodge, affiliated with Hostelling International, has clean but darkish dorms. The private room has a double bed and two twins. There's a shared kitchen and TV room, complimentary coffee and tea, laundry facilities and a sauna. Call for reservations after 4:30pm.

Kulana Artist Sanctuary (Map p274; ☎ 985-9055; www.panpolynesia.net/kulana; Volcano village; camping $15, s/d $30/40) Guests share the main house bathroom, kitchen and library, and in the cooperative spirit of the founder's vision, you're required to participate in easy caretaking tasks. It has a contemplative, communal atmosphere geared toward the creative, or spiritual seekers. Kulana truly lives up to its motto: 'no smoking, alcohol, drugs or drama.' Ask about monthly artist-in-residence rates from $300.

CAMPING

The park has two free drive-up campgrounds that are relatively uncrowded outside summer. Sites are first-come, first-served, with a limit of one week at each campground. Because of the elevation, nights can be crisp and cool.

Kulanaokuaiki Campground (Map p272; Hilina Pali Rd) About 3.5 miles off Chain of Craters Rd, is newer and less developed. It has three campsites plus toilets and picnic tables, but no water.

Namakanipaio Campground The park's busiest campground is between the 32- and 33-mile markers off Hwy 11, 3 miles west of the visitors center. Tent sites are in a small meadow that offers little privacy, but is surrounded by fragrant eucalyptus trees.

There are restrooms, water, fireplaces and picnic tables.

Namakanipaio Cabins (Map p274; bookings at Volcano House ☎ 967-7321; 4-person cabins $40) Windowless A-frame plywood palaces. Each of the 10 cabins has a double bed, two single bunks and electric lights, but no power outlets or heating. Volcano House provides linens but bring a sleeping bag to warm you through cold nights. Showers and toilets are shared. Check-in requires refundable deposits for keys ($12) and linen ($20).

Mid-Range & Top End   Map p274

My Island B&B (☎ 967-77216; www.myislandinnhawaii .com; 19-3896 Volcano Rd; s $50-85 d $65-100, house $135) On 7 acres of verdant rain forest, the owners, who are longtime residents run an old-style B&B in a historic 1886 house that's filled with fine art, koa furniture and over 300 record albums. The best options, especially for families, are the six spacious houses scattered across the property and in Volcano village (extra adults $20 per day). The rooms in the main house are rather cramped. The sociable hosts once ran a tour company and are more than willing to share their knowledge of Hawai'i.

Lehua Lodge (☎ 800-908-9764; www.volcanogallery .com; 11-3873 12th St; house $145) This airy, cedar loft is so perfect that you'll be tempted to stay indoors for your vacation. Downstairs, you'll find a bedroom, full kitchen and charming living room with rocking chair and soaring 20ft ceiling. The porch overlooks the lush ohia-fern forest that secludes the house. Upstairs, the romantic master bedroom features a sleigh bed, from which you can gaze through windows at the moon. Washer and dryer are available, and kids are welcome.

Volcano Rainforest Retreat (☎ 985-8696, 800-550-8696; www.volcanoretreat.com; 11-3832 12th St; cottage d incl breakfast $125-245) With four beautiful, private cedar cottages, this B&B is distinct in its focus on spiritual, restorative practices. Each cottage harmonizes functional structure with nature – one shaped into a cedar and redwood octagon, and two with a Japanese-style soaking tub. Reservations are a must. Massage, energy healing, counseling, personal-growth workshops and guided spiritual retreats are also offered.

Kilauea Lodge (☎ 967-7366; www.kilauealodge .com; Old Volcano Rd; r $135, cottage d $155-175 both incl breakfast) This longtime B&B offers a variety of solid accommodations with the country comfort you'd expect to find: working fireplaces, high ceilings, quilts and bath tubs. None of the rooms on the main property have private TVs or phones, but who needs them with a beautiful garden hot tub? Kilauea Lodge also features a fine restaurant (see below) run by owner-chef Albert Jeyte.

Volcano House (☎ 967-7321; www.volcanohouse hotel.com; 1 Crater Rim Dr; r $85-185) Perched on the rim of Kilauea Caldera, opposite the visitors center, Volcano House has a long, venerable history. Most lower-level rooms, however, look out onto a walkway, and even rooms on the upper floor might have only a partial view of the crater. The small rooms have a pleasant character, with koa furniture, vintage stationery and, importantly, heating. There are no TVs, but the hotel has a terrific game library. Reserve at least two months ahead.

EATING & DRINKING

The **dining room** and **snack bar** at Volcano House (see above) are the only restaurant options within the park, but the cafeteria-quality fare is overpriced. Go to Volcano village to eat and just warm yourself by the living-room fire (which has been burning since the 1870s!) or just order drinks at **Uncle George's Lounge** (☽ 4:30-9pm).

It's a long haul from the park to Volcano village restaurants, but otherwise you have no choice. For groceries, pickings are slim at both **Volcano Store** (☎ 967-7210; cnr Old Volcano & Haunani Rds; ☽ 5am-7pm) and **Kilauea General Store** (☎ 967-7555; Old Volcano Rd; ☽ 7am-7:30pm Mon-Sat, to 7pm Sun).

Kiawe Kitchen (☎ 967-7711; Cnr Old Volcano & Haunani Rds; mains $9-12; ☽ noon-2:30pm & 5:30-9:30pm Thu-Tue) A modern café with pleasant outdoor seating and a nice list of fine wines and Big Island microbrews. The house specialties are gourmet crispy-crust pizzas and baguette sandwiches featuring wood-fired meats.

Lava Rock Café (☎ 967-8526; Old Volcano Rd at 27-mile marker; mains $6-12; ☽ 7:30am-5pm Mon, to 9pm Tue-Sat, to 4pm Sun) Located behind Kilauea General Store, this is the favored breakfast spot in town. Steer clear of the saimin and order the French toast with *liliko'i* butter instead. Kids' menu available.

JP Café (☎ 985-7456; 19-4005 Haunani Rd; breakfasts $5, sandwiches & burgers $5-8; ☽ 6:30am-5:30pm Mon-Sat, 9am-5pm Sun) Just the basics, cooked in a kitchen probably smaller than your own, but it's decent for a quick meal or take-out.

Thai Thai Restaurant (☎ 967-7969; 19-4084 Old Volcano Rd; mains $12-16; ☺ 5-9pm) The owners, who hail from Thailand, offer tangy curries and noodles with plenty of vegetarian choices. Go wild: it's all fresh, tasty and spicy (if you like) and apportioned generously.

Kilauea Lodge (☎ 967-7366; www.kilauealodge .com; Old Volcano Rd near Wright Rd; mains $19-39; ☺ 5:30-9pm) In a rustic dining room with stone fireplace, amid a misty fern forest, Kilauea Lodge suits Volcano village perfectly. This is the only fine-dining restaurant in town, and you can expect upmarket mains like braised rabbit, venison, Parker Ranch steaks and fresh fish in papaya-and-ginger sauce. Reservations are advised.

GETTING THERE & AROUND

Driving nonstop, the national park is 29 miles (45 minutes) from Hilo and 97 miles (2½ hours) from Kailua-Kona. Either way, you'll drive on Hwy 11. Volcano village is a couple miles east of the park entrance.

KA'U

The Ka'u district encompasses the entire southern flank of Mauna Loa, acting as a buffer zone between touristy South Kona and the wilderness of Hawai'i Volcanoes National Park. This stretch of Hwy 11 is prone to flooding, washouts and road closures during heavy winter storms. Your only two cross-island alternatives are Saddle Rd and Hwy 19 between Hilo and Waimea, but during the worst storms, even Hwy 19 might be closed due to rock slides.

The district is sparsely populated, with only about 5000 people and three towns. You pass desertlike expanses of hardened lava and lush foothills, where macadamia nuts and island-favorite Ka'u oranges are grown. For travelers, rural seclusion, exotic beaches and a handful of unique B&Bs distinguish Hawai'i's southern coastline.

Past the 35-mile marker you'll see fewer trees and more lava, before the terrain becomes ranchland. In 2004, Kahuku Ranch ended its cattle operations adjacent to Hawai'i Volcanoes National Park, and the park acquired 116,000 acres on the slopes of Mauna Loa. Kilauea's Southwest Rift Zone

runs through 20 miles of the Ka'u Desert, *makai* of the road, all the way from the Kilauea summit to the coast. You've left the national park when the signs reading 'Caution: Nene Crossing' disappear.

PAHALA
pop 1400

Just past the 51-mile marker, you'll reach Pahala, a former sugar town. Ka'u Agribusiness once had 15,000 acres of cane planted for 15 miles in either direction from the town, but the mill closed for good in 1996. The company has since replaced the cane with groves of macadamia-nut trees.

There are two entrances to Pahala. The southern access is via Maile St, which winds north past the shuttered sugar mill, rickety homes, 'Beware of Dog' signs and junker cars rusting in yards. Alternatively, turn inland off Hwy 11 at Kamani St, which passes the hospital before heading directly into the commercial part of town.

'Commercial,' however, is an overstatement. All you'll find are a fire station, a gas station, a post office, a bank with an ATM and **Ka'u Hospital** (☎ 928-8331). The main reason to stop? Fresh, hot *malasada* from **Tex Drive Inn** (☎ 928-8200; malasada 85¢; meals $5; ☺ 7am-8pm Mon-Sat, to 6pm Sun). The restaurant is clean (including the restrooms) and the egg-and-meat breakfasts will tide you over for hours.

Wood Valley

About 4 miles inland from Pahala is a remote Buddhist temple and retreat center, **Nechung Dorje Drayang Ling** (Map p272). The weather-beaten temple, sitting quietly in an overgrown 25-acre property, was built in 1902 by Japanese sugarcane laborers who lived in the valley. The place can seem deserted and rather dilapidated, but a peaceful forest surrounds the temple and peacocks roam freely.

In 1975 a Tibetan lama, Nechung Rinpoche, took up residence here, and in 1980 the Dalai Lama visited to dedicate the temple. Since then, many Tibetan lamas have conducted programs here and the Dalai Lama himself returned for a visit in 1994. In addition to its Buddhist teachings, the center also lets outside groups conduct meditation, yoga and New Age spiritual workshops (see www.nechung.org). Temple monks also produce organic coffee that's exceptionally smooth and rich (and, at $35 per pound, likely to encourage slow sipping 'in the moment').

Wood Valley Temple & Retreat Center (Map p272; ☎ 928-8539, 928-6271; Nechung Dorje Drayang Ling; www.nechung.org; dm/s/d with shared bathroom $35/50/75) Here you'll find a meditation hall with two peaceful guest rooms on the upper floor, and simpler rooms and dorms below. A freestanding guesthouse with five double rooms is tucked back on the grounds. Food is not provided, but a kitchen and a dining room are available. Guests are welcome to join the morning services.

PUNALU'U

A small bay with a black-sand beach, Punalu'u was once a major Hawaiian settlement, and after Westerners arrived it became a key sugar port. Nowadays it's famous mainly for green sea turtles that trundle out from the sea to bask in the sun after gorging on *limu* (seaweed).

Punalu'u Beach Park, a county park located just south, has restrooms, showers, drinking water and a picnic pavilion. Be careful walking on the sands, which are used as nesting sites by hawksbill turtles. Don't approach these gentle giants because they're both an endangered species and very sensitive to human disturbance.

Most days, the waters are not ideal for swimming, and it's fun to watch *malihini* (newcomers) in tropical swimwear braving the icy, spring-fed waters. Fierce rip currents pull seaward near the pier and lots of coconut husks and driftwood float about. The most popular part of the beach is the northern pocket, lined with coconut palms and backed by a duck pond. The ruins of the Pahala Sugar Company's old warehouse and pier lie slightly to the north. The Kane'ele'ele Heiau ruins sit on a small rise.

The **campground** at Punalu'u Beach Park sits on a flat, grassy area overlooking the beach, but there's zero privacy. At night, you can drift off to sleep to the sounds of crashing surf. Come daybreak, it's overrun with picnickers. Permits (p178) are required.

To reach the beach, take either the turnoff to SeaMountain, Ka'u's only condo complex, or the one marked Punalu'u Park, less than 1 mile east.

WHITTINGTON BEACH PARK

Not far before Na'alehu there's a pull-off with a scenic lookout above Honu'apo Bay. From here you can see the cement pilings of the old pier, which was used for shipping sugar and hemp until the 1930s.

The turnoff to Whittington Beach Park is 1 mile beyond the lookout. Although there are tide pools to explore, there's no beach and the ocean is usually too rough for swimming. Endangered green sea turtles can sometimes be seen offshore; apparently they've been frequenting these waters for a long time, as Honu'apo means 'caught turtle' in Hawaiian.

Camping is allowed with a county permit (p178). The park is far enough from the highway to offer privacy, and has restrooms and sheltered picnic tables, but there's no potable water.

NA'ALEHU

With a population of 1000, Na'alehu is tiny, but it's famous for being the southernmost town in the USA. It's the Ka'u district's commercial and religious center, with a grocery store, a library, a police station, a post office, a gas station, an ATM and six churches. Na'alehu closes up early, so you shouldn't count on finding food or gas here if you're driving past at night.

Eating

Na'alehu Fruit Stand (☎ 929-9009; Hwy 11; sandwiches under $5, pizza $8-10; ☷ 8am-7pm Mon-Thu, to 8pm Fri & Sat, to 8pm Sun) Don't be fooled by the name: it's actually a one-stop produce store, bakery and deli. The ovens crank out bread in the morning, and pizzas to order starting at 11am. Local papaya, oranges and macadamia nuts are reasonably priced. At a few picnic tables out front, you can eat and 'talk story' with the good-natured proprietor and other locals.

Punalu'u Bakeshop & Visitor Center (☎ 929-7343; Hwy 11 near Ka'alaiki Rd; ☷ 9am-5pm) The Big Island's best-known sweet bread bakery has become a tourist landmark. You can indulgently sample many flavors of sweet bread, which you can have mailed to you back home. The lunch counter serves sandwiches, soups, salads and desserts. The onslaught of tourist paraphernalia is relentless, but the public restrooms are clean (what a find!).

Shaka Restaurant (☎ 929-7404; Hwy 11; breakfast & lunch $5-8, dinner $10-15; 🕙 10am-9pm Tue-Sun) This casual diner serves full, hearty meals, including eggs Benedict and French toast (made from Punalu'u sweet bread) for breakfast and meaty dinners. They offer a *na keiki* (childrens) menu, a full bar and live music on weekends.

WAI'OHINU

Before reaching South Point Rd, Hwy 11 winds down into a pretty valley and the sleepy village of Wai'ohinu, which sits nestled beneath green hills. The town is known for its landmark **Mark Twain monkeypod tree**, which was planted by the author back in 1866. The original tree fell in a 1957 hurricane, but hardy new trunks have sprung up and it's once again fully grown.

Sleeping

Most tourists stay along the Kona Coast or in Hilo, but you might be surprised at the B&B gems you'll find in Wai'ohinu.

South Point Banyan Tree House (☎ 929-8515; reservations 949-492-1258; www.southpointbth.com; cnr Pinao St & Hwy 11; r $150) A gargantuan banyan tree envelops this studio house on stilts, giving the impression you're in a tree house. Inside, the room is suffused with light from glass doors, skylights and windows face to face with the magnificent banyan. The airy room includes a queen-size bed, a sofa, a full kitchen, a washer/dryer, an outdoor hot tub and wraparound lanai. While it's located near Hwy 11, the thriving jungle of mango, lychee, *'ulu* (breadfruit) and banana trees outside provide ample privacy.

Macadamia Meadows B&B (☎ 929-8097, 888-929-8118; www.macadamiameadows.com; 94-6263 Kama'oa Rd; incl breakfast d $65-85, ste $120-135) For a close-up view of a working macadamia-nut farm, why not spend a few nights on site? Just a half-mile south of town, this contemporary home features clean, spacious guest rooms with cable TV, a microwave, a refrigerator, private entrances and lanai. The suites adjoin two bedrooms – ideal for families or groups. An added bonus: guests receive a free orchard tour, where you'll learn about Hawaii's macadamia-nut industry from friendly insiders (and also get to pick and taste a fresh nut).

Hobbit House B&B (☎ 929-9755; www.hi-hobbit.com/Hawaii/bnb; d $190) The aptly named Hobbit House is a whimsical, custom-designed house perched high on a bluff with a spectacular ocean view. The accommodations are very comfortable, with an antique four-poster bed, a double Jacuzzi, a full kitchen and lanai – while the sloping 'mushroom' roof, stained glass and slanted windows add a fairytale touch. The hosts moved from the mainland to Hawai'i over 25 years ago, and they're especially personable and familiar with the island. The remote setting and panoramic view make for a truly unique experience – but the steep half-mile drive up requires a 4WD. It's off Hwy 11, on the Ha'ao Springs Trail.

Shirakawa Motel (☎ 929-7462; www.shirakawamotel.com; 95-6040 Hwy 11; s/d $43/45, r with kitchenette $55-65) For just the basics, the 'southernmost motel in the USA' might be simple and weather-beaten, but it's a bargain. The deluxe kitchenette room comes with two

---

HIDDEN BIG ISLAND

- Private beaches down the **Road to the Sea** (p289)
- A hike to the summit of **Mauna Kea** (p246) or **Mauna Loa** (p282)
- A day trip on Mana/Keanakolu Rd to the **Hakalau Forest National Wildlife Refuge** (p233)
- Delectable sushi at **Sushi Rock** in Hawi (p227)
- **Mo'okini Heiau** at the island's remote northernmost tip (p226)
- The **Hobbit House B&B** overlooking the Ka'u coast (p287)
- Uncrowded beaches along **Kekaha Kai State Park** (p215)
- Traversing the Big Island on a **bicycle tour** (p182)
- An escape from the world at **Kona Village Resort** (p217)
- A yoga retreat at the **Yoga Oasis** (p270)

HAWAI'I (THE BIG ISLAND)

double beds, a full kitchen, a microwave, kitchen supplies and cable TV. Still family-run, the rooms sit beneath verdant hills right near the center of town. The longtime owners can tell you all about the Big Island 'back in the day.'

Getting There & Away

The Hele-On Bus (p184) runs one bus daily to Pahala, Punalu'u, Na'alehu, Wai'ohinu and Hawaiian Ocean View Estates on the No 23 Ka'u route ($3.75 to $5.25). From Ka'u to Hilo, take the No 7 Downtown Hilo bus, which originates in Wai'ohinu.

SOUTH POINT

South Point is the southernmost spot in the USA. In Hawaiian, it's known as Ka Lae, which means simply 'the point.' South Point has rocky coastal cliffs and a turbulent ocean. Yet this rugged coastline is the site where the first Polynesians landed, in desperate straits by some accounts. Much of the area now falls under the jurisdiction of Hawaiian Home Lands. There are no facilities.

To get here, take the South Point Rd between the 69- and 70-mile markers on Hwy 11. Along the mostly one-lane road, drivers must let each other pass (give the *shaka* – the Hawaiian hand greeting – if someone waves you ahead!). The winds are bracing here, as evidenced by tree trunks bent almost horizontal.

After a few miles of scattered houses, macadamia-nut farms and grassy pasture-land, you'll see the **Kama'oa Wind Farm**: rows of high-tech windmills in a pasture beside the road. With cattle grazing beneath, it's a surreal scene. Each of these wind-turbine generators can produce enough electricity for 100 families. It's thought, theoretically at least, that by using wind energy conversion, the state could produce more than enough electricity to meet its needs, but the wind farm is not operating at capacity.

About 4 miles south of the wind farm you'll pass a few abandoned buildings wasting away. Until 1965, this was a Pacific Missile Range station that tracked missiles shot from California to the Marshall Islands in Micronesia.

Ten miles down from the highway, South Point Rd forks. The road to the left goes to **Kaulana boat ramp**, while the right fork leads to the craggy coastal cliffs of Ka Lae.

Ka Lae

The confluence of ocean currents just offshore makes this one of Hawai'i's most bountiful fishing grounds. Locals fish off the cliff, with some of the bolder ones leaning out over steep lava ledges. Land ruins here include **Kalalea Heiau**, usually classified as a *ko'a* (a small stone pen designed to encourage fish and birds to multiply); look inside for a well-preserved fishing shrine.

An outcropping on the heiau's western side has numerous **canoe mooring holes** that were drilled long ago into the lava rock. Strong currents would pull the canoes out into deep turbulent waters where the enterprising ancient Hawaiians could fish, still tethered to the shore, without getting swept out to sea.

The wooden platforms built on the edge of the cliffs have hoists and ladders for the small boats anchored below; you may see a sea turtle or two gliding around in the relatively calm waters below the hoists.

There's a large unprotected *puka* (hole) in the lava directly behind the platforms where you can watch water rage up the sides and recede again with incoming waves. Keep an eye out for it, as it's not obvious until you're almost on top of it.

Walk down past the light beacon and continue along the wall to finally reach the southernmost point in the USA. There are no markers here, no souvenir stands, just crashing surf and lots of wind.

Green Sands Beach

Green Sands Beach, traditionally known as Papakolea, was formed by semiprecious olivine crystals chipped from the lava cliffs and worn smooth by a relentless and pounding surf. Olivine is a type of volcanic basalt that's rich in iron, magnesium and silica. Don't expect to see an emerald beach, however. The olivine sand is mixed with black sand, and it appears as a dull olive green. You can swim here, but waves are strong and pound the shore at full force.

To get here, go left where South Point Rd forks. You'll dead-end at a shack where you might see locals charging $5 for 'secure parking' in an impromptu lot. Avoid wasting your money, as no one can legally charge 'admission' to the public-access shoreline.

From here, it's a 2.5-mile hike along a rutted dirt road to the beach. If you have a high-riding 4WD vehicle, you could drive in, but the road is rough and you'll probably take about 25 minutes. It's a gentle and beautiful hike, though winds will whip around you.

Eventually you'll need to scramble down some cliffs to get to Green Sands Beach. Pick a calm day to visit, for the entire beach can be flooded during high surf. By now, this beautiful small beach is squarely on the beaten path. For a more remote setting, go for the Road to the Sea.

HAWAIIAN OCEAN VIEW ESTATES

Around the 76-mile marker, there's one last stop for food and gas before the long drive up to Honaunau. You won't find more than the necessities at the 'commercial center' of Hawaiian Ocean View Estates (HOVE), a subdivision with just over 2000 residents: a gas station, a post office, a hardware store, a supermarket and a couple of local eateries. This residential area is one of the last sunny expanses of land in Hawai'i to be totally free of resorts. Land here is relatively cheap, perhaps owing to the isolation and harsh lava-rock vista, but burglaries are frequent here. Controversial proposals for large developments occasionally pop up, but so far all have been defeated, to the relief of island environmentalists.

ROAD TO THE SEA

The Road to the Sea is hardly traveled, and it's no wonder: the unpaved 4WD-only road crosses loose lava rock, ledges and cracks. If you brave the journey, however, you'll

likely have the beaches to yourself. Bear in mind, whipping winds are not unusual (and on especially gusty days, flying sand can just about exfoliate your inner ears!).

To get here, turn *makai* at the row of three mailboxes between the 79- and 80-mile markers. Another landmark is a sign that reads 'Ka Ulu Malu Shady Grove Farm.' Set your odometer as soon as you turn. The road is private and barking dogs might give you a chase.

From here you'll cross 6 miles over a rudimentary, seemingly never-ending lava road. To reach the first and smaller of the two beaches takes 30 minutes, if you drive slowly, although it can be done in 20 minutes, if you're comfortable on rough terrain.

To reach the second beach, drive a half-mile back inland. Skip the first left fork that appears (it's a dead end) and take the second-left fork instead. Look for arrows painted on the lava rock. The road goes inland before heading toward the shore again, and the course isn't always readily apparent. There are many places you can lose traction or get lost. Almost a mile from the fork, you'll reach a red *pu'u* (hill). Park here and walk down to the ocean. If you decide to walk the whole distance, it's about 1.5 miles. Bring as much water as you can carry as it's hot and shadeless.

Neither beach is named, but both have exquisite black-and-green sand, similar to Green Sands Beach. Along the Kona Coast, you'll find calmer waters and convenient amenities, but finding these secluded spots can be a day's adventure.

HAWAI'I
(THE BIG ISLAND)

Maui

It's inevitable that one island was going to make the claim, but *Maui no ka 'oi* (Maui is the best) is virtually a mantra here.

So why *do* more people flock to Maui than any other Neighbor Island? For starters, the beaches are magnificent and stretch for miles, and the island boasts top-notch conditions for an oceanful of water sports, including world-class windsurfing and whale watching.

Exploring on land is equally awesome. You can hike the crunchy lunarlike surface of the world's largest dormant volcano, explore the salt-sprayed whaling town of Lahaina or tee off on the stunning greens that host the PGA season-opener. See for yourself why the cliffside Road to Hana, which switchbacks its way past roaring waterfalls and jungle valleys, is the most legendary drive in Hawaii.

Or perhaps you'd prefer to mellow out at a cushy resort or hillside B&B. Maui is an island for romantics. So many couples come here for their vows and honeymoons, that 'getting Maui'd' is another bit of local lingo. As for restaurants, Maui has several that hover near the top of trendy fine-dining magazine polls, and deservedly so.

Whatever brings you here, you won't run out of things to do. Have you ever stared up from the depths of a volcanic crater on a full-moon night? Kayaked past frolicking dolphins, snorkeled among sea turtles or dived into a sunken volcano? There's a slice of paradise for everyone on Maui.

MAUI

HIGHLIGHTS

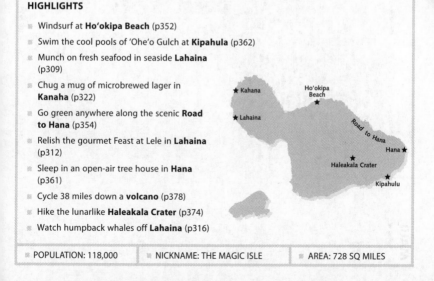

- Windsurf at **Ho'okipa Beach** (p352)
- Swim the cool pools of 'Ohe'o Gulch at **Kipahula** (p362)
- Munch on fresh seafood in seaside **Lahaina** (p309)
- Chug a mug of microbrewed lager in **Kanaha** (p322)
- Go green anywhere along the scenic **Road to Hana** (p354)
- Relish the gourmet Feast at Lele in **Lahaina** (p312)
- Sleep in an open-air tree house in **Hana** (p361)
- Cycle 38 miles down a **volcano** (p378)
- Hike the lunarlike **Haleakala Crater** (p374)
- Watch humpback whales off **Lahaina** (p316)

★ Kahana   Ho'okipa Beach ★

★ Lahaina

Road to Hana

Hana ★

Haleakala Crater ★

Kipahulu ★

POPULATION: 118,000	NICKNAME: THE MAGIC ISLE	AREA: 728 SQ MILES

MAUI

20 km
12 miles

0
0

PACIFIC OCEAN

PACIFIC OCEAN

PACIFIC OCEAN

21°00'N
20°50'N
20°40'N
20°30'N
21°00'N
20°50'N
20°40'N
20°30'N

156°50'W
156°40'W
156°30'W
156°20'W
156°10'W
156°00'W

156°50'W
156°40'W
156°30'W
156°20'W
156°10'W
156°00'W

Wai'anapanapa
State Park

Hana
Bay
Hana
Airport
Hana
Hamoa
Hana
Point
Ka'eleku
Kalahu
Point
Nahiku
Hana
Forest
Reserve
360
Waiohonu Stream
Waialua
Waihe'e
Bay
Oke'anae
Pu'a Ka'i'a State
Wayside Park
Ko'olau
Forest
Reserve
Waiho'i Valley
Palikea Stream
'Ohe'o
Gulch
Kipahulu
Honomanu
Bay
Ke'anae Valley
Waikamoi Stream
Waikamoi Stream
Kaumahina State
Wayside Park
Haleakala National
Park
Kipahulu
Forest
Reserve
Kaupo
Kaupo Gap
Pi'ilani Hwy
31

Waipi'o
Bay
Huelo Point
Hana Hwy
Huelo
Uaoa
Bay
Ho'okipa
Beach Park
Pa'uwela
Pa'uwela Point
368 365
398 390
Haiku
Makawao
36
378
Haleakala
Crater Rd
Pu'u Ulaula
(10,023ft)
377
Baldwin Ave
Kula Hwy
Kahikinui Forest
Reserve
Polipoli Spring State
Recreation Area
HA Baldwin
Beach Park
Pa'ia
Kahului
Airport
Kahului
Kahului Bay
Pu'unene
Haleakala Hwy
Hali'imaile
Pukalani
Kula
Waiakoa
Keokea
'Ahihi-Kina'u
Natural Area
Reserve
Ulupalakua
Ranch
37
Pi'ilani Hwy

West Maui
Forest
Reserve
'Eke Crater
(4751ft)
Pu'u Kukui
(5788ft)
'Iao Valley
State Park
West Maui Mountains
Kahakuloa
Waihe'e
Waihee
Wailuku
Waikapu
Kahului
Honoapi'ilani Hwy
340
340
30
30
380
311
Kahekili Hwy
Kuihelani Hwy
Mokulele Hwy
Kealia Pond National
Wildlife Refuge
Kihei
Wailea
Ma'alaea Bay
Makena
Pu'u Olai
(360ft)
La Perouse
Bay
Molokini
Crater

Honokohau
Honokohau Stream
Napili
Bay
Kapalua
Kapalua
West Maui
Airport
Napili
Kahana
Honokowai
Ka'anapali
Lahaina
Olowalu
Moke'ehia
Island
Ma'alaea
Ma'alaea Bay
Papawai
Point
30
30

Kaho'olawe
Pu'u Moiwi
(1161ft)
Kanapou
Bay

Climate

Maui's west coast is largely dry and sunny. The southeast coast and Kula uplands receive more rain and commonly have intermittent clouds. Temperatures vary more with elevation than season. Daytime highs vary only about 7°F year-round. Average daily temperatures in August hover around 80°F in Lahaina, Kihei or Hana, but only 50°F at Haleakala summit.

Maui gets the most rain between December and March, averaging 15in annually along the west coast and 69in in Hana. For a recorded weather forecast, call ☎ 877-5111. For a more extensive marine forecast, including surf conditions, call ☎ 877-3477.

National, State & County Parks

The star of Maui's parks, **Haleakala National Park** (www.nps.gov/hale) embraces the lofty volcanic peaks that gave rise to east Maui. With its stunning landscape of red cinder cones and gray lava, the park offers one-of-a-kind hiking and sightseeing, good birding and some of the best camping on Maui. The park's summit section (p377) contains stunning Haleakala volcano and most of the major sights. But this is a park with two faces, the lush coastal side standing in sharp contrast to the barren, lunarlike crater floor of Haleakala. In the Kipahulu section (p362), south of Hana, you can hike to towering waterfalls, swim in cascading pools and visit ancient Hawaiian archaeological sites.

Maui's second-most visited park is 'Iao Valley State Park (p335), outside Wailuku, where a towering green pinnacle rises from the valley floor, offering a picture-perfect scene.

For a glorious, unspoiled stretch of beach, head to Makena State Park (p349), the northern portion of which is a haunt for nude sunbathers. The most interesting oceanside park with camping, Wai'anapanapa State Park (p358), sits on a gem of a black-sand beach north of Hana and offers lava caves and a coastal trail to explore. If you want to discover a dreamy cloud forest, head Upcountry to Polipoli Spring State Recreation Area (p372), where a lightly trodden network of trails winds beneath lofty trees.

County parks on Maui are small, generally just a couple of acres along the beach, but some do offer camping.

CAMPING
National Parks

Camping is available in both the summit and Kipahulu sections of Haleakala National Park. For drive-up camping, reservations are not taken and there is no fee. Haleakala also has free backcountry camping on the crater floor, but that requires advance reservations. See p380 for more information on camping in the crater and also renting a cabin ($75 per night), reservations for which are awarded through a highly competitive lottery held months in advance (although last-minute vacancies sometimes occur).

A TALE OF CHIEFS & CONQUERORS

Before Western contact, Maui had three population centers: the southeast coast around Hana, the Wailuku area and the district of Lele (present-day Lahaina).

In the 14th century, Pi'ilani, chief of the Hana district, conquered the entire island. During his reign, Pi'ilani accomplished some impressive engineering feats. He built Maui's largest temple, Pi'ilanihale Heiau (p357), which still stands today, as well as an extensive islandwide road system. Almost half of Maui's highways still bear his name.

The last of Maui's ruling chiefs was Kahekili. During the 1780s, he was the most powerful chief in the islands, bringing both O'ahu and Moloka'i under Maui's rule. In 1790, while Kahekili was in O'ahu, Kamehameha the Great (see p31) launched a bold naval attack on Maui. Using foreign-acquired cannons and the aid of two captured foreign seamen, Isaac Davis and John Young, Kamehameha defeated Maui's warriors in a fierce battle at 'Iao Valley (p334).

An attack on his own homeland by a Big Island rival forced Kamehameha to withdraw from Maui, but the battles continued for years. When Kahekili died on O'ahu in 1794, his kingdom was divided. In 1795, Kamehameha invaded Maui again, and this time he conquered the entire island and brought it under his rule. In 1800, he established his royal court at Lahaina. It remained the capital of Hawai'i until Kamehameha III moved it to Honolulu in 1845.

MAUI IN...

Three Days

Spend the first day exploring the old whaling town of **Lahaina** (p301), capping it off with dinner at a waterfront restaurant. On the second day, head to **Haleakala National Park** (p374) to catch the sunrise and hike a bit of the crater. On day three, take a whale-watching or snorkeling **cruise** (p308) in the morning, have fun at one of Maui's gorgeous beaches in the afternoon, and in the evening choose between the **Old Lahaina Luau** (p312) or the **Feast at Lele** (p312).

Five Days

Take a full day to fully appreciate the drive down the abundantly lush **Road to Hana** (p354). On day five, spend the morning kayaking among the turtles and dolphins along the **south Maui coast** (p337), then kick around **Pa'ia** (p351) with its fun shops, enjoy a meal and explore the **Upcountry** (p366).

One Week

With one week, you've got time to play a round of golf at one of the island's luxury courses in **Kapalua** (p324) or **Wailea** (p340), go horseback riding in **Makena** (p348), spend a day **diving** (p294), or maybe try your hand at **windsurfing** (p297). And don't miss the slack-key guitar masters (p325) in Kapalua, either.

State Parks

Polipoli and Wai'anapanapa, the only state parks on Maui with camping, have campsites and cabins. Permits are required. The maximum length of stay is five consecutive nights per month at each park. Tent camping costs $5 per day for up to 10 people. Polipoli has one primitive cabin (closed Tuesday) and a rough access road that usually requires a 4WD vehicle. Wai'anapanapa has 12 very popular cabins, which must be reserved well in advance. Cabins at either park cost $45/55 for up to four/six people.

For state camping permits or cabin reservations, contact the **Division of State Parks** (☎ 984-8109; www.hawaii.gov/dlnr/dsp; Room 101, State Office Bldg, 54 S High St, Wailuku, HI 96793; ☺ 8am-3:30pm Mon-Fri).

County Parks

Kanaha Beach Park (p328), just north of Kahului airport, allows camping Thursday through Monday; Papalaua Wayside Park (p314), on Hwy 30 south of Lahaina, allows camping Friday through Wednesday. Camping is limited to three consecutive nights. Permits cost $3 per adult per day (50¢ for children under 18), and are available by mail or in person from the **Department of Parks & Recreation** (☎ 270-7389; www.co.maui.hi.us; 700 Halia Nakoa St, Wailuku, HI 96793) at the War Memorial Complex at Baldwin High School.

Activities

Let loose – you're on Maui! This island sports some of the world's best windsurfing, surfing and whale watching. It's ideal for snorkeling, kayaking, diving, hiking and golf, too. Whether you take to land or the water, whatever you decide to do, it's here.

WATER ACTIVITIES

Swimming

Maui has scores of wonderful beaches, with plenty of good swimming opportunities. The northwest coast from Ka'anapali (p317) to Honolua Bay (p325) and the southwest coast from Kihei (p337) through Wailea (p344) to Makena (p348) are largely fringed with sandy beaches. Water conditions on this sunny, western side of Maui are generally calmer and better suited for swimming than the windward northern and eastern coasts.

Snorkeling & Diving

Don a mask and fins and a whole other world opens. For dive and snorkel boat tours, the main destinations are the sunken volcanic crater of Molokini (p297) and the island of Lana'i. Although a few dive boats take snorkelers, and some snorkeling tours take divers, you're better off going out on a tour that's geared for the activity you're doing.

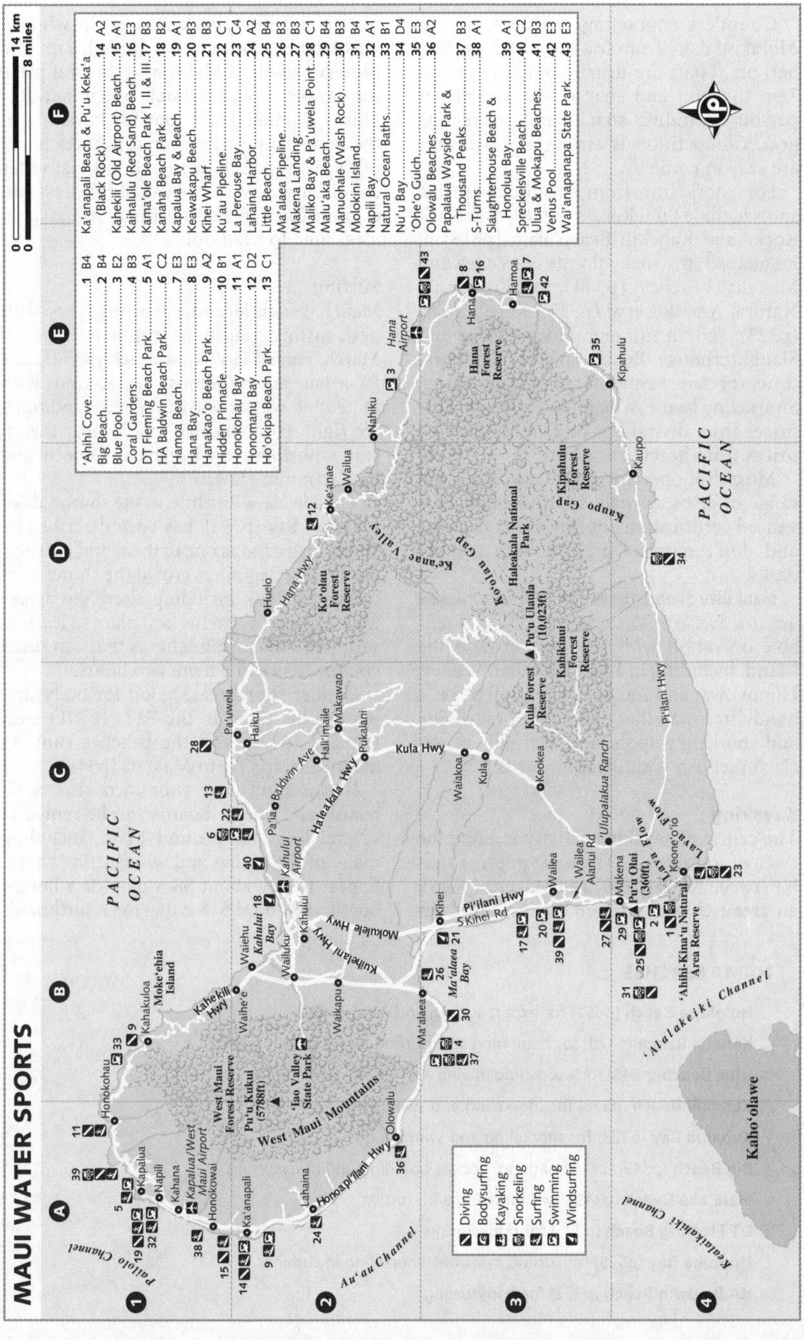

MAUI WATER SPORTS
0 — 14 km
0 — 8 miles
'Ahihi Cove....1 B4
Big Beach....2 B4
Blue Pool....3 E2
Coral Gardens....4 B3
DT Fleming Beach Park....5 A1
HA Baldwin Beach Park....6 C2
Hamoa Beach....7 E3
Hana Bay....8 E3
Hanakao'o Beach Park....9 A2
Hidden Pinnacle....10 B1
Honokohau Bay....11 A1
Honomanu Bay....12 D2
Ho'okipa Beach Park....13 C1
Ka'anapali Beach & Pu'u Keka'a (Black Rock)....14 A2
Kahekili (Old Airport) Beach....15 A1
Kaihalulu (Red Sand) Beach....16 E3
Kama'ole Beach Park I, II & III....17 B3
Kanaha Beach Park....18 B2
Kapalua Bay & Beach....19 A1
Keawakapu Beach....20 B3
Kihei Wharf....21 B3
Ku'au Pipeline....22 C1
La Perouse Bay....23 C4
Lahaina Harbor....24 A2
Little Beach....25 B4
Ma'alaea Pipeline....26 B3
Makena Landing....27 B3
Maliko Bay & Pa'uwela Point....28 C1
Malu'aka Beach....29 B4
Manuohale (Wash Rock)....30 B3
Molokini Island....31 B4
Napili Bay....32 A1
Natural Ocean Baths....33 B1
Nu'u Bay....34 D4
'Ohe'o Gulch....35 E3
Olowalu Beaches....36 A2
Papalaua Wayside Park & Thousand Peaks....37 B3
S-Turns....38 A1
Slaughterhouse Beach & Honolua Bay....39 A1
Spreckelsville Beach....40 C2
Ulua & Mokapu Beaches....41 B3
Venus Pool....42 E3
Wai'anapanapa State Park....43 E3
Diving
Bodysurfing
Kayaking
Snorkeling
Surfing
Swimming
Windsurfing
PACIFIC OCEAN
PACIFIC OCEAN
Pailolo Channel
Au'au Channel
'Alalakeiki Channel
Kealaikahiki Channel
Kaho'olawe
Moke'ehia Island
West Maui Forest Reserve
Pu'u Kukui (5788ft)
'Iao Valley State Park
West Maui Mountains
Honokohau
Kahakuloa
Kapalua
Napili
Kahana
Kapalua/West Maui Airport
Honokowai
Ka'anapali
Lahaina
Olowalu
Honoapi'ilani Hwy
Kahekili Hwy
Waihe'e
Waiehu
Kahului Bay
Wailuku
Kahului
Kahului Airport
Waikapu
Ma'alaea
Ma'alaea Bay
Kuihelani Hwy
Mokulele Hwy
Kihei
S Kihei Rd
Pi'ilani Hwy
Wailea
Wailea Alanui Rd
Makena
Pu'u Olai (360ft)
Keone'o'io
'Ahihi-Kina'u Natural Area Reserve
Lava Flow
'Ulupalakua Ranch
Pa'ia
Baldwin Ave
Haleakala Hwy
Hali'imaile
Makawao
Pukalani
Kula Hwy
Waiakoa
Kula
Keokea
Kula Forest Reserve
Kahikinui Forest Reserve
Pu'u Ulaula (10,023ft)
Haleakala National Park
Ko'olau Gap
Ke'anae Valley
Kaupo Gap
Kipahulu Forest Reserve
Pi'ilani Hwy
Pa'uwela
Haiku
Huelo
Hana Hwy
Ko'olau Forest Reserve
Ke'anae
Wailua
Nahiku
Hana Airport
Hana Forest Reserve
Hana
Hamoa
Kipahulu
Kaupo

MAUI

Countless snorkeling cruises leave for Molokini daily from Ma'alaea and Lahaina harbors. Boats are usually out from about 7am to noon and charge $40 to $50 per person, including snacks and snorkeling gear. Competition is strong, so discounts are easy to come by.

For snorkeling from the beach, prime spots include Pu'u Keka'a (p318), aka 'Black Rock,' and Kahekili Beach Park (p318) in Ka'anapali; the rocky points of Wailea and Makena beaches (p344); 'Ahihi-Kina'u Natural Area Reserve (p350); Kapalua Bay (p323); and, in summer, Honolua Bay and Slaughterhouse Beach (p325). The best time for snorkeling is in the morning. Snorkeling gear can be rented at reasonable prices from dive shops or at more inflated prices from hotel beach huts.

Most dive operators on Maui offer a full range of dives as well as refresher and advanced certification courses. Book directly, and don't monkey around with activity desks.

Maui Dive Shop (☎ 800-542-3483; www.mauidive shop.com; dives from $80, courses from $300) is a reliable operation with branches around the island, including in Kihei, Lahaina, Wailea, Honokowai and Kahana. The shop offers a handy free map that details the best diving and snorkeling spots, and also sells plasticized reef fish identification cards.

Kayaking
The center of kayaking activity is along the coast of south Maui. The most popular spot is between Kihei (p340) and Makena (p348), an area rich with marine life including sea turtles and humpback whales (in winter). Unspoiled La Perouse Bay (p350), a marine preserve south of Makena, is the best place for kayakers to see schools of spinner dolphins. Another good spot for kayaking in the calmer summer season is the area north of Kapalua (p325). Keep in mind that water conditions on Maui are usually clearest and calmest early in the morning, so that's an ideal time to head out.

Surfing
Maui has some legendary surfing spots, with peak surfing conditions from November to March. Famed Ho'okipa Beach (p352) near Pa'ia has surfing almost year-round, with incredible winter waves. When conditions are right, Honolua Bay (p325) near the island's northern tip can have some of the best action in Hawaii.

The Ma'alaea Pipeline, at the south side of Ma'alaea Bay (p336), has been described by *Surfer* magazine as one of the world's 10 best fast breaks. Beginners crowd the shores near Lahaina (p306), including along the breakwall. Lahaina is also the best place to learn to surf, and has surfing schools that can teach you the basics in a mere two hours.

Gentler shorebreaks good for bodysurfing can be found in the Pa'ia (p351) area, Kapalua (p323) and the beaches running from Kihei (p337) to Makena (p348).

If you don't have your own gear, surfboards and boogie boards can be rented at several locations around Maui, including many of the diving and windsurfing shops. Expect to pay about $8 a day for a boogie board and about $18 a day for a surfboard.

TOP 10 BEACHES
- **Ho'okipa Beach** (p352) for expert surfing and windsurfing
- **Kanaha Beach** (p328) for beginning windsurfing and kitesurfing
- **Ulua Beach** (p345) for snorkeling, diving and whale watching
- **Kahekili Beach** (p318) for snorkeling and swimming
- **Kapalua Bay** (p323) for snorkeling and swimming
- **Big Beach** (p349) for sunbathing, boogie boarding and bodysurfing
- **Malu'aka Beach** (p349) for snorkeling with turtles
- **DT Fleming Beach** (p325) for bodysurfing
- **Honolua Bay** (p325) for surfing in winter, snorkeling in summer
- **HA Baldwin Beach** (p352) for bodysurfing

Windsurfing

Maui is a mecca for windsurfers. Some of the world's best windsurfing is at Ho'okipa Beach (p352) near Pa'ia, though it's suitable for experts only. Those who aren't quite there yet head to nearby Spreckelsville Beach (p352). If you're new to the sport, start at Kanaha Beach (p328) in Kahului.

Overall, the island is known for its consistent winds, and windsurfers can find action in any month. Although trade winds can blow at any time of the year and flat spells could also hit anytime, generally the windiest time is June to September and the flattest from December to February.

Parts of the Kihei coast have slalom sailing in summer. At Ma'alaea Bay (p336) conditions are good for advanced speed sailing (the winds are usually strong and blow offshore toward Kaho'olawe). In winter, on those occasions when *kona* (leeward) winds blow, the Ma'alaea-Kihei area is often the only place windy enough to sail.

Most windsurfing shops are in Kahului and handle rentals, lessons, sell windsurfing gear, and book package tours that include your gear, accommodations and car.

Kiteboarding

On Maui all the action centers on 'Kite Beach,' the western end of Kanaha Beach Park (p328) in Kahului. Check with the **Maui Kiteboarding Association** (www.maui.net/~hotwind /mka.html) for the latest guidelines. See p58 for more information.

LAND ACTIVITIES
Hiking

Hands down, the most extraordinary trails are at Haleakala National Park (p374), where hikes, ranging from half-day walks to overnight treks, meander across the moonscape of Haleakala Crater. In the Kipahulu section of the national park, south of Hana, a trail leads to two towering waterfalls.

In Maui's Upcountry, Polipoli Spring State Recreation Area (p372) has an extensive trail system in cloud forest, including the daylong Skyline Trail that connects with Haleakala summit.

North of Wailuku are the scenic Waihe'e Valley Trail (p326) and Waihe'e Ridge Trail (p326), both of which branch off the Kahekili Hwy. Near Ma'alaea Bay, the challenging Lahaina Pali Trail (p337) follows an old footpath through the West Maui Mountains.

Several pull-offs along the Hana Hwy (p362) lead to short nature walks. There's also a historic coastal trail between Wai'anapanapa State Park (p358) and Hana Bay. From La Perouse Bay (p350), on the other side of the island, there's a strenuous coastline hike over an ancient lava footpath.

The **Sierra Club** (☎ 573-4147; www.hi.sierraclub.org /maui) sponsors guided hikes led by naturalists to various places on the island, mostly on Saturday. Nonmembers are asked to pay $5 each; carpooling to trailheads may be available.

Cycling & Mountain Biking

The key trails for mountain biking are in the Upcountry. Best is the ride on the Skyline Trail (p372), from Haleakala National Park into Polipoli Spring State Recreation Area, where several other bike trails wind through redwood forests. Of course the most trodden route of all is the guided Haleakala sunrise ride (p378) from the volcanic summit down to the coast.

THE MOLOKINI PLUNGE

Snorkelers and divers will be thrilled by steep walls, ledges, white-tipped reef sharks, manta rays, turtles and abundant fish at the largely submerged volcanic crater of Molokini, off Maui's southwest coast. Half of the crater rim has eroded away, leaving a crescent-moon shape that rises 160ft above the ocean surface.

Legends say that Molokini was created by a jealous Pele, goddess of volcanoes. When one of the goddess's lovers secretly married a *mo'o* (water lizard), an angry Pele chopped the lizard in half, leaving Molokini as its tail.

No underwater site draws more visitors. Don't fall for any discounted afternoon tours – go out early for the smoothest sailing and best conditions.

For the best deals, check the ads that abound in the Maui tourist magazines or comparison shop at the harbor the day before.

Horseback Riding

With its abundance of ranch land, Maui has some excellent trail rides. The most unusual ride meanders down into the barren hollows of Haleakala Crater via Sliding Sands Trail. Top-notch rides that take in greener pastures start from Makena (p350) and 'Ohe'o Gulch (p362).

Golf

With scenic ocean vistas and emerald mountain slopes, golfing just doesn't get much better. Kapalua (p324) and Wailea (p346) are the most prestigious places to play, while championship courses are also found at Ka'anapali (p319) and Makena (p348). At the other end of the spectrum, you can enjoy a fun round at the friendly Waiehu Municipal Golf Course (p327) and at lesser-known country clubs elsewhere around the island. Pick up the free tourist magazine *Maui Golf Review* for in-depth course profiles.

Tennis

The county maintains tennis courts in several towns. These counts are free to the public on a first-come, first-served basis. Numerous hotels and condos also have tennis courts for their guests. If you're looking to hone your game, you'll find there are full-service tennis clubs in Wailea (p346) and Kapalua (p324).

Getting There & Away

AIR

Most travelers disembark in central Maui at Kahului, which has the busiest airport in Hawaii outside Honolulu. North of Lahaina in west Maui, Kapalua Airport is a small airport serviced by prop planes and commuter aircraft. Tiny Hana Airport sees only a few flights a day, all by prop plane.

Hana Airport (HNM; ☎ 248-8208) A single terminal off the Hana Hwy, about 3 miles north of Hana in east Maui.

Kahului International Airport (OGG; ☎ 872-3830) For information on getting to and from Kahului's airport, see p332. There's a small **visitor information desk** (☎ 872-3893; ☽ 7:45am-10pm) in the baggage-claim area. Nearby are courtesy phones for contacting accommodations and ground transportation, plus racks upon racks of free tourist magazines and brochures. Near the departure gates are newsstands, gift shops, ATMs, snack bars, a restaurant (last chance for a bowl of saimin!) and a cocktail lounge.

Kapalua Airport (JHM; ☎ 669-0623) The terminal is off Hwy 30, about midway between Kapalua and Ka'anapali, within easy reach of Lahaina.

See p532 for airline contact details and more information on flights to Maui, including from the mainland and abroad.

For interisland travel, choose between **Hawaiian Airlines** (☎ 800-367-5320; www.hawaiianair.com) or **Aloha Airlines** (☎ 800-367-5250; www.alohaairlines.com). All interisland flights from Maui, except Hawaiian Airlines' daily service to Kaua'i, go through Honolulu, meaning you'll eat up half a day in transit if you are going anywhere other than O'ahu. There are at least a dozen daily flights to Honolulu and scads from there on to other islands. See p532 for more on interisland flights.

BOAT

Interisland ferries to Moloka'i and Lana'i depart from Lahaina Harbor. For information on ferry schedules and ticket prices, see p404 for sailings of the *Moloka'i Princess* and p388 for Expeditions' handy Maui–Lana'i ferry.

Getting Around

If you really want to explore Maui and get to off-the-beaten-path sights, you'll need your own wheels. Public transportation is limited to the main towns and tourist resorts.

Be aware that most main roads are called highways whether they're busy four-lane thoroughfares or just quiet country roads. What's more, islanders refer to highways by name, rarely by number. If you ask someone how to find Hwy 36, chances are they aren't going to know – ask for the Hana Hwy instead.

MAUI FOR KIDS

The **Maui Ocean Center** (p336) falls over backward to dazzle kids. There's a microworld viewable through glass portholes at kids' heights, a touch pool with pencil urchins and cushion stars, and interactive exhibits that resonate with whale songs. Also tops for *na keiki* (children) fun are:

- Boogie boarding (p294) on the beach
- Catching a **whale-watching tour** (p300)
- Riding the **sugarcane train ride** (p308) from Lahaina
- Walking the moonlike surface of **Haleakala** (p374)

ROAD DISTANCES & DRIVE TIMES

Average driving times and distances from Kahului are as follows. Naturally allow more time during weekday morning and afternoon rush hours, and all day on weekends.

destination	miles	time
Haleakala Summit	36	1½ hr
Hana	51	2 hr
Honolua Bay (via Kahekili Hwy)	26	1½ hr
Ka'anapali	26	50 min
Kaupo (via Kula)	45	2 hr
Kihei	12	25min
La Perouse Bay	21	50 min
Lahaina	23	40 min
Ma'alaea	8	20 min
Makawao	14	30 min
'Ohe'o Gulch (via Hana)	61	2¾ hr
Pa'ia	7	15 min
Polipoli Spring Campground	24	1¾ hr
Wailuku	3	15 min

The best map for getting around is the encyclopedic *Ready Mapbook of Maui County*, but it's bulky. A good lightweight, foldout map is Nelles' *Maui, Molokai & Lanai*. The colorful Franko's *Maui, the Valley Isle* features water sports and is sold at dive shops; it is waterproof and rip-resistant.

TO/FROM THE AIRPORTS

With either of the following Kahului airport transfer services you can make advance reservations for your arrival to speed things along, and you must reserve in advance for your return to the airport. Both services have courtesy phones in the baggage-claim area.

Executive Shuttle (☎ 669-2300, 800-833-2303) is cheaper and less backlogged than the competition. Certainly on your return to the airport, when you have to call for a pickup, these are the people to go with. The price depends on the destination and the size of the group. For example, the cost for two people from Kahului airport is $18 to Wailuku, $23 to Kihei, $25 to Wailea, $35 to Lahaina and $45 to Kapalua. For a single person, deduct about $3 from those fares, and for each additional person up to eight, add about $3.

Speedi Shuttle (☎ 661-6667, 800-977-2605; www.speedishuttle.com) is the largest airport-transfer service on Maui. Fares tend to be 10% to 20% higher than those charged by Executive.

Kahului airport taxi dispatchers are near the exit of the baggage claim area. Approximate fares are Wailuku, $13; Kihei, $25; Pa'ia–Ha'iku area, $20 to $30; Lahaina, $50; and Ka'anapali, $60.

Taxi fares from the Kapalua/west Maui airport average $15 to Ka'anapali and $20 to most other places along the west Maui coast.

Most resorts on the Ka'anapali coast offer free shuttles to/from the Kapalua airport.

BICYCLE

Cyclists on Maui face a number of challenges: narrow roads, heavy traffic, an abundance of hills and mountains, and the same persistent winds that so delight windsurfers.

Maui's stunning scenery may entice hard-core cyclists, but casual riders hoping to use a bike as a primary source of transportation around the island may well find such conditions daunting.

Getting around by bicycle within a small area can be a reasonable option for the average rider, however. For example, the tourist enclave of Kihei is largely level and now has cycle lanes on two main drags, S Kihei Rd and the Pi'ilani Hwy.

The full-color *Maui County Bicycle Map* ($6), available from bicycle shops, shows all the roads on Maui that have cycle lanes and gives other nitty-gritty details. For information on bicycle rentals, see specific destinations around the island.

BUS

Maui has limited bus services, but the routes interconnect and will take you a bit further afield than it appears at first glance. You can, for instance, take a public bus from Kahului to Lahaina, then hop on the resort shuttle from Lahaina to Ka'anapali. What you can't do by bus is explore any remote places, or even some heavily visited areas such as Pa'ia, Hana and Kula.

Maui Public Transit System (Roberts Hawaii ☎ 871-4838, Maui County ☎ 270-7511; www.co.maui.hi.us/bus) has four routes: Kahului–Lahaina, Kahului–Wailea, Kahului–Wailuku and Ma'alaea–Wailea. All operate Monday to Saturday. Schedules are subject to change.

The three longest routes are provided by Roberts Hawaii and have schedules that dovetail with one another. There are no transfers; you have to buy a new ticket when you board the second bus. Monthly passes ($45) and day passes ($10), sold on buses, are good for all routes.

Roberts' Route A operates between Wailea and Ma'alaea, a 30-minute trip with stops in Kihei. It is $2 one way between the Ma'alaea Harbor Village shopping center and Uwapo Rd in Kihei, or $1 between Uwapo Rd and the Shops at Wailea. At the Pi'ilani Village shopping center in Kihei, Route A connects to Route C with service to Kahului. At Ma'alaea Harbor Village, Route A connects to Route B with service to Kahului and Lahaina. Buses run once an hour about a dozen times a day; the first bus leaves Wailea at 6:55am, the last at 6:55pm.

Roberts' Route B operates from Wal-Mart in Kahului to the Wharf Cinema Center in Lahaina, with a stop at Ma'alaea. From Kahului it takes 15 minutes to get to Ma'alaea and one hour to Lahaina. The one-way fare is $2 from Lahaina to Ma'alaea, and $1 from Ma'alaea to Kahului. Buses run six times a day, every two hours on the half-hour, with the first bus leaving Wal-Mart at 7:30am.

Roberts' Route C runs from Queen Ka'ahumanu Center in Kahului to the Shops at Wailea, with stops at Wal-Mart in Kahului and the Pi'ilani Village shopping center in Kihei. From Kahului it's 40 minutes to Kihei and an hour to Wailea. The one-way fare is $2. Buses run five times a day, with the first bus leaving the Queen Ka'ahumanu Center at 7:20am.

Maui County operates other routes around Wailuku and Kahului, serving 22 stops, including all of the major shopping centers, the hospital and government offices. These buses are mainly geared for local shoppers and are free.

The **Akina West Maui Shuttle** (☎ 879-2828; www .akinatours.com) operates once an hour between Lahaina and Ka'anapali. Buses head south from Ka'anapali's Whalers Village shopping center at 55 minutes past the hour from 8:55am to 9:55pm, and north from Lahaina Harbor at 30 minutes past the hour from 9:30am to 10:30pm. The one-way fare is $1.

Free resort shuttles take guests between hotels and restaurants in the Ka'anapali (p321) and Wailea (p348) areas.

CAR & MOTORCYCLE

See p536 for more information on the national car-hire chains, including their toll-free numbers and Websites. **Alamo** (☎ 871-6235), **Avis** (☎ 871-7575), **Budget** (☎ 871-8811), **Dollar** (☎ 877-7227), **Hertz** (☎ 877-5167) and **National** (☎ 871-8851) all have booths at Kahului airport. Alamo, Avis, Budget, Dollar and National also have offices on Hwy 30 in Ka'anapali and will pick you up at Kapalua Airport. Dollar is the only rental agency serving Hana Airport.

In addition to the national chains, there are a few local agencies on the island. In return for lower rates, you'll generally get an older car:

Kihei Rent A Car (☎ 879-7257, 800-251-5288; www .kiheirentacar.com; 96 Kio Loop, Kihei) Family-owned and offers 24hr roadside assistance. Rates start at $25/155 per day/week for 'beaters,' such as 10-year-old Nissan Sentras.
Maui Cruisers (☎ 249-2319, 877-749-7889, in Canada ☎ 800-488-9083; www.mauicruisers.net; 1270 Pi'ihana Rd, Wailuku) Rents out used compact cars from $29/150/560 per day/week/month, all inclusive of taxes.

For information on renting a wheelchair-accessible van, call **Accessible Vans of America** (☎ 800-303-3750; www.accessiblevans.com), which has a branch in Kihei.

The minimum age to rent a moped is 18; to rent a motorcyle it's 21.

Hawaiian Riders rents mopeds from $29 a day and motorcycles from $100 a day in both Lahaina (☎ 661-1970; 196 Lahaina-luna) and Kihei (☎ 891-0889; Kama'ole Shopping Center, 2463 S Kihei Rd).

TAXI

Taxi fares are regulated by the county. The minimum flag-down fare is $2.50, and each mile is about $2. Some bigger companies, with service throughout the island, are **Island-wide Taxi** (☎ 874-8294) and **Sunshine Cabs of Maui** (☎ 879-2220).

TOURS

Those without a car can catch some of the island's main attractions by joining a guided tour.

Boat

Maui has enough dinner cruises, sunset sails and charter sailboats to fill a book. Most leave from Lahaina and Ma'alaea Bay, although a few depart from south Maui.

KARL LEHMANN

West Maui (p314) at night

Aerial view of snorkellers at Honolua Bay
(p325), Maui

ANN CECIL

ANN CECIL

A vehicle on the scenic Hana Highway
(p354) with the Ke'anae Peninsula in
the distance, Maui

ANN CECIL

Waves crash about the rocks on the
Maui (p290) coastline

Kahakuloa Head (p327) dominates
the coast off the Kahekili Hwy, Maui

ANN CECIL

PETER HENDRIE

Road crossing and clouds near the summit at
Haleakala National Park (p374), Maui

Tourists off West Maui sight a North Pacific humpback whale (p316)

KARL LEHMANN

The best tours are the whale-watching cruises, which operate from December to mid-May, when the humpbacks are hanging around. Recommended is the nonprofit **Pacific Whale Foundation** (☎ 249-8811, 800-942-5311; www.pacificwhale.org), which operates naturalist-led tours from Ma'alaea and Lahaina. Trips include whale watching in season, as well as wild dolphin ecoadventures and snorkel tours year-round. Some proceeds benefit marine-conservation projects.

For snorkel and dive tours to Molokini crater, see p297.

Bus & Van

The most popular tours are the drive to Hana, which runs down the Hana Hwy and includes Kipahulu, and the trip to Haleakala National Park. Both are full-day tours. The going rate for the Haleakala tour is about $60 for adults, $35 for children. For the Hana trip, it's about $80 for adults, $45 for children. Because of road conditions, both of these trips are done in minivans or half-sized buses, so the tours tend to be more personal and less crowded than those found elsewhere.

'Ekahi Tours (☎ 877-9775, 888-292-2242; www.ekahi .com) is a family-run operation that runs a variety of personalized tours focusing as much on culture as sightseeing, including a tour of Kahakuloa village (adult/child $70/50) that includes a visit to a working taro patch.

Other reliable operators:
Polynesian Adventure Tours (☎ 877-4242, 800-622-3011; www.polyad.com)
Roberts Hawaii (☎ 539-9400, 800-831-5411; www .robertshawaii.com)
Valley Isle Excursions (☎ 661-8687, 877-871-5224; www.tourmaui.com)

Helicopter

Numerous helicopter companies take off from the Kahului heliport for trips around the island. Some cross the channel and tour Moloka'i's spectacular north shore as well.

Companies advertise in the free tourist magazines, which are available everywhere, and prices are competitive. Typical 30-minute tours of the West Maui Mountains cost around $125 and one-hour circle-island tours cost about $230. Be aware that not every seat is a window seat; ask about seating policies before making reservations to avoid disappointment.

Some established companies:
Alex Air (☎ 871-0792)
Blue Hawaiian (☎ 871-8844, 800-745-2583)
Sunshine Helicopters (☎ 871-0722, 800-469-3000)

LAHAINA

pop 17,975
Lahaina has long been the pulse of Maui. From the days when the first rowdy whalers rolled ashore, this is where all the action's been. Today the streets still bustle with visitors and the nights hop with people out for a good time. The old wooden storefronts that once housed saloons, dance halls and brothels are now crammed with art galleries, restaurants and souvenir shops.

Sightseeing attractions hail back to the whaling era as well – homes of missionaries, prisons for sailors and graveyards for both. Still, that's just one side of Lahaina. Even without its fascinating history, this town would be a drawcard. It boasts an ideal coastal setting and a scenic mountain backdrop. With soft breezes wafting off the water and sunset views of Lana'i, it's easy to see why people flock here.

Yes, there are crowds and it's often boisterous but, hey, that's part of the fun. There's no better place on Maui to linger over a drink, catch dinner or spend a night on the town.

HISTORY

Lahaina was once a royal court for Maui chiefs and was the breadbasket of west Maui. It served as the capital of Maui and even briefly as the capital of all of Hawaii (p293). In the early 1820s the first whalers arrived in Lahaina. Missionaries landed in their wake and the two were soon at each other's throats. Shortly after his arrival in 1823, William Richards, Lahaina's first Protestant missionary, converted Maui's native governor, Hoapili, to Christianity. Under Richards' influence, Hoapili passed laws against drunkenness and debauchery. But after months at sea, the whalers weren't looking for a prayer service when they pulled into port. To most sailors, there was 'no God west of the Horn.'

In 1826, when the English captain William Buckle of the whaler *Daniel* pulled into Lahaina, he was outraged to discover

LAHAINA

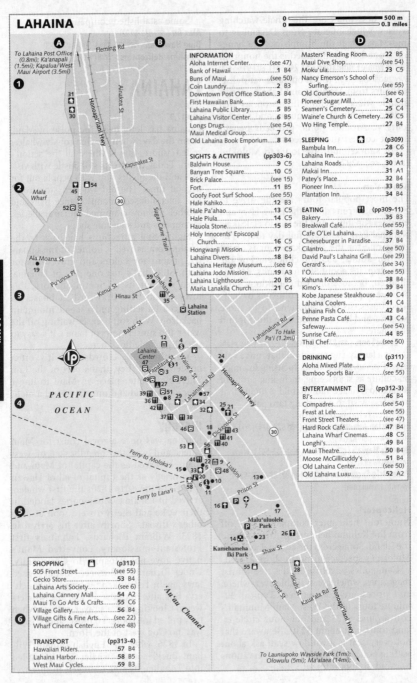

0		500 m
0		0.3 miles

INFORMATION
Aloha Internet Center............(see 47)
Bank of Hawaii..........................**1** B4
Buns of Maui...........................(see 50)
Coin Laundry............................**2** B3
Downtown Post Office Station..**3** B4
First Hawaiian Bank...................**4** B3
Lahaina Public Library...............**5** B5
Lahaina Visitor Center..............**6** B5
Longs Drugs............................(see 54)
Maui Medical Group...................**7** C5
Old Lahaina Book Emporium......**8** B4

SIGHTS & ACTIVITIES (pp303-6)
Baldwin House............................**9** C5
Banyan Tree Square..................**10** C5
Brick Palace.............................(see 15)
Fort..**11** B5
Goofy Foot Surf School............(see 54)
Hale Kahiko..............................**12** B3
Hale Pa'ahao............................**13** C5
Hale Piula................................**14** C5
Hauola Stone............................**15** B5
Holy Innocents' Episcopal
   Church...................................**16** C5
Hongwanji Mission....................**17** C5
Lahaina Divers..........................**18** B4
Lahaina Heritage Museum........(see 6)
Lahaina Jodo Mission...............**19** A3
Lahaina Lighthouse...................**20** B5
Maria Lanakila Church..............**21** C4

Masters' Reading Room............**22** B5
Maui Dive Shop........................(see 54)
Moku'ula..................................**23** C5
Nancy Emerson's School of
   Surfing..................................(see 55)
Old Courthouse........................(see 6)
Pioneer Sugar Mill....................**24** C4
Seamen's Cemetery..................**25** C4
Waine'e Church & Cemetery....**26** C5
Wo Hing Temple......................**27** B4

SLEEPING (p309)
Bambula Inn..............................**28** C6
Lahaina Inn...............................**29** B4
Lahaina Roads...........................**30** A1
Makai Inn..................................**31** A1
Patey's Place.............................**32** B4
Pioneer Inn...............................**33** B4
Plantation Inn...........................**34** B4

EATING (pp309-11)
Bakery......................................**35** B3
Breakwall Café.........................(see 55)
Cafe O'Lei Lahaina....................**36** B4
Cheeseburger in Paradise.........**37** B4
Cilantro....................................(see 50)
David Paul's Lahaina Grill.........(see 29)
Gerard's...................................(see 34)
I'O...(see 55)
Kahuna Kebab..........................**38** B4
Kimo's......................................**39** B4
Kobe Japanese Steakhouse......**40** C4
Lahaina Coolers........................**41** C4
Lahaina Fish Co........................**42** B4
Penne Pasta Café......................**43** C4
Safeway...................................(see 54)
Sunrise Café.............................**44** B5
Thai Chef.................................(see 50)

DRINKING (p311)
Aloha Mixed Plate....................**45** A2
Bamboo Sports Bar...................(see 55)

ENTERTAINMENT (pp312-3)
BJ's..**46** B4
Compadres...............................(see 54)
Feast at Lele............................(see 55)
Front Street Theaters...............(see 47)
Hard Rock Café........................**47** B4
Lahaina Wharf Cinemas............**48** C5
Longhi's....................................**49** B4
Maui Theatre.............................**50** B4
Moose McGillicuddy's...............**51** B4
Old Lahaina Center...................(see 50)
Old Lahaina Luau.....................**52** A2

SHOPPING (p313)
505 Front Street.......................(see 55)
Gecko Store..............................**53** B4
Lahaina Arts Society................(see 6)
Lahaina Cannery Mall...............**54** A2
Maui To Go Arts & Crafts.........**55** C6
Village Gallery..........................**56** B4
Village Gifts & Fine Arts...........(see 22)
Wharf Cinema Center...............(see 48)

TRANSPORT (pp313-4)
Hawaiian Riders........................**57** B4
Lahaina Harbor.........................**58** B5
West Maui Cycles......................**59** B3

To Lahaina Post Office
(0.8mi); Ka'anapali
(1.5mi); Kapalua/West
Maui Airport (3.5mi)

Fleming Rd

Honoapi'ilani Hwy

Alnakea St

Kapunakea St

Sugar Cane Train

Mala
Wharf

Ala Moana St

Pu'unoa Pl

Kenui St

Hinau St

Limahana Pl

Lahaina
Station

Baker St

Lahainaluna Rd

To Hale
Pa'i (1.2mi)

Honoapi'ilani Hwy

Lahaina
Center

Papalaua St

Waine'e St

Lahainaluna Rd

Dickenson St

Luakini St

PACIFIC
OCEAN

Ferry to Moloka'i

Ferry to Lana'i

Prison St

Malu'uluolele
Park

Shaw St

Kamehameha
Iki Park

'Au'au Channel

Kaua'ala Rd

Ilikahi St

Front St

To Launiupoko Wayside Park (1mi);
Olowulu (5mi); Ma'alaea (14mi);

MAUI

a new 'missionary taboo' against womanizing. Buckle's crew came to shore seeking revenge against Richards, but a group of Hawaiian Christians came to Richards' aid and forced the whalers back to their boat.

The next year, after Governor Hoapili arrested the captain of the *John Palmer* for allowing women to board his ship, the angry crew shot a round of cannonballs at Richards' house. The captain was released, but laws forbidding liaisons between seamen and indigenous women stayed.

After Governor Hoapili's death, laws prohibiting liquor and prostitution were no longer strictly enforced, and whalers began to flock to Lahaina. In 1846, almost 400 ships pulled into port. Among the sailors who roamed Lahaina's streets was Herman Melville, who later penned *Moby-Dick*.

When the whaling industry fizzled in the 1860s, Lahaina became all but a ghost town. In the 1870s sugar came to Lahaina and it remained the backbone of the economy until tourism took over in the 1960s.

ORIENTATION
The focal point of Lahaina is its bustling small-boat harbor, backed by the old Pioneer Inn and Banyan Tree Sq. The main drag and tourist strip is Front St, which runs along the shoreline.

INFORMATION
Bookstores
Old Lahaina Book Emporium (☎ 661-1399; 834 Front St; ☼ 10am-9pm, to 6pm Sun) Maui's largest independent bookstore, with new and used volumes, plus vintage Hawaiiana.

Emergency
Police (☎ 244-6400) For nonemergencies.
Police Fire & Ambulance (☎ 911)

Internet Access
Aloha Internet Center (☎ 661-5192; Lahaina Center, 900 Front St; per 15 min $4, per hr $13; ☼ 11am-8pm) Come here if you need a quiet space.
Breakwall Café (☎ 661-7220; 505 Front St; per min 20¢; ☼ 7am-2pm Mon-Sat) Friendliest café around, and if you have your own laptop you can use their wi-fi connection free.
Buns of Maui (☎ 661-5407; Old Lahaina Center, 880 Front St; per min 10¢; ☼ 8am-5pm) Only your computers, but you can't beat the price. Huge frosted cinnamon buns and good java to boot.

Laundry
Coin laundry (Limahuna Pl, opp the Bakery; ☼ 24hr)

Library
Lahaina Public Library (☎ 662-3950; 680 Wharf St; ☼ noon-8pm Tue, 9am-5pm Wed & Thu, 10:30am-4:30pm Fri & Sat)

Media
Maui Time (☎ 661-3786; www.mauitime.com; 505 Front St) This weekly has entertainment listings for Lahaina and the rest of the island.

Medical Services
The Maui Memorial Hospital in Wailuku (p333) is the nearest hospital to Lahaina in case of emergencies.
Longs Drugs (☎ 667-4384; Lahaina Cannery Mall; ☼ 8am-10pm Mon-Fri, to 9pm Sat & Sun) Lahaina's largest pharmacy.
Maui Medical Group (☎ 249-8080; 130 Prison St; ☼ 7:30am-9pm Mon-Fri, 8am-noon Sat & Sun) This clinic handles nonemergencies.

Money
Both banks have 24-hour ATMS.
Bank of Hawaii (☎ 661-8781; Old Lahaina Center, 880 Front St)
First Hawaiian Bank (☎ 661-3655; 215 Papalaua St)

Post
Lahaina Post Office (☎ 661-0904; 1760 Honoapi'ilani Hwy, Lahaina, HI 96761; ☼ 8:30am-5pm Mon-Fri, 9am-1pm Sat) You'll have to go a couple of miles north of town near the Lahaina Civic Center to pick up general-delivery mail (held 30 days) sent to Lahaina.
Downtown post office station (132 Papalaua St, Old Lahaina Center; ☼ 8:15am-4:15pm Mon-Fri) More convenient if you're in town, but longer lines and fewer parking spaces.

Tourist Information
Lahaina Visitor Center (☎ 667-9193; www.visit lahaina.com; 648 Wharf St; ☼ 9am-5pm) This friendly volunteer-staffed information desk is inside the old courthouse at Banyan Tree Sq.

SIGHTS
Nearly half of Lahaina's best sights are clustered around the harbor, and most of the rest are either on Front St or within a couple of blocks of it. This makes Lahaina an ideal town to explore easily on foot. See also p306 for our recommended walking tour of Lahaina.

Banyan Tree Square

The largest banyan tree in the USA is so sprawling that it appears to be on the verge of pushing the old courthouse, which shares the square, clear off the block. Planted as a seedling in 1873 to commemorate the 50th anniversary of the first missionary arrival in Lahaina, the tree now stands more than 60ft high. It has 16 major trunks and scores of horizontally stretching branches reaching across the better part of an acre. Local kids like to use the aerial roots to swing from branch to branch. With its shaded benches, the square makes a nice spot to take a break from the crowds on Front St.

Old Courthouse

Behind the banyan tree looms Lahaina's **old courthouse** (648 Wharf St), built in 1859. The location overlooking the harbor was no coincidence. Smuggling was so rampant during the whaling era that the island government decided this was the ideal spot to house the customs operations, the courthouse and the jail – all neatly wrapped into a single building. It also held the governor's office and in 1898 the US annexation of Hawaii was formally concluded here.

Today the old jail in the courthouse basement is used by the nonprofit **Lahaina Arts Society** (☎ 661-0111; ☽ 9am-5pm) and the cells that once held drunken sailors now display fine artwork. It's a fun place to walk through. One of the cells has fascinating period photos showing the courthouse and banyan tree the way they looked a century ago. All exhibits are by island artists and include paintings, jewelry, pottery, woodcarvings and quality basketwork.

Lahaina Heritage Museum (☎ 661-3262; admission free; ☽ 9am-5pm), operated by the volunteers of the Lahaina Town Action Committee, offers a glimpse into Lahaina's history. The main exhibit changes every few months, but always on display are native Hawaiian items such as a chief's kava bowl, calabashes, octopus lures, ceremonial war clubs, stone oil lamps and poi pounders. The museum is on the building's upper floor.

Wo Hing Temple

One of the most unique structures on Front St is the two-story **Wo Hing Temple** (☎ 661-5553; 858 Front St; admission $1; ☽ 10am-4pm), which opened in 1912 as a meeting hall for the fraternal order of Chee Kung Tong, a Chinese benevolent society.

After WWII, many of its members moved to O'ahu seeking better business opportunities, and as Lahaina's ethnic Chinese population declined, so too did the building. It was restored and turned into a museum in 1984. Inside you'll find cultural artifacts, period photos, a ceremonial dancing-lion costume and a Taoist shrine, as well as a collection of opium bottles found during a cleanup of the grounds.

Whatever you do, don't miss the tin-roof cookhouse out back, which has been set up as a little theater to show fascinating films of old Hawaii shot by Thomas Edison in 1898 and 1906, soon after he invented the motion-picture camera. These grainy B&W shots set to a backdrop of slack-key-guitar music create a poignant image of old Hawaii, with *paniolo* (cowhands) running their cattle, cane workers in the fields and everyday street scenes.

Hale Pa'ahao

Hale Pa'ahao (Stuck-in-Irons House), Lahaina's old **prison** (☎ 667-1985; admission free; ☽ 10am-4pm), was built in 1852 by convicts who dismantled the old harborside fort and carted the stones here to construct the 8ft-high prison walls.

Inside, one of the whitewashed cells has an authentic-looking 'old seadog' mannequin with a recorded story about 'life in this here calaboose.' In another cell, you'll find a list of offenses and arrests for the year 1855. The top three offenses were drunkenness (330 arrests), adultery and fornication (111), and 'furious riding' (89). Others include profanity, lascivious conduct, aiding deserting sailors and drinking 'awa (kava moonshine). Hawaiians could collect bounties by turning in sailors who jumped ship or fooled around with local women.

There's also a copy of a 16-year-old seaman's diary, vividly describing his time spent in the prison.

Hale Kahiko

With its three *pili* (thatched) houses, **Hale Kahiko** (Lahaina Center; admission free; ☽ 9am-6pm) replicates an ancient Hawaiian village. Despite the irony of being at the rear of a shopping center, the site offers an insightful glimpse of what life was like in Hawaii before Western development swept the landscape. Look at the entrance for a brochure that provides more historical background.

The buildings have been authentically constructed, using ohia-wood posts, native thatch and coconut-fiber lashings. The grounds are planted in native flora that Hawaiians relied upon for food and medicinal purposes. Each *hale* (house) had a different function; one was used as family sleeping quarters, another as a men's eating house (traditional *kapu* – taboos – forced men and women to eat separately), and the third as a workshop where women made tapa. Inside you'll find everyday implements from the period, such as gourd containers, woven baskets and poi pounders.

Baldwin House

Dating from 1834, **Baldwin House** (☎ 661-3262; 696 Front St; adult/family $3/5; 🕙 10am-4pm) is the oldest Western-style building in Lahaina. This two-story house was home to Reverend Dwight Baldwin, a missionary doctor who also used it as Lahaina's first medical clinic. The exterior of the coral and rock building originally looked like the Masters' Reading Room next door, but it has since been plastered over. The weighty walls beneath the plaster are a full 24in thick, which keeps the house cool year-round.

It took the Baldwins 161 days to get to Hawaii from their native Connecticut. These early missionaries traveled neither fast nor light, and the house still holds the collection of china and furniture they brought with them around the Horn. Also on display are some fine Hawaiian quilts. The entrance fee includes a brief tour.

Waine'e Church

Built in 1832, **Waine'e Church** (535 Waine'e St) was the first stone church in Hawaii, though it's had problems standing its ground. The steeple and bell collapsed in 1858. In 1894 the church was torched by royalists because its minister supported the annexation of Hawaii. A second church, built to replace the original, burned to the ground in 1947, and the third was blown away in a storm a few years later. One could get the impression that the old Hawaiian gods didn't take kindly to the house of this foreign deity! The fourth version has been standing since 1953 and still holds regular Sunday services.

The adjacent **cemetery** is more interesting than the church. Here lie several notables: Governor Hoapili, who ordered the original church built; Queen Keopuolani, a wife of Kamehameha I; and Reverend William Richards, Lahaina's first missionary.

Library Grounds

The area around the **public library** (p303) was once the site of a royal taro field. Kamehameha III himself sometimes worked in the mud here to prove to his subjects that he believed in the dignity of labor.

This was also the location of the first Western-style building in Hawaii, the **Brick Palace**, erected by Kamehameha I so he could keep watch on arriving ships. Despite the grand name, this 'palace' was a modest two-story structure built around 1800 by two ex-convicts from Botany Bay. All that remains today is the excavated foundation, found on the *makai* (seaward) side of the library.

The nearby **Hauola Stone** is a water-worn lava stone on the shoreline. The ancient Hawaiians believed this flat, seat-shaped stone emitted healing powers to those who sat upon it. To spot it, look to the right as you face the ocean – it's the middle of three stones. In the 14th and 15th centuries royal women sat here while giving birth to the next generation of chiefs and royalty.

About 100ft south of the Hauola Stone stands the **Lahaina Lighthouse**, which lays claims to being the oldest lighthouse in the Pacific. Commissioned in 1840 to aid whaling ships pulling into Lahaina, it shone with a beam fueled by sperm-whale oil. The current structure dates from 1916.

Lahaina Jodo Mission

Enjoy a quiet moment at this **Buddhist mission** (12 Ala Moana St), where a 12ft-high bronze Buddha sits serenely in the courtyard looking out across the Pacific toward its homeland in Japan. Nearby is a lofty pagoda and a 3-ton temple bell, Hawaii's largest, which is rung 11 times at 8pm daily.

Hale Pa'i

The site of the first printing press in Hawaii is at **Hale Pa'i** (☎ 661-3262; 980 Lahainaluna Rd; admission by donation; 🕙 10am-3pm Mon-Fri), a cottage at the side of Lahainaluna High School, 1.5 miles from Hwy 30 at the end of Lahainaluna Rd.

MAUI

The main purpose of the press was to make the Bible available to Hawaiians, but it was also used to produce other works, including the first Hawaiian botany book and, in 1834, Hawaii's first newspaper. The old Ramage press was so heavily used that it fell apart in the 1850s, but several of the items printed from it are on display. If you want to get a feel for the work, you can use a replica of the original equipment to handpress your own copy of a page from the first Hawaiian primer. Reprints of amusing 'Temperance Maps' ($5) drawn by an early missionary make a curious souvenir.

Launiupoko Wayside Park

About 2.5 miles south of Lahaina at the 18-mile marker, this is a popular place to watch the sun set behind Lana'i. On the park's small stretch of gray sand, a children's wading pool fills up at high tide. The park has showers, toilets and picnic tables.

ACTIVITIES

Lahaina is not known for its beaches, which are largely shallow and rocky. For swimming and snorkeling, head up the coast to neighboring Ka'anapali (p317).

For boat tours, whale watching and other cruises, see p308.

Diving

Diving boats leave from the harbor with programs suited for all levels, including novices.

Maui Dive Shop (☎ 661-5388, 800-542-3483; www .mauidiveshop.com; Lahaina Cannery Mall; dives from $80, courses from $300; ☺ 8am-9pm) is a reliable full-service dive shop.

Lahaina Divers (☎ 667-7496, 800-998-3483; www .lahainadivers.com; 143 Dickenson St; dives from $100; ☺ 6am-8pm) offers a full menu of dives, including daily 'discover scuba' dives for non-certified divers that go to a reef crawling with turtles.

Surfing

The section of beach south of the **505 Front St** shopping center is a favorite spot for young surfers. Surfers also take to the waters just offshore from **Launiupoko Wayside Park**, and a couple of local surfing competitions take place there during the year.

Several places in Lahaina offer surfing lessons for beginners. Most guarantee you'll be able to stand and ride a wave after a two-hour lesson, or it's free. Rates vary depending upon the number of people in the class and the length of the lesson, but for a two-hour lesson expect to pay about $55 in a small group, $175 for a private lesson.

Goofy Foot Surf School (☎ 244-9283; www.goofy footsurfschool.com; 505 Front St; ☺ 8am-5pm) does a fine job of combining fundamentals with fun. In addition to lessons, it runs daylong surf camps and specialized clinics.

Nancy Emerson, who was winning international surfing contests by the time she was 14, runs **Nancy Emerson's School of Surfing** (☎ 244-7873; www.surfclinics.com; 505 Front St; ☺ 8am-5pm), the oldest surfing school on the island.

WALKING TOUR

Lahaina's fascinating history comes to life on this 1.5-mile walking tour that takes you to pivotal historical sites from the days of ancient Hawaii through to the missionary and whaling eras. You'll need a few hours to explore the churches, cemeteries and museums, and poke around at a leisurely pace.

Take a stroll around **Banyan Tree Sq** (**1**; p304), investigate the **old courthouse** (p304) and enjoy the view from the harbor before

Start Banyan Tree Sq
Finish Pioneer Inn
Duration 2-3 hours
Distance 1.5 miles

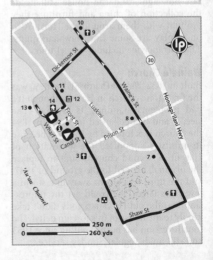

starting your walk at the west side of the square. The four cannons you see opposite the old courthouse were raised from the wreck of a Russian ship that sank in Honolulu Harbor in 1816. In a comic twist, they now point directly at Lahaina's small-boat harbor, which is jam-packed with sunset sailboats, fishing vessels and windjammers.

At the corner of Wharf and Canal Sts, look for a reconstructed section of coral wall from a **fort (2)** built in 1832 to keep rowdy whalers in line. At the height of its use, the fort had 47 cannons, most salvaged from sunken foreign ships. A nearby public market was nicknamed 'Rotten Row' for all its drunks, gamblers and licentious women. Each day at dusk, a Hawaiian sentinel beat a drum to alert sailors to return to their ships. Those who didn't make it back in time ended up imprisoned in the fort. In 1854, the fort was dismantled and its coral blocks were used to build the new prison.

Continue up Canal St, which borders the square and was once part of a canal system that ran through Lahaina. An enterprising US consul officer built this section of the canal in the 1840s to allow whalers easier access to freshwater supplies – for a fee. Because of problems with mosquitoes, most of the canal system was filled in long ago. Incidentally, Hawaii had no mosquitoes until the whalers brought them in from North America in their water barrels.

Turn right on Front St to reach **Holy Innocents' Episcopal Church (3**; 561 Front St), which has an interior splashed in a Hawaiiana motif. Paintings on the koa altar depict a fisher in an outrigger canoe and Hawaiian farmers harvesting taro and breadfruit. Above the altar is a Hawaiian Madonna and Child. Until the turn of the 20th century, the church property was the site of a vacation home belonging to Hawaii's last monarch, Queen Lili'uokalani.

Just south of the church you'll find a grassy building foundation, which is all that remains of **Hale Piula (4)**, Lahaina's halfhearted attempt at a royal palace. Construction on the palace was started in the 1830s but never completed – Kamehameha III preferred to sleep in a Hawaiian-style thatched house, and at any rate the capital was moved to Honolulu halfway through the project. The structure was later dismantled and the stones used to build the harborside courthouse.

Across the street is **Malu'uluolele Park (5)**, which once contained a pond with a central island, Moku'ula, that was one of the most sacred royal compounds in Hawaii. It was home to several kings and the site of an ornate burial chamber. Despite its history, the pond was buried and today it's a county park with basketball courts, tennis courts, a baseball field and not a hint of its fascinating past. But that may eventually change, as preservationists hope to return at least some of the site to its pre-Western state.

Turn left on Shaw St, then left on Waine'e St to reach **Waine'e Church (6**; p305). Stroll the old cemetery adjacent to the church, where several of the most important figures in 19th-century Maui are buried. Many of the old tombstones have evocative inscriptions and photo cameos.

Next up, as you continue north, is **Hongwanji Mission (7**; 551 Waine'e St), a Buddhist temple dating to 1904. Although it's usually locked, you can glance in through the glass doors at the gilded altar.

You'll find one of Lahaina's more notorious sights, **Hale Pa'ahao (8**; p304), on the corner of Prison St. Here you can take a peek into the old prison cells where drunken whalers once served time for debauchery and other misdeeds.

Continue north along Waine'e St to Dickenson St to reach **Maria Lanakila Church (9)**, Maui's first Catholic church, which dates to 1846 and has a tile-work portrait of Father Damien. Adjacent to the church is the **Seamen's Cemetery (10)**, which despite its name has only one seaman's tombstone that can be identified. However, historical records indicate that numerous sailors from the whaling era were buried here, including a shipmate of Herman Melville's from the *Acushnet*.

From here, walk down Dickenson St toward the harbor. On the corner of Front and Dickenson is the **Masters' Reading Room (11)**, which during Lahaina's whaling heyday was an officers club for captains. From here captains could keep an eye on rabble-rousing in the harbor across the road. The original construction of coral and stone block remains intact, and it now houses the offices of the Lahaina Restoration Foundation, a group instrumental in preserving Lahaina's historical sites. Next door, on the same property, is the **Baldwin House (12**; p305), a missionary house that's now a museum.

MAUI

Cross the road to return to the harbor, stopping to view the **Brick Palace** (**13**; p305) and the Hauola Stone (p305), two waterfront sights at the rear of the library.

Now is a good time to treat yourself to a cold drink at the atmospheric **Pioneer Inn** (**14**; p311), the most prominent landmark on the harborfront. For half a century this veranda-wrapped building was Lahaina's only hotel; Jack London once slept here. It's got a whaling-era atmosphere, with swinging doors, ship figureheads and signs warning against womanizing in the rooms. Actually, the inn was built in 1901, long after the whaling boom had passed, but nobody seems to notice or care.

LAHAINA FOR CHILDREN
Kids will find plenty to catch their interest here. The **banyan tree** (p304) is a cool sight and those dangling aerial roots invite at least one Tarzan-style swing. The **sugarcane train** (p308) makes a popular family outing. Or let the *na keiki* (children) try their hand at surfing, taking a lesson from kid-friendly **Goofy Foot Surf School** (p306). And there are plenty of other water activities. Head to neighboring **Ka'anapali** (p319) for fun on the beach and good snorkeling. In the winter the whale watching (see below) is awesome.

TOURS
One glimpse of the harbor is all it takes to understand where the action is in this town. Lahaina Harbor brims with catamarans and other vessels catering to the tourist trade. You'll find scores of day cruises, from whale-watchers and glass-bottomed boats to daylong sails to Lana'i.

Atlantis Submarine (☎ 667-2224, 800-548-6262; www.atlantisadventures.com; adult/child $80/40; ☻ departures 8am-2pm) See the world from a porthole aboard this 65ft sub. The sub dives to a depth of about 130ft to see coral, fish and sunken ships. Tours leave from Lahaina Harbor.

Pacific Whale Foundation (☎ 879-8811, 800-942-5311; www.pacificwhale.org; adult/child $27/15) This nonprofit foundation offers several cruises, all with a bent on learning more about the marine environment. In winter their whale-watchers sail out of Lahaina Harbor eight times a day; catch the 7am cruise and you'll not only save 30% of the regular fare but also get the calmest seas. In the unlikely event you don't spot whales, your next trip is free and kids under age six are always free.

Reefdancer (☎ 667-2133; Lahaina Harbor; adult/child 1 hr $33/19, 1½ hr $45/25; ☻ departures 10am-2:15pm)

A glass-bottomed boat with a submerged lower deck lined with underwater viewing windows.

Sugarcane train (☎ 667-6851; 975 Limahana Pl; www.sugarcanetrain.com; adult/child $16/10; ☻ 9am-5pm, four times daily) The century-old sugarcane train once carried cane from the fields to Lahaina's sugar mill, and now carries tourists on a 30-minute ride between Lahaina and Ka'anapali. The train's got character, but the ride's a bit pokey and there's not that much to see, so it's an experience best enjoyed by steam-train buffs and kids.

Trilogy Excursions (☎ 661-4743, 888-225-6284; www.sailtrilogy.com; adult/child $170/85) A top-notch operation with active catamaran tours that let you get your feet wet. The traditional daylong (6am to 4pm) trip from Lahaina to Lana'i's Hulopo'e Beach includes a barbecue lunch, volleyball on the beach and snorkeling time, or catch the 10am boat that adds on dinner and sails back to Lahaina amid the sunset. In winter there's whale watching along the way and you can spot spinner dolphins all year. Discounts are given for online booking.

FESTIVALS & EVENTS
Lahaina Town Action Committee (☎ 667-9194, 888-310-1117; www.visitlahaina.com) provides updated details on Lahaina events.

Chinese New Year (falls between mid-January and mid-February) Front St turns into a street festival with colorful lion dances and lots of firecrackers.

Ocean Arts Festival (weekend in mid-March) Celebrates the migration of humpback whiles with Hawaiian music, hula and games at Banyan Tree Sq.

Banyan Tree (mid-April) The tree gets its own two-day birthday party, complete with a frosted cake and a serenade of live music.

International Festival of Canoes (mid-May to last Saturday in May; www.mauicanoefest.com) Master carvers from around the Pacific descend on Lahaina to carve outrigger canoes, with the whole process from log to launch taking place right in town; culminates with a parade down Front St and the launching of the canoes.

Fourth of July Parade on Front St and a fireworks show over the harbor.

Ole Longboard Classic (second Saturday in August) Maui's premier long-board surfing event is held at Launiupolo Park.

A Taste of Lahaina (mid-September) Maui's big culinary blast features cooking demonstrations by Maui's top chefs, tasting booths, entertainment and a kids' zone.

Mardi Gras of the Pacific (Halloween night) Attracts a whopping 30,000 revelers for music, dancing and costume competitions; the action is right on Front St, which is closed to traffic.

Banyan tree (first Saturday in December) Lahaina lights its favorite tree with thousands of colorful lights; accompanied by music, food booths and a craft show.

SLEEPING

Despite the flood of tourists that fill its streets, Lahaina doesn't have that many places to stay. The nearest campground (p314) is in Olowalu, 5 miles south of town.

Budget

Patey's Place (☎ 667-0999; www.alternative-hawaii.com /affordable/maui.htm; 761 Waine'e St; dm $25, s/d $55/60, with shared bathroom $45/50; P ⬛) A branch of the Big Island hostel by the same name, this casual little operation is Lahaina's only hostel. Patey's occupies an aging building, but it's got a fresh coat of paint and central location. There's a dorm for men and a dorm for women, each sleeping five to six people, as well as five private rooms. Guests share a common kitchen and living room and the place has coin-operated laundry facilities and lockers. Internet use is $6 per hour.

Mid-Range

Bambula Inn (☎ 667-6753, 800-544-5524; www.maui .net/~bambula; 518 Ilikahi St; r $85, studios $110-120; P ❀) You'll feel like part of the family at this delightful place, nestled in a garden of banana trees and flowers. The bright, cheerful studios have private lanai. Only the most expensive unit has air-con, but all are cooled sufficiently by ceiling fans. As a bonus, there's snorkel gear to borrow and free sunset cruises on the family sailboat, with whale sightings practically guaranteed during winter. French and German are spoken.

Lahaina Inn (☎ 661-0577, 800-669-3444; www .lahainainn.com; 127 Lahainaluna Rd; r incl breakfast $120-130, ste $170; P ❀) Walking into this little century-old inn is like stepping back in history. Its 12 guest rooms were pain-

---

THE AUTHOR'S CHOICE

Plantation Inn (☎ 667-9225, 800-433-6815, www.theplantationinn.com; 174 Lahainaluna Rd; with breakfast r $160-210, ste $220-250; P ❀ ⬛) Hands down the classiest place to stay in Lahaina, this two-story Victorian-style inn beams with period elegance. Its plantation charm is accented with rocking chairs on the porch and antique furnishings and four-poster beds in the rooms. A generous continental breakfast is provided at Gerard's (p311), the French restaurant downstairs at the inn.

---

stakingly restored and decorated to recreate their original character. They're small but delightfully atmospheric, and each has hardwood floors, floral wallpaper, antique furnishings and a lanai. To keep the period ambience intact, there's no TV in the rooms. Parking costs $5.

Makai Inn (☎ 662-3200; www.makaiinn.net; 1415 Front St; r $75-130; P) Right on the water at the north end of town, this family-run place is a real gem. Although it's an older condo complex, the rooms are bright and breezy, with Hawaiian prints on the walls and unsurpassed oceanfront lanai. The tropical garden in the central courtyard would be the envy of any top-end resort. All units have full kitchens; the main price difference is the distance from the ocean – the cheapest place is just 40ft from the water! There's no minimum stay. Ask about discounts for longer visits.

Pioneer Inn (☎ 661-3636, 800-457-5457; www.pioneer innmaui.com; 658 Wharf St; r $120-165; ste $165-185; ❀ ⬛) It can be noisy from the traffic and the raucous bar, but this historic two-story hotel couldn't be more in the middle of the action. Unfortunately, the funky old harbor-front rooms for which the inn was famous are gone. Instead, small motel-style rooms face either Front St, Banyan Sq or the inn's courtyard. Considering the size of the rooms and the less-than-soundproof walls, the rates are a bit pricey, though you might find a deal online.

Lahaina Roads (☎ 667-2712, 800-669-6284; www .klahani.com; 1403 Front St; units $150; P ⬛) North of the town center, near the Lahaina Cannery Mall, this modern condominium complex has roomy one-bedroom units with a sofa bed in the living room that can sleep up to four. All units are oceanfront, just a stone's throw from the water, and you can enjoy the view from your private lanai.

EATING

Lahaina is chock-full of places to eat, ranging from unpretentious little cafés to some of Maui's most acclaimed dinner restaurants. No visit to Maui would be complete without enjoying a dinner on Front St, where the restaurants hang over the ocean and sport unforgettable sunset views. Keep in mind that so many folks staying in Ka'anapali pour into Lahaina at dinnertime that the traffic often jams up. Give yourself extra time, and call ahead to make reservations.

MAUI

TOP 10 EATS

- **David Paul's Lahaina Grill** (p311), Lahaina
- **Pacific'O** (p311), Lahaina
- **I'o** (p311), Lahaina
- **Sansei Seafood Restaurant & Sushi Bar** (p343), Kihei
- **Roy's Kahana Bar & Grill** (p322), Kahana
- **Hali'imaile General Store** (p368), Hali'imaile
- **Mama's Fish House** (p354), Pa'ia
- **Who's the Boss?** (p334), Wailuku
- **Moana Bakery & Café** (p353), Pa'ia
- **Mañana Garage** (p331), Kahului

Budget

Bakery (☎ 667-9062; 991 Limahana Pl; snacks $1.50-5; ☯ 5:30am-2pm Mon-Fri, to 1pm Sat, to noon Sun) Don't be deterred by its stark warehouse appearance – on the other side of the rickety screen door you'll enter Lahaina's best bakery. You can get crispy French breads, flaky turnovers and huge muffins, plus sandwiches made to order and fresh salads.

Cilantro (☎ 667-5444; Old Lahaina Center, 880 Front St; mains $3.50-9; ☯ 10:30am-9pm, to 10pm Fri & Sat) Mexican food is as fresh as it comes at this restaurant where slices of green avocado and sprigs of cilantro brighten the plates. Try the tacos filled with lemon-herb chipotle rotisserie chicken or head straight for the top-of-the-line Margarita shrimp combo plate.

Kahuna Kebab (884 Front St; sandwiches $4-9; ☯ 11am-10pm) Tucked into a courtyard off Front St, this popular local eatery attracts surfers with its killer wrapped-'ahi (yellowfin tuna) sandwich. It also does a nice job with veggie wraps, chicken kebabs and pita sandwiches. Order at the window and chow down at one of the shaded café tables.

Sunrise Café (☎ 661-8558; 693-A Front St; mains $5-9; ☯ 6am-4pm) Looking for a place to have an early breakfast near Lahaina harbor? This little hole-in-the-wall café cooks up a spicy breakfast burrito, decadent chocolate pancakes and Belgian waffles piled sky-high with tropical fruit. Salads and sandwiches round out the lunch menu.

Safeway (☎ 667-4392; Lahaina Cannery Mall, 1221 Honopi'ilani Hwy; ☯ 24hr) Supermarket with take-out salads and a deli.

Mid-Range

Café O'Lei Lahaina (☎ 661-9491; 839 Front St; lunches $7-10, dinner mains $15-21; ☯ 10:30am-9:30pm) A standout in the run of oceanfront restaurants lining Front St, this breezy place is cozier than its neighbors and offers a more inspired menu. At lunch, choose from creative salads with organic Ha'iku veggies, focaccia sandwiches and mains such as blackened mahimahi (a white-fleshed fish) with papaya salsa. At dinner, there's a changing menu of fresh seafood dishes.

Thai Chef (☎ 667-2814; Old Lahaina Center, 880 Front St; mains $9-16; ☯ lunch Mon-Fri, dinner nightly) Winner of the 'Best Thai Restaurant on Maui' vote by readers of the island's daily newspaper, this intimate little restaurant is worth searching out. The spring rolls served with a pineapple dipping sauce are heavenly, while the Chiang Mai chicken bursts with the fragrance of fresh cilantro and mint. Fried bananas topped with coconut ice cream make the perfect finale. No alcohol is served, but you can bring your own bottle.

Lahaina Fish Co (☎ 661-3472; 831 Front St; mains $10-25; ☯ lunch & dinner) Perched on a balcony above the shoreline, you could almost stick out a pole and catch your own fish. Fortunately, the work is done for you. The fish is fresh, the servings generous and the sunset view second to none. Lots of dishes to choose from, but if you want to walk away with the best value, order the generous fish-and-chips, which costs just $10.

Kimo's (☎ 661-4811; 845 Front St; lunch $7-12, dinner $16-26; ☯ lunch & dinner) You get your oceanfront, your sunset view, and the place is large and lively enough that the kids can relax and be themselves. All the usual fresh fish, steak and chicken dinners come with warm carrot muffins, sourdough rolls and a Caesar salad. Lunch covers the gamut, from cheeseburgers to the catch of the day.

Cheeseburger in Paradise (☎ 661-4855; 811 Front St; mains $8-12; ☯ 8am-11pm) No place on the waterfront draws a larger crowd than this energetic open-air restaurant that's built its reputation on Black Angus cheeseburgers served up with Jimmy Buffett–style music. If a juicy burger doesn't catch your fancy, this little slice of paradise also makes decent

Cajun chicken sandwiches, vegetarian burgers and specialty salads.

Penne Pasta Café (☎ 661-6633; 180 Dickenson St; appetizers $2-6, mains $7-14; ☯ lunch Mon-Fri, dinner Sat & Sun) It's a simple place on a side street rather than the main drag, but that helps keep prices low, and you can dine alfresco at streetside tables. The Italian menu is health-oriented, with a range of traditional pastas or gluten-free brown-rice pasta, as well as cheese flatbreads and bountiful salads. For dessert, don't the miss the tiramisu.

Kobe Japanese Steakhouse (☎ 667-5555; 136 Dickenson St; dinner $10-26; ☯ 5:30-11:30pm) Watch the Japanese chefs yield their flying knives at this lively teppanyaki (open-grill cooking) restaurant. Choose from chicken, steak, seafood or tofu for the main course, all accompanied with appetizer, soup, rice and tea.

Lahaina Coolers (☎ 661-7082; 180 Dickenson St; breakfast & lunch $7-11, dinner mains $12-25; ☯ 8am-midnight) This open-air restaurant relies heavily on Maui-grown produce. For island flavor, try the 'local pizza,' a medley of Portuguese sausage, pineapple, Kula tomatoes and Maui onions. The rest of the menu ranges wildly from vegetarian shepherd's pie to demiglazed filet mignon.

Top End

David Paul's Lahaina Grill (☎ 667-5117; 127 Lahainaluna Rd; mains $26-39; ☯ from 6pm; ☒) This sophisticated chef-driven restaurant, in historic Lahaina Inn, has drawn accolades from leading gourmet magazines. The New American menu mixes local ingredients with tastes from around the continent and the Pacific Rim. House specialties include tequila shrimp with firecracker rice, seared 'ahi crusted in Maui onions and Kona coffee-roasted rack of lamb. There's no surer bet for a fine meal in Lahaina.

Pacific'O (☎ 667-4341; 505 Front St; lunch $10-15, dinner $20-30; ☯ 11am-4pm & 5:30-10pm) Here you'll find beachside tables, superb contemporary Pacific cuisine and an award-winning wine list. Start off with the coconut seafood chowder, brimming with rock shrimp and Maui herbs, then move on to adventurous dinner mains like Indonesian painted fish with grilled pineapple. Lunch is a tamer affair, with salads and sandwiches – but the same ocean view.

I'o (☎ 661-8422; 505 Front St; mains $18-28; ☯ dinner) Adjacent to its sister restaurant Pacific'O, this is chef James McDonald's venture into nouveau Hawaiian cuisine. I'o is unquestionably the favorite top-end oceanfront dinner restaurant in Lahaina. The innovative menu includes such delights as prawns in passion fruit, blue crab cakes with goat cheese and filet mignon with Maui fern shoots. The dining room makes postmodern aquarium chic work, and if you dine early you'll overhear the Feast at Lele luau (p312) out back.

Gerard's (☎ 661-8939; 174 Lahainaluna Rd; mains $27-50; ☯ 6-9pm; ☒) A candlelit setting and authentic French fare characterize this romantic dinner restaurant. It's easy to see why this is where islanders come to celebrate wedding anniversaries. The menu includes traditional favorites like duck foie gras, rack of lamb and escargot with wild mushrooms, but you'll find plenty of fresh Hawaiian seafood, including Kona lobster, as well. A superb wine list and delectable Maui-berry homemade sorbets top it off.

DRINKING

Aloha Mixed Plate (☎ 661-3322; 1285 Front St; ☯ 10:30am-10pm; ℗) This peppy beach shack at the north side of town offers a fun slice of Hawaii that's hard to find elsewhere on Maui. Dig your toes into the sand as you enjoy a rainbow-colored tropical drink, perhaps with liliko'i (passion fruit) puree and vodka, or an old-fashioned pina colada brimming with rum. The pupu (snacks) menu has tantalizing treats – don't miss the chutney coconut prawns. If you come at around sunset and you'll be able to overhear Old Lahaina Luau's music next from door for free!

Best Western Pioneer Inn (☯ 11am-10pm) This century-old landmark, with its whaling-era atmosphere and harborside veranda ideal for people watching, is the most popular place for a drink in Lahaina. Guitarists playing soft-rock or country music add to the mood at sunset. Get $2 Buds from 3pm to 6pm.

Bamboo Sports Bar (☎ 667-0361; 505 Front St; ☯ 11am-2am) Known as the place 'where locals hang loose,' this is where everyone, tourists and islanders alike, comes to watch sports on big-screen satellite TV and shoot a game of pool. Or down a few cold beers along with Asian-style pupu that include sushi and Thai salads.

ENTERTAINMENT

Front St is the heart of Lahaina's nightlife and much of what's happening on the island after dark happens here, as has been the case since the whaling days. Check the *Maui Scene* magazine in Thursday's *Maui News* or the free weekly *Maui Time*. Typically, night-spots in Lahaina don't have a cover charge, unless there's a big-name performer.

Nightclubs

Moose McGillicuddy's (☎ 667-7758; 844 Front St) Head here if you want to dance up a storm. With its two dance floors, the place hops with DJs and live music from 9pm to 2am. The decor kicks back to the Beach Boys era, with old license plates, movie posters and other Americana kitsch galore. Honeymooners, frat boys and everyone else rub shoulders here. Happy hour (from 3pm to 6pm) features draft beers for a mere $1 and mai tais (alcoholic drinks made from rum, grenadine, and lemon and pineapple juices) for $2.

Hard Rock Cafe (☎ 667-7400; Lahaina Center, 900 Front St) There's not much that's Hawaiian about this rock-themed chain restaurant, but it does get jiggy to the island's best reggae on Monday from 10pm. Also live rock on Friday and Saturday nights. Long happy hours: 3pm to 6pm and 10pm to midnight.

Cheeseburger in Paradise (☎ 661-4855; 811 Front St) This waterfront eatery looming over the ocean is as breezy and open-air as it gets. You can hear the music from a block away, and everything here says tropics, from the rattan on the lanai to the frosty margaritas. There's live music from 4:30pm to 11pm, typically country and soft-rock sounds.

Compadres (☎ 661-7189; 1221 Honoapi'ilani Hwy) There's not much atmosphere at this Mexican restaurant at the Lahaina Cannery Mall,

but the place really comes to life with salsa music and dancing every Saturday night from 10pm.

Longhi's (☎ 667-2288; 888 Front St) This upscale Italian restaurant with its art deco decor and koa-wood dance floor has live music and dancing from 9:30pm on Friday. It tends to draw an older, well-heeled crowd.

Pacific'O (☎ 667-4341; 505 Front St) With a romantic setting on the waterfront, this intimate candlelit restaurant has live jazz from 9pm to midnight on Friday and Saturday.

BJ's (☎ 661-0700; 730 Front St) On the inland side of Front St, BJ's still boasts a view of the ocean and has live music from 7:30pm to 10pm. Incidentally, this was where the legendary 1970s Blue Max club partied.

Many restaurants have live music in the evening, including seaside **Kimo's** (☎ 661-4811; 845 Front St), which has Hawaiian-influenced music, and the next-door **Café O'Lei Lahaina** (☎ 661-9491; 839 Front St), which often has a slightly jazzier theme.

Luau, Hula & Theater

Lahaina lays claim to some of the best shows on the island. Its two luau have few rivals anywhere in Hawaii (reservations are essential) and catching one is a sure bet to highlight a vacation.

Feast at Lele (☎ 667-5353; www.feastatlele.com; 505 Front St; adult/child $95/65; ⏰ 6-9pm) Cooked up by the award-winning chef at I'o restaurant, this luau is an intimate affair on the beach. Four dance performances in Hawaiian, Tongan, Tahitian and Samoan styles are each matched to a food course. With the Hawaiian music, you're served *kalua* (cooked in an earthen pit) pork, poi and taro; with the Tongan, lobster and octopus salad; and so on. A true gourmet feast.

'Ulalena (☎ 661-9913; www.ulalena.com; 880 Front St, Old Lahaina Center; adult/child $50/28; ⏰ 7:30pm Mon-Sat) Along the lines of a Cirque du Soleil–style show, this extravaganza has its home at the 700-seat Maui Theatre. The theme is Hawaiian history and storytelling; the medium is modern dance, brilliant stage sets, acrobats and elaborate costumes. All in all, an entertaining, high-energy performance.

Lahaina Cannery Mall (☎ 661-5304) This shopping center at the north side of town hosts free *na keiki* hula shows at 1pm on Saturday and Sunday and free Polynesian dance performances at 7pm on Tuesday.

THE AUTHOR'S CHOICE

Old Lahaina Luau (☎ 667-4332; www.old lahainaluau.com; 1251 Front St; adult/child $85/55; ⏰ 5:15-8:15pm) No other luau on Maui comes close to matching this one for its authenticity, presentation and all-around aloha. The hula troupe is first-rate and the feast is superb as well, with high-quality Hawaiian fare and none of the long lines you'll find at a resort-hotel luau. It's held on the beach near the Lahaina Cannery Mall.

Cinemas

Multiscreen theaters showing first-run movies include **Lahaina Wharf Cinemas** (Wharf Cinema Center, 658 Front St) and **Front Street Theaters** (Lahaina Center, 900 Front St). For showtimes at either, call ☎ 249-2222.

SHOPPING

Lahaina has numerous arts and crafts galleries, some with high-quality collections and others with mediocre works. 'Art night,' from 7pm to 10pm on Friday, is when Lahaina galleries have openings, occasionally with entertainment and hors d'oeuvres.

Banyan Tree Sq is the focal point for several events. On weekends it's the site of an arts and crafts fair, with Hawaiian music and entertainment throughout the day.

Lahaina Arts Society (☎ 667-9193; 648 Wharf St) The best place to start any artwork browsing is at this gallery in the old courthouse on Banyan Tree Sq. This society, which represents more than 100 island artists, is a nonprofit collective so you'll find some of the best prices in Lahaina. The art varies, but some of Maui's best-known artists got their start here, and there are some gems among the collection.

Village Gifts & Fine Art (☎ 661-5199; Front & Dickenson Sts) This little shop in the Masters' Reading Room sells jewelry, prints, wooden bowls and silkscreened fabrics. A portion of the proceeds helps support the Lahaina Restoration Foundation.

Gecko Store (☎ 661-1078; 703 Front St) A fun shop dedicated to guess what? Yep, everything here – T-shirts, toys, jewelry, you name it – crawls with cute little geckos. You'll be amazed what geckos can do.

Maui to Go Arts & Crafts (☎ 662-0799; 505 Front St) Features an extensive collection, from pineapple-design wind chimes and nostalgic Hawaiian reproductions to fine hand-blown glass and crafted koa bowls.

Village Gallery (☎ 661-4402; 120 Dickenson St) This substantial art gallery carries Hawaiian-influenced oils, watercolors and prints, and also has changing exhibits featuring well-known island artists. Much of the work is museum quality.

GETTING THERE & AWAY

Most flights to Maui land at Kahului airport (p298). Ferries to Lana'i (p387) and Moloka'i (p403) dock at Lahaina Harbor.

The Honoapi'ilani Hwy (Hwy 30) connects Lahaina with Ka'anapali and points north, and with Ma'alaea to the south and Wailuku to the east. To get to Lahaina from the airport in Kahului, take Hwy 380 south to Hwy 30; by car or taxi, the drive takes about 45 minutes.

GETTING AROUND
To/From the Airport

Most visitors rent cars at Kahului airport, then drive to Lahaina; see p300. **Executive Shuttle** (☎ 669-2300, 800-833-2303) provides the best and cheapest taxi service between Lahaina and the Kahului airport, charging $30 for one person, $35 for two and $2 more for each additional person up to six.

Bicycle

West Maui Cycles (☎ 661-9005; 1087 Hinau; per day $20-50, weekly rental $100-200; ☒ 8:30am-5:30pm Mon-Sat, 10am-4pm Sun) rents a variety of quality road performance and hybrid bikes.

Bus

The Maui Public Transit System (p298) connects Kahului and Lahaina six times a day ($3, one hour) with a stop at Ma'alaea, where connections can be made to Kihei and Wailea. Buses leave from the Wharf Cinema Center every two hours between 8:30am and 6:30pm.

The Akina West Maui Shuttle (p300) connects Lahaina and Ka'anapali ($1, 25 minutes). Buses operate once an hour throughout the day and stop en route at the Lahaina Cannery Mall.

Car & Motorcycle

Hawaiian Riders (☎ 662-4386; 196 Lahainaluna; ☒ 8am-5:30pm) rents mopeds from $29 a day, Harley-Davidson motorcycles from $100.

PARKING

Much of Front St has free on-street parking, but there's always a line of cruising cars. Your best bet is the large parking lot at the corner of Front and Prison Sts, where there's free public parking with a three-hour limit. There are also a few private parking lots, averaging $5 per day, with the biggest one being Republic Parking on Dickenson St. Otherwise, park at one of the shopping centers and get your parking ticket validated for free by making a purchase.

MAUI

Taxi
Ali'i Cab (☎ 661-3688), **LA Taxi** (☎ 661-4545) and **Rainbow Taxi** (☎ 661-0881) operate out of Lahaina.

WEST MAUI

West Maui snares the lion's share of tourists. Its heartbeat is unquestionably Lahaina (p301), which boasts a wealth of historic sites along with top-rated restaurants and entertainment. Running north from Lahaina you'll find beautiful beaches backed by a run of resort communities beginning with the bustling high-rises at Ka'anapali and ending 10 miles later at Kapalua (p324), one of the world's classiest golf destinations.

Beyond Kapalua the development ceases, the beaches are quiet and the coast is rugged. The narrow Kahekili Hwy (p326), which runs along the remote back side of west Maui, passes through quintessentially rural terrain with a couple of hillside ranches and a village so small it doesn't even have a store.

LAHAINA TO MA'ALAEA
The stretch between Lahaina and Ma'alaea has pretty mountain scenery, but during winter most people are craning their necks to look seaward as they drive along the highway. The popular bumper sticker 'I brake for whales' says it all, as this is a prime whale-watching road.

During winter, humpback whales occasionally breach as close as 100yd from the coast here. Forty tons of leviathan suddenly exploding straight up through the water can be a real showstopper! Unfortunately, some drivers whose heads are jerked oceanward by the sight hit their brakes and others don't, making for high rear-ender potential.

Olowalu
Olowalu, which means 'many hills,' has a lovely setting, with cane fields backed by the West Maui Mountains. There's little to mark the village other than Olowalu General Store and a seemingly misplaced French restaurant.

SIGHTS & ACTIVITIES
When the water is calm you'll undoubtedly see a line-up of cars. There's lots of **snorkeling** in the water between the 13- and 14-mile marker, south of the general store. The coral reef is large and shallow, so the potential is there, but it's often silty enough to leave snorkelers disappointed.

A dirt road starting behind the general store leads to the **Olowalu Petroglyphs**. Go around the north side of the store, park just beyond the water tower and look for the signposted gate. A 400yd walk leads up this hot, open road to the petroglyphs. It's easy to follow; just keep the cinder cone straight ahead of you as you go. As with most of Maui's extant petroglyphs, these figures are carved into the vertical sides of cliffs rather than on horizontal lava like on the Big Island. Most of the Olowalu figures have been damaged, but you can still make some out.

SLEEPING & EATING
Camp Pecusa (☎ 661-4303; www.maui.net/~norm/tenting .html; 800 Olowalu Village Rd; campsite per person $6) The safest coastal camping on Maui is at this low-profile 'tent ground' run by the Episcopal Church, half a mile south of Olowalu General Store. Camping is along the shaded beach. The beach isn't suitable for swimming, but there's good snorkeling out on the reef. There is a solar-heated shower, a couple of outhouses, drinking water and picnic tables, and a caretaker lives on the grounds. No alcohol is allowed, and there's a maximum stay of seven nights. Reservations are not accepted, but space is usually available. All check-ins must be by 5pm.

Chez Paul (☎ 661-3843; Olowalu Village Rd; mains $29-38; ☯ 5:45-9pm) Conveniently located on the way to nowhere, as Chez Paul likes to say, this fine French restaurant has been building its stellar reputation since 1968. Old-fashioned artwork and white linen add ambience, but it's the classic French dishes like rack of lamb, crispy duck, and fresh fish poached in champagne that packs those pretty tables. Reservations are recommended. The restaurant is next to the Olowalu General Store.

Papakua Wayside Park
Between the 11- and 12-mile markers, this is a narrow county park squeezed between the road and the water, but it does have firepits, toilets and tent camping (for permit information, see p294) under kiawe. Campers should take note that this place can buzz all night with the sound of traffic passing by, so unless you're hard of hearing you'll be

WEST MAUI

0 _____ 5 km
0 _____ 3 miles

INFORMATION
Bank of Hawaii..............................(see 35)
Laundry..(see 35)
Main Post Office............................**1** B4
Whalers General Store....................(see 35)

SIGHTS & ACTIVITIES
Bellstone (Pohaku Kani)................**2** C3
Boy Scouts' Camp Mahulia..........**3** D4
Hale Pa'i.......................................**4** B5
Haleki'i-Pihana Heiau State
  Monument..................................**5** D4
Kapalua Dive Company..................(see 30)
Kapalua Golf Academy...................(see 16)
Lookout...**6** D6
McGregor Point Light Beacon........**7** D6
Maui Ocean Center........................(see 37)
Mendes Ranch...............................**8** D4
Nakalele Blowhole.........................**9** C3
Nakalele Point Light Station..........**10** C3
Natural Ocean Baths......................**11** C3
Olowalu Petroglyphs......................**12** B6
Plantation Golf Course...................**13** B3
Turnbull Studios & Sculpture Garden..**14** D3
Ukumehame Beach Park.................**15** C6

Village Golf Course........................**16** B3
Waiehu Municipal Golf Course.......**17** D4

SLEEPING
Camp Pecusa.................................**18** B6
Guesthouse....................................**19** B5
Hale Kai..**20** A4
Hale Napili....................................**21** B3
House of Fountains.........................**22** B5
Kahana Sunset................................**23** B3
Kapalua Bay Hotel.........................**24** B3
Kuleana Maui.................................**25** A4
Mahina Surf...................................**26** B3
Napili Kai Beach Resort..................**27** B3
Napili Shores.................................**28** B3
Noelani..(see 26)
Papalaua Wayside Park...................**29** C6
Ritz-Carlton Kapalua......................**30** B3

EATING
Chez Paul......................................**31** B6
Farmers Market..............................(see 32)
Fish & Poi......................................(see 28)

Honokowai Marketplace.................(see 33)
Honokowai Okazuya & Deli...........**32** A4
Java Jazz & Soup Nutz...................**33** A4
Ma'alaea Grill................................(see 37)
Pizza Paradiso...............................(see 33)
Plantation House Restaurant..........**34** B3
Reilly's..(see 35)
Roy's Kahana Bar & Grill...............(see 35)
Sansei Seafood Restaurant & Sushi
  Bar..(see 24)
Vino..(see 30)

DRINKING
Fish & Game Brewing Company &
  Rotisserie....................................(see 35)

ENTERTAINMENT
Lehua Lounge.................................(see 24)

SHOPPING
Kahana Gateway.............................**35** B3
Kaukini Gallery & Gift Shop...........**36** D3
Ma'alaea Harbor Village.................**37** D6

MAUI

better off camping at Camp Pecusa, further north in Olowalu. Dive and snorkel boats anchor offshore at **Coral Gardens**. This reef also creates **Thousand Peaks** toward its west end, with breaks favored by long-boarders and beginning surfers.

Further north at the 12-mile marker is **Ukumehame Beach Park**. Shaded by ironwood trees, this sandy beach is OK for sunbathing or taking a quick dip, but because of the rocky conditions most locals stick with picnicking and fishing.

In the other direction, the pull-off for the western end of the **Lahaina Pali Trail** (p337) is just south of the 11-mile marker, on the *mauka* (inland) side of the road. Keep an eye out as it can be hard to spot.

Scenic Viewpoints

A couple of inconspicuous roadside lookouts lie just south of the 10-mile marker, but they're unmarked and difficult to negotiate in traffic – don't even consider them unless you're heading south and don't have to cross lanes. The best bet is to stop instead at **Papawai Point** between the 8- and 9-mile markers, which is signposted 'scenic point' and has a good-sized parking lot. Because the point juts into the western edge of Ma'alaea Bay, a favored humpback nursing ground, it's one of the best places on Maui for coastline whale watching. It's also a good place to stop and enjoy the sunset.

LAHAINA TO KA'ANAPALI

There are a couple of beach parks on the stretch between Lahaina and Ka'anapali, as well as nearby B&Bs.

Sights & Activities

Wahikuli Wayside Beach Park, about 2 miles north of Lahaina, occupies a narrow strip of beach flanked by the highway. With a gift for prophecy, the Hawaiians named it Wahikuli (noisy place). The beach is mostly backed by a black-rock retaining wall, though there's a small sandy area. If you don't mind traffic noise, the swimming conditions are usually fine, and when the water's calm, you can snorkel near the lava outcrops at the park's south end. There are showers, restrooms, parking and picnic tables.

Hanaka'o'o Beach Park is a long, sandy beach, just south of Ka'anapali Beach Resort, with full facilities. The beach has a sandy bottom, and water conditions are usually quite safe for swimming. However, southerly swells, which sometimes develop in summer, can create powerful waves and shorebreaks, while the occasional *kona* storm can kick up rough water conditions in winter. You can snorkel down by the second clump of rocks on the south side of the beach park, but it doesn't compare with sites further north. Hanaka'o'o Beach is also called 'Canoe Beach,' as local canoe clubs store their outriggers here.

Sleeping

The following B&Bs are in a residential neighborhood between Lahaina and Ka'anapali, and within walking distance of Wahikuli State Wayside Beach Park.

Guesthouse (☎ 661-8085, 800-621-8942; www.maui guesthouse.com; 1620 Ainakea Rd; s/d incl breakfast $115/130; P ⊠ 🖳 ⚫) This upscale B&B is a romantic option, with four roomy suites, each with either a hot tub or a Jacuzzi, and everything from a private lanai to chocolate kisses on the pillow. Privacy is easy to come by here, and it would make an ideal place for a honeymoon. The house is smoke-free, and guests have access to a kitchen and laundry facilities.

WHALE OF A TAIL

Come in the winter and you're in for the sight of your life. That's when humpback whales (p48) cruise the waters along the western coastline of Maui, and are visible right from the beach. This area is the main Hawaiian birthing grounds for these awesome creatures. They like to stay in shallow waters when they have newborn calves, as a safeguard against shark attacks. Ma'alaea Bay (p336) is a favorite nursing ground and the waters abound with whales performing acrobatic breaches and tail slaps. Around Lahaina, where the waters are busy with human activity, whales generally stay well offshore. The best bet for whale spotting is to go south at least as far as Launiupoko Wayside Park (p306). Maui's finest shoreline whale-watching stretches are from Olowalu to Ma'alaea Bay (p316) and from Keawakapu Beach (p339) to Makena Beach (p348).

House of Fountains (☎ 667-2121, 800-789-6865; www.alohahouse.com; 1579 Lokia St; r/studios/ste incl breakfast $95/115/145; P ⛔ ⛎) A touch of luxury at affordable prices. These tropical-style accommodations are loaded with amenities and there's a guest kitchen, ocean-view sundeck and Jacuzzi. German is spoken.

KA'ANAPALI
Ka'anapali boasts all the trappings of resort vacationing, from cushy hotels and seaside dining to a plethora of activities in and out of the water.

In the late 1950s, Amfac, owner of Lahaina's Pioneer Sugar Mill, earmarked 600 acres of relatively barren sugarcane land for development. Now Ka'anapali is lined with a dozen high-rise oceanfront hotels and condominium complexes, two 18-hole golf courses, 40 tennis courts and a full-service shopping center.

Ka'anapali boasts 3 miles of sandy beach and scenic views across the 'Au'au Channel to Lana'i and Moloka'i. While Ka'anapali is certainly not in a 'getaway' in the sense of avoiding the crowds, it has its quieter niches. The north side of Pu'u Keka'a (also known as Black Rock), for instance, and the condos up around the golf course are less busy than the central beach area.

Sights
WHALERS VILLAGE MUSEUM
Simply put, this little **museum** (☎ 661-5992; Level 3, Whalers Village, 2345 Ka'anapali Pkwy; admission

free; ⏰ 9am-9:30pm) is one of the best whaling museums to be found anywhere. Take time to soak up the first-rate presentation, which combines authentic period photos, whaling ship logs and detailed interpretive boards that sound the depths of whaling history. It's all rounded out with exhibits of harpoons, the model of a whaling barque, whale jawbones and a wild array of scrimshaw.

In the 19th century, whales were considered a 'floating gold mine' of oil, spermaceti, blubber and baleen. A lot of the character of the whalers comes through, and you'll get a feel for how rough and dirty the work really was. Wages were so low that sailors sometimes owed the ship money by the time they got home and had to sign up for another four-year stint just to pay off the debt. Haunting seafaring songs sung by New England whalers play in the background. Films on whales play in a little theater next to the museum shop, which sells excellent scrimshaw carvings.

If the museum has your interest piqued, you'll find a full-size **sperm whale skeleton** hanging at the front entrance to the shopping center to round out the experience.

KA'ANAPALI BEACHES
Ka'anapali is really two beaches, with Pu'u Keka'a the dividing mark. The stretch north of Pu'u Keka'a to Honokowai is Ka'anapali Beach, while everything south of Pu'u Keka'a to the Hyatt is officially Hanaka'o'o Beach. Still, since the resort was built, the whole

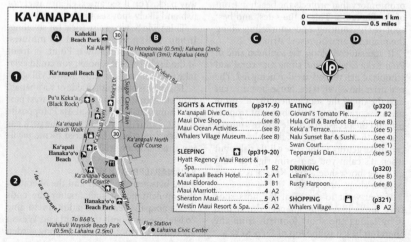

KA'ANAPALI

SIGHTS & ACTIVITIES	(pp317-9)	EATING	(p320)
Ka'anapali Dive Co	(see 6)	Giovani's Tomato Pie	7 B2
Maui Dive Shop	(see 8)	Hula Grill & Barefoot Bar	(see 8)
Maui Ocean Activities	(see 8)	Keka'a Terrace	(see 5)
Whalers Village Museum	(see 8)	Nalu Sunset Bar & Sushi	(see 4)
		Swan Court	(see 1)
SLEEPING	(pp319-20)	Teppanyaki Dan	(see 5)
Hyatt Regency Maui Resort & Spa	1 B2	DRINKING	(p320)
Ka'anapali Beach Hotel	2 A1	Leilani's	(see 8)
Maui Eldorado	3 B1	Rusty Harpoon	(see 8)
Maui Marriott	4 A2		
Sheraton Maui	5 A1	SHOPPING	(p321)
Westin Maui Resort & Spa	6 A2	Whalers Village	8 A2

strip, north and south, tends to just get called Ka'anapali Beach.

Public beach parking is ridiculously limited to a few slots at the resort hotels and the Whalers Village shopping center (tell the attendant you're going to the beach and need one of the free public parking spots). If these spots are full, Whalers Village provides three hours of free parking if you spend more than $10 at one of its shops or restaurants. Or better yet, park for free at Kahekili Beach Park to the north or at Hanako'o Beach Park to the south and stroll along the shore.

Ka'anapali Hanaka'o'o Beach

This is the heart of the action, with the vibrant stretch in front of the Whalers Village shopping center dubbed 'Dig Me Beach.'

As for water conditions, much of the stretch between the Sheraton and the Hyatt can be dangerous, particularly on the point in front of the Marriott, where strong currents sometimes develop. As a general rule, waters are rougher in winter, though actually the worst conditions can occur in early summer if there's a southerly swell.

Be careful in rough surf, as the waves can pick you up and bounce you onto the coral reef that runs from the southern end of the Westin down to the Hyatt. In calm weather you can snorkel the reef. Check with the hotel beach huts for water conditions.

Pu'u Keka'a

Pu'u Keka'a (Keka'a Point) is the rocky lava promontory that protects the beach in front of the Sheraton. This is the safest and best spot for swimming and snorkeling along the main Ka'anapali resort strip.

If you snorkel along the southern side of Pu'u Keka'a, you'll find some nice coral and schools of fish that are used to being fed. The real prize, however, is the horseshoe cove cut into the tip of the rock, where there's more pristine coral, along with abundant tropical fish and the occasional turtle. There's often a current to contend with off the point, which can make getting to the cove a little risky, but when it's calm you can swim right around into the horseshoe. Pu'u Keka'a is also a popular shore-dive spot.

If you want to see what the horseshoe cove looks like, you can peer down into it by taking the short footpath from the Sheraton beach to the top of Pu'u Keka'a.

> ### LEAP INTO THE DEEP
>
> According to traditional Hawaiian beliefs, Pu'u Keka'a, the westernmost point of Maui, is a place where the spirits of the dead leaped into the unknown to be carried to their ancestral homeland.
>
> The rock is said to have been created during a scuffle between the demigod Maui and a commoner who questioned Maui's superiority. Maui chased the man to this point, killed him, then froze his body into stone and cast his soul out to sea.
>
> A different kind of soul jumps into the water today. You'll often find a line of adventurous teens waiting for their turn to leap off the rock for a resounding splash into the cool cove below.

Kahekili Beach Park

This idyllic golden-sand beach, backed by swaying palms, is Ka'anapali's hidden jewel. It has fantastic snorkeling and although it's open ocean, the water is usually calm and perfect for swimming. And unlike the main Ka'anapali strip, there are no crowds, access is easy and there's plenty of free parking.

Snorkeling is so good here that the **Pacific Whale Foundation** (☎ 879-8811; donations accepted; ⏰ 1hr snorkel tours at 10am Fri, Sat & Mon) leads free guided snorkeling tours. Or just strike out on your own. You can snorkel north to Honokowai Point and then ride the mild current, which runs north to south, all the way back. You'll see an excellent variety of fish and likely spot sea turtles as well.

This wide beach is also ideal for strolling. If you walk north for about 20 minutes, you'll come to Honokowai Point, in front of the Embassy Suites hotel; you could even take a lunch break in Honokowai village.

The park is at the north side of Ka'anapali. From the Honoapi'ilani Hwy, turn west past the 25-mile marker onto Kai Ala Pl (opposite Pu'ukoli'i Rd), then bear right. The park has showers, restrooms, a covered picnic pavilion and barbecue grills.

KA'ANAPALI BEACH WALK

Stroll between the Hyatt and the Sheraton, the opulent hotels that anchor the ends of Ka'anapali Beach. In addition to fine coastal scenery, both the Hyatt and Westin are worth a detour for their dazzling garden statuary and landscaping replete with free-form pools, rushing waterfalls and swan ponds. A walk through the Hyatt's rambling lobbies is a bit like museum browsing – the walls hang with everything from heirloom-quality Hawaiian quilts to wooden temple toys, Thai bronzes and Papua New Guinea war shields.

At the southern end of the walk the grace-ful 17ft-high bronze sculpture *The Acrobats*, a work by Australian John Robinson, makes a dramatic silhouette against the sunset. If you walk along the beach in the early evening, you'll often be treated to enter-tainment, most notably from the beachside restaurants at Whalers Village (p317) and from the Hyatt, which holds its luau (p319) on the oceanfront.

Activities

WATER ACTIVITIES
Ka'anapali Dive Co (☎ 667-4622; www.kaanapali diveco.com; Westin Maui Resort & Spa; dive $80; ☉ 9am-5pm) offers an introductory dive for novices that starts with instruction in a pool and ends with a guided dive from the beach.

Maui Ocean Activities (☎ 667-2001; www.maui watersports.com; Whalers Village; kayak rentals $15; ☉ 8am-4:30) has kayak rentals; gives surfing lessons ($59) and windsurfing lessons ($69), both about 90 minutes; and rents a slew of gear from beach umbrellas to hobie cats.

LAND ACTIVITIES
Ka'anapali Golf Courses (☎ 661-3691; www.kaanapali -golf.com; 2290 Ka'anapali Pkwy; green fees South/North Course $105/130, after 2:30pm $65/80; ☉ first tee time 6:30am) consists of two courses. The Ka'anapali North Course, designed by Robert Trent Jones, is tournament grade with greens that emphasize putting skills. The Ka'anapali South Course is a bit shorter and more of a resort course. The setting (bordering condos and the road) isn't as tranquil as the Kapalua course but it tends to be less windy down this way and the rates are a relative bargain.

Courses
Whalers Village (☎ 661-4567; www.whalersvillage .com; 2435 Ka'anapali Pkwy) offers lei-making classes, children's crafts, hula lessons and the like. The schedule changes throughout the year, so look for the calendar of events posted at the shopping center or ask at your hotel.

Festivals & Events
The **Maui Onion Festival**, at Whalers Village the first weekend in August, heats up with raw onion–eating contests (participants get free breath mints!) and cooking demonstrations by some of Maui's best chefs.

Sleeping
See p316 for mid-range B&Bs between La-haina and Ka'anapali.

TOP END
All of the following accommodations are in the Ka'anapali resort, either on the beach or within walking distance of it.

Hyatt Regency Maui Resort & Spa (☎ 661-1234, 800-233-1234; www.maui.hyatt.com; 200 Nohea Kai Dr; r/ste from $320/850; P X 🖎) You'll be struck by the lavishness of this place as soon as you step into the lobby atrium with its orchids, palm trees, huge Ming vases and $2 million worth of artwork. But don't think that makes it highbrow. The Hyatt is heaven for kids, with parrots in the palms and a meandering pool with swim-through grottoes and a 150ft water slide. For grown-ups, there's a swim-up bar and a pampering full-service spa.

Ka'anapali Beach Hotel (☎ 661-0011, 800-262-8450; www.kbhmaui.com; 2525 Ka'anapali Pkwy; r/ste from $195/260; P X 🖎) The most Hawaiian-influenced of Ka'anapali's resorts, this hotel has an enviable location, with a wide sandy stretch of beach out front and Pu'u Keka'a just minutes away. While it's the oldest of Ka'anapali's seaside hotels, it's also the smallest, which makes it pleasantly low-key. There's lots of aloha here. The only down-side is that some of the rooms aren't as spiffy as you might like. Parking is $6.

Maui Eldorado (☎ 661-0021, 800-688-7444; www .outrigger.com; 2661 Keka'a Dr; studios/1-bedroom units from $220/270; P X 🖎) Set on the golf course, this place offers the conveniences of condo living and less hustle and bustle than the beachside resorts. Consider the studios, which are very big and have kitchens set completely apart from the bedroom area, and don't bother paying extra for the ocean view. The hotel often has good deals on its website, which can make it a real bargain.

Westin Maui Resort & Spa (☎ 667-2525, 800-228-3000; 2365 Ka'anapali Pkwy; r/ste from $350/900; P X 🖳 🖎) A good choice for the health-conscious, every single room here is smoke-free and the in-house spa specializes in treatments with tropical fragrances. The grounds are replete with waterfalls, free-form pools and garden statuary. When you're done hanging out on the beach, you can go back to your room and log on to high-speed Internet. There's also a business center.

Sheraton Maui (☎ 661-0031, 800-782-9488; www .sheraton-hawaii.com; 2605 Ka'anapali Pkwy; r/ste from $350/790; P ⌘ ☒ ☮) This sleek resort breathes elegance and enjoys Ka'anapali's best beach locale, right in front of Pu'u Keka'a. The rooms have rich wood tones, Hawaiian prints and dataports, and the grounds have night-lit tennis courts, a fitness center and a fun lava-rock swimming pool. Online deals can sometimes ease the price bite.

Eating
BUDGET
The Whalers Village shopping center has a small basement-level **food court**, with Chinese fast food and the usual pizza-by-the-slice and burger fare.

MID-RANGE
Hula Grill & Barefoot Bar (☎ 667-6636; Whalers Village; appetizers & grill menu $6-13, dinner mains $10-29; ◷ 11am-10:30pm) Right on the beach under coconut-frond umbrellas, this fun place is distinguished by its kiawe (mesquite wood) grill and wood-fired pizzas. Enjoy inventive *pupu* like spicy coconut calamari and *kalua* pork pot-stickers on the bistro side, or make dinner reservations in the more formal dining room for lobster, fresh fish and steak.

Nalu Sunset Bar & Sushi (☎ 667-1200; Maui Marriott; sushi from $5, mains from $13; ◷ 5-10:30pm) Japanese food with sunset views. Start with the volcano roll with spicy seared *'ahi*. Then cool down with tamer fare like teriyaki chicken. Or swing by from 5pm to 8pm Monday to Thursday for the all-you-can-eat *pupu* buffet ($14). There's live music Wednesday and Friday nights.

Giovani's Tomato Pie (☎ 661-3160; Ka'anapali Pkwy & Honopi'ilani Hwy; mains $11-20; ◷ dinner) This family-friendly restaurant overlooking the golf course offers good-value Italian fare. You can get buffalo wings, pizzas large enough to satisfy four people and a full range of pasta dishes, from ravioli to shrimp scampi.

Keka'a Terrace (☎ 661-0031; Sheraton Maui, 2605 Ka'anapali Pkwy; mains $10-14; ◷ lunch) This open-air, ocean-view restaurant, surrounded by koi ponds, is a good lunch choice. Try the

fish taco with Spanish rice or go for one of the island-style plate lunches.

TOP END
Swan Court (☎ 661-1234; Hyatt Regency Maui Resort & Spa, 200 Nohea Kai Dr; breakfast buffet $21, dinner mains $30-45; ◷ 6:30-11:30am & 5:30-10pm) The setting doesn't get much more romantic than this, overlooking a swan pond with meditative waterfalls and an Oriental garden. Breakfast is a grand spread with sinful pastries and a savory omelet station, while dinner features seafood with a Hawaii Regional flair.

Teppanyaki Dan (☎ 661-0031; Sheraton Maui, 2605 Ka'anapali Pkwy; dinner $24-45; ◷ 6-9:30pm Tue-Sat) Chefs prepare traditional teppanyaki meals right at your table. The only difference from dining in Japan is that here the ingredients are fresh Hawaiian. Choose from seafood options like Kona lobster or hibachi butterfly fish, or go for the juicy steak.

Drinking
Leilani's (☎ 661-4495; Whalers Village; ◷ 11am-midnight) This open-air bar on the waterfront is a good place to have a few drinks while watching the sweaty, suntanned multitudes parade by. Also a decent *pupu* menu.

Rusty Harpoon (☎ 661-3123; Whalers Village) Long happy hours (2pm to 6pm and 10pm to 1:30am) attract the crowds, as do elevated views over the beach and big-screen satellite TVs.

Entertainment
The Ka'anapali hotels feature a variety of entertainment, including music in their lounges and restaurants, hula shows, dinner theater and Polynesian revues.

HULA & LIVE MUSIC
Ka'anapali Beach Hotel (☎ 661-0011; 2525 Ka'anapali Pkwy) 'Maui's most Hawaiian hotel' cheerfully entertains anyone who chances by between 6:30pm and 7:30pm with a free hula show.

Sheraton Maui (☎ 661-0031; 2605 Ka'anapali Pkwy) Beachside torch-lighting and a cliff-diving ceremony from Pu'u Keka'a take place at sunset, followed by music with hula dancing from 6pm to 8pm at the hotel's Lagoon Bar.

Hula Grill & Barefoot Bar (☎ 667-6636; Whalers Village) Beachside restaurant/bar with live Hawaiian music from 3pm to 9:30pm.

Hyatt Regency Maui Resort & Spa (☎ 661-1234; 200 Nohea Kai Dr) There's a free torch-lighting ceremony at 6:15pm, followed by Hawaiian music until 9:30pm in the Weeping Banyan Lounge.

Westin Maui (☎ 667-2525; 2365 Ka'anapali Pkwy) The hotel's poolside bar and grill has live Hawaiian entertainment to 9pm.

Whalers Village (☎ 661-4567; 2435 Ka'anapali Pkwy) Ka'anapali's shopping center has live Hawaiian music, hula and Polynesian dance performances several evenings a week, as well as live jazz from 2:30pm to 5pm on Sunday.

LUAU & DINNER SHOWS

Drums of the Pacific (☎ 667-4727; Hyatt Regency Maui Resort & Spa, 200 Nohea Kai Dr; adult/child/teen $80/27/50; ⏰ 5-8pm) This luau includes an *imu* ceremony (the unearthing of a roasted pig from an underground oven), an open bar, a Hawaiian-style buffet dinner and a South Pacific dance and music show.

Kupanaha: Maui Magic for all Ages (☎ 667-0128; Ka'anapali Beach Hotel, 2525 Ka'anapali Pkwy; adult/child/teen $70/20/50; ⏰ Tue-Sat) Illusionists work their magic at this dinner show, which also includes Hawaiian legends through hula and chants.

Shopping

Whalers Village (☎ 661-4567; 2435 Ka'anapali Pkwy; ⏰ 9:30am-10pm) shopping center has more than 50 shops:

ABC store (☎ 667-9700) For beach mats and sundries.

Dolphin Gallery (☎ 661-3223) Has designer jewelry, Hawaiian sculpture and Asian fine arts.

Honolua Keiki (☎ 661-1778) Buy kids clothing here.

Honolua Wahine (☎ 661-3253) Get your bikinis next door.

Na Hoku (☎ 667-5411) One of Hawaii's oldest jewelers, specializes in Hawaiian floral and marine life designs.

Tropical Palm (☎ 661-1939) Has a good selection of aloha wear for both men and women.

Getting There & Around

The Akina West Maui Shuttle (p298) connects Lahaina and Ka'anapali ($1, 25 minutes). Stops are made at several places in Ka'anapali, including the Whalers Village shopping center, Maui Marriott and the Hyatt Regency Resort & Spa.

The free **Ka'anapali Trolley** (☎ 667-0648) runs between the Ka'anapali hotels, Whalers Village and the golf course about every 20 minutes between 10am and 10pm. Drivers take an hourlong break at noon and 6pm, so plan around it.

HONOKOWAI

Honokowai gets knocked about by comparison with its ritzier neighbors – Ka'anapali to the south and Kahana to the north. And indeed, to the degree that Ka'anapali is a planned community, Honokowai is an unplanned one, consisting mainly of a stretch of assorted condos squeezed between the shoreline and Lower Honoapi'ilani Rd. But don't write the place off – it's convenient, affordable and low-rise, and the ocean views here are every bit as fine as in the upscale resorts elsewhere along this coast. And you can find quiet niches and plenty of aloha.

Sights & Activities

Honokowai Beach Park, in the center of town, is good for picnics, but it's largely lined with a submerged rock shelf and has poor swimming conditions with shallow water. Water conditions improve at the south side of town, and you can walk along the shore right on down to the glorious Kahekili Beach Park that marks the northern end of Ka'anapali.

Sleeping

Hale Kai (☎ 669-6333, 800-446-7307; www.halekai .com; 3691 Lower Honoapi'ilani Rd; 1-/2-bedroom units from $120/150; 🏊) This delightfully old-fashioned place on the water's edge has louvered windows to catch the trades and a Hawaiian lava-rock facade. Guests can literally step off their lanai and onto the beach. Even the pool is shoreline here, with a splash of saltwater. If you need two bedrooms, request a loft unit – they're just $5 more and are loaded with character.

Mahina Surf(☎ 669-6068, 800-367-6086; www.mahina surf.com; 4057 Lower Honoapi'ilani Rd; 1-/2-bedroom units from $140/170; 🏊) A cheery place with spacious, well-appointed units, this low-rise complex is nicely set around a large grassy yard with a heated pool. All units have private oceanfront lanai perfect for whale watching and sunset views. Ask about discounts.

Noelani (☎ 669-8374, 800-367-6030; www.noelani -condo-resort.com; 4095 Lower Honoapi'ilani Rd; studios $130, 1-/2-/3-bedroom units from $165/240/300; 🏊) Aloha atmosphere, plenty of palm trees and two freshwater pools add to the allure at this good-value condominium. Each unit is right on the beach and you can listen to the surf from the ocean-facing lanai. All have an extra sofa bed, and all but the studios have a washer-dryer. Look online for discounts.

MAUI

Kuleana Maui (☎ 669-8080, 800-367-5633; www
.kuleanaresorts.com; 3959 Lower Honoapi'ilani Rd; 1-bedroom
units from $115; 🛋) If you're looking for a quiet
location, this modern condominium buffered in palm-shaded gardens is a winner.
And despite the reasonable rates, the units
are attractively furnished with Hawaiian
touches and all the expected amenities. Plop
down an extra $15 for an ocean view and you
won't regret it.

Eating
Java Jazz & Soup Nutz (☎ 667-0787; Honokowai Marketplace, 3350 Lower Honoapi'ilani Rd; breakfast & lunch
$5-9, dinner $10-26; 🕒 breakfast, lunch & dinner; 🌐) As
bohemian as you'll find this side of Green-
wich Village, this arty café brews a potent
java and has a menu as eclectic as its decor.
Lunch features gourmet sandwiches, while
at dinner the chef ventures into Mediter-
ranean-influenced cuisine. If you've got a
sweet tooth, don't miss the chocolate-chip
pancakes.

Honokowai Okazuya & Deli (☎ 665-0512; 3600
Lower Honoapi'ilani Rd; mains $6-10; 🕒 10am-2:30pm &
4:30-9pm Mon-Sat) Forget *loco moco* (a dish of
rice, fried egg and hamburger patty topped
with gravy). Upscale plate lunches are the
specialty at this Japanese-style deli. The
mahimahi with lemon, capers and rice is
a long-running favorite but the salads and
stir-fry Kula veggies are winners as well.

Pizza Paradiso (☎ 667-2929; Honokowai Marketplace, 3350 Lower Honoapi'ilani Rd; mains $7-20; 🕒 11am-
10pm; 🌐) You'll find top-notch pizza at this
Italian café, as well tasty meatball sandwiches smothered in caramelized onions
and award-winning tiramisu.

For fresh fruits and vegetables, visit the
farmers market (🕒 7-11am Mon, Wed & Fri), which
sets up north of Honokowai Beach Park.

KAHANA
Kahana, the stretch immediately north of
Honokowai, is a trendy area with several
high-rise condominium complexes and a
couple of the best restaurants in west Maui.

Information
The **Kahana Gateway shopping center** (4405
Honoapi'ilani Hwy) has a gas station, a **Bank of
Hawaii** (☎ 669-3922), a **coin laundry** (last wash
8pm daily) and the little **Whalers General Store**
(☎ 669-3700; 🕒 6:30am-11pm) for basic groceries
and sundries.

Sights & Activities
The sandy **beach** that fronts the village has
reasonable swimming conditions. For snorkeling, a good area is along the rocky outcropping at the north side of the Kahana
Sunset condos. You can park at the seaside
Pohaku Park and walk north a couple of
minutes to access the beach.

Sleeping & Eating
Kahana Sunset (☎ 669-8700, 800-669-1488; www
.kahanasunset.com; 4909 Lower Honoapi'ilani Rd; 1-bedroom
units $130-240, 2-bedroom units $195-370; 🛋) This
three-story condominium complex, on its
own little private stretch of the beach, is nestled in landscaped gardens. The architecture
has Balinese accents, the lanai are huge and
the units are spacious with a touch of luxury
and generous amenities. There's a freestyle
heated pool and a separate children's pool.

Roy's Kahana Bar & Grill (☎ 669-6999; Kahana Gateway, 4405 Honoapi'ilani Hwy; mains $26-33; 🕒 dinner; 🌐)
A branch of the renowned Roy's in Honolulu
(p65), this restaurant centers around an ex-
hibition kitchen and features superb Hawaii
Regional Cuisine. Top appetizers ($8 to $14)
are the spicy blackened 'ahi and the Hawaii
Kai blue crab cakes. Move on to such yummy
mains as sake-seared sea bass or Roy's classic
honey-mustard beef short ribs. If you've still
got room, the chocolate soufflé is a decadent
treat you won't soon forget.

Reilly's (☎ 667-7477; Kahana Gateway, 4405 Honoapi'ilani Hwy; mains $21-33; 🕒 lunch & dinner; 🌐)
It takes some moxie to set up right next to
Roy's, but this fine-dining restaurant, complete with a piano bar and two chef-owners
from the prestigious Culinary Institute of
America, has been winning awards left and
right. Some of the best steaks on Maui,
including a filet mignon with a cabernet-
reduction sauce that melts in your mouth. A
standout among the appetizers ($6 to $14) is
the pina-colada tempura shrimp.

The **Fish & Game Brewing Company & Rotisserie**
(☎ 669-3474; Kahana Gateway, 4405 Honoapi'ilani Hwy;
🕒 11am-1:30am; 🌐) also has a solid pub menu
($5 to $10), with fried calamari, barbecued
ribs and oysters on the half-shell.

Drinking
Fish & Game Brewing Company & Rotisserie
(☎ 669-3474; Kahana Gateway, 4405 Honoapi'ilani Hwy;
🕒 11-1:30am; 🌐) Maui's only microbrewery
has rich dark woods and a glass wall over-

looking the brewing operation. The beers range from a light, crisp Honolua lager to Wild Hog, a robust, full-bodied black stout with a creamy finish. Sample them all with six 3.5oz glasses ($6).

NAPILI

Napili Kai Beach Resort, built in 1962, was the first hotel north of Ka'anapali. To protect the bay, as well as its investment, Napili Kai organized area landowners and petitioned the county to create a zoning bylaw restricting all Napili Bay buildings to the height of a coconut tree. The law was passed in 1964, long before the condo explosion took over the rest of west Maui, and consequently Napili today is one of the more relaxed niches on the coast. Most of Napili's condos are on the beach and for the most part are away from the road and the sound of traffic. It's easy to see why it's popular.

Sights & Activities

Napili Beach is a beautiful, curved, golden-sand strand, with excellent swimming and snorkeling when it's calm. Big waves occasionally make it into the bay in the winter, attracting bodysurfers, but also creating strong rips.

Sleeping

Napili Kai Beach Resort (☎ 669-6271, 800-367-5030; www.napilikai.com; 5900 Lower Honoapi'ilani Rd; r/studios from $190/220, 1-/2-bedroom ste from $360/480; 🐾 🗩) Spread across several acres, this beachside resort at the northern end of Napili Bay brims with hospitality. The units tastefully blend Polynesian decor with Asian touches like Japanese shoji doors. Each unit has a dataport and private lanai, and some units are disabled accessible. Deals include a fifth night free.

Hale Napili (☎ 669-6184, 800-245-2266; www.maui .net/~halenapi; 65 Hui Dr; studios $110-150, 1-bedroom units $175) The Hawaiian management couldn't be friendlier at this well-maintained little condo complex smack on the beach. Step off your lanai and you're in the sand. There are only 18 units, so it books up quickly. Three-day minimum stay.

Napili Shores (☎ 669-8061, 800-688-7444; 5315 Lower Honoapi'ilani Rd; www.outrigger.com; studios $175-240, 1-bedroom units $210-250; 🗩) This condo boasts a palm-filled resort setting with solar-heated pools, a hot tub and lawn croquet. Some of the well-appointed units are

reserved for nonsmokers, and all have voice mail and dataports. There are often good discounts on the website.

Eating

Fish & Poi (☎ 442-3700; Napili Shores, 5315 Lower Honoapi'ilani Rd; mains $13-21; 🕑 dinner Tue-Sun) Teak furnishings and a view of a koi pond set the mood at Napili's best restaurant. Hawaiian comfort food goes upscale here with *'ahi poke* on crisp sweet potatoes, tempura-style fish-and-chips and macadamia-crusted chicken. Kids will like the *keiki* menu of burgers and grilled cheese, and parents will like the price ($3 to $5).

Entertainment

Napili Kai Beach Resort (☎ 669-1500; 5900 Honoapi'ilani Rd; adult/child $10/5; 🕑 5pm Tue) The resort hosts a recommendable hula performance by a local *na keiki* troupe.

KAPALUA

It's a safe bet if you're staying in Kapalua, you love golf and don't mind paying for the best. Golf isn't the only thing Kapalua has going for it, by any means, but it is, after all, the resort's raison d'être. Elite golfers toss all sorts of accolades Kapalua's way. Not only is it Maui's premier golf destination, but *Golf Digest* magazine has named Kapalua one of its top 10 golf resorts in the USA.

The Kapalua resort development includes the upscale Kapalua Bay and Ritz-Carlton hotels, some luxury condos, superb restaurants, three golf courses and a world-class tennis club. Nestled in pineapple fields and fronting the ocean, it's a classy, uncrowded development – the most exclusive in Maui – and it has beautiful beaches as well.

Sights

KAPALUA BEACH

This white-sand crescent beach at Kapalua Bay has a clear view of Moloka'i across the channel. Long rocky outcrops at both ends of the bay make Kapalua Beach the safest year-round swimming spot on this coast. There's good snorkeling on the right side of the beach, where you'll find lots of large tangs, butterfly fish and orange slate-pencil sea urchins. Not only do tourists like to sun on the beach here, but endangered monk seals have been known to take to the sand on sunny days – give them a wide berth.

MAUI

Take the drive immediately north of Napili Kai Beach Resort to get to a parking area where there are restrooms and showers. A tunnel from the parking lot leads under the Bay Club restaurant to the beach.

ONELOA BEACH
This wide, white-sand beach fronts the lower links of the Ironwoods golf course. Aptly named (Oneloa means 'Long Sand'), it extends half a mile along Oneloa Bay. On calm days swimming is safe close to shore, but when there's any sizable surf, strong rip currents can be present.

Makaluapuna Point, the northwest point of Oneloa Bay, is topped by a curious formation known as the **Dragon's Teeth**. The lava rock here has been cut by the whipping surf into 3ft-high spikes that bear an uncanny resemblance to pointed teeth. It's a fun site to walk to and only takes about 15 minutes return. En route you'll pass the Honokahua burial site, a 13.6-acre native burial grounds; you can skirt along the outside of this area but do not enter any of the sites marked 'Please Kokua,' which are easily visible islets of overgrown native vegetation at the edge of manicured golf greens.

To get to the Makaluapuna Point end of the beach, drive north to the very end of Lower Honoapi'ilani Rd (near its intersection with Office Rd), where you'll find beach parking and a monument giving more details on the burial site. The trail to the Dragon's Teeth leads from the monument along the north edge of the golf course.

Activities
Kapalua Dive Company (☎ 669-3448; www.kapalua dive.com; Ritz-Carlton Kapalua; dives $55, kayak tours $60; ☑ 9am-5pm) offers a range of water activities. They rent boogie boards for $3 per day and good-quality mountain bikes for $25 a day.

Kapalua Golf (☎ 669-8044, 877-527-2582; www .kapaluamaui.com; 2000 Village Rd; Village/Bay/Plantation course green fees before 1:30pm $180/190/230, after 1:30pm $80/85/90; ☑ first tee 7am) comprises three of the island's top championship golf courses. The Village is Kapalua's stunning mountain course, rising from sea level to nearly 800ft in the first six holes. The Bay course is the tropical ocean course, meandering through palms past a lava peninsula and a couple of bays. The Plantation course incorporates a rugged natural landscape to

the max, winding through rolling hills and deep gorges.

Want to hone your golf skills? **Kapalua Golf Academy** (☎ 669-6500; www.kapaluagolfacademy .com; 1-hr clinic $30, lessons per hr $70-90, golf school from $330; ☑ 8am-6pm) is Hawaii's top golf academy. Staffed by PGA pros, facilities include an indoor hitting bay with video analysis. Programs are matched to players of all levels. You can join the daily afternoon clinic, take private and group lessons or sign up for the more intensive golf school.

Kapalua Tennis (Tennis Garden ☎ 669-5677, Village Tennis Center ☎ 665-0112; www.kapaluamaui.com; 100 Kapalua Dr; resort guests/nonguests per person per day $10/12, racquet rental $6; ☑ 8am-6pm) is Hawaii's largest full-service tennis club, with 20 Plexipave courts and an array of clinics. If you're on your own, give the club a ring and it'll match you with other players for singles or doubles games.

Tours
Maui Pineapple Company (☎ 669-8088; 2½-hr tour $29; ☑ 9:30am & 12:30am Mon-Fri) opens its fields for pineapple-plantation tours led by long-time workers, who will give you the lowdown on pineapple growing and its history in Hawaii. Reservations are required, as are covered shoes. The price includes picking your own pineapple to take home.

Festivals & Events
Mercedes Championship (early January) PGA Tour's season-opening takes place at the Plantation course with the biggest names in golf teeing off for a $5 million purse.
Kapalua Wine & Food Festival (mid-July; www.kapalua maui.com) Held over four days, featuring renowned winemakers and Hawaii's hottest chefs for a culinary extravaganza of cooking demonstrations and wine tasting.

Sleeping

Kapalua Bay Hotel (☎ 669-5656; www.kapaluabay hotel.com; 1 Bay Dr; r/ste from $390/940; ▨ ▨) This stylish beachfront resort breathes elegance, from the stunning open-air lobby to the plantation decor in the guest rooms. Welcome lei, complimentary golf and even free massage are part of the pampering that's lavished on guests here. It's a class act. Demonstrations of Hawaiian arts take place daily.

Kapalua Villas (☎ 669-8088, 800-545-0018; www .kapaluavillas.com; 500 Office Rd; 1-/2-/3-bedroom units from $200/300/430; ▨ ▨) If you have a small group this is the way to go. Three luxury condominium complexes comprise the Kapalua Villas. The one-bedroom units sleep up to four, the others six to eight. Cheaper rates are for fairway views. The Bay Villas are closest to the beach, but the Ridge Villas, which are up on the golf course, also have ocean views. Amenities include free tennis and discounted golf.

Eating

Sansei Seafood Restaurant & Sushi Bar (☎ 669-6286; Kapalua Shops; à la carte $4-19, mains $16-24; ☾ dinner) At Maui's top sushi restaurant, dine on innovative appetizers like sautéed halibut cheeks with fresh asparagus, or go with traditional sushi and sashimi. Mains run the gamut from Japanese noodles to Colorado T-bone steaks. If you come between 5:30pm and 6pm, all food is discounted 25%.

Plantation House Restaurant (☎ 669-6299; 2000 Plantation Club Dr; breakfast & lunch $5-15, dinner mains $16-30; ☾ 8am-3pm & 5:30-9pm) Pure country club, this open-air restaurant has reliably good food and a grand view across the fairways clear down to the ocean. And where else can you get breakfast served until 3pm? Favorites include the Moloka'i French toast and smoked salmon Benedict. Dinner is more upscale, blending Hawaiian and Mediterranean influences.

Vino (☎ 661-8466; Village Course Clubhouse; lunch $8-16, dinner mains $16-28; ☾ lunch & dinner) Contemporary Italian food and a superb wine selection are the hallmarks at this popular restaurant near the Ritz-Carlton. Run by sansei chef DK Kodoma, the menu includes traditional favorites like calamari fritto and braised lamb shank, as well as fresh local seafood. For dessert, don't miss the classic Italian ricotta cheesecake.

Entertainment

Masters of Hawaiian Slack-Key Guitar Concert Series (☎ 699-3858; www.slackkey.com; Ritz-Carlton Kapalua; admission $35; ☾ 6 & 8:30pm Tue) Top slack-key guitarists Cyril Pahinui, Ledward Kaapana and Dennis Kamakahi are monthly guests at this exceptional concert series, and George Kahumoku Jr, a slack-key legend in his own right, is the weekly host. Call for reservations; the cozy theater has only 125 seats.

Lehua Lounge (☎ 669-5656; Kapalua Bay Hotel, 1 Bay Dr; ☾ 4:30-9:30pm) For a memorable experience, swing by this open-air lounge in the Kapalua Bay Hotel lobby, which offers a spectacular sunset view. There's a $4 happy hour tropical-drink special and hula dancing with soothing Hawaiian music.

NORTHERN BEACHES

Kapalua marks the end of development on the west Maui coast. From here on, it's all rural Hawaii, with golf carts giving way to pickup trucks and old cars with surfboards tied on top. The coast gets more lush and scenically rugged as you go along. Quickly you meet the beginning of the Kahekili Hwy, and it's possible to continue around on this coastal road to Wailuku.

DT Fleming Beach Park

This long, sandy beach shaded by ironwood trees, at the north end of Kapalua, is good for surfing and bodysurfing, with winter providing the biggest waves. The shorebreaks can be tough, however, and this beach is second only to Ho'okipa for injuries. Take notice of the sign warning of dangerous currents – the beach has seen a number of drownings over the years. The reef on the right is good for snorkeling, but only when it's very calm.

Fleming, which takes its name from the Scotsman who first developed this area's pineapple industry, is a county beach park with restrooms, picnic facilities and showers. Look for the blue shoreline access sign after the 31-mile marker on Hwy 30.

Slaughterhouse Beach & Honolua Bay

Slaughterhouse Beach (Mokule'ia Bay) and Honolua Bay, about a mile north of Fleming Beach, offer great conditions for several water sports. The bays are separated by the narrow Kalaepiha Point and together form the Honolua-Mokule'ia Bay Marine Life Conservation District. Fishing is prohibited,

MAUI

as is collecting shells, coral and sand. In the winter, both bays see heavy surf and sand erosion.

Honolua Bay faces northwest, and when it catches the winter swells, it has some of the most awesome surfing anywhere in the world. It's so good that it's made the cover of surfing magazines.

Slaughterhouse Beach is a hot bodysurfing spot during the summer. Its attractive white-sand crescent is good for sunbathing and exploring – look for glittering green olivine crystals in the rocks at the south end of the beach.

In summer, snorkeling is excellent in both bays, and you can sometimes see spinner dolphins. Both sides of Honolua Bay have good reefs with abundant coral, while the midsection of the bay has a sandy bottom. When it's calm, you can snorkel around Kalaepiha Point from one bay to the other, but forget it if there have been heavy rains, as Honolua Stream empties into Honolua Bay, and the runoff clouds the water.

Slaughterhouse Beach, at the 32-mile marker, has public parking and a concrete stairway leading down to the beach.

KAHEKILI HIGHWAY

The Kahekili Hwy (Hwy 340) curves around the undeveloped northeastern side of the West Maui Mountains. It's ruggedly scenic, with deep ravines, eroded red hills and rock-strewn pastures sloping down to lava sea cliffs and aquamarine ocean. The route is pastoral and quiet, with a couple of waterfalls, blowholes and one-lane bridges. You'll likely spot cowhands on horseback and lazy egrets riding the backs of cows.

It's about 22 miles in all from the southern end of the road at Wailuku to its northern end in Honokohau. Like its counterpart to the south (the Pi'ilani Hwy around the southern flank of Haleakala), the Kahekili Hwy is shown either as a black hole or an unpaved road on most tourist maps. The road, however, is paved its entire length – though much of the drive is very winding and narrow, with blind curves and the occasional sign warning of falling rocks.

Traffic crawls in both directions, but it's easiest to approach it from the highway's southern end, outside Wailuku (p332). The road between Honokohau and Kahakuloa is two lanes and easy going, while the section between Kahakuloa and Waihe'e is mostly one lane (with two-way traffic) and has a few hair-raising cliffside sections without shoulders. While the posted speed limit on most of the road is 15mph, in some sections it's a mere 5mph.

But taking it slowly is the whole point anyway. Allow at least 1½ hours, not counting stops, and gas up before starting out.

Waiehu & Waihe'e

Waiehu Beach Rd turns into Kahekili Hwy at the northern end of Wailuku and heads through the little towns of Waiehu and Waihe'e. The old-fashioned **Waiehu Municipal Golf Course** (☎ 243-7400; 200 Halewaiu Rd; greens fee $45-50), near the shore, is an easily walkable, no-frills course.

Waihe'e Valley Trail, also known as Swinging Bridges, is a moderate 4-mile trail that runs alongside an irrigation ditch over two suspension foot bridges with wooden planks and groaning cables (fun!) to a gentle stream and, further uphill, an artificial dam pool. It takes about two hours return. Because it's on private property, same-day hiking permits should be obtained from **Wailuku Agribusiness** (☎ 244-9570; Hwy 30, Waikapu; ⊙ from 7am Mon-Fri). Several people have been injured or killed in flash floods along this trail, so turn back immediately if it starts to rain. To get to the trailhead, follow Waihe'e Valley Rd inland from near the 5-mile marker for just under half a mile, where there's a small parking lot on the right. Walk 100yd up to the top of the road, where there's a T-junction; the trailhead is on your right. Just walk through the gate and you're on your way.

Just before the 7-mile marker, a paved one-lane road heads up to the Boy Scouts' Camp Mahulia and the start of the **Waihe'e Ridge Trail**, a lightly trodden route offering varied scenery and breathtaking views of the interior and coast. The trailhead, one mile up, is marked with a Na Ala Hele sign and a squeeze-through opening in the fence. The well-defined trail is 2.5 miles one way and takes about two hours return. It starts in pasture and climbs into cool forest reserve land, and though it's a bit steep, it's a fairly steady climb and not overly strenuous. The trail ends at the 2563ft peak of Lanilili, where the ridge-top views are similar to those you'd get from a helicopter.

Waihe'e to Kahakuloa

Back on highway, near the 7-mile marker, is **Mendes Ranch** (☎ 871-5222; www.mendesranch.com; 3530 Kahekili Hwy; rides $90-130), a working cattle ranch. Horseback trail rides go to rain forest and sea-cliff overlooks; some include a ranch-style barbecue lunch.

Next you'll pass a **waterfall** on the left, rain permitting. For another view, stop at the pull-off about 170yd north of the 8-mile marker and look down into the ravine below; you'll see a picture-perfect waterfall framed by double pools.

Continuing around beep-as-you-go hairpin turns, the highway gradually levels out atop sea cliffs. Before the 10-mile marker is **Turnbull Studios & Sculpture Garden** (☎ 667-2787, 800-781-2787; ☺ by appointment), where you can glimpse Bruce Turnbull's grand bronze and wood creations by peering through the gates.

Just before the 14-mile marker, the hilltop **Kaukini Gallery & Gift Shop** (☎ 244-3371; ☺ 10am-5pm) has works by island artists, with watercolors, native-fiber baskets, pottery and much more. Cold drinks are sold here too, and there's a good bird's-eye view of Kahakuloa village from the grounds.

Kahakuloa Village

Kahakuloa lies at the base of a small green valley with cliffs standing like centurions around the bay. Although it contains only a few dozen simple homes, Kahakuloa (Tall Lord) has two churches. The little tin-roof **Catholic mission** sits hillside at the southern end of town, just off the road, and the **Protestant church**, sporting a green wooden exterior and red-tile roof, hunkers down on the valley floor further north. The town doesn't have any shops, but villagers often set up roadside stands selling shave ice, fruit and banana bread.

Heading up out of the valley, at the northern edge of town, a pull-off provides a good view of the village and the rugged coastline. The rise on the south side of Kahakuloa Bay is **Kahakuloa Head**, 636ft high, once one of chief Kahekili's favorite cliff-diving spots. As you climb out of the valley, the terrain is hilly, with rocky cattle pastures punctuated by tall sisal plants. At a number of pull-offs, you can stop and explore. Lush pastures beg you to traipse down the cliffs and out along the rugged coastline.

Bellstone & Ocean Baths

That huge boulder with concave marks on the inland side of the road just past the 16-mile marker is **Pohaku Kani**, a bellstone. If you hit it with a rock on the Kahakuloa side where the deepest indentations are, you might be able to get a hollow sound. It's pretty resonant if you hit it right, but it takes some imagination to hear it ring like a bell.

Just opposite, a couple of vague 4WD tracks lead off toward the coast. Park and head right (south) to reach an overlook; from there you can plan how to navigate your way down the lava cliffs into the **natural ocean baths** at the ocean's edge. Bordered by lava rock and encrusted with semiprecious olivine minerals, incredibly clear, calm pools sit in the midst of roaring surf. Some have natural steps, but take care not to sit near any blowholes. If the area is covered in silt from recent storm runoffs, or the waves look too high, forget about it – it's dangerous.

Nakalele Point

From impromptu parking areas between the 39- and 38-mile markers, a brief walk leads out to a **light station** at the end of Nakalele Point. The coastline here has interesting pools, arches and other formations worn out of the rocks by the pounding surf. Continue walking along the coast (there's no trail) for another 15 minutes until you reach the impressive **Nakalele Blowhole**; if you see only a little sputtering, that's because you haven't found *the* big blowholes – keep going. During the winter season, you can sometimes spot humpbacks breaching offshore.

As you continue north along the highway, Moloka'i comes into view, and the scenery is very lush on the way to **Honokohau Bay**, the furthest point north on Maui.

CENTRAL MAUI

Your first look at Maui will likely be here, on the windswept flatlands that separate Maui's two mountain masses. Somewhat paradoxically, central Maui lays claim to both the island's largest urban sprawl and its most fertile agricultural land. Fields of waving sugarcane stretch clear across the plains from Kahului to Ma'alaea, and it's this area that has earned Maui its former nickname, the Valley Isle.

Kahului, to the north, is the commercial end of it all with a plethora of shopping centers, Maui's gateway airport and its deepwater shipping port. Virtually everything that comes to Maui comes through Kahului, so it's not surprising that highways branch out in all directions like spokes on a wheel.

Wailuku, the county seat, is the more distinctive and less hurried end of it all. This is an older town with a handful of historical sites, some interesting curio shops and tempting ethnic restaurants. It's also the gateway to lush 'Iao Valley State Park, one of Maui's most-visited scenic spots.

KAHULUI
pop 20,150
OK, there's no mistaking it: Kahului is not a tourist mecca. With its run of stores, offices and strip malls, Kahului is simply the place where islanders come to shop and do business and it makes no pretense to be anything else.

Still, like any city, if you dig a little deeper, you'll find more to your liking. You have to go island-style to have fun here. Mingle with easy-going locals at the Saturday morning swap meet, discover a hole-in-the-wall vendor making Hawaii's best sherbet (called *guri-guri*) or catch a slack-key guitarist performing on the lawn of the Maui Arts & Cultural Center.

History
In the 1880s, Kahului became the headquarters of Hawaii's first railroad, which was built to haul sugar from the fields to the refinery and harbor. In 1900, an outbreak of bubonic plague hit Kahului, and in an attempt to wipe it out, the settlement that had grown up around Kahului Harbor was purposely burned to the ground.

Present-day Kahului is a planned community developed in the early 1950s by the Alexander & Baldwin sugar company. It was called 'Dream City' by cane workers, who had long dreamed of moving away from the dusty mill camps into a home of their own. These first tract houses are still found at the southern end of town.

Orientation
The airport is on the east side of town, connected to central Kahului by Keolani Pl, which leads to both the Haleakala Hwy

(Hwy 37) and the Hana Hwy (Hwy 36). Ka'ahumanu Ave (Hwy 32) is Kahului's main artery, connecting the town to neighboring Wailuku (p332). Dairy Rd, to the south, links to both Lahaina (take Hwy 380) and Kihei (take Hwy 311).

Information
Bank of Hawaii (☎ 871-8250; 27 S Pu'unene Ave) Convenient location and a 24-hour ATM.

Borders Books & Music Café (☎ 877-6160; Maui Marketplace, 270 Dairy Rd; ☽ 9am-10pm, to 11pm Fri & Sat) Good selection of maps, Hawaiiana books and international newspapers.

Kahului Post Office (☎ 871-2487; 138 S Pu'unene Ave, Kahului, HI 96732) General delivery mail is held 30 days.

Kahului Public Library (☎ 873-3097; 90 School St; ☽ 1-8pm Tue, 10am-5pm Wed-Sat)

Kinko's (☎ 871-2000; Dairy Center, 395 Dairy Rd; per min 20¢; ☽ 11am-11pm Mon-Fri, 9am-9pm Sat & Sun) For Internet access.

Longs Drugs (☎ 877-0041; Maui Mall, 70 E Ka'ahumanu Ave; ☽ 8am-10pm Mon-Fri, to 9pm Sat & Sun) The town's largest pharmacy, with both over-the-counter and prescription drugs.

Maui Visitors Bureau (☎ 872-3893; www.visitmaui .com; Kahului Airport; ☽ 7:45am-10pm) Has a staffed booth in the airport's arrivals area. Pick up free tourist magazines and brochures from the racks nearby.

Wow-Wee Maui's Café (☎ 871-1414; 333 Dairy Rd; per min 20¢; ☽ 6am-6pm) For Internet access.

Sights
KANAHA BEACH PARK
A hot windsurfing and kiteboarding spot, Kanaha Beach draws a crowd when the wind is right. This beach is the best place in Maui for beginners to learn, and many windsurfing shops (p330) give their lessons here. That said, boarders can be fiercely territorial, so it's best not to go without a local introduction.

Kanaha is OK for swimming, though most people prefer the cleaner waters on the other side of the island in Kihei (p338). You'll find restrooms, showers and shaded picnic tables. But the airport noise can be annoying and the picnic and camping sections, at the eastern end of the beach, have a reputation for theft and violence.

The shoreline access sign can be found down by the car-hire lots at the airport, or if you're coming from downtown Kahului, take Amala Pl.

KANAHA POND BIRD SANCTUARY

The first stop Audubon tours make when they arrive on Maui is at **Kanaha Pond** (Hwy 37, near its junction with Hwy 36; admission free; ☉ dusk-dawn), a haven for the endangered black-necked stilt, a wading bird that feeds along the pond's marshy edges. It's a graceful bird in flight, with long orange legs that trail behind. Even though the entire stilt population in Hawaii is estimated at just 1500, the birds can commonly be spotted here.

The pond is an unlikely respite in the midst of suburbia, beneath the flight path for the airport and just beyond the highway where trucks go barreling along. An observation deck just beyond the parking lot is good for spotting stilts, coots, ducks

and black-crowned night herons. Upon entering the sanctuary, close the gate behind you and walk in quietly, you should be able to make several sightings right along the shoreline.

It's possible to hike on the sanctuary's service roads from September to March – when the birds aren't nesting – by obtaining a free permit from the **Department of Land & Natural Resources** (☎ 984-8100; Room 101, State Office Bldg, 54 S High St, Wailuku; ☉ 8am-4:30pm Mon-Fri).

MAUI ARTS & CULTURAL CENTER

The $32 million **Maui Arts & Cultural Center** (MACC; ☎ 242-2787, tour reservations ext 228; www.mauiarts.org; 1 Cameron Way; admission free; ☉ tour 11am Wed) is the main concert venue on the island. Free

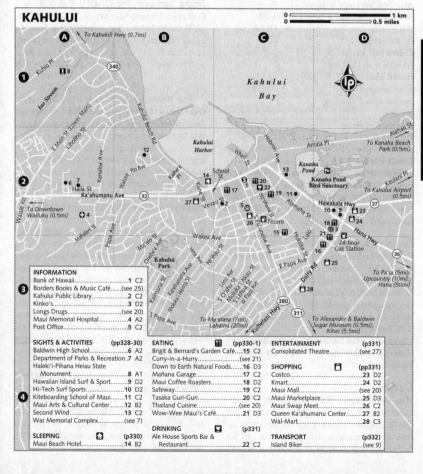

KAHULUI

0 — 1 km
0 — 0.5 miles

Kahului Bay

To Kahekili Hwy (0.7mi)

Iao Stream

Kuhio Pl

340

Kahului Harbor

Kahului Beach Rd

E Main St (Lower Main)

Liholiho St

Kanaloa Ave

Wailoa Pio Ave

Kahee Pl

Kane St

School St

Wharf St

Hobron Ave

Amala Pl

Kanaha Pond

To Kanaha Beach Park (0.5mi)

Alahao St

To Kahului Airport (0.5mi)

Keolani Pl

Kaahumanu Ave

32

Vevau St

Puunene Ave

Ka'ahumanu Ave

Haleakala Hwy

37

Hana Hwy

36

Haila St

To Downtown Wailuku (0.5mi)

Wakea Ave

Mahalani St

Papa Ave

Maalani St

Onehee Ave

Mahele St

Hina Ave

Ni'ihau St

Lono Ave

Kamehameha Ave

Kanaha Ave

Molokai Hema St

S Oahu St

Molokai Akau St

S Lehua St

W Papa Ave

S Papa Ave

Kahului Park

Lalo St

E Papa Ave

Dairy Rd

24-hour Gas Station

To Pa'ia (5mi); Upcountry (10mi); Hana (50mi)

380

311

Kuihelani Hwy

To Ma'alaea (7mi); Lahaina (20mi)

To Alexander & Baldwin Sugar Museum (0.5mi); Kihei (5.5mi)

MAUI

INFORMATION	
Bank of Hawaii	1 C2
Borders Books & Music Café	(see 25)
Kahului Public Library	2 C2
Kinko's	3 D2
Longs Drugs	(see 20)
Maui Memorial Hospital	4 A2
Post Office	5 C2

SIGHTS & ACTIVITIES	(pp328-30)
Baldwin High School	6 A2
Department of Parks & Recreation	7 A2
Haleki'i-Pihana Heiau State Monument	8 A1
Hawaiian Island Surf & Sport	9 D2
Hi-Tech Surf Sports	10 D2
Kiteboarding School of Maui	11 C2
Maui Arts & Cultural Center	12 B2
Second Wind	13 C2
War Memorial Complex	(see 7)

SLEEPING	(p330)
Maui Beach Hotel	14 B2

EATING	(pp330-1)
Brigit & Bernard's Garden Café	15 C2
Curry-in-a-Hurry	(see 21)
Down to Earth Natural Foods	16 D3
Mañana Garage	17 C2
Maui Coffee Roasters	18 D2
Safeway	19 C2
Tasaka Guri-Guri	20 C2
Thailand Cuisine	(see 20)
Wow-Wee Maui's Café	21 D3

DRINKING	(p331)
Ale House Sports Bar & Restaurant	22 C2

ENTERTAINMENT	(p331)
Consolidated Theatre	(see 27)

SHOPPING	(pp331)
Costco	23 D2
Kmart	24 D2
Maui Mall	(see 20)
Maui Marketplace	25 D3
Maui Swap Meet	26 C2
Queen Ka'ahumanu Center	27 B2
Wal-Mart	28 C3

TRANSPORT	(p332)
Island Biker	(see 9)

tours (reservations required) include both the concert halls and the grounds, which have remains of Pa Hula Heiau, a temple that once stood here. The center's **Schaefer International Gallery** (11am-5pm Tue-Sun) has changing exhibits of works by both island and international artists.

Activities
WINDSURFING
Windswept Kahului is the base for Maui's main windsurfing operations. Daily rentals start around $50, with discounts for longer rentals. Introductory windsurfing classes last a couple of hours and cost around $80. The business is very competitive, so ask about discounts. Shops that sell and rent gear and arrange lessons:

Hawaiian Island Surf & Sport (871-4981, 800-231-6958; www.hawaiianisland.com; 415 Dairy Rd; 8:30am-6pm)

Hi-Tech Surf Sports (877-2111; www.htmaui.com; 425 Koloa St; 9am-6pm)

Second Wind (877-7467, 800-936-7787; www.secondwindmaui.com; 111 Hana Hwy; 9am-6pm Mon-Sat, 10am-5:30pm Sun)

KITEBOARDING
On Maui, the kiteboarding action centers on Kite Beach, the western end of Kanaha Beach Park.

Kiteboarding School of Maui (873-0015; www.ksmaui.com; 22 Hana Hwy; course $300; 8:30am-5pm) is the premier kiteboarding operation on Maui. Instructors are certified by the International Kiteboarding Organization.

Festivals & Events
Maui Film Festival (mid-June; www.mauifilmfestival.com) This weeklong festival shows dozens of film premieres at the Maui Arts & Cultural Center.

Ki Ho'alu Slack-Key Guitar Festival (late June) One of Hawaii's premier slack-key guitar festivals, bringing in big-name musicians from throughout the state, takes place at the Maui Arts & Cultural Center.

Starboard Hawaii State Windsurfing Championships (July) Windsurfing slalom competitions are held at Kanaha Beach Park.

Sleeping
Maui Beach Hotel (877-0051, 800-367-5004; www.castleresorts.com/MBH; 170 Ka'ahumanu Ave; r from $105;) With its faux-Polynesian decor and free airport shuttle, this is the better of Kahului's two hotels, both of which sit side

by side on a busy commercial strip that hardly conjures up images of vacationing in Hawaii.

Kanaha Beach Park allows camping (see p294 for permits and fees), but sites are directly beneath the flight path with planes rumbling overhead from dawn until midnight. It's not only a noisy option, but folks down-and-out on their luck sometimes hang out here and personal safety is also an issue. Bottom line: there are better places to camp.

Eating
Kahului has some good places to eat that are worth a trip to town.

BUDGET
Tasaka Guri-Guri (871-4513; Maui Mall, 70 E Ka'ahumanu Ave; scoop 50¢, quart $5; 10am-6pm Mon-Sat, to 8pm Fri, to 4pm Sun) Looking for a treat to break the heat? Join the crowd here for tangy homemade tropical sherbets. The *guri-guri*, as it's called, is so popular that locals pick some up on the way to the airport to take to friends whenever they go off-island.

Wow-Wee Maui's Café (871-1414; 333 Dairy Rd; kava $4, snacks $1-7; 6am-6pm;) Known for their scrumptious Wow-Wee Maui chocolate bars, this hip café has kava (also called 'awa in Hawaiian) drinks (yes, they're legal) served in a coconut shell. Bagels and sandwiches share the menu, but everybody comes for the intoxicating combination of kava and chocolate.

Curry-in-a-Hurry (877-3328; 333 Dairy Rd; meals $4-8; 11am-2pm & 6-9pm Tue-Sat) It's just a little shack next to Wow-Wee Maui's, but it serves some of the island's healthiest fare with an accomplished Ayurveda cook dishing out Indian vegetarian food. The menu changes daily, but coconut curry, tofu tandoori, samosas and basmati rice are staples.

Maui Coffee Roasters (877-2877; 444 Hana Hwy; snacks $1-6; 7am-6pm Mon-Fri, 8am-5pm Sat, to 2:30pm Sun;) The island's best coffee deal will set you back just 50¢ a cup. Locals linger over pastries, not to mention newspapers and chess sets.

If you need to pick up groceries, **Safeway** (877-3377; 170 E Kamehameha Ave; 24hr) supermarket is in the town center. Or if you prefer health food, **Down to Earth Natural Foods** (877-2661; 305 Dairy Rd; 7am-9pm Mon-Sat, 8am-8pm Sun) has Maui's largest selection, including a take-out deli and salad bar.

MID-RANGE

Brigit & Bernard's Garden Café (☎ 877-6000; 335 Hoohana St; lunch $6-15, dinner $10-18; 🕙 10:30am-3pm Mon-Fri, 5-9pm Wed-Fri; 🗷) This little caterer's café has a shady outdoor patio, full bar and a surprisingly extensive menu, with everything from Caesar salads and fresh fish to heavy European favorites like Wiener schnitzel and pasta carbonara.

Thailand Cuisine (☎ 873-0225; Maui Mall, 70 E Ka'ahumanu Ave; mains $8-15; 🕙 lunch & dinner; 🗷) The solid menu of well-prepared Thai dishes includes a mouth-watering Penang curry redolent with lime and sweet basil and a 'Kukui evil prince' that will set your senses on fire.

TOP END

Mañana Garage (☎ 873-0220; 33 Lono Ave; lunch $9-15, dinner $18-28; 🕙 11am-9pm Mon-Tue, to 10:30pm Wed-Sat; 🗷) This is the hottest place in town, with a Latin-influenced menu, bright Caribbean decor and a following that packs the house. The blackened fish tostada and guava-glazed barbecue ribs are house specials on an extensive menu that also includes vegetarian options. Excellent dinner discounts of up to 50% may be available, but the nights change so call for details.

Drinking

Ale House Sports Bar & Restaurant (☎ 877-9001; 355 E Kamehameha Ave) Knock back your brews here while watching the game on big-screen TV. It's a popular spot for folks who've moved to Maui from the mainland and come in droves to watch mainland sports events on the tube. Local flavor, but not unwelcoming to visitors. Also pool and darts.

Mañana Garage (☎ 873-0220; 33 Lono Ave; 🕙 11am-9pm Mon-Tue, to 10:30pm Wed-Sat; 🗷) Cheery and bright, this bar at the side of the restaurant dining room attracts a hip crowd, with islanders and vacationers in equal measure. There's live Latin music most evenings (but no dancing). Come on Tuesday for the $2 margaritas.

Entertainment

Maui Arts & Cultural Center (MACC; box office ☎ 242-7469; www.mauiarts.org; 1 Cameron Way) This modern center boasts two indoor theaters and a large outdoor amphitheater – all with excellent acoustics – and is the venue for film festivals, community theater, performances by the Maui Symphony Orchestra and Hawaiian cultural organizations. MACC is also *the* place in Maui for big-name concerts, playing host to the likes of UB40, blink-182 and the Brothers Cazimero, one of the state's most popular Hawaiian music duos.

Queen Ka'ahumanu Center (☎ 877-4325; 275 Ka'ahumanu Ave) This shopping center hosts free performances by dancers of the Old Lahaina Luau (p312). Call for showtimes.

Borders Books & Music Café (☎ 877-6160; Maui Marketplace, 270 Dairy Rd; 🕙 9am-10pm, to 11pm Fri & Sat) Bring the kids for *na keiki* storytime on Wednesday mornings. Also, there's live Hawaiian music on Saturday afternoons. All events are free.

Consolidated Theatre (☎ 878-3456; Queen Ka'ahumanu Center, 275 Ka'ahumanu Ave) Shows first-run movies.

Shopping

Kahului has Maui's only big-box discount chains and the lion's share of its shopping malls. The mainland discount stores **Costco** (☎ 877-5241; 540 Haleakala Hwy; 🕙 11am-8:30pm Mon-Fri, 9:30am-6pm Sat, 10am-6pm Sun), **Wal-Mart** (☎ 871-7820; 1011 Pakaula St; 🕙 6am-11pm) and **Kmart** (☎ 871-8553; 424 Dairy Rd; 🕙 8am-11pm) are all on or near Dairy Rd. The island's two largest malls, **Queen Ka'ahumanu Center** (☎ 877-4325; 275 Ka'ahumanu Ave; 🕙 9:30am-9pm Mon-Fri, to 7pm Sat, to 5pm Sun) and the **Maui Marketplace** (☎ 873-0400; 270 Dairy Rd; 🕙 most stores 10am-9pm Mon-Sat, to 7pm Sun), are nearby.

Better yet, skip the mall and head to the **Maui Swap Meet** (Pu'unene Ave; admission 50¢; 🕙 5:30am-1pm Sat), a friendly island scene where you buy direct from craftspeople and local farmers. You'll not only find a wide variety of fresh-picked fruit, veggies and flowers but everything from T's and batik skirts to bamboo wind chimes, jewelry and homemade jams. This place glows with aloha and the prices are unbeatable.

TOP FIVE SHOPPING EXPERIENCES

- **Maui Crafts Guild** (p354), Pa'ia
- **Maui Swap Meet** (p331), Kahului
- **Lahaina Arts Society** (p313), Lahaina
- **Hana Coast Gallery** (p362), Hana
- **Hot Island Glass** (p369), Makawao

Getting There & Around
TO/FROM THE AIRPORT

Most people pick up rental cars (p300) at Kahului airport. See p299 for shuttle transport and taxi fares.

BICYCLE

Island Biker (☎ 877-7744; 415 Dairy Rd; per day $30; ☯ 9am-5pm Mon-Sat) rents quality mountain bikes.

BUS

The Maui Public Transit System (p299) connects Kahului with Ma'alaea, Kihei, Wailea and Lahaina; buses run every two hours. There are also free buses that run around Kahului and connect to Wailuku six times a day between 7am and 6pm.

HALEKI'I-PIHANA HEIAU STATE MONUMENT

One of Maui's most important historical sites, **Haleki'i-Pihana Heiau** (Map p315; Hea Pl; admission free; ☯ sunrise-sunset) consists of the remains of two adjoining temples atop a knoll with a commanding view across the plains of central Maui.

It was here that Kahekili, the last ruling chief of Maui, lived. This was also the birth place of Keopuolani, wife of Kamehameha I. After the decisive battle of 'Iao in 1790, Kamehameha I came to these heiau (an ancient stone temple) to worship his war god Ku, offering what is thought to have been the last human sacrifice on Maui.

Haleki'i (House of Images), the first heiau, has stepped stone walls that tower above 'Iao Stream, which was the source for the stone used in the temple construction. A *pili* grass building and a couple of *ki'i* (deity images) have been reconstructed at Haleki'i.

The pyramidlike mound of **Pihana Heiau** is directly ahead, just a five-minute walk, but watch out for thorns if you're wearing flipflops. Pihana, which means 'gathering place of supernatural beings,' is partially overgrown with kiawe, wildflowers and weeds. Much larger than Haleki'i, this temple was the one used for human sacrifices.

A certain mana still emanates from the site. To imagine it all through the eyes of the Hawaiians 200 years ago, ignore the surrounding industrial warehouses and tract homes and concentrate instead on the wild ocean vistas.

To get to the monument, two miles northeast of central Wailuku, take Waiehu Beach Rd (Hwy 340) and turn inland onto Kuhio Pl three-quarters of a mile south of the intersection of Hwys 340 and 330. Then head left onto Hea Pl and drive up through the gates. The heiau are less than half a mile from Hwy 340.

WAILUKU
pop 17,625

Wailuku is unabashedly local – there's nothing touristy in the whole town. An ancient religious and political center, one translation of its name means 'waters of slaughter,' after

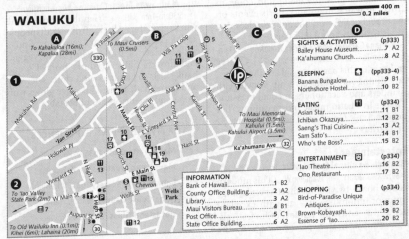

WAILUKU

SIGHTS & ACTIVITIES   (p333)
Bailey House Museum.....................7 A2
Ka'ahumanu Church......................8 A2

SLEEPING   (pp333-4)
Banana Bungalow.........................9 B1
Northshore Hostel......................10 B2

EATING   (p334)
Asian Star.............................11 B1
Ichiban Okazuya........................12 B2
Saeng's Thai Cuisine...................13 A2
Sam Sato's.............................14 B1
Who's the Boss?........................15 B2

ENTERTAINMENT   (p334)
'Iao Theatre...........................16 B2
Ono Restaurant.........................17 B2

SHOPPING   (p334)
Bird-of-Paradise Unique
  Antiques.............................18 B2
Brown-Kobayashi........................19 B2
Essense of 'Iao........................20 B2

INFORMATION
Bank of Hawaii..........................1 B2
County Office Building...................2 A2
Library.................................3 A2
Maui Visitors Bureau....................4 B1
Post Office.............................5 C1
State Office Building....................6 A2

To Kahakuloa (16mi);
Kapalua (28mi)

To Maui Cruisers (0.5mi)

To Maui Memorial Hospital (0.5mi);
Kahului (1.5mi);
Kahului Airport (3.5mi)

To 'Iao Valley State Park (2mi)

To Old Wailuku Inn (0.1mi);
Kihei (6mi); Lahaina (20mi)

the bloody battles that took place in the surrounding 'Iao Valley. Kahekili built his royal palace at the valley entrance. Because of its rich history, Wailuku has several sites on the National Register of Historic Places, including the Bailey House Museum, Ka'ahumanu Church and the 'Iao Theatre on N Main St.

Although its heyday is long passed, unassuming Wailuku is still home to Maui's government. The town's central area serves as the county capital, complete with a few midrise government buildings, while the backstreets are lined with a colorful hodgepodge of older shops and neighborhood restaurants.

Its antique and pawn shops can make for interesting browsing, and thanks to the combination of low rent and hungry government employees there are several good lunchtime eating options at prices that shame Maui's more touristed towns. There is one caveat – the town can get rough at night. The public parking lot on W Main St is an after-dark hangout rife with drug dealing and fights that gets more police calls than any other spot on Maui – so steer clear.

Information

The county and state office buildings are adjacent to S High St, near its intersection with Main St.

Bank of Hawaii (☎ 871-8200; 2105 Main St) Has a 24-hour ATM.

Maui Memorial Hospital (☎ 244-9056; 221 Mahalani St; ☉ 24hr) This is the island's main hospital, with 24-hour emergency services.

Maui Visitors Bureau (MVB; ☎ 244-3530, 800-525-6284; www.visitmaui.com; 1727 Wili Pa Loop; ☉ 8am-4:30pm Mon-Fri) Essentially an administrative office, so you'll find better information and more brochures at the airport booth (p328).

Wailuku Post Office (☎ 244-1653; 250 Imi Kala St; ☉ 8am-4:30pm Mon-Fri, 9am-noon Sat)

Sights
BAILEY HOUSE MUSEUM

This worthwhile little **museum** (☎ 244-3326; 2375-A E Main St; adult/child $5/1; ☉ 10am-4pm Mon-Sat) occupies the former home of missionary Edward Bailey, who came to Wailuku from Boston, Massachusetts, in 1837. The second story of the house remains much the same as it was in missionary days, decorated with antiques and some of the works that Bailey, an accomplished engraver, created.

The Hawaiian collections on the ground floor are the real prize of the museum. The museum boasts a superb collection of handcrafted bowls made from native woods and other ancient artifacts including stone adzes, feather lei and tapa cloths. There's also a display of spears, shark-tooth daggers and other weapons similar to those used in the bloody battles at nearby 'Iao Valley.

Friendly Maui Historical Society volunteers run the museum. If you're lucky enough to catch Uncle Sol, a spry octogenarian and an accomplished ukulele player, he loves to talk story and is a wealth of information on local history.

KA'AHUMANU CHURCH

Established in 1832, **Ka'ahumanu Church** (cnr Main & High Sts) is the oldest Congregational church in Maui. The church was named in honor of Queen Ka'ahumanu, who cast aside the old gods and burned temple idols, allowing Christianity to flourish. She visited Wailuku and in her ever-humble manner requested that the church bear her name.

This present building was erected in 1876 by missionary Edward Bailey atop a former heiau site and royal compound. The old clock in the steeple, brought around the Horn in the 19th century, still keeps accurate time. Hymns are sung in Hawaiian at Sunday morning services but at other times the church is usually locked.

Festivals & Events

Hulafest Week (mid-January) A slew of competitions, from surfing meets to foot races and golf tournaments.

Hula Bowl Maui (late January; www.hulabowlmaui.com) Maui plays host to the classic East versus West college all-star football game at the War Memorial Complex stadium.

Maui County Fair (late September; www.calendarmaui.com) Held at the War Memorial Complex, this is a venerable county fair with agricultural exhibits, rides, ethnic foods and a dazzling orchid display.

Sleeping
BUDGET

Wailuku has two hostels. Both places are in older, termite-gnawed buildings that occasionally get a fresh coat of paint but are otherwise spartan. Because of frequent management changes it's hard to predict what your experience will be like. Best advice: size the places up when you arrive and don't dish out money for a lengthy stay in advance.

Banana Bungalow (☎ 244-5090, 800-846-7835; www.mauihostel.com; 310 N Market St; dm $18, r with shared bathroom $32; ⌨) A backyard Jacuzzi and barbecue facilities are offset by cramped dormitories and uncomfortable mattresses. Still, the common amenities are the plus here, and include a group kitchen, coin laundry, shed for storing windsurfing gear and free airport shuttle and island tours.

Northshore Hostel (☎ 242-0895, 866-946-7835; www.northshorehostel.com; 2080 E Vineyard St; dm $18, s/d with shared bathroom $38/50; ⌨) Traditionally more popular with international travelers, Northshore is the smaller of the two hostels but sports a common kitchen and gear storage.

MID-RANGE

Old Wailuku Inn (☎ 244-5897, 800-305-4899; www.mauiinn.com; 2199 Kaho'okele St; r $120-180; ❄) Step back into the 1920s in this elegant period home, built by a wealthy banker. Authentically restored by its friendly innkeepers, the inn retains the antique furniture and native hardwood floors of earlier times, while discreetly adding modern amenities. Each room is unique, but all are large and comfy with traditional Hawaiian quilts warming the beds. It's a sure winner.

Eating
BUDGET

Sam Sato's (☎ 244-7124; 1750 Wili Pa Loop; mains $4-7; ❂ 7am-2pm Mon-Sat) Dry noodles (which are not really dry, but cooked with a soy-based sauce) and saimin noodle soups are the specialties at this popular eatery. Sato's makes *manju* (Japanese cakes filled with sweet bean paste) that Honolulu residents rave about.

Ichiban Okazuya (☎ 244-7276; 2133 Kaohu St; mains $5-8; ❂ 10am-2pm & 4-7pm Mon-Fri) Little more than a tin-roof shed, this place tucked behind the government buildings has been dishing out tasty Japanese-style plate lunches to office workers for half a century, so you'd better believe they have the recipes down pat. It's take-out, but there's an inviting picnic table shaded by an old mango tree out back.

MID-RANGE

Who's the Boss? (☎ 244-6816; 2051 Main St; mains $6-12; ❂ 10am-2:30pm Mon-Fri) This perky bistro blends the talents of the French owner of Chez Paul and his wife, a Vietnamese chef. Fresh fish with papaya salsa, creative sand-wiches and oversized salads are standards. It's Wailuku's busiest restaurant, and for good cause – you can enjoy the same type of gourmet food served at Chez Paul's dinner restaurant for a fraction of the cost.

Asian Star (☎ 244-1833; 1764 Wili Pa Loop; mains $6-12; ❂ 10am-9:30pm) An excellent Vietnamese restaurant with an extensive menu, Asian Star specializes in classics like *pho* noodle soup and *banh hoi* (a Vietnamese rice-paper wrap chock-full of goodies and garnished with mint). True, the atmosphere here in the industrial loop is minimal, but service is congenial.

Saeng's Thai Cuisine (☎ 244-1567; 2119 Vineyard St; mains $7-13; ❂ lunch, dinner) Good Thai food in an alluring open-air setting is what you'll find at Maui's oldest Thai restaurant. There are aromatic curries, fresh seafood, a masterful pad thai and lots of veg dishes.

Entertainment

Ono Restaurant (☎ 244-5117; 2102 Vineyard St) A good place to have a drink, with live jazz on the weekends.

'Iao Theatre (☎ 242-6969; N Market St) Restored after years of neglect, the 1928 art deco theater hosts local drama group productions.

Shopping

In the block of N Market St running north from Main St you'll find a run of pawnshops, galleries and antique shops, some of them intriguingly cluttered affairs stocking a mishmash of Hawaiiana items.

Brown-Kobayashi (☎ 242-0804; 38 N Market St) For Japanese lacquerware and Asian antiques.

Bird-of-Paradise Unique Antiques (☎ 242-7699; 56 N Market St) Poke around for kimono and glassware here.

Essense of 'Iao (☎ 244-5244; 1980 Main St) If you want to bring home a little jungle fragrance, the handmade candles, soaps and body oils are scented with plumeria, eucalyptus and wild ginger.

Getting There & Around

The Maui Public Transit System (p298) runs free loop buses between Wailuku and Kahului from 7am to 6pm. Wailuku stops include the state office building, the hospital and the post office.

'IAO VALLEY ROAD

In 1790 Kamehameha I attacked Kahului by sea and routed the defending Maui warriors up into precipitous 'Iao Valley. Those unable to escape over the mountains were slaughtered along the stream. The waters of 'Iao Stream were so choked with bodies that the area was called Kepaniwai (Dammed Waters).

Today 'Iao Valley State Park encompasses much of the upper valley along the stream. 'Iao Valley Rd leads droves of tourists every day into the park, passing a few sights along the way.

Tropical Gardens of Maui

These **gardens** (☎ 244-3085; 200 'Iao Valley Rd; adult/child $3/free; ☺ 9am-4:30pm Mon-Sat), which straddle both sides of 'Iao Stream, are easily the best of Maui's many gardens. They have a superb orchid collection, endemic Hawaiian plantings, brilliant bromeliads, fragrant gingers, a lily pond and a Zen-like bamboo grove with a trickling waterfall. Plaques with interesting background information identify many of the plants. See if you can find the world's largest orchid!

Kepaniwai County Park

Another mile further, this **park** ('Iao Valley Rd; ☺ 7am-7pm) is dedicated to Hawaii's varied ethnic heritage. After years of neglect, the park has been spruced up. There is a traditional *hale*, a New England-style missionary home, a Filipino farmer's hut, Japanese gardens with stone pagodas, and a Chinese pavilion with the requisite statue of Sun Yat-sen. 'Iao Stream runs through the park, bordered by picnic shelters with barbecue pits. The place is cheerfully alive with families picnicking here on weekends.

Up at the west end of Kepaniwai County Park is the **Hawaii Nature Center** (☎ 244-6500; 875 'Iao Valley Rd; adult/child $6/4; ☺ 10am-4pm), a nonprofit educational facility with interactive kid-oriented exhibits that let youngsters take to the air on the wings of a dragonfly, come nose to nose with a happy-face spider and the like. The center also leads two-hour **rainforest walks** ($25); reservations are required.

'Iao Valley State Park

Nestled in the mountains, 3 miles out of central Wailuku, this **park** (admission free; ☺ 7am-7pm) extends clear up to Pu'u Kukui (5788ft), Maui's highest and wettest point. The valley is named after 'Iao, the beautiful daughter of Maui. **'Iao Needle**, a rock pinnacle that rises 2250ft, is said to be 'Iao's clandestine lover, captured by Maui and turned to stone. A monument to love, this is the big kahuna, the ultimate phallic symbol.

Clouds often rise up the valley, forming a shroud around the top of 'Iao Needle. A stream meanders beneath the needle, and the steep cliffs of the West Maui Mountains form a picture-postcard backdrop. After a two-minute walk from the parking lot, you'll reach a bridge where most people stop to photograph 'Iao Needle. However, just before the bridge, the walkway that loops downhill by the stream leads to the nicest photo angle – one that captures the stream, bridge and 'Iao Needle together. There are two other short paths, starting opposite each other over the bridge. The lower one leads down along 'Iao Stream, while the upper one leads steeply up to a sheltered lookout with another fine view of 'Iao Needle.

PU'UNENE

Pu'unene is given over to sugarcane fields and centered around a mill run by the Hawaiian Commercial & Sugar (C&S) Company. When the mill is in operation, the air hangs heavy with the sweet smell of molasses.

The power plant next to the mill burns residue sugarcane fibers (called bagasse) to run the mill machinery that extracts and refines the sugar. With a capacity of 37,000 kilowatts, it's one of the world's largest biomass power plants.

> ### DETOUR: OLD PU'UNENE
>
> A little slice of a bygone plantation village is hidden behind the sugar mill in Pu'unene. There, a long-forgotten church lies abandoned in a field of waving cane, across from the village's old schoolhouse. But the place isn't a ghost town. Out back, just beyond the school, is an old shack that's served as a used bookstore since 1913. It's a bit musty and dusty, but still sells books for a mere dime. To get there turn off Mokulele Hwy (Hwy 311) onto Hansen Rd and take the first right onto Pu'unene Ave, continuing past the old Pu'unene Meat Market building (c 1926) and the mill. Turn left after half a mile, just past a little bridge. After the pavement ends, turn right and drive behind the old school to reach the bookstore.

MAUI

Pu'unene's main attraction is the **Alexander & Baldwin Sugar Museum** (☎ 871-8058; cnr Pu'unene Ave & Hansen Rd; adult/child $5/2; ◷ 9:30am-4:30pm Mon-Sat, also Sun Feb-Apr, Jul & Aug), an intriguing little museum in the former home of the mill's superintendent. Exhibits give the skinny on the sugarcane biz and include a working scale model of a cane-crushing plant.

Most interesting, however, are the images of people. The museum traces how Samuel Alexander and Henry Baldwin gobbled up vast chunks of Maui land, how they fought tooth and nail with an ambitious Claus Spreckels to gain access to Upcountry water, and how they dug the extensive irrigation systems that made large-scale sugarcane plantations viable.

Representing the other end of the scale is a turn-of-the-20th-century labor contract from the Japanese Emigration Company stating that the laborer shall be paid $15 a month for working 10 hours a day in the field, 26 days a month. Illuminating period photos and artifacts of plantation life are also on display.

KEALIA POND NATIONAL WILDLIFE REFUGE

A bird-watcher's oasis, the **Kealia Pond NWR** (☎ 875-1582; Mokulele Hwy; ◷ 8am-4:30pm Mon-Fri) harbors native waterbirds year-round and hosts migratory ducks and shorebirds from October to April. In the rainy winter months, Kealia Pond swells to more than 400 acres, making it one of the largest natural ponds in Hawaii. In summer it shrinks to half that, giving it a skirt of crystalline salt and accounting for its name (Kealia means 'salt-encrusted place').

You can view much of the pond right from N Kihei Rd, between Kihei and Ma'alaea (there are several places to pull off on the roadside), as well as from the refuge's visitor center off Mokulele Hwy (near the 6-mile marker). In both places, you're almost certain to spot wading Hawaiian black-necked stilts, Hawaiian coots and black-crowned night herons – all native waterbirds that thrive in this sanctuary. What's special about the visitor center site, adjacent to a long-abandoned catfish farm, is that you can get much closer to the birds and in winter it's the best place to see visiting osprey, a majestic fish hawk that dive-bombs for its prey in the old fishponds.

MA'ALAEA BAY

Ma'alaea literally means 'beginning of red dirt,' but once there you'll swear it means 'windy.' Ma'alaea Bay runs along the south side of the isthmus between the twin mountain masses of west and east Maui.

Sights

The state-of-the-art **Maui Ocean Center** (☎ 270-7000; www.mauioceancenter.com; 192 Ma'alaea Rd; adult/child $20/13; ◷ 9am-5pm, to 6pm Jul & Aug) is not only a feast for the eyes but a great place to learn about Hawaiian marine life. The Maui Ocean Center is the largest tropical aquarium in the USA, and is dedicated to indigenous Hawaiian marine life. The variety and brilliance of the fish and coral is nothing short of dazzling.

Exhibits start with creatures of the shallowest intertidal waters and progress into deep ocean life. The center filters seawater from the adjacent bay through its tanks, providing a nutrient-rich environment that allows coral (it boasts the world's largest aquarium collection) and fish to thrive. The extensive 'living reef' section focuses on the sealife you might see while snorkeling in Hawaiian waters, with interpretive displays identifying sunshine-bright butterfly fish, rainbow-colored wrasses, menacing moray eels and other tropical fish.

Hands down the most impressive sight is the enormous main tank with a see-through acrylic tunnel that allows you to walk right through the center as schools of fish, gliding eagle rays and reef sharks encircle you. It's as close as you can get to being underwater without donning dive gear. The 'Hawaiians and the sea' exhibit offers insights into ancient fishing techniques and the relationship of indigenous people with their environment. For a meditative experience, don't miss the mesmerizing column of free-floating jellyfish, a sort of living lava lamp. Elsewhere are interactive displays on whales, as well as a touch pond that will thrill kids and a sea turtle pool where injured turtles are treated for eventual release into the wild.

Activities
WINDSURFING & SURFING

Prevailing winds from the north funnel between the mountains straight out toward Kaho'olawe, creating strong midday gusts and some of the best **windsurfing** conditions on Maui. In fact, these are the strongest winds on the island. In winter, when the wind dies down elsewhere, windsurfers still fly along Ma'alaea Bay.

The bay also has a couple of hot surfing spots. The **Ma'alaea Pipeline**, south of the harbor, freight-trains right and is the fastest surf break in all Hawaii. Summer's southerly swells produce huge tubes. Ma'alaea Bay is fronted by a continuous 3-mile stretch of sandy **beach**, running from Ma'alaea Harbor south to Kihei, which can be accessed at several places along N Kihei Rd.

HIKING
Inland of the bay, the historic 19th-century route of the **Lahaina Pali Trail** zigzags steeply up through kiawe and native dryland sandalwood trees. After the first mile it passes into open, sun-baked scrub, from where you can see Haleakala and the fertile central plains. Ironwood trees precede the crossing of Kealaoloa Ridge (1600ft), after which you descend through Ukumehame Gulch. Look for postcard views of Kaho'olawe and Lana'i, stray petroglyphs and *paniolo* graffiti. Stay on the footpath all the way down to Papalaua Beach and don't detour onto 4WD roads. The 5.5-mile trail should take about 2½ hours each way.

You can hike in either direction, but starting off early from the east side of the mountains keeps you ahead of the blistering sun. The trailhead access road, marked by a Na Ala Hele sign, is on Hwy 30, about 100yd south of the intersection of Hwy 380, near Ma'alaea. If you prefer to start at the west end or want to have a ride waiting for you when you finish, the trailhead is 200yd south of the 11-mile marker on Hwy 30.

Eating
There are a few restaurants and a good homemade ice-cream shop in the **Ma'alaea Harbor Village** shopping center adjacent to the ocean center.

Getting There & Away
Ma'alaea has some of Maui's best bus service. Buses run by Maui Public Transit System (p298) connect Ma'alaea Harbor Village shopping center with Lahaina, Kahului, Kihei and Wailea. Service depends on the route, but buses operate from around 7:30am to at least 5:30pm.

THE AUTHOR'S CHOICE

Ma'alaea Grill (Map p315; ☎ 243-2206; Ma'alaea Harbor Village; lunch $7-11, mains $15-21; ☷ 10:30am-3pm Mon, to 9pm Tue-Sun; ☷) This place has it all: a fantastic harbor view, attentive service and excellent food. Fresh seafood, organic salads and hearty sandwiches shore up the menu. At lunch, the seared *'ahi* sandwich on focaccia is guaranteed not to disappoint. At dinner, try the blackened mahimahi with fresh papaya salsa.

SOUTH MAUI

South Maui offers a mixed plate of aquatic adventures and beaches, all enjoying the sunny, dependably dry conditions off Haleakala's leeward slopes. The three communities that make up south Maui sport three distinctive characters. Kihei is Maui's biggest middle-class beach destination, lined with condominium complexes and replete with all the conveniences one needs for a vacation at the beach. Wailea (p344) boasts the island's most upscale beach destination with lavish resorts and designer golf courses. Makena (p348), the least developed, is the haunt of those seeking solitude, with a scattering of exclusive homes and Maui's best-known clothing-optional beach.

KIHEI
pop 19,850
Fringed with sandy beaches its entire length and gleaming in near-constant sunshine, it's no secret why visitors flock here. The town itself might not be a beauty but the scenery from the beach is some of the finest in Hawaii. From the soft sands of Kihei you'll be treated to picturesque views of Lana'i and Kaho'olawe, as well as of west Maui, which, because of the deep cut of Ma'alaea Bay, looks like a separate island from here.

It's hard to believe, but just three decades years ago Kihei was little more than a stretch of undeveloped beach with a scattering of homes and a church or two. Since the 1970s, developers have pounced on Kihei with such intensity that S Kihei Rd, which runs the full length of Kihei, is now lined with condos, gas stations, shopping centers and fast-food places in such congested disarray that it's the example most often cited by antidevelopment forces on Hawaii's other islands. To them, Kihei is what no town wants to become.

While Kihei may not win any prizes for aesthetics, it has advantages for visitors: the sheer abundance of condos means that Kihei's rates are among the cheapest in Maui, the nightlife is booming, and the dining scene is better than ever.

Orientation

Pi'ilani Hwy (Hwy 31) runs parallel to and bypasses the start-and-stop traffic of S Kihei Rd. Half a dozen crossroads connect the two, making it easy to zip in and out of Kihei efficiently. The place is becoming more bicycle-friendly, with bike lanes found on the Pi'ilani Hwy, as well as on S Kihei Rd.

Information

American Savings Bank (Map p338; ☎ 879-1977; 1215 S Kihei Rd; ♥ 9am-6pm Mon-Fri, to 1pm Sat) 24-hour ATM.

Cyberbean Internet Café (Map p341; ☎ 879-4799; Kihei Town Center; ♥ 7am-9pm Mon-Sat, 8am-8pm Sun; per min 20¢) Several computers, few waits and decent coffee.

Hale Imua Internet Stop (Map p341; ☎ 891-9219; Kama'ole Shopping Center, 2463 S Kihei Rd; per 15 min $3, then per min 15¢; ♥ 8am-9pm)

Kihei Post Office (Map p338; ☎ 879-1987; 1254 S Kihei Rd)

Lipoa Laundry Center (Map p338; Lipoa Center, 40 E Lipoa St; ♥ 8am-8pm Mon-Sat, to 5pm Sun)

Longs Drugs (Map p338; ☎ 879-2033; 1215 S Kihei Rd; ♥ 8am-10pm Mon-Fri, to 9pm Sat & Sun) Kihei's largest pharmacy.

Urgent Care Maui Physicians (Map p338; ☎ 879-7781; 1325 S Kihei Rd; ♥ 7am-10pm) This clinic accepts walk-in patients.

Sights

Kihei's southern beaches are postcard perfect, with ideal conditions for swimming and sunbathing. This is a case of the further south you go, the better it gets. At the northern end of Kihei, around Kihei Wharf, swimming is not advised, although windsurfers, kayakers and canoeists find water conditions more than suitable for their purposes. Snorkeling is fine at Keawapaku Beach, but for the best conditions, snorkelers and divers should head to Wailea and Makena instead.

MAI POINA 'OE IA'U BEACH PARK

At the northern end of Kihei, it has a long sandy beach and full facilities. Sunbathing is good in the morning before the wind picks up, while windsurfing is best in the afternoon; many people take windsurfing lessons here, and outrigger canoes and kayaks launch from the beach.

KALEPOLEPO BEACH PARK

Local families love to take their *na keiki* to play in the calm, shallow waters at this beach park, bordering the south side of the Hawaiian Islands Humpback Whale National Marine Sanctuary. It's essentially a big swimming pool, because the beach is encircled by the stone walls of **Ko'ie'ie Fishpond**.

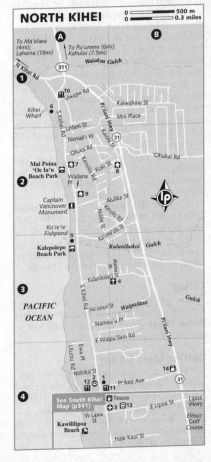

The most intact fishpond remaining on Maui, Ko'ie'ie was built in the 16th century to raise mullet for the *ali'i* (royalty). The 3-acre fishpond is on the National Register of Historic Places. The best view of the fishpond is from the back steps of the marine sanctuary, where the whale-watching scope is set up.

KALAMA PARK
This one's best suited for playing on land. Opposite Kihei Town Center, Kalama Park has ball fields, tennis and volleyball courts, an in-line skating rink, a playground, picnic pavilions, restrooms and showers. The park is long and grassy, but the beach is shallow and unappealing for swimming.

KAMA'OLE BEACH PARKS
Kama'ole is one long beach divided into three sections (Kam I, II and III) by rocky points. All three are pretty beaches with golden sands and full facilities.

Water conditions vary with the weather, but swimming is usually good. For the most part, these beaches have sandy bottoms with a fairly steep drop, which tends to create good conditions for bodysurfing, especially in winter.

For snorkeling, the southern end of Kama'ole Beach Park III has some nearshore rocks harboring a bit of coral and a few tropical fish, though there are better snorkeling beaches to the south.

KEAWAKAPU BEACH
Stretching between the southernmost Kihei hotels and Mokapu Beach at the beginning of the Wailea resorts, sandy Keawakapu Beach is more scenic and less crowded than roadside Kihei beaches. Morning snorkeling is fairly good at the rocky outcrops that form the northern and southern ends of the beach, and you can rent snorkel gear at the northern end, near the Maui Oceanfront Inn.

There's a fine view from the beach, and during the winter, whales cavort in the surrounding waters and sometimes come quite close to shore. With its cushiony soft sand, it's also a favorite place for people doing sunrise yoga and wake-up strolls.

To get to the south side of Keawakapu Beach, go south on S Kihei Rd until it ends at a beach parking lot. Near the middle of the beach, there's a parking lot at the corner of Kilohana and S Kihei Rd; look for a blue shoreline access sign on the *makai* side of the street. At the northern end, beach parking can be found at the side of Mana Kai Maui. There are outdoor showers at all three places.

HAWAIIAN ISLANDS HUMPBACK WHALE NATIONAL MARINE SANCTUARY
The **marine sanctuary headquarters** (Map p338; ☎ 879-2818, 800-831-4888; www.hihwnms.nos.noaa.gov; 726 S Kihei Rd; ◷ 10am-4pm Mon-Fri) has a little visitor center with simple displays on whales, sea turtles and other endangered marine life, but that's not why people come here.

This is a prime whale-watching spot, and the center's oceanfront lanai makes a great spot for sighting the humpback whales that frequent the bay during the winter. A free scope is set up for viewing.

DAVID MALO'S CHURCH
Philosopher David Malo, who built this church in 1853, was the first Hawaiian ordained to the Christian ministry and co-author of Hawaii's first constitution. While most of Malo's original church was dismantled, a 3ft-high section of the walls still stands beside a palm grove. Pews are lined up inside the stone walls, where open-air services are held at 9am on Sunday by **Trinity Episcopal Church-by-the-Sea** (100 Kulanihako'i St).

Activities

DIVING & SNORKELING

Maui Dive Shop (Map p341; ☎ 879-3388; www.mauidive shop.com; 1455 S Kihei Rd; dives from $80, courses from $300; ☼ 6am-9pm), the main outlet of this is-landwide diving chain, is a good spot to rent or buy water-sports gear, including boogie boards, snorkels, fins and wet suits.

Maui Dreams Dive Co (Map p341; ☎ 874-5332, 888-921-3483; www.mauidreamsdiveco.com; 1993 S Kihei Rd; dives from $60, courses from $250; ☼ 7am-5pm), a family-run, five-star PADI outfit, gets en-thusiastic reviews for its personal attention and environmentally friendly approach.

KAYAKING & CANOEING

South Pacific Kayaks & Outfitters (Map p341; ☎ 875-4848, 800-776-2326; www.mauikayak.com; Rainbow Mall, 2439 S Kihei Rd; 1-/2-person kayaks per day $30/40, tours $55-90; ☼ 8am-5pm), a long-established operation, not only rents kayaks, but leads a variety of adventurous kayak tours in the 'Ahihi-Kina'u Natural Area Reserve area.

If you just want to spend an hour or two on the water, **Blue Hawaiian Water Sports** (Map p341; ☎ 875-8486; www.mauisports.biz; 2980 S Kihei Rd; 1-/2-person kayaks per hr $10/15; ☼ 9am-5pm) is right on the beach at the Maui Oceanfront Inn, where you can hop in a kayak and paddle away.

Kihei Canoe Club (Map p338; Kihei Wharf; www.kiheicanoeclub.com; donation $25) invites visitors to share in the mana by joining members in paddling their outrigger canoes on Tuesday and Thursday mornings. No advance regist-ration is necessary; just show up at the wharf at 7:30am. The donation helps offset the cost of maintaining the canoes and entitles you to join them each Tuesday and Thursday for the rest of the month.

Festivals & Events

Whale Day is typically held on the second Saturday in February at Kalama Park. This one's for kids, with a parade, games, story-telling and other fun things.

Sleeping

You'll find only a scattering of B&Bs and hotels – no mistake about it, Kihei is con-doville. The town has scores of condos and the competition keeps the prices honest. Some condominium complexes maintain a front desk or a daytime office that handles bookings, but others are booked only via rental agents. One thing to keep in mind –

in many places along S Kihei Rd, the traffic is noisy, so when you book, avoid rooms close to the road.

The following rental agents handle Kihei condos:

Bello Realty (☎ 879-3328, 800-541-3060; www.bello maui.com; PO Box 1776, Kihei, HI 96753)

Kihei Maui Vacations (☎ 879-7581, 800-541-6284; www.kmvmaui.com; PO Box 1055, Kihei, HI 96753)

Resort Quest Maui (☎ 879-5445, 800-822-4409; www.resortquestmaui.com; 2511 S Kihei Rd, Kihei, HI 96753)

BUDGET

Ocean Breeze Hideaway (Map p338; ☎ 879-0657, 888-463-6687; www.hawaiibednbreakfast.com; 435 Kalalau Pl; r incl breakfast $75) In the home of a friendly couple who know the island inside and out, this B&B has two comfortable rooms, one with a queen bed and a glimpse of the ocean, the other with two twin beds. Each has a private entrance and refrigerator.

MID-RANGE

Two Mermaids on the Sunny Side of Maui B&B (Map p341; ☎ 874-8687, 800-598-9550; www.twomermaids.com; 2840 Umalu Pl; poolside studios $115, 1-/2-bedroom units $140/180, all incl breakfast; ☒ ☒) You couldn't feel more at home than at this welcoming B&B. One unit has a private hot tub and deck and both have kitchenettes and cheerful tropical decor. Families are welcome and the inviting backyard pool has a shallow section for kids. One of the owners is a justice of the peace, and she can provide wedding packages for those looking for a getaway honeymoon.

Nona Lani Cottages (Map p338; ☎ 879-2497, 800-733-2688; 455 S Kihei Rd; r $85, cottage from $105) The scent of plumeria fills the air and the friendly hosts make lei from the flowers grown out back. Rooms in the main house are downright cushy. The cottages (for up to four) are simpler but have all the neces-sities, including kitchen and lanai. In high season, rooms have a four-night minimum, cottages a seven-night minimum.

Kihei Kai Nani (Map p341; ☎ 879-9088, 800-473-1493; www.kiheikainani.com; 2495 S Kihei Rd; 1-bedroom units $110; ☒ ☒) This low-rise complex, op-posite Kama'ole Beach Park II, has roomy one-bedroom units. Don't be fooled by the affordable price; this inviting place has well-equipped units with private lanai and lit-tle extras like free local calls. Guests gather around the barbecue grills for evening cook-outs – a great way to meet the neighbors.

Mana Kai Maui (Map p341; ☎ 879-2778, 800-367-5242; www.crhmaui.com; 2960 S Kihei Rd; r $125, 1-bedroom units $230; 🏊 🖳) You won't find a better sunset view than at this complex perched on a point above Keawapaku Beach. And you can swim and snorkel from the beach right outside the door. The place boasts all the conveniences of a condo as well as the

pluses of a hotel, with a front desk and a full-service restaurant.

Kama'ole Beach Royale (Map p341; ☎ 879-3131, 800-421-3661; www.mauikbr.com; 2385 S Kihei Rd; 1-/2-bedroom units from $115/140; 🏊 🖳) Opposite Kama'ole Beach Park I, this condo is quieter than most because it's set back from the road. Pick one of the top-floor units, well

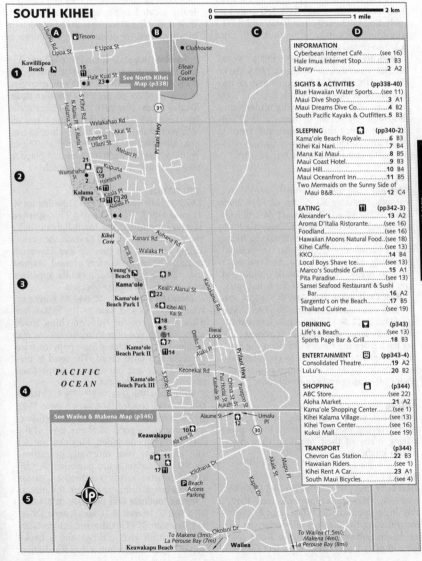

SOUTH KIHEI

0 ——————— 2 km
0 ——————— 1 mile

INFORMATION
Cyberbean Internet Café..........(see 16)
Hale Imua Internet Stop..............1 B3
Library..2 A2

SIGHTS & ACTIVITIES   (pp338-40)
Blue Hawaiian Water Sports....(see 11)
Maui Dive Shop.............................3 A1
Maui Dreams Dive Co.....................4 B2
South Pacific Kayaks & Outfitters.5 B3

SLEEPING   (pp340-2)
Kama'ole Beach Royale.............6 B3
Kihei Kai Nani............................7 B4
Mana Kai Maui............................8 B5
Maui Coast Hotel.........................9 B3
Maui Hill...................................10 B4
Maui Oceanfront Inn..................11 B5
Two Mermaids on the Sunny Side of
    Maui B&B..............................12 C4

EATING   (pp342-3)
Alexander's...............................13 A2
Aroma D'Italia Ristorante........(see 16)
Foodland...................................(see 16)
Hawaiian Moons Natural Food..(see 18)
Kihei Caffe................................(see 13)
KKO...14 B4
Local Boys Shave Ice................(see 13)
Marco's Southside Grill.............15 A1
Pita Paradise...........................(see 13)
Sansei Seafood Restaurant & Sushi
    Bar......................................16 A2
Sargento's on the Beach..........17 B5
Thailand Cuisine.......................(see 19)

DRINKING   (p343)
Life's a Beach...........................(see 13)
Sports Page Bar & Grill.............18 B3

ENTERTAINMENT   (pp343-4)
Consolidated Theatre.................19 A2
LuLu's......................................20 B2

SHOPPING   (p344)
ABC Store.................................(see 22)
Aloha Market............................21 A2
Kama'ole Shopping Center........(see 1)
Kihei Kalama Village.................(see 13)
Kihei Town Center....................(see 16)
Kukui Mall................................(see 19)

TRANSPORT   (p344)
Chevron Gas Station..................22 B3
Hawaiian Riders.......................(see 1)
Kihei Rent A Car........................23 A1
South Maui Bicycles...................(see 4)

Tesoro
E Lipoa St
Kawililipoa Beach
Uluru Rd
Lipoa St
15
Hale Kuai St
3   23
See North Kihei Map (p338)
Clubhouse
Elleair Golf Course
S Kihei Rd
N Alalai Pl
Halama St
N Alanui Pl
Welakahao Rd
Akai St
Pi'ilani Hwy
Kahele St
Uilani St
Mehani Pl
31
21
Waimahaihai St
2
Kupuna
Halelani Pl
16
Keala Pl
Kalama Park
13   20
Alahele Pl
4
Kihei Cove
Kanani Rd
Auhana Rd
Il'ilili Rd
Walaka Pl
Young's Beach
9
Kama'ole
Keali'i Alanui St
22
Kama'ole Beach Park I
6   Kihei Ali'i Kai St
Kanaloanui Rd
18
5
@1
7
Kama'ole Beach Park II
14
Iliwai Loop
Alaku Pl
PACIFIC OCEAN
Kama'ole Beach Park III
Keonekai Rd
Kihei Rd
Ohina St
Puu Hoolai St
Kaithole St
Aukahi St
Pi'ilani Hwy
Papanoo St
See Wailea & Makena Map (p346)
Alaume St
Umalu Pl
12
30
Keawakapu
Ala Koa St
10
8   11
17
Kilohana Dr
Beach Access Parking
Kapili Dr
Maui Pl
Alake St
To Makena (3mi); La Perouse Bay (7mi)
Okolani Dr
Keawakapu Beach
Wailea
To Wailea (1.5mi); Makena (4mi); La Perouse Bay (8mi)

MAUI

worth the extra $10, which have unob-structed ocean views. Units are spacious and well-furnished and the rooftop barbecue area is a superb place to watch the sunset.

Wailana Inn (Map p338; ☎ 874-3131, 800-399-3885; www.wailanabeach.com; 14 Wailana Pl; studios $100-140) This gay-friendly place has a dozen studios with a tasteful decor that outshines other places in its price range. Although it's not a condo, the units still have full amenities including kitchenette and lanai, and there's a clothing-optional rooftop deck with a hot tub and broad ocean views.

Maui Oceanfront Inn (Map p341; ☎ 879-7744, 800-263-3387; www.mauioceanfrontinn.com; 2980 S Kihei Rd; r/ste from $100/160; 🗷) The rooms may be tiny but the place has an enviable location right on Keawakapu Beach. Having undergone a thorough renovation to the tune of $7 mil-lion, the rooms sport an agreeable tropical decor and modern amenities such as data-ports. It's comfortable, if a bit cramped.

TOP END
Maui Hill (Map p341; ☎ 879-6321, 877-997-6667; www.aston-hotels.com; 2881 S Kihei Rd; 1-/2-bedroom units $280/350; 🗷 🗷) Regally set on a hillside opposite Keawakapu Beach, these Mediter-ranean-style villas prove that condo living can be luxurious – nothing has been spared outfitting the spacious units. And you don't have to break the bank: book online and you'll save up to a third off the listed rates.

Maui Coast Hotel (Map p341; ☎ 874-6284, 800-895-6284; www.mauicoasthotel.com; 2259 S Kihei Rd; r/ste from $195/240; 🗷 🗷) This modern seven-story hotel has large well-appointed rooms. It's set back from the road, away from the traf-fic, and guests have access to compliment-ary laundry facilities and tennis courts. Ask about off-season and senior discounts.

Eating
Kihei has some fun dining options, but those staying awhile are likely to be pre-paring many of their meals in their own condo kitchens.

BUDGET
Kihei Caffe (Map p341; ☎ 879-2230; 1945 S Kihei Rd; mains $3-8; ⏰ 5am-3pm) Opposite Kalama Park, this little open-air breakfast spot is great for watching the throngs of beachgoers go by. Homemade cinnamon rolls, Kona cof-fee and early hours make it perfect for jet-lagged travelers who wake up *way* too early. Fresh salads and sandwiches at lunch.

Home Maid Bakery (Map p338; ☎ 874-6035; Azeka Makai; pastries 50¢-$3; ⏰ 6am-4pm) You wouldn't know by looking at it, but this unpreten-tious bakery sells the island's best coconut turnovers and yummy *manju*.

Local Boys Shave Ice (Map p341; Kihei Kalama Village, 1913 S Kihei Rd; shave ice $4 ⏰ 11am-5pm) Conven-iently located opposite Kalama Park, this little stall is the place for a refreshing delight of soft shaved ice drenched in a rainbow of syrups.

Foodland (Map p341; ☎ 879-9350; Kihei Town Center) and **Safeway** (Map p338; ☎ 891-9120; 277 Pi'ikea Ave, Pi'ilani Village) are both 24-hour supermarkets. If you want to go organic, **Hawaiian Moons Natural Foods** (Map p341; ☎ 875-4356; Kama'ole Beach Center, 2411 S Kihei Rd; ⏰ 8am-8pm, to 6pm Sun) sells everything from island produce to trail mix. **Kihei Farmers Market** (Map p338; 61 S Kihei Rd; ⏰ 1:30-5:30pm Mon, Wed & Fri) is a good place to pick up fruits, cheeses and vegetables.

MID-RANGE
KKO (Map p341; ☎ 875-1007; 2511 S Kihei Rd; pupu $8-13, mains $10-17; ⏰ 8am-midnight) This spirited restaurant and bar has torch lights blazing nightly and the sun sets beyond the ocean-facing lanai to the tune of live Hawaiian music. The menu centers around seafood including a tasty fish quesadilla appetizer and fresh-catch dinner specials.

Alexander's (Map p341; ☎ 874-0788; Kihei Kalama Village, 1913 S Kihei Rd; meals $8-11; ⏰ 11am-9pm) This is *the* spot for fish-and-chips, made with your choice of mahimahi, 'ahi or ono (wahoo). Try the sides of hush puppies, fried zucchini and corn bread. The food is pre-pared for take-out, but there are simple lanai tables where you can eat.

Stella Blues (Map p338; ☎ 874-3779; Azeka Mauka, 1279 S Kihei Rd; breakfast $5-10, lunch & dinner $7-22; ⏰ 7:30am-midnight; 🗷) Agreeable contempor-ary decor and a good meal any time of the day. The jalapeño-laden Mexican omelet will jump-start your morning, or mellow out with macadamia-nut pancakes. A var-iety of creative salads, sandwiches, pastas and vegetarian dishes shores up the menu.

Marco's Southside Grill (Map p341; ☎ 874-4041; 1445 S Kihei Rd; breakfast $6-11, lunch & dinner $10-26; ⏰ 7:30am-10pm; 🗷) This atmospheric restaur-ant, with high arch ceilings and a back-drop of classic Italian music, has fine Italian fare, wood-oven-fired pizzas and superb Hawaiian seafood. The salads are huge and the Reuben sandwich is second to none.

Horhito's Mexican Cantina (Map p338; ☎ 891-6394; Lipoa Center, 41 E Lipoa St; combo plates $10-14; ☒ lunch & dinner; ☒) This is the real deal, with an accomplished Mexican chef, friendly staff and generous servings. Best of all, it doesn't skimp on the spices. The specialty here is the fajitas, though the menu runs the gamut.

Aroma D'Italia Ristorante (Map p341; ☎ 879-0133; Kihei Town Center, 1881 S Kihei Rd; mains $9-19; ☒ dinner Mon-Sat) Just like Mama used to make...if yo mama was Italian. Aroma started with just six tables and is now a bustling, full-grown dinner restaurant with an old-world decor and traditional recipes to match. Delicious pastas, mouth-watering chicken parmigiana and superb antipasto.

Vietnamese Cuisine (Map p338; ☎ 875-2088; Azeka Makai, 1280 S Kihei Rd; mains $8-15; ☒ 10:30am-9:30pm) Try the savory *banh hoi*, the Vietnamese version of a burrito flavored with basil and mint. Tasty *pho* soups, wok dishes and noodle plates round out the menu at south Maui's best Vietnamese restaurant.

Pita Paradise (Map p341; ☎ 875-7679; Kihei Kalama Village, 1913 S Kihei Rd; mains $7-19; ☒ 11am-9:30pm Mon-Sat, dinner Sun) Eat outdoors on a breezy patio. The lamb kebab with herb-roasted potatoes is a great choice and the baklava ice cream is to die for. It also serves excellent salads.

Thailand Cuisine (Map p341; ☎ 875-0839; Kukui Mall, 1819 S Kihei Rd; mains $8-15; ☒ lunch Mon-Sat, dinner daily; ☒) The shopping mall setting isn't special, but the food at this family-run eatery is top rate. The extensive menu includes sweet and spicy coconut curries, papaya salad, shrimp rolls and several vegetarian offerings. Classical Thai dancers perform at dinner Monday to Thursday.

TOP END
Sansei Seafood Restaurant & Sushi Bar (Map p341; ☎ 879-0004; Kihei Town Center; appetizers $3-14, mains $16-30; ☒ dinner; ☒) This is the trendiest place in town, but worth the wait for a table. The creative Japanese-Hawaiian menu rolls out everything from traditional *'ahi* sashimi to seared *'opakapaka* (pink snapper) in a white truffle sauce. Not to be missed is the award-winning mango crab salad roll. And despite its loyal following, Sansei offers deals – come between 5:30pm and 6pm and all food, including sushi, is 25% off.

Sarento's on the Beach (Map p341; ☎ 875-7555; 2980 S Kihei Rd; appetizers $9-15, mains $29-45, ☒ dinner) Right on the beach, you can almost feel the salt spray at this elegant open-air restaurant. The menu is award-winning. Not surprisingly, seafood is the forte, with everything from chilled shrimp gazpacho to lobster-and-crab cioppino. It's all rounded out with one of Maui's best wine lists. Pricey, but guaranteed to be a memorable night.

Drinking
Sports Page Grill & Bar (Map p341; ☎ 879-0602; Kama'ole Beach Center, 2411 S Kihei Rd) If life won't be complete without the playoffs on the big screen, this is the place. The TVs compete with live music Tuesday through Sunday nights. Be forewarned: the place gets a bit smoky; it's one of the few places in Maui where smokers can still light up.

KKO (Map p341; ☎ 875-1007; 2511 S Kihei Rd; ☒ 8am-midnight) Come here for happy-hour specials from 2pm to 5pm daily and all-day Friday; there's also sports TV.

Kihei Kalama Village (Map p341; 1913 S Kihei Rd), opposite Kalama Beach, houses the main cluster of Kihei's watering holes. A favorite is **Life's a Beach** (Map p341; ☎ 891-8010), a brightly painted, Bob Marley-lovin' shack with neon palm trees, live music, DJs and a breezy beach view; it's the home of the $1 mai tai from 4pm to 7pm.

Entertainment
Kihei's nightlife scene is hopping, and there's something happening every night, with weekends seeing the most action.

Hapa's Night Club (Map p338; ☎ 879-9001; Lipoa Center, 41 E Lipoa St; admission $5-8; ☒) Maui's hottest dance spot, Hapa's rocks on Monday to the guitar work of local legend Willie K; hosts the gay community on 'ultra fab' Tuesday; does an aloha jam on Wednesday;

TOP FIVE ENTERTAINMENT SPOTS
- **Hapa's Night Club** (see above), Kihei
- **Lulu's** (p344), Kihei
- **Maui Arts & Cultural Center** (p329), Kahului
- **Old Lahaina Luau** (p312), Lahaina
- **Casanova** (p369), Makawao

MAUI

grooves to salsa on Sunday; and has top live bands Thursday to Saturday. Everybody comes here, tourists and locals alike.

Horhito's Mexican Cantina (Map p338; ☎ 891-6394; Lipoa Center, 41 E Lipoa St) Next door to Hapa's, this friendly restaurant has live music, mostly jazz, on Thursday and Sunday nights. Plenty of drink specials too.

LuLu's (Map p341; ☎ 879-9944; 1941 S Kihei Rd) No problem finding LuLu's – you can hear this boisterous place a mile away. Ultracasual, it's got a kitsch-cluttered bar where drinks flow freely, a poolroom where you can shoot some stick and a good *pupu* menu. Wednesday through Saturday there's live music from 4pm to 7pm and DJs with dancing from 10pm to 2am.

Marco's Southside Grill (Map p341; ☎ 874-4041; 1445 S Kihei Rd) For a mellower and more elegant scene, Marco's has piano music nightly. Linger over a drink in a Spanish leather chair as the bartender works the 24-karat beer-tap pulls.

Sansei Seafood Restaurant & Sushi Bar (Map p341; ☎ 879-0004; Kihei Town Center) If you want to belt out your own tunes, you can sing to laser karaoke here from 10pm to 2am on Thursday and Friday.

Consolidated Theatre (Map p341; ☎ 875-4910, Kukui Mall; 1819 S Kihei Rd) This multiscreen cinema shows first-run movies.

Shopping

Friendly Isles Woodcarving (Map p338; 61 S Kihei Rd) At the same site as the Kihei Farmers Market, here you can watch master woodcarver Tevita whittle a log down into a *ki'i* image.

ABC store (Map p341; ☎ 879-6305; 2349 S Kihei Rd; ☒ 6am-11pm) This tourist-oriented convenience store sells liquor, cheap beach mats, suntan lotion and other practical beach items.

Kihei overflows with souvenir shops of all sorts. Near the public library, **Aloha Market** (Map p341; S Kihei Rd) is an outdoor collection of stalls selling cheapo T-shirts, swimwear, island jewelry etc. **Kihei Kalama Village** (Map p341; 1913 S Kihei Rd), opposite Kalama Park, has more of the same.

Getting There & Around

BICYCLE

South Maui Bicycles (Map p341; ☎ 874-0068; 1993 S Kihei Rd; day/week $30/130; ☒ 8:30am-5pm Mon-Sat) rents well-maintained Trek road bikes.

BUS

The Maui Public Transit System (p299) serves Kihei with two bus routes.

One route connects Kihei with Wailea and Ma'alaea. Stops include Kama'ole Beach III, Kama'ole Shopping Center, Pi'ilani Village shopping center, and Uwapo Rd and S Kihei Rd. It runs every hour, with the northbound bus leaving Kama'ole Beach III on the hour from 7am to 7pm, and the southbound bus leaving Kama'ole Beach III on the hour from 7:45am to 7:45pm. Fares are $1 to $2. From Ma'alaea you can connect to public buses bound for Lahaina.

The second route is a 40-minute express linking Kahului with Kihei's Pi'ilani Village shopping center five times a day; leaving Pi'ilani Village for Kahului every two hours from 8:42am to 4:42pm.

WAILEA
pop 5200

Wailea breathes money and you'll be struck by the contrast with the commercialism of Kihei to the north – everything here is green, manicured and precise. Wailea has swank hotels on the beach, low-rise condo villas, a shopping center, a trio of golf courses and a tennis club that's been nicknamed 'Wimbledon West.'

Wailea's lava-rock coastline is broken by attractive golden-sand beaches that lure swimmers, snorkelers and sunbathers. From Wailea and neighboring Makena, there are good views of Lana'i, Kaho'olawe and Molokini, and during winter there's superb shoreline whale watching.

Orientation & Information

If you're heading to Wailea from Lahaina or Kahului, be sure to take the Pi'ilani Hwy (Hwy 31) and not S Kihei Rd, which can be a tedious drive through congested traffic. Wailea's main road is Wailea Alanui Dr, which turns into Makena Alanui Dr after Polo Beach and continues south to Makena.

The **Shops at Wailea** (3750 Wailea Alanui Dr; ☒ 9:30am-9:30pm) has an ATM, as do many of the hotels.

Sights

Wailea's beaches begin with the southern end of Keawakapu Beach in Kihei and continue south toward Makena. They are all lovely strands with free public access, showers and restrooms.

While Wailea's beaches generally have good swimming conditions, occasional high surf and *kona* storms can create dangerous shorebreaks and rip currents at all of them. Size up conditions carefully before going in, and read any posted warning signs. See p346 for water-sports lessons and gear hire.

ULUA & MOKAPU BEACHES

Located between the Wailea Marriott and the Renaissance Wailea Beach Resort, Ulua Beach is a little gem. The first road south of the Renaissance will take you to the beach parking lot.

When it's calm, Ulua Beach has Wailea's best easy-access snorkeling. Head straight for the coral at the rocky outcrop on the right side of Ulua Beach, which separates it from its twin to the north, Mokapu Beach. Snorkelers can spot long needlefish, bright yellow butterfly fish, schools of convict tangs and dozens of other tropical fish. Snorkeling is best in the morning before the winds pick up and before the crowds swarm the area. When the surf's up, forget snorkeling – go bodysurfing instead.

Pacific Whale Foundation leads **free guided snorkeling tours** at 9am Tuesday and Thursday; no reservations necessary, just show up and bring your own snorkeling gear.

WAILEA BEACH

The largest and widest of Wailea's beaches, this slopes gradually, making the inshore waters good for swimming. When the water's calm, there's good snorkeling around the rocky point on the south side of the beach. Divers entering the water at Wailea Beach can follow an offshore reef that runs down to Polo Beach. At times, there's a gentle shorebreak suitable for bodysurfing.

Beach access is from the road running between the Four Seasons Resort and the Grand Wailea Resort, both of which front Wailea Beach.

POLO BEACH

Although fronted by a condo development and the Fairmont Kea Lani, the south end of Polo Beach is seldom crowded.

When there's wave action, boogie boarders and bodysurfers usually find a good shorebreak here. When the waters are calm,

the rocks at the north end of the beach are good for snorkeling. At low tide, the lava outcropping at the south end of the beach has some interesting little tide pools that harbor spiny sea urchins and small fish.

To get to Polo Beach, turn down Kaukahi St after the Kea Lani. There's a beach parking lot on the right, near the end of the road.

PALAUEA BEACH

Just off Makena Rd, Palauea Beach is a quarter-mile south of Polo Beach. A fair number of people use the beach for surfing, bodysurfing and boogie boarding. It's more secluded and less frequented than Polo Beach, but otherwise it's much the same, without the development.

Kiawe trees block the view of the beach from the roadside, but Palauea is popular with locals. You'll find it by looking for the line of cars along the roadside.

PO'OLENALENA BEACH

Beyond all the development of the Wailea resort strip lies this lovely long crescent with two Hawaiian names: Po'olenalena Beach and Paipu Beach. For added confusion the beach is also known locally as Changs, for the family that once farmed at the south end of Po'olenalena, near the current-day Makena Surf condos.

This beach is well-used by local families on weekends, but it's rarely crowded and the shallow, sandy bottom and calm waters make for excellent swimming. There's good snorkeling off both the southern and northern lava points, but be careful not to damage the live coral or disturb the sea turtles. **Haloa Point**, a bit further north, is a popular scuba-diving spot.

The beach parking lot is on Makena Alanui Rd, a quarter-mile south of its intersection with Makena Rd. The only facilities consist of a pit toilet.

WAILEA BEACH WALK

For a delightful stroll, take the shoreline path that runs for 1.3 miles from the Renaissance Wailea Beach Resort to the Fairmont Kea Lani, connecting the Wailea beaches and resort hotels that front them. The path winds above the jagged lava points that separate the beaches and is landscaped with native Hawaiian flora.

MAUI

The walk is a winner any time of the year, but in winter it's one of the best walks in all of Hawaii for spotting humpback whales – on a good day, you may be able to spot more than a dozen of them frolicking in the waters offshore. Forgot your binoculars? Just drop a coin in the telescope north of the Wailea Marriott.

Some of the luxury hotels you'll pass along the walk are worth strolling through as well, most notably the Grand Wailea Resort, which is adorned with $30 million worth of artwork. In front of the Wailea Point condos are the foundations of three Hawaiian house sites dating to AD 1300; this is also a fine spot to watch the sun set.

Activities

Maui Ocean Activities (☎ 667-2001; www.mauiwatersports.com; Grand Wailea Resort; kayak rentals $15; 🕑 8am-4:30pm) has kayak rentals; gives surfing lessons ($60) and windsurfing lessons ($70); and rents gear ranging from beach umbrellas to hobie cats.

Wailea Golf Club (☎ 875-7450, 800-332-1614; www.waileagolf.com; 100 Golf Club Dr; green fees $105-155; 🕑 1st tee time 7am) consists of three championship courses. The Emerald course is a tropical garden that consistently ranks top; the rugged Gold course takes advantage of volcanic landscapes; and the Blue course is marked by an open fairway and challenging greens. Wailea Golf Club is the home of the Senior Skins Game and the LPGA Skins Game.

Wailea Tennis Club (☎ 879-1958, 800-332-1614; 131 Wailea Ike Pl; per hr $30-35; 🕑 7am-7pm) is an award-winning complex with 11 Plexipave courts, a dress code, lessons, clinics and equipment rentals.

Festivals & Events

The internationally acclaimed **Xterra World Championship** (www.xterraplanet.com), held in late October, is an off-road triathlon that begins with a 1-mile swim off the Wailea Marriott, follows with an 6.8-mile trail run and tops it off with a grueling 18.65-mile bike ride up the slopes of Haleakala.

Sleeping

MID-RANGE

Eva Villa (☎ 874-6407, 800-824-6409, in Germany 0800 182 1980; www.mauibnb.com; 815 Kumulani Dr; units $130-145) Vacation like a millionaire in this sparkling hilltop villa on the slopes above Wailea. The welcoming hosts have planted the grounds with fruit trees and the gardens hide a koi pond and Jacuzzi. Poolside on the ground floor are a studio and a two-bedroom suite; adjacent to the house is a cozy cottage with a wraparound lanai. After dark, slip up to the rooftop sundeck for fantastic stargazing.

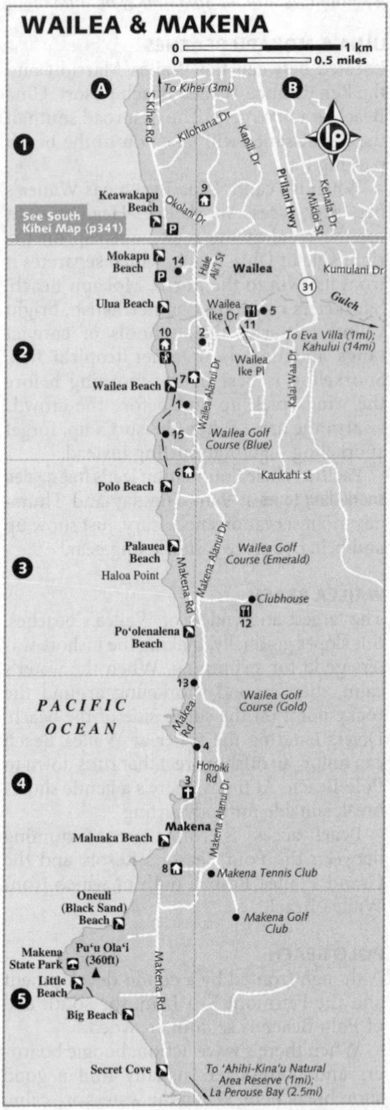

MAUI

TOP END

Grand Wailea Resort Hotel & Spa (☎ 875-1234, 800-888-6100; www.grandwailea.com; 3850 Wailea Alanui Dr; r $480-900; 🔀 🔊) Maui's most extravagant resort – the lobbies are replete with sculptures and artwork, while the grounds are given over to tropical gardens and spouting fountains. Some of it has an upscale Hawaiiana motif; all of it is unabashedly opulent. A 2000ft-long system of water slides and waterfall grottoes will thrill kids of any age. The place is family-friendly – if the kids need a break from the pool, or you just want to slip away on your own, the hotel's Camp Grande program offers lots of fun activities.

Palms at Wailea (☎ 879-5800, 800-688-7444; www.outrigger.com; 3200 Wailea Alanui Dr; 1-/2-bedroom units from $240/270; 🔀 🔊) The good life without all the ritzy trappings found at the beachfront resorts. Instead, you'll find privacy, acres of gardens and spacious well-equipped condo units with large lanai. And you'll probably have the pool all to yourself! Not surprisingly, it's a favorite among return visitors.

Wailea Marriott (☎ 879-1922, 800-367-2960; www.waileamarriott.com; 3700 Wailea Alanui Dr; r $340-530; 🔀 🔊) Wailea's first hotel, this low-key operation has been renovated and has some nice Polynesian accents including a koi pond, majestic banyan trees and an open-air tropical lobby. Book online and you can typically save about a third off the rack rates.

Fairmont Kea Lani (☎ 875-4100, 800-659-4100; www.kealani.com; 4100 Wailea Alanui Dr; ste $430-850, oceanfront villa $1200-1800; 🔀 🔊) A swank resort with fanciful Moorish-style architecture, the Kea Lani resembles something out of *Arabian Nights* and boasts luxury fit for a sheik. The roomy suites have private lanai and marble bath, while oceanfront villas come with their own plunge pools.

Eating

BUDGET

Caffe Ciao (☎ 875-4100; Fairmont Kea Lani; sandwiches $10; 🕐 6:30am-10pm) This deli may be a bit pricey, but the food's good and it's a convenient place to pick up a picnic lunch for the beach. Best are the sandwiches, which are stacked high enough to make a meal for two.

MID-RANGE

Longhi's (☎ 891-8883; Shops at Wailea; breakfast & lunch $4-15, dinner $24-34; h8am-10pm) Open-air and with a sea view, this award-winning restaurant is a favorite at breakfast, when it bakes its own pastries and serves a knock-out Italian frittata. At dinnertime, Longhi's grills up Wailea's best steaks. There are lots of seafood options as well.

SeaWatch (☎ 875-8080; 100 Wailea Golf Club Dr; breakfast & lunch $5-13, dinner $24-30; h8am-10pm) Head up here if you want to escape the hotel scene. At breakfast, everyone comes for the eggs Benedict with lox. At other times you'll find tasty sandwiches, salads, seafood and steaks, some with a Pacific Rim accent. Sit on the veranda for a panoramic ocean view across the fairway.

Tommy Bahama's Tropical Café (☎ 875-9983; Shops at Wailea; lunch $9-18, dinner $25-36; 🕐 11am-10pm) OK, the decor may be faux-tropical, but the lunch menu is divine, especially the beer-battered grouper fish, mango-chicken salad and the signature coconut shrimp. Dinner is pricier, but equally creative, or you can sidle up to the bar and order up the best cheeseburger to be found for miles.

TOP END

Joe's Bar & Grill (☎ 875-7767; 131 Wailea Ike Pl; mains $18-38; 🕐 5:30-9:30pm) Run by the owners of the famed Hali'imaile General Store, Joe's has become celebrated in its own right. The emphasis is on solid American standards adorned with Pacific accents, including a

MAUI

popular New York steak served with Kula vegetables. Go Hawaiian for dessert, with a decadent pineapple cake topped with glazed macadamia nuts.

Spago (☎ 874-8000; Four Seasons Resort; mains $29-50; ☽ 6-9:30pm) This trendy oceanfront restaurant offers a fine sunset view and a creative fusion of Californian and Hawaiian cuisine. The spicy 'ahi poke, served in a sesame-miso wrap that looks like an ice-cream cone, is a delicious starter you won't find elsewhere. For mains, the mahimahi in cabernet sauce with Moloka'i yams, and the seared scallops with mai-tai sauce are sure bets.

Entertainment

All of the Wailea hotels have some sort of live music, most often jazz or Hawaiian, in the evenings.

Four Seasons Resort (☎ 874-8000; 3900 Wailea Alanui) The lobby lounge has Hawaiian music and hula performances from 5:30pm to 7:30pm nightly and a hodgepodge of jazz, contemporary and flamenco guitar later in the evening.

Wailea Marriott (☎ 879-1922; 3700 Wailea Alanui) There's hula from 6pm to 9pm in the hotel's Kumu Bar and live Hawaiian music in its Mele Mele Lounge from 9pm to 11pm.

Longhi's (☎ 891-8883; The Shops at Wailea) This is the place to go for dancing on Saturday nights, with live music until 1:30am.

Shopping

Shops at Wailea (☎ 891-6770; 3750 Wailea Alanui Dr; ☽ 9:30am-9pm) This two-story shopping center has dozens of shops, most flashing such as names as Prada, Gucci and Tiffany. Among the more interesting shops:

Na Hoku (☎ 891-8040) Hawaiian jeweler specializing in island floral and marine life designs.

Célébritiès (☎ 875-6565) A gallery with art by the likes of John Lennon and David Bowie.

Honolua Surf Co (☎ 891-8229) Hip surfer-motif Ts, shorts and aloha shirts.

Martin & MacArthur (☎ 891-8844) Top-quality Hawaiian-made wood carvings, paintings and other crafts.

Maui Waterwear (☎ 891-1939) A full line of tropical swimwear.

Noa Noa (☎ 879-9069) Hand-batiked Indonesian clothing.

Getting There & Around

The Maui Public Transit System (p298) operates buses between Wailea and Kihei every hour. The first bus leaves the Shops at Wailea at 6:55am and runs along S Kihei Rd before heading up to the Pi'ilani Village shopping center and Ma'alaea. From Ma'alaea you can connect to buses bound for Lahaina. Five times a day an express bus runs between Wailea and Kahului, leaving Wailea every two hours from 8:20am to 4:20pm.

A free **shuttle bus** (☎ 879-2828) runs around the Wailea resort every 30 minutes from 6:30am to 8:30pm, connecting most of the hotels, condos, shopping center and golf courses. But be forewarned: it stops short of the Fairmont Kea Lani.

MAKENA
pop 475

Makena was just a sleepy seaside village until the 1980s when the Seibu Corporation bought 1800 acres here from 'Ulupalakua Ranch, and developed it into a resort with a golf course and luxury hotel.

A lack of water has slowed further growth. Developers would like to drill wells on Haleakala's slopes to provide water for hundreds of new luxury homes and condominiums. Upcountry farmers, concerned that further development will drain the watershed they rely on, have been vocal in opposition, as have environmentalists who don't want to see Makena's raw nature spoiled. For now it's at a standoff, but this is sure to remain one of the most heated issues on Maui.

Thankfully, much of Makena remains wild and free. The dominant shoreline feature is Pu'u Ola'i, a 360ft cinder hill a mile south of the landing. Just beyond Pu'u Ola'i are two knockout beaches at Makena State Park. Big Beach is a huge sweep of glistening sand and a prime sunset-viewing locale. Little Beach is a secluded cove and Maui's most popular nude beach.

Sights & Activities
MAKENA BAY

To explore the older side of Makena, turn right onto Makena Rd after the Makena Surf condos and go about a mile to Makena Bay. **Makena Landing** has boat-launching facilities, showers and toilets. When seas are calm, there's good snorkeling along the rocks at the south side of the landing. This is also one of the most popular spots on Maui for kayaking, and many tours leave from here.

South of the landing is the **Keawala'i Congregational Church**, one of Maui's earliest missionary churches. The current building was built in 1855 with 3ft-thick walls made of burnt coral rock. The graveyard has a fine bayside view and old tombstones with cameo photographs, many of Hawaiian cowboys laid to rest in the '20s and '30s.

Makena Rd ends shortly after the church at a cul-de-sac on the ocean side of Maui Prince Hotel.

MALU'AKA BEACH

Dubbed 'Turtle Beach,' this golden-sand beach fronting the Maui Prince Hotel has rocky outcrops that provide decent snorkeling. There's some coral here but the real prize is the sheer abundance of sea turtles, which feed at the south end of the beach. Viewing the turtles can be a treat, but be sure to give them a wide berth.

There are beach parking lots and restrooms at both ends of the beach. At the north side, there's the lot opposite Keawala'i Congregational Church. Or, after driving south past the Maui Prince Hotel, take the first sharp right, where there's additional parking for about 60 cars.

Kai Kanani (☎ 879-7218; www.kaikanani.com; Maui Prince Hotel; adult/child from $39/19; ☒ 8am-5pm), a beach shack fronting the hotel, has a catamaran tour that gets you over to Molokini for snorkeling in just 15 minutes – the quickest service on the island.

MAKENA STATE PARK

Makena State Park, south of the Maui Prince Hotel, incorporates Big Beach, Little Beach and Oneuli Beach. In the late 1960s, this was the site of an alternative-lifestyle encampment that took on the nickname 'Hippie Beach.' The tent city lasted until 1972, when police finally evicted everyone on health code violations. More than a few of Maui's now-graying residents can trace their roots on the island to those days.

Only recently incorporated into the state park system, Makena may eventually have full beach facilities, but for now, it remains in a natural state except for a couple of pit toilets and picnic tables.

Oneuli (Black Sand) Beach

Look for the first Makena State Park access sign and the dirt road leading to this little salt-and-pepper-sand beach. A lava shelf along the shoreline makes for poor swimming, but families come here on the weekends for fishing and picnics. Kayakers take to the water here as well, and it can be a good spot for seeing turtles poking their heads out of the water as they feed along the shore.

Big Beach

Big Beach is the sort of scene that people conjure up when they dream of a Hawaiian beach – beautiful and expansive, with virtually no development on the horizon.

The Hawaiian name for Big Beach is Oneloa, literally 'Long Sand.' The golden sands stretch for over half a mile and are as broad as they come, with clear turquoise waters. But the open ocean beyond can have powerful rip currents and dangerous shorebreaks during periods of heavy surf. When waters are calm you'll find kids boogie boarding here, but at other times breaks are for experienced bodysurfers only.

The turnoff to the main parking area is a mile past the Maui Prince Hotel. A second parking area lies a quarter-mile to the south. You can also park alongside the road and walk in; watch for kiawe thorns in the woods behind the beach. Thefts and broken windshields are unfortunately commonplace, particularly from rental jeeps and convertibles. Don't leave anything valuable in your car.

Little Beach

As it is hidden by a rocky outcrop that juts out from Pu'u Ola'i (the cinder cone that marks the north end of Big Beach), most visitors don't even know Little Beach is there. But take the short trail up the rock that links the two beaches and bam, there it is, spread out in front of you.

Little Beach, also known as Pu'u Ola'i Beach, is a popular nude beach, despite a rusty old sign and many arrests to the contrary. Citations for nude sunbathing (which is, in fact, illegal) cost a pretty penny. All the uproar over nudity here probably has less to do with any Hawaiian cultural issues than with the fact that it's one of the few openly gay meeting places on Maui. The crowd here is mixed, about half gay and half straight.

Little Beach fronts a sandy cove that usually has a gentle shorebreak ideal for bodysurfing and boogie boarding. Snorkeling along the rocky point is good when the water is calm.

MAUI

SECRET COVE

Well, once it was secret. Now a favorite for getaway weddings, it's a toss-up whether you'll have this little pocket cove all to yourself or it'll be packed to the brim with tuxes and tulle. But this lovely postcard-size beach of golden sand with a straight-on view of Kaho'olawe is certainly worth a peek.

The cove is a quarter-mile after the southernmost Makena State Park parking lot. The entrance is through an opening in a rock-lava wall, marked with a blue-and-white shoreline sign just south of house No 6900.

Sleeping & Eating

Maui Prince Hotel (☎ 874-1111, 800-321-6248; www.mauiprince.com; 5400 Makena Alanui Dr; r $320-490, ste from $600) It looks like a fortress from the outside, but the interior incorporates a fine sense of Japanese aesthetics. The five-story hotel surrounds a courtyard with waterfalls, running streams, carp ponds and raked-rock gardens. All 310 rooms have at least partial ocean views.

Hakone (☎ 875-5888; Maui Prince Hotel; mains $26-45, 6-9pm Mon-Sat) This refined restaurant features Japanese haute cuisine with Hawaiian flourishes. The specialty here is the *rakuen kaiseki* ($60), a traditional Kyoto-style dinner with half a dozen courses impeccably presented by kimono-clad waitresses.

BEYOND MAKENA

Makena Rd continues as a narrow paved road for 3 miles after Makena State Park. The road goes through the 'Ahihi-Kina'u Natural Area Reserve before deadending at La Perouse Bay.

Sights & Activities

'AHIHI-KINA'U NATURAL AREA RESERVE

This rugged 2045-acre preserve includes the protected waters of 'Ahihi Bay and Cape Kina'u, created when Maui's last lava flow spilled out to the sea in 1790. Here you'll find abundant *'a'a* (rough, jagged lava).

Snorkeling is great in the reserve. Just about everyone heads to the little roadside cove 170yd south of the first reserve sign – granted it offers decent snorkeling, but there are better, less-crowded options. Instead, drive 350yd past the cove and look for a large clearing on the right. Park here and follow the coastal footpath south for five minutes to

reach a black-sand beach with fantastic coral, clear water and few visitors. Enter the water from the left side of the beach where access is easy, snorkel in a northerly direction and you'll immediately be over large coral heads that harbor an amazing variety of fish. Huge rainbow parrotfish abound here and it's not unusual to see turtles and the occasional reef shark (generally harmless).

LA PEROUSE BAY

This is an astounding natural area with archaeological remains of the early Hawaiian village Keone'o'io – mainly house and heiau platforms – scattered among the lava patches. Volunteers patrol the area to discourage car break-ins and educate visitors.

Keep an eye open for spinner dolphins, which commonly come into the bay during the day. For expert kayakers, surfers and divers only, the bay offers a real challenge, and the sealife is amazing. However, strong offshore winds put snorkeling and swimming out of the question.

The paved road ends just short of La Perouse Bay at the **La Perouse Monument**, which commemorates French explorer Jean François de Galaup La Perouse who landed here in 1786. Although it may be possible to drive all the way to the bay on the 4WD road, you're better off parking just after the asphalt ends and walking along the coast; the bay is just a few minutes' walk away.

Just before the monument, **Makena Stables** (☎ 879-0244; www.makenastables.com; trail ride $145) offers morning-long horseback rides up the volcanic slopes led by a cowboy historian whose stories are as fascinating as the terrain; it's worth every penny.

From La Perouse Bay, it's possible to continue along the **King's Hwy (Hoapili) Coastal Trail**. This ancient footpath follows the coastline across jagged lava flows (wear hiking boots). It's a dry area with no water, little vegetation and it can get very hot. The first part of the trail is along the sandy beach at La Perouse Bay. Right after the trail emerges onto the lava fields, it's possible to take a spur trail for three-quarters of a mile down to the light beacon at the tip of Cape Hanamanioa. Alternatively, walk inland to the Na Ala Hele sign and turn right onto the King's Hwy as it climbs through rough *'a'a* lava inland for the next 2 miles before coming back to the coast to an older lava flow at Kanaio Beach.

EAST MAUI

East Maui begins in the windsurfing haven of Pa'ia and flows south down the winding coastal road to the tranquil village of Hana, the most celebrated drive in Hawaii. And it doesn't stop there. After Hana, the road continues to the cool pools of 'Ohe'o Gulch, in the coastal Kipahulu section of Haleakala National Park, and becomes an adventurous romp around the south side of the island.

PA'IA

pop 2500

Pa'ia is an old sugar town with a fresh coat of paint. In the early 20th century, the town boasted 10,000 residents, most of whom lived in plantation camps on the cool slopes above the now-defunct Pa'ia sugar mill.

During the 1950s, there was an exodus to Kahului, shops closed, and Pa'ia began to collect cobwebs. In the '60s, hippies seeking paradise found themselves here, followed by windsurfers who discovered nearby Ho'okipa Beach. Dubbed the 'windsurfing capital of the world,' Pa'ia now has as many international windsurfers as it once had sugarcane workers.

No longer just a quick stop on the way to Hana, Pa'ia has blossomed into a lively, interesting destination. Its old wooden storefronts, now splashed in cheery tones of rosy pink, sunshine yellow and sky blue, house

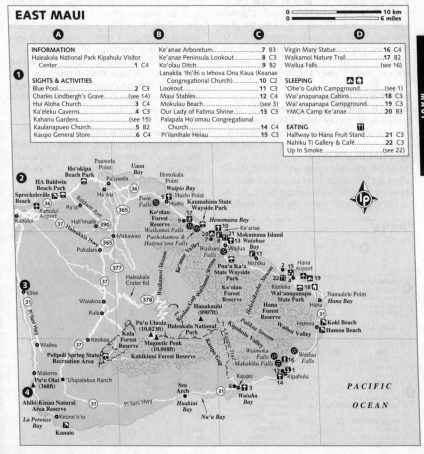

EAST MAUI

0 ——— 10 km
0 ——— 6 miles

INFORMATION		
Haleakala National Park Kipahulu Visitor Center...**1** C4	Ke'anae Arboretum.........................**7** B3	Virgin Mary Statue........................**16** C4
	Ke'anae Peninsula Lookout..........**8** C3	Waikamoi Nature Trail..................**17** B2
	Ko'olau Ditch.................................**9** B2	Wailua Falls.............................(see 16)
	Lanakila 'Ihi'ihi o Iehova Ona Kaua (Keanae	
SIGHTS & ACTIVITIES	Congregational Church)...............**10** C2	**SLEEPING**
Blue Pool...**2** C3	Lookout..**11** C3	'Ohe'o Gulch Campground.........(see 1)
Charles Lindbergh's Grave............(see 14)	Maui Stables................................**12** C4	Wai'anapanapa Cabins.................**18** C3
Hui Aloha Church...........................**3** C4	Mokulau Beach.............................(see 3)	Wai'anapanapa Campground........**19** C3
Ka'eleku Caverns............................**4** C3	Our Lady of Fatima Shrine............**13** C3	YMCA Camp Ke'anae....................**20** B3
Kahanu Gardens.............................(see 15)	Palapala Ho'omau Congregational	
Kaulanapueo Church.......................**5** B2	Church..**14** C4	**EATING**
Kaupo General Store.......................**6** C4	Pi'ilanihale Heiau.........................**15** C3	Halfway to Hana Fruit Stand.........**21** C3
		Nahiku Ti Gallery & Café..............**22** C3
		Up In Smoke..............................(see 22)

MAUI

an array of shops geared for visitors. You'll find plenty to catch your interest – eclectic clothing shops, quality galleries, surf shops and an ever-growing variety of scrumptious restaurants.

Orientation & Information

The Hana Hwy (Hwy 36) runs straight through the center of Pa'ia. This is the last real town before Hana and the last place to gas up your car. Pa'ia is also a link to the Upcountry via Baldwin Ave, which runs to Makawao passing the old sugar mill en route. Everything in town is within walking distance.

The **coin laundry** (129 Baldwin Ave; 🕑 6am-9pm) and **post office** (☎ 579-8866; 120 Baldwin Ave) are opposite each other. **Bank of Hawaii** (☎ 579-9511; 35 Baldwin Ave) has a 24-hour ATM. **Livewire Café** (☎ 579-6009; 137 Hana Hwy; per min 15¢, 20-min minimum; 🕑 6am-10pm Sun-Thu, to midnight Fri & Sat) is a great place to surf the Net while enjoying superb pastries and coffee – and with 15 stations there's never a wait.

Sights & Activities

Sailboards Maui (☎ 579-8432; 22 Baldwin Ave; boogie boards/sailboards per day $8/20; 🕑 9am-6pm) is the place to rent sailboards and boogie boards.

HO'OKIPA BEACH PARK

Ho'okipa, which has long been one of Maui's prime surfing spots, has established itself as Hawaii's premier windsurfing beach. Winter has the biggest waves for board surfers,

and summer has the most consistent winds for windsurfers. During shoulder-season weather conditions, the unspoken agreement is that surfers go out in the morning and windsurfers launch in the afternoon.

Strong currents, dangerous shorebreak and razor-sharp coral make this is an area for experts only. For spectators, though, it's great, attracting the world's top windsurfers. Ho'okipa is just before the 9-mile marker; look for the line of cars on the lookout above the beach. The park has restrooms, showers and picnic pavilions.

SPRECKELSVILLE BEACH

Spreckelsville Beach, by the golf course between Kahului airport and Pa'ia, is a long stretch of rocky shore composed of sandy strands punctuated with lava outcrops. It's one of the windiest places on the north shore, making it a prime windsurfing spot for beginners, particularly in summer.

To get there, turn toward the ocean on Nonohe Pl, which runs along the west side of the Maui Country Club. Turn right where the road ends and look for the blue shoreline-access sign.

HA BALDWIN BEACH PARK

HA Baldwin Beach Park, a big county park about a mile west of Pa'ia, has a long sandy beach with good bodysurfing and boogie boarding. Swimming and snorkeling may be possible before the afternoon winds pick up. The park also has showers, restrooms,

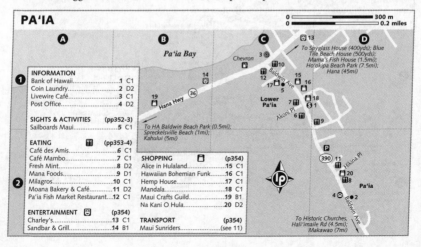

PA'IA

INFORMATION	
Bank of Hawaii	1 C1
Coin Laundry	2 D2
Livewire Café	3 C1
Post Office	4 D2

SIGHTS & ACTIVITIES	(pp352-3)
Sailboards Maui	5 C1

EATING	🍴 (pp353-4)
Café des Amis	6 C1
Café Mambo	7 C1
Fresh Mint	8 D2
Mana Foods	9 D1
Milagros	10 C1
Moana Bakery & Café	11 D2
Pa'ia Fish Market Restaurant	12 C1

ENTERTAINMENT	🎭 (p354)
Charley's	13 C1
Sandbar & Grill	14 B1

SHOPPING	🛍 (p354)
Alice in Hulaland	15 C1
Hawaiian Bohemian Funk	16 C1
Hemp House	17 C1
Mandala	18 C1
Maui Crafts Guild	19 B1
Na Kani O Hula	20 D2

TRANSPORT	(p354)
Maui Sunriders	(see 11)

Pa'ia Bay

To Spyglass House (400yds); Blue Tile Beach House (500yds); Mama's Fish House (1.5mi); Ho'okipa Beach Park (7.5mi); Hana (45mi)

To HA Baldwin Beach Park (0.5mi); Spreckelsville Beach (1mi); Kahului (5mi)

To Historic Churches, Hali'imaile Rd (4.5mi); Makawao (7mi)

picnic tables and a well-used baseball and soccer field. A word of caution: crime and drunken nastiness are not unheard of here. Look for the turnoff at the 6-mile marker.

Festivals & Events

Top international windsurfing events take place at Ho'okipa Beach:

Aloha Classic Windsurfing Championships (November)
High-Tech, Ezekiel, Lopez Surfbash (first weekend in December) Maui's largest surf contest is held at Ho'okipa Beach, with competing short-boarders, long-boarders and boogie boarders.

Sleeping

Pa'ia has no hotels, but it does have sleeping options. If you're looking to stay longer, you can sometimes find private rooms by checking bulletin boards around Pa'ia.

Ho'okipa Haven (☎ 579-8282, 800-398-6284; www.hookipa.com; 62 Baldwin Ave No 2A; r & studios from $55) This established vacation rental service books dozens of private places in Pa'ia and the Upcountry. German is spoken and last-minute specials can be found online.

Chameleon Vacation Rentals Maui (☎ 575-9933, 866-575-9933; www.donnachameleon.com; r & cottages from $60) Managed by a friendly, ecominded booking agent, it has everything from oceanfront cottages to rustic cabins in Pa'ia, Ha'iku and further along toward Hana.

Spyglass House (☎ 579-8608, 800-475-6695; www.spyglassmaui.com; 367 Hana Hwy; r $90-150) Wonderfully eccentric and surfer-casual, this friendly place sports porthole windows, stained glass and plenty of hidden nooks and crannies. Set back from the highway and right on the ocean, rooms in the original Spyglass House are better furnished than those in the adjacent garden addition. Guests have access to a kitchen, Jacuzzi and barbecue grills.

Blue Tile Beach House (☎ 579-8608, 800-475-6695; www.beachvacationmaui.com; 363 Hana Hwy; r $90-150, ste $250) You'll find cushy rooms with fabulous ocean views at this exclusive house, which fronts its own beach. Managed by the folks at Spyglass, the six units share a spacious, fireplaced living room and a full kitchen. The upstairs suite, with its own Jacuzzi and sauna, is perfect choice for honeymooners.

Eating

Any excuse for stopping in Pa'ia around mealtime will do – the food is almost universally wonderful. Nothing better awaits you in Hana (or even comes close), so stock up on picnic supplies and take-out.

BUDGET

Café des Amis (☎ 579-6323; 42 Baldwin Ave; breakfast $3-8, lunch & dinner $6-14; ☯ 8:30am-8:30pm) You can't walk by this place without being pulled in by the aromatic scents wafting out the door. The savory fare includes spicy Indian curry wraps with mango chutney and mouth-watering crepes (both dinner and dessert style). Wash it all down with a fruit smoothie, or bring your own wine.

Fresh Mint (☎ 579-9144; 115 Baldwin Ave; mains $6-13; ☯ 11am-9pm) Spotless and tidy, this cheery, lime green place has only a dozen tables, so arrive early. It's authentic Vietnamese fare, but totally veg, offering up unique recipes as well as familiar dishes like pad Thai and summer rolls. The 'soy fish,' simmered in caramel-pineapple sauce and served in a clay pot is great. The banana fritter with coconut tapioca makes a fine finale.

Mana Foods (☎ 579-8078; 49 Baldwin Ave; ☯ 8:30am-8:30pm) This large, down-to-earth health food store has everything from organic juices to fresh-baked breads and a salad bar.

MID-RANGE

Moana Bakery & Café (☎ 579-9999; 71 Baldwin Ave; breakfast & lunch $6-12, dinner $12-29; ☯ 8am-9pm) With a kitchen overseen by a French pastry master, Moana has terrific croissants and breakfast fare. Lunch and dinner is a creative fusion of offerings with everything from Hana Bay crab cakes and North Shore saimin to demiglazed rack of lamb.

Café Mambo (☎ 579-8021; 30 Baldwin Ave; mains $5-15; ☯ 8am-9pm) This casual restaurant, with tall leatherback chairs, serves breakfasts until noon; the chocolate cream waffle dripping with real maple syrup is one decadent delight. At dinner order the crispy *kalua* duck fajita, topped with guacamole and feta cheese – absolutely delicious. Mambo also packs box lunches in coolers for the Road to Hana (for two people $15; call ahead).

Pa'ia Fish Market Restaurant (☎ 579-8030; 2A Baldwin Ave; meals $9-15; ☯ 11am-9:30pm) When a place packs in a local crowd, you know the fish is fresh. The specialty here is fish-and-chips but there are full plate meals as well – choose from *'ahi, ono, opah* (moonfish) or whatever just came off the boat. It's all on display in a refrigerated cooler.

MAUI

Milagros (☎ 579-8755; 3 Baldwin Ave; lunch $7-10, dinner $12-18; ☽ 8am-10pm) This justifiably popular Tex-Mex café has sidewalk dining on a prime people-watching corner. Recommended are the fish tacos with heavenly salsa. It's also a good place to linger over a late-afternoon beer.

TOP END

Mama's Fish House (☎ 579-8488; 799 Poho Pl; mains $32-50; ☽ 11am-2:30pm & 5-9:30pm) At Kuʻau Cove, 2 miles east of Paʻia center, Maui's top seafood restaurant combines a fine ocean view with impeccably prepared fish. It's so fresh that each day's menu names the person who caught the fish and the place it was caught. The *onaga* (red snapper), sautéed in coconut milk and served with grilled banana, poi and Molokaʻi sweet potatoes, is a delightful medley of Hawaiian flavors. Lunch is served here, but come for dinner, when the beachside tiki torches are lit and the scene is as romantic as it gets. Reservations are essential.

Entertainment

Sandbar & Grill (☎ 579-8742; 89 Hana Hwy) Paʻia's main watering hole has entertainment nightly, with a DJ some nights, live music other times. There's also a good *pupu* menu; the *kalua* pork wontons make a perfect complement to a frosty beer.

Charley's (☎ 579-9453; 142 Hana Hwy) This combo pizzeria, restaurant and bar is the place to watch. A hangout of country-music icon Willie Nelson when he's on the island, it has live music and dancing most nights.

Moana Bakery & Café (☎ 579-9999; 71 Baldwin Ave) This happening place has jazz and blues on Friday, Latin rhythm on Sunday and vintage Hawaiian tunes on Wednesday.

Livewire Café (☎ 579-6009; 137 Hana Hwy) The square in front of this cybercafé is often the scene of live music of the folk guitar and blues type, and the occasional art show.

Shopping

Paʻia has unique shops and you can browse without any of the hustle and bustle found in the more heavily touristed towns.

Maui Crafts Guild (☎ 579-9697; 43 Hana Hwy) This collective of 21 artists and craftspeople operates the island's best gallery. Everything sold here is handmade on Maui. Located on the *makai* side of the road, as you come into town from Kahului, it sells patterned silks,

woodwork, glass, jewelry, pottery, natural fiber baskets and more.

Na Kani O Hula (☎ 573-6332; 105 Baldwin Ave) Catering to hula *halau* (troupes), the shops sells *ʻuliʻuli* (gourd rattles containing seeds and decorated with feathers), *puʻili* (bamboo sticks used in hula performance), gourd drums and the like – any of which would make a fascinating gift to take home.

Mandala (☎ 579-9555; 29 Baldwin Ave) Very nice silk clothing, Buddhas, Asian crafts and Indonesian fabrics are sold at this diverse shop.

Hemp House (☎ 579-8880; 16 Baldwin Ave) Hemp clothing, hemp soap, hemp lotion, hemp Frisbees…you get the picture.

Other fun shops:

Alice in Hulaland (☎ 579-9472; 19A Baldwin Ave) Hats, hula dolls and curios.

Hawaiian Bohemian Funk (☎ 579-9109; 19B Baldwin Ave) Apparel, jewelry and natural cosmetics.

Getting Around

Maui Sunriders (☎ 579-8970, 866-500-2453; www .mauibikeride.com; 71 Baldwin Ave; per day $30; ☽ hours vary) rents 21-speed Trek mountain bikes. The price includes a bike rack, should you want to drive your bike around the island.

THE ROAD TO HANA

The Hana Hwy rates as the most spectacular coastal drive in Hawaii. A cliff-hugger, the narrow road winds its way deep into lush valleys and back out above a rugged coastline, snaking around more than 600 twists and turns along the way. One-lane bridges mark dozens of waterfalls, some tiny and Zen-like, others sheer and lacy. The 54 bridges to Hana have 54 poetic Hawaiian names taken from the streams and gulches they cross – names like Heavenly Mist, Prayer Blossoms and Reawakening.

The valleys drip with vegetation. African tulip trees add bright splashes of orange to the verdant rain forests, bamboo groves and fern-covered hillsides. Built in 1927 using convict labor, the road follows the royal trail system constructed by Chief Piʻilani in the 15th century.

It would take about two hours to drive straight through from Kahului to Hana. But this is not a drive to rush. If you're not staying over in Hana, get an early start to give yourself a full day. Those with time to explore will find short trails to hike, mountain pools to dip in and a couple of historic sites to check out, all just a few minutes beyond the road.

Please pull over if local drivers are behind you. They have places to get to and move at a different pace.

Twin Falls

At Hwy 36's intersection with Hwy 365, which occurs just after the 16-mile marker, the Hana Hwy changes numbers to Hwy 360 and the mile markers begin again at zero.

After the 2-mile marker on Hwy 360, you'll see a dirt parking area on your right next to a fruit stand marking the start of the walk to Twin Falls. It takes about 25 minutes to walk to the falls and back. It's a pleasant-enough scene and a worthy walk if you're hanging around this area and looking for something to do. But if you're on the way to Hana, don't stop here now – there are better waterfalls further down the road.

Huelo

The Door of Faith Rd, a one-lane road half a mile past the 3-mile marker, leads down to historic **Kaulanapueo Church** (1853), made from coral and stone. The church is likely to be locked, however, so if you're short on time, this one can be easily bypassed. There's no beach access here, as the road deadends at gated homes.

Ko'olau Forest Reserve

After Huelo, the vegetation becomes increasingly lush as the highway snakes along the edge of the Ko'olau Forest Reserve. Ko'olau, which means 'windward,' catches the rain clouds. The coast in this area gets 60in to 80in of rain a year, while a few miles up on the slopes the annual rainfall is an impressive 200in to 300in. The reserve is heavily forested and cut with numerous gulches and streams. From here, there seems to be a one-lane bridge and waterfall around every other bend.

Many of the dirt roads leading inland from the highway are the maintenance roads for the **Ko'olau Ditch**, which parallels the highway. The century-old system is capable of carrying 450 million gallons of water a day through 75 miles of ditches and tunnels from the rain forest to the dry central plains. If you want to take a closer look, stop at the small pull-off just before the bridge

that comes up immediately after the 8-mile marker. Just 50ft above the road you can see a hand-hewn stone-block section of the ditch on your right.

As you leave the village of **Kailua**, you'll notice Norfolk pines up on the hillside, followed by a grove of painted eucalyptus trees with rainbow-colored bark that were introduced from Australia. After that, is a long stretch of bamboo.

Waikamoi Trail & Waterfalls

Further on, a half-mile past the 9-mile marker, there's a wide dirt pull-off with space for a few cars to park below the **Waikamoi Nature Trail**. This peaceful 30-minute trail loops through tall trees with wonderful fresh scents and lots of birdsong. You're welcomed by a sign that reads: 'Quiet. Trees at Work.' The grand reddish trees are *Eucalyptus robusta*. Note the huge climbing philodendron vines wrapped around them – the vines provide an apt illustration of the etymology of 'philodendron,' a Greek word meaning 'lover of trees'! Keep an eye out for occasional metal spikes and tree roots that protrude along the path. From the ridge at the top, there's a good view of the winding Hana Hwy.

Waikamoi Falls is at the bridge just before the 10-mile marker. One waterfall and a pool are near the road. It's possible to walk a short way up to a higher waterfall, but the rocks can be slippery, and the bottom waterfall is prettier anyway. Past Waikamoi, bamboo grows almost horizontally out from the cliffs, creating a canopy effect over the road.

At the 11-mile marker is **Puohokamoa Falls**, another attractive little waterfall. This one doesn't have public access, but you can get a good view of it right from the bridge.

Haipua'ena Falls, half a mile after the 11-mile marker, is a gentle little waterfall with a wonderful pool deep enough for swimming. Most people don't know this one's here, as you can't see the pool from the road. There's space for just one or two cars on the Hana side of the bridge. To reach the falls, walk upstream for a couple of minutes. Wild ginger grows along the path, and ferns hang from the rock wall behind the waterfall, making for quite an idyllic setting.

Shortly after the 12-mile marker, **Kaumahina State Wayside Park** has picnic tables and toilets. A two-minute walk up the hill under the park's tall eucalyptus trees provides a broad ocean vista, with Ke'anae Peninsula to the southeast.

Honomanu Bay

For the next several miles, the scenery is particularly magnificent, opening up to a new vista as you turn round each bend. If you're on this road after heavy rains, you can expect to see waterfalls galore crashing down the mountains.

Just after crossing the bridge at the 14-mile marker, an inconspicuous road heads down to **Honomanu Bay** and a rocky black-sand beach used mostly by surfers and fishers. The water's usually too turbulent for swimming, but on very calm days it's possible to snorkel here.

Ke'anae

You've made it halfway to Hana! Ke'anae Valley, which extends down from the Ko'olau Gap in Haleakala Crater, averages 150in of rain a year. Ke'anae Peninsula was formed by a later eruption of Haleakala that flowed through Ko'olau Gap down Ke'anae Valley. Outlined by its black-lava shores, the peninsula still wears its birthmark around the edges. Unlike its rugged surroundings, the peninsula is very flat, like a leaf floating on the water.

Ke'anae Arboretum, three-quarters of a mile past the 16-mile marker, is unkempt and disappointing. Introduced tropical plants include painted eucalyptus trees and golden-stemmed bamboo, whose green stripes look like the strokes of a Japanese *shodo* artist. A short paved path leads up past heliconia, ti, banana, guava, breadfruit, ginger and other fragrant plants to dozens of varieties of Hawaiian taro in irrigated patches. Be forewarned: swarms of mosquitoes can make the walk miserable.

The road that leads down to Ke'anae Peninsula is just beyond the Ke'anae Arboretum. **Lanakila 'Ihi'ihi o Iehova Ona Kaua** (Ke'anae Congregational Church) is an attractive old stone church, built in 1860, about half a mile down. This is one church, made of lava rocks and coral mortar, whose exterior hasn't been covered over with layers of whitewash, and rather than being locked tight you'll find open doors and a guest book. Surrounding the church, **Ke'anae** is a quiet little village with colts and goats roaming freely. At the end of the road is a scenic coastline of jagged rock and pounding waves. The rock island down the coast is **Mokumana Island**, a seabird sanctuary.

There's a good view of Ke'anae village, with its squares of planted taro fed by Ke'anae Stream, at **Ke'anae Peninsula Lookout**, an unmarked pull-off just past the 17-mile marker on the *makai* side of the Hana Hwy; look for the bright yellow tsunami speaker.

SLEEPING

YMCA Camp Ke'anae (☎ 248-8355; www.mauiymca .org; 13375 Hana Hwy; campsite or dm $16, cottage $115) Set on a knoll overlooking the coast, the Y has cabins that sometimes fill with groups, but otherwise are available to individuals as hostel-style dorms. It's purely a bunk-bed deal; you have to bring your own sleeping bag, food and cookware. Kitchen facilities are not available, though there are simple outdoor grills. If you have your own tent, you can pitch it on the grounds. There are also two cottages, each with two bedrooms, kitchenette and a lanai with spectacular ocean views. Advance reservations are required; there's a three-night limit. It's between the 16- and 17-mile markers.

Wailua

Shortly after the Ke'anae Peninsula Lookout, you'll pass a couple of roadside fruit stands. Best is **Halfway to Hana** (☎ 248-8301; south of 21-mile marker; ☉ 8:30am-4pm), which has been here for two decades selling fresh-baked banana bread, fruit slices, snacks and cool drinks.

Take Wailua Rd seaward a quarter mile after the 18-mile marker to reach **Our Lady of Fatima Shrine**. This little white-and-blue chapel, built in 1860, is also known as the Coral Miracle Church. The coral used in the construction came from a freak storm that deposited coral rocks onto a nearby beach. After the church was completed, another rogue storm hit the beach and swept all the leftover piles of coral back into the sea, or so the story goes. The current congregation now uses **St Gabriel's Mission**, the larger and newer church out front.

From Wailua Rd you can also get a peek of the long cascade of **Waikani Falls** if you look back up toward the Hana Hwy. Wailua Rd deadends half a mile down, though you won't want to go that far, as driveways blocked off with logs and milk crates prevent cars from turning around.

Waysides

Back on the Hana Hwy, just before the 19-mile marker, **Wailua Valley State Wayside** lookout comes up on the right. It has a broad view into Ke'anae Valley, which appears to be a hundred shades of green. You can see a couple of waterfalls, and if it's clear, you can look up at Ko'olau Gap, a break in the rim of Haleakala Crater. If you climb up the steps to the right, you'll find a good view of Wailua Peninsula, but there's a better view of it at a large paved turnoff a quarter-mile down the road.

Halfway between the 22- and 23-mile markers is **Pua'a Ka'a State Wayside Park**, where a tranquil waterfall empties into a pool before flowing down into a ravine. The park has restrooms, a pay phone, shaded streamside picnic tables and a pool large enough for swimming.

EATING

Before the 29-mile marker is the **Nahiku Ti Gallery & Café** (☎ 248-8800; ❧ 6am-5pm), serving decent coffee and pies to a reggae beat. But it's the barbecue stand next door, **Up in Smoke** (dishes $4-6; ❧ 10am-5pm, closed Thu), that draws the crowds here for their delicious fresh fish kebabs and *kalua* pig sandwiches, grilled right on the spot.

'Ula'ino Road

This road leads *makai* from the Hana Hwy to three worthwhile sights. The Ka'eleku Caverns are on the paved part of the road, half a mile from the Hana Hwy. The other sights can be a bit more challenging to get to. Even when it's very dry, you probably won't be able to go the entire 3 miles of 'Ula'ino Rd without a 4WD, but you can usually get as far as Kahanu Gardens, and then walk in the rest of the way to the Blue Pool.

KA'ELEKU CAVERNS

These **caves** (☎ 248-7308; www.mauicave.com; 1-hr walking tour at 11am $29, 2½hr wild adventure tour at 1pm $70; ❧ closed Sun), with ceilings reaching 40ft high, are so formidable that they once served as a slaughterhouse – 17,000lb of cow bones had to be removed before they were opened to tours! Now you can wind your way through the underground lava tubes, formed by ancient lava flows. Rain or shine, tours are led through this fragile ecosystem of stalactites and stalagmites. The main tour

is an easy walk, mostly over smooth cinders. If you're feeling adventurous, join the 'wild' tour that wiggles through tight spaces and climbs up into hidden niches. All gear is provided, including flashlights and hard hats. Reservations are advised.

KAHANU GARDENS

The 122-acre **gardens** (☎ 248-8912; www.ntbg.org; self-guided tour adult/child $10/free; ❧ 10am-2pm Mon-Fri) is a combination botanical garden and historical site under the jurisdiction of the National Tropical Botanical Garden (a non-profit group dedicated to the conservation of rare and medicinal plants). Kahanu Gardens features ethnobotanical collections from the tropical Pacific. Most interesting is the canoe garden, landscaped with plants brought to Hawaii by the early settlers in their outriggers. The property boasts a variety of Polynesian trees, including the Pacific's largest known collection of *'ulu* (breadfruit).

The grounds are also the site of **Pi'ilanihale Heiau**, the largest temple in Hawaii, with an immense stone platform reaching 450ft in length. The history of this astounding heiau is shrouded in mystery, but there's no doubt that it was an important religious site for Hawaiians. Archaeologists believe construction began as early as AD 1200 and the heiau was built in sequences. The final grand scale was the work of Pi'ilani (the heiau's name means House of Pi'ilani), the 14th-century Maui chief who is also credited with the construction of many of the coastal fishponds and taro terraces in the Hana area.

The gardens and heiau, on Kalahu Point, are 1.5 miles down 'Ula'ino Rd. The road is crossed by a streambed immediately before reaching the gardens; if it's dry you should be able to drive over it OK, but if it's been raining heavily don't even try.

BLUE POOL

Past Kahanu Gardens, 'Ula'ino Rd quickly becomes rough. Major dips in the road pass over another streambed that clearly calls for 4WD vehicles, especially if it has been raining hard recently. You may have to park off to the side of the road and walk the final mile to the coast.

When you get to the water's edge, turn left and strike out across the beach boulders for five minutes or so until you see paradise on earth at this beautiful waterfall. (Unless, of course, things are very dry, in which case you might not see much more than a trickle.)

Blue Pool is of spiritual significance to native Hawaiians. Be sure to stop and read the signboard on 'Ula'ino Rd, opposite Ka'eleku Caverns, which the local *'ohana* (family) has posted with guidelines on visiting the site.

Wai'anapanapa State Park

This is a wonderful park with lots to offer, including interesting grottoes and a stunning black-sand beach set against cobalt blue waters.

The road into Wai'anapanapa State Park is just after the 32-mile marker, half a mile south of the turnoff to Hana Airport. The road ends at a parking lot above Pailoa Bay, which is surrounded by a scenic coastline of low rocky cliffs. A short path from the parking lot leads down to the black-sand beach. There's usually strong rips here but when it's very calm the area around the sea arch is good for snorkeling. Check it out carefully, though, people have drowned here.

Two impressive lava-tube **caves** are just a five-minute walk from the parking lot along a loop path. On the outside, the caves are covered with ferns and flowering impatiens. Inside, they're dripping wet and cool. Wai'anapanapa means 'glistening waters,' and should you be tempted to take a dip in the cave pools, the clear mineral waters will leave you feeling squeaky clean. On certain nights of the year, the waters in the caves turn red. Legend says it's the blood of a princess and her lover who were killed in a fit of rage by the princess's jealous husband after he found them hiding together here. Less romantic types attribute the phenomenon to swarms of tiny bright-red shrimp called *'opaeula*, which occasionally emerge from subterranean cracks in the lava.

A **coastal trail**, which runs parallel to the ancient King's Hwy, leads south about 2 miles from the park to Kainalimu Bay, just north of Hana Bay. Some of the original smooth lava stepping-stones are still in place along the trail and there are gorgeous coastal views along the way. Beyond the park cabins, the trail passes blowholes and goes over a bridge before reaching **temple ruins** after a three-quarter-mile walk. As the trail fades, keep following the coast over old lava fields. Once you reach the boulder-strewn beach

at Kainalimu Bay, it's about a mile further to Hana center.

SLEEPING

Tent **camping** is free with a permit. The facilities are good, but remember this is the rainy side of the island, so it can get wet at any time. Sites are on a shady lawn with an ocean view. The dozen **housekeeping cabins**, which book up months in advance, are across the park. See p294 for details on permits, fees and reservations.

HANA

pop 1875

Separated from Kahului by 54 bridges and almost as many miles, Hana sits isolated, like an island unto itself. Lying beneath the rainy slopes of Haleakala, Hana is cradled on one side by lush green pastures and on the other by a black lava coastline.

Still, Hana is not a grand finale to the magnificent Hana Hwy, and people expecting great things are often disappointed. While the setting is pretty, the town itself doesn't overwhelm the senses – it's actually quite simple and sedate. What makes Hana special is more apparent to those who stop and stay awhile. There's an almost timeless rural character, and though 'Old Hawai'i' is an oft-used cliché elsewhere, it's hard not to think of Hana in such terms.

People in Hana cling to their traditional ways and the village has one of the most Hawaiian communities in the state. Many of its residents have Hawaiian blood and a strong sense of *'ohana*. If you spend time around here you'll hear the words 'auntie' and 'uncle' a lot.

Hana has always drawn its share of celebrities. The late George Harrison had a home here, Oprah Winfrey recently bought land in the area, and Kris Kristofferson and his family are active members of the Hana community.

History

In ancient times, Hana was the heart of one of Maui's largest population centers, with the village itself thought to have been reserved for the *ali'i*. It was from Hana that the 14th-century chief Pi'ilani set out to conquer the central plains of Wailuku; he then marched on to Lele (present-day Lahaina) and united Maui under his rule.

Curiously, the paths he took became such important routes that even today half of Hana's highways still bear his name.

In 1849, a whaler by the name of George Wilfong bought 60 acres of land for planting sugar and changed Hana's landscape for the next century. He used spare blubber pots and a team of oxen to squeeze the juice out of the cane, but couldn't find enough indigenous Hawaiians willing to work on his fledgling plantation. Then, in 1850, a new legislative act allowed for the importation of overseas labor. Chinese, Japanese and Portuguese laborers were brought in to work the sugarcane fields. Hana soon became a booming plantation town, complete with a narrow-gauge railroad connecting the fields to the Hana Mill. In the 1940s, Hana could no longer compete with larger sugar operations in central Maui, so the mill shut down.

Enter San Francisco businessman Paul Fagan, the owner of Pu'u O Hoku Ranch (p410) on Moloka'i, who purchased 14,000 acres in Hana in 1943. Starting with 300 Herefords, Fagan converted the cane fields to ranch land. A few years later, Fagan opened a six-room hotel as a getaway resort for his well-to-do friends and had his minor-league baseball team, the San Francisco Seals, do spring training here. That's allegedly when visiting sports journalists gave the town its moniker, 'Heavenly Hana'. Today, Hana Ranch still has a few thousand head of cattle worked by *paniolo*.

Orientation & Information

Geographically and economically, Hana Ranch and the hotel are the hub of town. Hana closes up early. If you're going to be heading back late, get gas in advance – the sole **gas station** is only open until 6:30pm.

Hana Ranch Center (Mill St) is the commercial center of town. It has a **post office** (☎ 248-8258); a tiny **Bank of Hawaii** (☎ 248-8015; ☽ 3-4:30pm Mon-Thu, to 6pm Fri); and the **Hana Ranch Store** (☎ 248-8261; ☽ 7am-7:30pm), which sells groceries, liquor and general supplies. There's no ATM at the bank, but **Hasegawa General Store** (☎ 248-8231; 5165 Hana Hwy; ☽ 7am-7pm Mon-Sat, 8am-6pm Sun) has one. The **Hana Community Health Center** (☎ 248-8294; 4590 Hana Hwy) is on the north side of town.

MAUI

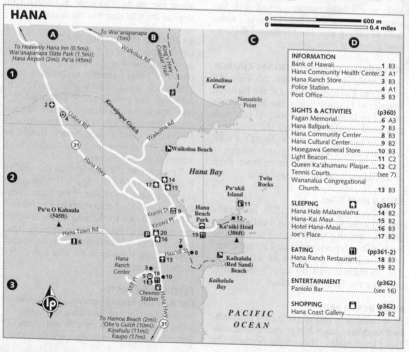

HANA

0 ____ 600 m
0 ____ 0.4 miles

To Wai'anapanapa (1mi)

To Heavenly Hana Inn (0.5mi); Wai'anapanapa State Park (1.5mi); Hana Airport (2mi); Pa'ia (45mi)

King's Hwy Coastal Trail

Waikoloa Rd

Kainalimu Cove

Nanualele Point

Kawaipapa Gulch

Uakea Rd

31

Waikoloa Rd

Waikoloa Beach

Hana Bay

Twin Rocks

17

14
15

Pu'ukii Island

Keanini Dr 9
Keawa Pl

Hana Beach Park

11

Pu'u O Kahaula (545ft)

Hana Town Rd

6

P 20
16

19

Ka'uiki Head (386ft)

Hau'oli St 8

13

Kaihalulu (Red Sand) Beach

Hana Ranch Center

3
5 18
1 10

Mill Pl

Chevron Station

Hana Hwy

Kaihalulu Bay

To Hamoa Beach (2mi); 'Ohe'o Gulch (10mi); Kipahulu (11mi); Kaupo (17mi)

31

PACIFIC OCEAN

LP

Sights

HANA CULTURAL CENTER

This **cultural center** (☎ 248-8622; www.hookele
.com/hccm; 4974 Uakea Rd; admission $2; ☺ 10am-4pm)
is a good place to get a sense of Hana's
roots. The small, community-run museum
displays quilts, Hawaiian artifacts, wooden
carvings, period photographs and a couple
of reconstructed thatched *hale*.

The grounds contain the old Hana police
station and three-bench **courthouse**, which
dates back to 1871. Although it looks like
a museum piece, the court is still used on
the first Tuesday of each month; a judge
shows up to hear minor cases such as traffic
violations, sparing Hana residents the need
to drive all the way to Wailuku.

HASEGAWA GENERAL STORE

The century-old **general store** (☎ 248-8231;
5165 Hana Hwy; ☺ 7am-7pm Mon-Sat, 8am-6pm Sun)
was once Hana's best-known sight. After
it burned down in 1990, it relocated under
the rusty tin roof of the town's old theater
building. While some of its character was
lost along with its eclectic inventory, the
store is still haphazardly packed with just
about everything from bags of poi and aloha
dolls to fishing gear and the record that immortalized the store in song.

WANANALUA CONGREGATIONAL CHURCH

South of the Hotel Hana-Maui, this looks like
an ancient Norman church. On the National
Register of Historic Places, the building was
erected in 1838 with thick walls of lava rock
and coral mortar to replace the congregation's original grass church. There's a little
cemetery at the side with graves randomly
laid out rather than lined up in rows. Even
at rest, Hana folks like things casual.

FAGAN MEMORIAL

After Paul Fagan died in 1959, his family
erected a memorial on Lyon's Hill, Fagan's
favorite spot for watching the sunset. The
huge hilltop cross is now Hana's most dominant landmark and makes for a fine vista.
The 15-minute trail up Lyon's Hill starts
opposite the Hotel Hana-Maui.

HANA BEACH PARK

At the southern end of Hana Bay, this **black-
sand beach** has a snack bar, showers, restrooms
and picnic tables. Hana folks occasionally
come down here with ukuleles, guitars and a
few beers for impromptu evening parties.

When water conditions are very calm,
snorkeling and diving are good out in the
direction of the light beacon. Currents can
be strong, and snorkelers shouldn't go beyond the beacon. Surfers head to **Waikoloa
Beach**, at the northern end of the bay.

Ka'uiki Head, the 386ft cinder hill on the
south side of Hana Bay, was the site of an
ancient fort, and, according to legend, home
to the demigod Maui. The islet at the tip of
the point, which now holds the light beacon, is **Pu'ukii** (Image Hill). The name can be
traced to a huge deity image that the great
king Umi erected here in the 16th century
to ward off invaders. In 1780, the Maui chief
Kahekili successfully fought off a challenge
by Big Island chiefs at Kauiki Head.

Queen Ka'ahumanu, one of the most powerful women in Hawaiian history, was born
in a cave here in 1768. A **trail** to a plaque
noting the queen's birth starts along the hill
at the side of the wharf at Hana Beach Park,
starting in ironwood trees and passing by
a tiny red-sand beach. The path takes only
about five minutes to walk, but watch your
step, as the trail can be a bit crumbly.

KAIHALULU (RED SAND) BEACH

On the south side of Kauiki Head, this gorgeous little cove has sand eroded from the red
cinder hill and beautiful turquoise waters.
The beach is favored by nude sunbathers.
Although the cove is partly protected by a
lava outcrop, the currents can be dangerous if the surf is up. Water drains through
a break on the left side, which should be
avoided. Your best chance of finding calm
waters is in the morning.

The path to the beach is at the end of
Uakea Rd beyond the ballpark. It starts across
the lawn at the lower side of the Hana Community Center, where a steep 10-minute trail
continues down to the beach. The curious
can also find an interesting overgrown Japanese cemetery – a remnant of the sugarcane
days – along the way at the east side of the
community center.

Festivals & Events

East Maui Taro Festival (last weekend in March; www
.tarofestival.org) This three-day event at Hana Ballpark
is Hana's big annual bash and one of the most quintessentially Hawaiian events on the island, with poi-making

demonstrations, outrigger canoe races, a taro pancake breakfast and hula dancing; certainly a fun time to be here, but book your accommodations well in advance.

Hana Relays (second Saturday in September; www.virr .com) A relay road race that begins in Kahului and follows the Hana Hwy 52 miles to town.

Sleeping

In addition to accommodations in Hana, there are cabins and tent camping at Wai'anapanapa State Park (p358), just north of Hana, and camping at 'Ohe'o Gulch (p362), about 10 miles south near Kipahulu.

BUDGET

Joe's Place (☎ 248-7033; www.joesrentals.com; 4870 Uakea Rd; r without bathroom $45, r $55) It may come as a surprise to find one of Maui's best budget accommodations smack in the middle of Hana. It's straightforward, with a dozen basic rooms, but it's spotlessly clean and guests have access to a full kitchen, TV room and barbecue grills. And to top it off, the friendly manager is a wealth of knowledge on the area – ask him to show you the article on Joe's that appeared in, of all places, the *Wall Street Journal*.

MID-RANGE

Hana Hale Malamalama (☎ 248-7718; www.hana hale.com; Uakea Rd; studios $160, cottages from $185) Built in a natural setting above a restored stone fishpond, this is one of the most atmospheric places to stay in Maui. It's spread over several acres, with seven unique units in all, including the 'Treehouse Cottage,' perched on stilts in a junglelike setting, and the 'Bamboo Inn' replete with tropical bamboo decor and fine ocean views. Going natural here doesn't mean giving up comforts: all units have two-person whirlpool bathtubs and kitchens.

Hana Lani Treehouses (☎ 248-7241; www.maui .net/~hanalani/treetop.htm; PO Box 389, Hana, HI 96713; r $90, treehouses $100) This is the real deal, built on platforms in the tree tops with no electricity or running water. Instead, the tree houses have tiki torches, bamboo outhouses with hot showers, hammocks and camp-style kitchens. The experience is pure Robinson Crusoe, much closer to camping out than staying in a hotel – essentially just mosquito screens and a roof separate you from the rest of the jungle. There are rooms in the main house for the less wild at heart.

Heavenly Hana Inn (☎ 248-8442; www.heavenly hanainn.com; Uakea Rd; 1-/2-bedroom ste $190/260) On the north side of town you'll find this little slice of Japan, an authentic *ryokan*-style inn that looks like it dropped right out of Kyoto. The suites are roomy with a separate sitting area and each has its own private entrance. Shoji doors, fresh-cut flowers, a tearoom and a happy Buddha in the garden are just part of the serene decor.

Hana Kai-Maui (☎ 248-8426, 800-346-2772; www .hanakai.com; 1533 Uakea Rd; studios $145, 1-bedroom units $145-195) Units in this condominium complex have a splendid ocean view from the lanai and it's just a short walk to the beach. There are more distinctive places to stay in Hana, but if you want a full kitchen and the conveniences of condo living, this is the place. Ask about fifth-night-free deals and weekly discounts.

Hana Ali'i Holidays (☎ 248-7742, 800-548-0478; www.hanaalii.com; PO Box 536, Hana, HI 96713; houses $80-300) Hana's largest vacation rental agency manages more than a dozen places, running the gamut from simple studio condos to cushy beachfront houses with ocean-view lanai.

Hana Accommodations (☎ 248-7868, 800-228-4262; www.hana-maui.com; houses $75-150) This agency has four properties on the south side of Hana, near Hamoa Beach, ranging from a Japanese-style studio with an efficiency kitchen to a modern three-bedroom home.

TOP END

Hotel Hana-Maui (☎ 248-8211, 800-321-4262; www .hotelhanamaui.com; 5031 Hana Hwy; r $380-430, cottages $500-1200; ☒ ☒) One of Maui's more exclusive getaway hotels, this pampering place has an engaging low profile that resembles a plantation estate. Everything's very airy and open, rich with Hawaiian accents, from island art in the lobby to traditional quilt bedspreads. Rooms have bleached hardwood floors, tiled baths, and French doors opening to trellised patios. If that's not relaxing enough, there's complimentary morning yoga and a full-service spa offering Hawaiian massage and seaweed wraps.

Eating

Hana has a couple of small grocery stores with a limited selection, but if you're staying awhile you're better off picking up supplies in Kahului before heading down.

MAUI

Tutu's (☎ 248-8224; burgers $4, plates $7; ⏰ 8am-4pm) You don't always have to pay a fortune for an ocean view. Join the local crowd at this fast-food grill fronting Hana Beach Park, where you'll find good picnic fare and tables by the bay.

Hana Ranch Restaurant (☎ 248-8255; Hana Ranch Center; lunch buffet $14; ⏰ 11:30am-3pm) The best lunch deal in town is the buffet here, which has a fresh salad bar, fried fish and other hot dishes for less than a cheeseburger would cost at the Hotel Hana-Maui.

Hotel Hana-Maui (lunch $15-19, dinner $30-35; ⏰ 11am-2:30pm & 6:15-9pm) Casual elegance characterizes this open-air restaurant serving Pacific regional cuisine. Enjoy dishes such as hoisin barbecue quail and ginger-seared ʻahi. The best time to come is on Friday, when there's a dinner buffet ($45) accompanied by a hula show. Forget lunch, which is more mundane and terribly overpriced.

Entertainment

Paniolo Bar (⏰ 6:30-8:30pm Fri-Sun) This hotel lobby bar hosts Hawaiian entertainment on weekends. Some nights it's a ukulele player, on other nights guitarists and hula dancers.

Shopping

Hana Coast Gallery (☎ 800-637-0188) At the north side of the Hotel Hana-Maui, this is worth a visit, even if you're not shopping, just to see the museum-quality wooden bowls, paintings, sculpture and Hawaiian featherwork.

Hana Cultural Center (☎ 248-8622; 4974 Uakea Rd; ⏰ 10am-4pm) Has a gift shop selling simple handicrafts.

BEYOND HANA

From Hana, the road continues on to Kipahulu, passing ʻOheʻo Gulch, the southern end of Haleakala National Park. This incredibly lush stretch is perhaps the most beautiful part of the entire drive down from Paʻia.

From Hana to Oheo, the road is narrow and winding. Between the hairpin turns, one-lane bridges and drivers trying to take in all the sights, it's a slow-moving 10 miles (allow at least 45 minutes).

You'll get extra coastal views by detouring along the 1.5-mile **Haneoʻo Rd** loop, which runs past a couple of beaches and ancient shoreline fishponds. The turnoff is just before the 50-mile marker.

Koki Beach

This beach is at the base of a red cinder hill less than half a mile from the start of the loop. Most of Koki's sand washes away in winter, leaving a rocky shoreline. Local surfers who know the coastline sometimes surf here, but rocks and strong currents make it hazardous for newcomers.

The offshore rock topped by a few coconut trees is **Alau Island**, a seabird sanctuary. The trees were planted years ago by Hana residents so that they'd have coconut milk to drink while fishing off the island.

Hamoa Beach

A little further is a lovely gray-sand beach that's used by the Hotel Hana-Maui, but is accessible to everyone. James Michener once said it was the only beach in the North Pacific that looked as if it belonged in the South Pacific. When the surf's up, there's good surfing and bodysurfing, though be aware of rip currents. When seas are calm, swimming in the cove is good. Public access is down the steps just north of the hotel's bus-stop sign. There are showers and restrooms.

Wailua Falls

As you continue south, you'll see waterfalls cascading down the cliffs, orchids growing out of the rocks, and lots of breadfruit and coconut trees. There's even a statue of the Virgin Mary tucked into a rock face on the side of the road. Wailua Falls at the Wailua Bridge, which comes up soon after the 45-mile marker, is a stunning 100ft drop visible from the road. Everybody stops here to take photos and you'll usually find a few vendors selling banana bread, jewelry and the like.

ʻOheʻo Gulch

The most visited area in the Kipahulu section of **Haleakala National Park** (admission per car per week $10; ⏰ 24hr), ʻOheʻo Gulch is cut by a lovely series of waterfalls and wide pools, each one tumbling into the next one below. When the sun shines, the pools make good swimming holes. A 2-mile trail runs up the streambed, rewarding hikers with picture-perfect views of the falls.

HISTORY

Not so long ago, ʻOheʻo Gulch was dubbed the 'Seven Sacred Pools' in a tourism promotion scheme. There are actually 24 pools extending from the ocean all the way up to Waimoku Falls and they were never sacred – but they sure are splendid. They also have a rich history. A large Hawaiian settlement once spread throughout the Oheo area, and archaeologists have identified the stone remains of more than 700 structures. The early villagers cultivated taro and sweet potatoes in terraced gardens along the stream.

One of the expressed intentions of Haleakala National Park is to manage its Kipahulu area 'to perpetuate traditional Hawaiian farming and ho'onanea' – a Hawaiian word meaning to pass the time in ease, peace and pleasure. Parts of the park are being returned to their original use.

INFORMATION
The park's **visitor center** (☎ 248-7375; www.nps .gov/hale; ☉ 9am-5pm) offers a variety of programs, depending on the time of year and the staff available on any given day. Typically, 15-minute cultural history talks and demonstrations are given daily on the half hour between 12:30pm and 3:30pm. See p364 for guided tours. You'll find restrooms near the parking lot and bottles of drinking water can be purchased at the visitor center. Food and gas are not available.

SIGHTS & ACTIVITIES
Lower Pools
The **Kuloa Point Trail**, a 20-minute half-mile loop, runs from the Kipahulu visitor center down to the lower pools and back, passing some interesting interpretive signs along the way. At the junction with Pipiwai Trail, go right. A few minutes down, you'll come to a broad grassy knoll with a beautiful view of the Hana coast. On a clear day, you can see the Big Island, 30 miles away across 'Alenuihaha Channel. This would be a fine place to break out a picnic lunch.

The large freshwater pools along the trail are terraced one atop the other and are connected by gentle cascades. They're usually calm and great for swimming, though the water's brisk. The second big pool below the bridge is a favorite. If it's been raining heavily and the water is flowing too high and fast, the pools are closed and signs are posted.

Still, heavy rains falling on the upper slopes can bring a sudden torrent here at any time. If the water starts to rise, get out immediately. People have been swept out to sea

from these pools by flash floods. The ocean below is not inviting at all – the water is quite rough, and gray sharks frequent the area!

Actually, most of the injuries that occur here come from falls on slippery rocks. Also hazardous are submerged rocks and ledges in some of the pools, so check carefully before jumping in.

And here's a little-known oddity: Oheo is home to a rare goby fish called 'o'opu, which spends the first stages of its life in the ocean, but returns to breed in the upper stream. The fish, which has a face that resembles a frog, works its way up the chain of pools and waterfalls by using its front fins as suction cups on the rocks.

Waterfall Trails
The **Pipiwai Trail**, which starts on the *mauka* side of the visitor center, leads up to Makahiku Falls (half a mile) and Waimoku Falls (2 miles). Or take a little shortcut by picking up the trail from the pedestrian crossing across the highway. To see both falls, allow about two hours return. The upper section is muddy, but boardwalks cover some of the worst bits.

Along the path, you'll pass large mango trees and lots of guava before coming to an overlook after about 10 minutes. **Makahiku Falls**, a long bridal-veil waterfall that drops into a deep gorge, is just off to the right. Thick green ferns cover the sides of 200ft basalt cliffs where the fall cascades. The scene is quite rewarding for such a short walk.

To the left of the overlook, a worn path continues up to the top of the falls, where there's a popular skinny-dipping pool. At midday the pool is quite enjoyable, but by late afternoon the sun stops hitting it and the mosquitoes move in. Rocks above the falls will keep you from going over the edge as long as the water level isn't high; a cut on one side lets the water plunge over the cliff. But if the water starts to rise, get out immediately – a drop over this sheer 184ft waterfall could, obviously, be fatal.

Back on the main trail, you walk under guava and banyan trees, cross Palikea Stream (killer mosquitoes thrive here, too) and enter the wonderland of the **Bamboo Forest**, where thick groves bang together musically in the wind. Beyond them is **Waimoku Falls**, a thin, lacy 400ft waterfall dropping down a sheer rock face. When you come out of the first

MAUI

grove, you'll see the waterfall in the distance. The pool under Waimoku Falls was partially filled in by a landslide during a 1976 earthquake, so it's not terribly deep. At any rate, swimming is not recommended because of the danger of falling rocks.

If you want to take a dip, you'll find better pools to swim in along the way. About 100yd before Waimoku Falls, you'll cross a little stream. If you go left and walk upstream for 10 minutes (there's not really a trail; just walk alongside the stream), you'll come to an attractive waterfall and a little pool about neck deep. There's also an inviting pool in the stream about halfway between Makahiku and Waimoku Falls.

TOURS

If you have a little bit more time, join one of the ranger-led hikes up into the bamboo forest; they start from the visitor center and last about an hour, but starting times vary with the day of the week, so call ahead.

The **Kipahulu Ohana**, a group of native Hawaiian farmers, has restored 2.5 acres of ancient taro patches and if you happen to be there on the first Tuesday of the month, they take visitors on a taro patch tour at 1pm, also departing from the visitor center.

SLEEPING

The national park maintains a primitive **campground** half a mile southeast of the Kipahulu visitor center. The campground is Hawaiian style – a huge open pasture - set amid the stone ruins of an ancient village. There are some incredible places to pitch a tent on grassy cliffs right above the coast and the pounding surf.

In winter, you'll usually have the place to yourself. It gets busier in summer, but even then it's large enough to handle everyone who shows up. Facilities include pit toilets and a few picnic tables and grills but *no* water. Permits aren't required, though camping is limited to three nights each month.

GETTING THERE & AWAY

A lot of people leave the 'Ohe'o Gulch area in midafternoon to head back up the Hana Hwy. Some of them, suddenly realizing what a long trek they have ahead, become very impatient drivers.

You might want to consider leaving a little later, which would give you more time to sightsee and enable you to avoid the rush. Getting caught in the dark on the Hana Hwy does have certain advantages. You can see the headlights of oncoming cars around bends that would otherwise be blind, and the traffic is almost nonexistent.

There are no shortcuts back, but there's usually another option. From Kipahulu, the Pi'ilani Hwy (don't be misled by the term 'highway' – it's just a dirt road in places) heads west through Kaupo and to the Upcountry. It's usually passable and it shouldn't be done in the dark. Also, it's going to take as long as turning around and going back up the Hana Hwy, so if you opt for the Pi'ilani Hwy, take it as an adventure, not a time-saver. The Kipahulu visitor center posts the road conditions.

For details on the drive, see the Pi'ilani Hwy section (p365).

Kipahulu

The little village of Kipahulu lies less than a mile south of Oheo. At the turn of the 20th century, Kipahulu was one of several sugar-plantation villages in the Hana area. It had a working mill from 1890 to 1922. Following the closure of the mill, unsuccessful attempts were made to grow pineapples here. Then ranching took hold in the late 1920s.

Today, Kipahulu has both exclusive estates and more modest homes. Fruit stands are set up here and there along the roadside; some are attended by elderly women who string lei and sell bananas, papayas and woven *lauhala* (pandanus-leaf) hats. This is the end of the line for most day visitors who have pushed beyond Hana.

SIGHTS

Aviation hero Charles Lindbergh made his home here during the last years of his life. He began visiting in the 1960s, built a cliffside home in Kipahulu in 1968, and died of cancer in Hana in 1974. Lindbergh is buried in the graveyard of **Palapala Ho'omau Congregational Church**. The inscription on his simple grave (If I take the wings of the morning and dwell in the uppermost parts of the sea...) is taken from Psalm 139. The church itself, with its 26in-thick walls and simple wooden pews, dates from 1864. It's known for its window painting of a Polynesian Christ draped in the red and yellow feather capes worn only by Hawaii's highest chiefs. The churchyard is a peaceful place, with sleepy cats lounging around, waiting for a nice warm car hood to sprawl out on.

Would-be visitors sometimes get the location mixed up with St Paul's Church, which sits on the highway three-quarters of a mile south of Oheo; the dirt drive down to Palapala Ho'omau Church is a quarter-mile beyond that, on the *makai* side of the road immediately after the 41-mile marker.

ACTIVITIES

If you want to get off the road and into the wilderness, native Hawaiian–owned **Maui Stables** (☎ 248-7799; www.mauistables.com; 3-hr ride $150; departures 9:30am & 1pm), between the 40- and 41-mile markers, offers trail rides up the slopes from Kipahulu.

PI'ILANI HIGHWAY

As it continues past Kipahulu, the road changes its name to the Pi'ilani Hwy (Hwy 31), curving along the southern flank of Haleakala. It's 25 ruggedly scenic miles between Kipahulu and Tedeschi Vineyards.

Someday in an asphalt future, this may well be a real highway with cars zipping along in both directions. For now, it's an unspoiled adventure. Here you can beat your own path to unnamed beaches and ancient heiau and catch views up Kaupo Gap before heading back to civilization. Signs such as 'Motorists assume risk of damage due to presence of cattle' and 'Narrow winding road, safe speed 10mph' give clues that this is not your standard highway.

The hardest part is finding out if the road is currently open and passable, although it usually is. Many tourist maps mark it as impassable, and car-hire agencies say that just being on it is a violation of their contract. Nevertheless, most of it is paved, and the stretch between Upcountry and Kaupo has even been upgraded in recent years.

The only tricky section is five unpaved miles after the 39-mile marker leading to the Kaupo area from Kipahulu. Depending on when it was last graded, standard cars can usually make it easily, though it may still rattle your bones. But after hard rains, streams flow over the road, making passage difficult, if not dangerous. A 4WD vehicle, or at least a high-riding car with a manual transmission, will minimize your chances of bottoming out.

Flash floods sometimes wash away portions of the road, making it impossible to get through until it's repaired. The **county public works department** (☎ 248-8254; ☺ 6:30am-3pm Mon-Fri) fields calls about road conditions, or ask at the **visitor center** (☎ 248-7375; ☺ 9am-5pm) at 'Ohe'o Gulch.

The best way to approach the drive is with an early-morning start, when the road is so quiet you'll feel like the last soul on earth. Take something to munch and plenty to drink, and check your oil and spare tire. It's a long haul to civilization if you break down, and the tow charge can run to hundreds of dollars. In the 'Ohe'o Gulch area, you might find a fruit stand, but gas stations and other services are nonexistent beyond Hana.

Kaupo

As the road winds around from Kipahulu, it skirts the edge of rocky cliffs and the vegetation picks up. First the road is shaded with big mango trees, banyans, bougainvillea and *wiliwili* trees with red tiger-claw blossoms. Then you'll see increasing numbers of *hala* (pandanus) and guava trees as the road bottoms out into gravel.

The village of Kaupo is around the 35-mile marker. However, don't expect a developed village in any sense of the word, as Kaupo is basically a scattered community of *paniolo* – many of them third-generation ranch hands – who work the Kaupo Ranch.

Kaupo Gap is a deep and rugged valley providing the only lowlands on this section of coast. As it was once heavily settled, it has three historic heiau as well as two 19th-century churches. While the road curves in and out, it's well worth stopping and enjoying a picturesque view of the church across the bay. Kaupo Ranch cattle were once shipped from a landing in the bay, and you can still see steps leading down into the water on a rock jutting out into the ocean.

Loaloa Heiau, the largest temple, is a registered national historical monument. All three heiau sites are *mauka* of **Hui Aloha Church**, which is a three-quarter-mile east of Kaupo General Store. Beside the rocky black-sand **Mokulau Beach**, this attractive whitewashed church, built in 1859 and restored in 1978, is surrounded by a stone wall and a few windswept trees. The area was an ancient surfing site. Mokulau, which means 'many small islands,' is named for the rocks just offshore.

MAUI

Kaupo General Store (☎ 248-8054; ⊗ 10am-5pm Mon-Sat), on the east side of the gap, is 'the only store for 20 miles' and sells snacks and drinks. Opening hours can be a bit flexible, however, so it's best not to count on it.

Kaupo to 'Ulupalakua Ranch

Past Kaupo village, you'll be rewarded with awesome views of Kaupo Gap, a large gap that opens up from the rim of majestic Haleakala. Then *makai* of the 31-mile marker, a very rough but short 4WD road passes through a gate and runs down to the ocean at **Nu'u Bay**, favored by locals for swimming when the water is calm. Spinner dolphins sometimes play offshore. If you snorkel or dive here, be sure to stay within the protected bay, as strong currents and riptides inhabit the open ocean beyond.

After another mile, there's a wide turnoff on the *mauka* side of the highway. From here you can walk out to dramatic **Huakini Bay**, where you can sit on smooth boulders and watch the violent surf. As the road continues, it runs in and out of numerous gulches and crosses a few bridges, gradually getting closer to the coast. Striations of lava testify to centuries of volcanic upheaval.

After the 29-mile marker, keep an eye out for a natural lava **sea arch**. Continue driving until it disappears from sight, then spot a turnout on the *makai* side. Park and take the worn footpath down through pastoral green fields to the cliff's edge, where you can see the arch close up and blowholes spout along the coast.

The road continues to rise, improving after the 23-mile marker. A few miles south of 'Ulupalakua Ranch, it crosses an expansive **lava flow**, dating from 1790, Haleakala's last eruption. This flow, which is part of the Kanaio National Area Reserve, is the same one that covers the La Perouse Bay area (see the South Maui section). Just offshore is the crescent island of Molokini with Kaho'olawe beyond. The large grassy hills between here and the sea are volcanic cinder cones. There's such a wide-angle view that the ocean horizon is noticeably curved, and sunsets are bewitching here.

As you approach Tedeschi Vineyards, groves of fragrant eucalyptus trees replace drier and scrubbier terrain. It's open rangeland here; cattle graze beside the road and occasionally mosey across in front of you.

UPCOUNTRY

Resplendent with rolling hills, emerald pastures and grazing horses, the cool green highlands on the western slopes of Haleakala make up Maui's Upcountry.

Surprisingly, more land on Maui is used for grazing dairy and beef cattle than for any other purpose, and a fair chunk of Upcountry is occupied by ranches. Haleakala Ranch covers vast spreads to the north, while 'Ulupalakua Ranch encompasses thousands upon thousands of acres to the south. Not surprisingly, ranching culture is thick on the ground in these parts, especially in Makawao, an old *paniolo* town.

Here, too, is Maui's garden land. Upcountry soil is so rich it produces more than half of the cabbage, lettuce, onions and potatoes grown in Hawaii and almost all of the commercially grown proteas and carnations. And if the heat along the beach is getting to you, a break in the Upcountry can be positively refreshing as the days are cooler up here and the nights are outright brisk.

You'll drive through a slice of the Upcountry just to get to Haleakala National Park, but this area is worth a visit for its own sake. On the mountainside above Kula you'll find the delightful cloud forests of Polipoli. Other Upcountry sightseeing spots include art galleries, historic churches, landscaped botanical gardens – even a winery with a tasting room. Spend at least a day up here and you won't regret it – or better yet, get to know Upcountry more intimately by staying at one of the area's cozy B&Bs.

PA'IA TO MAKAWAO

Baldwin Ave (Hwy 390) rolls uphill for 7 miles from Pa'ia (p351) up to Makawao, starting amid sugarcane fields near the old Pa'ia Sugar Mill and then traversing pineapple fields interspersed with little open patches where cattle graze.

There are two churches along Baldwin Ave. The **Holy Rosary Church** (945 Baldwin Rd), with its memorial statue of Father Damien, comes up first on the right, and the attractive **Makawao Union Church** (1445 Baldwin Ave), a stoneblock building with stained-glass windows, is further along on the left. Makawao Union Church, built in 1916, is on the National Register of Historic Places.

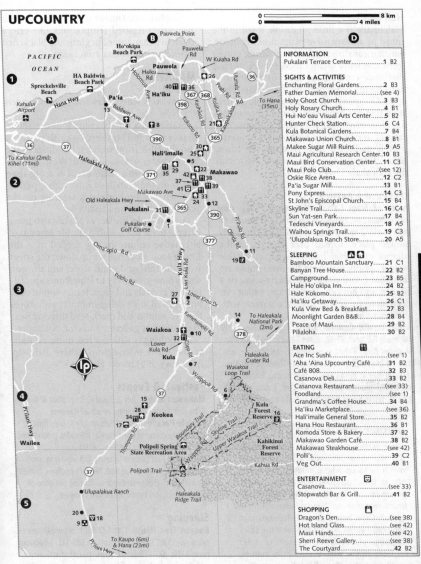

UPCOUNTRY

PACIFIC OCEAN

0 — 8 km
0 — 4 miles

INFORMATION
Pukalani Terrace Center...............1 B2

SIGHTS & ACTIVITIES
Enchanting Floral Gardens............2 B3
Father Damien Memorial..........(see 4)
Holy Ghost Church.......................3 B3
Holy Rosary Church.....................4 B1
Hui No'eau Visual Arts Center.......5 B2
Hunter Check Station...................6 C4
Kula Botanical Gardens.................7 B4
Makawao Union Church...............8 B1
Makee Sugar Mill Ruins...............9 A5
Maui Agricultural Research Center.10 B3
Maui Bird Conservation Center.....11 C3
Maui Polo Club........................(see 12)
Oskie Rice Arena.......................12 C2
Pa'ia Sugar Mill.........................13 B1
Pony Express.............................14 C3
St John's Episcopal Church..........15 B4
Skyline Trail.............................16 C4
Sun Yat-sen Park.......................17 B4
Tedeschi Vineyards....................18 A5
Waihou Springs Trail..................19 C3
'Ulupalakua Ranch Store.............20 A5

SLEEPING
Bamboo Mountain Sanctuary......21 C1
Banyan Tree House.....................22 B2
Campground..............................23 B5
Hale Ho'okipa Inn.......................24 B2
Hale Kokomo.............................25 B2
Ha'iku Getaway..........................26 C1
Kula View Bed & Breakfast..........27 B3
Moonlight Garden B&B...............28 B4
Peace of Maui...........................29 B2
Pilialoha..................................30 B2

EATING
Ace Inc Sushi............................(see 1)
'Aha 'Aina Upcountry Café..........31 B2
Café 808..................................32 B3
Casanova Deli...........................33 B2
Casanova Restaurant.............(see 33)
Foodland..................................(see 1)
Grandma's Coffee House.............34 B4
Ha'iku Marketplace..................(see 36)
Hali'imaile General Store.............35 B2
Hana Hou Restaurant.................36 B1
Komoda Store & Bakery..............37 B2
Makawao Garden Café...............38 B2
Makawao Steakhouse...............(see 42)
Polli's.....................................39 C2
Veg Out..................................40 B1

ENTERTAINMENT
Casanova................................(see 33)
Stopwatch Bar & Grill................41 B2

SHOPPING
Dragon's Den...........................(see 38)
Hot Island Glass.......................(see 42)
Maui Hands.............................(see 42)
Sherri Reeve Gallery.................(see 38)
The Courtyard..........................42 B2

MAUI

Past Hali'imaile Rd, just after the 5-mile marker, is Kaluanui, the former plantation estate of sugar magnates Harry and Ethel Baldwin. It now houses the **Hui No'eau Visual Arts Center** (☎ 572-6560; www.huinoeau.com; 2841 Baldwin Ave; gallery admission $2; ☻ 10am-4pm Mon-Sat). Famed Honolulu architect CW Dickey designed the two-story plantation home with

Spanish-style tile roof in 1917. The nonprofit arts club founded here in the 1930s offers prestigious classes in printmaking, pottery, woodcarving and other visual arts. Visit the gallery and extensive grounds, which include stables turned into art studios, and a 150-year-old tree that's a unique hybrid of Cook and Norfolk Island pines.

Hali'imaile

Hali'imaile is a little pineapple town in the midst of an expansive plantation. Its name, which means 'fragrant twining shrub,' comes from the *maile* plants used for lei-making that once covered the area. In addition to housing the headquarters of the Maui Pineapple Company, the town has an old general store that has been turned into Upcountry's top restaurant and a friendly guesthouse that rates as one of Maui's best budget options.

Hali'imaile Rd runs through the town, connecting Baldwin Ave (Hwy 390) with the Haleakala Hwy (Hwy 37).

SLEEPING & EATING

Peace of Maui (☎ 572-5045, 888-475-5045; www .peaceofmaui.com; 1290 Hali'imaile Rd; s/d with shared bathroom $50/55, 2-bedroom cottage $125; 🖳) This aptly named place, spread over 2 acres at the edge of quiet Hali'imaile, is an unbeatable budget option. Rooms in the main house are small but comfortable. Guests have use of a kitchen and hot tub. The cottage, which can sleep up to six, is pure luxury, complete with an ocean-view lanai.

Hali'imaile General Store (☎ 572-2666; 900 Hali'imaile Rd; lunch $9-12, dinner $20-29; ⏱ lunch Mon-Fri, dinner daily) Treat yourself to an exuberant mix of Hawaiian and Asian influences at this atmospheric restaurant featuring high ceilings and plantation-era decor. Lunch plays it safe, with Kula garden salads and a variety

---

DETOUR: OLINDA ROAD

For a scenic country drive head off into the hills above Makawao along Olinda Rd, which picks up where Baldwin Ave leaves off, drifting up past Makawao's **rodeo grounds** and the **Maui Polo Club**, which holds matches on Sunday afternoons in the fall. From here there are clearings with fine ocean views and air rich with the spicy fragrance of eucalyptus trees. Four miles up from town, past the 11-mile marker, you'll pass the **Maui Bird Conservation Center**, which breeds endangered birds. The mile-long **Waihou Springs Trail** begins roadside 4.8 miles up and makes an enjoyable 45-minute return walk if you want to get out and stretch. Near the top of Olinda Rd, turn left onto Pi'iholo Rd to wind back down into town.

---

of sandwiches. Dinner dishes add flair with perfectly prepared temptations like crispy duck in a mango-pecan glaze and blackened chicken with banana-rum sauce.

MAKAWAO

pop 6330

Makawao is where Hawaiian *paniolo* meets the New Age.

Started as a ranching town in the 1800s, Makawao is still bordered by cattle pastures, and the false-front wooden buildings in the town center retain an Old West appearance. The town's main event is a big-time rodeo on the Fourth of July, with a parade of cowhands on horseback wearing *palaka* (checked shirts) and festive lei.

All that aside, the face of Makawao is more diverse these days, with a sizable amount of alternative culture having seeped in – the health food store has set up down the street from the feed and grain store, and the gun shops have given way to storefronts specializing in crystals and yoga. It may sound odd, but all in all, it's a delightful mix; with stores that sell saimin and crack seed thriving next to creative art galleries and chic boutiques.

Everything is within a few minutes' walk of the main intersection, where Baldwin Ave (Hwy 390) meets Hwy 365.

Festivals & Events

Makawao Rodeo (July 2, 3 and 4) Takes place at the Oskie Rice Arena with roping events all day long.
Paniolo Parade (starts at 9am on July 3) Goes right through the center of town; park at the rodeo grounds and take the free shuttle to the town center.
Upcountry Fair (second Saturday and Sunday in June) Traditional agricultural fair with livestock auctions, farmers market, crafts, chili cookoff, ethnic dancing and good ol' country music; held at the Eddie Tam Complex.

Sleeping

Banyan Tree House (☎ 572-9021; www.banyantree house.com; 3265 Baldwin Ave; cottage $85-115, 3-bedroom home $380; 🖳) This former plantation manager's classic home filled with antiques. The place is lush and cool, shaded by banyan and monkeypod trees, and organic vegetable gardens nestle the lovely pool. Rent the entire home or one of the four charming cottages, each with a kitchen.

Hale Ho'okipa Inn (☎ 572-6698; www.maui-bed -and-breakfast.com; 32 Pakani Pl; r incl breakfast $95-125, 2-bedroom ste $145-165) About a mile southwest of town center, this richly historic craftsman-style house, built in 1924, has four guest rooms furnished with antiques and art. Most romantic is the 'rose room,' with its own lanai entrance and a claw-foot bathtub.

Eating
BUDGET
Makawao Garden Café (☎ 573-9065; 3669 Baldwin Ave; lunch $6-8; ☑ 11am-4pm) Tucked back in a little courtyard at the north end of Baldwin Ave, this owner-run café makes an excellent chicken Caesar salad and creative sandwiches such as grilled eggplant and goat cheese on focaccia. Definitely the place for lunch.

Komoda Store & Bakery (☎ 572-7261; 3674 Baldwin Ave; pastries 60¢-$2; ☑ 7am-5pm Mon, Tue, Thu & Fri, to 2pm Sat) Just south of the main intersection, this family-run bakery is famous throughout the islands for its mouth-watering cream puffs and *liliko'i* (passion fruit) malasadas.

Casanova Deli (☎ 572-0220; 1188 Makawao Ave; mains $3-6; ☑ 7am-6pm Mon-Sat, 8:30am-6pm Sun) Makawao's best breakfast option, this Italian deli has buttery croissants, fluffy omelets and strong coffee, as well as good sandwiches and deli fare. Take it all out on the roadside deck and watch the world flow by.

MID-RANGE & TOP END
Polli's (☎ 572-7808; 1202 Makawao Ave; $8-17; ☑ 7am-10pm, 8am-10pm Sun) This old standby Tex-Mex restaurant is usually full of folks watching surf videos and stuffing themselves with tacos, fajitas and Polli's popular baby back

ribs. It gets packed with cyclists coming down from Haleakala for lunch, but is more of a local hangout at night.

Casanova Restaurant (☎ 572-0220; 1188 Makawao Ave; pizza $10-18, mains $20-24; ☑ dinner) This popular dinner restaurant has a full Italian-influenced menu, ranging from superb kiawe-fired pizzas to rigatoni *fra diavola*, the latter a delightful medley of seafood, capers and spicy tomato sauce.

Makawao Steakhouse (☎ 572-8711; 3612 Baldwin Ave; mains $21-30; ☑ dinner) When nothing but a steak will do, there's no better place to go than a steakhouse in the midst of ranchland. The atmosphere matches the menu, with old-fashioned pine walls brimming with *paniolo* paintings and period photos.

Entertainment
Casanova (www.casanovamaui.com; admission $5-20) East Maui's hottest music spot, Casanova brings in mainland performers and some of Hawaii's top musicians. DJs spin midweek, followed by live bands – anything from salsa or blues to Jawaiian and Cuban jazz – on weekends. Dress to impress, they say.

Stopwatch Bar & Grill (☎ 572-1380; 1127 Makawao Ave) This friendly smoke-free sports bar is the place to go for dancing to live rock bands on Friday and Saturday nights and sports TV any time of the day.

Shopping
Sherri Reeve Gallery (☎ 572-8931; 3669 Baldwin Ave) A wonderful collection of works by local artist Sherri Reeve, ranging from handpainted T-shirts and tanks to full-scale watercolors of Maui scenes.

Dragon's Den (☎ 572-2424; 3681 Baldwin Ave) Need a lift? Get your Chinese herbs, smudge sticks and lapis lazuli heart stones here.

Courtyard (3620 Baldwin Ave) You'll find a cluster of interesting galleries here, the most notable being **Hot Island Glass** (☎ 572-4527), where you can watch glassblowers from 11:30am to 4:30pm Tuesday through Sunday, and **Maui Hands** (☎ 572-5194), which has sensual crafts and fine handmade jewelry.

HA'IKU
pop 4500
A number of roads lead through Ha'iku, a scattered community that stretches from Makawao down the slopes to the Hana Hwy. Alexander & Baldwin grew its first 12 acres

MAUI

of sugarcane near Ha'iku in 1869, and the village once had a sugar mill and a pineapple cannery. Today, the old cannery houses a few local eateries and quirky shops.

Today, Ha'iku is seeing a bit of a revival. Its rural character and its proximity to Makawao and Ho'okipa have attracted a number of new residents, including windsurfers, artists and New Age folks. The area has some wonderful B&Bs and makes a reasonably convenient base for exploring the whole island. The intersection of Ha'iku and Kokomo Rds marks the center of town.

Sleeping
BUDGET
Bamboo Mountain Sanctuary (☎ 572-4897; www .maui.net/~bamboomt; 1111 Kaupakalua Rd; s/d $55/75, 2-bedroom ste $150) This place radiates serenity with quiet verandas overlooking bamboo groves and Buddhas in the garden. Tucked into the woods a couple of miles from the ocean, the sanctuary blends the influences of Zen Buddhism and classic yoga. Amenities include a communal kitchen (vegetarian food only) and an ocean-view hot tub. Those interested can join morning *zazen* (Zen meditation). The sanctuary is sometimes closed during retreats.

Hale Kokomo (☎ 572-5613; www.bbonline.com/hi /kokomo; 2719 Kokomo Rd; r without/with bathroom incl breakfast $50/$60, ste $80) This Victorian-style house has a pleasant character with hardwood floors, bamboo blinds and walls adorned with Hawaiian prints. Rooms are cozy, each with a fridge. Run by a Swiss couple, breakfast is European-style with cheese and lots of fruit and there's a living room with a fireplace where you can relax in the evening.

MID-RANGE
Pilialoha (☎ 572-1440; www.pilialoha.com; 2512 Kaupakalua Rd; with breakfast s/d studios $90/95, cottage $110/130) A quiet setting and attention to detail characterize Pilialoha, where you'll find welcoming hosts, roses on the tables and tasteful decor. The charming two-bedroom cottage has a private deck overlooking a eucalyptus grove. Or soothe your weary muscles in the studio's Japanese-style soaking tub. Both have full amenities, including a washer-dryer.

Ha'iku Getaway (☎ 575-9362, 800-680-4946; 1765 Ha'iku Rd; www.haikugetaway.com; studios/ste/cottages from $75/95/135) This contemporary house offers the comforts of home. All three units

have cooking facilities, gas barbecues and more. The studio is compact with a futon-style bed, the suite can sleep four and the roomy two-bedroom garden cottage accommodates six.

Eating
Hana Hou Restaurant (☎ 575-2661; Ha'iku Marketplace; 810 Ha'iku Rd; $6-14; ☯ 10am-10pm Mon-Sat, to 7am Sun) In pidgin, the name means 'do it again,' and sure enough, people come back again and again for the backyard barbecue served at picnic tables. You can enjoy Hawaiian food like *laulau* (bundles of pork or beef with salted fish that are wrapped in leaves and steamed) here, or sit down to burgers and beer, and on some nights Brother Francis accompanies it all with Hawaiian tunes.

Veg Out (☎ 575-5320; Ha'iku Town Center, 810 Kokomo Rd; $3-9; ☯ 10:30am-7:30pm Mon-Fri, 11:30am-6pm Sat) This casual vegetarian eatery has a loyal following and *muy delicioso* fajitas smothered in pineapple salsa and guacamole. The pesto goat-cheese pizza is a winner too.

PUKALANI
pop 7380
Sunny Pukalani, literally 'heavenly gate,' may be a nice place to live, but it's little more than a gas-up-and-stock-up town for the stream of traffic that passes through each day making a beeline for Haleakala. There's even a bypass road that allows visitors to skip it altogether.

Orientation & Information
Upcountry's largest town, Pukalani is 2 miles from Makawao along Hwy 365. If you're coming from Kahului, take the Haleakala Hwy (Hwy 37), which climbs for 6 miles through cane fields before reaching Pukalani. To come into town, take the Old Haleakala Hwy exit, where the bypass highway begins. The Old Haleakala Hwy is Pukalani's main street.

Pukalani Terrace Center (Old Haleakala Hwy & Pukalani St) has a **coin laundry**, a **post office** (☎ 572-0019) and a **Bank of Hawaii** (☎ 572-7242) with a 24-hour ATM. A couple of gas stations are on the Old Haleakala Hwy.

Activities
Pukalani Golf Course (☎ 572-1314; www.pukalani golf.com; 360 Pukalani St; greens fees $45-60) A mile

west of Pukalani Terrace Center, this golf course has 18 holes, sweeping views and a driving range that stays open late.

Eating

Foodland (☎ 572-0674; Pukalani Terrace Center, Old Haleakala Hwy & Pukalani St; ☒ 24hr) This supermarket is a convenient stop for those heading up the mountain for the sunrise, or coming down for supplies.

Ace Inc Sushi (Pukalani Terrace Center; sushi $4-7; ☒ 10am-4pm) This independent stall inside the Foodland supermarket rolls out unbeatably fresh sushi made to order for take-out. It makes a great quick lunch if you're on your way to Haleakala.

'Aha 'Aina Upcountry Café (☎ 572-2395; 7 Aewa Pl; meals $5-11; ☒ 7am-2pm Tue-Sat, to 1pm Sun) Right along the Old Haleakala Hwy, this little café is the place to get breakfast, which is served until closing. The menu is all over the map, with Belgian waffles, *huevos rancheros* and good ol' *loco moco*.

KULA

pop 9730

It's cooler in Kula, refreshingly so. Perched at an average elevation of 3000ft, the Kula region is Maui's agricultural heartland, producing a bounty of salad greens, tomatoes and squashes that thrive in the sunny days, cool evenings and rich volcanic soil. Kula strawberries are divine, and no gourmet cook in Hawaii would ever want to be without sweet Kula onions.

During the California gold rush of the 1850s, Hawaiian farmers in Kula shipped so many potatoes off to West Coast miners that the area became known as 'Nu Kaleponi,' the Hawaiian pronunciation for New California. In the late 19th century, Portuguese and Chinese immigrants began to move in to farm the Kula area after they had worked off their contracts on the sugar plantations.

Kula grows the majority of Hawaii's proteas, large bright flowers. Some look like oversized pincushions, others like feathers, and still others have spinelike petals. Kula's also the source of almost all of the carnations used in lei throughout the islands, and many of the chrysanthemums. In spring, you'll find a burst of color right along the roadside as well, as the purple blossoms of the jacaranda tree and the yellow flowers of the gold oak bloom in profusion.

Sights & Activities

All of Kula is a garden, but if you want to take a closer look, you can visit several established walk-through botanical gardens, each with their own special appeal.

MAUI AGRICULTURAL RESEARCH CENTER

University of Hawai'i maintains this 20-acre **garden** (☎ 878-1213; 424 Mauna Pl; admission free; ☒ 7am-3:30pm Mon-Thu) on the slopes above Waiakoa village. It's here that Hawaii's first proteas were established in 1965. You can walk through rows of them, as well as dozens of new hybrids under development. Nursery cuttings from the plants here are distributed to protea farms across Hawaii, which in turn supply fresh flowers to the US mainland, Japan and Europe. Some sections of the research center garden are used for experiments in plant pathology, but the rest of the garden is open to the public (Friday is the day set aside for pesticide spraying).

To get here, follow Copp Rd (between the 12- and 13-mile markers on Hwy 37) for half a mile and turn left on Mauna Pl.

KULA BOTANICAL GARDEN

Cool and shady, this mature, naturalized **garden** (☎ 878-1715; 638 Kekaulike Ave; adult/child $5/1; ☒ 9am-4pm) has acres of theme gardens, including native Hawaiian specimens and a 'taboo garden' of poisonous plants. Because a stream runs through it, the garden supports a wide variety of vegetation. It can be a bit overgrown, but that's part of its charm. The garden is certified by the state to rehab injured nene, which can be seen in a cage-free aviary behind the orchid house.

ENCHANTING FLORAL GARDENS

Sunny and open, this roadside **garden** (☎ 878-2531; 2505 Kula Hwy; adult/child $5/1; ☒ 9am-5pm) near the 10-mile marker has wide paved paths for easy strolling. The garden features both tropical and cool-weather flowers, presented a bit like an oversized home garden, with neat orderly rows of colorful blooms.

HOLY GHOST CHURCH

The octagonal **Holy Ghost Church** (☎ 878-1261; Lower Kula Rd; ☒ 8am-5pm), a hillside landmark in Waiakoa, is on the National Register of Historic Places. Built in 1895 by Portuguese immigrants, the church features a beautifully ornate interior that looks like it came

MAUI

right out of the Old World, and indeed much of it did. The altar was carved by renowned Austrian woodcarver Ferdinand Stuflesser, shipped in pieces around the Cape of Good Hope, then hauled by oxen up to Waiakoa. If you want to learn more, open up the history binder near the guest registry at the back. Finding the church is easy as the distinctive white building is readily visible from the highway.

Sleeping
Kula View Bed & Breakfast (☎ 878-6736; 600 Holopuni Rd; studio incl breakfast $85) This studio unit above a country home offers views of the distant ocean. You'll find everything you'll need for your time in Upcountry, including warm jackets for the Haleakalea sunrise. Breakfast includes organic fruit from the backyard and guests have their own private entrance.

Eating
Kula Sandalwoods Restaurant (☎ 878-3523; Haleakala Hwy; mains $5-10; ⊙ 6:30am-2:30pm Mon-Fri, to noon Sun) A chef from the prestigious Culinary Institute of America makes this a treat. At breakfast the eggs Benedict is a standout; at lunch don't miss the tangy *kalua*-pig sandwich. Excellent salads feature garden-fresh Kula greens. To top it off there's an ocean view and quick service. The restaurant is less than a mile north of Haleakala Crater Rd.

Café 808 (☎ 878-6874; Lower Kula Rd, Waiakoa; $4-8; ⊙ 6am-8pm) Island *grinds* (food) is what you'll find at this popular local eatery a quarter-mile south of the Holy Ghost Church. Its down-home menu is as wide and long as its kitchen. Show up before 11am for banana pancakes or an omelet with home fries. Folks come for miles around for the hamburger steak topped with onions and mushrooms.

Sunrise Market & Protea Farm (☎ 878-1600; Haleakala Crater Rd; $2-5; ⊙ 7:30am-4pm in winter, 7am-4:30pm in summer) Stop here, a quarter-mile up from the intersection of Hwys 378 and 377, to pick up post-sunrise java, bakery items, sandwiches and fruit salads. Then stroll out back to view its protea garden.

POLIPOLI SPRING STATE RECREATION AREA
Polipoli Spring State Recreation Area is high up in Kula Forest Reserve on the western slope of Haleakala. The park is in coniferous

forest and has picnic tables, camping and a network of little-used hiking and mountain biking trails. It's not always possible to get all the way to the park without a 4WD, but it's worth driving part-way for the view.

Access is via Waipoli Rd, off Hwy 377, just under half a mile before its southern intersection with Hwy 37. Waipoli is a narrow, switchbacking one-lane road through groves of eucalyptus and open rangeland (watch for cattle on the road). Layers of clouds often drift in and out; when they lift, you'll get panoramic views across green rolling hills to the islands of Lana'i and Kaho'olawe.

Except for the bird calls, everything is still here. When the clouds are heaviest, visibility is measured in feet. The road has some soft shoulders, but the first 6 miles are paved. After the road enters the forest reserve, it reverts to dirt. When it's muddy, the next four grinding miles to the campground are not even worth trying in a standard car.

The whole area was planted during the 1930s by the Civilian Conservation Corps (CCC), a Depression-era work program. Several of the trails pass through old CCC camps and stands of redwood, cypress, cedar and pines. In fact, it all looks somewhat like the northern California coast.

Activities
WAIAKOA LOOP TRAIL
The trailhead for the Waiakoa Loop Trail starts at the hunter check station 5 miles up Waipoli Rd, which is all paved. Walk three-quarters of a mile down the grassy spur road on the left to a gate marking the trail. The hike, which starts out in pine trees, makes a 3-mile loop. You can also connect with the Upper Waiakoa Trail at a junction about a mile up the right side of the loop.

UPPER WAIAKOA TRAIL
The Upper Waiakoa Trail is a strenuous 7-mile trail that begins off Waiakoa Loop at an elevation of 6000ft, climbs 1800ft, switchbacks and then drops back down 1400ft. It's stony terrain, but it's high and open, with good views. Bring plenty of water.

The trail ends on Waipoli Rd between the hunter check station and the campground. If you want to start at this end of the trail, keep an eye out for the trail marker for Waohuli Trail, as the Upper Waiakoa Trail begins across the road.

HIDDEN MAUI

- Enjoying a drink at Kapalua Bay's **sunset hula show** (p325)
- Hiking through the cloud forests of **Polipoli** (p372)
- Picnicking at **Secret Cove** (p350) in Makena
- Snorkeling at **'Ahihi-Kina'u Natural Area Reserve** (p350)
- Walking to the surf-sharpened **Dragon's Teeth** (p324)

BOUNDARY TRAIL

This is a 4-mile marked and maintained trail that begins about 200yd beyond the end of the paved road. Park to the right of the cattle grate that marks the boundary of the Kula Forest Reserve. This is a steep downhill walk that crosses gulches and drops deep into woods of eucalyptus, pine and cedar, as well as a bit of native forest. In the afternoon, the fog generally rolls in and visibility fades.

SKYLINE TRAIL

This otherworldly trail is the major link in a hiking route that begins at a lofty elevation of 9750ft in Haleakala National Park and leads down to Polipoli campground at 6200ft, a total distance of 8.5 miles. It takes about four hours to walk.

To get to the trailhead, go past Haleakala summit and take the road to the left just before Science City. The Skyline Trail, which is actually a dirt road used to maintain Polipoli Spring State Recreation Area, starts here in open terrain made up of cinders, lava bombs and vents. After three crunchy miles, it reaches the tree line (8500ft) and enters native *mamane* (a native tree with bright yellow flowers) forest. In the winter, *mamane* is heavy with clusters of delicate yellow flowers that look like sweet-pea blossoms.

If the clouds treat you kindly, you'll have broad views all the way between the barren summit and the dense cloud forest. Eventually the trail meets the Polipoli access road, where you can either walk to the paved road in about 4 miles, or continue via the **Haleakala Ridge Trail** and **Polipoli Trail** to the campground. The Skyline Trail is also fun to do on a mountain bike.

Sleeping

Tent camping requires a permit from the state (see p294), but facilities are limited. There are restrooms, but no showers or drinking water. Fellow campers are likely to be pig hunters. Otherwise the place can be eerily deserted, and damp. Come prepared – this is cold country, with winter temperatures frequently dropping below freezing at night.

From the campground, it's another half-mile walk down a forest trail to the one housekeeping **cabin**. Unlike the other state cabins, this one has gas lanterns and a wood-burning stove but no electricity or refrigerator. See p294 for reservations details.

KEOKEA

Around the turn of the 20th century, Keokea was home mainly to Hakka Chinese who farmed the remote Kula region. Although there's not much to it, Keokea is the last real town before Hana if you're swinging around the southern part of the island. It has a coffee shop, gas pump, a small general store and an art gallery.

Sights

The village's green-and-white **St John's Episcopal Church** was built in 1907 to serve the Chinese community, and it is still marked with Chinese characters. For a time, Sun Yat-sen, father of the Chinese nationalist movement, lived on the outskirts of Keokea. A statue of Sun Yat-sen and a small **park** dedicated to him can be found on the *makai* side of Hwy 37 beyond Grandma's Coffee House. On a clear day, you'll enjoy great views of west Maui and Lana'i from the roadside.

Sleeping & Eating

Moonlight Garden B&B (☎ 878-6977, 866-878-6297; www.maui.net/~mauimoon; 213 Kula Hwy; 1-/2-bedroom cottage $125/130) This delightful place is within walking distance of Keokea village center. The two freestanding cottages sit amid fruit trees and stands of bamboo, and have decks with views out to the sea. Both cottages are spacious with full kitchen, washer-dryer, hammocks and tasteful island decor, and the one-bedroom cottage has a fireplace.

Grandma's Coffee House (☎ 878-2140; Hwy 37; pastries $2, deli fare $6-8; ☾ 7am-5pm) This cheery little café has homemade pastries, Kula salads, sandwiches and fresh dark-roasted Maui coffee. Grandma's family has been

MAUI

growing coffee beans since 1918. If you want to see what coffee trees look like, just walk out to the side porch, and you'll be eye-to-eye with the bright red beans. It's also the place to pick up picnic fare if you're headed around the Pi'ilani Hwy to Hana.

'ULUPALAKUA RANCH

From Keokea, Hwy 37 winds south through ranch country with good views of Kaho'olawe and the little island of Molokini. Even on overcast days, you can often see below the clouds to sunny Kihei on the coast.

In the mid-19th century, 'Ulupalakua Ranch was a sugar plantation owned by whaling ship captain James Makee. King David Kalakaua, the 'Merrie Monarch,' was a frequent visitor who loved to indulge in late-night rounds of poker and champagne. The 20,000-acre ranch now has about 6000 head of cattle, as well as small herds of merino sheep and Rocky Mountain elk.

Sights

Established in the middle of 'Ulupalakua Ranch in 1974, **Tedeschi Vineyards** (☎ 878-6058; www.mauiwine.com; tours & tastings free; ☷ 9am-5pm, tours 10:30am & 1:30pm) offers tastings of its products. Most interesting is the Maui Blanc pineapple wine, which is surprisingly light and dry for a fruit wine. Sticking with the tropical theme, it also produces a pineapple–passion fruit wine. Less of a splash are the grape wines. Attached to the tasting room and gift shop is a fascinating little **exhibit** on ranch history. Free tours of the grounds and the winery operation are given.

Opposite the winery, you can see the remains of the three stacks of the **Makee Sugar Mill**, built in 1878.

Festivals & Events

Traditionally held on the last Saturday in April at Tedeschi Vineyards, '**Ulupalakua Thing** (www.ulupalakuathing.com) is a feast for the senses that brings Maui's top chefs on board to whip up their latest and greatest creations. You can sample their fare, listen to live entertainment and sip wine while relaxing on the winery lawn.

Eating

'**Ulupalakua Ranch Store** (☎ 878-2561; burgers $7; lunchtime grill ☷ 11am-1:30pm, store ☷ 9am-5pm) Op-

posite the ranch headquarters, 5.5 miles south of Keokea, this store has a deli and lunchtime grill with take-out salads, hormone-free beef burgers and, occasionally, elk burgers. The store also sells cowboy hats, bandannas and jeans, as well as souvenir T-shirts and knickknacks. Say howdy to the life-sized wooden cowboys on the front porch.

Getting There & Away

After the vineyard, it's another 25 dusty, bumpy miles to Kaupo along the spectacular Pi'ilani Hwy (p365).

HALEAKALA NATIONAL PARK

As inspiring as it is awesome, Haleakala has long been the soul of Maui. Ancient kahuna came to the summit to worship, Mark Twain praised its healing solitude, and visitors still find mystic experiences here. For many people no visit to Maui is complete without making the requisite pilgrimage at dawn to watch the sun rise above the huge crater.

Haleakala has something for everyone. Often (but erroneously) called the world's largest dormant volcano, Haleakala Crater (which again is a misnomer, as it's actually a craterlike basin) measures a whopping 7.5 miles wide, 2.5 miles long and 3000ft deep – more than enough to swallow the entire isle of Manhattan.

From the crater's rim there are stunning views of its lunarlike surface. But the adventure needn't stop at the viewpoints – with a good pair of hiking boots you can walk into the crater on trails that meander around cinder cones and peer up at towering walls. Or go light on your feet and take a horseback ride to the crater floor.

In its prime, Haleakala probably reached a height of 12,000ft before water erosion carved two large river valleys out of the rim. The gaps, Ko'olau Gap on the northwest side and Kaupo Gap on the southeast, are dominant features in the crater wall. Cinder cones on the crater floor were added in later eruptions. The latest flow of lava poured out in 1790 – which on the geological clock means Haleakala could just be snoozing.

Early morning is usually the best time for viewing the crater (see p376). Later in the day, warm air generally forces clouds higher and higher until they pour through the two gaps in the crater's rim and into the crater itself. Although sunrises get top billing, sunset can be nearly as impressive.

Haleakala National Park stretches from the volcano summit down to the pools of 'Ohe'o Gulch (p362) in its Kipahulu section on the coast south of Hana. There are separate entrances to both sections of the park, but there's no passage between them.

INFORMATION

Haleakala National Park (www.nps.gov/hale; 7-day entry pass per car $10, per person on foot, bicycle or motorcycle $5) never closes, and the pay booth at the park entrance opens well before dawn and stays open late. Annual national park passes ($50) can be purchased at the gate, as can a $20 annual tri-park pass that's valid for all three of Hawaii's national parks (the other two are Hawai'i Volcanoes National Park and Pu'uhonua o Honaunau National Historical Park, both of which are on the Big Island).

The park's **headquarters** (☎ 572-4400; ☀ 8am-4pm) are less than a mile up the highway from the park boundary. You can call ahead for recorded information on activities, camping permits and general park conditions. The office has detailed brochures, provides camping permits and sells books on geology and flora and fauna. A few silversword grow in front of the building, and occasionally a pair of nene wander around the parking lot. These endangered birds are much too friendly for their own good; do not feed them and be careful coming in and out of the parking lot – most nene deaths are the result of being hit by cars. There are no views at park headquarters; this is simply an information and rest room stop.

For views and more, the real **visitor center** (p377) is up near the summit.

You can get drinking water at park headquarters, but no food is sold in the park. Bring something to eat, particularly if you're going up for the sunrise; you don't want a growling stomach to rush you all the way back down the mountain before you've had a chance to explore the sights.

It's a good idea to check on weather conditions (☎ 877-5111) before driving up. It's not uncommon for it to be cloudy at Haleakala when it's clear on the coast. A drizzly sunrise is a particularly disappointing nonevent after getting out of bed at 4am. Always bring warm clothing, as overnight predawn temperatures dip below freezing, and even at the height of the day, when the clouds blow in, it can turn suddenly cool.

SIGHTS

For information on driving Haleakala Crater Rd, see p381.

Hosmer Grove Trail

Hosmer Grove, three-quarters of a mile before park headquarters, has an inviting half-mile loop trail that begins at the edge of the campground. Not only is it a birder's delight, but anyone looking for a little greenery after hiking the crater will love this shaded woodland walk.

The trail starts in a forest of lofty introduced trees, then passes into native Hawaiian shrub land. The exotics in Hosmer Grove were introduced in 1910 in an effort to develop a lumber industry in Hawaii. They include incense cedar, Norway spruce, Douglas fir, eucalyptus and various tyoes of pines. Although the trees adapted well enough to grow, they didn't grow fast enough at these elevations to make tree harvesting practical. Thanks to this failure, today there's a park here instead.

HOUSE OF THE RISING SUN

According to legend, the goddess Hina was having problems drying her tapa cloth because the days were too short. Her son Maui, the prankish demigod for whom the island is named, decided to take matters into his own hands. One morning he went up to the mountaintop and waited for the sun. As it came up over the mountain Maui lassoed the rays one by one and held tight until the sun came to a halt. When the sun begged to be let go, Maui demanded that as a condition for its release it hereafter slow its path across the sky. The sun gave its promise, the days were lengthened and the mountain became known as Haleakala, 'House of the Sun.' To this day there are about 15 more minutes of daylight at Haleakala than on the coast below.

MAUI

Native plants include 'akala (Hawaiian raspberry), mamane, pilo, kilau ferns and sandalwood. The 'ohelo, a berry sacred to the volcano goddess Pele, and the pukiawe, which has red and white berries and evergreen leaves, are eaten by nene.

There are wonderful scents and birdcalls along the trail. The native 'i'iwi and 'apapane, both sparrow-size birds with bright red feathers, are fairly common. The 'i'iwi has a very loud squeaking call, orange legs and a curved salmon-colored bill. The 'apapane is a fast-moving bird with a black bill, black legs and a white undertail. It feeds on the nectar of ohia flowers, and its wings make a distinctive whirring sound.

Ring-necked pheasants sometimes get flushed out along the trail. You might also see – or at least hear – the melodious laughing thrush, also called the spectacle bird for the circles around its eyes that extend back like a pair of glasses.

Waikamoi Preserve

Waikamoi Preserve is a 5230-acre reserve adjoining Hosmer Grove. In 1983, Haleakala Ranch conveyed the land's management rights to the Nature Conservancy through a permanent conservation easement.

The preserve's native koa and ohia rain forest provides the last stronghold for 76 species of rare native plants and forest birds. You're apt to see the 'i'iwi, the 'apapane and the yellow-green 'amakihi. You might also catch a glimpse of the yellow-green 'alauahio (Maui creeper) or the 'akohekohe (Maui parrotbill), both endangered species found nowhere else.

The only way to see the preserve is to join a **guided hike**. The National Park Service offers free three-hour, 3-mile guided hikes that enter the preserve from Hosmer Grove campground at 9am on Monday and Thursday. Hikes are sometimes canceled because of weather conditions, so call ahead. The Nature Conservancy occasionally leads hikes through the preserve as well, but only for school and community groups.

Leleiwi Overlook

Leleiwi Overlook (8840ft) is midway between park headquarters and the summit visitor center. From the parking lot, it's a five-minute walk across a gravel trail to the overlook, from where you can see the West Maui Mountains and both sides of the isthmus connecting the two sides of Maui. You also get another angle on Haleakala Crater. The trail has plaques identifying some interesting native plants, such as the silver-leafed hinahina, found only at Haleakala, and the kukae-nene, a member of the coffee family.

A SUBLIME SPECTACLE

Sunrise at Haleakala is an unforgettable experience, one that Mark Twain called the 'sublimest spectacle' he'd ever seen. As you drive up the mountain in the dark, the only sights are twinkling town lights, a sky full of stars, and a distant fishing boat or two on the dark horizon.

About an hour before sunrise, the night sky begins to lighten and turn purple-blue, and the stars fade away. Ethereal silhouettes of the mountain ridges appear.

Plan to arrive at the summit about 30 or 40 minutes before the actual sunrise. The gentlest colors show up in the moments just before dawn. The undersides of the clouds lighten up first, accenting the night sky with pale silvery slivers and streaks of pink.

About 20 minutes before sunrise, the light intensifies on the horizon in bright oranges and reds, much like a sunset. Be sure to turn around for a look at Science City, whose domes turn a blazing pink. For the grand finale, the moment when the disk of the sun appears, all of Haleakala takes on a fiery glow. It feels like you're watching the earth awaken.

Temperatures hovering around freezing and a cold wind are the norm at dawn and there's often a frosty ice on the top layer of cinders, which crunch underfoot. If you don't have a winter jacket or sleeping bag to wrap yourself in, be sure to bring a warm blanket from your hotel. This will give you the option of sitting outside in a peaceful spot to take it all in rather than huddling for heat at the crowded visitor center.

The best photo opportunities occur before the sun rises. Every morning is different, but once the sun is up, the silvery lines and the subtleties disappear. If you wake up late or traffic is slow, pull over at one of the lower crater overlooks before first light erupts instead.

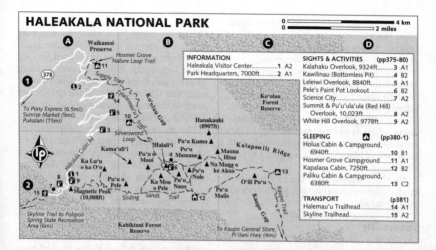

HALEAKALA NATIONAL PARK

0 —————————— 4 km
0 —————————— 2 miles

INFORMATION
Haleakala Visitor Center..............1 A2
Park Headquarters, 7000ft..........2 A1

SIGHTS & ACTIVITIES   (pp375-80)
Kalahaku Overlook, 9324ft............3 A1
Kawilinau (Bottomless Pit)............4 B2
Leleiwi Overlook, 8840ft...............5 A1
Pele's Paint Pot Lookout..............6 B2
Science City.................................7 A2
Summit & Pu'u'ula'ula (Red Hill)
  Overlook, 10,023ft.....................8 A2
White Hill Overlook, 9778ft...........9 A2

SLEEPING   (pp380-1)
Holua Cabin & Campground,
  6940ft....................................10 B1
Hosmer Grove Campground.........11 A1
Kapalaoa Cabin, 7250ft..............12 B2
Paliku Cabin & Campground,
  6380ft....................................13 C2

TRANSPORT   (p381)
Halemau'u Trailhead...................14 A1
Skyline Trailhead.......................15 A2

In the afternoon, if weather conditions are right, you might see the **Brocken specter**, an optical phenomenon that occurs at high elevations. Essentially, by standing between the sun and the clouds, your image is magnified and projected onto the clouds. The light reflects off tiny droplets of water in the clouds, creating a circular rainbow around your shadow.

Kalahaku Overlook

Whatever you do, don't miss this one. Kalahaku Overlook (9324ft), about a mile above Leleiwi Overlook, offers a bird's-eye view of the crater floor and the ant-sized hikers on the trails snaking around the cinder cones below. At the observation deck, information plaques give you the skinny on each of the volcanic formations that punctuate the crater floor. For photography, afternoon light is best.

The 'ua'u (Hawaiian dark-rumped petrel) nests in burrows in the cliff face at the left side of the observation deck between May and October. Even if you don't spot the birds, you can often hear the parents and chicks making their unique clucking sounds. Of the fewer than 2000 'ua'u remaining today, most nest right here at Haleakala, where they lay just one egg a year. These seabirds were thought to be extinct until seen again in the crater during the 1970s.

A short trail below the parking lot leads to a fenced enclosure containing lots of silversword, from seedlings to mature plants.

Haleakala Visitor Center

The **visitor center** (☉ 6am-3pm in summer, 6:30am-3pm in winter) on the rim of the crater (9745ft) is the main sunrise-viewing spot. The center has displays on geological and volcanic evolution and a recording explaining what you see on the crater floor 3000ft below. There are books and postcards, and a ranger is usually on duty. There are restrooms.

Before dawn, the parking lot fills up with everyone coming to see the sunrise show. Brief natural and cultural history talks are given at the summit visitor center at 9:30am, 10:30am and 11:30am. Park rangers also lead a moderately strenuous two-hour hike that goes about a mile down Sliding Sands Trail; meet at the trailhead at 9am on Tuesday and Friday. Guided hikes along the 12-mile Sliding Sands–Halemau'u Trail are led once or twice a month.

Summit

The **Pu'u'ula'ula (Red Hill) Overlook**, at 10,023ft, is Maui's highest point. Congratulations! The 37-mile drive from sea level to the summit of Haleakala you've just completed is the highest elevation gain in the shortest distance anywhere in the world.

The summit building at the overlook has panoramic wraparound windows, and on clear days you can see the Big Island, Lana'i, Moloka'i and even O'ahu. When the light's right, the colors of the crater from the summit are spectacular, with an array of shades in greens, grays, reds and browns.

The summit building is half a mile uphill from the visitor center. You may see 'lava bombs,' hardened molten lava expelled long ago from the crater's volcanic vents.

Dozens of silversword have been planted around the summit building, making this the best place to see these luminous silver-leafed plants in various stages of growth. Found only on Hawaii's high volcanic areas, silversword grow for four to 25 years before shooting up one glorious stalk with hundreds of blooms, and then going to seed and dying.

Nearby, **Magnetic Peak**, with its iron-rich cinders, has an uncanny ability to mess with your compass.

Science City

On the Big Island's Mauna Kea, scientists study the moon. Here at Haleakala, appropriately enough, they study the sun. Science City, just beyond the summit, is off-limits to visitors. It's under the jurisdiction of the University of Hawaii, which owns some of the domes and leases other land for a variety of private and government research projects.

Department of Defense-related projects here include laser technology related to the 'Star Wars' project, satellite tracking and identification, and a deep-space surveillance system. The Maui Space Surveillance System (MSSS), an electro-optical state-of-the-art facility used for satellite tracking, is the largest telescope anywhere in use by the Department of Defense. The system is capable of identifying a basketball-size object flying in space 20,000 miles away.

In 2004, the Faulkes Telescope, a joint operation of the University of Hawai'i and a UK-based educational foundation, became operational. Dedicated to raising interest in astronomy among students, the telescope is fully robotic and can be controlled in real time via the Internet from classrooms in both the UK and Hawaii.

ACTIVITIES

All park programs offered by the National Park Service are free. Ranger-led **walks** through Waikamoi Preserve (p376) and from the summit visitor center (p377) are held throughout the year. Evening **stargazing programs** and full-moon hikes are offered between June and September, when the weather is warm enough (p375).

Hiking

Hiking the crater floor offers a completely different angle on Haleakala's lunar landscape. Instead of peering down from the rim, you're looking up at the walls and towering cinder cones. It looks so much like a moonscape that US astronauts trained here before going to the moon. Speaking of which, hiking here on full-moon nights is magical.

The crater floor is a very still place. The sound of cinders crunching underfoot is often the only noise to reach your ears, except for the occasional bark of a pueo (Hawaiian owl) or honking of a friendly nene. Ring-necked pheasants are also likely to be startled by your approach and swiftly dart up from the crater floor.

The weather at Haleakala can change suddenly from dry, hot conditions to cold, windswept rain. Although the general rule is sunny in the morning and cloudy in the afternoon, fog and clouds can blow in at any time. Be prepared for temperatures that can drop into the 50s (°F) during the day and the 30s at night – at any time of year. Hikers without proper clothing risk hypothermia. The climate also changes radically as you walk across the crater floor. In the 4 miles between the Kapalaoa and Paliku cabins, rainfall varies from an annual average of 12in to 300in. December to May is the wet season.

The 27 miles of trails inside the crater are reliably marked at junctions. To protect the fragile environment, always keep to the center of established trails and do not be tempted off them, even for well-trodden shortcuts through switchbacks. One of the most popular full-day outings is the vigorous 11.5-mile hike that starts down Sliding Sands Trail and returns via Halemau'u Trail.

With the average elevation on the crater floor at 6700ft, the relatively thin air means that hiking can be quite tiring. The higher elevation also means that sunburn is more likely. Take sunscreen, rain gear, a first-aid kit and plenty of water.

SLIDING SANDS TRAIL

Sliding Sands, the summit trail into the crater, starts at the south side of the visitor-center parking lot at 9740ft and descends steeply over loose cinders down to the crater floor. The trail leads 9.5 miles to the Paliku cabins and campground, passing the

Kapalaoa cabin at 5.8 miles after roughly four hours.

The first 6 miles of the trail follow the south wall. There are great views on the way down, but virtually no vegetation. About 2 miles down (at 1400ft), a steep spur trail leads past silversword plants to **Ka Lu'u o ka O'o** cinder cone, about half a mile north. Four miles down, after an elevation drop of 2500ft, the trail intersects with the first of three spur trails leading north into the cinder desert, which after about 1.5 miles meets the Halemau'u Trail.

As you strike out across the crater floor for 2 miles to Kapalaoa, verdant ridges rise on your right, eventually giving way to ropy *pahoehoe* (quick, smooth-flowing lava). From Kapalaoa cabin to Paliku, the descent is gentle and the vegetation gradually increases. Paliku (6380ft) is beneath a sheer cliff at the eastern end of the crater. In contrast to the crater's barren western end, this area receives heavy rainfall, with ohia forests climbing the slopes.

HALEMAU'U TRAIL

If you're not up for a long hike, consider doing just part of the Halemau'u Trail. Even hiking just the first mile gives a fine view of the crater with Ko'olau Gap to the east, and it's fairly level up to this point. If you were to continue on the trail and hike down 1400ft and 2 miles of switchbacks, then walk another mile across the crater floor to Holua cabin and campground, the 8-mile return would make a fine day hike and be a good workout. But start early before the afternoon clouds roll in and visibility vanishes.

At 6940ft, Holua is one of the lowest areas along this hike, and you'll see impressive views of the crater walls rising a thousand feet to the west. A few large **lava tubes** here are worth exploring: one up a short, steep cliff behind the cabin, and the other a 15-minute detour further along the trail.

If you have energy, push on just another mile to the colorful cinder cones, being sure to make a short detour onto the **Silversword Loop**, where you'll see these plants in various stages of growth. If you're here in summer, you should be able to see the plants in flower, with their 6ft-tall stalks ablaze with hundreds of maroon and yellow blossoms. But be careful – half of all silverswords today are trampled to death as seedlings,

mostly by careless hikers who wander off trails. The trail continues another 6.3 miles to the Paliku cabin.

The trailhead to Halemau'u is 3.5 miles above park headquarters and about 6 miles below the summit visitor center. There's a fair chance you'll see nene in the parking lot. If you're camping at Hosmer Grove, you can take the little-known, unexciting **Supply Trail** instead, joining the Halemau'u Trail at the crater rim after 2.5 miles.

EXPLORING THE CINDER DESERT

Almost all hiking trails lead to the belly of the beast. There's no way to see this amazing area without backtracking. Three major spur trails connect Sliding Sands Trail, from near Kapalaoa cabin, with the Halemau'u Trail between Paliku and Holua cabins. As the trails are not very long, if you're camping you may have time to do them all.

The spur trail furthest west takes in many of the crater's most kaleidoscopic cinder cones, and the viewing angle changes with every step. If you prefer stark, black and barren, both of the other spur trails take you through 'a'a (rough, jagged lava) and *pahoehoe* lava fields, with the one furthest east lying splattered with rust-red cinders.

All three trails end up on the north side of the cinder desert near **Kawilinau**, also known as the Bottomless Pit. Legends say the pit leads down to the sea, though the park service says it's just 65ft deep. Truth be told, there's not much to see, as you can't really get a good look down the narrow shaft. Don't miss the short loop trail to sit for a while in the saddle of **Pele's Paint Pot Lookout**, the crater's most jaw-dropping vantage point.

KAUPO TRAIL

From the Paliku campground, it's possible to continue another 8.5 miles down to Kaupo on the southern coast. The first 4 miles of the trail drop 2500ft in elevation before reaching the park boundary. It's a steep rocky trail through rough lava and brushland, with short switchbacks alternating with level stretches; it can be worth coming this far just for the coastal views.

The last 4.5 miles pass through Kaupo Ranch property on a rough jeep trail with no shade cover as it descends to the bottom of Kaupo Gap, exiting into a forest where feral pigs snuffle about. Here trail markings

MAUI

become vague, but once you reach the dirt road, it's another 1.5 miles to the end at the east side of the Kaupo General Store.

The 'village' of Kaupo (p365) is a long way from anywhere, with very little traffic. Still, what traffic there is – largely sightseers braving the circle-island road and locals in pickup trucks – moves slow enough along Kaupo's rough road to start conversation. If you have to walk the final stretch, it's 8 miles to the 'Ohe'o Gulch campground.

This is a strenuous hike, and because of the remoteness and the ankle-twisting conditions, it's not advisable to hike alone. According to legend, the demigod Maui used this route, hiking uphill as he made his way up into the volcano to harness the sun. Note that no camping is allowed on Kaupo Ranch's property, so most people spend the night at the Paliku campground and then get an early start.

Cycling & Mountain Biking

Each morning before dawn, groups of cyclists gather at the top of Haleakala for the thrill of coasting 38 miles down the mountain, with a 10,000ft drop in elevation.

Generally, it's an all-day affair (eight to 10 hours), starting with hotel pickup at around 2:30am, a van ride up the mountain for the sunrise, and about 3½ hours of biking back down. It's not a nonstop cruise, as cyclists must periodically pull over for cars following behind, and the primary exercise is squeezing the brakes – you'll need to pedal only about 400yd on the entire trip!

It's a competitive market, and the going rate is around $100, which includes bike, helmet, transportation and meals. Bikes are generally modified with special safety breaks, and each group is followed by an escort van. Pregnant women, children under 12 and those shorter than 5ft tall are usually not allowed to ride, but exceptions are not unknown. Keep in mind that the road down Haleakala is narrow and winding with lots of blind curves, and there are no bike lanes.

Cruiser Phil's (☎ 893-2332, 877-764-2453; www .cruiserphil.com), **Maui Downhill** (☎ 871-2155, 800-535-2453; www.mauidownhill.com), **Maui Mountain Cruisers** (☎ 871-6014, 800-232-6284; www.mauimountaincruisers .com) and **Mountain Riders** (☎ 242-9739, 800-706-7700; www.mountainriders.com) all offer the sunrise bike tour.

In addition to the guided tours, other companies will rent you a mountain bike with assorted gear, give you a van ride to Haleakala summit, and then leave you on your own to bike down at your own pace. Be careful on the road if you choose this option. Drivers are almost certain to notice a pack of two dozen yellow-rainsuit-clad bikers, but a single cyclist is less visible. The going rate is around $60.

Companies offering this 'unguided' option include **Haleakala Bike Co** (☎ 575-9575, 888-922-2453; www.bikemaui.com), **Upcountry Cycles** (☎ 573-2888, 800-373-1678; www.bikemauihawaii.com) and **Maui Sunriders** (☎ 579-8970, 866-500-2453; www.mauibikeride.com).

Horseback Riding

Pony Express (☎ 667-2200; www.ponyexpresstours.com; Haleakala Crater Rd; $155) is in a eucalyptus grove, 2.5 miles up Hwy 378 from Hwy 377. The most interesting of several trail rides offered is the ride down the Sliding Sands Trail, which starts at the summit of Haleakala. The narrated 7.6-mile ride takes about four hours and includes a picnic lunch on the crater floor. Reservations are required.

SLEEPING

Accommodations are kept primitive, but are still popular. Backcountry campsites have pit toilets and limited nonpotable water supplies that are shared with the crater cabins. All water needs to be filtered or chemically treated; conserve it, as water tanks occasionally run dry. Fires are allowed only in grills. Other campfires are prohibited, and you must take out all trash. No food, electricity or showers are available anywhere.

Remember that sleeping at an elevation of 7000ft is nothing like camping on the beach. Without a waterproof tent and a winter-rated sleeping bag, forget about it. In case of genuine emergencies, rangers can sometimes be found at Paliku or Holua ranger cabins – but don't count on it.

Camping

Hosmer Grove campground boasts a primo setting, in a small field adjacent to lofty trees and beside the trailhead to one of Maui's best birding trails. The campground (at 6800ft) tends to be a bit cloudy and damp but there's a covered picnic pavilion where you can seek shelter if the rains start. In addition to the picnic tables, campers will find grills, toilets and running water. Camping is free and permits are not required, though there's a three-day camping limit per month. It's busier in summer than in winter and is often full on holiday weekends. Hosmer Grove is just after the park entrance and offers the only drive-up camping in the mountainous section of Haleakala National Park (the other drive-up campground is in the Kipahulu section of the park; p362).

Two **backcountry campgrounds** lie inside Haleakala Crater. One is at Holua, 4 miles down the Halemau'u Trail at the base of steep cliffs, and the other is at Paliku, below a rain-forest ridge at the trail's end. Weather can be unpredictable at both. Holua is typically dry after sunrise, until clouds roll back in the late afternoon. Paliku is in a grassy meadow, with skies overhead alternating between stormy and breathtakingly sunny. Do not camp near the cabins.

Permits (free) are required for crater camping. They are issued at park headquarters on a first-come, first-served basis between 8am and 3pm on the day of the hike. Camping is limited to three nights in the crater each month, with no more than two consecutive nights at either campground. Permits can go quickly if large groups show up, a situation that is more likely to occur in summer. Group size is limited to 12 people.

Cabins

Three **rustic cabins** (up to 12 people for $75) lie along trails in the crater. The cabins – one each at Holua, Kapalaoa and Paliku – were built by the CCC in the 1930s, and each has a wood-burning stove, two propane burners, some cooking utensils, 12 bunks with sleeping pads (but no bedding), pit toilets and a limited supply of water and firewood.

Hiking distances to the cabins from the crater rim range from 4 miles to 10 miles. The driest conditions are at Kapalaoa, in the middle of the cinder desert off the Sliding Sands Trail. Those craving lush rain forest will find Paliku serene. Holua has unparalleled sunrise views. There's a three-day limit per month, with no more than two consecutive nights in any cabin. Each cabin is rented to only one group at a time.

The problem here is the demand, which is so high the park service holds a monthly lottery to award reservations! To enter, your reservation request must be received two months prior to the first day of the month of your proposed stay (eg requests for cabins on any date in July must arrive before May 1). Your chances increase if you list alternate dates within the same calendar month and choose weekdays rather than weekends.

Only written (no phone) reservation requests (Haleakala National Park, PO Box 369, Makawao, HI 96768, Attn: Cabins) are accepted for the lottery. Include your name, address, phone number, specific dates and cabins requested. Only winners are notified. Cancellations occur creating vacancies, sometimes at the last minute but occasionally a few weeks in advance as well. You can check for vacancies in person at park headquarters at any time, but calls (☎ 572-4400) regarding cancellations are accepted only between 1pm and 3pm, and you'll need to have a credit card handy to secure the cabin if there is a vacancy. On the plus side, if you get a vacancy anytime within three weeks of your camping date, the cabin fee drops to $60 a day.

GETTING THERE & AROUND

Haleakala Crater Rd (Hwy 378) twists for 11 miles from Hwy 377 near Kula up to the park entrance, then another 10 miles to Haleakala summit. It's a good paved road all the way, but it's steep and winding. You don't want to rush it, especially when it's dark or foggy. Watch out for cattle wandering freely across the road.

The drive to the summit takes about 1½ hours from Pa'ia or Kahului, two hours from Kihei and a bit longer from Lahaina. If you need gas, fill up the night before, as there are no services on Haleakala Crater Rd. Loosen your gas tank cap about a quarter-turn before starting your ascent to prevent vapor lock.

On your return from the summit, you'll see all of Maui unfolding below, with sugarcane and pineapple fields creating a patchwork of green on the valley floor. The highway snakes back and forth, and in some places as many as four or five switchbacks are in view all at once. Put your car in low gear to avoid burning out your brakes. Be careful of cyclists.

Note bicycles are allowed only on paved roads within the park, so as not to disturb the fragile ecosystem.

KAHO'OLAWE

The uninhabited island of Kaho'olawe, 7 miles off the southwest coast of Maui, looms on the horizon as a symbol of the separation of native Hawaiians from their land and a focal point in the Hawaiian-rights movement.

Kaho'olawe was used by the US military as a bombing target from WWII until 1990. Though the bombing has stopped, the island remains off-limits because of the stray ammunition that peppers Kaho'olawe and its surrounding waters.

Kaho'olawe is 11 miles long and 6 miles wide, with its highest point the 1477ft Luamakika. The island is dry and arid, and because of the red dust that hangs in the air, Kaho'olawe often appears to have a pink tinge when viewed from Maui.

PATHWAY TO TAHITI

Kaho'olawe has played an important role in Hawaiian history. The channel between Lana'i and Kaho'olawe, as well as the westernmost point of Kaho'olawe itself, is named Kealaikahiki, meaning 'pathway to Tahiti.' When early Polynesian voyagers made the journey between Hawai'i and Tahiti, they lined up their canoes at this departure point.

More than 500 archaeological sites have been identified. They include several heiau (an ancient stone temple) and ku'ula (fishing shrine) stones dedicated to the gods of fishers. Pu'umoiwi, a large cinder cone in the center of the island, contains one of Hawaii's largest ancient adze quarries.

PRISONERS & OPIUM

Since ancient times, Kaho'olawe had been under the rule of Maui. From 1830 to 1848, Kaulana Bay, on the island's northern side, served as a place of exile for Maui men accused of petty crimes. Kaho'olawe's secluded southwestern side was used for decades by smugglers importing Chinese opium. To avoid detection, they would unload their caches at Honokanai'a Bay (known as Smugglers Bay) on arrival from China and then return later in fishing boats to pick up the illicit goods.

INTO THE DUST BOWL

Kaho'olawe, now nearly barren, was once a lush, green and forested island.

The first attempt at ranching was made in 1858, when a Scotsman, RC Wyllie, leased the entire island from the territory of Hawaii, but the sheep he brought over were diseased and the venture failed. The sheep that did survive were left to roam freely, causing serious damage to native plants. Over the years, the territory granted leases to other ranchers. Cattle were first brought over around 1880, and sheep were tried again. Land mismanagement was the order of the day.

By the early 1900s feral goats, pigs and sheep had dug up, rooted out and chewed off so much of Kaho'olawe's vegetation that the island was largely a dust bowl. Angus MacPhee, a former manager of Maui's 'Ulupalakua Ranch, ran Kaho'olawe's most successful ranching operation, which lasted from 1918 to 1941. When MacPhee got his lease, Kaho'olawe looked like a wasteland. MacPhee rounded up 13,000 goats, which he sold on Maui, and built a fence across the width of the entire island to keep the remaining goats at one end. He then planted grasses and ground cover. Once the land was again green, MacPhee started raising cattle for the Honolulu market, and though it was not easy, MacPhee, unlike his predecessors, was able to make it profitable.

A BOMBING TARGET

In 1939 Kaho'olawe Ranch subleased part of the island to the US army for bombing practice and moved the cattle to Maui. Following the attack on Pearl Harbor in 1941, the US military took control over all of Kaho'olawe and began bombing the entire island. Ranch buildings and water cisterns were used as targets, reducing them to rubble.

Of all the fighting that took place during WWII, Kaho'olawe was the most bombed island in the Pacific. After the war, civilians were forbidden to return to Kaho'olawe; MacPhee was never compensated for his losses. In 1953 a presidential decree gave the US navy official jurisdiction over Kaho'olawe, with the stipulation that when Kaho'olawe was no longer 'needed,' the live ammunition would be removed and the island would be returned to Hawaiian control.

THE KAHO'OLAWE MOVEMENT

In the mid-1960s Hawaii politicians began petitioning the federal government to cease its military activities and return Kaho'olawe to the state of Hawaii. In 1976, in an attempt to attract greater attention to the bombings, small groups of native Hawaiians sailed out and occupied the island. Despite arrests, other occupations followed.

During one of the 1977 crossings, group members George Helm and Kimo Mitchell mysteriously disappeared in the waters off Kaho'olawe. Helm had been an inspirational Hawaiian-rights activist, and with his death the Protect Kaho'olawe 'Ohana movement sprang up. Helm's vision of turning Kaho'olawe into a sanctuary of Hawaiian culture became widespread among islanders.

In 1980, in a court-sanctioned decree, the navy reached an agreement with Protect Kaho'olawe 'Ohana that allowed the them regular access to the island. The decree restricted the navy from bombing archaeological sites. In 1981 Kaho'olawe was added to the National Register of Historic Places as a significant archaeological area. For nearly a decade, the island had the ironic distinction of being the only such historic place that was being used by its government as a bombing target.

In 1982 the 'Ohana began to go to Kaho'olawe to celebrate *makahiki*, the annual observance to honor Lono, god of agriculture and peace. But the military continued to bomb parts of the island. In what many Hawaiians saw as the crowning insult to their heritage, the US military offered Kaho'olawe as a bombing target to foreign nations during biennial Pacific Rim exercises.

In an unanticipated backlash against the military, the exercises brought recognition of what was happening to Kaho'olawe into a broader arena. An international movement against the bombing, led by environmentalist and union groups in New Zealand, Australia, Japan and the UK, resulted in those countries withdrawing from the Kaho'olawe exercises. The plan was scrapped.

In the late 1980s Hawaii's first native Hawaiian governor, John Waihee, and other state politicians became more outspoken in their demands that Kaho'olawe be returned to Hawaiians. In October 1990, as Hawaii's two US senators, Daniel Inouye and Daniel Akaka, were preparing a congressional bill to stop the bombing, President George Bush issued an order to halt military activities. The senators' bill, which became law the next month, required the island to be cleared of munitions and restored to its prewar condition.

THE NAVY SETS SAIL

In 1994, a Memorandum of Understanding between the state of Hawaii and the US navy established standards for a cleanup, which stated that 100% of surface munitions would be taken away and 30% of subsurface munitions would be cleared. However, there was a catch; the federal law that authorized the cleanup had a time limit of 10 years, regardless of the results.

After an expenditure of over $400 million, the cleanup finished in 2003, and the navy shipped off the island. The government estimated that only 77% of Kaho'olawe's land had been cleared of surface ordnance, and a mere 9% of the island cleared of bombs down to a depth of 4ft.

In 2004, jurisdiction over Kaho'olawe was finally transferred from the US navy back to the state of Hawaii. The state's **Kaho'olawe Island Reserve Commission** (www.kahoolawe.hawaii.gov) is in the process of developing a long-term plan, but in the meantime there's still much to be done.

LENDING A HAND

Today there's no public access to the island of Kaho'olawe unless you're a member or guest of **Protect Kaho'olawe 'Ohana** (PKO; www.kahoolawe.org), whose mission is to heal Kaho'olawe, pay respects to the spirits of the land and revitalize the island's cultural and natural resources. The PKO visits the island for a few days a month, usually around the time of the full moon, to clean up historic sites and work on revegetation projects. The group welcomes volunteers, for whom paying a $85 fee covers expenses, including the boat ride and food. You'll need to bring your own sleeping bag, tent and personal supplies. Log onto the website for full details and schedules.

Lana'i

Lana'i's promo dub, 'The Private Island,' is more than just hype geared to attract wealthy vacationers. Castle & Cooke owns 98% of the island. Just two decades ago, the company had Lana'i covered in pineapples, which at one point were so thick on the ground that they counted for 20% of the world's commercial production. But in the early 1990s the company reinvented itself (and Lana'i), ending its pineapple operations and throwing its resources into two luxury resorts.

The last of the pineapple fields have given way to golf greens and Lana'i has emerged as an exclusive vacation destination. Thanks in part to billionaire Bill Gates, who rented out both hotels in their entirety to host his wedding, Lana'i has become a trendy getaway destination for corporate CEOs. Beyond the resorts some things haven't altered all that much. The center of Lana'i remains Lana'i City – not a city at all, but merely a little town of tin-roofed houses that's home to almost all of the island's residents. Its pace is still relaxingly S-L-O-W.

Lana'i can be interesting to explore, but many of the sights are along rutted dirt roads that require a 4WD vehicle. Not surprisingly, visiting can be quite expensive. An easy way to get a little taste of the good life is to take the ferry over from Maui in the morning, snorkel at Hulopo'e Bay, treat yourself to lunch at the Manele Bay Hotel, then take the boat back in the afternoon.

HIGHLIGHTS

- Dive **Cathedrals** (p394) near Pu'u Pele rock
- Stroll **Shipwreck Beach** (p396)
- Savour venison for dinner at the Formal Dining Room at the **Lodge at Koele** (p392)
- Have a Mai tai on the lanai at **Manele Bay Hotel lounge** (p395)
- Relax under the shady pines at **Lana'i City Community Park** (p391)
- Experience **Manele Bay Hotel** (p395)
- Hit the **Munro Trail** (p397)
- Mountain bike to the **Garden of the Gods** (p397)
- Notch up a round of free golf with locals in **Lana'i City** (p391)
- Snorkel with spinner dolphins off **Hulopo'e Beach** (p394)

★ Shipwreck Beach

★ Garden of the Gods

Lodge at Koele ★

★ Munro Trail

★ Lana'i City

Manele Bay Hotel ★ ★ Hulopo'e Beach

★ Cathedrals (Hulopo'e Bay)

POPULATION: 3200	NICKNAME: THE PRIVATE ISLAND	AREA: 140 SQ MILES

Climate

Relative to the other islands (p521), Lana'i is rather dry, but even the island's drier areas can get soaked with heavy rainfall during winter storms. Lana'i City has a mild climate. Evenings can be brisk, with temperatures dipping to around 50°F in winter. Average temperatures range from 66°F in winter to 73°F in summer. Rainfall averages less than 40in annually in Lana'i City, and about 15in along the coast. When it's overcast in Lana'i City, chances are that Manele Bay will be sunny.

Activities

Lana'i has no national, state or county parks, but its finest beach, Hulopo'e Beach,

is run by the Lanai Company as a public park (for camping, see p395). Much of the island is undeveloped, however.

Lana'i's terrain is dominated by a ridge running from northwest to southeast, which reaches a height of 3370ft at Lana'ihale and offers good hiking opportunities.

Lana'i's top activity is golfing. Both of Lana'i's resorts have world-class 18-hole designer golf courses that have rated among the top 10 in the USA by *Golf Digest* magazine. Or go local-style at Hawaii's only free golf course (p391).

Snorkeling and swimming are fantastic at Hulopo'e Beach (p394), and if you're there in the morning you can often watch dolphins frolicking just offshore.

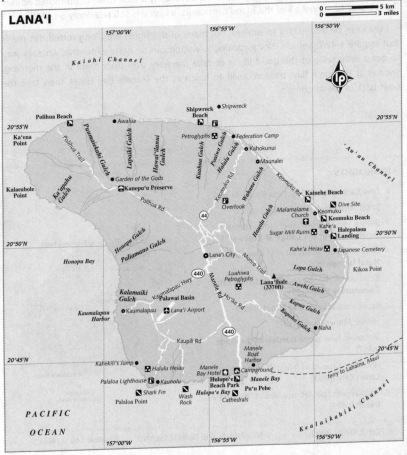

Mountain bike rentals are available at the Lodge at Koele (p391). The island offers plenty of dirt roads and trails, from beginner to advanced, but expect challenging hills as well as dusty and sometimes muddy conditions.

Almost all organized activities on the island are coordinated through the resorts. These include tennis, horseback riding and scuba diving.

Getting There & Away

You can get to Lana'i by air or boat.

AIR

There are no direct flights to Lana'i from the mainland; most people fly to Honolulu or Maui first. See p532 for informa-tion on trans-Pacific flights from the USA and abroad. Lana'i airport (LNY) is about 3.5 miles southwest of Lana'i City. **Island Air** (☎ 800-652-6541; www.islandair.com) provides the only scheduled air service to Lana'i. There are seven flights a day. All flights to Lana'i are from Honolulu. If you're coming from Maui, or any island other than O'ahu, you'll need to go via Honolulu. For more information on interisland flights, see p535.

BOAT

Expeditions (on Maui ☎ 661-3756, 800-695-2624; www.go-lanai.com; one-way fare adult/child $25/20) runs a passenger ferry five times daily between Maui and Lana'i. Not only is it much cheaper than flying, but if you take the boat in winter there's a fair chance of seeing whales along

---

CHANGING TIMES

Archaeological studies indicate Lana'i was never heavily settled. Since ancient times, it has been under the rule of its more dominant neighbor Maui. In 1778, when Big Island chief Kalaniopu'u was routed in a failed attempt to invade Maui, he took his revenge on tiny Lana'i and sent warriors under the command of Kamehameha the Great. Kamehameha's troops were brutal, killing everyone they found.

In 1823 a missionary named William Ellis became the first Westerner to step ashore. He guessed the island's population to be around 2000. Although the early missionaries did not spend a lot of time on Lana'i, they still had some influence. After they introduced the heretofore unknown concept of adultery to Hawai'i, Maui women accused of that criminal offense were banished in the 1830s to barren northwest Lana'i as punishment.

In the 1850s the Mormons moved in and set up a community at Palawai Basin, south of present-day Lana'i City. They intended to establish a 'City of Joseph,' but the community floundered until 1861 when a new charismatic elder, Walter Gibson, arrived. Mormons from around the islands poured in, as did money to buy Palawai Basin. At the height of it all, there was one Mormon for every Lana'ian.

Gibson, a shrewd businessman, handled the financial matters for the community and slyly made the land purchases in his own name, rather than in the church's. In 1864, after refusing to transfer the title of his Lana'i holdings to the mother church, he was excommunicated by Brigham Young. This suited Gibson just fine. He held onto the prime Lana'i real estate he had cornered, and Lana'i's Mormon congregation eventually left for La'ie on O'ahu.

Gibson left the land to his daughter, who in 1888 established the Maunalei Sugar Company. A landing at Kahalepalaoa on Lana'i's east coast was developed, a water-pumping station went up at nearby Keomuku, the area was planted with sugarcane and the whole shebang was connected by a little railroad. By 1901, however, the pumps were drawing saltwater, the whole enterprise folded and the land was sold off to cattle ranching interests. Ranching wasn't wildly successful either.

Enter Jim Dole, who in 1922 paid $1.1 million for Lana'i, a mere $12 an acre. Dole's Hawaiian Pineapple Company, which was already making big bucks on O'ahu, poured millions of dollars into Lana'i to turn it into a plantation island. It built Lana'i City, dredged Kaumalapau Bay to make it a deepwater harbor, put in roads and water systems, cleared the land and planted pineapples. By the end of the 1920s production was in full swing. Although it took a dive during the Great Depression, the pineapple industry bounced back and was the backbone of the economy until the 1980s.

LANA'I IN...

Three Days
Start your first day with a breakfast buffet at the **Manele Bay Hotel** (p395), then snorkel the crystal waters off Hulopo'e Beach (p394). In the afternoon, wander around the streets and shops of **Lana'i City** (p389) and watch the sun set behind the Norfolk pines. On the second day, play a round of golf at one of the world-class resort courses or at the local free course, depending on how deep you want to dig into your pocket. On day three, rent a mountain bike or 4WD and explore the **Garden of the Gods** (p397).

Five Days
Take the scenic **Munro Trail** (p397), then relax over dinner and a drink at **Henry Clay's Rotisserie** (p392). Stroll **Shipwreck Beach** (p396), enjoy a game of tennis or take a swim before dinner and follow that with a splurge at the candlelit **Formal Dining Room** (p393).

One Week
With a week, you've got time to play golf on both resort courses, scuba dive and thoroughly explore Lana'i's dusty back roads. Go out to **Polihua Beach** (p397), discover the ruins at **Kaunolu** (p398) and go **horseback riding** (p391) into the cool pastures above Lana'i City.

---

the way. The boat leaves Lahaina Harbor (p313) from the pier in front of the Pioneer Inn at 6:45am, 9:15am, 12:45pm, 3:15pm and 5:45pm, arriving at Manele Boat Harbor in Lana'i about an hour later. The return boat leaves Lana'i at 8am, 10:30am, 2pm, 4:30pm and 6:45pm. Reservations can be made by phone in advance. Tickets are sold at Expeditions' booth at the Lahaina pier between 9am and 4pm; outside those hours, or if boarding at Lana'i, buy your ticket right on the boat.

Getting Around

Lana'i has only one town, Lana'i City, in the center of the island. Outside Lana'i City there are only three paved roads: Keomuku Rd (Hwy 44), which extends northeast to Shipwreck Beach; Kaumalapau Hwy (Hwy 440), which extends west past the airport to Kaumalapau Harbor; and Manele Rd (also Hwy 440), which flows south to Manele and Hulopo'e Bays. If you really want to go far afield you'll need to hire a 4WD Jeep. Many of Lana'i's dirt roads were built to service the pineapple fields of yesteryear; their conditions vary from good to impassable, largely depending on the weather.

The University of Hawaii's *Moloka'i/Lana'i* map shows the topography of Lana'i as well as its geographical and archaeological sites. Nelles' *Maui, Moloka'i & Lana'i* map is less detailed, but it's user-friendly. A handy

free foldout map, *The Island of Lana'i* – which shows Lana'i City, the grounds of the two resorts and the island's main roads – can be picked up free at the hotels. Lana'i City Service (below) provides customers with its *Jeep Safari Drive Guide*, a basic sketch map with off-road directions to major sights.

TO/FROM THE AIRPORT
The resorts provide a shuttle van service (opposite) that meets guests at the airport and ferry dock. Nonguests can use the shuttle for a fee, or call a taxi (opposite) in advance of your arrival.

CAR
The only car rental company on the island, **Lana'i City Service** (Map p390; ☎ 565-7227, 800-533-7808; fax 565-7087; 1036 Lana'i Ave, Lana'i City; ☼ 7am-7pm), is an affiliate of Dollar (p537). Having a monopoly on Lana'i translates into steep prices. Unlike Dollar affiliates on other islands, this one requires a one-day deposit to make a booking and there are no discounts available. Compact cars rent for $60 a day, 4WD Jeep Wranglers for $130. The Jeeps are usually available on short notice, but the cars can be in short supply and sometimes need to be booked more than a week in advance. Customers arriving by air can use the red airport courtesy phone for free pickups.

While Lana'i has many dirt roads in fine condition, Lana'i City Service restricts all its

DRIVING TIMES		
From Lana'i City		
destination	miles	time
Garden of the Gods	6	25 min
Hulopo'e Beach	8	25 min
Kaumalapau Harbor	7	20 min
Keomuku	8	25 min
Lana'i Airport	3.5	15 min

cars to paved roads – only the 4WD Jeeps may be driven on dirt roads. Even then, the company decides on a day-to-day basis which dirt roads you can and can't drive on, depending on the weather and the current condition of the ruts and washouts. Keep in mind if you do go off the beaten path and get stuck, it can be a long walk back to town and you can expect to pay an exorbitant amount in towing and repair fees.

SHUTTLE
The resort shuttle van goes between the Manele Bay Hotel, Hotel Lanai and the Lodge at Koele, as well as to the airport and ferry dock. Shuttles run about every 30 minutes throughout the day in peak season, hourly in the slower months. The first usually heads out about 7am, the last around 11pm. Anyone can use the shuttle for a daily fee of $25 (for hotel guests, the cost is added to their hotel bill; nonguests pay at one of the hotels when the bus stops).

TAXI
Rabaca's Limousine Service (☎ 565-6670) charges $6 per person between the airport and Lana'i City and $10 per person between Manele Bay and town, with a two-person minimum. Advance reservations are a good idea.

LANA'I CITY

pop 3000
If you want to see what Hawaii used to be like, Lana'i City is it. This former plantation town, sitting on a cool central plateau beneath the slopes of Lana'ihale, glows with small-town charm. The whole town radiates around a central park, which is shaded by stately Norfolk pines. Step into any of the shops and restaurants surrounding the park and you'll find some of the friendliest people on the planet. Despite its outpost location, it's hard not to think of Lana'i City as a slice of the sort of rural America that has been virtually lost back on the mainland.

Very little in the town center looks different from the way it would have 50 years ago. The buildings date back to the plantation era. Even the two banks are in elementary wooden structures that are little more than shacks – there's not much need for security here. Yes, some of the old plantation buildings house new shops, but the facades are the same and the majority are still owned and operated by Lana'i families. The resorts simply haven't spilled into town.

This is a great place to unwind the clock. Here you'll wake to the sound of crowing roosters, and there is no rush-hour traffic.

HISTORY
Lana'i City was built in the 1920s as a plantation town for field workers and staff of the Hawaiian Pineapple Company. The first planned city in Hawaii, the town was built in the midst of the pineapple fields, with shops and a theater surrounding the central park, rows of plantation houses lined up beyond that and a processing plant on the edge of it all. Fortunately it was done with a little pizzazz. Dole hired New Zealander George Munro, a naturalist and former ranch manager, to oversee much of the work, and he planted the tall Norfolk and Cook Island pines that give the town its green character.

ORIENTATION
The town is laid out in a sensible grid pattern, and almost all shops and services border Lana'i City Community Park, which marks the center of town. Most activities take place at or near the Lodge at Koele, about a mile north of the park.

INFORMATION
There's no local daily newspaper or tourist office, but community notices, including rental housing ads and the movie theater schedule, are posted on bulletin boards outside the post office and grocery stores. You can sneak a virtual peek at www.visitlanai.net or www.lanaionline.com.

LANA'I

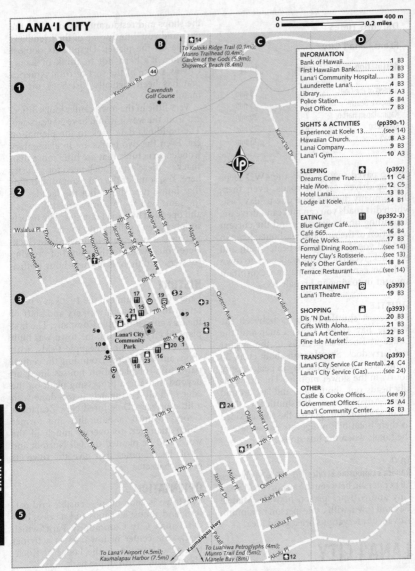

LANA'I CITY

INFORMATION	
Bank of Hawaii	1 B3
First Hawaiian Bank	2 B3
Lana'i Community Hospital	3 B3
Launderette Lana'i	4 B3
Library	5 A3
Police Station	6 B4
Post Office	7 B3

SIGHTS & ACTIVITIES	(pp390-1)
Experience at Koele 13	(see 14)
Hawaiian Church	8 A3
Lanai Company	9 B3
Lana'i Gym	10 A3

SLEEPING	(p392)
Dreams Come True	11 C4
Hale Moe	12 C5
Hotel Lanai	13 B3
Lodge at Koele	14 B1

EATING	(pp392-3)
Blue Ginger Café	15 B3
Café 565	16 B4
Coffee Works	17 B3
Formal Dining Room	(see 14)
Henry Clay's Rotisserie	(see 13)
Pele's Other Garden	18 B4
Terrace Restaurant	(see 14)

ENTERTAINMENT	(p393)
Lana'i Theatre	19 B3

SHOPPING	(p393)
Dis 'N Dat	20 B3
Gifts With Aloha	21 B3
Lana'i Art Center	22 B3
Pine Isle Market	23 B4

TRANSPORT	(p393)
Lana'i City Service (Car Rental)	24 C4
Lana'i City Service (Gas)	(see 24)

OTHER	
Castle & Cooke Offices	(see 9)
Government Offices	25 A4
Lana'i Community Center	26 B3

Bank of Hawaii (☎ 565-6426; 460 8th St) Has a 24-hour ATM.

First Hawaiian Bank (☎ 565-6969; 644 Lana'i Ave) Has a 24-hour ATM.

Lana'i Community Hospital (☎ 565-6411; 628 7th St) Offers 24-hour emergency medical services.

Launderette Lana'i (☎ 565-7628; cnr Fraser & Houston Sts; ⏰ 6am-9pm) Self-service coin laundry.

Library (☎ 565-7920; cnr Fraser Ave & 7th St; ⏰ 9am-4:30pm Mon-Wed & Fri, 2-8pm Thu)

Post Office (☎ 565-6517; 620 Jacaranda St; ⏰ 9am-4:30pm Mon-Fri, 10am-noon Sat)

SIGHTS

Lana'i City has no museums, though in some ways the whole town resembles one.

Stroll around **Lana'i City Community Park**, soak up the local color and talk story with the old-timers. Or swing by on Saturday morning when the park turns into a festive little **community market** where you can get Hawaiian and Filipino *grinds* (food) and buy handicrafts. Occasionally someone brings a guitar and does some singing. On Sunday mornings, swing by the **Hawaiian church** and you'll be serenaded with choir music.

ACTIVITIES

The public recreation complex in Lana'i City, which includes **Lana'i Gym** (☎ 565-3939; cnr Fraser Ave & 7th St; admission free; ☻ 8am-4:30pm Mon & Thu-Sat), has a 75ft-long pool, a basketball court and a couple of tennis courts. The **activities desk** (☎ 565-7300; ☻ 6:30am-6:30pm) at the Lodge at Koele also rents mountain bikes for $40 per day.

Golf

Experience at Koele (☎ 565-4653; guests/nonguests $185/230; ☻ 8am-6:30pm) has been rated by *Conde Nast* readers as the No 1 golf resort in the world. With a signature 17th hole dropping 250ft to a wooded ravine, it can prove as challenging as it is beautiful – it once took Jack Nicklaus eight shots just to get off the tee. Designed by Greg Norman, the course sprawls beneath the mountains and offers splendid views of the neighboring islands. This is as good as it gets.

Cavendish Golf Course, a local nine-hole course on the north side of Lana'i City, is a popular recreation spot for islanders. Anyone can play; simply bring your clubs and begin. There are no dress codes and no fees, though there is a donation box where visitors can make an offering.

Koloiki Ridge Trail

This 5-mile return hike begins at the back of the Lodge at Koele and leads up to one of the most scenic parts of the Munro Trail (p397). It takes about 2¾ hours return and offers bird's-eye views of remote valleys and Maui and Moloka'i.

Begin by taking the paved path to the golf clubhouse and from there walk uphill on the signposted path. Past the Norfolk pines you'll reach a hilltop bench with a plaque bearing the poem 'If' by Rudyard Kipling. Enjoy the view and then continue through the trees until you reach a chain-link fence.

LANA'I FOR KIDS

Activities for children are centered at resorts. A fun place to start is the **Stables at Ko'ele** (see above), which has pony rides, or join one of the hotel's family-oriented guided hikes. Still, the lion's share of activities geared for children are at the Lodge's sister hotel, the beachside **Manele Bay Hotel** (p395), which runs a *na keiki* (children's) camp. Other top spots for kids:

- **Hulopo'e Bay** (p393) Don a mask and see those cool fish
- **Hulopo'e Beach** (p394) Explore the tide pools
- **Manele Bay Hotel** (p395) Visit the koi ponds on its grounds

---

Go around the right side of the fence and continue up the hillside toward the powerlines. At the top of the pass, follow the trail down through the thicket of guava trees until you reach an abandoned dirt service road, which you'll turn left on. You'll soon intersect with the **Munro Trail** (p397); turn right on it and after a few minutes you'll pass Kukui Gulch, named for the candlenut trees that grow there. Continue along the trail until you reach a thicket of tall sisal plants; about 50yd after that bear right to reach Koloiki Ridge, where you'll be rewarded with panoramas.

Horseback Riding

The **Stables at Koele** (☎ 565-7300; group rides $65-140; ☻ 7am-5pm, group rides 9am & 1:30pm) offers a variety of trail rides, ranging from an 1½-hour ride that goes up the hill about the Lodge for sweeping views of Maui and Moloka'i, to a four-hour trail ride that includes a gourmet picnic lunch. Pony rides for children are available ($10 per 10 minutes).

FESTIVALS & EVENTS

The annual **Pineapple Festival** (www.visitlanai.net /lanaievents.html), held on the first Saturday in July, celebrates the island's pineapple past with local food, game booths and live music at Lana'i City Community Park. The first week of October sees the **Aloha Festivals**, when Lana'i gathers enough folks to have a little parade in the town center and there are various dances and cultural events.

LANA'I

TOP THREE SLEEPS

- **Lodge at Koele** (below)
- **Manele Bay Hotel** (p395)
- **Hotel Lanai** (below)

SLEEPING

Hotel Lanai (☎ 565-7211, 800-795-7211; www.hotel lanai.com; 828 Lana'i Ave; r $105-135, studio cottage $175) This quaint little lodge is the real deal. Built by Jim Dole in 1923 to house plantation guests, its engaging ambience is a throwback to an earlier era. All ten fully restored rooms have pine furnishings, pedestal sinks and patchwork quilts; the more expensive ones have front porches overlooking Lana'i City. Only drawback: the walls are thin, so request a room away from the restaurant. There's a one-bedroom cottage in the rear.

Hale Moe (☎ 565-9650; www.lanaibandb.com; 502 Akolu Place; r incl breakfast $80-90) Ocean-view lanai and big rooms with comfortable beds await guests at this contemporary home at the south side of town. The host is active in Lana'i's art community and can give you the lowdown on what's happening on the island. She can also arrange for guests to rent the neighbor's jeep for a mere $40 a day.

Dreams Come True (☎ 565-6961, 800-566-6961; www.dreamscometruelanai.com; 547 12th St; B&B r incl breakfast $100, vacation home per night $380) Period plantation house furnished with Asian antiques. Rooms have whirlpool baths and canopied beds. Guests share a common living room and a full kitchen. The owners can arrange vacation rentals of nearby homes.

THE AUTHOR'S CHOICE

Lodge at Koele (☎ 565-7300, 800-321-4666; www.islandoflanai.com; r/ste from $400/730) This pampering resort, on a rise above town, affects the aristocratic demeanor of an overgrown plantation estate, complete with afternoon tea, lawn bowling and croquet. The 'great hall' lobby brims with an eclectic collection of antiques, artwork and upholstered furnishings, and also boasts Hawaii's two largest stone fireplaces. The guest rooms have a casual elegance with hand-crafted four-poster beds, private lanai and marble bathrooms. Add impeccable service and there's little wonder why the hotel is one of the highest-rated in Hawaii.

EATING
Budget

Coffee Works (☎ 565-6962; 604 Ilima Ave; $1.50-4; 5am-4pm Mon-Fri, 10am-6pm Sat & Sun) For Lana'i's best cup of coffee head to this low-key, local hangout. They've got excellent croissants, caffe lattes and carrot cake.

Café 565 (☎ 565-6622, 408 8th St; breakfast & lunch $6; 10am-3pm & 5-8pm Mon-Fri) A Philly cheese steak on Lana'i? Why not! This place specializes in sub sandwiches loaded with fresh tomatoes and fried onions. Sit outside at shaded picnic tables.

TOP THREE EATS

- **Henry Clay's Rotisserie** (below)
- **Formal Dining Room** (opposite)
- **Blue Ginger Café** (below)

Mid-Range

Blue Ginger Café (☎ 565-6363; 409 7th St; breakfast & lunch $5-8, dinner $10-14; 6am-8pm, to 9pm Fri & Sat) This unpretentious little bakery-café with cement floors and plastic chairs serves up three square meals a day. The food is good and the folks are as friendly as any you'll ever come across. At dinner, don't miss the fresh mahimahi (a white-fleshed fish) smothered in capers and onions.

Pele's Other Garden (☎ 565-9628; cnr 8th St & Houston St; lunch $5-8, dinner $10-19; 10am-2:30pm Mon-Fri & 5-8pm Mon-Sat) An aromatic combination of an Italian deli, pizzeria and bistro. There are even café tables on the front porch where you can sit and watch the Lana'i City traffic trickle by. At night, tablecloths, low lights and jazz set the mood.

Terrace Restaurant (☎ 565-7300; Lodge at Koele; breakfast & lunch $10-20; 7am-9:30pm) The Lodge's lobby-side restaurant overlooks the hotel's gardens. Breakfast menu items include blue crab cakes and smoked pâté on a bagel. There are salads and sandwiches at lunchtime. Head elsewhere for dinner, though.

Top End

Henry Clay's Rotisserie (☎ 565-4700; Hotel Lanai, mains $19-29; dinner) The island's most bustling dinner spot combines fresh ingredients

THE AUTHOR'S CHOICE

Formal Dining Room (☎ 565-7300; Lodge at Koele; mains $43-52; ⏱ 6:30-9:30pm) This is the place for a splurge. Lana'i's top-rated restaurant serves a mouth-watering rack of lamb with cherry sauce, as well as local fish and venison from Lana'i's Axis deer. Prices are steep, but the food and service live up to the bill and the setting with a crackling fireplace has few rivals. As the name implies, men are required to wear a jacket – but one can be borrowed from the front desk.

with a Cajun flair. The namesake chef shows off his New Orleans roots with memorable dishes such as duck confit with garlic cassoulet or Creole eggplant over angel-hair pasta. The charming dining room has a fireplace, high ceilings and hardwood floors.

ENTERTAINMENT

People go to bed early in Lana'i, so there's no riveting nightlife, but **Lodge at Koele** (☎ 565-7300, 800-321-4666; www.islandoflanai.com) has mellow Hawaiian music in its 'great hall' lobby every evening from 7pm until 10pm. The bar at **Henry Clay's Rotisserie** (☎ 565-4700; Hotel Lanai), which usually stays open until around 10pm, is the place to go for a drink. **Lana'i Theatre** (☎ 565-7500; 456 7th St), the island's cozy little cinema, shows first-run feature films every night but Thursday.

SHOPPING

Gifts with Aloha (☎ 565-6589; 363 7th St; ⏱ 9:30am-6pm Mon-Sat) A good place for classy koa-bead jewelry, aloha shirts, tropical-print dresses and Hawaiian music CDs.

Dis 'N Dat (☎ 565-9170; 418 8th St; ⏱ 10am-5:30pm Mon-Sat) A fun shack with an incredibly eclectic collection from little Buddhas to wind chimes and antique jewelry.

Lana'i Art Center (☎ 565-7503; 339 7th St; ⏱ noon-4pm Mon-Sat) Run by volunteers, this place sells locally made arts and crafts.

Pine Isle Market (☎ 565-6488; 356 8th St; ⏱ 8am-7pm Mon-Sat) Pick up groceries and sundry items at this general store.

TOP THREE ENTERTAINMENT SPOTS

- **Lodge at Koele** (above) Hawaiian music in the 'great hall'
- **Hale Ahe Ahe** (p395) A drink at the Manele Bay Hotel
- **Lana'i Theatre** (above) A bag of popcorn and a movie

GETTING THERE & AROUND

The resort shuttle (p389) stops at the Hotel Lanai and the Lodge at Koele. Lana'i's only car rental office (p388) is in town. The **activities desk** (☎ 565-7300; ⏱ 6:30am-6:30pm) at the Lodge at Koele rents mountain bikes for $40 per day.

MANELE & HULOPO'E BAYS

The center of all of Lana'i's water activities lies 8 miles south of Lana'i City at Hulopo'e Beach and Manele Bay. Manele Harbor is a scenic crescent-shaped harbor backed by sheer cliffs. Its protected position not only provides a popular sailboat anchorage, but also makes Lana'i one of the easier islands to sail to from Honolulu (although 'easy' is a relative term – the waters can be quite rough). Overland it's a cinch to get there: simply take Manele Rd (Hwy 440), which terminates right at the beach. If you're coming in from Maui, this is where the ferry arrives. From the bay it's just a ten-minute walk to Hulopo'e Beach.

SIGHTS & ACTIVITIES

Manele and Hulopo'e Bays are part of a marine life conservation district, which prohibits the removal of coral and rocks and restricts many fishing activities. Water activities can be dangerous during *kona* (leeward) storms, when winds produce strong currents and swells.

Manele Harbor

In the early 20th century, cattle were herded down to Manele Bay for shipment to Honolulu, and you can still see the remains of a cattle chute if you walk around the point at the end of the parking lot. Stone ruins from a fishing village and concrete slabs from the days of cattle ranching are up on the hill above the parking lot, though the ruins are largely overgrown with thorny kiawe.

Off the parking lot are rest rooms, showers, drinking water, picnic tables and a little harbormaster's office. Coral is abundant near the cliff sides, where the bottom quickly slopes off to about 40ft. Beyond the bay's western edge, near Pu'u Pehe rock, is **Cathedrals**, the island's most spectacular dive site with splendid grottoes.

Hulopo'e Beach

Lana'i's only easy-to-access beach is a beauty. Everybody loves it – locals taking the *na keiki* (children) for a swim, tourists on daytrips from Maui, and the spinner dolphins who frequent the bay during the early morning hours.

This gently curving white-sand beach is long, broad and protected by a rocky point to the south. On the north side of the bay, the Manele Bay Hotel sits on a low seaside terrace. Even with the hotel, this is a pretty quiet beach. Generally, the most action occurs when the tour boats from Maui pull in.

For some of Lana'i's best **snorkeling**, head to the left side of the bay, where there's an abundance of coral and reef fish. Also in that direction, just beyond the sandy beach, you'll find a low lava shelf with tide pools to explore. Here, too, you'll find a protected shoreline splash pool ideal for children, with cement steps leading down to it. It looks as if all the kids on Lana'i rushed down to scrawl their names in the cement when it was poured in 1951.

The beach park has solar-heated outdoor showers, rest rooms, water fountains, picnic tables, pay phones and campsites (opposite).

Pu'u Pehe

From Hulopo'e Beach, a short path leads south to the end of the point that separates Hulopo'e and Manele Bays. The area has fascinating geological formations. The point is actually a volcanic cinder cone that's sharply eroded on its seaward edge. The lava has rich rust-red colors with swirls of gray and black, and its texture is bubbly and brittle – so brittle that huge chunks of the point have broken off and fallen onto the coastal shelf below. You'll also see a small sea arch just beneath the point.

Pu'u Pehe is the name of the cove to the left of the point as well as the rocky islet just offshore. This islet, also called Sweetheart's Rock, has a tomb-like formation on top that figures into Hawaiian legend.

It is said that an island girl named Pehe was so beautiful that her lover decided to make their home in a secluded coastal cave, lest any other young men in the village set eyes on her. One day when he was up in the mountains fetching water, a storm suddenly blew in and by the time he rushed back down, powerful waves had swept into the cave, drowning Pehe. The lover carried Pehe's body to the top of Pu'u Pehe, where he erected a tomb and laid her to rest within. Immersed in grief, he then jumped into the surging waters below and was dashed back onto the rock, joining his lover in death.

Other Activities

The **Challenge at Manele** (☎ 565-2222; guests/non-guests $185/230; ⏰ 7:10am-6:30pm), designed by Jack Nicklaus, offers spectacular hole plays along seaside cliffs and high ratings from golf enthusiasts.

DETOUR: LUAHIWA PETROGLYPHS

Lana'i's highest concentration of ancient petroglyphs are carved into three dozen boulders spread over three dusty acres on a remote slope overlooking the Palawai Basin.

To get to this seldom-visited site, head south from Lana'i City along Manele Rd. Midway between the 7- and 8-mile markers, turn left onto the wide dirt road that comes up immediately after a gray roadside shed. There's also a cluster of six Norfolk pines at the turn. You're now on Ho'ike Rd. Head for the water tower on the ridge, taking a sharp left after 1 mile. Stay on this road for half a mile and then take the jog to the right. About a third of a mile down this road, you'll come to a large cluster of boulders on the right. Park off to the side and walk up to the boulders.

Many of the rock carvings are quite weathered, but you can still make out linear and triangular human figures, dogs and a canoe or two. Other than gusts of wind, the place is eerily still and quiet. You can almost feel the presence of the ancients here – honor their spirits and don't touch the carvings, which are very fragile.

SPIRITS IN THE NIGHT

According to legend, Lana'i was a land of *akua* (spirits), rumored to be flesh-eaters, and they alone roamed the island until the 15th century. It was at this time that Kaululaʻau, the young prince of Maui, lived in what is today the town of Lahaina. He was a mischievous child. After he tore out the breadfruit trees that his father Kaʻakaleneo had just planted, the elders decided to banish him to uninhabited Lana'i, an almost certain death.

Not one to be easily intimidated, Kaululaʻau learned to trick the evil spirits of Lana'i. To avoid being ambushed at night, he convinced the *akua* that he slept in the surf, though when darkness fell he slipped off to the shelter of a cave. Night after night, the *akua* returned to the beach and rushed out to look for the prince in the waves. The longer they searched, the more exhausted they got, until finally the pounding surf overcame them. Kaululaʻau continued his pranks until all 400 of Lana'i's *akua* had either perished or fled to Kaho'olawe.

Kaululaʻau's family had given him up for dead when Mauians noticed a light from a fire across the 'Au'au Channel, which separates Maui and Lana'i. When they went over to investigate, they found Kaululaʻau alive and well, and the island devoid of spirits. Kaululaʻau was brought back to Maui a hero.

Need some free time to tee off? **Pilialoha Keiki Camp** (☎ 565-2398; Manele Bay Hotel; per day $60; ☯ 9am-3pm) runs a drop-off day program for kids aged 5 to 12, with crafts, lunch and outdoor activities around the bay.

SLEEPING

Manele Bay Hotel (☎ 565-7700, 800-321-4666; www.islandoflanai.com; r $400-730, ste from $1200) This place is pure luxury. Perched above the island's finest beach, its tropical lobbies are adorned with artwork, antiques and Italian marble floors. Many rooms overlook sculptured gardens and koi ponds. Top-rated golf, snorkeling, swimming (as well as a pampering spa) are just some of the many activities guests have to choose from. Ask about golf packages and fifth-night-free discounts.

Camping is allowed at Hulopoʻe Beach. Pick up permits from the **Lanai Company** (☎ 565-2970; registration fee $5, campsite per person $5) inside the Castle & Cooke office in Lana'i City. Sometimes you can get permits without advance reservations if the campground's not full – but keep in mind that it's commonly booked up weeks in advance, especially during summer and on weekends throughout the year. The maximum stay is three nights.

EATING

The **Manele Bay Hotel** (☎ 565-7700) is the only dining option outside Lana'i City.

Hulopoʻe Court (Manele Bay Hotel; continental/full breakfast buffet $16/24; ☯ 7-11am) An unbeatable way to start the day is with a scrumptious buffet at this open-air restaurant. You can also order á la carte, but expect to run up a similar tab. The grand setting includes high ceilings with showy chandeliers, ornate Chinese vases and a fine view of the ocean.

Manele Clubhouse (Challenge at Manele golf course; lunch $9-16, dinner $20-30; ☯ 10am-3:30pm daily, 5:30-9pm Thu-Mon) Excellent sandwiches and salads and a bay view from across the greens make this a top lunch choice. Try the pad Thai or the grilled mahimahi sandwich.

Ihilani Restaurant (Manele Bay Hotel; appetizers $20-25, mains $25-45; ☯ 6-9:30pm Tue-Sat) The hotel's elegant French-Mediterranean restaurant serves up such temptations as honey-glazed duck and seared Hawaiian snapper with baby artichokes. While it's a fine-dining venue, it's not stuffy – jackets are optional and the place is open-air with an ocean view.

ENTERTAINMENT

The Manele Bay Hotel lounge, **Hale Ahe Ahe** (☯ 5pm-midnight), has live music in the evenings from Tuesday to Saturday. Sip cocktails in the lounge or on the lanai.

KEOMUKU RD

From Lana'i City, Keomuku Rd (Hwy 44) heads north past the Lodge at Koele, quickly rising into the cool upland hills, where fog and cloud cover drift above grassy pastures. Along the way are impromptu overlooks, offering straight-on vistas of the undeveloped southeast shore of Moloka'i and its tiny islet

LANA'I

Mokuho'oniki, in great contrast to Maui's Ka'anapali high-rises off to your right.

As the road gently slopes down to the coast, the scenery is punctuated by interesting rock formations sitting atop the eroded red earth, similar to those found at Garden of the Gods in northwest Lana'i. Further along, a shipwreck comes into view. After 8 miles, the paved road ends near the coast. To the left, a dirt road leads to Shipwreck Beach, while turning right onto Keomuku Rd takes you to Keomuku Beach or, for the truly intrepid, all the way to Naha.

SHIPWRECK BEACH

Shipwreck Beach covers 9 miles of Lana'i's northeast shore, starting from Kahokunui at the end of Hwy 44 and stretching toward Polihua Beach on the northwest shore. True to its name, there are a couple of shipwrecks here, as well as a coastline that's fun for beachcombing. Lots of driftwood washes up on this windswept beach. Some of the pieces are identifiable as the sun-bleached timbers of shipwrecks – hulls, side planks, perhaps even a gangplank if your imagination is active. A low rock shelf lines much of the shore, so the shallow, murky waters are not great for swimming.

A dirt road runs left from the highway past some old wooden beach shacks called Federation Camp, which are used by fisherfolk. Park here before the sand gets too deep and then continue along the beach.

It's likely to be just you and the driftwood as you walk along, the sand gradually changing colors. In some places, it's a colorful, chunky mixture of rounded shells and bits of rock that look like some sort of beach confetti. Up on the slopes, some of the beach *pohuehue* (morning glory) is entwined with a plant that looks something like yellow-orange fishing line. This is Lana'i's official flower, a leafless parasitic vine called *kauna'oa*.

After walking north for about 10 minutes, you'll reach the site of a former lighthouse on a lava-rock point, though only the square cement foundation remains. From here you'll get a good view of a rusting **WWII liberty ship** (cargo ship) that washed up on the reef.

From the lighthouse foundation, white trail markings lead directly inland about 100yd to a cluster of fragile **petroglyphs**. The simple figures are etched on large boulders on the right side of the path. Keep your eyes open here for wild animals – sightings of mouflon sheep on the inland hills are not uncommon. Males have curled-back horns, and dominant ones travel with a harem.

It's possible to walk another 6 miles all the way to Awalua, but there's not much else to see besides another shipwreck. The hike is windy, hot and dry, although the further down the beach you go, the prettier it gets.

KEOMUKU TO NAHA

Keomuku Beach, a barren stretch of shore that runs from Kahokunui south to Halepalaoa Landing, is best suited for those scratching for something different to do. There's not really much to see other than a few marginal historical sites, scattered groves of coconuts and lots of kiawe.

Keomuku Rd, the 4WD-only dirt road that heads south from the end of Hwy 44, is likely to be either dusty or muddy, but if you catch it after it's been graded, it's not bad. Going the full 12 miles down to Naha, at the end of the road, can take as long as two hours one way when the road is rough; half of that when conditions are better.

Less than a mile down the road is **Maunalei**. An ancient heiau (stone temple) once sat there until the ill-fated Maunalei Sugar Company took it apart and used its stones to build a cattle fence. Some islanders believed it was the temple desecration that caused the company's wells to turn salty and kill the sugarcane, dooming the fledgling business.

Another 4 miles along is **Keomuku**, the center of the short-lived sugarcane plantation. There's little left to see other than the reconstructed **Ka Lanakila o Ka Malamalama Church**, originally built in 1903. The ruins of a couple of fishponds lie along the coast, but they're not easily visible.

Another heiau at **Kahe'a**, 1.5 miles south of Keomuku, was also dismantled by Maunalei Sugar Company, this time to build a

---

LANA'I'S BEST BEACHES

- **Hulopo'e Beach** (p394) for swimming and snorkeling
- **Manele Bay** (p393) for diving
- **Shipwreck Beach** (above) for beachcombing

railroad to transport the sugar to **Halepalaoa Landing**, south of Kahe'a. Kahe'a, meaning 'red stains,' was a *luakini*, where human sacrifices were made. From here the road to **Naha** gets rougher and doesn't offer much for the effort, but should you want to continue, it's about 4 miles further.

ROAD TO GARDEN OF THE GODS

The dirt road into northwest Lana'i starts north of Lana'i City, just past the Lodge at Koele, reached by turning left between the tennis courts and stables, then following the signs through former pineapple fields. The section of road leading straight through Kanepu'u Preserve up to the Garden of the Gods is a fairly good, albeit dusty, route that usually takes about 20 minutes from town. To travel onward to Polihua Beach is another matter, however; the road down to the beach is rocky, narrow and is suitable only for a 4WD, and even at that it's sometimes impassable. Depending on when the road was last graded, the trip could take anywhere from 20 minutes to an hour.

KANEPU'U PRESERVE

About 5 miles northwest of Lana'i City, this diverse native dryland forest is the last of its kind in all of Hawaii. Although Castle & Cooke retains title to the land, it has granted the Nature Conservancy an easement to the 590-acre forest in perpetuity. It's home to 49 species of native plants, including the endangered *'iliahi* (Hawaiian sandalwood) and *nau*, a fragrant Hawaiian gardenia. You'll glimpse many of them on the self-guided interpretive trail that takes just 10 minutes.

Native dryland forests once covered 80% of Lana'i and were also common on the leeward slopes of other Hawaiian islands, but feral goats and cattle made a feast of the foliage. Credit for saving this ecosystem goes to ranch manager George Munro, who fenced hoofed animals out in the 1920s.

GARDEN OF THE GODS

There's no garden at the Garden of the Gods, but rather a dry and barren landscape of strange wind-sculpted rocks in rich shades of ocher, pink and sienna. The colors change with the light, pastel in the early morning and late afternoon. How godly the garden appears depends on who's looking. Some people just see rocks, while others find the formations hauntingly beautiful.

POLIHUA BEACH

On the northwestern tip of the island, Polihua is a broad, 1.5-mile-long white-sand beach. Although it's gorgeous, strong winds kicking up the sand often make it uncomfortable, and water conditions are treacherous year-round.

Polihua means 'eggs in the bosom' and refers to the green sea turtles that used to nest here en masse. After a long hiatus, the now-endangered turtles are making a comeback.

MUNRO TRAIL

The Munro Trail is an exhilarating 8.5-mile adventure that can be hiked, mountain biked or negotiated in a 4WD vehicle. Those making the journey under their own steam should be prepared for steep grades and allow all day. If you're driving and the dirt road has been graded recently, give yourself two to three hours. However, be aware that the road can become very muddy (particularly in winter and after heavy rainstorms) and Jeeps often get stuck. It's best to consider this as a fair-weather outing only. Drivers also need to watch out for sheer drop-offs.

The trail is named after George Munro, who planted the trees both here and elsewhere around Lana'i in order to provide an island watershed. He selected species that draw moisture from the clouds and fog, both of which are fairly common in the high country.

LANA'I

To start the trail, head north on Hwy 44, the road to Shipwreck Beach. About a mile past the Lodge at Koele, turn right onto a paved road lined with Norfolk pines, which ends in half a mile at a cemetery. The Munro Trail starts at the left of the cemetery. It passes through sections planted with eucalyptus and climbs along the ridge, where the path is draped with ferns and studded with Norfolk pines.

Before the Munro Trail was upgraded to a dirt road, it was a footpath. It's along this trail that islanders tried to hide from Kamehameha the Great when he went on a rampage in 1778. Ho'okio Battleground, where Lana'ians made their last stand, is just above Ho'okio Gulch, about 2.5 miles from the start of the trail.

The trail looks down upon a series of deep ravines that cut across the eastern flank of the mountain, and it passes Lana'ihale, which at 3370ft is the highest point on Lana'i. On a clear day, you can see all of the inhabited Hawaiian Islands except Kaua'i and Ni'ihau from various points along the route. Do not stray off the main trail as it descends for 6 miles onto the central plateau. Keep the hills to your left and turn right at the big fork in the road. Once you hit the cattle grate, pavement is not far away. The trail ends back on Manele Rd (Hwy 440) between Lana'i City and Manele Bay.

KAUMALAPAU HWY

KAUMALAPAU HARBOR

Lana'i's commercial harbor is approximately 7 miles west of Lana'i City at the end of Kaumalapau Hwy (Hwy 440), which heads west out of town past the airport. Kaumalapau Harbor was built for shipping pineapples, and now is used by cargo boats bringing supplies to the island. You can often find people fishing from the boulder jetty for *awa* (milkfish), a tasty fish that's a common catch in the bay. Scuba divers sometimes use the bay as well – the deep waters at Kaumalapau are extremely clear. As along most of the southwest coast, Kaumalapau has sheer coastal cliffs.

KAUNOLU

The site of an early Hawaiian fishing village abandoned in the mid-19th century, Kaunolu boasts the greatest concentration of ruins on Lana'i. It was a vacation spot of Kamehameha the Great, who came here to fish the prolific waters of Kaunolu Bay.

Kaunolu Gulch separates the two sides of the bay. Most of the house foundations sit on the eastern side. **Halulu Heiau**, on the western side, once dominated the whole scene. The temple included a *pu'uhonua* (place of refuge), where *kapu* (taboo) breakers could be absolved from their death sentences. There are petroglyphs, including some on the southern side of the heiau. However, most of the sites are too overgrown with kiawe to be recognizable.

Beyond the heiau ruins, the Palikaholo sea cliffs rise more than 1000ft. Northwest of the heiau, there's a high natural stone wall along the perimeter of the cliff. Look for a break in the wall at the cliff's edge, where there's a sheer 90ft drop. This is **Kahekili's Jump**, named after a high-ranking Hawaiian chief. There's a ledge below it that makes diving into the ocean here a bit death-defying. Apparently, Kamehameha used to amuse himself by making upstart warriors leap from this cliff. More recently, it has been the site of the world-class Red Bull cliff-diving championships.

To get here, follow the Kaumalapau Hwy (Hwy 440) past the airport, turning left at your first opportunity onto a pot-holed dirt road that circles around the south side of the airport. The turnoff to Kaunolu is marked by a painted water pipe; turn right onto this dirt road, which leads south in the direction of the Palaloa lighthouse. Unless the road has gotten long-overdue attention, expect ruts deep enough to swallow a jeep, but you may be able to make it part of the way and walk the last mile or so.

Moloka'i

MOLOKA'I

Kaua'i may be the oldest of the main Hawaiian islands, but Moloka'i is the most mysterious. According to the ancient chants, Moloka'i was a child of Hina, goddess of the moon and mother to Maui – a powerful little *keiki* (child) in other words – and you'll feel an enigmatic transcendence permeating life here.

Commonly called 'the most-Hawaiian island,' because almost half of its population claims native Hawaiian ancestry, it might also be called 'the most-religious island,' for there are churches, believers and gospel *everywhere*. This is most-clearly felt in tourism, as the locals here are actively anti-development, but welcoming to individuals, especially those showing genuine *aloha 'aina* (love of the land).

Moloka'i is only sparsely populated, which fosters a laid-back lifestyle intrinsically connected to the land – fishing, hunting, ranching and agriculture are still major occupations in Hawaii's last rural stronghold. Traditionally the island was also a place of refuge for Hawaiians who broke *kapu* (taboos), or were somehow outside the mainstream, and Moloka'i has a long tradition of transvestitism that continues today.

If a stroll along Hawaii's longest beach, or watching the sunrise over distant Haleakala on Maui, is just your speed, then this is the place. Only here can you hike down a cliffside trail to an historic leprosy settlement, and only here can you drive over the entire island without hitting a single stoplight. Welcome to Moloka'i – the island preserving the past for the future to envy.

HIGHLIGHTS

- Jump gigantic boulders at **Make Horse Beach** (p427)
- Swing at **Dixie Maru Beach** (p428)
- Sate the sweet tooth at **Kanemitsu Bakery** (p409)
- Sink some sunset cocktails at **Hotel Moloka'i's** (p408) oceanfront bar
- Explore the **Moa'ula Falls** (p415) in Halawa Valley
- Rent a 'tentalow' at private **Kaupoa Beach Village** (p426)
- Hike in **Kamakou Preserve** (p416)
- Post-a-Nut from **Ho'olehua** (p418) with Auntie Peggy
- Get set for an historical hike down to **Kalaupapa Peninsula** (p421)
- Do some summer snorkeling at **Twenty-Mile Beach** (p402)

Make Horse Beach ★
Dixie Maru Beach ★
Kaupoa Beach Village ★
Kalaupapa Peninsula ★
Ho'olehua ★
Kanemitsu Bakery ★
Hotel Moloka'i ★
Kamakou Preserve ★
Moa'ula Falls ★
Twenty-Mile Beach ★

MOLOKA'I

| POPULATION: 7404 | NICKNAME: THE FRIENDLY ISLE | AREA: 260 SQ MILES |

Climate

At Kaunakakai, the average daily temperature is 70°F in winter, and 78°F in summer. The average annual rainfall is 14 inches. Still, these statistics say nothing of Moloka'i's microclimates, which include arid, rolling ranchland in the west; rugged and dense rainforest rising to mountains around Kamakou in the middle; and the lush, rainy north and east coasts.

For the National Weather Service's recorded weather and marine forecasts, call ☎ 552-2477.

State & County Parks

Everyone who comes to Moloka'i visits – or should visit – the leprosy settlement on the Kalaupapa Peninsula, within Kalaupapa National Historical Park (p421). Adjacent to this historic site on the peninsula's 'topside' is Pala'au State Park (p420), Moloka'i's only state park.

Moloka'i counts One Ali'i Beach Park (p407) and Papohaku Beach Park (p429) among its few county parks.

CAMPING

Camping is allowed at isolated, soggy Pala'au State Park near the Kalaupapa trailhead and Waikolu Lookout (p416) a remote and primitive site just outside Kamakou Preserve. Permits ($5, five-day maximum stay) are technically required. Permits may be obtained from the **state-park caretaker** (☎ 567-6923), whose home is immediately north of the mule stables on the road to Pala'au State Park. Division of State Parks offices on other islands issue advance permits.

One Ali'i and Papohaku Beach Parks are the only county parks where you can camp. The latter is Moloka'i's number-one place, in terms of space, setup and scenery, for camping. The westerly stretch of Papohaku Beach is particularly attractive, albeit windy. The less-appealing, side-of-the-road One Ali'i Beach Park is closer to Kaunakakai, and handy for early-morning ferry departures.

Required permits (adult/child $3/50¢) for these county parks are issued by the **Department of Parks & Recreation** (Map p407; ☎ 553-3204; Mitchell Pauole Center, Ainoa St; ⏰ 8am-4pm Mon-Fri) in Kaunakakai. Permits are limited to three consecutive days; if you want to camp longer, you should return to the county-parks office every three days for a new permit.

You can also camp at private Waialua Pavilion & Campground (p413), in East Moloka'i, and beside the Kapuaiwa Coconut Grove (p407) in Kaunakakai. The latter books up far in advance, so contact **Hawaiian Homelands** (☎ 560-6104; PO Box 2009, Kaunakakai, HI 96748; permits $20) as soon as is practical to

---

MOLOKA'I IN...

Three Days

Hop on the ferry from Maui, cruising into town to stock up on cocktail-hour fixings for sunset on your lanai. Chill heavily, adjusting to Moloka'i time. Follow up with a morning snorkel and swim at **Twenty-Mile Beach** (p413), via a road trip into **Halawa Valley** (p415). Catch the sunset at **Kaunakakai Wharf** (p407). On your last day, **Kalaupapa Peninsula** (p421) awaits.

Five Days

Follow the three-day itinerary, perhaps hiking to **Moa'ula Falls** (p415) while in Halawa Valley. On day four, pamper yourself with brunch at **Kaupoa Beach** (p426), if it's Sunday, or breakfast at **Hula Shores** (p410), if it's not. Explore the **west-end beaches** (p427), catching the 'green flash' at sunset if you're lucky. En route be sure to Post-A-Nut at the **Ho'olehua post office** (p418). You won't need luck to experience the green on a hike through the inimitable **Kamakou Preserve** (p416), Moloka'i's rain forest, on your final day.

One Week

Follow the five-day itinerary, adding a horseback ride through **Pu'u O Hoku Ranch** (p414) on day six. Rent a kayak or bike on day seven, strap on the snorkel equipment and explore the southeastern coast. Squeeze in a sunset at **Mo'omomi Beach** (p419) and dinner at **Kamuela Cookhouse** (p418).

reserve it. Permits for the entire site, which has electricity, water, picnic tables, rest rooms and showers, are issued to just one group at a time, with native Hawaiians given priority.

Activities

Moloka'i has wild ocean waters, rough trails, remote rainforests and a burgeoning number of outdoor adventures. You can rent gear, go on (or tailor) tours, and get activity information from the two general outfitters here, Molokai Outdoor Activities (p405) and Molokai Fish & Dive (p405), both in Kaunakakai (p408).

WATER ACTIVITIES

Moloka'i has 32 miles of barrier reef with decent snorkeling; the most-popular strip is the beach around the 20-mile marker on Moloka'i's southeastern end. Known as Twenty-Mile Beach (p413), this beach is also good for swimming. Rock Point (p413), not far north of here, and Halawa Beach (p415), at the northern end of the road, are popular surfing spots.

For swimming in protected coves and unbeatable vistas, head straight for the west-end beaches (p428). Papohaku Beach is the broadest and longest sandy beach in Hawaii, but high winds make it unsafe for swimming. Dixie Maru Beach, the most southwesterly beach accessible by car, is a lovely bay for swimming and snorkeling. Quiet Kawakiu Beach, the most northwesterly beach you can reach by car, is a beautiful crescent with fine coastal views and good swimming when seas are calm. Just south of here is small, picture-perfect Make Horse Beach.

Papa Hemingway would have had a field day with the incredible sportfishing in Moloka'i waters, especially around the Penguin Banks of the southwestern tip; charters leave from the Kaunakakai Wharf (p407).

LAND ACTIVITIES

Like the island itself, the hiking here is pristine, remote and rugged, with little traffic. The most-popular hike is down the mule trail to the Kalaupapa Peninsula (p421). You can enjoy the epic views and go solo as far as the beach at the foot of the cliffs, but to

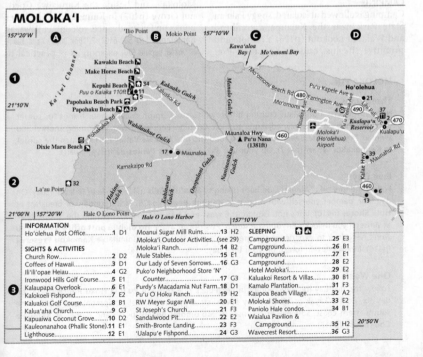

MOLOKA'I

explore the leprosy settlement proper, you must go on a tour (see p422).

The Nature Conservancy's Kamakou Preserve (p416) features unique rainforest hikes in the island's untamed interior and out to scenic valley overlooks. Backcountry trails to waterfalls and remote valleys do exist on the east side of the island and the north shore, but going without a local friend is inadvisable. The longer you hang around here, though, the more doors will be opened.

Adventurous cycling awaits along miles of dirt roads or cruise up the picturesque north shore. See p405 for rental outfits. Horseback-riding on the lush north shore is possible at Pu'u O Hoku Ranch (p414) or saddle up on the wide open range at the Moloka'i Ranch (p425).

A Hawaiian island without an 18-hole golf course? Not to worry, the nine-hole Ironwood Hills Golf Club (p420) is such a honey you'll want to play it twice. There's also a more-formal nine-hole course (soon to be 18) at Kaluakoi Villas called Kaluakoi Golf Course (p427). Free, public tennis courts are found at the Mitchell Pauole Center (p408).

Getting There & Away

If you have time, taking the ferry from Maui is a more sociable and scenic experience than flying – the afternoon boat catches the sunset almost year-round, and in winter, breaching whales glorify the scene.

AIR

Moloka'i (Ho'olehua) Airport (MKK; ☎ 567-6140) is pretty teeny: you claim your baggage on a bench outside. However, there are car-rental booths, a snack bar and a cocktail lounge, pay phones and a visitor information desk that is occasionally staffed. Look for free Moloka'i newspapers here; off-island papers are also for sale.

Island Air (☎ 567-6115, 800-652-6541; www.islandair .com), Aloha's commuter airline, flies directly to Moloka'i eight times a day from Honolulu, and twice from Kahului (Maui). The commuter air terminal in Honolulu is a 10-minute walk through and out the interisland terminal. **Hawaiian Airlines** (☎ 567-6510, 800-882-8811; www.hawaiianair.com) flies from Honolulu to Moloka'i every afternoon. Flights to/from any other island require stopping, and most

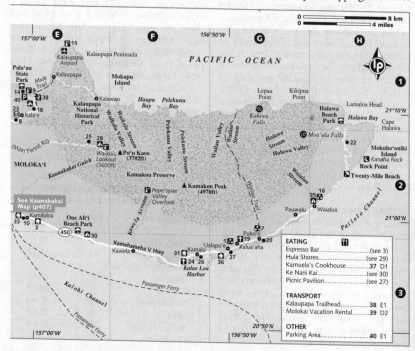

EATING 🍴
Espresso Bar.......................(see 3)
Hula Shores.......................(see 29)
Kamuela's Cookhouse...........**37** D1
Ke Nani Kai.......................(see 30)
Picnic Pavilion...................(see 27)

TRANSPORT
Kalaupapa Trailhead.............**38** E1
Molokai Vacation Rental........**39** D2

OTHER
Parking Area......................**40** E1

likely changing planes, in Honolulu. Delays and cancellations of interisland flights are fairly common.

Unscheduled, on-demand puddle-jumpers are the most economical way to fly between Moloka'i and Honolulu. They are like a budget-traveler's aerial tour, since they usually cruise at around 1000ft. They only leave when there are enough folks to go (usually three to four – perfect for a group). About four of these small air carriers make the Moloka'i flight:

George's Aviation (☎ 866-834-2120, on O'ahu ☎ 306-4284) One-way/return to Honolulu $50/90.

Molokai Air Shuttle (☎ 567-6847, on O'ahu ☎ 545-4988) One-way/return to Honolulu $55/90.

Pacific Wings (☎ 567-6814; www.pacificwings.com) Flies once daily to Honolulu (return $90). There's also a daily scheduled flight from Honolulu to Kalaupapa (return $140).

Paragon Air (☎ 866-946-4744, on Maui ☎ 244-3356; www.paragon-air.com) Flies between Maui, Moloka'i and Lana'i (return $95) and runs a daily tour from Maui to the Kalaupapa Peninsula ($225).

BOAT

Molokai Princess (information ☎ 667-2585, reservations ☎ 662-3355; www.molokaiferry.com; adult/child $40/20, book of six tickets $185) departs Kaunakakai Wharf for Lahaina (Maui), from Monday to Saturday at 5:30am and 2:30pm, with an additional Sunday departure at 3pm. In the other direction, the ferry leaves Lahaina at 6:30am Monday to Saturday and daily at 5:15pm. The crossing through the Pailolo Channel takes about 1¾ hours, but can seem longer when the passage is choppy; perhaps that's why it's nicknamed Pakalolo Channel (marijuana is proven to ease nausea). Tickets can be purchased at ticket booths at the Kaunakakai Wharf or in Lahaina by cash or credit card. You can also buy tickets online or by phone using a credit card.

Getting Around

Renting a car here is essential, if you intend to explore the island in earnest. But Moloka'i is not the place to off-road on the innumerable dirt spurs and tracks, just to see what's there. Many dirt paths that seem like possible roads are just driveways into someone's backyard. All in all, folks aren't too keen on strangers cruising around on their private turf and the *pakalolo* (marijuana) growing here and there tends to make people skittish.

On the other hand, if there's a fishpond you want to see, and someone's house is between the road and the water, it's usually easy to strike up a conversation and get permission to cross. Moloka'i people are receptive and friendly to those people genuinely interested in Hawaiian ways. If you're lucky they might even share a little local lore and history with you, particularly the old-timers.

The University of Hawaii's joint *Moloka'i/Lana'i* map shows Moloka'i's topography; it's sold at stores in Kaunakakai. A more user-friendly lightweight fold-out map is Nelles' *Maui, Molokai, Lanai*. The bulky *Ready Mapbook of Maui County*, which includes coverage of Moloka'i and Lana'i, is an invaluable resource for adventurers.

TO/FROM THE AIRPORT & FERRY

Several national car-rental chains (p537) are represented at the airport. If you rent a car from an agency without an airport office, they'll send someone to shuttle you into town to pick up your vehicle.

Driving out of the airport, you're greeted by a sign reading, 'Aloha! Slow Down – This is Moloka'i.' Indeed, after a few days here, 40 mph feels way fast. At the stop sign, turn right to reach Moloka'i's main road, stretching from east to west. Westward from Kaunakakai, it's called Hwy 460 (Maunaloa Hwy). Eastward from Kaunakakai, it's Hwy 450 (Kamehameha V Hwy). East of the airport toward Kaunakakai, Hwy 470 (Kala'e Hwy) branches off Hwy 460, and heads up to the Kalaupapa Peninsula overlook.

You'll find no traffic lights and no taxis on mellow Moloka'i, but there are

ROAD DISTANCES & DURATIONS FROM KAUNAKAKAI

destination	miles	time
Halawa Valley	27	1½ hr
Ho'olehua Airport	6.5	10 min
Kalaupapa Trailhead	10	20 min
Maunaloa	17	30 min
Papohaku Beach	21.5	45 min
Puko'o	16	20 min
Twenty-Mile Beach	20	30 min

a couple of companies who do provide shuttle services for set fees. To be assured of a ride from the airport or ferry dock, make advance reservations. There's a three-person minimum. **Molokai Off-Road Tours & Taxi** (☎ 553-3369) and **Molokai Outdoor Activities** (☎ 553-4477, 877-553-4477; www.molokai -outdoors.com) have shuttles from the airport to Kaunakakai ($22 per person), or Moloka'i Ranch and west-end condominiums ($20 per person).

It takes about 20 minutes to walk from the dock into Kaunakakai, though rental car agencies will meet you at your ferry if you arrange it; catching the ferry after dropping off your rental car is easy as most agencies will usually give you a ride to the dock.

BICYCLE

Molokai Outdoor Activities (Map pp402-3; ☎ 553-4477, 877-553-4477; www.molokai-outdoors.com) rents out bikes per hour/day/week for $13/26/113. Bikes come with free helmets and locks; car racks are an additional $5 a day. Expert **Molokai Bicycle** (Map p407; ☎ 553-3931; www.bike hawaii.com/mol okaibicycle; 80 Mohala St; ⏱ 3-6pm Tue & Thu, 9am-2pm Sat) is a small Kaunakakai operation renting out rigid and front-suspension mountain bikes and road bikes ($15 to $24 per day, $70 to $100 per week). Rentals include helmet, lock and water bottle. Car racks, child carriers and jogging strollers are available. Shop hours are limited, but you can make arrangements to pick up a bike at other times, including at the airport or ferry.

CAR & MOPED

Keep in mind that rental vehicles are not allowed 'off-road,' meaning any dirt road, and there can also be restrictions on camping.

As there are only a few companies operating on Moloka'i, it's best to book well in advance, especially if you're planning a weekend visit.

Island Kine Auto Rental (☎ 553-5242, 553-5342, 866-627-7368; www.molokai-car-rental.com; 242 Ilio Rd), a local outfit, rents out nice, shiny new compacts from around $30 per day, all inclusive. Trucks and 4WD vehicles are also available. The office is in Kaunakakai, but the staff cheerfully pick up clients at the ferry dock and airport. By the time you read this, they should have moved to the

main intersection in town, just across from the Chevron.

You can save some money by renting an older, kinda-scruffy car from **Molokai Rent-a-Car** (☎ 553-3929, 866-239-3929; 82 Ala Malama) for $26/150 per day/week. Head here if you don't have a major credit card.

Budget (☎ 567-6877) and **Dollar** (☎ 567-6156) both have offices at the airport. See p537 for toll-free reservation numbers and general rental information.

Molokai Outdoor Activities (Map pp402-3; ☎ 553-4477, 877-553-4477; www.molokai-outdoors.com) arranges car rentals with optional racks for bikes, kayaks and surfboards. Theoretically it rents Yamaha mopeds (per 24hr/week $40/165), but don't get your hopes up.

There are gas stations only at Kaunakakai and Maunaloa.

TOURS

Advance arrangements are always helpful, and often necessary. Many charter boats and family-owned tour companies don't maintain offices; you just call them up, arrange your tour and hook up at the wharf or wherever you're staying. Most tours have at least a three-person minimum. Sailing and whale-watching charters (winter only), as well as scuba boats, mostly leave from Kaunakakai Wharf.

Based at the Hotel Moloka'i, **Molokai Outdoor Activities** (Map pp402-3; ☎ 553-4477, 877-553-4477; www.molokai-outdoors.com; Kamehameha V Hwy) offers a slew of tours led by friendly island residents. For any activity it doesn't offer directly, it can contact someone who does. It also arranges tours plus flight-and-ferry combinations, making it possible to visit Moloka'i from Maui or Honolulu on a day jaunt. Interesting, active tours include a 9-mile bike-kayak-snorkel trip along the east coast ($141), a sunset paddle down the east coast, landing at the Hotel Moloka'i bar ($41), and a waterfall hike into Halawa Valley ($75). A 'round the island' whirlwind, and a more-rewarding east-end cultural tour (including lunch $141) are also offered. It also arranges surfing lessons, boat charters, whale-watching and the tour to Kalaupapa Peninsula – but be mindful that these tours are always cheaper when you book directly.

Working in conjunction with Moloka'i Ranch, **Molokai Fish & Dive** (Map p407; ☎ 553-5926,

522-0184; www.molokaifishanddive.com; Ala Malama Ave; ☺ 8am-6pm Mon-Sat, 8am-2pm Sun) is the other big tour leader on Moloka'i. In addition to daily kayak ($75 to $85) and downhill-biking tours ($45), it also leads morning and afternoon hikes into Halawa Valley ($75) and scuba diving trips (1/2 tank $125/275). Horseback riding is another option.

If you want to get off road with a local guide, try a half-/full-day 4WD tour ($54/130) with **Molokai Off-Road Tours & Taxi** (☎ 553-3369).

Because so much of the Moloka'i coastline is only accessible by boat, a north-shore charter (summer only) can be rewarding as it lets you see and experience impenetrable parts of the island. If you're traveling in a group, mo' bettah, as you can tailor tours to your specifications. All boats leave from Kaunakakai Wharf. Try one of these personable outfits:

Alyce C Sportfishing Charters (☎ 558-8377; www .alycecsportfishing.com) Fishing charters start at $300 for the whole boat for a half day, with a captain who knows where the fish are, and shares the catch in nice, manageable filets. Also does whale-watching jaunts and round-island runs.

Bill Kapuni's Snorkel & Scuba Adventures (☎ 553-9867) Scuba (two-tank dive $125) and snorkel ($65) tours with a PADI dive master, who also knows a lot about the craft of building ancient Hawaiian canoes. Whale-watching, sunset, fishing and north-shore charters, too.

Ma'a Hawai'i – Moloka'i Action Adventures (☎ 558-8184, 870-2721; PO Box 1269, Kaunakakai, HI 96748) Get outdoors with Captain Walter Naki: deep sea fishing, bow hunting, hiking secret spots and north shore boat tours all offered.

Molokai Charters (☎ 553-5852) Two-hour sunset sail ($40) and a four-hour sail ($50) on a 42ft sloop includes whale-watching in season. A full-day snorkeling trip to Lana'i is $90.

KAUNAKAKAI

pop 2726

Kaunakakai (or 'town' as it's called locally, since it's Moloka'i's only real town) takes much of its character from what it doesn't have. There's not a single elevator, no neon and no strip malls. There's too little parking and no public restroom either – the stuff of many a community meeting.

Most of the island's businesses line Ala Malama Ave, the town's broad main street, where stores have aging wooden false fronts

that give Kaunakakai the air of an old Wild West town, and an almost timeless quality. There's a couple of restaurants and banks, a bakery, post office, pharmacy and one of just about everything else a small town needs. The tallest point is the church steeple.

INFORMATION
Emergency
Police, Fire & Ambulance (☎ 911)

Internet Access
Stanley's coffee shop gallery (Map p407; ☎ 553-9966; Ala Malama Ave; per 10 min $1; ☺ 6am-3:30pm Mon-Sat) Faxes and printing, too.

Laundry
Neither of these places sells laundry detergent, so bring or beg your own.
Ohana Launderette (Map p407; Kamoi St; ☺ 6am-9pm)
The Laundramat (Map p407; Makaena Pl; ☺ 7am-9pm)

Library
Kaunakakai Library (Map p407; ☎ 553-1765; Ala Malama Ave; ☺ noon-8pm Mon & Wed, 9am-5pm Tue, Thu & Fri) A silent-as-a tomb space to browse off-island newspapers and magazines.

Media
In lieu of a daily newspaper, bulletin boards around Kaunakakai are the prime source of news and announcements. The board next to the Bank of Hawaii is extensive, but others line Ala Malama Ave.
Dispatch (☎ 552-2781; www.aloha.net/~mkkdisp) Free weekly published each Thursday; watch the events calendar for local happenings.
Molokai Advertiser-News (☎ 558-8253) Free weekly published on Wednesday.

Medical Services
Molokai Drugs (Map p407; ☎ 553-5790; Molokai Professional Bldg, Kamoi St; ☺ 8:45am-5:45pm Mon-Sat) Sells some books and maps, along with pharmaceuticals.
Molokai General Hospital (☎ 553-5331; 280 Puali St, Kaunakakai; ☺ 24hr) Emergency services.

Money
Banks with 24hr ATMs are one of Kaunakakai's few concessions to the modern world. **Bank of Hawaii** (Map p407; ☎ 888-643-3888; www.boh.com; Ala Malama Ave) is the largest.

Post
Post Office (☎ 553-5845; Ala Malama Ave)

MOLOKA'I

KAUNAKAKAI

INFORMATION		Molokai Bicycle.......................**11** B2		Misaki's.............................**20** B1
Bank of Hawaii.........................**1** A2		Molokai Fish & Dive...............**12** B1		Molokai Drive-Inn..................**21** B2
Department of Parks &		Molokai Surf...........................**13** C2		Molokai Pizza Café................**22** A2
Recreation...........................**2** D1		Swimming Pool..................(see 10)		Outpost Natural Foods.........**23** A1
Library.......................................**3** A2		Tennis Courts.........................**14** D1		Oviedo's...............................**24** C1
Molokai Drugs.........................**4** C2				
Molokai Visitors Association.....**5** C2		SLEEPING 🛏 (pp408-9)		DRINKING 🍷 (p410)
Ohana Launderette..................**6** C2		Friendly Isle Realty.................**15** B1		Molokai Wines & Spirits.........**25** B1
Stanley's coffee shop gallery....**7** B1				
The Laundramat.......................**8** A1		EATING 🍴 (pp409-10)		SHOPPING 🛍 (p410)
		Friendly Market.......................**16** B1		Kamakana Fine Arts Gallery....**26** A2
SIGHTS & ACTIVITIES (pp407-8)		Kamoi Snack-N-Go..................**17** C2		
Kamehameha V House.............**9** A3		Kanemitsu Bakery..................**18** B1		TRANSPORT (p410)
Kaunakakai Gym.....................**10** D1		Mango Mart Deli.....................**19** B1		Molokai Rent-A-Car..............**27** B1

Tourist Information

Molokai Visitors Association (MVA; ☎ 553-5221, 800-553-0404, outside Hawaii ☎ 800-800-6367; www .molokai-hawaii.com; 4 Kamoi St) Efficient office has good B&B information and the lowdown on what's happening around the island.

SIGHTS

The days when pineapple was loaded from **Kaunakakai Wharf** are gone, but the harbor still hums with activity. A commercial interisland barge chugs in, skippers unload catches of mahimahi, and a buff guy paddles his outrigger canoe. At dusk, the scene becomes sunkissed. On the western side of the wharf, near the canoe shed, are the stone foundations of oceanfront **Kamehameha V house** (Map p407), now overgrown with grass. The house was called 'Malama,' which today is the name of Kaunakakai's main street, leading from the harbor through town.

As Moloka'i was the favorite island playground of King Kamehameha V, he had the royal 10-acre **Kapuaiwa Coconut Grove** (Map pp402–3) planted near his sacred bathing pools in the 1860s. Standing tall, about a

mile west of downtown, its name means 'mysterious taboo.' The regal grove is today under the management of Hawaiian Home Lands (HHL). Be careful where you walk (or park), because coconuts can drop.

Across the highway is **Church Row** (Map pp402–3), where a quaint white church with green trim sits next to a quaint green church with white trim etc. Any denomination that attracts a handful of members receives its own little tract of land here.

Walk down to the **beach** at night in Kaunakakai and you may spot what looks like ghosts walking on the water. Spooky, but less so when you realize these are actually local fishers, who walk far out onto the shallow coastal reef carrying lanterns. 'Torch fishing' is good here, when the wind dies down, and lantern light stuns the prey.

Three miles east of town, **One Ali'i Beach Park** (Map pp402–3) is used mainly for picnics, parties and camping, as the water is shallow and swimming conditions are poor. Two memorials erected in the park commemorate the 19th-century immigration of Japanese citizens to Hawaii.

ACTIVITIES

While things to do in Kaunakakai proper are limited, it *is* the place to rent gear or arrange tours.

Molokai Fish & Dive (Map p407; ☎ 553-5926, 522-0184; www.molokaifishanddive.com; Ala Malama Ave; ☺ 8am-6pm Mon-Sat, 8am-2pm Sun) rents out snorkel sets ($10), boogie boards ($12), and rods and reels ($10 to $14). It also sells all manner of camping equipment and runs tours (see p405). Some tours leave from Molokai Fish & Dive, but others depart from the Moloka'i Ranch (p425), with whom they work closely.

Molokai Outdoor Activities (Map pp402-3; ☎ 553-4477, 877-553-4477; www.molokai-outdoors.com; Hotel Moloka'i, Kamehameha V Hwy; ☺ 8am-5:30pm) also rents out kayaks, snorkel sets, surfboards, fishing poles, tennis rackets and just about anything else you might need. See p405 for their laundry list of tours.

Surfboards and boogie boards can be rented from **Molokai Surf** (Map p407; ☎ 553-5093; Kamehameha V Hwy; ☺ 9:30am-5pm Mon-Sat). All of the places mentioned so far offer surfing lessons ($50 to $75 per hour). In terms of swimming, however, the Kaunakakai area is a dud, with silty and shallow waters.

Kaunakakai Gym (☎ 553-5141; Mitchell Pauole Center; ☺ 11am-3pm Mon-Fri, 10am-3pm Sat) has an indoor swimming pool. There are also two outdoor tennis courts here available free to the public. You're not likely to have to fight the crowds for a court.

FESTIVALS & EVENTS

Two of Moloka'i's most notable special events are culture-rich affairs worth catching if you're in the area.

Molokai Ka Hula Piko (May) Papohaku Beach Park hosts this free hula festival featuring dance, music and chants.

Moloka'i Hoe (mid-October) Grueling outrigger canoe race that sets off from remote Hale O Lono Point, with six-person teams paddling furiously across the 41-mile Kaiwi Channel to O'ahu.

SLEEPING

For cottages, houses and condos **Molokai Vacation Rental** (☎ 553-8334, 800-367-2984; www .molokai-vacation-rental.com; PO Box 1979, Kaunakakai, HI 96748; cnr of Maunaloa & Kala'e Hwys) has a decent selection in all price ranges. **Friendly Isle Realty** (Map p407; ☎ 553-3666, 800-600-4158; www .molokairesorts.com; 75 Ala Malama Ave, Kaunakakai) also handles vacation rentals.

TOP FIVE SLEEPS

- **Kaupoa Beach Village** (p426), Moloka'i Ranch
- **Moanui Beach House** (p411)
- **Papohaku Beach Park** (p429), camping
- **Hotel Moloka'i** (below)
- **Pu'unana Dunbar Beachfront Cottage** (p413)

Budget

Camping is permitted at **One Ali'i Beach Park** (p407), but sites enjoy little privacy, thanks to floodlights and late-night carousing. If you like to plan in advance, you might also camp at **Kapuaiwa Coconut Grove** (see p401 for permit details).

Mid-Range

Ka Hale Mala (☎ /fax 553-9009; www.molokai-bnb .com; apt with/without breakfast $80/70, extra person from $15) This spacious four-room apartment is the ground level of a two-story house, east of Kaunakakai and before the 5-mile marker. The spotless 900-sq-ft apartment has exposed-beam ceilings, fully equipped kitchen, TV, VCR and large lanai overlooking the garden. Guests can harvest veggies and fruit, from figs to tangelos, here. A full gourmet breakfast may include such specialities as taro or poi (fermented taro) pancakes. The space can sleep four, which can work out economically for a small group.

A'ahi Place Bed & Breakfast (☎ 553-8033; www .molokai.com/aahi; PO Box 2006, Kaunakakai, HI 96748; cottage d $75, incl breakfast $85, extra person $20) This very simple, clean cedar cottage is in a small subdivision, uphill from the Molokai Shores condos. Kind of like a camp cabin (with lots of wood and indirect light), this place has a full kitchen, two full-sized beds, a washing machine and garden lanai. It's an open space best suited for one or two people. The continental breakfast includes fresh fruit, baked breads and coffee. There's a three-night minimum stay, or a $30 surcharge. Ask about weekly discounts.

Hotel Moloka'i (Map pp402-3; ☎ 553-5347, 800-535-0085; www.hotelmolokai.com; Kamehameha V Hwy; standard/oceanfront r $90/140, oceanfront room with kitchenette $150; ☒) These two-story Polynesian-style buildings look cooler from the outside than they are inside. Dark, hot and queerly angled, it's worth upgrading to an ocean view or 2nd-story unit; just steer clear of the standard rooms, some of which abut the trash heap. But the private lanai provides relief, and the oceanfront pool, bar and restaurant, with sunsets and stargazing, make this place. The staff are super, too. It's about 2 miles east of town. For the on-site Molokai Outdoor Activities desk, see p408.

Top End
Molokai Shores (Map pp402-3; ☎ 553-5954, 800-535-0085; www.marcresorts.com; Kamehameha V Hwy; 1-/2-bedroom oceanfront units $170/210; ☒) Like a starter apartment out of university – all mustard linoleum and worn brown carpet – these condos, about 1.5 miles east of town belie the fresh, tropical air that makes islands so special. Not all units are *that* bad and the 3rd-floor digs have high cathedral ceilings at least. Each has a full kitchen, cable TV, lanai and ceiling fans. Go online for discounts.

EATING
Moloka'i is kind of like Cuba: you don't visit for the food. Here, approaching eating as necessity rather than potential pleasure will help you face the carnivorous, carb-heavy menus that are so typical; renting a condo with kitchen facilities is a workable solution for food lovers.

Budget
Molokai Drive-Inn (Map p407; ☎ 553-5655; Kamehameha V Hwy; meals $3-7; ☒ 6am-10pm) Folks flock to this town landmark for plate lunches with grilled *'ahi* (yellow-fin tuna) or shrimp ($7.50), mounds of greasy fried saimin (local noodle soup) with veggies ($2.70), burgers ($3.50) and milkshakes. Breakfast is a flat $5 and comes with two eggs, hash browns and a choice of meat product, from Spam to Portuguese sausage. Serious talking-story and gossip entertains while you wait.

Kanemitsu Bakery (Map p407; ☎ 553-5855; Ala Malama Ave; ☒ bakery open 5:30am-6:30pm Wed-Mon) The one, the only, this is the bakery responsible for the Moloka'i sweet bread sold on all the other islands. The Danish pastries, croissants and doughnuts are tasty too. The cinnamon apple crisp ($1) is a favorite. Skip the attached restaurant, though.

Mango Mart Deli (Map p407; ☎ 553-8170; Ala Malama Ave; sandwiches $4-6; ☒ 8am-8pm Mon-Sat, to 6pm Sun) Big, tasty sandwiches, including a vegetarian sub overflowing with good stuff like sprouts and avocado, are standards here. All types of cold cuts and good cheese (eg Jarlesberg, Brie) are sold by the pound.

Kamoi Snack-N-Go (Map p407; ☎ 553-5790; Molokai Professional Bldg, Kamoi St; scoops $1.70-2.60; ☒ 9am-9pm Mon-Sat, noon-9pm Sun) Hawaii has its share of great ice cream: here it's a couple-dozen flavors of the gourmet, Honolulu-made Dave's. Snacks and drinks are also sold here.

Most of Kaunakakai's other eateries are old-fashioned lunch counters on Ala Malama Ave. At **Oviedo's** (Map p407; ☎ 553-5014; Ala Malama Ave) you can fill up 'on Hawaii's best Filipino food,' according to a native son, for $5. Atmospheric **Stanley's coffee shop gallery** (Map p407; ☎ 553-9966; Ala Malama Ave; snacks $2-4; ☒ 6am-3:30pm Mon-Sat) is good value, with homemade muffins piping hot from the oven ($1.50), saimin ($2.75) and terrific coffee. The milkshakes ($3.25) are extra thick.

Self-Catering
Outpost Natural Foods (Map p407; ☎ 553-3377; 70 Makaena Pl; ☒ 9am-6pm Mon-Thu, 9am-5pm Fri, 10am-5pm Sun) Here you'll find bulk grains, granola and trail mix, plus dried fruit, yogurt and fresh produce, some of it organic. Lots of juices and prepared foods are available for take-out.

Friendly Market (Map p407; ☎ 553-5595; Ala Malama St; ☒ 8:30am-8:30pm Mon-Fri, to 6:30pm Sat) has Moloka'i's best grocery selection, and

---

TOP FIVE EATS
- **Puko'o Neighborhood Store 'N' Counter** (p413) is close to secluded beaches and has terrific plate lunches and the best people-watching
- **Kamuela Cookhouse** (p418) has juicy steaks, to-die-for desserts and an 'all in the family' feeling
- **Molokai Drive-Inn** (left) is manna for food-strapped Moloka'i with fresh fish plate lunches and huge breakfasts
- **Kaupoa Beach Village** (p426) offers Sunday brunch plus easy access to their private beach
- **Hula Shores** (p410) for a divine breakfast and huge salads

MOLOKA'I

not far behind is **Misaki's** (☎ 553-5505; Ala Malama Ave; ◯ 8:30am-8:30pm Mon-Sat, 9am-noon Sun) – check out the discounted stuff in aisle one.

Mid-Range & Top End
Molokai Pizza Cafe (Map p407; ☎ 553-3288; Kaunakakai Pl; meals $7.50-15, small/medium/large pizza from $9.50/15/18; ◯ 10am-10pm Mon-Thu, 10am-11pm Fri & Sat, 11am-10pm Sun) The savory pizza here has won many hearts. The herb sauce has it going on, and you'll love it if you're a fan of thick-crust pizza. The late hours are a bonus, as are the rides for kids and free soda refills. Sub sandwiches, salads, pasta, catch of the day and ribs are all on the menu.

Hula Shores (Map pp402-3; ☎ 553-5347, 800-535-0085; www.hotelmolokai.com; Hotel Moloka'i, Kamehameha V Hwy; breakfast & lunch $5-8, dinner $14-20; ◯ breakfast, lunch & dinner) Sunset views of Lana'i, tiki torches, and waves lapping at the shore (splashing your table legs even), make this Moloka'i's most-atmospheric restaurant. It's the best breakfast spot in town too, with all manner of fruit and/or nut pancakes ($5.25 to $6.75) and build-your-own omelettes ($6.25 to $7.75). At lunch you can order burgers and sandwiches, while at dinner, there are many salads, steaks galore ($13 to $17) and interesting catches of the day (at market prices) served with tomato-ginger glaze, or lemon butter and capers.

DRINKING
For local vibe and lapping wave soundtrack, head to **Hula Shores** (☎ 553-5347, 800-535-0085; www.hotelmolokai.com; Hotel Moloka'i, Kamehameha V Hwy), Moloka'i's top drinking spot replete with daily happy hour from 4 to 6pm. **Stanley's coffee shop gallery** (☎ 553-9966; Ala Malama Ave) feels straight out of Seattle with its luscious coffee drinks of all flavors, funky decor and funny habitués.

Molokai Wines & Spirits (Map p407; ☎ 553-5009; Ala Malama Ave; ◯ 9am-10pm, to 10:30pm Fri & Sat) carries a good assortment of imported beers, Hawaiian microbrews and inexpensive wines.

ENTERTAINMENT
Mom always said it's in poor taste to state the obvious, but…there's not much to do here after you watch the sun go down.
Hotel Moloka'i (Map pp402-3; ☎ 553-5347, 800-535-0085; Kamehameha V Hwy; www.hotelmolokai .com; ◯ noon-2am) Crowd around the poolside bar to enjoy local musicians playing mellow

Hawaiian guitar from 4pm to 6pm. 'Aloha Fridays' are popular with visitors and locals, making this the hottest spot on the island.

Kanemitsu Bakery (Map p407; ☎ 553-5855; Ala Malama Ave; ◯ closed Tue) offers night owls the opportutiy to slip down the alley behind Ala Malama Ave at 10pm to buy hot loaves from the taciturn night-shift baker.

Other than this, the **baseball field** (Map p4070) in Kaunakakai is the most active spot on the island. For some local flavor, you could go down and cheer on the Moloka'i Farmers as they compete against their high-school rivals, the Lana'i Pinelads, or check out the 4-H livestock competition.

SHOPPING
Kamakana Fine Arts Gallery (Map p407; ☎ 553-8520; www.kamakanagallery.com; Upstairs, Molokai Center, 110 Ala Malama Ave; ◯ 9:30am-5:30pm Mon-Fri, 7:30am-2:30pm Sat) Browsing this gallery gives you an idea of the eclecticism of Moloka'i's creativity. There are over 80 local artists represented here, proffering pretty lahuala (hala-leaf) woven items, handcrafted jewelry, lots of lei, etched glassware, pottery and Hawaiian instruments.

Molokai Fish & Dive (☎ 553-5926, 522-0184; www .molokaifishanddive.com; Ala Malama Ave; ◯ 8am-6pm Mon-Sat, 8am-2pm Sun) Racks upon racks of island T-shirts are sold here, plus postcards, books and maps. It also stocks water-sports gear, camping equipment, fishing tackle, sunscreen and almost anything else you might need on Moloka'i.

GETTING THERE & AROUND
There is no public transportation into Kaunakakai from the ferry or the airport, but you can hire a taxi or a car with prior arrangement. Kaunakakai is a walking town and almost everything is easily reached on foot. Parking is limited on Ala Malama Ave proper, so you might try one of the side streets (eg Makaena Pl) or the Mitchell Pauole Center lot.

EAST MOLOKA'I

The 27-mile drive from Kaunakakai to Halawa Valley, along the Kamehameha V Hwy (Hwy 450), ranks as of one of Hawaii's most scenic. It takes about 1½ hours each way, but you might stretch it out by snorkeling at Twenty-Mile Beach, swimming around the 21-mile marker, or enjoying a leisurely picnic at Halawa Beach Park. It's a good paved road from start to finish. There is no gas after Kaunakakai, so check your gauge.

The road starts out hugging the ocean, passing homesteads, heiau (ancient stone temple) and fishponds, before turning into a one-lane ribbon at around the 20-mile marker, curving at the whim of the golden-sand beach that dominates the vista up this way. Once the road turns inland, the terrain grows lush, with ancient groves of primary forest rising to pasture and mountains beyond. More coastal views, and the odd silver waterfall dropping down the mountainsides, provide eye candy here. The last part of the road is narrow, with lots of hairpin bends and scenic coastal views, as you wind up to a cliff-top view of Halawa Valley.

The majority of Moloka'i's vacation rentals and B&Bs are on this southeastern stretch of the coast.

KAWELA

A grassy strip wedged between the road and sea in Kawela, shortly before the 6-mile marker, **Kakahai'a Beach Park** has a couple of picnic tables, and is a peaceful spot for a leg stretch or snack. This park is the only part of **Kakahai'a National Wildlife Refuge** (http://pacific islands.fws.gov/wnwr/mkakahaianwr.html) open to the public. Most of the 40-acre refuge is inland from the road. It includes marshland, with a dense growth of bulrushes and an inland freshwater fishpond that has been expanded to provide a home for endangered birds, including the Hawaiian stilt and coot.

KAMALO

Only two of the four Moloka'i churches that missionary and prospective saint, Father Damien, built outside of the Kalaupapa Peninsula (p421) are still standing. One of them is **St Joseph's Church**, a small village about 10 miles east of Kaunakakai (the other is Our Lady of Seven Sorrows, p412). This simple, one-room wooden church, dating from 1876, has a steeple and a bell, five rows of pews and some of the original wavy glass panes. A lei-draped statue of Father Damien and a little cemetery are beside the church. Only the tsunami warning speaker brings the scene into the 21st century.

Just over three-quarters of a mile after the 11-mile marker, a small sign, on the *makai* (seaward) side of the road, notes the **Smith-Bronte Landing**, the site where pilot Ernest Smith and navigator Emory Bronte safely crash-landed their plane at the completion of the world's first civilian flight from the US mainland to Hawaii. The pair left California on July 14, 1927, destined for O'ahu and came down on Moloka'i 25 hours and two minutes later. A little memorial plaque is set among the kiawe trees and grasses, in the spot where they landed.

Tucked back on a 5-acre leafy lot across from St Joseph's Church, the studio cottage at the **Kamalo Plantation & Moanui Beach House** (☎ 558-8236; www.molokai.com/kamalo; cottage d $85, 2-bedroom house $140, both incl continental breakfast) affords lots of privacy. There's a full kitchen, lanai and abundant beach toys. These friendly folks also rent out the fabulous **Moanui Beach House** up the road, with incredible views towards Maui and ample lanai to enjoy them. The modern house features cathedral ceilings, great beds and a full kitchen. There's a two-night minimum stay at the cottage, three at the house.

'UALAPU'E

A half mile beyond Wavecrest Resort condo development, at the 13-mile marker, you'll spot **'Ualapu'e Fishpond** on the *makai* side of the road. This fishpond has been restored and restocked with mullet and milkfish, two species that were raised here in ancient times. After this, look to your left for the defunct **Ah Ping Store** and its old gas pump at the roadside. This classic building, of faded green wood with a red tin roof, was a Chinese-owned grocery store in the 1930s.

You'll definitely feel away from it all at **Wavecrest Resort** (www.wavecrestaoao.com; 1-bedroom units per day/week $70/550, 2-bedroom units $110/700; 🌊), a big ocean-facing condo complex. Units vary depending upon the owners' taste, but all are spacious and quiet. Each has a roomy living room with a sofa bed, a full kitchen, an entertainment center and lanai. Breezes blow right through the oceanfront units, which enjoy great views of Maui and Lana'i. A $40 surcharge applies for stays of less than a week. Units are rented either directly through the owners via the website, or through Molokai Vacation Rentals or Friendly Isle Realty (p408).

MOLOKA'I

KALUA'AHA

The village of Kalua'aha is less than 2 miles past Wavecrest. The ruins of **Kalua'aha Church**, Molokai's first Christian church, are a bit off the road and inland but just visible, if you keep an eye peeled. It was built in 1844 by Moloka'i's first missionary, Harvey R Hitchcock. **Our Lady of Seven Sorrows Church** (☙ service 7:15am Sun) is a quarter of a mile past the Kalua'aha Church site. The present Our Lady of Sorrows is a reconstruction from 1966 of the original wood-frame building, constructed in 1874 by the missionary Father Damien. From the church parking lot, a fine view of an ancient **fishpond** and the hazy high-rise-studded shores of west Maui provide an incongruous backdrop.

'ILI'ILI'OPAE HEIAU

'Ili'ili'opae is Moloka'i's biggest and best-known heiau, and is thought to be the second largest in Hawaii. It also might possibly be the oldest religious site in the state. Over 300ft long and 100ft wide, the heiau is about 22ft high on the eastern side, and 11ft high at the other end. The main platform is strikingly level. Historians believed the original heiau may have been three times its current size, reaching out beyond Mapulehu Stream.

Although once a site of human sacrifice, 'Ili'ili'opae is today silent except for the chittering of birds. African tulip trees line the trail to the site, a peaceful place filled with *mana* (spiritual power), and whose stones still seem to emanate vibrations of a dramatic past. A good place to sit and take it all in is on the northern side, up the steps to the right of the heiau. Remember, however, that it's disrespectful to walk across the top of the heiau. In doing so you may succumb to heat exhaustion, too, and perhaps even twist an ankle more easily than you think.

Visiting this heiau is a little tricky, since it's on private property and the trail to it was almost completely overgrown at the time of research. To avoid disappointment, you might check with the MVA (p407) in Kaunakakai to see if you need advance permission to visit. Tours led by locals were on the docket last we checked.

The turnoff to the heiau is on the inland side of the highway, just over half a mile past the 15-mile marker, immediately after Mapulehu Bridge. It starts on a dirt drive on the east side of the creek. After a 10-minute walk, a footpath leads alongside a wall, and then off to the left opposite a house, where signs point you into the jungle and across a streambed. The heiau is only another two minutes' walk. Watch out for vicious local dogs along the way.

PUKO'O

You might go 'oh-oh' when you stumble on Puko'o. Once the seat of local government (complete with a courthouse, a jail, a wharf

---

FISHPONDS

Along the road to Halawa Valley, look *makai* (seaward) every so often and you'll see evidence of a highly developed system of early aquaculture. Indeed, Moloka'i's southeast coast is strung with Hawaii's largest concentration of ancient fishponds, which numbered over 60 at one time.

One type of fishpond was inshore and totally closed off from the sea. The other was created by a scallop-shaped stone wall that was parallel to the beach, and formed a shoreline enclosure. According to legend, fishponds were the work of the *menehune*, Hawaii's mythical race of little people, who made them appear virtually overnight.

Constructed from the 13th century onward, the enclosures were built of lava rock upon the reefs, and fitted with slatted sluice gates. These gates allowed small fish into the pond, where they were hand-fed with breadfruit and sweet potatoes. Fattened fish were then trapped and easily scooped up with a net.

Many fishponds were strictly for the *ali'i* (royalty or chiefs), with commoners forbidden to eat the fish raised in them. The system worked until the mid-1800s, when overgrazing by cattle and sheep resulted in widespread erosion, and the clay that washed down from the mountains choked the ponds. Over the years, efforts have been made to restock a few of the fishponds, mostly with mullet and milkfish. One of the most impressive and easily visited is the **Kalokoeli fishpond**, behind Molokai Shores condos, east of Kaunakakai.

and post office) the center of island life shifted to Kaunakakai, when the plantation folks built that more centrally located town. Nowadays, Puko'o is a sleepy, slow-paced place just sitting in a bend on the road, but has little surprises like the cozy **beach** accessible just before the Puko'o Neighborhood Store 'N' Counter, near the 16-mile marker. Take the short, curving path around the small bay, where fish leap out of the water, and you'll come to a sweet beach with swimmable waters, backed by kiawe and ironwood trees.

You get a load of placid ocean views at **Hilltop Cottage** (☎ 558-8161, cell phone ☎ 336-2076; www.molokaihilltopcottage.com; Kamehameha V Hwy; cottage d $150), a fresh, breezy cottage with a wraparound lanai that's almost as big as the living space. Located on a rise before the 18-mile marker, halfway between Puko'o and Waialua, the one-bedroom cottage has a full kitchen that is tastefully furnished and Swiss clean. There's a two-night minimum stay to avoid a hefty surcharge, and car-rental packages are available.

Honomuni House (☎ 558-8383; www.molokai-aloha.com/honomuni; Kamehameha V Hwy; cottage d $85) is a snug, garden guest cottage that's just beyond the Honomuni Bridge on the mauka (inland) side of the highway, before the 18-mile marker. Surrounded by grand trees and expansive lawn, these studio-style digs have a full kitchen, a bathroom and an outdoor deck and shower. The living room area has a sofa bed and TV. Seasonal fruits are provided. Save a bundle by booking for a week or more.

Puko'o Neighborhood Store 'N' Counter (☎ 558-8498; Kamehameha V Hwy, Puko'o; 🕗 8am-6:30pm, grill closed Mon) is a well-stocked little grocery store, near the 16-mile marker, and has fresh produce, eggs and video rentals. But come here for the counter – it's the only place to get a meal at the east end of the island. The fresh fish specials and hearty plate lunches (around $7) compete for Moloka'i's best and the filling chili bowl ($2.95) is *ono* (delicious). Breakfast options include pancakes or omelettes ($5). There are shaded picnic tables for chowing down.

WAIALUA

If you don't slow it down, you'll miss wee Waialua, a little roadside community just past the 19-mile marker. The attractive **Waialua Congregational Church**, which marks the center of the village, was built of stone in 1855. Nearby Waialua Beach is the site of Molokai's *keiki* surf competitions.

About 1200 yards after the 19-mile marker, begin looking for the remains of a stone chimney, a remnant of the **Moanui Sugar Mill**, which processed sugar until the mill burned down in the late 1800s. The ruins are about 50ft inland from the road, just before a stand of tall ironwood trees. Onward north from there, the road is spaghetti-thin, winding its way through land forlorn and mysterious, with the turquoise surf just below.

If you want beach over this way, look no further than the 20-mile marker, from where a stretch of white sand called **Twenty-Mile Beach**, pops up right along the thin roadside. There are pull-offs for parking, and when other Moloka'i beaches are rough, this is the area for swimming and snorkeling. However, when the tide is low, it's sometimes too shallow for snorkeling inside the reef. Snorkeling is much better beyond the reef, but, unless it's very calm, the currents can be dangerous. Many tourists end up with fins dangling in hand, just looking at the white caps and not daring to venture in.

The pointy clutch of rocks sticking out, as the road swings left before the 21-mile marker, is called, appropriately enough, **Rock Point**. This popular surf spot is the site of local competitions and it's the place to go if you're looking for east-end swells. For our money, the best swimming out here is about 500 yards beyond the 21-mile marker.

Sleeping

Waialua Pavilion & Campground (☎ 558-8150; vacate @aloha.net; HC 1, Box 780, Kaunakakai, HI 96748; tent site per person $15) The Congregational Church maintains this spiffy campground right on the ocean. Who cares if it's enclosed by a chain-link fence? There's a shower, a toilet and picnic tables here. Groups occasionally book the grounds, so call in advance to confirm that space is available.

Dunbar Beachfront Cottages (☎ 558-8153, 800-673-0520; www.molokai-beachfront-cottages.com; 2-bedroom cottages $140) The layout and furnishings are simple and functional at these two vacation cottages on secluded private beaches in Kainalu, around the 18-mile marker. Each cottage sleeps four people and comes with a fully equipped kitchen, TV, VCR, ceiling fans, a laundry, lanai and barbecue grills. The Pu'unana unit sits up high and has lots of windows taking in the delicious sea views. There's a three-night minimum stay and $75 cleaning charge.

WAIALUA TO HALAWA

After the 21-mile marker, the road starts to wind upwards. This is where the driving starts to get hairy and the vistas more varied. Tall grasses right at the edge threaten to reclaim the road, while ironwood trees and spiky sisal plants dot the surrounding hills. It's a good paved road – the problem is there's not always enough of it. In places, including some cliff-hugging curves, this road is only wide enough for one car, and you'll need to do some horn tooting. The road levels out just before the 24-mile marker, where there's a view of the bulbous islet of **Mokuho'oniki**, a seabird sanctuary.

The fenced grassland in this area is part of **Pu'u O Hoku Ranch** – at 14,000 acres, it's Molokai's second-largest ranch. Founded by Paul Fagan of Hana, the name means 'where hills and stars meet' – Jimmy Stewart and JFK are among the famous faces to have visited here. This is a certified organic farm; among the goodies grown is *'awa* (kava).

A hidden grove of sacred *kukui* (candlenut trees) on the ranch property marks the grave of the prophet Lanikaula, a revered 16th-century *kahuna* (priests, healers and sorcerers). One of the reasons the battling armies of Maui and O'ahu steered clear of Moloka'i for centuries was the powerful reputations of *kahuna* like Lanikaula, who were said to have been able to pray their enemies to death. Many islanders claim to have seen the night lanterns of ghost marchers bobbing

along near the grove. There's a little pull-off in the heart of the grove – dare to stop.

The ranch offers guided **horseback riding** (☎ 558-8109; www.puuohoku.com; 1hr/2hr rides $55/75) through wooded trails and windswept pastures. Their 4-hour ride to the beach for snorkeling ($120) is terrific in the winter, when humpback whales are migrating. There's a minimum of two people, and making reservations 24 hours in advance is appreciated.

After passing the 25-mile marker, the jungle closes in, and the scent of eucalyptus fills the air. About 1.25 miles after the 25-mile marker, there's a turnoff with a panoramic view of **Halawa Valley** and **Moa'ula Falls**; walk down the road a bit more for an even better vista. In the winter, this is a good place to watch for whales breaching.

There are lots of 'beep as you go' hairpin bends on the one-lane road that leads down to the valley, but the road is in good condition and the incline is reasonably gradual. No worries.

Sleeping & Eating

Pu'u o Hoku Ranch (☎ 558-8109; www.puuohoku.com; 2-bedroom cottage per day/week $150/1100; 4-bedroom cottage $165/990, extra guest per night $20) These comfortable digs, on spectacular grounds, have full kitchens, lanai, and views for days – perfect for a memorable romantic interlude or family getaway, especially the 4-bedroom unit with a fireplace. Also available is an entire lodge, with a fireplace, a swimming pool and sleeping accommodations for 22. Rates are based on two- and four-person occupancy for the smaller or bigger cottage, respectively; a two-night minimum stay required.

The little **store** right at the ranch gate sells kava, Snickers and sodas.

MOLOKA'I FOR KIDS

Moloka'i isn't the most kid-friendly island. Rough water conditions here make for dicey swimming, few diversions mean children can bore easily, and you have to be at least 16 years old to visit the Kalaupapa Peninsula. That said, here are some ideas for traveling with *na keiki* (children) here:

- **Rent a house** (p408) Provides running-around room, beach or lawn space, plus a TV and VCR, usually
- **Fly a kite** (p427) The friendly folks at the Big Wind Kite Factory offer free sport kite flying lessons
- **Kawakiu Beach** (p428) The protected area here is usually good for swimming
- **Hike to Moa'alu Falls** (opposite) Guided trips into the back of Halawa Valley are fun for the whole family

HALAWA VALLEY

Halawa Valley once had three heiau, two of which are thought to have been used for human sacrifice, and you'll probably feel the charge down here, though little remains of the sites. In the mid-19th century, the fertile valley had a population of about 500 people and produced most of Moloka'i's taro, as well as many of its melons, gourds and fruits. Taro production declined over the years, coming to an abrupt end in 1946, when a massive tsunami swept up Halawa Valley, wiping out the farms and much of the community. A second tsunami washed the valley clean in 1957. Only a few families now remain in Halawa.

Sights & Activities

Sunday services are still occasionally held in Hawaiian at the valley's little wooden **church**, where visitors are welcome anytime (the door remains open). It's a peaceful place to take five.

Halawa Beach was a favored surfing spot for Moloka'i chiefs, and remains so today for local kids. This beach park has double coves separated by a rocky outcrop, with the north side a bit more protected than the south. When the water is calm, there's good swimming and folks launch sea kayaks here, but both coves are subject to dangerous rip currents when the surf is heavy. There can also be strong currents whenever Halawa Stream, which empties into the north cove, is flowing heavily.

Halawa Beach Park has rest rooms and running water – treat water before drinking. Although pretty, the place has an eerie, foreboding quality and locals may show some hostility to outsiders. On the flip side, if you're received well, you might ask to be shown the way to 250-foot **Moa'ula Falls**, which are the twin falls to the back of the valley, reached via a 2-mile trail. Otherwise you can take a tour with Molokai Outdoor Activities or Molokai Fish & Dive (p405).

CENTRAL MOLOKA'I

Central Moloka'i takes in the Ho'olehua Plains, which stretch from Mo'omomi Beach in the west to the former plantation town of Kualapu'u. Extraordinarily fitting for the heart of Moloka'i, this part of the island also

has forested interiors leading to Kamakou Preserve, a unique rain forest that includes the island's highest mountain. On the north side of central Moloka'i is Kalaupapa Peninsula, the site of Hawaii's infamous leprosy colony.

Certainly the most-trodden route in central Moloka'i is the drive up Hwy 460, past the Kamakou Preserve mountain-road turnoff, and onto Hwy 470, past the coffee plantation, restored sugar mill museum, mule stables and the trailhead down to Kalaupapa Peninsula. The road ends at Pala'au State Park, site of the Kalaupapa Overlook, where you'll find one of the most captivating views on Moloka'i.

KAMAKOU

One of the profound, secret sides of Moloka'i lives in these mountains, which form the spine of the island's east side that reaches up to Mt Kamakou (4961ft), the island's highest peak. Hawaiian women used to hike up to the top of Kamakou to bury the afterbirth of their babies. According to folklore, this ritual would lead the newly born children to reach great heights in life. These days, islanders come to the forest to pick foliage for lei, as well as to hunt pigs, deer and goats.

The steep mountains here effectively prevent rain clouds from entering Moloka'i's central plains. Incredibly, more than 60% of Molokai's water supply comes from these forests. In the 1960s, a 5-mile-long tunnel was bored into the western side of Waikolu Valley. It now carries up to 28 million gallons of water daily to the Kualapu'u Reservoir.

The Nature Conservancy's Kamakou Preserve is a near-pristine rain forest that is home to more than 250 native plants (over 200 endemic) and some of Hawaii's rarest birds. With its mountaintop perch, Kamakou offers some splendid views of the northshore valleys unfolding below. The forest is a treasure and sufficient rationalization to upgrade to a 4WD rental.

Orientation

Kamakou is protected in its wilderness state in part because the rutted dirt road leading to it makes it hell to reach. A 4WD is essential and that's not just cover-your-ass guidebook jive. In dry weather, some people do make it as far as the lookout in a car, but if it's been raining at all, it's not advisable to

MOLOKA'I

try. In places where the road is narrow, a stuck car can block the whole road and it's ugly trying to maneuver out of that mud – especially due to the drop-off just at the road's edge. During the rainy season the road tends to get progressively more rutted until it's regraded in summer.

The 10-mile mountain road leading up from the highway to Waikolu Lookout takes about 45 minutes to drive, depending on road conditions. Start the journey by driving north from Kaunakakai on Hwy 460. Turn right about 1300 yards after the 3-mile marker, immediately before Manawainui Bridge. The paved road ends shortly at the Kalamaula hunters' check box. Although it starts out fairly smoothly, the road deteriorates as it goes along.

The landscape starts off shrubby, dry and dusty, later turning to dark, fragrant woods of tall eucalyptus, with patches of cypress and Norfolk pines. Although there's no evidence of it from the road, the Kalamaula area was once heavily settled. It was here that Kamehameha the Great knocked out his two front teeth in grieving the death of a female high chief, whom he had come to visit.

The **Moloka'i Forest Reserve** starts about 5.5 miles down the main road. A short loop road on the left leads to a former Boy Scout camp that's now used by The Nature Conservancy. After another 1.5 miles, there's an old water tank and reservoir off to the left. Another 2 miles brings you to the Sandalwood Pit, and one mile past that to Waikolu Lookout and Kamakou Preserve.

Sights

SANDALWOOD PIT

The centuries-old **Lua Na Moku Iliahi** ('Sandalwood Measuring Pit') is nothing more than a grassy depression on the left side of the road. Today it takes imagination to see the whole picture, as years of water erosion have rounded the sides of the hull-shaped hole. In the early 19th century, shortly after the lucrative sandalwood trade began, the pit was hand dug to the exact measurements of a 100ft-long, 40ft-wide and 7ft-deep ship's hold, and filled with fragrant sandalwood logs cleared from the nearby forest.

In the frenzy to make a quick buck to pay for alluring foreign goods, the *ali'i* forced the *maka'ainana* (commoners) to abandon their crops and work the forest. When the

pit was full, the wood was strapped onto the backs of the laborers, who hauled it down to the harbor for shipment to China. The sea captains made out like bandits, while Hawai'i was stripped of its sandalwood forests. After all the mature trees were cut down, the *maka'ainana* pulled up virtually every new sapling, in order to spare their children the misery of another generation of forced harvesting.

WAIKOLU LOOKOUT

At 3600ft, Waikolu Lookout provides a spectacular view into Waikolu Valley and out to the ocean beyond. Even if you're not able to spend time in Kamakou Preserve, get to this **lookout** if you can. Morning is best for clear views. If it's been raining recently, you'll be rewarded with numerous waterfalls streaming down the cliff sides. Waikolu means 'three waters' – presumably named for the three drops in the main falls.

A remote, grassy **camping area** is directly opposite the lookout. If you can bear the mist and cold winds that sometimes blow up from the canyon, especially during the afternoon and evening, this could make a base camp for hikes into the preserve. The site has pit toilets but no water supply or other amenities. No open fires are allowed and permits are required (see p401).

KAMAKOU PRESERVE

In 1982 Moloka'i Ranch conveyed to The Nature Conservancy the rights to manage the **Kamakou Preserve** (☎ 553-5236; http://nature.org/wherewework/northamerica/states/hawaii/preserves/art2355.html), which starts immediately beyond the Waikolu Lookout. Its 2774 acres of native ecosystems include cloud forest, bogs, shrub land and habitat for many endangered plants and animals.

Much of the preserve is forested with 'ohi'a lehua, a native tree with fluffy red blossoms, whose nectar is favored by native birds. It is home to two rare avian species that live only on Moloka'i, the Moloka'i creeper and Moloka'i thrush, as well as the bright red 'apapane (Hawaiian honeycreeper), yellow-green 'amakihi (bird) and pueo (Hawaiian owl). Other treasures include tree ferns, native orchids and silvery lilies.

The road deteriorates quickly from the preserve entrance. Don't even think about driving it without a 4WD. Even with a 4WD,

If you're not used to driving in mud and on steep grades, it can be challenging. There are a few spots where it would be easy to flip a vehicle. The Nature Conservancy asks visitors to sign in and out at the preserve entrance. Check out the sign-up sheet, where visitors write short entries on everything from car breakdowns to trail conditions and bird sightings. Occasionally, portions of the preserve are closed. At such times, notices are posted.

Activities

As Kamakou is a rain forest, trails in the preserve can be very muddy. Rain gear is a good idea, and you should bring ample drinking water. The **Pepe'opae Trail** affords a stunning view of Pelekunu Valley. Along the way, an extensive boardwalk allows hikers to access a nearly undisturbed Hawaiian montane bog, a miniature forest of stunted trees and dwarfed plants; the boardwalk protects the fragile ecosystem from being trampled. From the terminus at **Pelekunu Valley Overlook**, you'll enjoy a view of majestic cliffs, and if it's not too cloudy, you can see down the valley out to the ocean. The area receives about 180 inches of rain each year, making it one of the wettest regions in the Hawaiian Islands.

There are two ways to reach the Pepe'opae Trail. The easiest is to walk from Waikolu Lookout about 2.5 miles along the main jeep road to the main trailhead. It's a nice forest walk that takes just over an hour. There are some side roads along the way, but they're largely overgrown and it's obvious which is the main road. You'll eventually come to the 'Pepe'opae' sign that marks the start of the trail, which then branches to the left and heads east for 1 mile to the overlook.

The second and far-rougher way is to take the **Hanalilolilo Trail**. This trail, which is muddy and poorly defined, begins on the left side of the road about five minutes' walk past the Waikolu Lookout, shortly after entering the preserve. The Hanalilolilo Trail climbs 500ft through a rain forest of moss-covered 'ohi'a trees and connects with the Pepe'opae Trail after 1.5 miles. Turn left on the Pepe'opae Trail, and it's about a half-mile walk up to the summit overlooking Pelekunu Valley. Give yourself a good half-day to complete the entire hike back to the entrance.

HIDDEN MOLOKA'I

- Get that Swiss Family Robinson feeling at remote **Hale O Lono Point** (p426)
- The wild cliffs and bluffs of **Mo'omomi Beach** (p419)
- Talking story at **Molokai Drive-Inn** (p409)
- Kukui grove at **Pu'u O Hoku Ranch** (p414)
- The beach at the 16-mile marker near **Puko'o** (p412)
- The verdant hush along **Pepe'opae Trail** (left)
- Whale-watching from the **Maui–Molokai ferry** (p404)
- Star-gazing from your lanai (constellation books sold at Big Wind Kite Factory, p427)
- The entire island, brah!

Guided hikes with **The Nature Conservancy** (Molokai Preserves; ☎ 553-5236; www.nature.org; suggested donation $25), which offer insights into the preserve's history and ecology, are conducted on the first or second Saturday of the month. Transportation is provided to/from the preserve. Also ask about volunteer workdays, if you're seriously interested.

KUALAPU'U

Kualapu'u is the name of both a 1017ft hill, and the little village at the crossroads that has grown up north of it. At the base of the hill is the world's largest rubber-lined reservoir, which can hold up to 1.4 billion gallons of water piped in from the rain forests of eastern Moloka'i. The reservoir is presently the only source of water for the Ho'olehua Plains and the dry west end.

Del Monte set up headquarters here in the 1930s, and Kualapu'u developed into a pineapple-plantation town. The center of Del Monte's activities covered the spread between Kualapu'u and the nearby Ho'olehua homesteads. Pineapple ruled for nearly 50 years, but when Del Monte pulled out of Moloka'i in 1982, the economy crumbled.

While farm equipment rusted in overgrown pineapple fields, small-scale farming began developing more intensely, planting watermelons, dryland taro, macadamia nuts, sweet potatoes, seed corn, string beans and onions. The soil is so rich here, some feel Moloka'i has the potential to be Hawaii's 'breadbasket.' Still, there's nothing like a cash crop to give the local economy a jolt. In the case of Kaulapu'u, it was a java jolt: in 1991 coffee saplings were planted on formerly fallow pineapple fields, and now cover some 600 acres.

Stop by **Coffees of Hawaii** (☎ 567-9023, 800-709-2326; www.molokaicoffee.com; cnr Hwys 470 & 490) for free samples of several types of rich Moloka'i brews at the company shop and café, which sells packaged beans (16oz for $12). You can also take a 45-minute guided walking tour through the **coffee fields** (adult/child $7/3.50; ☽ 9:30 & 11:30am Mon-Fri), weather permitting. You're required to call ahead and make reservations to let the guides know you're coming.

Duck inside the screen door of **Kamuela Cookhouse** (☎ 567-9655; Hwy 490; breakfast & lunch $6-10, dinner $8-17; ☽ 7am-8pm), a down-home, friendly place with some of the best food on Moloka'i. The folks who just bought the historic restaurant are sticking with the winning formula of wholesome, hearty food served with aloha. Try the tender grilled mahimahi with ginger butter ($11) or the aromatic prime rib ($15, Thursday only). If you can, finish with the homemade chocolate mac-nut pie, or a slab of *liliko'i*-orange (passion fruit–orange) cheesecake. Breakfasts and plate lunches are equally as huge.

Espresso Bar (☎ 567-9241, 800-709-2326; snacks $2-5; ☽ 7am-4pm Mon-Fri, 8am-4pm Sat, 10am-4pm Sun) sells plain sandwiches, bagels and salads, plus any coffee drink you might desire at fair prices. Cooling off with a beer here after the Kalaupapa Peninsula hike is highly recommended.

HO'OLEHUA

Ho'olehua is the dry plains area that separates eastern and western Moloka'i. Here, in the 1790s, Kamehameha the Great trained his warriors in a year-long preparation for the invasion of O'ahu.

Ho'olehua was settled as an agricultural community in 1924, as part of the first distribution of land under the Hawaiian Homes Commission Act (p34), which made public lands available to native Hawaiians. By 1930, over half of Moloka'i's ethnic-Hawaiian population was living on homesteads.

The first homestead was attempted closer to the coast, at Kalaniana'ole, but it failed when the well water pumped to irrigate crops turned brackish. Many of those islanders then moved north to Ho'olehua, where homesteaders were already planting pineapple, a crop that required little water.

As the two giants Dole and Del Monte established operations in Moloka'i, homesteaders found it increasingly difficult to market their own pineapples and were eventually compelled to lease their lands to the plantations. Today, a more reliable water supply allows the cultivation of more diversified crops, including coffee, sweet potato, papaya and herbs. The wheels of government turn slowly, but native Hawaiians continue to receive land deeds in Ho'olehua in accordance with the Hawaiian Homes Act.

Orientation & Information

Three roads run east to west, with minor crossroads going north to south. Farrington Ave is Ho'olehua's main street, with a fire station, Episcopal church and Moloka'i's high school. The post office is on Pu'u Pe'elua Ave, just south of where it intersects with Farrington Ave. Pu'u Kapele Ave leads westward and then merges into another paved road that heads beachward, but dead ends at the Western Space & Missile Center, a radio receiving station for the US air force. Here, a bunch of odd metal towers and wire cables make it look as if grown-up kids have been mucking around with a giant Erector Set.

MAIL HOME SOME ALOHA

Peggy, the friendly postmaster of the **Ho'olehua post office** (☎ 567-6144; Pu'u Peelua Ave; ☽ 7:30am-11:30am & 12:30pm-4:30pm Mon-Fri) stocks baskets of unhusked coconuts that you can address and mail off as a unique (even edible!) 'postcard.' These coconuts, which the postmaster gathers on her own time, are offered free for this 'post-a-nut' purpose, and she keeps some felt pens on hand so you can jot down a message on the husk. Priority mail postage for an average-sized coconut to anywhere in the USA costs from $5. International deliveries are also possible.

Sights & Activities

PURDY'S MACADAMIA NUT FARM

The Purdy family runs the best little **macadamia-nut farm tour** (☎ 567-6601; admission free; ☺ 9:30am-3:30pm Mon-Fri, 10am-2pm Sat) in all of Hawaii. Unlike tours on the Big Island that focus on processing, Mr Purdy takes you into his orchard and personally explains how the nuts grow. A single macadamia tree can simultaneously be in different stages of progression – with flowers in blossom, tiny nuts just beginning and clusters of mature nuts. It's slow going, with a tree not bearing mature clusters until it's 10 years old.

Purdy's 1.5 acres of mature trees are nearly 75 years old and grow naturally: no pesticides, herbicides, fertilizers or even pruning. Everything is done in quaint Moloka'i style: You can crack open macadamia nuts on a stone with a hammer, and sample macadamia blossom honey scooped up with slices of fresh coconut. Macadamia nuts and honey are for sale.

To get to the farm, turn right onto 490 from Hwy 470. After 1 mile, take a right onto Lihi Pali Ave, just before the high school. The farm is a third of a mile up, on the right.

MO'OMOMI BEACH

This remote **beach**, located on the western edge of the Ho'olehua Plains, is ecologically unique. Managed by The Nature Conservancy, it stands as one of the few undisturbed coastal sand-dune areas left in Hawaii. Among its native grasses and shrubs are at least four endangered plant species that exist nowhere else on earth. It is one of the few places in the populated islands where green sea turtles still find suitable breeding habitat. Evidence of an adze quarry and the fossils of a number of long-extinct Hawaiian birds have been unearthed here, preserved over time by Mo'omomi's arid sands.

Mo'omomi is not lushly beautiful, but windswept, lonely and wild. In short, totally enchanting and worth the trouble it takes to get there. Follow Farrington Ave west, past the intersection with Hwy 480, until the paved road ends. Mo'omomi Ave, which is sometimes an alternate route, is usually closed and signposted as such.

From there, it's 2.5 miles farther along a red-dirt road that is in some areas quite smooth and in others deeply rutted. In places, you may have to skirt the edge of the road and straddle a small gully. It's ordinarily passable in a standard car, although the higher the vehicle the better. Rental-car contracts will forbid it, however, and it's definitely best to have a 4WD. After rain, it quickly becomes muddy.

If it gets too rough, there's a spot halfway down this last stretch, where you can pull off to the right and park. If you get lost in the maze of dirt roads, just keep heading toward the sea and look for the picnic pavilion that announces you've found **Mo'omomi Bay**, with a little sandy beach used by sunbathers. The rocky eastern point, which protects the bay, provides a fishing perch, and further along the bluffs, a sacred ceremony might be underway. The picnic pavilion, belonging to the Hawaiian Home Lands, has toilets, but bring your own drinking water.

The broad, white-sand beach that people refer to as Mo'omomi is not here – it's at **Kawa'aloa Bay**, a 20-minute walk further west. The wind, which picks up steadily each afternoon (brace yourself), blows the sand into interesting ripples and waves. The narrower right side of Kawa'aloa Bay is partially sheltered; however, the whole beach can be rough when the surf is up, and swimming is discouraged.

There's a fair chance you'll have Kawa'aloa to yourself, but if you don't you can always walk further on to one of the other sandy coves. Most of the area that is west of here is open ocean with strong currents. The high hills running inland are actually massive sand dunes – part of a mile-long stretch of dunes that back this part of coast. The coastal cliffs, which have been sculptured into jagged abstract designs by wind and water, are made of sand that has petrified due to Mo'omomi's dry conditions. The entire stretch of coast makes a superb spot to watch the sun set, coloring the cliffs in successive shades of golden green.

Because of the fragile ecology of the dunes, visitors should stay along the beach and on trails only. Visitors are not allowed to take any natural objects, including flora, rocks and coral. Foot access is allowed without a permit via the route described, although visitors with a 4WD vehicle can also get a gate key from The Nature Conservancy and drive directly to Kawa'aloa Bay (a permit application and $25 key deposit are required).

MOLOKA'I

The **Nature Conservancy** (☎ 553-5236; www .nature.org; suggested donation $25) leads monthly guided hikes of Mo'omomi, usually on the fourth Saturday of the month. Transportation is provided to and from the preserve. As it's common for hikers to fly over from other islands to join in, the pickup run includes Moloka'i airport. Reservations are required and spots fill up well in advance.

KALA'E

Four miles northeast of Hwy 460 is the sugar mill built by Rudolph W Meyer, an entrepreneurial German immigrant. Meyer was en route to the California gold rush when he stopped off in the islands, married a member of Hawaiian royalty and landed a tidy bit of property in the process.

He eventually found his gold in potatoes, which he grew and exported to the Californian miners. He also served as overseer of the Kalaupapa leprosy settlement and as manager of King Kamehameha V's ranch lands.

In the 1850s, Meyer established his own ranch, and exported cattle from Pala'au village. In one infamous incident, after finding his herd declining, he had all the men of Pala'au charged with cattle rustling, and sent off to jail in Honolulu. In 1876, when a new reciprocity treaty gave Hawaiian sugar planters the right to export sugar duty-free to the US, Meyer turned his lands over to sugar, and built the mill. It operated for only a decade.

Sights & Activities
R W MEYER SUGAR MILL
The mill, which is on the National Register of Historic Places, is the last of its kind. A lot of time and money has gone into authentic restorations, including the rebuilding of a 100-year-old steam engine, a mule-powered cane crusher, and other rusting machinery abandoned a century ago.

The **museum** (☎ 567-6436; adult/concession $2/1; ⏲ 10am-2pm Mon-Sat), beside the parking lot, contains a small display of Moloka'i's history with period photos, a few Hawaiiana items and a 10-minute video. Meyer and his descendants are buried in a little family plot out back.

This is also the Moloka'i campus for **Elderhostel** (☎ 877-426-8056; www.elderhostel.com) educational travel programs for seniors.

IRONWOOD HILLS GOLF COURSE
There are no polo shirts here, just a delightfully casual **golf course** (☎ 567-6362; green fees for 9/18 holes $18/23, pull/electric carts from $3/11, golf-club rental from $7; ⏲ 7am-5pm), with crabgrass growing in the sand pits and local golfers who actually look like they're having fun. Originally built by Del Monte for its employees, the course is down the red dirt road at the edge of the pasture, immediately south of Meyer Sugar Mill.

PALA'AU STATE PARK

Pala'au State Park, at the northern end of Hwy 470, is a must-visit for the bird's-eye view from the Kalaupapa Overlook. If you're planning on heading down to Kalaupapa itself, a side trip to the overlook is probably best done before you hike, so as not be anticlimactic. Nearby, a five-minute walk through a grove of ironwoods leads to a phallic-shaped rock. Both trails are easy to follow and are just a couple of minutes from the parking lot. The park has camp sites, picnic areas and lovely stands of paper-bark eucalyptus.

Sights & Activities
KALAUPAPA OVERLOOK
The Kalaupapa Overlook provides a scenic overview of the Kalaupapa Peninsula from the edge of a 1600ft cliff. It's like an aerial view without the airplane. Kalaupapa residents use the term 'topside' to refer to all of Moloka'i outside their peninsula, and seen from here, the reason is obvious. Because of the angle of the sun, the best light for photography is usually from late morning to mid-afternoon.

The lighthouse, at the northern end of the peninsula, once boasted the most-powerful beam in the Pacific. The 700,000-candle-power Fresnel crystal lens cast its light until 1986, when it was taken down and replaced by an electric light beacon.

Interpretive plaques identify significant landmarks below and explain Kalaupapa's history as a leprosy colony. The village where all of Kalaupapa's residents live is visible, but Kalawao, the original settlement and site of Father Damien's church and grave, is not.

Kalaupapa means 'flat leaf,' an accurate description of the lava-slab peninsula that was created when a low shield volcano poked up out of the sea, long after the rest of Moloka'i had been formed. The dormant Kauhako Crater, visible from the overlook, contains a little lake that's more than 800ft deep. At 400ft, the crater is the highest point on the Kalaupapa Peninsula.

There's a vague **trail** of sorts that continues directly beyond the last plaque at the overlook. Simply follow this trail for 20 minutes or so until it peters out. Few people go this way, and it's very peaceful – if you're lucky, you may even spot deer crossing the trail.

The path, on a carpet of soft ironwood needles, passes through a thickly planted forest of ironwood and eucalyptus, dotted here and there with Norfolk pines. These diagonal rows of trees were planted during a CCC (Civil Conservation Corps) reforestation project in the 1930s. The trees create a canopy over the trail, and there's little undergrowth to obscure the way.

KAULEONANAHOA

Kauleonanahoa (the penis of Nanahoa) is Hawaii's premier **phallic stone**, poking up in a little clearing inside an ironwood grove. The legend goes that Nanahoa hit his wife Kawahuna in a jealous rage and when they were both turned to stone, he came out looking like this. Nature has endowed it well, but the explanatory plaque confirms rumors it has been 'carved to some extent'. Reputedly women who bring offerings of lei and dollar bills to the rock cock and stay overnight here return home pregnant, but evidently there's no danger in having a look.

Sleeping

A quarter of a mile before the overlook, the **camping area** is usually quite peaceful, even deserted. It's basically just a field next to a concrete picnic pavilion, affording no privacy, especially when local families show up to barbecue and celebrate. At night, apart from the trickle of passing traffic, the only sounds come from roosters and the braying of mules from the nearby stables. Clouds start gathering in the late afternoon and, by midnight, your tent may well be drenched; this is less likely during the summer dry season. Still, it rains here a lot. There are rest rooms, but no potable water. Look for the pavilion past the mule stables, which are around the 5-mile marker. See p401 for site fees and permit information.

KALAUPAPA PENINSULA

Kalaupapa Peninsula is electrifying, spreading out beautifully between glittering seas at the base of seemingly impenetrable, majestic cliffs. The peninsula's remoteness makes it feel exceptionally lonely and cut off, which is why it served as a leprosy settlement for more than a century. The peninsula has been designated the Kalaupapa National Historical Park and is managed by the Hawaii Department of Health and the **National Park Service** (www.nps.gov/kala). It is unique in that many of the people whose histories are being described are still living on the site. These are tragic stories of relocation and forced removal from their homes and families.

Access to the peninsula is only by mule, on foot or by small plane and is one of Moloka'i's major attractions. It's also a pilgrimage of sorts for admirers of Father Damien (Joseph de Veuster), the Belgian priest who devoted the latter part of his life to helping people with leprosy, before dying of the disease himself. He is being proposed for sainthood. He has our vote. Check out the movie *Molokai: The Story of Father Damian,* starring Peter O'Toole and Kris Kristofferson, to learn about the heroic deeds of Father Damien.

HISTORY

Ancient Hawaiians used Kalaupapa as a refuge when caught in storms at sea. The peninsula held a large settlement at the time of early Western contact, and the area is rich in archaeological sites, currently under investigation. A major discovery in 2004 indicated that Kalaupapa heiau had major ritual significance, with possible astronomical purposes.

In 1835, doctors in Hawaii diagnosed the state's first case of leprosy, one of many diseases introduced by foreigners. Before modern medicine, leprosy manifested itself in dripping, foul-smelling sores. Eventually, patients experienced loss of sensation and tissue degeneration that could lead to fingers, toes and noses becoming hideously deformed or falling off altogether. Blindness was common. Alarmed by the spread of the disease, King Kamehameha V signed into law an act that banished people with leprosy to Kalaupapa Peninsula, beginning in 1865.

MOLOKA'I

Hawaiians call leprosy *mai ho'oka'awale,* which means 'separating sickness,' a disease all the more dreaded because it tore families apart. Kalaupapa Peninsula is surrounded on three sides by some of Hawaii's roughest and most shark-infested waters, and on the fourth by the world's highest sea cliffs. Some patients arrived in boats, whose captains were so terrified of the disease they would not land, but instead dropped patients overboard. Those who could, swam to shore; those who couldn't perished.

Once the afflicted arrived on Kalaupapa Peninsula, there was no way out, not even in a casket. The original settlement was in Kalawao, at the wetter eastern end of the peninsula. Early conditions were unspeakably horrible, with the strong stealing rations from the weak and women forced into prostitution or worse. Lifespans were invariably short, and desperate.

Father Damien arrived at Kalaupapa in 1873. He wasn't the first missionary to come, but he was the first to stay. What Damien gave them most of all was a sense of hope. The priest put up more than 300 houses – each little more than four walls, a door and a roof, but still a shelter to those cast here. Damien was a talented carpenter, and some of the solid little churches he built around Moloka'i and the Big Island still stand. Damien also nursed the sick, wrapped bandages on oozing sores, hammered coffins and dug graves. On average, he buried one person a day. In 1888, he installed a water pipeline over to the sunny western side of the peninsula, and the settlement moved from Kalawao to where it remains today.

Damien's work inspired others. Brother Joseph Dutton arrived in 1886 and stayed 44 years. In addition to his work with the sick, he was a prolific writer who kept the outside world informed about what was happening in Moloka'i. Mother Marianne Cope arrived a year before Damien died. She stayed 30 years, helping to establish a girls' home and encouraging patients to live life to the fullest. She is widely considered to be the mother of the hospice movement. Damien died in 1889 at the age of 49. In 1995, he was beatified by Pope John Paul II and is now a candidate for sainthood.

Over the years, some 8000 people have come to the Kalaupapa Peninsula to live out their lives. The same year that Father Damien arrived, a Norwegian scientist named Dr Gerhard Hansen discovered *Mycobacterium leprae,* the bacteria that causes leprosy, thus proving that the disease was not hereditary, as was previously thought. Even in Damien's day, leprosy was one of the least contagious of all communicable diseases: only 4% of human beings are even susceptible to it.

In 1909, a fancy medical facility called the US Leprosy Investigation Station opened at Kalawao. However, the hospital was so out of touch – requiring patients to sign themselves in for two years, live in seclusion and give up all Hawaiian-grown food – that even in the middle of a leprosy colony, it attracted only a handful of patients. It closed a few years later.

Since the 1940s, sulfa antibiotics have been used to successfully treat and control leprosy, but the isolation policies in Kalaupapa weren't abandoned until 1969. Today, fewer than 100 patients are living on Kalaupapa Peninsula, the vast majority of them senior citizens (at the time of research, the youngest was 67, the oldest 92). They are, of course, free to leave, but they choose to stay. When you see this wildly beautiful peninsula for yourself, it's not hard to understand why. Many rightly feel that this is their only home, and have long fought against being bought out by the government and displaced from their land.

While the state of Hawaii officially uses the term 'Hansen's Disease' for leprosy, many Kalaupapa residents consider that to be a euphemism that fails to reflect the stigma they have suffered and continue to use the old term 'leprosy.' The degrading appellation 'leper,' however, is offensive to all.

INFORMATION

Old state laws requiring everyone who enters the settlement to have a 'permit,' and be at least 16 years old, are no longer a medical necessity, but they continue to be enforced in order to protect the privacy of the patients. There's no actual paper permit. Your reservation with Damien Tours or Molokai Mule Ride acts as your permit. Only guests of Kalaupapa residents are allowed to stay overnight. That said, you *can* hike down to the base of the cliffs and play on the beautiful chocolate-sand beach, located outside the settlement, without prior arrangement.

SIGHTS & ACTIVITIES

On typical tours, the village looks nearly deserted, though here and there people might be mowing lawns, or repotting their crotons. The sights are mainly cemeteries, churches and memorials. Visitors are not allowed to photograph the residents. Kalaupapa is a tourist attraction, but its people are not.

A stop at a small store for snacks and drinks is made towards the beginning of the tour, followed by a short visit to a simple **visitor center**, where photographs of the original settlement are on display, and books and videos are for sale. Groups then travel across the peninsula to Kalawao.

St Philomena Church (better known as Father Damien's Church), in Kalawao, was built in 1872. You can still see where Damien cut open holes in the floor so that the sick who needed to spit could attend church and not be ashamed. The graveyard at the side contains Damien's gravestone and original burial site, although his body was exhumed in 1936 and returned to Belgium. In 1995, his right hand was reinterred here.

The view from Kalawao is one of the island's finest. It's one of the world's finest, with the highest *pali* (cliffs) on earth, measuring 3300ft, with an average gradient of 58 degrees, folding out in successive ripples, like a geological accordion, towards the northeast. The **rock island** just offshore is the legendary home of a giant shark. From some angles, it looks like a shark's head coming straight up out of the water, while from other angles it looks like a dorsal fin. This is your lunch spot and a favorite movie location: *Jurassic Park II* and *III*, *Robert Louis Stevenson* and *Mark Twain* were all shot here.

The **hiking trail** down to Kalaupapa starts on the east side of Hwy 470, just north of the mule stables. The 3-mile hike along the mule trail takes just over an hour going down, slightly longer going up. It's best to begin hiking by 8am, before the mules start to go down, to avoid walking in fresh dung, though you have no choice on the return trip. The steep narrow trail, with 26 switchbacks, is matted in places but is not terribly strenuous. Look for guava at the top of the trail.

The deserted, sensuous **beach** at the bottom of the trail has great *pali* views and hostile surf, undertow and some say sharks, so take care. Here you'll find pristine cocoa-colored sand and *opihi* (edible limpet) the size of silver dollars. It's imperative to be respectful of this special place: you cannot venture beyond the beach unless you're on a tour, and the divine powers will have your hide if you take anything but photos or leave anything but footprints.

TOURS

Bus Tours

Everyone who comes to the Kalaupapa Peninsula, must visit the settlement with **Damien Tours** (☎ 567-6171; $30; ☘ tours Mon-Sat). Richard Marks, who runs Damien Tours, is a wry storyteller, opinionated oral historian and the third generation of his family to live on Kalaupapa. Reservations must be made in advance (call between 4pm and 8pm), and bring your own lunch. The tours pick up visitors both at the airport and the bottom of the trail. At the time of research, visitors arriving by mule could not ride in the school bus driven by Richard (thus missing the best banter).

Tours last 3.5 hours and are uncomfortably rushed. What irony to come to the most-remote part of the most Hawaiian of islands, only to be constantly admonished to hurry up. This is because everyone is beholden to the tyranny of the outbound airplane schedule. Consider that these tours were once eight hours, and you'll realize how fast you have to move, and how many sights you miss. Capping the maximum number of tour participants might go some way toward ameliorating the problem.

Mule Rides

One of the best-known outings in the islands is the mule ride down the *pali* to Kalaupapa. While the mules move none too quickly – actually, hiking down can be faster – there's a certain thrill in trusting your life to these sure-footed beasts, while descending 1600ft on 26 narrow cliff-side switchbacks.

Molokai Mule Ride (☎ 567-6088, 800-567-7550; www.muleride.com; per person $150; ☘ Mon-Sat) is the only outfit offering rides. Because the number of saddles is limited, tours can fill up quickly; make reservations well in advance. Tours begin at the mule stables at 8am sharp, for a short riding lesson from real *paniolo* (Hawaiian cowboys). At around 8:30am, riders hit the trail, which begins opposite the stables. The mules arrive in Kalaupapa around 10am, and shortly thereafter

MOLOKA'I

the bus tour of the peninsula begins. The whole shebang includes lunch, and lands back at the stables at around 3:30pm. Wear loose trousers, close-toed shoes and a windbreaker. Airport transfers are available for $9 per person (two-person minimum).

GETTING THERE & AROUND

The switchback mule trail down the *pali* is the only land route to the peninsula, either on foot (p423) or by riding a mule (p423); the other option for getting to Kalaupapa is by air. No matter how you get there, you cannot wander around by yourself, and must join Damien Tours (p423) to visit the settlement. Molokai Outdoor Activities (p405) sells combination tours that allow you to hike (or ride) in and fly out.

Air

Kalaupapa has a little air strip at the edge of the peninsula and air service via small prop planes. The beauty of flying in are the views you get en route of the *pali* and towering waterfalls. Passengers must first book a tour with Damien Tours before buying air tickets.

Pacific Wings (☎ 567-6814, on Maui ☎ 873-0877, 888-575-4546; www.pacificwings.com; return $70) flies daily from Honolulu to Kalaupapa (departing at 8:40am, 30 minutes). The return flights leave Kalaupapa at 1:45pm.

Paragon Air (on Maui ☎ 244-3356, on the Neighbor Islands & US mainland ☎ 866-946-4744; www.paragon-air.com) offers flight packages from Maui ($225 per person) that include Damien Tours reservations and lunch. They also offer a fly-in and mule-ride package ($290) that departs from Kahului, Kapalua/West Maui or Hana airports.

WEST END

High, dry grassy rangeland with a buttoned-up feel, thanks to all the 'Private Property, Trespassers Will Be Prosecuted' signs, western Moloka'i is different in climate, landscape and tenor from the rest of the island. Points west are reached via the good, paved Maunaloa Hwy (Hwy 460). Primary roads also go to and around Kaluakoi Resort and down to Papohaku and Dixie Maru beaches. Moloka'i Ranch owns most of this part of Moloka'i, and access

here is at their whim, requiring special permission. Of course, paying guests, either on one of their tours, or in their accommodations, enjoy the most free rein here.

In the 1850s, Kamehameha V acquired the bulk of Moloka'i's arable land, forming Moloka'i Ranch, but overgrazing eventually led to the widespread destruction of native vegetation and fishponds. After his death, the ranch became part of the Bishop Estate, which quickly sold it off to a group of Honolulu businesspeople.

A year later, in 1898, the American Sugar Company, a division of Moloka'i Ranch, attempted to develop a major sugar plantation in central Moloka'i. The company built a railroad system to haul the cane, developed harbor facilities, and installed a powerful pumping system to draw water. However, by 1901 the well water used to irrigate the fields had become so saline that the crop failed. The company then moved into honey production on such a large scale that at one point Moloka'i was the world's largest honey exporter. In the mid-1930s, however, an epidemic wiped out the hives and the industry. Strike two for the industrialists.

Meanwhile, the ranch continued its efforts to find 'the crop for Moloka'i.' Cotton rice and numerous grain crops all took their turn biting Moloka'i's red dust. Finally pineapple took root as the crop most suited to the island's dry, windy conditions. Plantation-scale production began in Ho'olehua in 1920. Within 10 years, Moloka'i's population tripled, as immigrants arrived to toil in the fields.

In the 1970s, overseas competition brought an end to the pineapple's reign on Moloka'i. Dole closed its operation in 1976 and the other island giant, Del Monte, later followed suit. These closures brought hard times and the highest unemployment level in the state. Then cattle raising, long a mainstay, suddenly collapsed. In a controversial decision in 1985, the state, after finding a incidence of bovine tuberculosis, ordered every head of cattle on Moloka'i to be destroyed. Moloka'i Ranch has since restocked some of its herd, but the majority of the 2- smaller cattle owners called it quits.

Moloka'i Ranch still owns some 64,000 acres, about 40% of Moloka'i, and more than half of the island's privately held land. Many locals resent the ranch for restricting

THE MOLOKA'I PLAN

The Moloka'i Plan called for the preservation of Moloka'i's rural lifestyle and the maintenance of agriculture as the basis of the island's economy. It also called for all resort development to be low-rise and limited to the west end. The plan has been widely accepted as the guiding code for land use on Moloka'i, and is referred to whenever there are disputes over development – which is often.

Some critics say that the final compromise draft approved by Maui County officials – Moloka'i is part of Maui County – is too weak to protect west-end archaeological sites, and too strong in its support of Moloka'i Ranch as the key to revitalization. A diversified economy, not a greater reliance on tourism, is what opponents propose. The latest fight is over the admittance of cruise ships into Moloka'i, and so far opponents have successfully kept them at bay. You'll see 'no cruise ships' signs on front lawns and 'cruise ships pollute' on cars' rear bumpers.

access to land, and the pursuit of a number of traditional outdoor activities.

In the 1990s the ranch operated a small wildlife-safari park, where many shutterbug tourists snapped pictures of exotic animals, and trophy hunters paid $1500 a head to shoot African eland and blackbuck antelope. Rumors abound of how local activists, long resistant to the type of tourist-oriented development that has all but consumed neighboring Maui, made life so difficult for the ranch that the safari park was shut down. Some of the remaining animals were tragically killed before they could be transported to off-island zoos by an accidental overdose of tranquilizers, just another note in the island's troubled history.

Several years ago, the old plantation town of Maunaloa was bulldozed, levelling all but a few buildings, and new houses mimicking old, plantation-style homes were erected. This drove up rents and drove out some small businesses, again provoking the ire of island residents. The newest owners of Moloka'i Ranch – an international group flying under the banner of Molokai Properties – are taking a different tack, trying to engage, rather than isolate, the locals.

MAUNALOA

The long mountain range that comes into view on the left past the 10-mile marker is Maunaloa, which means 'long mountain.' Its highest point, at 1381ft, is Pu'u Nana. In addition to being the site of Hawaii's first hula school and one of the Hawaiian Islands' most-important adze quarries, Maunaloa was also once a center of sorcery. In short, a powerful place in Hawaiian history and culture.

The name Maunaloa not only refers to the mountain range but also to the town at the end of the road. Built in the 1920s by Libby, McNeill & Libby, this little plantation town was the center of the company's pineapple activities on Moloka'i. Dole, which acquired Libby, McNeill & Libby in 1972, closed down operations in Maunaloa in 1975.

Maunaloa is kind of a sad little place – one of the only spots in Moloka'i where people aren't smiling spontaneously. Moloka'i Ranch owns the land that the town sits on, which exists mostly for the tourist industry, giving it a superficial feel. These days about 230 people live in the area, most working for the ranch. With 8000 head of cattle, Moloka'i Ranch is actually the second-largest working cattle ranch in the state, but tourists are the main cash crop.

Information

All of Maunaloa's businesses lie along Maunaloa Hwy, the town's main street. The little rural **post office** (☎ 552-2852) is opposite the grocery store. The village **gas station** (☉ 7am-5pm Mon-Fri, 9am-5pm Sat, noon-4pm Sun) is the only one outside of Kaunakakai.

Sights & Activities

Moloka'i Ranch Headquarters & Logo Shop (☎ 552-0184; ☉ 6am-7pm) is on your immediate right, after Hwy 460 makes its final turn into town. Step inside for exhibits on ranch history, or to make bookings at the activity desk. Activity fees for guests are high, and for nonguests they are even steeper; if things are slow, discounts may be negotiable.

The ranch offers 2½-hour guided **horseback rides** (per person $80; ☉ 9:30am daily, 1pm Mon & Thu-Sat). The rides cross ranch pasture

DETOUR: HALE O LONO POINT

Just outside Maunaloa, veer off Hwy 460, blowing by tony Moloka'i Ranch on your right until the asphalt peters out and turns to crushed gravel. A sign points the way to **Hale O Lono Point**, a forlorn, fairly violent coastal landscape. After 3.4 miles of tolerable road and rolling ranchland, turn left. The driving is a little hairy for the next 1.2 miles to the point, with some deep gullies, but nothing too heinous, even for a regular car.

Just under a half mile farther on you'll hit a small protected swimming area and a fish-rich harbor with folks casting from the jetty into turbulent waters. This is the setting off point for the annual **Moloka'i Hoe** (http://holoholo.org/hoe) outrigger canoe race. The brutal 41-mile crossing through the Ka'iwi Channel from Molka'i to O'ahu tests the mental and physical endurance of the 6-person teams, the quickest of which made it in 4:50:31. If you're in Moloka'i in mid-October, do not miss this event. Drive around the harbor and you'll be greeted by an intense flotsam sculpture, with everything from a rusty anchor to human hair thrown together. You'll also see why this hostile stretch of coast is a favorite spot for ATV (All Terrain Vehicle) fans: rugged, deserted and way off the beaten track, if you've made it this far, you'll likely make some Hawaiian friends.

providing ocean and Lana'i views. With a two-person minimum, this is a romantic option for couples. For the more adventurous, there's a **paniolo roundup** (per person $80; 9:30am Mon-Sat, 1pm Mon & Thu-Sat), complete with barrel racing, pole vending and cattle herding. Guided hikes led by knowledgeable cultural guides cost $30 to $125. The most-fantastic adventures to be had here are on the back of mountain bikes, whether you're racing downhill on a gravity ride, or pedaling along the tops of the highest sea cliffs in the world ($35-100). Other ranch activities include kayaking, ocean fishing, archery and special kids' adventures and classes. Some of these tours are led in conjunction with Molokai Fish & Dive (p406).

Festivals & Events
Every June Moloka'i Ranch hosts the **He Makana Aloha** performing-arts competition and festival (free).

Sleeping
Moloka'i Ranch (660-2824, 888-627-8082; www.molokairanch.com; 8 Maunaloa Hwy; beach/lodge accommodation packages incl meals from $170/200;) Exquisite views from quilt-covered, canopy beds, tubs with braided rugs at its claw feet, rope hammocks slung between palm trees: this place defines rustic luxury. Accommodations are at the lodge hotel or, better yet, out at remote, private Kaupoa Beach Village, where each deluxe 2-bedroom canvas bungalow has a lanai, fine linens, solar-powered lights, ceiling fan, hot shower, and composting toilet. The village has pavilions where chefs

prepare buffet-style meals. Shuttles connect the two installations.

A visit to Moloka'i Ranch is very much a package tour. Ranch staff pick up guests at the airport, check them in at the ranch's Maunaloa headquarters, and then take them by van along the ranch's roads to the camp. Although the ranch offers visitors a chance to play a bit of *paniolo*, guests generally don't see much of Moloka'i outside the ranch gates – then again, the ranch owns almost half of the entire island. Package deals are available online.

Eating
Paniolo Café (552-2625; 1 Maunaloa Hwy; meals $3.50-8; 11am-7:30pm) This very casual place with cafeteria ambience does classic plate lunches ($5.50 to $7) like *loco moco* (a mound of rice with a hamburger and fried egg on top, and the whole mess smothered in gravy), chicken *katsu* (deep-fried chicken strips) and teriyaki beef, plus saimin with Spam ($3.50) or a tasty whole roasted chicken ($8). Skip the hamburgers. For everyday supplies, **Maunaloa General Store** (8am-6pm Mon-Sat) has a reasonable selection of groceries, plus wine and beer.

Maunaloa Room (660-2725, 877-726-4656; www.molokairanch.com; Maunaloa Hwy; breakfast $4-12, dinner $21-28; breakfast & dinner) offers upscale à la carte items like glazed tofu ($21 – that's some pricey bean curd!) and *mahi* with pineapple chutney ($26), plus nightly specials like all-you-can-eat Wok Night ($20).

The best eating deal out here is **brunch** ($20; 11am-1pm Sun) at secluded Kaupoa Beach, replete with omelets cooked to order, catch of the day, rainbows of tropical fruits and salads, pastries, potatoes, the works. For reservations (essential), call **Moloka'i Ranch** (☎ 660-2824).

Entertainment

At Moloka'i Ranch's lodge, the Paniolo Bar is one of Moloka'i's only bars. Cocktails and *pupu* are served in a genteel cowboy atmosphere. **Maunaloa Town Cinemas** (☎ 552-2707; 1 Maunaloa Hwy; bargain matinees before 6pm $5, night admission $6.50) shows first-run movies.

Shopping

Big Wind Kite Factory & Plantation Gallery (☎ 552-2364; www.molokai.com/kites; 120 Maunaloa Hwy; ☺ 8am-5pm Mon-Sat, 10am-2pm Sun) The island's most-interesting shop makes and sells colorful kites in all shapes and styles. Most days you can watch the kitemakers at their craft, fashioning whimsical tropical fish and other island-influenced designs. Free sport kite-flying lessons are available upon request.

An extension of the kite factory is the eclectic **gift shop** next door, which not only has Moloka'i's best book selection, but also sells travel hammocks (the bomb), Civil War ephemera, wood carvings from Bali, scrimshaw carvings from Moloka'i deer, and jewelry.

KALUAKOI RESORT

In the 1970s, Moloka'i Ranch joined with Louisiana Land & Exploration Company to form the Kaluakoi Corporation, which proposed developing western Moloka'i into a major suburb of Honolulu, complete with a ferry service. The plan called for 30,000 private homes on the heretofore uninhabited west coast. A vocal antidevelopment movement boomed quicker than the buildings could, however, and the plan was scrapped.

In its place, a somewhat more-modest plan was hatched for the development of Kaluakoi Resort. Only 200 of the condo units, one 18-hole golf course, and one of the four planned hotels, were ever built. The 290-room hotel never really took off and the occupancy rate was so low that part of it was turned into condos. Things worsened after September 11, 2001. The house lots have been subdivided, but fewer than 100 houses have been built, mostly starter

castles scattered along the edge of the beach and up on the bluff.

Later, mismanagement by a Japanese corporation effectively ran the resort with its 18-hole golf course into the ground. The greens turned brown, and things looked deserted for a while. Now that's all ready to change, as Moloka'i Ranch has bought most of the resort property.

Sights & Activities

Visitors today can still have the beaches pretty much to themselves, but that surely won't last. Indeed, at the time of research they were readying to reopen the back nine of the **Kaluakoi Golf Course** (☎ 552-0255; ☺ 7:30am-4pm).

Turning off Hwy 460 before Maunaloa, at the 15-mile marker, a road leads down to the resort and main west-end beaches. **Kepuhi Beach** is the white-sand beach in front of the old Kaluakoi Hotel. Swimming conditions are often dangerous here. Not only can there be a tough shorebreak but strong currents can be present even on calm days. During the winter, the surf breaks close to shore, crashing in waves that are half water, half sand. Experienced surfers take to the northern end of the beach.

A five-minute hike up to the top of **Pu'u o Kaiaka**, a 110ft-high promontory at the southern end of Kepuhi Beach, rewards strollers with a nice view of Papohaku Beach. At the top, you'll find the remains of a pulley that was once used to carry cattle down to waiting barges for transport to O'ahu slaughterhouses. There was also a 40ft heiau on the hilltop until 1967, when the US army bulldozed it. To get to the parking lot, turn off Kaluakoi Rd onto Kaiaka Rd, proceeding a half mile to the road's end.

In the opposite direction, **Make Horse Beach** supposedly takes its name from days past, when wild horses were run off the cliff north of here. *Make* (mah-*kay*) means 'dead' in Hawaiian. This pretty little white-sand beach is a local favorite, and more secluded than the one in front of Kaluakoi Hotel. It's an idyllic spot for sunbathing and sunset, but usually not for swimming. On the calmest days, daredevils leap off the giant boulder at the beach's southern end.

To get here, turn off Kaluakoi Rd onto the road to Paniolo Hale condos and then turn left toward the condo complex. You can park just beyond the condos and walk the last quarter of a mile down to the golf course, or brave the deeply rutted dirt road to its end, where there's a parking area. Once at the golf course, cross a narrow stretch of fairway, and you're on the beach.

Kawakiu Beach, further north along the shoreline, is a broad crescent beach of white sand and bright turquoise waters. To get there, turn off Kaluakoi Rd onto the road to the Paniolo Hale condos, but instead of turning left down to the condos, continue straight toward the golf course. Where the paved road ends, there's space to pull over and park, just before crossing the greens. You'll come first to a rocky point at the southern end of the bay. Before descending to the beach, scramble around up here for a scenic view of the coast, south to Papohaku Beach and north to 'Ilio Point.

When seas are calm, usually in summer, Kawakiu is generally safe for swimming. When the surf is rough, there are still areas where you can at least get wet. On the southern side of the bay, there's a small, sandy-bottomed wading pool in the rocks. The northern side has an area of flat rocks over which water slides, to fill up a shallow shoreline pool.

In 1975, Kawakiu was a focus of Moloka'i activists, who began demanding access to private, and heretofore forbidden, beaches. The group, Hui Alaloa, marched to Kawakiu from Mo'omomi in a successful protest that convinced Moloka'i Ranch to provide public access to this secluded west-end beach. Except for weekends, you may well have the place to yourself.

Sleeping & Eating

Ke Nani Kai (off Kaluakoi Rd; 1-/2-bedroom units from $115/145; 🏊) Set on manicured grounds adjacent to superlative Papohaku Beach and nine holes of golf, the best of these condos are arguably the nicest on Moloka'i. Each has a full kitchen, lanai, washer and dryer, a bath with a tub and cable TV; most have a sofa bed in the living room, making this an economical option for small groups. For $20 more you get (distant, partial) ocean views. Book through Friendly Isle Realty or Molokai Vacation Rental (p408).

Paniolo Hale (studios from $95, 1-bedroom unit from $120; 🏊) Big, airy lanai at these spiffy condos look over leafy, quiet grounds, giving it the best atmosphere of all the west-end complexes. Although individually owned, the units are very well furnished in a casual, yet quality, tropical style with hardwood floors, lots of light and loads of space. Book through **Molokai Vacation Rental** (p408).

Kaluakoi Villas (☎ 552-2721, 800-367-5004; www .castleresorts.com; 1131 Kaluakoi Rd; studio/1-bedroom unit from $135/160; 🏊) *The Shining* anyone? These villas – too quiet, too deserted, grass invading the parking lot – are part of the old Kaluakoi Hotel and it's a bit eerie. The beach location is good, and the oceanfront swimming pool is a plus, but units only have kitchenettes and you're far from everything. Go for the deeply discounted Internet offers, or not at all.

The old Kaluakoi Hotel's sundries shop is open for business, selling wine, beer and a few convenience foods at inflated prices. Making a trek up to the Maunaloa General Store (p426) will pay off when buying supplies or groceries in bulk.

WEST END BEACHES

From Moloka'i's west-end beaches, the twinkling lights of O'ahu are just 26 miles away. The view is of Diamond Head to the left, Makapuu Point to the right. The very best constellation books are sold at Big Wind Kite Factory (p427) if you want to gaze skyward with intent.

Beautiful **Papohaku Beach** lays claim to being Hawaii's longest beach. It's 2.5 miles of quintessential paradise and vast enough to hold the entire population of Moloka'i without getting crowded. There's seldom more than a handful of beachgoers, even on

---

TED NUGENT'S DREAM DESTINATION?

Hounds and camouflaged trucks are common sites in hunting-happy Moloka'i. The Axis deer that run free here are descendants of eight deer sent from India in 1868 as a gift to King Kamehameha V. Feral pigs, introduced by the early Polynesian settlers, still roam the upper wetland forests, and feral goats inhabit the steep canyons and valley rims. All wreak havoc on the environment and are hunted as game animals. Drive carefully, especially around Kaunakoi Rd, where the deer run thick.

MOLOKA'I'S BEST BEACHES

- **Dixie Maru** (right) Very intimate slice of sand with calm waters and decent snorkeling

- **Make Horse Beach** (p427) Where the golf course meets the sea and local spearfishers and thrill seekers are frequently found

- **Kawakiu Beach** (opposite) Best fits the Hawaiian stereotype: soft white sand, azurexaters and that laidback paradise feeling

- **Papohaku Beach** (below) Glittering ocean and miles of golden sand are perfect for a romantic sunset visit while there's no swimming on offer

- **Twenty-Mile Beach** (p413) Easy access combines with worthwhile snorkeling

- **Mo'omomi Beach** (p419) Get way off the trodden track at this secluded spot

Beach, stretching north. The large concrete tunnel at the south end of the beach was used to load sand onto barges for shipping to Honolulu. The sand was used in construction, and in building up Waikiki beaches until environmental protection laws stopped sand-mining operation in the early 1970s.

The next three beach-access points lead to rocky coastline, suitable for fishing. The gold-sand beach at the end of the road, which the ancient Hawaiians knew as Kapukahehu, is now called **Dixie Maru**, after a ship that went down in the area long ago. Dixie Maru is the most-protected cove on the west shore, and the most-popular **swimming** and **snorkeling** area. The waters are generally calm, except when the surf is high enough to break over the mouth of the bay. The sand is an interesting confetti mix of waterworn coral bits and small shells. There's a tree swing here calling your name, and you can, reportedly, see the famous 'green flash' (the green color results from atmospheric refraction of the setting or rising sun) during sunset from here.

Sleeping

Papohaku Beach Park is a choice site for camping; it's often peaceful – the surf lulling you to sleep, and the birds waking you up. However, boisterous families with young kids and pick-up trucks move in here, especially on weekends. The beach also attracts down-and-outers, but the vibe is low-key.

Sites are grassy and level. Secure your tent carefully, as the wind sometimes blows with hardy gusts. The camping area has two sections; they are watered by timed sprinklers on different days of the week, so pay attention to the sign that tells which area is watered on which days – there's nothing more depressing than finding your tent and belongings soaked! See p401 for permit information.

sunny days, and at times you can walk the shore without seeing another soul. With soft golden sands gleaming in the sun, and wisps of rainbows tossed up in the crashing surf, it's a gorgeous place for barefoot strolling.

So where is everybody? Well, for one, it can be windy, with gusts of sand continually smacking you in the face. But the main drawback is the water itself, which is usually too treacherous for swimming. There's not a lick of shade either.

The first access point, which is the most developed of the seven turnoffs from Kaluakoi Rd with parking lots, is **Papohaku Beach Park**, a grassy park with campsites, indoor *and* outdoor showers, picnic facilities, changing rooms, toilets and water fountains.

From the third access point, off Papapa Place, there is a broad view of Papohaku

NI'IHAU

Long closed to outsiders, Ni'ihau, 'The Forbidden Island,' has more successfully spurned change than any other Hawaiian island, and perhaps no other island so captivates the imagination as this social experiment dating back to the 1860s.

HISTORY

Captain Cook anchored off Ni'ihau on January 29, 1778, two weeks after 'discovering' Hawaii. Cook noted in his log that the island was lightly populated and largely barren – a description that's true today. His visit was short, but it had a lasting impact. It was on little Ni'ihau that Cook introduced two things that would quickly change the face of Hawaii. He left two goats, the first of the grazing animals that would devastate the islands' native flora and fauna. And his men introduced syphilis, the first of several Western diseases that would strike the Hawaiian people.

In 1864 Elizabeth Sinclair, a Scottish widow, bought Ni'ihau from King Kamehameha V for $10,000 in gold. He originally tried to sell her the 'swampland' of Waikiki, but she passed it up for the 'desert island.' Interestingly, no two places in Hawaii today could be further apart, either culturally or in land value. Mrs Sinclair brought the first sheep to Ni'ihau from New Zealand and started the ranching operation that her great-grandsons continue today.

LIFESTYLE & CULTURE

Ni'ihau is the only island where the primary language is still Hawaiian. It has no paved roads, no airport and no islandwide electricity. The entire island, right down to the church, belongs to the Ni'ihau Ranch, which is privately owned by the non-Hawaiian Robinson family. The Robinsons are highly protective of Ni'ihau's isolation and its people. They provide shelter, food staples and medical care, plus higher education for residents, in a privatized sort of socialism.

Most of Ni'ihau's 250 residents live in Pu'uwai ('heart' in Hawaiian), a settlement on the dry western coast. Each house in the village is surrounded by a stone wall to keep grazing animals out of the gardens. It's a simple life; water is collected in catchments, and the toilets are in outhouses.

Business is conducted in Hawaiian, as are Sunday church services. The two Robinson brothers who manage the ranch speak Hawaiian fluently. There is a schoolhouse where three teachers hold classes from kindergarten through 12th grade for the island's 50 students. Although courses are taught solely in Hawaiian up to the fourth grade, students learn English as a second language.

ENVIRONMENT

Ni'ihau is the smallest of the inhabited Hawaiian Islands, with a total land area of 70 sq miles and 45 miles of coast. The island is semi-arid, lying in the lee of Kaua'i. Ni'ihau's 860-acre Halalii Lake is the largest in Hawaii, though even during the rainy winter season, it's only a few feet deep. In summer, it sometimes dries up to a mud pond.

Of the approximately 50 Hawaiian monk seals that have taken up residence in the populated Hawaiian islands, more than 30 live on Ni'ihau. About half of all Hawaii's endangered coots, the 'alae ke'oke'o, breed on Ni'ihau. Introduced creatures also proliferate on Ni'ihau.

Ni'ihau shells – lustrous, colorful and delicate sea jewels strung into exquisite and coveted lei costing anywhere from $125 to $25,000 – are unique to this small island; in late 2004, protective legislation was before the governor so that only items made of 100% Ni'ihau shells and crafted entirely in Hawaii could carry the label Ni'ihau.

ECONOMY & POLITICS

The island economy has long depended on sheep and cattle ranching, which has always been a marginal operation on windswept Ni'ihau. Major droughts in recent decades have taken a toll on the herds, and consequently the place has been through some hard times. Ni'ihau only receives an average of 12in of rain annually.

Ranch activities, which once provided most of the work on Ni'ihau, are no longer commercially viable. Consequently, the Robinsons have been looking toward the federal government as a potential source of income and employment. For several years Ni'ihau has leased sites to the government that are used for the placement of unmanned radars linked to missile-tracking facilities on Kaua'i.

In addition, since 1999, military special operations forces have staged periodic training maneuvers on Ni'ihau, using the uninhabited southern end of the island. The operations are small-scale, typically with teams of a dozen soldiers practicing a mock rescue operation or the like. There are ongoing negotiations to increase the military presence on Ni'ihau as part of the testing program for new US weapons technology. The hope is that the military, as a secretive tenant, won't interfere with the rest of Ni'ihau's affairs.

Ni'ihau is 17 miles from Kaua'i and is connected by a weekly supply boat that travels between the two islands. The boat docks in Kaua'i at Kaumakani, headquarters of Ni'ihau Ranch and the Robinson family. Kaumakani is also home to a settlement of Ni'ihauans who prefer to live on Kaua'i, though many of them still work for the Robinsons. Politically, Ni'ihau falls under the jurisdiction of Kaua'i county.

SNAPSHOT: NI'IHAU TODAY

Ni'ihau is by no means a living-history museum of Hawaiians stuck in time. Although it's got a foot in the past, it takes what it wants from the present. The supply boat brings soda pop as well as poi (fermented taro), and the island has more dirt bikes than outrigger canoes. Ni'ihau residents are free to go to Kaua'i to shop, have a few beers (Ni'ihau itself is dry) or just hang out. What they are not free to do is bring friends from other islands back home with them. Those Ni'ihauans who marry people from other islands, as well as those whom the Robinsons come to see as undesirable, are rarely allowed to return.

Still, for the most part, Ni'ihauans accept that that's the way things are. Some of those who leave are critical, but those who stay don't appear to be looking for any changes. To outsiders, Ni'ihau really is an enigma. Some romanticize it as a pristine preserve of Hawaiian culture, while others see it as a throwback to feudalism. The Robinsons view Ni'ihau as a private sanctuary and themselves as the protectors of it. It's that kind of paternalism that often rubs outside native Hawaiian groups the wrong way, though for the most part Ni'ihauans don't seem to share those sentiments, and they resist outside interference.

VISITING NI'IHAU

Although outsiders are not allowed to visit Ni'ihau, the Robinsons have 'opened up' the island – at least to a degree – via expensive helicopter flights and hunting excursions. Either of the following trips can be arranged at the **Gay & Robinson headquarters** (☎ Kaua'i 335-3500, 877-441-3500; http://gandrtours-kauai.com; 2 Kaumakani Av, Kaumakani, Kaua'i). See p504.

■ **Niihau Helicopters** (per person $300) Has no set schedule; tours should be arranged well in advance. Half-day tours take off from Port Allen airport in Kaua'i. The helicopter – an Agusta 109A, not one of the big-window type of choppers used on other aerial tours – makes a stop at a beach (location depends on weather), where lunch is provided and the snorkeling is revelatory. The pilot flies over much of Ni'ihau but avoids the population center of Pu'uwai village.

■ **Niihau Safaris** (per hunter/observer $1810/400) Provides everything you'll need (rifle, license, transportation, guide and preparation and shipping of trophies) to hunt Polynesian boar and feral sheep mostly, but also wild eland, Barbary sheep and wild oryx. Organizers promote this as 'useful harvesting of game' and obey norms of free-chase hunting.

You can also scuba dive the waters around Ni'ihau (but cannot set foot on the island), with several dive operators in Kaua'i; a typical three-tank dive costs around $280. See p464, p491, p495 and p502. Snorkeling is also an option via catamaran tours out of Port Allen (p502).

Kaua'i

Imagine that the adventure gods and vacation goddesses got together to conjure a place of cliff-hanging hikes, pristine beaches, thundering waterfalls and rainbow-hooded valleys. They made sure the seas were clear and warm, and added a couple of mountains, swaths of rain forest and soil so fertile the sweetest stuff on earth could grow there. On these fundamentals, all agreed.

Problems arose, however, because one goddess was a surfer and one god was a dad with three kids. One enjoyed 300-thread-count sheets, while another liked waking to birds singing in the woods. Before long, the floodgates burst wide and everyone weighed in on the fantasy island's design – spiritual nooks, ribbons of river, a tremendous canyon, edible delights – until there were so many divergent opinions it looked like an EU plenary session. 'Enough!' boomed the alpha god. 'We'll just throw it all together.' And so Kaua'i was born.

Kaua'i is famous for many reasons. It's so green, locals say if you plant a broomstick it will grow. Rimming the north of the island, the legendary Na Pali Coast has some of the world's highest cliffs and most rewarding trekking. And honeymooners have been loving in Kaua'i since Elvis tied the knot in *Blue Hawaii*. Kaua'i is famous for kayaking and superlative day hikes, intimate accommodations, and miles upon miles of beaches, many of them secluded.

'Paradise' is a word you'll hear often in Kaua'i, and if you can visit only one of the fabulous five main islands of Hawaii, make it this dream destination.

HIGHLIGHTS

- Rope-jump at **Kipu Falls** (p452)
- Relax on North Shore beaches: **Ke'e** (p485), **Hanalei** (p179) or **Hideaways** (p475)
- Savour gourmet, organic and vegan cuisine, all in **Kapa'a** (p466)
- Quench your thirst with smoothies or *noni* (Indian mulberry) shots at roadside stands in **Kapa'a** (p466), **Moloa'a** (p468) or **Kilauea** (p472)
- Backcountry in **Waimea Canyon** (p509) or **Alaka'i Swamp** (p514)
- Unwind with a Thai, tandem or hot-rock massage in **Kapa'a** (p480)
- Hike to **Hanakapi'ai Falls** (p488)
- Visit a **Hindu temple** (p457) near Wailua
- Paddle or hike the **Na Pali Coast** (p486)
- Swim with dolphins and sea turtles at **Ha'ena Beach** (p485)

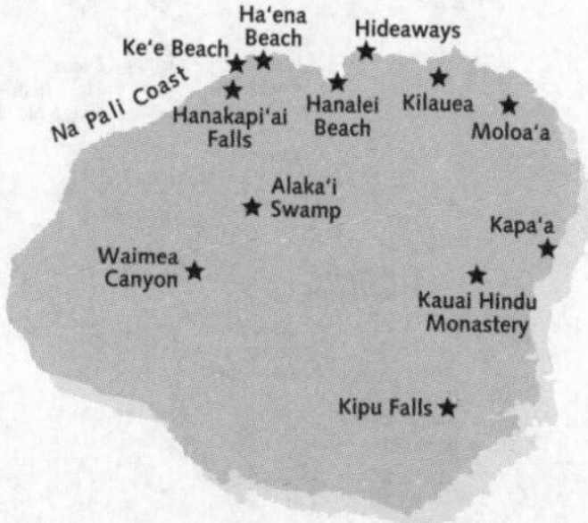

(map with labels: Ha'ena Beach, Ke'e Beach, Hideaways, Na Pali Coast, Hanakapi'ai Falls, Hanalei Beach, Kilauea, Moloa'a, Alaka'i Swamp, Kapa'a, Waimea Canyon, Kauai Hindu Monastery, Kipu Falls)

| POPULATION: 59,950 | NICKNAME: THE GARDEN ISLE | AREA: 558 SQ MILES |

Climate

'No rain, no rainbows' reads a Kaua'i bumper sticker and visitors should be prepared to get wet, particularly on the Eastside and North Shore. Mt Wai'ale'ale (5148ft), almost smack in the middle of the island, is considered the wettest place on earth, averaging 486in of rain annually. The upside is that the rain is usually warm, short-lived and produces rainbows. Summer is generally drier than winter, but it rained every day while researching this book in June, and blue skies happen in winter, too.

Climatic variances here mean the sun is almost always beaming down on the South Shore or Westside, making these attractive beach destinations. Since the island is only 33 miles wide and 25 miles from north to south, you can zip into the sun quickly. At higher elevations (eg Waimea Canyon, on helicopter flights), things can get chilly.

The National Weather Service provides recorded **local weather information** (☎ 245-6001) and **marine forecasts** (☎ 245-3564). For more details on weather, including climate charts, see p521.

State & County Parks

Kaua'i is a bonanza for hikers, campers, and even mountain bikers, who will revel in the miles of trails and coastline maintained in over a dozen parks.

Spending time at county beach parks, many located on idyllic beaches, is irresistible. Lydgate (p454) and Hanalei (p479) are both popular for water sports.

CAMPING

For more nature time, there are beautifully located campsites sprinkled throughout the island at state and county parks, plus several backcountry camps near Waimea Canyon (p510). Additionally, there are cabins (p514) at Koke'e State Park, providing easy access to trailheads.

Whether you hoof the entire 11 miles or opt for a shorter jaunt, the Na Pali Coast State Park treks (p486) are world-class and offer phenomenal camping, for those willing to work for it. Koke'e State Park (p510) and adjacent Waimea Canyon State Park (p509) are riddled with trails and backcountry camping to challenge the hardy, plus more

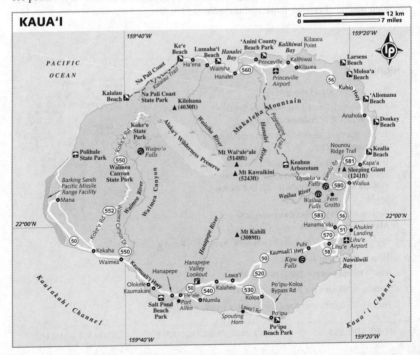

manageable day hikes. The parks straddle awesome Waimea Canyon, known as the 'Grand Canyon of the Pacific.' Polihale State Park (p509), with its drive-up beach camping, attracts casual campers and partiers.

The county also maintains several recommendable coastline parks with campsites, among them Ha'ena (p484), 'Anini (p473) and Lucy Wright Beach Parks (p506), all of which front pretty beaches. Anahola (p468) and Hanamau'lu (p451) tend to attract a rougher, shadier crowd and are not recommended for solo or female campers.

For camping supplies and rentals, see p478 and p504.

State Parks

Permits are required to camp in Koke'e and Polihale (per campsite per night $5) and Na Pali Coast State Parks ($10). Camping is limited to five consecutive nights within a 30-day period (ie you only have five total nights on the entire Kalalau Trail in the Na Pali Coast Park). You can camp in Hanakoa Valley on the Kalalau Trail, but not for two consecutive nights. The same holds true for Hanakapi'a Valley.

You can obtain permits in person or by mail from the **Division of State Parks** (☎ 274-3444; www.hawaii.gov/dlnr/dsp/index.html; Suite 306, State Offices, 3060 Eiwa St, Lihue, HI 96766; ☽ 8am-3:30pm Mon-Fri) and at state park offices on other islands. Up to five may be listed on each permit, but a picture ID for each person must be shown. You can download the permit application or send a letter to the office specifying the park(s) at which you want to stay and the dates you wish to stay at each park. Your application must include a photocopy of each camper's ID, with the ID number and birth date. You can apply for a permit as early as a year in advance, and many people do, particularly for Na Pali Coast campsites in summer. So apply for your permits as soon as is practical, and if your plans change once you get the permit, be sure to cancel, as you'll be tying up an empty site and preventing someone else from camping.

Remote backcountry camping in Waimea Canyon is available to hardcore hikers. The **Division of Forestry & Wildlife** (DOFAW; Map p444; ☎ 274-3433; www.hawaiitrails.com; Suite 306, State Offices, 3060 Eiwa St, Lihue, HI 96766; ☽ 8am-4pm Mon-Fri) issues free, backcountry camping permits

---

ISLAND OF LUCK & MYSTERY

Major historical moments in Kaua'i's earliest history occurred in and around Wailua (p452), the site of Kaua'i's royal court. In the 12th century or so, during the second wave of Tahitian immigration to Kaua'i, a chief named Moikeha landed his fleet of double-hulled canoes at Wailua.

Moikeha was received at the royal court by *ali'i nui* (high chief) Puna, Kaua'i's elder statesman. Puna bequeathed his daughter to Moikeha in marriage, and upon Puna's death Moikeha became the *ali'i nui* of Kaua'i. Instrumental in the future development of Kaua'i, Moikeha introduced taro and sweet potatoes, and sent his son Kila back to Tahiti to fetch the *pahu hula*, a sharkskin drum essential in hula temples and still used today.

Kaumuali'i was the last chief to reign over an independent Kaua'i. Although he was a shrewd leader and Kaua'i's warriors were fierce, it was apparently the power of Kaumuali'i's *kahuna* (priests) that protected him from the advances of Kamehameha the Great. In 1796 Kamehameha, who had conquered all the other main Hawaiian islands, sailed from Oahu with an armada of war canoes toward Kaua'i. A mysterious storm suddenly kicked up at sea, compelling him to turn back to Oahu, and he never reached Kaua'i's shores.

During the next few years both Kamehameha and Kaumuali'i continued to prepare for war by gathering foreign weaponry and trying to ally foreign ships to their causes. In 1804 Kamehameha and his warriors again massed on the shores of Oahu, ready to attack Kaua'i. However, on the eve of the invasion, an epidemic of what was probably cholera struck the island of Oahu, decimating the would-be invaders and forcing yet another delay.

While Kamehameha's numerically superior forces had Kaumuali'i unnerved, Kaumuali'i's uncanny luck had a similar effect on Kamehameha. In 1810 they reached an agreement that recognized Kaumuali'i as *alii nui* of Kaua'i, but ceded the island of Kaua'i to the Kingdom of Hawai'i. It was essentially a truce and the plotting continued, with Kaumuali'i never fully accepting Kamehameha's ultimate authority.

KAUA'I IN...

Three Days

Rise early and hit the **North Shore** (p469): swim with wildlife at **Ha'ena Beach Park** (p484) and hike the first leg of the **Kalalau Trail** (p486) to Hanakapi'ai. Play at the waterfalls, then hike out and snorkel at **Ke'e Beach** (p485). Eat, drink and get merry in **Hanalei** (p478). On day two visit must-see waterfalls, like **Wailua** (p452), **Opaeka'a** (p456) and **Kipu** (p452), paddling up the **Wailua River** (p452) or hiking the **Moalepe & Kuilau Trails** (p457). Dedicate your last day to **Waimea Canyon** (p509) and **Koke'e State Park** (p510), where hiking and breathtaking vistas await.

Five Days

Firstly, follow the three-day itinerary. On the fourth day, get some sun, swim, snorkel and boogie board around **Po'ipu** (p492). Take a surfing lesson at Po'ipu before heading east to explore secret coves of **Maha'ulepu Beach** (p495). Take day five easy, visiting the **Kilauea Lighthouse** (p470) and poking around nearby beaches, such as **Secret** (p473), **Larsens** (p469) or **Moloa'a Beach** (p469). Relax with a massage (p465) then splash out for dinner at **A Pacific Cafe** (p463) or **Café Hanalei** (p476).

One Week

Follow the five-day itinerary. Spend another day pursuing your favorite activity (p436): horseback riding, sea or river kayaking, windsurfing, scuba diving, hiking, fishing, snorkeling or mountain biking. On your final day, wrap things up with some culture, visiting the **Kaua'i Museum** (p445) and the **International Surfing Hall of Fame** (p446). Lunch in quaint **Hanapepe** (p503), and head west to catch the sunset at **Polihale State Park** (p509).

for four sites in Waimea Canyon, two sites (Sugi Grove and Kawaikoi) in the Koke'e State Park area, and the Waialae site near the Alaka'i Wilderness Preserve. This last option, with its high concentration of endangered and native bird populations, is primo turf for birders. Camping is limited to four nights in the canyon, three nights in the Koke'e area and two nights in the Alaka'i Wilderness Preserve within a 30-day period. You can reserve a permit a maximum of 30 days in advance by phone, but you'll still need to collect the permit in person, with proper ID.

County Parks

The county maintains seven campgrounds on Kaua'i. Moving clockwise around the island, these are: Ha'ena, Hanalei, 'Anini, Anahola, Hanamau'lu, Salt Pond and Lucy Wright Beach Parks. Camping permits cost $3 per night per adult camper (children under 18 free) and can be applied for six consecutive nights, for a total of 60 nights in a calendar year.

Each campground is closed one day a week – to clean up and prevent people from squatting permanently. Haena and Lucy Wright are closed Monday; 'Anini and Salt Pond are closed Tuesday; Hanamau'lu is closed Wednesday; and Anahola is closed Thursday. All county campgrounds have showers and toilets, and most have covered picnic pavilions and barbecue grills.

Like most things in Kaua'i, enforcement of permit compliance is laid-back. If you just set up camp and pay the rangers when they come around, it will cost $5 per person. However, if you're caught out without a permit, they *can* ask you to move. Permits are issued in person or by mail (at least one month in advance) at the **Division of Parks & Recreation** (Map p444; ☎ 241-6660; www.kauaigov.org; Suite 150, Lihu'e Civic Center, 4444 Rice St, Lihu'e, HI 96766; permits issued ☒ 8:15am-4pm Mon-Fri).

Following are two handy satellite offices that also issue permits:

Kalaheo Neighborhood Center (☎ 332-9770; 4480 Papalina Rd, Kalaheo; ☒ 8:30am-12:30pm Mon-Fri)
Kapa'a Neighborhood Center (Map p453; ☎ 822-1931; 4491 Kou St, Kapa'a; ☒ 8:30am-12:30pm Mon-Fri)

Activities

This island is an adventure hound's playground, offering a staggering array of activities on land and sea. If you don't do

KAUA'I

something in Kaua'i you've never done before, you're missing the point. Not to worry if you're traveling with the wee ones, since most outfitters accommodate children with special gear, pricing and activity options; see p448 for child-friendly ideas. Most outfitters are concentrated in Hanalei (p478), Kapa'a (p463) and Po'ipu (p492).

WATER ACTIVITIES
Swimming
Swimming is best on the North Shore in summer (try Ke'e Beach, p485, or Hanalei Bay, p479) and the South Shore in winter (above all at Po'ipu, p492). If rough seas and surf – endemic here – make you nervous, there are public pools in Kapa'a (p464) and

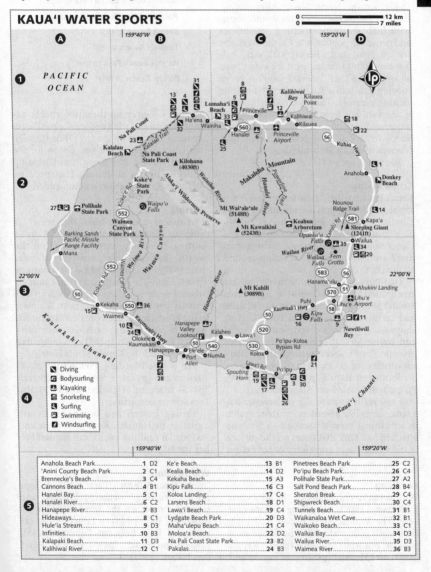

KAUA'I WATER SPORTS

0 — 12 km
0 — 7 miles

Legend:
- ⟋ Diving
- ⟋ Bodysurfing
- ⟋ Kayaking
- ⟋ Snorkeling
- ⟋ Surfing
- ⟋ Swimming
- ⟋ Windsurfing

Anahola Beach Park	1	D2	Ke'e Beach	13	B1	Pinetrees Beach Park	25	C2
'Anini County Beach Park	2	C1	Kealia Beach	14	D2	Po'ipu Beach Park	26	C4
Brennecke's Beach	3	C4	Kekaha Beach	15	A3	Polihale State Park	27	A2
Cannons Beach	4	B1	Kipu Falls	16	C3	Salt Pond Beach Park	28	B4
Hanalei Bay	5	C1	Koloa Landing	17	C4	Sheraton Break	29	C4
Hanalei River	6	C2	Larsens Beach	18	D1	Shipwreck Beach	30	C4
Hanapepe River	7	B3	Lawa'i Beach	19	C4	Tunnels Beach	31	B1
Hideaways	8	C1	Lydgate Beach Park	20	D3	Waikanaloa Wet Cave	32	B1
Hule'ia Stream	9	D3	Maha'ulepu Beach	21	C4	Waikoko Beach	33	C1
Infinities	10	B3	Moloa'a Beach	22	D2	Wailua Bay	34	D3
Kalapaki Beach	11	D3	Na Pali Coast State Park	23	B2	Wailua River	35	D3
Kalihiwai River	12	C1	Pakalas	24	B3	Waimea River	36	B3

Waimea (p504), and protected swimming areas at Lydgate (p454) and Salt Pond Beach Parks (p503).

Snorkeling

Snorkeling also unlocks the underwater world; check out marine delights at the shore dives in the next section, plus 'Anini Beach (p473) on the North Shore. Alternatively, head to Po'ipu (p492) on the South Shore, with high sea turtle–spotting possibilities and dense fish populations. On the Westside, try Salt Pond Beach Park (p503), with shallow conditions that are good for kids. Shops all over Kaua'i sell 'snorkel food' in order to whip fish into a feeding frenzy for your viewing pleasure. This is not only harmful to the fish, but soils the water; see p56 for more on diving and snorkeling responsibly. Shops renting snorkel gear are ubiquitous (corrective masks are available, too).

For tours, see p441.

Scuba Diving

Kaua'i has amazingly clear waters and many top scuba-diving spots here, including Koloa Landing (p493), Po'ipu Beach Park (p494), Ke'e Beach (p485), Tunnels (p483) and Cannons Beach (p484) are shore dives. Boat dives are also on offer, including around Ni'ihau (p431).

Two-tank shore dives with equipment cost around $85, boat dives $100, night dives around $80, introductory dives start at $100 and certification courses cost $400. Most shops allow you to do certification theory and coursework at home, and open-water dives on Kaua'i. Recommended shops offering certification courses and all types of dives are located in Kapa'a (p464), Koloa (p490) Po'ipu (p495) and Port Allen (p502).

If you really want to slip underwater but a tank seems like a burden, consider snuba, in which you breathe through an air hose attached to a tank that floats on the surface of the water. Tours are offered out of Po'ipu (p495).

Kayaking

With seven rivers, including the only navigable one in Hawai'i, kayaking is all the rage here. The Wailua River paddle and hike, ending at a 200ft waterfall, is by far the most popular; outfitters in Lihu'e (p451), Kapa'a (p464) and Hanalei (p480) rent kayaks and

---

TOP 10 BEACHES

- Hideaways (p475)
- Larsen's Beach (p469)
- Ke'e Beach (p485)
- Hanalei Beach Park (p484)
- 'Anini County Beach Park (p473)
- Polihale State Park (p509)
- Secret Beach (p473)
- Tunnels Beach (p483)
- Ha'ena Beach Park (p484)
- Po'ipu Beach (p494)

---

run tours. Sign on for the unforgettable, 18-mile Na Pali seafaring endurance paddle (in summer only) in Po'ipu (p495) or Hanalei; the latter is also where you put in for the dreamy Hanalei Bay route. Short trips up Hulei'a Stream, Kalihiwai, Hanapepe or Waimea Rivers are also recommended.

Surfing

Old-timers grumble that the secret is out, but the world is stoked with Kaua'i's surfing. Generally, surfing is best on the North Shore in winter, especially Hanalei Bay (p479), Tunnels (p483) or Cannons (p484), and the south coast in summer, where hugely popular Po'ipu Beach (p494) crowds up. Pakalas (p505), near Waimea, is the Westside's hottest break. Transitional swells happen on the Eastside, when surfers hit Kealia Beach (p467) or Wailua Bay (p452) behind the Kapa'a Sands Hotel.

For boogie boarding, Po'ipu's the place: Brennecke's (p495) is best and Shipwreck (p495) is second. Hanalei Bay (p479) also sees some good action.

Surfing lessons and board rentals are available in Hanalei, Kapa'a, Wailua and Po'ipu. To find the swells, call the **surf hotline** (☎ 335-3720).

Windsurfing

'Anini County Beach Park (p473) is tops for windsurfing (including lessons) and speed sailing when the wind is up, or try Nawiliwili Bay (p446) in Lihu'e. More experienced folks frequent Tunnels (p483), Maha'ulepu Beach (p495) or Salt Pond Beach Park (p503).

Fishing

Fishing is a mainstay sport and diversion on Kaua'i. Charter fishing boats depart from Nawiliwili's small boat harbor (p446) Kapa'a (p464) and 'Anini Beach (p473). Ask about sharing the catch if you want to keep what you hook – not all charters spread the wealth. Freshwater bass fishing in private reservoirs or rainbow trout in Koke'e State Park (p510) is another option.

To cast independently, you'll need a freshwater license from the **DOFAW** (Map p444; ☎ 274-3344; Suite 306, 3060 Eiwa St, Lihu'e; 7/30 days $10/20, seniors free) or consider using the established guides at **Cast & Catch** (☎ 332-9707; half-day charter for half-anglers $250).

LAND ACTIVITIES

Not much of a water person? No worries! Kaua'i has some of the most dazzling and gratifying hiking around, as well as mountain biking, horseback riding, golf and tennis. Exhilarating soft adventures can be had on zipline tours, where you get strapped into a harness, don a pair of gloves, and zoom via gravity and a pulley mechanism high above the ground surrounded by beautiful forest and waterfall scenery.

Hiking

With the largest concentration of trails on Kaua'i, Koke'e State Park has everything from easy day hikes delivering phenomenal canyon vistas (p513) to nail-biters (p513) ending in splendid Na Pali valley views. Like what you see? Then hit the spectacular 11-mile Kalalau Trail (p486), justly famous as a must-do for trekkers. Ribbons of trail snake through the Kapa'a–Wailua area, too, most notably the Moalepe and Kuilau Ridge Trails (p457), the Nounou Ridge Trail (p458) and the Powerline Trail (p458).

The **Sierra Club** (☎ 651-0682; www.hi.sierraclub .org/kauai/kauai.html) in Kaua'i leads guided hikes (suggested donation $3) ranging from strolls up the Sleeping Giant to overnighters in Waimea Canyon. Advance registration may be required; look for upcoming hikes in the 'Community Calendar' section of the *Garden Island*. Koke'e Museum (p512) also has guided hikes.

Cycling & Mountain Biking

Over 80 miles of trail island wide are also open for mountain biking (including the Powerline Trail, p458, and Waimea Canyon Trail, p510); visit the DOFAW (p435) for a free leaflet that lists trails open to cyclists and to purchase their useful topographical map. For more maps, see p526. For rainforest tours, see p441.

Horseback Riding

Alternatively, let a horse do the work: horseback-riding tours are offered by professional ranches with beautiful animals in Princeville (p475), Po'ipu (p496) and Kalihiwai (p473). No experience is required; call to arrange private rides (minimum two riders).

Golf

Take it from the pros: Kaua'i has superlative golfing. Of the nine courses here, over half were designed by either Jack Nicklaus or Robert Trent Jones Jr, while two others are endearing municipal courses. The championship Princeville courses (p475) are recognized as among the country's most challenging.

Tennis

Tennis anyone? Aside from many hotels offering court use to their guests, there are tennis clubs in Lihu'e (p447), Princeville (p475) and Po'ipu (p496). Court rental costs around $20 per hour, racket rentals are $5 an hour. Free, municipal courts pepper the island as well.

Getting There & Away

AIR

All scheduled passenger flights to Kaua'i land at **Lihu'e airport** (LIH; ☎ 245-2831). The following carriers fly nonstop from the US mainland (see p532 for airline contact details):

Alaska Airlines Daily from Los Angeles.
Aloha Airlines Daily from Oakland.
American Airlines Daily from Los Angeles.
United Airlines Daily from Los Angeles and San Francisco.
US Airways Daily from San Francisco.

For travel between islands, choose **Hawaiian Airlines** (☎ 838-1555) or **Aloha Airlines** (☎ 245-6618). All interisland flights from Kaua'i, except Hawaiian Airlines' and Aloha's (on Island Air) daily service to Maui, go through Honolulu, meaning you'll eat up half a day in transit if you are going anywhere other than O'ahu. There are at least a dozen daily flights to Honolulu and scads om there on to other islands. Aloha flights Kapalua and Kahalui, Maui – plus those to Moloka'i and Lana'i with continuing service to Kahalui, Maui – use Island Air, which is infamous for late and cancelled flights. Nevertheless, Island Air has the last Honolulu–Lihu'e–Honolulu flight of the day (leaving Honolulu at 8pm and Lihu'e at 9pm), giving you just a little more vacation time on Kaua'i.

Kaua'i also has a small airport in Princeville (p474) on the North Shore, from where helicopter tours depart (see p442).

Getting Around

You'll want to rent a car. Kaua'i does have limited bus service connecting most towns, but it won't take you to major destinations, like Kilauea Point, Waimea Canyon or Koke'e State Park. Furthermore, bus travelers in these parts can be downright weird.

Kaua'i has one belt road running three-quarters of the way around the island, from Ke'e Beach in the north, to Polihale in the west; the Na Pali Coast is only accessible by boat or on foot, and even then only partway. Few roads mean congestion, especially between Lihu'e and Kapa'a where tedious rush-hour traffic is common. To combat traffic, a 'contra-flow' lane is created weekdays from 6am to 8:30am on Hwy 56 in the Wailua area; this turns a northbound lane into a southbound lane by reversing the flow of traffic, so that commuters to Lihu'e have an extra lane open. Metered parking in Lihu'e costs 25¢ for 30 minutes. Driving

ROAD DISTANCES & TIMES

From Lihue

destination	miles	time
Anahola	14	25 min
Hanalei	31	1 hr
Hanapepe	16	30 min
Kapa'a	8	15 min
Ke'e Beach	40	1¼ hr
Kilauea Lighthouse	25	40 min
Po'ipu	10	20 min
Port Allen	15	25 min
Princeville	28	45 min
Waimea	23	40 min
Waimea Canyon	42	1½ hr

in Kaua'i at night, where street lamps are few, is difficult.

Explorers should pick up the *Ready Mapbook of Kauai* ($11), a 67-page atlas sold in bookstores and Long's Drugs that shows virtually every spur, dirt and 4WD road, plus beaches and their access points. Kaua'i's most detailed topographical map ($5), available from the DOFAW (p435), shows the island's network of trails. You can request a copy to be sent to you by sending a check or money order for $6 (for foreign addresses add $1) to the Lihu'e DOFAW office.

TO/FROM THE AIRPORT

The Kaua'i Bus does not stop at Lihu'e airport. Beckon a taxi by using the 'to call taxi' phone outside the terminal; they're speedy. Approximate fares from the airport include: Coconut Plantation ($17), Kapa'a ($20) and Po'ipu ($30). Car-rental booths are lined up on the other side of the airport road, opposite the arrival/departure gates.

BICYCLE

Get on your bike and ride: there's some picturesque coastal pedaling north from Kapa'a (p464) to Anahola, along the south shore near Po'ipu (p498) and in the Hanalei Bay area (p483). Bicycle rentals are available in these towns.

BUS

Kaua'i Bus (☎ 241-6410; ⏱ 7am-5pm Mon-Sat) has two main routes (see table right). Trips are short: the bus from Lihu'e to either Hanalei or Kekaha takes 1¼ hours, and only 25 minutes from Lihu'e to Kapa'a. Schedules are available on the bus or at the Kaua'i Visitors Bureau (p445). No large backpacks, boogie boards or strollers are allowed on the bus – carry-on size limit is 9x14x22 inches – but bicycles can be accommodated on racks in front. The single-trip fare is $1.50 (student or senior 75¢); you must have exact change (bills accepted) when you board. Monthly passes ($15) for unlimited rides can be purchased at Lihu'e Civic Center (Map p444).

CAR

Consider hiring a 4WD, which will allow you to seek adventures off-road at places like Koke'e State Park and Polihale Beach; rates are about $100 per week more than a regular compact car. The following agencies

KAUA'I BUS ROUTES

route	main stops	frequency
Kekaha-Lihu'e-Kekaha	Kekaha Neighborhood Center; Waimea; Hanapepe; Kalaheo; Lawa'i; Kukui Grove; Lihu'e Big Save	9 Mon-Fri, 4 Sat
Kekaha-Po'ipu-Lihu'e	Kekaha Neighborhood Center; Koloa; Po'ipu Rd	1 morning bus Mon-Fri, 1 afternoon departure Sat
Hanalei-Lihu'e-Hanalei	Hanalei Center; Princeville Shopping Center; Kilauea Food Mart; Kealia Beach; Kapa'a Big Save; Wilcox Hospital; Lihu'e Big Save; Kukui Grove	8 Mon-Fri, 4 Sat
Lihu'e Extension	Kukui Grove; Nawiliwili; Lihu'e Big Save; Wilcox Hospital; Rice Shopping Center	8 Mon-Fri

have hire-car booths at Lihu'e airport (for details, including toll-free numbers and websites, see p537):
Alamo (☎ 246-0646)
Avis (☎ 245-3512)
Budget (☎ 800-527-0700)
Dollar (☎ 800-342-7398, 742-8351)
Hertz (☎ 245-3356)
National (☎ 245-5636)
Thrifty (☎ 800-847-4389, 283-0898)

There are many local hire-car agencies that are reliable, economical and keep more of your tourist dollars in Kaua'i. The following offer airport pick-ups and may rent to travelers under 25 and/or those without a credit card:
Hawaiian Riders (Map p493; ☎ 742-9888; www.hawaiianriders.com; 2320 Po'ipu Rd, Po'ipu) Jeeps and exotic cars (per day from $150).
Island Cars (Map p443; ☎ 246-6000; www.islandcars.net; 2983 Aukele St, Lihu'e) Daily/weekly rates start at $24/129.
Rent-A-Wreck (Map p443; ☎ 632-0741; www.rentawreck.com; Harbor Mall, 3501 Rice St, Lihu'e) Not local exactly, but still cheaper than the big boys at $33/175 per day/week.

MOTORCYCLE
No helmet law and wide, open roads make motorcycle rentals, particularly Harley Davidsons, popular. You must have a motorcycle license or endorsement, and some agencies require previous Harley experience. Rates hover around $100/170 for 10/24 hours:
Hawaiian Riders (Map p493; ☎ 742-9888; www.hawaiianriders.com; 2320 Po'ipu Rd, Po'ipu) Also rents mopeds (per day $50).

Street Eagle (Map p443; ☎ 241-7020; 877-212-9253; www.streeteagle.com; 3-1866 Hwy 50, Lihu'e)
Two Wheels Rentals (Map p443; ☎ 246-9457; www.2wheels.com; 3486 Rice St, Lihu'e)

TAXI
Taxis charge $2 at flag fall and $2 per subsequent mile, metered in 25¢ increments. Taxi companies include **Akiko's Taxi** (☎ 822-7588), in the Lihu'e-Kapa'a area; **North Shore Cab** (☎ 826-4118), based in Princeville; and **Southshore Cab** (☎ 742-1525), on Kaua'i's south side.

TOURS
Boat
Catamaran and raft tours either depart from Port Allen (p502) or Waimea (p507). In winter, whale watching is compulsory. Check out the aerial feats of migrating humpbacks on the North Shore, at Ha'ena Beach Park, Kilauea Point or take a boat tour from Port Allen or Waimea.

Bus & Van
Most adventurous of all, **Aloha Kauai Tours** (☎ 245-6400, 800-452-8113; www.alohakauaitours.com; 1702 Haleukana St, Lihu'e) has 4WD tours, including a full-day Koke'e Park–Waimea Canyon circuit (adult/child $125/90), which visits harder-to-reach places like the Kilohana Crater, and a 5½ hour mountain bike/hike tour (adult/child 9-12/child 5-8 $100/75/50) on the Westside ending in a remote beach beyond Maha'ulepu. It also offers snorkel and rain-forest tours.

Several companies offer full- and half-day whirlwind van tours, taking in major sites, including Koloa, Waimea Canyon and Po'ipu on the western swing and the Fern Grotto, Hanalei and Ke'e Beach on the northeastern swing. Prices depend on your departure point: Lihu'e is the cheapest, then Po'ipu and Princeville. Full-day tours start at adult/child $62/43, half-day tours at $41/29. Reliable companies include the following:

Kauai Paradise Tours (☎ 246-3999; kauaiaufdeutsch @msn.com; full-day tour $88) Specializes in tours narrated in German.

Polynesian Adventure Tours (☎ 246-0122, 800-622-3011; www.polyad.com)

Roberts Hawaii (☎ 539-9400; www.robertshawaii.com)

Helicopter

Sure the buzz of these 'Kaua'i mosquitoes' swooping in is a nuisance when you're communing with the heavens on the rim of Waimea Canyon, but dang! the views are mind-boggling. Dipping into the canyon or zipping along the Na Pali Coast, helicopters deliver different views from those on land or sea, and are a terrific alternative for visitors with mobility issues. While some wilderness hikers resent the intrusion of helicopters into otherwise serene areas, almost anyone with a deep appreciation of nature secretly wonders what it looks like from up there.

If you're keen to do a chopper tour, arrange it early in your trip as they're sometimes cancelled due to bad weather. Walking in (rather than making an advanced reservation) means you can wait until a sunny day with the best visibility; this isn't always feasible, however, as tours do book up. Choose a company that uses noise-canceling headphones and helicopters with large windows. Passengers in middle seats often feel cheated due to lower visibility. While overall these outfits have outstanding safety records, accidents do happen: in 2003 a Jack Harter helicopter crashed over Mt Wai'ale'ale, killing the pilot and all four passengers.

The going rate is around $160 for a 45-minute 'circle-island tour' that zooms by the main sights, but tours of under an hour feel rushed. Various 'ultimate splendor' tours, usually lasting an hour or slightly more, are around $200. Ask about discounts and peruse the freebie tourist magazines for coupons. All of the following operators depart from and accept bookings at Lihu'e airport, except where noted:

Air Kauai (☎ 246-4666, 800-972-4666; www.airkauai .com)

HeliUSA Airways (☎ 826-6591, 866-936-1234; www .heliusahawaii.com) Books and flies from Princeville Airport; handy if you're on the North Shore.

Inter-Island Helicopter (☎ 335-5009, 800-335-5567; http://hawaiian.net/~interisland; 1-3410 Kaumuali'i Hwy) Pricier flights from Hanapepe, but the only outfit that flies without doors and lands at a waterfall.

Jack Harter Helicopters (☎ 245-3774, 888-245-2001; www.helicopters-kauai.com)

Safari Helicopters (☎ 246-0136, 800-326-3356; www .safariair.com)

Will Squyres (☎ 245-8881, 245-7541, 888-245-4354; www.helicopters-hawaii.com; cnr Hwy 56 & 570, Lihu'e)

LIHU'E

pop 12,000

Train your eyes skyward for early morning rainbows, watch for chickens crossing the road and don't be intimidated by all those mud-splattered monster trucks. Welcome to Lihu'e, the county capital and arrival point for virtually all travelers to Kaua'i. The biggest Kaua'ian city has a small-town feel, introducing visitors to the intimate vibe for which the Garden Isle is famous. Indeed, even first-timers will feel like instant 'ohana (family) here.

Home to the state and county offices and megastores, like Home Depot and WalMart – which locals either love or loathe – Lihu'e is where you can take care of business. While there are several good restaurants, a worthwhile museum and a fine swimming beach, this town is kind of like a laundromat: useful, but not much fun. An afternoon here is all you'll need, and you'll find better accommodations up or down the coast.

HISTORY

Lihu'e got its start as a plantation town back in the day when sugar was king and the massive old mill along Hwy 50 at the south entrance to town was Kaua'i's largest. Though it closed in 2001, ending more than a century of operations, it's still Lihu'e's most impressive building. Now the entire area, but Lihu'e especially, is experiencing a retail boom, providing employment for those that lost work when the mill closed.

ORIENTATION

Lihu'e is surrounded on all sides by highways: Hwy 56 (Kuhio Hwy) to the west and Hwy 51 (Kapule Hwy) to the east, while Hwy 570 (Ahukini Rd) and Rice St are the north and south borders respectively. Hwy 56 leads you straight to the south shore, while Hwy 570 feeds right into the airport.

There are no bus services to/from the airport, so most people drive or catch a taxi into town (p440). Cutting through the heart of town, Rice St is Lihu'e's main drag. Here you'll find many convenient services and government offices. Many more services are strung along Hwy 56 from Wailua to Kapa'a (see p452).

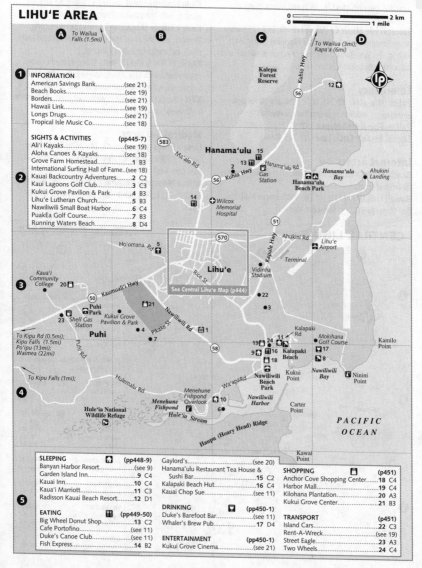

LIHU'E AREA

INFORMATION
American Savings Bank................(see 21)
Beach Books................................(see 19)
Borders......................................(see 21)
Hawaii Link................................(see 19)
Longs Drugs...............................(see 21)
Tropical Isle Music Co................(see 18)

SIGHTS & ACTIVITIES (pp445-7)
Ali'i Kayaks...............................(see 19)
Aloha Canoes & Kayaks.............(see 18)
Grove Farm Homestead.................1 B3
International Surfing Hall of Fame..(see 18)
Kauai Backcountry Adventures.......2 C2
Kaui Lagoons Golf Club.................3 C3
Kukui Grove Pavilion & Park..........4 B3
Lihu'e Lutheran Church.................5 B3
Nawiliwili Small Boat Harbor..........6 C4
PuakEa Golf Course......................7 B3
Running Waters Beach...................8 D4

SLEEPING (pp448-9)
Banyan Harbor Resort.................(see 9)
Garden Island Inn.........................9 C4
Kauai Inn..................................10 C4
Kaua'i Marriott...........................11 C3
Radisson Kauai Beach Resort.......12 D1

EATING (pp449-50)
Big Wheel Donut Shop.................13 C2
Cafe Portofino...........................(see 11)
Duke's Canoe Club.....................(see 11)
Fish Express..............................14 B2
Gaylord's..................................(see 20)
Hanama'ulu Restaurant Tea House &
  Sushi Bar...............................15 C2
Kalapaki Beach Hut.....................16 C4
Kauai Chop Sue.........................(see 11)

DRINKING (pp450-1)
Duke's Barefoot Bar....................(see 11)
Whaler's Brew Pub......................17 D4

ENTERTAINMENT (pp450-1)
Kukui Grove Cinema...................(see 21)

SHOPPING (p451)
Anchor Cove Shopping Center.......18 C4
Harbor Mall...............................19 C4
Kilohana Plantation.....................20 A3
Kukui Grove Center.....................21 B3

TRANSPORT (p451)
Island Cars................................22 C3
Rent-A-Wreck............................(see 19)
Street Eagle..............................23 A3
Two Wheels...............................24 C4

INFORMATION

Bookstores

Beach Books (Map p443; Harbor Mall, 3501 Rice St; 8:30am-7:30pm Mon-Sat) Cheap new and used beach reading.

Borders (Map p443; ☎ 246-0862; Kukui Grove Center, 4303 Nawiliwili Rd; 9am-10pm Mon-Thu, to 11pm Fri & Sat, to 8pm Sun) This large chain has a big book selection and café, plus CDs, DVDs and videos, many of local interest.

Tropical Isle Music Co (Map p443; ☎ 245-8700; www .tropicislemusic.com; Anchor Cove Shopping Center, 3416 Rice St; 9am-9pm) Staggering selection of Hawaii- and Kaua'i-specific books, CDs and videos.

Emergency

Police (Map p443; ☎ 241-1771; 3060 Umi St) For non-emergencies, incident reporting and information.
Police, Fire & Ambulance (☎ 911)
Sexual Assault Crisis Line (☎ 245-4144)

Internet Access

Beach Books (Map p443; per 15 min $3) Has one computer for Internet access.
Hawaii Link (Map p443; ☎ 246-9300; Harbor Mall, 3501 Rice St; per hr $12; 9am-6pm Mon-Fri)

Laundry

Lihu'e Laundromat (Map p444; ☎ 332-8356; Rice Shopping Center, 4303 Rice St; 6am-9pm)

Media

Garden Island (www.kauaiworld.com) Kaua'i's slim daily newspaper lists events and is handy for plugging into island issues.
Kaua'i Independent (www.thekauai.com) Very left-leaning, with good monthly events calendar.
Kaua'i Visitor Magazine (www.kauaivisitor.com) Monthly, with the usual advertorial and discounted tour offers, but useful for daily TV listings.
KKCR (91.9FM & 90.9 FM North Shore) Fantastic community radio with varied programming, including blues, reggae, salsa, Hawaiian and Grateful Dead shows.
KVIC (channel 3) Available in almost all hotels and resorts, a televised loop of tourist information.

Medical Services

Long's Drugs (Map p443; ☎ 245-7771; Kukui Grove Center, 3-2600 Kaumuali'i Hwy; 8am-9pm Mon-Sat, 8am-6pm Sun)
Wilcox Memorial Hospital (Map p443; ☎ 245-1010, TTY 245-1133; 3420 Kuhio Hwy) Emergency services 24 hours.

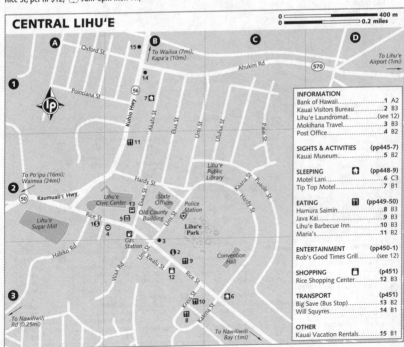

Sweetheart's Rock in Pu'u Pehe cove (p394) at dusk, Manele Bay, Lana'i

Overlooking Hulopo'e Bay, from Manele Bay (p393), Lana'i

Garden of the Gods (p397), Lana'i

A mule ride (p423) down the cliffs to Kalau-papa Peninsula, Moloka'i

ERIC L WHEATER

KARL LEHMANN

Kepuhi Beach (p427), one of several white-sand beaches on Moloka'i's sunny West End

ANN CE

An ancient Hawaiian fishpond (p412) near Kaunakakai, Moloka'i

Money

Banks with 24-hour ATMs:
American Savings Bank (Map p443; ☎ 246-8844; Kukui Grove Center, 3-2600 Kaumuali'i Hwy)
Bank of Hawaii (Map p443; ☎ 245-6761; 4455 Rice St)

Post

Main Post Office (Map p444; ☎ 800-275-8777; 4441 Rice St, Lihue, HI 96766; ⏰ 8am-4:30pm Mon-Fri, 9am-1pm Sat) Receives poste restante (general delivery) mail for a maximum 30 days.

Tourist Information

Kauai Visitors Bureau (Map p444; ☎ 245-3971, 800-262-1400; www.kauaivisitorsbureau.org; Suite 101, 4334 Rice St) Offers monthly calendar of events, bus schedules and list of Sunshine Markets. Order a free 'vacation planning kit' online or by calling the 800 number. For brochures and other printed tourist information, the airport has a better selection.

Travel Agencies

Mokihana Travel (Map p444; ☎ 245-5338; Suite 3, 3016 Umi St; ⏰ 8am-5pm Mon-Fri, to noon Sat) Professional, efficient agency sells interisland flights, plus international phone cards.

SIGHTS
Kaua'i Museum

More than poi (fermented taro) pounders and Hawaiian quilts, a quick hour spent in this interesting **museum** (Map p444; ☎ 245-6931; www.kauaimuseum.org; 4428 Rice St; adult/child 6-12/youth 13-17/senior $7/1/3/5, 1st Sat of month free; ⏰ 9am-4pm Mon-Fri, 10am-4pm Sat) will give you an insightful overview of Kaua'i's history. For a more in-depth experience, make reservations for a **guided tour** (tour $10; ⏰ 10am Mon, Wed & Thu).

Straightforward, well-written displays explain Hawai'i's volcanic genesis and the formation of the island chain from the ocean floor, as well as Kaua'i's unique ecosystems, emphasizing native flora and fauna. Early Hawaiian artifacts (tapa bark cloth, wooden bowls, ceremonial leis etc) are also in the collection here, though will likely disappoint if you've visited the fine Bishop Museum in O'ahu (p97).

Upstairs, the collection is Kaua'i-specific, and covers the arrival of missionaries, sugar and the mélange of folks imported to work the fields. In a socioeconomic commentary that still rings true, a replica of a plantation worker's spartan shack sits opposite the spacious bedroom of an early missionary's house, furnished with a koa (Hawaiian

timber tree) four-poster bed and Hawaiian quilts. Hawai'i's multiethnic roots and vastly unequal distribution of land can be traced to this period of the sugar and pineapple empire. Anyone interested in 'the Forbidden Island' won't want to miss the photographs of Ni'ihau, which give outsiders a rare peek into that protected isle.

If you run out of time before seeing the entire museum, ask for a free re-entry pass when you leave. An adjacent gallery has rotating exhibits of contemporary art. Be sure to browse the Edith King Wilcox Gift Shop (p451), too.

Wailua Falls

This strikingly scenic 80ft waterfall (Map p434) is just north of Lihu'e. Indeed, this gushing double waterfall (Wailua means 'two waters') misting the surrounding tropical foliage is fantastic, especially after heavy rains when it becomes one wide cascade. At these times you can literally watch fish being thrown out beyond the powerful waters for a flying dive into the pool below.

This is not a waterfall to explore from the top, hence the sign at the parking lot near a closed path reading: 'Slippery rocks at top of falls. People have been killed.' There are plenty of stories of people sliding off the rocks, some miraculously grabbing roots and being rescued, and others not so lucky.

A third of a mile before the road's end, at a large dirt pull-off (parking lot), an eroded trail leads to the base of the falls. Because the trail is as slippery as an incumbent politician (and as hazardous), it's not open to the public, but from this pull-off you get a fine view of a second waterfall to the southeast.

To get there from Lihu'e, follow Hwy 56 north and turn left onto Ma'alo Rd (Hwy 583), which is a narrow paved road that weaves through sugarcane fields and ends at the falls after 4 miles.

Lihu'e Lutheran Church

Atop a curvy country lane just off Hwy 50 is Hawaii's oldest Lutheran **church** (Map p443; ☎ 245-2145; 4602 Ho'omana Rd; ⏰ services 8am & 10:30am Sun). It's a quaint, clapboard house of worship, with some surprises. Crossing the threshold, bright birds-of-paradise and gardenia-scented air intoxicate, but things turn queerer as you enter the church proper, with its slanted floor reminiscent of a ship's deck and balcony like a captain's bridge. These and other architectural details are thanks to the German immigrants who built this church, styling it after the boat that brought them over in the late 19th century. Completed in 1983, this building is actually a faithful reconstruction of the 1885 original, which was leveled in Hurricane Iwa in 1982.

Fancying an afterlife with a view, the immigrants themselves now lie at rest in the church cemetery on a knoll overlooking the cane fields in which they toiled. Visitors are welcome to stroll amid the graves and take pictures inside and out, except during Sunday service.

Kalapaki Beach

Surfers trot toward the swells with boards at the ready, while mainlanders bask on the sands of this beach (Map p443), Lihu'e's best. Sheltered by points and breakwaters at Nawiliwili Bay and lined with coconut palms, this beach off Hwy 51 lies in front of the Kaua'i Marriott (p449). It's also called Marriott Beach, but is open to the general public (free beach parking is close to the water at the hotel's north side). Swimming is usually good, even in winter. The **beach hut** here rents snorkel gear, surfboards and kayaks, and a variety of restaurants (p449), from casual to 'bust out the credit card,' lines the beach. This is a good chill-out spot before catching your flight out.

Fronting the beach is the **International Surfing Hall of Fame** (Map p443; ☎ 632-2270; adult/child under 12 $10/free; ☼ 9am-9pm). In existence since the '60s, but without a bricks-and-mortar home, this long-overdue tribute to the world's greatest surfers exhibits boards, memorabilia and original art in cool digs replete with thatched roof and piped-in surfing tunes. The museum screening room shows classic surf movies, too.

Nawiliwili Beach Park

A footbridge from Kalapaki Beach crosses Nawiliwili Stream to Nawiliwili Beach Park (Map p443), from where you can see the light beacon on Kukui Point; at the far end of the parking lot you can also see the lighthouse on the more distant **Ninini Point**. Right at the mouth of the stream under ironwood trees is a simple shelter with a wooden sign reading 'Pine Tree Uptown' – it's an

impromptu neighborhood open-air bar of sorts. Old-timers gather here during the day with beers to 'talk story' and play music.

The other sight in these parts is the massive cruise ships calling in at **Nawiliwili Harbor**; smaller boats, including deep-sea fishing charters and kayak tours, leave from the nearby small-boat harbor. Recommended outfitters include:

True Blue Charters (☎ 245-9662; www.trueblue charters.com; 4-/6-hr shared deep-sea fishing charter per person from $100/130; ☼ Dec-Mar 2-hr whale-watching tour adult/child $50/35)

Wild Bill's (☎ 822-5963; 4-hr shared deep-sea fishing charter per person $115)

Menehune Fishpond Overlook

After 0.5 miles twisting up Hulemalu Rd, you'll come to an overlook with the Menehune Fishpond (Alakoko Fishpond; Map p443) fanning out below. In the background are the misty cliffs of Haupu Ridge, sloping down into the 238 acres of the **Hule'ia National Wildlife Refuge**, (pacificislands.fws.gov/wnwr /khuleianwr.html) along the north side of Hule'ia Stream.

Once planted with taro and rice, the area now provides breeding and feeding grounds for endemic water birds. The fishpond, created by a stone wall that runs along a bend in Hule'ia Stream, was said to have been built overnight by Kaua'i's legendary *menehune* (little people). The stone wall is now covered by a thick green line of mangrove trees. Morning is the best time for viewing the fishpond, as in the afternoon you look into the sun.

The refuge is closed to the public, but kayak tours along Hule'ia Stream drift through it; though the views from above are better, the mana (spiritual essence) is more powerful at eye level. **Island Adventures** (☎ 245-9662; www .kauaifun.com; 2½ hr adult/child $59/39, 4½ hr adult/child $89/69) does trips from Nawiliwili Harbor. You'll get 2.5 miles of paddling along Hule'ia Stream, with a swim and rope-swing jaunt at the end. The longer tour hikes down to a set of waterfalls and includes lunch.

If you continue about a mile past the fishpond overlook and then turn right onto Puhi Rd, you'll arrive at Hwy 50, opposite Kauai Community College. Continue about 2.5 miles and you'll hook up with Kipu Rd; a left turn will take you to the dirt path to **Kipu Falls** (p452).

Ninini Point

This place delivers 360-degree sensations: jets directly above swoop in for a landing and waves crash against the rocks below. Looking east, soaring cliffs cut off rainbows and, closer in, golfers tee off near a beckoning scoop of beach. These terrific views from Ninini Point are made more so by its 100ft **lighthouse** marking the northern entrance to Nawiliwili Bay. Here, Hawaiians still fish, pick *opihi* (an edible limpet) and gather *limu* (an edible seaweed).

The road to the lighthouse begins off Hwy 51, just over 0.5 miles south of the intersection with Hwy 570 and marked with two concrete slabs. You'll pass a guard gate (usually empty) and through Hole 12 of the Mokihana Golf Course, for a total of just over two miles, most of it rutted dirt road, before you reach the short spur to the lighthouse. This is all completely open to the public.

To get to **Running Waters Beach** (the little slice of sand visible from Ninini Point) return to Hole 12 and park in the lot just before it, then follow the signs for Shore Access. Turn right at Whaler's Brew Pub (p450) and descend to its parking lot, where you'll see another Shore Access sign to your left. It's a steep, quick walk to the beach below, where the sand is golden and the surf runs in and out of naturally carved channels in the volcanic rock. You'll probably have the beach to yourself, and it makes a wonderful picnic spot. Wading beyond ankle depth is not advisable here. You can also reach this beach (but not the lighthouse) by driving through the Marriott (p449), following signs to Whaler's Brew Pub.

Grove Farm Homestead

A bit musty and memory filled, is **plantation museum** (Map p443; ☎ 245-3202; Nawiliwili Rd; 2-hr tour adult/child under 12 US$5/2; ☺ tours 10am & 1pm Mon, Wed & Thu). The preserved farmhouse was built in 1864 by George Wilcox, the son of missionaries Abner and Lucy Wilcox, and it feels suspended in time, with rocking chairs sitting dormant on a covered porch, and books with no readers lining the shelves of the old home's library. Reservations are required.

Kilohana Plantation

Formerly the 1930s sugar plantation estate of Gaylord Parke Wilcox, once big boss man of Grove Farm Homestead, **Kilohana** (Map p443; ☎ 245-9593; www.luaukilohana.com; Hwy 50; admission free; ☺ 9:30am-9:30pm, to 5pm Sun) is a tourist magnet thanks to its famous luau (p451), Gaylords restaurant (p450) and one-stop upscale shopping (p451).

The 15,000-sq-ft, Tudor-style mansion built by Wilcox has been painstakingly restored and its legacy as distinguished historic house on Kaua'i recaptured. Antique-filled rooms and Oriental carpets laid over hardwood floors lead you past cases of poi pounders, koa bowls and other Hawaiiana to one shop-cum-gallery after another. Behind the main house is **Kilohana Clayworks** pottery shop, where you can watch potters at work.

Carriages pulled by Clydesdale horses **tour** (adult/child US$12/6; ☺ 11am-5pm) the 35-acre grounds, including gardens and livestock barns, giving a sense of the plantation's purpose back in old Kaua'i.

Kilohana is 1.5 miles west of Lihu'e on Hwy 50.

ACTIVITIES

You can play tennis for free at county tennis courts in central Lihu'e at Lihu'e Park (Map p444), and across from Kaua'i Community College in Puhi Park (Map p443). You can also hit the nicely kept courts at **Ala Lani Spa & Tennis Club** (Map p443; ☎ 245-3323; Kaua'i Marriott; court rental per hr $20).

You could spend your entire vacation at the challenging golf courses in Lihu'e, which include the following:

Kauai Lagoons Golf Club (Map p443; ☎ 241-6000; Kaua'i Marriott; green fees Mokihana/Kiele $85/130, off-peak cheaper, club rental $35) Two Jack Nicklaus-designed 18-hole par-72 courses.

Puakea Golf Course (Map p443; ☎ 245-8756, 866-773-5554; www.puakeagolf.com; near Kukui Grove Center; green fees incl cart before/after 1pm $125/65, club rental $30/20) Lush cliffs of Mt Ha'upu serve as a backdrop.

FESTIVALS & EVENTS

Here is a selection of Kaua'i's most exciting special events; for a complete list, visit www.kauaivisitorsbureau.com.

E Pili Kakou I Ho'okahi Lahui (late January; ☎ 246-4752; www.epilikakou.org) Popular annual two-day hula retreat at the Kaua'i Marriott where you can participate in classes or just watch.

Annual Waimea Town Celebration (mid-February; ☎ 335-2824) Free fun on the Westside includes a rodeo, canoe races, and lei and ukelele competitions.

KAUA'I FOR KIDS

Kaua'i is such a wicked destination for kids, with so much to do, even grown-ups get jealous. If you need a break, give a shout to **Babysitters of Kauai** (☎ 632-2252; www.babysittersofkauai.com; per hr $15, 3 hr minimum).

In addition to general fun stuff (snorkeling, swimming, helicopter tours, luau, etc), Kaua'i has some specific activities and attractions perfect for the younger set, including the following:

- **Playtime** at Kamalani Playground & Kamalani Play Bridge (p454)
- **Children's Garden** at Na 'Aina Kai Botanical Garden (p470)
- **Knowhow** at Kaua'i Children's Discovery Museum (p462) – summer day camps are offered here, too
- **Amusements** at Fun Factory (p462)
- **Gaming** at ComputerWeb (p462)
- **Eating** at Mango Mama's (p472)
- **Safe water fun** at Po'ipu Beach Park (p494), Baby Beach (p492), Salt Pond Beach Park (p503), Lydgate Beach Park (p454) and Queen's Bath (p475)
- A **boat tour** of the Na Pali Coast with Holo Holo Charters (p502). For kids aged two and up
- **Tubing** down the old Lihu'e sugar irrigation ditch (p451)
- **Hiking** the Canyon Trail (p513); Kuilau Trail (p457); or the Kalalau Trail along the Na Pali coast to Hanakapi'ai (p487)

Annual Kaua'i Polynesian Festival (late May; ☎ 335-6466; www.kauaipolyfest.com) This four-day event featuring loads of food, cultural workshops, and dance exhibits and competitions is held at picturesque Kukui Grove Pavilion & Park.

Concert in the Sky (July 4; ☎ 246-2440) Feast on island foods and enjoy live entertainment all day before the grand finale fireworks show set to music; held at Lihu'e's Vidinha Stadium.

Heiva I Kauai-Iorana Tahiti (early August; ☎ 822-9447, 822-4556) Dance troupes from as far as Tahiti, Japan and Canada join groups from Hawaii in this Tahitian dance competition at the Kukui Grove Pavilion; drumming contests, too.

Annual Eo e Emalani I Alaka'i (early October; ☎ 335-9975; www.aloha.net/~kokee; admission free; ⏰ 10am) Hula Halau from all over Hawaii participate in this outdoor dance festival at the Kokee Museum; royal procession, music and crafts are also featured.

Lights on Rice Parade (early December; ☎ 246-1004; admission free; ⏰ 6:30pm) A dazzling array of floats bedecked with lights parade along Rice St in Lihu'e in this popular event.

SLEEPING

The pickings are slim for sleeping in Lihu'e, especially for solo travelers who won't find decent value there. Travelers with mid-range or top-end budgets will find a better selection, though more distinctive properties are

still found outside town. If you're on a shoestring or just want a bunk to lay your head, consider moving up the coast to Kapa'a (p465).

Budget   Map p444
Motel Lani (☎ 245-2965; 4240 Rice St; r standard/deluxe $34/52; ❄) This Bates Motel–type place hiding behind tropical foliage at a busy intersection may seem off-putting, but is Lihu'e's best budget choice. Darkish and shaggy outside, the six rooms at this family-run motel are basic but clean, and each has a small refrigerator. Upgrading to 'deluxe' gets you a slightly bigger room with a TV. There's a two-day minimum stay or a $2 surcharge. No credit cards.

Tip Top Motel (☎ 245-2333; tiptop@aloha.net; 3173 Akahi St; r $50; ❄) Is this Lihu'e or Lima? The parking-lot view from the cinderblock rooms make the Tip Top seem straight out of Latin America. White cement inside and out, its 12 rooms sport worn comforters and zero charm. As a last budget resort, this place works, but isn't recommended for women travelers or families.

Mid-Range   Map p443
Garden Island Inn (☎ 245-7227, 800-648-0154; www.gardenislandinn.com; 3445 Wilcox Rd; with kitchenette

ground fl r $85, upper fl d $95-105, ste $135; [icon]) You'll feel the aloha in this super-friendly place with 21 spiffy rooms. Ground-floor units are nicely appointed with overhead fans, quality double beds and rattan furniture, making them good value. Rooms on the 2nd and 3rd floors are more inviting still, with bigger living space, lanai (balcony) and views. Kalapaki Beach is just up the street, and many shops and good restaurants are within walking distance.

Kauai Inn ([phone] 245-9000; www.kauaiinn.com; 2430 Hulemalu Rd; r with kitchenette incl breakfast $80-110; [icon]) This peaceful property en route to the Menehune Fishpond Overlook is Kaua'i's oldest hotel. Originally the Fairview Hotel (founded in 1890 in a different location), such luminaries as Lee Marvin and John Wayne stayed here. After it was leveled by Hurricane Iniki, the McKnight family spent nearly a decade restoring the 48 rooms. The cheapest rooms are serviceable, but dark; upstairs units are better, with carpet and tiled floors, sitting area and bathtubs. Each room is unique, so look at a few before choosing.

Banyan Harbor Resort ([phone] 245-7333, 800-422-6926; www.vacation-kauai.com; 2411 Wilcox Rd; 1-/2-bedroom units $115/145; [icon]) Families looking for spacious, comfortable digs might consider this condo complex near Kalapaki Beach. The big, open units have terrific amenities – a gourmet dinner party for six is doable in the well-equipped kitchen; washer and dryer makes cleanup easy. Up to four people can squeeze into the one-bedroom unit, six might get by in a two-bedroom unit. All condos have lanai, but those on the ground floor don't get light, while others look at the parking lot.

Top End
Kaua'i Marriott
Map p443

Kaua'i Marriott ([phone] 245-5050, 800-220-2925; www.marriotthotels.com; Kalapaki Beach; r $330-445; [icon]) This sprawling, upmarket hotel is the best of the Eastside biggies, and the most Hawaiian-feeling: nene (Hawaiian geese) look upon koi-stocked ponds, the koa canoe *Princess* gleams in the lobby and room decor is stylishly tropical with orchid bedspreads and native botanical prints. Even the cheaper room views are attractive, and Kalapaki Beach is right out the door. The restaurants (p450) are fine and the 26,000-sq-ft pool is Hawaii's biggest. Look for online booking specials.

Radisson Kauai Beach Resort (Map p443; [phone] 245-1955, 888-805-3843, www.radisson-kauai.com; 4331 Kauai Beach Dr; r $250-360; [icon] [icon]) Frequent business travelers will feel at home on Radisson's beachfront property: the rooms are quite standard in their beigeness, with small sitting area and teeny lanai. You would have to get a great online deal or package to make this one worth it – luckily, they abound and savvy travelers can shave off $100 at least from these rack rates.

EATING
Budget

Hamura Saimin (Map p444; [phone] 245-3271; 2956 Kress St; noodles $3.50-4.25; [icon] 10am-11:30pm Mon-Thu, to late Fri & Sat, 10am-9:30pm Sun) Ask any Eastsider where to eat and without fail they'll exclaim 'Hamura Saimin!' You're in old Kaua'i once the screen door slams behind you at this simple Japanese noodle shop run by three generations of the same family. Expect to wait for a vacant stool along the winding counter while folks slurp away at their fresh, healthy and *ono* (good) saimin. Load on extras, like chopped egg, green onion or Spam. **Holo Holo Shave Ice** ([icon] 1-4pm Mon-Fri) is here for your sweet tooth.

Fish Express (Map p443; [phone] 245-9918; 3343 Kuhio Hwy; lunch $6-7.50; [icon] 10am-7pm Mon-Sat, to 5pm Sun, lunch to 3pm) 'Eat at Fish Express!' Eastsiders exclaim again. Just south of Wilcox Memorial Hospital, this popular place makes killer fresh-fish lunches (take-out only). Choose from inventive items, like grilled ono with orange-tarragon sauce or macadamia-encrusted *'ahi* (yellowfin tuna) in *liliko'i* (passion fruit)-dill sauce, which come with rice and salad ($7.50). Outside of lunch hours, snag something from the deli case: generous sashimi trays are $6 and nine types of *poke* (marinated raw fish) and fresh fish are sold by the pound.

Kalapaki Beach Hut (Map p443; [phone] 246-6330; 3474 Rice St; breakfast & burgers $4-7; [icon] 7am-7pm) Yet another local blue-ribbon winner, this casual place facing Kalapaki Beach has big breakfasts – egg and cheese sandwiches are good on the go or sample an omelet sautéed with fresh ono – and inventive fast food for lunch (try the 'local boy' burger with Portuguese sausage, green onion and kimchi). There's a kids' menu and veggie options too, but the best part is the upstairs dining porch with unadulterated ocean views. Yum!

Java Kai (Map p444; ☎ 632-0801; 4302 Rice St; breakfast $6-7, drinks $1.35-4; ☷ 6am-7pm Mon-Fri, to 3pm Sat, to 1pm Sun) This locally owned and operated café chain has a complete breakfast menu served until 1pm. It's the place to go for your morning jolt, any time of day. A full range of coffee drinks, iced or hot, is on tap, as are fresh juices, frappés and smoothies.

Kauai Chop Suey (Map p443; ☎ 245-8790; Harbor Mall, 3501 Rice St; lunch $7, dinner $7-10; ☷ lunch Tue-Sat, dinner Tue-Sun). This straightforward Chinese place (read: all business, little atmosphere) has flavorful standards, like sweet-and-sour chicken ($10), and more creative options like fried tofu with black mushrooms ($9) and shrimp with bitter melon ($8.25). Vegetarians can choose widely from the menu.

TOP 10 EATS

- **Blossoming Lotus** (p466)
- **'Anini Beach Lunch Shak** (p474)
- **Hamura Saimin** (p449)
- **A Pacific Cafe** (p463)
- **Hanapepe Cafe** (p504)
- **Postcards Cafe** (p482)
- **Fish Express** (p449)
- **Kountry Kitchen** (p466)
- **Ono Char Burger** (p468)
- **Kalaheo Coffee Co & Café** (p501)

Mid-Range & Top End

Duke's Canoe Club (Map p443; ☎ 246-9599; Kaua'i Marriott; appetizers $7-9, mains $17-29; ☷ dinner) The open-air layout overlooking Kalapaki Beach, oil lamps and meandering, koi-stocked stream give this place knockout atmosphere. Toothsome appetizers, like spicy sugarcane shrimp in chili sauce and mac-nut and Dungeness-crab wontons, start off the extensive menu. Mains include herb-roasted prime rib and seven-spiced 'ahi with papaya-mustard vinaigrette. Live music happens nightly from 6:45pm. Convenient parking is behind the Kalapaki Beach Hut, where a footbridge crosses the stream to Duke's.

Maria's (Map p444; ☎ 246-9599, 246-9122; 3142 Kuhio Hwy; à la carte $5-9, dishes $12-13; ☷ 11am-9pm Mon-Fri, noon-9pm Sat) Cooking aromas from south of the border envelop you at this sunny, cozy place offering Mexican fare with cheery service. Small tables and *artesanía* (handicrafts) add to the intimate feel while you chow on a $10 chicken burrito (the food is authentic Mexican, the prices less so), or choose from 11 different combinations mixing up tostadas, enchiladas, tacos and quesadillas with varied fillings (a couple vegetarian), and rice and beans on the side. Wash it all down with Maria's sangria or a Mexican beer.

Cafe Portofino (Map p443; ☎ 245-2121; Kaua'i Marriott; appetizers $8-12, mains $14-28; ☷ dinner) Even Martha Stewart voted for this noted Italian restaurant with great Kalapaki Beach and bay views as the place for a romantic interlude. Among several house specialities is a traditional osso buco if you're craving veal shank, or give the kinder, gentler vegetable lasagna a go. Save room for the homemade gelato. A live harpist performs nightly, adding loads of ambience.

Gaylord's (Map p443; ☎ 245-9593; www.gaylords kauai.com; lunch $8-11, dinner $20-34; ☷ lunch Mon-Sat, brunch Sun, dinner nightly) 'Country-club sedate' best approximates the ambience and food at this famous place where the menu will delight Granny (rack of lamb, tenderloin tips, etc). The scant offerings for vegetarians are more interesting, like the fire-grilled veg Napoleon with goat cheese ($12). Sunday brunch, with tasty selections like Belgian waffles with *liliko'i* ($11), is your best bet if you want to experience dining here.

Lihu'e Barbecue Inn (Map p444; ☎ 245-2921; 2982 Kress St; lunch $5-12, dinner $19-24; ☷ 10:30am-1:30pm Mon-Sat, 5-8:30pm Mon-Thu, 4:30-9pm Fri & Sat) Diner atmosphere doesn't keep the local crowds away from this 'special night out' place; choose from scores of menu items, including stuffed mahimahi (dolphin), seared salmon with mango chutney or mac nut–encrusted chicken.

DRINKING & ENTERTAINMENT
Bars & Nightclubs

Duke's Barefoot Bar (Map p443; ☎ 246-9599; Kaua'i Marriott; ☷ 11am-midnight) Leave your shoes at the door at this chill place right on Kalapaki Beach. A good mix of Hawaiian, rock and pop music livens things up nightly, and there's a casual burgers-and-sandwiches bar menu served until 11pm.

Whaler's Brew Pub (Map p443; ☎ 245-2000; 3132 Ninini Pt; ☷ 11:30am-2am Mon-Sat, DJs from 10pm Thu-Sat) For beers and a bitchin' view, head to this microbrewery at the end of the road through the Kaua'i Marriott. Overlooking Nawiliwili Harbor and the lighthouse on Ninini Point, you can sample a handful of beers brewed on-site; there's a simple bar menu by day, and dancing and DJs by night.

Rob's Good Times Grill (Map p444; ☎ 246-0311; Rice Shopping Center, 4303 Rice St; ☽ 9pm-2am) The atmosphere might be a little hokey, but a young, energetic crowd comes out to boogie to a live DJ Thursday through Saturday (Friday is the hottest). Sunday through Tuesday is karaoke and Wednesday is country line dancing; yeehaw! There are typically whopping drink specials, like $3 Coronas.

Luau

Luau extravaganzas (hula, chanting, dancing with fire and other Polynesian-inspired demonstrations by talented performers with all-you-can eat Hawaiian buffet and open bar – mai tais, wine and beer usually) are on offer at the following places:

Radisson Kauai Beach Resort (Map p443; ☎ 335-5828; www.luau-hawaii.com; 4331 Kauai Beach Dr; adult/child/teen $57/27/37; ☽ 5:15pm Thu & Sun)

Kilohana Plantation (Map p443; ☎ 245-9593; www .luaukilohana.com; Hwy 50; adult/child/teen $60/31/56; ☽ 5:30pm Tue & Thu) Historic plantation setting is a bonus here.

Cinemas

Kukui Grove Cinema (Map p443; ☎ 245-5055; Kukui Grove Center, 3-2600 Kaumuali'i Hwy; adult/child $6/4, before 5pm $4) Catch a movie at this fourplex.

SHOPPING

Kilohana Plantation (Map p443; www.luaukilohana .com; Hwy 50) For sheer variety and presentation, the shops here can't be beat. Here you can browse one of Kaua'i's widest collections of arts and crafts. Finely strung Ni'ihau shell lei, scrimshaw, dolls, woodcarvings and contemporary paintings by local artists are crammed into every room in the house, including the closets and bathrooms. For more details, see p447.

Edith King Wilcox Gift Shop (Map p444; Kaua'i Museum, 4428 Rice St) Based at the Kaua'i Museum (p445), this is a shopping treat, with a broad selection of Hawaiiana books, and a small collection of koa bowls and other handicrafts. You can enter the shop, free of charge, through the museum lobby.

Shopping malls in Kaua'i not only house useful services and recommendable restaurants, but they also serve as landmarks for when locals give directions. You'll so often hear 'turn right at Big Save,' it's worth knowing the names and locations of important emporia and what shops they hold:

Kukui Grove Center (Map p443; ☎ 245-7784; 3-2600 Kaumuali'i Hwy) Sears, Long's Drugs (p444), Borders (p444), K-Mart, Radio Shack and various banks.

Harbor Mall (Map p443; ☎ 245-6255; 3501 Rice St) Ali'i Kayaks (p452), Beach Books (p444), Hawaii Link (p444), Kauai Chop Suey and Rent-A-Wreck (p440).

Anchor Cove Shopping Center (Map p443; ☎ 246-0634; 3416 Rice St) Aloha Kayaks & Canoes (p452), Crazy Shirts, International Surfing Hall of Fame (p446) and Tropical Isle Music (p444).

Rice Shopping Center (Map p444; 4303 Rice St) Lihu'e Laundromat (p444) and Rob's Good Time Grill (p451).

GETTING AROUND

The Kaua'i Bus (p440) connects Lihu'e to Kalapaki Beach with very limited service on Routes 100, 400 and 500 (five departures Monday to Friday and four departures on Saturday). The Lihu'e Extension (Route 700) runs hourly buses from Kukui Grove Center to the Garden Island Inn/Kalapaki Beach from 8am to 3pm Monday to Friday.

In Lihu'e, pick up buses at the Big Save Supermarket at the northeast side of the Lihu'e Civic Center or the First Hawaiian Bank in Kukui Grove Center.

AROUND LIHU'E
Hanama'ulu

Hanama'ulu is a sleepy little village between Lihu'e and Wailua along Hwy 56. It's significant in Hawaiian folklore as the birthplace of Kaua'i's legendary hero Kawelo, depicted in folktales as a skillful warrior and champion spear thrower.

Three-quarters of a mile from the village, **Hanama'ulu Beach Park** lies inside Hanama'ulu Bay, a deep, protected bay with a partial boulder breakwater. The park has campgrounds with full facilities, but it's more of a sketchy local hangout than a destination and is not recommended for solo women travelers. The waters are occasionally off-limits because of pollution; park users are often polluted, too. For information on obtaining camping permits, see p435. Get to Hanama'ulu Beach Park from Hwy 56, by turning *makai* (seaward) at the 7-Eleven onto Hanama'ulu Rd. After a quarter mile, turn right onto Hehi Rd. As you enter the park, you'll first go under the highway bridge and then the picturesque arched trestle of an abandoned railroad bridge.

Locals flock to this crossroads of Hwy 56 (Kuhio Hwy) and Hanama'ulu Rd for copious portions of Japanese food at the **Hanama'ulu Restaurant Tea House & Sushi Bar** (Map p443; ☎ 245-2511, 245-3225; 3-4291 Kuhio Hwy; mains $7-9.50, special platters $15-17, Sun dinner buffet adult/child 7-12 $21/15, child under 7 for each year $1; 🕑 11:30am-9:30pm Tue-Sun). The all-you-can-eat Sunday dinner buffet is a real crowd-pleaser, as are the private, screen-enclosed rooms, varied plate lunches and Japanese beer. Next door, the **Big Wheel Donut Shop** (Map p443; ☎ 245-2536; Old Hanama'ulu Trading Post; 🕑 4am-to late) sells poofy glazed donuts for 60¢ each.

Also in Hanama'ulu is **Kauai Backcountry Adventures** (Map p443; ☎ 245-2506, 888-270-0555; www.kauaibackcountry.com; Hwy 56; tour per person zipline $110, tubing $85) offering adventures down the old irrigation ditch near Lihu'e.

Kipu Falls

It's hot and you're craving freshwater. It's time for **Kipu Falls**, a short drive and hike from Lihu'e. This waterfall and swimming hole – replete with thrilling 20ft rope jump – has long been a low-key, local favorite (you'll see 'Locals Only!' and 'No Haole!' graffiti around). Now the word is out and locals are ticked. To minimize visitor impact, come early or late on a weekday, leave the weekends to residents and keep it clean.

To get there, take Kipu Rd off Hwy 50 at the 3-mile marker. A dirt path leading to the falls is just under one mile along, before the one-lane bridge. A five-minute walk on the path takes you to the falls. Don't leave anything of value in your car. Returning to Lihu'e, you can take more scenic Hulemalu Rd (turn right off Kipu Rd 0.75 miles from the falls path), which takes you past the **Menehune Fishpond** and hooks up with Wa'apa Rd near Nawiliwili.

EASTSIDE

On that rare occasion when you hear locals complaining, it's likely to be about Eastside traffic. Chock-a-block with strip malls and shopping complexes, the Eastside is Kaua'i's commercial heart, running from Lihu'e through Wailua and Waipouli to Kapa'a.

Still, the Eastside is more endearing than it sounds, with colonnades of coconut palms and peeks of rolling surf ameliorating all that stop and go. Many important services, including most good-value accommodations, are on the centrally located Eastside, making it an attractive base for travelers.

WAILUA

There are strip malls and condos ad nauseam driving the 3-mile stretch of Hwy 56 (Kuhio Hwy) from Wailua to Kapa'a. But look on the side streets, toward the mountains and along the coast, and you'll discover lovely B&Bs, parks, beaches and activities galore. This area, midway between the North Shore and Koke'e State Park, is a good base for exploring the rest of Kaua'i.

Relics of Kaua'i's royal days (p435) – known as the 'Seven Sacred Heiau', running from the mouth of the Wailua River up to the top of Mt Wai'ale'ale – can be visited. Six of these heiau sites are located within a mile of the river mouth. Five are visible, while the sixth is abandoned in a field on the northern side of the Wailua River. All date to the early period of Tahitian settlement.

Orientation & Information

In promotional materials, this stretch is sometimes referred to as the 'Coconut Coast'; in local circles, it's known as traffic hell. You can circumnavigate it by taking the Kapa'a By-Pass Rd, which cuts northeast at Coconut Plantation and dumps you onto Hwy 581 near the center of Kapa'a town.

Pop into the **Tin Can Mailman** (☎ 822-3009; tincan.mailman@verizon.net; Kinipopo Shopping Village, 4-356 Kuhio Hwy; 🕑 11am-7pm Mon-Fri, noon-4pm Sat), which has delightful Hawaiiana oddities, like vintage LPs, maps, photos and postcards, '50s-era paper dolls and cruise menus. It also stocks an impressive variety of rare, new and used books.

Sights
WAILUA RIVER STATE PARK
This state park straddling the Wailua River includes most of the seven sacred heiau, the Fern Grotto, a riverboat (p459 for tours) basin and public boat ramp. Most importantly, it's the setting-off point for the celebrated Wailua River kayak trip.

EASTSIDE

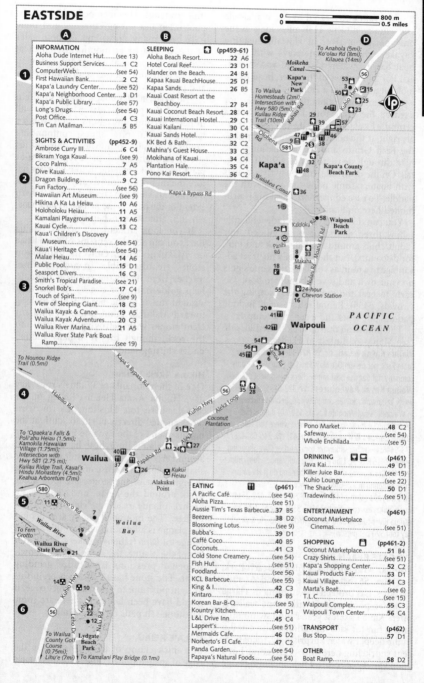

0		800 m
0		0.5 miles

INFORMATION
Aloha Dude Internet Hut......(see 13)
Business Support Services.............1 C2
ComputerWeb.......................(see 54)
First Hawaiian Bank......................2 C2
Kapa'a Laundry Center..........(see 52)
Kapa'a Neighborhood Center......3 D1
Kapa'a Public Library.............(see 57)
Long's Drugs.......................(see 54)
Post Office.................................4 C3
Tin Can Mailman.........................5 B5

SIGHTS & ACTIVITIES (pp452-9)
Ambrose Curry III.........................6 C4
Bikram Yoga Kauai...............(see 54)
Coco Palms...............................7 A5
Dive Kauai.................................8 C3
Dragon Building...........................9 C2
Fun Factory..........................(see 56)
Hawaiian Art Museum.............(see 9)
Hikina A Ka La Heiau.................10 A6
Holoholoku Heiau.....................11 A5
Kamalani Playground.................12 A6
Kauai Cycle.............................13 C3
Kaua'i Children's Discovery
  Museum............................(see 54)
Kaua'i Heritage Center..........(see 54)
Malae Heiau............................14 A6
Public Pool..............................15 D1
Seasport Divers........................16 C3
Smith's Tropical Paradise.......(see 21)
Snorkel Bob's...........................17 C4
Touch of Spirit.......................(see 9)
View of Sleeping Giant..............18 C3
Wailua Kayak & Canoe..............19 A5
Wailua Kayak Adventures..........20 C3
Wailua River Marina.................21 A5
Wailua River State Park Boat
  Ramp...............................(see 19)

SLEEPING (pp459-61)
Aloha Beach Resort...................22 A6
Hotel Coral Reef......................23 D1
Islander on the Beach...............24 B4
Kapaa Kauai BeachHouse............25 D1
Kapaa Sands............................26 B5
Kauai Coast Resort at the
  Beachboy............................27 B4
Kauai Coconut Beach Resort......28 C4
Kauai International Hostel..........29 C1
Kauai Kailani..........................30 C4
Kauai Sands............................31 B4
Kauai Sands Hotel.....................31 B4
KK Bed & Bath.........................32 C2
Mahina's Guest House................33 C3
Mokihana of Kauai....................34 C4
Plantation Hale........................35 C4
Pono Kai Resort.......................36 C2

EATING (p461)
A Pacific Café.......................(see 54)
Aloha Pizza..........................(see 51)
Aussie Tim's Texas Barbecue......37 B5
Beezers.................................38 D2
Blossoming Lotus.....................(see 9)
Bubba's.................................39 D1
Caffè Coco..............................40 B5
Coconuts................................41 C3
Cold Stone Creamery...............(see 54)
Fish Hut...............................(see 51)
Foodland..............................(see 56)
KCL Barbecue.........................(see 55)
King & I.................................42 C3
Kintaro.................................43 B5
Korean Bar-B-Q.......................(see 5)
Kountry Kitchen......................44 D1
L&L Drive Inn..........................45 C4
Lappert's..............................(see 51)
Mermaids Cafe.........................46 D2
Norberto's El Cafe.....................47 C2
Panda Garden.........................(see 54)
Papaya's Natural Foods............(see 54)
Pono Market...........................48 C2
Safeway................................(see 54)
Whole Enchilada......................(see 5)

DRINKING (p461)
Java Kai................................49 D1
Killer Juice Bar.......................(see 15)
Kuhio Lounge.........................(see 22)
The Shack..............................50 D1
Tradewinds............................(see 51)

ENTERTAINMENT (p461)
Coconut Marketplace
  Cinemas..............................(see 51)

SHOPPING (pp461-2)
Coconut Marketplace..................51 B4
Crazy Shirts..........................(see 51)
Kapa'a Shopping Center..............52 C2
Kauai Products Fair.....................53 D1
Kauai Village............................54 C3
Marta's Boat...........................(see 6)
T.L.C...................................(see 15)
Waipouli Complex.......................55 C3
Waipouli Town Center.................56 C4

TRANSPORT (p462)
Bus Stop.................................57 D1

OTHER
Boat Ramp................................58 D2

The Wailua River, fed by Mt Wai'ale'ale and estimated to be 11¾ miles long, is the only navigable river in Hawaii, meaning kayakers share the waterways with river-boat barges, water-skiers and wakeboarders. For good views of the river, head to the lookout at 'Opaeka'a Falls (p456).

Kayaking the Wailua River is popular for a reason: the 7-mile round trip is easy, with a centrally located launch site and kayak rentals right at the boat ramp. The route passes the Fern Grotto and has a mile-long side hike through dense forest to a 200ft waterfall. On the downside, this busy river crawls with boaters, some none-too-swift with the paddle. To ease congestion, kayaking is prohibited here on Sunday.

You can do the kayak trip independently (allow three hours) or on a guided tour (adult/child around $85/70, – ask and look for discounts), but there's really no great advantage to a tour, as you'll see the same sights on your own and save a bundle to boot. Go early to beat the crowds (see Escaping the Crowds, p455). Rental rates usually include paddles, life vests and a car-rack setup.

The following outfits are on the Eastside (see Map p453 unless marked):

Wailua Kayak & Canoe (☎ 821-1188; Wailua River State Park; per person Oct-May/Jun-Sep $40/50) The only company right at the boat ramp; check equipment carefully.
Wailua Kayak Adventures (☎ 822-5795, 639-6332; www.kauaiwailuakayak.com; Hwy 56, behind Coconuts in Waipouli; single/double kayaks $30/60) Boat is put securely on your car so you can take it where you wish.
Aloha Canoes & Kayaks (Map p443; ☎ 246-6804, 877-473-5446; www.hawaiikayaks.com; Anchor Cove Shopping Center, 3416 Rice St, Lihu'e; double hull canoe adult/child $60/49) Get a group of eight together and do it Hawaiian style: paddling in a double-hull canoe.
Ali'i Kayaks (Map p443; ☺ 241-7700, 877-426-2544; www.aliikayaks.com; Harbor Mall, 3501 Rice St, Lihu'e; Wailua River tour with lunch adult/child $90/70, Kalapaki Bay tour $20 per person)

LYDGATE BEACH PARK
Popular with families, Lydgate Beach Park, on Hwy 56 between the 5- and 6- mile markers, has protected swimming in a large seawater pool created with stone walls. It offers Kaua'i's safest year-round swimming, and is fun for kids and adults, who can dip in the deeper water. Surprisingly, there's decent snorkeling here, too – zero coral, but a good variety of colorful fish, including large

unicorn tangs. The open ocean beyond the pool often has strong currents, and there have been many drownings on both sides of the Wailua River mouth, just north of Lydgate. The park has a lifeguard, changing rooms, restrooms, showers, drinking water and picnic pavilions.

The **Kamalani Play Bridge**, at the southern extent of the park, is reason alone to pull in here. A community-built, giant wooden labyrinth with spiral slides, confounding ramps and stairs to nowhere, plus kid art strewn throughout, this place fosters serious playtime. Adults will dig it, too: go early before the munchkin crowds arrive and check out the 2nd-story sea views. At the northern extent of the park is the **Kamalani Playground**, which is almost as enchanting.

If you look straight out across Wailua Bay, you can see the remains of **Kukui Heiau** on Alakukui Point. Only its foundation stones are discernible. In ancient times torches were lit on the point at night to help guide outrigger canoes. If you walk straight down to the beach while looking toward Alakukui Point, you may find ancient stones with petroglyphs carved into the rock, though they're usually hidden under shifting sands.

Hikina Akala Heiau
One of the remnants of Wailua's royal heyday, Hikina Akala Heiau ('Rising of the Sun'), is here, too. This long, narrow temple is aligned directly north to south at the northern end of the Lydgate Beach parking lot. The heiau is thought to have been built around AD 1200. Boulders still outline the shape, so you get a sense of its original size, though most of the stones are long gone. Walk around the heiau, and you'll see a bronze plaque reading: 'Hauola, City of Refuge.' The mounded grassy area behind the plaque is all that remains of this former refuge for *kapu* (taboo) breakers. About 10ft left of the plaque, the stone with the bowl-shaped depressions is an adze grinding stone. The stone hasn't always been in this upright position; to grind a correct edge, it would have been laid flat. There are some flat stone salt pans on the grounds.

MALA'E HEIAU
In a thick clump of trees growing on the edge of an abandoned cane field, this **temple**

is just 40ft off the highway, across from the Holiday Inn. Although this is Kaua'i's largest heiau, covering 2 acres, it's choked with grasses and Java plum trees, and almost impossible to explore. However, there are plans to eventually incorporate it into Wailua River State Park, hopefully accompanied by a restoration effort.

In the 1830s missionaries converted Deborah Kapule, the last Kaua'ian queen, and she converted the interior of Mala'e Heiau into a cattle pen. Except for these alterations, it's relatively well preserved, thanks largely to its impenetrable overgrowth. The stone walls, which encompass an altar, reach up to 10ft high and extend 8ft wide.

SMITH'S TROPICAL PARADISE
The hour-long loop trail through theme gardens at **Smith's Tropical Paradise** (☎ 821-6895/6; www.smithskauai.com/paradise.html; adult/child under 12 $5.25/2.50; Wailua Marina; ⏱ 8:30am-4pm) offers the cheapest landscaped flora experience on the Eastside. Three evenings a week, there's a luau and Polynesian show here (p461).

COCO PALMS
Palm trees swaying majestically on the *mauka* (inland) side of Hwy 56 beckon you through a dilapidated gate to the famous Coco Palms, Kaua'i's first resort hotel and an island landmark. It was built on the site of Kaua'i's ancient royal court in a historic 45-acre coconut grove. The 'tropical theme'

hotel looked like a movie set, with lagoons, thatched cottages and torch-lit paths. In fact, the hotel's outdoor chapel was built in 1954 for the movie *Sadie Thompson* with Rita Hayworth. The highest-profile onscreen wedding here was when Elvis Presley wed Joan Blackman in *Blue Hawaii*. At its height, the Coco Palms was *the* place for mainland couples to get hitched, as well as a playground for Hollywood leading males and their ingenues. The resort was ripped apart by Hurricane Iniki and still looks it, sitting empty and in disrepair, but the kindly caretaker is usually game to show folks around.

HIGHWAY 580
Hwy 580 (Kuamo'o Rd) starts at the traffic light on Hwy 56 at Coco Palms. It winds inland passing heiau, historical sites, towering 'Opaeka'a Falls and Wailua Homesteads before ending at Keahua Arboretum, the starting place for a couple of worthwhile hiking trails (p457). The main through-road is Hwy 581 (Kamalu Rd), which connects with Hwy 580 at its southern end and with Olohena Rd at its northern end. Together, Kamalu Rd and Olohena Rd form Hwy 581.

Holoholoku Heiau
This *luakini* (temple used for human sacrifices) is 0.25 miles up Hwy 580 on the left. Like all of the Wailua heiau, this one was an enclosure-type construction, with its stone walls built directly on the ground rather than

---

ESCAPING THE CROWDS

The Kaua'i crowd flow is funny – you can go to a picture-perfect beach and have it all to yourself, but set out for a day hike and it's packs of screaming children and clueless weekend warriors jackknifed across the trail. Here are some tips for beating the crowds:

- **Start early** – For popular trails, such as Ke'e Beach to Hanakapai'ai (p486), hit the trail around 7am.

- **Go late** – Spouting Horn (p492), the 30-minute quickie walk up Kalalau Trail to the first views of the cliffs (p486) and the Kilauea Lighthouse (p470) can all be experienced fast, right before dark falls.

- **Rent gear the night before** – Rent for 24 hours the day prior, especially for kayaks, and you can put in before everyone else.

- **Camp or rent a house on the beach** – Allows you to put Nos 1 and 2 into practice easily.

- **Stay near trailheads** – If hiking is your thing, stay at the YWCA or Koke'e Lodge cabins (p514) in Koke'e State Park.

- **Go to offbeat beaches** – Maha'ulepu Beach (p495), Donkey Beach (p467), Running Waters Beach (p447), Anahola Beach (p468) or Moloa'a Beach (p468).

on terraced platforms. This whole area used to be royal property, and here on the west side of the grounds, against the flat-backed birthstone, queens gave birth to future kings. This stone is marked by a plaque that reads 'Pohaku Ho'ohanau' (Royal Birthstone). Another stone a few yards away, marked 'Pohaku Piko,' was where the *piko* (umbilical cords) of the babies were left. Above the temple where Hawaiian royals were born, steps lead to a hilltop cemetery where later-day Japanese laborers lie at rest.

Poli'ahu Heiau

Perched high on a hill overlooking the meandering Wailua River, this temple is named after the snow goddess Poli'ahu, one of Pele's sisters. This relatively well-preserved heiau is thought to have been of the *luakini* type. Poli'ahu Heiau is immediately before the 'Opaeka'a Falls lookout, on the opposite side of the road.

Immediately south of Poli'ahu Heiau, on the same side of Hwy 580, look for a 'Falling Rocks' sign that marks a short and rutted dirt drive leading to a **bellstone**. In old Hawaii, the Wailua River was a naval entrance, and the bellstone at this lookout was thought to have been used by sentries to warn of attacks and ring out royal birth announcements.

Because of the road's angle, it's easiest to approach coming downhill from Poliahu. There are actually two stones at the end of the drive, one with an all-too-perfect petroglyph whose age is suspect. Archaeologists question just which stone may have been the bellstone. Although you can find depressions in them, they may be the result of modern-day poundings by people trying to check out the resonance for themselves.

A short path down from these rocks leads to a vista of the river, where you can see cattle grazing on the banks below.

'Opaeka'a Falls

High and broad, this waterfall usually flows as a double cascade, though after a heavy rain the two sides often merge. The peaks of the Makaleha Mountains form a scenic backdrop; look for white-tailed tropical birds soaring in the valley below the falls. This easily viewed waterfall can be seen from a signposted viewpoint 1.5 miles up Hwy 580 from Wailua. For the best angle, walk up the sidewalk past the parking lot

toward the bridge. Cross the road for a good overhead view of the Wailua River and don't miss the groovy pedestrian-crossing sign.

Wailua Homesteads

This suburb sprang up when early homesteaders, taking advantage of multi-acre parcels courtesy of the government (see p34), used the land to graze cattle. The Dole Company once grew pineapples up here, like almost everywhere in Hawaii. Today pastoral Wailua Homesteads is a mix of residential homes, where locals breed fighting cocks, and B&Bs, tucked away on large, landscaped lots.

Kamokila Hawaiian Village

Perched on the bank of the Wailua River, this re-created Hawaiian **village** (☎ 823-0559; self-guided tour adult/child $5/3; ☉ 9am-5pm), with various grass huts, an assembly house, a shaman's house and other structures, approximates a traditional indigenous settlement. A small map gives you the gist of each building's purpose. As you walk around, you might recognize the village as that used in the movie *Outbreak*.

This, small, down-home operation run by a Hawaiian family also offers **outrigger canoe tours** (adult/child $30/20) on the Wailua River that include a paddle, short hike and waterfall swim. This is an interesting variation on the regular Wailua River kayak trip (p459), as it leaves from the village and guarantees a Hawaiian guide.

Kamokila is on the south side of Hwy 580, opposite 'Opaeka'a Falls, at the end of a narrow 0.5-mile-long paved road.

KAUAI'S HINDU MONASTERY

Devotees provide hilarious commentary while giving tours through this 51-acre **monastery** (☎ 822-3012; www.himalayanacademy.com /hawaii; 107 Kaholalele Rd; donations welcome; ❧ tours 9am, 3-4 per month) perched above the Wailua River. Not only does this tranquil haven boast meditative spots tucked into wildly tropical landscaping with 200 types of *ti* (native plant whose leaves are used to make hula skirts) among other fascinating foliage, it's also home to the world's largest single-pointed quartz crystal. This 50-million-year-old, six-sided sucker is huge. Weighing 750 pounds and standing over three feet tall, it electrifies the air in the **Kadavul Temple** (❧ meditation 9am-noon), where it lives.

The highlight of the tour is the **Iraivan Temple**, a monumental work-in-progress that is being entirely hand carved from granite by a village of artisans founded in Bangalore, India, specifically for this project. The scale is tremendous: the dome alone weighs 8½ tons and took three people four years carving full-time to complete. The crafting, shipping and assembling of this structure will be particularly interesting for artists, architects and engineers. The 'Great Crystal' will move here when the temple is completed in 2012.

Call or go online for tour dates, as they change monthly, and don't miss the **gift shop**

(p461). To get here, take Hwy 580 (Kuamoo Rd) from where it begins at the intersection with Hwy 56 (Kuhio Hwy) for 4.3 miles and turn left at Kaholalele Rd. You can also visit the monastery's **Sacred Rudraksna Forest** (7345 Kuamo'o Rd; admission free; ❧ 6am-6pm).

COCONUT PLANTATION BEACH

The Eastside's main resort development is Coconut Plantation on Hwy 56, between the 6- and 7-mile markers, with four hotels, a condominium and a shopping center. It fronts a half-mile-long beach, but water activities are restricted due to the low lava shelf that runs along most of the beach and the strong currents that prevail beyond. The best section for swimming and surfing is in front of the Kauai Sands Hotel (p460), where there's a break in the shelf. You can occasionally spot monk seals basking on the shore. The large field between the resorts here is popular with golden plovers and other migratory birds.

Activities

HIKING

Moalepe & Kuilau Ridge Trails

For the effort, these two trails are among the most visually rewarding on Kaua'i. Together they make an easy 9-mile hike or bike, with sweeping views of lush valleys, mist-covered mountains and the sparkling ocean beyond. You can start either at the marked trailhead on the right just before Hwy 580 crosses the stream at the Keahua Arboretum, 4 miles up from the junction of Hwys 580 and 581, or at the end of Hwy 581 (Olohena Rd) where it bends into Waipouli Rd. There's parking at both spots; don't leave anything of value in your car.

DETOUR: 'OPAEKA'A FALLS HIKE

To hike to the base of 'Opaeka'a Falls for a swim – only for the fit and best done with a buddy – take the trailhead 700yd past the viewpoint entrance. Head downhill to the river and cross it, hanging on to the great fallen tree to your left (upriver). Make sure you have a good handhold, as the river flows fast and the rocks slippery. Follow the discernible trail across the rock shelf to the forest where there's a fork (a cairn here helps on the return): right goes to the top of the falls for an overhead cascade view, left goes uphill to a clearing. Go left, cross the clearing to another cairn, and follow the uphill trail into the woods. After about 50yd, it will seem you can't go any further as the trail plummets down to the right. Look closely for the ropes that will help you down an incredibly steep slope to the next level part of trail, from where it's an easy jaunt to the base of the falls. Allow about 40 minutes each way. Only do this hike in dry conditions and don't hotdog in or around these falls – one slip could be fatal.

The trail from Keahua Arboretum starts up a wide dirt path also used by horses and the occasional renegade dirt biker. Along the way, birdsong emanates from the dense native vegetation, including koa trees, 'ohi'a lehua (native tree with red pom-pom–like flowers) and thickets of ti. The sheaths of peeling eucalyptus bark here look and feel like human skin. In the upper reaches, the lush, fern-covered hillsides provide broad vistas of the mountains. Guava trees and wild thimbleberries grow along the path.

The hike climbs to a broad ridge offering views into patchwork valleys clear down to the coast. You can see Kapa'a to the east and the island's uninhabited central region to the west. It takes about 40 minutes to walk the 1.25 miles up to a clearing on the ridge top, where picnic tables and a view of Mt Wai'ale'ale make for pleasurable refueling.

Beyond the clearing, to the right past the picnic area, the Kuilau Ridge Trail continues as a narrow footpath with even more spectacular views. It ends in about a mile at the Moalepe Trail. If you don't want to go that far, at least walk a little of it, as some of the best views, including cliffs cleaved by waterfalls, are along the next half mile.

If you go left at the connection with the Moalepe Trail, you'll come to a viewpoint after about 10 minutes. If you go right on Moalepe, you'll come out on Olohena Rd in Wailua Homesteads after about 2.25 miles. It's all well signposted.

Powerline Trail

In the 1930s electric transmission lines were run along the mountains between Princeville and Wailua, and a 13-mile maintenance route now called the Powerline Trail was created. There is occasional talk of turning it into a real inland road, but environmental concerns make it unlikely to happen anytime soon. The hike takes a full day and is only recommended in dry weather.

The south end of the trail begins across the stream at the Keahua Arboretum, at the end of Hwy 580 (Kuamo'o Rd). After fording the stream, look for the trailhead on your right after cresting the hill. Dark and steep at first, the trail passes into sunlight, providing views of the Makaleha Mountains and Mt Kawaikini. Alternating ocean, mountain and valley views dominate for the next several miles. After about two hours of hiking, you'll

come to a steep ascent and a lookout, at the trail's highest point. The remaining 6 miles to Princeville make for mostly dull, flat walking, in land shared with hunters and their hounds; it's best to turn around here.

Nounou Ridge Trail

This trail climbs up the Sleeping Giant to a summit on the giant's upper chest, affording views of the east coast and the highland valleys. It's a well-maintained trail that takes 1½ to two hours round-trip and provides a hardy workout thanks to its pitch.

There are two marked trailheads. The trail on the western side (3 miles round-trip) is a shaded forest trail of tall trees and moss-covered stones. Access is on Kamalu Rd (Hwy 581), near house No 1068. Walk through a metal gate marked as a forestry right-of-way and up along a small cattle pasture to the trailhead. While you can't park at the trailhead, you can park and access the trail at the end of Lokelani Rd, which is off Kamalu Rd a bit further north.

The trail on the eastern side (3.5 miles roundtrip) is more exposed and has better views. It begins at a parking lot a mile up Haleilio Rd in the Wailua Houselots neighborhood. The trail is steeper and has switchbacks almost to the ridge and wide vistas. This is a wonderful trail to do early in the morning, when it's relatively cool and you can watch the light spread across the valley. The packed trail can get slippery when wet; look for a walking stick, which hikers sometimes leave near the trailhead.

The eucalyptus trees at the trailhead soon give way to a tall, thick forest of Norfolk pines. About five minutes into the woods, right after the Norfolk pines begin, there's a fork. Veer left up the path with the large rock beside it. The trail then passes through thick strawberry guava bushes that can grow up to 15ft high; in places, creating a canopied, tunnel-like effect. Strawberry guava is considered the sweetest of any guava; pop the small red fruits whole.

A few minutes' walk below the summit, the eastern and western trails merge on the ridge. Continue up to the right past some hala (pandanus) trees. The summit sports a picnic-table shelter, perfect for getting out of the passing showers that can create incredible valley rainbows. To the west, there's a 180-degree view of Wailua and the Makaleha

Mountains. Below, to the east, you can see Kapa'a, Coco Palms and the Wailua River. To the right of the riverboat docks and inland from the Aloha Beach Resort, you can see Mala'e Heiau as a dark-green square in the midst of an abandoned cane field.

If you go south across the picnic area, the trail hesitantly continues. About five minutes' walk up, there's a good viewpoint from a rocky area. The ridge continues up the giant's chin. Should it tempt you, size it up carefully – it's sharp, and loose rocks and slides are visible.

GOLF
The well-regarded public **Wailua County Golf Course** (☎ 241-6666; green fees weekday/weekend & holiday $32/44, optional cart/club rental $16/from $15) is an 18-hole, par-72 course off Hwy 56 north of Lihu'e. It's so heavily played that morning tee times are taken up to a week in advance. After 2pm the green fees drop by half and play is on a first-come, first-served basis.

Tours
Every bus tour itinerary includes the 2-mile riverboat tour up the Wailua River to the Fern Grotto, making it Kaua'i's busiest tourist attraction. The riverboats are big with wide, flat bottoms – very simple, covered barges with tourists packed on like cattle. The grotto, a large musty cave beneath a fern-covered rock face, makes for a pretty respite while kayaking, but is not a must-see.

Smith's Motor Boat Service (☎ 821-6892; www .smithskauai.com; adult/child under 12 $15/7.50) leaves the Wailua River Marina, on the south side of the river, every 30 minutes between 9am and 3:30pm. Smith's also has a ticket booth on the north bank of the river.

Sleeping
Though not beachside, Wailua B&Bs represent some of the best value on Kaua'i. Our recommendations are all in the Wailua Homesteads area, about 3 miles from the coast in a rural setting. All of these are within a couple of miles of the intersection of Hwys 581 (Olohena Rd) and 580 (Kuamo'o Rd).

BUDGET
Lani Keha (☎ 822-1605; fax 823-6308; 848 Kamalu Rd; s/d $55/65, ste $80) Set back on a large grassy expanse at the base of Sleeping Giant, this place is value packed. The three rooms have a king bed, and share the living room, dining room and lanai. The suite has lush mountain views and a kitchenette. Groups can rent the entire house at special rates.

Rosewood Bed & Breakfast (☎ 822-5216; www .rosewoodkauai.com; 872 Kamalu Rd; r $45-55) The bunkhouse here has three comfortable, unique rooms that share one bathroom and outdoor shower. The bonus is the kitchenettes, in-room sinks and barbecue. For more details, see The Author's Choice below.

Other options include:
House of Aleva (☎ 822-4606; 5509 Kuamo'o Rd; s/d incl tax & breakfast $50/55) Quaint home with a spiritual vibe; can't beat the price, but guests share space with the owners – not everyone's cup of tea.
Peacock Inn (☎ 822-1558; 6581 Kuamo'o Rd; apt $65) Funky one-bedroom apartment run by friendly locals with lots of lore.

MID-RANGE
B&Bs
Aloha Country Inn (☎ 822-0166; alohacountryinn@ hawaiian.net; 505 Kamalu Rd; r $75-90) Need a place to relax, stretch out and recuperate after doing the Na Pali Coast? Look no further than the distinct, sprawling rooms in this

---

THE AUTHOR'S CHOICE

Rosewood Bed & Breakfast (☎ 822-5216; www.rosewoodkauai.com; 872 Kamalu Rd; cottage $115, 2-bedroom cottage $135; 🖥) A perennial favorite for its well-equipped digs at fair prices, this nonsmoking place is terrific value. For couples, the studio cottage nestled in the exuberantly landscaped garden makes a nice, romantic getaway. The king bed with lush linens cooled by ceiling fans doesn't hurt. Whip up breakfast in bed in the kitchenette. The homey, 2-bedroom cottage is great for families, with its gadget-filled kitchen, master bedroom with gleaming en-suite bath, and darling upstairs room with twin beds. A screened dining area faces a private garden, plus there's a lanai and washer/dryer. A stylish guest room ($85) upstairs in the owners' home has a king bed, tiled bath with sunken tub, and mountain views. These accommodations come with breakfast on your first/last day. There's a three-night minimum; no credit cards.

classy house. Super quiet, hardwood floors and kitchenettes on steroids are just some of the perks in this gold standard of private accommodation. Bathrooms are bigger than many Manhattan apartments – one even has a Jacuzzi for soaking dem tired bones. A two-bedroom house and a couple of cottages, all with the same attention to detail, are also available.

Magic Sunrise Hawaii (☎ 821-9847; www.magic sunrisehawaii.com; 139 Royal Dr; r $50-75, cottages $90-145; ☒) Many travelers (especially Europeans) dig this tranquil, Swiss-run place with a distinctively New Age flavor. Three playful, pastel rooms with bamboo beds, mosquito nets and Indian prints are in the main house. Also on the colorful, spacious grounds are a one-bedroom unit with a lanai overlooking the mountains, and a two-bedroom cottage that holds up to five people comfortably. All guests have kitchen access. Retreats and workshops are occasionally held here.

Rainbows End (☎ 823-0066; www.rosewoodkauai .com; 6470 Kipapa Rd; cottage $115) Way up on a quiet road tucked into a misty mountain valley, this cute little cottage is small but comfortable, with funky details like inlaid mahogany floors, original artwork and stained-glass windows. A nice alternative for a family, the cottage has a futon sofa, small kitchenette, living room, comfy bedroom with a queen bed and a bathroom with a claw-foot whirlpool tub (yes!). One drawback is that if it's raining anywhere on Kaua'i, it will be raining here.

Inn Paradise (☎ 822-2542; www.affordable-paradise .com/kauai87_e.html; 6381 Makana Rd; d from $70) Take in rolling green pastures while enjoying a morning coffee on your shared lanai at this place that offers a good combination of privacy, value and comfort. Each of the three sunny units has private entrance and nice touches, like Persian carpets and Hawaiiana wall prints. From kitchenette to full-blown kitchen, each unit permits cooking. The most expensive King Kaumuali'i unit ($90) is like a small house, with living room, two bedrooms and one bath; it sleeps up to four people but can be connected with another suite to accommodate six.

Hotels & Condos
Kapaa Sands (☎ 822-4901, 800-222-4901; www.kapaa sands.com; 380 Papaloa Rd; studio/2-bedroom unit from $110/150; ☒) Friendly, modern and with a

killer beachfront locale, the 24 condo units are good value. All have kitchens, lanai, breeze-catching louvered windows and at least a partial ocean view. The two-bedroom units, which accommodate four people comfortably, are the sweetest deal. There's a three- /seven-day minimum stay in low/ winter season.

Islander on the Beach (☎ 822-7417, 800-922-7866; www.islanderkauai.com; 484 Kuhio Hwy; r from $150; ☒ ☒) Designed to keep you playing outside instead of in, this airy hotel on six nicely landscaped acres has an upscale tropical feel, but still exudes casualness. The pool overlooking the beach is quite nice indeed. All rooms are plush, with big fluffy beds, refrigerator, coffeemaker and lanai, but upgrading to an oceanfront unit for $210 a night is worth considering. Kids under 18 stay free.

Plantation Hale (☎ 822-4941, 800-775-4253; www .plantation-hale.com; 484 Kuhio Hwy; condo units $165-185; ☒ ☒) These popular rooms-cum-condos on the highway side of Coconut Plantation are part of the Best Western chain and often booked solid. The units have modern layouts featuring a full kitchen, lots of bathroom and closet space, and lanai. The one-bedroom units sleep up to four, which could suit two very close couples.

Kauai Coconut Beach Resort (☎ 822-3455, 800-760-8555; www.kcbresort.com; 484 Kuhio Hwy; r $165-215) Undergoing a complete overhaul at the time of research, this beachside hotel at the quieter north end of Coconut Plantation will likely be stellar when it is completely renovated. By the time you read this, it should be reopened as The Courtyard by Marriott.

TOP END
Aloha Beach Resort (☎ 823-6000, 800-823-5111; www.abrkauai.com; 3-5920 Kuhio Hwy; garden-/ocean-view r $240/310, cottages from $375) Don't balk at the rack rates for this comfortable hotel adjacent to Lydgate Beach Park, because going online or working through a travel agent can slash them by half. Then what results is fair value, with spacious, amply furnished rooms. Request the Pikake Wing, which has larger rooms with two queen beds and a big-screen TV, or go all out for one of the cottages tucked away on the verdant, manicured grounds.

Kauai Coast Resort at the Beachboy (☎ 822-3441, 877-977-4355; www.kauaicoastresort.com; 484 Kuhio Hwy; r from $180, 1-/2-bedroom units from $225/310; ☒ ☒)

ERIC L WHEATER

Mist on Kaua'i's rocky Na Pali Coast (p486)

Ha'ena Beach Park (p484), Kaua'i

ANN CECIL

ANN CECIL

Kaua'i's westernmost town, Kekaha (p508), with Ni'ihau island in the distance

ANN CECIL

The swimming pool at Princeville Hotel
(p474), Kaua'i

MARK NEWMA

KARL LEHMANN

Sunset along the Kalalau Trail (p486) on the
Na Pali Coast, Kaua'i

Hanakoa Stream in the Na Pali Coast
State Park (p486), Kaua'i

A tour boat (p459) cruises along Wailua River surrounded by lush greenery, Kaua'i

ANN CECI

Big and bustling, it's popular with families and bubbly groups of vacationing bachelorettes. The condos have fully equipped kitchens, a washer/dryer and movies on demand, plus there's a kiddie pool on the grounds. There's a full spa, tennis courts and proper lobby bar.

Eating & Drinking

Kintaro (☎ 822-3341; 4-370 Kuhio Hwy; appetizers $3.50-6, meals $11-20; ☾ 5:30-9:30pm Mon-Sat) Quantity and quality is a winning combination no matter what your business, and this superlative Japanese restaurant has it right. The sushi bar is excellent, interesting appetizers, like sake-marinated mushrooms over escargot, are a must-try and the plentiful sukiyaki dinners make a yummy fill-up. Herbivores: try the veggie tempura.

Aussie Tim's Texas Barbecue (☎ 822-0300; www.aussietims.com; 4-361 Kuhio Hwy; meals $8-15; ☾ 4-9pm Tue-Fri, 1-9pm Sat & Sun) Fast gaining fame for its authentic barbecue – including slow-roasted ribs – one of its secrets (aside from the sauce) is that it only uses Meyer Ranch beef (hormone-, antibiotic- and additive-free) and free-range chickens. Smoked leg of lamb and game dishes also star.

Several nearby eateries also serve *ono grinds* (good food):

Korean Bar-B-Q (☎ 823-6744; Kinipopo Shopping Village, 4-356 Kuhio Hwy; plates $7; ☾ 10:30am-9pm Wed-Mon, 4:30-9pm Tue) More local than Korean, with good plate lunch at honest prices.

Whole Enchilada (☎ 822-4993; 4-356 Kuhio Hwy; meals $5-10; ☾ 11am-8pm Tue-Sat) Prodigious, fresh Mexican food with great prices. Finally.

THE AUTHOR'S CHOICE

Caffé Coco (☎ 822-7990; 4-369 Kuhio Hwy; salads & wraps $5-10, platters $12-20; ☾ 11am-9pm Tue-Fri, 5-9pm Sat & Sun) Tucked into a leafy corner where rustling bamboo and hip music serenade diners, the atmosphere and food here rock. Fresh, tangy ingredients create a winning melody of taste and texture in menu staples, like tofu veggie peanut wraps and Moroccan spiced 'ahi with banana chutney. Sinful desserts, like chocolate mocha cake, washed down with whatever's your pleasure from the espresso bar, are irresistible. Music nightly in the garden; BYOB ($5 corkage).

Coconut Marketplace (484 Kuhio Hwy) mall kiosks sell tasty vittles from 11am until around 9pm. The aromas of **Aloha Pizza** (☎ 822-4511; pizza $5.50-23) will lure you toward delectable calzone and pizza, including a sublime artichoke-garlic version. **Fish Hut** (☎ 821-0033; meals $8) specializes in fresh 'ahi and ono (white-fleshed wahoo) served with coleslaw and fries, plus shrimp, fish-and-chips. There's also a branch of Lappert's for ice cream.

Entertainment

Lihu'e has two of Kaua'i's most energetic nightclubs, with a healthy mix of tourists and locals. Otherwise the luau are the big nighttime events.

NIGHTCLUBS

Tradewinds (Coconut Marketplace; ☾ 10-2am) A fun, diverse crowd spreads out at a casual bar, with daily happy hour from 2pm to 7pm. Tropical ambience, darts, karaoke and dancing Wednesday nights make this a favorite hangout.

Kuhio Lounge (☎ 823-6000; Aloha Beach Resort, 3-5920 Kuhio Hwy; admission $5; ☾ after 10pm) A good place for a drink any night. On Friday it becomes the area's hottest dance spot with locals and tourists shaking that groove thang.

LUAU & HULA

Kauai Coconut Beach Resort (☎ 822-3455; Coconut Plantation; luau adult/child 3-11/under 17 $59/26/38; ☾ 6pm Tue-Sun) A luau with an open bar, all-you-can-eat dinner and a Polynesian revue. You can glimpse spinning fireballs and other festivities from the hotel parking lot. The culinary curious can stop by at 10:45am to watch the *imu* (oven) preparation, when the pig is stuffed with hot rocks and buried.

Smith's Tropical Paradise (☎ 821-6895; Wailua Marina; luau adult/child 3-6/7-13 $60/19/30; ☾ 5pm Mon, Wed & Fri) The heavily touristed musical and dancing comes with mai tais and a dinner buffet featuring *kalua* pig and Jello.

Coconut Marketplace (☎ 822-3641; ☾ 5pm Wed) Free hula shows are performed here.

CINEMAS

Coconut Marketplace Cinemas (☎ 821-2324; shows before 6pm $4) Screens first-run movies.

Shopping

Kauai's Hindu Monastery shop (☎ 822-3012; www.himalayanacademy.com/hawaii; 107 Kaholalele Rd);

KAUA'I

9am-noon) Stock up on enlightened souvenirs – choose from chanting CDs, alarm clocks with the Great Crystal on the face, granite lingams and tiger-eye Ganesh figurines. See also p457.

Coconut Marketplace (⊙ 9am-9pm Mon-Sat, 10am-6pm Sun) Chock-full of boutiques, art galleries and gift shops, including an outlet of **Crazy Shirts** (☎ 822-0100).

Getting Around

You need your own transport to reach any sites not on the main stretch of Kuhio Hwy. The **Kaua'i Bus** (☎ 241-6410) offers limited service between Wailua and Lihu'e, and Wailua and Hanalei, Monday to Friday. Main stops are at Coconut Marketplace going north and Aussie Tim's Texas Barbecue going south.

WAIPOULI

Waipouli is the mile-long commercial strip between Coconut Plantation and Kapa'a. Its biggest draw (of all things!) is its shopping centers, which contain some of Kaua'i's best places to eat and largest supermarkets.

Information

There are ATMs inside the Foodland supermarket in the Waipouli Town Center and Safeway in Kauai Village.

ComputerWeb (☎ 821-0077; www.computerweb.com; Kauai Village, 4-831 Kuhio Hwy; per 10 min $2; ⊙ 9am-9pm Mon-Sat) Internet, laptop connections and cutting-edge gaming at this friendly store.

Kapaa Laundry Center (☎ 822-3113; Kapa'a Shopping Center, 4-1101 Kuhio Hwy; ⊙ 7:30am-9:30pm) Wash your togs to the soothing sounds of piped-in slack-key tunes.

Kapa'a Post Office (☎ 800-275-8777; Kapa'a Shopping Center, 4-1101 Kuhio Hwy; ⊙ 8am-4pm Mon-Fri, 9am-2pm Sat)

Sights

On clear days, you can see the outline of the **Sleeping Giant** atop Nounou Ridge from a marked viewpoint just north of the Waipouli Complex. According to legend, the amicable giant fell asleep on the hillside after gorging on poi at a luau. When his *menehune* friends needed his help, they tried to rouse him by throwing stones. But the stones bounced from the giant's full belly into his open mouth. The stones lodged in the giant's throat, he died in his sleep and turned into rock. Now he rests, stretched out on the ridge with his head in Wailua and his feet in

Kapa'a. At an elevation of 1241ft, the giant's forehead is the highest point on the ridge.

Poke around in Kauai Village, Waipouli's largest shopping center, and you'll find the **Kaua'i Heritage Center** (☎ 821-2070; admission free; ⊙ 9am-5pm Mon-Sat), which displays handmade wood carvings, feather leis, bamboo nose flutes and other traditional Hawaiian crafts. One-day workshops ($25, reservations required) in hula, lei making and chanting are on offer.

If too much rain is driving you and the kids nuts, get thee straight to the **Kaua'i Children's Discovery Museum** (☎ 823-8222; www.kcdm .org; Kauai Village; adult/child $5/4; ⊙ 9am-5pm Tue-Sat), where hands-on play with interactive exhibits unlocks secrets of the natural and technological world. From June to August, it offers a day camp (two-hour session $14, per day $40) for kids aged five to 10, and there's a gift shop with educational toys.

Another rainy-day option is **Fun Factory** (Waipouli Town Center; games 50¢-$1; ⊙ 10am-10pm, to midnight Fri & Sat), with loads of video games, rides and games of skill.

Activities

For hiking trails up Nounou Ride, see p458.

Submit to Kaua'i's surfing Svengali at **Ambrose's** (☎ 822-3926; ambrose.curry@verizon.net; 770 Kuhio Hwy; lessons per hr $25), where your mind and body will be coached in the ways of the wave; lessons 'for the obtuse' are given in waters he has been riding for over 35 years. Post-lesson you can buy a board shaped by Señor Curry or take home a piece of his art.

Also teaching newbies is the **Wailua Bay Surf Company** (☎ 823-1129, 645-1067; www.wailua baysurfcokauai.com; 5111 Nounou Rd; 2-hr lesson $45).

Sleeping

Mokihana of Kauai (☎ 822-3971; 796 Kuhio Hwy; condo units $72; ♿) These beachfront time-shares are supreme value, especially if you get on the rental office's sublet list (published every April and October) and then rent directly from the owners. It's most feasible in the low season, when rates drop to just $43. Each unit has a kitchen and lanai, plus room to roam. Don't book units ending in 12 or 14, as you'll abut the laundry room. Ground-floor units are wheelchair accessible.

Kauai Kailani (condo units $72-85) The nearby sister property has 58 two-bedroom time-share units handled by the front desk at Mokihana of Kauai. These condos have fully equipped kitchens, two twin beds in one room and a queen bed in the other; rates are good for up to four people, and the same sublet list mentioned above advertises rentals here.

You can make advance reservations for either Mokihana of Kauai or Kauai Kailani through **Hawaii Kailani** (☎ 360-676-1434; www .hawaii-kailani.com/index.php; Suite 100, 1201 11th St, Bellingham, WA 98225).

Eating
BUDGET
Papaya's Natural Foods (☎ 823-0190; Kauai Village, 4-831 Kuhio Hwy; dishes $5-8, salad per lb $7; ☾ 9am-8pm Mon-Sat, deli to 7pm) Chow down on voluminous portions of yummy baked tofu and veggies, punchy Kung Pao tofu or faux chicken, or load up at the well-provisioned salad bar. There's a full café and courtyard dining that attracts interesting characters. This is also Kaua'i's biggest health-food store.

King & I (☎ 822-1642; Waipouli Plaza, 4-901 Kuhio Hwy; mains $7-11; ☾ 4:30-9:30pm) This friendly, family-run restaurant sets the Kaua'ian standard for Thai food with a lengthy menu featuring goodies such as curries popping with kaffir lime and lemongrass, fiery or not, as you like. Vegetarians will find loads of options, like flavorful eggplant and tofu in chili oil or a mound of traditional pad Thai with tofu.

Panda Garden (☎ 822-0092; Kauai Village, 4-831 Kuhio Hwy; lunch specials $6-9, mains $8-12, 4-course dinner $14-17; ☾ 10:30am-9:30pm, from 4pm Wed) Kaua'i's best Sichuan restaurant has Chinese standards, but also more inventive dishes, like garlic spinach with egg-white sauce and cold ginger chicken. You can munch outdoors at tables almost in the parking lot.

KCL Barbecue (☎ 823-8168; Waipouli Complex, 4-971 Kuhio Hwy; dishes $4-8; ☾ 10am-10pm) For a meal on the run, try this hole-in-the-wall local eatery, with delicious chicken katsu and over 100 other dishes; great value.

Giant supermarket chain, **Safeway** (☎ 822-2464; Kauai Village, 4-831 Kuhio Hwy; ☾ 24 hr) has a huge selection. There's a deli counter, a shockingly good bakery with superb lemon doughnuts and multi-grain breads, a fish counter with unbeatable sesame-'ahi poke and a respectable wine selection. Another option is **Foodland** (Waipouli Town Center; ☾ 6am-11pm), which is smaller.

MID-RANGE & TOP END
A Pacific Cafe (☎ 822-0013; fax 822-0054; Kauai Village, 4-831 Kuhio Hwy; mains $19-25, 3-course tasting menu $45; ☾ 5:30-9:30pm) This high-energy restaurant bustles with attentive wait staff and loud diners enjoying legendary Pacific Rim cuisine. The menu is continually evolving to include intriguing items, like miso-glazed butterfish and fire-roasted *ono* on rock-shrimp risotto. The dim-sum sampler offers delicious tidbits, like mushroom and goat-cheese wontons, or try the *hamachi* sashimi with black truffle sauce à la carte. Save room for unbelievably good chocolate crème brûlée or *liliko'i* cheesecake. Reservations are recommended.

Coconuts (☎ 823-8777; 4-919 Kuhio Hwy; mains $14-21; ☾ 4-10pm Mon-Sat) Don't let the kitschy façade fool you: this lively place cranks out consistent, island-influenced food that people love. The fresh catch in kaffir-lime broth is a winner, as is the wasabi-encrusted *ahi*. The marriage of flavors in the smoked pork chop with pineapple chutney works well. Also recommended is the molten chocolate cake. Reservations are not accepted, so dine early or late.

Shopping
Marta's Boat (☎ 822-3926; www.martasboat.com; 770 Kuhio Hwy; ☾ 10am-6pm Mon-Sat) Whimsical Marta's has soft and sexy threads from the Paris, LA and New York crops. Distinctive lingerie and frocks shine, but jewelry and excruciatingly cute little-girl clothes also enchant. No bargains here, folks.

TOP FIVE SHOPS

- **Marta's Boat** (above)
- **Tin Can Mailman** (p452)
- **T.L.C.** (p467)
- **Kauai Fine Arts** (p503)
- **Sunshine Markets** (p491)

KAPA'A

This is one of those funny little towns where historic and contemporary Hawaii meet in a fun, functional relationship. In 'Kapa'a' town,' old-timers talk story with dread-locked youth over lattes, while tourists cycle past restored wooden fronts of old shops now selling crystals or garden burgers. You can hear the surf when it's pounding, and rainbows are de rigueur. As unimposing as it feels, this old plantation town is one of Kaua'i's largest. Budget accommodations and affordable, delectable restaurants attract travelers and off-beat types to Kapa'a, adding to the town's upbeat and colorful vibe.

Information

Aloha Dude Internet Hut (☎ 822-3833; www.aloha dude.net; 4-1387 Kuhio Hwy; per 15 min $3; ☼ 8:30am-7:30pm)

Business Support Services (☎ 822-5504; fax 822-2148; 4-1191 Kuhio Hwy; Internet access per hr $10; ☼ 8am-6pm Mon-Sat, from 10am Sun) Cheaper Internet access, plus fax, copies and stamps.

First Hawaiian Bank (☎ 822-4966; 4-1366 Kuhio Hwy) Has a 24-hour ATM.

Sights

KAPA'A COUNTY BEACH PARK

This county beach park is a one-mile-long ribbon of beach beginning at Kapa'a's north end, where there's a ball field, picnic tables and a public pool. At the south end of the beach, near the Pono Kai Resort, is a nice sandy area.

A pretty, shoreline foot-and-bicycle **path** runs the length of the beach park, crossing over a couple of old bridges where families and old-timers drop fishing lines. The path makes an appealing alternative to walking along the highway to and from town.

HAWAIIAN ART MUSEUM

This **museum** (☎ 823-8381; www.huna.org; Suite 11, Dragon Bldg, 4504 Kukui St; ☼ by appointment) contains the personal collection of Serge Kahili King, the founder of Aloha International and a renowned *huna* healer (ancient Hawaiian world view and healing process using the mind, body and spirit). While the museum (strong on Hawaiiana) can only be visited by appointment, there are free **talk story sessions** at 5pm on Wednesday that focus on Hawaiian culture, as well as hula classes and *huna* healing circles. Visit the website for current offerings.

Activities

Kapa'a is one of Kaua'i's centers for renting sports equipment, especially for kayaking the Wailua River (p452), and for arranging scuba dives.

There are free tennis courts in Kapa'a New Park and a public **swimming pool** (☎ 822-3842; admission free; ☼ 10am-4:30pm Thu-Mon) at Kapa'a County Beach Park.

DIVING & SNORKELING

Diving out of Kapa'a means driving or boating to dive sites. But if you're staying in the area, it's convenient. For popular dive sites and typical prices, see p438.

Dive Kauai (☎ 822-0452, 800-828-3483; www.divekauai .com; 1038 Kuhio Hwy; ☼ 8am-5:30pm Mon-Sat, 9am-3pm Sun) Super-friendly; one of Kaua'i's top dive outfits.

Seasport Divers (☎ 823-9222, 800-685-5889; www .seasportdivers.com; 4-976 Kuhio Hwy) Rents gear, leads dives, including to Ni'hau, and offers certification courses. Snorkel gear is available.

Snorkel Bob's (☎ 823-9433; www.snorkelbob.com; 4-734 Kuhio Hwy; basic snorkel sets per day/week $2.50/9, good ones $8/32, boogie boards $6.50/26; ☼ 8am-5pm Mon-Sat) The cool thing about Snorkel Bob's is you can rent gear on Kaua'i and return it on the Big Island, O'ahu or Maui.

SURFING

The best breaks around here are at Kapa'a Sands, fronting the hotel of the same name, in Wailua Bay and a mile up the coast at Kealia Beach (particularly in winter). When the sets are rolling in, there's good boogie boarding at either break. Surfboard rentals are $20/100 per day/week and boogie boards are $4/15 at Seasport Divers (p464). For lessons, see p462.

FISHING

Setting out from the small boat ramp at the end of Kaloloku Rd, off Hwy 56, is gregarious **Hawaiian Style Fishing** (☎ 635-7335; half-day charter per person $100), which works out of a locally built, owned and operated boat.

CYCLING

A smooth 6-mile coastal pedal starts in Kapa'a, running along Kealia Beach and on to Anahola (p468), before turning into a single track for another 9 miles. Many of the island trails open to mountain bikers are easily accessed from Kapa'a (see p439).

Kauai Cycle (☎ 821-2115; www.bikehawaii.com/kauai cycle; 1379 Kuhio Hwy, Kapa'a; 18-speed cruiser per day/ week $15/75, quality mountain bike with front suspension $20/95, full suspension $35/150; ☼ 9am-6pm Mon-Fri, to 4pm Sat) rents bikes maintained by knowledgeable cyclists.

BODYWORK & YOGA

For a mind and body experience, try **Touch of Spirit** (☎ 823-6144; Suite 8, Dragon Bldg; massage per hr $35-95, body wraps $65-95; ⏰ 10am-5pm Mon-Fri). Hot-rock massage, reflexology, facials, herbal body wraps, waxing, reiki, and tarot and psychic readings ($35) are all offered.

Also in the building is **Bikram Yoga Kauai** (☎ 822-5053; Suite 10, Dragon Bldg; 90 min class 1/5 $15/65). For more bodywork options island-wide, see p480.

Tours

If you're interested in learning about the town's sugar and pineapple boom days, hook up with a 90-minute **Kapa'a History Tour** (☎ 245-3373; PO Box 1778, Lihu'e; adult/child $15/5; ⏰ 10am Tue, Thu & Sat). Advance reservations are required.

Sleeping

BUDGET

Mahina's Guest House (☎ 823-9364; www.mahinas .com; 4433 Panihi Rd; s $55-85, d $60-95) Four-bedroom house across from the beach. It's a casual, peaceful place for women travelers. Rooms are spacious, with hardwood floors, lots of closet space and sunrise views from your bed. Some have partial sea views, all have full sea soundtrack. Guests share kitchen, bathroom, dining and living room, telephone, stereo and laundry facilities. There's a good library, and you can walk to shops and the bus. All in all, this shared accommodation allows independent travelers to live local style in safe, happy surroundings.

Hibiscus Hollow (☎ 823-0925; cgliddle@hawaiilink .net; 4906 Laipo Rd; d/tr/q incl tax $50/60/65) This cheery little studio attached to the home of Greg and Sue Liddle is a sweetheart of a deal. Nothing grand, but it has a good kitchenette, barbecue, TV, VCR, phone and a little lanai. Up to four people can squeeze in here.

K.K. Bed & Bath (☎ 822-7348, 800-615-6211 ext 32; www.kkbedbath.com; s/d/tr $40/50/60) Reserve early to snag one of these two rooms in a converted storehouse behind the home of local lay historian Richard Sugiyama. Set in a tranquil patch of grass and garden, the comfortable units are spacious and well equipped, with TV, microwave, fridge, phone and small eating area. Rooms are wheelchair accessible. This popular familial place is just half a block from the beach and a short jaunt to the center of Kapa'a town.

Kapaa Kauai BeachHouse (☎ 822-3424; www .kauai-blue-lagoon.com; 4-1552 Kuhio Hwy; s/d bunk in dorm $23/35, r $50) This hostel is a mixed bag. The cheap carpet and worn bath mat decor is kinda icky, as are the three toilets and two showers for the entire place, which accommodates over 30 people. If you email a reservation, make sure you confirm with a phone call. On the upside, it's so close to the ocean you'll feel the salt spray, there are two lanai and the bunks are doubles, with a curtain you can draw for some privacy. Good kitchen facilities are shared with a fascinating combination of veterans, drifters, surfers and seers. Overall, it's the best value for solo travelers, but has its blemishes.

Kauai International Hostel (☎ 823-6142; www .hostels.com/kauaihostel; 4532 Lehua St; dm/r $20/50) 'I should have slept in my car,' was how one traveler summed up the spare, rough-around-the-edges rooms. The sometimes dodgy characters in residence don't help. Still, it's the only cheap game in town when the better Kapaa Kauai BeachHouse is full.

MID-RANGE & TOP END

Rosewood Vacation Rentals (☎ 822-5216; www.rose woodkauai.com; studio/2-bedroom unit $85/225, plus cleaning fee) Manages a complex of three homes in spitting distance from the beach. All are beautifully equipped and furnished, with private lanai. The older 'Big Kahuna' house has a luxurious, deep bathtub that faces the ocean and is better laid out, but not as modern as the two-bedroom 'Love Shack.' The 'Surf Shack' is a darling studio, with privacy via the landscaping and screening.

Pono Kai Resort (☎ 822-9831, 800-456-0009; www
.ponokai-resort.com; 4-1250 Kuhio Hwy; 1-/2-bedroom
units from $135/150; ⊠ ⚏) More intimate than
many, this 219-unit beachfront condo is
within walking distance of town. Each of
the roomy, well-equipped units has a full
kitchen, a living room with queen sofa bed,
cable TV and lanai. There are tennis courts
and a decent swath of beach. More economical units with kitchenette are available.
Alternatively, snag an ocean-view double for
an extra $45. Ask about weekly discounts.

Hotel Coral Reef (☎ 822-4481, 800-843-4659; fax
822-7705; 1516 Kuhio Hwy; r $65-100) Nicely located
facing the ocean and a little spit of beach,
the rooms are plain and fairly small. Those
with lanai and tile are better than standard
rooms in the main building with worn carpet. Those in the seaside building are best.

Eating
BUDGET
Mermaids Cafe (☎ 821-2026; 4-1384 Kuhio Hwy; mains
$9; ⏱ 11am-9pm) 'Killer dude!' is one reac-
tion to the overflowing plates of coconut
curry (with tofu or chicken), 'ahi wraps with
wasabi cream sauce or secret cilantro sauce
and satay wraps served at this great little
owner-run place. Wash down all this sub-
limely simple food with a hibiscus lemonade
or Thai iced tea at the outside tables. You'll
come back for more.

Kountry Kitchen (☎ 822-3511; 1485 Kuhio Hwy;
meals $4-8; ⏱ 6am-2pm) Come to this down-
home place hungry: the fluffy mac-nut
pancakes are the size of dinner plates; the

THE AUTHOR'S CHOICE

Blossoming Lotus (☎ 822-7678; www.blos
sominglotus.com; Ground Fl, Dragon Bldg; mains $7-
14; ⏱ 11am-3pm & 6-9:30pm) It's mind-boggling how food without meat, dairy, eggs
or even honey can taste so rich. Assuage all
doubts and dine exquisitely at this 'vegan
world fusion' emporium where the divine
coconut curry comes piled on a bed of
quinoa, and the bountiful glory wrap with
grilled tofu is like a rainbow bursting from
a tortilla. Carefully crafted teas and giant
cookies top it all off. If you like the vittles
here, check out the cookbook, available
only at the restaurant or online at www
.veganfusion.com.

---

build-your-own omelettes are served with
all the sides and the cup of coffee is bottomless. The staff make you feel like 'ohana;
breakfast served all day, lunch from 11am.

Pono Market (☎ 822-4581; 4-1300 Kuhio Hwy; plate
lunch $6; ⏱ 7am-7pm Mon-Fri, to 6pm Sun) Diminutive
store and deli counter that serves generous
plate lunches and deliciously fresh sushi rolls
with plenty of aloha. Locals are always hanging around here noshing on kalua pig with
poi, and the sushi is packaged and ready to
go to the beach. Teriyaki chicken, lomilomi
(salmon), poke and abalone or scallop salad
($10.99 per lb) are staples. The hard-to-resist
big cookies are baked fresh daily.

Beezers (☎ 822-4411; 4-1380 Kuhio Hwy; items $3-
8; ⏱ 11am-10pm) Banana splits, malted milkshakes and ice-cream sundaes are staples at
this old-fashioned ice-cream shop brimming
with nostalgic 1960s decor. Sundaes bear
names like peppermint twist and Mustang
Sally, and not much else on the menu – hot
dogs, pastrami sandwiches and ice-cream
sodas – approaches current-day trends. A
regular old ice-cream cone will set you back
$3.25.

Bubba's (☎ 823-0069; www.bubbaburger.com; 4-
1421 Kuhio Hwy; burgers $3-5; ⏱ 10:30am-9pm) From
100% Kaua'i beef to vegan taro burgers, this
is fresh, wholesome fast food.

MID-RANGE
Norberto's El Cafe (☎ 822-3362; 4-1373 Kuhio Hwy;
dinner $13-16; ⏱ 5-9pm Mon-Sat) Kaua'i's original
Mexican restaurant makes all menu items
without lard. Bonus: margaritas and Mexican brews.

Drinking
Java Kai (☎ 823-6887; 4-1384 Kuhio Hwy; drinks $1.50-
4.50; ⏱ 6am-6pm) Jumping coffee joint that's
the place to get zonked on all manner of java
drinks and meet and greet the good folks of
Kapa'a. Disregard the baristas throwing attitude, grab a sidewalk table and settle in.

Shack (☎ 823-0200; 4-1639 Kuhio Hwy; burgers $6-7,
beers $4; ⏱ noon-2am) Twelve beers on tap (yes,
Guinness, too), multiple TVs to catch the big
game and bar food, including huge salads.
Merry makers flock here, especially on $2
pint Thursday.

Killer Juice Bar (cnr Hwy 56 & Kou Rd; ⏱ 9am-5pm)
Truly just a shack by the side of the road, it
has wonderfully thick fruit smoothies, plus
fresh bread and produce.

Shopping

This little town packs a shopping wallop.

T.L.C. (☎ 822-0004; neptoon@hawaiian.net; 1592 Kuhio Hwy; �) 10am-6pm Mon-Sat) For good quality, fun and flirty second-hand togs.

Kauai Products Fair (☎ 246-0988; www.kauai productsfair.com; �) 9am-5pm Thu-Sun) Handicrafts (including pottery, jewelry, batik clothing) and produce are sold at this crafts fair on the north side of town.

KAPA'A TO KILAUEA

Flowing north from Kapa'a, the road and vistas open up beautifully, with bejeweled ocean and distant bays on one side, and electric-green sugarcane and the jagged peaks of the Anahola Mountains on the other. A couple of scenic lookouts just north of Kapa'a have such great views it's as if you're beholding Kaua'i for the first time. Sunsets can be particularly picturesque at low tide, when waves break over the shallows and fishers are out with their throw nets.

Kealia Beach

This long, pretty beach is at the 10-mile marker. During transitional swells, it's a hot surf spot. After rainstorms, the sand may be heavily littered with tree limbs carried down Kealia Stream, which empties at the beach's south side.

Donkey Beach

An easy 10-minute walk down from the highway takes you to golden Donkey Beach. Passing the 'Nudity is against the law: violators will be prosecuted' sign en route is your first clue that this long, windy beach has long been known as Kaua'i's main nudist beach. It's also a popular gay beach (though it draws a mixed crowd).

Technically, nude sunbathing is illegal on Kaua'i, and the police have occasionally rolled in and busted those in the buff – as if the island didn't have bigger problems. Tolerance is episodic, so doff clothing at your own risk.

Summer swells are rideable here, but from October to May dangerous rip currents and a powerful shore break take over. It's so windy the ironwood trees lean away from the shore and those right at the beach are so blown over they almost look like shrubs (which make for lousy shade, so bring sun protection). *Naupaka* and *ilima*, native ground-creeping flowers, add dashes of color in the sand.

To get to the beach, stop at the paved parking lot at the ocean side of Hwy 56, about halfway between the 11- and 12-mile markers; look for the small 'Public Shoreline Access' sign. From there just follow the path down to the beach.

HAWAIIAN HOMES & LANDS

Even before the current 'Californication' of Kaua'i, where walled compounds are being hastily constructed by temporary residents who split their time between here and the mainland, land issues have been flash points. Bumper stickers reading 'Keep Hawaiian Lands in Hawaiian Hands' and 'Locals Only: We Grew Here, You Flew Here' are common sights on Kaua'i and are your first tip that paradise has its warts.

Independence activists Sondra and Michael Grace know those warts well: after waiting years to receive land under the Hawaiian Homes Commission Act (see p34), the Graces, along with a handful of other indigenous Hawaiian families, occupied homesteads in the Hawaiian Home Lands area of Anahola.

In 1991, in spite of possessing a quit claim deed, the government sent in sheriffs, the National Guard and bulldozers, and levelled the small community. Fourteen of the homesteaders, peacefully chanting in a circle, were arrested for trespassing. They were quickly released, but the Graces had a second homestead bulldozed by the government and continue to fight for indigenous Hawaiian land rights. According to some estimates, between 30,000 and 40,000 people have died while on the Hawaiian Home Lands waiting list.

To learn more about the fight for independence and the Hawaiian land controversy, visit www .hawaiiankingdom.org and check out the documentary video *Anahola*, by Nicholas Rozsa, which tells the story of the Anahola demolition, with interviews from a wide cross-section of Hawaiian society and leadership. The Graces keep this film and many other resources on hand at their B&B (see the boxed text, p468).

Anahola

pop 1932

You'll miss this small village if you're not looking for it, but find it, scratch below the surface and enigmatic Anahola will slowly reveal itself as one of Kauaʻi's most captivating pockets. Being among the few that stay in Anahola is a good way to start.

Grouped together at the side of Hwy 56, just south of the 14-mile marker, is Anahola's modest commercial center, with the post office, a burger stand and a small convenience store.

SIGHTS & ACTIVITIES

A county park on Hawaiian Home Lands (p467), **Anahola Beach Park** sits at the south side of Anahola Bay. This wide bay, fringed with a nice sandy beach, was an ancient surfing site, and its break is still popular with surfers today. To get there, turn off Hwy 56 onto Kukuihale Rd at the 13-mile marker, drive a mile down and then turn onto the dirt beach road.

Alternate access to this beach is via Aliomanu Rd (First) at the 14-mile marker, which dead ends at the southern stretch of secluded **ʻAliomanu Beach**, from where you can beach stroll north for a couple of miles. To get to the northern part of this intimate beach by car, turn onto Aliomanu Rd (Second), just past the 15-mile marker on Hwy 56. Turn left onto Kalaelea View Dr, go 0.5 miles and turn right at the beach access sign. This great beach is accessed via a short trail; look for the rope swing to your left.

For a massage, contact Andrew Crawford at **Moonbath Massage** (☎ 651-2018; wacx65@hotmail .com; PO Box 831, Anahola 96703; per hr $45). **TriHealth Ayurveda** (☎ 828-2104, 800-455-0770; www.oilbath .com; PO Box 340, Anahola, HI 96703; treatments $100-245) offers traditional Ayurvedic therapies, including synchronized oil massage (two therapists) plus steambath; streaming hot oil poured on your forehead; and hot oil rhythmically poured over your entire body.

SLEEPING & EATING

Anahola Beach Park For camping permit information, see p436.

Ono Char Burger (☎ 822-9181; Hwy 56; burgers $5-7; ☉ 10am-6pm Mon-Sat, 11am-6pm Sun) Even Chuck Norris and Steve Tyler recognize Ono Char as Kauaʻi's best burger joint. Try the 'old fashioned' with cheddar, onions and sprouts, or the 'local girl', smothered in Swiss cheese, pineapple and teriyaki sauce. Crispy thin fries and melt-in-your-mouth onion rings are compulsory extras. The chocolate milkshakes are the real deal – and that's from someone who knows her shakes.

Hole in the Mountain

More like a sliver in the mountain these days, this once-obvious sight was largely filled in by a landslide. Legend says the original hole was created when a giant threw his spear through the mountain, causing the water stored within to gush forth as waterfalls. Slightly north of the 15-mile marker, look back at the mountain, down to the right of the tallest pinnacle, and on sunny days you'll be able to see a smile of light coming through a slit in the rock face.

Koʻolau Road

Koʻolau Rd is a peaceful, scenic loop drive through rich green pastures, dotted with soaring white egrets and bright wildflowers. It makes a nice diversion and is the way to get to untouristed Moloaʻa Beach or Larsen's Beach (no facilities at either). Koʻolau Rd connects with Hwy 56 0.5 miles north of the 16-mile marker and again 180yd south of the 20-mile marker.

Pre- or post-beach, fuel up at the **Moloaʻa Sunrise Fruit Stand** (☎ 822-1441; Hwy 56 & Koʻolau Rd; drinks $2-5.50, sandwiches $5-6; ☉ 7:30am-6pm Mon-Sat, 8am-6pm Sun). The frosties (100% frozen fruit puree) and smoothies are decadent, and the fresh sandwiches burst from multigrain bread slices. Try the turkey breast, cucumber and local chèvre number or jazz your body with $2 *noni* shots.

KAUA'I

MOLOA'A BEACH

This pretty little beach with plenty of shade is cleaved by Moloa'a Stream: to the north is a shallow protected swimming area good for families; to the south is rougher water, but with more sand to spread out. The views of green hills and diminutive cliffs rolling toward the crescent-shaped bay are a slow, but sure, intoxicant. To get here, follow Ko'olau Rd and turn onto Moloa'a Rd (1.25 miles and 1 mile coming from the south and north respectively). The road ends 0.75 miles down at a few beach houses and a little parking area. The whole bay can have strong currents when the surf is rough.

LARSEN'S BEACH

This long, golden-sand beach is good for solitary strolls and beachcombing. Although shallow, snorkeling can be good when the waters are very calm, which is usually only in the summer. Beware of a vicious current that runs westward along the beach and out through a channel in the reef.

Very much a local beach, when the tide is low, you might share Larsens with Hawaiian families collecting an edible seaweed called *limu kohu*. The seaweed found here is considered to be some of the finest in all of Hawaii. Otherwise, it will be you, the sand and the waves. Boulder hop around the point at the western end of the beach to access supremely private sands.

The turnoff to Larsen's Beach is on Ko'olau Rd, a little more than a mile down from the north intersection of Ko'olau Rd and Hwy 56, or just over a mile north of the intersection of Moloa'a and Ko'olau Rds. Turn toward the ocean on the dirt road there (easy to miss if you're coming from the south: look for it just before the cemetery) and take the immediate left. It's 1 mile to the parking area and then a five-minute walk downhill to the beach.

NORTH SHORE

Aaaah, the North Shore, where the unhurried life is complemented by the incredible scenery of deep mountain valleys, rolling pastures, ancient taro fields, white-sand beaches and the rugged Na Pali Coast. Most folks zoom to the northern extent, romp at the beach and turn around. Take a local tip

and do it slow – whether you're hiking or just poking around – to really get the idea.

A drive along the North Shore takes in the seabird sanctuary at Kilauea and a couple of small coastal villages before reaching the resort complex of Princeville, with its condos and golf courses. But it's the area beyond, from the Hanalei Bridge to Ke'e Beach at the road's end, that best embodies the North Shore spirit. This is Kaua'i without mass tourism, and its appeal lies not in creature comforts, but in stunning natural beauty.

Rainy days, common on the lush North Shore, can be almost dreamlike. The tops of the mountains become shrouded in clouds that alternately drift and lift, revealing a series of plunging waterfalls. In winter it might rain for days on end, but in summer it usually means quick showers followed by rainbows. Keen eyes might see a moonbow (a rainbow colored with moonbeams) on the full moon.

KILAUEA
pop 2092

Making the slow, magical transformation into a place to go to rather than just pass through, the former-sugar-plantation town of Kilauea is a charmer. The main attractions not to be missed are still the picturesque lighthouse and seabird sanctuary at Kilauea Point (the most-visited site on the North Shore), but hanging around here is becoming an attractive option, too.

Sights & Activities
ROCK QUARRY BEACH

Also known as Kahili Beach, Rock Quarry is a broad sandy beach, with a pretty fringe of ironwood trees. Fairly remote, this beach has rich fishing and, on occasion, surf turf. If the waves are big enough to ride, swimmers should take extreme caution with strong near shore currents.

Public access is via Wailapa Rd, which begins midway between the 21- and 22-mile markers on Hwy 56. Follow Wailapa Rd north for less than 0.5 miles beyond Hwy 56 and then turn left on the unmarked dirt road that begins at a bright-yellow water valve. The dirt road, which continues for 0.5 miles before ending at the beach, is rough. Compact cars can do it, but pick your way slowly over and around the crevasses.

NORTH SHORE

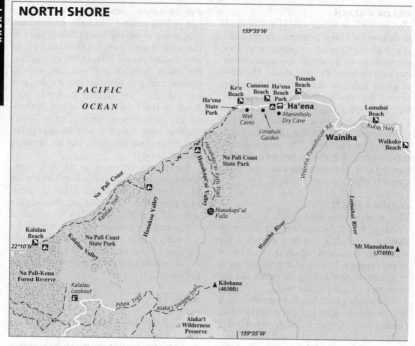

NA 'AINA KAI BOTANICAL GARDENS

Plant enthusiasts should make a point of touring these **Botanical Gardens** (☎ 828-0525; www.naainakai.com; 4101 Wailapa Rd; 3-hr tour $35; ☼ 9am Tue-Thu). Promoted as a sculpture garden (there are 70 too-precious, life-sized bronzes sprinkled throughout), the real attractions are the Poinciana maze, rare plants, informed docents and decadent structures on this 240-acre former estate. Request the three-hour 'Formal & Wild Forest Garden' riding tour, if you have mobility issues. To get the best bang for your buck, call about the 'Founder's Tour,' usually held once a week and led by the gentleman farmer whose handiwork you'll be touring. To reach the gardens, turn right onto Wailapa Rd, between the 21- and 22-mile markers on Kuhio Hwy; the garden is just over 1300yd down on your right.

The **children's garden** here is a real marvel. There's a wooden playground, fort, covered wagon, graffiti wall, and a giant Jack-in-the-Beanstalk fountain and wading pool.

Opening times and admission policies were not yet set at time of research.

CHRIST MEMORIAL EPISCOPAL CHURCH

After turning onto Kolo Rd, just past the 23-mile marker on Hwy 56, look immediately for the striking Christ Memorial Episcopal Church. Built in 1941 of lava rock, the headstones (also of lava rock) in the churchyard are much older, dating back to when the original Hawaiian Congregational Church stood on this site.

KILAUEA POINT

This national **wildlife refuge** (☎ 828-0383; pacific islands.fws.gov/wnwr/kkilaueanwr.html; adult/child under 16 $3/free; ☼ 10am-4pm, closed federal holidays) is the northernmost point of the inhabited Hawaiian Islands. Topped by a **lighthouse** built in 1913, it's picture-postcard material. Park staff at the **visitors center** are very knowledgeable and will train the telescope there on nesting birds. Also see them if transportation for the disabled is required to reach the lighthouse.

Even if birds bore you, it's worth driving to the end of Kilauea Rd for the stunning view of the lighthouse (with the biggest clamshell lens in the world) and cliffs beyond. The

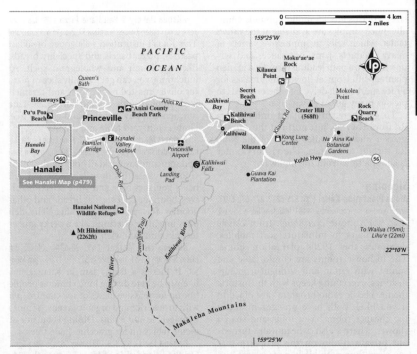

refuse itself is not open to the public. Binoculars are loaned free at the lighthouse; in addition to birds, scan for sea turtles, frolicking spinner dolphins in spring and summer, and humpback whales in winter.

Four species of birds come to Kilauea to nest, but most leave after their young have been reared. Red-footed boobies, the most visible, are abundant on the cliffs to the east of the point, where they build large stick nests in the treetops. Boobies nest from February to September, with their peak egg-laying occurring in spring.

Wedge-tailed shearwaters arrive by March and stay until November, nesting in burrows they dig into Kilauea Point. Other readily spotted species are the red-tailed and white-tailed tropic bird, from March to October. If you're lucky, you'll spot a pair flying in loops, performing their courtship ritual.

Laysan albatrosses are at Kilauea from around December to July. Some nest on Moku'ae'ae Rock, straight off the tip of the point. Other albatross nesting sites lie on the grassy clearing to the west of Kilauea Point. Look out beyond this clearing to

see Secret Beach (p473), divided into three scalloped coves by lava fingers.

Great frigate birds nest on the Northwestern Hawaiian Islands, not Kaua'i, but these aerial pirates visit Kilauea Point year-round to steal food from other birds. You won't see the distinctive red throat balloon that the male puffs out to attract females, though, as they're here to feed, not breed. Frigate birds, which have a wingspan of 7ft and a distinctive forked tail, soar with a mesmerizing grace. Golden plovers (the legendary birds believed to have led the ancient Polynesian mariners to these islands) arrive from the Arctic in August and stay through spring.

Some of Kaua'i's estimated 100 nene, the endangered Hawaiian goose that was reintroduced here in 1982, can also be spotted.

GUAVA KAI PLANTATION

This **plantation** (☎ 828-6121; www.guavakai.com; Kuawa Rd; admission free; ☺ 9am-5pm) cultivates 480 acres of guava trees that produce juice for Ocean Spray and other juice companies. Harvest yields of this big hybrid, whose fruit grows to half a pound (twice the normal size), are close to 4.5 million pounds annually. Juice samples are available at the **visitors center**, which sells an impressive variety of guava products, jams, hot sauces and syrups. There's a path leading through a garden planted with tropical flowers that makes for a nice short stroll; delve into the orchards to pick as many guava as you like.

To get there, turn inland onto Kuawa Rd from Hwy 56, just north of the 23-mile marker and 0.25 miles south of the Kolo Rd turnoff to Kilauea. The visitors center is about a mile from the highway.

Sleeping
Aloha Plantation Kauai (☎ 828-6872, 877-658-6977; www.garden-isle.com/aloha; 4481 Malulani Rd; r $50-60, studio $90) Antique *everything*, from classic barber chairs to miniature surf mobiles, decorates this 1920s plantation home. The in-house rooms are comfortable and sunny, with rattan and wrought-iron furnishings; everything keeps with the historic theme (classic radio programs are piped in if you like). Both have private entrances; the cheaper room has a toilet and shared shower. There's also a beautifully turned-out private studio on the property that can sleep four, with kitchenette, stereo and DVD player. An outdoor cooking area, plus a Jacuzzi, are for guest use.

Bird Song Cottage (☎ 828-1458, 652-1431; www .kauaibirdsongcottage.com; house $125) This intensely romantic and classy home away from home sits on six secluded acres in Kilauea. Two lanai (one facing the ocean, the other the sea), high ceilings and lots of windows make the most of the phenomenal location. Full kitchen, quality linens, gorgeous granite bath, loads of outdoor space – including a fruit orchard and organic veggie garden – will make you swoon.

Eating
Mango Mama's (☎ 828-1020; cnr Hwy 56 & Ho'okui Rd; drinks $3-5, sandwiches $3-6.50; ⏱ 7am-6pm Mon-Sat) Fresh and sassy, this place done up in pink zebra stripes sets the standard for little roadside joints. It has smoothies, tempeh burgers and *noni* shots like the rest, but has superior ambience. A pint-sized kiddie dining area, reading material and lots of tropical foliage create a shady haven that encourages lingering over your bagel with avocado and Vegemite. So what if *everything* is pink?

Kilauea Bakery & Pau Hana Pizza (☎ 828-2020; Kong Lung Center, Kilauea Rd; pizza $7-20; ⏱ 6:30am-9pm) This Kaua'i institution sells gooey breakfast pastries, pizza, bagels and speciality breads, like sourdough and wholegrain spelt. At lunchtime, you can get the daily slice of pizza (eg olives, roasted red peppers and caramelized onions) with a salad for $6.25. Late lunchers can buy one slice and get one free. Grab a courtyard table and dig in.

Farmers Market (☎ 828-1512; Kong Lung Center, Kilauea Rd; deli items $4-7; ⏱ 8:30am-8:30pm, to 8pm Sun) Did someone say cocktail hour on the lanai? Good, because this upscale grocer and deli has a gourmet beer and wine selection, olives, boutique cheeses, flat breads and other goodies for grownup snacking. The deli does inventive offerings, like a perky ginger teriyaki tofu sandwich.

Kilauea Fish Market (☎ 828-6244; Kilauea Rd; plates & wraps $8-11, poke per lb $7; ⏱ 11am-7pm Mon-Sat) If there's a traffic jam in Kilauea, it's likely to be here during lunch hour as people line up for massive plates of soy cilantro 'ahi with brown rice and organic greens, or more manageable 'ahi wraps. Dining is outside at picnic tables under graceful shade trees.

Banana Joe's (☎ 828-1092; Hwy 56; ⏱ 9am-6pm) On the inland side of Hwy 56 near the 24-mile marker, look for this yellow fruit shack for local products, like organic salad mix ($4.25 a giant bag), papaya and pineapple salsas ($5), honey, Hanalei poi, and feta and goat cheeses ($6). Fresh veggies and fruit grown on the adjacent 6-acre plot are also sold here.

Entertainment
Kilauea Theater & Community Events Center (☎ 828-0438; Kong Lung Center, ⏱ showtimes 5:30 & 7pm) Screens classic and first-run movies, and hosts occasional live performances.

Getting There & Around
Kolo Rd, the main turnoff into Kilauea, is 585yd beyond the 23-mile marker. Kilauea Rd starts opposite the church and ends 2 miles later at Kilauea Point. After 0.5 miles, you'll reach historic Kong Lung Center, with restaurants, shops and the theater.

KALIHIWAI
Kalihiwai Rd was a loop road going down past Kalihiwai Beach, connecting with the highway at two points, until the tidal wave

KAUA'I

of 1957 washed out the Kalihiwai River bridge. The bridge was never rebuilt, and now there are two Kalihiwai Rds, one on each side of the river.

Sights & Activities
KALIHIWAI BEACH
The section of Kalihiwai Rd 0.5 miles west of Kilauea leads down a mile to Kalihiwai Beach, a stretch of white sand cut through by the Kalihiwai River that empties into a wide, deep bay. Kayakers (see p438) launch here for the one-hour scenic paddle up to the Kalihiwai Valley. The pretty, broad beach is popular for many activities, such as swimming, boogie boarding, bodysurfing and, when the northwest swells roll in, some daredevil surfing along the cliff at the east end of the bay. The beach has no facilities. As you take Kalihiwai Rd back up to the highway, look to the left as soon as you see the 'Narrow Bridge' sign; you'll spot a picturesque waterfall that's partially hidden in a little valley.

SECRET BEACH
More like the 'Secret's Out Beach,' this gorgeous golden-sand beach backed by sea cliffs and jungle-like woods has been 'discovered.' While it's still a beauty frequented by Kaua'i's alternative community, 'secret' is definitely a misnomer. Perhaps reverting to its Hawaiian name, Kauapepa Beach, which is how it appears on some maps, would be appropriate.

To get there, turn down Kalihiwai Rd 0.5 miles west of Kilauea and then turn right onto the first dirt road, which is 180yd from Hwy 56. The road ends at a parking area 585yd down. Don't leave anything of value in your car. The well-defined trail begins from the parking lot. After two minutes' walk it leads downhill through ironwood trees and mixed jungle growth. All in all, the trail only takes about 10 minutes and deposits you at the western end of this long, sandy beach. While this part of the beach is quite idyllic, if you're up for a stroll or feel the need for more privacy, walk along the beach in the direction of Kilauea Lighthouse.

The beach has open seas, with high winter surf and dangerous currents prevailing from October to May. In summer water conditions are much calmer, and swimming and snorkeling can be good.

HORSEBACK RIDING
You can sate your appetite for North Shore landscapes on a scenic horseback ride at the **Silver Falls Ranch** (☎ 828-6718; www.silverfalls ranch.com; end of Kamo'okoa Rd; 90-min trail ride $80, 2-/3-hr ride $100/120). The super-friendly professionals here lead daily rides, with lunch and swimming at a remote waterfall. The grounds are exquisite, with blooming orchids, old-growth trees and water elements enhancing the ride.

Sleeping
Accommodations around here include **Hale Ho'o Maha** (☎ 828-1341; www.aloha.net/~hoomaha; 2883 Kalihiwai Rd; d $75), where everything, down to the muumuu-draped hostess and the shag rugs, exude *That '70s Show*. The two rooms each have two double beds (bonus: four travelers can stay at the double price) and share an entire darkish house, including common rooms, bath and kitchen.

'ANINI
If you're looking for an all-round great beach, with facilities, swimming, snorkeling, surf and windsurfing (lessons too), 'Anini is it. To get there, cross Kalihiwai Bridge (look and listen for the thundering waterfall here), turn onto the second Kalihiwai Rd and then bear left onto 'Anini Rd. It's about 1.5 miles from the highway to the beach.

There has been talk of connecting Princeville with 'Anini by a direct coastal road, but local resistance has kept the talk just that. For now, 'Anini's deadend street means little traffic, keeping this area unhurried and quiet. Still, 'Anini is growing, and a number of exclusive homes, including many vacation rentals and Hollywood getaways, have shot up.

Sights & Activities
Over a mile of clean beach lined with almond shade trees defines **'Anini County Beach Park**. Divided into day-use, windsurfing and camping areas, it's a popular spot, with gentle breezes and calm (for Kaua'i) waters. Facilities include restrooms, showers, changing rooms, drinking water, picnic pavilions and barbecue grills.

Swimming and snorkeling are good in the day-use area and in front of the camping area; conditions are best when the tide is high. A pretty good spot is opposite the midpoint of Kauai Polo Club's fence or at the far end of 'Anini Rd. The snorkeling is shallow, but the long barrier reef means lots of fish. Be careful over here because the 'Anini Channel cutting across the reef creates dangerous rip currents. The protected lagoon west of the channel provides safer water conditions.

'Anini Beach also has good windsurfing. You can give it a go with **Windsurf Kauai** (☎ 828-6838; windsurfkauai@aol.com; 3-hr lesson $7, board rental 30 min/3 hr $25/45/50; ☻ 9am & 1pm Mon-Fri), which offers lessons and rents boards with gear

Fishing boats out of 'Anini include the following:

'Anini Fishing Charters (☎ 828-1285; www.kauai fishing.com; charter 4 hr shared per person $95, private for up to six anglers $475)

North Shore Charters (☎ 828-1379; similarly priced)

Sleeping

'Anini has idyllic camping right on the water, with shaded tent sites. It's relatively spacious for a beach park, although it crowds up on weekends, when local families arrive. See p436 for how to obtain a permit.

Well-equipped, spacious vacation homes just across the road from the beach include (rates quoted here are weekly, excluding cleaning fees):

'Anini Hale (☎ 826-6167; www.aninihale.com; 3657 'Anini Rd; 2-bedroom cottage/house $750/1500) Luxurious house with ocean views shares a large lot with a mountain-facing cottage.

'Anini Beach Hideaway (☎ 828-1051; www.anini beachhideaway.com; 3635 'Anini Rd; 1-bedroom house from $875) Its spacious lawn is good for kids.

'Anini Beach Hale (☎ 828-6808, 877-262-6688; www .yourbeach.com; 3629 'Anini Rd; 2-bedroom house $1400) Lots of windows and large lanai; perfect for two couples.

Noho Kai (☎ 821-1454, 800-769-3285 ext 00; www .nohokai.com; 3617 'Anini Rd; 3-bedroom house $1775) Huge front and back lanai, plus all bedrooms open onto a private lanai, too.

Eating

If you're anywhere near 'Anini, don't miss the chance to eat at the **'Anini Beach Lunch Shak** (☎ 635-7425; meals $3.75-7; ☻ 10:30am-3pm Tue-Sat). The fresh-fish tacos – *ono, ahi,* it doesn't matter – flautas and burritos served from this lunch truck kick ass. Try the pharaoh-style double-wrap taco or the heftier Sara special, and spike it with one of 24 bottled

hot sauces or the truck's special cilantro-jalapeño sauce (50¢).

PRINCEVILLE
pop 1698

No need to mince words: Princeville is one giant resort. A planned community spread over 11,000 acres on a promontory between 'Anini Beach Park and Hanalei Bay, it is Kaua'i's biggest development by far. It has a dozen condo complexes, a luxury hotel, hundreds of private homes, championship golf courses, tennis courts, restaurants, a shopping center and a little airport (used only by helicopter tours, p442).

While Princeville stands in sharp contrast to the free-spirited North Shore communities that lie beyond, the design tries to tread lightly with low-rise condos and relatively uncrowded development. Princeville makes a good day trip for swimming at Queen's Bath, relaxing at Hideaways, and taking in unbeatable coastal and valley views. Fun, family activities and tours are another draw.

History

Princeville traces its roots to Robert Wyllie, a Scottish doctor who later became foreign minister to Kamehameha IV. In the mid-19th century Wyllie bought a large coffee plantation in Hanalei and began planting sugar. When Queen Emma and Kamehameha IV came to visit in 1860, Wyllie named his plantation and the surrounding lands Princeville in honor of their son, Prince Albert. The plantation later became a cattle ranch.

Orientation & Information

Kuhio Hwy changes from Hwy 56 to Hwy 560 at the 28-mile marker in front of Princeville. The 10-mile stretch from here to Ke'e Beach at the end of the road is one of the most scenic drives in all of Hawaii.

Princeville Center, the shopping center just past the entrance to Princeville, has the main cluster of services for the North Shore, including a small medical clinic, banks, a library, a **post office** (☎ 800-275-8777; ☻ 10:30am-3:30pm Mon-Fri, to 12:30pm Sat) and shops.

Sights
PRINCEVILLE HOTEL

This place is all about the views of Hanalei Bay and the Bali Hai mountains. If your jaw doesn't drop upon entering the opulent lobby with floor-to-ceiling windows and 180-degree views of Bali Hai, have your pulse checked. All the giant urns, chintz sofas, chandeliers and miles of marble inside are no match for the glorious eye candy outside.

The luxury hotel was erected amid enormous controversy in 1985. Locals, who were ticked at losing one of their favorite sunset spots, nicknamed the bluff-side building 'the Prison.' The original hotel was indeed dark and inward-looking, and it so failed to incorporate its surroundings that the owners closed it down in 1989. Over the next two years the hotel was gutted and virtually rebuilt. While it stuns from the inside, the bummer is that you can see this hulk of a complex from almost every beach north of here.

BEACHES

Princeville has a magnificent secluded lozenge of sand called **Hideaways** (aka Pali Ke Kua). When calm, there's good swimming and snorkeling, and it's perfect for sunset anytime. To get there, park in the public lot just after the guardhouse at the Princeville Hotel and take the path between the fences. After several minutes, the trail becomes unbelievably steep, with stairs and ropes to aid your descent. For roomier play, head to **Pu'u Poa Beach**, between the Princeville Hotel and the mouth of the Hanalei River. High surf, common in winter, can generate dangerous currents at both beaches.

QUEEN'S BATH

This delightful lava-rock pool right on the shoreline provides a natural protected swimming and snorkeling hole. The surf splashes in softly or with a crash, periodically flushing clean the ice-blue pool, which is so salty you float along effortlessly. It's a nice spot, and popular, too. Look for turtles and monk seals just beyond the pool.

To get here, enter the Princeville Resort area and drive just under 1.5 miles before turning right onto Punahele Rd. Park in the area at the end of the road and take the trail to the right. It's about a 10-minute walk to the bottom. About halfway down, you'll pass a gushing waterfall, but be careful rinsing off here, as leptosperosis (p541) lurks. When you reach the shore, turn left and walk over the rocks for five minutes.

Activities
HIKING
The south road leads to the trailhead for the **Powerline Trail**, but this hike is more rewarding starting from Keahua Arboretum (see p458).

GOLF
The Robert Trent Jones Jr–designed championship links at the **Princeville Golf Club** (☎ 826-5070; www.princeville.com; 5-3900 Kuhio Hwy; green fees Prince/Makai $150/110, club rental $35) are legendary, especially the 18-hole par-72 Prince, which is Kaua'i's highest-rated course. The 27-hole par-72 Makai isn't too shabby either. Green fees include cart and day pass to the spa. There are 'matinee specials' at both courses if you tee off after noon and deeper discounts as the day goes on. Collared shirts are required.

TENNIS
You can hit at either the **Princeville Tennis Club** (☎ 826-3620; www.princeville.com; 5-3900 Kuhio Hwy; court per person per hr $15) or the **Hanalei Bay Resort Tennis Club** (☎ 826-6522; Hanalei Bay Resort; court per person per hr $6).

Tours
Saddle up for a horseback ride at **Princeville Ranch Stables** (☎ 826-6777, 826-7473; www.princeville ranch.com; Hwy 56; 3-/4-hr tour $110/120; ☺ tours Mon-Sat) between the 26- and 27-mile markers. It crosses ranch lands to a waterfall for a picnic and swim. There's also a 90-minute bluff ride ($65), and for the adventurous, a 90-minute cattle drive (yes, you actually drive the cattle, $120).

Across the road is **Princeville Ranch Adventures** (☎ 826-7669, 888-955-7669; www.adventureskauai .com), with half-day zipline, kayaking and hiking tours ($80 to $110), all of which include lunch and waterfall romping.

Sleeping
Princeville's condo complexes are either perched on cliffs or beside the golf course. Sometimes you can find condo residents renting rooms for about $50 a day; check the bulletin board outside Foodland in Princeville Center and the *Garden Island* newspaper classifieds.

Most condo complexes are represented by a number of different rental agents, who usually offer cheaper prices than direct bookings at a front desk. Get all the details before booking, however, as there can be cleaning fees, minimum stays and other restrictions. The following agents have fairly extensive Princeville rentals:

Oceanfront Realty (☎ 826-6585, 800-222-5541; www.oceanfrontrealty.com; PO Box 223190, Princeville, HI 96722) Its online specials are pretty good deals.

Century 21 All Islands (☎ 826-7211, 800-828-1442; www.c21allislands.com; PO Box 223700, Princeville, HI 96722)

North Shore Properties (☎ 826-9622, 800-488-3336; www.hanaleinorthshoreproperties.com; PO Box 607, Hanalei, HI 96714) Handles many properties in Hanalei, too.

MID-RANGE

Sealodge (☎ 826-6751; Kamehameha Ave; 1-bedroom unit from $100; 🏊) The great sunrise views across the expansive coral reef of 'Anini compensate for the tight digs at this older complex perched high on the cliffs. Let the waves rock you to sleep and don't miss the beach below. Units can be booked through the rental agents listed earlier.

Pali Ke Kua (☎ 826-9394, 800-535-0085; www.marc resorts.com; 1-/2-bedroom unit $200/240; 🏊) This upscale property with subdued style is a good choice, especially if you connect with one of the various discount schemes that can cut rates by as much as 50% (check online). The Marc Resorts office here also handles a couple of simpler units for $125 in the nearby Hale Moi complex.

Cliffs at Princeville (☎ 826-6219, 800-622-6219; www.castleresorts.com/CLF; 3811 Edward Rd; units $120-150; 🏊) Refurbished, large condos with front and rear lanai are the draws at this complex with a less dramatic setting than others around Princeville.

TOP END

Hanalei Bay Resort (☎ 826-6522, 800-922-7866; www.hanaleibaykauai.com; 5380 Honoiki Rd; r $185-275, studios $215-240, 1-bedroom unit $350-390; 🏊) The views from this resort of Bali Hai and Hanalei Bay are its reason for being. Choose from hotel-style rooms or condos, but be sure to upgrade for just a few dollars more for a unit with an ocean view. This place is popular with honeymooners.

Princeville Hotel (☎ 826-9644, 800-325-3589; www.princeville.com; 5520 Ka Haku Rd; r $450-675, ste $775-4800; 🏊 🏊) Deluxe, over-the-top rooms have king beds, marble bathrooms with deep soaking tubs and phenomenal coastal views,

and modern gadgets like liquid-crystal windows between the bedroom and bath that morph from clear to opaque with the flick of a switch. It's all an exercise in decadence. Check out deep discounts online. The pool is the most magnificent in Kaua'i.

Eating

Dining choices here are limited to the eateries in the Princeville Hotel or Hanalei Bay Resort. If you're here and hungry, you might push onto Hanalei, with a wider selection.

BUDGET

The following slim pickings are in Princeville Center:

Foodland (☎ 826-9880; 🕐 6am-11pm) Cheap bakery and deli with takeaway items for an economical lunch, plus groceries.

Lappert's (☎ 826-7393; single scoop $3.10; 🕐 10am-9pm) Creamy, flavorful ice cream.

Paradise Bar & Grill (☎ 826-1775; sandwiches $7-8.50; 🕐 11am-11pm) Casual place with burgers and fried things mostly, and a full bar.

Princeville Chevron Gas Station (🕐 6am-10pm, to 9pm Sun) Locally raised, hormone-free, grass-fed beef is delivered to the shop here on Friday.

MID-RANGE & TOP END

Café Hanalei (☎ 826-2760; Princeville Hotel; breakfast $6-10, lunch $12-20, dinner $21-35, 3-course prix fixe $52; 🕐 6:30am-2:30pm & 5:30-9:30pm) Any meal at this terrace restaurant with staggering Hanalei Bay views is sure to impress, but dinner will be unforgettable. Rev up with an oyster 'martini' appetizer spiked with fiery pepper vodka, chased with a rack of lamb marinated in Kaua'i coffee or lemongrass-crusted 'ahi. The prix fixe is good value. Or drop in for dessert: the signature chocolate baby cake or chocolate tower filled with passion-fruit mousse are stunners.

La Cascata (☎ 826-2761; Princeville Hotel; dinner mains $24-36, 3-course prix fixe $52; 🕐 6-10pm) The views of Bali Hai might be slightly better here than at Café Hanalei, but the food isn't as inventive. La Cascata has upscale, haute starters, like seared foie gras and 'ahi and roasted beet tartare. Mains are mostly fancy pasta, and heavy meats and game. The crispy-skin *onaga* (snapper) with wild mushrooms stands out.

Bali Hai Restaurant (☎ 826-6522; Hanalei Bay Resort; breakfast & lunch $7-12; dinner mains $17-32; 🕐 breakfast, lunch & dinner) Another feast for your eyes awaits at this restaurant with open-air dining room taking in all of Hanalei Bay. For breakfast, the speciality is fried eggs, Portuguese sausage, poi pancakes and taro hash browns. Dinner brings fish mains, like blackened *ono* with spicy mango chutney, or broiled with coconut milk and peanut-satay sauce. Cheaper eats are served at the Happy Talk Lounge (see below).

Entertainment

Surprisingly, Princeville has one of the most happening dance clubs on Kaua'i, with (egad!) real live music.

Landing Pad (☎ 826-9561; Princeville Airport; admission $3-5; ⏰ 9pm-2am Wed-Mon) Drop in for local reggae or rock bands on Friday or Saturday; Thursday is DJ and dancing.

Happy Talk Lounge (☎ 826-6522; Hanalei Bay Resort) The same (or better) views as the more expensive and sedate Bali Hai Restaurant, plus a tasty bar menu ($7 to $15), and live jazz from 4pm to 7pm Sunday and Hawaiian music most other nights.

Living Room (☎ 826-9644; Princeville Hotel) A spectacular view of Hanalei Bay thanks to its bodacious location and glass walls makes a fine place for a sunset drink and sushi rolls. The lovely live entertainment from 7:30pm to 10:30pm swaddles this lounge in ambience.

Luau (☎ 826-2788; Princeville Hotel; adult/child 6-12 $63/30; ⏰ 6pm Mon & Thu) Includes an *imu* ceremony, Hawaiian food, live music and dance.

TOP FIVE ENTERTAINMENT SPOTS

- **Landing Pad** (see above)
- **Tahiti Nui** (p482)
- **Happy Talk Lounge** (see above)
- **Sushi & Blues** (p483)
- **Kuhio Lounge** (p461)

Getting Around

The **Princeville Chevron gas station** (⏰ 6am-10pm Mon-Sat, to 9pm Sun) is the last place heading west toward Ke'e Beach to buy gas (with pump prices at least 10¢ higher than anywhere else on Kaua'i), so make sure you check your tank before heading off to Hanalei or Hae'na.

HANALEI VALLEY

Just beyond Princeville, on Hwy 56, the **Hanalei Valley Lookout** provides a spectacular bird's-eye view of the valley floor with its meandering river and spread of patchwork taro fields. It's a beautiful scene, and while many people pull in, jump out, snap photos and move on, chilling here really lets you grasp the grace of the place. From the lookout, off to your lower right-hand side you can see the North Shore's first one-lane bridge, which opened in 1912. Visible to the south are the twin peaks of Hihimanu ('beautiful' in Hawaiian).

Hanalei Bridge and six other one-lane bridges between Hanalei River and the end of the road are the only link between this part of the North Shore and the rest of the island. Not only picturesque, they protect the North Shore from development, as big cement trucks and heavy construction equipment are beyond the bridges' limits. Over the years, developers have introduced numerous proposals to build a two-lane bridge over the Hanalei River, but North Shore residents have successfully beaten them down. It happens infrequently, but during unusually heavy rains the road between the taro fields and the river can flood, and the Hanalei Bridge remains closed until the water subsides.

If you like what you saw from the lookout, head into the Hanalei Valley by turning left onto 'Ohiki Rd immediately after the Hanalei Bridge. This 2-mile **scenic drive** through the **Hanalei National Wildlife Refuge** (http://pacificislands.fws.gov/wnwr/khanaleinwr.html) parallels the Hanalei River, passing taro fields, banana trees, bamboo thickets, *hau* (hibiscus) trees and wild ginger, all encompassing 917 acres of the valley, stretching up both sides of the Hanalei River.

Prior to Western contact, the valley was planted in taro, but in the mid-1800s rice paddies were planted to feed the Chinese laborers working in the cane fields. The rice grew so well that by the 1880s it became a major export crop. The demand for rice eventually waned, and while taro once again predominates, what you see is only 5% of that original acreage planted in taro. The wetland taro farms in the refuge produce two-thirds of Hawaii's commercially grown poi taro, and also create habitat for endangered waterbirds.

This is a bird-watching hotspot. From the roadside, you can spot snow-white egrets and night herons, as well as some of the valley's endangered waterbirds, including the Hawaiian coot, the Hawaiian stilt, the Hawaiian duck and the Hawaiian gallinule, with its bright-red bill.

You can delve into the refuge to see 360-degree views via the challenging **Hanalei–Okolehau Trail**. Allow at least three hours for the 4.5-mile round-trip. The signposted trailhead is 0.75 miles down 'Ohiki Rd across from the parking area. Cross the bridge at the start of the trail and curve around, keeping right. After five minutes, turn left at the fork, heading uphill on a 4WD dirt road that eventually turns to a choked forest path, from where it's another 1.75 miles of doggedly steep hiking and scrambling to the top of Kauka'opua hill and the pay-off views. Alternatively, you can **kayak** (p480).

RULES OF THE ROAD

The North Shore has special rules of the road thanks to all one-lane bridges. When two cars approach an empty one-lane bridge from opposite directions, the car that reaches the bridge last yields to the entire line-up of approaching cars, rather than alternating one car in each direction.

HANALEI

Pulling away from the Hanalei Bridge, you parallel the lazy Hanalei River, drifting past fields of taro in seven shades of green and tall grasses bending in the wind. The pace immediately slows, there are no buildings in sight and time feels suspended. It wouldn't be surprising if a mischievous *menehune* jumped from the roadside growth.

Backed by lofty mountains and fronted by a lovely bay, the village took a beating during Hurricane Iniki, losing many old wooden buildings. Fortunately, most of the reconstruction was done in a period style matching the town's original character, which remains friendly, casual and slow. If outdoor adventures are your thing, consider basing yourself here.

Orientation & Information

Nearly anything you might desire can be found in Hanalei Center or **Ching Young**

Village (www.chingyoungvillage.com). The North Shore's main general store since the 19th century, the old Ching Young Store (now a shop called Evolve Love) has grown into this shopping center. Across the street is the Hanalei Center.

There are no banks west of Princeville, but there's an ATM in the Ching Young Village's Big Save supermarket.

Akamai Computer Center (☎ 826-1042; per hr $12; ⏰ 10am-5pm Mon-Fri) Next to Hanalei Wake Up Cafe, has Internet access.

Bali Hai Photo (☎ 826-9181; Ching Young Village; per hr $9; ⏰ 8am-8pm Mon-Fri, 9am-5pm Sat, 10am-5pm Sun) Cheaper Internet access.

Post Office (☎ 800-275-8777; 5-5226 Kuhio Hwy) In the village center.

Sights

WAI'OLI HUI'IA CHURCH & MISSION HOUSE MUSEUM

Hanalei's first missionaries, the Reverend and Mrs William Alexander, arrived in 1834 in a double-hulled canoe. Their church, hall and mission house are in the middle of town, set on a huge manicured lawn with a beautiful mountain backdrop.

The pretty green wooden **church** retains an airy Pacific feel, with large, outward-opening windows and high ceilings. The doors remain open during the day, and visitors are welcome. A Bible printed in Hawaiian and dating to 1868 is displayed on top of the old organ. The Wai'oli Church Choir, the island's best, sings hymns in Hawaiian at the 10am Sunday service.

Wai'oli Mission Hall, to the right of the church, was built in 1836. The hall, which originally served as the church, was built of coral lime and plaster with a distinctive steeply pitched roof to handle Hanalei's heavy rains.

Behind the church and hall is the **Wai'oli Mission House** (☎ 245-3202; admission by donation; ⏰ 9am-3pm Tue, Thu & Sat). The Alexanders spent their first three years living in a grass hut here, but couldn't adjust to living Hawaiian style, so they built this big New England house. It was home to other missionaries over the years, most notably Abner and Lucy Wilcox, whose family became the island's most predominant property holders. The main part of the house, built in 1837, has old wavy glass panes, some nice woodwork and interesting architectural features. Period furnishings are also on display. The Mission House was closed for repairs at the time of research, with an uncertain reopening date.

To get to the inconspicuous parking lot, turn inland immediately before Hanalei School and then left on the dirt driveway opposite the water hydrant.

HANALEI BAY

Hanalei means 'Crescent Bay,' and that it is – a large, perfectly shaped bay, and one of Hawaii's most scenic. The best beaches here are at Hanalei Beach Park and Pinetrees Beach Park; there's another public beach on Weke Rd near Aku Rd. Each of the three beaches has restrooms, showers, drinking water, picnic tables and grills. Hanalei Beach Park is the best place for catching the sunset, because you can see Bali Hai from there. It's also a popular summer anchorage for sailboats.

On the opposite side of the road, midway between the beach pavilion and Hanalei Beach Park, the big brown house with the wraparound porch is the private old **Wilcox Home**, which traces its roots to early Hanalei

missionaries Abner and Lucy Wilcox. The remains of a narrow-gauge railway track once used to haul Hanalei rice lead to the long pier jutting into the bay.

Incidentally, if the road names here sound familiar, it means you're beginning to learn the names of Hawaiian fish – each road along the beach is named after a different one.

Hanalei Beach Park

It's no wonder the long beach shaded by ironwood trees at Hanalei Beach Park is so popular. There really is something for everyone: winter surfing and summer swimming and snorkeling, camping and kayaking, plus a sandy-bottom beach with a gentle slope. As always, take extreme caution during periods of high surf as dangerous shore breaks and rip currents are common then.

The mouth of the Hanalei River and a small boat ramp (with kayaks) are at the eastern end of the park. That part of the beach is called **Black Pot**, after the big iron pot that was once hung there for impromptu cookouts.

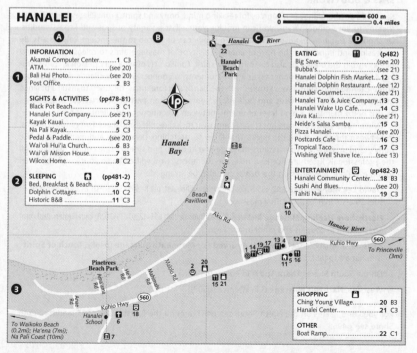

HANALEI

0 _____ 600 m
0 _____ 0.4 miles

INFORMATION
Akamai Computer Center..........1 C3
ATM....................................(see 20)
Bali Hai Photo.......................(see 20)
Post Office.............................2 B3

SIGHTS & ACTIVITIES (pp478-81)
Black Pot Beach......................3 C1
Hanalei Surf Company............(see 21)
Kayak Kauai...........................4 C3
Na Pali Kayak.........................5 C3
Pedal & Paddle.......................(see 20)
Wai'oli Hui'ia Church...............6 B3
Wai'oli Mission House.............7 B3
Wilcox Home...........................8 C2

SLEEPING (pp481-2)
Bed, Breakfast & Beach...........9 C2
Dolphin Cottages..................10 C2
Historic B&B.........................11 C3

EATING (p482)
Big Save...............................(see 20)
Bubba's................................(see 21)
Hanalei Dolphin Fish Market....12 C3
Hanalei Dolphin Restaurant....(see 12)
Hanalei Gourmet....................(see 21)
Hanalei Taro & Juice Company..13 C3
Hanalei Wake Up Cafe............14 C3
Java Kai...............................(see 21)
Neide's Salsa Samba..............15 C3
Pizza Hanalei.......................(see 20)
Postcards Cafe.......................16 C3
Tropical Taco.........................17 C3
Wishing Well Shave Ice...........(see 13)

ENTERTAINMENT (pp482-3)
Hanalei Community Center......18 B3
Sushi And Blues....................(see 20)
Tahiti Nui.............................19 C3

SHOPPING
Ching Young Village..............20 B3
Hanalei Center......................21 C3

OTHER
Boat Ramp............................22 C1

Hanalei River
Hanalei Beach Park
Hanalei Bay
Weke Rd
Beach Pavilion
Aku Rd
Hanalei River
Kuhio Hwy (560)
To Princeville (3mi)
Pinetrees Beach Park
Hee Rd
Amama Rd
Malolo Rd
Mahimahi Rd
Anae Rd
Kuhio Hwy (560)
Hanalei School
To Waikoko Beach (0.2mi); Ha'ena (7mi); Na Pali Coast (10mi)

KAUA'I

Pinetrees Beach Park
Pinetrees has some of the bay's highest winter surf and is the site of various surfing contests, including the Pinetrees Longboard Classic. Held in late-April, it features ageing surfers on old-school wooden boards. A section, known locally as **Toilet Bowls**, on Ama'ama Rd has restrooms and showers. Gaze on million-dollar views here.

Waikoko Beach
This beach (no facilities), protected by a reef on the western bend of Hanalei Bay, has a sandy bottom and is shallower and calmer than the middle of the bay. Pull off the highway around the 4-mile marker. Winter surfing is sometimes good off Makahoa Point, the western point of the bay; surfers call this break **Waikokos**.

Activities
Active travelers will be stoked with the outdoor adventures around Hanalei. With so much surfable coastline, plus the gorgeous

Na Pali Coast hike nearby, it's not surprising that some of the best outdoor outfitters are here, too. If you're keen for a tour, lessons or good rental gear, this is the place. Try the following:

Pedal & Paddle (☎ 826-9069; www.pedalnpaddle.com; Ching Young Village; ☽ 9am-6pm; rents tents day/week $12/35, sleeping bags $3/10, backpacks $5/20) And more.

Kayak Kauai (☎ 826-9844; www.kayakkauai.com; Kuhio Hwy; ☽ 8am-5pm; rents the above, plus stoves day/week $6/24, foam sleeping pads $4/16) Stores gear and cars for $5/10 (day/week).

KAYAKING
Meandering up the Hanalei River and through the Hanalei National Wildlife Refuge makes a killer kayak trip. The lush riverfront is canopied by overhanging trees in places, and the 6-mile round-trip journey is way less congested than kayaking on the Wailua River. How far you'll be able to go depends on the water level in the river.

If you want to get hardcore, consider the 18-mile Na Pali Coast trip. This strenuous

---

SPAS & BODYWORK

Kaua'i has an abundance of resources for relaxing mind, body and spirit. From Pilates and raindrop therapy to kava-ginger wraps, you can indulge yourself at a variety of spas and fitness studios. Or choose a traditional *lomilomi* massage. *Lomilomi* can be traced to the ancient Polynesians. By increasing and improving the flow of energy, this type of massage aims to release tension and blocks within the body, but also the mind and spirit. *Lomilomi* is often a very personal, transforming experience. The practitioner takes a few moments to connect with the client's energy before administering long, continuous strokes with the hands and forearms – destined to instill a balance of energy. Breathing exercises and hula movements are often part of the masseur's repertoire, as this helps maintain a high level of energy between practitioner and client.

Other massages on offer are hot stone (warm river rocks are rolled and placed on various chakras, in between the toes, along the neck), Thai (intense stretching, pressuring and manipulating the body), tandem (where two masseurs massage you at once) and side-by-side couple massage. All the professionals listed are licensed massage therapists, who will come to your condo or hotel for an extra fee. Massages on the beach can also be arranged.

- **David Lee Monasevitch** (☎ 635-5965; david@hawaiilink.net; per hr $65) Swedish Esalen, deep tissue, Shiatsu, *lomilomi* and Thai massage.
- **Northshore Healing Massage** (Robert & Marisa Duggan; ☎ 651-4299, 651-7928; kauaihealers@aol.com) Specializing in couples and tandem massage.
- Eastside, in Anahola see **Trihealth Ayurveda** or **Moonbath Massage** (p468). **Touch of Spirit** is in Kapa'a (p465).
- On the South Shore, **Anara Spa** is in Po'ipu (p496).
- Westside, **Hart-Felt Massage** is in Waimea (p507).

For yoga and Pilates on the North Shore see p481, around the Eastside see p465, and for South Shore see p496.

paddle is only possible from May to September due to rough seas. Even in the summer calm, you should take motion-sickness preventatives the day before. The put-in is at Ha'ena (lots of dolphins and turtles), and the take-out at Polihale, where a van picks you up to return to Hanalei, meaning you circumnavigate Kaua'i in a day. When conditions are right, you'll enter several caves, including (if you're lucky), the Double Door Cave with freshwater cascade pouring through the cave roof. Guides love tips.

Kayak Kauai (☎ 826-9844; www.kayakkauai.com; Kuhio Hwy; rents single kayaks day/week $28/112, double kayaks $52/208; ☽ 8am-5pm) Hawaii's biggest outfitter. For the Hanalei River paddle, you put in right outside the shop. Tours include a Na Pali Coast thriller ($175), Blue Lagoon kayak and snorkel ($60), or open-ocean paddle on the South Shore (winter; $115). It also rents snorkel gear (day/week $8/20) if you want to get a closer look at all those sea turtles.

Na Pali Kayak (☎ 826-6900, 866-977-6900; www.kauaivacation.com/napali_kayak_tours.html; tour $175) The Na Pali Coast trip is the only tour these folks lead and their guides have over a decade of experience paddling these waters. A guaranteed adventure.

Pedal & Paddle (☎ 826-9069; www.pedalnpaddle.com; Ching Young Village; rents single kayaks day/week $15/60, double kayaks $35/140; ☽ 9am-6pm) Kayak rentals include all equipment and gear to secure it to your car. Check out the clear-bottomed kayaks ($45) for use at Hanalei or 'Anini. Snorkel sets are $5/20 (day/week), plus it rents boogie boards (day/week $5/20), beach chairs and umbrellas.

SURFING & WINDSURFING
Hanalei Bay swells are generally best in winter, but Hawaiian ocean weather is fickle, so you never know.

Hanalei Surf Company (Hanalei Center, 5-5161 Kuhio Hwy; surfboards day/week $15/65, boogie boards $5/20; ☽ 8am-9pm) An established outfit; fins are a couple of dollars more. Call the shop to set up surfing lessons. It also has economical snorkel sets.

Hawaiian Surfing Adventures (☎ 482-0749; www.hawaiiansurfingadventures.com; 2-hr lesson $75, board rentals day/week $20/100) Gives one-on-one lessons in Hanalei Bay; for two or more students the price drops to $55 per person.

Kayak Kauai (☎ 826-9844; www.kayakkauai.com; Kuhio Hwy; surfing lessons per hr $50, rents boogie/surfboards per day $6/20; ☽ 10am & 2pm) If you rent gear for four days, you get three more days free.

Windsurf Kauai (☎ 828-6838; windsurfkauai@aol.com; 2-hr lesson $60) Also gives winter lessons in Hanalei Bay and 'Anini (p473).

YOGA & PILATES
Yoga Hanalei (☎ 826-9646; upstairs, Hanalei Center; 1/3/5 90-minute classes $15/40/52) Different levels of Ashtanga and Bikram, including a silent Bikram class.

Mary Jane's Pilates in Paradise (☎ 826-0342; mjpilates@verizon.net; Ching Young Village, Hanalei; 1-hr group classes per hr $10-30) Kicking Pilates, gyrotonic and gyrokenisis classes, plus teacher training. Private classes are $60 to $70 per hour.

Sleeping
You can camp on Friday, Saturday and holidays with a permit from the county (p436).

Historic B&B (☎ 826-4622; www.historicbnb.com; 5-5067 Kuhio Hwy; r with shared bath incl breakfast $85, r incl breakfast $105) Quaint, serene, within walking distance of everything, this is the perfect place to stay in Hanalei. If you can actually get one of the rooms, that is. Housed in Kaua'i's oldest Buddhist temple (built in Lihu'e in 1901 and moved here in 1985), this little inn has three rooms with shoji sliding doors, decorated Japanese style. The cheaper rooms have queen beds, the third has a king bed. Choose between American- or Japanese-style breakfast. Guests have use of a refrigerator and microwave oven. Because sound travels easily here, small children are not allowed.

Bed, Breakfast & Beach (☎ 826-6111; www.bestofhawaii.com/hanalei; r incl breakfast $85-135) This contemporary three-story house is steps from the beach and has great views from the wraparound lanai. The three rooms here have fluffy linens, hardwood floors and shared living space; the $95 unit comes with private lanai. Alternatively, check out the modern rooms at their nearby Plantation Guest House ($130), all with private entrance, ocean view and shared lanai.

Hale Reed (☎ 415-459-1858; www.hanalei-vacation.com; 4441 Pilikoa St; 2-bedroom apt/3-bedroom house per week from $900/$1300) Very well-maintained and located place, with an immaculate garden apartment sleeping four with patio, good outdoor space and full kitchen. Upstairs three-bedroom unit (sleeps 10) has fantastic light, a great wraparound lanai and comfortable, roomy layout. Units can be rented separate or together (from $2500 a week).

Other options:

Ohana Hanalei (☎ 826-4116; www.hanalei-kauai.com; PO Box 720, Hanalei, HI 96714; studio $85, incl taxes) Quick beach access and bonuses, like cable TV, telephone and cooking facilities.

Dolphin Cottages (☎ 826-9622, ask for Jodi; Kuiho Hwy; cottages $1000 per week) Fully equipped cottages right on the river behind Dolphin Restaurant sleep four to six comfortably.

Hanalei Cottage & Hanalei House (☎ 338-1625, 800-992-7866; www.waimea-plantation.com; 1-bedroom cottage from $335 per night, 6-bedroom house from $700) Two sparkling, beautifully furnished oceanfront properties with paradisiacal tropical views and quality everything.

Eating
BUDGET

Hanalei Taro & Juice Company (⏱ 10:30am-5pm Mon-Sat) Permanently parked in a grassy lot at the entrance to town, it specializes in Hanalei-grown taro products. Vegetarian or turkey sandwiches on taro buns ($6) make a nice meal, and the taro mochi dessert (50¢) is a treat.

Wishing Well Shave Ice (shave ices small/large $2/2.50; ⏱ noon-5pm Tue-Sun) Van vendor makes refreshing shave-ice treats in tropical flavors and has $2 ice-cream scoops. There are a couple of picnic tables where you can eat.

Java Kai (☎ 826-6717; Hanalei Center; ⏱ 6:30am-6pm) Take your coffee and tempting pastries on the lanai at casual Java Kai.

Hanalei Wake Up Cafe (☎ 826-5551; cnr Kuhio Hwy & Aku Rd; breakfast $5-7; ⏱ 6-11:30am) Have a wholesome early breakfast (omelettes, pancakes, French toast, etc). Disregard the chilly service and skip the coffee.

Or grab something to go:

Big Save (☎ 826-6652; Ching Young Village; ⏱ 7am-9pm) The only supermarket west of Princeville, with the prices to show for it.

Bubba's (☎ 826-7839; Hanalei Center; burgers $3-5; ⏱ 10:30am-8pm) Local chain serving inexpensive dogs, burgers and fish sandwiches.

Hanalei Dolphin Fish Market (☎ 826-6113; 5-5016 Kuhio Hwy; ⏱ 10am-7pm) Gigantic 'ahi sushi rolls ($6), poke (per lb $11-14) and clam chowder (per pint $5) make a great picnic. Fresh fish, too (per lb $10-17).

Tropical Taco (☎ 827-8226; www.tropicaltaco.com; 5-5088 Kuhio Hwy; dishes $3-7; ⏱ 11am-5pm Mon-Sat) Big burritos (including the Fat Jack, a deep-fried version), soft or crispy tacos; bland beans are saved by hot sauce.

MID-RANGE & TOP END

Postcards Cafe (☎ 826-1191; www.postcardscafe.com; Kuhio Hwy; mains $16-22; ⏱ 6-9pm) Postcards' reputation for creative, healthy fare is rock solid. Sure, everyone cringes at the prices, but they also keep coming back for more of the signature, Asian-influenced local food. Start off with some porcini-encrusted scallops followed by tofu with roasted cashews in tamari ginger and you'll be converted, too. Though the menu is largely vegetarian, engaging fish mains, like fish with spicy pineapple-sage sauce (market price), are also offered.

Hanalei Gourmet (☎ 826-2524; www.hanaleigourmet.com; Hanalei Center; meals $14-23; ⏱ 8am-9:30pm) Jump into the mix at this energetic bar and restaurant serving well-prepared island-style food, like a ginger chicken sandwich with pineapple aioli, mac-nut fried chicken and daily fish specials, all served with soup or salad. Voluminous portions mean you might be taking some of that wicked Caesar salad home with you. Picnickers: check out the deli at the side.

Pizza Hanalei (☎ 826-9494; Ching Young Village; pizza from $12/17/23; ⏱ 11am-9pm) The pizzas are made with care and it shows. Choose from whole-wheat or white crust with any imaginable topping, from spinach and olive pesto to pepperoni or jalapeños. Meat lovers dig the leaden Lizzy Special with pepperoni, Canadian bacon and sausage. There's a loaded special for vegetarians, too. Mitigate the steep prices with a plain/pepperoni slice, or the lunchtime special with slice, salad and drink ($6).

Neide's Salsa Samba (☎ 826-1851; dishes $9-17; 5-5161 Kuhio Hwy; ⏱ lunch & dinner) Unique flavors and a quiet veranda are the main attractions at this little owner-run restaurant serving Mexican and Brazilian fare. In addition to the usual Mexican dishes, like huevos rancheros and burritos, you can gorge on traditional Brazilian offerings, such as panqueca, a veggie or chicken crepe stuffed with pumpkin. Neide also makes a fantastic passion-fruit margarita.

Hanalei Dolphin Restaurant (☎ 826-6113; 5-5016 Kuhio Hwy; mains $18-27; ⏱ 11am-9:30pm) Upscale, riverside restaurant drawing crowds from Princeville serves the likes of ginger chicken, veggie casseroles and loads of shrimp dishes. For atmosphere without the fuss or price tag, sidle up for some pupu (snacks) and chichi cocktails, served all day long.

Entertainment

Tahiti Nui (☎ 826-6277; Kuhio Hwy; ⏱ 11am-2am) What's not to love about this tropical bar with big people-watching lanai? Generous happy hours (4pm to 6pm Monday to Saturday, all day Sunday), mouth-watering *pupu* ($8 to $11), groovy live music (from 8pm) *and* you can smoke.

Sushi & Blues (☎ 826-9701; www.sushiandblues.com; Ching Young Village; ☼ 6pm-2am) You can hit the dance floor and enjoy rocking sushi, with live blues and jazz nightly.

Hawaiian Slack-Key Guitar Concerts (☎ 826-1469; Hanalei Community Center; adult/child $10/8; ☼ 4pm Fri & 3pm Sun) For local culture and tunes.

Getting Around

Pedal & Peddle (☎ 826-9069; www.pedalnpaddle .com; Ching Young Village; ☼ 9am-6pm) rents cruisers (day/week $10/40) and mountain bikes ($20/100), alternatively, you could try **Kayak Kauai** (☎ 826-9844; www.kayakkauai.com; Kuhio Hwy; ☼ 8am-5pm), also with cruisers ($15/60) and mountain bikes ($20/80).

If driving west, the last chance to fill your tank is at Princeville (p477).

AROUND HANALEI
Lumaha'i Beach

The gorgeous mile-long stretch of beach where Mitzi Gaynor promised to wash that man right out of her hair in the 1958 musical *South Pacific* is a broad white-sand beach with lush jungle growth on one side and tempestuous open ocean on the other. This is a good beach for exploring. Around some of the lava outcrops you can find green sand made of the mineral olivine.

There are two ways onto Lumaha'i. The first and more scenic is a three-minute walk that begins at the parking area 0.75 miles past the 4-mile marker. The trail slopes to the left at the end of the retaining wall (take the other steep trail from the 'no beach access sign' to reach a shoreline rock shelf perfect for a private picnic). Seek shelter from the wind at the lava point at the eastern end here. These rocks are popular for sunbathing and being photographed, but size it up carefully, as people have been washed away by high surf and rogue waves.

Lumaha'i has dangerous shore breaks – this is not a beach to turn your back on. It's particularly treacherous in winter, though there are strong currents year-round. Because of the numerous drownings that have occurred here over the years, Lumaha'i has been nicknamed Luma*die* by locals. Indeed, a touching memorial remembered two visitors killed by a rogue wave here just a month before research.

Back on the road, there are a couple of **lookouts** with views down onto Lumaha'i. The first is at the 5-mile marker, though the next one that pops up around the bend has a better angle.

The other access onto Lumaha'i Beach is along the road at sea level at the western end of the beach, just before crossing the Lumaha'i River Bridge. The beach at this end is lined with ironwood trees. Across the way is pastoral Lumaha'i Valley, all grazing horses and rainbows.

Wainiha

Ancient house sites, heiau sites and old taro patches reach deep into Wainiha Valley, a narrow valley with steep green walls. This valley is said to have been the last hideout of the *menehune*. In fact, as late as the mid-19th century, 65 people in the valley were officially listed as *menehune* on the government census!

A stellar place to stay is **River Estates** (☎ 826-5118, 800-399-8444; www.riverestate.com; 2/3-br house $175, extra person $25), a complex of three immaculate homes that can be rented together (sleeping up to 20) or separately. Everything is high-class here, the grounds are expansive, ensuring privacy and the romantic honeymoon cottage is on the river's edge.

The **Wainiha General Store** (☎ 826-6251; 5-6600 Hwy 560; ☼ 10:30am-7:30pm) is the last place to grab groceries and beer before the end of the road. Just past the store, **Auntie's Rentals** (☎ 826-5566; 5-6935 Hwy 560; 1-bedroom cottage day/week $125/750) has a couple of older plantation-style cottages across from a long stretch of pretty beach (rough waters, though). Big picture windows and lanai give you the most of the ocean or mountain views.

HA'ENA

Ha'ena has houses on stilts, little beachfront cottages, a few vacation homes, a YMCA camp, large caves, campsites and beautiful sandy beaches. It also has the only hotel beyond Hanalei. If you're looking for the classic vacation where you disconnect from worries of the modern age, this is perfect.

Sights & Activities
TUNNELS BEACH

Tunnels is a big horseshoe-shaped reef that has great diving and snorkeling when the water is calm, which is generally limited to the summer. There's a current as you head into deeper water. When conditions are right, you can start snorkeling near the east point and let the current carry you westward. It's more adventurous (and less crowded) than Ke'e Beach, and the coral is beautiful.

Approaching the parking area midway between the 8- and 9-mile markers, you'll notice trucks with board racks and surfboard lawn art. That's because this beach has a rad tubular winter surf break at the outer corner of the reef (hence the name Tunnels) that tempts both windsurfers and board surfers; dangerous rip currents that prevail from October to May make it suitable for experts only.

You can walk from Tunnels to Ha'ena Beach Park.

HA'ENA BEACH PARK
Ha'ena Beach is a beautiful curve of white sand, but take care from October to May when strong rip currents and shore breaks are the norm. To the right, you can see the horseshoe shape of Tunnels outlined by breaking waves. To the far left is **Cannons**, a particularly good wall dive, with crevices and lava tubes sheltering all sorts of marine life. You'll wonder how sea turtles can be endangered, there are so many coasting in these waters; playful dolphins visit early in the morning.

MANINIHOLO DRY CAVE
Three large sea caves – one dry, two wet – which were part of the coast thousands of years back, are on the inland side of the road between Ha'ena and Ke'e Beach. According to legend, the caves were created when the goddess Pele dug into the mountains looking for a place on Kaua'i's North Shore to call home.

Maniniholo Dry Cave, across from Ha'ena Beach Park, is a deep broad cave that you can walk into. Drippy and creepy, a constant seep of water from the cave walls keeps the interior damp and humid.

LIMAHULI GARDEN
Most of Limahuli is still lush, virgin forest. The National Tropical Botanical Garden, a nonprofit organization that preserves and propagates rare plants, owns 1000 acres of Limahuli Valley, including a towering waterfall.

Limahuli Garden (☎ 826-1053; www.ntbg.org; admission $15; 🕒 9:30am-4pm Tue-Fri & Sun) contains collections of Hawaiian ethnobotanical and medicinal plants and other endangered native species. There are also ancient stone terraces planted with taro. Endemic trees include the endangered *Kokio hauheleula*, which has a red hibiscus-like blossom. A 3.25-mile loop trail (self-guided) winds through the most interesting parts of the garden.

The garden is just before the stream that marks the boundary of Ha'ena State Park.

Sleeping
The county beach park has campsites, covered picnic tables, restrooms and showers. Many hikers from the Kalalau Trail camp here, using it as a base before starting the trail. It's a bit over a mile to the trailhead, and this is a safer place to park a car than the end of the road if you're going on to Kalalau. See p436 for camping permit information.

Hanalei Colony Resort (☎ 826-6235, 800-628-3004; www.hcr.com; Hwy 560; 1-/2-bedroom from $180/215; 🖳 😠 🖳) This low-rise condo complex is on Tunnels Beach just before the 8-mile marker and has the secluded feel befitting the only hotel for miles. Each unit has a full kitchen and lanai, but no TV, stereo or phone, enhancing the solitary feeling here. Though this isn't the fanciest complex on Kaua'i, the remote, rock-star location conveys a feeling of privilege. This makes a superb recuperation spot after hiking the Na Pali Coast – you'll be loving that Jacuzzi. For weekly stays, the seventh night is free.

Kauai YMCA-Camp Naue (☎ 826-6419; fax 246-4411; off Hwy 560; campsite & dm per person $12) Be kind to your budget and at these simple beachside bunkhouses, before the 8-mile marker, each with screened windows, cement floors and multiple bunks. No linens are provided. You can also pitch a tent. The camp is geared to groups but accepts individual travelers if there's room. There are showers, but the kitchen is reserved for large groups. Call ahead to see if there's room. The camp is a 10-minute walk from Tunnels Beach.

Eating & Drinking
Na Pali Art Gallery & Coffee House (☎ 826-1844; Hanalei Colony Resort; snacks $2-3; 🕒 7am-5pm) Whips up excellent coffee drinks, all hot or iced as you like. Browse nice Ni'ihau shell jewelry as you caffeinate.

Tunnels Bar & Grill (Hanalei Colony Resort; ⊙ 11am-sunset) A phenomenal beachside location – was readying to open at the time this book was being researched.

HA'ENA STATE PARK

Commonly called 'the beach at the end of the road,' Haena State Park's Ke'e Beach is a marvel. Framing the far side of the beach is the distinctive 1280ft cliff that marks the start of the Na Pali Coast. Almost everyone calls it Bali Hai, its name in the movie *South Pacific*. To the ancient Hawaiians it was known as Makana, meaning 'gift,' which sums it up perfectly. Come here for sunset and pull up a tree-root seat.

Sights & Activities
WET CAVES
Two wet caves are within the boundaries of Ha'ena State Park. The first, **Waikapala'e Wet Cave**, is just a few minutes' walk uphill from the main road along a rutted dirt drive opposite the visitor parking overflow area. The second, **Waikanaloa Wet Cave**, is right on the south side of the main road.

Both caves are deep, dark and dripping, with pools of very cold water. Divers sometimes explore them, but the caves can be dangerous, so only go with an experienced local diver.

KE'E BEACH
Snorkeling is good at Ke'e Beach, which has a variety of tropical fish. A reef protects the right side of the cove and, except on high surf days, it's usually calm. The left side is open and can have a powerful current, particularly in winter. When it's really calm – generally only in summer – snorkelers cross the reef to the open ocean where there's great visibility, big fish, large coral heads and the occasional sea turtle. It makes the inside of the bay look like kid stuff, but check it out carefully because breaking surf and strong currents can create dangerous conditions. We know more than one snorkeler who shredded herself here. When the tide's superlow, you walk far out on the reef without getting your feet wet and peer into tide pools.

There are several ways to behold the Na Pali Coast from here. One way is to walk the first 30 minutes of the Kalalau Trail (p486). Another is to take the short walk out around the point at the left side of the beach, toward the heiau. Or, simply walk down the beach to the right for a few minutes and look back as the cliffs unfold, one after the other.

Showers, drinking water, restrooms and a pay phone are tucked back in the woods behind the parking lot.

KAULU PAOA HEIAU
To make the five-minute walk through almond trees to Kaulu Paoa Heiau, take the path on the western side of the beach. Follow the stone wall as it curves uphill, and you'll reach the heiau almost immediately. The overgrown section at the foot of the hill is one of the more intact parts of the heiau, but keep walking up the terraces toward the cliff face. Surf pounding below, vertical cliffs above – what a spectacular place to worship the gods!

Beneath the cliff face, large stones retain a long flat grassy platform. A thatched-roof *halau* (a longhouse used as a hula school) once ran the entire length of the terrace. It was here that dances to Laka, the goddess of hula, were performed. In ancient Hawai'i this was Kaua'i's most sacred hula school, and students aspiring to learn hula came from all of the Hawaiian islands.

Fern wreaths, rocks wrapped in *ti* leaves, lei and other offerings to Laka are still placed in crevices in the cliff face. Under no circumstances should these be disturbed. This site is sacred to Hawaiians and should be treated with respect. Night hula dances are still performed here on special occasions.

LOHIAU'S HOUSE SITE
Difficult to find and even harder to envision, Lohiau's house site is just a minute's walk above the beach parking lot. At the Kalalau Trail sign, go left along the barely discernible dirt path to a vine-covered rock wall. This overgrown level terrace runs back 54ft to the bluff and is said to have been the home of Lohiau, a 16th-century prince.

Legend says that the volcano goddess Pele was napping one day under a *hala* tree on the Big Island when her spirit was awakened by the sound of distant drums. Her spirit rode the wind toward the sound, searching each island until she finally arrived at Ke'e Beach. Here above the heiau she found Lohiau beating a hula drum, surrounded by graceful hula dancers.

Pele took the form of a beautiful woman and captured Lohiau's heart. They became lovers and moved into this house. In time Pele had to go back home to the Big Island, leaving lovesick Lohiau behind. His longing quickly got the better of him, and he died on this site from grief.

NA PALI COAST STATE PARK

The Moreno Glacier in Argentina; lava sizzling the sea on the Big Island: Some natural wonders in this world are so beautiful they're hard to get your mind around. Na Pali, which in Hawaiian, means simply 'the cliffs,' is one of those places. These aren't Hawai'i's highest cliffs (those are in Moloka'i, p421), but they are the grandest.

Na Pali Coast State Park encompasses the rugged, corrugated 22-mile stretch between the end of the road at Ke'e Beach in the north and the road's opposite end at Polihale State Park in the west. It has the most sharply fluted coastal cliffs in Hawaii.

History

Kalalau, Honopu, Awa'awapuhi, Nu'alolo and Miloli'i are the five major valleys on the Na Pali Coast. Since the first waves of Tahitian settlers, these deep river valleys contained sizable settlements. When winter seas prevented canoes from landing on the northern shore, trails down precipitous ridges and rope ladders provided access.

In the mid-19th century missionaries established a school in Kalalau, the largest valley, and registered the valley population

at about 200. Influenced by Western ways, people gradually began moving to towns, and by century's end the valleys were largely abandoned.

The Na Pali valleys, with limited accessibility, fresh water and abundant fertility, have long been a natural refuge for people wanting to escape one scene or another, like modern-day 'Kalalau outlaws,' who drop out back here.

Sights & Activities

Hiking the 11-mile Kalalau coastal trail into Hanakapi'ai, Hanakoa and Kalalau Valleys is a backpacking adventure rated among the world's most beautiful.

You can access valleys beyond Kalalau while kayaking (p480 and p495) the Na Pali Coast. A couple of strenuous hikes in Koke's State Park, on the opposite side of the island, go to cliff-tops with gorgeous views into Awa'awapuhi and Nualolo Valleys (p513) for a different take on the Na Pali Coast.

KALALAU TRAIL

Kalalau is Hawaii's premier trail. Here, it's common to meet hikers who have trekked in Nepal or climbed to Machu Picchu. The Na Pali Coast is similarly spectacular, a place of singular beauty.

The Kalalau Trail is basically the same ancient route used by the Hawaiians who once lived in these remote north-coast valleys. The trail runs along high sea cliffs, and winds up and down across lush valleys before it finally ends below the steep fluted

---

SWEAT-FREE NA PALI COAST

Let's face it: not everyone is a triathlete or conditioned trekker. If the knees or biceps aren't what they used to be, or vacation time is short, you can still enjoy the grandeur of this place. Whatever the reason, don't miss seeing the Na Pali Coast, even if it means you can't hike or kayak through the unique landscape.

Here are some ideas:

- Walk a few minutes west on **Ke'e Beach** (p485), scurrying over rocks for a better view. Highly recommended in early-morning light.
- Cruise up to the **Kalalau Lookout** and the **Pu'u o Kila Lookout** in Koke'e State Park (p512).
- Take a **helicopter tour** (p442).
- Take a **catamaran** or **raft tour** from Port Allen (p502) or Waimea (p507). The bonus here is snorkeling in the rich waters north of Polihale State Park. Consider leaving from Waimea for shorter travel times.
- Buy the **screen saver**. They're sold everywhere!

pali of Kalalau. The scenery is breathtaking, with sheer green cliffs dropping into brilliant turquoise waters.

Orientation & Information

The state parks office in Lihu'e can provide a basic Kalalau Trail brochure with a map. Information is also posted at the Ke'e Beach trailhead.

The hike itself can be divided into three parts:

Ke'e Beach–Hanakapi'ai Valley (2 miles)
Hanakapi'ai Valley–Hanakoa Valley (4 miles)
Hanakoa Valley–Kalalau Valley (5 miles)

The first 2 miles of the trail to Hanakapi'ai Valley are insanely popular: 500,000 people hike it annually, and it shows in the eroded trail edges, muddy passages with ankle-deep puddles and, in summer especially, boisterous children. No permit is required for this hike to Hanakapi'ai Valley. See p455 for how to get more solitude here.

Hardy hikers in good shape can walk the 11-mile trail straight through in about seven hours. Until the Hanakoa Valley campground reopens, however, it's not possible to (legally) break the trip beyond Hanakapi'ai. In winter there are generally only a few people at any one time hiking all the way in to Kalalau Valley, but foot traffic is thick in summer. Weekends are busiest.

Even if you're not planning to camp, a permit is officially required to continue on the Kalalau Trail beyond Hanakapi'ai. Free day-use hiking permits are available from the **Division of State Parks** (p435), which also issues the required camping permits for Hanakapi'ai and Kalalau valleys. Camping along the entire Kalalau Trail is limited to five nights total. For more details on permits and the need to reserve them in advance, see p435.

An attractive way to combine kayaking and hiking the coast: Kayak Kauai and Na Pali Kayak (p480) will paddle with you and your gear to Kalalau campground (you supply the permit), for around $125 per person. Local guys will hike in your gear for around $80, allowing you to nimbly make your way to Kalalau; ask around in Hanalei.

Ke'e Beach to Hanakapi'ai Valley

The 2-mile trail from Ke'e Beach to Hanakapi'ai Valley is a delightfully scenic hike. Morning is a good time to go west, and the afternoon to go east, as you have the sun at your back and good light for photography. The trail weaves through *kukui* and *'ohi'a* trees and then back out to clearings with fine coastal views. There are orchids, wildflowers and a couple of Zen-like waterfalls en route. The black nuts embedded in the clay are *kukui* (candlenuts), polished smooth by the scuffing of innumerable hiking shoes.

Just 0.25 miles up the trail, you catch a fine view of Ke'e Beach and the surrounding reef. After 30 minutes, you come to a finger of cliff with your first view of the Na Pali Coast on one side and Ke'e Beach on the other. Even if you weren't planning on a hike, it's well worth coming this far.

WARNING

The Kalalau Trail is a hike into rugged wilderness and hikers should be well prepared. In places, the trail runs along steep cliffs that can narrow to little more than a foot in width, which some people find unnerving. However, hikers accustomed to high-country trails don't consider it unduly hazardous. Like other Hawaiian trails, the route can be muddy and slippery if it's been raining – look for walking sticks at the trailhead.

Accidents happen. Most casualties along the Kalalau Trail are the result of people fording swollen streams, walking after dark on cliff-edge trails, or swimming in treacherous surf. Keep in mind that the cliffs are composed of loose and crumbly rocks; don't try to climb the cliffs, and don't camp directly beneath them, as goats commonly dislodge stones that can tumble down on top of you. Still, for someone who's cautious and aware, this can be a hike into paradise.

There's no shortage of water sources along the trail, but all drinking water must be boiled or treated. Bring what you need, but travel light. You don't want extra weight shifting on stream crossings or along cliff edges. Pack out what you pack in. Garbage and jettisoned weight from departing campers is a serious problem at Kalalau, and it cannot be overstated: take your detritus with you. Shoes should have good traction. If you bring a sleeping bag, make it a light one.

Hanakapi'ai has a sandy beach in the summer, but it's sometimes not accessible across a flooded river. In winter the sand washes out, and it becomes a beach of boulders, some of them sparkling with tiny olivine crystals. The western side of the beach has a small cave with dripping water and a miniature fern grotto.

The ocean is dangerous here, with unpredictable rip currents year-round. It's particularly treacherous during winter high-surf conditions, but summer trades also bring very powerful currents. Hanakapi'ai Beach is matched only by Lumahai for the number of drownings on Kaua'i. A sign at the time of research put the number of Hanakapi'ai deaths at 82.

If you're just doing a day hike and want to walk further, it makes more sense to head up the valley to Hanakapi'ai Falls than it does to continue another couple of miles on the coastal trail.

Hanakapi'ai Valley to Hanakoa Valley

A 10-minute walk up the Kalalau Trail from Hanakapi'ai Valley on the way to Hanakoa Valley, there's a nice view of Hanakapi'ai Beach. From there the trail goes into bush, and the next coastal view is not for another mile. This is the least scenic part of the trail.

Craggy cliffs begin to tower overhead following some well-cut, but hot and exposed switchbacks that climb 800ft in elevation. Here the trail traverses rocks where rivulets of water tumble over the cliff face into a pool. The trail keeps climbing past the 3-mile marker; this final section of the switchbacks over rocks and mud can be fairly brutal, and the grade is steep. Soon the trail reaches its highest point at Space Rock, a prominent boulder overlooking the coast.

Winding from waterfall gulch to ridge and back again, the trail then passes through several mini valleys within the greater Ho'olulu Valley, finally reaching Waiahuakua Valley. Old Hawaiian stone terraces announce the trail's entrance into Hanakoa Valley, passing a helipad and hunting shack.

Hanakoa Valley to Kalalau Valley

This is the most difficult part of the trail, although without question the most beautiful. Make sure you have at least three hours of daylight left.

About a mile out of Hanakoa Valley, you'll reach the coast again and begin to get fantastic views of Na Pali's jagged edges. There are some very narrow and steep stretches along this section of the trail, so

---

DETOUR: HANAKAPI'AI FALLS

The 2-mile hike from Hanakapi'ai Beach to Hanakapi'ai Falls – a side trip off the Kalalau Trail – takes about 2½ hours return. Because of some tricky rock crossings, this trail is rougher than the walk from Ke'e Beach to Hanakapi'ai Beach. Due to the possibility of flash floods in the narrow valley, the Hanakapi'ai Falls hike should only be done in fair weather.

The trail itself is periodically washed out by floodwaters, and sections occasionally get redrawn, but the path is not that difficult to follow, as it basically goes up the side of Hanakapi'ai Stream. The trail is not well maintained, and in places you may have to scramble over and around tree trunks and branches.

There are trails on both sides of the stream, but the main route heads up the stream's western side. About 50yd up, there are old stone walls and guava trees. Big old mango trees along the way might have fruit for the picking. Ten minutes' walk from the trailhead, you'll find thickets of green bamboo interspersed with eucalyptus. Also along the trail is the site of an old coffee mill, though all that remains is a little of the chimney.

The first of five stream crossings is about 25 minutes' walk up, at a sign that warns: 'Hazardous. Keep away from stream during heavy rainfall. Stream floods suddenly.' Be particularly careful of your footing on the rocky upper part of the trail. Some of the rocks are covered with a barely visible film of slick algae – it's like walking on ice.

Hanakapi'ai Falls is spectacular, with a wide pool gentle enough for swimming. Directly under the falls, the cascading water forces you back from the rock face – a warning from nature, as rocks can fall from the top. This is a very peaceful place to spend a little time meditating. It's a beautiful lush valley, though it's not terribly sunny near the falls because of the incredible steepness.

be cautious of your footing. A little past the halfway mark, you'll get your first view into Kalalau Valley.

The large valley has a beach, a little waterfall, a *heiau* site, some ancient house sites and some interesting caves that are sometimes dry enough to sleep in during the summer. The scene here is very communal, with drum circles and new friends sharing campfire stories par for the course.

An easy 2-mile trail leads back into the valley to a pool in Kalalau Stream where there's a natural water slide. Valley terraces where Hawaiians cultivated taro until 1920 are now largely overgrown with bitter Java plum, and edible guava and passion fruit. Feral goats scurry up and down the crumbly cliffs and drink from the stream.

Kalalau Valley has fruit trees, including mango, papaya, orange, banana, coconut, guava and mountain apple. During the 1960s and '70s people wanting to get away from it all tried to settle in Kalalau, but forestry rangers eventually routed them out. Rangers still swoop in by helicopter every six months or so to check camping permits; those caught without permits are forced to hike back out immediately.

Getting There & Away

There's space for parking at Ke'e Beach at the trailhead. Unfortunately, break-ins to cars left overnight here are all too common. Some people advise leaving cars empty and unlocked to prevent smashed windows. It's generally safer to park at the campground at Ha'ena Beach Park. Whatever you do, don't leave valuables in a locked car.

You could store everything in Hanalei or Wainiha and take a taxi to the trailhead. Kayak Kauai (p480) stores gear and cars. **North Shore Cab** (☎ 826-4118) charges about $20 for a taxi from Hanalei to Ke'e Beach. En route to Ha'ena from Hanalei, Wainiha General Store (p483) stores bags for $3 a day.

SOUTH SHORE

'Sunny Po'ipu' is Kaua'i's main beach resort area and the slogan isn't just propaganda: dark storm clouds can be dumping rain in Kapa'a, but invariably, the sun will be shining in Po'ipu (which is tricky because *po'ipu* means 'completely overcast' in Hawaiian).

For most of the year, including winter, there are calm waters good for swimming and snorkeling. During summer the surfers roll in with the swells.

To get to Po'ipu and Koloa from Lihu'e, take Hwy 50 (Kaumuali'i Hwy) and turn off onto Hwy 520 (Maluhia Rd). Immediately after turning down Maluhia Rd, you enter the fairy-tale **Tree Tunnel**, a mile-long stretch of road canopied by swamp mahogany trees, a type of eucalyptus. When the 900 trees were planted in 1911, the tunnel was more than double its current length, but most of the tunnel was lopped off when Hwy 50 was rerouted.

The cinder hill to the right about 2 miles down Maluhia Rd is Pu'u o Hewa. From its top, the ancient Hawaiians raced wooden *holua* (sleds) down paths covered with oiled *pili* grass. To add even more excitement to this popular spectator sport, the Hawaiians crossed two sled paths near the middle of the hill. The paths were approximately 5ft wide; the eagle-eyed might be able to see the 'X' on the hillside where they crossed. Hewa means 'wrong' or 'mistake.' The hill's original name was lost when a surveyor jotted 'Puu o Hewa' (Wrong Hill) on a map he was making.

KOLOA
pop 1942

The village of Koloa, 3 miles inland from Po'ipu, was the site of Hawaii's first sugar plantation. These days this sleepy town is largely a retail diversion for the Po'ipu resort hordes, although an effort is underway to promote Koloa's historical essence; look for 'Koloa Heritage Trail' maps in brochure racks around here. Most travelers just blow through Koloa en route to Poi'pu, but lunch options are better here.

Koloa was once a thriving plantation village and commercial center until it largely went bust after WWII. While its history is sugar, its present is tourism. Today, with its aging wooden buildings and false storefronts, Koloa has the appearance of an Old West town. The former fish markets, barber shops, bathhouses and beer halls have become boutiques, galleries and restaurants.

History

Hawaii's first sugar plantation was started in Koloa in 1835, but the raw materials had arrived long before; sugarcane came with the original Polynesian settlers, and the earliest Chinese immigrants brought small-scale refinery know-how. However, large-scale production did not begin until William Hooper, an enterprising 24-year-old Bostonian, arrived in Kaua'i in 1835 and made inroads with the *ali'i* (local chiefs).

With financial backing from Honolulu businesspeople, he leased land in Koloa from the king and paid the *ali'i* a stipend to release commoners from their traditional work obligations. He then hired Hawaiians as wage laborers, and Koloa became Hawaii's first plantation town. In 1888 workers were typically given a three- to five-year contract in which they had to work 10 (field hands) or 12 hours (factory workers) a day, six days a week. The wage? Nine dollars a month.

Orientation & Information

Koloa Rd (Hwy 530), which runs between Lawa'i and Koloa, is the best way to leave Koloa if you're heading west – it's a pleasant rural drive through pastures and cane fields. Hapa Rd, off Weliweli Rd, connects Koloa and Po'ipu and makes a great bike ride (for rentals, see p498).

First Hawaiian Bank (☎ 742-1642; 3506 Waikomo Rd) At the east end of town.

Koloa Country Store & Cafe (☎ 742-1255; 5356 Koloa Rd; per hr $10; ☽ 8am-8pm Mon-Sat, 9am-5pm Sun) Has Internet access and all kinds of java drinks.

Post office (☎ 800-275-8777; 5485 Koloa Rd) Serves both Koloa and Po'ipu.

Sights

OLD KOLOA HISTORIC BUILDINGS

Until recently the building that houses **Crazy Shirts** (☎ 742-7161; ☽ 10am-9pm) was the Yamamoto General Store. Check out the huge monkey-pod tree planted by Mr Yamamoto in 1925 alongside. Before the theater across the street burned down, moviegoers would line up at Yamamoto's for crack seed (a local snack) and soft drinks. A couple of wooden sculptures by the late Maui artist Reems Mitchell sit on the sidewalk in front of the store. In the courtyard behind, you'll find the site of the former town hotel, along with a little **historical display** that includes a Japanese bath and some period photos.

At the east side of town is the **Koloa Jodo Mission** (☎ 742-6735; 2480 Waikomo Rd), which dates back to 1910. The Buddhist temple on the left is the original, while next to it is a newer and larger temple where services are now held. During services, the smell of incense and the sound of beating drums fills the air. Obon (Japanese Festival of the Dead) dances are held here each June.

St Raphael's Catholic Church, Kaua'i's oldest Catholic church, is the burial site of some of Hawaii's first Portuguese immigrants. The original church, built in 1854, was made of lava rock and coral mortar with walls 3ft thick – a type of construction that can be seen in the ruins of the adjacent rectory. When the church was enlarged in 1936, it was plastered over, and it now has a more typical whitewashed appearance. To get

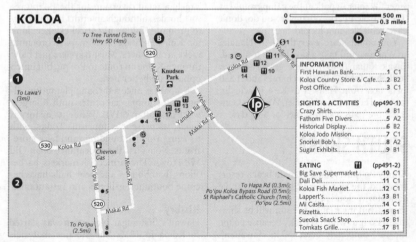

KOLOA

0 ———— 500 m
0 ———— 0.3 miles

To Tree Tunnel (3mi);
Hwy 50 (4mi)

To Lawa'i
(3mi)

Knudsen Park

Malihia Rd

Weliweli Rd

Yamada Rd

Makai Rd

Koloa Rd

Koloa Rd (530)

Chevron Gas

Po'ipu Rd

Mission Rd

Makai Rd (520)

To Po'ipu
(2.5mi)

To Hapa Rd (0.3mi);
Po'ipu Koloa Bypass Road (0.5mi);
St Raphael's Catholic Church (1mi);
Po'ipu (2.5mi)

Waikomo Rd

Ohuohu St

INFORMATION
First Hawaiian Bank................1 C1
Koloa Country Store & Cafe......2 B2
Post Office................3 C1

SIGHTS & ACTIVITIES (pp490-1)
Crazy Shirts................4 B1
Fathom Five Divers................5 A2
Historical Display................6 B2
Koloa Jodo Mission................7 C1
Snorkel Bob's................8 A2
Sugar Exhibits................9 B1

EATING 🍴 (pp491-2)
Big Save Supermarket................10 C1
Dali Deli................11 C1
Koloa Fish Market................12 C1
Lappert's................13 B1
Mi Casita................14 C1
Pizzetta................15 B1
Sueoka Snack Shop................16 B1
Tomkats Grille................17 B1

there from Koloa Rd, turn onto Weliweli Rd, then right onto Hapa Rd and proceed 0.5 miles to the church.

SUGAR EXHIBITS

Any sugarologists in the crowd? This **field**, on Koloa Rd opposite Sueoka Store, is for you. In a tiny, clumped garden, you'll find a dozen varieties of sugarcane all twisted together and labeled with faded interpretive markers. The stone smokestack in another corner of the field is a relic from one of Koloa's early mills and dates back to 1841.

In the center of the field, the principal ethnic groups that worked the plantations are immortalized in a **sculpture**. The Hawaiian wears a *malo* (loincloth) and has a poi dog by his side. The Chinese, Korean, Japanese, Portuguese, Filipino and Puerto Rican groups are likewise in indigenous field dress. You may notice that the plaque on the wall curiously makes reference to a haole (Caucasian) overseer – present-day islanders found the depiction of this Caucasian plantation boss seated on a high horse so unacceptable that he was actually omitted from the sculpture at the 11th hour.

Activities

A handful of outfitters is based in Koloa. Some are notable, such as **Fathom Five Divers** (☎ 742-6991, 800-972-3078; www.fathomfive.com; 3450 Poipu Rd), a five-star PADI dive operation. For snorkel gear, there's **Snorkel Bob's** (☎ 742-2206; www.snorkelbob.com; 3236 Poipu Rd), which also rents boogie boards (day/week $6.50/26).

Free municipal **tennis courts** are found in Knudsen Park.

Eating

The following places to eat are strung along Koloa Rd (Hwy 530) near its intersection with Maluhia Rd (Hwy 520).

Sueoka Snack Shop (☎ 742-1112; 5392 Koloa Rd; snacks $1.50-4.50, plate lunch $4; ⏲ 9am-3pm) Jump in line at this take-out window at the side of the Sueoka Store (open 7am to 9pm) for sandwiches and saimin; skip the burgers. Good

---

SUNSHINE MARKETS

For island-grown fruits and vegetables, many organic, that are fresher than grocery store produce, catch a farmers market, known locally as Sunshine Markets. From passion fruit to edible flowers and herbs, shopping these markets is a sense sensation. Arrive early because once the whistle blows people rush in, scooping things up quickly. Depending on the location, it can all wrap up within an hour or so.

Monday

- noon at Knudsen Park, Maluhia Rd, Koloa (Map p490)
- 3pm at Kukui Grove Center, Hwy 50, Lihu'e (Map p443)

Tuesday

- 2pm at Hwy 560, on the western outskirts of Hanalei (Map p479)
- 3:30pm at Kalaheo Neighborhood Center, Papalina Rd, Kalaheo (p436)

Wednesday

- 3pm at Kapa'a New Park, Olohena Rd, Kapa'a

Thursday

- 3:30pm at Hanapepe Town Park, behind the fire station
- 4:30pm at Kilauea Neighborhood Center, Keneke St, Kilauea

Friday

- 3pm at Vidinha Stadium, Hwy 51, Lihu'e (Map p443)

Saturday

- 9am at Kekaha Neighborhood Center, Elepaio Rd, Kekaha
- 9am at Christ Memorial Episcopal Church, Kolo Rd, Kilauea (p470)

plate lunches include a tasty mahimahi plate. Too bad there's nowhere to eat it, though.

Pizzetta (☎ 742-8881; 5408 Koloa Rd; pizza $9-19, mains $10-17; ☒ 11am-10pm) This buzzing pizzeria is the most happening place (in one of the oldest buildings) in town. Thin-crust gourmet pizza, like fire-roasted vegetables with feta cheese, are novel, or try a tarragon-chicken *panini* ($7) during lunch or eggplant lasagna during dinner. There's a children's menu, happy hour (3pm to 5:30pm) and pizza by the slice ($3 to $4, until 6pm). Folks in Po'ipu dig their free delivery service (orders over $20 from 5pm).

Mi Casita (☎ 742-2323; 5470 Koloa Rd; appetizers $6-9.50, meals $5.50-12; ☒ 11am-9pm Mon-Sat, 4:30-9pm Sun) For filling, home-style Mexican fare, this bright little family-run restaurant is great. Meals include rice and beans, plus tacos, *chili rellenos* (stuffed green peppers) or enchiladas. Roll away from the table after a *quesadilla suiza*, tortillas stuffed with chicken and cheese smothered in cream sauce ($12). A fat, tasty chicken burrito is only $6.

Tomkats Grille (☎ 742-8887; 5396 Koloa Rd; plate lunch $10-13, dinner $15-19; ☒ 7am-midnight) Lunch crowds dig into mounds of beer battered, deep-fried mahimahi at this popular hangout. Burgers and grilled sandwiches, like teriyaki chicken come with fries. Dinner means catch of the day or steaks, mostly. The happy hour (3pm to 6pm), with $2 beers and $4 margaritas, is a big hit. All food can be ordered for take-out.

Lappert's (☎ 742-1272; ☒ 11am-10pm) For ice cream.

Just up the road:

Koloa Fish Market (☎ 742-6199; 5482 Koloa Rd; lunch $4-7; ☒ 10am-6pm Mon-Fri, to 5pm Sat) Bento boxes, sushi, plate lunch and fresh fish.

Dali Deli (☎ 742-8824; 5490 Koloa Rd; snacks $3-7; ☒ 8am-3pm Mon-Fri) A friendly place, with coffee, bagels, quiche, soup and salads.

Big Save Supermarket (cnr Waikomo Rd & Koloa Rd; ☒ 6am-11pm) Koloa's only grocery store.

PO'IPU
pop 1075
Poi'pu, about 3 miles south of Koloa down Po'ipu Rd, is Kaua'i's largest collection of hotels and condos fronted by undulating golden-sand beaches. There are vacation rentals and cottages, too. Po'ipu is fabulous for a day at the beach, but not much else; its most popular attraction is the **Spouting Horn blowhole** (see below).

Orientation
There's no town, so reaching other sights means driving. If you want to skip Koloa en route to Po'ipu, take the Po'ipu–Koloa Bypass Rd (Ala Kin'oike Hwy) off Hwy 520.

Sights
PRINCE KUHIO PARK
This park is about 0.5 miles down Lawa'i Rd, across from Ho'ai Bay. Here you'll find **Ho'ai Heiau** and a **monument** honoring Prince Jonah Kuhio Kalaniana'ole, born nearby in 1871 and the Territory of Hawaii's first delegate to the US Congress. It was Prince Kuhio who spearheaded the Hawaiian Homes Commission Act, which set aside 200,000 acres of land for indigenous Hawaiians, many of whom are still waiting for it. You'll also find the remains of a fishpond and an ancient Hawaiian house platform.

BABY BEACH
A protected swimming area just deep enough for children is off Hoona Rd, east of Prince Kuhio Park. Look for the beach access post that marks the pathway between the road and the beach. For big kids, deeper water with fewer rocks is a short stroll west down this narrow beach.

LAWA'I BEACH
This beach (also called Beach House) opposite Lawa'i Beach Resort is rich snorkel turf, especially during winter. It's a little rocky with just a roadside strip of sand, but the water is usually quite clear and there's an abundance of tropical fish, including orange-shouldered tangs, rainbow parrotfish, raccoon butterfly fish and white-spotted puffer fish. When the surf's up in summer, the snorkelers share the beach with surfers. Across from the beach are restrooms, a shower and public parking. Oh! And another groovy pedestrian crossing sign, too.

SPOUTING HORN BEACH PARK
A geyser of water suddenly shoots 25ft into the air with a basso whooshing sound like a whale breathing. Or there's a ho-hum spurt of water watched by a swarm of bored tourists. How much water surges through Spouting Horn all depends on the waves, tides

and overall force of the sea rushing into the lava tube. Nevertheless, it's still popular.

Coming during high tide gives you more chance of seeing impressive aquatic displays here, which can reach 30ft when the surf is truly up. You can avoid the tour-bus crowd by arriving in the late afternoon, which is also the best time to see rainbows dancing in the spray. To get here, turn right off Po'ipu Rd onto Lawa'i Rd, just past Po'ipu Plaza, and continue for 1.75 miles.

NATIONAL TROPICAL BOTANICAL GARDEN
The sound of rustling palms and crashing waves ride on gardenia scented winds at the **National Tropical Botanical Garden** (NTBG; ☎ 742-2623; www.ntbg.org; 4425 Lawa'i Rd; admission free; ⏱ 8:30am-5pm), opposite Spouting Horn Beach Park. With a mission of propagating tropical and endangered plant species and researching ethnobotanical and medicinal plants, this exuberant garden is worth a look, even if plants aren't your thing. Ten acres surrounding the **visitors center** are lush with multihued hibiscus blossoms, sprays of orchids, *ti* plants, topiaries and palms, and

are free for the wandering. Benches tucked away here and there foster stolen kisses. The **gift shop** sells exquisite feather jewelry.

The NTBG owns much of the remote Lawa'i Valley east of the Spouting Horn area, including the **Allerton Garden**, started in the 1870s by Queen Emma, who built a summer getaway cottage there. Chicago industrialist Robert Allerton bought the property in the late 1930s and significantly expanded the decorative gardens in the 100-acre, seaside estate. Visits to Allerton Garden are only by **guided tour** (2½-hr tour $30; ⏱ 9am, 10am, 1pm & 2pm Mon-Sat). Reservations are required; meet at the visitors center. This tour is also available in Japanese.

The NTBG's **McBryde Garden**, in the upper part of the valley, can be visited on a self-guided tour ($15). No reservations are required, you just hop on a **tram** (⏱ every 30 min, 9:30am-2:30pm Mon-Sat, returning on the hr 10am-4pm) from the visitors center to the valley.

KOLOA LANDING
Koloa Landing, at the mouth of Waikomo Stream, was once Kaua'i's largest **port**. Sugar

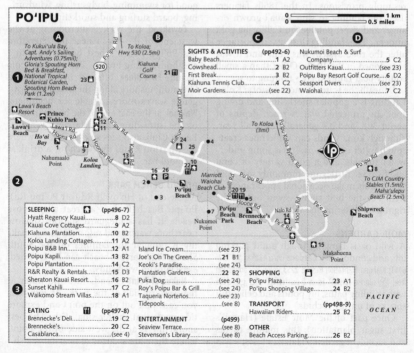

HURRICANE INIKI

From Allende's Chile to the World Trade Center, September 11, 2001 is a bad day in history. So it was for Kaua'i, in 1992 when Hurricane Iniki made a direct hit on the island. The most powerful storm to hit the state in a century, Iniki blew in with gusts of 165 miles an hour, felling trees by the thousands and damaging an estimated 50% of buildings on Kaua'i. Thirty-foot waves washed away entire wings of beachfront hotels and 1300 homes were totally destroyed – Po'ipu and Princeville were particularly hard hit.

Miraculously, only two people died, but the total value of the damage to the island was $1.6 billion. The tourist industry took awhile to bounce back, but is again thriving. What isn't are a couple of Kaua'i's native bird species, which have not been spotted since Iniki.

grown on Koloa Plantation was shipped from here, and whalers called at Koloa Landing to resupply provisions. In the 1850s farmers used the landing to ship Kaua'i-grown oranges and sweet potatoes to California gold miners. The landing lost its importance after the road system was built, and it was abandoned in the 1920s. Other than a small county boat ramp, there's nothing to see.

Beneath the water is another story; Koloa Landing is a popular snorkeling and diving spot. Its protected waters reach depths of about 30ft, and it's generally calm all year, although kona winds can sometimes create rough water conditions. It has some underwater tunnels, and a good variety of coral and fish. Sea turtles are commonly seen, and monk seals make occasional appearances as well. For the best sights, swim out to the right after entering the water.

MOIR GARDENS

A wild oasis hanging tough amid parking lots and condos, **Moir Gardens** (Pa'u A Laka; ☎ 742-6411; Kiahuna Plantation Resort, 2253 Poipu Rd; admission free; ☾ sunrise-sunset) is a beautiful old garden with winding paths, lily ponds and delightful shocks of unruly orchids.

Once part of the Moir Estate (Hawaii's first sugar plantation), this mature cactus and succulent garden – Hawaii's finest – was

preserved in its entirety, with the Kiahuna Plantation Resort built around its perimeter. The old lava-stone plantation house, which fronts the gardens, is also here. The plantation house, now Plantation Gardens restaurant (p498), was a wedding gift to Hector and Alexandra Knudsen Moir in 1933.

The Moirs were avid, in-tune gardeners who switched to drought-tolerant plants before it was fashionable. In 1948 the Brooklyn Botanical Garden ranked Moir Gardens one of the 10 best cactus-and-succulent gardens in the world, in the same league as the Royal Gardens of Monaco. The amazing variety of exotic textures and colors makes it a serene place to stroll, even though you never lose sight of the condos or the sound of humming vacuum cleaners.

PO'IPU (SHERATON) BEACH

The long ribbon of golden sand running from the Sheraton Kauai Resort east to Po'ipu Beach Park is known simply as Po'ipu or Sheraton Beach. It's actually three attractive crescent beaches separated by narrow rocky points. The turquoise waters are good for swimming, bodysurfing, windsurfing, board surfing and snorkeling.

Cowshead, the rocky outcropping at the west end of the beach near the Sheraton, has Po'ipu Beach's best boogie-boarding and bodysurfing breaks. Top surfing spots include **First Break**, offshore in front of the Sheraton; inshore along the beach are slow, gentle waves more suitable for beginners. **Waiohai**, at the east end of the beach in front of the sprawling new Marriott Waiohai Beach Club, also sees swells. Detour where the Marriott kisses the beach for a drink at the pool bar.

PO'IPU BEACH PARK

At the end of Ho'owili Rd (off Po'ipu Rd), Po'ipu Beach Park is a great all-purpose beach. It has a lifeguard station, shallow nearshore waters and safe swimming, making it popular for families on the South Shore. This narrow beach can be crowded, especially on weekends.

Nukumoi Point extends into the water at the western side of the park. At low tide, you can walk out on the point and explore tide pools that shelter small fish. The best snorkeling is at the west side of the point, where there are swarms of near-tame fish.

Beach facilities include restrooms, showers and picnic tables, and there's a cool playground for kids. Beach toys can be rented across the street at Nukumoi Beach & Surf Company (p495).

BRENNECKE'S BEACH

This beach with a good shore break is the top spot for bodysurfing and boogie boarding. However, it breaks really close to shore, making it dangerous for novices. While it's best when surf is highest, which is generally in summer, there's some respectable action in winter as well. Beware of strong rips that are present with high surf. The beach is only a small pocket of sand and the waters can get crowded. For safety reasons, fins are not allowed and surfboards are prohibited.

SHIPWRECK BEACH

Shipwreck Beach, the pleasant golden-sand beach fronting the Hyatt Regency Kauai, also has ace bodysurfing and boogie boarding. A couple of challenging nearshore surf breaks attract local board surfers as well. The water conditions here are for the experienced, and the pounding shore-break and high surf make for dangerous swimming.

MAHA'ULEPU BEACH

This **beach** (🕑 7:30am-6pm, to 7pm summer), just a couple of miles beyond Shipwreck Beach, has lovely white sands, sheltered coves, tide pools, petrified sand dunes and sea cliffs. At various times of the year Maha'ulepu is good for surfing, windsurfing, boogie boarding and snorkeling. Hiking and exploring here is enticing whenever. Come before bulldozers arrive to clear the way for future resorts.

Before Westerners ever showed up, this area was heavily settled, and many important historic sites lie buried beneath the cane fields and shifting sands. Along the beach, people still claim to see ghost marchers coming in from the sea at night.

The property is owned by Grove Farm and access hours are strictly enforced. The 'road' is rough and deeply rutted. To get there, drive past the Hyatt Regency Kauai and continue on the cane road for 1.5 miles and turn right where it dead-ends at a gate. Continue past the gravel plant, and after 585yd you'll come to a gatehouse; from there it's 0.5 miles to the beach parking area. Two short trails to the beach begin at the parking area and lead to a popular windsurfing spot and a good place from which to explore.

If you walk east along the beach for about 10 minutes you'll reach scenic **Kawailoa Bay**, which is surrounded by sand dunes to the west and protected by jutting sea cliffs to the east. The bay has a lovely beach, and it's not uncommon to find Hawaiians net-fishing in the waters along the shore. Monk seals call in here sometimes, with a new calf recently added to the brood.

Activities

SNORKELING & DIVING

Dive boats and catamaran cruises usually depart from Kukui'ula Bay, a small boat harbor about 0.5 miles east of Spouting Horn. **Seasport Divers** (☎ 742-9303, 800-685-5889; www .seasportdivers.com; Po'ipu Plaza, 2827 Po'ipu Rd; led dives shore 1-/2-tank $75/100, boat 1-tank $125, night $80, Ni'ihau 3-tanks $275) leads dives. Snorkelers can hop on dive boats, too ($65).

KAYAKING

Outfitters Kauai (☎ 742-9667, 888-742-9887; www .outfitterskauai.com; Po'ipu Plaza; 🕑 reservations taken 8am-9pm) rents double kayaks (day $80) and offers kayak tours, including the standard Wailua River circuit (adult/child $94/72), a Kipu Falls kayak, hike and zipline tour that includes a pretty two-mile paddle on Hule'ia River (adult/child $130/100) and a 12-hour Na Pali Coast tour (summer only, $185).

SURFING

Po'ipu has killer breaks and reliable sun. If you sign up for lessons, check how big your class will be. Four is maximum density. **Margo Oberg's Surfing School** (☎ 332-6100, 888-742-6924; 2-hr lesson $48) leads highly regarded classes designed by this World Cup surfing champion at Po'ipu Beach. Also teaching at Poi'pu Beach is **Kauai Surf School** (☎ 742-8019; www.kauaisurfschool.com; 2-hr lesson $60). Classes meet at Nukumoi Surf Company.

Nukumoi Beach & Surf Company (☎ 742-8019; www.nukumoi.com; 2100 Hoone Rd; rents boards soft-top hr/day/week $5/20/60, hard $7.50/30/80, boogie boards day/week $5/15, snorkel gear day/week $5/15; 🕑 7:45am-7pm Mon-Sat, 10:30am-6:30pm Sun) is right across from Po'ipu Beach Park.

Seasport Divers (☎ 742-9303, 800-685-5889; www .seasportdivers.com; Po'ipu Plaza, 2827 Po'ipu Rd; rents surf boards day/week $20/100, boogie boards day/week from $4/15, snorkel sets day/week from $4/15) also rents gear.

HORSEBACK RIDING

You can access beautiful coastal lands that others can't while on horseback rides with **CJM Country Stables** (☎ 742-6096; www.cjmstables .com; ☺ tours Mon-Sat). Choose from a 2- /3-hour secret beach ride ($75/85) or a 3½-hour ride with a swim and picnic at the beach ($95), both in the secluded Maha'ulepa Beach area. The stables are in Po'ipu, along the main dirt road 1.5 miles east of the Hyatt Regency Kauai.

GOLF & TENNIS

If you like to golf, you'll groove on Po'ipu. The economical **Kiahuna Golf Club** (☎ 742-9595; www.kiahunagolf.com; 2545 Kiahuna Plantation Dr; before/ after 11am $65/55, club rental from $20) is an 18-hole par-70 Robert Trent Jones Jr course. Prices include cart and drop even lower after 2:30pm weekdays.

More exclusive is the **Poipu Bay Resort Golf Course** (☎ 742-8711; nonguests $140, club rental $40), an 18-hole, par-72 course adjacent to the Hyatt Regency Kauai. Tee times after 3pm cut the standard price by over half. Carts are included in the rate. This course has hosted the PGA Grand Slam for over a decade.

The friendly **Kiahuna Tennis Club** (☎ 742-9533; kiahunatennisclb@aol.com; 2290 Poip'u Rd; court rental per person per hr $10; ☺ 8am-6pm), with tennis courts, pool (cool waterslide!) and the reasonable **Casablanca Restaurant & Bar** (☎ 742-2929; ☺ 7:30am-10pm Mon-Sat, 8:30am-5pm Sun), makes for good, family fun.

BODYWORK & YOGA

Anara Spa (☎ 742-1234, 800-554-9288; www.anaraspa .com; Hyatt Regency Kauai, 1571 Po'ipu Rd; massage per hr $75-250, treatments $65-75) offers all manner of massages, herbal wraps, body scrubs and polishing in a lush, indulgent setting.

Oceanfront Yoga (☎ 639-9294; www.aloha-yoga .com; Po'ipu Beach Park; 90-minute class $12; ☺ 8:30am Mon, Wed & Fri) holds Hatha yoga outside.

Tours

South Shore sunset cruises are offered by **Capt Andy's Sailing Adventures** (☎ 335-6833, 800-535-0830; www.capt-andys.com; Lawa'i Rd; adult/child $59/40).

Outfitters Kauai (☎ 742-9667, 888-742-9887; www .outfitterskauai.com; Po'ipu Plaza; ☺ reservations taken 8am-9pm) is one of the only outfits offering mountain-bike tours: a 13-mile downhill screamer along Waimea Canyon Rd (adult/ child $80/60).

Sleeping

The **Poipu Beach Resort Association** (☎ 742-7444; www.poipubeach.org; PO Box 730, Poipu, HI 96756) can mail a brochure listing most of Po'ipu's accommodations, or check its website for information.

The following vacation rental companies have scads of places:

Gloria's Vacation Rentals (☎ 742-2850, 800-684-5133; www.gloriasvacationrentals.com; PO Box 1258, Koloa, HI 96756) Good variety in all price ranges; an easy-to-navigate website.

Grantham Resorts (☎ 742-2000, 800-325-5701; www.grantham-resorts.com; Waikomo Stream Villas, 2721 Po'ipu Rd) Homes, hideaways and condos.

Kauai Vacation Rentals (☎ 245-8841, 800-367-5025; www.kauaivacationrentals.com; 3-3311 Kuhio Hwy, Lihu'e, HI 96766)

R&R Realty & Rentals (☎ 742-7555, 800-367-8022; www.r7r.com; 1661 Pe'e Rd, Po'ipu, HI 96756) Specializes in condos.

MID-RANGE

Koloa Landing Cottages (☎ 742-1470, 800-779-8773; www.koloa-landing.com; 2704B Hoonani Rd; studio $95, 2-/4-person cottage $110/140) These five cozy and festive cottages across the street from Koloa Landing are maintained with abundant aloha. Each unique cottage is tucked into lush landscaping, and has TV, phone and full kitchen, with nice touches like *lauhala* mats and bamboo wind chimes. Additional cleaning fees apply. Reserve in advance, as it's within walking distance of Po'ipu's best breaks and snorkeling and is often booked out solid. It also rents a large, homey two-bedroom, two-bath house in Koloa ($195). Ask about discounts.

Poipu B&B Inn (☎ 742-1146, 800-808-2330; www .poipu-inn.com; 2720 Hoonani Rd; r incl breakfast $125-150, condo unit & house $110-125) The four rooms in this 1933 plantation home near Koloa Landing are country-cute – lots of white wicker and carousel horses – and comfortable. Each has a king bed, kitchenette and tiled bath (two have soaking whirlpool units). The big lanai is a treat – too bad it overlooks the road. It also rents condos and 1- /2- /3-bedroom homes in Po'ipu.

Po'ipu Plantation (☎ 742-6757, 800-634-0263; www.poipubeach.com; 1792 Pe'e Rd; B&B r $110-175, 1-/2-bedroom unit from $115/165; ☒) The nine condo-style units and four B&B rooms feel further from the beach than they are, but have some interesting features. The modern, comfortable condos are standard, sleep four, have fully equipped kitchens and lanai, but share a hot tub and barbecue area. The smaller B&B rooms are in a 1930's house; best to upgrade to the Ali'i Suite, with ocean view, whirlpool tub and fireplace adding atmosphere.

Kauai Cove Cottages (☎ 742-2562, 800-624-9945; www.kauaicove.com; 2672 Puuholo Rd; studio from $95) The interiors of these studio cottages on a nondescript street near Koloa Landing is where the charm lies. Canopy beds, reams of mosquito netting, lots of bamboo and an open layout make these good for a couple. The patios are small, but the kitchen is well equipped and the hardwood floors feel good on beached-out feet. Ask about the good-value, private Palm Room (from $85) and Garden Suite (from $105) that are located in a subdivision up the road.

Waikomo Stream Villas (☎ 742-7220, 800-325-5701; www.grantham-resorts.com; 2721 Poipu Rd; 1- or 2-bedroom unit $100-165; 🏊) The price is definitely right for these clean, modern condos on pretty grounds within walking distance of the best Po'ipu beaches. Each of the 60 units is fully loaded with lanai, a well-equipped kitchen, one or two bedrooms, separate living room, cable TV, VCR, stereo and washer/dryer. Upgrade to a two-bedroom for an open, split-level layout with lots of light. Four-night minimum stay.

TOP END
Gloria's Spouting Horn Bed & Breakfast (☎ 742-6995; www.gloriasbedandbreakfast.com; 4464 Lawai Beach Rd; s & d incl breakfast $325; 🏊) Justly famous for its ocean perch near Spouting Horn, this B&B pays exquisite attention to detail and makes a tempting romantic splurge. Each of the three guestrooms has a wooden canopy bed with sumptuous linens, private ocean-front lanai, a deep, delicious bathtub and fluffy robes. All spitting distance from the foaming surf, this place is dreamy, relaxing and exclusive. There's a three-day minimum stay, and no credit cards.

Po'ipu Kapili (☎ 742-6449, 800-443-7714; www.poipukapili.com; 2221 Kapili Rd; 1-/2-bedroom unit from $210/280; 🏊) Epitomizing functional luxury, this condo complex shines. The 60 units are extremely roomy and tastefully furnished, with lots of wood, ceiling fans, fully equipped kitchen, dining room, ocean views and big, lush beds. Private lanai lead off the bedrooms. Every unit has a large bathtub in

a spacious bathroom. The complex has tennis courts, barbecue area, and an extensive book and video library. All units are wired with digital cable and Internet access. Five-day minimum stay.

Hyatt Regency Kauai (☎ 742-1234, 800-554-9288; www.kauai.hyatt.com; 1571 Po'ipu Rd; r $425-650, ste $1200-4000; 🏊 🏊) Po'ipu's most exclusive hotel is a class act, with airy lobbies adorned with antiques and orchids, and a central building looking straight onto the ocean. Inside, the big, super comfortable rooms are well coordinated, with designer tropical decor in muted tones, CD players and overhead fans. The Hyatt is also home to the world-famous Anara Spa (p496), has a 150ft waterslide and hosts special *na keiki* (childrens') activities at Camp Hyatt. There are six restaurants, and the bar overlooking the ocean is killer.

Kiahuna Plantation (☎ 742-6411, 800-688-7444; www.outrigger.com; 2253 Po'ipu Rd; 1-/2-br units from $225/365; 🏊) The fresh, airy units are spread across acres of quiet, garden-filled grounds between Po'ipu Rd and a nice bit of Po'ipu Beach. Each has a fully equipped kitchen, living room and large lanai; the one-bedroom unit sleeps four adults, the two-bedroom units, six adults. Third-floor units are best; try for one overlooking Moir Garden. There are summer and holiday programs for kids. Online discounts available.

Sheraton Kauai Resort (☎ 742-1661, 800-782-9488; www.starwood.com/hawaii; 2440 Ho'onani Rd; r $325-595; 🏊 🏊) Divided by Ho'onani Rd and split into two sections, not all of the Sheraton's rooms are on Po'ipu Beach. In fact, until you reach the pricey Deluxe Garden category ($475), you'll be across the road. Families flock to this place for its proximity to Po'ipu Beach, the in-room movies and Playstation, and two kiddie pools. Also here is the **Keiki Aloha Club** (☎ 742-4012; 🕘 9am-4pm Mon, Wed, Fri).

Eating
BUDGET
Taqueria Norteños (☎ 742-7222; Po'ipu Plaza, 2827 Po'ipu Rd; meals $2.50-5; 🕘 11am-10pm Thu-Tue) 'Where there's a line, you should dine', and the axiom holds water at this inexpensive Mexican take-out window. Nothing fancy mind you, but a veggie/beef burrito at $3/3.80 or two enchiladas with rice and beans for $4.50 is value. Save room for sugary *buñuelos*, a traditional fried-pastry dessert ($2.30).

Island Ice Cream (Po'ipu Plaza, 2827 Po'ipu Rd; scoop $3-4; ⓨ 10am-8pm) Serves shave ice, too.

Puka Dog (☎ 742-6044; Po'ipu Shopping Village; hot dogs $6; ⓨ 11am-6pm Mon-Sat) Get a damn good hot dog at this leafy, bamboo shack embedded in the mall. Choose from Polish sausage or veggie dog and slather with your choice of funky (mango, pineapple, coconut?!) or traditional relish. It's the secret garlic-lemon sauce that does it. Wash it all down with freshly squeezed lemonade.

Brennecke's Deli (☎ 742-1582; 2100 Hoone Rd; sandwiches $4-6; ⓨ 8am-9pm) Don't be put off by the convenience-store vibe because it makes fat, tasty sandwiches, tailored to your tastes. Choose from seven types of bread, including a yummy onion and dill roll, and a laundry list of cheese, protein (including taro burgers or honey ham) and load on the veggies. Perfect for a picnic.

Joe's on the Green (☎ 742-9696; Kiahuna Golf Course Rd; breakfast $5-8, lunch $7-9; ⓨ 7am-5:30pm, to 8:30pm Wed & Thu) Run here with the locals for the early bird special ($5, served until 9am Monday to Saturday), or arrive leisurely for some Hawaiian sweet-bread French toast or stick-to-your-ribs biscuits and gravy. Reubens and burgers figure prominently during lunch, which segues nicely into happy hour (3pm to 5:30pm). Live Hawaiian music accompanies dinner on Wednesday and Thursday.

MID-RANGE & TOP END

Keoki's Paradise (☎ 742-7535; Po'ipu Shopping Village; café menu $5-11, dinner $17-25; ⓨ café menu 11am-midnight, dinner 5-10pm) Tiki torches and faux waterfalls inside temper the mall atmosphere outside here, where the café menu is your best bet. Try *panko*-crusted calamari, Thai shrimp sticks or the grilled chicken Caesar. The fresh fish at dinner, served with hoisin lime vinaigrette or baked in a garlic and basil glaze, is the most interesting. Save room for the wicked hula pie ($6).

Plantation Gardens (☎ 742-2121; Kiahuna Plantation; appetizers $8-15, mains $18-27; ⓨ pupu 4pm, dinner 5:30-10pm) Zesty, Pacific Rim flavors (eg fish wontons in mango-ginger sauce or shrimp steamed in *ti* leaves) dominate at this restaurant overlooking the cactus gardens at Kiahuna Plantation. The veranda with garden views is the place to be. Be kind to your budget by keeping to drinks and *pupu*.

Roy's Poipu Bar & Grill (☎ 742-5000; www.roys restaurant.com; Po'ipu Shopping Village; appetizers $7-

12, mains $19-25; ⓨ 5:30-9:30pm) The darling of foodies and in-flight magazines as *the* place for Hawaii regional cuisine, this branch of Roy's empire is in vogue. Signature appetizers include shrimp and asparagus crepes with chèvre. Mains are all about sauces, like the pesto-steamed whitefish with cilantro-ginger-peanut oil and grilled shrimp with smoked tomato *beurre blanc*. There's a long, intriguing wine list.

Brennecke's Beach Broiler (☎ 742-7588; www .brenneckes.com; 2100 Hoone Rd; dinner $17-24; ⓨ 11am-10pm) Upstairs and overlooking the beach, best visited for its happy hour (3pm to 5pm) with pub grub and $4 mai tais.

Tidepools (☎ 742-6260; Hyatt Regency; mains $23-30; ⓨ 6-10pm) The most interesting restaurant at the Hyatt Regency Kauai has a romantic setting with open-air thatched huts, tinkling waterfalls and a sprawling carp pond. Choose from crab cakes with passion-fruit salsa, 'ahi sashimi and steamed mussels to start, followed by its signature macadamia nut–crusted mahimahi in a ginger-butter sauce. A special *keiki* (child) menu is also available.

Entertainment

Hyatt Regency Kauai (☎ 742-1234, 800-554-9288; www.kauai.hyatt.com; 1571 Po'ipu Rd) For entertainment in Po'ipu, it's got to be the Hyatt. The Seaview Terrace, just off the lobby, is darned stunning with its…sea view. There's live Hawaiian music from 6pm to 8pm nightly; on Tuesday and Saturday the entertainment includes hula dancing (7pm), other days it's a torch lighting (6:15pm). It's all free, plus the cost of your cocktails, of course. The Hyatt also hosts a luau at 6pm on Thursday and Sunday (adult/child 6 to 12/child 13+ $65/33/50). There's live jazz from 8pm to 11pm in the Hyatt's hyper-atmospheric **Stevenson's Library** (☎ 742-1234; ⓨ 6pm-1am) lounge and bar, plus a pool table and cribbage boards. Let the wagering begin! Proper resort attire required.

A free **Polynesian dance show** (☎ 742-2831; ⓨ 5pm Tue & Thu) is performed at Poipu Shopping Village.

Getting Around

Outfitters Kauai (☎ 742-9667, 888-742-9887; www .outfitterskauai.com; Po'ipu Plaza; ⓨ reservations taken 8am-9pm) rents cruiser/mountain/full suspension bikes for $20/30/40 a day. Bicycle rentals include a helmet and lock. For car, motorcycle or moped hire, see p440.

WESTSIDE

Is the West the best? You'll feel the difference as soon as you cross over into the red, hot landscape of Kaua'i's Westside. It's rural and uncrowded, with rolling hills of sugarcane and coffee plants pushing out of rust-red dirt separating a handful of small towns that exude aloha. You'll hear folks refer to the Westside, known for the ruggedly spectacular scenery of Waimea Canyon and Koke'e State Park, as 'the most Hawaiian' in Kaua'i. These are must-see sights for all Kaua'i visitors, and orgasmic for hiking and camping freaks.

From Lihu'e to Polihale State Park, the furthest point accessible by car on the Westside, it's 38 miles along Hwy 50 (Kaumuali'i Hwy).

KALAHEO

An old, sleepy Portuguese community where the tallest building is still the Iglesia Ni Cristo steeple, Kalaheo is quintessentially local in flavor. Poi dogs bark from tiny backyard cages, local boys roar by in big, off-road trucks and everyone calls their neighbor by name.

While Kalaheo is off the main tourist track, it has some reasonably priced accommodations, is within driving distance of Po'ipu Beach and makes a convenient base for exploring Kaua'i's Westside sights.

The town's main shops, post office and restaurants are clustered around the intersection of Hwy 50 and Papalina Rd.

Sights

KUKUIOLONO PARK
Kukuiolono means 'light of Lono,' referring to the torches that Hawaiians once placed on this hill to help guide canoes safely to shore. More recently this was part of pineapple baron Walter D McBryde's estate, but he ceded it to the people of Kaua'i upon his death in 1928.

To get here, turn left onto Papalina Rd from Hwy 50 in Kalaheo center. Entering the park, you pass through an old stone archway. A tidy little Japanese garden is at the far end of the parking lot.

HIDDEN KAUA'I

- **Running Waters Beach** (p447)
- **Kauai's Hindu Monastery** (p457)
- **'Aliomanu Beach** (p468)
- **Kamalani Play Bridge** (p454)
- **Kapa'a By-Pass Rd** (p452)
- **'Anini Beach Lunch Shak** (p474)
- Trailblazing around **Maha'ulepu Beach** (p495)
- **Double Door Cave** (p480)
- **Funky pedestrian crossing signs** (456 and p492) There are more. Can you spot them?
- Skipping over the **Swinging Bridge** (p503)
- Feeding chickens at **Kukuiolono Golf Course** (p501)

PU'U ROAD SCENIC DRIVE
Pu'u Rd is a scenic side-loop with small ranches, grand mango trees shading hidden drives and fine coastal views. It's a winding country road, only one lane with some blind curves, but nothing tricky if you go slow and honk on the hairpins. And it's so quiet, you may not even encounter another car.

After leaving Kukuiolono Park, turn right onto Pu'u Rd to start the drive. It's just over 3 miles back to Hwy 50 this way. About half-way along, you'll look down on Port Allen's oil tanks and the town of Numila, with its old sugar mill.

Down the slope on the west side of the road are coffee trees, part of a total of 4000 acres that have been planted between Koloa and 'Ele'ele. The coffee, on McBryde Sugar Company property, is one of the company's grander schemes for diversifying crops on land formerly planted solely in sugarcane.

HANAPEPE VALLEY LOOKOUT
The scenic lookout that pops up shortly after the 14-mile marker offers a view deep into Hanapepe Valley. The red-clay walls of the cliffs are topped by bright-green cane like a sugar frosting. This is but a teaser of the dramatic vistas awaiting at Waimea Canyon.

While old King Sugar may dominate the scene surrounding Hanapepe Valley, glance

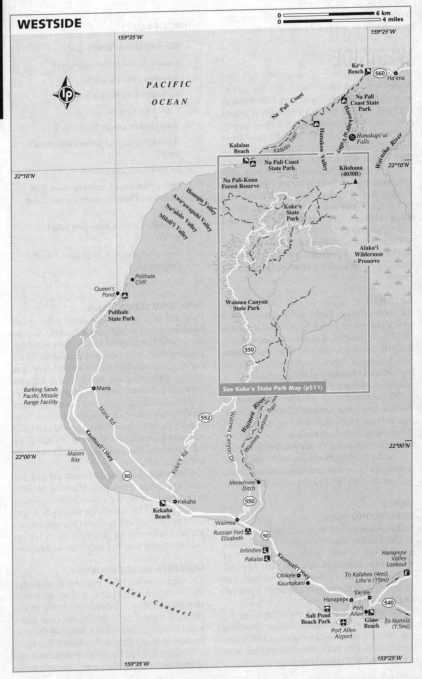

WESTSIDE

PACIFIC OCEAN

0   6 km
0   4 miles

159°35'W   159°25'W

Ke'e Beach   560   Ha'ena

Na Pali Coast

Na Pali Coast State Park

Hanakoa Valley

Hanakapi'ai Valley

Hanakapi'ai Falls

Kalalau Trail

Waininha River

Kalalau Beach

Na Pali Coast State Park

Kilohana (4030ft)

22°10'N

Na Pali-Kona Forest Reserve

Koke'e State Park

Honopu Valley
Awa'awapuhi Valley
Nu'alolo Valley
Miloli'i Valley

Alaka'i Wilderness Preserve

Polihale Cliff

Queen's Pond

Polihale State Park

Waimea Canyon State Park

Barking Sands Pacific Missile Range Facility

Mana

550

See Koke'e State Park Map (p511)

Mana Rd

Kaumuali'i Hwy

Waimea River

552

Waimea Canyon Trail

Waimea Canyon Dr

Koke'e Rd

22°00'N

Majors Bay

50

Kekaha

550

Menehune Ditch

Kekaha Beach

Waimea

Russian Fort Elizabeth

50

Infinities
Pakalas

Kaumuali'i Hwy

Olokele
Kaumakani

Hanapepe Valley Lookout

To Kalaheo (4mi); Lihu'e (15mi)

Kaulakahi Channel

Hanapepe   'Ele'ele

Salt Pond Beach Park

Port Allen

540

Glass Beach

To Numila (1.5mi)

Port Allen Airport

159°35'W   159°25'W

toward the opposite side of the road and you'll see the island's newest commercial crop – endless rows of coffee trees.

Activities

There are free tennis courts in Kalawai Park.

Kukuiolono Golf Course (☎ 332-9151; Kukuiolono Park; green fees adult/child $8/3, pull carts $2; ☯ 6:30am-6:30pm) is an unassuming, nine-hole, par-36 golf course with grand hilltop views and earthy appeal (bags of chicken feed for the fowl on the fairway and super-friendly locals are just the start). Grab a bucket of balls ($2) and hit the driving range, with its gorgeous sea and coffee plantation views. No tee times: first come, first served. Check out the cheap vittles at the **snack bar** (☯ 8am-3:30pm), with more views.

Sleeping

Kalaheo Inn (☎ 332-6023, 888-332-6023; www.kalaheo inn.com; 4444 Papalina Rd; studio/1-/2-bedroom $55/65/105) Friendly and comfortable, this motel-turned-traveler's haunt right in the center of town has 14 units, each different, giving you a lot of choice. Most rooms have fully equipped kitchens (some have kitchenettes), all have TV, VCR and good, firm beds. The biggest three-bedroom units ($130) are extremely homey and can work out very economically for groups. Ask about discounts for longer stays.

Aloha Estates (☎ 332-7812; www.kalaheo-plantation .com; 4579 Pu'u Wai Rd; d $55-75) Skip the worn and dark cheapest digs at this 75-year-old plantation home and head upstairs for bright, fresh suites ($65) with kitchenettes, the smaller of which have a private bathroom. For an extra $5, you can step up again to a room with full kitchen (shared bathroom) or the delightful Magnolia suite, with bathroom, kitchenette and private lanai overlooking a garden. The cheery, flexible hosts offer discounts for a week or more. Two-night minimum or a $10 surcharge.

Bamboo Jungle House (☎ 332-5515; 888-332-5115; www.kauai-bedandbreakfast.com; 3829 Waha Rd; r/ste incl breakfast $110/130) Talk about whimsical luxury! This place has a lap pool, bordered by a volcanic rock waterfall spilling into a Jacuzzi and wild tropical plantings that you can appreciate from your private lanai. The three units each have private entrance, mosquito nets and CD player. The suite has a

kitchenette. Sounds of paradise accompany you everywhere on this distinct property.

Classic Vacation Cottages (☎ 332-9201; www .classiccottages.com; 2687 Onu Pl; studios $45-65, 1-/2-/3-bedroom $75/80/100) The rooms at this rambling place of adjacent properties a mile up from Hwy 50 are older, but very accommodating, especially for bigger groups. Every unit is different; some are dark, others less so, but all have kitchen, cable TV, DVD and ceiling fans. Some have phones, others have washers and dryers. Up to seven people can hunker down in the three-bedroom house.

Eating

Bread Box (☎ 332-9000; 4447 Papalina Rd; ☯ 4am-to late Tue-Sat) The definitive hole-in-the-wall, this bakery sells aromatic fresh breads, tasty macadamia-nut rolls ($1.50) and what may well be the last 25¢ cup of coffee in America. Come early for the good stuff.

Kalaheo Coffee Co & Café (☎ 332-5858; www .kalaheo.com; 2-2436 Hwy 50; breakfast $4-7, lunch $5-8; ☯ 6am-2:30pm Mon-Fri, 6:30am-2pm Sat & Sun) Don't zoom through town without stopping at this café for a gooey mac-nut sticky bun or sublime cinnamon knuckle (either $2.75), washed down with a robust cup of coffee. Breakfast is more imaginative than most: try the gigantic bagel Benny, which piles turkey, a poached egg and hollandaise sauce on half a bagel, or the veggie tofu wrap. Lunch salads, like Oriental vegetable salad and a pasta-herb-chicken number, eclipse the sandwiches.

Shipwreck Subs (☎ 651-9132, 635-6562; 4414 Papalina Rd; 6-/13-inch sub $4.50/9.50; ☯ 11am-6pm) Sandwiches to compete with NYC's finest deli are the staple here. Choose from any cold cut you can imagine, plus five types of cheese and loads of veggies. Great to pick up en route to Koke'e State Park trailheads. Big Island Tropical Dreams ice cream (scoop $3) is also here.

Brick Oven Pizza (☎ 332-8561; Hwy 50; 10-/12-/15-inch pizza from $9.50/13/20; ☯ 11am-10pm Tue-Sun) There is good reason this classic pizzeria has been around since 1977. Real brick-oven pies with either regular or whole-wheat crust come with surprises, such as a truly vegetarian version piled with premium veggies and stock-free sauce. The Gordon Biersch is on tap (mug/pitcher $3.30/13.50), and kids are given raw pizza dough to muck around with.

Other options in town include:

Camp House Grill (☎ 332-9755; Hwy 50; breakfast $5-6, dinner $10-12; ☺ 6:30am-9:30pm) Local joint with diner atmosphere and reasonably priced food. Lunch and dinner emphasize barbecue.

Kalaheo Steak House (☎ 332-9780; 4440 Papalina Rd; dinner $17-25; ☺ 6-10pm) Dig into the beef, from a 12oz sirloin to an insanely huge 24oz prime rib. All dinners come with a green salad and bread.

'ELE'ELE & NUMILA

What residential 'Ele'ele has going for it is a shopping center at the 16-mile marker, with a supermarket, bank, post office, laundry and a few restaurants. The best restaurant is **Grinds Cafe** (☎ 335-6027; www.grindscafe.net; breakfast $4-7, lunch $4.50-9; ☺ 5:30am-6pm), which has good pastries and sandwiches. There's a kids' menu or build a pizza from the laundry list of extras, like artichoke hearts and barbecued chicken.

Hwy 540 is an alternate route that leads off Hwy 50 just after Kalaheo and connects back to Hwy 50 at 'Ele'ele. After passing through fields of coffee trees, it swings by Numila, a former cane town with tin-roof wooden houses surrounding a defunct sugar mill. At the southwest edge of Numila is the **Kauai Coffee Company** (☎ 335-0813, 800-545-8605; www.kauaicoffee.com; Hwy 540; ☺ 9am-5:30pm), Hawaii's biggest coffee operation. The little **museum** (admission free) with simple displays is just a mechanism to get you to buy product, which you can sample for free at the café on premises. The *malasadas* (warm Portuguese fried and sugary dough, 60¢) and coffee cakes ($1.25) here go quick.

PORT ALLEN

Port Allen, immediately south of 'Ele'ele on Hanapepe Bay, is one of Kaua'i's busiest recreational boat harbors. The Port Allen Marina Center just up from the harbor has most of the tour offices, plus the **West Side Copy Center** (☎ 335-9990; 4353 Waialo Rd; per hr $6; ☺ 8am-6pm Mon-Fri, 8am-noon Sat), with Internet access, and **Kauai Coffee Cafe** (☎ 335-5333; 4353 Waialo Rd; sandwiches $4-6; ☺ 6:30am-2pm), with coffee, smoothies, wraps and *panini* sandwiches.

Sights

Dig your toes into drifts of it or scoop it up by the handful at this little cove just east of Port Allen covered in colorful bits of sea glass. The smooth, pebble-like nuggets covering **Glass Beach** wash in from a long-abandoned dump site nearby, worn and weathered after decades of wave action. Sometimes the glass is deep, other times it's largely washed out to sea. There is terrific exploring east along the rocky coast pocked with tide pools and strewn with odd flotsam. Don't miss the Japanese cemetery with a view on the path above the beach.

To get to the little cove, take Aka'ula St, the last left before entering the Port Allen commercial harbor, go past the fuel storage tanks and then curve to the right down a rutted dirt road that leads 100yd to the beach.

Activities

For a real adrenaline high, take an ultralight lesson with **Birds in Paradise** (☎ 822-5309; www.birdsinparadise.com; Burns Field, Puolo Rd; 30-min/1-hr lesson $96/165). You can also do a round-the-island lesson on one of these powered hang gliders for $300. Take the road for Salt Pond Beach Park to reach the airport.

Tours

The majority of Kaua'i's catamaran and raft tours leave from this harbor, as do the scuba-dive boats of **Mana Divers** (☎ 335-0881; www.manadivers.com; Bay 3, Port Allen Boat Harbor, 4310 Waialo Rd), which offers boat dives, night dives and certification courses.

There are many choices for boat cruises. In summer the scenic Na Pali Coast circuit is the star, while in winter everyone braves the seas for whale watching. Morning trips generally have calmer seas and lots of dolphins. Book as early in your trip as possible, as high surf or foul weather can cancel tours (or at least the snorkeling part). Seasickness is part of the experience: take remedies 24 hours before departure.

The major difference in tours is the type of boat: either a catamaran, raft on steroids or motorized cruiser. Rafts are the most exhilarating, bouncing along the water and entering caves (in mellower weather), but can be hard on the back, have no bathrooms and force you to eat lunch on your lap. These also have the smallest capacity – about 15 passengers – ensuring a smaller tour. The tours to Ni'ihau have longer travel times, but offer unparalleled snorkeling.

The standard, five-hour Na Pali snorkel tours cost around $120/90 per adult/child, including lunch and snorkel gear; five-hour sunset trips are around $90/70; and two-hour whale-watching tours are $75 per person.

The following offices are in Port Allen Marina Center, except where noted:

Holo Holo Charters (☎ 335-0815, 800-848-6130; www .holoholocharters.com; ⏲ 6am-8pm) Na Pali catamaran tours, plus Ni'ihau snorkel tour (adult/child 6-12 $169/119) and cabin cruiser tour suitable for even the littlest kids (adult/child 2-12 $99/69). It's the only company with a catamaran tour where you actually sail as opposed to motor (adult/child $119/85).

Capt Andy's Sailing Adventures (☎ 335-6833, 800-535-0830; www.capt-andys.com) The usual catamaran tours, plus a raucous raft trip (adult/child $100/60) and a two-hour sunset cruise out of Po'ipu (p496).

Blue Dolphin Charters (☎ 335-5553, 877-511-1311; www.kauaiboats.com) Offers sunset tours. Look for heavily discounted offers in the tourist mags; bring snacks as food is skimpy.

Kauai Sea Tours (☎ 826-7254, 800-733-7997; www .kauaiseatours.com; Aka'ula St, Port Allen) Rigid hull raft and catamaran tours; scuba-diving option on the latter for $25 more.

HANAPEPE
pop 2153

For the town exuding the most spunk and character, many visitors vote for Hanapepe. Once one of Hawaii's best-preserved historic towns (parts of the TV miniseries *The Thorn Birds* was filmed here because it so resembled the dusty Australian outback of days past), Hurricane Iniki changed all that. About half of Hanapepe's old wooden buildings were destroyed, but the essence of an unhurried, traditional town remains.

The turnoff into Hanapepe is marked by a sign on Hwy 50.

Sights & Activities

Be sure to take a stroll (or skip for full effect) over the **Swinging Bridge**, which crosses the Hanapepe River; the path begins opposite the Koa Wood Gallery. Its funky old predecessor fell victim to Iniki, but in a community-wide effort this new bridge was erected in 1996.

SALT POND BEACH PARK

Kaua'i has long been famed for its *alae* salt, a sea salt with a red tint that comes from adding a bit of that iron-rich earth you see everywhere. The salt is made by letting seawater into shallow basins called salt pans, letting it evaporate and scraping off the

---

---

dried crystals. Indigenous Hawaiians still make salt this way down on the coast south of Hanapepe.

Salt Pond Beach Park is just beyond the salt ponds. It has a sandy beach popular with families, a lifeguard daily, covered picnic tables, barbecue grills, showers and campsites (see below). Water in the cove gets up to 10ft deep and is very good for swimming laps – four times across equals 0.5 miles. Both ends of the cove are shallow and good for kids. You might see folks windsurfing here, too.

To get here, turn left just past the 17-mile marker onto Lele Rd, then right onto Lokokai Rd; the beach is about a mile from the highway.

Tours

En route to Salt Pond Beach Park, Lokokai Rd is also the way to Burns Field, from where **Inter-Island Helicopter** (☎ 335-5009, 800-335-5567; http://hawaiian.net/~interisland/; 1-3410 Kaumuali'i Hwy; flights regular/waterfall $180/250) tours depart; look for its office on Hwy 50, next to Lappert's.

Sleeping & Eating

There are campsites in Salt Pond Beach Park (see p436 for permit information).

Hanapepe Cafe (☎ 335-5011; 3830 Hanapepe Rd; lunch $6-10, dinner $8-17; ☺ lunch Tue-Sat, dinner Fri & Sat) Cool art and chatty locals infuse this vegetarian café with loads of energy, making the delicious food even more so. Specials, served with homemade focaccia and salad, change daily: The crepe du jour might be ratatouille with creamy pesto, while the pasta is a dynamic puttanesca. Veggie lasagna gussied with caramelized onions and goat cheese is another good choice. Portions are big. The apple pie is unequivocally the best ever. Dinner brings linens, candlelight and live guitar music.

Green Garden (☎ 335-5422; 1-3843 Hwy 50; meals $13-25; ☺ 5-9pm Wed-Mon) This is one of the oldest restaurants on this side of the island. Salad bar and soup come with dinner mains in the teriyaki prime rib and broiled *ono* with peppercorns vein. Vegetarian selections, like baked tofu with shiitake and button mushrooms, are more interesting. If you're up for dessert, don't miss the *liliko'i* chiffon pie – famous here since the 1950s. The retirement-home atmosphere is a turnoff, though.

Get your shave ice and crack seed at **Hawaiian Hut Delights** (☎ 335-3781; Hanapepe Rd; ☺ noon-5pm Mon-Fri, 10am-4pm Sat) and your ice cream at **Lappert's** (☎ 335-6121; www.lapperts.com; 1-3555 Hwy 50; ☺ 10am-6pm). This is the ice-cream chain's factory, where all that cold, yummy stuff is made.

OLOKELE & KAUMAKANI

Olokele exists only for the Olokele Sugar Company, the last remaining sugar producer on Kaua'i, and Kaumakani exists only as the headquarters of **Gay & Robinson** (☎ 335-2824; www.gandrtours-kauai.com; 2 Kaumakani Av), owners of this plantation and the island of Ni'ihau (p430).

The road to Gay & Robinson headquarters and the sugar mill, which comes up immediately after the 19-mile marker, is shaded by tall trees and lined with classic, century-old lampposts. Taking this short drive offers a glimpse into plantation life. Everything is covered with a layer of red dust from the surrounding fields. Quite a few indigenous Ni'ihauans live in this area, many of them working for the Robinsons.

At the end of the road is a simple **visitors center** (admission free; ☺ 8am-4pm Mon-Fri, 11am-3pm Sat), which is more gift shop than anything.

More interesting are the two-hour **mill tours** (☺ 8:45am & 12:45pm Mon-Fri), especially when the mill is actually munching the cane and cranking out the sugar, which isn't always the case. Gay & Robinson also offers a 3½-hour **4WD-tour** (☺ 8:30am & 12:30pm Mon-Fri, reservations required) on its private ranch lands.

If Ni'ihau intrigues you, you might jump on a helicopter or a safari tour (see p431).

WAIMEA

Travelers have always favored Waimea (literally 'reddish water'). Polynesians populated this river valley upon arriving and it was subsequently the site of an ancient Hawaiian settlement. It was here that Captain Cook first came ashore on the Hawaiian Islands and where Kaumuali'i welcomed the first missionaries to Hawaii in 1820. In 1884 Waimea Sugar moved in, and Waimea bloomed into a plantation town. The old sugar mill, now abandoned, sits along the highway on the west side of town.

Today travelers still come to engaging, attractive Waimea, the Westside's biggest town, using it as a base for exploring Waimea Canyon and Koke'e State Park. Waimea Canyon Dr (Hwy 550) and Koke'e Rd (Hwy 552) head north from town to Koke'e State Park.

Information
First Hawaiian Bank (☎ 338-1611; 4525 Panako Rd) On Waimea's central square.
Na Pali Explorer (☎ 338-9999, 877-335-9909; www.napali-explorer.com; Kaumuali'i Hwy; Internet per hr $6) For digital mail and Internet access.
Post Office (☎ 800-275-8777; 9911 Waimea Rd)
West Kauai Medical Center (☎ 338-9431; Waimea Canyon Dr) Has 24-hour emergency-room services.
Westside Sporting Goods (☎ 338-1411; 9681 Kaumuali'i Hwy; ☺ 9:30am-5:30pm Mon-Fri, to 4:30pm Sat) Stocks camping and hiking supplies, including fleece sleeping bags ($15), camp-stove fuel, *tabi* (reef-walking sandals) and first-aid kits.

Sights
WEST KAUAI TECHNOLOGY & VISITORS CENTER
The state-funded **center** (☎ 338-1332; 9565 Kaumuali'i Hwy; admission free; ☺ 9:30-5pm Mon-Fri, 9am-noon Sat) has some interesting photo and artifact displays on local history from a technology perspective, and a great assortment of books for sale. Volunteers from the

center lead two-hour **walking tours** (donations accepted; 🕑 9:30am Mon, reservations preferred) of historic Waimea.

HISTORIC TOWN CENTER

Among the wooden buildings with false fronts giving downtown its classic style is the neoclassical **First Hawaiian Bank** (1929) and the Art Deco **Waimea Theatre** (1938).

The **statue** of Captain Cook in the center of town is a replica of the original statue by Sir John Tweed that stands in Whitby, England. The great navigator, clutching his charts and decked out in his finest captaining threads, now watches over traffic on Hwy 50.

Waimea Foreign Mission Church (cnr Huakai & Makeke Rds) was originally a thatched structure built in 1826 by the Reverend Samuel Whitney, the first missionary to Waimea. The present church was built of sandstone blocks and coral mortar in 1858 by another missionary, the Reverend George Rowell.

In 1865 Reverend Rowell had a spat with some folks in the congregation and went off to build the **Waimea Hawaiian Church** (Hwy 50; 🕑 service 8:30am Sun), a wooden frame church that was downed in the 1992 hurricane, but has been rebuilt. Sunday services include hymns sung in Hawaiian.

RUSSIAN FORT ELIZABETH

The remains of this fort (1815–64) stand above the east bank of the Waimea River. Hawaiian laborers started building the fort

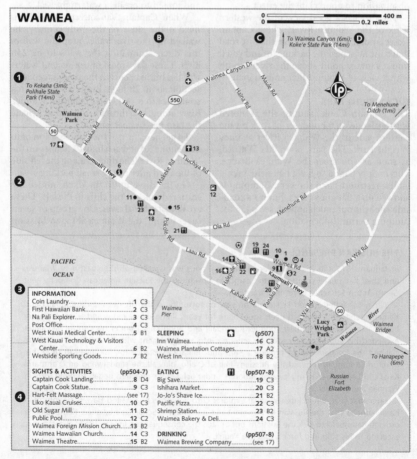

in 1815 under the direction of Georg Anton Schaeffer, a representative of the Russian-American Company. The alliance between the Russians and Kauai's King Kaumuali'i proved to be a short-lived one, and the Russians were tossed out in 1817, the same year the fort was completed. It remained occupied by Hawaiian forces until 1864 when it was decommissioned. See the boxed text, p506.

You can take a short walk through this curious period of Kaua'i's history. The most intact part of the fort is the exterior lava-rock wall (*kapu*, to climb), which is 8ft to 10ft high in places and largely overgrown with scrub. The seaward side was designed like the points of a star, but it takes close observation to appreciate the effect.

The fort has a good view of the western bank of the Waimea River, where Captain Cook landed. Bear right down the dirt road that continues past the parking lot and you'll find a vantage point above the river mouth with a view of Waimea Pier and Ni'ihau.

LUCY WRIGHT PARK

The Captain Cook landing site is noted with a plaque on a nondescript rock on the western side of the Waimea River at Lucy Wright Park. The park is on Ala Wai Rd, as soon as you cross the Waimea Bridge. This county park also has a ball field, picnic tables, restrooms and showers. Camping is allowed on a flat grassy area, but it's a roadside site without much appeal; see p436 for camping permit information.

WAIMEA PIER

Until Port Allen was built, Waimea served as the region's main harbor. It was a major port of call for whalers and traders during the mid-19th century, and plantations started exporting sugar from Waimea later on in the century. Picturesque Waimea Pier, off Pokole Rd, is now used for pole fishing, crabbing and picnicking.

MENEHUNE DITCH

The Menehune Ditch is a stone and earthen aqueduct constructed prior to Western contact. Kaua'i's legendary little people, the *menehune*, are said to have built the ditch in one night. The ditch was an engineering masterpiece, with rocks carefully squared and joined to create a watertight seal.

When Captain Vancouver visited Waimea at the close of the 18th century, he walked up the river valley atop the wall of this ditch, estimating the walls to be 24ft high. These days most of the ancient waterway lies buried beneath the road, except one section about 2ft high. Even today, the ditch continues to divert water from the Waimea River along, and through, the cliff to irrigate the taro patches below.

To get here, turn at the police station onto Menehune Rd and go almost 1.5 miles up the Waimea River. The ditch is along the left side of the road after a very small parking area.

On the drive up to the ditch, notice the scattered holes in the cliffs to the left. These are **Hawaiian burial caves**. One group of seven caves behind the Waimea Shingon Mission

---

THE RUSSIAN PRESENCE

In January 1815 a Russian ship loaded with seal skins was wrecked off the coast near Waimea, and chief Kaumuali'i confiscated the cargo. In November the Russian-American Company sent Georg Anton Schaeffer to retrieve the skins.

When Schaeffer arrived in Hawaii he saw opportunity in the rift between Kaumuali'i and Kamehameha – the two had been squabbling for years, lining up weapons and allies, as Kamehameha threatened to finally conquer Kaumualii and bring Kaua'i under his control. Schaeffer exceeded his authority, however, by entering into an agreement with Kaumuali'i in which he claimed the Russians would provide a ship and military assistance for the invasion of O'ahu. In return, Kaumuali'i offered the Russians half of O'ahu, plus all the sandalwood on O'ahu and Kaua'i. In September 1816 Hawaiian laborers under Schaeffer's direction began to build forts in Waimea and Hanalei.

Later that year, when Russian naval explorer Otto von Kotzebue visited Hawaii, he informed Kamehameha that the Russian government did not endorse Schaeffer's alliance. Kamehameha ordered Kaumuali'i to kick the Russians out or face the consequences. In May 1817 Schaeffer was escorted to his ship and forced to leave Kaua'i.

was explored by Wendell Bennett of the Bishop Museum in the 1920s. At that time, each of the caves held a number of skeletal remains, some in canoe-shaped coffins and others in hollowed-out logs.

Activities

Just before the entrance to the fort, immediately after the 21-mile marker, you'll notice cars parked on the side of the highway. This is the access point to the popular surf break called **Pakalas**. Park here and take the short dirt path to the beach, and you'll be treated to mellow, predictable swells to the east of the stone jetty and a long stretch of gorgeous gold-sand beach backed by swaying palms to the west. Another break over this way called **Infinities** has its fans.

Hart-Felt Massage (☎ 338-2240; www.hartfeltmassage.com; Waimea Plantation Cottages, No 40, Waimea; massage $40-115; ☺ 9am-6pm Mon-Sat) offers oil raindrop therapy, trager therapy (deep relaxation through rocking and bouncing), massage, herbal body wraps, salt scrubs, facials and other treats.

Tours

Two outfitters doing Na Pali Coast boat tours are based in Waimea:

Liko Kauai Cruises (☎ 338-0333, 888-732-5456; www.liko-kauai.com; Waimea Rd) Tours by an indigenous Ni'ihauan on a boat built in Kaua'i; departs from Kikiaola Harbor in Kekaha, so has the shortest travel time to the Na Pali Coast.

Na Pali Explorer (☎ 338-9999, 877-335-9909; www.napali-explorer.com; Kaumuali'i Hwy) Super-friendly outfit has 26ft and 48ft rafts doing snorkel and scenic trips. It also rents snorkel gear, boogie boards and other beach toys.

Sleeping

Inn Waimea (☎ 338-0031; www.innwaimea.com; 4469 Halepule Rd; r $75-95; ☐) Close to the heart of Waimea, this lovely old missionary home with four guest rooms masterfully combines historic character with modern comforts. Rooms are spacious, crisp and cozy and have a coffeemaker, refrigerator, cable TV, phone and high-speed Internet access. Upstairs rooms have views, and the shared living room and lanai contribute to the familial feel. The cheapest room is wheelchair accessible, while the suite has a king bed and a Jacuzzi. Weekly discounts are available. These folks also rent three cottages nearby.

Waimea Plantation Cottages (☎ 338-1625, 800-992-7866; www.waimea-plantation.com; 9400 Kaumuali'i Hwy; r $120-150, 1-/2-/3-br cottages from $185/230/265; ☐ ☒) From the outside, these plantation workers' homes dating from the early 1900s differ little from locals' homes on adjacent side streets: the wooden cottages, clustered around a coconut grove, are cutesy-rustic down to their tin-roof porches and little lanai. Each unit boasts cable TV, stereo and full kitchen. There are ocean-facing four- and five-bedroom houses for rent here (from $380). The hotel rooms don't have nearly the same appeal as the cottages. The 27-acre property backs onto a decent, if murky, cocoa-colored beach. This popular place sometimes overbooks, so reconfirm.

Across from the Waimea Theatre, **West Inn** (☎ 338-1107) was prettying itself to open at the time of publication; this should be Waimea's most economical accommodation when it's done.

Eating & Drinking
BUDGET

Jo-Jo's Shave Ice (9740 Kaumuali'i Hwy; shave ice $2-4; ☺ 10am-6pm) Towering cones of shave ice are sold in 60 tantalizing tropical flavors, like lychee, tamarind and rum. Or opt for a triple-flavored version – the liliko'i/guava/mango combination is hands-down the local favorite.

Waimea Bakery & Deli (☎ 338-1950; 9875 Waimea Rd; snacks $2-5; ☺ 7am-2pm) Inexpensive sandwiches, burgers, breakfast burritos and pastries are strengths among the long and varied menu, and the coffee is decent as well. Hours are somewhat elastic at this very laid-back place.

You can stock up on groceries and picnic fixings at the local **Big Save** (☺ 7am-9pm) or **Ishihara Market** (9946 Kaumuali'i Hwy; ☺ 6am-8:30pm Mon-Fri, 7am-8:30pm Sat & Sun), a grocery store with a good deli selling take-out sushi and green salads.

MID-RANGE

Pacific Pizza (☎ 338-1020; 9850 Kaumuali'i Hwy; pizza $7-16; ☺ 11am-9pm) Traditional or wacky, it's all done here, including a pie with basil, olives, mushrooms, salmon and spicy Thai sauce. Beer, wine, salads and wraps round things out.

Shrimp Station (Kaumuali'i Hwy; dishes $4.75-12; ☺ 11am-5pm) Follow your nose to this little side-of-the-road lunch window serving fresh, aromatic shrimp plates. Varieties include coconut and sweet chili. Each comes with a half-pound of the buggers and two scoops of rice.

Waimea Brewing Company (☎ 338-9733; www .waimea-plantation.com/brew; Waimea Plantation Cottages, 9600 Kaumuali'i Hwy; appetizers $3.50-13, dishes $9-25; ☺ 11am-9pm) When the equipment is working, the USA's westernmost microbrewery serves eight house beers, including Na Pali Pale Ale, Pakala Porter and its flagship Waialeale Ale, a light golden brew. The open setup is pleasant, as is the live music in the evening. Pub fare will fill you up and desserts (including seven kinds of cheesecake) will make you smile.

KEKAHA

Kekaha is Kaua'i's westernmost town. As you continue toward Polihale, it's a rural scene, with the inland cliffs getting higher and the ravines deeper. Corn and sunflowers, which are planted for seed production, grow in fields along the road. Cattle and cattle egrets feed in the pastures. Kekaha has great beaches, or rather it has one long glorious stretch appropriate for the sunset if you can't make it to Polihale State Park.

This is open ocean, and when the surf is high there can be dangerous currents; when there's no swell, it's good for swimming. Ni'ihau and its offshore islet, Lehua, are visible from the beach. There's a very inconspicuous shower just inland from the highway between Alae and Amakihi Rds; restrooms and picnic tables are nearby. Free tennis courts are at the junction of Hwys 552 and 50.

A few blocks inland from the beach is Kekaha Rd, which runs parallel to the highway. This is downtown Kekaha, folks, with a post office and a couple of stores. The village's most dominant feature is its old sugar mill, visible from just about everywhere, including the beach.

On its eastern end, Kekaha Rd comes out to Hwy 50 near the Kikiaola Small Boat Harbor, a state harbor with a launch ramp.

Sleeping & Eating

Two good websites for finding places to lay your head in Kekaha are the **Kekaha Info Page** (www.aloha.net/~inazoo/index.htm.htm) and **Kekaha Oceanside** (www.kekahaoceansidekauai.com).

Mindy's (☎ 337-9275; mindys@hgea.org; 8842 Kekaha Rd; d from $65) Hikers anticipating heavy time on the Waimea Canyon and Koke'e park trails might make this sunny 2nd-story apartment their base. There's a big old deck for kicking back, a full kitchen, bed space for four ($5 for each extra person) and nice extras, like TV, phone and stereo. Complimentary fruit and coffee are provided. Reserve well in advance.

Obsessions (☎ 337-2224; Waimea Canyon Plaza, cnr Hwy 552 & Kekaha Rd; breakfast & lunch $4-7; ☺ 8:30am-6pm Mon-Fri, 6:30am-3pm Sat & Sun) Luckily (because it's the only game in town) this little place grills a mean *panini*. From the bread for the French toast to the homegrown salads, everything is homemade here. Even the coffee comes from the owner's 5-acre coffee patch. The menu includes five different flavors of fluffy pancakes, various omelets, sandwiches and salads.

Also in the Waimea Canyon Plaza is the **Menehune Food Mart**, which has limited groceries, wrapped sandwiches and a few simple hot items, and **Aloha Ice Cream**, selling Lappert's delights.

Entertainment

Waimea Theatre (☎ 338-0282; ☺ 7:30pm) Good movies, including art and classic flicks, are shown here.

BARKING SANDS

Ooh, are the locals hopping mad about this one: after the September 11 terrorist attacks, the US Navy base at **Barking Sands Pacific Missile Range Facility** closed public access to its beach at Majors Bay. Not only did this violate the Hawaiian custom of keeping coastline open for everyone, it shut surfers off from some of their favorite winter swells. Following public outcry, the Navy reopened a piece of the coast, but only to Kaua'i residents without felony convictions. Call ☎ 335-4229 for access information.

The missile-range facility at Barking Sands (so-called because on sunny, windy days, the moving sands make sounds said to be similar to barking dogs) provides the aboveground link to a sophisticated sonar network that tracks more than 1000 sq miles of the Pacific. Established during WWII, it's been developed into the world's largest underwater listening device. The supersensitive equipment even picks up the songs of humpback whales – the base has gathered the most comprehensive collection of humpback whale soundtracks ever recorded.

The naval presence on Kaua'i is not without controversy. While the Navy is Kaua'i's largest employer, it also occupies and prohibits access to indigenous Hawaiian territory. Furthermore, new US military initiatives suggest that the naval presence in Kaua'i is likely to be expanded, a move viewed with mixed emotions. Indeed, at the time of writing the Navy was negotiating an easement and lease for 6300 additional acres adjacent to the existing facility.

POLIHALE STATE PARK

If you want remote, come to the beautiful long **white-sand beach** at Polihale. It's not deserted – when it's raining everywhere else, beachgoers head this way – but it's out there, down 3.5 miles of washboard dirt road and cut off from points north by the Na Pali cliffs. It's also a prime spot for hot-rodding around the beach in big trucks – veterans of Polihale know to drop their tire pressure to 20lbs to be able to get traction in the sand.

It's a gorgeous spot, particularly at sunset, with aqua-colored water that often comes to shore in huge explosive waves. Expert surfers and boogie boarders shred at Polihale (and get munched doing it), but strong rip currents make the waters treacherous for swimming. Bring sun protection, as shadeless Polihale roasts all day long.

Polihale State Park is about 5 miles from the Barking Sands military base. Turn left 0.75 miles north of the base entrance at the (subtle) sign for the park onto a wide dirt road that passes through abandoned sugarcane fields. The road is bumpy but passable.

After almost 3.5 miles, at a large spreading tree in the middle of the road, a turnoff leads to the only safe swimming spot in the area. To get there, turn right at the tree, and then after a 0.25 miles, follow the road up the hill to the right to the base of the dunes. Walk a couple of minutes north along the beach and you'll come to **Queen's Pond**, where a large semicircle of reef comes almost to shore, creating a protected pool. When the seas are calm, the reef blocks the ocean currents. But when surf breaks over the reef and into the pool, a dangerous rip runs toward an opening at the reef's southern end. The rest of the beach is bordered by open sea.

To get to the state park facilities, go back to the tree at the main cane road, turn left and continue another mile. A turnoff on the left leads to a camping area with restrooms, outdoor showers, drinking water and a picnic pavilion. Further down, other camping areas are in the dunes just above the beach amid thorny kiawe trees (see p436 for camping permit information). Due to its remoteness, Polihale attracts a motley crowd of locals and adventurers, Hawaiians and hippies. It's got a festive, renegade feel; if you're looking for contemplative solitude, this probably isn't the place.

At the very end of the beach is **Polihale Cliff**, marking the western end of the Na Pali Coast. Combined with the untamed ocean and vast expansive beach, it's a magnificent sight. There's a terraced heiau toward the base of the cliff. It was originally on the beach, but over the years ever-shifting sands have added a 300ft buffer between it and the sea. Bushwhacking to the heiau through wasp nests and tangled brush isn't worth it.

WAIMEA CANYON STATE PARK

Waimea Canyon is nicknamed the 'Grand Canyon of the Pacific.' While the slogan smacks of promotional hype, it's not a bad description. Although it's smaller and 200 million years younger than the famous Arizona canyon, Waimea Canyon is certainly grand.

The canyon's colorful river-cut gorge is 2785ft deep. The river flowing through it, the Waimea, is 19.5 miles long, Kaua'i's longest. All in all, it seems incredible that such an immense canyon could be tucked inside such a small island.

The view of the canyon is usually a bit hazy. The best vistas come on sunny days after it's been raining heavily – at such times the earth's a deeper red and waterfalls cascade throughout the canyon, providing unbeatable scenery. Bring lots of film or an empty digital camera card.

Orientation

The southern boundary of Waimea Canyon State Park is about 6 miles up the road from Waimea. Waimea Canyon Dr and Koke'e Rd merge nearby. Koke'e Rd (Hwy 552), which climbs up from Kekaha, also has scenic views, but not of the canyon. Waimea Canyon Dr (Hwy 550) starts in downtown

Waimea. The road is 19 miles long, ultimately ending at lookouts with terrific views into Kalalau Valley on the Na Pali Coast.

The views start about a mile up from Waimea and get better as the road climbs. There are plenty of scenic lookouts. The one at 1.75 miles up looks down on the Waimea River and the taro patches irrigated by the Menehune Ditch. About 2.5 miles up, there are good views out to Kekaha Beach with Ni'ihau in the background. From there on, it's all canyon views.

Sights

ILIAU NATURE LOOP

The marked trailhead for the 10-minute Iliau Nature Loop comes up shortly before the 9-mile marker. This is also the trailhead for the longer Kukui Trail (see right). There's a bench with a view at the start of the trail, but take a three-minute walk to the left and you'll be rewarded with a top-notch vista into Waimea Canyon. After heavy rainfall, waterfalls explode down the sheer rock walls across the gorge.

The trail is named for the *iliau*, a plant endemic to Kaua'i's Westside, which grows along the trail and produces stalks up to 10ft high. Like its cousin the silversword, *iliau* grows to a ripe old age. Then for a grand finale it bursts open with blossoms and dies.

SCENIC LOOKOUTS

The most scenic of the lookout points along this stretch of Waimea Canyon Rd, **Waimea Canyon Lookout** is signposted 585yd north of the 10-mile marker. This takes in sweeping views of Waimea Canyon from a perch of 3400ft. The prominent canyon running in an easterly direction off Waimea is Koai'e Canyon, which is accessible to backcountry hikers (see right).

As you continue up the road, the 800ft **Waipo'o Falls** can be seen from a couple of small unmarked lookouts before the 12-mile marker and then from a lookout opposite the picnic area shortly before the 13-mile marker. The picnic area has barbecue pits, restrooms, drinking water, a pay phone and Camp Hale Koa, a Seventh Day Adventist camp.

Pu'u Hinahina Lookout (3640ft) is at a marked turnoff between the 13- and 14-mile markers. There are two lookouts close to the parking lot. One has a fine view down

Waimea Canyon clear out to the coast, while the other has a view of Ni'ihau.

Activities

For serious hikers, there are trails that lead deep into Waimea Canyon. During weekends and holidays, all of these trails are fairly heavily used by pig hunters.

The trailhead for the **Kukui Trail** is shortly before the 9-mile marker. This trail continues from the Iliau Nature Loop (see left) at a sign-in box. From there, the Kukui Trail makes a steep 2000ft descent down the western side of Waimea Canyon, 2.5 miles to the Waimea River. Wiliwili Camp is at the end of the trail.

Koai'e Canyon Trail begins at Kaluaha'ulu Camp, 0.5 miles up the Waimea River from the end of the Kukui Trail. From there, it runs east for 3 miles along the southern side of Koai'e Canyon. There are some good swimming holes along the way and at the trail's end for cooling off. Avoid this trail during stormy weather due to the danger of flash flooding. The canyon's fertile soil once supported an ancient Hawaiian settlement, and the long-abandoned remains of a heiau and some house sites are still discernible. The Koai'e Canyon Trail passes Hipalau Camp and ends at Lonomea Camp.

A third trail in this area is the 8-mile **Waimea Canyon Trail**, which runs south from Wiliwili Camp to the town of Waimea, ending on Menehune Rd. Much of the trail is along a 4WD road that leads to a hydroelectric power station. While there's public access along the route, the trail passes over private property, so no camping is allowed. There are a number of river crossings, making the trail best done only during dry weather.

Sleeping

All four camps on the canyon trails are part of the forest reserve system. Although they have simple open-air shelters, there are no facilities, and the stream water needs to be treated before drinking. See p435 for camping permit information.

KOKE'E STATE PARK

Winding your way up Koke'e Rd, the air turns crisp and pine scented, with expansive ocean views unfolding below. Still, better views await at the Kalalau Viewpoints up the road, one of the most popular spots to

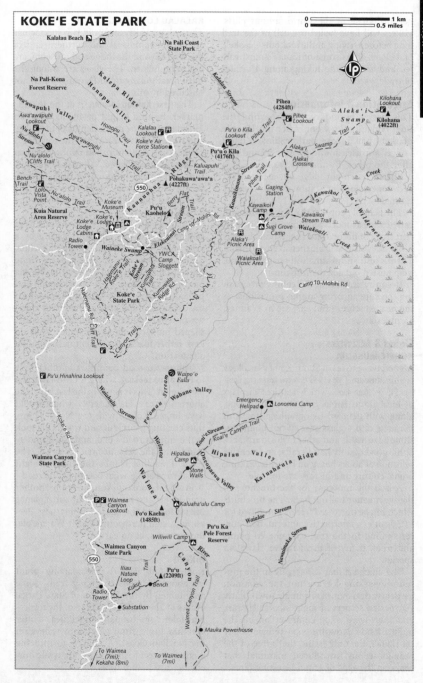

KOKE'E STATE PARK

0 ——————— 1 km
0 ——————— 0.5 miles

Kalalau Beach

Na Pali Coast
State Park

Na Pali-Kona
Forest Reserve

Awa'awapuhi
Lookout

Nu'alolo
Stream

Awa'awapuhi Valley

Kalepa Ridge

Honopu Valley

Honopu Trail

Awa'awapuhi Trail

Kalalau
Lookout

Koke'e Air
Force Station

Kaluapuhi
Trail

Pohakuwa'awa'a
(4227ft)

Pihea
(4284ft)

Pihea
Lookout

Kilohana
Lookout

Alaka'i
Swamp

Kilohana
(4022ft)

Kalalau Stream

Pu'u o Kila
Lookout

Pihea Trail

Pu'u o Kila
(4176ft)

Alaka'i
Crossing

Alaka'i Swamp

Nu'alolo
Cliffs Trail

Bench
Trail

Lolo
Vista Point

Nu'alolo Trail

Kuia Natural
Area Reserve

Koke'e Museum

Koke'e
Lodge

Koke'e
Lodge
Cabins

Radio
Tower

550

Kaunuohua Ridge

Pu'u
Kaohelo

Waineke Swamp

Koke'e
Trail

Halemanu

Halemanu-Koke'e Trail

Koke'e
State Park

Halemanu Rd

Berry Flat Trail

Elekeninui Stream

YWCA
Camp
Sloggett

Koke'e
Stream

Kumuwela

Kumuwela Ridge Rd

Camp 10-Mohihi Rd

Kawaikōī
Stream

Kawaikoi
Camp

Sugi Grove
Camp

Alaka'i
Picnic Area

Waiakoali
Picnic Area

Gaging
Station

Kawaikoi
Stream Trail

Waiakoali

Creek

Kawaikōī

Pihea Trail

Kauaikinana Stream

Alaka'i Swamp Trail

Alaka'i Wilderness Preserve

Creek

Cliff Trail

Halemanu Rd

Canyon Trail

2

Pu'u Hinahina Lookout

Waialae Stream

Waipo'o
Falls

Wahane Valley

Po'omau Stream

Waimea

Koke'e Rd

Emergency
Helipad

Lonomea Camp

Koai'e Stream

Koai'e Canyon Trail

Hipalau
Camp

Stone
Walls

Osteopaewa Valley

Hipalau Valley

Kaluaha'ula Ridge

Waimea Canyon
State Park

P Waimea
Canyon Lookout

Po'o Kaeha
(1485ft)

Kaluaha'ulu Camp

Waialae Stream

Pu'u Ka
Pele Forest
Reserve

Wiliwili Camp

Nawaimaka Stream

Waimea
River
Canyon

Waimea Canyon
State Park

550

Iliau
Nature
Loop

Kukui Trail

Bench

Pu'u
(2209ft)

Radio
Tower

Substation

Waimea Canyon Trail

Mauka Powerhouse

To Waimea
(7mi);
Kekaha (8mi)

To Waimea
(7mi)

get a glimpse of the world-famous cliffs. Hikers will have heard the call of the trail long before arriving at the lookouts – Koke'e State Park offers some of Kaua'i's most varied and challenging hiking along 45 miles of trail.

Orientation & Information

This park's boundary starts beyond the Pu'u Hinahina Lookout. After the 15-mile marker, you'll pass park cabins, Koke'e Lodge, a museum and a campground one after the other. By the way, Koke'e Lodge is not an overnight lodge but a restaurant and concessionaire station for the nearby cabins.

The helpful people at the Koke'e Museum can provide a lot of basic information on current trail conditions and suggestions for day hikes; they also sell inexpensive trail maps. There's also an information board and trail map posted outside the museum.

If you're staying in the cabins or camping, be sure to bring ample provisions, as the nearest stores (and gas) are in Waimea, 15 miles away.

Sights & Activities

KOKE'E MUSEUM

A good place to learn about Kaua'i's ecology is this **museum** (☎ 335-9975; www.kokee.org; donation $1; ☒ 10am-4pm), which features displays of local flora, fauna, climate and geology, along with detailed topographical maps of the area, and a glass case of poi pounders, stone adze heads and other historic artifacts. Some good quality handicrafts, an extensive selection of books heavy on Hawaiiana, flora, fauna, culture and history are for sale.

Ask at the museum for the brochure to the short **nature trail** out back. The brochure, which can be borrowed free or purchased for $1.50, offers interpretive information corresponding to the trail's numbered plants and trees, many of them native Hawaiian species.

The chickens that congregate in the museum's parking lot are not the common garden variety but *moa* (jungle fowl). Early Polynesian settlers brought *moa* to Hawaii, and they were once common on all the main islands. Now the *moa* remain solely on Kaua'i, the only island that's free of the mongoose, an introduced mammal that preys on the eggs of ground-nesting birds.

KALALAU LOOKOUTS

The Kalalau Valley lookouts, two spectacular coastal viewpoints at the northern end of the road beyond the lodge and museum, are not to be missed. The views are among the most breathtaking in all Hawaii – when not obscured by mist, that is.

The first, **Kalalau Lookout**, is at the 18-mile marker. From a height of 4000ft, you can look deep into the green depths of the valley and straight out to sea. When the weather is cooperative, late-afternoon rainbows sweep so deeply into Kalalau Valley that the bottom part of the bows curve back inward. Bright-red *apapane* birds feed from the flowers of the *'ohi'a lehua* trees near the lookout railings.

Kalalau Valley was once the site of a large settlement and was joined to Koke'e by a very steep trail that ran down the cliffs. Today the only way into the valley is along the coastal Kalalau Trail (p486) from Ha'ena on the North Shore or by kayak (p480 and p495). One legend says that rain has sculpted the cliffs into the shapes of the proud chiefs who are buried in the mountains; the cone-shaped pinnacles along the valley walls do look rather like a row of sentinels standing at attention.

The paved road continues another mile to **Pu'u o Kila Lookout**, where it dead-ends at a parking lot. This is actually the last leg of the aborted Koke'e–Ha'ena Hwy, which would have linked Koke'e with the North Shore, thus creating a circle-island road. One look at the cliffs at road's end, and you'll understand why the scheme was scrapped. The Pihea Trail that climbs the ridge straight ahead runs along what was to be the road.

From this lookout, you can enjoy another grand view into Kalalau Valley and a glance inland toward the Alaka'i Wilderness Preserve. A sign here points to Mt Wai'ale'ale, the wettest spot on earth.

HIKING

Koke'e State Park is the starting point for about 45 miles of hiking trails, some maintained by the Division of State Parks, others by the DOFAW. Three of the trails – Nu'alolo, Awa'awapuhi and Pihea – offer breathtaking clifftop views into valleys on the Na Pali Coast. A couple go into the swampy bogs of Alaka'i Swamp, while others are easy nature trails.

Be aware that pig and goat hunters use some of these trails during the hunting season, so you might want to bust out the brightly colored clothing. The camping sites here are strewn with the detritus of ignorant, lazy or disrespectful users (in this case that includes hunters). Please take your trash with you.

Halemanu Road Trails

The starting point for several scenic hikes, Halemanu Rd is just north of the 14-mile marker. Whether or not the road is passable in a non-4WD vehicle usually depends on recent rainfall. The wet, clay roads here make for a skid fest, providing no traction when wet, so even if you can drive in, if it starts raining, you might not be able to get out.

The first hike is **Cliff Trail**, a short, simple walk to an overlook peering into Waimea Canyon. From there, you can continue on the **Canyon Trail**, a steep, but not too strenuous 1.75 miles one way that follows the canyon rim, passes Waipo'o Falls and ends at **Kumuwela Lookout**, with views down the canyon to the ocean beyond. From the falls to the lookout is the most spectacular part (take care crossing the river, and skip doing so if the water level is anywhere close to your knees), with panoramic canyon views and a full-on shot of the towering waterfalls. Take a lunch. On either trail, keep your eyes peeled for wild goats scrambling along the canyon walls.

A little further down Halemanu Rd is the start of **Halemanu–Koke'e Trail**. This easy 1.25-mile (each way) nature trail passes through a native forest of koa and ohia trees that provide a habitat for native birds, including the 'i'iwi, 'apapane, 'amakihi and 'elepaio. One of the common plants found on this trail is banana *poka*, a member of the passion-fruit family and a serious invasive pest. It has pretty pink flowers, but it drapes the forest with its vines and chokes out less aggressive native plants.

Nu'alolo & Awa'awapuhi Trails

The Nu'alolo and Awa'awapuhi Trails each go out to the very edge of sheer cliffs, allowing you to peer down into valleys that are otherwise accessible only by boat. The valley views are extraordinary. Bring plenty of water, as there's none along the way. Edible plants on the trail include blackberries, thimbleberries, guava and passion fruit.

These trails connect via the 2-mile **Nu'alolo Cliffs Trail**, which is also very scenic and offers numerous viewpoints into Nu'alolo Valley, plus a little valley waterfall. The Nu'alolo Cliff Trail connects the Nu'alolo Trail near the 3.25-mile mark to the Awa'awapuhi Trail a little short of the 3-mile mark.

You can combine the three to make a hard-core day hike of about 10 miles. Then you'll have to either hitch a ride or walk an additional 2 miles back down the road to where you started.

Prolific, wild goats are readily spotted along the cliff walls. Capable of breeding at five months of age, the goats have no natural predators in Hawaii, and their unchecked numbers have caused a fair amount of ecological damage.

ALAKA'I SWAMP LIFE

As the only major island free of the dastardly egg-eating mongoose, it's not surprising Kaua'i boasts the largest number of native bird species in Hawaii. This is clearly a boon for birders, who will revel in the remote Alaka'i Swamp, which has the greatest concentration of Kaua'i's native forest bird species. Many of these species are endangered, some having fewer than 100 birds remaining.

The Kaua'i 'o'o, the last of four species of Hawaiian honeyeaters, was thought to be extinct until a nest with two chicks was discovered in Alaka'i Swamp in 1971. However, the call of the 'o'o – that of a single male – was last heard in 1987.

The swamp is a unique ecosystem – here trees grow knee-high – with 10 times more native birds than introduced birds. (Elsewhere in Hawaii, introduced birds outnumber natives many times over.) Thanks to the swamp's high elevation, it's also one of the few places in Hawaii where mosquitoes don't flourish. Hallelujah!

While up in Koke'e State Park, you might also keep en eye out for the hoary bat, one of only two native Hawaiian mammals (the monk seal is the other).

The 3.75-mile **Nu'alolo Trail** starts between the cabins and Koke'e Lodge. The trail begins in cool upland forest and descends 1500ft, ending with a fine view from Lolo Vista Point, a lookout on the valley rim.

The trailhead for the **Awa'awapuhi Trail** begins at a parking area just after the 17-mile marker. The trail descends 1600ft, ending after 3.25 miles at a steep and spectacular *pali* overlooking Awa'awapuhi and Nu'alolo Valleys. Just after the 2.5-mile marker is the jaw-dropping **Awa'awapuhi Viewpoint** right at cloud level. To reach it, jog to the right just before the 3-mile marker, where the Nu'alolo Cliff Trail comes in. Awa'awapuhi means 'valley of ginger,' and *kahili*, a pretty yellow ginger, can be seen on this hike.

Kawaikoi Stream Trail

This trail, a scenic mountain stream trail of about 3 miles return, begins between the Sugi Grove and Kawaikoi campgrounds, off Camp 10–Mohihi Rd. It starts out following the southern side of Kawaikoi Stream, then heads away from the stream and makes a loop, coming down the northern side of the stream before reconnecting with the southern side. If the stream is running high, don't make the crossing.

Kawaikoi Stream is popular for rainbow-trout fishing, which is allowed during an annual open season in August and September. Fishing licenses (p439) are required.

Camp 10–Mohihi Rd is up past the Koke'e Museum on the right. Like many the dirt roads, when it's dry, it can accommodate ordinary cars, at least part way. However, when the road is really wet and rutted, even 4WD vehicles can have difficulty.

Pihea Trail

The Pihea Trail starts from the Pu'u o Kila Lookout (p512) and combines coastal views with an opportunity to see some of the Alaka'i wilderness without getting sucked down by bog. The beginning of the trail was graded in the 1950s, before plans to make this the last leg of the circle-island road were abandoned.

The first mile of the trail runs along the ridge, offering fine views into Kalalau Valley, before coming to the Pihea Lookout, a viewpoint that requires a steep scramble to reach. The Pihea Trail then turns inland through wetland forest and, at about 1.75

miles, crosses the Alaka'i Swamp Trail. If you turn left there, you can continue for 2 miles through Alaka'i Swamp to Kilohana Lookout. If you go straight instead, you'll reach the Kawaikoi Campground in about 2 miles.

Alaka'i Swamp Trail

If you're not an avid hiker, the Alaka'i Wilderness Preserve, which is so inaccessible even invasive plants haven't been able to choke out the endemic swamp vegetation, is not for you. Those who do venture this far off the beaten track, however, will be treated to plentiful native bird species and utter solitude.

Parts of the swamp receive so little sunlight that moss grows thick and fat on all sides of the trees. Most people that see this swamp view it from a helicopter, but it's possible to walk through a corner of it.

This rough 3.5-mile trail starts off at Camp 10–Mohihi Rd and goes through rain forest and bogs before reaching Kilohana Lookout, perched on the rim of Wainiha Pali. If it's not overcast – and that's a big 'if' considering this is the wettest place on earth – hikers will be rewarded with a sweeping view of the Wainiha and Hanalei Valleys to the north. While most of the trail has been spanned with boardwalks, this can still be an extremely wet and slippery trail, and in places you can expect to have to slog through mud. It's certainly a trail that's best suited for hiking in the relatively drier summer season.

If your car can't make it down Camp 10–Mohihi Rd, your best bet is to park near the Kalalau Lookout and approach the Alaka'i Swamp Trail via the Pihea Trail.

Sleeping

Koke'e Lodge (☎ 335-6061; PO Box 819, Waimea, HI 96796; cabin $35-45) The 12 cabins in Koke'e State Park are managed by the lodge, which is actually a restaurant (p515). The oldest cabins are a little tired and have just one large room, but are a bargain. Newer are the two-bedroom cedar cabins. Each cabin, old and new, has one double and four twin beds, and a kitchen with a refrigerator and oven, as well as linens, blankets, a shower and woodstove. Of the newer cedar cabins, No 2 Lehua is particularly comfortable and has a wheelchair ramp. State park rules limit stays to five days. The cabins are often booked up well in advance, but cancellations do occur, and you can occasionally get a cabin at the last moment. At the time of research new management had just taken over this installation, but park staff insist that 'nothing is going to change.'

YWCA Camp Sloggett (☎ 245-5959; www.camping kauai.com; campsites per person $10, bunk beds $20, cottage s/d $65) Right in Koke'e State Park, the Y has a 1-bedroom cottage, a bunkhouse that holds 40 and a cement-slab platform for tent camping. Guests must provide their own linens for the bunkhouse, but there are bathrooms with hot showers and a kitchenette. Tent campers have a barbecue pit for cooking, and use of the showers and toilets in the bunkhouse. No reservations are needed for the bunkhouse and tent sites, while the cottage has a two-night minimum stay and needs to be reserved. It also has a lodge that sleeps 10, which could work for groups or families. Camp Sloggett is about 0.5 miles east of the park museum down a rutted dirt road that's usually OK for cars.

CAMPING

The Koke'e campgrounds are at an elevation of almost 4000ft, and nights are crisp and cool. Take a sleeping bag and warm clothing.

The most accessible camping area is the Koke'e State Park Campground, which is north of the meadow, just a few minutes' walk from Koke'e Lodge. The campsites are in an uncrowded grassy area beside the woods, and have picnic tables, drinking water, restrooms and showers. Permits are required; see p435 for details.

Further off the main track, Kawaikoi and Sugi Grove campgrounds are about 4 miles east of Koke'e Lodge, off the 4WD Camp 10–Mohihi Rd in the forest reserve adjacent to the state park. Each campground has pit toilets, picnic shelters and fire pits. You'll need to carry in or treat the stream water. These forest reserve campgrounds have a three-night maximum stay and require camping permits (free) in advance from the DOFAW (see p435).

Eating

Koke'e Lodge (☎ 335-6061; snacks $3-7; ⏰ 9am-3:30pm) This is the only place to eat north of Waimea. It serves smoked-salmon quiche, granola and other breakfast fare all day long, plus hearty soups (try the Portuguese bean), sandwiches and interesting salads, like the Moroccan with couscous, hummus and Mediterranean veggies. The attached **gift shop** (⏰ 9am-4pm), sells candy bars, potato chips and a few canned-food items.

NORTHWESTERN HAWAIIAN ISLANDS

On a map of the Pacific, the rocks and shoals of the Northwestern Hawaiian Islands are just a speckle of dots stretching from Kaua'i nearly 1300 miles across the ocean in an almost straight northwesterly line.

There are 10 island clusters in all, encompassing 33 islands. These include atolls, each with a number of low sand islands formed on top of coral reefs, as well as some single-rock islands and a reef that is largely submerged. From east to west, the clusters are: Nihoa Island, Necker Island, French Frigate Shoals, Gardner Pinnacles, Maro Reef, Laysan Island, Lisianski Island, Pearl and Hermes Atoll, the Midway Islands and Kure Atoll. The total land area of the Northwestern Hawaiian Islands is just under 5 sq miles.

All of the islands except Kure Atoll (a state seabird sanctuary) and the Midway Islands are part of the Hawaiian Islands National Wildlife Refuge (NWR). Established in 1909 by President Theodore Roosevelt, it is the oldest and largest of the national wildlife refuges. In 1988, the Midway group was given a separate refuge status as the Midway Atoll NWR.

Visitors aren't allowed on the Northwestern Hawaiian Islands without permits, and these are granted only in the rarest of circumstances. Human activities are simply too disturbing to the fragile ecosystem. The only human habitation in the Hawaiian Islands NWR is at Tern Island, and that is for wildlife researchers.

When it comes to wildlife, the Northwestern Hawaiian Islands are home to around 15 million seabirds, all of which find room for at least a foothold. Eighteen seabird species nest on these islands, feeding on the abundant fish in the submerged reefs. The avian population includes frigate birds, boobies, albatross, terns, shearwaters, petrels, tropic birds and noddies. Screeching black-and-white sooty terns are the most abundant, numbering several million.

The Laysan duck, Laysan finch, Nihoa finch and Nihoa millerbird, endemic to Laysan and Nihoa Islands respectively, are all endangered or threatened species. This is not because their numbers are declining, but because these species exist in only one place on earth and are therefore susceptible to habitat disruption or to the introduction of new diseases and predators. One rat from a shipwrecked boat, weed seed from a hiker's boot or an oil slick washing ashore could mean the end of the species.

The endangered Hawaiian monk seal (p47), which exists only in Hawaii and has a total species population of about 1300, uses Kure Atoll, the French Frigate Shoals and Laysan, Lisianski, Nihoa and Necker Islands as its main pupping grounds.

THE FRENCH FRIGATE SHOALS

The French Frigate Shoals consist of a 135ft rock, La Perouse Pinnacle, named after the French explorer who almost wrecked on the reef, as well as 13 sand islands. One of them, 37-acre Tern Island, is the field headquarters for the Hawaiian Islands NWR. Most of Tern Island is covered by an airfield from the days when the US coastguard had a radio navigation station there. The old coastguard barracks now house two US Fish & Wildlife Service refuge managers and up to a dozen volunteers. Of the green sea turtles that nest in the Hawaiian Islands, 90% do so at the French Frigate Shoals.

LAYSAN ISLAND

Despite its small area (not quite 1.5 sq miles), Laysan is the biggest of the Northwestern Hawaiian Islands. The island also looms large as an illustration of how human interference can wreak havoc on island ecology.

Prior to the 19th century, millions of Laysan albatross (gooneys) lived on the island. From 1890 to 1904, human settlers arrived to mine Laysan for guano – the phosphate-rich bird droppings used as fertilizer – which led to the construction of houses, the introduction of pack mules and the docking of large ships. All this compromised the birds' habitat. Hundreds of thousands of albatross eggs were collected for their albumen, a substance used in photo processing. As each albatross lays just one egg a year, an 'egging' sweep could destroy an entire year's hatch. In one six-month period alone, 300,000 birds were killed for their feathers, used by milliners to make hats for fashionable ladies.

Pet rabbits virtually destroyed the island's vegetation, leading to erosion. The loss of native food plants spelled the end of three endemic land birds: the Laysan flightless rail, Laysan honey-creeper and Laysan millerbird. The Laysan duck reached the brink of extinction, with just six remaining in 1911, but has made a modest comeback, numbering about 300. Its only habitat is the brackish lagoon in the island's center. The Laysan finch, whose population once numbered only 100 (thanks to the rabbits), is again common on Laysan Island. A cousin of the honeycreeper, it has become carnivorous and feeds on the eggs and carcasses of seabirds.

About 160,000 pairs of Laysan albatross now live on the island, still one of the world's largest colonies. Albatross sometimes court for five seasons before mating. Once they do mate, pairs stay together for life and sometimes live for 30 years.

NECKER & NIHOA

Necker and Nihoa, the two islands closest to the main Hawaiian Islands, were probably settled more than a thousand years ago. Archaeological remains of stone temple platforms, house sites, terraces and carved stone images suggest that the early settlers were from the French Marquesas. Necker and Nihoa are rugged, rocky islands, each less than a quarter of a square mile. Nihoa is the tallest of the Northwestern Hawaiian Islands, with sheer sea cliffs and a peak elevation of 910ft.

Two land bird species live on tiny Nihoa and nowhere else. The Nihoa finch, which like the Laysan finch is a raider of other birds' eggs, has a population of a few thousand. The gray Nihoa millerbird, related to the Old World warbler family, is rare and secretive. It wasn't even discovered until 1923 and was so named because it eats miller moths; approximately 400 birds remain.

MIDWAY ISLANDS

The Midway Islands are best known as the site of a pivotal WWII battle between Japanese and American naval forces. Postwar, Midway served as a naval air facility with 3000 personnel.

In 1996 the military transferred jurisdiction of Midway to the US Fish & Wildlife Service and began an extensive cleanup program to remove contaminants left over from the military occupation and to rid Midway of non-native plants. The Fish & Wildlife Service then created a management policy dubbed 'from guns to goonies,' aiming to blend wildlife protection with low-impact tourism. It contracted with a private company, the Midway Phoenix Corporation, which developed the island for ecotourism, renovating the former officers' quarters into a hotel, arranging flights and running tours geared for divers and naturalists. To minimize environmental impact, all activities were guided and no more than 100 visitors were allowed on Midway at any one time.

Although the money generated from tourism helped defray the cost of operating the refuge, the costs were much higher than expected and Midway Phoenix pulled out in 2002 after chalking up huge losses. The Fish & Wildlife Service hopes to find a new vendor to resume operations, but until that happens, all public access to Midway has ceased. When, or even if, it will resume is anyone's guess.

More than a million seabirds nest on Midway, including the world's largest colony of Laysan albatross, which are so thick between November and July that they virtually blanket the ground. Sand Island, the largest in the three-island Midway Atoll, measures about 2 miles in length and a mile across. It contains a smattering of early-20th-century relics, including the remains of a trans-Pacific cable station dating to 1903 and WWII-era anti-aircraft guns.

VIRTUAL VISITS

To learn all about Midway, and to find out whether tourism has started up again (don't hold your breath), go online at the **US Fish & Wildlife Service site** (midway.fws.gov).

Other websites to check out are those of the **Hawaiian Islands National Wildlife Refuge** (pacificislands.fws.gov) and the **Northwestern Hawaiian Islands Coral Reef Ecosystem Reserve** (www.hawaiireef.noaa.gov).

DIRECTORY

Directory

CONTENTS

PRACTICALITIES

- Electricity: Voltage is 110/120V, 60 cycles, as elsewhere in the USA.

- Laundry: Most accommodations have inexpensive coin-operated washers and dryers; other convenient laundry locations are listed in individual island chapters.

- Newspapers & Magazines: Hawaii's daily, the *Honolulu Advertiser,* is available throughout the islands.

- Radio & TV: Hawaii has about 50 radio stations; all the major US TV networks are represented, as well as cable channels offering tourist information and Japanese-language programs.

- Video System: Video systems use the NTSC standard, which is not compatible with the PAL system.

- Weights & Measures: As on the mainland, distances are measured in feet, yards and miles; weights in ounces, pounds and tons.

ACCOMMODATIONS

Hawaii has a wide variety of accommodations in all price ranges – from camping to condominiums and everything in between. There is also a handful of inexpensive hostels and state park cabins; cheap campsites are located around each island.

Some lodging places have high- and low-season rates, usually in effect from mid-December to mid-April. Holidays (p526) always command premium prices. When demand peaks, including during special events (p524) year-round, lodgings book up well in advance. Off-season, rates are a bit cheaper and finding a choice room is a bit easier. You are as likely to find special deals off-season as you are to pay posted 'rack rates' during the peak winter season. The only exception to this rule is at family-friendly resorts during the summer. If there is a distinct variation between high- and low-season rates, it's noted in individual reviews. Sometimes rates fluctuate depending on if it's a weekday or weekend.

For last-minute deals, check out:

- www.expedia.com
- www.orbitz.com
- www.priceline.com
- www.travelocity.com

Our reviews indicate rates for single occupancy (s), double (d) or simply the room (r), when there's no difference in the rate for one or two people. A double room in our budget category usually costs $75 or less; mid-range doubles cost $75 to $195; top-end rooms start at $195. Unless noted, breakfast is *not* included, bathrooms are private and all lodging is open year-round; rates generally don't include taxes of a whopping 11.41%.

For an explanation of the icons used in this book see the Quick Reference on inside front cover.

A reservation guarantees your room, but most reservations require a deposit, after which, if you change your mind, the establishment will only refund your money if they're able to rebook your room within a certain period. Note the cancellation policies and other restrictions before making a deposit.

Assume smoking is not permitted inside.

B&Bs, Inns & Guesthouses

Some Hawaiian B&Bs are little more than spare bedrooms in family households; others are romantic hideaways. Most B&Bs discourage unannounced drop-ins, and for that reason, some do not appear on maps in our book. Same-day reservations are usually hard to get. B&B rates generally begin at around $60, although the average is closer to $100 and the most exclusive properties begin at $150. Many require a minimum stay of two or three days. Many B&Bs offer continental breakfast or provide food for guests to cook their own.

Many B&Bs are booked through agencies, including the following:
Affordable Paradise Bed & Breakfast (☎ 261-1693; www.affordable-paradise.com; 332 Kuukama St, Kailua, HI 96734) Books reasonably priced B&Bs and cottages.
All Islands Bed & Breakfast (☎ 263-2342, 800-542-0344; www.all-islands.com) Books scores of host homes.
Bed & Breakfast Hawaii (☎ 822-7771, 800-733-1632; www.bandb-hawaii.com; Box 449, Kapaa, HI 96746) A larger statewide service.

If you're traveling with children, note that some B&Bs are not geared to accept children as guests. Be sure to ask about these kinds of policies before making reservations.

Camping & Cabins

Hawaii has lots of public campgrounds, but no full-service private campgrounds. In general, national park camping is better than at state parks, which are better than at county

parks. Sites are less busy during the week than on weekends.

Although theft and violence has decreased, campers should be conscious of their surroundings. People traveling alone, especially women, need to be particularly cautious (see p531). The less you look like a tourist, the less likely you are to be targeted; always be careful with your valuables. Choose your park carefully; some are merely pit stops along the road frequented primarily by drinkers. For the most part, the further you are from population centers, the less likely you are to run into hassles. (Thieves and drunks aren't big on hiking.)

Two national parks allow camping: Haleakala National Park on Maui (p380) and Hawai'i Volcanoes National Park on the Big Island (p283). Both stunning parks have drive-up and wilderness camping areas; getting a space is seldom a problem. Haleakala also rents cabins inside the volcanic summit, with advance reservations.

The five largest islands offer camping at state parks. The parks usually have picnic tables, barbecue grills, drinking water, toilets and showers. Maintenance of the facilities varies greatly. You may obtain permits ($5 per night per site) from any Division of State Parks office. The main office, **Division of State Parks** (☎ 587-0300; room 310, 1151 Punchbowl St; postal address Box 621, Honolulu, HI 96809; www.hawaii.gov/dlnr/dsp; ☒ 8am-3:30pm Mon-Fri), handles reservations for all islands.

County parks vary. Some have wonderful white-sand beaches and good facilities, while others are unappealing roadside rest areas. Just because camping is allowed doesn't mean you'd *want* to camp there.

The state and counties also oversee some basic housekeeping cabins. For more specifics, see the O'ahu (p75), Big Island (p177), Maui (p293), Lana'i (p395), Moloka'i (p401) and Kaua'i (p434) chapters.

Condominiums

More spacious than hotel rooms, condominiums are individually owned apartments furnished with everything a visitor needs – from a kitchen to washers and dryers (usually) to lanais. They're almost always cheaper than all but the bottom-end hotel rooms, especially if you're traveling with a group. Most units have a three- to seven-day minimum stay. The weekly rate is often six times the daily rate and the monthly is three times the weekly.

Most condos are rented through agencies, which are listed in individual island chapters. To often save money, try booking directly first, then go through the agencies. You can also do your own web searches for online classifieds. Don't forget to ask about cleaning fees, which will be tacked onto your bill and vary depending on how long you stay.

Hostels

Hawaii has only three hostels associated with **Hostelling International** (HI; www.hiusa.org). Two are in Honolulu (p104) and another is near Hawai'i Volcanoes National Park on the Big Island (p283). Otherwise there are a number (although not an overwhelming number) of private hostel-style places around the islands. Few provide pristine digs; some are mere crash pads that don't compare favorably with the back seat of your car. Most are spartan, offer a common kitchen and Internet access and have bulletin boards thick with useful postings. Dorm beds generally cost under $20. You can find some listed at www.hostelhandbook.com online.

Hotels

Hotels commonly undercut their standard published 'rack rates' to remain as close to capacity as possible. While some hotels simply offer discounted rates, others throw in a free hire car. Ask about specials before booking. Within a particular hotel, the main thing that impacts room rates is the view and floor. An ocean view can cost 50% to 100% more than a parking-lot view (euphemistically called a 'garden view'). The higher the rate, usually the quieter the room.

Resorts

If you're celebrating a special event, a lull-you-into-submission resort might be just the ticket. These pleasure palaces are designed to meet your every need and keep you on property every minute of the day. There are a myriad of dining options, multiple swimming pools, children's programs and fitness centers. At the priciest ones, beach sands are without blemishes, coconut trees are trimmed of drooping fronds and every aspect of your experience is controlled (in an oh-so-seamless way). If that sounds a tad contrived, try it – you might get hooked.

ACTIVITIES

You name it, you can probably do it outdoors in Hawaii. The sheer number of activities offered is almost as endless as the horizon. And you don't have to be an aficionado to participate. Most outfitters and tour organizers offer lessons for beginners. So go ahead, learn to paddle an outrigger canoe or hop in a kayak and hug the coastline looking for endangered sea turtles. Swim or float in protected coves; body-surf the breaking waves. Don a snorkel and watch the underwater show unfold beneath you. And while Hawaii will never be mistaken for the Great Barrier Reef, scuba diving is hugely popular in these parts.

As for surfing, that quintessential Hawaiian pastime, visitors can hang ten and watch world-class athletes strut their stuff during competitions (see p524) or they can find their sea legs with the help of a buff instructor. Same goes for kiteboarding, boogie boarding and windsurfing.

Don't want to get wet? Try whale watching in winter or a sunset catamaran cruise. On dry land, Hawaiian golf courses are almost in a class unto themselves. Tennis is also a huge draw; although most hotels and resorts have their own courts, there are plenty of public courts.

Hiking is phenomenal in Hawaii, and conditions range from parched desertlike trails to muddy rain-forest paths. There are rigorous hikes and hourlong loops, both rewarding. Great horseback riding and mountain biking is available on each island.

Nine out of 10 repeat visitors polled would say that Kaua'i is the most action- and adventure-oriented island, and since O'ahu is so dominated by Honolulu and Waikiki, that O'ahu is the least. But such simplistic analysis belies the depth of play available on any given Sunday on any given island. For further details, see Hawaii Outdoors (p55).

BUSINESS HOURS

Unless there are variances of more than a half-hour in either direction, the following are 'normal' opening hours for entries in this book:

Banks 8:30am-4pm Mon-Fri; some banks open to 6pm Fri and 9am-noon Sat

Bars & Clubs to midnight daily; some clubs to 2am Thu-Sat

Businesses 8:30am-4:30pm Mon-Fri; some post offices open 9am-noon Sat

Restaurants breakfast 6-10am; lunch 11:30am-2pm; dinner 5-9:30pm
Shops 9am-5pm Mon-Sat, some also open noon-5pm Sun; major shopping areas and malls keep extended hours

CHILDREN (NA KEIKI)

Hawaii has adventure activities galore and all the necessary perks to stave off kiddy crankiness: splashy beaches, food for the finicky, video arcades, fruit falling from trees and loads of bugs to mess around with. Hawaii also offers tons of accessible cross-cultural opportunities, many available through hotels and resorts. Nevertheless, enjoyable family travel entails some logical gymnastics and juggling to keep boredom at bay. When the going gets tough, bust out the chocolate macadamia nuts or stop for shave ice.

Successful travel with young children requires planning and effort. Try not to overdo things; even for adults, packing too much into the time available can cause problems. Include children in the trip planning; if they've helped to work out where you will be going, they will be much more interested when they get there. Consult Lonely Planet's *Travel with Children,* which has lots of valuable tips and interesting anecdotal stories.

Many activities require that children be of a certain height in order to participate; unless Junior is 6ft tall and six years old, it's always best to inquire. For specific ideas about what to do with the kids, where to do it, see p122 for O'ahu, p229 for the Big Island, p298 for Maui, p391 for Lana'i, p414 for Moloka'i and p448 for Kaua'i.

If you're traveling with infants and come up short, **Baby's Away** (☎ 800-996-9030 on the Big Island, ☎ 800-496-6386 on O'ahu, ☎ 800-942-9030 on Maui; www.babysaway.com) rents cribs, strollers, playpens, high chairs and more. The easiest and most reliable way to find babysitters is to ask the hotel concierge.

Practicalities

Na keiki are welcome most everywhere in Hawaii (except at some smaller B&Bs). Children under 17 or 18 often stay free when sharing a room with their parents and using existing bedding. But it's always safest to ask. Cots and roll-away beds are usually available (for an additional fee) at hotels and resorts.

Because children are seen as well as heard in Hawaii, many restaurants have children's menus with significantly lower prices. Let's face it: chicken wings and hot dogs take less preparation than seared *'ahi* (yellowfin tuna). High chairs are usually available, but it pays to inquire ahead of time.

Most car-hire companies (p537) lease child-safety seats, but they don't always have them on hand; reserve in advance if you can.

For details about activities, see Hawaii Outdoors (p55).

CLIMATE CHARTS

Average temperatures in Hawaii differ only about 7°F from winter to summer. Near the coast, average highs are about 83°F and lows around 68°F. And yet, it snows on Mauna Kea and Mauna Loa on the Big Island in winter (and sometimes on Haleakala).

Hawaii's mountains trap trade winds blowing from the northeast, blocking clouds and bringing abundant rainfall to the island's windward sides. Windward Hilo on the Big Island is the rainiest city in the USA. Conversely, those same mountains block wind and rain from the southwesterly, or leeward, sides, where it's the driest and sunniest.

During *kona* (leeward) weather, winds blow from the south, turning snorkeling spots into surfing spots and vice versa. *Kona* storms usually occur in winter and are very unpredictable. See also p13.

COURSES

Some resorts and shopping centers, for example Whaler's Village on Maui (p319), offer free or low-cost classes and workshops in hula, traditional Hawaiian arts and the like. Since many schedules are unpredictable, keep your ears and eyes open. The hotel concierge is always a good source of local information. For a few more ideas, check out the Waimea 'Ukulele & Slack Key Guitar Institute (p232), the East Hawaii Cultural Center (p254) and the Volcano Art Center (p276), all on the Big Island. On Maui, the Hui No'eau Visual Arts Center (p367) is always great.

So-called alternative-lifestyle workshops for mediation, tai chi, Pilates and yoga classes take place around the islands. They predominate on Kaua'i (p480) but you'll also find some on the Big Island (p257).

The main venue for courses is the **University of Hawai'i** (UH; www.hawaii.edu), which has its main campus at Manoa on O'ahu and a

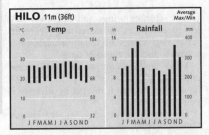

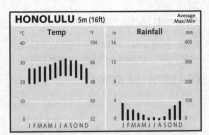

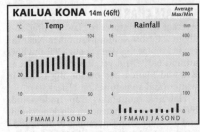

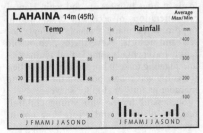

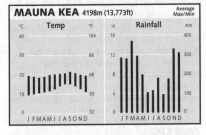

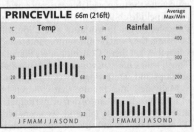

smaller campus in Hilo on the Big Island. UH offers full-time university attendance and summer-school courses. The summer session consists primarily of two six-week terms. For a catalog, contact the **Summer Session office** (☎ 956-5666; www.summer.hawaii.edu; Room 101, Krauss Bldg, 2500 Dole St, Honolulu, HI 96822).

CUSTOMS

Each visitor is allowed to bring 1L of liquor and 200 cigarettes duty-free into the USA, but you must be at least 21 years old to possess the former and 18 years old to possess the latter. In addition, each traveler is permitted to bring up to $100 worth of gift merchandise into the USA without incurring any duty.

Most fresh fruits and plants are restricted from entry into Hawaii, and customs officials are militant. In order to help prevent the pestilent spread of invasive alien species (see Responsible Tourism, p54),

it's also important to clean shoes and outdoors gear before bringing it to the islands. Because Hawaii is a rabies-free state, the pet quarantine laws are draconian, but you may be able to slice the time and expense to 30 days ($655) or 5 days ($225). For complete details, contact the **Hawaiian Department of Agriculture** (☎ 808-483-7151; www.hawaiiag.org).

DANGERS & ANNOYANCES

Although Hawaii is generally a safe place, tourism is its biggest industry by far, and as such, officials want to ensure visitors remain safe and happy. Concern about visitors' negative experiences in Hawaii has led state officials to establish the **Visitor Aloha Society of Hawaii** (VASH; ☎ 808-926-8274; www.visitoralohasociety ofhawaii.org), an organization providing aid to visitors who become the victims of accidents or crimes while vacationing in Hawaii.

For health concerns, see the Health chapter (p540).

Drugs

Pakalolo (marijuana) is still a billion-dollar underground industry (and Hawaii's most profitable crop), but the use of 'ice' (crystal methamphetamine) has become rampant since the 1990s, especially in rural communities. Some attribute the ice epidemic to dropping prices for the drug and crackdowns on marijuana cultivation. Whatever the cause, ice-related crime is rising and social-service agencies are struggling to provide treatment for addicts.

Scams

The main scams directed towards visitors in Hawaii involve fake activity-operator booths and timeshares booths. Salespeople at the latter will offer you all sorts of deals, from free luaus to sunset cruises, if you'll just come to hear their 'no obligation' pitch. *Caveat emptor.*

Theft & Violence

The islands are notorious for rip-offs from parked rental cars. It can happen within seconds, whether from a secluded parking area at a trailhead or from a crowded parking lot. Best not to leave anything valuable in your car any time. If you must, at least pack things well out of sight *before* you've pulled up to the place where you're going to leave the car. Many locals leave their car doors unlocked all the time to avoid paying for broken windows.

Other than rip-offs, most hassles are from drunks. Be tuned in to the vibes on beaches at night (see also Women Travelers, p531) and in places where young men hang out to drink, such as public campgrounds (p519). As expected, watch your belongings in hostels.

Overall, violent crime is lower in Hawaii than in most mainland cities. However, there are some pockets of resentment against tourists as well as off-islanders moving in. O'ahu tends to be worse than the other islands. A few stats are revealing: while the murder rate is at its lowest since 1956 and serious juvenile crime stands at record lows, aggravated assaults rose 10% in 2003.

Tsunami

Tsunami (incorrectly called tidal waves – the Japanese term *tsunami* means 'harbor wave') are not common, but when they hit they can be severe. Generated by earthquakes, typhoons or volcanic eruptions, the largest tsunami ever to hit Hawaii was in 1946. Waves reached a height of about 55ft, entire villages were washed away and 159 people died. Since that time, Hawaii has installed a warning system, aired through yellow speakers mounted on telephone poles around the islands. They're tested on the first working day of each month at 11:45am for about one minute.

Hawaii has had a tsunami every 10 years or so over the past century, killing more people statewide than all other natural disasters combined and causing millions of dollars in property damage. If you're in a low-lying coastal area when one occurs, immediately head for higher ground. The front section of the telephone books show maps of areas susceptible to tsunami and safety evacuation zones.

For a complete discussion of ocean safety, see p58.

DISABLED TRAVELERS

Many of the major resort hotels and tourist areas have elevators, TTD-capable phones, wheelchair-accessible rooms and other features to smooth the day. Beyond that, few generalizations can be made islandwide. For specifics, contact the **Commission on Persons with Disabilities** (☎ 586-8121; Room 101, 919 Ala Moana Blvd, Honolulu, HI 96814; www.hawaii.gov/health/dcab) about its three-part *Aloha Guide to Accessibility*. Part I contains general information and is obtainable free by mail. Parts II and III ($15) detail beach, park, shopping-center and visitor-attraction accessibility and list hotels with wheelchair access or specially adapted facilities.

Seeing-eye and guide dogs are not subject to the same quarantine as other pets, provided they meet the Department of Agriculture's minimum requirements (see p522).

Hawaii Wheelchair Vans (☎ 871-7785, 800-303-3750; Suite 121A, 355 Hukilike St, Kahului, HI 96732) books accessible accommodations, rents accessible vans and arranges various activities for disabled travelers on O'ahu and Maui. If you're not leaving the driving to them, don't forget to pack your disabled-parking placard.

For a list of services available to disabled passengers by airline, go to www.everybody.co.uk/airindex.htm.

On the mainland USA, the **Society for the Advancement of Travel for the Handicapped** (SATH; ☎ 212-447-7284; www.sath.org; Suite 610, 347 Fifth Ave, New York, NY 10016) publishes a quarterly magazine and has various information sheets on travel for the disabled.

DISCOUNTS

Glossy tourist magazines are distributed freely, replete with discount coupons for activities and restaurants. They're well worth perusing, perhaps while you're waiting for your baggage by the airport carousel.

Students with valid identification generally receive discounts into museums and such. Since Hawaii is a popular destination for retirees, lots of senior discounts are available. The applicable age has been creeping lower as well. The nonprofit American Association of Retired Persons (AARP) is a good source for travel bargains. For information on joining this advocacy group for Americans 50 years of age and older, contact **AARP** (☎ 888-687-2277; www.aarp.org; Membership Center, 3200 E Carson St, Lakewood, CA 90712).

EMBASSIES & CONSULATES

US embassies abroad:

Australia (☎ 02-6214 5600; 21 Moonah Pl, Yarralumla, Canberra, ACT 2600)
Canada (☎ 613-238 5335; 490 Sussex Dr, Ottawa, Ontario K1N 1G8)
France (☎ 33 1 43 12 22 22; 2 Av Gabriel, 75008 Paris)
Germany (☎ 030-8305 0; Neustädtische Kirchstrasse 4-5, 10117 Berlin)
Ireland (☎ 353 1 668 8777; 42 Elgin Rd, Ballsbridge, Dublin 4)
Italy (☎ 39 06 46741; Via Veneto 119/A, 00187 Rome)
Japan (☎ 03-3224 5000; 10-5, Akasaka 1-chome, Minato-ku, Tokyo)
Netherlands (☎ 070-310 9209; Lange Voorhout 102, 2514 EJ The Hague)
New Zealand (☎ 04-462 6000; 29 Fitzherbert Tce, PO Box 1190, Thorndon, Wellington)
UK (☎ 020-7499 9000; 24/31 Grosvenor Sq, London W1A 1AE)

Consulates in Honolulu:

Australia (☎ 524-5050; 1000 Bishop St)
Germany (☎ 946-3819; 252 Paoa Pl)
Italy (☎ 531-2277; Suite 201, 735 Bishop St)
Japan (☎ 543-3111; 1742 Nuuanu Ave)
Netherlands (☎ 531-6897; Suite 702, 745 Fort St Mall)
New Zealand (☎ 547-5117; Suite 414, 900 Richards St)
Philippines (☎ 595-6316; 2433 Pali Hwy)

EMERGENCIES

Dial ☎ 911 for police, fire and ambulance emergencies. The inside front cover of island phone books lists other vital service agencies, such as poison control, coastguard rescue, and suicide and crisis lines.

If you lose your passport, contact your consulate in Honolulu (see left); a complete list of consulate phone numbers can be found in the Yellow Pages.

For lost or stolen traveler's checks or credit cards, notify the bank or relevant company immediately (see p527). For any other theft, especially if you intend to file an insurance claim, contact the police to make an incident report.

As for heli-rescues of stranded hikers, don't count on it. Cell-phone coverage is spotty in remote areas and Lonely Planet doesn't want to imply that hikers are a phone call away from getting out of trouble. Having said that, **Travelguard** (☎ 800-844-7181) provides evacuation insurance for hikers.

See also Medical Services (p527).

FESTIVALS & EVENTS

With its good year-round weather, Hawaii has a seemingly endless number and variety of festivals and events. The following is an overview of major festivities, each of which is detailed in Festival & Events sections throughout the individual island destination chapters. Surf the Hawaii Visitors and Convention Bureau's (HVCB) complete events calendar at www.calendar.gohawaii.com. For holidays, see p526.

JANUARY–MARCH
NFL Pro Bowl (O'ahu) early January
Hula Bowl (O'ahu) January
Chinese New Year (statewide) mid-January to mid-February
Cherry Blossom Festival (mostly on O'ahu) February to early March
St Patrick's Day Parade (Waikiki, O'ahu) March 17
Merrie Monarch Festival (Hilo, the Big Island; p259) starts Easter Sunday

MAY
May Day (especially on O'ahu) May 1
Molokai Ka Hula Piko (Moloka'i; p408)

JUNE
Pan-Pacific Festival (Honolulu, O'ahu) first weekend of June

King Kamehameha Hula Competition (Honolulu, O'ahu) late June

JULY
Transpacific Yacht Race (Honolulu, O'ahu) early to mid-July
Rodeos (Waimea on the Big Island, p232, and Makawao on Maui, p368)

SEPTEMBER–NOVEMBER
Aloha Week (statewide) mid-September to early October
Princess Kaiulani Commemoration Week (Waikiki, O'ahu) third week in October
Kona Coffee Cultural Festival (Kailua-Kona, the Big Island; p192) early November
Triple Crown of Surfing (North Shore of O'ahu) November through December

DECEMBER
Pearl Harbor Day (Honolulu, O'ahu) December 7
Bodhi Day (statewide) December 8

FOOD

Reviews in the Eating section for each destination are broken down into three price categories: budget (for meals costing $10 or less), mid-range (where most main dishes cost $10 to 20) and top end (where most dinner mains cost more than $20). These price estimates do not include taxes, tips or beverages.

For details about Hawaiian specialties and delicacies, see p63.

GAY & LESBIAN TRAVELERS

Despite the contradictory attitudes of Hawaiians (p38) – a heritage of Polynesian tolerance stands in contrast to some contemporary Hawaiian elders' stated prejudice against homosexuality – Hawaii remains a popular destination for gay and lesbian travelers. The state has strong legislation to protect minorities and a constitutional guarantee of privacy that extends to sexual behavior between consenting adults (p38).

Gay Hawaii is not an in-your-face kind of place; public hand-holding and other outward signs of affection between gays is not commonplace. But everyday queer life on the Neighbor Islands is rife with low-key picnics and potlucks. Hidden B&Bs are the norm, not the exception. Without question, the main gay scene is in Waikiki on O'ahu.

Contact the **Gay & Lesbian Community Center** (☎ 951-7000; www.thecenterhawaii.org; Box 22718, Honolulu, HI 96823), a good source of information on local issues. The center has support groups, movie nights, a community newspaper and a library. The monthly **Odyssey** (www.odysseyhawaii .com), free at gay-friendly businesses throughout Hawaii, covers the island-side gay scene.

For general information, surf the following sites:
- www.gay.com
- www.gayhawaii.com
- www.gayjourney.com
- www.rainbowhandbook.com

MORE THAN ONE KIND OF RAINBOW IN HAWAII

You might have to dig a bit outside Waikiki for overt signs of gay life, but once your gaydar taps into a steady flow of same-sex venues, you'll feel oh-so-pretty and gay. Check out www.purpleroofs .com for a complete listing of gay-friendly accommodations, including the following:

- **Waikiki Grand** (p129)
- **Wailana Inn** (p342)

- **Kalani Oceanside Retreat** (p270)

Gay-friendly hangouts include the following:
- **Cabana at Waikiki** (p128)
- **Angles Waikiki** (p136)
- **In-Between** (p136)
- **Hapa's Night Club** (p343)

- **Hula's Bar & Lei Stand** (p135)
- **Fusion Waikiki** (p136)
- **Lava Zone** (p268)

Gay-friendly beaches include the following:
- **Queen's Surf Beach** (p126)
- **Little Beach** (p349)

- **Kehena Beach** (p270)
- **Donkey Beach** (p467)

Pacific Ocean Holidays (☎ 923-2400, 800-735-6599; Box 88245, Honolulu, HI 96830; www.gayhawaiivacations .com) arranges packages.

HOLIDAYS

Also see Festivals & Events (p524).
New Year's Day January 1
Martin Luther King Jr Day third Monday of January
Presidents Day third Monday of February
Easter in March or April
Memorial Day last Monday of May
King Kamehameha Day June 11
Independence Day July 4
Admission Day third Friday of August
Labor Day first Monday of September
Columbus Day second Monday of October
Election Day second Tuesday of November
Veterans Day November 11
Thanksgiving fourth Thursday of November
Christmas Day December 25

INSURANCE

It's expensive to get sick, crash a car or have things stolen from you in the USA. For hire-car insurance see p537 and for health insurance see p540. To protect yourself from items that may be stolen from your car, consult your home-owner's (or renter's) insurance policy before leaving home.

INTERNET ACCESS

If you usually access your email through your office or school, you'll find it easier to open a free account with **Yahoo!** (www.yahoo .com) or **Hotmail** (www.hotmail.com).

If you bring a laptop from outside the USA, invest in a universal AC and plug adapter. Also, your PC card modem may not work once you leave your home country – but you won't know until you try. The safest option? Buy a reputable 'global' modem before leaving home. Ensure that you have at least a US RJ-11 telephone adapter that works with your modem. For more technical help, visit www.teleadapt.com.

On the main islands cybercafés and business centers offer inexpensive online computer access. When accommodations provide free Internet access for those traveling without laptops, this is noted with an 🖳 . See also the relevant Information sections in individual destinations in this book.

Even if your hotel room does not have a modem port on its phone, you can plug into the main line as long as you remember to set

your machine to dial for an outside line first. Some luxury hotels may provide wireless Internet access for guests, so ask.

See p16 for Internet resources.

LEGAL MATTERS

You have the right to an attorney from the very first moment you are arrested. If you can't afford one, the state must provide one for free. The **Hawaii State Bar Association** (☎ 537-9140, 800-808-4722) makes attorney referrals, but foreign visitors may want to call their consulate for advice.

In Hawaii, anyone driving with a blood alcohol level of 0.08% or higher is guilty of driving 'under the influence,' which carries severe penalties. Driving while on any substance, be it beer, buds or barbiturates, is a decidedly bad idea. As with most places, the possession of marijuana and narcotics is illegal in Hawaii.

Hawaii's **Department of Commerce & Consumer Affairs** (☎ 587-1234) offers information on your rights regarding refunds and exchanges, time-share contracts and car hire.

According to the letter of the law, hitch-hiking is illegal statewide.

THE LEGAL AGE FOR...

▪ Drinking: 21
▪ Driving: 16
▪ Sex: 16
▪ Voting: 18

MAPS

First things first: the maps in this book are sufficient for quite a bit of exploring! And staying within the family for another minute, Lonely Planet's *Honolulu & Oahu City Map* is invaluable. Serious hikers should also consult Lonely Planet's *Hiking in Hawaii*.

If you want to beat your own path, the *Ready Mapbook* series is extremely useful. These atlas-style books (about $10 each) cover virtually every road on each of the main islands. (Lana'i and Moloka'i are included in the book for Maui.)

United States Geological Survey (USGS; ☎ 888-275-8747; www.usgs.gov) publishes full-island and detailed sectional maps; be careful to note that some were drawn decades ago. USGS maps can be purchased on Kaua'i at the Kauai Museum (p445) and the Koke'e State Park museum (p512); on O'ahu at the **Pacific Map Center** (☎ 545-3600; 560 N Nimitz, Honolulu), and on the Big Island at Hawai'i Volcanoes National Park (p271). Individual island chapters list bookstores that sell maps under Information sections.

Divers and snorkelers should try **Franko's Maps** (www.frankosmaps.com), a series of laminated, waterproof maps (about $7) of each island showing snorkeling and diving spots.

MEDICAL SERVICES

Overall, Hawaii is a very healthy place to live and visit. It ranks first of all the 50 US states in life expectancy, currently about 76 years for men and 81 years for women. The longer you stay, the healthier you'll feel. If you get really sick here, try to do it in a major city. The following are major island hospitals:

Hilo Medical Center (Map p250; ☎ 974-4700; 1190 Waianuenue Ave, Big Island)

Kona Community Hospital (☎ 322-9311; www.kch .hhsc.org; 79-1019 Haukapila St, Kealakekua, Big Island)

Lana'i Community Hospital (Map p390; ☎ 565-6411; 628 7th St, Lana'i)

Maui Memorial Hospital (Map p332; ☎ 244-9056; 221 Mahalani St, Wailuku, Maui)

Molokai General Hospital (Map p407; ☎ 553-5331; 280 Puali St, Kaunakakai, Moloka'i)

Straub Clinic & Hospital (Map p90; ☎ 522-4000; 888 S King St, Honolulu, O'ahu)

Wilcox Memorial Hospital (Map p443; ☎ 245-1010; 3420 Kuhio Hwy, Kaua'i)

See also Emergencies, p524, and the Health chapter, p540.

MONEY

The US dollar is the only currency used in Hawaii. The dollar (commonly called a buck) is divided into 100 cents. Coins come in denominations of one cent (penny), five cents (nickel), 10 cents (dime), 25 cents (quarter) and the rare 50-cent piece (half dollar). Notes come in one-, five-, 10-, 20-, 50- and 100-dollar denominations.

See the Quick Reference inside the front cover for exchange rates, and Getting Started (p13) for information on costs.

ATMs, Cash & Checks

ATMs are great for quick cash influxes and can negate the need for traveler's checks

entirely, but watch out for ATM surcharges. Most banks charge around US$1.50 per withdrawal.

The **Bank of Hawaii** (www.boh.com) and **First Hawaiian Bank** (www.fhb.com) both have extensive ATM networks that will give cash advances on major credit cards and allow cash withdrawals with affiliated ATM cards. Most ATMs in Hawaii accept bank cards from both the Plus and Cirrus systems. Look for ATMs outside banks, and in large grocery stores, shopping centers, convenience stores and gas stations.

If you're carrying foreign currency, it can be exchanged for US dollars at the Honolulu International Airport and larger banks around Hawaii.

Personal checks not drawn on a Hawaiian bank are generally not accepted.

Credit Cards

Major credit cards are widely accepted in Hawaii, including at car-hire agencies and most hotels, restaurants, gas stations, grocery stores and tour operators. Many B&Bs and some condominiums – particularly those handled through rental agencies – do not accept credit cards, however.

Tipping

In restaurants, good waiters are tipped at least 15%, while dissatisfied customers make their ire known by leaving 10%. There has to be real cause for not tipping at all. Taxi drivers and hairstylists are typically tipped about 10% and hotel bellhops about $1 per bag.

Traveler's Checks

Traveler's checks provide protection from theft and loss. Keeping a record of the check numbers and those you have used is vital for replacing lost checks, so keep this information separate from the checks themselves. For refunds on lost or stolen travelers checks, call **American Express** (☎ 800-992-3404) or **Thomas Cook** (☎ 800-287-7362).

Foreign visitors carrying traveler's checks will find things infinitely easier if the checks are in US dollars. Most mid-range and top-end restaurants, hotels and shops accept US dollar traveler's checks and treat them just like cash. If, however, you're camping and dining on *loco moco*, you won't be able to do much with a traveler's check but sop up spilled grease.

DIRECTORY

PHOTOGRAPHY

For a very complete short course on photographic ins and outs, dos and don'ts, consult Lonely Planet's *Travel Photography*.

Both print and slide film are readily available in Hawaii. Disposable underwater cameras costing about $10 are sold everywhere and deliver surprisingly good snaps.

If you're in Hawaii for any length of time, have your film developed here, as the high temperature and humidity greatly accelerate the deterioration of exposed film. Longs Drugs is one of the cheapest places for developing film and it offers frequent free second-set deals. All the main tourist enclaves have one-hour print shops.

Don't even think about taking snaps of military installations.

With the implementation of high-powered X-ray at many airports, don't pack film into checked luggage or carry-on bags. Instead carry your film in a baggie to show separately to airport security officials (known as a hand check). Remember to finish off the roll in your camera and take it out, too, or those photos may end up foggy.

For video information, see p518.

POST

Mail delivery to and from Hawaii usually takes a little longer than similar services on the US mainland via the **US postal service** (USPS; ☎ 800-275-8777; www.usps.gov).

First-class mail between Hawaii and the mainland goes by air and usually takes three to four days. For 1st-class mail sent and delivered within the USA, postage rates are 37¢ for letters up to 1oz (23¢ for each additional ounce) and 23¢ for standard-size postcards.

International airmail rates for letters up to 1oz are 60¢ to Canada or Mexico, 80¢ to other countries. Postcards cost 50¢ to Canada or Mexico, 70¢ to other countries.

You can have mail sent to you c/o General Delivery at most big post offices in Hawaii. On O'ahu, all general-delivery mail addressed to Honolulu or Waikiki is delivered to the main post office adjacent to Honolulu International Airport. General delivery mail is usually held for up to 30 days. Most hotels will also hold mail for incoming guests.

SENIOR TRAVELERS

Hawaii is a very popular destination for retirees, and lots of senior discounts are available. For instance, Hawaii's biggest hotel chain, Outrigger, offers across-the-board discounts.

The nonprofit American Association of Retired Persons (AARP) is a good source for travel bargains. For information on joining this group, contact **AARP** (☎ 800-424-3410; www .aarp.org).

Elderhostel (☎ 617-426-8056, 877-426-8056; www .elderhostel.org) is a great nonprofit organization offering educational programs for those aged 55 and older. One- and two-week programs are offered (see p530).

SHOPPING

Hawaii has a lot of fine craftspeople, and quality handicrafts can be readily found on all the islands. Save some money so you can spend it here. The best way to distinguish authentic Hawaiiana from the fake stuff is to shop at well-respected art galleries and artist's cooperatives. A sampling of these includes: the granddaddy of them all, the Bishop Museum on O'ahu (p97), the Volcano Art Center on the Big Island (p276) and the Hu'i No'eau Visual Arts Center (p366) and Maui Crafts Guild (p354), both on Maui. On Kaua'i, the little town of Hanapepe (p503) has a number of fine galleries.

See the Culture chapter (p43) for more information on Hawaiian arts.

Ni'ihau shell lei (p41), garlands made from the tiny shells that wash up on the island of Ni'ihau, are one of the most prized and expensive Hawaiian souvenirs.

Music shops carry recorded traditional and contemporary Hawaiian music (p522). Hula musical instruments such as nose flutes and gourd rattles are uniquely Hawaiian and make interesting gifts.

Hawaii's island-style clothing is colorful and light. The classiest aloha shirts are of lightweight cotton with subdued colors (like those of reverse-fabric prints). Crazy Shirts outlets sell quality T-shirts with home-grown Hawaiian designs, some dyed with coffee, hemp, beer or Kaua'i red dirt.

Food items are always a hit back home. Macadamia nuts, Kona coffee, *liliko'i* (passion fruit) or *poha* (gooseberry) preserves and mango chutney all make convenient gift items. Find them at the ubiquitous ABC Stores. As for pineapples, they're not only heavy and bulky, they're likely to be just as cheap at home. Hawaii is a good place to pick up Japanese cooking ingredients that might be difficult to find back home.

Flowers such as orchids, anthuriums and proteas make good gifts if you're flying straight home. Proteas stay fresh for about 10 days and then can be dried. Foreign visitors should check with their airline in advance, however, as there are commonly restrictions against taking agricultural products across international borders (see p522).

SOLO TRAVELERS

Travel, including solo travel, is generally safe and easy. In general, women need to exercise more vigilance in large cities than in rural areas. Everyone, though, should avoid hiking, cycling long distances or camping alone, especially in unfamiliar places. For more safety advice, see Women Travelers (p531) and Dangers & Annoyances (p522).

TELEPHONE

Always dial '1' before toll-free (☎ 800, 888, etc) and domestic long-distance numbers. Some toll-free numbers may only work within the state or from the US mainland, for instance, while others may work from Canada, too. But you'll only know if it works by making the call.

Pay phones are readily found in shopping centers, beach parks and other public places. Calls made from one point on an island to other point on that island are considered local and cost 25¢ or 50¢. Calls from one island to another are always long distance and more expensive. Hotels often add a hefty service charge of $1 for calls made from a room phone.

Private prepaid phone cards are available from convenience stores, supermarkets and pharmacies. Cards sold by major telecommunications companies such as AT&T may offer better deals than upstart companies.

Cell (Mobile) Phones

The USA uses a variety of mobile-phone systems, 99% of which are incompatible with the GSM 900/1800 standard used throughout Europe and Asia. Check with your cellular service provider before departure about using your phone in Hawaii. Verizon has the most extensive cellular network on the islands, but AT&T, Cingular and Sprint also have decent coverage. Cellular coverage is quite good on O'ahu, but more spotty on some of the Neighbor Islands. Coverage is downright nonexistent in many remote regions and on hiking trails.

Long-Distance & International Calls

To make international calls direct from Hawaii, dial ☎ 011 + country code + area code + number. (An exception is to Canada, where you dial ☎ 1 + area code + number, but international rates still apply.)

For international operator assistance, dial ☎ 0. The operator can provide specific rate information and tell you which time periods are the cheapest for calling.

If you're calling Hawaii from abroad, the international country code for the USA is ☎ 1. All calls to Hawaii are then followed by the area code ☎ 808 and the seven-digit local number. Also dial the area code when making a call from one island to another (eg O'ahu to Maui).

TIME

Hawaii does not observe daylight saving time. It does, though, have about 11 hours of daylight in midwinter (December) and almost 13½ hours in midsummer (June). In midwinter, the sun rises at about 7am and sets at about 6pm. In midsummer, it rises before 6am and sets after 7pm.

And then there's 'Hawaiian time,' which is either a slow-down-the-clock pace or a euphemism for being late.

When it's noon in Hawaii, it's

2pm in Los Angeles (same day)
5pm in New York (same day)
10pm in London (same day)
7am in Tokyo (next day)
8am in Melbourne (next day)
10am in Auckland (next day)

TOILETS

Relatively speaking, it's not hard to go in Hawaii. There are hundreds of hotels and resorts, into which you can wander freely and avail yourself of the facilities without fear of being stopped. In addition, an overwhelming number of beaches generally have well-developed facilities, which include toilets, showers and changing rooms.

TOURIST INFORMATION

Hawaii Visitors & Convention Bureau (☎ 800-464-2924; www.gohawaii.com; Suite 801, 2270 Kalakaua Ave, Waikiki, HI 96815) will mail tourist information.

Additional tourist offices include:

O'ahu Visitors Bureau (☎ 524-0722, 877-525-6248; www.visit-oahu.com; Suite 1520, 733 Bishop St, Honolulu 96813)

Big Island Visitors Bureau Hilo (☎ 961-5797, 800-525-6284; www.bigisland.org; 250 Keawe St, Hilo 96720); Waikoloa (☎ 886-1655; 250 Waikoloa Beach Dr, Waikoloa 96738)

Maui Visitors Bureau (☎ 244-3530, 800-525-6284; www.visitmaui.com; 1727 Wili Pa Loop, Wailuku) Also represents Lana'i and Moloka'i.

Destination Lana'i (☎ 565-7600, 800-947-4774; www .visitlanai.net)

Moloka'i Visitors Association (☎ 553-3876, 800-800-6367; www.molokai-hawaii.com; Kamehameha V Hwy, Kaunakakai 96748)

Kauai Visitors Bureau (☎ 245-3971, 800-262-1400; www.kauaivisitorsbureau.org; Suite 101, 4334 Rice St, Lihu'e)

TOURS

See p532 for package tours and p535 for cruises to the Hawaiian Islands.

A number of companies operate half-day and full-day sightseeing bus tours on each island. Specialized adventure tours like whale-watching cruises, bicycle tours down Haleakala, snorkeling trips to Lanai and boat cruises along the Kona Coast are also available. All of these tours can be booked after arrival in Hawaii. For details, consult the Activities sections near the front of island destination chapters.

Helicopter tours go to some amazing places, with flights over active volcanoes, along towering coastal cliffs and even above inaccessible waterfalls. Prices vary depending on the destination and the length of the flight, with a 45-minute tour averaging $125 per passenger. Morning flights often have the clearest weather and the smoothest air conditions, but cloudy weather can occur at any time, so keep an eye on the weather forecast. For details, see the Tours section near the front of each island chapter.

If you want to visit another island while you're in Hawaii but only have a day or two to spare, consider an island-hopping tour to the Neighbor Islands. The largest company specializing in 'overnighters' is **Roberts Hawaii** (on O'ahu ☎ 523-9323, from the Neighbor Islands & US mainland ☎ 800-899-9323; www.robertsovernighters.com). You can also do a working volunteer tour on the island of Kaho'olawe (p382).

Elderhostel (☎ 617-426-7788, 877-426-8056; www .elderhostel.org) offers educational programs for those aged 55 or older. Many of these focus on Hawaii's people and culture, while others explore the natural environment. The fee is about $650/1300 for one-/two-week programs, including accommodations, meals and classes, but excluding airfare.

Earthwatch International (☎ 800-776-0188; www .earthwatch.org) projects in Hawaii focus on activities such as restoring mountain streams and assisting in humpback whale research. The cost is around US$2400 for programs that last about two weeks. Meals and accommodations are included, but airfare is not.

VISAS

Since the establishment of the Department of Homeland Security following the events of September 11, 2001, immigration now falls under the purview of the **Bureau of Citizenship & Immigration Service** (BCIS; www.bcis.gov).

Getting into the US can be a bureaucratic nightmare, depending on your country of origin. To make matters worse, the rules are rapidly changing. For up-to-date information about visas and immigration, check with the **US State Department** (http://unitedstatesvisas.gov /visiting.html).

Most foreign visitors to the USA need a visa. However, there is a Visa Waiver Program through which citizens of certain countries may enter the USA for stays of 90 days or less without first obtaining a US visa. The list is frequently changing, but currently it includes Andorra, Australia, Austria, Belgium, Brunei, Denmark, Finland, France, Germany, Iceland, Ireland, Italy, Japan, Liechtenstein, Luxembourg, Monaco, the Netherlands, New Zealand, Norway, Portugal, San Marino, Singapore, Slovenia, Spain, Sweden, Switzerland and the UK. Under this program you must have a return ticket (or onward ticket to any foreign destination) that is nonrefundable in the USA. Note that you will not be allowed to extend your stay beyond 90 days.

Because the **Department of Homeland Security** (DHS; www.dhs.gov) is continually modifying its requirements, even those with visa waivers may be subject to enrolment in the US-Visit program. This program may require that visa recipients have a machine-readable passport and/or a digital scan of their fingerprints. Contact the DHS for current requirements.

Regardless, your passport should be valid for at least six months longer than your intended stay and you'll need to submit a recent photo (50.8mm x 50.8mm) with the visa application. Documents of financial stability and/or guarantees from a US resident are sometimes required, particularly for those from developing countries. Visa applicants may be required to 'demonstrate binding obligations' that will ensure their return home. Because of this requirement, those planning to travel through other countries before arriving in the USA are generally better off applying for their US visa in their home country rather than while they are on the road.

The validity period for a US visitor visas depends on your home country. The actual length of time you'll be allowed to stay in the USA is determined by the BCIS at the port of entry. If you want to stay in the USA longer than the date stamped on your passport, go to the Honolulu office of the **Citizenship & Immigration Service** (☎ 532-3721; 595 Ala Moana Blvd, Honolulu) before the stamped date to apply for an extension.

WOMEN TRAVELERS

Hawaii presents few unique problems for women travelers and may be more relaxed and comfortable than many mainland destinations. The one area in which women – especially solo travelers – might feel uneasy is in local bars. In any culture the world over, a scene involving bunches of men knocking back liquor can get dicey, so proceed to local watering holes with a group or with your wits fully about you.

If you're camping, opt for secure, well-used camping areas over isolated locales where you might be the only camper. County parks and their campgrounds (see p519) are notorious for late-night beer binges and some are known for long-term squatting and may be unpleasant for solo travelers. Women walking alone on beaches after dark should stay alert to any nefarious, drunken vibes floating their way.

WORK

US citizens can pursue work in Hawaii as they would in any other state – the problem is finding a decent job. Foreign visitors in the USA on tourist visas are not legally allowed to take up employment.

Finding serious 'professional' employment is difficult since Hawaii has a tight labor market. The biggest exceptions to this rule are for teachers and nurses. Waiting on tables at restaurants or cafés is probably what you can expect. Folks with language, scuba, fishing or guiding skills might investigate employment with resorts. But if you think you're going to get a housekeeping or groundskeeping job at a megaresort, think again; many of these jobs go to locals.

Check notice boards in larger cities, at hostels (which often offer room and board in exchange for work), at coffee shops and cafés, and at natural food stores. Also check the *Honolulu Advertiser*'s classified job ads (www.honoluluadvertiser.com) and continue surfing at www.jobshawaii.com. The **State Department of Labor & Industrial Relations** (☎ 586-8700; www.dlir.state.hi.us; 830 Punchbowl St, Honolulu, HI 96813) can be a good resource.

For volunteer work, contact the **Sierra Club** (www.hi.sierraclub.org) or **Malama Hawaii** (www.malamahawaii.org). Additionally, the **National Park Service** (☎ 808-985-6092; www.nps.gov/volunteer) has a program allowing volunteers to work at Hawai'i Volcanoes National Park (p271) on the Big Island and Haleakala National Park (p374) on Maui.

Transportation

GETTING THERE & AWAY

The vast majority of all visitors to Hawaii arrive by air because Hawaii is a tiny dot in the middle of the Pacific Ocean. Folks traveling between the US mainland and Asia, Australia, New Zealand or the South Pacific are usually allowed to make a stopover in Honolulu. Virtually all international flights, and the majority of domestic flights, arrive at Honolulu International Airport (p114). For information on tours to Hawaii, see p530.

ENTERING THE COUNTRY

A passport is required for all foreign citizens except Canadians, who only need to show proof of residence. Residents of most other countries need a tourist visa. It's always advisable to confirm this information since it changes rapidly. See p530 for details.

AIR

US domestic and international airfares vary tremendously depending on the season, general tourism trends to the islands, and how much flexibility the ticket allows for flight changes and refunds. Since nothing determines fares more than demand, when things are slow, airlines lower their fares to fill more seats. There's a lot of competition, and at any given time any one of the airlines could have the cheapest fare.

THINGS CHANGE...

The information in this chapter is particularly vulnerable to change. Check directly with the airline or a travel agent to make sure you understand how a fare (and ticket you may buy) works and be aware of the security requirements for international travel. Shop carefully. The details given in this chapter should be regarded as pointers and are not a substitute for your own careful, up-to-date research.

Airports & Airlines

Because of the sheer distance, travelers arriving from Europe will often need to change planes on the US mainland. Major gateway airports include the following:

Atlanta International Airport (ATL; ☎ 800-897-1910; www.atlanta-airport.com)

Chicago O'Hare International Airport (ORD; ☎ 773-686-2200; www.ohare.com)

Denver International Airport (DEN; ☎ 303-342-2000; www.flydenver.com)

Los Angeles International Airport (LAX; ☎ 310-646-5252; www.los-angeles-lax.com)

New York JFK International Airport (JFK; ☎ 718-244-4444; www.panynj.gov)

San Francisco International Airport (SFO; ☎ 650-876-2222; www.flysfo.com)

The vast majority of incoming flights from overseas and the US mainland arrive on O'ahu at **Honolulu International Airport** (HNL; ☎ 836-6413; www.honoluluairport.com). Airlines flying into Honolulu:

Air Canada (☎ 888-247-2262; www.aircanada.ca)

Air New Zealand (☎ 800-262-1234; www.airnz.co.nz)

Air Pacific (☎ 800-227-4446; www.airpacific.com)

Alaska Airlines (☎ 800-252-7522; www.alaskaair.com)

Aloha Airlines (☎ 800-367-5250; www.alohaairlines.com)

American Airlines (☎ 800-223-5436; www.aa.com)

China Airlines (☎ 800-227-5118; www.china-airlines.com)

Continental (☎ 800-523-3273; www.continental.com)

Delta (☎ 800-221-1212; www.delta.com)

Hawaiian Airlines (☎ 800-367-5320; www.hawaiianair.com)

Japan Airlines (☎ 800-525-3663; www.japanair.com)

Korean Airlines (☎ 800-438-5000; www.koreanair.com)
Northwest-KLM (☎ 800-225-2525; www.nwa.com)
Philippine Airlines (☎ 800-435-9725; www.philippine air.com)
Qantas Airways (☎ 800-227-4500; www.qantasusa .com)
United (☎ 800-241-6522; www.ual.com)
US Airways (☎ 800-428-4322; www.usairways.com)

There is an increasing number of direct flights from the US mainland to Kaua'i, the Big Island and Maui on various airlines. See the Getting There & Away sections near the front of individual island chapters for details. To reach Lana'i (p393) or Moloka'i (p410), you'll have to fly via Honolulu or Maui.

Neighbor Island airports include:

Hilo International Airport (ITO; ☎ 935-5707; Hawai'i)
Kahului Airport (OGG; ☎ 872-3830; Maui)
Kona International Airport at Keahole (KOA; ☎ 329-3423; Hawai'i)
Lana'i Airport (LNY; ☎ 565-6757; Lana'i)
Lihu'e Airport (LIH; ☎ 245-2831; Kaua'i)
Moloka'i Airport (MKK; ☎ 567-6140; Moloka'i)

Tickets

Fares change infinitely faster than the trade winds. The best deals are often found on the Internet. Start searching at www.travelo city.com, www.expedia.com or www.orbitz .com.

Once in Hawaii, you'll find discounted fares to virtually any place around the Pacific. Larger travel agencies that specialize in discount tickets include **King's Travel** (☎ 593-4481; www.kingstravel.com; 725 Kapiolani Blvd, Honolulu) and **Panda Travel** (☎ 734-1961; www.pandaonline .com; 1017 Kapahulu Ave, Honolulu).

Round-the-world (RTW) tickets allow you to fly on the combined routes of two or more airlines and can be a good deal if you're coming from a great distance and want to visit other parts of the world in addition to Hawaii. **British Airways** (☎ 800-247-9297; www .britishairways.com) and **Qantas Airways** (☎ 800-227-4500; www.qantas.com.au) offer the best plans through programs called oneworld Explorer and Global Explorer, respectively.

Circle Pacific tickets are essentially a take-off on RTW tickets, but instead of moving in one general direction, they allow you to keep traveling in the same circular direction. Because you start and end at a city that borders the Pacific, these tickets are most practical for travelers who live in or near the Pacific region. Contact **Air New Zealand** (☎ 800-262-1234; www.airnz.co.nz) or **Continental** (☎ 800-523-3273; www.continental.com), whose program is Circle Micronesia. Continental's flights originate in Los Angeles, San Francisco and Honolulu.

US Mainland

Competition is high among airlines flying to Honolulu from major mainland cities. Typically, the lowest return fares from the US mainland to Hawaii are about $600 from the east coast and $400 from the west coast. Sometimes package-tour companies offer the best airfare deals, even if you don't want to buy the whole 'package.'

Most mainland flights fly into Honolulu. American, Continental, Delta, Northwest-KLM and United fly to Honolulu from both the east and west coasts. But there are also direct flights to Maui, Kaua'i and the Big Island. United, US Airways, Alaska Airlines and American all fly into Kaua'i from either Los Angeles or San Francisco, for instance.

Hawaiian Airlines has nonstop flights to Honolulu from Los Angeles, Las Vegas, Seattle, Phoenix, Portland, San Francisco, San Diego and Sacramento. It also has nonstop flights to Maui from Los Angeles, San Francisco and Seattle.

Aloha Airlines offers flights to Honolulu from Las Vegas, Sacramento, Oakland and Orange County. It also flies to Maui from Oakland, Reno, Las Vegas and Orange County and to the Big Island (Kona) from Oakland and Las Vegas.

For those with limited time, package tours can sometimes be the cheapest way to go. Basic ones cover airfare and accommodations, while deluxe packages include car hire, island hopping and all sorts of activities. If you're going to Hawaii on a short getaway, packages may cost little more than what airfare alone would have cost. Although costs

---

DEPARTURE TAX

Taxes and fees for US airports are normally included in the price of tickets when you buy them, whether they're purchased in the USA or abroad. There are no state taxes to pay when leaving Hawaii.

TRANSPORTATION

vary, one-week tours with airfare and no-frills hotel accommodations usually start around $500 from the US West Coast, $800 from the US East Coast, based on double occupancy. **Pleasant Hawaiian Holidays** (☎ 800-742-9244; www.2hawaii.com) has departures from various US mainland points. **Sun Trips** (☎ 800-786-8747; www.suntrips.com) offers packages from Oakland, California.

And then there's the Air Tech Space-Available FlightPass, which certainly can be the cheapest way to fly between the West Coast and Hawaii. **Air Tech** (☎ 212-219-7000; www.airtech.com) offers super deals by selling standby seats at $129 one way. If you provide the staff with a two- to four-day travel window, they'll get you a seat at a nice price. Currently, flights to Honolulu, Kaua'i, and Maui depart from San Francisco and Los Angeles

The nonstop flight time to Hawaii is about 5½ hours from the west coast or 11 hours from the east coast.

Australia
Hawaiian Airlines flies nonstop between Sydney and Honolulu. Qantas flies to Honolulu from Sydney and Melbourne (via Sydney, but without changing planes). Return fares range seasonally from A$900 to A$1400.

Canada
Air Canada offers direct flights to Honolulu from Vancouver and also other Canadian cities via Vancouver. The cheapest return fares to Honolulu are about C$800 from Vancouver, C$1100 from Calgary or Edmonton, and C$1400 from Toronto.

Japan
Japan Airlines flies to Honolulu from Tokyo, Osaka, Nagoya and Fukuoka. Return fares vary according to departure city and season but, with the exception of busier holiday periods, they're generally around ¥40,000 for a ticket valid for three months.

Fares to Honolulu on All Nippon Airways (ANA), which also depart from Sapporo and Kumamoto, are sometimes steeply discounted to ¥70,000.

Continental and Northwest-KLM have several flights to Honolulu from Tokyo and Osaka; ticket prices are comparable to those offered by Japan Airlines.

Micronesia & New Zealand
Continental has nonstop flights from Guam to Honolulu with return fares from about US$1100. Air New Zealand flies from Auckland to Honolulu for about NZ$1650 return.

South Pacific Islands
Hawaiian Airlines flies to Honolulu from Tahiti and American Samoa. From American Samoa return fares are about US$600; from Tahiti to Honolulu, return fares are about US$700.

Air New Zealand offers return tickets from Fiji to Honolulu via Auckland for about NZ$1370. It also flies to Honolulu from Tonga, the Cook Islands and Western Samoa for around NZ$870 (from Western Samoa) or NZ$1080 (from Tonga and the Cook Islands) return.

Southeast Asia
Northwest-KLM flies to Honolulu from Hong Kong, Bangkok, Manila, Seoul and Singapore. Thai Airways, Korean Air, China Airlines, Singapore Air and Philippine Airlines also offer numerous flights between Southeast Asian cities and Honolulu.

Although there are some seasonal variations, the standard return fares are about US$1000 from Manila, US$1200 from Seoul and Bangkok, US$1400 from Hong Kong and US$1600 from Singapore.

Those fares, however, are the standard published fares, and bucket shops in places such as Bangkok, Singapore and Hong Kong should be able to come up with much better deals – often at around half the price of the standard fares.

UK & Continental Europe
The most common route to Hawaii from Europe is west via New York, Chicago or Los Angeles. If you're interested in heading east with stops in Asia, it may be cheaper to get a RTW ticket instead of returning the same way.

The lowest return fares with American Airlines from London, Frankfurt and Paris to Honolulu are usually around €800. United, Delta and Continental have a similarly priced service to Honolulu from some European cities.

London is arguably the world's headquarters for bucket shops specializing in discount tickets. Two good, reliable agents for cheap tickets in the UK:

STA Travel (☎ 020-240 9821; www.statravel.co.uk; 33 Bedford St, Covent Garden, London)

Trailfinders (☎ 020-7628 7628; www.trailfinders.co.uk; 1 Threadneedle St, London)

SEA

In recent years, a handful of cruise ships has begun offering tours that include Hawaii. Most cruises last 10 to 12 days and have fares that start at around US$150 a day per person, based on double occupancy – though discounts and promotions can bring that price down to under US$100 a day. Airfare to and from the departure point costs extra.

Most Hawaiian cruises include stopovers in Honolulu, Maui, Kaua'i and the Big Island. Cruise lines include the following:

Holland America Cruise Line (☎ 877-724-5425; www .hollandamerica.com) Typically departs for Honolulu from San Diego, Seattle or Vancouver.

Princess Cruises (☎ 800-568-3262; www.princess .com) Offers the most cruises; operates between Honolulu and Tahiti.

You can also get to Hawaii by private yacht. If you don't have one of your own, and you're hoping to get on a crew, start poking around the Honolulu ports in early spring. Experienced crew should try www .boatcrew.net, a well-organized site with a database of boats leaving from various mainland ports. Membership is US$10 per month (or US$100 per year).

GETTING AROUND

AIR

Only Moloka'i and Lana'i have a regular ferry service from Maui at the present time (although plans for a 'superferry,' p536, are just getting underway), so you'll likely be island-hopping by plane.

The major airports handling most interisland traffic include: Honolulu (on O'ahu), Kahului (on Maui), Kona and Hilo (both on the Big Island) and Lihue (on Kaua'i). See p532 for details.

Airlines in Hawaii

Hawaiian Airlines (right) and Aloha Airlines (right), the two major interisland carriers, offer frequent flights in full-bodied planes

between the five major airports. Their advantage over the smaller carriers is frequency and dependability of service. Island Air (below), an affiliate of Aloha Airlines, is the largest commuter airline and offers a very extensive schedule, but it's infamous for late and cancelled flights.

Less-frequent flights also go into Lana'i; to Ho'olehua and Kalaupapa, both on Moloka'i; to Kapalua (west Maui) and Hana, both on Maui; and to Waimea-Kohala, on the Big Island. In addition to being served by Island Air, the smaller airports are also served by Pacific Wings and Molokai Air Shuttle, which use prop planes. These carriers often have more competitive fares, but companies can come and go. Their best advantage? They fly lower to the ground, so you'll almost feel like you're on a sightseeing plane.

The advance reservations versus walk-up policies vary by commuter company.

Air Passes

The three largest carriers – Hawaiian Airlines, Aloha Airlines and Island Air – generally have interisland airfares of $80 to $115, depending on which flight you catch. The lower-priced fares are usually for flights leaving early in the morning or late in the day.

Aloha Airlines offers lower interisland fares ($70 to $90 one way) for those who join its frequent flyer program or book tickets in advance via the Internet. Aloha and Island Air offer American Automobile Association (AAA) members a 25% discount off standard ticket fares on all of their interisland flights. The fare is applicable to AAA cardholders *and* those traveling with them. Other schemes come up from time to time, so it's always smart to ask about current promotional fares. Generally, it's quite simple, though: the further you fly, the more it costs.

Aloha Airlines (☎ 800-367-5250, on O'ahu ☎ 484-1111; www.alohaairlines.com) Flies nearly 125 daily routes on 737s between Honolulu, Kaua'i, Maui and the Big Island.

George's Aviation (☎ 866-834-2120, on O'ahu ☎ 306-4284) Flies charter prop planes between Honolulu and Moloka'i.

Hawaiian Airlines (☎ 800-367-5320, on O'ahu ☎ 838-1555; www.hawaiianair.com) Flies nearly 135 daily routes on DC-9s between Honolulu, Kaua'i, Moloka'i, Lana'i, Maui and the Big Island.

Island Air (☎ 800-367-5250; www.islandair.com) Flies small 18- and 37-passenger planes between Honolulu, Moloka'i, Lana'i, Maui and the Big Island.

Moloka'i Air Shuttle (☎ 567-6847, on O'ahu ☎ 545-4988) Flies prop planes between Honolulu and Moloka'i.

Pacific Wings (☎ 888-575-4546; www.pacificwings .com) Flies prop planes from Molokai to Honolulu and Maui.

Paragon Air (☎ 866-946-4744, on Maui ☎ 244-3356; www.paragon-air.com) Flies prop planes between Maui, Moloka'i and Lana'i.

BICYCLE

For the intrepid traveler who doesn't mind blistering heat, strong headwinds and challenging traffic, cycling is an adventurous way to get around.

Realistically, though, it's best suited for well-conditioned cyclists. Furthermore, dedicated cycle lanes are relatively rare on the islands. And to make matters worse, Hawaii's roads also tend to be narrow, and many of the main coastal routes are heavily trafficked. But please, if you want to cycle, by all means do.

Bicycle-hire shops are located on all the islands. It's most feasible to cycle on Kaua'i, although it will entail backtracking because Kaua'i's ring road does not go all the way around the island. The Big Island might feel *really* big when experienced under pedal power, unless you are training for an Iron-man competition. Cycling around Maui as a primary method of transport means you'll have to deal with serious traffic congestion, while cycling on O'ahu entails confronting big-city issues in Honolulu and Waikiki.

If you bring your own bike to Hawaii, which costs upwards of US$100 on flights from the mainland, it will cost an additional US$25 to transport it on interisland flights. The bicycle can be checked at the counter, the same as any baggage, but you'll need to prepare the bike by wrapping the handlebars and pedals in foam or by fixing the handlebars to the side and removing the pedals.

In general, bicycles are required to follow the same state laws and rules of the road as cars. For island-specific cycling information, see the Activities and Getting Around sections of the island destination chapters. See also p61.

BOAT

In response to the increasing costs of interisland flights, a new ferry service has sprung up. Beginning in mid- to late 2006, a new **Hawaii Superferry** (www.hawaiisuperferry.com) will operate a four-story, state-of-the-art catamaran between Honolulu and Kaua'i (three hours to Nawilili Harbor; thrice weekly), Maui (three hours to Kahului; daily service) and the Big Island (four hours to Kawaihae; four trips weekly). Fares are expected to be about $42 to $60 per person and per vehicle, which makes the price about half of what it would cost to fly. Fares to the Big Island are projected to be $10 higher.

Currently passenger ferries also operate between Maui and Lana'i (p393), and between Maui and Moloka'i (p410).

Norwegian Cruise Line (☎ 800-327-7030; www .ncl.com) is the only company that operates a cruise between the Hawaiian Islands that starts and ends in Hawaii. The seven-day interisland cruise makes a quick stop in Kiribati (it must because it's a foreign-registered ship) before calling on Maui (Kahului Harbor), Kaua'i (Nawiliwili Harbor), Hilo and Honolulu. Longer 10- and 11-day itineraries include Kona on the Big Island. Staterooms for the seven-day route start at $800.

BUS

O'ahu's excellent islandwide public system, called TheBus (p115), makes O'ahu the easiest island to navigate without a car. Schedules are frequent, service is reliable and fares are just $1.50 per ride regardless of your destination.

The Big Island has limited public-bus service, and what it does have is geared primarily for commuters. While these buses can get you between major towns, they're not practical for short sightseeing hops; service is infrequent. Nonetheless, it's called the Hele-On Bus (p197).

The limited Kauai Bus (p115) can take visitors between the major island towns and as far north as Hanalei, but it doesn't cover many of the main tourist destinations such as Waimea Canyon. The Maui Public Transit System (p313) has fairly limited service and isn't really practical for getting around.

CAR

Statistically speaking, over 60% of all visitors to Hawaii rent their own vehicles. And that figure rises to 85% for US visitors to Neighbor Islands. So to most of you, we say: read on.

TRANSPORTATION

The minimum age for driving in Hawaii is 18 years, though car-hire companies usually have higher age restrictions. If you're under age 25, you should call the car-hire agencies in advance to check their policies regarding restrictions and surcharges.

Automobile Associations

American Automobile Association (AAA; Map p84; ☎ 593-2221, from Neighbor Islands ☎ 800-736-2886; www.aaa-hawaii.com; 1130 N Nimitz Hwy, Honolulu) has its only Hawaii office in Honolulu. It provides members with maps and other information. Members also get discounts on car hire, air tickets, some hotels, some sightseeing attractions, as well as emergency road service and towing (☎ 800-222-4357). For information on joining, call ☎ 800-564-6222. AAA has reciprocal agreements with automobile associations in other countries, but be sure to bring your membership card from your country of origin.

Driver's License

An international driving license, obtained before you leave home, is only necessary if your country of origin is a non-English-speaking one.

Fuel & Towing

Fuel is readily available everywhere except on the drive to Hana. Expect to pay at least 50¢ more per US gallon than on the mainland. For example, when mainland gas costs an average of $1.90, you'll pay anywhere from $2.25 to $2.75 per US gallon in Hawaii. Still, for Europeans and Canadians, it will be less expensive than at home.

If you get into trouble with your car, towing is mighty expensive in Hawaii and therefore to be avoided at all costs. Figure the fees at about $65 to start, plus $6.50 per mile you must be towed. How to avoid it? Don't drive up to Mauna Kea in anything but a 4WD car, for instance, and don't even drive 4WD vehicles in deep sand. Most hire companies officially prohibit use of their cars on dirt roads.

Hire

Cars for hire are readily available except on Lana'i and Moloka'i, where you'll want to make as early a reservation as possible. With advance reservations (highly recommended), the daily rate for a small car ranges

from $35 to $50, while typical weekly rates are $175 to $250. (Rates for mid-size cars or even 4WD vehicles are often only a tad higher.) If you belong to an auto club or a frequent-flier program, you may get a discount, so ask. It always pays to shop around between hire companies. You can often snag great last-minute deals via the Internet.

Rental rates generally include unlimited mileage, though if you drop off the car at a different location from where you picked it up, there's usually a hefty additional fee.

Having a major credit card greatly simplifies the hire process. Without one, some agents simply will not rent vehicles, while others require prepayment, a deposit of $200 per week, pay stubs, proof of return airfare and more.

Toll-free numbers for the following companies operating in Hawaii work from the US mainland:

Alamo (☎ 800-327-9633; www.alamo.com)

Avis (☎ 800-321-3712; www.avis.com) Avis has a multi-island hire-car deal at a discounted rate as long as you rent for a minimum of five days total.

Budget (☎ 800-527-0700; www.budget.com) Budget produces great driving tour guides to O'ahu ($17) and Maui (including Moloka'i, $20).

Dollar (☎ 800-800-4000; www.dollarcar.com) Dollar is the primary hire agency on Lana'i. It's one of the more liberal agencies renting to folks under the age of 25.

Hertz (☎ 800-654-3131; www.hertz.com)

National (☎ 800-227-7368; www.nationalcar.com)

There is a handful of smaller agencies (see the Getting Around section of each island destination chapter), but for the most part, big companies offer newer, more reliable cars and fewer hassles.

Insurance

Liability insurance covers people and property that you might hit. For damage to the actual rental vehicle, a collision damage waiver (CDW) is available for about $15 a day. If you have collision coverage on your vehicle at home, it might cover damages to car rentals; inquire before departing. Additionally, some credit cards offer reimbursement coverage for collision damages if you rent the car with that credit card; again, check before departing. Most credit-card coverage isn't valid for rentals of more than 15 days or for exotic models, jeeps, vans and 4WD vehicles. For recorded information on your legal rights, call the state **Department of Commerce & Consumer Affairs** (☎ 808-587-1234 ext 7222).

Road Conditions & Hazards

Drivers under the influence of alcohol, marijuana, or 'ice' (crystal methamphetamine) are a hazard, no matter if it's 11am or 11pm. The crime of driving while intoxicated (DWI) is legally defined as having a blood alcohol level of greater than 0.08%. See also p526.

Sections of some roads, including the Road to Hana (p354) and the Kahekili Hwy (p326), may be washed out after significant periods of rain. It's always best to inquire before setting out (see p529). The most useful driving maps are the *Ready Mapbook* series (p526).

Stay alert for one-lane-bridge crossings: one direction of traffic usually has the right of way while the other must obey the posted yield sign. Downhill traffic must yield to uphill traffic where there is no sign.

A word of warning: street addresses on some Hawaiian highways may seem quirky, but there's a pattern. You'll often see hyphenated numbers, such as 4-734 Kuhio Hwy. That's because the first part of the number identifies the district breakdown that the post office uses, and the second part identifies the street address within that district. The numbers are in a numerical order but they can throw you because 4-736 may be followed by 5-002 as a new district starts.

Road Rules

As with mainland USA, driving is (mostly) on the right-hand side of the road. If it's an unpaved or poorly paved road, locals tend to hog the middle stripe until an oncoming car approaches.

Drivers at a red light can turn right after coming to a full stop and yielding to oncoming traffic, unless there's a sign at the intersection prohibiting the turn. Island drivers usually just wait for the next green light.

A popular bumper sticker here reads: 'Slow down. This is not da mainland.' Locals will tell you there are three golden rules for driving on the islands: don't honk your horn, don't follow too closely and let people pass whenever it's safe to do so. Any cool moves like this are acknowledged by waving

the *shaka* (Hawaiian hand greeting) sign. Horn honking is considered rude unless required for safety, or for urging complacent cattle off the road.

Hawaii requires the use of seat belts for drivers and front-seat passengers. Heed this, as the ticket is stiff. State law also strictly requires the use of child-safety seats for children aged three and under, while four-year-olds must either be in a safety seat or secured by a seat belt. Most car-hire companies lease child-safety seats for around $5 a day, but they don't always have them on hand; reserve one in advance if you can.

Speed limits are posted *and* enforced. If you're stopped for speeding, expect a ticket, as the police rarely just give warnings. Most accidents are caused by excessive speed.

HITCHING

Hitchhiking, though technically illegal statewide, is relatively common, sometimes necessary and even convenient, although Lonely Planet does not recommend it. It can be an efficient, cheap way to get around, but is not without risks, obviously. Hitchhikers should size up each situation carefully before getting in cars, and women should be especially wary of hitching alone (see p531).

Hitchhiking is never entirely safe anywhere in the world. Travelers who decide to hitchhike should understand that they are taking a serious risk. People who do choose to hitchhike will be safer if they travel in pairs and let someone know where they are planning to go.

MOPED & MOTORCYCLE

Motorcycle hire is not common in Hawaii, but mopeds are a transportation option in some resort areas like Kihei-Wailea and Kaanapali-Kapalua, on Maui, and on Kaua'i. You can legally drive either vehicle in Hawaii as long as you have a valid driver's license issued by your home country. The minimum age for renting a moped is 16; for a motorcycle it's 21.

There are no helmet laws in the state of Hawaii. Even the most cautious riders will likely seize the opportunity to be bathed in tropical breezes as they lean into turns down the Kohala or Puna coasts. Please be careful and remember that hire agencies often provide free helmets. Also remember that the windward sides of the islands generally require hardcore foul-weather gear, since it rains early and often.

State law requires mopeds to be ridden by one person only and prohibits their use on sidewalks and freeways. Mopeds must always be driven in single file and may not be driven at speeds in excess of 30mph. Bizarrely, mopeds can be more expensive to rent than cars.

TAXI

All the main islands have taxis, with fares based on mileage regardless of the number of passengers. Since cabs are often station wagons or minivans, they're a good value for groups (a particularly smart idea if the designated driver decides to join the partying). Rates vary, as they're set by each county, but average around $2.50 at flag-down, then about $2 per additional mile. Outside of Honolulu and Waikiki, and at most hotels and resorts, travelers will have to call ahead to book for a taxi. Pick-ups from remote locations (for instance, after a long through-hike) can sometimes be arranged in advance.

Health

CONTENTS

Hawaii encompass an extraordinary range of climates and terrains, from the freezing heights of volcanic summits to tropical rain forests. Because of the high level of hygiene, infectious diseases will not be a significant concern for most travelers, who will experience nothing worse than mild sunburn.

BEFORE YOU GO

INSURANCE

The USA offers possibly the finest health care in the world. The problem is that, unless you have good insurance, it can be prohibitively expensive. It's essential to purchase travel health insurance if your regular policy doesn't cover you when you are overseas.

Bring any medications you may need in their original containers, clearly labeled. A signed, dated letter from your physician describing all medical conditions and medications, including generic names, is also handy.

If your health insurance does not cover you for medical expenses abroad, consider supplemental insurance. Check the Subwwway section of the Lonely Planet website (www.lonelyplanet.com/subwwway) for more information about insurance. Make sure you find out in advance if your insurance will make payments directly to providers or reimburse you later for overseas health expenditures.

MEDICAL CHECKLIST

- acetaminophen (eg Tylenol) or aspirin
- anti-inflammatory drugs (eg ibuprofen)
- antihistamines (for hay fever and allergic reactions)
- antibacterial ointment (eg Neosporin) for cuts and abrasions
- steroid cream or cortisone (for poison ivy and other allergic rashes)
- bandages, gauze, gauze rolls
- adhesive or paper tape
- scissors, safety pins, tweezers
- thermometer
- pocket knife
- DEET-containing insect repellent for the skin
- permethrin-containing insect spray for clothing, tents and bed nets
- sun block

RECOMMENDED VACCINATIONS

No special vaccines are required or recommended for travel to the USA. All travelers should be up-to-date on routine immunizations, listed below.

Vaccine	Recommended for	Dosage	Side effects
tetanus-diphtheria	all travelers who haven't had booster within 10 years	one dose lasts 10 years	soreness at injection site
measles	travelers born after 1956 who've had only one measles vaccination	one dose	fever; rash; joint pains; allergic reactions
chicken pox	travelers who've never had chicken pox	two doses a month apart	fever; mild case of chicken pox
influenza	all travelers during flu season (Nov-Mar)	one dose	soreness at the injection site; fever

INTERNET RESOURCES

There is a wealth of travel health advice on the Internet. The World Health Organization publishes a superb book, called *International Travel and Health*, which is revised annually and is available online at no cost at www.who.int/ith. Another website of general interest is MD Travel Health at www.mdtravelhealth.com, which provides complete travel health recommendations for every country, updated daily, also at no cost.

It's usually a good idea to consult your government's travel-health website before departure, if one is available:

Australia (www.smartraveller.gov.au)
Canada (www.hc-sc.gc.ca/english/index.html)
UK (www.dh.gov.uk/PolicyAndGuidance/HealthAdviceForTravellers/fs/en)
USA (www.cdc.gov/travel)

IN HAWAII

AVAILABILITY & COST OF HEALTH CARE

For immediate medical assistance anywhere in Hawaii, call ☎ 911. In general, if you have a medical emergency, the best bet is to find the nearest hospital and go to its emergency room. If the problem isn't urgent, you can call a nearby hospital and ask for a referral to a local physician, which is usually cheaper than a trip to the emergency room. In Hawaii the nearest hospital could be a fair distance away, so the best choice may be an expensive stand-alone, for-profit urgent-care center. Also keep in mind that medical helicopter evacuation may not always be possible from remote areas. See p527 for a list of major hospitals on all islands.

Pharmacies are abundantly supplied, but you may find that some medications that are available over-the-counter in your home country require a prescription in the USA, and, as always, if you don't have insurance to cover the cost of prescriptions, they can be shockingly expensive.

INFECTIOUS DISEASES

In addition to more common ailments, there are several infectious diseases that are unknown or uncommon outside the North American mainland. Most are acquired by mosquito or tick bites, or environmental exposure. Currently Hawaii is rabies-free.

Dengue Fever

Dengue is transmitted by aedes mosquitoes, which bite preferentially during the daytime and are usually found close to human habitations, often indoors. They breed primarily in artificial water containers such as jars, barrels, cisterns, metal drums, plastic containers and discarded tires. As a result, dengue is especially common in densely populated, urban environments. In Hawaii the last outbreak of this mosquito-borne disease was in 2002. For updates, consult the **Hawai'i State Department of Health website** (www.state.hi.us/doh).

Dengue usually causes flulike symptoms, including fever, muscle aches, joint pains, headaches, nausea and vomiting, often followed by a rash. There is no treatment for dengue fever except to take analgesics such as acetaminophen/paracetamol (eg Tylenol) – do not take aspirin as it increases the likelihood of hemorrhaging – and drink plenty of fluids. See a doctor to be diagnosed and monitored. Severe cases may require hospitalization for intravenous fluids and supportive care. There is no vaccine. The cornerstone of prevention is insect protection measures.

Giardiasis

This parasitic infection of the small intestine occurs throughout the world. Symptoms may include nausea, bloating, cramps and diarrhea, and may last for weeks. To protect yourself, you should avoid drinking directly from waterfalls, ponds, streams and rivers, which may be contaminated by animal or human feces. The infection can also be transmitted from person to person if proper hand washing is not done. Giardiasis is easily diagnosed by a stool test and readily treated with antibiotics.

Leptospirosis

Leptospirosis is acquired by exposure to water contaminated by the urine of infected animals such as rats and feral pigs. Outbreaks often occur at times of flooding, when sudden overflow may contaminate water sources downstream from animal habitats. Even an idyllic waterfall may, in fact, be infected with leptospirosis. The initial symptoms, which resemble a mild flu, usually subside uneventfully in a few days, but a minority of cases are complicated by jaundice or meningitis. It can also cause hepatitis and renal failure, which might be fatal. Diagnosis is through blood tests and the disease is easily treated with doxycycline. There is no vaccine. You can minimize your risk by staying out of bodies of freshwater (eg pools, streams) that may be contaminated, especially if you have any open cuts or sores. Because hikers account for many of the cases of leptospirosis in Hawaii, the state posts warning signs at trailheads. If you're camping, water purification is essential.

West Nile Virus

These infections were unknown in the USA until a few years ago, but have now been reported in almost every state. Humans in Hawaii have not been affected so far, but the rising number of reported cases in California – as well as documented cases of West Nile virus in Maui birds – is cause for concern. The virus is transmitted by culex mosquitoes, which are active in late summer and early fall and generally bite after dusk (see also 'Mosquito Bites,' opposite). Most infections are mild or asymptomatic, but the virus may infect the central nervous system, leading to fever, headache, confusion, lethargy, coma and sometimes death. There is no treatment for West Nile virus.

For the latest update on the areas affected by West Nile, go to the **US Geological Survey website** (http://westnilemaps.usgs.gov).

ENVIRONMENTAL HAZARDS

Vog, a visible haze or volcanic smog from active volcanoes, is usually dispersed by trade winds and is not generally hazardous. When it occasionally hangs over the islands, though, it can create breathing problems for some.

See p57 for advice on ocean safety.

Altitude Sickness

Acute Mountain Sickness (AMS), aka 'altitude sickness,' may develop in those who ascend rapidly to altitudes greater than 7500ft, as on Mauna Kea (see p275) and Mauna Loa (see p249) on the Big Island. Being physically fit offers no protection. Those who have experienced AMS in the past are prone to future episodes. The risk increases with faster ascents, higher altitudes and greater exertion. Symptoms may include headaches, nausea, vomiting, dizziness, malaise, insomnia and loss of appetite.

Severe cases may be complicated by fluid in the lungs (high-altitude pulmonary edema) or swelling of the brain (high-altitude cerebral edema).

The best treatment for AMS is descent. If you are exhibiting symptoms, do not ascend. If symptoms are severe or persistent, descend immediately. When traveling to high altitudes, it's also important to avoid overexertion, eat light meals and abstain from alcohol. If your symptoms are more than mild or don't resolve promptly, see a doctor. Altitude sickness should be taken seriously; it can be life-threatening when severe.

Bites & Stings

Hawaii has no established snake population in the wild, although snakes have been sighted recently in the wild, especially in sugarcane fields.

Leeches are found in humid rain-forest areas. They do not transmit any disease but their bites are often intensely itchy for weeks afterwards and can easily become infected. Apply an iodine-based antiseptic to any leech bite to help prevent infection.

Bee and wasp stings mainly cause problems for people who are allergic to them. Anyone with a serious bee or wasp allergy should carry an injection of adrenaline for emergency treatment. For others pain is the main problem – apply ice to the sting and take painkillers.

Commonsense approaches to these concerns are the most effective: wear long sleeves and pants, hats and shoes (rather than sandals) to protect yourself.

MAMMAL BITES

Do not attempt to pet, handle or feed any animal, with the exception of domestic animals known to be free of any infectious disease. Most animal injuries are directly related to a person's attempt to touch or feed the animal.

Any bite or scratch by a mammal, including bats or feral pigs, goats etc, should be promptly and thoroughly cleansed with large amounts of soap and water, followed by application of an antiseptic such as iodine or alcohol. It may also be advisable to start an antibiotic, since wounds caused by animal bites and scratches frequently become infected.

MARINE ANIMALS

Marine spikes, such as those found on sea urchins, scorpion fish and Hawaiian lionfish, can cause severe local pain. If this occurs, immediately immerse the affected area in hot water (as high a temperature as can be tolerated). Keep topping up with hot water until the pain subsides and medical care can be reached. The same advice applies if you are stung by a cone shell.

Marine stings from jellyfish and Portuguese man-of-war (aka 'bluebottles,' which have translucent, bluish, bladder-like floats) also occur in Hawaii's tropical waters. Even touching a bluebottle a few hours after it's washed up onshore can result in burning stings. Jellyfish are often seen eight to 10 days after a full moon when they float into shallow nearshore waters such as at Waikiki; the influx usually lasts for three days. If you are stung, first aid consists of washing the skin with vinegar to prevent further discharge of remaining stinging cells, followed by rapid transfer to a hospital; antivenoms are widely available.

Despite extensive media coverage, the risk of shark attack in Hawaiian waters is no greater than in other countries with extensive coastlines. Avoid swimming in waters with runoff after heavy rainfall (eg around river mouths) and those areas frequented by commercial fishing operators. Do not swim if you are actively bleeding, as this attracts sharks. Check with lifeguards about local risks. Keep in mind that your chances of being hit by a falling coconut on the beach are greater than of shark attack, though!

MOSQUITO BITES

When traveling in areas where West Nile or other mosquito-borne illnesses have been reported, keep yourself covered and apply a good insect repellent, preferably one containing DEET, to exposed skin and clothing. In general, adults and children over 12 should use preparations containing 25% to 35% DEET, which usually lasts about six hours. Children between two and 12 years of age should use preparations containing no more than 10% DEET, applied sparingly, which will usually last about three hours. Neurologic toxicity has been reported from DEET, especially in children, but appears to be extremely uncommon and generally related to overuse. DEET-containing compounds should not be used on children under age two.

Insect repellents containing certain botanical products, including oil of eucalyptus and soybean oil, are effective but last only 1½ to 2 hours. Products based on citronella are not effective.

Visit the **Center for Disease Control's website** (CDC; www.cdc.gov/ncidod/dvbid/westnile/qa/prevention .htm) for prevention information.

SPIDER BITES

Although there are many species of spiders in the USA, the only ones that cause significant human illness are the black widow, brown recluse and hobo spiders. It is a matter of debate which of these species are conclusively found in Hawaii. The black widow is black or brown in color, measuring about 15mm in body length, with a shiny top, fat body, and distinctive red or orange hourglass figure on its underside. It's found usually in woodpiles, sheds and bowls of outdoor toilets. The brown recluse spider is brown in color, usually 10mm in body length, with a dark violin-shaped mark on the top of the upper section of the body. It's active mostly at night, lives in dark sheltered areas such as under porches and in woodpiles, and typically bites when trapped. The symptoms of a hobo-spider bite are similar to those of a brown recluse, but milder.

If bitten by a black widow, you should apply ice and go immediately to emergency. Complications of a black widow bite may include muscle spasms, breathing difficulties and high blood pressure. The bite of a brown recluse or hobo spider typically causes a large, inflamed wound, sometimes associated with fever and chills. If bitten, apply ice and see a physician.

Cold

Cold exposure may be a problem in certain areas. To prevent hypothermia, keep all body surfaces covered, including the head and neck. Synthetic materials such as Gore-Tex and Thinsulate provide excellent insulation. Because the body loses heat faster when wet, stay dry at all times. Change inner garments promptly when they become moist. Keep active, but get enough rest. Consume plenty of food and water. Be especially sure not to have any alcohol. Caffeine and tobacco should also be avoided.

HEALTH

Watch out for the 'Umbles' – stumbles, mumbles, fumbles, and grumbles – which are important signs of impending hypothermia. If someone appears to be developing hypothermia, you should insulate them from the ground, protect them from the wind, remove wet clothing or cover with a vapor barrier such as a plastic bag, and transport immediately to a warm environment and a medical facility. Warm fluids (but not coffee or tea) may be given if the person is alert enough to swallow.

Diving & Snorkeling Hazards

Divers, snorkelers and surfers should seek specialized advice before they travel to ensure their medical kit contains treatment for coral cuts and tropical ear infections, as well as the standard problems. Divers should ensure their insurance covers them for decompression illness – get specialized dive insurance through an organization such as **Divers Alert Network** (DAN; www.diversalertnetwork .org). Have a dive medical before you leave your home country – there are certain medical conditions that are incompatible with diving that your dive operator may not always ask you about.

Heat

Travelers should drink plenty of fluids and avoid strenuous exercise when the temperature is high.

Dehydration is the main contributor to heat exhaustion. Symptoms include feeling weak, headache, irritability, nausea or vomiting, sweaty skin, a fast, weak pulse and a normal or slightly elevated body temperature. Treatment involves getting out of the heat and/or sun, fanning the victim and applying cool wet cloths to the skin, laying the victim flat with their legs raised and rehydrating with water containing ¼ teaspoon of salt per liter. Recovery is usually rapid and it is common to feel weak for some days afterwards.

Heatstroke is a serious medical emergency. Symptoms come on suddenly and include weakness, nausea, a hot, dry body with a body temperature of over 106°F, dizziness, confusion, loss of coordination, fits and eventually collapse and loss of consciousness. Seek medical help and commence cooling by getting the person out of the heat, removing their clothes, fanning and applying cool, wet cloths or ice to their body, especially to the groin and armpits.

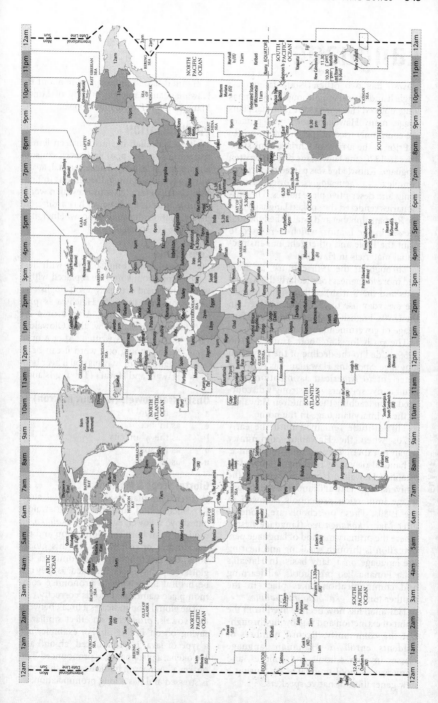

Language

Hawaii has two official state languages: English and Hawaiian. Although English has long replaced Hawaiian as the dominant language, many Hawaiian words and phrases are commonly used in speech and in print.

Prior to the arrival of Christian missionaries in 1820, the Hawaiians had no written language. Knowledge was passed on through complex oral genealogies, stories, chants, songs and descriptive place names. The missionaries rendered the spoken language into the Roman alphabet and established the first presses in the islands, which were used to print the Bible and other religious instructional materials in Hawaiian.

Throughout the 19th century, as more and more foreigners (particularly the Americans and the British) settled in the islands, the everyday use of Hawaiian declined. In the 1890s, English was made the official language of government and education.

The push for statehood, from 1900 to 1959, added to the decline of the Hawaiian language. Speaking Hawaiian was seen as a deterrent to American assimilation, thus adult native speakers were strongly discouraged from teaching their children Hawaiian as the primary language in the home.

This attitude remained until the early 1970s when the Hawaiian community began to experience a cultural renaissance. A handful of young Hawaiians lobbied to establish Hawaiian language classes at the University of Hawai'i, and Hawaiian language immersion preschools followed in the 1980s. These preschools are modeled after Maori *kohanga reo* (language nests), where the primary method of language perpetuation is through speaking and hearing the language on a daily basis. In Hawaii's 'Aha Punana Leo preschools, all learning and communication takes place in the mother tongue – *ka 'olelo makuahine*.

Hawaiian has now been revived from the point of extinction and is growing throughout the community. Record numbers of students enroll in Hawaiian language classes in high schools and colleges, and immersion school graduates are raising a new generation of native speakers.

If you'd like to discover more about the Hawaiian language, get a copy of Lonely Planet's *South Pacific Phrasebook*.

PRONUNCIATION

Written Hawaiian has just thirteen letters: five vowels (**a**, **e**, **i**, **o**, **u**) and seven consonants (**h**, **k**, **l**, **m**, **n**, **p**, **w**). The letters **h**, **l**, **m** and **n** are pronounced much the same as in English. Usually every letter in Hawaiian words is pronounced. Each vowel has a different pronunciation depending on whether it is stressed or unstressed.

Consonants

p/k	similar to English, but with less aspiration; **k** may be replaced with **t**
w	after **i** and **e**, usually a soft English 'v;' thus the town of Hale'iwa is pronounced 'Haleiva,' After **u** or **o** it's often like English 'w,' thus Olowalu is pronounced as written. After **a** or at the beginning of a word it can be as English 'w' or 'v,' thus you'll hear both Hawai'i and Havai'i (The Big Island).

Unstressed vowels (without macron)

a	as in 'ago'
e	as in 'bet'
i	as the 'y' in 'city'
o	as in 'sole'
u	as in 'rude'

Glottal Stops & Macrons

Written Hawaiian uses both glottal stops ('), called *'okina*, and macrons (a straight bar above a vowel, eg **ā**), called *kahako*. In modern print both the glottal stop and the macron are often omitted. In this guidebook, the macrons have been omitted, but glottal stops have been included, as they can be helpful in striving to pronounce common place names and words correctly.

The glottal stop indicates a break between two vowels, producing an effect similar to saying 'oh-oh' in English. For example, *'a'a*, a type of lava, is pronounced 'ah-ah,' and Ho'okena, a place name, is pronounced 'Ho-oh-kena.' A macron inidicates that the vowel is stressed and has a long pronunciation.

Glottal stops and macrons not only affect pronunciation, but can give a word a completely different meaning. For example, *ai* (with no glottal) means 'sexual intercourse,' but *'ai* (with the glottal) means 'food.' Similarly, the word *ka'a* (with no macron over the second **a**) means 'to roll, turn or twist,' but *ka'ā* (with a macron over the second **a**) is a thread or line, used in fishing.

Compound Words

In the written form, many Hawaiian words are compound words made up of several different words. For example, the word *humuhumunukunukuapua'a* can be broken down as follows: *humuhumu-nukunuku-a-pua'a* (literally, trigger fish snout of pig), meaning 'the fish with a snout like a pig.' The place name Waikiki is also a compound word: *wai-kiki* (literally, freshwater sprouting), referring to the freshwater swamps once found in the area. Some words are doubled to emphasize their meaning, much like in English. For example, *wiki* means 'quick,' while *wikiwiki* means 'very quick.'

Common Hawaiian Words

For more Hawaiian words, see the Glossary on p548.

aloha – love, hello, welcome, goodbye
hale – house
heiau – religious temple
kane – man
kapu – taboo, restricted
lu'au – traditional Hawaiian feast
mahalo – thank you
mahimahi – dolphin fish, popular in restaurants
mauka – a directional, toward the mountains
makai – a directional, toward the sea
'ono – delicious, tasty
pau – finished, completed
poi – staple food made from taro
'ukulele – four-stringed musical instrument, used in modern Hawaiian music (literally, 'leaping flea,' because of the action of the fingers when playing)
wahine – woman

PIDGIN

Hawaii pidgin is a distinct language, spoken by over 500,000 people. It developed on sugar plantations where the *luna* (foreman) had to communicate with field laborers from many foreign countries. Early plantation pidgin used a very minimal and condensed

form of English as the root language, to which elements from Cantonese, Hawaiian and Portuguese were added. It became the second language of first-generation immigrants and many Hawaiians.

As this English-based pidgin evolved, it took on its own grammatical structure and syntax. Many words were pronounced differently and combined in ways not found in English. Rather than a careless or broken form of English, it evolved into a separate language, called Hawaii Creole by linguists.

Today, there is ongoing controversy about the validity of pidgin, with opponents saying that it erodes standard English and becomes a barrier to social and educational advancement. Proponents argue that pidgin is a rich and vibrant language that should not be looked down upon or banned from schools, and that pidgin speakers are often unjustly seen as less intelligent.

In recent years many award-winning plays, books and poetry have been written in pidgin by local authors who are passionate in their determination to keep pidgin alive in the community.

Common Pidgin Words & Phrases

brah – shortened form of *bradah* (brother); also used as 'hey you'
broke da mout – delicious, as in 'My auntie make broke da mout kine fish!'
buggahs – guys, as in 'Da buggahs went to without me!'
bumbye – later on, as in 'We go movies bumbye den (then).'
bummahs – bummer; an expression of disappointment or regret
chicken skin – goose bumps
cockaroach – to steal, as in 'Who went cockaroach my slippahs?'
da kine – whatchamacallit; used whenever you can't think of the word you want
Fo' real? – Really? Are you kidding me?
funny kine – strange or different, as in 'He stay acking (acting) all funny kine.'
geev 'um – Go for it! Give it all you got!
Howzit? – Hi, how's it going? As in 'Eh, howzit brah?'
How you stay? – How are you doing these days?
kay den – 'O.K. then,' as in 'Kay den, we go beach.'
laydahs – Later on. I'll see you later, as in, 'Kay den, laydahs.'
no ack – (Literally, 'no act.') Stop showing off, cool it.
rubbah slippahs – (rubber) thongs, flip-flops
talk story – any kind of casual conversation
to da max – a suffix that adds emphasis to something, as in 'Da waves was big to da max!'

Glossary

'a'a – type of lava that is rough and jagged

adzuki bean – often used as a topping for shave ice (in paste or as whole beans)

'ahi – yellowfin tuna

'ahinahina – silversword plant with pointed silver leaves

ahu – stone cairns used to mark a trail; or an altar or shrine

ahupua'a – traditional land division, usually in a wedge shape that extends from the mountains to the sea

aikane – friend

'aina – land

'akala – Hawaiian raspberry; also called a thimbleberry

akamai – clever

'akepa – endangered crested honeycreeper

aku – bonito (skipjack tuna)

akua – god, spirit, idol

'alae ke'oke'o – endangered Hawaiian coot

'alala – Hawaiian crow

ali'i – chief, royalty

aloha – the traditional greeting meaning love, welcome, good-bye

aloha 'aina – love of the land

'ama'ama – mullet

'amakihi – small, yellow-green bird; one of the more common native birds

anchialine pool – contains a mixture of seawater and freshwater

'a'o – Newell's shearwater (a seabird)

'apapane – bright red native Hawaiian honeycreeper

'aumakua – protective deity, deified ancestor or trustworthy person

awa – milkfish

'awa – see *kava*

'awapuhi – wild ginger

banh hoi – Vietnamese version of fajitas

'elepaio – a brownish native bird with a white rump, common to O'ahu forests

fuku-bonsai – Hawaiian-style potted dwarf trees

goza – rolled-up straw mats used at the beach

hala – pandanus tree; the leaves are used in weaving mats and baskets

hale – house

hana – work; a bay, when used as a compound in place names

haole – Caucasian; literally, 'without breath'

hapa – portion or fragment; person of mixed blood

hau – indigenous lowland hibiscus tree whose wood is often used for making canoe outriggers (stabilizing arms that jut out from the hull)

Hawai'i nei – all the Hawaiian Islands taken as a group

heiau – ancient stone temple, a place of worship in Hawaii

Hina – Polynesian goddess (wife of Ku, one of the four main gods)

holoholo – to walk, drive or ramble around for pleasure

holua – sled or sled course

honu – turtle

ho'olaule'a – celebration, party

ho'onanea – to pass the time in ease, peace and pleasure

huhu – angry

hui – group, organization

hukilau – fishing with a seine (a large net), involving a group of people who pull in the net

hula – Hawaiian dance form, either traditional or modern

hula 'auana – modern hula, developed after the introduction of Western music

hula kahiko – traditional hula

hula halau – hula school or troupe

hula ohelo – a hula dance style in which the some of the dancer's motions imitate sexual intercourse

humuhumunukunukuapua'a – rectangular trigger-fish; Hawaii's unofficial state fish

'i'iwi – a bright red Hawaiian honeycreeper with a curved, salmon-colored beak

'iliahi – Hawaiian sandalwood

'ili'ili – small stones

'ilima – native plant, a ground cover with delicate yellow-orange flowers

'io – Hawaiian hawk

issei – first-generation Japanese immigrants

kahili – a feathered standard, used as a symbol of royalty

kahuna – knowledgeable person in any field; commonly a priest, healer or sorcerer

kahuna nui – high priest

kama'aina – person born and raised or a longtime resident in Hawaii; literally, 'child of the land'

kanaka – man, human being, person; also native Hawaiian

Kanaloa – god of the underworld

kane/Kane – man; also the name of one of four main Hawaiian gods

kapa – see *tapa*

kapu – taboo, part of strict ancient Hawaiian social and religious system

kaukau wagon – lunch wagon

kaunaoa – a groundcover vine with yellow tendrils used to make lei

kava –a mildly narcotic drink ('awa in Hawaiian) made from the roots of *Piper methysticum*, a pepper shrub

keiki – child

ki – see *ti*

kiawe – a relative of the mesquite tree introduced to Hawaii in the 1820s, now very common; its branches are covered with sharp thorns

ki'i – image, statue (often of a deity)

kilau – a stiff, weedy fern

kipuka – an area of land spared when lava flows around it; an oasis

ko – sugarcane

ko'a – fishing shrine

koa – native hardwood tree often used in making native crafts and canoes

kohola – whale

koki'o ke'oke'o – native Hawaiian white hibiscus tree

kokua – help, cooperation

kona – leeward side; a leeward wind

konane – a strategy game similar to checkers

ko'olau – windward side

Ku – Polynesian god of many manifestations, including god of war, farming and fishing (husband of Hina)

kukui – candlenut tree and the official state tree; its oily nuts were once burned in lamps

kupuna – grandparent, elder

ku'ula – a stone idol placed at fishing sites, believed to attract fish

Laka – goddess of the hula

lama – native plant in the persimmon family

lanai – veranda

lau – leaf

lauhala – leaves of the hala plant used in weaving

lei – garland, usually of flowers, but also of leaves or shells

limu – seaweed

lio – horse

loko i'a – fish pond

lolo – stupid, feeble-minded

lomi – to rub or soften

lomilomi – traditional Hawaiian massage

Lono – Polynesian god of harvest, agriculture, fertility and peace

loulu – native fan palms

luakini – a type of *heiau* dedicated to the war god Ku and used for human sacrifices

mahalo – thank you

mahele – to divide; usually refers to the missionary-initiated land divisions of 1848

mai ho'oka'awale – leprosy; literally, 'the separating sickness'

mai'a – banana

maile – native plant with twining habit and fragrant leaves; often used for lei

maka'ainana – commoners; literally, 'people who tend the land'

makaha – a sluice gate, used to regulate the level of water in a fish pond

makahiki – traditional annual wet-season winter festival dedicated to the agricultural god Lono

makai – toward the sea

makaku – creative, artistic imagination

malihini – newcomer, visitor

malo – loincloth

mamane – a native tree with bright yellow flowers; used to make lei

mana – spiritual power

manini – convict tang (a reef fish); also used to refer to something small or insignificant

mauka – toward the mountains; inland

mele – song, chant

menehune – 'little people' who built many of Hawaii's fishponds, heiau and other stonework, according to legend

milo – a native shade tree with beautiful hardwood

moa pahe'e – a game, similar to 'ulu maika, using wooden darts and spears

mokihana – an endemic tree or shrub, with scented green berries; used to make lei

mo'i – king

mo'o – water spirit, water lizard or dragon

mu – a 'body catcher' who secured sacrificial victims for the heiau altar

muumuu – a long, loose-fitting dress introduced by the missionaries

naupaka – a native shrub with delicate white flowers

Neighbor Islands – the term used to refer to the main Hawaiian Islands outside of O'ahu

nene – a native goose; Hawaii's state bird

nisei – second-generation Japanese immigrants

niu – coconut palm

noni – Indian mulberry; a small tree with yellow, smelly fruit that is used medicinally

nuku pu'u – a native honeycreeper with a yellow-green underbelly

ogo – seaweed

'ohana – family, extended family

'ohi'a lehua – native Hawaiian tree with tufted, feathery, pom-pom-like flowers

'okole – buttocks

olo – traditional long, wooden surfboard

one hanau – birthplace, homeland

'o'o ihe – spear throwing

pahoehoe – type of lava that is quick and smooth-flowing

pakalolo – marijuana; literally, 'crazy smoke'

palaka – Hawaiian-style plaid shirt made from sturdy cotton

pali – cliff

palila – endemic honeycreeper

paniolo – cowboy

panquela – Brazilian crepe stuffed with pumpkin

pau – finished, no more

Pele – goddess of fire and volcanoes; she's said to live in Kilauea Caldera

piko – navel, umbilical cord

pili – a bunchgrass, commonly used for thatching houses

pilo – native shrub in the coffee family

pohaku – rock

pohuehue – morning glory

poi – staple Hawaiian starch made of steamed, mashed taro

Poliahu – goddess of snow

po'ouli – endangered endemic creeper

pua aloalo – a hibiscus flower

pueo – Hawaiian owl

puhi – eel

pu'ili – bamboo sticks used in hula performances

puka – any kind of hole or opening; small shells that are made into necklaces

pukiawe – native plant with red and white berries and evergreen leaves

pulu – the silken clusters encasing the stems of hapu'u ferns

pupu – snack or appetizer; also a type of cowry shell

pu'u – hill, cinder cone

pu'uhonua – place of refuge

raku – a style of Japanese pottery characterized by a rough, handmade appearance

rakusen kaiseki – multicourse chef's tasting menu

ryokan – traditional Japanese inn

rubbah slippah – rubber thongs

sansei – third-generation Japanese immigrants

shaka – hand gesture used in Hawaii as a greeting or sign of local pride

tabi – Japanese reef-walking shoes

talk story – to strike up a conversation, make small talk

tapa – cloth made by pounding the bark of paper mulberry, used for early Hawaiian clothing (*kapa* in Hawaiian)

ti – common native plant; its long shiny leaves are used for wrapping food and making hula skirts (*ki* in Hawaiian)

tiki – see *ki'i*

tutu – grandmother or grandfather; also term of respect for any member of that generation

'ua'u – dark-rumped petrel

ukulele – a stringed musical instrument derived from the 'braguinha,' which was introduced to Hawaii in the 1800s by Portuguese immigrants

'uli'uli – gourd rattle containing seeds and decorated with feathers

'ulu maika – ancient Hawaiian bowling game

unagi – eel

wahine – woman

wikiwiki – hurry, quick

wiliwili – the lightest of the native woods

zazen – Zen meditation

zendo – communal Zen meditation hall

Behind the Scenes

THIS BOOK

This 7th edition of *Hawaii* was written by a team of authors led by Kim Grant. Kim wrote all of the front and back chapters, with the exceptions of History, The Culture and Food & Drink. Luci Yamamoto wrote The Culture and Food & Drink, as well as the Big Island chapter. Glenda Bendure and Ned Friary (Maui, Lana'i), Michael Clark (O'ahu) and Conner Gorry (Moloka'i, Kaua'i) contributed tirelessly to this title. Nanette Napoleon wrote the History and Language chapters. The Health chapter was largely based upon text written by Dr David Goldberg. Some text and maps for this title were updated and adapted from *Hiking in Hawaii 1* by Sara Benson and Jennifer Snarski, *Maui 1* by Sara Benson and *Hawai'i: The Big Island 1* by Conner Gorry and Julie Jares. Ned Friary and Glenda Bendure were the coordinating authors and Sara Benson was the contributing author on the previous edition of this book.

THANKS FROM THE AUTHORS

Kim Grant We've been incredibly fortunate to have Commissioning Editor Sam Benson navigating this Matson-style ocean liner. An author at heart, and Hawaii specialist by design, no one was more qualified than she. Sam made our lives flow as smoothly as the hips of an experienced hula dancer. *Mahalo* to Conner, Michael, Ned, Glenda and Luci who are serious about their work so that you, dear reader, can have some serious fun. I raise a cup of Kona espresso to my fine colleagues.

Glenda Bendure & Ned Friary A special thanks to all of the people who worked with us on this

project – we appreciate their patience and input. Thanks also to Bill Heyde for the lowdown on Maui behind the scenes, Catie Hausman for providing a kid's angle on Maui, Allen Tom from the Hawaiian Islands Humpback Whale National Marine Sanctuary, and Bert Webster and Joan Rusconi for their support.

Michael Clark Of all who made researching O'ahu a joy, my special thanks to Gage, Carol and Jesse Perrin, Zabia, Ropato Rob Kay, Eunice Leung, Patricia Card, Camila and Cara Chaudron, Serena Cutler, Grant Marcus, Kay Caldwell, Guy Kellogg, Adrienne Valdez, Dixie Thompson, Ed and Michelle Smith, Phil Uesato, Karen Sinn (Hawaiian Historical Society) and Maura Jordan (O'ahu Visitors Bureau). A big *mahalo* to fellow author Kim Grant and to Sam Benson at Lonely Planet for editorial aloha. And a special dedication to Janet, Melina and Alex – next time we'll all go sailing!

Conner Gorry A guide like this never sees the light of day without a lot of help from my friends. In Kaua'i thanks to Ambrose Curry III, Richard and Sarah, Syam Tadavarthy and the gente at Kayak Kauai, Rosemary Smith, Earl Kline and especially, Williamm and Lisa. At home, the folks at the Centro Memorial Martin Luther King provided, yet again, fantastic support throughout, particularly since my good buddy Apagón couldn't let me alone. Sam Benson at Lonely Planet sets the standard – thanks, boss! And to my husband Joel Suárez-Gorry, who makes *un otro mundo* possible every day. *Te quiero siempre* *JSR*.

THE LONELY PLANET STORY

The story begins with a classic travel adventure: Tony and Maureen Wheeler's 1972 journey across Europe and Asia to Australia. There was no useful information about the overland trail then, so Tony and Maureen published the first Lonely Planet guidebook to meet a growing need.

From a kitchen table, Lonely Planet has grown to become the largest independent travel publisher in the world, with offices in Melbourne (Australia), Oakland (USA) and London (UK). Today Lonely Planet guidebooks cover the globe. There is an ever-growing list of books and information in a variety of media. Some things haven't changed. The main aim is still to make it possible for adventurous travelers to get out there – to explore and better understand the world.

At Lonely Planet we believe travelers can make a positive contribution to the countries they visit – if they respect their host communities and spend their money wisely. Every year 5% of company profit is donated to charities around the world.

Luci Yamamoto *Mahalo* to my editor, Sam Benson, for the chance to see an old landscape with new eyes; to Bobby Camara for defining the true meaning of 'local' and for holding me to impeccable standards; to Doug Codiga for being my volcano companion; to Glenn Kunimura for the road-to-the-sea adventure; to Grant Matsushige for the insider's Mauna Kea summit tour; to Tom, Nancy and Judi for endless support and patience; and to MJP for all else.

CREDITS

Hawaii 7 was commissioned and developed in Lonely Planet's Oakland office by Sara Benson. David Zingarelli provided invaluable assistance along the way. Kerryn Burgess contributed to the brief. Cartography for this guide was developed by Alison Lyall and the Project Manager was Chris Love. The book was coordinated by Martine Lleonart (editorial), Owen Eszeki (cartography) and Jim Hsu (layout). Martine was assisted by Victoria Harrison, Kristin Odijk, Jackey Coyle and Meg Worby. Owen was assisted by Wayne Murphy, Emma McNicol and Barbara Benson. Jim was assisted by Adam Bextream, Indra Kilfoyle, Suzannah Shwer and Yvonne Byron. Sally Darmody and Kate McDonald gave valuable help and advice during layout. Candice Jacobus designed and prepared the artwork for the cover. The language chapter was complied by Quentin Frayne. Jennifer Garret and Stephanie Pearson provided valuable advice throughout.

THANKS FROM LONELY PLANET

Many thanks to the travelers who used the last edition and wrote to us with helpful hints, useful advice and interesting anecdotes:

A Alois Ackermann, Matt Aemisegger, Trygve Anderson, Kellie Avery **B** Max Barolo, Kurt & Monique Bergwerff, Megan Berkle, Sarah Blanchard, Rick Byrne **C** Ruth Campbell, Claudia Caramanti, Walter Chapko, Jennifer Charpentier, Anthony Chung, Pierpaola Conte, R.S. Coon **D** Polly Davis, Felipse Dawsey, Louise Dean, Tony DeYoung, Virginia DiPiazza, Sian Douthwaite, Christian Durrer, Zybnek Dvorak **E** Michael Easker **F** Margaret Finger, Dario Frigo **G** Jonathan Gaines, Rhona Gardiner, Jim Gibson, Ronalie Green, Veronica Green, Damaris Gueting, Gretchen Guidotti, Alex Guild **H** Cecilia Han, Lindsay Hanson **I** Jo Ingle **J** Marie Jenks, Lindsay Jones, Tim Julou **K** Kyle Kajihiro, Eve Karasik, Ted Karasik, Kimberly Kinchen, Steve Koenig, Jerzy Krupinski **L** Laura LaLonde, Ian Lamont, Tracy Latimer, Justus Leerling, Mikelson Leong, Christine Lepschy, Harold Leszinski, Sarah Lieberman, Gunilla Lindblad **M** Martin Maranus, Anja Maria, Bob Martin, Jeff Matsuda, Kate Matthams, Sarah McCowatt, Gerrard Meneaud, Bill Michael, Trish Mihalek, Patick Milligan, Sara Elida Mills, Ariane Minnaar, Maureen Moore, Gerome Mortelecque **N** Zsolt Robert Nagy, Barbra Newton, Dion Nissenbaum **P** Lois Palumbo, Susan Proboski, Eulalia Marti Puig **R** Bernice Robins, James Ryan, Jim Ryan, S Ryan **S** Antonio Scarica, Mark Schlagboehmer, U Schläpfer, James Sears, Gary Sinclair, Sharon Sinclair, Nanhi Singh, Michael Smith, Glen Stevens, Kazuaki Sugiyama, Richard Sugiyama **T** Kathryn Taback, Christoph Tmej **V** Mattia Vaccari **W** Monika Weber, Krissy Williams, Sally Wood **Y** Mary Anne Yonk, Jim Yu **Z** Uri Zwick

ACKNOWLEDGMENTS

Many thanks to the following for the use of their content:

Globe on back cover © Mountain High Maps 1993 Digital Wisdom, Inc.

SEND US YOUR FEEDBACK

We love to hear from travelers – your comments keep us on our toes and help make our books better. Our well-travelled team reads every word on what you loved or loathed about this book. Although we cannot reply individually to postal submissions, we always guarantee that your feedback goes straight to the appropriate authors, in time for the next edition. Each person who sends us information is thanked in the next edition – and the most useful submissions are rewarded with a free book.

To send us your updates – and find out about Lonely Planet events, newsletters and travel news – visit our award-winning website: **www.lonelyplanet.com/feedback**

Note: We may edit, reproduce and incorporate your comments in Lonely Planet products such as guidebooks, websites and digital products, so let us know if you don't want your comments reproduced or your name acknowledged. For a copy of our privacy policy visit www.lonelyplanet.com/privacy

Index

INDEX

INDEX

564

MAP LEGEND
ROUTES

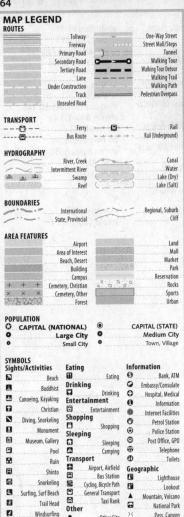

Tollway	One-Way Street
Freeway	Street Mall/Steps
Primary Road	Tunnel
Secondary Road	Walking Tour
Tertiary Road	Walking Tour Detour
Lane	Walking Trail
Under Construction	Walking Path
Track	Pedestrian Overpass
Unsealed Road	

TRANSPORT
Ferry — Rail
Bus Route — Rail (Underground)

HYDROGRAPHY
River, Creek — Canal
Intermittent River — Water
Swamp — Lake (Dry)
Reef — Lake (Salt)

BOUNDARIES
International — Regional, Suburb
State, Provincial — Cliff

AREA FEATURES
Airport — Land
Area of Interest — Mall
Beach, Desert — Market
Building — Park
Campus — Reservation
Cemetery, Christian — Rocks
Cemetery, Other — Sports
Forest — Urban

POPULATION
CAPITAL (NATIONAL) — CAPITAL (STATE)
Large City — Medium City
Small City — Town, Village

SYMBOLS
Sights/Activities
Beach, Buddhist, Canoeing, Kayaking, Christian, Diving, Snorkeling, Monument, Museum, Gallery, Pool, Ruin, Shinto, Snorkeling, Surfing, Surf Beach, Trail Head, Windsurfing, Winery, Vineyard, Zoo, Bird Sanctuary

Eating
Eating

Drinking
Drinking

Entertainment
Entertainment

Shopping
Shopping

Sleeping
Sleeping, Camping

Transport
Airport, Airfield, Bus Station, Cycling, Bicycle Path, General Transport, Taxi Rank

Other
Other Site, Parking Area, Picnic Area

Information
Bank, ATM, Embassy/Consulate, Hospital, Medical, Information, Internet Facilities, Petrol Station, Police Station, Post Office, GPO, Telephone, Toilets

Geographic
Lighthouse, Lookout, Mountain, Volcano, National Park, Pass, Canyon, Shelter, Hut, Waterfall

LONELY PLANET OFFICES

Australia
Head Office
Locked Bag 1, Footscray, Victoria 3011
03 8379 8000, fax 03 8379 8111
talk2us@lonelyplanet.com.au

USA
150 Linden St, Oakland, CA 94607
510 893 8555, toll free 800 275 8555
fax 510 893 8572, info@lonelyplanet.com

UK
72–82 Rosebery Ave,
Clerkenwell, London EC1R 4RW
020 7841 9000, fax 020 7841 9001
go@lonelyplanet.co.uk

Published by Lonely Planet Publications Pty Ltd
ABN 36 005 607 983

© Lonely Planet 2005

© photographers as indicated 2005

Cover photographs: Row of surfboards, Waikiki, O'ahu, APL Corbis (front); Vintage postcard, Linda Ching/Lonely Planet Images (back). Many of the images in this guide are available for licensing from Lonely Planet Images: www.lonelyplanetimages.com

All rights reserved. No part of this publication may be copied, stored in a retrieval system, or transmitted in any form by any means, electronic, mechanical, recording or otherwise, except brief extracts for the purpose of review, and no part of this publication may be sold or hired, without the written permission of the publisher.

Printed through SNP SPrint Singapore Pte Ltd at
KHL Printing Co Sdn Bhd, Malaysia.

Lonely Planet and the Lonely Planet logo are trademarks of Lonely Planet and are registered in the US Patent and Trademark Office and in other countries.

Lonely Planet does not allow its name or logo to be appropriated by commercial establishments, such as retailers, restaurants or hotels. Please let us know of any misuses: www.lonelyplanet.com/ip

Although the authors and Lonely Planet have taken all reasonable care in preparing this book, we make no warranty about the accuracy or completeness of its content and, to the maximum extent permitted, disclaim all liability arising from its use.